D1070485

HISTORY

OF

Bourbon, Scott, Harrison and Nicholas

COUNTIES,

KENTUCKY.

WITH AN OUTLINE SKETCH OF

THE BLUE GRASS REGION,

By ROBERT PETER, M. D.

EDITED BY WILLIAM HENRY PERRIN.

Illustrated.

CHICAGO:
O. L. BASKIN & CO., HISTORICAL PUBLISHERS, LAKESIDE BUILDING.

1882.

This Volume Was Reproduced
From An Original Edition
In The
Fort Worth Public Library
Fort Worth, Texas

SOUTHERN HISTORICAL PRESS
% The Rev. S. Emmett Lucas, Jr.
P. O. Box 738
Easley, South Carolina 29640

ISBN 0-89308-142-6

PREFACE.

OUR history of Bourbon, Scott, Harrison and Nicholas Counties, after months of arduous toil, is now completed. Every important field of research has been minutely scanned by those engaged in its preparation ; no subject of universal public value has been omitted, save where protracted effort failed to secure trustworthy results. We are well aware of our inability to furnish a perfect history from meager public documents, inaccurate private correspondence and numberless conflicting traditions, but claim to have prepared a work fully up to the standard of our promises. Through the courtesy and the generous assistance met with everywhere, we have been enabled to rescue from oblivion the greater portion of important events that have transpired in Bourbon, Scott, Harrison and Nicholas Counties in past years. We feel assured that all thoughtful people in the counties, at present and in future, will recognize and appreciate the importance of the undertaking, and the great public benefit that has been accomplished.

It will be observed that a dry statement of facts has been avoided ; and that the rich romance of border incident has been woven in with statistical details, thus forming an attractive and graphic narrative, and lending beauty to the mechanical execution of the volume, and additional value to it as a work for perusal.

To those who have assisted our corps of writers in gathering material or furnished us data of historical value, we acknowledge our indebtedness ; and to Dr. Robert Peter, of Lexington ; Mr. F. L. McChesney, of Paris ; Mr. S. F. Gano, of Georgetown ; Mr. L. G. Marshall, of Cynthiana and Mr. J. A. Chappell, of Carlisle, our thanks, for able contributions, are specially due.

THE PUBLISHERS.

CONTENTS.

PART I.

GENERAL MATTER AND BOURBON COUNTY HISTORY.

SCOTT COUNTY.

HARRISON COUNTY.

NICHOLAS COUNTY.

APPENDIX.

PART II.

BIOGRAPHICAL SKETCHES.

ADDENDA.

ILLUSTRATIONS.

VIEWS.

PORTRAITS.

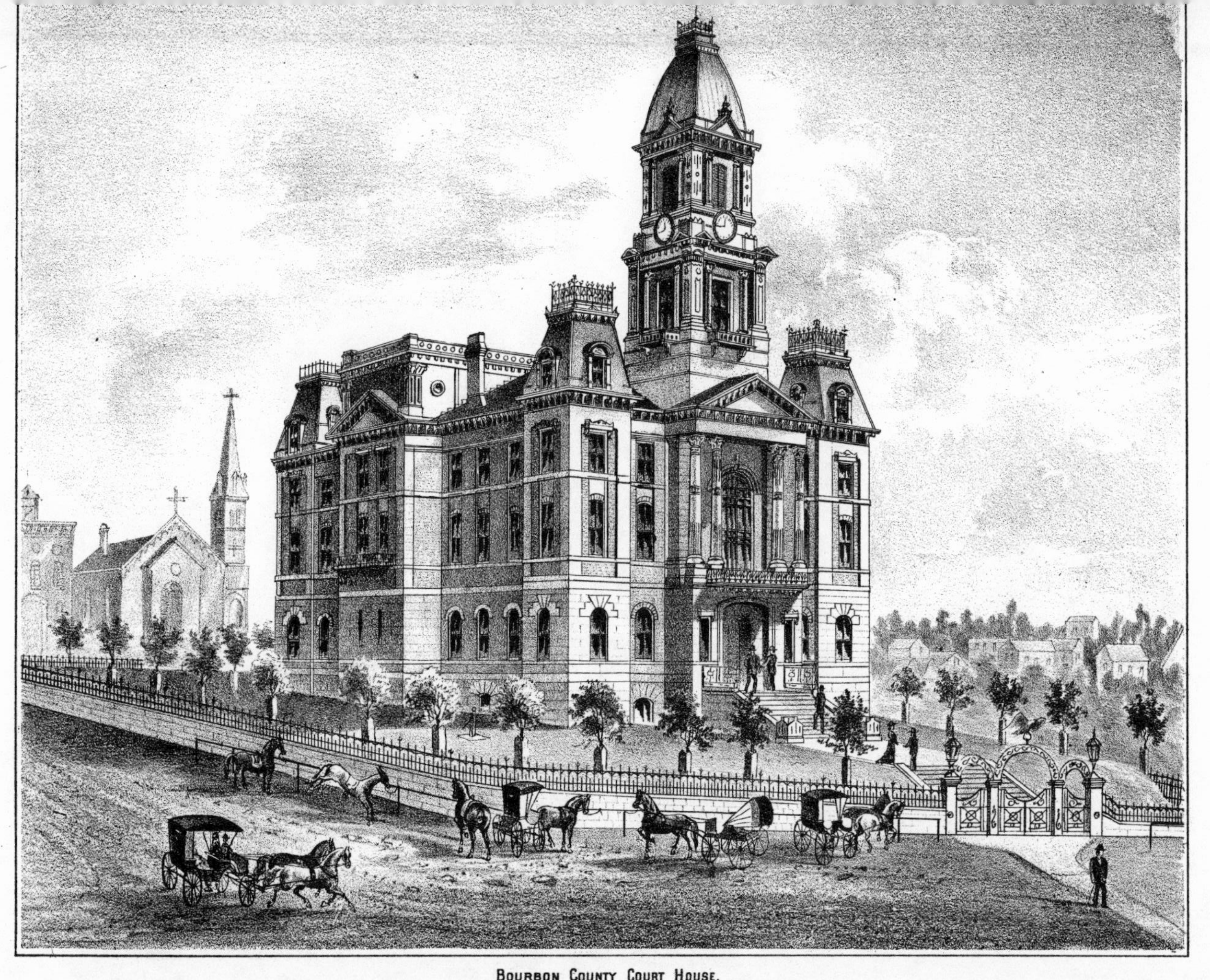

Bourbon County Court House.

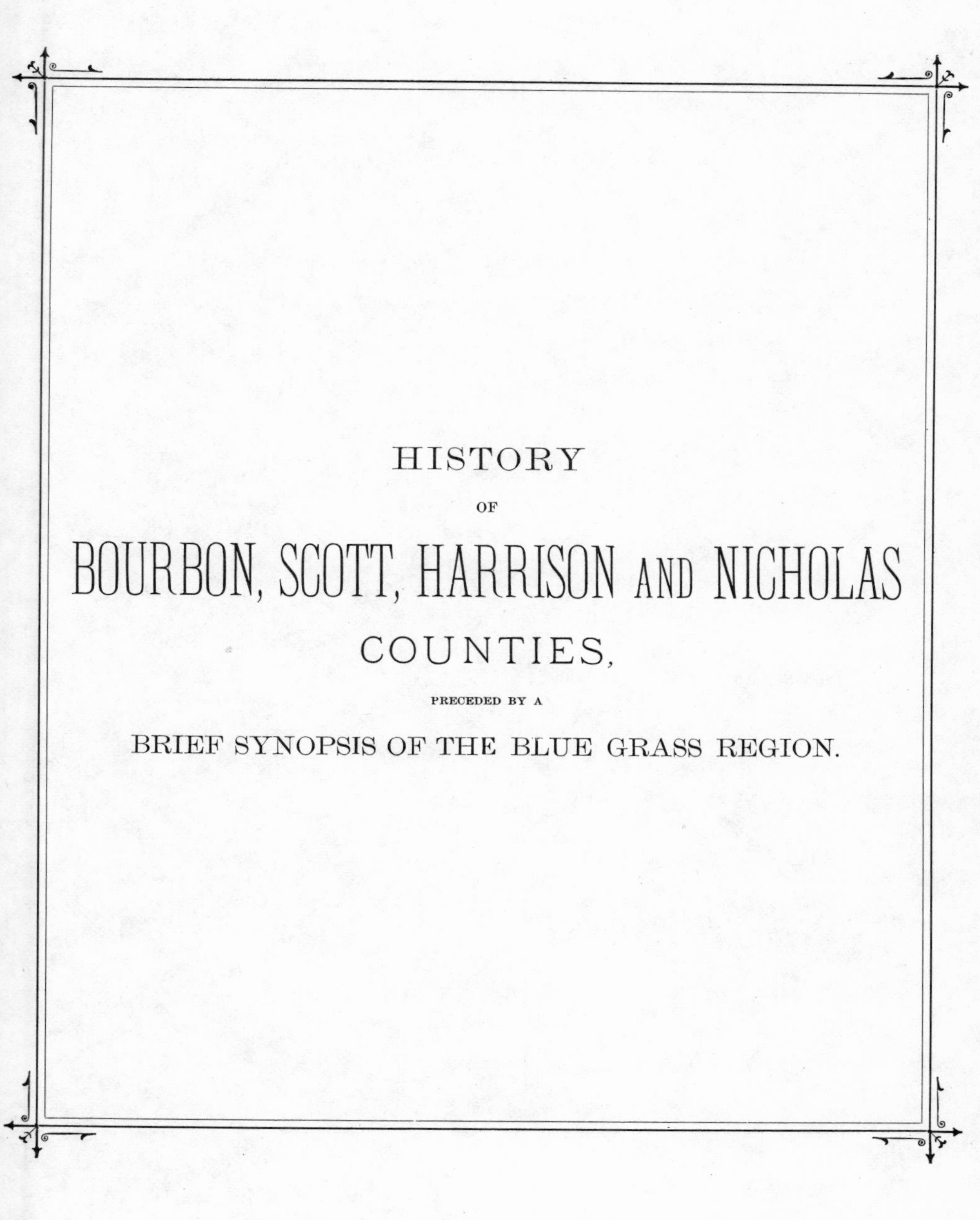

HISTORY

OF

BOURBON, SCOTT, HARRISON AND NICHOLAS

COUNTIES,

PRECEDED BY A

BRIEF SYNOPSIS OF THE BLUE GRASS REGION.

SYNOPSIS OF THE BLUE GRASS REGION.*

ORIGIN OF THE BLUE GRASS—ITS AGRICULTURAL EXCELLENCE—NOURISHING PROPERTIES OVER OTHER GRASSES—SOILS OF THE BLUE GRASS REGION—WHY THE BLUE GRASS SOIL IS FERTILE—THE EXTENT OF THE BLUE GRASS REGION BY COUNTIES.

"The verdant hills
Are covered o'er with growing grain,
And white men till the soil
Where once the red man used to reign."

WE are told by our early historians that the first pioneers in Central Kentucky were astonished at its very great fertility; not as shown in luxuriant blue grass, which now characterizes this region, but in the tall canebrakes which covered it, unbroken, except by the buffalo trails which traversed them, and in the mighty forest growth and great abundance of game.

It was the favorite hunting-ground of many savage tribes, but the exclusive property of no single one. And, probably, because of its productiveness of game, it was also "the dark and bloody ground" of the savages who contended for its rich spoils.

The introduction of live stock by the white settlers caused the gradual extermination of the cane, which was almost the only undergrowth on the rich land, and its place was soon monopolized, all over the region, by what has now a world-wide reputation as "Kentucky blue grass." So that, at this time, the cane is found, growing only in spots, which are inaccessible to grazing animals, which are very fond of its leaves and young shoots—a forage said to be very nourishing and fattening to them.

But whence came the blue grass? The late Dr. John Torrey, of New York, one of the most learned and experienced botanists of our country, stated his belief that this grass had been introduced into this country from England (See "Natural History of New York"); and this seemed to be quite a prevalent belief with our farmers and the early settlers; strengthened by the fact that this blue grass, from time immemorial, had been recognized as the "smooth-stalked meadow-grass," or "spear grass," of England, known to botanists as the *Poa pratensis.*

In corroboration of this belief, Dr. Samuel Martin, of Clark County, Ky., published a statement in the agricultural part of the report of the United States Commissioner of Patents, for 1854 (p. 190), to the effect that the seed of this grass was brought from England by a family which accompanied Daniel Boone to Boonesboro and sowed in a garden at that place. But, spreading in a troublesome manner, it was dug up and thrown over the fence, and, from this spot, spread all over the State.

The venerable Dr. Martin, more recently, in 1867, gave a more detailed account of this legend, to the Farmers' Club, at Lexington (See *Farmers' Home Journal*), as follows: "In the party accompanying Boone to Kentucky, in 1769, was an Englishman, whose wife had tied up in the corner of her handkerchief, some seeds she had brought from England. These she sowed in her garden at Boonesboro. The grass increased so rapidly that she pulled it up, and threw it into an adjoining lot. Here it took root and flourished, and next year, Dr. Martin's father bought from the woman a bushel of the seed for $2.25; and in this way was it introduced into this country."

Oral traditions are, proverbially, unreliable. One of the English names for this grass is "green meadow grass;" a name which is quite appropriate, for its color is a delicate and handsome *green*, and never, at any time of its growth, is it *blue*, and the present writer thinks it is possible that the grass seed sown at Boonsborough was of "*orchard grass* (*Dactylis glomerata*), which is the

*In considering the history of the four counties to which this volume is devoted, a sketch, from a scientific standpoint, of the famous and world-renowned Blue Grass Region, of which these counties form a part, is highly appropriate, and we give it as the opening chapter of our work. This sketch was written at our request by Dr. Robert Peter, of Lexington, Chemist to the State Geological Survey, and one of the ablest scientists of Kentucky. It is well worthy of a careful perusal.—ED.

bluest of our grasses, and not the seed of what is now known as blue grass. Seed of this orchard grass, brought from Virginia, and sown about the beginning of the present century, on the lawn of the farm of the late Col. Samuel Meredith—where the writer now resides—produced a vigorous growth, and has maintained its supremacy through all the varying seasons which have intervened, even against the encroachments of the blue grass, which, although it would soon displace it in the open pasture ground subject to grazing, cannot master it in the shade of trees or shrubbery. It seems probable to the writer that the name, "blue grass," which is quite appropriate as applied to the orchard grass, but not at all suitable to the smooth-stalked Poa, was really first given to the former grass; and that the blue grass of Dr. Martin's legend was orchard grass, and not the green meadow grass of our present rich pastures.

This last-named grass seems to be as persistent and valuable, in favorable localities in England, as it is in Kentucky. In the elaborate work on "British Husbandry," published in 1834, in the Library of Useful Knowledge, "*Poa pratensis*, or smooth-stalked poa," is said to be "one of the most useful of grasses, for it vegetates in the driest soils" (never very dry in England), "supports its verdure during winter, and in the spring throws out numerous shoots for early pasture." But, by the reports of English agricultural chemists and of farmers, it does not appear to be more nourishing in England than some other species of Poa, and, but for its winter-growing property, is not distinguished as a superior pasture grass, as it is in Kentucky. It seems to require the abundant phosphates, alkalies, lime, etc., of the blue limestone soil of Kentucky, to fully develop its superior excellence.

Whether or not this grass was ever introduced from England, it is a fact, established by the pioneer explorers of Alaska, and other of our Northern regions, that it is found growing wild there. Prof. Asa Gray, of Harvard, now one of our oldest and most learned botanists, states that it is indigenous in the mountain regions, from Pennsylvania northward. Indeed, it is to be found almost everywhere north of 40° north latitude, and farther south, in suitable situations. It is the June grass of New York and the New England States; spreading over the whole Northern Hemisphere, no doubt, wherever it meets with suitable conditions; sometimes flourishing in a luxuriant sod, where these are favorable, and dwindling into an inconspicuous, weedy growth, where circumstances are not congenial.

Long droughts and extreme heat are unfavorable to it. It cannot thrive, generally, in the Southern States, and Prof. E. W. Hilgard, of the University of California, tells us that it is unsuited to the dry climate of that State, and only to be kept alive, with great difficulty, in lawns, by assiduous irrigation. The present season in Kentucky (1881), remarkable for its high temperature in July and August (the thermometer, on many days, showing more than 100° Fahrenheit in the shade, and 140° in the sun), together with its continued drought during these two months, severely tried its powers of endurance. The whole plant—leaves, stems, roots and running root-stocks, seemed entirely dead and was completely dried up at the latter end of August; so that the usually beautiful and green blue grass pastures of the early summer presented the browned and sunburnt aspect of the arid plains of Colorado, and the trampling of the animals of the farm raised a cloud of dust, just as on a dry summer road.

But, although much of it was killed which was in the open sunshine, the great recuperative powers of this grass responded to the autumn rains, especially under the shade of trees. Moderate showers, which fell on September 1, 4 and 7, speedily changed the dreary aspect of the fields, and, from the matted sod, which seemed to be utterly dead, green spires of grass appeared throughout the surface, which needed only continued moisture to renew the verdant carpet of the pastures.

Blue grass not only spreads rapidly, by means of its creeping, superficial root-stocks, which cover the ground in a dense mat or sod, and protect the soil from washing, but its abundant seeds are ever ready to germinate. Indeed, over all the open ground, in the so-called blue grass region of Kentucky, this grass spreads, uncared for, in a brief space of time. Thus it is propagated, without cultivation, overcoming all but the most robust and persistent of the weeds of the pasture.

It begins to make a new or increased growth early in spring, ripens its seeds in June, then rests and remains comparatively dormant during the usually hot and dry weather of July and August. Starting anew, after the autumn rains have moistened and cooled the soil, it makes a quick and vigorous growth during the milder and moister fall season. It preserves its verdure, withstands the severest cold of winter, and even grows during the whole of that season, except when the ground is frozen hard, and one of its greatest benefits to the farmer of this region is, that it generally supplies such abundant and nutritive winter pasture, especially when it has been preserved for that purpose, that in ordinary mild seasons, on the sheltered soil of the thinned-out native forest, which has been sown with this grass, called woods or woodland pastures, the animals of the farm are frequently wintered on this alone, without any other protection than that of the trees, and with no fodder nor corn only during deep snows or prolonged hard frosts; thus, saving a great expense in labor and provender.

Stock are all quite fond of it, and many bullocks and sheep are raised and fattened on this alone. Even the hogs of Kentucky require no other food until they are ready for the fattening pen.

Testimony as to the remarkable nourishing, developing and fattening power of the blue grass and other vegetable products of Central Kentucky is abundant. Indeed, the vigor and luxuriance of the vegetable growth, and the superior development of the animals of the farm, are now acknowledged by the world at large. Even man himself seems to take on a higher development in this favored region. The native Kentuckian has, from early times, been noted for his size and strength, and this traditional opinion was fully sustained, during the late civil war, in the actual measurement of United States Volunteers of different nationalities.

In an interesting pamphlet, published in 1876, by Prof. N. S. Shaler, giving "A General Account of the Commonwealth of Kentucky," prepared for the Centennial Exhibition at Philadelphia, is a table (p. 23) giving the results of the official measurements of more than a million white men, volunteers to the United States Army, compiled from the report of the Sanitary Commission by B. A. Gould, in which it is shown that the men from Kentucky and Tennessee, of whom 50,333 were measured, exceeded those from other States of the Union, as well as those from Canada and the British Provinces, and from England, Scotland, Ireland, Germany and Scandinavia, in average height, weight, and in their proportion of tall men, and their weight to the cubic inch; while they also excelled all others, except the Scandinavians, in circumference of the skull and chest.

As to the favorable influences of the blue grass region on the live stock of the farm, much testimony could be presented. The late Dr. D. D. Owen, in Vol. 2, of his Reports of the Geological Survey of Kentucky (p. 30), speaking of the remarkable development of stock pastured on the Blue Limestone Region generally, adds: "For the most part, they are almost a year in advance in bulk, weight and form, to the stock raised on the soils derived from the carboniferous group;" that is, on the coal fields.

In the annual report, for 1880, of the Kentucky Commissioner of Agriculture, Mr. C. E. Bowman, a gentleman of great experience and extensive information in Kentucky farming, we find the following paragraphs (p. 21), viz.:

Live Stock.—"As a stock-raising district, Kentucky has not its equal in the world. Her horses, mules, cattle, sheep and hogs are produced in their most perfect form and development. * * * The South and West look to its great annual sales of short-horns for their supplies of breeding animals, and the East to its annual horse sales for their supplies of fast trotters and fleet-footed coursers. Many of her best bloods have found the way across the ocean, with a view to improving the studs and herds of Great Britain."

These remarks, which apply particularly to the Blue Grass Region, are corroborated by the observations of a well-informed English traveler in America, who republished, in the present year (1881), his views and experiences, in No. 196 of Harper's Franklin Square Library, under the title of "To-day in America," by Joseph Hatton, Esq., etc., etc. On page 14 of this interesting work, after remarking in terms of admiration on the superior qualities of Dr. Herr's celebrated horse, "Mambrino King," he adds: "We saw many good horses of the trotting family in Kentucky. Indeed, here we saw the best of the trotters that we met anywhere in the country, and we noticed them carefully wherever we went. * * * We visited a number of breeding stables about Lexington and Frankfort, both of trotters and race horses, and we saw a great many fine horses here, and also about Louisville. There is much blood in the State, and a great number of fine horses; more than we found in the same area in the country through which we passed."

Indeed, the fame of Kentucky fine horses is world-wide. The horse, recently proved to be the swiftest in the world —Maud S.—was raised in the Blue Grass Region.

In this relation, we quote from the Second Annual Report of the Kentucky Commissioner of Agriculture, W G. Davie, Esq., in 1879, from an article on the "Thoroughbred Horse in Kentucky," by Mr. B. G. Bruce, the able editor of the *Kentucky Live Stock Record*, published in Lexington, who is good and reliable authority on this subject: "If you examine the thoroughbred horse, you will, on investigation, find a superior animal organization —his bones are more solid, his tendons stronger and better defined, his muscles more firm and elastic—in fact, as his form and quality are so much superior, it results that he is much more active, much more fleet and much more powerful, than any other variety of the horse tribe. * * * A square inch of bone from a thoroughbred horse is much heavier than a square inch from a cart horse, the latter being more porous and calcareous, resembling pumice stone, while the thoroughbred is solid, partaking more of the close-grained nature of ivory. The same will apply to the tendons and muscles. * * * Kentucky has, for years, bred more first-class blood horses than all the States combined. The State breeds them in greater numbers, and has a climate, soil and provender better adapted to the production of the higher types of animals than any section of America."

The author goes on to show what experience has fully demonstrated; that blood alone, if not maintained by favorable external conditions, is not sufficient to maintain the greatest perfection of animal development, and to hint at the probable influence of soil and geological formations. "If you take Kentucky horses," he adds, "or cattle, to Pennsylvania and the Eastern States, their posterity begin to undergo a change in the first generation; in the second, it is still greater; and, in the tenth or twelfth remove, they are no longer the same breed of animals. * * * Animal formation is modified by the vegetable formations of which it is the result, and the vegetable formations are modified by the elements of the soil from which they derive their nourishment. Not only the forms of animals, but their physical systems, their secretions and excretions, are affected by the different geological formations from which they derive, through its vegetation, the elements of their organization."

Experience on the turf and the road seems to demonstrate that there are, in the peculiar soil and underlying rock strata of Central Kentucky, or especially in the Blue Grass Region, influences and agencies which give greater hardness and solidity to the bone, strength to the muscle, power to the nerve and capacity to the lungs not generally found associated in other regions.

Causes of the peculiar agricultural excellence of the Blue Grass Region.—The peculiar excellence of the animal products of this region is evidently not due to the blue grass or other provender, *per se;* but is to be attributed to agencies which make the vegetable food more than usually rich and nourishing.

Blue grass grows abundantly in other localities, and corn, and oats, and other provender; but they do not show that superior developing power over animal life which they exhibit in this favored region. Farmers of other parts of the country have eagerly sought the seed of the "true Kentucky blue grass," but they have found that, unless their soils and other local conditions are congenial to the highest development of this grass, they fail to obtain the results which it gives in the Blue Limestone Region of Kentucky. The climate and all the meteorological conditions may be the same as in its home in Kentucky, but the soil and the rock substratum may not possess the store of mineral fertilizers which enrich those of Central Kentucky.

Experience of nearly a century of cultivation of this rich soil, without the use of artificial fertilizers, has demonstrated in it a very extraordinary durability of productiveness. Fortunately, we have a pretty reliable record for comparison, in a publication made on September 16, 1797, in the columns of the old *Kentucky Gazette*, by the Lexington Emigration Society, in which they made a statement of the average produce of an acre of their new rich land, at that early period, as follows: Wheat, on corn ground, 25 bushels; wheat, on fallow, 35 bushels; corn, 60 bushels; potatoes, 250 bushels; hemp, 800 pounds; tobacco, 2,000 pounds; hay, 6,000 pounds.

These figures were probably as favorable as could honestly be presented at that time, and, it is interesting to see that the eighty-four years of cultivation of our soil, without the use of any manures or fertilizers, have not reduced our products lower than we now obtain them. Time and the long-continued cultivation have removed most of that deep vegetable mold; the remains of ages of previous vegetable growth and decay, which covered the ground in those early days, to a considerable depth, with a black vegetable mold, like that of the surface of a well-manured garden, and contributed much soluble food for plants; and our old fields are now of a brownish color; yet they still yield, in good seasons, crops which are not so greatly below those above quoted, as might have been expected, and rest in fallow, or in a clover rotation, or in pasture grass, wonderfully renews their productiveness. Our farmers, in good seasons, yet obtain their fifty to sixty bushels of corn to the acre, and their twenty-five or more bushels of wheat, and, on plowed-up pasture land, secure much more than 800 pounds of hemp.

There was a time when the black vegetable mold, commonly called *Humus*, was believed to be the essential fertilizing principle of the soil. The French chemist, Grandeau, as his *matiere noire*, still attaches great importance to this ingredient of the soil, but since the time of Carl Sprengel, who first pointed out the indispensable necessity of some of the mineral ingredients of the soil to plant and animal nourishment, and the popular writings of Liebig have commended the mineral theory to the agriculturists of the world, they now look to the soil and to the rocks, out of which it has been produced by disintegration, for many of the essential elements of fertility.

The late Prof. Agassiz, more wisely than he thought, perhaps, told the farmers of Massachusetts, "that the question, fundamental to all others in the *stock* business, is the *rock* question."

Soils of Blue Grass Region.—All soils are produced by the decay or disintegration of rocks. Those of Kentucky have mostly been formed, in the course of long geological epochs, under the action of the atmospheric agencies, out of the rock strata on which they at present lie, and hence they partake greatly of the character of those rocks. Soils of such an origin are called Sedentary soils, and are not usually deep, or of frequent occurrence on the globe. They are hardly known over the broad expanse of our continent north and west of Kentucky, or over the northern portion of Europe and Asia, the most of that extensive area being covered by a mixed deposit of clay, sand, gravel and bowlders, called the "Drift," made up of the debris of Northern rock strata which have been broken or ground up, and carried, during long periods of refrigeration, by the action of immense glaciers, which covered the Northern Hemisphere, and by the floods of water which poured from them.

This mixed deposit, made up, largely, of coarse and hard silicious materials, which so generally covers the country of the great Northwest, that scientific observers of that region have asserted, that the soil is not affected by its underlying rock stratum, does not seem to have crossed the valley of the Ohio to enter Kentucky. Thus, the rich soil which had been produced from our ancient limestone and other rocks in the long periods during which they have been raised above the ocean level, has remained undisturbed and unburied up to the present day.

The rock strata, out of which the soil of the Blue Grass Region was produced, belong to an exceedingly ancient geological formation, which was, evidently, at first laid down as a calcareous mud, hardening gradually into rock in the course of a long period, under the deep waters of a warm ocean which swarmed with the lower forms of marine animal life.

Dr. D. D. Owen, in the first volume of his Reports of the Geological Survey of Kentucky, thus describes our blue, shelly limestone: "So prolific, indeed, is the blue limestone in fossil remains, that continuous beds may be traced, in which the imbedded shells and corals are so closely cemented, that it would be difficult to place the finger on a spot without touching some of these organic relics. The contemplation of these must fill the mind of the observer with the profoundest reflections. Here is spread before his eyes more than 500 feet of solid rock, deposited at the bottom of a primeval ocean, far more ancient than the coal formation that furnishes our fossil fuel; the age of which can, in fact, be traced through nine vast (overlying) geological formations, each many hundred feet in thickness, each the sepulcher of myriads of extinct races, that peopled the earth in succession. * * * In the fossiliferous strata of the blue limestone of Kentucky, we behold, indeed, one of the oldest and deepest-seated of the stratified sedimentary formations, over which many miles (in thickness) of sedimentary particles subsided, during a long cycle of geological events; yet here, in the heart of Kentucky, do we find it reaching the surface, filled with exuviæ of the earliest organized marine existences, whose elements now contribute, in connection with the mineral matter of which it is composed, to eliminate a soil, fertile and prolific, on which now wave the luxuriant harvests of an enterprising people."

In a spirit of prophecy, he predicted (Vol. 2, of same work, p. 43) that "the time will come, as our means of transportation shall be more extended and cheap, when many of the inferior sandy soils, and stiff, cold tenaceous clay lands of Kentucky will be manured with these fossiliferous limestones." And this he believed before the great richness of some of the limestone layers, in phosphates, had been fully ascertained.

Although the general reader is supposed to know little of the significance of the several chemical elements of soils, we will here, by placing side by side the constituents of two Kentucky soils, analyzed by the writer, try to enable him to judge of the peculiar excellency, in composition of our Central Kentucky soils.

Composition of two Kentucky soils.—One, No. 681, of Kentucky Geological Reports: A very rich and fertile soil from the Blue Grass Region; the other, No. 644, of same reports: A poor, exhausted soil from a less favored geological formation:

COMPOSITION IN 100 PARTS.	No. 681. Rich Soil.	No. 644. Poor Soil.
Organic and volatile matters (humus, etc.)......	10.365	2.309
Alumina (the earth of clay).....................	5.395	1.745
Oxide of iron..................................	7.110	1.420
Oxide of manganese,...........................	.620	.040
Carbonate of lime.............................	1.995	.097

Magnesia	1.234	.191
Phosphoric acid (P2 O5)	.333	.078
Sulphuric acid (S O3)	.093	.021
Potash	.762	.075
Soda	.106	.030
Sand and insoluble silicates	72.035	93.495

By comparing the relative proportions of the more essential ingredients of these two soils, viz., the phosphoric acid, potash, lime and magnesia, as well as their very different proportions of inert "sand and insoluble silicates," the reader can easily judge of their relative value.

It may be remarked that very few soils on the surface of the globe excel or equal No. 681 in richness of composition. These facts may enable us to understand one reason:

Why our blue grass soil is so fertile.—But many other indispensable conditions aid, which will be briefly stated: 1. Favorable climatic and meteorological ones. The present exceedingly dry and hot summer season (of 1881) fully demonstrates that, without the usual forty-four to forty-five inches of annual rainfall, properly distributed throughout the season of growth, the native richness of our soil and blue grass could not be developed. 2. Our soil, derived from the slow solution and wasting of a limestone, which had, evidently, been deposited under the water of a deep ocean at a distance from any shore, is full of organic remains, and is wholly made up of materials in the very finest state of division. In the greater number of these soils, analyzed by the present writer, that silicious portion, usually stated as "sand and insoluble silicates," will pass easily through the finest bolting cloth.*

It is so very fine, indeed, that the popular opinion is that the soil of the Blue Grass Region, contains no sand, and sand for building purposes must be hauled from a distance. It is so fine that it presents some of the plastic properties of clay, but yet is so permeable that water penetrates it with great rapidity, and excess of surface water readily escapes. This state of very fine division of the soil is a very great aid to fertility, causing it to be eminently absorptive and retentive of moisture, and of the fertilizing gases and vapors of the atmosphere, as well as of the rich remains of decomposing organic bodies. By the greater surface which its fine particles present to the rootlets of plants, it greatly aids in the supply of their nourishment, while the development and penetration of these essential organs is facilitated. 3. Much of our blue grass soil is naturally under-drained, by numerous clefts and caverns in the underlying limestone, through many of which underground streams constantly flow, and, in the bottoms of some of the sink-holes, along the course of these cavern-channels, cool springs boil up. 4. The subsoil and under-clays of the blue grass soils are found to be very rich in the mineral elements of plant food, and although, when brought up to the surface in quantity, they may not benefit it, until they have been exposed for a considerable time to the atmosphere and have acquired *humus*, yet they furnish to deep-rooted plants, such as clover, and to trees, much moisture and fertilizing elements. 5. But the most influential condition of all is the underlying blue limestone, of the Lower Silurian formation, which, from its soft and decomposable beds and marls, constantly supplies the superincumbent soil with essential fertilizing elements.

*It passed through a wire seive having 1,600 meshes to the centimetre square.

As early as 1848, the attention of the present writer was attracted to this limestone as a probable cause of the great and durable productiveness, without manures, of our blue grass soil, from which there was, annually, an immense exportation of animal and vegetable products, without a corresponding exhaustion of the soil. Some of his analyses of limestone, from the hard grey crystalline layers, obtained, in blasting a well in Lexington, and from nearer the surface, gave him, to his great surprise, from one-third of 1 per cent up to as much as 3 per cent of phosphoric acid. These results, with some remarks on the importance of this fact, to our agriculture, and the continued productiveness of our soil, were published by him in the Albany *Cultivator*, for April, 1849.

More recently, by analyzing some of the softer and more porous layers of this limestone, in the vicinity of Lexington, in a considerable number of samples, he has found the presence in them all of phosphoric acid, varying in proportions from those above mentioned, up to as much as 30 per cent in one unique sample. In eleven samples, the analyses of which are given in Vol 5 (new series), of Kentucky Geological Reports, in his Chemical Report, under Fayette County, the percentage of phosphoric acid was found by him to vary from a little more than 5 per cent up to nearly 22 per cent. No doubt, these rich phosphatic layers, if to be found in sufficient extent, might be utilized as fertilizers on poorer soils, in accordance with the prediction of the late Dr. Owen. It is probable that more extensive investigation will show that this indispensable ingredient of the bones of animals, of the seeds of plants, indeed, of all vegetable and animal tissues, will be found more abundant and generally diffused, throughout the decomposable layers of

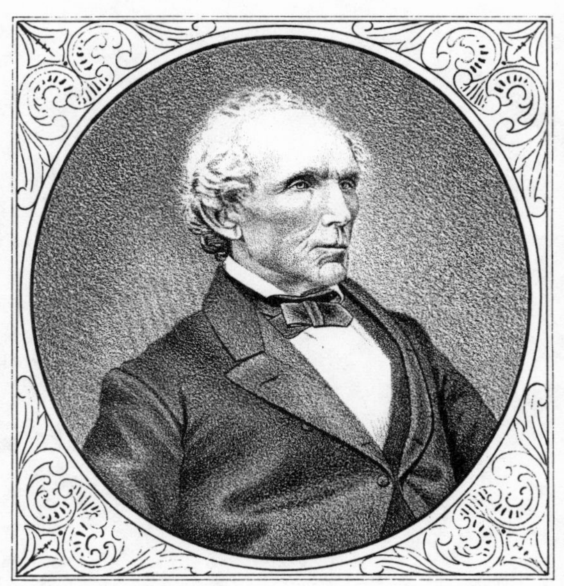

Garrett Davis

the blue Silurian limestone, or even those of the Upper Silurian limestone, than is now generally suspected.

The necessity of phosphates to all plant nourishment makes them indispensable in artificial fertilizers. They are generally obtained from animal bones, guano, or fossil phosphates, which are usually ground up and treated with sulphuric acid, to render them more soluble. The present price of mineral phosphoric acid is about 3 cents per pound; a limestone containing 20 per cent of this acid, then, would be worth about $12 a ton, where transportation is not too costly. Hitherto, however, while this valuable acid is found generally diffused throughout our limestone layers, very rich ones have not been discovered of sufficient extent for commercial purposes.

How the blue limestone substratum fertilizes the soil of the Blue Grass Region.—We hope, without the use of technical terms, to make this plain to the intelligent reader. The atmospheric water, falling as rain, etc., always brings with it, in solution, a certain quantity of carbonic acid, which exists in the atmosphere in small proportion; this gas being a constant product of all animal respiration, as well as of all decaying organic substances, animal or vegetable.

Penetrating the soil, which always contains decaying organic substances, it meets with more of this gas, and acquires other acids from these substances; so that the water in the soil always contains a notable quantity of dissolved acids. Coming in contact with the limestone rock, this acidulated watery solution continually dissolves out, not only the carbonate of lime, which forms the greater weight of the rock, but also carbonate of magnesia and phosphate and sulphate of lime, and small proportions of the alkalies—potash and soda—which it always contains. Hence, this water, when it comes again to the surface, in springs, or collects in wells, is always what is called "hard water," because it contains lime and magnesian salts, which curdle a soap solution. When this hard water is boiled, the gaseous solvent of these earthy salts, the carbonic acid, is driven off by the heat, and a crust or earthy deposit is formed, these salts being insoluble in the water free from carbonic acid. Even free exposure to the air, by permitting the escape of this gaseous acid, causes the deposit of these earthy salts, and the formation of icicle-like stalactites in caves, and incrustations and petrifactions of various kinds.

By this continued action of the carbonated water, our beds of limestone are gradually dissolved and washed away, possibly to aid in the formation of new rocks at lower levels, or to furnish materials for coral reefs or marine shells, in the Gulf of Mexico; while the earthy and silicious insoluble residue of the dissolved limestone layers remains, forming the present soil.

We need only examine an old limestone fence or wall, which has been exposed for some years to the weather, to witness the effects of the solvent action of the atmospheric waters, which action is much more rapid under the soil; and when we calculate the quantity of limestone which is thus annually carried away in solution, we can understand that, in the untold ages since the blue limestone strata were first raised above the level of the primeval ocean, probably hundreds of feet of thickness of the solid limestone, thus partly dissolved and removed by atmospheric waters, may have contributed to form, by its undissolved residue, the rich blue grass soil, which now covers the remaining rock in considerable thickness.

One thousand parts of clear spring water, taken in the dry season, from the "Big Spring," which boils up at the bottom of a deep sinkhole on the writer's farm, six and a half miles from Lexington, gave on analysis, more than a fourth of one part of solid saline matters (0.2733 to the 1,000), consisting of the ingredients of the dissolved limestone, including some of its phosphates and a little common salt, potash, etc.

Water of this character, and probably richer in saline matters, especially in dry seasons, continually moistens the blue grass soil, conveying to the growing vegetation on the surface, in solution, several of the indispensable elements of plant nourishment, taken from the limestone substrata, such as phosphoric and sulphuric acids, potash, soda, lime, magnesia, iron and silica. As fast as pure water escapes, by evaporation from the green surfaces of the plants, leaving the saline matters behind in their tissues, more of the soil water penetrates through the rootlets, to keep up the supply and increase the amount of solid saline matters. "Mr. Lawes, of England, found, in the moist climate of that country, common farm plants, such as wheat, barley, beans, peas and clover, exhaled, during five months of growth, more than two hundred times their (dry) weight of water."

This evaporation of the pure water from the soil solution which enters the tissue of plants, is greater in our warmer and drier climate than in England; but, calculating on this basis, the production of a ton of hay, if grown only in five months, would require the exhalation of 400,000 pounds of water, which, if taken from soil water alone, of the degree of hardness of our spring water, would leave more than 108 pounds of ash ingredients, which is nearly as much as the hay would leave after being burnt. So that very little demand for mineral ingredients need be made, by special root action, on the soil, the productiveness being greatly maintained by the soil water supplied, measurably, from the rock, without soil exhaustion. Thus does our rich blue limestone continually renovate the soil which lies on it, and hence it is that manures have been greatly neglected in the Blue Grass Region, and phosphatic fertilizers and lime, especially, are found to exert little influence on our best new lands.

Why the Kentucky blue grass is so nourishing.—It was at one time believed, by vegetable physiologists and chemists, that vegetables exerted a selected power over the mineral ingredients of the soil in which they grew, to such an extent, at least, that the ash left after the burning of their combustible matters, although different in composition in different species, would be found to be always similar, or nearly so, for the same species, whatever may have been the nature of the soil on which it grew. And the manufacturers of fertilizers still base their formulæ of ingredients, for the several farm crops to be manured, generally, upon the ash analyses of those crops. But it is now known, that, although different vegetables show preferences as to the mineral ingredients of their food, and as to their quantity, so that, when grown on the same soil and under the same conditions, different plants, growing side by side, will give ashes quite various in relative quantity and composition; yet, they are all under the influence of physical and chemical conditions, which may introduce—as was partly explained above, in relation to hard limestone water—various mineral ingredients in more than the usual or normal proportions, and, often in much greater quantities than may be essential to their healthy development. The plants, acting by capillary attraction on the soil water, like a sponge, and the water of the absorbed solution being evaporated from the leaves and green parts, deposits in the vegetable tissues a quantity of the dissolved saline matters, which bears a proportion to the amount of soil water absorbed.

The writer has verified this fact in some marked instances: 1. In the ash analyses of thirty different samples of leaf tobacco, grown on different soils in Kentucky, in Cuba and in Florida (See appendix to his Chemical Report, in Vol. 4, old series, of Reports of Kentucky Geological Survey). In these different samples the total ash contents varied from 13.16 per cent, in the Simpson County leaf, to 17.79 per cent in that of Daviess County. The potash varied from 20.50 per cent, in Mason County, to 35.38 per cent in Bracken County; the lime varied from 16.70 per cent, in Owen County, to 35.18 per cent in Mason County; the phosphoric acid varied from 1.74 per cent, in Larue County, to 6.14 per cent in Barren County; the sulphuric acid varied from 1.26 per cent, in Barren County, to 6.69 per cent in Owen County.

Other ingredients showed similar variations in proportions, proving that the amount and composition of the mineral ingredients varied greatly, according to the local conditions of soil, water, etc., etc.

Another verification was obtained by the writer, in the comparative ash analyses of entire hemp plants, grown, severally, in the *very dry* season of 1874, and in the *very moist* season of 1873; both on the same soil. (See Vol. II, of Reports of Kentucky Geological Survey, new series, p. 137.) Both samples were collected, roots, leaves and all, in the month of September, when the plants were at their maturity and ready for cutting. Sample A, grown in the very dry season, was not more than six to seven feet in height. Sample B, grown in the very moist season, was about twelve feet high. The percentage of ash, to the air-dried plants, in Sample A, was 4.223; in Sample B, only 2.563, carbonic acid being deducted in both cases.

The chemical composition, as calculated into 100 parts of the ash of these two samples also varied. The ash of B, grown in the moist season, contained smaller proportions of lime, magnesia, sulphuric acid and silica, and larger proportions of potash, soda and phosphoric acid than that of Sample A, grown in the dry season.

Bnt the signification of these differences of proportions can better be seen when a comparison is made of the relative quantities of these several ash ingredients to 100 parts of the dried hemp plants, as follows:

	A.	B.
Lime	1.624	0.802
Magnesia	.361	.154
Potash	1.582	1.121
Soda	.016	.037
Phosphoric acid (P2 O5)	.366	.363
Sulphuric acid (S O3)	.096	.042
Chlorine	.041	.013
Silica	.134	.031
Per cent of ash to dried plants	4.223	2.563

This table shows the effects of the greater transpiration of the hard soil water in the dry season than in the moist; for, while there was a smaller proportion of ash ingredients in the hemp which had a luxuriant growth, because of the regular supply of pure atmospheric water in the moist season, which, measurably, kept down, or diluted, the soil water, the difference in weight of the ash was mainly occasioned by greater quantities of lime, magnesia and silica, in the plant of the dry season, and not by any material variations in the proportions of the alkalies or phosphoric acid; and this variation was evidently caused by the greater exhalation of water and carbonic acid from the larger quantity of soil solution, which entered the plant and left these insoluble materials, in excess, in its tissues, during the dry season. But these very materials, which seem to be in excess, in the plant grown in the dry season, perform their functions as mineral fertilizers, when sufficient moisture, and other necessary conditions, are present, as is fully shown in the luxuriant growth on the same soil, of the plants of the moist season. No doubt these mineral ingredients, in the soil water, and the water of our springs, derived from the limestone rock substratum, are mainly instrumental in giving to the blue grass soil its great and durable productiveness, and these substances are indispensable, not only to vegetable growth, but also to animal growth and development.

It is probable, therefore, from the foregoing facts, that the ashes of the rich Kentucky blue grass would be found, on analysis, to contain more of these essential elements of vegetable and animal nourishment than those of the same grass grown under less favorable conditions.

In another comparative examination, of two samples of Indian corn, similar results were obtained by the writer. (See Vol. 4, Kentucky Geological Survey, old series, p. 315.) Sample No. 1 was from an exhausted field, based on sandstone rock, in Breckinridge County, Ky., which yielded about eight to twelve bushels per acre. Sample No. 2 was from a field in the Blue Grass Region of Kentucky, which yielded about seventy-five bushels to the acre; both in a rather unfavorable season. The percentage of ash in the dried corn was: In Sample No. 1, only 0.980; in Sample No. 2 it was 1.412. The percentage of earthy phosphates, in Sample No. 1, was 0.2077; in Sample No. 2, it was 0.3723.

Evidently, when fed in equal weights, to animals, the corn of the rich field would be more nourishing to bone and muscle, than that of the poor field. On examination, there was also found to be a larger proportion of oil, in the product of the rich field, and the larger quantity of earthy phosphates, no doubt, corresponded with a greater proportion of nitrogenous or flesh-forming principles in that.

Calculating the quantities of mineral fertilizers furnished to the two crops by the soils, we find that the twelve bushels of the poor field obtained only about eleven pounds and three-quarters; while the seventy-five bushels received from the rich field as much as nearly 106 pounds. The abundance of these mineral fertilizers, supplied to the soil of the Blue Grass Region, as above described, is, evidently, a principal cause of the great productiveness of the blue grass soil, as well as of the high nutritive quality of its vegetable products. The beneficial influence of hard limestone water, in the nutrition of animals of the farm, where the ordinary food did not supply quite enough of the earthy salts for the needs of the animal economy, in the formation of bone, muscles, etc., was fully proved many years ago by the celebrated agricultural chemist, Boussingault. The ash of the ordinary Indian corn is generally deficient in lime, as food for animals, according to his experience, and, he found by actual comparative weighings, that those animals which used the hard water with such food, thrived better and grew faster than others supplied with purer water.

It will be seen in the foregoing facts and conclusions, that the peculiar richness of our blue grass pastures, is not in the blue grass *per se*, but is dependent on the soil, which is abundantly supplied with the indispensable mineral elements of vegetable and animal nutrition, derived from the decomposable layers of the underlying blue limestone, which contain an inexhaustible supply of these materials, and which constantly yield them to the soil, by the agency of the carbonated waters of the atmosphere, giving a soil water, or rock solution, which makes the blue grass farmer measurably independent of ordinary commercial fertilizers, so far as the phosphates and other fixed ingredients of plant food are concerned. Experiments with phosphates, plaster of paris, lime, etc., on our rich soil, show, generally, by the little effect they produce, that it already is well supplied with these essential ingredients.

The Extent of the Blue Grass Region.—Of the 40,000 square miles of area of the State of Kentucky, the Great Central, or Blue Grass Region, underlaid, mainly, by the so-called blue limestone of the Lower Silurian, or Cambrian formation, contains about 10,000 square miles, or about one-fourth of the area of the State.

Other geological formations, in the other parts of the State, have produced very fertile soils, for various crops, and, on some of them, the blue grass also flourishes; but this central portion has acquired the popular cognomen of the Blue Grass Region, by distinction.

By reference to the geological map of Kentucky, it will be seen, that this includes, in whole or in part, more than thirty counties; of which the central southern counties are more uniformly the richest. And no soils in the world exceed, in this respect, some of those of Woodford, Clark, Bourbon, Fayette, Mercer, Jessamine and parts of Mason, Scott and other counties, in this great central region of our State.

The primeval forest growth on these rich lands, as given by the late Dr. Owen, are, pignut hickory, sugar tree, hackberry, ash, walnut, mulberry, buckeye, box elder, etc., etc., and the original undergrowth was dense cane-brakes and pea-vines, with papaw, etc., etc. Prof. Shaler states: "The best soil may be known by its growth of blue ash, large black locusts and black walnuts. These are characteristic," he says, "and never to be found together, save on the best soils."

Much difference is to be observed in the various beds of the Lower Silurian formation. Some are of soft limestone with marly layers, full of the remains of the animals which inhabited the primeval ocean, under which they were slowly deposited in the course of a long period of time. These form the best soils, and contain the very rich phosphatic irregular deposits, which have been described above. In all of these softer beds, the mineral elements of plant food and animal nourishment abound, in a condition favorable for solution in the atmospheric waters, or in the acids of vegetable sap present in the rootlets of plants.

Other beds of this formation, however, are harder and less soluble in the waters of the atmosphere and the soil; like the so-called Kentucky marble, a close-grained, hard limestone, of difficult decomposition, not containing many fossils and often flinty, with very little marly partings in its bedding; or the fine granular buff magnesian limestone, which admirably resists the action of the atmospheric agencies, and hence is well suited for architectural purposes; but, like the Kentucky marble, forms rather a poor soil as compared with those above noted.

Another notable bed of rock, in this Lower Silurian region, not favorable to the production of very rich soil, is what was called by Dr. Owen, the Mudstone, or rotten sandstone layer, passing through portions of Boone, Kenton, Campbell, Gallatin, Pendleton, Bracken, Mason, Owen, Grant, Harrison, Nicholas, Scott, Fayette, Garrard and Washington Counties, and producing what is called, in some localities, "sobby beech land." The forest growth of the soil formed of these mudstone layers is principally beech, and, on the better portions, hickory, oak, tulip poplar, and, sometimes, sugar-tree, walnut and hackberry. That portion of this formation, which passes through Fayette County, is covered by a soil which would be considered quite good in any other region not so remarkable for great fertility as is the usual blue grass soil.—*Robert Peter, M. D.*

PART I.

HISTORY

OF

BOURBON, SCOTT, HARRISON & NICHOLAS COUNTIES.

CHAPTER I.

BOURBON, SCOTT AND OTHER COUNTIES—THEIR GEOLOGICAL FORMATION—THE BLUE LIMESTONE OF KENTUCKY—TIMBERS AND SOILS OF BOURBON COUNTY—CANE RIDGE LANDS—TOPOGRAPHY, ETC., OF SCOTT—SOILS AND TIMBERS OF HARRISON AND NICHOLAS.

THE preceding article gives a general sketch of the Blue Grass Region from a scientific standpoint, and will be found of peculiar interest to all dwellers in this favored section. In the pages following, our researches will be confined to the northern belt of the blue grass, comprising Bourbon, Scott, Harrison and Nicholas Counties. As Bourbon originally embraced the greater part, or this entire section, the history of all of these counties will be given together down to the date of separation of each from the parent stock, when they will be taken up separately and followed in detail, from that period to the present time. But few finer portions of country may be found; none richer in historical association than the Blue Grass Region of Kentucky, and particularly that part to which this volume is devoted. More than a century has passed away since the first white man gazed upon this fertile region; since Daniel Boone, from the mountain-summit, like Moses from Pisgah's top, viewed "the landscape o'er," then the home and hunting-ground of rival tribes of hostile savages. In that hundred years what changes have come over the scene! The thirteen Colonies that threw off the galling yoke of the haughty Briton, have expanded into a greater nation than any Cæsar ever ruled. The aboriginal tribes have been driven beyond the great Father of Waters, the wilderness of Central Kentucky has "budded, blossomed and brought forth fruit," and has become the home of a prosperous and intelligent people.

The Counties of Bourbon, Scott, Harrison and Nicholas—the Northern belt of the Blue Grass Region—embrace within their territory some of the finest lands in the State. Originally the land was covered with a rich, black, vegetable mold, the accumulation of ages, which made it a perfect hot-bed of fertility. But, after clearing up of the forests, and as the heat of the sun and the full influence of atmospheric agencies were brought to bear upon the naked earth, this gradually changed, and at the present time we find, in the blue grass lands, "a soil varying from a rich dark brown color, to a light yellowish, or reddish brown, in the upper soil, and a light brownish or reddish yellow in the subsoil." Geographically, the counties we are describing are situated a little north of the center of the State, and are watered and drained by the Licking River, and its numerous tributaries, except Scott, which is mostly drained by tributaries of the Kentucky River. Farming and stock-raising are the principal pursuits of the people outside of the cities and towns, and some of the finest stock-farms in the State are to be found in these counties. Considerable grain and hemp are cultivated, and tobacco is extensively grown in Harrison and Nicholas Counties, and in a more limited way in Bourbon and Scott.

One of the most important features of a country is its geological structure, and upon this feature depend the pursuits of its inhabitants and the genius of its civilization. Agriculture is the outgrowth of a fertile soil; mining results from mineral resources; and from navigable waters spring navies and commerce. "Every great branch of industry requires for its successful development the cultivation of kindred arts and sciences. Phases of life and modes of thought are thus induced which give to different communities and States characters as various as the diverse rocks that underlie them. In like manner, it may be shown that their moral and intellectual qualities depend on material conditions. Where the soil and subjacent rocks are profuse in the bestowal of wealth, man is indolent and effeminate; where effort is required to live, he becomes enlightened and virtuous; and when, on the sands of the desert, labor is unable to procure the necessaries and comforts of life, he lives a savage."*

A writer upon the subject says: "Geology traces the history of the earth back through successive stages of development to its rudimental condition in a state of fusion. Speculative astronomy extends it beyond this to a gaseous state, in which it and the other bodies of the solar system constituted a nebulous mass, without form and motion. When, in the process of development, motion was communicated to the chaotic matter, huge fragments were detached from its circumference, which formed the primary planets. These retaining the rotary motion of the sun, or central mass, in turn threw off other and smaller fragments, thus forming the secondary planets, as in the case of the moon, which attends the earth. All these bodies are similar in form, have a similar motion on their axis, move substantially in a common plane and in the same direction—the result of the projectile force which detached them from the parent mass. These facts are strong evidence that the sun and the planetary system that revolves around it were originally a common mass, and became separated in a gaseous state, as the want of cohesion among the particles would then favor the dissevering force. From the loss of heat, they next passed into a fluid, or plastic state—the point in the history of the earth where it comes within the range of geological investigation. While in this condition, it became flattened at the poles, a form due to its diurnal rotation and the mobility of its particles. At a further reduction of temperature, its melted disc was transformed into a crust of igneous rock. A great many facts render it almost certain that the vast nucleus within this enveloping crust is still an incandescent mass. Compared with its enormous bulk, the external covering is of only filmy thickness, the ratio of the two being as the pulp and peel of an orange. In this world-crucible are held in solution the sixty-one elementary substances, which, variously combining, produce the great variety of forms, energies and modes of being, which diversify and enliven terrestrial nature. From the same source the precious metals have been forced into the superincumbered rocks, whither the miner descends and brings them to the surface. Volcanoes are outlets for the tremendous forces generated in these deep-seated fires. As an evidence of their eruptive power, Vesuvius sometimes throws jets of lava, resembling columns of flame, 10,000 feet in height. The amount of lava ejected at a single eruption from one of the volcanoes of Iceland has been estimated at 40,000,000,000 tons, a quantity sufficient to cover a large city with a mountain as high as the tallest Alps. By the process of congelation, which has never ceased, the rocky crust which rests on this internal sea of fire is now supposed to be from thirty to forty miles in thickness. The outer or upper portion of it was the most universal geological formation, and constituted the floors of the primitive oceans. The rocks composing it are designated unstratified, because they occur in irregular masses, and igneous from having originally been melted by intense heat. The vast cycle of time extending through their formation and reaching down to the introduction of life on the globe constitutes the *Azoic age*. The earth's surface, consisting of arid wastes and boiling waters, and its atmosphere reeking with poisonous gases, were wholly incompatible with the existence of plants and animals. By the continued radiation of heat, the nucleus within the hardened crust contracted, and the latter, to adapt itself to the diminished bulk, folded into huge corrugations, forming the primitive mountain chains and the first land that appeared above the face of the waters. The upheaval of these vast plications was attended with depressions in other parts of the surface, constituting the valleys and basins of of the original rivers and oceans. Through the agency of water, the uplifted masses were disintegrated, and the resulting sediment swept into the extended depressions. Here it settled into parallel layers, and constitutes the stratified rocks. In some localities, these are entirely wanting; in others, many miles in depth, while their average thickness is supposed to be from six to eight miles. The plain, separating the stratified from the unstratified rocks, runs parallel with the oldest part of the earth's crust. When solidification commenced, it was the surface, and, as induration advanced toward the center, the crust thickened by increments on the inside, and therefore the most recently formed igneous rocks are the farthest below the surface. Stratification commenced at the same plane, and extended in an upper direction, and hence the most recent deposits are nearest the surface, when not displaced by disturbing causes. In the silent depths of the stratified rocks are the former creations of plants and animals, which lived and died during the slow, dragging centuries of their formation. These fossil remains are fragments of history, which enables the geologist to extend his researches far back into the realms of the past, and not only determine their former modes of life, but study the cotemporaneous

* Davidson.

history of their rocky beds, and group them into systems. The fossiliferous rocks are not only of great thickness, but frequently their entire structure is an aggregation of cemented shells, so numerous that millions of them occur in a single cubic foot. Such has been the profusion of life that the great limestone formations of the globe consist mostly of animal remains, cemented by the infusion of mineral matter. A large part of the soil spread over the earth's surface has been elaborated in animal organisms. First, as nourishment, it enters the structure of plants and forms vegetable tissue. Passing thence as food into the animal, it becomes endowed with life, and when death occurs it returns to the soil, and imparts to it additional elements of fertility."

Of all the geological formations, the blue limestone is the most important to this section of the country, as being the basis of the famous blue grass lands. It has been pretty well demonstrated, that where the blue limestone exists, there the genuine blue grass will flourish, and where the former is lacking, the latter is, to a great degree, devoid of the strongly nourishing qualities it possesses when growing upon a blue limestone soil. Of the blue limestone, Dr. Peter, whose sketch of the Blue Grass Region forms the introduction to this volume, says: "This formation (the blue limestone) has usually been considered equivalent to the Lower Silurian strata of Murchison. In this region it is almost entirely calcareous, being generally composed of thin beds of dark blue-gray fossiliferous limestone, alternating with thin layers of marly shale or clay; or, in its lower members, such as are exhibited on the Kentucky River, at Frankfort, and at several other places on the river above, for many miles, appearing in more massive, thick layers of buff granular magnesian limestone—an excellent building-stone, which was used in the construction of the Clay Monument at Lexington—and the light, bluish-gray or yellowish, brittle and sparry layers, which has been called Kentucky marble, and polished for ornamental and useful purposes. Attempts have been made to compare the rocks of this formation with those of New York and Pennsylvania; but, as in regard to all the Western strata, the much greater prevalence of calcareous matter in the rocks of the west and south, as compared with those of the north and east, renders this task somewhat difficult. It is believed, however, that what has been called, in Ohio and Kentucky, the blue limestone formation, commences above, with the equivalents of the Hudson River groups and the Utica slate, of the New York geologists, and continues downward, in its equivalency, including their Trenton, Black River, Bird's-eye, and Chazy limestones, to the equivalent of their calciferous sandstone, which is probably our buff magnesian limestone above mentioned. The so-called Kentucky marble bears a close resemblance to the New York Bird's-eye limestone.

"This formation is one of great importance in Kentucky, being the basis of our far-famed blue grass lands. 'The whole of the slightly curved undulating triangular area, having its base on the Ohio River, between Garrett's Landing in Trimble County, and the eastern limits of Mason County, with its apex curving a little west of south, to the Turkey Neck Bend of the Cumberland River, embracing the axis of the great blue limestone in Kentucky.' The main surface exposure of this formation, however, is better described by Dr. Owen in the Kentucky Geological Survey, as existing in a great curved triangular area, the southern apex of which terminates in Lincoln County, and from which only a narrow strip, or axis, occasionally to be observed in the deep cuts of the valleys, can be traced through Casey, Russell and Cumberland Counties, to the Cumberland River, in Monroe County.

"From the present appearance of this elevated table-land of Central Kentucky and Ohio, underlaid by the blue limestone formation, it seems that in former geological ages, the solid crust of the earth was elevated in this region as though by the operation of an internal force, so that the various super-imposed strata was raised into a mountain, the top of which, as calculated by the celebrated Sir Ch. Lyell, was about three thousand five hundred feet above the level of the ocean; and that subsequently, denuding agencies have worn away the summit of this mountain down to its present height of about fourteen hundred feet above the sea level at Cincinnati, leaving the lowest formation—the blue limestone—in the highest central area of the present table-land, and all other super-imposed strata with the upper exposed edges regularly disposed around it—just as would appear the several coats of an onion, if a wooden peg was pushed from the center to cause an exterior protrusion, and then the summit of the elevation was cut off with a knife. In Kentucky, however, a break, or seperate axis of elevation, runs down southward as described above, from the apex of the curved triangular area of the blue limestone in Lincoln County, through Casey, Russell and Cumberland Counties, to Monroe County, and into Tennessee."

Of Bourbon County we copy the following from the State Geological Survey: "Bourbon County contains as fine a body of genuine blue grass lands as can be found in the State, lying, for the most part, level or gently undulating, except the Flat Rock region adjoining Bath, which is more broken. It is all based on the blue limestone formation. In the western part of the county the prevalent beds are thin blue and gray *Leptæna* and *Chætetes* layers underlaid by the *testudinaria* beds, and overlaid by strata containing a small variety of *A. capax* and *Leptæna filitexta* (?).

"The northwest part of the county land supports a growth of blue and black ash, honey-locust, walnut, sugar-tree, wild cherry, buckeye and box-elder; undergrowth, hawthorn, young elm, mulberry, hackberry, besides young trees of many of the species previously cited. In Cane Ridge, burr oak grows very large.

"The superiority of this soil is clearly shown by the analysis of Dr. Peter's No. 568. It excels even the fine Woodford soil in the amount of phosphoric acid. The sub-soil, shell-earth, and under-clay, Nos. 570 and 571, contain the most extraordinary percentage of that substance, and the shell under-earth, No. 571, is, besides, richer in potash than any soil, sub-soil or under-clay that has yet been analyzed. This shell-earth is full of fragments, the even tolerably perfect specimens of *A. capax* and *O. testudinaria;* and the nearest underlying rock is charged with the same fossil shells, weathering rough, with some cherty segregations, under which is a smoother and thinner-bedded bluish-gray limestone rusty surfaces, of which about five feet are exposed in the quarries where rocks are obtained for the stone fences.

"The soil derived from these upper shell beds is a remarkably fine, loose, mellow, calcareous loam peculiarly adapted for blue grass. It is not quite so light a soil as the best hemp soil of Woodford, but yields crops of hemp but little inferior to those of that county. It is found so well adapted for grasses that the farms here are almost exclusively grazing farms raising only what little grain is necessary to feed stock occasionally in winter.

"The other variety of Bourbon soil collected for analysis is from 'Cane Ridge,' the sample being taken from William Buckner's farm, among the huge burr-oak timber which forms a marked feature in the growth of timber of this part of the county, associated with sugar-tree, honey-locust, buckeye and box-elder. The under-clay has much decomposing gravel, iron ore disseminated; the underlying rocks belong to the upper series of the blue limestone formation of Kentucky, characterized by *Favosites maxima, O. lynx, O. occidentalis, Leptæna* alternata, the branching *Chætetes;* the latter are abundant in the beds immediately underlying the Buckner farm, along with the O. occidentalis. The soil is very deep, with here and there large blocks of reddish gray limestone, lying half-buried in the soil, and nearly concealed by the luxuriant sod and tall growth of blue-grass, singularly congenial to this soil. Nos. 574, 575, 576 and 577, of Dr. Peter's report, exhibit the composition of this variety of Bourbon soil. By consulting these it will be seen that the soil is nearly equal in the amount of phosphoric acid to the variety just cited, but the sub-soil and under-clay, though still rich in that acid, fall short of the amount found in the sub-soils and under shell-earth of the Cooper's Creek lands, and the amount is less, instead of greater, than in the surface soil.

"Four varieties of limestone, underlying the Cooper's Creek and Cane Ridge lands, have received a chemical examination, and the result will be found in Dr. Peter's report under the head of Nos. 572, 573, 578 and 579. The first two contain the largest amount of the mineral food of plants, and *A. capax* bed No. 572 being, on the whole, the most valuable for agriculture; though No. 573 contains the largest amount of sulphuric acid. They all, however, bespeak the fertility of the derivative soil."

Of these examinations, No. 572 is from Capt. William P. Hume's farm, Bourbon County. A crystalline, coarse, granular, light-gray limestone, containing many shells, corals; very much eroded and cellular on the exterior, when it is of a brown color. Composition, dried at 212° Fahr.:

Carbonate of lime	81.340–45.645 of lime.
Carbonate of magnesia	.979
Alumina and oxides of iron and manganese	.640
Phosphoric acid	.221
Sulphuric acid	.324
Potash	.104
Soda	.177
Sand and insoluble silicates	16.646
	100.431

No. 573 is from the same farm, is "shell limestone near the surface." A gray limestone full of fossils, shells and composition, dried at 212° F.:

Carbonate of lime	94.680–53.13 of lime.
Carbonate of magnesia	.980
Alumina and oxide of iron and manganese	1.120
Phosphoric acid	.196
Sulphuric acid	.592
Potash	.166
Soda	.233
Insoluble silicates	1.086
Loss	.947
	100.000

No. 578, is from the Cane Ridge lands, and taken from William Buckner's land, in Bourbon County. A limestone principally made up of pure large crystalline grains; composition, dried at 212° F.:

Carbonate of lime	97.540–53.735 per cent of lime.
Carbonate of magnesia	.699
Alumina and oxides of iron and manganese.	.287
Phosphoric acid	.093
Sulphuric acid	.180
Potash	.065
Soda	.206
Insoluble silicates	1.446
	100.516

"In the early settlement of the country," says the Geological Survey, "an abundant, general, large, undergrowth

Henry Clay Sr.

of cane gave name to the cane ridge of land, which is about a mile wide, lying between the waters of Stoner and Hinkston.

"The farms of Bourbon are generally laid down in blue-grass, affording pasture for large herds of celebrated stock—the staple commodity of the county.

"On the divide between the waters of the Licking and Kentucky Rivers, there is a narrow strip of sobby, beech land, like that extending through the adjacent part of Fayette, and ranging nearly north and south.

"Near the toll-gate, on the Flat Rock Turnpike, the *A. capax* beds appear in perfection, and in the surface rock in the high grounds, some seventy to eighty feet above the market house in Paris, and one hundred and fifty to one hundred and sixty feet above the forks of Houston and the Stoner Branch of the Licking Rivers, some distance below the *capax* beds are some earthy marlites resembling the graptolite beds in the hills about Cincinnati, near the water works; but none of these fossils were discovered, as yet, in this rock, only a cast of bi-valve (modiola ?). The rocks are here dipping to the east from a half to one degree."

Of Scott County, the State Survey says: "The soil in the neighborhood of Georgetown, in Scott County, is derived from a gray sub-crystalline member of the blue limestone formation weathering reddish grey, and containing *Atrypa capax* and *modesta*. The surface of the county is level and the farms in a high state of cultivation; this character of soil and country extends for about four miles north of Georgetown, when the country becomes more broken, the hills assuming a peculiar rounded contour.

"The growth three-quarters of a mile north of Georgetown, is sugar-tree, thick and shellbark hickory, black locust, wild cherry and oak, and little or no poplar. This is on the second bottom of Elkhorn Creek. Four miles north, where the surface becomes more broken and hilly, the principal timber is beech, white oak, small and large hickory; the rocks are more shaly, and the intervening layers more argillaceous.

"Fourteen miles north of Georgetown, the silicious mudstone appears, and gives more or less character to the country north, even as far as the Ohio River, as heretofore described in remarks on Owen, Grant, Gallatin and Boone Counties.

"The rocks on the North Elkhorn, in the western part of this county, are the *Orthis testudinaria* and *Chætetes lycoperdon* beds of the blue limestone, such as occur in the Frankfort section from one hundred to one hundred and forty feet above the Kentucky River. East of Georgetown, gray and blue *Leptæna* layers of the blue limestone prevail; one which is semi-crystalline, is almost entirely composed of such shells. The beds are generally from two to six or eight inches thick. The higher beds contain *A. capax* and small varieties of *Chætetes lycoperdon*. The prevalent *Leptæna* appears to be *L. filitexta*.

"The geological and consequent agricultural character of the southern part of Scott County, partake of that of adjacent portions of Woodford, Franklin and Bourbon Counties; while the northern part is more broken, and the soil is derived more, or in part, from the silicious mudstones. Both varieties have been collected for chemical analysis."

We give two of these as follows: No. 748—From a woodland pasture; James F. Robinson's farm near Georgetown, on the Elkhorn Creek. The primitive forest growth sugar-tree, white oak, black walnut, wild cherry and black locust. Dried at 212° Fahr.—with the following comp.:

	Grains.
Organic and volatile matters	1.540
Alumina, oxides of iron and manganese	.494
Carbonate of lime	3.663
Magnesia	.101
Sulphuric acid	.045
Potash	.071
Soda	.113
Silica	.087
	6.114

No. 749 is the same soil, but taken from an old adjoining field forty-five years or more in cultivation. Dried at 212° Fahr.—following comp.:

	Grains.
Organic and volatile matters	1.470
Alumina, oxides of iron and manganese	.253
Carbonate of lime	4.497
Magnesia	.076
Sulphuric acid	.045
Potash	.058
Soda	.049
Silica	.130
	6.578

"The blue limestone formation of Harrison County seems to be traversed by veins containing some sulphuret of lead, accompanied with sulphate of barytes, as near the Kentucky River on the southern confines of Woodford County. The soil of the southwestern part of Harrison County is a dark crumbling soil, based on a mulatto subsoil derived from rough weathering sub-crystalline, close-grained, light gray limestone, containing *Leptæna Cincinnatiensis*, under which are limestones containing fragments of *Asaphus* (*Isotelus*) *gigus* in large quantities, and *Pleurolomaria* (*Turbo?*) bilex of Cour. This description of soil commences four miles north of Cynthiana, and extends to the southern and western limits of Harrison County, at an elevation of about one hundred feet above the South Fork of the Licking River. Very little of the silicious mudstone was observed in Harrison County."

The following analysis is of soil from Mr. James Miller's farm, three miles south of Cynthiana—woods pasture; forest growth, large black walnut, sugar-tree, white oak, blue ash and poplar. Dried at 212° Fahr., and had the following composition:

	Grains.
Organic and volatile matters	1.217
Alumina, oxides of iron and manganese, etc.	.563
Carbonate of lime	2.580
Magnesia	.072
Sulphuric acid	.062
Potash	.185
Soda	.070
Silica	.098
	4.847

"On the western edge of Nicholas County, on the slopes of the Hinkston waters, the country is rather broken. but the soil of the upland over the red under-clay, with gravel iron ore, must be productive under an efficient system of farming. The upper part of the formation on the Hinkston hills is an ash gray, earthy—a kind of marlite. These strata alternate with dark gray, blue sericea and ceralline beds of limestone, the whole resting about two-thirds of the way down the slope on an orthoceras bed of limestone. The derivative soil in dry weather has the peculiar crisp grain indicative of the rich retentive calcareous clay, but it is stiff and muddy in wet weather. In some of the slopes near Carlisle, the beds of silicious mudstone crop out, especially on the west and southwest slopes.

"There is little or no beech timber up the Hinkston, but this kind of lumber is abundant on the east side of the Maysville Turnpike, and on Beaver Creek and east of the line adjoining Harrison County, near Headquarters. The water that runs off from the slopes of the ridges about seventy feet above the valleys, over the outcrop of the silicious mudstone, where this description of rock has been laid bare by the washing of the hill sides, is highly charged with magnesia, much of which is probably in the state of chloride, as re-agents indicate a large proportion of both ingredients. This water is also milky from suspended particles of either extremely fine silex or clay. There are many facts which go to show that this description of water acts injuriously both on man and stock, if habitually used, as explained elsewhere."

Further facts of a geological character will be given in other chapters of this work upon the separate counties, whose history is given herewith.—*W. H. Perrin.*

CHAPTER II.

THE MOUND-BUILDERS AND THE PRE-HISTORIC TIMES—EARLIEST INHABITANTS OF THE COUNTRY—THEIR MONUMENTS AND FORTIFICATIONS—RELICS IN THE NORTH BELT OF THE BLUE GRASS REGION—THE INDIANS—THEIR OCCUPATION OF THE DARK AND BLOODY GROUND.

"——back in the by-gone times
Lost 'mid the rubbish of forgotten things."

ACCORDING to the researches of archæologists, a race of people inhabited this country long prior to its occupancy by the Indians whom Columbus found in possession of it at the time of his discovery. But of this people, little is known beyond conjecture; concerning their existence, authentic history is silent. Aside from the rearing of the mounds and earthworks, which extend from the Lake Superior region to New Mexico, and thence into South America, no records exist of their progress and achievements. The antiquarian finds in their works no inscriptions which can unfold the mysteries of by-gone centuries. He finds only moldering skeletons, the scattered remnants of vessels of earthenware, rude weapons of war, axes made of stone, and other implements equally rude. A thousand interesting queries naturally arise respecting these nations that now repose under the ground, but the most searching investigation can only give us vague speculations in answer. If we knock at their tombs, no spirit comes back with a response, and only a sepulchral echo of forgetfulness and death reminds us how vain is the attempt to unlock the mysterious past upon which oblivion has fixed its seal. Who were these people; whence did they come, and whither did they go? We know not. Generation after generation lived, moved, and are no more. Time has strewn the track of its ruthless march with the fragments of their mighty works, but not even their names (other than Mound-Builders) have an existence in the speculations of those who come after them.

Some writers upon the pre-historic races of America have discovered evidences convincing to themselves, that the Mound-Builders came from Asia, and that their advent was made at different times from different portions of that division of the globe. But at what period or periods they came to this continent is but speculation. From the comparatively rude state of the arts among them, it is universally believed that the time was very remote. What finally became of them is another of the vexing questions that have been extensively discussed, with but little satisfactory results. The fact that their works extend into Mexico and Peru, has induced the belief that it was their posterity that dwelt in these countries when they were first visited by the Spaniards. The Mexican and Peruvian works, with the exception of their magnitude, are similar. Relics common to all of them have been occasionally found, and it is believed that the religious uses which they subserved were the same. There is little doubt that these people were idolators, and writers upon the subject have conjectured that the sun was an object of adoration. The mounds were generally built in a situation affording a view of the rising sun. When inclosed with walls, their gateways were toward the east. The caves in which they were occasionally found buried opened in the same direction. Whenever a mound was partially inclosed by a semi-circular pavement, it was on the east side, and when bodies were buried in graves, as was frequently the case, they lay east and west; and finally, medals have been found in a number of mounds opened in different parts of the United States, upon which was represented the sun and his rays of light. All these evidences go far toward proving the Mound-Builders sun-worshipers. Nothing, however, definite or conclusive, will ever satisfactorily penetrate the obscurity that has settled over this "peculiar people," and their religious and social customs, until the last trump awakes the sleeping nations, and not only the sea, but these mysterious mounds, give up their dead.

The works of the Mound-Builders constitute the most interesting class of antiquities found within the limits of the United States. They consist of the remains of what were apparently villages, altars, temples, idols, cemeteries, monuments, camps, fortifications and pleasure grounds. The farthest relic of this strange people discovered in a northeastern direction was near Black River, on the south side of Lake Ontario. From this point they extend in a southwestern direction by way of the Ohio, the Mississippi, Mexican Gulf, Texas, New Mexico and Yucatan, into South America. Commencing in Cattaraugus County, N. Y., there was a chain of these forts and earthworks, extending more than fifty miles southwesterly, and not more than four or five miles apart, evidently built by a people rude in the arts and few in numbers. "One of the most august monuments of remote antiquity to be found in the whole country, may still be seen in West Virginia, near the junction of Grave Creek and the Ohio River. According to actual measurement, it has an altitude of ninety feet, a diameter at the base of one hundred feet, at the summit of forty-five feet, while a partial examination has disclosed within it the existence of many thousands of human skeletons."* In the State of Ohio, where these ancient works and mounds have been surveyed and carefully examined, are found some of the most extensive and interesting that occur in the United States. At the mouth of the Muskingum, among a number of curious works, was a rectangular fort containing forty acres, encircled by a wall of earth ten feet high, and perforated with openings resembling gateways. In the mound near the fort were found the remains of a sword, which appeared to have been buried with its owner. Near the side of the body was a plate of silver, which had perhaps been the upper part of a copper scabbard, portions of which were filled with iron rust, doubtless the remains of a sword.

The Cahokia mound of Missouri, though scarcely so high, is larger at the base than that of West Virginia, mentioned above. It covers twelve acres, and has an altitude of about eighty feet. No thorough exploration of it has been made. The plow has reduced its terraces somewhat and the rain has gullied its sides, but the evidence seems conclusive that it was originally composed of four platforms, rising one from the other as they approach the highest, which formed the center. It is not improbable that it was the site of a camp, and that the platforms were designed to protect the lodges from the attacks of enemies. A work, known as the "Bourneville Inclosure," in Ross County, Ohio, is thus described by Messrs. Squier and Davis, two eminent archæologists: "This work occupies the summit of a lofty, detached hill, twelve miles westward from the city of Chillicothe, near the village of Bourneville. The hill is not far from four hundred feet in perpendicular height, and is remarkable, even among the steep hills of the West, for the general abruptness of its sides, which, at some points, are absolutely inaccessible, * * * * The defenses consist of a wall of stone, which is carried round the hill a little below the brow; but at some places it rises, so as to cut off the narrow spurs, and extends across the neck that connects the hill with the range beyond." Nothing, however, like a true wall exists there now, as we learn from local authority, but the present appearance is rather what might have been "expected from the falling outward of a wall of stones, placed, as this was, upon the declivity of a hill." The area inclosed by this wall was 140 acres, and the wall itself was two miles and a quarter in length. Trees of the largest size now grow upon these ruins. On a similar work in Highland County, Ohio, Messrs. Squier and Davis found a large chestnut tree, which they supposed to be 600 years old. "If," they say, "to this we add the probable period intervening from the time of the building of this work to its

*Pre-Historic Times.

abandonment, and the subsequent period up to its invasion by the forest, we are led irresistibly to the conclusion that it has an antiquity of at least one thousand years. But when we notice, all around us, the crumbling trunks of trees, half hidden in the accumulating soil, we are induced to fix on an antiquity still more remote." Mr. Knapp, agent of the Minnesota Mining Company, some years ago, counted 395 annular rings on a hemlock tree which grew on one of the mounds of earth thrown out of an ancient copper mine, occupied at some remote period by this race of people. Mr. Foster, a writer upon the subject, notes the great size and age of a pine stump, which must have grown, flourished and died since the works were deserted; and Col. Whittlesey, of the Ohio Geological Survey, not only refers to living trees, now flourishing in the gathered soil of the abandoned trenches, upward of three hundred years old, but says: "On the same spot, there are the decayed trunks of a preceding generation or generations of trees that have arrived at maturity and fallen down from old age."

The antiquities of the Mound-Builders and the relics they have left behind them are considered in two great divisions, viz.: Implements (including ornaments) and Earthworks. The earthworks have again been divided, by American archæologists, into seven classes: 1, Defensive inclosures; 2, sacred and miscellaneous inclosures; 3, sepulchral mounds; 4, sacrificial mounds; 5, temple mounds; 6, "animal" mounds; and 7, miscellaneous mounds. The defensive inclosures, as already shown, were upon the tops of hills and elevations, where they were more easy of defense. The sacred inclosures are generally found on "the broad and level river bottoms, seldom occurring upon the table-lands, or where the surface of the ground is undulating or broken."* The sepulchral mounds are almost innumerable in the United States, and are literally numbered by thousands and tens of thousands. They vary from six to eight feet in height, generally stand outside the inclosures, and are mostly round, though sometimes elliptical or pear-shaped. The sacrificial mounds are peculiar to the New World. Says Dr. Wilson: "This remarkable class of mounds has been very carefully explored, and their most noticeable characteristics are their almost invariable occurrence within inclosures; their regular construction in uniform layers of gravel, earth and sand, and their covering a symmetrical altar of burnt clay or stone." The temple mounds are pyramidal structures, truncated, and generally having graded avenues to their tops. In some instances they are terraced, or have successive stages. The animal mounds are principally, though not wholly, confined to Wisconsin. In that State are thousands of this class, in shape representing men, beasts, birds and reptiles, all wrought with persevering labor upon the surface of the soil. The miscellaneous mounds are found in many localities throughout North America. Of the temple mounds of this State, Collins, in his history of Kentucky, says: "The temple, or terraced, mounds are said to be more numerous in Kentucky than in the States north of the Ohio River—a circumstance which implies an early origin and application of the familiar phrase, '*sacred soil.*' The striking resemblance which these temple mounds bear to the *teocallis* of Mexico has suggested the purposes to which they were devoted, and the name by which they are known. Some remarkable works of this class have been found in the counties of Adair, Trigg, Montgomery, Hickman, McCracken, Whitley, Christian, Woodford, Greenup and Mason. The temple mound near Lovedale, in Woodford County, is a very interesting specimen of this class—an octagonal work, with graded ascents at each of the northern angles; and there is a work of curious design near Washington, in the county of Mason, which, though differing in form from the preceding, is obviously a specimen of the *teocalli* class. There is also a temple mound in Greenup County, which has excited a good deal of interest. It forms part of a connected series of works, communicating by means of parallel embankments, and embracing the chief structural elements peculiar to this class of works. On a commanding river terrace stands one of the group of this series—an exact rectangle, 800 feet square, with gateway, bastion, ditch and hollow-way, with outworks consisting of parallel walls leading to the northeast and to the southwest, from opposite sides of the rectangular inclosure. The work has many of the salient features of an extensive fortification, and appears to have been designed for purposes of military defense; and yet there is nothing to forbid the supposition that its sloping areas were also devoted to the imposing rites of a ceremonial worship."

The relics of this lost race are, as Mr. Collins says, numerous in Kentucky, and the central portion of the State contains a number of very interesting works. Some of these have been explored by scientific men. Prof. Rafinesque, an eminent archæologist, and at one time Professor of Natural History in Transylvania University at Lexington; a man whose opinions on the remains in the Mississippi Valley are often quoted by historians, and are much respected, visited and surveyed some of the ancient works in Fayette County in 1820. A map and plate drawn by him of the remains near Lexington, is to be seen now in the Smithsonian Institute. In an article in the *Western Review*, he says: "I have visited, with a friend, the ancient monument or fortification situated about two and a half miles from Lexington in an easterly direction, and above the head of Hickman Creek, and we have ascertained

*Lubbock.

that it is formed by an irregular circumvallation of earth surrounded by an outside ditch. The shape of this mound is an irregular polygon of seven equal sides. The whole circumference measures about sixteen hundred of my steps, which I calculated at nearly a yard, or three feet each, or altogether, 4,800 feet—less than a mile. The different sides measure as follows: West side, 360 feet; southeast side, 750 feet; east-southwest side, 660 feet; east-northeast side, 1,080 feet; northeast side, 600 feet; northwest side 600 feet." Of his examination of another group of mounds in Fayette County, Prof. Rafinesque, in an article in the *Western Review*, of 1820, says: "I visited this group of mounds a few days ago, in company with two gentlemen from Lexington. They are situated about six miles from this town, in a north-northeast direction, on the west and back part of Col. Russell's farm, which lies on the road leading from Lexington to Cynthiana. The ground on which they stand is a beautiful level spot, covered with young trees and short grass, or fine turf on the south side of a bend of North Elkhorn Creek, nearly opposite of Opossum Run, and close by Hamilton's farm and spring, which lie west of them. They extend as far as Russell's Cave, on the east side of the Cynthiana road.

"No. 1, which stands nearly in the center, is a circular inclosure 600 feet in circumference, formed of four parts. No. 2 lies northeast of No. 1, at about two hundred and fifty feet distance, and is a circular, convex mound 175 feet in circumference, nearly four feet high, surrounded by a small outward ditch. No. 3 lies nearly north of No. 1, and at about two hundred and fifty feet distance from No. 2. It is a singular and complicated monument, of an irregular square form. No. 4, are two large *sunken* mounds, connected with No. 3. No. 5 is a monument of an oblong square form, consisting of the four usual parts of a parapet, an inward ditch, a central area and a gateway. This last stands nearly opposite the gateway of No. 3, at about one hundred and twenty-five feet distance, and leads over the ditch to the central area. No. 6 is a mound without a ditch, 190 feet in circumference and five feet high. No. 7 is a stone mound on the east side of Russell's Spring, and on the brim of the gully. No. 8 is a similar stone mound, but rather smaller, lying north of No. 7, at the confluence of Russell's Spring with the North Elkhorn."

A chain of mounds extend through Bourbon County in nearly a northwest direction, and from their position to each other, were probably used for purposes of communication. From coals and ashes found upon them, just below the surface, it is supposed that beacon fires were kindled upon them as a kind of telegraphic signals. In a bend of Stoner Creek, a short distance below Paris, is a ditch still plainly visible, which was cut across the narrow neck of land, at the entrance to the bend. Two mounds are situated in this bend, one inside and the other outside the ditch. That outside has been opened and found to contain human bones. When the country was first settled, there was a causeway or ditch, extending from the ditch across the bend above mentioned a mile and a half, to a large mound, which stood on elevated ground. A fortification at the junction of the Stoner and Hinkston, six miles north of Paris, is now nearly obliterated, owing to the fact that it is on low ground subject to overflow. A similar fortification is situated three miles from this, on Hinkston Creek, which has two mounds in connection with it—one inside and one outside the fortification, somewhat like that described on the Stoner.

A very interesting mound is located in Harrison County, and is one of the largest in the State. It is near the little village of Claysville, and covers nearly half an acre of ground, being about one hundred feet in diameter at the base east and west, seventy-five feet north and south, and about twenty-five feet high. A large sycamore tree, some four feet in diameter stands upon the summit of it, and is probably, from appearances, five hundred years old.

In Nicholas County is the remains of a burying-ground five miles south of the Upper Blue Licks, which is supposed to have been of this mysterious people, from the large size of bones unearthed. It has been pretty well demonstrated by several writers that the Mound-Builders were a race large in stature. The writer was present at the opening of a mound in Ohio, a few years ago, from which three skeletons were taken. The bones of one—the largest—were in an excellent state of preservation, and judging from the length of the thigh bone, must have belonged to a man full seven feet in height. The burying-ground above alluded to is thus described: "The elevation or mound is now but little above the level of the surrounding country, and embraces nearly an acre. It is covered with fragments of human bones, some of them of giant size. A lower jaw-bone, exhumed about 1867, with the teeth all perfect, was readily fitted over the jaw of a large man. A thigh bone, also, when laid upon the thigh of a man six feet high, projected several inches beyond the cap of the knee. Articles resembling beads have been dug from the mound; fragments of earthenware are scattered all over it." A very singular remain is near the Upper Blue Licks Springs, which consists of a space more than one hundred feet square, paved with large stones, smoothly dressed and well laid. They were brought some distance, as no stones of their size are to be found within a mile of the place. Thus, all over the country, are found these silent monuments, which

> "——like the one
> Stray fragment of a wreck, which thrown
> With the lost vessel's name, ashore,
> Tells who they were that live no more."

The Indians are supposed by many writers to be, not only the successors, but the conquerors of the Mound-Builders. The question of their origin has long interested archæologists, and is one of the most difficult they have been called on to answer. One hypothesis is that they were an original race, indigenous to the Western Hemisphere. Those who entertain this view think their peculiarities of physical structure preclude the possibility of a common parentage with the rest of mankind. Prominent among these distinctive traits is the hair, which in the red man is round, in the white man oval, and in the black man flat. In the pile of the European, the coloring matter is distributed by means of a central canal, but in that of the Indian it is incorporated in the fibrous structure. Since, therefore, these and other ethnological features are characteristic only of the aboriginal inhabitants of America, it is inferred that they are indigenous to this part of the globe.

A more common supposition, however, is that they are a derivative race, and sprang from one or more of the ancient peoples of Asia. In the absence of all authentic history, and even when tradition is wanting, any attempt to point out the particular theater of their origin must prove unsatisfactory. They are perhaps an offshoot of Shemitic parentage, and some imagine, from their tribal organization and faint coincidence of language and religion, that they were the descendants of the ancient Hebrews. Others, with as much propriety, contend that their progenitors were the ancient Hindoos, and that the Brahmin idea, which uses the sun to symbolize the Creator of the universe, has its counterpart in the sun-worship of the Indians. They also see in the Hindoo polytheism, with its thirty thousand divinities, a theology corresponding with the innumerable minor Indian deities, of which birds, quadrupeds, reptiles and fishes are made the symbols. The Persians, and other primitive oriental stocks, and even the nations of Europe, if the testimony of different antiquarians could be accepted, might claim the honor of first peopling America.

Though the exact place of origin may never be known, yet the striking coincidences of physical organization between the oriental types of mankind and the Indians, point unmistakably to some part of Asia as the place whence they emigrated. Instead of eighteen hundred years, the time of their roving in the wilds of America, as determined by Spanish interpretation of their pictographic records, the interval has perhaps been thrice that period. Their religions, superstitions and ceremonies, if of foreign origin, evidently belong to the crude theologies prevalent in the last centuries before the introduction of Mahometanism or Christianity. Scarcely three thousand years would suffice to blot out perhaps almost every trace of the language they brought with them from the Asiatic cradle of the race, and introduce the present diversity of aboriginal tongues. Like their oriental progenitors, they have lived for centuries without progress, while the Caucasian variety of the race, under the transforming power of art, science and improved systems of civil polity, have made the most rapid advancement. At the time of their departure eastward, a great current of emigration flowed westward to Europe, making it a great arena of human effort and improvement. Thence proceeding farther westward, it met, in America, the midway station in the circuit of the globe, the opposing current direct from Asia. The shock of the first contact was the beginning of the great conflict which has since been waged by the rival sons of Shem and Japheth. The first thought of the Indian, when hostilities commenced on the Atlantic border, was to retire westward. It was from beyond the Alleghanies, according to the traditions of their fathers, they had come, and in the same undefined region they located their paradise, or happy hunting-ground. To employ an aboriginal allegory, "the Indians had long discerned a dark cloud in the heavens, coming from the east, which threatened them with disaster and death. Slowly rising at first, it seemed shadow, but soon changed to substance. When it reached the summit of the Alleghanies, it assumed a darker hue; deep murmurs, as of thunder, were heard; it was impelled westward by strong wind, and shot forth forked tongues of lightning."

The movement of this cloud typified the advance of labor, science and civilization, and before it the Indian is still retreating. Step by step he has been pressed backward before the advancing tide of immigration. His council-fire paled in the growing dawn of the nineteenth century, and then went out forever on the Atlantic slope. "The anointed children of education were too powerful for the tribes of the ignorant." There is much in the character of the Indian to loathe, and much, too, to inspire us with admiration and sympathy. When stung to madness at our broken pledges and encroachments upon their hunting-grounds, they essayed to resent our oppression, we made it an excuse to wantonly murder them. Who can blame them for fighting for the graves and homes of their fathers? The pale-faces would do the same. But the strong conquered, and the weak were vanquished; the Indians were driven backward, and shrinking before a power they could not stay, they have disappeared, and their war-cry has died away in the distant west. "Slowly they climbed the distant mountains and must soon hear the roar of the last wave that will settle over them forever."

When first visited by the whites, Kentucky was the favorite hunting-ground of many different tribes of Indians, but it is not known that any of them ever resided permanently within its borders. Annually, during the hunting season, the Delawares, Wyandots, Shawnees, and other tribes from beyond the Ohio, and the Catawbas, Cherokees and Creeks, from the south country, came here to hunt the deer, elk and buffalo, which, in great numbers, roamed the forests, grazed upon the natural pastures, and frequented the salt-impregnated springs so common in this section. However, their visits were periodical, and, when the hunt ended, they returned with the trophies of the chase, to their own towns. But in the coming of the pale-faces they foresaw the destruction of these beautiful hunting-grounds, and determined to drive the white invaders hence. The fierce contests which occurred between them and the first white settlers were numerous, of long continuance, and often disastrous to the latter, ere the final expulsion of the savages from the territory, that, in these sanguinary struggles, was re-baptized the "Dark and Bloody Ground." The heroic deeds of the pioneer fathers are inscribed upon hundreds of battle-fields. Assuredly, if a community of people ever lived who were literally cradled in war, it was the early inhabitants of Central Kentucky. From the first exploration of the country by Daniel Boone up to the year 1794, they were engaged in one incessant battle with the savages. Trace the path of an Indian incursion anywhere through the great valley of the West, and it is found dyed with Kentucky's blood, and its battle-fields white with the bones of her children.

The counties of Bourbon, Scott, Harrison and Nicholas have been the scene of some of the stirring events alluded to above. The following thrilling incident occurred in Bourbon on Cooper's Run in April, 1787. A widow, of the name of Skaggs, lived in a lonely spot with her family, consisting of two grown sons, three grown daughters (one of them married and the mother of an infant), and a daughter about half grown. One night their cabin, which was a double one, was attacked by a band of Indians, four of the inmates killed, one of the girls carried off a captive, while one of the sons and the married daughter with her infant made their escape. The neighborhood was aroused, and at daylight the next morning thirty men, well armed and well mounted, under Col. Edwards, started in pursuit of the savages. A light snow had fallen, and they were enabled to follow the trail at a gallop. When the Indians found they were pursued, and likely to be overtaken, they tomahawked their captive and left her lying by their trail where she was found by the pursuers before life became extinct, but she died in a few minutes after they came up. They soon overtook the savages, when a fight commenced, but by a strategy on their part in leaving two of their number to hold the whites in check, the main body succeeded in making their escape; the two left behind were killed.

Another incident, and which is said to have been the last of its kind enacted in Bourbon County, was somewhat as follows: A party of Indians, about twenty in number, made an incursion into the neighborhood to steal horses. A squad of hunters followed them, and came up with them encamped upon the Stoner a few miles from Paris. They fired into their camp, killing one and wounding several others, when the Indians fled, but soon returned and a fight took place, which lasted until the ammunition of the whites gave out, and they were forced to retreat leaving their foes in possession of the field. But one of the whites were killed, a man named Frank Hickman, whose skeleton was afterward recognized by the initials on his knee-buckles.

McClelland's Station, which stood upon the present site of Georgetown, was the scene of several skirmishes with Indians, which is more fully given in the history of Georgetown. In the year 1778, a party of Indians stole a number of horses in Scott (rather what is now Scott) and were pursued by Capt. Herndon with a few companions, but they succeeded in escaping with their booty. Many such incidents as the above occurred not only in Scott, but in all the surrounding country. In 1788, three horses were stolen from Jacob Stucker by Indians, in which two of the savages were killed by the whites, who pursued them, and another wounded, and the horses recovered.

Ruddel's Station, which some authorities locate in Bourbon County, and others just over the line in what is now Harrison County, was captured in 1780 by a large force of Canadians and Indians, under the notorious Col. Byrd, a British officer. His force amounted to some six hundred men—white and red—with six pieces of artillery, said to be the first cannons that ever awoke the echoes of the Kentucky hills. On the 22d of June (1780), this formidable force appeared before Ruddel's, and Col. Byrd demanded its surrender to His Britanic Majesty's forces, at discretion. Capt. Ruddel complied on the condition that the prisoners be placed under charge of the English instead of the savages. But when the gates were thrown open, the Indians rushed in, seized the first white person they met, claiming them as individual prisoners. When Col. Byrd was remonstrated with by Capt. Ruddel for this disregard of the conditions of surrender, he acknowledged his inability to control his savage allies. The scenes which ensued after the capture are almost indescribable, and are unsurpassed except in savage warfare. Wives were separated from their husbands, and mothers from their young children, without hope of ever being re-united. After the prisoners were secured and the booty divided, the savages proposed to move against Martin's Station, in Bourbon County, but Col. Byrd refused, unless the prisoners should be given into his charge—the Indians to take for their share, the property, which was agreed to. Martin's Station was then captured without opposition. The savages were so elated with these successes, that they were anxious to proceed at once against Bryant's Station and Lexington, but for some inexplicable reason Col. Byrd refused, and the expedition returned north of the Ohio River. Higgins' block-house, near where Cynthiana now stands, had its incidents of thrilling interest and border warfare. On the 12th of June, 1786, it was attacked by a large party of Indians, in which several of the inmates were severely wounded. But upon the arrival of help from Hinkston and Harrison's Stations, the Indians fled, without being able to capture the station.

The most thrilling event that occurred within the four counties, however, transpired in Nicholas. It was on the sacred soil of Little Nicholas, that the famous battle of Blue Licks was fought, one of the most disastrous battles to the whites that ever took place in Kentucky. It was fought on the 19th of August, 1782, on the old State road, about half a mile from the Lower Blue Licks, between a large force of Indians under the infamous renegade, Simon Girty, on their return from Bryant's Station in Fayette County, where they had been repulsed, and a small party of whites, from that section, which had been sent in pursuit of them. The following account of it is from Collins, which he accredits to McClung's historical sketches: "Col. Daniel Boone, accompanied by his youngest son, headed a strong party from Boonesboro; Trigg brought up the force from Harrodsburg, John Todd commanded the militia around Lexington. Nearly a third of the whole number assembled were commissioned officers, who hurried from a distance to the scene of hostilities, and, for the time, took their place in the ranks. Of those under the rank of Colonel, the most conspicuous were Majs. Harlan, McBride, McGary and Levi Todd, and Capts. Bulger and Gordon. Todd and Trigg as senior Colonels took the command. A tumultuous consultation, in which every one seems to have had a voice, terminated in a unanimous resolution to pursue the enemy without delay. It was well-known that Gen. Logan had collected a strong force in Lincoln, and would join them at furthest in twenty-four hours. It was distinctly understood that the enemy was at least double, and, according to Girty's account, more than treble their own numbers. It was seen that their trail was broad, and obvious, and that even some indications of a tardiness and willingness to be pursued, had been observed by their scouts, who had been sent out to reconnoiter, and from which it might reasonably be inferred that they would halt on the way, at least march so leisurely, as to permit them to wait for the aid of Logan. Yet so keen was the ardor of officer and soldier, that all these obvious reasons were overlooked, and in the afternoon of the 18th of August, the line of march was taken up, and the pursuit urged with that precipitate courage which has so often been fatal to Kentuckians. Most of the officers and many of the privates were mounted.

"The Indians had followed the buffalo trace, and, as if to render their trail still more evident, they had chopped many of the trees on either side of the road with their hatchets. These strong indications of tardiness made some impression upon the cool and calculating mind of Boone, but it was too late to advise retreat. They encamped that night in the woods, and on the following day reached the fatal boundary of their pursuit. At the Lower Blue Licks, for the first time since the pursuit commenced, they came within view of an enemy. As the miscellaneous crowd of horse and foot reached the southern bank of Licking, they saw a number of Indians ascending the rocky ridge on the other side. They halted on the appearance of the Kentuckians, gazed at them for a few moments in silence, and then leisurely disappeared over the top of the hill. A halt immediately ensued, and a dozen or twenty officers met in front of the ranks for consultation. The wild and lonely aspect of the country around them, their distance from any point of support, with the certainty of their being in the presence of a superior enemy, seems to have inspired a seriousness bordering upon awe. All eyes were now turned upon Boone, and Col. Todd asked his opinion as to what should be done. The veteran woodsman, with his usual unmoved gravity, replied: 'That their situation was critical and delicate; that the force opposed to them was, undoubtedly, numerous and ready for battle, as might readily be seen from the leisurely retreat of the few Indians who had appeared upon the crest of the hill; that he was well acquainted with the ground in the neighborhood of the Lick, and was apprehensive an ambuscade was formed at the distance of a mile in advance, where two ravines, one upon each side of the ridge, ran in such a manner that a concealed enemy might assail them at once both in front and flank, before they were apprised of the danger. It would be proper, therefore, to do one of two things: either to await the arrival of Logan, who was now undoubtedly on his march to join them, or if it was determined to attack without

"EVERGREEN" RESIDENCE OF M.M. CLAY, PARIS, KY.

delay, that one-half of their number should march up the river, which there bends in an elliptical form, cross at the rapids and fall upon the rear of the enemy, while the other division attacked in front. At any rate, he strongly urged the necessity of reconnoitering the ground carefully before the main body crossed the river.'

"Such was the counsel of Boone, and although no measures could have been much more disastrous than that which was adopted, yet it may be doubted if anything short of an immediate retreat upon Logan, could have saved this gallant body of men from the fate which they encountered. If they divided their force, the enemy, as in Estill's case, might have overwhelmed them in detail; if they remained where they were without advancing, the enemy would certainly have attacked them, probably in the night, and with a certainty of success. They had committed a great error at first in not waiting for Logan, and nothing short of a retreat, which would have been considered disgraceful, could now repair it. Boone was heard in silence and with deep attention. Some wished to adopt the first plan; others preferred the second, and the discussion threatened to be drawn out to some length, when the boiling ardor of McGary, who could never endure the presence of an enemy without instant battle, stimulated him to act, which had nearly proved destructive to his country. He suddenly interrupted the conversation with a loud whoop, resembling the war-cry of the Indians, spurred his horse into the stream, waved his hat over his head and shouted aloud: 'Let all who are not cowards, follow me!' The words and the action together produced an electrical effect. The mounted men dashed tumultuously into the river, each striving to be foremost. The footmen were mingled with them in one rolling and irregular mass. No order was given, and none was observed. They struggled through a deep ford as well as they could, McGary still leading the van, closely followed by Majs. Harlan and McBride. With the same rapidity they ascended the ridge, which, by the trampling of buffalo foragers, had been stripped bare of all vegetation, with the exception of a few dwarfish cedars, and which was rendered still more desolate in appearance by the multitude of rocks blackened by the sun, which were spread over its surface. Upon reaching the top of the ridge, they followed the buffalo trace with the same precipitate order, Todd and Trigg in the rear, McGary, Harlan, McBride and Boone in front. No scouts were sent in advance; none explored either flank; officers and soldiers seemed alike demented by the contagious example of a single man, and all struggled forward, horse and foot, as if to outstrip each other in the advance. Suddenly the van halted. They had reached the spot mentioned by Boone, where the two ravines head on each side of the ridge. Here a body of Indians presented themselves and attacked the van. McGary's party instantly returned the fire, but under great disadvantage. They were upon a bare and open ridge, the Indians in a bushy ravine. The center and rear ignorant of the ground, hurried up to the assistance of the van, but were soon stopped by a terrible fire from the ravine which flanked them. They found themselves as if in the wings of a net, destitute of proper shelter, while the enemy were in a great measure covered from their fire. Still, however, they maintained their ground. The action became warm and bloody. The parties gradually closed, the Indians emerged from the ravines, and the fire became mutually destructive. The officers suffered dreadfully. Todd, Trigg, Harlan, McBride and young Boone were already killed.

"The Indians gradually extended their line, to turn the right of the Kentuckians, and cut off their retreat. This was quickly perceived by the weight of the fire from that quarter, and the rear instantly fell back in disorder, and attempted to rush through their only opening to the river. The motion quickly communicated itself to the van, and a hurried retreat became general. The Indians instantly sprang forward in pursuit, and falling upon them with their tomahawks, made a cruel slaughter. From the battle ground to the river, the spectacle was terrible. The horsemen severally escaped, but the foot, particularly the van, which had advanced farthest within the wings of the net, were almost totally destroyed. Col. Boone, after witnessing the death of his son and many of his dearest friends, found himself almost entirely surrounded at the very commencement of the retreat. Several hundred Indians were between him and the ford, to which the great mass of the fugitives were bending their flight, and to which the attention of the savages was principally directed. Being intimately acquainted with the ground, he, together with a few friends, dashed into the ravine which the Indians had occupied, but which most of them had now left to join in the pursuit. After sustaining one or two heavy fires, and baffling one or two small parties, who pursued him for a short distance, he crossed the river below the ford, by swimming, and entering the wood at a point where there was no pursuit, returned by a circuitous route to Bryant's Station. In the meantime, the great mass of the victors and vanquished crowded the bank of the ford. The slaughter was great in the river. The ford was crowded with horsemen and foot and Indians, all mingled together. Some were compelled to seek a passage above by swimming; some, who could not swim, were overtaken and killed at the edge of the water. A man by the name of Netherland, who had formerly been strongly suspected of cowardice, here displayed a coolness and presence of mind equally noble and unexpected. Being finely mounted, he had outstripped the great mass of fugitives, and crossed the river in safety. A dozen or twenty horsemen accompanied him, and having placed the river between them and the enemy, showed a disposition to continue their flight, without regard to the safety of their friends who were on foot, and still struggling with the current. Netherland instantly checked his horse, and, in a loud voice, called upon his companions to halt, fire upon the Indians, and save those who were still in the stream. The party instantly obeyed; and facing about, poured a close and fatal discharge of rifles upon the foremost of the pursuers. The enemy instantly fell back from the opposite bank, and gave time for the harassed and miserable footmen to cross in safety. The check, however, was but momentary. Indians were seen crossing in great numbers above and below, and the flight again became general. Most of the foot left the great buffalo trace, and plunging into the thickets, escaped to Bryant's Station. But little loss was sustained after crossing the river, although the pursuit was urged keenly for twenty miles. From the battle ground to the ford, the loss was very heavy."

Such was the fatal battle of Blue Licks, which for the small number engaged, is one of the severest recorded in Indian warfare. Like the defeat of Braddock three-quarters of a century before, the disaster was attributable to a refusal to accept good counsel and sensible advice. Had the counsel of Boone been followed, instead of the example of the hot-headed McGary, and the little army have fallen back on Logan, with this re-enforcement they would have been strong enough to have defeated the Indians instead of themselves being defeated. Of the one hundred and eighty-two whites engaged in the battle, sixty were killed, and three were taken prisoners, who after a long and dreary captivity were exchanged and liberated, and returned to their homes. When the battle was over and the pursuit ended, the Indians, fearing the whites might rally and with re-enforcements turn upon them, collected the spoils as quickly as possible, and continued their march to the Ohio River, which they crossed without further molestation from their enemies. Col. Logan arrived at the battle ground the second day after the battle, but the enemy had disappeared, and he did not deem it prudent to pursue. He performed the sad and melancholy duty of burying the dead, after which he disbanded his men and returned home.

The foregoing incidents are illustrative of the life our pioneer ancestors lived in this country. All their adventures, hair-breadth escapes and narrow risks, would form a large volume of thrilling interest. Only a few have been given, however, to embellish these pages, and show what it cost to make the blue grass section a paradise.—*Perrin.*

CHAPTER III.

SETTLEMENT OF BOURBON COUNTY BY THE WHITES—THEIR EARLY TRIALS AND HARDSHIPS—ORGANIZATION OF THE COUNTY—ITS NAME, COUNTY SEAT, PUBLIC BUILDINGS, ETC.—COUNTY OFFICERS—THE CENSUS FROM 1790 TO 1880—DIVISION INTO PRECINCTS.

FROM across the ocean, the colonists of a new and powerful people came and effected a lodgment at isolated spots on the Atlantic coast. They achieved in time their independence, but could not pay their soldiers for their long and faithful service in the war for liberty. As a partial remuneration, wild lands were donated to them in the distant territories of the "far west," of which Kentucky was then the frontier. These Revolutionary land grants brought many adventurous individuals hither, and Kentucky became at once the center of attraction. More than a century ago the whites took possession of the territory now embraced in Bourbon and the surrounding counties. The lands were wrested from the savages with little regard for hereditary titles. The Indians sought to hold their favorite hunting-grounds, and for years held in check the tide of immigration. The story of this long and sanguinary struggle is "an oft told tale." The line of settlements firmly established along the Ohio, from Pittsburgh to the Falls, began to advance, and, with every step, slowly pressed back the Indian race to extinction.

Settlements were made in Bourbon County as early as 1776, but were not permanent. Collins says in his history of Kentucky, that the first corn raised in Bourbon County was by John Cooper, near Hinkston Creek, in 1775. That he lived alone there in his cabin, and was killed by the Indians on the 7th of July, 1766; also, in the same year, Michael Stoner, Thomas Whitledge, James Kenny, and several others, "raised corn, a quarter of an acre to two acres each." Thomas Kennedy built a cabin on Kennedy's Creek, a short distance south of Paris, in 1776, but left in the fall, going back to Virginia, where he remained until 1779, when he returned, and settled permanently on the little creek which still bears his name. While upon his first visit, he assisted Michael Stoner, who owned a large body of land on what is now Stoner Creek, to clear a piece of ground and build a cabin. During the time they were thus engaged, they lived for three months without bread or salt. Stoner was a man of some prominence and wealth, and was among the very first settlers of the county.

Hon. James Garrard was among the early settlers of the county, and a man of considerable prominence. He was twice Governor of Kentucky, and held other important positions, with honor and credit to the people whom he represented. The following is inscribed upon the monument erected to his memory by the State: "This marble consecrates the spot on which repose the mortal remains of Col. James Garrard, and records a brief memorial of his virtues and his worth. He was born in the county of Stafford, in the colony of Virginia, on the 14th day of January, 1749. On attaining the age of manhood, he participated with the patriots of the day in the dangers and privations incident to the glorious and successful contest which terminated in the independence and happiness of our country. Endeared to his family, to his friends, and to society, by the practice of the social virtues of Husband, Father, Friend and Neighbor; honored by his country, by frequent calls to represent her dearest interests in her Legislative Councils; and finally by two elections, to fill the chair of the Chief Magistrate of the State, a trust of the highest confidence and deepest interest to a free community of virtuous men, professing equal rights, and governed by equal laws; a trust, which for eight successive years, he fulfilled with that energy, rigor and impartiality which, tempered with Christian spirit of God-like mercy and charity for the frailty of men, is best calculated to perpetuate the inestimable blessing of Government and the happiness of Man. An administration which received its best reward below, the approbation of an enlightened and grateful country, by whose voice, expressed by a resolution of its General Assembly, in December, 1822, THIS MONUMENT of departed worth and grateful sense of public service, was erected, and is inscribed."

Gov. Garrard died at his residence, "Mount Lebanon," near Paris, on the 19th of January, 1822, in the seventy-fourth year of his age. He was an exemplary member of the church, and a man of great practical usefulness. His death was sincerely mourned, not only by the people of the county, but by those of the State at large.

James Douglass, probably the first surveyor in this region, and who visited Central Kentucky as early as 1773, finally settled in Bourbon. He is said to have been a member of the first Grand Jury, of the first Court of Quarter Sessions held after Kentucky was admitted into the Union as a State. A colony, consisting of the Millers, McClellans, Thompsons, McClintocks and others, settled in the neighborhood of Millersburg in 1778; but, like many of the early settlers of this section, they were forced to leave on account of Indians. They returned, however, the following year, and erected a block-house where Millersburg now stands. John Martin built a cabin, which was afterward changed into a block-house, about three miles south of Paris. Ruddel's Station, of historic fame, is supposed by many to have been in what is now Ruddel's Mills Precinct, but Collins says it was situated just over in Harrison County. Houston's cabin, on the present site of Paris, was also fortified, or changed into a block-house, the better to afford protection to the scattered settlers. Thus, amid dangers and hardships, the whites obtained a foothold in what now forms Bourbon County. In the chapters devoted to the towns, villages and election precincts, additional facts and particulars will be given of the settlement of each neighborhood.

Every age and land and country have had their great men, whose names have been enshrined in poetry and song, in history and romance. Britain boasts of Alfred the Great, and France of Henry the Fourth; America sings the praises of Washington, Franklin and Jefferson, and why should not Kentucky embalm the name of Daniel Boone? The laurels that bloom around the tomb of this old pioneer should never fade from the minds of Kentuckians. Though it is not known that he ever had his abode in either of the counties treated of in this volume, yet there is not a spot of Central Kentucky but he was familiar with, and in one of the precincts of Bourbon County sleeps a brother of the old Kentucky Indian fighter. We deem it highly appropriate in this work to give a brief sketch of the man, who, without violence to the subject, might be termed the discoverer, as well as the first settler of Kentucky. He was born in Pennsylvania February 11, 1731, and was the first white man who ever made a permanent settlement within the limits of the present State of Kentucky. But little is known of his early life, or of his career prior to his emigration to Kentucky. His father removed to North Carolina when he was but a boy, and there Daniel remained until forty years of age. The glowing descriptions that reached the pine barrens of North Carolina, of the rich lands beyond the Cumberland Mountains, excited in him a desire to visit this "favored clime." In 1769, he left his home, and with five others, of whom John Findlay* was

*Findlay had been on a hunting, trapping and trading expedition to Kentucky, prior to his coming with Boone.

one, he started to explore the country of which he had heard so favorable an account. They built a cabin on the banks of Red River, to shelter them from the rigor of winter, and spent their time hunting and trapping. Boone, in company with a man named Stuart, was surprised and captured by the Indians, in December, but they effected their escape after seven days' captivity. On regaining their camp, they found it deserted. The fate of its inmates were never fully ascertained. A few days after this, they were joined by Squire Boone, a younger brother of Daniel, and a companion, who had followed them from North Carolina. In a second excursion, Boone and Stuart were again assailed by the Indians, when the latter was killed, but Boone was fortunate in making his escape. Their only remaining companion, becoming disheartened at the perils by which they were surrounded, returned home, leaving the two brothers alone in the wilderness. Their ammunition finally running short, Squire Boone was sent back to the settlements for a fresh supply, and for months Daniel was left alone to battle with the wild beasts and Indians. In July, 1770, the younger Boone returned, with ammunition, and together they continued to range the forests until the spring of 1771, when they retraced their steps to North Carolina. For nearly three years, Boone had been absent from his family, and, during that time, he had not tasted bread nor salt, nor seen the face of a white man, except those of his brother and friends who had been killed.

Boone was so well pleased with the country he had seen that he determined to sell his farm and remove, with his family, to Kentucky. Disposing of his property, he started for his El Dorado, on the 25th of September, 1773. At a place called Powell's Valley, he was joined by five other families and forty men, well armed. With this addition to his force, he proceeded on his journey with confidence. When near the Cumberland Mountains, the party was attacked by a large force of Indians, and, though the savages were defeated, it was not without a loss to the whites of six men killed and wounded. This so discouraged them that they retreated to the settlements, on Clinch River, where they remained until 1775, when Boone, in company with a few men, made another visit to Kentucky, in the service of Col. Richard Henderson, leaving his wife and family at the settlements on Clinch River. They arrived on the 25th of March, and, on the 1st of April, they commenced building a fort, which was afterward called Boonesboro. Here they were several times attacked by Indians, and lost some five or six men, killed and wounded. As soon as the fort was completed, Boone removed his family hither. "From this time, the little garrison was exposed to incessant assaults from the Indians, who appeared to be perfectly infuriated at the encroachments of the whites, and the formation of settlements in the midst of their old hunting-grounds. The lives of the emigrants were passed in a continued succession of the most appalling perils, which nothing but unfailing courage and indomitable firmness could have enabled them to encounter. They did, however, breast this awful tempest of war, and bravely and successfully, and in defiance of all probability, the small colony continued steadily to increase and flourish, until the thunder of barbarian hostilities rolled gradually away to the north, and finally died in low mutterings on the frontiers of Ohio, Indiana and Illinois."* In these exciting times, Boone stood the central figure in that band of hardy pioneers, who bore the shock of the dreadful struggle, which gave a yet more terrible significance and a still more crimson hue to the history of the old dark and bloody ground.

In July, 1776, Boone's daughter was captured by the Indians. They were pursued by Boone, with eight men, and, on the third day, were overtaken, and his daughter rescued, uninjured. During this period, they lived in constant peril and anxiety. The fort was attacked, in April, by an overwhelming force of Indians, but were finally defeated and driven off. In July, it was again attacked by 200 warriors, and again they were defeated, with loss. Boone himself was captured in January, 1778, at Blue Licks, where he had gone to make salt for the garrison. He remained a prisoner until June following, when he contrived to make his escape and returned to Boonesboro. After his escape from the Indians, the fort was attacked by a large force of savages, commanded by Canadian officers well skilled in modern warfare. But, after a siege of nine days, they gave up the matter, and retired, having sustained quite a heavy loss. From this time, he enjoyed a period of peace and quiet, until August, 1782, a time rendered memorable by the disastrous battle of Blue Licks, in which Boone participated, and in which a son was killed. He almost miraculously escaped the slaughter of this ill-fated battle. He accompanied Gen. George Rogers Clark on his expedition against the Indian towns, but of his service in this affair little is known, except that he was one of the number engaged in it.

In the treaty of peace between the United States and Great Britain, in 1783, Boone saw the standard of civilization planted in the wilderness. "He had laid out the larger part of his little property to procure land warrants, and, having raised about $20,000, on his way from Kentucky to Richmond, he was robbed of the whole, and thus left destitute of the means of procuring more. Unac-

*Collins' Kentucky.

quainted with the technicalities of the law, the few lands he was able afterward to locate, were, through his ignorance, swallowed up and lost by better claims. Dissatisfied with these impediments to the acquisition of the soil, he left Kentucky, and, in 1795, he was a wanderer on the banks of the Missouri, a voluntary subject of the king of Spain."* The remainder of his life was devoted to the society of his children. He died at the house of his son-in-law, Flanders Callaway, at Charette Village, on the Missouri River, September 26, 1820, aged eighty-nine years. The Legislature of Missouri was in session when the event occurred, and resolved that, in respect to his memory, the members would wear the usual badge of mourning for thirty days, and voted an adjournment for that day. On the 13th of September, 1845, his remains were, according to a resolution of the Kentucky Legislature, brought to Frankfort and interred in the State Cemetery, and there they repose, awaiting the final resurrection.

The early pioneers of Bourbon and the surrounding Counties were a hardy, fearless and self-reliant people; they were a quiet people, simple in their habits and accomplishments, and devoid of all reckless extravagance. Fresh from the scenes of the Revolutionary struggle—a free people—their manhood elevated, they shrank from no difficulty, but, with a stern, unflinching purpose, they went forth to subdue the wilderness and subject it to the use of man. They lived in comparative social equality, the almighty dollar did not form a Chinese wall between the rich and poor; a man was esteemed, not for his money bags, but for his actual merit. Aristocratic distinctions were left beyond the mountains, and the first society lines drawn were to separate the very bad from the general mass. No punctilious formalities marred their social gatherings, but all were happy and enjoyed themselves in seeing others happy. The rich and poor dressed alike, the men generally wearing hunting shirts and buck-skin pants, and the women attired themselves in coarse fabrics, the produce of their own fair hands. Silks, satins and fancy goods that now inflate our vanity and deplete our purses, were then unknown. The cabins were furnished in the same style of simplicity. The bedsteads were home-made, and often consisted of forked sticks driven into the ground, with cross poles to support the clap-boards or the cord. One pot, kettle and frying-pan were the only articles considered indispensable, though some included the tea-kettle. A few plates and dishes, upon a shelf in one corner, was as satisfactory as is now a cupboard full of china, and their food was as highly relished from a puncheon-slab as it is at the present day from an oiled walnut table. Some of the wealthiest families had a few splint-bottomed chairs, but, as a general thing, stools and benches answered the places of lounges and sofas, and, at first, the green-sward or smoothly-leveled earth, served the double purpose of floor and carpet. Whisky toddy was considered good enough for the finest party, the woods furnished an abundance of venison, and corn-pone supplied the place of every variety of pastry.

The credit of subduing the wilderness and transforming it into an Eden of loveliness was not the work of man alone. The women did as much, in their way, as the men themselves. They were the help-meets, as well as the companions, of the men, and bore their part, uncomplainingly, in all the hardships of border life. They assisted in planting, cultivating and harvesting the crops, as well as attending to their household duties. They were happy and contented, and, we dare to say, yearned far less for the frivolities of fashionable life than do their fair descendants. A hundred years, however, have brought with them marvelous changes, not only in the face of the country, but in the usages of society, and grand improvements have been made in our manners and customs. We have grown older, in many respects, if not wiser, and could not think of living on what our ancestors lived on. The corn-dodgers and wild meat they were glad to get would appear to us but a frugal repast, and would cause our Grecian noses to go up in lofty disdain. But this is an age of progress and improvement, and these observations are made by way of contrasting the past and present. The pioneers who bore the brunt of savage warfare, and made this country an earthly paradise, have long since passed to their final account, but their trials and hardships are remembered, and their names deserve to be "written in characters of living light upon the firmament, there to endure as radiant as if every letter was traced in shining stars."

The rich lands of Central Kentucky were settled rapidly after the close of the Revolutionary war. The influx of emigrants brought hither by the extravagant reports of the first visitors to this "land of corn and wine," and military land warrants of Revolutionary soldiers soon served to people the Licking and Elkhorn country. So rapidly did the country settle up that the fast-increasing population required increased civil rights and more perfect territorial organization.

Kentucky was, originally, a part of Fincastle County, Va. It was afterward made an individual county of the Old Dominion, and so remained for several years. But its territory was large, and its citizens remote from the seat of government, and, as soon as the number of inhabitants

*Collins.

required it, changes were made, by a division of the unwieldly county. In the month of November, 1780, by an act of the General Assembly of Virginia, the county of Kentucky was divided into three districts, which were designated, respectively, Fayette, Lincoln and Jefferson Counties. The next county formed was Nelson, in 1784, from a part of Jefferson. In the following year (1785), Bourbon was formed from the territory of Fayette, thus being the fifth county erected in what now comprises the State of Kentucky, and was created seven years before Kentucky became a member of the Federal Union. Bourbon, at the time of its formation as a county, extended north to the Ohio River, and covered a large area since divided into a number of counties. The first division of her territory occurred in 1788, when Mason was set off; in 1793, the formation of Harrison took off a large slice, and, in 1799, Bourbon and Mason contributed jointly to the formation of Nicholas. Thus liberally has Bourbon given of her territory for the creation of new counties, until the frequent drafts made have brought her down to her present area. As now bounded, Harrison lies on the north, Nicholas and Montgomery on the east, Clark on the south, and Fayette and Scott on the west. The county was named in honor of the House of Bourbon, whence had descended the monarch of France, reigning at the time of our Revolution and at the time the county was organized, and Paris, the seat of justice, received its name, doubtless, from France's gay capital.

The formation of a county, a hundred years ago, and the organization of its different departments—judicial, civil and political—is a somewhat interesting study to the readers of the present day. Rumaging through the old records at the court house, we, with the assistance of Judge Turney, unearthed the first book of the Bourbon County Court, in which is recorded the proceedings of that august body. The first entry bears the date of May 16, 1786, and is in a plain, old-fashioned hand, still perfectly legible, though the book is old, musty and stained with age. As a matter of interest and curiosity to our readers, we copy some of these early proceedings, "in the original," as we might say, no effort being made to improve the phraseology. The first record of the court proceedings is as follows:

MAY COURT, 1786.

At Colonel James Garrard's in Bourbon County Tuesday the sixteenth day of May Anno Domini one thousand seven hundred and eighty-six and in the tenth year of the Commonwealth*

A new commission of the peace dated the twelfth day of January one thousand seven hundred and eighty-six to this county directed to James Garrard* Thomas Swearingen, John Edwards, Benjamin Harrison, John Hinkson, Alvin Mountjoy, Thomas Warring, Edward Waller, and John Gregg, Gentlemen was produced and read whereupon the said James Garrard took the oath of fidelity and the oath of a justice of the peace which were administered to him by John Edwards† Named in the said Commission And then the said James Garrard Gent. administered the aforesaid oathes to Benjamin Harrison, John Hinkson Alvin Mountjoy, Thomas Warring, Edward Waller, and John Gregg, Gent. who took the same respectively.

A Majority of the Justices Commissioned being present John Edwards is appointed Clerk to the Court of this County who thereupon entered into Bond with his securities in the penalty of one thousand pounds for the execution of his office and took the oath required by Law.

Absent John Hinkson Gent.

A Commission from his excellency the Governor of this State‡ to Benjamin Harrison§ Gent. to be Sheriff of this County was produced by the said Harrison who took the oath of fidelity and the Oath of Office and together with John Edwards and John Hinkson his securities entered into Bond for the due performance thereof according to Law. Present John Hinkson Gent.

The Court being then opened by the Sheriff proceeded to business.

At a Court held for Bourbon County at the house of James Garrard Gent. on Tuesday the Sixteenth day of May one thousand seven hundred and eighty-six in the tenth year of the commonwealth.

Present James Garrard, John Hinkson, Alvin Mountjoy, Thomas Warring, Edward Waller, & John Gregg Gent.

On the motion of John Edwards Clerk of this Court John Machir is admitted as Deputy Clerk who took the oath prescribed by law.

John Allen Esquire produced a commission of his fitness to act as an Attorney at Law and had the oath prescribed by law administered to him whereupon he is admitted to practice as an Attorney at Law in this Court.

On the motion of William Bennet administration of the Estate of Josheway Bennet deceased is granted to him whereupon he took the oath required by Law and together with David Hughes his security entered into and acknowledged Bond in the penalty of two hundred pounds for his due. admin of said decedants Estate.

Ordered that John Strode, John Constant, Edward Wilson, and Van Swearingen or any three of them being first sworn before a Justice of the peace for this County appraise in Current money the slaves (if any) and personal estate of Joshua Bennet deceast and return the appraisement to the Court.

Absent James Garrard Gent.

Ord' James Garrard Gent. is by the Court recommended to his excellency the Governor as a proper person to act as Surveyor of this County.

Absent Alvin Mountjoy Gent. present James Garrard Gent.

On the motion of Benjamin Harrison, Gent. Sheriff Robert Hinkson was admitted and sworn as deputy Sheriff.

James Garrard, John Hinkson, Thomas Warring, Edward

[*The Commonwealth alluded to is that of Virginia.—ED.]

[*Afterward Governor of Kentucky.—ED.]

[†First United States Senator from Kentucky.—ED.]

[‡Virginia.—ED.]

[§For whom Harrison County was named.—ED.]

Waller and John Gregg Gent. are sworn Commissioners of Oyer and Terminer for this county.

Absent James Garrard Gent.

James Garrard Gent produced a commission from his Excellency the Governor to be surveyor of this County whereupon he took the oath required by Law and together with William Routt and John Edwards his securities entered into and acknowledged Bond in the penalty of three thousand pounds for the due performance of said office.

Present James Garrard Gent.

Ordered that Edward Waller, John Waller, Miles Conway and Henry Lee or any three of them be appointed to examine the fitness of those persons nominated by James Garrard Gent. as deputy surveyors.

Ordered that court be adjourned till to morrow morning ten o'clock. The minutes of these proceedings were signed thus—

James Garrard.

Such is a complete record of the proceedings of the first day of the first court ever held in Bourbon County. Without encumbering our pages with the proceedings in detail, we will make a few extracts by way of illustrating the past and present in court matters as well as in the general history of the county. On the second day of court, Edmund Lyne, Henry Lee, Miles Conway, Andrew Hood, John Grant, William Routt, George Reading, Sr., Abraham Bird and John Waller were recommended in a petition to the Governor "as proper persons to be added to the commission of the peace of this County." Upon the same day, "Benjamin Harrison, Sheriff of the county, protested to the court that he would not be answerable for the escape of any prisoner for want of a gaol—ordered that it be certified." Also upon the same day, Miles Conway, Edward Dobbins and Henry Lee were appointed to view "the best and most convenient way for a road from the mouth of Limestone on the top of the Hill," etc.

The second session of court was held at the house of John Kizer, beginning on the 20th of June, 1786. Among the proceedings we notice that it is "Ordered that Edmund Lyne Gent be appointed overseer of the road from the Lower blue licks to Johnson's Fork of Licking, and that the titheables residing at the Licks assist him in keeping the same in repair." It was also "Ordered that Thomas Warring Gent take in a list of the titheables north of main Licking, that John Hinkson Gent take in a list of the titheables between main Licking and Hinkson's fork, and on the water's of Stoner's fork below Cooper's Run, John Gregg Gent in the forks of Stoner and Hinkson, Alvin Mountjoy Gent on Houston's fork and Cooper's Run; and James Garrard Gent east of Houston's Fork and southeast of the main road, leading from Lexington to Limestone, and return their respective lists to the court." And the following: "The court proceeded to fix the rates of Liquors, Diet and provender as follows (to Wit): West India Rum at twenty-four shillings per gallon, Continent rum at fifteen shillings per gallon, Brandy at fifteen shillings per gallon, Whiskey at ten shillings per gallon, Wine at twenty-four shillings per gallon, for a warm Dinner one shilling and six pence. For a could dinner one shilling, Breakfast with Tea, Coffie or Chocolate one shilling and three pence, breakfast without Tea, Coffey or Chocolate one shilling, for corn per gallen six pence, Pastrage for twenty-four hours six pence, Stablage and Hay or fodder for twenty-four hours one shilling, Lodging in Clean Sheats six pence. Ordered that the Ordinary Keepers in this County take pay according to the above rates and no more."

The third session of court, commencing July 18, 1786, was held at John Kizer's; the fourth session, beginning August 15, 1786, was held at Fairfield*; the September and October terms were likewise held at Fairfield. At the November term, the place of meeting was established at the mouth of Houston, under the following order, which forms a part of the records of that session:

Ordered that the place for holding Court for this County be established at the Confluence of Stoner and Houston forks of Licking, and that Alvin Mountjoy, John Grant and James Matson, Gentlemen, be appointed to procure two acres of land at said place for the purpose aforesaid, and also that they let to the lowest bidder the building of a Court house, which shall be a frame, thirty-two by twenty feet, with a shingle roof and finished in the necessary manner, and a jail sixteen feet square, of hewn logs twelve inches square.

Teste, John Edwards, C. B. C.

The next records we fished up after this old book, were a little different in their character. The following is a specimen:

For value received I promise to pay to Mr. Hugh McClintock bearer, fifteen pounds current money of Virginia, on or before the first day of April next, as witness my hand and seal at Limestone the third day of February 1786.

Signed, Ebenezer Platt. [Seal.]

Teste, Daniel Boone.

Attached to the note is the following in Daniel Boone's own hand writing:

Sir as capt platt hath Left his store house and all other conserns on My hands in order to Rase the cash I Will oblige myself to pay the cash at the time the note seacifies or before witness my hand this 3 Day of febury 1786. Daniel Boone.

It seems the old pioneer did not "Rase the cash," at the time the note "seacifies or before," and, that it was finally sued on, judging from the following "verdict," which is recorded on the back of it:

We, the jury, do find for the plaintiff sixteen pounds and eleven pence damages. Signed,

Aquilla Standerford, Foreman of Jury.

*We can find no one who remembers anything of Fairfield.

✓ The following is another interesting specimen :

The Commonwealth of Virginia to the Sheriff of Bourbon County Greeting. You are hereby Commanded to take Thom Theobold if he be found within your Bailiwick and him safely Keep so that you have his body before the Justices of aforesaid County at the Court House thereof on the third Tuesday in November next to answer John Troutman of a Plea Trespass on the Case, Damages, two hundred pounds, and have then there this Writ. Witness,

JOHN EDWARDS, Clerk of said Court House.

7th of September, 1789. In the xv year of the Commonwealth. JOHN EDWARDS, CLK.

On the back of this ironclad document is the following indorsement:

Executed on Thos Theobold and he has not give security, because he run in a house and armed himself with a shot gun after the writ was served. GEORGE MOUNTJOY.

It seems that this service of a writ was not altogether satisfactory to the majesty of the law, as it is crossed out and the following entry made just below it :

Executed and broke Custiday. GEORGE MOUNTJOY.

An old note was also found given by Simon Kenton to John Nichols for "three pounds, thirteen shillings and eight pence," dated July 12, 1786. Upon the back of this note is the indorsement—

To dangerous to go where Kenton is.

It seems the note became due when Kenton was out among the Indians, and the valiant officer concluded it "*to* dangerous" to go after him.

The machinery of the courts and the new county was, at length, with the aid of the lubricating oil of frontier wisdom, fully put in motion, and, in a short time, the different departments were running smoothly. As we have seen, John Edwards was the first Clerk. He was a man of considerable prominence, and was afterward, upon the admission of Kentucky as a State, the first United States Senator. Benjamin Harrison was the first Sheriff, James Garrard the first surveyor, and John Allen the first attorney admitted to the bar. But without going into further details of these early proceedings and early officers, we will give the first county officers elected under the present Constitution. They are as follows : William M. Samuels, County Judge ; Richard Brown, County Clerk ; James M. Arnold, Circuit Clerk ; Joshua Irvin, Sheriff ; W. W. Alexander, County Attorney ; Joseph Porter, Jailer ; John M. Taylor, Assessor ; W. W. Fothergill, Coroner ; William Garth, Surveyor, and A. M. Brown, School Commissioner. The present officers of the county, and of the different courts are as follows ; Circuit Judge, Hon. B. F. Buckner ; Commonwealth's Attorney, Hon. C. J. Bronston ; Clerk, Joseph M. Jones ; Master Commissioner, R. H. Hanson ; Sheriff, John B. Northcott. Criminal and Chancery term second Monday in January. Regular terms, third Monday in April and October. Judge of Court of Common Pleas, C. S. French. First Monday in March and July. Judge of County Court, Hon. Matt. Turney ; County Attorney, Ben. G. Patton ; Clerk, James M. Hughes ; Sheriff, John B. Holladay ; Assessor, Claude Paxton ; Surveyor, L. B. M. Bedford ; Jailer, Joseph McCarney ; Master Commissioner, R. H. Hanson ; Circuit Clerk, Joseph M. Jones ; Treasurer, C. V. Higgins, Jr. ; School Commissioner, W. H. Sockhart. Bourbon Quarterly Court, Hon. Matt Turney, Judge ; Clerk, P. M. Miller ; Constable, J. M. Taylor.

The first court house of the county, and which we have already alluded to, by giving the original order of the court for its erection, was built according to the specifications given in that order, viz. : "a frame, thirty-two by twenty feet," etc. It stood on the "Court House Square," and after years of service was replaced by a commodious building. It was sold to John Allen, when the new one was finished, who moved it to his farm a short distance from town. It was first occupied by the court, October 16, 1787. At a term of the court held in February, 1797, an order was made for the new court house as follows :

The Commissioners appointed to draft a plan for a court house have proceeded to sketch out the present one, which they now offer for the consideration of the court, and have fixed on the center of the Public Square as the most convenient spot for the house to stand on. Given under our hands this 20th day of February, 1797. Signed, John Allen, John Metcalfe, Charles Smith and David Hickman, which is accepted by the court. And it is ordered that Charles Smith, James Duncan and Thomas Jones, gentlemen, be appointed commissioners to let out, and superintend the building of the same to the lowest bidder after the time and place has been advertised three weeks in the *Kentucky Herald*.

This building was commenced immediately and was finished and occupied during the year 1799. The stone foundation was built by Thomas Metcalfe, afterward Governor of the State, and who lived in Nicholas County, but his uncle, John Metcalfe, built the superstructure. Collins says of Gov. Metcalfe :

As a mason, he built of stone several court houses—at West Union, Adams Co., Ohio; at Greensburg, Greene Co., Ky., and others, and laid the foundation of that at Paris, Bourbon Co., which was burnt down May 8, 1872. From his trade and his great earnestness afterward as a public speaker, he received the sobriquet of the "Old Stone Hammer," by which he was familiarly and proudly known for forty-five years.

As we have said, John Metcalfe, an uncle of the Governor, built the edifice, the carpenter's work being done by a Mr. McCord. The history of Paris, published by Keller & McCann, a few years ago, says :

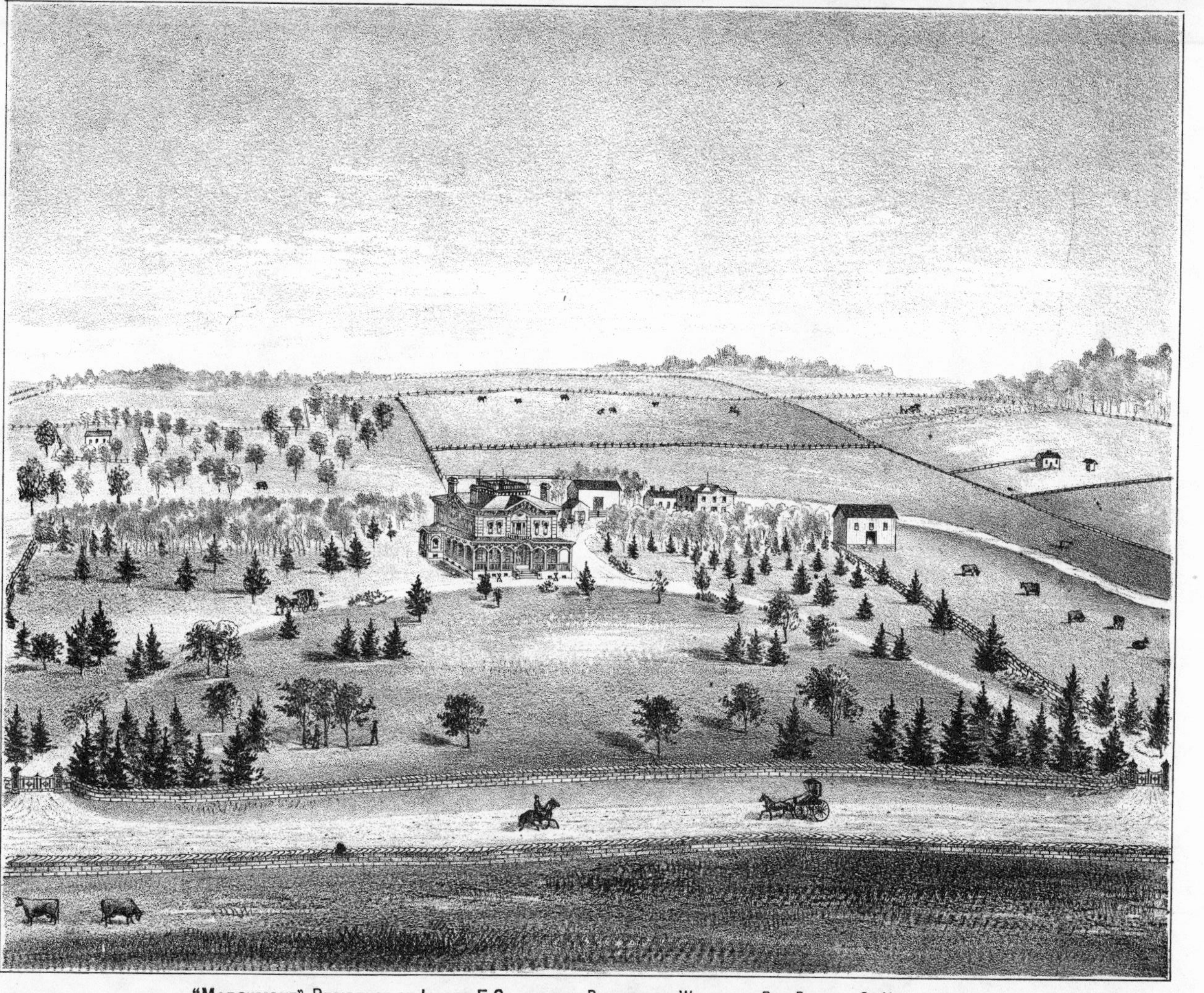

"MARCHMONT" RESIDENCE OF JAMES E. CLAY, NEAR PARIS, ON THE WINCHESTER PIKE, BOURBON CO. KY.

This house was built to rival the great stone temple of justice at Lexington. For years it was the pride and boast of the Bourbons, and, in 1816, when the little box cupola was removed and in its stead the magnificent spire that went down in its ruins in 1872 was erected, the heart of the nation was supposed to be happy. Those of our citizens whose memories carry them back to that day, inform us that the boys stood and gazed upon this imposing structure with awe, and only ceased to look and wonder when their necks seem to break with pain, and their heads swim with the floating clouds. The bell that hung in this steeple was purchased in Philadelphia by Hugh Brent, Esq., for $50. It had seen service on the high seas, and bore the date of 1730.

Memoria in æterna of this historic bell, and the destruction of the old court house by fire, we give the following paraphrase, of which the original poem, entitled the "Court House Bell," was written upon a very similar catastrophe, by Judge O. F. Pearre, of Pontiac, Ill., in 1874:

"In Philadelphia the bell was bought,
'Out West,' to Paris, the bell was brought.

* * * * *

"Placed on high in the Court House steeple,
And sold to the county—a bell for the people.

"As of yore, it did its duty well,
In its new position of 'Court House Bell.'

"It called the lawyers to wordy fray—
They came to spout and remained to *prey*.

"It startled the ear of the Court House rats,
As it summoned the Magistrative cats;

"Saying, 'walk to your council chamber please,
And examine the state of the public cheese.'

"It spoke when the political hacks came by,
To preach for truth some ancient lie.

"It rang for joy when the first glad ray
In the East proclaimed our Natal Day.

"It shrieked aloud when the fire-fiend came,
And called the people to fight the flame.

"Solemn and slow was its measured toll,
As it rang the knell of the parting soul.

"Slow and solemn its measured beat,
When funeral pall and marching feet

"Went by with the dead, and the last farewell
Was heard from the throat of the sobbing bell.

"But on May the eighth of 'seventy- (two) four,'
It rang at noon to ring no more.

"And the tones that came from the quivering bell
Were the tones of its own funeral knell.

* * * * *

"Of lurid, hungry flames that clasped
The city's heart within their grasp;

* * * * *

"With a tiger's spring and a tongue of flame,
Across the chasm the fire-fiend came.

"On the Court House roof, with fiery claws,
He sprang as the springing lion draws

"His prey to the earth, then clasped the bell
To his fiery breast, till it, tottering, fell

"To the earth below, with burning beam
And blazing rafter, till a stream

"Of molten metal came out to tell
The end of the Paris Court House bell."

The present court house, which, Phœnix-like, has arisen from the ashes of the old one, is a model of beauty and elegance. It was built in 1873–74, the first session of court being held in it in October, 1874. An act was passed by the Legislature, empowering the County Court to issue $100,000 in bonds, for the erection of the building. The bonds were issued by the court, and Joseph Mitchell, William Shaw and George C. White, appointed Commissioners to superintend the work, which was begun early in the year 1873. The supervising architect was A. C. Nash, of Cincinnati; the carpenter's work was done by Thomas Pollock; the foundation and stone work by McGrain, Woods and Farrell; the stone was furnished by Collins & Stevenson, from the Cane Ridge quarry; the brick was made by J. M. Thomas and J. H. Bradshaw, and laid by G. W. Sidener and Robert Ransdall; the freestone work was done by Finnigan & Son, of Cincinnati; the galvanized iron and slate by Dunn & Witt, and the wrought and cast iron by M. Clements, of the same city; the plastering was done by William Haye, of Paris; the plumbing was done by T. F. Donnelly, of Lexington; the painting and graining by Charles A. Daugherty, of Paris; the tiling by M. Finnigan & Son. The clock was made by E. Howard & Co., of Boston, Mass., and the bell by Meneely & Kimberly, of Troy, N. Y. The benches of the circuit court room were furnished by J. T. Hinton, the chairs by George W. Davis, and the registers and furnace by J. J. Shaw, all of Paris.

The following description from the *Western Citizen*, of October 30, 1874, is an appropriate conclusion to the sketch of this model structure: "The architecture is chaste and tasteful, surpassed by few public buildings in this country, and reflects great credit on the architect, Mr. A. C. Nash, of Cincinnati, who also ranks it as one of his most successful specimens. The style of architecture is French *renaissance*. The building is of brick, and elaborately and tastefully trimmed with freestone. The cornices are of iron; the roof covered with slate, and gracefully topped out with an elegant and symmetrical tower, one hundred and thirteen feet above the ground line, in which is placed the clock and bell. The building is three stories, and contains rooms for circuit court, county and Circuit Clerk's and Sheriff's offices ; and also offices for County Judge and County Attorney, jury rooms, etc. Also the necessary fire and burglar proof vaults for the safe keeping of all State and county papers. The ground plan is one hundred and fifteen feet from front to rear, and eighty-two feet across the wings, having a large and spacious hall from front to rear, the county offices being on each side. The hall floors are of iron, concreted and laid with the best English tiling, in neat and appropriate patterns, the base being in Egyptian marble. The hall is fifteen feet and four inches in width, and is spanned at intervals with neat, plain arches, resting upon appropriate corbels, etc. The stairways are of wrought iron, spacious, and of handsome design.

"On the second floor is situated the Circuit Court room ; its dimensions sixty-two feet by sixty-eight, with a gallery sixteen by sixty-two feet ; the ceiling being twenty-eight feet six inches above the floor, and neatly ornamented with a large ventilating center piece of stucco ; also the angles, with walls and ceiling, coved and neatly finished—the walls blocked and colored in imitation of stone work. The Judge's stand, platform and canopy are of handsome design ; gallery, front railing around the bar, the furniture, gas-fitting and heating are all in keeping with the design. The room is, without exception, the handsomest court room in the State."

The total cost of the building, including furnishing, interest on bonds, etc., is not far short of $125,000.

The first jail or county prison was erected in the winter of 1786–87. It was built of logs, hewn twelve inches square, which made a very formidable structure one hundred years ago, and which was considered a rather safe lodging for evil-doers, but at the present day it would not long hold "boy-burglars," much less our more experienced criminals. This was superseded in a few years by one built of stone, which "stood upon the corner of the square, opposite the Northern Bank building." The present jail building was erected in 1878–79, and is a substantial edifice. It is of stone, and cost about $15,000, though according to estimates the cost was not to exceed $12,660. The plans were designed by H. P. McDonald, and the building was erected by Peter Pfeiffer. It is built on the modern prison style, and fitted up with the latest and most approved "furniture," and everything necessary for the *safety* of boarders and occupants.

The county farm and poor house comes rightly under the title of public buildings, and in this connection will receive a few words. "The poor ye have with ye alway," we were told, and their care is a sacred duty of the county. To the shame of the wealthy, grand old county of Bourbon be it written, that she is lamentably careless and negligent in the care of poor. A gentleman said to us: "I would die before I would go the county's poor house ; it is a shame and disgrace to a county of the wealth this possesses to provide no better than it does for the poor." We have visited a number of such institutions in Ohio and Illinois, and have usually found them a *home* for the poor and helpless—institutions creditable alike to the counties in which they are located and the people who support them.

The Bourbon County Poor Farm consists of about one hundred and fifty acres of land near Ruddel's Mills, on Hinkston Creek. The improvements are a Superintendent's house, frame, two stories high, with an L, and five houses for paupers, which are cheap, two-room cottages. John Reynolds is Superintendent ; John Current, Commissioner of the Poor. The county gives the Superintendent the use of the land, pays him a salary, and furnishes everything to run the institution. The buildings will accommodate about fifty persons, and the care of the paupers cost about $100 apiece annually. James Ingles managed the farm for twenty-four years, and the cost of running it is said to have been much less than now, the cost now being about $5,000 a year. It is divided into two departments—white and colored, and at the present time there are eighteen whites and sixteen blacks being cared for. The colored department has accommodations for about thirty persons. This was originally a separate institution, but both whites and blacks are now under the same management. All of the inmates dependent on the county for support do no labor on the farm. The farm is in excellent repair, having a good stone fence nearly all around it. In the past there has been an average of about forty inmates per year.

Incidents of some interest occur occasionally within the unenviable precincts of the place. As, for instance, about the year 1870, a marriage took place in it, and the high contracting parties are still inmates. A man named Shields has been an inmate for fifty years. Henry Towles, who once owned several thousand acres of land in the county, and could ride for seven miles in a straight line upon his own land, died, it is said, as keeper of the poor house. Richard Samuels, now an inmate, is a son of Judge Samuels, first County Judge under the new constitution of the State.

The population of Bourbon County for the several decades since its formation, is as follows : In 1790, when its territoral limits were almost limitless, its population was 7,837 ; in 1800, 12,825 ; in 1810, 18,009 ; in 1820, 17,664 ; in 1830, 18,436 ; in 1840, 14,478 ; in 1850, 14,-456 ; in 1860, 14,860 ; in 1870, 14,863 ; and in 1880, 15,-

958. The difference in population is attributable to the change of territoral limits. We find from an old record that the county was assessed for £550 sterling in 1790. Its annual assessment has increased since then. At the time of its organization, the county, although of large dimensions, had but few inhabitants, and hence did not require many divisions of its territory. As the poplation increased, however, for the sake of convenience, the county was divided into a number of districts, for election and other purposes, necessary to facilitate its business, and aid in the administration of its affairs. But, without going into a discussion of these divisions and subdivisions made from time to time, it is only necessary to add, that, at present, the county is divided into eight election precincts, as follows, viz.: Paris, No. 1; Millersburg, No. 2; Flat Rock, No. 3; North Middletown, No. 4; Clintonville, No. 5; Hutchinson, No. 6; Centerville, No. 7; and Ruddel's Mills, No. 8. Each of these precincts has two Magistrates and a Constable, before and by whom the petty business of the county is transacted. The magistrates from the different precincts form the County Court, and at present the board is composed of the following gentlemen: Paris (No. 1), John M. Daniels and Thomas Isgrigg; Millersburg (No. 2), J. W. Miller and N. A. Jameson; Flat Rock (No. 3), T. M. Squires and B. F. Wilson; North Middletown (No. 4), James W. Mitchell and W. P. Schooler; Clintonville (No. 5), John Cunningham and George W. Morrow; Hutchinson (No. 6), J. S. Kenney and J. W. Beatty; Centerville (No. 7), James M. Barlow and H. Hawkins; Ruddel's Mills (No. 8), George W. Wyatt and W. B. Smith.

In the early history of Bourbon County, as at the present time, there was more or less of party strife. Bourbon County was formed just after the close of the Revolutionary war, when the people had for some time been divided into Whigs and Tories. Afterward came the "Old Court," "New Court," "Federal" and "Republican" or "Democratic" parties. These parties had their day, and then had their time to—die. The war of 1812, and the accompanying events, wiped out the old Federal party that had so bitterly opposed Mr. Jefferson. The war measures of Mr. Madison, and the then Republican party in Congress were strongly supported by the citizens generally. But as time passed on, and politicians became better educated to the business of wire-pulling, partyism grew, "and waxed strong." The Presidential election of 1824 was attended with unusual excitement. It was more exciting, perhaps, than any election that had ever taken place in the country. At this election the Presidential candidates were Henry Clay, Gen. Jackson, of Tennessee, John Quincy Adams, of Massachusetts, and William H. Crawford, of Georgia. These candidates had each his friends, who supported their favorite from personal motives, as well as from party consideration and party discipline. Mr. Clay carried his State, but was overwhelmingly defeated for the Presidency. Neither of the candidates had a majority of the votes in the Electoral College, according to the constitutional rule, but stood, Jackson in the lead, Adams second, Crawford third and Clay fourth, the latter being dropped from the canvass when it came to the count. Upon the House of Representatives devolved the duty of making choice of President. Each State, by its Representatives in Congress, cast one vote. Mr. Clay was Speaker of the House of Representatives, and, it is supposed, that, through his influence, the Kentucky delegation cast the vote of its State for Mr. Adams, instead of for Gen. Jackson. By this little stroke of policy, Mr. Clay was instrumental in organizing political parties that survived the generation in which he lived, and ruled, in turn, the destinies of the republic for more than a quarter of a century. At the next Presidential election, party lines were closely drawn, between Mr. Adams and Gen. Jackson, and the result of a hot and bitter contest was the election of the hero of New Orleans, by both the electoral and popular vote. For several years after the political power and official patronage had passed into the hands of Old Hickory, parties were known throughout the country as Jackson and anti-Jackson parties. These, with some modification and changes, finally became the Whig and Democratic parties, the latter of which has retained its party organization down to the present day, and is still one of the great political parties of the period. In 1856, upon the organization of the Republican party, in which organization the Whig party lost its identity, the county has been Democratic. Notwithstanding the great number of negroes added to the voting population, by virtue of the Fourteenth and Fifteenth Amendments to the national Constitution, the county still rolls up Democratic majorities.—*Perrin.*

CHAPTER IV.

PIONEER CHRISTIANITY — EARLY MEETINGS AND THE BUILDING OF CHURCHES — THE CANE RIDGE REVIVAL — EDUCATIONAL HISTORY—STATE AID TO SCHOOLS—EXTRACTS FROM STATE SUPERINTENDENT'S REPORT — COLORED SCHOOLS — THE PRESS, ETC.

"And lifted up our hearts in prayer
To God, the only Good."—*Gallagher*.

IT is to the credit of the early settlers of the county that they were a moral and God-fearing people, and that the introduction of the Gospel was coeval with their settlement in the wilderness. There were no churches, but each settler's cabin served as a temple of worship, and when the weather permitted, their

"Temples then were earth and sky;
None other did they know."

Often on the Sabbath Day, the scattered settlers would congregate at the most conveniently located house, when some one accustomed "to lead in meetin' " would read a chapter from the Bible, and after a hymn, offer prayer. The services, though simple in character, were fervent and sincere, and no doubt found favor with Him who declared that "where two or three are gathered together in My Name, there am I in their midst." When chance brought a minister to the neighborhood, the people were notified for miles around, and came to hear "the glad tidings of great joy." As their numbers increased and their means permitted, church buildings were erected, church societies were organized, and preachers engaged to point out to the sinner, as well as the believer, the way unto eternal life.

It is not possible, at this day, to designate the spot on which stood the first church building ever erected in Bourbon County, or the denomination to which it belonged. The Presbyterians, Baptists and Methodists established churches in an early day, and several church buildings were erected in the county prior to 1800. The minister came "as one crying in the wilderness," gathered the lost sheep into the fold, and organized churches in the different neighborhoods. To the honor and credit of the county be it recorded, that she has liberally supported the claims of the Gospel, as evidenced in the number of handsome church buildings to be found in her midst. It is not inappropriate in this connection to give a brief sketch of the Cane Ridge meeting mentioned in religious history in connection with what is known as the "Great Kentucky Revival." It took place in 1801, at the Old Cane Ridge Church, in the east part of Paris Circuit, under the ministrations of the Rev. Barton W. Stone, a preacher widely known, and esteemed throughout Central Kentucky, and who was Pastor of the Cane Ridge Church at the time. The sketch is taken from an old work published in 1848, by Elder Levi Purviance, and will recall to the minds of many still living an incident that is fast fading away with the rolling years, and that would soon be forgotten. It is as follows :

"The great meeting at Cane Ridge commenced on Friday before the third Lord's Day of August, 1801. From the commencement the roads were literally crowded with wagons, carriages, horsemen, and people on foot, all pressing to the appointed place, until by the Sabbath Day the grove that was then open near Cane Ridge meeting-house, was filled with wagons, tents and people. It was supposed that there were between twenty and thirty thousand people present. Elder Stone in his journal remarks : 'A particular description of this meeting would fill a large volume, and then the half would not be told.' For the sake of the present and future generations, I will attempt a faint description : From the very commencement, an uncommon solemnity appeared to rest on the countenances of the people. Not unfrequently several preachers would be speaking within the bounds of the encampment without any interruption to each other. Wagons, stumps and logs were used for stands. The preaching and exhortations were interesting and impressive. Salvation free to all mankind was proclaimed, and the willingness of Jesus to save all that would come was urged universally by the speakers. 'The Word of God was quick and powerful, and sharper than a two-edged sword.' Many sinners were cut to the heart, and fell prostate under an awful guilt and condemnation for sin. This was not confined to any one class. The moral, genteel and well-raised ; the giddy and profane, the wicked, the drunkard and the infidel ; the poor and also the rich, as well as the proud and vain, with all their gaudy attire, were brought down by the spirit of the Almighty, and they appeared to have forgotton everything in this world in view of their souls' eternal salvation.

"I recollect having seen a small girl, not more than ten

or eleven years of age, held up by a friend that stood in a wagon, while she invited sinners to the Savior. All who heard her seemed to be astonished at her eloquence and judgment manifested in inviting sinners to God. It appeared that from the mouths of children 'God had ordained strength; He took the weak things of the world to confound the mighty,' and by this means the most stubborn sinners were brought to bow to the Savior. At this meetting, and in this revival, there was a most solemn and interesting spirit of prayer manifested. In crowds, tents and wagons, you could hear fervent prayer. I have gone from the camping-ground into the woods, and it was difficult to get away from prayer. For more than a half mile, I could see people on their knees before God in humble prayer.

"This was not a sectarian meeting, although it was held at a Presbyterian meeting-house. Baptists, Methodists and Presbyterians were simultaneously engaged. Perfect friendship, unanimity and brotherly kindness prevailed. They had come together, to the help of the Lord against the mighty, and 'Zion was terrible as an army with banners.' The meeting lasted six days—the last sermon that was delivered on the occasion was by a Methodist preacher by the name of Samuel Hitt. It is known only to God how many were converted at this meeting. There were no means by which even to ascertain how many professed religion. The object of the meeting was not to build up any sect or party, but to bring sinners to the Savior. When the meeting was over, the people returned to their homes and friends. There were many there from Ohio, and some from Tennessee, and the excitement spread with the people, and the young converts joined the churches of their choice. The good work of reformation went on with irresistible force, and appeared like carrying everything before it. Many were persuaded that the glorious millennial day had commenced, and that the world would soon become the kingdom of our Lord Jesus Christ. But alas! That enemy of God and man, SECTARIANISM, raised its hydra head, and 'made war upon the saints of the Most High God and overcame them,' and the fair prospects of Zion were in some degree blasted. A cruel jealousy began to show itself among the leaders; some concluded that the spoils were not equally divided; others, that their craft was in danger. Notwithstanding the pride and selfishness of little-minded men raised a barrier in the way of the work, and in some degree obstructed it, yet, where the people continued humble and devoted to God, the good cause advanced, and sinners were converted to the Christian religion. But the bodily exercise, as it was called, seemed to change its manner of operation. The falling exercise became not so common, and the jerks succeeded. These, if possible, were harder to account for than the former, and it is impossible for me fully to describe them. The first I saw affected with them were very pious, exemplary persons. Their heads would jerk back suddenly, frequently causing them to give a yelp, or make some other involuntary noise. After this, nearly all classes became subject to them. The intelligent and the ignorant; strong, athletic men, and weak, effeminate persons were handled alike by them. Sometimes the head would fly every way so quickly that their features could not be recognized. I have seen their heads fly back and forward so quickly that the hair of the females would be made to crack like a carriage whip, but not very loud. A stranger looking on would have supposed that they would be killed instantly. Some wicked persons have taken them, while ridiculing them, and have been powerfully operated upon by them; others have taken them while trying to mimic them, and had them in good earnest. One thing that appeared almost miraculous was, that among the hundreds I have seen have them, I never knew or heard of one being hurt or injured by them."

Such is an historical sketch of one of the greatest religious revivals, perhaps, on record. It was not confined alone to the Cane Ridge Church, but extended all over Central Kentucky, and into Ohio and Tennessee. The same writer says: "I have no doubt many of my readers will pronounce it a delusion. Some of that day called it so; others called it the work of the devil, and some witchcraft." Another writer, William Rogers, of Cane Ridge, says of this same revival: "When, early in the month of April of the year in question (1801), a phenomenon in the religious history of the West, made its appearance in the south of Kentucky, more than one hundred miles from Cane Ridge. It was, in the language of that day, styled—'The falling exercise.' The accounts of it narrated were wondrous to our ears. In the month of May, the strange work was witnessed in the two churches of Cane Ridge and Concord, the former in Bourbon, the latter in Nicholas County, and both at the time under the pastorate of the Rev. Barton W. Stone, a young man of much purity, and high respect for learning, for talent and amiability of manners, in the Presbyterian ranks. The exercise in question soon spread in all directions, and meetings for public worship were kept up with but little intermission, not only in these two churches, but throughout the great West. The Rev. Stone was a regular and distinguished actor in many of them. The interest and the exercise was truly astounding, and thousands were the converts of that summer. Many a tall son and daughter of worldly pride was made to bear submission to Prince Messiah."

A few words of Barton W. Stone, one of the most remarkable preachers of his day, in Kentucky, is a fitting conclusion to the history of this wonderful revival. He was born in Maryland December 24, 1772, and was a son of John Stone, who died when he was very young. His mother, after her husband's death, removed to Virginia, and settled in what was then termed the backwoods, in Pittsylvania County, eight miles below the Blue Mountains, where the future great preacher received his early education in the private schools of the neighborhood, and which he afterward completed at Guilford Academy, in North Carolina. While pursuing his studies he was converted, and in 1793 became a candidate for the ministry in the Presbyterian Church, in Orange County, North Carolina. Before he was licensed to preach, however, he became discouraged, and determined to give up the idea of the ministry and engage in some other calling. Under this determination he visited his brother in the State of Georgia, and, while there, was chosen Professor of Languages in the Methodist Academy, near Washington, in 1795. In the following spring, he resigned his professorship, returned to North Carolina, attended the Orange Presbytery, and received his license to preach. Soon afterward he went to Tennessee, and finally made his way through the wilderness to Kentucky, and commenced preaching at Cane Ridge and Concord, in Bourbon County. He continued to labor in these churches until 1798, when they gave him a regular call, which he accepted, and was installed as their pastor. He preached for them several years, and during his pastorate occurred the great revival already noticed. But the liberality of his doctrine was at length complained of by the more rigid and Calvinistic, and, in 1803, the matter was brought before the Synod at Lexington. Foreseeing that the Synod would most likely decide against him, he, and four others, withdrew from its jurisdiction, and sent in their protest to the proceedings. The Synod, however, proceeded to pass on them the sentence of "suspension," for the crime of departing from the doctrines of the Confession of Faith. Upon this action of the Synod, he severed his connection with his congregations, and with his companions, formed what they termed the "Springfield Presbytery," but soon gave it up, as it savored of partyism, and then took the name of CHRISTIAN—the name given by divine appointment first at Antioch. Having divested themselves, to use his own words, "of all party creeds and party names, and trusting alone in God, and the words of His grace, we became a by-word and laughing-stock to the sects around us; all prophesying our speedy annihilation."

Mr. Stone continued to live a useful life. He finally became identified with the Christian Church (called, in derision, sometimes, Campbellites), and was one of its faithful ministers until his death. In the fall of 1834, he moved with his family to Jacksonville, Ill. In October, 1844, he made a visit to his children, relatives and friends living in Missouri, from which he never returned. He died on the 9th of November, at the residence of Capt. Samuel A Bowen, in Hannibal, Mo., at the age of 71 years. Thus passed away an able minister, a zealous Christian, and an exemplary man.

The sketches of the great revival of religion, and of Mr. Stone, are given as a part of the history of Bourbon County. In the chapters devoted to the city of Paris, and to the different villages and election precincts, a full and complete history will be given of all the churches and religious denominations existing in the county, or that have existed since its settlement, so far as can be obtained. Hence, we only allude to the subject here in general terms, and pass to other matters claiming our attention.

The common schools should interest every individual, not only of this county, but of the whole State. It is by education that communities attain civilization and refinement, and the child of the poor man rises to honor and greatness. In our own free country, and under the influence of our free schools, the poorest may become eminent and renowned. Without education, Henry Clay, the "mill-boy of the slashes," never could have become the leader of statesmen, nor James A. Garfield have risen from the canal-boat to the Presidential chair.

In the early settlement of this section, there were a great many drawbacks in the way of general education. The people were mostly poor, and money, or other means of remunerating teachers scarce; there were no school-houses, nor was there any public school fund. All persons, of both sexes, who had physical strength enough to labor, were compelled to take their part in the work of securing a support, the labor of the female being as heavy and important as that of the men; and this continued so for years. In the last place, both teachers and books were extremely scarce. Taking all these facts together, the wonder is that they had any schools at all. But the pioneers of Central Kentucky deserve the highest honors for their prompt and energetic efforts in this direction. Just so soon as the settlements would justify, schools were begun at each one. The teacher or pupil of to-day has no conception of getting an education under difficulties. There are, perhaps, however, a few aged people still living in Bourbon County who may remember some of the early difficulties that stood in the way of learning.

The first steps of Kentucky to extend the fostering aid of State patronage to the interests of general education, were taken more than three-quarters of a century ago. On the 10th of February, 1798, an act was approved by the State Legislature donating and setting apart of the public lands of the Commonwealth 6,000 acres each for the benefit and support of Franklin, Salem and Kentucky Academies, and for Lexington and Jefferson Seminaries. Similar acts were approved December 21, 1805, and January 27, 1808, embracing like provisions, and extending them to all the existing counties of the State. "Within twenty years," says Collins, "from the passage of the act of 1798, the following additional academies and seminaries were endowed with the grant of 6,000 acres each: Shelby, Logan, Ohio, Madison, New Athens, Bethel, Bourbon, Bracken, Bullitt, Fleming, Hardin, Harrison, Harrodsburg, Lancaster, Montgomery, Newport, Newton, Rittenhouse, Stanford, Washington, Winchester, Woodford, Somerset, Transylvania, Greenville, Glasgow, Liberty, Rockcastle, Lebanon, Knox, Boone, Clay, Estill, Henry, Greenup, Grayson, Warren, Breckinridge, Caldwell, Gallatin, Henderson, Union, Adair, Allen, Daviess and Pendleton."

One of the early laws of Kentucky, pertaining to the subject ef education, was, "that all the lands, lying within the bounds of this commonwealth, on the south side of Cumberland River, and below Obed's River, now vacant, etc., shall be reserved for the endowment and use of seminaries of learning throughout this commonwealth." The County Courts of the several counties were authorized to have surveyed, located and patented within their respective counties, or within the above reserve, or elsewhere in the State, 6,000 acres each, for seminary purposes, and all such lands were exempted from taxation. Noble as were the grants in purpose and plan, but little actual benefit was derived from them—at least, not half the benefit that should have been. Under subsequent unwise acts, the lands were allowed to be sold by county authorities, and the proceeds prodigally expended, and, in many cases, recklessly squandered. The proceeds from the sale of these lands, are, in some counties, wholly lost sight of; in other counties, they remain in the hands of trustees appointed, and forgotten or neglected by an indifferent public, while in other counties these funds are still held by trustees for their original uses. "But, for the want of wise laws and more competent and guarded management," says a recent writer, "a great plan and its means of success for the establishment and support of a system of public seminaries of a high order in each county was rendered an accomplished failure."

Many laws were enacted providing for a general system of public schools, but most of them were so framed as to amount to little, or were altogether impracticable. In December, 1821, an act was passed which provided that "one-half the net profits of the Bank of the Commonwealth should be distributed in just proportions to the counties of the State for the support of a general system of education, under legislative direction." A writer upon our school system makes this pertinent observation: "It is a singular phenomenon of the history of internal economy of our State for seventy years, that our main attempts at internal improvement and public education at State expense and under State superintendence have been embarrassed, or defeated almost wholly, by the misdirection and mismanagement of incompetent legislation."

It may not be uninteresting to the reader to know the history of our "permanently-invested school-fund." Its origin was somewhat as follows: By an act of Congress, approved June 23, 1836, that body apportioned about $15,000,000, of surplus money in the Treasury to the several older States, in the form of a loan, of which the share of Kentucky was $1,433,757. This fund was asked for and received by our State, with the expectation and intention of devoting it to school purposes, although no provision of the law imposed upon the State this obligation, yet, by different acts of the Legislature, the original fund was cut down until only $850,000 was finally set apart as the financial basis of our educational system. This is the origin of our school fund, and, for many years, we derived our only public school revenues from it, and a portion of it is still derived from the same source. By accumulation of unexpended surplus, from year to year, and the continual additions of this to the principal, this permanent fund is now about $1,500,000. This fund afterward suffered, however, by the ill-advised system of internal improvements, into which the State had embarked, and by which she was lavishing her finances on a multitude of isolated experiments, with little probability of finishing any of them. From this reckless fever of internal improvement, the revenues of the school fund were the first to suffer. As early as 1840, the Commissioners of the Sinking Fund declined payment of the interest on the school bond, due by the State, when a deficit occurred in the Treasury, and the Legislature sustained the action on the plea, that, as it was in the nature of a debt due herself, by the State, there was no loss of credit it refusing payment or repudiation.

But, without going into a general discussion of the school laws of Kentucky and the system of public education in the State, it is enough to say, and it is not out of place, either, that her educational system is lamentably deficient, and not to be compared with those of other States of the Union, whose natural resources of wealth are much less than Kentucky's, and whose native intelligence is no greater. There is no reason why the State of Kentucky should not have as good a system of education as any State in the whole Union. No other State of like area is richer in natural wealth; none of like population contains more eminent genius or more native intelligence. As an item of interest to our readers, and by way of contrasting our school system and the funds for its support, we give the following from the last report of the Ohio Board of Education:

The receipts of school moneys for the year	$11,243,210 38
Total expenditures for schools for the year	3,531,885 14
Leaving school fund balance	$7,711,325 24

The following is the exhibit of Kentucky's school fund:

State bonds, bearing 6 per cent interest	$1,327,000 00
Bank of Kentucky stock	73,500 00
Total	$1,400,500 00
Amount paid for schools, from October 11, 1880, to October 10, 1881	$766,138 46

In addition to the above, the revenues of the school fund are increased by an annual tax of 20 cents on the hundred dollars of property; a tax on the capital stock of certain banks in the State; fines, forfeitures, etc., and tax on billiard tables; a tax on dogs of $1 each, where a housekeeper has more than two; the proceeds of sales of certain carriers, over and above charges, amounting, in the aggregate, to near $1,000,000 more. With the vast resources of wealth, Kentucky, as a State, possesses, she might as well have a permanent school fund of $10,000,000 as to have the insignificant sum given above.

Notwithstanding the early disadvantages of the school laws, and the many inconveniences under which Bourbon and the adjoining counties labored, schools were established in the different neighborhoods and settlements, as soon as the population became sufficiently large to support them. Of these early schools little is now known. They were of the old-time subscription plan, and taught for so much per scholar. The teachers were scarcely up to the standard required at the present day. In the early times, if a man was incapable of filling any other position, he usually resorted to teaching school. It was something like an incident that came to the writer's notice in Illinois a few years ago. A young man concluded he was smart enough to teach school, and went to the County Examiner to procure a certificate. That officer proceeded to examine him, but found him very deficient, and declined to give him the required authority. The young man, however, importuned him to such an extent, that at last he wrote out the coveted document, sealed it, and bade him carry it to the trustees of his district. When opened by them, it was found to read: "This is to certify that Mr. Blank is qualified to teach a common school in Blank Township, and a —— common one at that." So it was with the early teachers in this section; they were not capable of teaching any but a *very common* school. It is not known who was the first teacher in Bourbon County, nor where the first school was taught; neither is it known where the first schoolhouse stood, nor when built. These particulars, so far as attainable, are given in other chapters, and hence extended mention of them is omitted in this connection. Suffice it to say, that schools were established, as necessity required them, in different parts of the county, until each settlement boasted of an institution of learning; and educational facilities, extensive for that early day, were enjoyed by the pioneers and their children.

There are, at the present time thirty-five school districts in Bourbon County, as we learn from Mr. W. H. Lockhart, County School Commissioner, devoted to the whites, in all of which there are schoolhouses, and in which schools are taught each year. In addition to these, there are five high schools in Paris, eight in the county, and one common school in Paris. The number of white children of school age in the county, 2,585; amount paid teachers for the year ending October 10, 1881, $4,841.06. Of the high schools and colleges in Paris and in the county, full and complete sketches will be found in other chapters of this work.

In support of our common schools, an educational system that has no equal among the nations of the earth, too much cannot be said. Ours is the first instance in the world's history, where a civil government took measures to confer upon all the blessings of education. Never before was embodied in practice a principle so comprehensive in its nature, and so fruitful in good results, as that of training a nation of intelligent people by educating *all* of its youth. It is this system of universal education that forms the bulwark of our liberty and independence. Take away our common schools, and we sink back into ignorance and despotism—the slaves of our educated rulers and sovereigns. The Czar of Russia can only by education and a familiarity with international law, domestic affairs, finance, commerce, and the organization of armies and navies, hold his scepter over seventy millions of subjects. The glory of England springs from the fostering aid she extends to her great universities, wherein are educated and trained for their positions in the House of Lords the army, navy and

James Scott

church, the sons of her nobility, who lead and rule the ignorant masses. But in this land of liberty and freedom, every man is born a king and heir to liberal education, and to all the highest trusts of the State and Republic. It has been thoroughly demonstrated in history that an ignorant people can be governed. But it is only an intelligent and educated people who can govern themselves.

From the annual report of the State Superintendent of Public Instruction, we may make the following extracts, which will be found of interest to our readers. The report says: "No candid mind will refuse to concede that the common school system has a firmer grasp upon the heart of Kentucky than ever before. It is discussed by every fireside, and on every street corner and highway; it is forced upon every candidate for legislative honors, and enlists the eloquent advocacy of our representative public men. Ten years ago, the people cared but little who was State Superintendent of Schools. Nine men out of ten could not have told who were candidates for the position, or who held the office. The matter is reversed, and the Superintendent has became a central figure, around whom public interest surges and shouts. Ten years ago, a man in the blue-grass country, worth $10,000, would as soon have thought of sending his children to the poor-house as to the public school. The public school was generally regarded as a charity devised for the education of paupers, but not to be countenanced by the rich, save as a benefaction to the poor. The schools were *common* in the sense of low, vulgar and inferior. The very accent with which the adjective was pronounced, indicated the contempt in which men of means regarded it. Our citizens have learned to regard it as common, in the sense of a community of interest, as the laws are common—*the common law*—as the State is common—the commonwealth, the common weal. Now, the idea of conferring a benefit upon the indigent, has given place to the true one, namely, to prepare citizens for the intelligent exercise of their suffrages, and to protect society from the penalties of ignorance.

"The wealthiest counties are becoming its best friends, and tax-payers are voting levies upon themselves to improve the quality and to extend the term of the schools. Half a million dollars are annually raised, by the election of the people, to supplement the public bonus. Tasteful and comfortable schoolhouses are fast taking the place of those old shams and shames, in which the children of the poor erstwhile were corraled. Eighteen hundred have been built within the last eight years. A home supply of teachers, furnished from our best young men and women, are taking the place of impecunious tramps and shiftless natives. The system is no longer an infirmary for the lame and halt and feeble. Incompetents to be provided for, no more are pensioned upon the bounty afforded by the school fund. It is not now a 'stepping-stone' to professions, a temporary expedient, accepted until something better turns up, or is turned up. Men and women among us are choosing it for their life-work, and emulating each other in their aspirations and achievements of *a profession*, which confers honor, and whose prizes are to be coveted, and whose badges are to be worn with pride. Cities and towns vie with each other in maintaining graded schools better than our average Western colleges, with their half-starved faculties.

"He who fails to see these tokens of revived interest is wilfully and wantonly blind. These and other signs of the times augur that an auspicious period is at hand, when the benefits of education will crush the bale of ignorance, and intelligence hold the ballots that fall into the Nation's urn of fate. The importance of our common-school system is apparent, when it is remembered that there are only 35,000 pupils in all the universities, colleges, seminaries and private academies of our State, while a quarter of a million of children flock to our seven thousand public schools. In half the counties, no schools are taught but common schools. In some of our counties of wealth and refinement, the public schools have absorbed all private enterprises because co-operative effort furnishes a superior quality of education. If our colleges decline in the number of matriculates, the cause is not to be found in diminished interest in education, but in the fact that our public schools are affording at home advantages formerly sought abroad.

* * * * * * *

"The expression of the popular will by a majority at the polls, in a fairly conducted election, is but the aggregate expression of American sovereignty. The people by their votes, determine who shall represent their sovereign will. How to wield this power for good is the supreme question for the State. An ignorant people, manipulated by corrupt leaders, become the worst of all tyrants. The idea that the majority can do no wrong, is only equaled by that monstrous political dogma of imperialism, 'the king can do no wrong.' No maxim ever embodied a more pernicious error than the pert or trite proverb, 'The voice of the people is the voice of God.' This can only be true when intelligence determines public questions, and patriotism executes its verdicts. See what corrupt ignorance, introduced to power, did for the States of the South! Consider what negro supremacy entailed upon South Carolina! The greatest crime of the century was the sudden enfranchisement of 4,000,000 unlettered Africans. Those who perpetrated this outrage upon our republican institutions, did it in the face of all the social science they had propagated. The North had emphasized the doctrine, that 'virtue and intelligence are essential to the perpetuity of the republic;' and yet, in an ill-advised hour of heated passion, rendered hot by the fires of civil war, they made a horde of ignorant slaves the peers of their intelligent masters, and thus provided the conditions that prostrated the South, and subjected its people to the most destroying despotism that ever ground into the dust a free citizenship. The only indemnity for this stupendous wrong is their education at the National expense. To require the people they impoverished by this act of folly to bear the burden of their education, would be a continued piece of injustice, which no political casuistry can justify, no species of sophistry disguise, and no maudlin philanthropy dignify with a decent apology.

"But Kentucky has 40,000 white voters who cannot read. Add to these 55,000 enfranchised negroes, and we have 95,000—one-third our entire electoral population—ignorant of the very means by which to acquaint themselves with the merits of questions submitted for their decision at the polls. Let this mighty census of ignorance increase, until it becomes the dominant majority—and grow it would, if left to itself, without State encouragement for its own improvement—and seat itself in power, and we have no reason to expect that Kentucky would escape the same or like disasters that have overtaken and overwhelmed every people that ever dared the fearful experiment. * * *

"Nothing for which the State pays money yields so large a dividend upon the cost as the revenue expended upon education. With it she supports more than 7,000 teachers, who impart instruction to 250,000 of her children. The influence of these school-rooms is silent, like all the great forces of the universe. But from the humble scene of the teacher's labors, there are shot into the heart of society the great influences that kindle its ardors for activity, which light civilization on its widening way, and which hold the dearest interest of humanity in its hand. The statistics are the smallest exponents of the worth of our schools. These are values that cannot be expressed in dollars and cents, nor be quoted in price-currents."

The foregoing extracts contain wholesome truths that should be well pondered, and should meet the hearty approbation of every thinking man and woman of the community, and excite in them a zealous support of the common schools. Acadamies, colleges and universities are well in their way, and are highly essential to the country, but the common schools are the foundation of our educational system; the safeguard of our liberties.

Compulsory education is a question attracting considerable attention throughout the country, and several States have already passed laws requiring parents and guardians to educate their children, and children placed in their charge. There is a growing sentiment in favor of compulsory education in Kentucky, and it is believed that a majority of the friends of the common-school system favor its introduction, but there is grave doubt upon the part of some as to the policy of such laws. A great good would be wrought however, if the wisdom of our legislators could devise some means to strengthen the boards of education in large towns and cities, whereby they might be enabled to prevent truancy. The instances are not few in which parents would welcome aid in this matter. Youthful idlers upon the streets should be gathered up by somebody and compelled to do something. If they learned nothing else, there would be at least this salutary lesson, that society is stronger than they, and without injuring them, will use its strength to protect itself.

Besides the white schools of the county, there are fourteen districts under the educational system inaugurated for the benefit of the colored people in the county, and one colored school in the city of Paris, with a total of fifteen schoolhouses, as shown by the records of Mr. Lockhart, School Commissioner. The school age of colored children is from six to sixteen years; there are 1,020 colored school children in the county, and there was paid to their teachers for the year ending October 10, 1881, $1,023.70. It is highly creditable to the colored people that they are taking an interest in the cause of education that is yearly increasing. The fund from which their children are educated is derived from the taxes paid by the colored people of the State, and, great or small, their taxes all go into their school fund.

The following extracts from the State Superintendent show the interest the colored people are taking in educating their children: "The colored school system has more than met the expectation of its projectors and friends, and is rapidly, by gratifying development, disappointing the prophecies of its enemies. The colored people are now taking hold of it with that enthusiasm and earnestness so characteristic of the race when their interests are at stake, and their claims to notice recognized by authority. They are exhibiting a most commendable zeal in supplementing the fund, and are really doing more to make the most of the opportunities tendered them by the State than the whites. They have, in a number of counties, organized and conducted institutes, and have a State association, whose exercises exhibit a surprising intelligence, and whose prudence in avoiding all complications with politics is worthy of all commendation. * * * * * There can exist no possible reason for the improvement of citizenship by education, conferred at the public expense upon the whites, which does not apply with equal force to the colored people, now that they have been clothed with the elective franchise. The negro is a voter, and to make him intelligent that he may advisedly exercise his sovereignty, is at once the duty and interest of the State, and nothing but the jaundiced eye of prejudice can fail to see this. It is too late to debate the propriety of the policy that conferred this exalted dignity upon him. * * * * * It will not do to say we did not make him a voter, and are not responsible for his citizenship. This delusive casuistry will not protect us from the consequences of his vicious ignorance. As well say we did not invite the epidemic to our midst, therefore, we will unheed the warnings of your Boards of Health, and let the pabulum of pestilence breed in our food sewers, miasmatic pools, and the haunts of filth."

The newspaper and the printing press of the present day constitute one of the most important features of the time and of the country, and a chronicle that said nothing of their power and influence would be considered, at least, incomplete. The daily paper, by the aid of the telegraph, which connects all points of civilization like spider-webs, gives us to-day all the news that transpired yesterday in the uttermost parts of the earth. And the county press, the faithful exponent of the county's interest, is the intellectual criterion for the masses, and the most popular channel of general information. It is also a true record of the county's history; the very advertisements in local papers eventually become historical facts, and it is to be regretted that so few persons seem to appreciate the value and importance of their county papers. And to-day journalism is recognized as a power in the land, a power before which the evil-doer and the corrupt official stand in awe. The legitimate press, holding as it does this acknowledged position, its history forms an interesting and worthy part of the history of the county. The subject, however, will be but briefly referred to here, and that in general terms, leaving the more minute details to be given in other chapters.

Suffice it, the first paper in Bourbon County was established in Paris previous to 1800, and was called the *Kentucky Herald*. It was published by Daniel Bradford, a brother to John Bradford, who established the *Kentucky Gazette* at Lexington, the first paper west of the Alleghany Mountains. There are now three newspapers published in the county, viz.: The *True Kentuckian* and *Western Citizen*, of Paris, and the *Bourbon News*, of Millersburg, full sketches of which will be found in the history of those cities.—*Perrin*.

CHAPTER V.

INTERNAL IMPROVEMENTS—TURNPIKES AND MACADAMIZED ROADS—THE MAYSVILLE AND OTHER TURNPIKES—STAGE COACHES—RAILROADS—KENTUCKY CENTRAL—PROJECTED ROADS—AGRICULTURE IN THE COUNTY—FAIR ASSOCIATIONS AND OFFICERS—CATTLE SHIPMENT—DISTILLERIES, ETC.

"Time—space—have yielded to my power."

THE roads and highways of a county or State constitute an important part of their internal improvements, Those of Bourbon County and of Central Kentucky are unsurpassed in any country. Turnpikes and macadamized roads pass in every direction and to every point of importance. Collins gives the origin of turnpikes in Kentucky as follows: "A turnpike road, or road on which *turnpikes* (i. e., toll-gates) are established by law, and which are made and kept in repair by the toll collected from travelers who use the road—the road itself being formed by throwing the earth from the sides to the center in a rounded form—is usually confounded with the modern macadamized or artificial road (invented by Macadam) of broken stone. No such road as the latter was made in Kentucky until 1829. By act of March 1, 1797, Joseph Crockett was appointed to erect a turnpike at some convenient place, and purchase as much land as may be necessary for that purpose, not exceeding two acres, or the road leading from Crab Orchard to Cumberland Gap, beyond where the road from Madison Court House intersects said road. The turnpike (toll-gate) was to be farmed out to the highest bidder, who should give bond and security, payable to the Governor of the State, for the faithful payment of his bid. He should 'have the right and privilege to receive the following tolls: For every person (except post-riders, expresses, women, and children under the age of ten years) 9 pence (12½ cents); for every horse, mare or mule, 9 pence; two-wheel carriage, 3 shillings; four-wheel carriage, 6 shillings ($1); and for every head of cattle *going to the eastward*, 3 pence (4⅙ cents). The surplus tolls, after paying for repairing the road, were to belong to the keeper of the turnpike (toll-gate).' Thus turnpike originally meant toll-gate, but now generally means the road itself on which the turnpike or toll-gate is established." From this small and insignificant commencement has originated as fine a system of roads as may be found anywhere. The limestone of this region has proven its value beyond controversy in the matter of road-building. Owing to the nature of the soil, the roads of the county, before they were macadamized, became almost impassable in winter. Limestone soil is more easily washed and cut into gullies by heavy rains than soil where the limestone does not exist. Hence, it became necessary to adopt some means of preserving the roads and preventing them from washing into gullies. No successful plan was invented until that of covering them with limestone. No amount of rain affects this covering, but on the contrary the rain assists in smoothing and leveling the surface and otherwise adding to its durability.

The first turnpike road ever built in the State passed through Bourbon County, and is still a popular highway, and also a road of almost unparalleled excellence. It was chartered as the Maysville & Lexington Turnpike Road. The career of this pioneer road was somewhat checkered and eventful, and were its history fully written it would form a rather readable narrative. It was chartered on the 4th of February, 1818, under an act "for the purpose of forming artificial roads," but years passed before it was built. It was incorporated anew January 22, 1827, with a capital stock of $320,000, to which, at any time within three years, the United States Government was authorized to subscribe $100,000, and the State of Kentucky the like sum. Gen. Metcalfe, afterward Governor of the State, then a Representative in Congress from the Maysville District, brought before Congress the subject of an appropriation for the proposed turnpike, but too late in the session to get the measure through. He, however, induced the Secretary of War to order a survey for the location of a "great leading mail road from Zanesville, in Ohio, through Maysville and Lexington, in Kentucky, and Nashville, Tenn., to Florence, Ala., *en route* to New Orleans." On the 12th of May following, Col. Long and Lieut. Trimble, of the United States Engineer Department, began the survey at Maysville. By a resolution of the Kentucky Legislature, adopted February 13, 1828, Congress was recommended to extend a branch of the National Road from Zanesville, Ohio, to Maysville, Ky., and thence through the States of Kentucky, Tennessee, Alabama and Mississippi, to New Orleans; and instructed her Senators in Congress, and requested her Representatives to use their utmost exertion to effect this object. A bill with an appropriation for this purpose passed the House of Representatives, but was defeated in the Senate in the spring of 1828. While the matter was thus delayed, Maysville took an initiatory step toward building this important road, procured from the Legislature, January 29, 1829, a charter for the Maysville & Washington Turnpike Road, which was but four miles in length. The necessary amount of stock was at once subscribed, and the "first spade of earth dug amid great rejoicing on the 4th of July following the passage of the act." The road was steadily pushed forward until its completion in November, 1830. This road was afterward finished through to Lexington, and became the "Maysville & Lexington Turnpike Road." Under this title, a bill passed the Lower House of Congress, on the 29th of April, 1830, "authorizing and directing the Secretary of the Treasury to subscribe, in the name and for the use of the United States, for 1,500 shares ($150,000) of the capital stock of the Maysville, Washington, Paris & Lexington Turnpike Road Company." It passed the Senate May 15, and, twelve days later (May 27) was vetoed by President Jackson. Kentucky, however, aided the enterprise, and took stock at different intervals, until her subscription amounted in the aggregate to $213,200, one-half the cost of the entire road. A new impulse had been given to the building of artificial roads, as "the only kind which can be permanent on Kentucky soil," in the winter of 1826–27. In his annual message to the Legislature, December 4, 1826, Gov. Desha took strong ground in favor of the road from Maysville to Louisville, "through the most important towns of Paris, Lexington, Frankfort, etc., etc."

This, as we have stated, was the first macadamized road through the county, and was built at a cost of $426,400, "including thirteen toll-houses and six covered bridges." Since its completion, a number of others have been built, until the county is a perfect net-work of pikes, diverging from Paris and connecting it with all important points. The following are the titles of some of them: Georgetown and Paris; Paris and Winchester; Paris and Clintonville; Paris and Flat Rock; Mount Sterling Pike; Bethlehem and Paris; North Middletown Pike; Paris and Jackstown; Cane Ridge Pike, and others. These roads are built on the general macadamized plan—the stone broken, usually, so as not to exceed six ounces in weight, and laid upon the road, according to probable wear, nine to ten inches deep, and one to three inches deeper in the center. Substantial bridges span many of the large streams where they are crossed by these roads, thus rendering high water no impediment to travel. The county has several iron, and a number of wooden bridges, and still there is room for a few more. The only objection that can be urged to the turnpike roads of the county, is the tax imposed upon those traveling over them, in the way of toll. The paying of toll is a nuisance that should be abated, and Paris and the county would do well, and find it to their interest, too, to take the matter into their own hands and make their roads all free.

The stage coach of the old regulation pattern seems almost a part of the turnpike road, and in the early days was the common mode of travel. The old vehicles were usually painted a kind of fawn color, ornamented profusely with red. The body was swung high above the wheels on heavy leather springs, so that every lurch of the coach seemed to threaten sure destruction to the passengers. While in the zenith of their glory, their arrival in town created far more of a sensation and a greater interest than the railroad trains do now. Everybody rushed out to see the stage and hear the news, and to catch a glimpse, if possible, of that great man, the driver. What a hero he was! In the innocency of our youth, he is the only man we ever remember having envied. Mark Twain gives an excellent pen portrait of him in his trip across the plains, but he had his day, and now he is laid on the shelf. The turnpike was not complete without a stage coach, nor the stage coach without a driver. Both are now gone with other relics of the olden time, and we are away on the "fast train" of internal improvement and development.

Railroads.—The railroads of Bourbon County are soon written. The history of the roads already built is brief and somewhat uninteresting; to projected roads more interest attaches, perhaps, than to those already in operation. The introduction and building of railroads form an interesting part of our history, and unquestionably hold the first place among the social forces of the present day. There is not a single occupation of interest which the railroad has not radically affected. Agriculture, manufactures, commerce, city and country life, banking, finance, law, and even government itself, have all felt its influence. But especially has it been a potent influence in providing the material organization for the diffusion of culture among the people, and thus preparing the conditions for a new step in social progress. Wholly unknown three-fourths of a century ago, the railroad has become the greatest single factor in the development of the material progress, not only of the United States and of the other civilized nations of the earth, but its blessings are being rapidly extended into the hitherto semi-civilized and barbarous portions of the globe.

Our progress and improvement in the building of railroads has kept pace with our advancement in everything else. None but a prophet could have foreseen the improvements that would be made in their construction in the first half century of their existence. As we travel over the great trunk lines in palace coaches, we may well wonder at the perfection of railroads, for certainly there is nothing more wonderful in our history. As we contemplate the subject, we are ready to exclaim, "What further improvements can be made in railroads!" Who can answer the question? The railroad system is the most stupendous monument to man's enterprise ever erected. It forms a perfect net-work of iron and steel in every portion of the country, running daily and nightly and continuously, thousands of locomotives and tens of thousands of of freight and passenger cars, loaded with tons and tons of the products of the country, with valuable merchandise from every part of the world, and with an almost innumerable number of precious human beings, dashing with lightning speed from city to city, and from State to State, from the Atlantic to the Pacific, and from the Lakes to the Gulf, representing a capital of at least $5,000,000,000. Ah, where is there another such (to quote from a circus bill) colossal combination? and we may add—monopoly.

The first railroad built in the West, and one of the first in the United States, was built on the present line from Lexington to Frankfort. It was originally chartered as the Lexington & Ohio Railroad, January 27, 1830. and was to extend from Lexington to Portland on the Ohio River, a village now included in the corporate limits of Louisville. This pioneer road, in its "primitive purity and innocence," was somewhat unique in its mechanical construction. The iron rails were soldered upon stone sills, which were laid lengthwise, instead of being spiked upon wooden cross-ties, as railroads are now built. It was finished to Frankfort in December, 1835, and its completion celebrated in a manner becoming so important an event. Although ranking as one of the oldest railroads of the United States, it was not fully completed through to Louisville until 1851, and by a consolidation of the two divisions of the road—that between Lexington and Frankfort, and between Frankfort and Louisville—in 1857, it became one road and company.

One of the first railroad projects that excited special interest in Paris and Bourbon County, was that known as the Charleston & Cincinnati Railroad. This trunk line was to extend from Charleston, S. C., to Cincinnati, Ohio, or from Cincinnati to Charleston (as might appear to its friends most convenient and practicable), passing through Lexington with diverging lines from the latter place to Louisville, Paris, Maysville, Newport, Covington, etc., etc., and almost every other town that wanted a railroad. The people took a lively interest in the matter, and flattering hopes were entertained of its successful and early completion. For several years, the agitation of the enterprise was kept up. Companies were formed and chartered by the Legislature, lines were surveyed, terminal and intersecting points suggested, and wind and gas enough expended to build several railroads. But it all amounted to nothing, and the interest in the project "grew smaller by degrees, and beautifully less," until finally the Charleston & Cincinnati Railroad died a natural death.

The Kentucky Central Railroad.—This road, so far, is the only culmination of railroad enterprise Bourbon County enjoys. Of all the railroad projects that have been agitated by her people, this, and its Maysville branch, are all that have been carried through to completion. These are much better than no railroad at all, but in the system, the experienced railroad man discovers vast room for improvement. The agitation of building a railroad from Paris to Covington, and from Paris to Lexington commenced as early as 1848. The county gave originally $150,000 in private subscriptions, and afterward voted $100,000 more. In 1853, the road was completed from Lexington to Paris, under the title of the "Lexington & Covington Railroad," and the first train passed between Lexington and Paris on the 22d of December of that year. In the fall of 1854, it was finished from Covington to Paris. and trains ran through from Covington to Lexington, The building of the entire road cost near $5,000,000.

The early years of the Kentucky Central were somewhat checkered, like many other railroad enterprises of that day. It was sold in 1859 by a decree of court, and bought by Boulder & Co. for $2,225,000. Afterward, the stockholders resisted the sale, and the matter was submitted to the United States Court at Covington, and the sale decided valid. A number of the old stockholders, John Bedford, Dr. Perrin and others then carried it to the Court of Appeals, which tribunal reversed the whole thing. Boulder & Co. next made an application to the Court of Appeals to have the case remanded back to the Court at Covington for a new hearing. In the meantime, however, a compromise was effected at 75 cents on the dollar for a new road. The title was also changed from "Lexington & Covington" to "Kentucky Central Railroad," by which it is still known. In 1880, the company sold out to M. E. Ingalls & Co., at 40 cents on the dollar. Recently, it was purchased by Mr. C. P. Huntington, of the Chesapeake & Ohio Railroad, at 60 cents on the dollar, who is the present owner. C. Alexander, one of the directors, owns most of the stock now held in Bourbon County. The present directory is composed of the following gentlemen: C. P. Huntington and George Bliss, of New York; Gen. John Echols, Virginia; C. Alexander, Paris, Ky.; E. H. Pendleton, B. S. Cunningham and M. E. Ingalls, Cincinnati, of whom M. E. Ingalls is President and Gen. Echols Vice President.

The Maysville Railroad.—This is now a division of the Kentucky Central and was commenced about the same time of the Lexington & Covington Railroad, and was originally known as the "Lexington & Maysville Railroad." Bourbon County contributed $200,000 to its building; Fayette and Mason voted alike amounts. After passing through various changes, full details of which will be found under the head of Nicholas County, it was purchased by the Kentucky Central, and is now operated as a division of the latter road. It should be a good paying line, but seems rather to always have been a somewhat poor investment to its owners.

The Kentucky Central Extension appears now to be a settled fact. It diverges from the main line at Paris, and passes through Winchester and Richmond, tapping the Knoxville Branch of the Louisville & Nashville system at or near Livingston, Ky., making the Kentucky Central proper about 170 miles in length. The estimated cost of the extension is $1,915,000. The following is from the last report (January, 1882) of President Ingalls, of the Kentucky Central: "The right of way was donated by Bourbon County, and exemption from taxation for twenty years was guaranteed by Clark County, and what was equivalent to $125,000 voted by Madison County in aid of same. The work is now in progress, and the board hope to have the line in operation by July 1, 1883. At the same time the extension was resolved on, it was decided to at once rebuild the main line and equipment, so as to be ready for the increase of business that was expected from the new line. The increase in gross earnings has been very satisfactory. They net all we could expect in the condition of the property and the extensive improvements we were making. After this current year, the property will be in such fine condition it can easily be operated for less than 60 per cent of its gross earnings."

This extension, when completed, will render the Kentucky Central one of the most valuable roads in the country, as the new line passes through coal fields and mineral regions, the best in the State, and hitherto with little or no railroad facilities. As work is now in rapid progress upon the different divisions of the extension, its completion may be expected at no distant day.

The Paris, Georgetown & Frankfort Railroad.—This is a project that has been agitated somewhat in this county, but as there is considerable opposition to the enterprise, its final completion, or building rather, for so far nothing has been done but the "wind work," seems just a little problematical. As a gentleman informed us,

"The road begins nowhere, ends nowhere, and there are no stations between." If built, the most it can ever be is a local feeder to some other road. Under the first proposition to build a road from Paris to Frankfort, the county agreed to give $400,000 ; it failed, and under the new order of things the county, we believe, proposes to give $100,000. The project is still being agitated, but time only will show to what result.

Agriculture.—This science is the great source of our prosperity, and is a subject in which we are all interested. It is said that gold is the power that moves the world and it might also be said that agriculture is the power that moves gold. All thriving interests, all prosperous industries, and all trades and professions, receive their means of support either directly or indirectly from agriculture. Its progress in Bourbon County for the last hundred years, is not the least interesting, nor the least important part of her history. The pioneers who commenced tilling soil here with a few rude implements of husbandry, laid the foundation of that perfect system of agriculture of the present. They were mostly poor and compelled to labor for a support, and it required brave hearts, strong arms, and willing hands—just such as they possessed—to conquer the difficulties with which they had to contend. The country was open to the raids of a savage foe. It often occurred that, while one-half of the male members were at work clearing the land or tending their small crops, the other half, with guns in hand, were standing guard to protect the laborers from the savages.

The tools and implements with which the pioneer farmer had to work were few in number and of a poor kind. The plow was the old "bar-share," some with and some without coulters; all had the wooden mold-board, and long beam and handles. Generally, they were of a size between the one and two horse plows, for they had to be used in both capacities. The hoes and axes were clumsy implements, and were forged and finished by the ordinary blacksmith. The hoes had no steel in them, and there was but little in the axes, and that little often of an inferior quality. If any of these were broken beyond the ability of the smith at the station to repair, a new supply had to be procured from the older settlements of the East. There was some compensation, however, for all these disadvantages under which the pioneer labored. The virgin soil of the now well-known and famous Blue Grass Region was so fruitful that it yielded bountiful crops, even under poor preparation and cultivation. The first little crop consisted of a "patch" of corn, potatoes, beans, pumpkins, and in some cases a few other "eatables." A small crop of tobacco was almost indispensable, and, if possible, a "patch" of flax was grown, from the lint of which the family clothing for summer wear was manufactured. This brought into use the spinning-wheel and the loom, implements which had been brought to the country by the pioneers, and which constituted the most important articles of housekeeping, as all the women and girls could spin and weave.

In the early history of the county, the pioneers were favored by the mildness of the climate, the abundance of wild game and the wonderful fertility of the land when brought into cultivation, which, as we have said, yielded the most bountiful crops. Step by step the hardy settlers made their inroads upon the heavy forests, enlarged their farms and increased their flocks and herds, until they had a surplus beyond their own wants and those of their own families. This directed attention to the question of markets, which hitherto had been confined to the Eastern cities, only accessible by overland transportation. But now the navigation of the Mississippi was looked to as a means of obviating these difficulties. Flat-boating out of the Licking River was tried, but its navigation proving perilous, the produce of the country was hauled to the Kentucky River, where boats were loaded by enterprising men with bacon, grain and whisky, and upon the spring tides floated out into the Ohio, thence to the Mississippi, and on to New Orleans, where the cargoes were disposed of, sometimes for cash, and sometimes exchanged for sugar, coffee and molasses, which were brought back with considerable labor and expense. After the victory of Gen. Wayne in 1794, which finally drove the Indians from Kentucky, the county rapidly settled, and markets were formed, formed for the surplus products nearer home.

The subject of negro slavery, as identified with the agriculture of the county, is deserving of some notice in this connection. Many of the early settlers, who were from Maryland and Virginia, brought negro slaves here with them. They were obtained by inheritance, or were purchased with their money, and were considered as much a part of the property of the owner as anything else which he possessed. As pertinent to the subject, we make the following extract from an article written by Dr. R. J. Spurr: "Without the labor of the negro, this region would have made much slower progress in its settlement, and the character of its population would probably have been very different. To negro slavery we are largely indebted for the chivalric character and open-handed hospitality of our fathers. * * * While the negro, as a slave, had some weaknesses, such as a lack of proper respect for the truth, a prospensity to petty pilfering, and a great fondness for alcoholic drinks, yet the masses were faithful to their owners, industrious and economical, and had at heart their welfare, prosperity and good name. They were good operatives on the farm, and, as a rule, were intrusted with the execution of the work to be done in the absence of the proprietor, taking great pride in accomplishing more and better work than was expected of them; the wife and children of the master were always safe under their protection. Where a man's circumstances compelled him to labor, he would make a 'hand' with the negroes, requiring no more work of them than he performed himself. The negro had his house to himself and family, all of whom were well fed, well clothed in domestic cloth, attended to in sickness by the family physician, and as carefully nursed as any other member of the family. Their supply of fuel for winter use was unlimited, and during cold weather they kept up rousing fires both day and night. Nearly all of them had their 'truck patches' of from a half to an acre of ground, and could raise such produce as suited their taste, sweet potatoes, tobacco and melons being their favorite crops. Saturday afternoon was usually given them to work their 'patches,' and at night the more thrifty would 'cobble' shoes, make brooms, cut cord-wood and do other odd jobs to make money, which, unfortunately, was too frequently spent for whisky. Flagrant violations of domestic law were occasionally visited with stripes; this punishment, however, was rarely resorted to, except here and there by a fiend in human shape, who had no fear of God nor respect for the opinions of men. This class were few in number, and were frowned upon by the more respectable class of society. Persons who had not known anything practically of slavery until they came to the country, so soon as their circumstances would permit, became the owners of slaves, and almost invariably proved to be the hardest task-masters.

"The slaves, with no cares pressing upon them, were the happiest people to be found in any commnnity. A failure of the crops, loss of stock, or pecuniary troubles, while sympathized in by them, caused none of that anxiety which the owner experienced. They were all, men and women, raised to habits of industry. They are *now* all FREEMEN, and the older ones, educated and accustomed to work, are rapidly passing away, while a new generation is coming on; reared with no restraints, they look upon work as one of the relics of slavery, and prefer anything, almost, to honest labor. Under this state of things, their future is not very bright nor flattering. Many of the slaves, belonging to the more conscientious of our citizens, were sufficiently educated to enable them to read the Bible, but the mass received no scholastic training. Their religious instruction, however, was not neglected. At family worship, they were brought into the house, the Scriptures read and explained to them, and encouragement to attend church given them. Many of them united with the various churches, whose records still show a considerable number of the colored population among the early membership, a majority of whom were noted for their strong abiding faith and strict moral deportment.

"There were cases in which servants proved incorrigible, and sooner or later this class found their way to the cotton fields of the far South. Negroes were never reared here as an article of merchandise, but for the use of their owner, and, if true and trusty, were very seldom parted with. Men were encouraged to take their wives at home, if a suitable woman was in the family. If not, they generally found one in the immediate vicinity, when they were allowed to go to see her every night in the week, and as a general thing they were more steadfast to their families than they are now. Husband and wife were always kept together when possible, and often at great sacrifice. When the owner of either husband or wife were about removing to a distant place, some trade would be made, either by purchase or exchange, to prevent their separation. In such cases, a man or woman would be parted with by the owner that otherwise money could not have bought."

Wheat was one of the early productions of the farmers. At first, there was a market for the small surplus, found in the new comers; but as it was more extensively produced, it, like other products of the country, was shipped to New Orleans; the price usually varying from 25 cents to 50 cents a bushel. The wheat crop was irregular then as now, sometimes yielding largely, and other years failing almost entirely. Some extraordinary crops would occasionally be produced, but at irregular periods. In harvesting the wheat crop, the sickle, or "reap-hook," was used, each reaper binding the grain he cut, the wages for which was from 50 cents to 75 cents per day, and to cut and bind an acre was considered a good day's work. It was not until about 1820–25 that the "cradle" came into use as an implement for cutting grain. It was thought by many to be a labor-saving machine, and expedited the harvesting of a crop, but others clung to the reap-hook as cheapest and best. About the year 1840, the reaper drawn by horses was introduced. A writer upon agriculture says: "The reaper, crude and imperfect at first, it came to us represented by oily-tongued men, who induced our farmers to buy it. The early harvester was a heavy tax, costing the farmer dearly and doing poor work. The improvements upon harvesters have all been paid for by the farmer, and not by the manufacturer; the latter made and sold them at a profit; the farmer bought them, but soon

"Pleasant Retreat" Residence of James Scott, Paris and North Middletown Pike, Ky.

saw something that suited him better, when he would buy it, throwing his old machine aside. The harvester, while costly, enables us to raise a larger acreage of grain, but probably at an equal cost per acre as when the sickle was used exclusively in harvesting. The manner in which the early farmers worked their land for wheat and corn was incalculable injury to it, the heavy rains of summer carrying away much of the loose soil."

Upon the early cultivation of wheat, Gov. Garrard, in an address delivered before the Bourbon County Agricultural Society, in 1838, said: "Attention was early turned to the culture of wheat for the supply of the New Orleans market, with flour. The crops of wheat proved profitable to the farmers for some years, and some of the exporters of flour were successful, while others sunk money, owing in part to the high price of wheat (six shillings per bushel), and in fact to the difficulty of navigating our streams. As soon as the citizens of Ohio came into competition with us in the Orleans market, we were compelled to relinquish it as unprofitable, owing to their being able to prepare and reach the market before us, and owing to their water power being preferable to ours, for both grinding and boating. The farmers finally declined the culture of wheat, except for home consumption."

Corn was the first of all crops raised by the pioneers. It was not cut up as it is now, but the blades were usually pulled off below the ears, cured, tied in bundles, stacked in the field or put away in the barn for horse-feed. After this was done, the tops were cut off just above the ears and put up in shocks, and during winter used to feed the cows. In the fall, when the corn was ripe, it was pulled from the stalk, hauled and thrown in a pile, and the neighbors invited in to help husk it. This was a gala time for the darkies, whose "corn-songs" are still remembered by the old people of the country. A sketch of the grasses of this section would be interesting if it could be relied on as correct. Of the famous blue grass, all that is known of its origin and introduction is given in a preceding article. Of native grasses there were but few varieties found here by the early settlers. Red clover was brought from the Eastern States somewhere between 1800 and 1810. Timothy, herd's grass, orchard grass, fox-tail, crab grass, etc., etc., were all brought here, either accidentally or otherwise, none of them being native of this region. In the early part of the century, rye was extensively produced. It was considered a valuable crop for more reasons than one; it was a valuable pasturage during the winter and spring for your stock; then to make a crop of grain to be fed down to hogs for the early markets; and when not thus disposed of, it was cut, and the grain made into whisky.

When the production of hemp was commenced in this community, the crop was pulled by hand, in the same manner as flax. It was manufactured into bagging, rope and twine for baling cotton, and found a market in the Southern States. Before the age of turnpikes, railroads and steam navigation, the marketing of hemp was a heavy undertaking, the usual mode being by wagons to Knoxville, Tenn., Decatur, Ala., Greenville, S. C., and other points, from where the wagons returned loaded with cotton. The first implement used in harvesting hemp was called the "strike-hook," somewhat like the grain sickle or reap-hook. About 1832, this was superseded by the "drag-hook," an implement still much in use. Hemp cradles have been tried, but have proved failures. Mowing machines are now considerably used, and with apparent success when in careful hands.

The water-rotting of hemp was prosecuted to some extent at one time, but it was soon abandoned on account of the work being so dirty and laborious. Previous to the water-rotting process, an effort was made to break unrotted hemp, but it was never successful, as the cordage made from such an article of hemp did not hold tar well, and was very liable to decay in warm climates. Many efforts have been made to get machinery that would economically break hemp, but none has been invented yet that proved successful, and the old "hand-break," now, as in the past, is principally relied upon.

The breeding and rearing of fine stock of all kinds has, from an early day, been a favorite pursuit throughout Central Kentucky, and has given to the Blue Grass Region a world-wide reputation. The subject, however, of blooded stock will be taken up in another chapter, where it will be treated at length by men perfectly familiar with it.

The following statistics from the Auditor's report for 1881, show something of the county's wealth and importance: Value of land as assessed, $5,740,403; average value of land per acre, $33.20; number of horses and mares, 3,679, value of same, $117,790; number of mules, 1,409, value of same, $53,862; number of sheep, 47,920, value of same, $90,975; number of hogs, 2,995, value of same, $6,227; number of cattle, 9,345, value of same, $274,518; total valuation of property, $7,788,472. Pounds of tobacco raised in the county, 121,800; pounds of hemp, 1,327,500; bushels of corn, 509,395; bushels of wheat, 161,350. In the address of Gov. Garrard's, already quoted from, he gives the following amount of stock and produce sold from eighty-four farms in Bourbon County, from the first of September, 1837, to the first of June, 1838: "Cattle, $76,000; hogs, $65,000; horses and mules, $23,000;

hemp and stock of various kinds (which were added together), $136,000, making a total of $300,000."

As showing something of the size and weight of Bourbon County cattle, a car-load was shipped from Paris, consisting of twelve head, December 15, 1874, by Bedford, Kennedy & Ferguson, which averaged 2,515 pounds. They were shipped to New York, and taken altogether are said to have been the largest ever received in a single lot in that market—the lightest weight being 2,150, and the heaviest, 2,995 pounds. They were thoroughbred Durhams, of the "1817 importation," were bred and raised by Alexander Brand, Esq., and sold by John A. Merrett and H. F. Burchard. The item went the rounds of the press at the time and was highly commented on throughout the country. So much interest did the shippers take in it, they had each steer photographed and grouped into a sort of portrait gallery.

Fairs.—The progress and growth of agriculture in the county, is more fully shown by a sketch of the fairs and associations that have existed, and are now in existence. Collins tells us that the first agricultural fair in Bourbon County was held in 1818, and that the present association held its first fair in 1836, and regularly every year since, except two years during the war, but another authority (Keller and McCann) takes issue with Mr. Collins, and says that if a fair was held in 1818, the proverbial "oldest inhabitant" knows nothing about it. Nor have we found anything nor learned anything of a fair held in 1818. There is little to be learned in regard to the early fairs of the county, as most of the early records have been destroyed. We find in an old copy of the *Citizen*, published in 1838, an address delivered by Gov. Garrard before the Bourbon County Agricultural Society, several extracts from which we have already given in the preceding pages. Without attempting to follow the association through all of its eventful history, from its organization to the present time, we will give a list of the officers and directors since the close of the war, which is as far back as we have been able to obtain reliable data. Beginning with the year 1866, the officers and directors were as follows: B. J. Clay, President; James Hall and Horace Miller, Vice Presidents; W. W. Mitchell, Treasurer, and B. F. Pullen, Secretary. Directors, James A. Cunningham, W. A. Parker, J. D. Butler, George M. Bedford, F. P. Clay, Val Hildreth, Joseph Ewalt, Jacob Spears and Joseph Mitchell.

In 1867, the following officers were elected: B. J. Clay, President; James Hall and George M. Bedford, Vice Presidents; W. W. Mitchell, Treasurer, and B. F. Pullen, Secretary. Joseph Mitchell, Horace Miller, James A. Cunningham, Val Hildreth, J. D. Butler, H. W. Rice, E. G. Bedford, J. W. Ferguson, John Cunningham, Dr. W. Fithian, were elected Directors. In 1868, B. J. Clay was re-elected President, and Joseph Mitchell and James Hall, Vice Presidents; B. F. Pullen, Treasurer, and J. A. Howerton, Secretary. Directors: J. A. Cunningham, Horace Miller, J. W. Ferguson, J. D. Butler, H. W. Rice, J. H. Ewalt, G. M. Bedford, E. G. Bedford, B. F. Bedford and E. B. Bishop. Annual membership was fixed at $4. In 1869, the same officers were elected, with the exception of J. W. Ferguson, who was elected Vice President in place of James Hall. Several changes were made in the directory, as follows: H. J. Rice, J. D. Butler, Horace Miller, B. F. Bedford, F. J. Barber, J. A. Cunningham, J. S. Kenney, Abram Renick, Joseph Ewalt and M. M. Clay.

The receipts were	$5,033 01
Expenditures	3,453 49
Balance	$1,579 52

In 1870, the annual meeting was changed from the second Saturday in April to the second Saturday in February, and the following officers elected: Same as last year, except James Hall was elected Vice President in place of Ferguson; J. W. Ferguson, H. M. Rosenberg, H. W. Rice, Joseph Scott, E. G. Bedford, F. J. Barber, J. D. Butler, J. S. Kenney, G. M. Bedford and James A. Cunningham, Directors. In 1871, B. J. Clay, President; Joseph Mitchell and J. W. Ferguson, Vice Presidents; B. F. Pullen, Treasurer, and James A. Howerton, Secretary. Directors: J. D. Butler, F. J. Barber, B. F. Bedford, Jr., E. G. Bedford, J. A. Cunningham, M. M. Clay, Joseph Ewalt, James Hall, J. S. Kenney and H. M. Rosenberg. In 1872, the old officers were re-elected, and a few changes made in the directory.

The total receipts were	$7,573 70
Expenditures total	7,545 48
Balance	$ 27 22

The same result followed the election of officers for 1873, and J. S. Kenney, E. G. Bedford, M. M. Clay, B. F. Bedford, S. P. Kennedy, James Cunningham, W. H. Renick, Harmon D. Ayres, H. C. Hutchcraft and Joseph Scott were elected Directors. In 1874, James Hall took the place of Joseph Mitchell as a Vice President—other officers were re-elected. A few changes were made in the directory. Same officers in 1875, with a few changes in the directory. In 1876, B. J. Clay was re-elected President; Joseph Mitchell and J. A. Howerton, Vice Presidents; Mr. Pullen was re-elected Treasurer, and W. A. Parker, Secretary; a few changes were made in the directory. In 1877, J. W. Ferguson took the place of J. A. Howerton as Vice President, and T. P. Muir was elected Secretary in place of

Mr. Parker, with a few changes in the directory. The old officers were re-elected in 1878, except C. M. Clay, Jr., who took the place of Ferguson as Vice President, with the following directory: F. Gano Hill, H. C. Hutchcraft, G. W. Morrow, J. Smith Kenney, B. F. Bedford, M. M. Clay, William Bedford, J. B. Kennedy, W. H. Renick and W. A. Parker. In 1879, C. M. Clay, Jr., was elected President; J. W. Ferguson and Joseph Mitchell, Vice Presidents; B. F. Pullen, Treasurer and W. A. Parker, Secretary, with but few changes in the directory. The old officers were all re-elected in 1880, and a few changes made in the directory. The same result was had in 1881, and in 1882, the following gentlemen were elected, viz.: J. W. Ferguson, President; B. F. Bedford and F. Gano Hill, Vice Presidents; B. F. Pullen, Treasurer; W. A. Parker, Secretary; and Brent Hutchcraft, H. C. Hutchcraft, M. M. Clay, John T. Hinton, John B. Kennedy, W. H. Renick, J. T. Hughes, H. C. Smith, George W. Morrow and J. W. Bedford were elected Directors.

Distilleries.—The manufacture of whisky is one of the most extensive and valuable interests, not only of Bourbon County, but of the entire Blue Grass Region. Indeed, the blue grass seems to have a beneficial effect on whisky, as it has on everything else that comes in reach of it. William Warfield, Esq., of Fayette County, tells us that the "peculiar suitability of blue grass pastures for beef-making" is unsurpassed; Mr. Ben Bruce, editor of the *Live Stock Record*, says: "No portion of America is so highly favored for the breeding and rearing of fine horses" as the Blue Grass Region of Kentucky. Dr. Peter, chemist to the State Geological Survey, is of the opinion that "even men take on a higher development," in this favored section; we all know that the beauty of the Blue Grass ladies has become proverbial; then why should not Blue Grass whisky be better? It is the universal opinion abroad, that all the Bourbon whisky shipped to every point is not only made in the Blue Grass Region, but is the product of Bourbon County alone, whence it receives its name. That whisky is a valuable commercial interest in this part of the State, and that the revenue derived from its sale and manufacture is large, is a fact beyond dispute; that it is a foe, bitter and relentless to Christian civilization, is a fact equally palpable.

It is not our province, however, as a historian, to discuss the evils of whisky, but to view it from a commercial standpoint. We were informed by a gentleman in Ohio, some time ago, that whisky would be sold as long as there was 8 cents profit on a 10-cent drink, and we have no doubt that so long as it is extensively sold, as it is now, it will be manufactured. Commercially then, it is one of the great business interests of this portion of Kentucky; next to fine stock, the most important, perhaps, and the most valuable.

From the very earliest settlement of the country, the manufacture of whisky has been numbered among its industries. The pioneers made whisky for the purpose of finding a market for their surplus grain. Since the day of the little log distillery, with a capacity of a few barrels per week, the business has grown and increased with the growth and development of the country. It is a significant fact, that of all the early manufacturing industries of Paris and Bourbon County, that of whisky alone has kept pace with the time. The hemp factories, the cotton mills, etc., are gone, and few of the present generation can point out the sites where erst they stood, but the distilleries are more flourishing than ever before.

It is not known at the present day, with any degree of certainty, perhaps, who started the first distillery in the county, or in what year the business was begun. Collins has the following upon the subject: "The first distillery in Bourbon County was near where the manufactory of W. H. Thomas stood in 1869, and was erected about 1790, by Jacob Spears, and others from Pennsylvania. Two negroes cut down the trees and hauled them to the distillery, while Mr. Spears cut the timber into suitable sizes, distilled, went to mill, and also attended a fine stallion he had brought with him. Others claim that Capt. John Hamilton, who run away from Pennsylvania on account of his participation in the 'whisky insurrection,' distilled in this region before Spears." We do not know if this is true, but no doubt it is, that the business commenced at least that far back. Emanuel Wyatt operated a small distillery in a very early day on land now owned by C. M. Clay; Benjamin Bedford also had a distillery very early. Robert Owen built a small distillery in the present precinct of North Middletown in 1806; and in what is now Centerville Precinct there were several distilleries built in early times. Thus the business was inaugurated in different parts of the county, and has increased and expanded to its present dimensions. An old gentleman informed us that those were the days of "honest whisky," when a bushel of grain would make two gallons of whisky that would retail at 25 cents a gallon. Then there was not so much red tape connected with making whisky as there is at present; "Uncle Sam" was not an interested partner as he is now, and anybody and everybody who felt a desire to do so were permitted to make it in the light of the sun, instead of having his operations veiled in "moonshine." But without dwelling longer upon the early manufacture of the article, we will devote a little space to the business as conducted at the present day.

There are seven distilleries in Bourbon County, now in successful operation, (and several others standing idle, owing to scarcity of grain the past year), owned and located as follows: White's Distillery at Paris; the Paris Distillery in Paris Precinct; Davies' Distillery at Millersburg; W. H. Thomas' in Paris Precinct; Ford & Bowen's at Ruddel's Mills; George Pugh's and Gus Pugh & Co.'s in the north part of the county.

White's Distillery, No. 14, Seventh District, is located in East Paris, on Stoner Creek. It was commenced by a man named Foley in 1855, but not completed until the following year. James A. Miller bought out Foley, and started it in operation in 1856, continuing the business until his death in the summer of 1860. In the following fall, Tarr, Hibler & White took charge of it and operated it for two years. Hibler sold out in 1863 to Tarr & White, and, in 1868, C. Alexander bought Tarr's interest. G. G. White bought out Alexander in 1877, and, in 1880, Mr. Ferguson bought a half interest in the concern, since which time the firm has been G. G. White & Co. The capacity of this distillery is four hundred bushels every twelve hours; the brand, "Chicken Cock," and there is a ready demand for the article; the manufacture of which amounts to about 9,000 barrels yearly. The storage capacity of the establishment is now 2,400 barrels, and the firm contemplate building a new warehouse soon of 1,800 to 2,000 barrels capacity. The article manufactured is "Sweet Mash Bourbon, Fire Copper," and all modern appliances are used, and thirty-five men are employed. The capacity for stock-feeding is 500 cattle and 800 hogs. Until the years 1880–81, all the grain used was purchased in the county; since that time most of it has been received from abroad. The main distillery building is 40x48 feet; boiler shed 42x50 feet. The concern is now mashing 600 bushels daily, though the usual quantity is 400 bushels. In 1881, the average was 4.14 gallons; in 1882, nearly 4½ gallons to the bushel. A cooper-shop is attached to the establishment.

Paris Distillery, No. —, Seventh district, is located in Paris Precinct, on the North Division of the Kentucky Central Railroad, and on the Paris & North Middletown Turnpike, one mile from Paris. It was built in 1868, and commenced operation in January, 1869, W. T. Buckner and George M. Bedford, proprietors, under the firm name of Buckner & Bedford. They continued until the summer of 1880, when they were bought out by Samuel Clay, Jr., & Co., who have since operated it. Under the proprietorship of Buckner & Bedford it made "sweet mash," but under the new firm it has changed to a "sour mash" establishment. The brand is "Paris Distillery—Hand Made." The capacity is 412 bushels; feed about 300 head of cattle, and employ in distillery proper some thirty hands. Storage capacity is about 15,000 barrels.

The Millersburg Distillery in the Seventh District, was completed February 1, 1882, and was built by William Davie. It is hand-made sour mash; with all the modern conveniences, has a daily capacity of 500 bushels, and annual product of 6,000 barrels. The distillery building proper is 70x145 feet, and was completed ready for business at an expenditure of about $40,000. Thirty hands are employed at an average of $2 per day wages. It is located on the Maysville Division of the Kentucky Central Railroad, in the village of Millersburg. Bonded capacity of the warehouse is 15,000 barrels, and the necessary corn-cribs, cooper-shops, etc., are attached. Pure water from wells, 24 to 30 feet, is used. Everything is complete, about the establishment, and the reputation of Bourbon whisky will be fully maintained. It is expected to use the products of the surrounding country in the manufacture of whisky. At the present writing (February, 1882), it is just getting down to business.

Ford & Bowen's Distillery is located at Kiser's Station, on the Kentucky Central Railroad, north of Paris. It was originally built by Mr. B. Bowen in 1857, the father of H. C. Bowen, and was run by him until 1867, with the "Bowen Brand," and is the second oldest sweet-mash distillery in the county. The building was formerly a cotton and woolen factory. B. Bowen first took in his son George, and son-in-law Thomas Duvall, as partners, which continued for three years, when the Bowens bought out Duvall, and in 1867 Mr. Bowen sold to his son George. The latter took George W. Wyatt into partnership, under the firm of Bowen & Wyatt. He afterward bought out Wyatt, and sold an interest to H. C. Clay and James K. Ford, when the firm became H. C. Clay & Co., and so remained until 1880, since when it has been as above, Ford & Bowen. The brand is "Peacock," which was established when the firm became H. C. Clay & Co. Capacity, 600 bushels of sweet mash every twenty-four hours. Capital invested, $50,000. Warehouse, built in 1880; capacity, 4,000 barrels; and brick house, built in 1881, of 8,000 barrels capacity; amount now in bond 6,000 barrels; cooper-shop attached, and about twenty hands altogether are employed.

H. C. Bowen's Distillery, No. 102, of the Seventh District, is located at Ruddel's Mills, on Stoner Creek, and was built by Howard & Bowen in 1868–69. About a year afterward, Mr. Howard died, and after several changes in firm in 1879, Mr. H. C. Bowen became sole proprietor. The warehouse was erected by the present owner, and has a capacity of 8,000 barrels; made in 1881, 3,400 barrels; now in bond 5,500 barrels; capacity, 444 bushels per day.

The distillery is located about two miles from Shawhan's Station, on the Kentucky Central Railroad, from which most of the shipments are made. Most of the grain is purchased in the county; cooper-shop attached, which makes from thirty-five to forty barrels per day. About twenty hands are employed, at an average of $2.00 per day wages. Capital invested, $50,000; brand, "H. C. Bowen," and is sweet-mash make.

W. H. Thomas' Distillery is five miles north of Paris, and three miles west of Kiser's Station. This is an old establishment, dating back to 1836–38, and was built by Jacob Spears, and has been owned and operated by several parties; has stood idle, and then been started up again, finally becoming the property of W. H. Thomas, the present proprietor. It makes pure copper whisky, and has storage capacity for about 2,500 barrels; a cooper-shop is attached, which makes the barrels used in the distillery. The brand of whisky made is "W. H. Thomas;" capacity, 54 bushels per day; and during the year 1881 there were made 900 barrels, it being a small establishment.

George Pugh's Distillery, is No. 13 of the Seventh Internal Revenue District of Kentucky, and was built by Jacob Wilson about 1800, and is the oldest distillery in the county now in operation. It was washed away during a time of high water, and re-built by John Ewalt. It lay idle for several years, and in the fall of 1856 George Pugh bought and re-built it and he and his sons have since run it. It is operated by water-power, and is a very small establishment, making only about one hundred and fifty barrels annually. It is in Ruddel's Mills Precinct, at the mouth of Townsend Creek, about eight miles from Paris. Has storage room for 700 barrels, and about 400 barrels in bond.

The distillery of J. S. Shawhan is a small establishment, located on the pike, about one and a half miles west of Shawhan Station, on the Kentucky Central Railroad. It was built by Mr. Shawhan in 1874, and made in 1881 only 232 barrels, and is at present standing idle.

Gus Pugh & Co.'s Distillery is No. 44, and is located about a quarter of a mile east of Shawhan Station. It was built in 1858 by Samuel Ewalt, and remodeled in 1872 by Gus Pugh—bought by him in 1870 of Ewalt. The brand is "Gus Pugh;" amount in bond, 300 barrels; capacity, 30 bushels per day; about 250 barrels annual production. The establishment is run by steam, and the production is the "hand-made sour mash." Like the last mentioned, it is a small establishment, doing but little business.—*Perrin.*

CHAPTER VI.

SHORT-HORN CATTLE INTERESTS — ADAPTABILITY OF BOURBON COUNTY FOR CATTLE RAISING — BREEDERS OF SHORT-HORNS: GEN. GARRARD, REV. GANO, THE CLAYS, AND OTHERS—IMPORTING OF CATTLE—THE NORTH KENTUCKY IMPORTING ASSOICIATION—THE SHORT-HORN RECORD, ETC., ETC.

And the flocks conceived before the rods, and brought forth cattle ringstreaked, speckled and spotted.—Gen., xxx, 39.

WHILE the Short-Horn cattle of Bourbon County are so numerous, so widely known and admired, and influence such a large trade, yet when one begins to ask, How shall I present, or rather preserve in a collated form all the material that would be interesting on this subject? it seems as though he must first unravel a labyrinth to reduce the matter to any system that will not weary with details, and yet present the truth.

It is hard to avoid the herd-book style, and yet prevent the other extreme of writing an encyclopedia on the subject. It is hard to divest one's self of all prejudice against certain crosses, and candidly give each breeder the share of space he deserves. It is hard to ascertain the facts connected with those who have bred good herds in times long gone by, and who have passed out of the arena as breeders near half a century ago, many of whom have crossed the river, where we trust they have found pastures ever green, and fountains that never dry; yet who have gone without leaving behind them any records of their plan of breeding, or their herds, except so far as from year to year, they and the purchasers from their herds choose to send the same to the herd-books. Realizing all these difficulties, it is with great hesitation that we crave the sympathy and forbearance of the breeders of this county, who may expect to find recorded here more than in the power of one person to achieve. But endeavoring to collate what will be of interest to them, we shall try and give impartially some of the leading incidents connected with the Short-Horn cattle of the county.

The Short-Horn cattle interests of Bourbon County are so interwoven with that of all the counties in this State, and also with that of the United States in general that it is hard to draw the county lines through the history. Fayette, Clark, Harrison, Montgomery and Scott, all, to a certain extent, have a common source as to their cattle supply.

Bourbon County has interchanged with these counties, and supplied the leading herds in each with some of the material that rendered them also noted for their fine cattle, besides supplying so many herds throughout the United States with either a start or a head, that it seems to one who knows the history of Short-Horns in that particular that it is a history of all the leading herds in the United States.

Situated about equal distance from Winchester, Lexington, Georgetown and Cynthiana—accessible by railroads from Cincinnati, Lexington and Maysville—this county is wonderfully located for convenience in breeding, selling and shipping cattle. Watered by beautiful streams flowing all the year round, the fields covered even in winter with a verdure that seems to have some mysterious power in producing bone, sinew and muscle, both to man and beast, situated at that degree of latitude that presents but few variations of temperature, where stock may graze in the open air twelve months in the year. It is not to be wondered that man, assisted so bountifully by nature, has been able to feed, cross up, sort out, select and build up herds that rival any ever produced in England or the United States.

It is owing to this, assisted by the fact that Bourbon County has been peopled by gentlemen of means and pride and ambition, who, having endeavored to obtain their start from the best to be had, have given their time, talents, study and fortunes to the improvement of Short-Horn cattle, that this county stands in the foremost ranks as the home of thoroughbred Short-Horns.

This county is especially noted as a producing county, whilst owing to the many high-priced cattle sold, and the custom of annual sales, many have been tempted to buy and speculate, and ship stock to the West to sell again. Only those will be noticed in the short space allotted to this subject who have established themselves as breeders, and, of course, it would be impossible to notice all the stock owned in the county, because almost every farmer in Bourbon County has now or has had during his life a Short-Horn bull or cow, either pedigreed or non-pedigreed.

The principles of breeding are so well known to all Short-Horn breeders that the following suggestions are presented with reluctance; yet before criticizing let the reader answer this question: What is the correct theory of breeding; and am I pursuing that one?

So many have allowed prejudice to control their ideas of crossing, that form has in many instances been sacrificed to blood. But this has only been of late years, so that the injury has not yet been felt as much as it will be unless they retrace their steps, while it is time. Happily, this is confined to but few herds.

Again, many breeders have pursued a fixed type and standard, endeavoring to breed up to a certain form, requiring a good pedigree, but always insisting that the animal shall be good also. This class of breeders are a blessing to the cattle interests of the country.

Others have embarked largely in paper pedigrees, believing that *blue* blood, if costly, is all that is necessary. It is needless to say that this class have already come to grief.

Others have good herds, but have been compelled by the demands of the public to discard bulls that they desired and use others that were more fashionably colored or bred, saying truly, "I am too old, and have not the means to fight against the fashion. I must have money, and I cannot use the bull I prefer simply because the animal traces to a tribe in England that were not Bates nor Booth." They have the sympathy of every honest breeder, and the time may yet come in their generation when the sole question shall be, Where can we find the best individual Short-Horn? It is still true to a certain extent, that "like produces like," yet if you select a cow from the herd of a breeder, who has for years been breeding to produce a type of fine bone, quick flesh-producing, even lines and great style, and breed the same to a bull from the herd of a breeder who has been seeking alone for size without regard to shape, or to a bull from another breeder who has only sought after blood, you will be apt to miss the mark in the offspring, and can have no assurance that it will be like either sire or dam.

When the size is desired to be enlarged, it should not be too abruptly done, and there is such a thing as obtaining animals too large and coarse. If you can get a cow of say 1,600 pounds, and a bull of 2,300 pounds of fine style, fine bone, and good shape, you have them heavy enough for all general purposes.

Short-Horns of a true type and good shape, that is to say, level backed, wide crops, wide hips, swelling sides, fine bone, fine tail, neat blood-like appearance, straight lines across the hips, straight from the point of the hock to point of hip near the tail, straight along the belly from the brisket to the end of the flank, smooth shoulders, not sinking at the girth, soft elastic skin, good handlers, placid, calm eye, short in the legs, short tapering horns, waxy horns well set on, quiet disposition, good milkers, clean, clear muzzle, solid colors, either red or roan, these have long been sought after, bred for and purchased when attainable, and breeders with pride in their stock have endeavored to produce them from the earliest known period in Short-Horn history, and it is not surprising that Bourbon County breeders have in the main owned many that were never defeated in the show ring. And as such stock has been the result of much trouble and experiment, so it has and ever will deservedly command high prices. Requiring several generations of judicious crossing, weeding out defects, meeting out to the breeders many blanks with the prizes, it is a fascinating pursuit, and is increasing daily the number of its votaries.

It is worth while to notice in passing the change in the colors of Short-Horns, most every one can remember that there was a time within their memory that Short-Horn cattle were uniformly white and roan, with here and there a red.

Take, for example, one of the leading herds of this county in 1851, 1852 and 1853, of fifteen head recorded in Volume II, A. H. B. Eight were roans and seven whites. The same breeder would not allow a white animal to be used on his herd for a *bonus* of $3,000 a year. Who knows but the style and fashion may change back again into its former channel? It is well to observe that the scarcer and more rare Short-Horns of peculiar qualities become, the higher prices they are held at in some quarters. While, on the other hand, it is with satisfaction that we observe many new beginners whose names appear at the annual sales, from New York to California, and Minnesota to Texas, indicating that the people, as a mass, are beginning to appreciate the value of an infusion of thoroughbred blood into scrub herds, and to at last acknowledge that a two-year-old thoroughbred, or even high grade, is equal to a three-year-old of common, mongrel stock.

Among the early breeders of Short-Horn cattle in Bourbon County, we find the name of Gen. James T. Garrard, the father of the late Charles Garrard, who was also a breeder. Gen. James T. Garrard's stock was sold by his executors in 1838, at which sale the bull Eclipse was sold for $688 to George Bedford and A. V. Bedford, and the bull Exception brought $1,830, and was knocked down to Brutus J. Clay and the Hutchcrafts.

As the importation of 1817 will always be an interesting theme to the older breeders, especially to those who have even now an admiration for the stock, and which at one time stood at the head of many of the best herds in the county, a catalogue of the herd of late Gen. James T. Garrard, of cattle bred by him, is given below, taken from a manuscript of the papers of Charles Garrard, and published in the Franklin *Farmer* February 17, 1838:

BULLS.

No. 1—Cornplanter, calved September 4, 1821; was got by the imported Tecumseh, out of cow No. 1.

No. 2—Champion, sire and dam as No. 1; calved January 22, 1823.

No. 3—Sportsman, calved February 3, 1824; got by No. 1, and out of cow No. 2.

No. 4—Denton, calved January 31, 1827; got by bull No. 2, and out of cow No. 1.

No. 5—Exchange, calved in 1827; got by bull No. 2, and out of Sylvia, full sister to cow No. 1.

No. 6—Misfortune, calved in March, 1828; got by bull No. 3, and out of cow No. 1.

No. 7—Comet, calved in December, 1829; was got by bull No. 3, and out of cow No. 1.

No. 8—Duroc, calved in 1828; was got by bull No. 3, and out of Sylvia, full sister to cow No. 1.

No. 9—Drone, calved in 1830; was got by bull No. 3, out of cow No. 1.

No. 10—Slider, calved May 31, 1832; was got by bull No. 8, and out of cow No. 1.

No. 11—Exception, calved February 16, 1833; was got by bull No. 5, and out of cow No. 9.

No. 12—Dentonio, calved in June, 1834; was got by bull No. 4, and out of cow No. 3.

No. 13—Hubback, calved in April, 1834; was got by bull No. 4, and out of cow No. 9.

No. 14—Albion, calved in April, 1835; was got by bull No. 10, and out of cow No. 8.

No. 15—Suwarrow, calved March 4, 1833; was got by bull No. 5, and out of cow No. 6.

No. 16—Experiment, calved March 16, 1837; was got by bull No. 11, and out of cow No. 8.

No. 17—A roan bull, calved March 6, 1836; was got by bull No. 11, and out of cow No. 8.

COWS AND HEIFERS.

No. 1—Lady Munday, calved in 1819; was got by imported San Martin, out of imported Mrs. Motte.

No. 2—My Smith Heifer, calved in 1820; was got by imported San Martin, out of Capt. Smith's imported Durham cow.

No. 3—Tulip, calved February 22, 1824; was got by Miranda, and out of cow No. 1. Miranda was gotten in England, and out of Capt. Smith's Teeswater cow.

No. 4—Hyacinth, calved February 6, 1826; was got by bull No. 2, and out of cow No. 3.

No. 5—Beauty, calved in 1826; was got by bull No. 3, and out of cow No. 1.

No. 6—Miss Durham, calved in 1828; was got by bull No. 3, and out of cow No. 5.

No. 7—Sprightly, calved January 31, 1828; was got by bull No. 3, and out of cow No. 3.

No. 8—Moss Rose, calved October 29, 1829; was got by bull No. 3, and out of cow No. 3.

No. 9—Cherry, calved October 31, 1829; was got by bull No. 6, and out of cow No. 7.

No. 10—Red Heifer, sold to Abm Smith; calved in 1831 or 1832; was got by bull No. 8, out of cow No. 6.

No. 11—Drucilla, calved in 1831; was got by bull No. 8, and out of cow No. 1.

No. 12—Flora, calved in 1831; was got by bull No. 8, and out of cow No. 3.

No. 13—Primrose, calved in 1832; was got by bull No. 8, and out of cow No. 3.

No. 14—Maria, calved in February; was got by Oscar, out of cow No. 8.

No. 15—Matilda, calved February 28, 1835; was got by bull No. 10, and out of cow No. 9.

No. 16—Snowdrop, calved August 26, 1835; was got by bull No. 11, and out of cow No. 12.

No. 17—Malvina, calved March 6, 1836; was got by Imp. Matchem, out of cow No. 9.

No. 18—Miss Reese, calved December 11, 1835; was got by bull No. 11, and out of cow No. 3.

No. 19—Mary Ann, calved March 24, 1837; was got by Imp. Matchem, and out of cow No. 3.

No. 20—Marchioness, calved February 11, 1837; was got by Imp. Matchem, and out of cow No. 14.

The care taken in the compilation of this catalogue, before the American Herd-Book was thought of, commends itself to every breeder, and is an example of the attention Gen. Garrard paid to his stock.

The bull Otley (4632), probably one of the best bulls ever in Kentucky, was imported in 1836, by Messrs. Dunn & Smith, and sold to Wasson & Shropshire, of Bourbon County, for $2,100. His calves were noted for fine hair, and being good handlers.

In 1840, the Fayette County Importing Company sold the stock they imported in 1839. Among the purchasers, we find the following:

Orlando (3225), sold to H. Clay, Jr., Bourbon....	$305 00
Miss Luck, sold to H. Clay, Jr., Bourbon.......	800 00
Lady Elizabeth, sold to H. Clay, Jr., Bourbon...	660 00

In 1850, the Earl of Seaham (1499), was imported by Messrs. Stevens & Sherwood, and bought by Rev. John A. Gano, Sr.

In 1853, the Northern Kentucky Association (so called because all its members were north of the Kentucky River), commissioned Charles T. Garrard, Nelson Dudley and Solomon Vanmeter, to import some cattle. They brought over twenty-four head, and these were sold shortly after their arrival. Brutus J. Clay was President of this association, and many Bourbon County men were members. At this sale, the following stock fell to Bourbon breeders:

The roan bull, Diamond (416), was sold to a company, viz., Brutus J. Clay, ½; J. Duncan, ¼; H. Clay, ⅛; G. M. Bedford, ⅛. Total for..................................	$6,001 00
Lady Stanhope, by Earl Stanhope, to B. J. Clay,	1,500 00
Gem, by Broker (9993), T. L. Cunningham....	825 00
Necklace, by Duke of Athol (10150), H. Clay, Jr.,	805 00
Bracelet, twin sister to Necklace, M. M. Clay..	750 00
Lady Caroline, by Newtonian, B. J. Clay.....	1,825 00
Orphan Nell, by Ruby (10760), J. Hill and J. A. Gano....................................	1,000 00

In 1853, there was an association in Scott County that imported and sold the following:

Venus, by Fair Eclipse (11456), J. Hill..........	$710 00
Rosamond, by Sir Charles Napier (10816) S. Corbin,	575 00
Cameo, by Arrow (9906), W. Boswell...........	450 00

Among the early importers, we find the name of James E. Letton. He imported the celebrated bull Locomotive (4242), and the cow Miss Severs. He began breeding about 1837, and was breeding in 1841.

Mr. James Matson imported John O. Gaunt (11621), and Javelin (11610), about 1852.

The Hutchcraft Brothers—John, James and Reuben—were breeding in 1840, and constituted a firm. They imported the bull Van Buren 1062, bred by Col. Craddock, in England.

Charles S. Brent was one of the pioneer breeders of Bourbon County, and continued as such down to 1851. He, at an early day, took the trip over the Alleghany Mountains to Philadelphia, and brought over several head from Col. Powell's stock.

It is said that stopping at a wayside tavern in the wilds of Pennsylvania, one of the cows that he had purchased dropped a calf, and, in the night, the crafty landlord, with an eye to improving the scrub stock of Pennsylvania Mountains, and not having the fear of the law or his Maker before his eyes, stole the calf, and substituted one of his own in stead. But the theft was discovered, and the calf belonging to the Short-Horn cow found hid in the hay, and restored to its natural dam.

Among other breeders of note we find Rev. John A. Gano, who is still living, hale and hearty, although age is beginning to show.

He began the Bellevue herd in 1835 or 1836. The source of his herd was Phœnix and Rosette, two heifers, by Oliver (2387), in calf to Goldfinder (2066) purchased from Maj. Ben Warfield, near Lexington, Ky., at $1,100, in 1835.

He also bought of Gen. James Garrard some of Excep-

Jonathan Owen

tion produce. In 1839, he purchased the young bull Chesterfield (3364) from J. G. Dunn's herd at $470. He also bred to Imp. Otley (4632). In 1845, he bought Crescent (11319) of Maj. George W. Williams. In 1847, he purchased Locum (11698) from James Duncan, and the same year bought of James Renick, the bull calf, Gen. Worth, by Ashland.

In 1850, he owned Gold Eagle (535). In 1853, purchased the imported bull, Earl of Seaham (10181) at $2,000, and the same year he bought at James Matson's sale Duchess and Lady Washington, both in calf to Imp. John O. Gaunt (11621) at about $850.

In partnership with J. Hill, he bought Imp. Orphan Nell in 1853 at $1,000 at North Kentucky Importing Association sale, and with Mr. Hill purchased, in 1854, Imp. Venus, at Scott County Importing Company's sale at $600, and the same year Rev. John A. Gano bought Ruby at sale of Kentucky Importing Company. Orphan Nell was of the celebrated Princess tribe, and produced many prize winners. This herd has varied in the course of the past forty years, and generally averaged about twenty to thirty breeders. Present size of herd about nine head, but Mr. Gano expects to increase it soon.

James Bagg, of Bourbon County, also imported some valuable stock, among which we note Imp. bull Oakum (763) calved in 1852. Imp. Milo (711), and the cow Imp. Amelia by Plato, from which descended so many valuable show animals. He also imported the cow Pomona by Bedford, Jr. Mr. Bagg is still living in Bourbon County about six miles from Paris.

Charles T. Garrard, a son of Gen. James T. Garrard, closed out the remainder of his herd in 1865, November 15. He had been breeding many years, and was one of the early pioneers in Short-Horn raising in this county. At his sale he sold the bull Exchange (3050), and sixteen cows and heifers, at an average of $156, most of the cows were 1817 stock.

Maj. George W. Williams, at the sale of Fayette County Importing Company, in 1840, purchased Fashion at $440, and Zela, a calf of Fashion's, at $445. He was the breeder of Romulus (12019), and, in 1841, bred the celebrated cow Lonan by Imp. Otley, from which have descended probably more show stock than from any other single cow, and whose produce brought such high prices at the celebrated sale of D. McMillan, Xenia, Ohio. At the sale of Maj. Williams, the cow Imp. Zelia by Norfolk passed into the hands of Col. B. N. Shropshire, who also owned Imp. Otley, and Annie Fisk. Mr. Shropshire died in 1878, and was a breeder of Short-Horns up to time of his death.

James S. Duncan, also one of the early breeders, a son of Maj. Jerre Duncan, bought Lonan at Maj. Williams' sale. He also founded the celebrated Nannie Williams family. He bred Perfection (810) from Lonan cow. Mr. J. S. Duncan died in 1849.

Maj. Jerre Duncan was an extensive breeder in 1850. His stock was principally Lonan's Nannie Williams, Ruby by young Sir Dimple, etc. His final sale was in August, 1867.

Brutus J. Clay was for the last forty years, and, up to the time of his death in 1878, one of the foremost of Kentucky breeders, an enthusiastic admirer of Short-Horns, possessing a fine estate, and a breeder on a large scale. For over forty years the President of the Bourbon County Agricultural Association, and also President of the North Kentucky Importing Company, and a liberal buyer of best stock, he soon formed a basis for the Auvergne herd that has produced many prize winners. He began breeding in 1837, and procured his start at Gen. Garrard's sale. The average number of head kept by him has been about one hundred. He owned Imp. Lady Caroline, Lady Stanhope, Imp. Susan. He also imported, in 1853, Locomotive (646). Lady Caroline was imported in 1853, and was descended from Lady Sarah by Satellite, the finest and highest priced cow at Mason's sale at Chilton. Animals used on this herd were Orontes 2d, Rover, Wissahikon, Duke of Bloomfield, London Duke, etc.; families embraced in this herd also were Imp. Lady Lettontons, Imp. Bracelets, Imp. Adelaide and Imp. Goodnesses, etc. From 1856 to 1861, this herd took five herd premiums at the United States and State fairs.

Henry Clay, who is still living at the advanced age of eighty-three years, began his herd in 1839 and 1840, and has been continuously so engaged ever since at his farm on the Winchester pike, about five miles from Paris. He bought two cows from the Fayette Importing Company at the sale in 1840. Lady Elizabeth brought $660, and from her has descended nearly all his herd. She is the source from whence sprang the celebrated Nelly Bly family that commanded an average of $1,261 per head for the females at J. H. Spear's sale at Tallula, Ill., in 1875.

He also bought the cow Miss Luck, who died in his hands leaving the bull Whig.

At his sale in 1867, he sold Burnside, 4618; Mozark, 5976, and thirty-four cows, mostly Lady Elizabeths and Imp. Ianthe stock. The average herd numbered about thirty head. The best bull raised by him was Havelock 2598.

Among the early breeders, we find H. W. Varnon. He obtained the start of his herd from Noah Spears, Jr., John A. Gano, Maj. Williams and James Matson. He owned

Imp. Javelin, 11610, and sold six bulls and twenty-five cows at his sale in 1856.

Ben C. Bedford began breeding Short-Horns in this county in 1840, and was quite a prominent breeder for many years, he obtained his start from Gen. James T. Garrard. Most of his stock in the years 1844 to 1854, were 1817.

He bred to Pioneer, 818; Perfection, 810, and Exchange, 483. He has been dead for several years, but left a son, Ben F. Bedford, who will be noticed further in the proper place.

Among the noted breeders of the present day, whose experience reaches back almost half a century, we find George M. Bedford, the proprietor of the Stoner herd, whose farm is situated about four miles from Paris on the North Middletown Turnpike, the home of so many prize-winners. He began breeding in 1838, when he obtained his first thoroughbred bull, and purchased his cow in 1842. He bought stock from R. How, of Nicholas County, and from Samuel Campbell, of New York. He has kept his herd up to almost seventy-five head. The best cow owned by him among so many was probably 56th Duchess of Goodness. He owned an interest in Imp. Diamond, and Imp. Sebastopol. In 1860, his herd netted him $1,000 in prizes, The 14th Duke of Thorndale, which stood long at the head of his herd, sold for $17,500 at public sale.

Edwin G. Bedford, the proprietor of Woodland Villa herd, about five miles from Paris on the Lexington pike where he still resides, began breeding Short-Horns in 1842 or 1843. He soon established a national reputation with his Laura family (1817's), and his London Duchess family (with odd numbers), the latter tracing direct to Imp. Miss Hudson by Hermes (8145), and being crossed with such noted animals as 14th Duke of Thorndale, 2d Duke of Geneva, Imp. Duke of Airdrie, 5th Duke of Geneva, 21st Duke of Airdrie, etc. At his sale in 1874, he sold all his London Duchess family, and B. F. Bedford became the purchaser at high prices of most of them. He also raised some noted stock from his Kitty Clover family and Cannondale Imp. Rosabella stock. He replenished his herd at the North Elkhorn Imp. Company sale, and has quite a good herd both in numbers and individual merit.

James Hall, the proprietor of Houston Dale herd has been one of the most successful breeders now living in Bourbon County. He began breeding in 1851, and procured the start for his herd from C. S. Brent at his sale in 1851, and also from the herds of William Warfield and Ben Warfield, near Lexington. The animals used on this herd were Sir George, Strafford, Princeton and the Rose of Sharon bulls, Duke of Mason, Lord of the Manor, Marmaduke and Oxford, Cambridge and the bull 43d London Duke, of London Duchess family. The tribes comprising this herd are Pomonas, Young Marys, Miss Wileys, Rose of Sharon, Cambrias, Phyllis, Galateas and Jessamine.

He has been very successful in the Jessamine family, breeding many prize-winners of a very even type and great style, inclining to fatten early, and of beautiful colors.

The basis of the pedigrees of Houston Dale have a strong infusion of blood from the tribes of such men as Thomas Bates, C. Mason, G. Crates, Mr. Charge, Robert and Charles Colling.

The Duke of Mason was full brother to Airdrie 3d, long at the head of A. Renick's herd. Marmaduke was a calf of Norma's; Lord of the Manor was by Muscatom, dam Grace.

Forty-third London Duke's sire sold for $17,500 at public sale, and his dam for $4,400.

Mr. Hall has raised exclusively to sell, frequently exhibiting his yearlings, and two-year-olds with great success, and then disposing of them, thus allowing the purchasers to procure some of his best. He has been enabled by private and public sale to keep his herd down to about thirty breeding cows.

In the long course of his breeding, he has had some prolific cows, one that produced twins four times, and on one of these occasions a heifer twinned with a bull proved to be a breeder, which is a rare freak of nature, as they are almost invariably free-martins. He at one time had three cows of respective ages, eighteen, eighteen and nineteen, which were all breeders. The highest price obtained from the sale of a cow from this herd was $3,000, for Grace 4th, at private sale.

Houston Dale farm is about one and a half miles from Paris, on the Ford's Mill road.

Ben F. Bedford, the proprietor of the Sweet Valley herd, located about four miles from Paris, on the Clintonville Pike, began breeding this herd in 1865, and used the best strains of blood attainable, and he has ever since been one of the most successful exhibitors at the leading fairs in this country. The herd was built up strongly from the Red Daisy or Desdemona family, which family trace back, in the English Herd-Book, as far as 1770, and came from Waistell's and Colling's herd. The sources of this herd were from the well-known stock of S. D. Martin and Hubbard Taylor, with the addition, in late years, of London Duchesses, Lady Knightly's Rose of Sharons and Goodnesses.

Mr. Bedford has endeavored to obtain the best blood, and to produce, by judicious crossing, animals for the show ring, and suitable for breeding purposes.

Franklin Bedford, a veteran breeder, began his present

herd in 1853, of Matson's stock, and the source of most of his stock were Imp. Rosabella, by Velocipede—family Imp. Ianthe family—and Imp. Pedigree by Mynheer. He has converted almost all the males into steers, and preserved the females until his herd has attained considerable proportions. He has been very successful in the production of beef cattle, which demonstrates the fitness of Short-Horns for that purpose. In 1877, he sold five steers three years old that averaged even 2,000 pounds, that went direct to England; four of them were Rosabella family, and the other Imp. Pedigree.

In 1876, he sold twelve head of three-year-olds, averaging 2,495 pounds.

John Cunningham, of Clintonville, has taken a great deal of interest in Short-Horns all his life, and has a herd of about thirty head. He began breeding in 1853; purchased Imp. Fannie, by Selim, at a cost of $1,000; also Imp. Deceiver 401. Both imported from Ireland, by Messrs. Wilson & Seawright, of Cincinnati, Ohio.

The best cow owned by him was the cow Dixie 1st; the Roan Duchess Bull, 2d Roan Duke of Oneida, stands at the head of his herd. His stock is principally of Imp. Illustrious, Rosemary and Phyllis families.

Cassius M. Clay, Jr., for a time partner with his father, the late Brutus J. Clay, controls the Auvergne herd, and is pursuing the same successful plan of breeding adopted by his father—to have good pedigrees, and animals individually of merit. Cassius M. Clay began breeding Short-Horns about 1871, and has devoted his time to the same ever since, in connection with farming a large estate—probably one of the most extensive in this State, and certainly presenting the true ideal of an "Old Kentucky Home," excelled by none. The source of his herd were the 4th and 2d Duchess of the Valley—the first a Craggs, and the second an Imp. Garland.

His present herd are also of other leading families—Agathas, Lady Carolines, Blooms, London Duchesses, Lady Elizabeths and Roan Duchesses.

He added the fine cow, Imp. Georgia Hillhurst, to his herd, from the North Elkhorn Importing Company's sale.

His herd numbers about fifty head. Among the fine show stock produced from this herd, we notice London Duke 23120.

Mr. Clay has also been elected to fill the position of President of the Bourbon County Agricultural Association, and from his experience in the halls of the Assembly of Kentucky, and his extensive knowledge of agriculture, he has proven himself a deserving officer.

Harvey W. Rice was quite a prominent breeder of Short-Horns, beginning about 1852, and selling his herd in 1871. He bred the cow Fashion, twin sister to Fancy, of Imp. Rosemary family. Fashion's gr. dam, Cambria, was the cow from which descended the celebrated Lonan family.

Fancy was the dam of the Kitty Clover family, so celebrated in Edwin Bedford's hands. At his sale in 1871, four bulls and twenty cows were sold, principally of the Cambria or Imp. Rosemary families.

The Glenwood herd deserves mention, both on account of its extent, and the fine stock composing it. Began by E. K. Thomas, with a herd of near forty, and in conjunction with Henry Smith, forming the firm of Thomas & Smith. Its success has been demonstrated by carrying off the grand prizes of $300 each, offered by the Bourbon County Agricultural Society for best cow and bull, taking the same tie three years in succession.

The herd is largely composed of Young Marys, which are noted for their size, style and color; also, Golden Pippin or Blooms, Adelaides, Jessamines, Imp. Pearlette, Desdemona, Rose of Sharon, Lady Knightly and London Duchesses. Thorndale Duke, which stood at head of herd in 1874, took nine first prizes in 1872–73.

Lewis Cunningham began breeding Short-Horns in 1867, procured his first start from Jerre Duncan's herd, at his sale in 1867; also, some from the herds of William and Abram Renick.

His stock have been principally Imp. Illustrious, Young Mary, Rose of Sharon, Red Roses, etc. He sold a heifer some years ago that crossed the ocean to fill a place in Lord Dunmore's herd, at the round sum of $3,400. Mr. Cunningham is one of the best posted men in the county in Short-Horn pedigrees; but, of late years, has reduced his herd to about ten head, called Sulphur Well herd.

J. W. Liver, owner of the Green Creek herd, began breeding Short-Horns in 1855, with stock of Imp. Illustrious and Young Mary families, purchased from William Renick and Isaac Van Meter; keeps about fifty head.

He once owned and used Lord Napier, whose sire and dam were imported.

His farm is situated near Clintonville, about seven miles from Paris.

O. H. Burbridge was at one time quite a breeder, and his name occurs frequently in the early volumes of the American Herd-Book. He was breeding in 1847, and bred to Lord Vane Tempest, Imp. John O. Gaunt, Imp. Javelin, etc. He obtained most of his stock from James Matson's herd. He has ceased breeding Short-Horns several years ago.

Joshua Barton, proprietor of the Hinkston herd, near Millersburg, had, as shown by his catalogue of 1879, quite a good lot of high-bred Short-Horns, of such families as Rose of Sharons, Cypresses, Myrtles, Seraphinas, Miss Flathers, Peris Irene, Young Mary, Phyllis, Frantic, etc.

The animal, at head of herd up to 1881, was 5th Lord Oxford 31738, and Norma's Duke.

J. E. Sudduth began breeding Short-Horns about 1868, and in 1873 had twenty-seven head, among which we notice the celebrated show bulls Dick Taylor and Washington, the latter taking eleven first premiums.

In 1880, having five years previously entered into partnership with R. B. Hutchcraft, the firm sold their stock, consisting of Young Marys, Jessamines, Rose of Sharons, etc.

The herd was kept at Stony Point Farm, about eight miles from Paris, on the Winchester pike. The name of herd is Stony Point herd; numbers about forty females. Bulls in use now are the Rose of Sharon bull, 5th Duke of Sycamore, 8497, and the Bates bull Oxford, of Fairview.

R. B. Hutchcraft has also kept at his farm, about four miles from Paris, on the Winchester pike, adjoining B. F. Bedford's, quite a nice herd of well-bred stock, and individually good. Mr. Hutchcraft is endeavoring to build up a herd that will be a credit to the county.

Col. W. E. Simms has probably the largest number of fashionably bred stock composing his herd to be found in Bourbon County.

He has spared no expense to procure the best blood, and in his herd you will find such as Lady Salis, Imp. Tuberoses, Imp. Princesses, Hilpas, Cypresses, Miss Wileys, Rose of Sharons, Imp. Georgie Oxford 3d.

The bulls used have been 14th Duke of Thorndale, 2d Duke of Oneida, 4th Duke of Hillhurst, the latter being owned by Col. Simms, and proving himself one of the best Duke's bulls in the country.

John Hill was one of the prominent breeders. At an early day, and in connection with Rev. John A. Gano, imported some well-bred stock, and maintained his interest in fine cattle until the day of his death in 1870.

He began breeding about 1840, and owned Imp. Irene and an interest in the Princess cow Imp. Orphan Nell, also in Imp. Venus, imported in 1853 from Cattley's herd in England. In 1870, his herd of fifty-six head were sold by his administrators, Irene 12th bringing $400; Irene 10th, $500; Irene 8th, $400, etc. His son, Capt. F. Gano Hill, has kept up a good herd on the farm ever since his father's death. The name of the herd is appropriately called "Hillburn Herd," and numbers now about fifty head; averages annual herd about thirty. The families represented there are Imp. Irene, Orphan Nell, Ianthe, Rose of Sharon, Jubilee, etc. Capt. Gano Hill buried two imported cows—May Lars 2d and Chilton Queen, the first costing $800, and the second $1,000.

Capt. Hill sold to A. J. Alexander from this herd a Jubilee heifer for $610, and she is now at Woodburn. The bulls used on this herd of note are Baron Bates, Baron J, and Chancery. "Hillburn" is near Centerville, about eight miles west of Paris.

Dr. William Kenney has now a well-bred Bates herd on his farm near Houston Station, nearly opposite E. G. Bedford's farm, consisting of about thirty head. His aim has been to secure good animals, and improve his stock by judicious crossing.

He used on this herd the Craggs bull, Duke of Brockton, and the Desdemona bull, Prince Climax 2d. The families in this herd are of the following tribes: Imp. Jane, Imp. Adelaide, Imp. Pansy, Imp. Agatha, Imp. Countess (or Craggs) Imp. Arabella, Imp. Mrs. Severs, etc.

His first catalogue was issued in 1876.

It is also worthy of note, and interesting to Short-Horn men, that the Short-Horn Record is being edited at Paris. Beginning as a private book, it soon assumed a national shape, and is at present edited by the well-known and popular Col. L. P. Muir, who has been so successful in the compilation of catalogues and management of public sales, his services being in demand in every State in the Union where Short-Horns are sold at public sale.

He has made Short-Horn pedigrees his study, especially for the past ten years, and it is with satisfaction we note the fact that he has been selected as editor of the Short-Horn Record, a book of which Kentucky breeders may well be proud, and which is calculated to inspire confidence in the public, from the fact that every pedigree now received and recorded there may be entitled a thoroughbred, and where errors are discovered the public is unhesitatingly informed of the fact.

This book reaches back as far as the English Herd-Book, and is being liberally patronized in the West, and its success is already determined.

In conclusion it may be said that whilst Short-Horns have fluctuated in prices as much as real estate, yet like real estate they have in the end proved a good investment. There are many new beginners stepping into the ranks deserving of mention, but that must be left to some future scribe, believing that new laurels will be added to the already noted herds of Bourbon County, and that this county will still continue to be one of the great centers from which supplies are to be sent to the North and West, and that stock raised here will still preserve untarnished the fame already justly given to the Bourbon County herds.
—*Irwin Taylor.*

CHAPTER VII.

WAR HISTORY OF BOURBON COUNTY—THE REVOLUTION AND INDIAN TROUBLES—OUR SECOND WAR WITH GREAT BRITAIN—CAPT. GARRARD'S COMPANY—TROUBLE WITH MEXICO—A COMPANY MADE UP BY CAPT. SIMMS—THE LATE WAR—INCIDENTS, ETC., ETC.

"Then the glad ears of each war-martyred son
Proudly shall hear the glad tidings 'well done.'
God will reward those dead heroes of ours,
And cover them over with beautiful flowers."
—*Carleton.*

THE first knowledge the Anglo-Saxon had of Kentucky was intermingled with "wars and the rumors of wars." When the pioneer, Boone, climbed

"The mountain there, and stood alone, alone!
Upon its top amid the rounding clouds,"

a mighty war with the mother country was upon the eve of breaking forth—a war that led the American people to freedom and liberty. Many of the Kentucky pioneers were soldiers who had fought in the Revolutionary army, and when they arrived in their new homes—homes that had been given them for gallant service—they were forced to fight the savages for their possession, often to the death. These contests between the white and red men are more particularly described in a preceding chapter. How many of the early settlers of this section were Revolutionary soldiers is not known, but it is believed that a large majority of them had taken part in the struggle for independence. According to Collins, there were known to be still living, in 1840, within the limits of Bourbon County, the following soldiers of the Revolution: Archibald Bell, William B. Branham, John Brest, Sr., George Bryan, Isaac Clinkinbeard, James Davis, John Debinler, Nathaniel Harris, Andrew Harves, Thomas Hays, Benjamin Henniss, John Hinkston, Joseph Jackson, Edward McConnell, William Scott, Sr., Abner Shropshire, Michael Smith, Joseph L. Stevens, Henry Towles, Henry Wilson and Henry Wiggington. This was quite an array of soldiers to be living sixty years after the scenes of their campaigns, and gives a pretty good idea of the number that must have been among the original settlers. After their settlement here, it was one long-continued struggle, as elsewhere mentioned, almost up to the beginning of our second war with England. Considering her population at the time, Kentucky furnished, perhaps, twice as many men during the war of 1812 as any other State in the Union, without it was Virginia. Not a battle nor a skirmish was fought during the whole period of the war in which Kentucky was not well and fully represented.

As in the war of the Revolution, so in the war of 1812, it is impossible to say how many soldiers Kentucky did furnish. This we do know that where life was to be risked and glory won, Kentuckians were always found. Collins gives the following list of a company that went from Bourbon County: "William Garrard, Captain; Edmund Basye, First Lieutenant; David M. Hickman, Second Lieutenant; Thomas H. McClanahan, Cornet; Charles S. Clarkson, First Sergeant; William Barton, Second Sergeant; John Clark, Third Sergeant; Benjamin W. Edwards, Fourth Sergeant; James Benson, First Corporal; William Walton, Second Corporal; Jesse Todd, Third Corporal; John S. Bristow, Fourth Corporal; Joseph McConnell, Farrier; Ephraim Wilson, Trumpeter; William Davis, Saddler.

"*Privates*—John Finch, William Beneer, David B. Langhorn, John Wynne, William Mountjoy, Samuel Henderson, Henry Wilson, William Jones, John Terrell, Walter Woodyard, Moses Richardson, Jacob Shy, Lewis Duncan, Robert Thomas, Jacob Counts, John Snoddy, Thomas Bedford, James Finch, Walker Thornton, Thomas Eastin, Gerrard Robinson, William M. Baylor, Alexander Scott, William Scott, James Clark, Roger P. West, Frederick Loring, Thomas Barton, Samuel J. Caldwell, John Baseman, Jesse Bowlden, John Funston, James Johnston, John Layson, William B. Northcutt, Jonathan Clinkinbeard, Thomas Webster, Abel C. Pepper, Beverly Brown, Edward Waller, Gustavus E. Edwards, Stephen Barton, Stephen Bedford, John M. Robinson, Jacob Sharrer, Isaac Sanders, James Brown, Henry Towles, John Metcalfe, Stephen Owen, James Conn, Jacob Thomas, William Allentharp, Nathaniel Hill, Strother J. Hawkins, Edward McGuire and Troy Waugh." This list purports to be taken from the original muster-roll of the company. It was cavalry, or, as designated, "State dragons." It served for one year, and was in "Maj. V. Ball's squadron." Thomas Bedford and Beverly Brown are reported as killed in action; Lieuts. Basye and Hickman, Joseph McConnell, Farrier, and privates Moses Richardson, Thomas Eastin, William Scott, Thomas Webster, G. E. Edwards, Stephen Barton and S. J. Hawkins were wounded. Sergt. John Clark died; fourteen are reported sick, thirty-nine frost-bitten, and three fit for duty. These casualties occurred between October 31 and December 31, 1812, inclusive.

But the data at hand is too meager, so far as connected with Bourbon County, to give an extended sketch of the part she took in it, beyond the fact that a majority of her able-bodied citizens were engaged in it at some time during its progress. The battle of the Thames ended the war in the Northwest, and the glorious victory of Gen. Jackson at New Orleans put a stop to it for good and all, and the news of peace, which had already been negotiated at Ghent, soon spread throughout the country. Thus quiet came once more to the people of the West. "It was time," says a writer upon the subject, "that Kentucky was allowed a little rest, for she may be said to have fought through the two first years of the war by herself. Virginia gave the Northwest to the nation, and her daughter, Kentucky, saved it from conquest by savage and foreign foes at the cost of her noblest blood." Peace settled down with her inestimable blessings, and almost for the first time within the memory of the white man, the dark and bloody ground was in a perfect state of quietude, and free from the dread of savage foes. War no more disturbed our peaceful pursuits, except at intervals as the faint sounds of savage yells and conflicts rolled along our frontiers, and only came to our ears as the low mutterings of thunder, from a distant storm cloud, whose lightnings could harm us not.

For several years the surviving soldiers of 1812 have been holding their annual re-unions at Paris, and as year by year is recorded upon the muster-roll of Time, their number is growing smaller. A few more rolling years, and the last of these old heroes will have answered the reveille for the last time. At the annual meeting held in 1881, there were present the following: Moore Johnson, from Mt. Sterling, aged eighty-six years; Thomas Jones, from Paris, aged eighty-nine; Thomas Casey, from Falmouth, aged eighty-five; Dr. C. C. Graham, from Louisville, aged ninety-seven; Zach Corbin, from Owen County, aged ninety; Enos B. Payne, from Newport, aged eighty-eight; Dr. G. H. Perrin, from Cynthiana, aged eighty-seven; Gilead Evans, from Nicholas County, aged eighty-seven; Dr. T. G. Chinn, from Lexington, aged eighty-four; Joshua Webb, from Madison County, aged eighty-nine; S. M. Berry, from Scott County, aged eighty-five; Samuel Jones, from Fleming County, aged ninety; and Thomas White, from Paris, aged eighty-nine. Since the annual meeting of 1880, the following old veterans had died: William Northcott, Kenton County, aged ninety-one years; Samuel Chinn, Clark County, aged ninety-three; William Rupard, Clark County, aged one-hundred and ten; Gen. William O. Butler, Carroll County, aged ninety; Maj. J. R. Curry, Harrison County, aged ninety-two; Hy. Lancaster, Garrard County, aged eighty-seven; Thomas Mount, ————, aged eighty-nine; William Boyd, Oldham County, aged eighty-five; Ayres Leforge, Fleming County, aged eighty-six; Hamilton Wilson, Newport, aged eighty-nine; and John Gillespie, Oldham County, aged one-hundred and one years.

An occasional misunderstanding with some obdurate tribe of Indians comprised our war experience, until the American eagle swooped down upon disrupted Mexico. The causes which led to this unpleasantness grew out of the admission of Texas into the American Union as a State, and may be termed but the forerunner of that great internecine war that commenced with the fall of Fort Sumter in 1861. That politics bore an important part in it there is no question. The majority of the Whig party opposed the measure of annexing Texas to the utmost of their power. Hon. Tom Corwin, of Ohio, made the ablest speech of his life, and said to have been one of the ablest ever made in the United States Senate, against the further prosecution of the war, just after the fall of Monterey. The Whig party—dominant in the North—believed it a measure for the extension of slavery, and upon that ground alone all the Northern members of the party opposed it. In the Presidential election of 1844, it was made a question at issue, and James K. Polk, the Democratic candidate—and whose party favored the annexation of Texas—was elected over Mr. Clay. This was taken as an indorsement of the measure by the people, and, accordingly, the "Lone Star" was admitted into the Union as a State. This led to open hostilities between the United States and Mexico, which began in the spring of 1846. In the declaration of war against Mexico, and the call for troops which followed, Kentucky was required to furnish four regiments of volunteers, comprising 2,400 men, but so great was the zeal of the people, that nearly 15,000 men responded to the call. The Louisville Legion, nine companies strong, reported to the Governor without delay, and were accepted. The four regiments furnished were officered as follows: First Regiment Cavalry, Humphrey Marshall, of Louisville, Colonel (Major General in the Confederate army in the late war); E. H. Field, of Woodford County, Lieutenant Colonel, and John P. Gaines, of Boone County, Major. Second Regiment, William R.

McKee, of Lexington, Colonel (killed at Buena Vista); Henry Clay, Jr., of Louisville, Lieutenant Colonel (killed at Buena Vista); C. H. Fry, of Danville, Major. Third Regiment, M. V. Thomson, of Georgetown, Colonel, (formerly Lieutenant Governor of the State); T. L. Crittenden, of Frankfort, Lieutenant Colonel (Major General in the Federal army during the late war); John C. Breckinridge, of Lexington, Major (Vice President of the United States under James Buchanan). Fourth Regiment, John S. Williams, Colonel (now United States Senator from Kentucky); William Preston, of Louisville, Lieutenant Colonel (Major General in the Confederate army); William T. Ward, of Greensburg, Major.

The Third Regiment (Col. Thomson) contained a company (Company H) from Bourbon County, under Capt. William E. Simms, while a number of men were scattered through the other regiments and companies. The following is the complete roll of the company: W. E. Simms, Captain; W. P. Bramlette, First Lieutenant; C. G. Campbell, Second Lieutenant; William Fisher, Third Lieutenant; Isaac H. Skillman, Orderly Sergeant; John H. Thompson, Second Sergeant; William Ewalt, Third Sergeant; L. C. Hughes, Fourth Sergeant; and James Taylor, Berry Kennedy, Reuben Sandford and William Samuels, Corporals. *Privates*—George W. Leonard, William Adair, Jackson Aubrey, John Anderson, P. N. Beathers, V. H. Bivens, D. C. Bonta, Benjamin F. Burden, Charles Barnett, Thomas P. Ball, William Briscoe, James Boswell, Foster Collins, Andrew Cole, J. G. Craddock, James Cravens, P. E. Coons, Joseph Delaney, Andrew Durgeon, Benjamin Ford, J. N. Fowl, Joseph Gipson, Isaac Gillespie, L. M. Howell, Harvey Humble, Caleb Hitchins, James Hutchinson, J. W. Hedges, James R. Henry, Francis Hulett, Perry Hughes, Leroy Hughes, Alfred Hulett, A. R. Fisher, Perry Hampton, J. M. B. Higgins, Joseph Hogg, J. W. Henry, James Innes, George M. Kenney, Jefferson Kenney, David Long, John T. Lloyd, M. W. Laughlin, Hugh Lowry, R. G. McDonald, John Norton, James McCracken, John Martin, Samuel Mullins, William Murphy, James Nunan, William H. Norton, Thomas Ryan, L. Ross, John B. Stivers, A. J. Speyers, Jacob Stokeley, John H. See, Robert Shidell, Samuel Scott, William Sharp, Joseph Stivers, Philip Swartz, Thomas H. Sample, John T. Henry, Claiborne H. True, Joseph Thompson, Henry Trimble, Jordan Thomas, Elias Way, John Watkins, W. T. Wells, Lewis Wyman, Burrell Wood, Andrew Waggott, Lenox Waggott, James Young, Henry Wilkins, Henry Sharp, Benjamin Utterback, Horatio Talbott, Joseph Williams, Francis Hall, Jesse Hall, W. T. Browning, W. E. Bush, John T. Turrey, Elijah True, Henry Trumbull.

This company was recruited to 108 men, and, as we have said, formed Company H, Third Regiment Kentucky Volunteers. The regiment under command of Col. Thomson was in the army of Gen. William O. Butler, and reached Mexico shortly after the capture of the city, where it was on active garrison duty for nearly a year. It behaved very well; about twenty died in Mexico, the remains of whom were brought home by Capt. Simms, and interred in the Paris Cemetery, where a handsome monument, erected by the county, marks their resting place.

The great civil war—the war between the States—was the next to disturb our peace and tranquillity. Less than a decade and a half passed, after the close of the Mexican war, before the great rebellion—as our Northern neighbors term it—broke upon the country. It is scarcely possible to write a correct, or a just history of this war, even after this long lapse of time. All the wars we had hitherto engaged in were waged against savages or foreign foes, but now we were called to measure strength among ourselves—literally, it was Greek meet Greek. A civil war was inaugurated without a parallel in the world's history. Of all the conflicts that have ever scourged our earth, a civil war, wherein the "brother betrays the brother to death, and the father the son, and children rise up against their parents, and cause them to be put to death," is the most dreadful. The rival houses of York and Lancaster, with their emblems of "White" and "Red," shook Old England to her center, filling her houses with mourning, her fields with carnage, and wasting the blood of her bravest and best, but when compared to our "war between the States," it pales into insignificance. Though the "pen were dipped in the gloom of earthquake and eclipse," it could not write a true history of those four dreadful years—1861–65. All the evils of war, and all the horrors of civil war were crowded into them, and the refined cruelties known to the civilization of the enlightened age in which we live were practiced by the opposing parties. But after four years of strife and bloodshed, the olive branch of peace again waved over us, and now fraternal love and prosperity smile upon the land from one end of the nation to the other. As we become naturalized to the new order of things, we find it a source of congratulation that the object of strife between the sections is forever removed, and will never cause another war on American soil. In the final union of "the Roses," England found the germ of her future greatness and glory, and in the harmonious blending of "the Blue" and "the Grey," who shall limit our own greatness and glory?

Our State being located upon the border, between the North and the South, it was but natural that our people should be divided in their opinions, as to the justice or injustice of the war, the acts of the National Government, and the project of setting up a new Republic. Thus divided in sentiment, the contending sections received many recruits (perhaps nearly an equal number, each) from Central Kentucky and from Bourbon County. Each, actuated by motives of the highest honor, with a firm, unswerving faith in the righteousness of their cause, rallied around their respective standards, and went forth to fight the battles of their country. Imbued with more than a Roman valor and patriotism, they bore uncomplainingly the privations of camp and field, and when the oft-repeated news was brought home of depleted and broken ranks, a similar spirit hurried on fresh legions to brace up the tottering columns. Bourbon County's valor was attested on many a hard-fought field, both in the ranks of the blue and the gray, and her sons were ever ready for posts of danger. Some, who went out to fight for the cause they deemed just and right, with only the benediction of a mother's prayers and tears, came not back to that mother's arms. They sleep in the swamps of the Chickahominy, on the banks of the Rapidan, at Shiloh, Chickamauga, Corinth, Stone River, Lookout Mountain, Fredericksburg, Chancellorsville and the Wilderness, and it is no reproach to their valor that they fell before foes who were as brave as themselves. Their memory is immortal; and beautiful as a crown of gold, the rays of the sunset lay upon the hilltops where they repose after their battles. Others, worn down with toil and exposure, dragged their wearied bodies home to die, and now sleep in the quiet churchyards, where, with each recurring anniversary, surviving friends gather together, moisten with tears the graves, and with loving hands lay immortelles upon the green hillocks above them. This is eminently proper. The custom of strewing floral mementoes on the graves of departed friends is time-honored and ancient. It is of Oriental origin, and we read that

> "In Eastern lands they talk in flowers,
> And tell in garlands their loves and cares,"

and that each little velvet petal that spreads itself to the light contains a mystical language more powerful and sympathetic in its nature than tongue can express. In ancient times, the people were as careful in guarding the memory of their dead, of embalming their virtues and erasing their errors, as they were mindful of their liberties. This sweet privilege, through the long roll of years that have passed, has fallen a blessed boon to our people, and they have felt it a duty to recall the virtues and heroic deeds of noble sons who endured the stern discipline of the camp, and dared the storm of battle for a cause in which their hearts and natures were enlisted, and with spring's first flowers they garland the spot where they slumber in glorified rest.

> "Winds of summer, oh! whisper low
> Over the graves where the daisies grow,
> Blossoming flowers and songs of bees,
> Sweet ferns tossed in the summer breeze—
> Floating shadows and golden lights,
> Dewy mornings and radiant nights—
> All the bright and beautiful things
> That gracious and bountiful summer brings,
> Fairest and sweetest that earth can bestow,
> Brighten the graves where the daisies grow."

Of the troops furnished to the National armies from this county, the Seventh Cavalry and the Fourth and Twenty-first Infantry received the larger number of men. Among the commissioned officers of the Seventh Cavalry, from Bourbon, were the following: A. B. and J. C. Masoner, Ruddel's Mills; Thomas L. Scott, Paris; H. H. Talbott, Paris; Rev. M. J. W. Ambrose, Paris; W. W. Bradley, Berry Station; Jesse Bryant, Berry Station; William M. Bell, Paris, and perhaps others. The Masoners were Quartermaster and Commissary of the Regiment; Rev. Ambrose was Chaplain, but resigned September 6, 1863. Jesse Bryant was promoted to Captain February 7, 1863, and to Major, but never mustered as such. Thomas L. Scott, promoted from Second to First Lieutenant, May 7, 1863, promoted to Captain, but not mustered as such—mustered out of service July 10, 1865. H. H. Talbott, promoted from Sergeant, Company C, to Second Lieutenant, Company A, wounded at Hopkinsville, December 16, 1864, and mustered out July 10, 1865; and William M. Bell, Second Lieutenant. W. W. Bradley entered the service as Captain of Company D, was promoted to Major February 6, 1863; to Lieutenant Colonel, September 17, 1864, and mustered out July 10, 1865. The following sketch of the Seventh Cavalry is from Gen. D. W. Lindsey's report as Adjutant General of Kentucky during the war:

"This regiment was organized at Paris, Ky., in August, 1862, under Col. Leonidas Metcalfe, and was mustered into service by Maj. L. Sitgraves, United States mustering officer. Before the regiment was thoroughly equipped or disciplined, they were ordered into active duty, and engaged in the battle of Big Hill, Ky., where they received the charge of the enemy under Gen. Kirby Smith, and lost many officers and soldiers in killed, wounded and prisoners. Owing to the enemy having possession of nearly the entire State, the organization of the regiment was much retarded. In October, 1862, under command of Col. Faulkner (Col. Metcalfe having resigned), the Seventh was placed upon active duty, and assigned to the Department

ELLEN CHALLENGER 4TH
THE CHAMPION COW OF KY.

AIRDRIE THORNDALE 6100 S. H. R.
THE CHAMPION BULL OF KY.

of the Cumberland. It was in all the early engagements in Southern Kentucky and Tennessee, and by their gallant bearing and soldiery conduct upon many well-fought fields won the commendation of the commanding General."

The regiment participated in the following-named battles, in which loss was sustained, in addition to several others not mentioned on the rolls, viz.: Big Hill, Richmond, Cynthiana and Hopkinsville, Ky.; Franklin, Triune and Nashville, Tenn.; La Fayette, Resaca, Ga.; Gainesville, King's Hill, Gadsden, Scottsville, Randolph and near Montgomery, Ala. The veterans and recruits of this regiment were transferred to the 6th Kentucky Veteran Cavalry.

The Fourth Kentucky Infantry drew quite a number of commissioned officers and privates from Bourbon. Among the officers were the following: R. M. Kelly, who was promoted from Captain of Company K to Major of the regiment March 23, 1862; to Lieutenant Colonel April 18, 1864; to Colonel, August 25, 1864; mustered out of the service August 16, 1865, and is now editor of the Louisville *Daily Commercial.* John T. Croxton was promoted from Lieutenant Colonel to Colonel March 23, 1862; to Brigadier General August 16, 1864; brevetted Major General, and resigned December 26, 1865. John A. Roberts, promoted from a private to Sergeant September 1, 1861; to Second Lieutenant, March 1, 1862; to First Lieutenant, March 27, 1863; to Captain, June 17, 1865, and mustered out August 17, 1865. C. V. Ray, promoted from Second to First Lieutenant January 12, 1862, and November 6, following, was appointed Adjutant. Elliott Kelly, commissioned First Lieutenant January 2, 1865. N. M. Kelly was First Lieutenant Company D, and died at Lebanon, Ky., January 12, 1862; and a large number of privates. This regiment was organized at Camp Dick Robinson, under Col. Speed S. Fry, and mustered into the United States service October 9, 1861, by Brig. Gen. George H. Thomas, United States mustering officer. The regiment saw hard service, and in the sketch of it, given in the Adjutant's report, published by Gen. Lindsey, of Frankfort, he bestows upon it much praise. He concludes his notice of it in the following words: "It received the praise and commendation of every general officer under whom it served, and the casualty list clearly shows it to have been ever foremost in the battle. It participated in the following among other battles in which loss was sustained, viz.: Mill Springs, Ky.; Corinth, Miss.; Rolling Fork, Ky.; Tullahoma, Tenn.; Chickamauga, Chattanooga, Mission Ridge, Lafayette, Mason's Church, Newnan, Ga.; Pulaski, Tenn.; Shoal Creek, Ala.; Lewisburg Pike, Franklin and Lynnville, Tenn., etc."

The Twenty-first Infantry also drew a large number of officers and privates from the county. Among the former were M. M. Clay, S. R. Sharrard, L. W. Dunnington, E. B. Davidson, J. B. Buckner, J. R. Jameson, and perhaps others. M. M. Clay entered the service as Captain of Company C, and resigned October 3, 1862. S. R. Sharrard, promoted from First Lieutenant to Captain October 3, 1862, and resigned April 7, 1864. L. W. Dunnington, promoted from Sergeant to Second Lieutenant April 12, 1864, transferred to Twenty-first Veteran Infantry, and mustered out of the service at Victoria, Tex., December 9, 1865. E. B. Davidson, promoted from Second to First Lieutenant Company C October 3, 1862; to Captain, April 12, 1864; transferred to Twenty-first Veteran Infantry, and mustered out at Victoria, Tex., December 9, 1865. John B. Buckner entered the service as Orderly Sergeant, promoted to Second Lieutenant October 3, 1862; to First Lieutenant April 12, 1864; transferred to Company C, Twenty-first Veteran Infantry, and promoted to Captain Company K January 18, 1865. J. R. Jameson, promoted from First Lieutenant to Captain February 27, 1862, and resigned June 12, 1863. The regiment contained, likewise, a large number of private soldiers from Bourbon. Indeed, Company C, Capt. Clay, was raised principally in Paris and the surrounding community.

The first commander of the Twenty-first was E. L. Dudley, of Lexington, who died February 20, 1862. The regiment saw much hard fighting during the war. The following extract is from its record in the Adjutant General's report: "After the retreat of Bragg from Kentucky, the regiment returned to Nashville, Tenn. On the 9th of December, 1862, it, with other regiments of the brigade, under command of Col. Stanley Matthews, while out for aging, were attacked near Dobbin's Ford by Wheeler's rebel cavalry. The conduct of the Twenty-first on that occasion was highly commended by the brigade commander, and the following-named non-commissioned officers and men were complimented in field orders by Gen. Rosecrans for their gallant conduct, viz.: Sergt. J. F. Morton, Company F; Corp. Henry Stahel, Company A; Corp. J. P. Hagan, Company F; Private George P. Montjoy, Company A; Private Cassius Keger, Company A; Private Edward Welch, Company A; Private William Murphy, Company A; Private R. B. Clusin, Company F; Private W. W. Oliver, Company F; Private John Morton, Company F; Private B. S. Jones, Company F."

It participated in the following battles, in which loss was sustained: Perryville, Stone River, Chickamauga, Rocky Face Ridge, Resaca, New Hope Church, Pine Top, Kenesaw Mountain, Smyrna, Atlanta, Jonesboro, Franklin and Nashville.

The following commissioned officers from Bourbon were in scattering regiments, viz.: Greenberry Reed, Captain in the Fortieth Infantry; C. B. Pettitt, First Lieutenant in same regiment; John W. Evans, Second Lieutenant in same regiment; Jesse Dennis, First Lieutenant in Fifty-third Infantry, and W. H. Drinkhard, First Lieutenant in the Fifty-fifth Infantry. John T. Farris, Quartermaster of Fifth Cavalry, afterward promoted to Major of Ninth Cavalry, and resigned November 10, 1862; John C. Brent, promoted from First Lieutenant Company B, to Major of Ninth Cavalry, February 9, 1863, and mustered out with the regiment. There may be other commissioned officers, that should be credited to Bourbon County, but we have scanned the Adjutant General's Report closely, and if such there be, he has overlooked them.

The Confederate army received perhaps a larger number of recruits from this county than the opposite side. Among the soldiers furnished to the South, were the following commissioned officers: Lieutenant Colonel, E. F. Clay; Major, Thomas Brent; Captains, James M. Thomas, R. G. Stoner, Harry Bedford, James Bedford, John Hope, —— Fowle, John B. Holladay, James Rogers, Hugh Henry, E. F. Spears; Lieutenants, James A. Allen, Samuel Hawes, William Talbott, A. J. Lovely and Harry Boesh, John P. Talbott and Charles Benton, Surgeons. Captain John Bradshaw was from Powell County, but is now a resident of this county. Col. E. F. Clay raised a company, of which he was Captain, of fifty or sixty men, which rendezvoused at Prestonburg. Capt. Clay was promoted to Lieutenant Colonel, and was wounded and taken prisoner at Puncheon Creek, in Magoffin County, Ky. Of his old company, William Talbott was First Lieutenant, Harry Clay, Second Lieutenant, and James Rogers, Brevet Lieutenant. The latter afterward resigned, and raised a company, of which he was made Captain. A. J. Lovely entered as private, was brevetted Lieutenant, and afterward promoted Captain in Commissary Department. This company was "D" of the "First Kentucky Rifles," John Williams, Colonel; and formed part of Gen. Humphrey Marshall's brigade.

Capt. J. M. Thomas raised a company principally in Bourbon and Nicholas Counties. He retired from the service at the end of a year, and W. T. Havens became Captain. He was a Sergeant in the company at the time of its organization. He is now editor of the Mount Sterling *Sentinel*. R. G. Stoner went in as captain of a company from Montgomery, and was afterward promoted to lieutenant-colonel of the regiment. John Hope raised a company, mostly in Bourbon, of which he was Captain. E. F. Spears was First Lieutenant, and afterward succeeded Hope as Captain. Samuel Hawes was Second Lieutenant, and was killed at Stone River. James A. Allen went out as Brevet Lieutenant, and was afterward promoted to Second Lieutenant; was severely wounded in the leg. This company was attached to Col. Roger Hanson's brigade.

Capt. W. E. Simms, who commanded a company in the Mexican war, entered the service as Colonel of the First Kentucky (Confederate) Cavalry. Col. Simms was elected to the Confederate Senate, when Col. Clay (at the time Lieutenant Colonel of the regiment), succeeded him in its command. Maj. Thomas Brent was killed near Lebanon, Ky. Capt. Harry Bedford was captured at Cynthiana, Ky. Capt. Holladay had a company from Nicholas County; he is now a citizen and Sheriff of Bourbon. He entered the service as Captain of his company, but was promoted to Major.

It is a more difficult matter to obtain correct data of the Confederate service, as there has been less published on the subject, than of the National service, the Adjutant General's Report of Kentucky, affording much valuable information pertaining to the forces in the service of the Government. In both sections we have only given the names of commissioned officers, so far as we could obtain them. The privates from the county would form, perhaps, two or three regiments, and their gallant and soldierly bearing is remembered by all who knew them. What more can be said of them—beyond the breathing of a prayer, that they may never be called to face each other again in such an unholy war.—*Perrin.*

CHAPTER VIII.

PARIS PRECINCT—BOUNDARIES, TOPOGRAPHY, PHYSICAL FEATURES, ETC.—THE PIONEERS—THEIR TOILSOME JOURNEYS—KENNEDY FAMILY—OTHER SETTLERS—EARLY INDUSTRIES—EDUCATIONAL AND RELIGIOUS—OLD CANE RIDGE CHURCH.

"But long years have flown o'er these scenes of the past,
And many have turned gray in the winter's cold blast;
While others only think of the time that is gone;
They are bent by the years that are fast rolling on."

WHEN first seen by white men, Central Kentucky was an unbroken wilderness. Dense forests overhanging the margins of crystal streams were unmolested by the pioneer's ax. The notes of myriads of songsters, the howl of wild beasts and the yell of savages alone awakened the silence that had brooded over them for centuries. But now came a change! The first wave of immigration rolled westward, precurser of an overwhelming tide destined to sweep everything before it. The fierce contest commenced between the pale-face and the Indian, and was waged with relentless fury, but the superior prowess of the white man prevailed, and his title to the "dark and bloody ground" was sealed with hundreds of human lives. The red sons of the forest have disappeared, and Cooper's "Last of the Mohicans," preserves in romance a story of the race. The plowshare levels their graves; their favorite hunting-grounds groan beneath the white man's harvests, and will know them no more forever. Fulfilled to the letter were the gloomy forebodings of the chief, when he spoke in the pale-face's council: "My people are like the scattered stalks that remain in the field when the tempest has passed over it. The Great Spirit ordained us for the forest, and our habitation is the shade. We pursue the deer for our subsistence, but they are disappearing before the pale-faces, and the red man must starve or leave the graves of his fathers, and make his bed with the setting sun." Thus has it been, and thus has the mellowing hand of Time served to

"Make their name sublime,
And departing, leave behind them,
Footprints on the sands of time."

The section to which this chapter is devoted, though small in extent, is not without traditional interest. Like every spot of Central Kentucky, it is entwined with historical association, and these associations and reminiscences, will be presented in a becoming form to our readers. They have been gathered from the most reliable sources now available, and are no doubt correct.

Paris Precinct, the Election Precinct No. 1 of Bourbon County, comprises the central part, and is as fine blue-grass land as the county contains, or as may be found, perhaps, in the entire blue grass region. Its configuration is good, save possibly a few bluffs contiguous to the water-courses. It would puzzle a mathematician to define the shape of Paris Precinct, or one of fertile imagination to give correctly its boundaries. As much as we can venture is, that it is bounded by Harrison County, and by Ruddel's Mills, Millersburg, Flat Rock, North Middletown, Clintonville, Hutchinson and Centerville Precincts. These extend round it, and we leave it to the reader to give to each the cardinal point of the compass, to which it is entitled. The precinct has an excellent system of natural drainage in its numerous water-courses. Stoner Creek or river is the largest stream, and flows nearly north through the center and through the city of Paris, where it furnishes water-power and supply to mills, distilleries, etc. It unites with the Hinkston near Ruddel's Mills, just before entering Harrison County. Kennedy's Creek is a tributary of Stoner, and flows in nearly the same direction, emptying into the latter a little south of Paris. Houston Creek enters the precinct from the west, near Houston Post Office, and unites with the Stoner at Paris. Clark's Branch is a small tributary of Houston, in the west part of the precinct. Flat Run flows north and empties into the Stoner near Ruddel's Mills. Cooper's Run in the northwest empties into the Stoner near Ewalt's Cross Roads; and Townsend's Creek passes through the northwest corner. The timber growth of Paris Precinct was that indigenous to this section of the State, and consisted chiefly of oak, hickory, black walnut, buckeye, ash, sugar maple, etc.

Like the most of Bourbon County, and of Central Kentucky, Paris Precinct was settled chiefly by Virginians, with now and then a family from Pennsylvania, Maryland, and North Carolina. To name him who erected the first cabin in what now forms this precinct, with any degree of certainty, is a task that no one, perhaps, can truly accomplish. The Kennedy family were early settlers, though it is not known that they were the first in the precinct. Thomas Kennedy was the first of the family to emigrate to Kentucky, and from him Kennedy's Creek took its name. From an old manuscript written by his son, Jesse Kennedy, in 1850, and now in possession of Mr. Frank Kennedy, we glean many facts of interest pertaining to the settlement of the family in Kentucky, and the journey of Mr. Kennedy through the wilderness, from his old home in Maryland. Thomas Kennedy, the pioneer, made his first trip to Kentucky on a "tour of inspection," in 1776, intending, if pleased with the country, to secure land for himself and two brothers, John and Joseph. He arrived at Boonesboro without accident or adventure, and there met with Michael Stoner, afterward an early settler himself in Paris Precinct. Stoner invited him to go and assist him in clearing a field and planting it in corn, which he did. This field was long known as "Strode's Field," and is now owned by Samuel Clay. At that time, the country was full of wild game, and fresh meat was plenty all the time. Buffalo were numerous and furnished all the settlers with meat. In the fall, Mr. Kennedy returned to Virginia, where his family then resided, intending to move out to Kentucky at once, but owing to various difficulties which interfered, he did not make the start until the fall of 1779, when he brought his family hither, consisting at the time of his wife and four children—three boys and a girl—the eldest being but seven years of age. His trip here shows the difficulties which stood in the way of the pioneers of this country a hundred years ago. He was a brick-mason and carpenter, and gathered together such tools as he might need, and property that he could not well do without, and placed them on a train—not of railroad cars, but pack-horses—and with his wife and little ones, and a few cattle, he commenced his journey through the wilderness toward the promised land. Although he did not wander forty years in the wilderness, yet his trials and tribulations while in it were great. Owing to the lateness of the season when he started, forage became scarce and his animals gave out and died by the wayside, and when he finally reached Boonesboro, they were all gone, except a mare and a little bull. Upon the latter he packed a bed, and upon the mare three of his children, while he and his devoted wife trudged on foot—he carrying his little girl upon his own back, and his wife carrying such things as she could. As his pack-horses, one by one, gave out, he hid his property in the forest, intending to return for it, but the unsettled state of the country prevented, and he thus lost it. To add to his troubles, the mare upon which his three boys were carried—the two smallest in willow-baskets swung across her back, and the large one riding upon her—fell down and broke the rider's leg, but without injuring the boys in the baskets. This was a distressing occasion. They were alone in the wilderness, but with that courage and fortitude born of desperation, they bandaged the boy's leg as best they could and continued their journey. In this forlorn condition they arrived at Boonesboro. After remaining there a short time, he joined a company under Capt. John Strode, and helped to build and settle Strode's Station, where he lived for four or five years. The winter of 1779–80, his first winter here with his family, was one of unusual severity. Much of the stock and wild game perished, and of the latter, that which lived through the winter became so poor that, to prevent starvation alone, forced the settlers to kill and eat it. In the spring of 1780, his wife died, and one of his children soon after followed her. He finally pre-empted land for himself and brothers, his own on Strode's Creek and theirs on Kennedy's Creek, and on which latter stream he, too, eventually settled, a few miles south of Paris. Amid many misfortunes which "followed so thickly as to tread on each other's heels," he lived and died on Kennedy's Creek, at an extreme old age. His son, Jesse Kennedy, lived with him, and devotedly watched over and cared for his aged parent until death relieved him of the solemn charge. Jesse served one year in the war of 1812, as master of a train of pack-horses, when he returned home and took charge of the homestead, and through his energy and untiring perseverence, he saved his father's property from sacrifice, cheered his declining years, and, after his death, accumulated considerable property for himself. He lived an honored and respected citizen of the community, and, to quote a stereotyped phrase, "died regretted by all who knew him." He has a son, Frank Kennedy, a lawyer in Paris.

The Bedfords were early settlers in Paris Precinct, and were from the Old Dominion. The pioneer of the family was Benjamin Bedford, who came to Kentucky about the year 1787, and stopped in Madison County, where he remained one season and raised a crop; then, in the following year, came to this section. His brother, Littleberry Bedford, came out in 1789 and located in this precinct, near where John T. Woodford now lives. He there erected a cabin, and, as he had purchased his land, supposed his title was good. He had not remained long on it, however, when Col. Gist rode up to him one day, and told him to cease further improvements, as he had a prior title, which he showed him. Col. Gist told him he need not leave the premises; that he might stay as long as he wished for an ear of corn per year. But Mr. Bedford was wise enough to see in this liberal offer a "consideration," and aware that as soon as he improved the place, he would be unceremoniously dispossessed, he wisely concluded not to remain, but to locate elsewhere. He moved to the place where Mrs. Patsey Clay now lives. Here he settled and remained until his death, which took place August 29, 1829, in his ninety-second year. He was a great hunter, and said to be the best shot in Kentucky, except Daniel Boone. He paid but little or no attention to agricultural pursuits, but, like many of the pioneers, spent his time mostly in hunting. Greenberry Bedford was another early settler in this neighborhood. He is said to have built the first *good* house in what is now Paris Precinct. Hitherto, none but cabins had been put up, and he lived in a very poor one for several years, when he erected a splendid house for the time. He hired a cabinet workman from Virginia to make his furniture, which was of the most substantial kind, and some of which is still in existence. He was a quiet man, peaceful among his neighbors, and highly respected by all. He came here and married a Miss Clay, and then returned to Virginia and brought out his negroes.

Michael Stoner and James Kenny are supposed to have settled in the present limits of the precinct as early as 1785. Stoner Creek was named for the former. He owned a large body of land on the west side of this stream, but also had fifty acres on the opposite side, which he gave to James Kenny in payment for "stocking" a shovel-plow for him. The land is now owned by J. D. Butler; his house is located on it, and it (the land), is worth several car-loads of shovel-plows. Stoner traded 1,000 acres, upon which he settled, to Samuel Clay for a negro woman, a horse and a gun. Stoner was afterward killed at a barn raising, by a log falling on him. Kenny was from Virginia, and settled near where J. D. Butler now lives. He had a son, Capt. James Kenny, who was in the war of 1812, and died of disease while in the service. A man named Bruce settled near Kenny. He had two negro women killed by the Indians, after which he went away and remained until more peaceful times. A man named Gass was also an early settler. He, Col. Gist, Kenny and Stoner, all had surveys on the west side of Stoner Creek Most of it is now owned by the Clay family, John T. Woodford and George W. Bedford. The Edwards family emigrated to Kentucky and settled in the present precinct about 1794–95. James Marvin came some time prior to the Edwards family, and located the land which Edwards afterward purchased. Jacob Langston, from Virginia, settled here previous to 1790, on the Robert Clark farm.

On the east side of the Stoner, one of the earliest settlers was Henry Leer, who came here from Virginia, but was originally from Holland. He settled among the very earliest, locating on the land now owned by his grandson, David Leer. His son Daniel succeeded him, and he, in turn, was succeeded by his son David, who now owns the place as above stated, it having been in the family ever since its original purchase. Josiah McDonald settled on what is now Flat Rock pike, near where the toll-gate stands, about the year 1790. Thomas Rogers settled near the mouth of Rogers' Creek. The place where Robert Clark now lives was once called Clark's Station. The Indians were numerous then, and hostile. The house was built bullet-proof, and part of it is yet standing, and forms the rear part of Mr. Clark's residence. John Honey came here in 1787, and was from Maryland. He settled on the farm now owned by Col. Lewis Muir. The old house is still standing, and has loop-holes, as the pioneers' houses were all built. It has been "weather-boarded" and modernized, however, since it served as a protection against prowling savages. David Caldwell came from Pennsylvania and settled on Houston Creek previous to 1800, where he died about the year 1828–29. He was a soldier in the Revolutionary war, and received an injury in one of his arms, which necessitated its amputation after he settled in Kentucky—an operation that was performed by Drs. Todd and Nicholas Warfield. He was a man highly respected in the community.

John Reed, William Galloway, Samuel Lyons and Lawrence Protzman were early settlers in the vicinity of Paris. The first three mentioned pre-empted the land on which the city is located. Reed was from Maryland, and made his pre-emption November 18, 1784. Galloway and Lyons were from Virginia, and made theirs in 1786. Protzman bought a portion of Reed's land and laid out a town, which he called Hopewell, now Paris. James Garrard, afterward Governor, John Edwards, Charles Smith, Edward Walker, Thomas West and James Duncan were also early settlers in the present precinct. Gov. Garrard settled about four miles north of Paris, at "Mount Lebanon," about 1780–85, and as noted elsewhere, the first session of court was held at his residence. Many other early settlers are entitled, doubtless, to mention in this chapter, but they are gone and forgotten in the long years that have passed, and no one now remembers them. Mr. Collins speaks of "Houston's Station," on the present site of Paris, but of it little or nothing is now known.

When the first emigrants came to what is now Paris Precinct, not only this immediate section, but nearly the entire State of Kentucky, was a wild region, claimed by numerous tribes of Indians, many of them hostile toward the whites. Our early history bears proof to this state of affairs, in the details given of the long and sanguinary struggle between the two races for supremacy in this rich and beautiful country. The savages let no opportunity to murder, plunder and massacre the whites pass unimproved, and hence the country contiguous to the early settlements, became a vast graveyard; while in more lonely spots, hunters and isolated settlers with their families, were wantonly butchered, their bodies left exposed, when their flesh became the food of wild beasts, their bones the sport of the storm. No early station nor settlement, perhaps, in Central Kentucky, is known, but has connected with it a tale of savage barbarity, of murder and bloodshed. The pioneer held his life in his hand; he stood ready at any moment to fight, and verily he found his lot cast in a land where he had plenty of it to do. It is said that the early settler of Kentucky slept with one eye open, and was far more likely to be found without his hat than his gun. These were the circumstances under which this country was reclaimed and wrested from the Indians. When we take a disinterested view of the matter, we have but little ground to blame the Indians for holding on to their hunting-grounds with such a death-like grip. The pale-faces, although they have not held the lands so long as did the savages, rather than be driven from their homes now, they would fight for them more fiercely than did the savages themselves. And yet the sequel has proven that it was ordained that the Anglo-Saxons should possess this country. The pioneers of Kentucky were but the advance guard—the picket line of the grand army that was to sweep away the last vestige of a crude and imperfect civilization. It was won at a fearful cost, however, but as we look over the beautiful blue grass lands, dotted with luxurious homes, we must admit that it is worth the price paid for it. But the "irrepressible conflict" with the savages was not the only trouble the pioneers had to contend with. From the time they left their comfortable homes beyond the mountains, this toil and privation commenced, and ended not (with many) until their lives ended, and with others until the savages met their Waterloo at the hands of Mad Anthony Wayne in 1794. As a proof of their hard life, the journey of Thomas Kennedy to the State affords ample illustration, and was but a type of that which fell to the lot of the pioneers generally.

Among the first improvements made in a newly-settled country are roads and mills. The savages have neither. Their roads are trails through the forest where men can only follow each other in single file. The first road through Paris Precinct was what was known as the "State road." This was merely the improvement of the old Buffalo trace. In the proceedings of the second session of court ever held in Bourbon County, we find the following of this old road: "The persons appointed to view the best way for a road from the mouth of Limestone in the wagon road on the top of the hill, made their report in these words: 'To extend from the mouth of Limestone down the river bottom to the first drain crossing the same, thence up the north side into a hollow, up said hollow into an old buffalo trace, thence with said trace into the wagon road.' Ordered that the same be established, that Edward Waller Gent., be appointed Assessor thereof, and that Thomas Warring, Gentleman, regulate the hands to assist him in opening and keeping the same in repair." This road crossed the Stoner, near White's distillery, "passed through a corner of the public square, and in a westerly direction along the Huston Cliffs, etc." Other roads were made, as necessity demanded, and improved from time to time, finally macadamized, until at the present day they are as fine a system of roads as any country possesses. The precinct has excellent turnpikes diverging from Paris in every direction. Among them are the Georgetown & Paris; Hume & Bedford; Paris & Townsend; Paris & Jackstown; Lexington, Paris & Maysville; Bethlehem & Paris; Paris & Clintonville; Paris & Winchestor; Paris & Harrod's Creek; Paris & Flat Rock, and Paris & North Middletown. The Lexington, Paris & Maysville pike is one of the oldest, not only in this county, but in the State, and has an interesting history, which is given in another chapter of this volume. The old style stage-coach, with its handsomely painted "body" and prancing team, was an almost inseparable part of the early turnpike road. But its day of usefulness is over; the locomotive has taken its place.

The first mill built in the present precinct of Paris is believed to be that known as Coulthard's, which, it is claimed, was built about 1785–90. It is on Stoner Creek, a short distance north of Paris, and is still in operation, although it has been several times improved and repaired. It was originally built by Abraham McJoy, and has been owned successively by a man named Bayler, Garrard, Hardin, Robert Palmer, Griggs, Goble, and in 1854 was bought by William Coulthard. In 1879, the firm became Coulthard & Honey, who still operate the old pioneer establishment. It is a stone building, two stories high, two run of buhrs, and does an extensive business. About forty years after the building of the Coulthard Mill, Spears & Garrard built a mill on the opposite side of the creek. It was a small affair, however, with but one run of buhrs. Previously, he had built a small distillery at the same place.

Another of the early mills, and by some claimed to be the first built in the precinct, was a small log structure erected by James Wright, Sr., and was both saw and grist mill, with two run of small buhrs. It finally became the property of his son, James Wright, who some years later rebuilt it in a very substantial manner, making it three stories high. The work was done by a man named Boone, who quarried the rock, hauled it and built the stone work, for the sum of *one hundred dollars!* The mill is on the Houston Creek, and on the south side of the Lexington & Maysville pike, about two miles from Paris. Robert Langston purchased the mill about 1854, and was the third owner. It is still running, and is in good condition. A man named Smith had a mill in the precinct at an early day. It is now run by a Mr. Spears. A little mill was built on Kennedy's Creek by one Michael Couchman, but of it we learned little of importance.

Ford's mill was another of the pioneer mills of the precinct, and was built by a man named Jourdan. He sold it in 1802 to a Mr. Brent, who, in 1811, had the road laid out to it; then sold the mill to Ford. He ran it until 1829, when Allison bought the site and built the Allison Mill, which ran until 1856, when it ceased business.

The manufacture of whisky was an early industry of the pioneers, and one that has not decreased in importance, even down to the present time. While the making of ardent spirits is considered by many as a business of somewhat questionable character, yet it is certainly a business that yields a large profit, and affords the country an immense source of revenue, and hence it is—honorable. Next to stock-raising, it is the most valuable industry in the Blue Grass Region. As we have said, the business was commenced at an early day. Capt. Kenny is said to have operated a distillery in the southern part of the precinct, as early as 1789–90, where he made apple brandy and whisky. Emanuel Wyatt had a distillery very early, on land now owned by Cassius M. Clay. John Tillett had a distillery on what is known as "Still House Branch" many years ago, upon land now owned by Samuel Clay. Ford commenced distilling at his mill in 1829, and continued the business for about ten years.

Of all the industries, however, carried on in Paris Precinct in early times, Benjamin Bedford appears to have conducted one of the most combustible nature, viz., that of a distillery and a powder-mill. Verily, a more *explosive* combination could not be formed. The powder manufactured in this establishment was used in the war of 1812, and the whisky—well, it was used as an antidote for snake-bites. A man named Spears built a small distillery very early, not far from where the Coulthard Mill stands. He afterward sold out to B. F. Rogers, who sold to Joseph Mitchell. In 1866, Worrall & Hutchison bought out Mitchell, and put up a large steam distillery of some three hundred bushels' capacity. This establishment was operated until 1869, when it failed, and, as a man informed us, "went to the demnition bow-wows."

A hemp factory was built about 1816–18, on what is now the Maysville & Lexington pike, by William Alexander. It was situated a half-mile from Paris, where William M. Taylor now lives, and continued in operation until 1856, when it ceased business. Another was built about the same time by Samuel Williams, on the Georgetown road, a short distance from Paris, which ran for a good many years. Samuel Pike also built a hemp factory, as early as 1827–28, about a mile and a half from Paris, which continued in operation until 1845. Still another was built on the east side of the Stoner, by William Woodward, on land now owned by William Shaw. It was built about 1822, and ran until 1826–27, when it ceased operation. All these factories made bagging, rope and twine, which were shipped South, where they found a ready market. About the year 1820, a cotton factory was built by Jefferson Scott, on the present Maysville & Lexington pike, on the farm now owned by Horace Miller. Its capacity was 720 spindles, and it continued in operation until 1831–32, when it closed business.

The Kentucky Central Railroad passes through Paris Precinct, and is of some benefit to the people. Its history is more fully given in another chapter. The Maysville Division diverges from the main line at Paris. With these two roads, the facilities for travel and transportation might be better than they are. It is, however, being greatly improved.

The early settlers of the precinct were alive to the necessity of education, and schools were established prior to 1800. One of the first schoolhouses of which we have any account was built on the east side of Stoner Creek, near where Clay's distillery now stands. Another was built on what is now the Flat Rock pike, near the second toll-gate. Still another near David Leer's place, which was built in about 1815. A new house has been erected upon its site, which is now in use. The other two mentioned have long since passed away, and there are no evidences left of their existence. Robert Langston, we are told, learned his letters from Col. William Wright, who cut them on a shingle—a rather novel text-book. There are now some half-dozen schoolhouses in the precinct outside of the city of Paris. These, however, are inadequate for the purposes for which they were designed. It is much to be regretted that every portion of the State pays so little attention to common school education. We have far too many academies, seminaries and colleges, and not half enough of common schools. Fewer private schools and more common schools is what is needed to improve our system of education.

The preaching of the Gospel in the precinct was coeval with its settlement by white people. The exact date of the formation of the first religious society is not now known. The first church edifice erected, is believed to have been old Mount Gilead Methodist Church, known as "Matheny's Meeting House," about three miles from Paris, on the Maysville pike, and was built in 1790. It was a log building, the logs were two feet in diameter, hewed, and were blue ash. It stood for many years a monument of pioneer Christianity. They were a strict sect, these old Methodists were, and believed not in the gaudy gewgaws and fashionable toggery with which we ornament our church pews at the present day. The male members of Matheny's meeting house wore their coats without collars, and buttoned up to the neck like a little boy's jacket, while the sisters dressed correspondingly plain. An incident is still remembered which illustrates the strict propriety in dress maintained in this pioneer church. A Miss Leer wore a "bombazine bonnet" to church one Sunday, which was beautifully quilted and elegantly "fixed up"—in a word, it was "a perfect love of a bonnet." But the minister did not think so. He watched for an opportunity, snatched it from her head, and casting it upon the ground, administered a scathing rebuke upon the ungodly extravagance of dress.

Among the original members of this old church were the Howard family, the Lowers, Brands, Carters, Hicks, Hannas and Leers. Daniel Leer was the first class-leader, and acted in that capacity for many years. Revs. John Whittaker and Christian Lowers were among the first preachers. The members of this church did not believe in slavery, it is said. Upon a certain occasion, Mr. Leer, the old class-leader, bought a negro woman upon the division of an estate, and the church raised a good-sized row over it. To avoid discipline, "he," said our informant, "stepped down and out."

Concord Universalist Church, or as it was known, "The First Universalist Church of Bourbon County," was organized originally some forty years ago. The church building was begun in 1845, and completed and dedicated May 30, 1847. The original members were Jesse Kennedy, Polly Kennedy, V. G. Wheat, W. A. Bacon, William L. Bacon, E. M. Kennedy, William Shaw and John Brown. The church prospered until the commencement of the war, when it was almost wholly broken up. About the year 1867, the building was sold under a degree of the court, bringing about $1,200. The purchaser designed turning it into a store or blacksmith's-shop, but it was burned shortly after its sale. It was situated about three miles from Paris, near C. M. Clay's, and was a frame building of substantial construction.

The Cane Ridge Church which is still standing in the east part of the precinct, on the Paris & Flat Rock pike, is believed by many to have been built prior to the old Mount Gilead Church. The Rev. Mr. Gano, however, places the date of its erection about 1794–95, and Elder Barton W. Stone became its pastor in 1798. It was then a Presbyterian Church, and among the original members were Joseph Luckey, Nathaniel Rogers, H. Wilson, John Frakes, John Irvin, David Jamison, —— Hall, William Maxwell, J. P. Campbell, David Purviance, and old Uncle Charley Spencer, an old colored man, than whom no more faithful member belonged to the church—none were more highly respected. Elder Stone continued its pastor for a number of years. It was at this church, in 1801, that the great revival meeting was held, at which there is said to have been present from twenty to thirty thousand people, and which is more fully described in a preceding chapter. Among the preachers since Elder Stone, are the following: Elders Frank Palmer, Samuel Rogers, Jacob Creath, John T. Johnson, John A. Gano, Sr., John Rogers, John I. Rogers, and John and Joshua Irvin. Elder Thomas Arnold is the present pastor. The original church, which was built of logs, as we have said, is still standing, although it has been somewhat modernized by being "weather boarded." In the revolution or reformation that followed Alexander Campbell, this church became a convert to the new faith, and since that period has been known as "Cane Ridge Christian Church." It was once very strong in numbers, but death and removals have greatly reduced its strength. A cemetery is adjacent, in which sleep many of the old members, and of the number, Elder Stone himself.

This comprises a complete sketch of Paris Precinct, so far as we have been able to obtain it, and we will leave the city of Paris to be treated of in a new chapter, and by a writer familiar with its history.—*Perrin.*

CHAPTER IX.

CITY OF PARIS—INTRODUCTORY—SELECTING A SITE FOR THE TOWN—THE ORIGINAL NAMES OF BOURBONTON AND HOPEWELL—EVERY-DAY LIFE OF THE SETTLERS—THE FIRST BRICK HOUSE—TAVERNS—THEATRICALS AND OTHER PASTIMES—SOME DISTINGUISHED PIONEERS.

"O, the pleasant days of old, which so often people praise !
True, they wanted all the luxuries that grace our modern days ;
Bare floors were strewed with rushes, the walls let in the cold,
O, how they must have shivered, in those pleasant days of old."
—*Brown.*

ALTHOUGH a century has not elapsed since the first settlement of this city, yet its early history is involved in obscurity. It is not known when the first house was built, or who was the first inhabitant, or why this particular locality was selected for the future city of Paris. One or two things are evident : The pioneers who came to this county did not do so to build cities, but came because they could obtain cheap lands. The soil was fertile ; the country marvelously beautiful and attractive, and none would locate in towns who had the means to purchase farms, which almost all possessed. The wants of the people of that day were few and simple. Their clothing was the handiwork of the thrifty house-wife, who was ever busy with the loom and the spinning wheel. And all through this region may yet be found—treasured as heirlooms, articles of exquisite workmanship, wrought by these pioneer mothers of Kentucky, who esteemed it their privilege and duty to share in the labors of the household, and whose sacrifices and industry and example laid the foundations of the future prosperity of the State. Corn, wheat, tobacco, flax, were the products of the soil. Almost every farm had its sugar camp, and the people made their own sugar, and from the ashes of burnt cobs they made their soda or saleratus. Except for needless luxuries they were self-sustaining. There was, therefore, no pressing necessity for large towns, with all their rush and bustle of trade. The blacksmith was, of course, indispensable ; but he could locate at any cross-roads ; and so, too, the carpenter was needed to rear the first rude structures in this then Western frontier of civilization ; and then, along the highway of travel the primitive tavern, with its accommodations for man and beast, became a necessity, and these, doubtless, formed the nucleus of the future city.

It is not known, nor is it important to know, why this particular locality was selected by the early settlers as a site upon which to build a town. Possibly, the town was an after-thought. Rocky, hilly, marshy in places, it may have been selected because it was not suited for agricultural purposes, and it would not have done, even at that early day, to have spoiled a blue grass farm to lay the foundations of a country town. That the proposed town was at the confluence of Stoner and Houston, two important creeks, which would yield an ample supply of water power near the large spring, which wells up a short distance from the mouth of Houston ; and that it was on the line of the buffalo trace, the then great thoroughfare of travel, were of themselves sufficient reasons for determining the location.

It appears from the records that the lands upon which this city stands was pre-empted by John Reed, of Maryland, on the 18th of November, 1784, and William Galloway and Samuel Lyons, of Virginia, in August, 1786. Lawrence Protzman afterward bought a portion of Reed's pre-emption, and laid it off into town lots.

Prior to the selection of a county-seat, the courts of Bourbon County had been held at James Garrard's, near Talbott's Station, at James Hutchison's, and at the residence of John Kiser, near the mouth of Cooper's Run. In November, 1786, the present site of Paris was selected by the court as the county seat, and the following order was made :

Ordered, That the place for holding courts for this county be established at the confluence of Stoner and Houston forks of Licking, and that Alvin Montjoy, John Grant and James Watson, gentlemen, be appointed to procure two acres of land at said place for the purpose aforesaid; and also, that they let to the lowest bidder the building of a court house, which shall be a frame of thirty-two by twenty feet, with a shingle roof, and finished in the necessary manner; and a jail sixteen feet square of hewn logs twelve inches square.

Teste: JOHN EDWARDS, C. B. C.

The buildings provided for in this order of court were erected during the next year, and the first court was held on Tuesday, October 17, 1787. This court house stood for ten or eleven years, but was sold, when a new one was built, to John Allen, who moved it to his farm on the Maysville road, one and a half miles northeast from town.

In 1789, the following act was passed by the Legislature of Virginia, establishing the town, which at that time was called Hopewell:

Be it enacted, That two hundred and fifty acres of land, at the court house in Bourbon County, as the same are laid off into town lots and streets by Lawrence Protzman, the proprietor thereof, shall be established a town by the name of Hopewell, and that Notley Conn, Charles Smith, Jr., John Edwards, James Garrard, Edward Waller, Thomas West, James Lanier, James Little, and James Duncan, gentlemen, are hereby constituted Trustees thereof.

The Trustees of said town, or a majority of them, are authorized to make such rules and orders for the regular building of houses thereon, as to them shall appear proper.

As soon as the purchasers of lots in the said town shall have built thereon a house sixteen feet square, at the least, with a brick or stone chimney, such purchasers shall then be entitled to, and have, and enjoy all the rights, privileges, and immunities which the freeholders and inhabitants of other towns in this State not incorporated, shall hold and enjoy.

At the session of the Virginia Legislature in 1790, the following act was passed amendatory to the above:

SECTION 1. *Whereas,* by an act of the assembly passed at the last session, entitled, "An act to establish a town in Bourbon County," two hundred and fifty acres of land at court house of said county of Bourbon, as laid off into lots and streets by a certain Lawrence Protzman, the then supposed proprietor thereof, was established a town by the name of Hopewell, of which Notley Conn, Charles Smith, Jr., John Edwards, James Garrard, Edward Waller, Thomas West, James Lanier, James Little and James Duncan, gentlemen, were constituted trustees, and whereas, since the passing of said act, many doubts have arisen who is the real proprietor of the said two hundred and fifty acres of land, and in consequence thereof the present holders of many of the said lots are disquieted, and the sale of the remainder thereof thereby prevented.

SEC. 2. *Be it therefore enacted by the General Assembly,* That from and after the passing of this act, the said two hundred and fifty acres of land, as laid off into lots and streets, shall be, and are hereby vested in the said Notley Conn, Charles Smith, Jr., John Edwards, James Garrard, Edward Waller, Thomas West, James Lanier, James Little and James Duncan, gentlemen, trustees, or a majority of them.

SEC. 3. The said trustees, or a majority of them, shall proceed to sell such of the said lots which now remain unsold, at public auction, for the best price that can be had, the time and place of which sale to be previously advertised two months in the *Kentucky Gazette* and convey the same to the purchaser, their heirs and assigns; subject, however, to the same rules, orders and conditions, as the said lots are subjected to by the said recited act.

SEC. 4. *And be it further enacted by the authority aforesaid,* That said trustees shall, as soon as the said sale shall be completed, return an account thereof to the court of the said county of Bourbon, to be there recorded, and the money arising from such sale shall be retained by them for the use and benefit of the person or persons in whom the title to the said two hundred and fifty acres of land shall hereafter be established, to be paid to such person or persons, or their legal representatives accordingly; *Provided nevertheless, and be it further enacted,* That in case the title of the said two hundred and fifty acres of land shall hereafter be established in any other person or persons than in the said Lawrence Protzman, the said trustees shall in such case convey such of the lots as were sold by him to the purchasers thereof, in fee simple, and the purchasers or holders of such lots, shall be subject only to account with the real proprietor thereof, for the value of the same when originally purchased as unimproved lots.

SEC. 5. *Be it further enacted,* that from and after the passing of this act the name of the said town shall be altered, and from thenceforth the same shall be established by the name of Paris; any law to the contrary notwithstanding.

There are conflicting statements as to the name of the place, although the above acts of the Virginia Legislature would seem to settle the matter definitely. Mr. Collins, the historian of Kentucky, says it was called Bourbonton, and a letter from the Treasury Department at Washington to the compilers of the volume entitled "Sketches of Paris," published here in 1876, corroborates the statement, and asserts that the post office was created January 1, 1795, with Thomas Eades as Postmaster, who was succeeded by William Paton, appointed July 1, 1800, and that the name was changed from Bourbonton to Paris, April 28, 1826, when James Paton, Jr., was appointed Postmaster.

Mr. James Paton, Sr., of this city, who is still living, and who was connected with the office from 1815 to 1837, is authority for the statement that there is some mistake as to the date of the change of name; that when he entered the office in 1815 it was known as Paris. He adds, however, that it had at one time been called Bourbonton, a fact which he had entertained by seeing the old way-bills in the office. From these statements and from the enactments of the Virginia Legislature, it seems clear that the town has borne the three names—Bourbonton, Hopewell and Paris. The selection of the last was peculiarly fitting. At the time the town was established there was a feeling of gratitude to France and to the Bourbons for the conspicuous part taken by the French people in the Revolutionary war, in which they contributed so largely to secure our National independence. Besides, the name of the county was Bourbon, given for the same reason, and it was, therefore, the more appropriate that the county-town should be called Paris; and this name was preferred and has been continued, carrying out in this instance, at least, the idea of the "survival of the fittest."

After the selection of Paris as the county seat, its population increased, and according to the census in 1790, six years after the settlement of the place, numbered 358. There is no reason to suppose that the early settlers indulged in any dreams of the future greatness of the town. If they did so, the illusion was rudely dispelled by the census of 1800, which showed a population of only 377, an increase in ten years of only nineteen inhabitants. The county, in the meantime, however, had increased with great rapidity.

The men of that day were not lacking in enterprise, for even then they looked forward to the opening of South Licking, and to carry out this purpose they secured the passage of an act through the Legislature in 1794, constituting John Edwards, Henry Clay, James Kenney, Charles Smith, William Garrard, William Kelley, William Boswell and James Smith, managers of a lottery, the object of which was to raise the sum of $2,800, to be used in opening the navigation of South Licking. Tickets were sold at $2, and the scheme was published for some time in the Lexington *Gazette*. We have been unable to ascertain whether the drawing ever took place, or the money was ever raised, or South Licking ever opened to navigation. The persons who were the managers of the lottery were leading and prominent citizens, showing that at that time there was not the same public sentiment against lotteries as now exists. In this respect, Paris was neither behind nor in advance of her sister towns; Georgetown had a lottery, and so also there were two in Lexington; one of the latter being for the benefit of the Dutch Presbyterian Protestant Church in that place.

In 1798, an act was passed by the Legislature, establishing Bourbon Academy, and "State aid" given to the institution, which donated for its benefit "six thousand acres of unappropriated lands."

In 1797, the publication of the *Kentucky Herald* was commenced. In an article published in 1855, in the *Citizen*, Mr. A. M. Brown, then the editor of that paper, states that James Stewart was the publisher. Other authorities are to the effect that it was published by Daniel Bradford, brother of the editor of the Lexington *Gazette*. It may be that both Stewart and Bradford were the joint publishers. The publication of the paper continued only one year. In March, 1797, the Legislature passed an act recognizing it as a medium of publishing laws or notices that required publication.

Very little is known of the habits or the every-day life of the early settlers. It is, however, clear, from the names which are mentioned, and from the prominent positions which many of them afterward held, that both the town and county was settled by some of the best citizens of Virginia and Maryland. It is probable that there were very few amusements in those days. There was no town hall. But, there was doubtless enough of social enjoyment and pastimes. The old-time quilting parties, the old-fashioned weddings, which were grand events, and the dance, probably the "Old Virginia Reel," and the Christmas festivities and holidays, and the crowning of the handsomest girl in the village, the "Queen of the May."

The facilities for obtaining news were not good. A post office was not established here until 1795, and the mails were by no means regular. There was very little local news. The inroads of the Indians, and their pursuit, were the chief topics of interest, and constituted the sensational news of the times, whilst their recital by the fireside at evening was, no doubt, listened to with most thrilling interest.

The erection of the second court house was begun in 1797, and the building was finished in 1799. The foundation was laid by Thomas Metcalfe, "Old Stone-hammer," afterward Governor of the State. His uncle, John Metcalfe, had the contract to erect the building. The carpentering work was done by a Mr. McCord. This house was destroyed by fire in 1872.

As soon as the county seat was located permanently in the place, and the town was laid off by Mr. Protzman, settlers were attracted here, who were on the lookout for suitable locations for merchandising and manufacturing. Mr. James H. McCann, who was born in Paris, in December, 1800, contributed some interesting facts, which appeared in "Sketches of Paris," a volume published in 1876, by G. R. Keller and J. M. McCann, and to whom we are also indebted for much information in regard to the early history of the place. From him we learn that the first settlers finding the bottoms an undesirable location for their purposes, they began to erect their houses on the higher ground. The first houses, it is believed, were built where the Bourbon House now stands, and along the road toward the Episcopal Church.

The first public house (or tavern) was erected of logs, on the lot now occupied by A. Shire's jewelry store, and was kept by Thomas West. It had no name like the hotels of to-day, but was known as "West's Tavern;" yet, in after years, when it was clapboarded, and washed over with a red-wash, it was known as "West's Red Tavern," and the only sign displayed was the "square and compass." The first hotel that bore a name was where the Bourbon House stands, and it was known as the "Indian Queen House," the sign displayed being a picture of a handsome Indian woman. The second hotel was kept by Thomas Eades in the Walker residence. The third was kept by Thomas Hughes, and stood just below the Citizens' Bank, occupying the site of the Stoker Hotel. The "Indian Queen

House" (portion of the present Bourbon House), was erected about 1804–5, and kept by Maurice Langhorn.

The first brick house erected in Paris was built by Thomas West, about 1796, extending from Pullen and Chamber's grocery (now L. Frank's dry goods store) to Ficklin's property, opposite the Court House door. It was in three divisions, two stories high. In after years the street was graded down, and these houses had to be entered by high steps, the first floors being perhaps eight or ten feet above the level.

The first regularly organized school was taught by Turner Lane (1796), in a little frame building, where the First Presbyterian Church stands, corner of Pleasant and Mulberry streets. He was superseded by John McCann (father of the venerable James H. McCann, now living), in 1800. The first Church organized was in 1787, by Rev. Andrew McClure, a Presbyterian minister, though the church building was not erected until 1789, and was not completely fitted up until several years afterward. It stood on the corner of Church and high streets, where James T. Davis' residence now stands. The first public burying-ground was known as the old "Dutch Graveyard," and adjoins the City School premises. The ground was donated by Lawrence Protzman. The first election of Town Trustees was held the first Friday in March, 1797, and the following gentlemen elected: John Metcalf, Daniel Duncan, William Kelly, Andrew Todd, Thomas Arnold and Richard Henderson. The Trustees before that time held their office by appointment by the Legislature.

The first bridge across Stoner at this point was built in 1795; was swept away in the fall of 1808, and was rebuilt the next year; this was torn away and replaced in 1833, by the one that stands firm yet, having been re-covered and otherwise repaired in 1875, and bids fair to last for several decades to come.

Paris in her earlier days seemed to have the same intellectual spirit animating her citizens as makes her famous for her educational institutions to-day. Establishing at the earliest day her academy and newspaper, it was but natural that she should have a public library, and as early as 1808 we find her with a chartered institution of this character. with the following gentlemen as Directors: William Garrard, Jr., Robert Trimble, William Kelly, Samuel Hanson and Benjamin Mills. The library was destroyed by fire in 1829.

The first grist-mill within the town limits was near the mouth of Houston, and was owned by John Allen, Esq. The first post office was kept by Thomas Eades (grandfather of Mrs. B. E. Knapp), at his tavern in the Walker residence. He was succeeded by William Paton, an uncle of our present City Clerk, the venerable James Paton, Sr., who assisted his uncle in the office for some time.

In 1810 the town records were torn up by some unknown person, and the first records after that contain a resolution of condemnation of the unknown vandal.

The first dramatic performance in Paris was in 1807, in the old Burr House, which is yet standing. The dancing room was transformed into a theater, there being no suitable hall in the town in which to give theatrical representations. The company was an amateur one, composed of a number of young men of the place, and during the winter gave several performances. Among the plays enacted was Shakespeare's sublime tragedy of Macbeth, which the young actors essayed to produce, showing that they had the utmost confidence in their histrionic ability. Our informant recalls the tragedy of Macbeth, as one of the pieces presented, from the boys using as by-words, when they would meet each other on the street, the expression, "when shall we three meet again?"

Another amateur society gave performances in 1815. Among the members were a young man named Mitchell, Ed. Hannegan, and James May, an Englishman, who had some experience as an actor. They produced the play entitled "Wild Oats." Hannegan, the young man referred to above, was at that time a clerk in a store; he was pale and delicate-looking, and rather handsome, and in the female parts, which were usually assigned to him, made a very handsome and presentable lady. He subsequently, we are informed, went to Indiana, and years afterward, when Hon. E. A. Hannegan, one of the most brilliant orators of his time, was elected United States Senator from that State, it was said that he had been a clerk in a store in this place. It is, therefore, not improbable, that the amateur actor of Paris was, thirty or thirty-five years after, the eloquent Senator from Indiana. James May, who was also a member, figured afterward in the most exciting criminal case in the county, on a charge of forgery, and was sentenced to imprisonment in the State Penitentiary.

In 1823 or 1824, the first regular theatrical company appeared in Paris, under the management of a man named Cargill. The company comprised three ladies and three gentlemen. The performances, which continued nightly for some weeks, were given in the dancing-room of the old Paris Hotel. Among the pieces presented was Maturin's Bertram, which was a great favorite with theater-goers at that day.

The first carriage was brought here by Mr. Thomas Arnold, the Clerk of the Circuit Court, in 1807. He was also the first who purchased a piano, about the same time. Judge Robert Trimble, Judge Benjamin Mills, Jesse Bledsoe and Daniel Duncan, although they were leading, well-to-do citizens of the town, and had large families of children, had no pianos. For many years afterward, there were very few carriages; no buggies. The gig seemed to be a favorite vehicle for travel. Maj. A. Throckmartin, afterward the proprietor of the Galt House, in Louisville, had, it is said, the finest turn-out of that day—an elegantly finished and showy gig, to which two horses were driven, one before the other, tandem style. But horseback riding was then the usual mode of travel; and these were romantic and delightful days, when the young men went visiting or to church, with their sweethearts riding on behind and affectionately circling them with their arms.

In the earlier days, travel was exceedingly dangerous, on account of the liability of travelers being waylaid by hostile Indians. In looking over the old newspaper files, we find that those returning to Virginia would advertise weeks ahead for persons to accompany them through the "wilderness," as it was then called. The first stage that ever passed through Paris was in 1808, conducted by George Walls, of Lexington; but this was only temporary. The first regular stage line was established by E. P. Johnson & Co., of Georgetown, in 1818. It was not until long after, in 1854, that the Kentucky Central Railroad was finished to Paris, and the town placed in easy access with the important trade centers of the country.

In those times, the same care was bestowed upon dress as at the present day; if anything, the young men dressed more elaborately, in fine broadcloths, with tastefully ruffled shirt-bosoms, high stocks and standing collars. Some of the older men, among them Mr. Raines, the father of John B. Raines, for many years Cashier of the Northern Bank, and Mr. Thornton, Capt. Abram Spears, and others, were not led away by the changes of fashion, but adhered to the old time style of knee-breeches, with stockings reaching up to the knees. And there was a courtliness and a dignity in the style which was in admirable keeping with the stateliness and pride of these gentlemen of the olden time, in any one of whom, no doubt, might have been found a fit prototype for the latter-day apostle of æstheticism.

From 1800 to 1810, the town made rapid progress, springing from 377 to 838 in population. In the meantime, the county had become very populous, the census showing a population of 18,009, larger than the county now has after the lapse of seventy-two years.

In 1812, the second war with Great Britain was begun, and the citizens of Bourbon County rushed forward with patriotic ardor in defense of their country. Capt. William Garrard's troops were composed largely of the young men of Paris. During the progress of the war, the deepest interest was manifested, and the most intense eagerness to hear the news. When the dreadful intelligence of Dudley's defeat was received, there was mourning everywhere; but when word came of victories, there were processions, and firing of muskets, and hurrahing, and other demonstrations of joy. The news of peace, and the victory at New Orleans, January 8, 1815, caused great and universal rejoicing.

It was not until 1823 or 1824 that, so far as can be learned, the first debating society was organized. Among the prominent members were George W. Williams, afterward a leading citizen of the county, and George Redmon, a shoemaker. The latter, especially, was a ready speaker, and took an active part in the debates and proceedings of the society.

Such, chiefly, was the beginning of Paris. The men who laid its foundations were men of strong will, of ability, of patriotism, and many of them of culture. The long array of prominent names shows that there were truly "giants in those days." James Garrard, the second Governor of the State, who was among the earliest settlers, was a man of massive frame, weighing upward of three hundred pounds. He had represented the county in the Virginia Legislature, when Kentucky was a part of Virginia. He was a member of the State Constitutional Convention; afterward held important political trusts, and was recognized as one of the leading men of the State. Judge Benjamin Mills was a prominent lawyer, and one of the Judges of the Appellate Court during the old and new court controversy. He was heavy set, rather below the usual height, and those who have seen him say, in appearance, he was very much like his son, Rev. T. A. Mills. Jesse Bledsoe is spoken of as one of the ablest men of his day. He was Circuit Judge of the Lexington District, United States Senator, and held other positions of honor and trust. Judge Robert Trimble was a man of splendid presence; in intellect, and in all that goes to make up true manhood in every respect, one of the first men of the State. He was one of the Judges of the Supreme Court. A splendid granite monument marks his last resting-place in the Paris Cemetery.

These distinguished men—except Governor Garrard—were all cotemporaries at the Paris bar, constituting a grand galaxy of legal ability unsurpassed in the State.

For many years, the history of Paris was only the record of ordinary, commonplace events. No startling murders, no great sensations, but everything moved on in the even tenor of its way. "Happy," it is said, "is that nation which has no history;" where everything passes along calmly and pleasantly and peacefully, undisturbed by the rude shocks of bloodshed, and of war. Where every man reposes in peace beneath his own vine and fig-tree. But here, as everywhere, that great struggle in which all humanity is engaged, the struggle for daily bread, has always been going on; it is the terrible life struggle, and some become weary and heart-sick, and fall by the way. The aggregate histories of all these people, as they toil year after year, earning scarcely enough to save their families from want; the sowing in peril that another may reap the rich harvest; if the life's history of each individual could be given, it would make a history of deeper interest than any which shall ever be written.

And there is another side—another history of the beautiful home-life; of noble deeds of charity, and of kindness; of patient waiting and self-denying sacrifices; the tender and ennobling attributes of our nature, as they show themselves in the gentle ministrations of kindness, and in deeds of which the world knows nothing; these are not written in ephemeral earthly histories, but in another book.—*F. L. McChesney.*

CHAPTER X.

CITY OF PARIS—EARLY PERIOD OF THE TOWN—ITS GROWTH—PIONEER POLITICS—IMPROVEMENTS OF THE CITY—WAR EXCITEMENT AND SOLDIERS—TRANSIENT PROSPERITY—BURNING OF THE COURT HOUSE—CENTRAL UNIVERSITY—TEMPERANCE MOVEMENT—CHOLERA, ETC., ETC.

MR. James H. McCann, who is now living, has a very distinct recollection of Paris as far back as 1805. There were, at that time, seventy-five or eighty buildings, situated mostly in the lower part of the town. From the best information that can be obtained, it is probable the *first* house built in Paris was the old log house on the northwest corner of High and Church streets, which was torn down last year. Some of these buildings are yet standing, among which are the old Burr House, now occupied by Mrs. Webb as a boarding-house, which was then a tavern, owned and kept by Mrs. James Duncan; the old Walker property, where Mr. Jeff Elgin now lives, is also one of the old landmarks; the two-story brick building, Dr. David Keller's residence, and the house adjoining were both built prior to that time, as was also a portion of the present Bourbon House; and the brick building lately occupied by Bayles & Davis. On High street, the town extended only to where Mr. James M. Hughes now lives. The ground now occupied by John T. Hinton's furniture store, the Adams Express, the post office and J. J. Shaw & Co.'s storehouse, and extending across Main street was then covered by a large pond of water, at times three or four feet deep, and had to be crossed on a log foot-bridge. It was the delight of the boys when it was frozen over, and it is said that wild ducks were killed upon the pond even after this time.

We are informed that the building—the residence and store—of Mr. Philip Nippert was built from the timber cut on the ground where it is situated.

The present residence of James Short, Sr., was then standing, and then, as now, the old Paris Mills was one of the institutions of Paris. The lower portion of the town was compactly built, many of the houses being of brick, and the old court house, then comparatively new, was regarded as a model of architectural beauty and symmetry. However, there was not much regard had for tasteful residences; many of the dwelling-houses were erected close to the streets. There were very few front yards with attractive walks, and beautified by evergreens and flowers. The people seemed to be of a more practical turn of mind, and regarded the ground they owned as more valuable for gardens than for showy front yards.

The growth of Paris, from this time forward, for many years, was not rapid. In 1830, the population was 1,217; in 1840, it had decreased to 1,197. In the meantime, the population of the county had also decreased. The small land-holders sold their farms, and went to the West, where land was cheap, and their little homesteads were absorbed in the larger farms of their wealthier and more prosperous neighbors. There was, therefore, no reason to expect an increase of the population of the town, which depended for its prosperity almost exclusively upon the local trade of the county.

From the very first organization of the county and town, the people took a lively interest upon all political questions. They were almost all politicians. "Stump-speaking" has always been the favorite way with the public men of Kentucky in which to reach the people, and almost all the men who have risen to prominence have won success because they were good speakers, most of whom secured their education in oratory upon the hustings. As early as 1792, a political society was organized in Paris, modeled after the Democratic society in Philadelphia, and was formed to oppose the then Federal party. In 1798, the celebrated resolutions of 1798, were passed by the Kentucky Legislature, and the people were much divided, and there was great excitement on the issues of that day. The "Alien and Sedition" law enacted about that time produced a feeling of intense opposition throughout the country, which resulted in hurling the old Federal party from power, and making the name of Federalist ever afterward odious with the people. All this section of Kentucky ranged itself with the Republican party in opposition to the Federalists. Then came on the war of 1812, and our people were unitedly in its favor; then followed the conflict between the old and new court parties, which was probably the fiercest ever known in the State. In 1824–25, came the contest for the Presidency, in which Adams, Clay, Crawford and Jackson were the candidates. There was no choice of President by the people, and the election was thrown into the House of Representatives of Congress, and through the influence of Mr. Clay, the vote of the State was cast for John Quincy Adams. This caused a permanent division and a strict drawing of party lines here into Whigs and Democrats, and in all the subsequent contests Bourbon County and Paris were always carried by the Whig party by a decided majority, and from that day until his death the people followed with an unfaltering devotion the political fortunes of Henry Clay. To give an idea of the political feeling then existing, a public dinner, given in Paris, in July, 1827, to Mr. Clay, was attended by 8,000 people.

As far back as 1830, there was much interest in the construction of turnpikes, and the feeling then manifested has brought forth abundant fruit, in giving to Bourbon County the most complete system of turnpike roads in the State. In that year there was much enthusiasm in favor of the Maysville & Lexington Turnpike road, which now constitutes our main street, and which, connecting with other roads extending hundreds of miles north and south, has not inaptly been called the "Broadway of the United States." To this road the citizens of Paris subscribed $30,500; in Lexington $13,000 was subscribed; in Millersburg, $5,200; in Nicholas County, $8,000, and $10,300 at Maysville. The Maysville & Lexington road bill passed Congress, but was vetoed by President Jackson. Collins' History of Kentucky contains the following "Practical Joke on the President," which was claimed, but, of course, groundlessly, to have some remote connection to the veto: "When President Jackson passed through Paris, in 1829, *en route* to Washington, to be inaugurated President, some Adams men changed the sign-board, east of town, so as to make the 'To Maysville' sign point to Mount Sterling. It is said, the General and party passed on toward the latter place some distance before discovering the mistake. It is added, that it was afterward claimed that this was, in great part, the cause of the old General's vetoing the Maysville road bill."

In 1851, the county of Bourbon subscribed $100,000 to the Lexington & Covington Railroad Company; individual subscriptions of stock were also made of $100,000. A like county subscription was also made to the Maysville & Lexington Railroad. Subsequently, the city of Paris subscribed $10,000 to the Covington & Lexington road. The Maysville & Lexington road, after being partially graded, and some other work done upon it, was abandoned, and was not finally completed until twenty years afterward, when the county subscribed $200,000 to aid in its construction. The Covington & Lexington road was finished to Paris in 1854. The road was afterward sold, and the stock of the county supposed to be lost. Subsequently, however, in a suit of the old owners against the heirs of an estate, who had purchased the road, the Court of Appeals decided to set aside the sale, and the title to the road reverted to its original owners. A compromise was affected by which a new company was organized, and this county accepted for its subscription $75,000 in stock, and this stock was sold last year for $45,000.

With the completion of the road to Covington, and the opening of new avenues of trade, the town and county both enjoyed, until the beginning of the late sectional war, an unwonted prosperity. There was a ready market for their stock and all their farm products. Indeed, the railroad, as is almost always the case, benefited the farmer more than it did the people of the town.

But the political excitement of 1860, followed by the terrible civil war, unsettled all business. In that year this county had given a large majority in favor of the Union candidates; but the feelings and interests and associations of a large majority of the people were with the South in its struggle. They deplored the war, and would have rejoiced could it have been averted, but when it begun and was followed up by the emancipation of the slaves, the white population, nine out of every ten, were in sympathy with the Southern people. In addition to this, the very flower of the young men had volunteered as soldiers in the Confederate army, Col. Roger W. Hanson's famous Second Kentucky Regiment and Gen. John H. Morgan's Cavalry being largely recruited from this section of the State. These people were in the anomalous position of being under Federal rule, yet sympathizing with the South. We state facts, and offer no comments. It was a civil war in which countrymen and townsmen and brothers were arrayed against each other, and that is the most dreadful of all wars. Paris and Bourbon County gave both to the Union and Confederate cause names which will be conspicuous in history. Judge Richard Hawes, the foremost citizen of his day in the county, at an advanced age, abandoned his home (which was seized by the Federal Government and used as a hospital), to avoid imprisonment, took refuge in Virginia, and was afterward made Governor of the Confederate Provisional Government of Kentucky. Col. William E. Simms was one of the Senators from the State in the Confederate Congress; Col. E. F. Clay, Maj. Thomas Y. Brent, Capt. J. Lawrence Jones, Capt. Daniel Turney, Capt. Ed. Taylor, Capt. J. M. Thomas, Capt. Ed. F. Spears, and others, made a record of brilliant service in the Confederate army. On the Union side were Gen. John T. Croxton, Col. Charles S. Hanson, Col. R. M. Kelly, Col. G. C. Kniffin, Maj. John Hall, Capt. M. M. Clay, Capt. Greenberry Reid, Capt. Thomas Vimont, and others, who bore a prominent part in the great struggle, and all of whom, both Confederate and Federal, are more particularly mentioned in a preceding chapter. Paris, fortunately, suffered very little from the ravages of war; no battle was fought in its immediate vicinity. In November, 1861, a serious affray occurred near the jail, at the bridge, between a squad of Union soldiers, belonging to the Eighteenth Kentucky Regiment, and Abram Spears and Daniel Hibler, two well-known and prominent citizens, in which the former was killed and the latter severely wounded, being shot through the breast, after having shot and killed a soldier named Ford. It was with some difficulty that Hibler was protected from the infuriated soldiers, but he was immediately arrested by Capt. Greenberry Reid, who happened at the time to be passing through the bridge, and was lodged in jail, where he remained until the following July, when he was released by Morgan's command. This affair, on account of the prominence of the parties engaged in it, caused very great excitement in the community. At that time, military rule was supreme. In October, 1861, the *Flag* suspended publication. In April, 1862, the grand jury found indictments against thirty-four citizens of the county who had entered the Confederate service, and against twelve others for invading the State to make war against it. On July 18, 1862, about sundown, Gen. John Morgan's forces reached Paris. A deputation of citizens had met Gen. Morgan on the road to Ruddel's Mills and surrendered the town. His advent here caused much rejoicing among the Southern sympathizers. But, a short time afterward, when he had left, an order was issued by the Federal authorities forcing Morgan's friends to pay for the acts of their favorite chieftain; and, in the carrying out of this order, assessments were levied upon a number of citizens of this section of of the State. September 1, Paris was again abandoned by the Union forces, and was taken possession of by the Confederates, who paroled all citizens who were attached to the Home Guards. The Provost Marshal issued an order making Confederate money receivable for all goods and produce sold. One merchant who refused to take the Confederate notes as money was placed under arrest. After remaining here a short time, the Confederates abandoned this section, and, after the battle of Perryville, withdrew their entire forces from the State.

It was not until the close of the war in 1865 that Paris made any considerable advance in population. The slaves had been emancipated, and rejoicing over their new-born freedom were restless under the restraints of farm-life, and came to the city by hundreds. Besides, there was an almost universal belief that with the destruction of slavery, Kentucky and other States where the institution had existed would enjoy a prosperity which they had never before realized. The prices of land, of houses, of everything, were inflated; money was plentiful; speculation was rife everywhere, and everything seemed to betoken an era of unexampled prosperity. In Claysville, a suburban town near Paris, one hundred houses were built in one week. In the meantime, railroad enterprises were infused with a new life. Action was taken looking to the completion of the Maysville & Paris Railroad, and the county, by a large popular majority, voted a subscription of $200,000 in aid of the enterprise. Another project, the Frankfort, Paris & Big Sandy Railroad was also agitated in 1871. A charter had been obtained from the Legislature in that year, and an application was made by Gen. John T. Croxton, the President of the company, to submit to a vote of the people of the county the proposition to subscribe $400,000 to the capital stock of the company. The Court, Judge Richard Hawes presiding, rejected the application. The contest was then transferred to the Legislature, and an amendment of the charter was asked making it mandatory upon the Court to submit the proposition to a popular vote. The question was thoroughly discussed, and although opposed by the Senator from this district and the Representative from the county, and the Railroad Committee in the House, of which Hon. J. C. S. Blackburn was Chairman, made a unanimous report against it, still the bill passed by a majority of thirteen votes; and in April, 1872, the Court, carrying out the mandatory act of the Legislature, submitted the proposition to the people, and it was carried by a

"WOOD LAWN." RESIDENCE OF JAMES HINTON NEAR PARIS. KY.

"PATTERSON DALE" RESIDENCE OF SAMUEL L. PATTERSON, PARIS PRECINCT, BOURBON CO. KY.

majority of 288 votes; for the subscription, 1,672; against 1,384. The contest was very exciting, the county being thoroughly canvassed by Gen. Croxton, F. L. McChesney, R. S. Henderson, Col. E. F. Clay, Capt. James M. Thomas and Frank Kennedy in favor of the proposition. Hon. W. A. Cunningham was the only one who spoke against the subscription, replying to F. L. McChesney, at Clintonville. A subscription of $350,000 was made to the road in Scott County, and $150,000 in Bath, with the private subscriptions, making in all $950,000; but the road was never built, and the subscription never called for. The financial crash of 1873 followed, and put an end to all enterprise; the growth of the city was checked; the value of property fell; business became paralyzed; the mechanics had very little to do; a feeling of depression pervaded every department of trade; and the city has not yet recovered from the effects of that disastrous financial crisis.

In 1870, the negroes were made voters, and first voted here at the August election in that year. At the polls, a partition was erected, and the whites voted on one side and the colored men on the other. Prior to 1869, two villages, Claysville and Ruckerville, had been within the city limits, and in anticipation of their enfranchisement, and to keep them from obtaining political control, an act had been passed by the Legislature, cutting them off from the city, and re-arranging its boundaries. Nothwithstanding this Legislation, the Republicans for several years carried the municipal elections, and elected Roger W. O'Connor, Mayor. Subsequently, the charter was amended so as to require the payment of a *per capita* tax before voting, and since that time the Democrats have carried the city at each election by a decided majority.

On May 8, 1872, the old court house was destroyed by fire, the work of an incendiary. The *True Kentuckian*, of May 15, contains the following description of the fire, written by the Hon. R. T. Davis:

About 10 o'clock Wednesday night, smoke issued from the court house; but as no danger was apprehended, and no particular attention paid to it, it was mistaken for clouds; but, as the volume increased, and the smoke-wreaths ascended faster, persons went over, and, on opening the door, were horrified at finding that the interior of that ancient structure was in flames, and everything demonstrating, beyond a doubt, that some ruthless hand had applied the incendiary torch to our halls of justice. The windows, which were open in the evening, were tightly closed by the vandal, in order that the flames might make such headway, and eat so deeply into the vitals of the building, as to defy all efforts to save it, when the incendiary's work should be discovered. Even the doors opening from the vestibule into the court room were closed, and every precaution taken by the as yet unknown burner to prevent an early discovery that might thwart his infamous design. When the inner door was opened, an appalling sight met the view; everything combustible was rapidly falling a prey to the devouring element; huge flame-tongues were darting, hissing, lapping and blighting everything they touched; struggling, as if obedient to a fire king, whose motto was "excelsior!" And now broke forth upon the still night air the fearful cry of "fire!" which soon brought crowds to the scene of conflagration, some manifesting deep concern, while by far the greater number looked calmly on.

The engine was soon brought into requisition, and our firemen bore down on the brakes manfully, with what appeared at first a prospect of success of subduing the flames. But no sooner did a stream of water extinguish the fire in one quarter than it burst forth in another.

Seeing that the old structure was doomed, the firemen ceased their efforts to save it, and directed their attention to the other buildings that were jeopardized by sparks and flying cinders, until the heat became so intense that those who manned the engine at the cistern, near the scene of the burning, were compelled to abandon their work, and, as they could do nothing more, drew off to watch the flames, which soon burst through the roof, and, in a few moments, fiery billows were roaring, tossing and seething around the base of the cupola, that symmetrical architectural work that towered aloft a "thing of beauty" and just pride of the Bourbons for more than half a century.

As the sheets of flame ascended, all eyes were directed to the old town clock, whose hands pointed to 10.50, the hour at which it ceased its labor, and whose face had been familiar to us from childhood, and wore the same look for all—a look as tender for those in squalid poverty as those in regal splendor. Like a faithful sentinel, it stood at its post, and faced the fiery enemy, until the supports gave way, and it was forced to yield to the fire-fiend who had decreed that with it "time should be no more."

When the old cupola sank down into the bed of fire, many of the spectators gave utterance to an involuntary exclamation, and a beautiful young lady burst into tears when the dear old fabric disappeared from view forever.

There was more and heavier timber used in the construction of the edifice than one would have supposed, being erected at a period when, to use the language of a friend, "timber was cheap and carpenters were honest." The fall of the cupola, and the other lumber brought in its descent, filled the air with millions of sparks, that circled, eddied, whirled and danced through the atmosphere, making a scene grand and beautiful beyond description, and the myriads of swallows that had been dislodged from their homes in the cupola, were confusedly darting hither and thither, reminding one of the dove sent from the ark, seeking a place to rest its wearied wings, but finding it not.

The morning after the fire dawned bright and beautiful upon our city; but the beauty was marred by the sad spectacle presented by the ruins of the old buildings, where the law had been expounded for threescore and ten years. Nothing was left of the old structure, wherein audiences had listened, with rapt delight, to the eloquence of Clay, Marshall, Breckinridge and others of the flower of Kentucky orators, but a shapeless mass of smoldering ruins. True, the old edifice was unsightly, and anything but a credit to a county possessed of so much wealth as Bourbon, but we deplore its loss, and say "peace to its ashes."

In 1873, an earnest effort was made to secure the location of Central University in Paris. Rev. L. H. Blanton, then of this city, now the Chancellor of the University, was the leading spirit in the movement, but was heartily seconded by a number of our public-spirited citizens. A magnificent subscription, reaching $110,000, was made, and offered as an inducement for the location of the University here, and in addition to this amount, it was believed that the interest upon the Garth Fund could also be diverted in the same direction. This would have increased the amount of the subscription to fully $140,000. Considerable feeling, however, had been engendered as to the location, and although Paris offered much the largest bid, the institution, by a vote of the Alumni Association, under whose auspices the enterprise was carried on, was located at Richmond. The response made for subscription was exceedingly liberal, and in the highest degree creditable to the people of our county.

In the latter part of November, the Murphy temperance movement was begun in Paris by Mr. I. N. Grubbs, of Pittsburgh, Penn., and George Leavenworth, a reformed drunkard, of Cleveland, Ohio. The meetings were held at the Baptist Church, and largely attended. Every night they would address immense audiences, and would be followed by brief remarks from local speakers. Leavenworth was an earnest and persuasive speaker, and certainly one of the most effective temperance lecturers in the country. During the meetings, which lasted more than two months, there were upward of one thousand signers to the pledge of total abstinence, all of whom enrolled themselves as members of the Christian Temperance Union. Such good order was never seen in Paris as on Christmas Day, 1877. There was a temperance dinner and supper in the dining-room of the Paris Hotel building, and no drunkenness seen anywhere. For a time, at least, all was quiet, and temperance held full sway in this city. The movement unquestionably was productive of good, but the results fell far short of the expectations of those actively engaged in it.

Paris, in its earlier days, was not a healthy city. In 1816, it was visited by what was called the "cold plague." The victims of the disease were first seized with a chilly fever, after which there were symptoms somewhat resembling cholera. Not being understood, it was especially fatal to old people. Among those who died were John Hildreth, Capt. James Kenney and Peter Cline and wife.

In 1833, the cholera first appeared in Paris. Business was suspended, and all who could get away left the town. The following is a list of those who died during the epidemic: Jonathan Willett, Thomas Burdin, Sophia (daughter of Dr. N. Warfield), Mrs. Lym, Thomas Hardwick, a daughter of Maj. George W. Williams, Mrs. Judith Bryan, Mrs. Gaither, Mrs. William M. Samuel, Mrs. Moore and son, Mrs. Hinton, Peter Sharrer, Sr., Mrs. Charles Brent, Parker (son of Mrs. Andrews), Jonathan Dearborn and son William, Erasmus Gill, Isaac Avery, Samuel D. Scott, Samuel Beeler, Mrs. Ann Kennedy, Mrs. James McCann, Peter Hizer, Mrs. Praul, Richard Samuel, George Davis, Mrs. James Paton, Richard Turner, a turnpiker (name unknown), Richard Holmes (a wagoner at John Mitchell's). Colored persons: Olivia, at William C. Lyle's; Julia, at N. Warfield's; Grace, at Mrs. Barker's; boy, at James H. McCann's; woman, at E. H. Herndon's; Jennie Jackson; Sarah Wallace; woman, at Mr. Cummins'; Marshall's woman; David, two men and woman at S. Pyke's; woman, at Mr. Waggoner's; Jenny, at Rev. Amos Clever's; Phœbe, at Jonathan Massie's; Gabriel, a stone mason; woman, at David Cline's; girl, at John Mitchell's; thirteen, at H. T. Duncan's factory. Citizens of the town who died in the country: George P. Bryant, Miss Susan Croxton, Dr. Davis, George W. Williamson, Mrs. John G. Martin, Elizabeth Leer, Mary Ann (daughter of Jonathan Massie), Mrs. Berkley.

At this time, Paris contained a population of about 1,200; and when this is borne in mind, the proportion of deaths from the scourge was very large.

In 1839, a disease known as the "Paris fever" prevailed, and a number of the citizens of the town were its victims, among whom were Benjamin Riggs, Hugh I. Brent, Joshua Smith, Sallie Davis, James Scott and others. The disease was supposed to have been caused by the miasma arising from the ponds and stagnant water about the town.

Again, in 1849, the cholera visited Paris, and the following taken from a slip which was sent out from the *Citizen* office, dated August 4, 1849, tells the story of its workings:

"The cholera has raged with great malignity and frightful mortality in Paris during the first few days of this week, but we are gratified to announce that the disease has abated in the violence and number of its attacks. The following is a list of the deaths since Thursday noon (July 26) to noon to-day: A. S. Pomeroy, Dyer Austin, Mrs. Thomas Rule; Old Cato, at Mrs. Keiningham's; Mrs. Green McIntyre; Aaron, son of N. B. Rion, Mrs. Squire Taylor, James Gardner's child; E. P. Watts, at A. Cummins'; negro woman at Mrs. Scott's; Squire Robinson; Ned, negro man of C. Talbutt's; James H. Wood, old Mrs. Lovely, Thomas R. Rule, John H. Thurston, Samuel McElroy, Dr. John A. Ingels; negro girl at Charles Talbutt's; George Elliott, James Heatherington, William Finlay, Mrs. Elizabeth Barker; Mary, daughter of George Northcutt; old negro woman, Smoot's mother; Charles, son of C. C. Daugherty ; George, son of Dr. L. G. Ray ; Dr. Quisenbury, Ezekiel Thurston (not cholera); Mrs. Sarah D. Scott, Charles Snyder (consumption); Mrs. Brent's negro boy, William T. Davis ; Henry, son of Mrs. Robinson ; Frank T., son of A. T. Sebree ; Mrs. Martha Potts (in Millersburg); Mrs. Barbara Lennox (in Millersburg); James Daugherty, Mrs. Ann Mitchell, Mrs. Israel N. Smith, Jesse P. Kern, negro girl of Mrs. Williams ; negro girl at David Kelley's ; Mrs. Samuel Clair ; Mr Sheppard (chair-maker); John McIntyre (in the country); Mrs. Catharine Hibler ; Judy Klizer, a free woman ; Stepney Barnett, free black ; Old Davy, negro man near town, and James Scott.

"The above is as accurate a list as we have been able to obtain, but we believe it to be very nearly correct. We hear of very few new cases within the last twenty-four hours. The whole number of deaths, since the 3d of July (when the first case of cholera occurred) to the 4th of August, in town and vicinity, sixty-five, which includes all the deaths of cholera and five or six other diseases. Owing to sickness, we have been unable to publish the *Citizen* this week. We hope, however, that we shall be able to renew our regular issues next week."

In addition to the above, the following also died : Mrs. Richard Talbott, child of William M. Taylor, Mrs. A. S. Pomeroy, Mrs. Robert S. Morrow, Mrs. Cheshire, Roger D. Williams (son of Maj. George W. Williams) of fever, Thomas Rule, Jr., Miss Harriet Robinson, Mrs. John Crosby, Miss Susan Daugherty, John Talbutt (son of Charles Talbutt), William Scroggin, Mrs. Willis Wills, Mrs. Dr. John A. Lyle, Miss Mary Chambers and others.

In 1852–53, the cholera again visited Paris, but was not so fatal as in 1833 and 1849.

In the fall and winter of 1873–74, the cerebro-spinal meningitis prevailed in Paris, and was very fatal. Among those who died were the following : Mrs. B. F. Massie, Oliver Shaw, Mrs. William Lair and child, William Clay, Miss Katie Holliday, Mrs. Mary Buckner, three children of Mrs. Merringer, Willie Gaper and Miss Ollie Stoker. About this time there were other deaths, among them the following : Mrs. B. F. Pullen, Mrs. J. S. Sweeney, Mrs. J. T. Hinton, Mrs. O. P. Carter, Miss Carrie Stuart, Miss Mary Ingels, Mrs. W. T. Poynter, Mrs. G. W. Williams and Mrs. Louisiana Rankins.

In 1873, the cholera appeared at Millersburg, and was very fatal. There were no cases in Paris. During the former epidemics, well water was generally used ; now almost every residence has a cistern, and it is claimed by some that the city owes its exemption from cholera in 1873 to the almost exclusive use of cistern water.—*McChesney.*

CHAPTER XI.

THE CHURCH HISTORY OF PARIS—INTRODUCTION OF THE GOSPEL—BUILDING OF THE FIRST CHURCHES—PRESBYTERIAN ORGANIZATION—OTHER DENOMINATIONS—THE BARNES REVIVAL—SOCIETIES, THE PRESS, ETC.

"How beautiful are the feet of them that preach the Gospel of peace and bring glad tidings of good things."

HAND in hand with the early settlers came the earnest and devoted preachers of the Gospel. The husbandman tilled the soil and the golden grain rewarded his industry, and in every household there was bread to supply the physical wants of man. But it is said, "that man shall not live by bread alone," and religion comes offering to satisfy the soul's hunger and the soul's thirst, and to give the bread, of which if any man eat he shall never hunger, and the water of which if any man drink he shall never thirst. And so in the early days, when the rude log house was built, the same hands erected the modest house of worship, where the Gospel of peace was proclaimed. First, in the county, so far as we can learn, came the Baptists; then the Presbyterians. Whilst there was wickedness then just as now, yet there seemed to be a strong religious element, transplanted here from the Valley of Virginia, which pervaded the whole community. But scarcely had the church gained a foothold than infidelity also appeared. Just before the close of the last century France had run wild, the Sabbath had been abolished, and the darkness of atheism had settled upon that people. At that time one of the most learned and brilliant of this school of infidels was Augustin Volney, the author of the "Ruins of Empires," whose whole life was devoted to the pulling down of all the altars of religion. It is not known why he came here, but about that time he became a resident of the county, and was industrious in sowing the seeds of infidelity; and the tares which were thus sown have grown up, and the baneful influence of his teachings have not passed away to this day. About the same time occurred in this county, that remarkable religious phenomenon, "the Shakes," the greatest revival which has ever occurred in the State, of which a full account is given elsewhere in the history of the county. In this connection we may state that we are informed on good authority that of all those who had the "Shakes," or spiritual "exercises," not one failed afterward to live a consistent Christian life.

The following full and accurate history of the Presbyterian Church, we reproduce from the "Sketches of Paris:"

Presbyterian Church.—The Presbyterians were the pioneers of religion in Paris, having established the first church in 1787, and continued ever since to sustain an organization, and to-day are sustaining two preachers, having two working congregations and owning two church buildings.

Rev. Andrew McClure, a man of devout and energetic disposition, was the first minister, and to him is due much of the honor for the firm hold his people have upon this community. He organized the church, was its first leader, and remained in charge until his death in 1793. The first official act of the session of the church, of which we have any record, bears date of September 25, 1809. The Ruling Elders then were Isaac Orchard, John Curry, James Alexander, Joseph Mitchell and William McConnell. It is probable that nearly all of these men were Elders when the church was organized.

In the spring of 1795, Rev. Samuel Rannells took charge of the church, and continued until his death in 1817. During Mr. Rannells' ministry, as well as Mr. McClure's, the church at Paris was connected with the church at Ruddel's Mills (or Stoner Mouth, as it was known), and after Mr. Rannells' death this connection was dissolved, and the Paris congregation sustained a minister for his whole time, having extended a call to the Rev. William Wallace, a young man of brilliant talents and ardent piety. He preached in Paris for some time before his ordination and installation as pastor. Under his ministration, the church was blessed with a revival, and more than one hundred persons were added to the membership. He died in 1818, after a pastorate of about one year.

At the death of Mr. Wallace, and for some time afterward, the pulpit was supplied by the Rev. James McChord, a man of extraordinary ability and one of the most eloquent speakers of his day. Mr. Ranck, in his history of Lexington, says he studied law with Henry Clay, but after mature deliberation abandoned that profession and attended a theological seminary in New York, where he took the foremost rank. His eloquence and energy built up a large congregation in Lexington, but he had his troubles, was removed, and died May 26, 1820, broken-hearted, aged thirty-five years. During the winter of 1819, or the spring of 1820, the Rev. John McFarland was called and installed pastor of the church. His pastorate extended through a period of eight years, and was terminated by his death on the 28th of July, 1828.

Rev. Mr. Pratt was engaged as pastor. During the following year, the pastor, assisted by Rev. John Black, conducted a meeting, during which thirty-four persons were added to the church, twenty-two of whom were colored. Again, in 1847, there was a considerable ingathering. Mr. Pratt's ministry closed during the spring or summer of 1852.

He was succeeded, in the fall of the same year, by Rev. E. B. Smith as pastor. Mr. Smith's ministry closed in the spring of 1856, and was followed by the Rev. Mr. Carrier, who seems to have labored as stated supply one year. In November, 1857, Rev. W. T. McElroy was invited to act as stated supply.

In January, 1858, a joint communion was held by the two churches, preaching alternately by the pastors. Twelve persons were received into the communion of the New-School Church, and a less number into the Old School, and the Synod of Kentucky on the part of the New School, having taken action looking to organic union of the two bodies. This action was consummated in the Paris church, in April, 1859, the joint session then meeting for the first time. The preachers employed during the four following years were Mr. Liggatt, Revs. E. W. Bedinger, Holloway and W. B. Browne.

In the spring of 1863, Rev. D. O. Davies was called, and installed pastor, and it was during his ministry that the war trouble sprang up, which resulted in the division of the church in 1866.

Mr. Davies continued pastor of the church in connection with the Southern General Assembly, until 1868, when he resigned the charge, and a call was extended to Rev. L. H. Blanton, now Chancellor of Central University, which was accepted and he was installed as pastor. In 1869–70, the present splendid church edifice was built, and in November, 1870, the church was dedicated, the dedicatory sermon being delivered by Rev. Dr. J. C. Stiles. About the same time the Synod of Kentucky met in Paris. During the pastorate of Dr. Blanton, the church membership was largely increased, and great activity was observable in the promotion of all the interests of the church. It was a working pastor, and an active, working, giving church. During the twelve years of Mr. Blanton's ministry, the large sum of $75,000 was collected, including the amount subscribed to build the church. The ladies were especially active, and prepared and published a book, entitled "Cooking in the Blue Grass," from the sale of which they realized several thousand dollars. Mrs. A. E. Randolph, now a missionary in China, went from this church, which has contributed liberally to the cause of foreign missions. Dr. Blanton resigned in 1880, and was succeeded by Mr. Sumrall, who served as stated supply for several months. In the spring of 1881, the congregation extended a unanimous call to Rev. Dr. E. H. Rutherford, of St. Louis, Mo. The call was accepted, and Dr. Rutherford in May, entered upon the duties of pastor. The following is a list of the present officers of the church: Ruling Elders, George W. Davis, A. W. Wright, D. M. Dodge, Joseph A. Howerton, John Gass, Joseph M. Jones and R. P. Dow. Deacons, Joseph Neely, David Kennedy, F. L. McChesney, Ed F. Spears, W. A. Johnson, George R. Bell, Victor K. Shipp, Emmett M. Dickson. Secretary and Treasurer, Joseph M. Jones. The Sunday school numbers about 125 pupils. Joseph A. Howerton, Superintendent; George W. Davis, Treasurer; W. A. Johnson, Secretary; Victor K. Shipp, Librarian; William Webb, Assistant Librarian.

In 1866, a division occurred in the Presbyterian Church, a portion uniting with the Southern General Assembly, and the remaining adhering to the Northern branch of the Church. The division of property was arranged without litigation, in a way satisfactory to the parties interested. The history of the church in connection with the Southern General Assembly has already been given. The other branch of the church retained possession of the building on the corner of Pleasant and Mulberry streets, which has since been repaired and handsomely improved. The following is a list of the pastors since the division: Rev. W. F. C. Webster, 1870–71; from spring of 1871 to fall of same year, Rev. G. W. Coons; from September, 1871, to April, 1874, Rev. C. F. Beach; from December, 1874, to 1878, Rev. R. W. Cleland. For some time after this, the church was without a regular pastor. Last year, Rev. Ernest McMillan was called to and accepted the pastorate of the church. The following are the officers: Elders, B. F. Harris, Dr. Joseph Fithian, James McClintock, Sr., Thomas I. Brent. Deacons, James Hall, George F. Smith, William H. Park. Superintendent Sunday School, George F. Smith; Librarian, George D. McClintock.

"The Baptist Church of Christ in Paris, in union with the Baptist Churches of the General Union, was constituted in the old court house on the 18th of February, 1818, upon the following members: Joel Prewitt, Rachel Johnson, James Pritchett, Pheba Pritchett, Agness Pullen, George

Bryan, Hannah Gorham and Nicholas Talbott, by Elders Jeremiah Vardeman and Davis Biggs.

"The first business meeting was held March 5, 1818. Elder Vardeman was Moderator, and Joel Prewitt, Clerk. The first Deacons were Nicholas Talbott, George Bryan and William S. Bryan, and Willis Young, First Stated Clerk.

"From this time to December, 1832, the number that had united with the church was 302 whites and 153 colored, of whom, among the whites, there are now living here or holding membership: Joseph Stephens, Washington Wheat, James Paton, Mrs. Grosjean, Mrs. Lucretia Feemster and Joseph Porter and wife.

"On April 18, 1818, George Bryan, William S. Bryan, James Pritchett and Joel Prewitt were appointed Commissioners to build a meeting-house for the church, and obtained a large lot at the intersection of the Winchester Turnpike road with Pleasant street, which was finished in March, 1822.

"Elder Vardeman continued pastor of the church from its organization to 1826, preaching one Saturday and Sunday of each month. The church was also supplied with preaching, during that time, by Elders John Holliday, Mason Owings, James D. Black, A. G. Curry, G. Gates and others.

"A revival commenced in the winter of 1827–28, under the preaching of Elder Vardeman and others, when 135 whites and 46 colored persons were received into the church.

"In 1839, Elder Vardeman moved to Ralls County, Mo., where he continued to preach until about a week before his death, which occurred in May, 1842, aged sixty-seven. His biographer says of him: 'This distinguished minister was one of a class somewhat rare in the annals of the church. He possessed the peculiar talent of bringing the leading truths of the Gospel home to the consciences of his hearers. His illustrations were singularly varied, his language strong, simple and well suited to convey clear thoughts to every class, even the most illiterate, while the deep fountains of feeling gushed from his own heart, and poured, like a shower of rain, over the minds of his hearers. In deep emotion, vivid conceptions of Gospel truth and the power of exciting sympathy, he resembled Whitfield. His voice was powerful, sonorous and clear. He commenced his ministry about the year 1801.'"*

The Deacons up to this time, in addition to those first named, were Jahab Wheat and Joseph Stephens; Clerks, Willis Young and Henry Croxton.

With 1832, commenced the "reformation," which caused a division in the church, and an act of separation from those claiming to be "Reformers" was adopted in December of that year.

In January, 1833, the church was re-organized, with about forty-eight white members. It has now a membership of about one hundred. From the time of its organization until a few weeks ago, the church has had a pastor—in 1833, Elder William Vaugh; 1836, R. T. Dillard; 1837, A. Goodell; 1838, G. C. Sedwick; 1842, J. W. Kenny; 1844, J. R. Davis; 1845, G. G. Goss; 1848, W. M. Pratt; 1849, T. J. Drane; 1849, E. D. Isbell; 1851, S. L. Helm; 1852, J. M. Frost; 1853, Y. R. Pitts; 1854, J. H. Yeaman, J. B. Link.

In 1857, the colored members of the church were organized into a separate church, under the name of the "African Church," by Elder J. B. Link and others, and have kept up their own organization ever since, and have been prosperous, having built a large and comfortable house of worship.

In 1858, Elder George Varden was chosen paster, and served until 1870. In 1865, the congregation determined to remove their house of worship from the old location, and rebuild in a more central position, sold the old building and lot, and purchased a lot on the corner of Locust and Main streets, upon which the present building was erected in 1867–68.

In 1870, Elder John Kingdon was chosen pastor; 1872, C. S. McCloud; 1873, Elder A. Myers supplied the church with preaching, and occasionally Elder Salin; 1874, Elder A. N. White, who continued several years. He was succeeded, in 1878, by Elder S. F. Taylor, who has recently resigned. The church is now without a pastor. The following are the officers: Deacons, James Paton, Sr., Joseph Stephens, Chester F. Croxton, James Bradshaw; Clerk, W. M. Goodloe. Sunday school—R. S. Henderson, Superintendent; William M. Goodloe, Treasurer; R. H. Hudson, Jr., Secretary; John Prewitt, Librarian; number of scholars, fifty-five.

Methodist Episcopal Church South.—The organization of the Methodist Church in Paris dates back to 1807. For about ten years, the preaching was in private houses, and mostly in the house now occupied by D. B. Flanigan, then owned by Morgan Francis. In 1817, mainly through the efforts of Peter Schwartzweiler, a brick church was built on the site on which the present building stands. The congregation being weakly, the building was not finished until 1820. Here the congregation worshiped until 1860, when the present building was erected. Several of the members of the congregation here, now living, contributed to the erection of the church, but the success of the undertaking was mainly due to the liberality and energy of Mr. John D.

* From "Sketches of Paris," furnished by Mr. James Paton, Sr.

Heame, then a merchant of this city, now of Covington, Ky.

Until 1865, Paris was only a circuit, having preaching only once or twice a month. In the fall of that year, it was made a station, and Rev. William F. Taylor appointed pastor. During the four years' pastorate of Mr. Taylor, the membership increased from seventy-five to one hundred and fifty-four. Rev. James C. Morris succeeded Mr. Taylor, remaining four years, and though many were added to the church, yet the membership decreased, owing to deaths, removals, etc., to one hundred and thirty-eight. Rev. W. T. Poynter followed Mr. Morris, remaining four years. During his pastorate the church was prosperous, and under his skillful management its financial plans were well executed, and he left the church in very good working order. He was followed by Rev. E. H. Pearce, who remained but one year, leaving the church about as he found it. Rev. Dr. James A. Henderson succeeded Mr. Pearce, and remained two years. He was followed by Rev. J. O. A. Vaught, who is the present pastor, now closing the second year of his pastorate, which is proving a prosperous year, more than forty persons having united with the church already.

Besides the above, nearly all the prominent ministers in the Kentucky Conference have preached in Paris—Cole, Lakin, Lindsay, Gunn, Bascom, Durbin, Stamper, Cartwright, Kavanaugh, Stribling, Ray, and many others.

The following is a list of the officers: Pastor, Rev. J. O. A. Vaught; Stewards—James McClure, Gray Smith, John Trundle, Selby Lillerton, E. P. Gamble and Edward R. Fithian; Trustees—H. M. Rucher and Dr. Wash. Fithian.

*St. Peter's Church.**—The first services of the Episcopal Church in Paris, of which there are any records, were conducted by clergymen from Lexington, Ky. As early as August 27, 1815, the Rev. John Ward, of Lexington, came to Paris and held service in the old court house, and on that occasion baptized an infant daughter of Walker and Sarah Thornton. That infant, long years ago, grew to womanhood, and is still living in the county and is well known as the poetess, Mrs. M. R. McAboy. This was the first baptism. After that time, up to the year 1830, occasional services were held, chiefly by clergymen from Lexington, among whom might be mentioned the Rev. G. T. Chapman, the author of a famous book of sermons on the principles and claims of the church.

During this period, no regular ministrations were sustained, nor does there seem to have been any further attempt made than to minister to certain persons who had preferences for the church on account of early associations in Virginia.

* Written by Rev. G. A. Weeks.

But in the year 1832 or 1833, a decisive attempt was made to establish a parish and erect a church edifice. This was done under the efficient leadership of the Rev. Amos Cleaver, who came to Paris from Philadelphia, then in the prime of his strength and energy. By indefatigable labor, covering a period of six years, he drew together a congregation of people, organized them into a parish, and completed a comfortable church edifice of brick. This church edifice was consecrated in due form and order under the name of St. Peter's Church, on the fifth day of August, 1838, by the Rt. Rev. B. B. Smith, Bishop of the diocese.

Soon after the consecration of the church, Mr. Cleaver saw fit to resign the charge of it, at least for a time, and the Rev. Francis B. Nash was chosen his successor, but did not long continue in the office, for, in the year 1840, Mr. Cleaver was recalled, and again entered upon the work which he had previously given up. He continued his second rectorship till some time in the year 1843.

During the ministry of Mr. Cleaver and Mr. Nash, a good many people were led to sympathize with the struggling parish and co-operate in its efforts, who did not become members of it. But some were baptized and confirmed.

Among the names of adults who received baptism at this time, mention might be made of Sarah A. Berkley, Mrs Cordelia Kelly, Mrs. Eliza J. Elliott (afterward Mrs. Garrett Davis), Mrs. Margaret T. Brent, Maj. Thomas Elliott, Caroline A. Scott, Amelia A. Timberlake. Of course, a much greater number of infants were baptized during the period.

Several of the adults named above were among the very first who received the rite of confirmation. Among the early confirmed we should also mention Mr. John Richards, Mrs. Mary A. Timberlake, Mrs. Elmira D. Brent, Mrs. Elizabeth L. Hart, Mr. William Hearne, Mr. Jefferson Scott, and, later, Mr. Hugh Brent. Some communicants had been confirmed elsewhere, as Mrs. M. Morray, Mrs. John Richards and Miss Nancy Marshall.

The first marriage under Mr. Cleaver's administration was that between John Alexander and Betsy Gass, and the second between Thomas Elliott and Eliza J. Morrow.

The first funeral was that of Matilda P. Hearne, an infant seventeen months old, and the second that of Charles E. Talbott, aged thirty years.

In the early part of the year 1843, Mr. Cleaver again gave up the charge of the church, and was succeeded by the Rev. J. Avery Shepherd.

The names of the rectors of the church succeeding

Messrs. Cleaver and Nash, with the time they continued in office, are as follows:

Rev. J. Avery Shepherd, about one year; Rev. G. G. Moore, about three years; Rev. H. H. Reid, about two years; Rev. T. H. Mitchell, about four years; Rev. J. Austin Merrick, about ten years; Rev. G. A. Weeks, about seventeen years, and who is the present incumbent. Under the ministrations of Messrs. Shepherd and Moore, there was a marked increase in the number of baptisms and confirmations.

After Mr. Reid's popular rectorship, he went abroad and was accidentally killed by a fall from a balustrade in a hotel in Italy.

Mr. Mitchell, in addition to his work in church, conducted a flourishing school, in which he did much good in instructing the youth of the parish. Mr. Merrick, by his efficiency as a disciplinarian, and by a strict adherence to church principles, imparted a churchly character to the parish which it never had received in such measure before. He and his good wife also did much for the instruction of the youth in a parish school. He resigned, at last, on account of chronic ill-health, and finally died in a charitable institution in the city of New York.

Among the laymen, now gone to their rest, who have been eminently useful in upholding the above named clergymen in their work, it may not be deemed invidious to mention the names of Dr. Harry Hopson and Hon. Robert T. Davis.

In the spring of 1870, the old church which Mr. Cleaver had built, was in the main taken down, and during the following summer and fall another of more elegant appearance and more complete in its appointments, erected in its place. This rebuilding was done at a cost of nearly $10,000, including all the furnishings. And as the building was now essentially a new church, it was reconsecrated on the 18th day of November, 1870. In its design as an ecclesiestical structure, it may be regarded as among the best in the diocese.

The parish has slowly advanced in strength from its beginning, and without doubt to-day stands on a stronger basis than ever before. Its baptisms and confirmations, reaching up into the higher hundreds, are an indication of the good it has done. "O, pray for the peace of Jerusalem; they shall prosper that love thee."

Officers of church at present time (February, 1882): Rev. George A. Weeks, Rector; Dr. David Keller, Senior Warden; Mr. William S. Taylor, Junior Warden; Harry Speers, Vestryman; W. W. Forman, Vestryman; O. A. Gilman, Vestryman; John C. Brent, Vestryman; Anderson Berry, Vestryman; James A. Stewart, Vestryman.

The following sketch of the early history of the Christian Church was written by Elder John A. Gano: "At the request of several brethren, members of the church in Paris, Ky., I write the following brief history of that church, in its origin, infancy and progress. For many years Elders Stone, Purviance, Dooley and others, in their itinerations, preached much in Bourbon County. The churches at Mount Carmel, Millersburg and Flat Run, at an early period, under their labors came into existence, nor should I fail to mention the efficient labors of those faithful ministers, Francis R. Palmer, Thomas Smith, Joel Haden and others, who, during the first quarter of the present century, throughout a considerable portion of Northern Kentucky, preached without any earthly compensation. Paris often shared in the benefit of these labors. It was not, however, until in September, 1827, when I came with Brother Thomas M. Allen to Paris to hold a meeting, that any encouraging movement toward the formation of a church took place. During that meeting he immersed Mrs. George W. Williams, and her mother, Mrs. Mary T. Webb. Later in the autumn of the same year, we held another meeting. Through the kindness of the magistracy we were permitted the use of that time-honored, grand old court house, all the meeting-houses in town being closed against us, until the good Baptist, Brother William Bryan, offered us the use of their house. As some of the members of his church objected, we preferred to use the court room and it was here, at this second meeting in the autumn of 1827, an effort was made to gather a church. On invitation several came forward to have their names enrolled, viz.: Mrs. Mary T. Webb, Mrs. George W. Williams, Mrs. H. Wilson, Mrs. M. Ashford, Miss M. Speak, and, perhaps, another. To encourage this little band, I had my name enrolled among them. Brother Allen and the writer preached either separately or together, monthly or oftener, for this little flock, which soon increased in numbers and influence. So many valuable additions, male and female, were made within a year that the church was organized on the same divine principles as the one in Jerusalem more than eighteen centuries ago. Mr. Allen was the influential and working man, and it was mainly through his instrumentality that the church prospered, and a good brick house of worship was erected in the year 1828. Brother T. M. Allen and John Rogers were present at the dedication of that building. Among the many generous contributors to aid in that work, I remember Mr. Hugh Brent, Sr., Mr. John L. Hickman, Sr., Mr. Daniel Duncan, George W. Williams, Esq., Mr. Samuel Pyke, Mr. Henry Wilson, Mr. Michael Ashford and Mr. Daniel Smedley. The first three were not members of the church. The others were, or soon

O. H. Burbridge

became such. After the completion of the house, Brother Allen became the regular preacher. My labors were still frequent and were successful. In those days we never thought of receiving any salary. Brother Allen visited Virginia in 1831, and was urged to preach monthly for the church in Paris, and consented to do so. I continued my labors with them until about 1835, and it was during this period that so many of the Baptist Church in Paris, embracing the preacher, Brother G. Gates, Brother Hiram Bledsoe, Brother William Bryan, and many others, discovering, on mutual consultation, with many of our brethren, the entire religious harmony existing between us, a cordial union was formed, 'on the foundation of apostles and prophets, Jesus Christ Himself being the chief cornerstone.' Our house became the place of worship, the brethren yielding up their former house to their quondam associates. Brother Allen removed to Missouri in 1836. Brother Aylett Raines succeeded me as the preacher in Paris, and, becoming permanently located here, did most efficient and successful service through a long series of years. The church has also had the labors of Elders R. C. Ricketts, David G. Burnett, John G. Tompkins, G. B. Moore, William S. Giltner, Dr. L. L. Pinkerton, O. P. Miller, L. Pyron, John Shackleford, David Walk, C. R. Marshall, and John S. Sweeney, the present pastor. A host of others have transiently visited and preached for this congregation, from the gifted Alexander Campbell, deceased, down to the many of humbler talents, both of the living and the dead.

"The church has continued to grow in members since its organization, and now has a membership of about four hundred. Elder John S. Sweeney is the pastor, having held the position for the past twelve years, and still retains a strong hold upon the affections and confidence of the congregation. He is a minister of decided ability, as is evidenced by his unusually long pastorate; longer, if we mistake not, than that of any other minister since the organization of the Christian Church in Paris.

"The following are the present officers of the church: Pastor, J. S. Sweeney; Elder, James M. Thomas; Deacons, J. T. Hinton, J. D. Butler, Horace Miller, W. T. Talbott, W. W. Gill; Treasurer, J. T. Hinton; Superintendent Sunday School, James M. Thomas. The Sunday school is largely attended, numbering upward of two hundred scholars. The old church building was torn down in 1859, and the present building erected and dedicated in June, 1859."

The Catholics of Paris and vicinity were occasionally visited prior to 1840 by missionary priests from Louisville and Cincinnati, among whom were Rev. Fathers Baden and Kenrick, afterward Archbishop of Baltimore, and others who labored hard in and around Paris. In 1850, Paris and the adjacent country were the fields of labor for Rev. Fathers McMahon, Force, Allen and Perry, of Lexington. Services were held in private houses throughout the county. Rev. Father Force bought the present lot on Main street, and in 1854 Rev. Father Allen, under the direction of the Right Rev. Bishop Carroll, built a small church, which still stands on the lot, for the accommodation of the congregation. In 1858, the frame church being entirely too small, the membership numbering about two hundred, Rev. Father Allen began the foundation of the new brick church, the corner-stone of which was laid in 1858.

Rev. Father Brandts, the successor of Rev. Father Perry, came to Paris in 1860. Seeing the want of a larger church, he commenced the erection of the present building, which was dedicated in 1865. The membership had then increased to about four hundred. In 1869, the congregation determined to enlarge the church, and means were provided for that purpose. The building of an addition was begun at once, and was finished in 1870. The total cost of the church building, including the addition, was about $25,000.

Father Brandts was succeeded by Rev. James McNerney, in 1876, who remained until 1877, when Rev. Ferdinand Brossart was appointed. On November 6, 1878, the present rector, Rev. James P. Barry took charge of the church.

The history of the church in Bourbon County may be summed up as follows: Some fifty years ago, the members were few and widely scattered, and had no regular church; consequently the Holy Sacrament of the Mass, as a matter of necessity, had to be offered up in some private residence. To-day, the Catholics of Bourbon have a resident priest at Paris, a neat church, a spacious cemetery, and a visitation convent with schools attached, boarding, academy and parochial. The Catholic population numbers one hundred and thirty families, or about one thousand persons.

The colored people have three new and substantial church buildings in Paris. The Methodist Church, finished within the last two or three years, is one of the most tasteful in the city. Rev. A. Price is its pastor. Rev. Elisha Green is pastor of the Colored Baptist Church, and Elder Julius Graves, of the Colored Christian Church.

For three weeks in March, 1882, Paris was the scene of the most wonderful religious revival which has ever occurred in its history. George O. Barnes, an evangelist, formerly a minister in the Presbyterian Church, but now cut loose from all church connection, held a series of meetings in the court house, which will accommodate 1,200 persons, and during the three weeks of his stay preached twice a day to crowded houses, and frequently hundreds were turned away unable to find sitting or even standing room. For several years, wherever Mr. Barnes has preached, there never has been a hall or church large enough to accommodate the throngs who wish to attend. Frequently the seats were filled an hour before the service began, and sometimes persons would remain from one service to another, without going to their homes. Such a deep religious interest never before pervaded the community. There are widely varying estimates of Mr. Barnes and his teachings. Some regard him as the most powerful preacher of the Gospel in the world, the Whitfield of the nineteenth century in eloquence, whilst a few are not favorably impressed by him, and regard his teachings as unsound and dangerous. His doctrines are sometimes severely criticised and his preaching condemned on account of the homely and so-called "slang" expressions used by him in the pulpit. But he rivets and holds enchained the attention of the audience from the opening to the closing word of his sermon. He never tires himself; while speaking, never moistens his lips with water; and never wearies his audience. His knowledge of Scripture is wonderful, and the great success of his labors is, in a measure, due to his deep earnestness, the simplicity of his language, his persuasive eloquence, and the absolute control he wields over those who listen to him. Holding that his commission as a minister of the Gospel is not only to preach, but to heal all manner of diseases, he prays with and anoints all the afflicted and suffering who come forward, and "trust as best they can in Jesus to heal them." Under his ministry, during the last three months, about three thousand persons have been anointed. In a poem entitled "Pulpit Eloquence," by Mrs. Amelia B. Welby, is given a picture of a preacher which so nearly describes Mr. Barnes that we reproduce it here:

"In stature majestic, apart from the throng,
He stood in his beauty, the theme of my song!
* * * * * * * * * *
Such language as his, I may never recall;
But his theme was salvation—salvation to all;
And the souls of a thousand in ecstasy hung
On the manna-like sweetness that dropped from his tongue;
Not alone on the ear his wild eloquence stole;
Enforced by each gesture it sank to the soul.
He spoke of the Savior—what pictures he drew!
The scenes of His sufferings were clear on my view;
The cross—the rude cross where He suffered and died,
The gush of bright crimson that flowed from His side,
The cup of His sorrows, the wormwood and gall,
The darkness that mantled the earth as a pall,
The garland of thorns, and the demon-like crews,
Who knelt as they scoffed Him—"Hail King of the Jews!"
He spake, and it seemed that his statue-like form
Expanded and glowed as his spirit grew warm;
His tone so impassioned, so melting his air,
As touched with compassion, he ended in prayer,
His hands clasped above him, his blue eyes upthrown,
Still pleading for sins that were never his own,
While that mouth, where such sweetness ineffable clung
Still spoke, though expression had died on his tongue.
O God! What emotions the speaker awoke!
A mortal he seemed, yet a deity spoke;
A man—yet so far from humanity riven!
On earth—yet so closely connected with heaven!"

Mr. Barnes is fifty-five years of age. He has preached twice every day for the past five years, and seems to gather strength by his labors. His labors closed here on the 29th of March, with altogether 621 confessions and 156 anointings, total, 777. The like has never been seen before in Paris.

In this chapter devoted to sketches of the Christian churches, it is not inappropriate to say a few words of those secret and benevolent societies which have done so much good in the community, and the grand aim of which is charity; a virtue that Paul declared was greater than faith and hope. First in order as in age, is the Masonic Institution.

Paris Lodge No. 2, A., F. & A. Masons, was organized in November, 1791. The charter was obtained from the Grand Lodge of Virginia, Kentucky at that time being a part of that State. The lodge at Paris was the second organized in Kentucky, the first lodge being in Lexington. All the lodges in the State remained under the jurisdiction of the Grand Lodge in Virginia until 1800, when the Grand Lodge of Kentucky was established. The lodge here has a long history, extending over a period of ninety-one years, and during that time has done a great work of charity. It is now in a flourishing condition, and bids fair to increase in all the elements of usefulness. The following are the present officers of the lodge: H. R. Blaisdell, W. M.; S. B. Kennedy, S. W.; Charles Offutt, J. W.; A. Shire, Secretary; B. F. Pullen, Treasurer.

Bourbon Lodge, No. 23, I. O. O. F., Paris, Ky., was organized, under dispensation, November 29, 1845, which was granted by John B. Hinkle, then Grand Master of Kentucky, to the following members of the order: P. G., J. V. Lovely, George Stoll, Joseph B. Cooper, R. P. Timberlake and W. S. Simpson. The first officers of the lodge were: J. V. Lovely, N. G.; L. B. Allison, V. G.; J. T. Davis, Treasurer; [an office which he has held for thirty-five years], and W. W. Fothergill, Secretary. The lodge has had a total membership, up to January 1, 1882, of 441. The membership, January 1, 1882, is 84. Deaths to same date, 35. The receipts of the lodge from its organization to January 1, 1882, aggregate $30,500. The total expenditures, including benefits, etc., $27,000; leaving a balance on hand of $3,500. In 1854–55, the Odd Fellows Hall, now opera house, was erected at a cost of about $10,000. In 1879, the hall was enlarged and otherwise improved. The lodge has property and funds to the amount of $16,000. The following persons are now the officers of the lodge: George Winter, P. G.; F. R. Armstrong, N. G.; Joseph Honey, V. G.; James T. Davis, Treasurer; J. J. McClintock, Secretary; manager of the opera house, J. Z. Croxton.

Peabody Lodge, No. 13, Knights of Pythias, was instituted September 23, 1870, and remained in existence one year, when it surrendered its charter and effects to the Grand Lodge of Kentucky. On the 13th day of February, 1873, it was again re-organized, and has continued unto the present day in a healthy and flourishing condition. The Knights of Pythias is an organization possessing peculiar attractions to the young men of our country, and to the middle-aged it is a haven wherein to pass the declining years of their lives, and, at the end thereof they can, through the agency of the endowment rank, leave a nice little competency to their loved ones. Of its membership here, B. F. Pullen is a Past Grand Chancellor, and A. J. Lovely is the Vice Grand Chancellor of Kentucky, at this time. The following members are the officers of Peabody Lodge, No. 13: E. S. Hedges, P. C.; A. C. Adair, C. C.; W. S. Taylor, V. C.; W. H. Lockhart, P.; A. C. Gatzeit, K. of R. and S.; J. G. Hanly, M. of E.; J. M. Daniels, M. of F.; W. M. Goodloe, M. of A.; J. H. Fuhrman, I. G.; J. W. Hite, O. G.; Charles Offutt, Trustee; A. J. Lovely, D. D. G. C.

Stoner Lodge, No. 559, Knights of Honor, was organized March 31, 1877, with the following charter members: B. F. Pullen, J. T. Nichols, Benjamin G. Paton, J. G. Hanly, Joseph M. Jones, O. A. Gilman, Dr. J. Ed. Ray, J. McCarney, Irwin Taylor, O. P. Carter, George H. Shawhan, Matt. Turney, J. S. Kenney, T. K. Marsh, J. D. McClintock, John W. Jameson, W. A. Cunningham, G. W. Allison, R. M. Adair, F. C. Lewis, G. M. Davis, Ed. Taylor, J. M. Grinnan, A. S. Stout, B. R. Hutchcraft, M. C. Chapline, F. R. Armstrong, Dan. Turney, C. A. Kenney, A. J. Lovely. Since that time, eighteen have been initiated into the order. This lodge has lost only one member since its organization, by death, Dr. L. D. Barnes, recently deceased, whose family have received $2,000 insurance. The officers, at present, of this lodge are: Henry Spears, Past Dictator; Judge Matt. Turney, Dictator; J. G. Hanly, Vice Dictator; Dudley Talbott, Assistant Dictator; W. W. Forman, Guide; F. L. McChesney, Chaplain; F. R. Armstrong, Reporter; A. J. Lovely, Financial Reporter; Henry Spears, Treasurer; Hugh Henry, Guardian; O. P. Carter, Sentinel; O. A. Gilman, Joseph M. Jones and Dr. J. Ed. Ray, Trustees. F. L. McChesney, Representative to Grand Lodge.

Paris has enjoyed unusual literary advantages. The "Lecture Association," for four or five years, brought here the most distinguished lecturers in the country, among whom were Mrs. Livermore, Henry Ward Beecher, Theodore Tilton, Robert Collyer, Rev. T. DeWitt Talmage, Olive Logan, Miss Helen Potter, Josh Billings and others. The association was financially a success, and, although no lecturers have been engaged for two years, has not been disbanded, and has a handsome surplus fund in its treasury. The "Paris Literary Society" has, for a number of years, been one of the institutions of Paris, and has done much to aid in the cultivation of a higher literary taste on the part of our people. Owing to the absence of some of its members it was not re-organized this season. The Paris Historical Society is a new organization, under the auspices of the Presbyterian Church (S. G. A.). It has held several interesting meetings, and bids fair to contribute much to the improvement of the young people of the city. The exercises comprise essays on historical and other subjects, readings, recitations, and vocal and instrumental music by the members of the society.

The Press.—The first paper ever published in Paris, as elsewhere stated, was the *Kentucky Herald.* It was established in 1797, by Mr. James Stewart, and was printed in a log house on High street. It however did not succeed, and, after a sickly existence of about one year, it died. No other paper was published until in 1808, when the *Western Citizen* was established by Messrs. Grimes & Johnson. In early times, printers were under the necessity of making their own ink, an art which few of them understood. Whilst this operation was in progress in the *Citizen* office, the fire used for the purpose communicated to some papers, and before it could be extinguished, the early files of the paper were destroyed. It is, therefore. impossible to ascertain the exact date of the first issue. The oldest number, seen by A. M. Brown, the editor of the paper in 1855, bore date, Thursday, November, 3, 1808, and was the thirtieth number of the first volume of the paper. Supposing a number to have been issued each week, this would bring the date of the 1st to the 7th day of April of that year. The number referred to was a curiosity; it was printed on foolscap paper, the pages measuring seven by twelve inches. This was smaller, however, than the ordinary size, for in the same issue this reference to the paper used appears: "We are this week reduced to the necessity of printing on *writing* paper, in consequence of having been disappointed in receiving a supply of the usual size." We have before us a copy of the paper, published in 1811, containing four columns to the page, and measuring nine and a half by fifteen and a half inches, besides the margin. This was probably the size of the paper at the beginning.

Early in 1809, the *Citizen* was purchased by Mr. Joel R. Lyle, who had before that been engaged as tutor in the "Bourbon Ladies' Academy and Boarding School," conducted by the Rev. John Lyle. Mr. Lyle was not then a practical printer, but in the course of his long connection with the office, acquired a knowledge of the business. He continued the editor of the paper until the summer of 1829, when a severe illness compelled him to resign his post to his son, William C. Lyle. The business was conducted under his name, however, until the 1st of January, 1832. For several years prior to this date, the paper was published under the name of Lyle & Keenon. Mr. Adam C. Keenon, now of Frankfort, for many years the Public Binder, was the partner ostensibly, but his brother, John C. Keenon, who was a practical printer, received the profits. Mr. K. learned the business in the *Citizen* office, and in 1817 published a paper in Cynthiana called the *Guardian of Liberty*, which was continued for a year or two. In this connection, it may be mentioned that Bishop H. H. Kavanaugh, of the Methodist Episcopal Church, worked in the office when a boy. Mr. J. L. Walker entered the office and commenced learning the printing business about the first of April, 1828. On the 1st of January, 1832, he and William C. Lyle became the owners of the office, and it was conducted under the name of Lyle & Walker.

It cannot be ascertained in what house the *Citizen* had its birth. After Mr. Lyle became the editor, the office was for some time in the second story of the stone house, on the corner of Broadway and High streets, and was entered by a stairway on the outside. It was afterward removed to the one-story stone house on the corner of High and Church streets, used before as a blacksmith-shop. It was again removed to the stone house on Broadway, second door from the corner. In 1841, the office was established in the building, corner of Main and Church streets, where it remained until 1877, when it was removed to its present location.

In its earlier years, the *Citizen* supported the principles of the Republican party, as opposed to those of the Federalists; was a warm advocate of the war with England in 1812; in the fierce struggle between the Old and New Court parties took the side of the Old Court party; supported Mr. Adams and Mr. Clay in opposition to Gen. Jackson; and when parties became divided under the names of Whig and Democrat, was found consistently advocating the principles of the former. For a number of years, when under the control of Messrs. Lyle & Walker, the paper was edited with signal ability by Mr. A. M. Brown, who afteward went to Missouri. Mr. Joel R. Lyle died in 1849. The following sketch of Mr. Lyle was given by one who knew him: "He was a man of strong, active and well-informed mind, and conducted his paper with ability and spirit. He was possessed of a rich and genial humor, which made him a pleasant companion, while his integrity of character, and his warm and devoted piety, secured to him the respect and confidence of all who knew him. His personal appearance is amongst the earliest recollections of our boyhood. In those days, it was the custom in the Presbyterian Church for the leaders of the music, or clerks as they were called, to stand up in front of the pulpit while singing. Mr. Lyle and Ebenezer Sharpe, one of the best men we ever knew, were the leaders of the music in the church on High street. They were both very fleshy, realizing Shakspeare's description of the fourth stage in man's life, and we remember them as they stood up there, thirty years ago, with their round, protuberant stomachs, and with voices uncommonly rich, mellow and powerful, sang the songs of praise they both loved so well, and of which they never wearied while on earth. William C. Lyle died in January, 1874. He stood high as a citizen, was respected by all while living, and his death was sincerely mourned. Mr. John L. Walker died in 1873. He was for many years an office-bearer in the Presbyterian Church, first as Deacon, and afterward as a Ruling Elder. He possessed the confidence and respect of all who knew him.

In 1867, the *Citizen* was published by John R. Johnson & Co. In February, 1868, F. L. McChesney and Lemuel T. Fisher became the publishers, and the politics of the paper was changed, and from that time forward it has been a consistent advocate of Democratic principles. In 1873, Mr. Fisher sold his interest, and William A. Johnson became one of the proprietors, and remained with the paper until 1878, when he disposed of his interest to the present publishers. The *Citizen* is now conducted by F. L. McChesney, and his son, James R. McChesney. [Mr. McChesney is too modest to say the *Citizen* is a good paper, but we have no such conscientious scruples, and take this opportunity to tell the people of Paris and Bourbon County that in the *Citizen* and *True Kentuckian*, they have two as good newspapers as may be found in Central Kentucky, and if they don't support them well they deserve to be bumped. This is not an advertisement, but a gratuitous expression of sentiment.—Ed.]

In 1817, a young man named Lilly started a paper in Paris. Its name was the *Instructor*. It lived but a short time. It is stated that the paper was afterward removed to Millersburg. The editor died with consumption soon after.

A paper called the Paris *Register* was published here awhile, about the years 1827–28, by Messrs. Clay & Benning. We have before us as we write No. 7, Vol. I, dated December 1, 1827. It was a New Court, Relief and Jackson paper. It survived a year or two. Mr. Thomas Clay, one of the proprietors, was the brother of Green Clay, of this county. Mr. Benning was the same man who was afterward killed at Lexington by Charles Wickliffe.

The *Kentucky Flag* was established here in 1854, by Samuel Pike. Col. Pike was recognized as an experienced editor, and the *Flag*, under his control, became one of the leading Democratic papers in the State. It was especially a popular campaign paper. Col. Pike was succeeded by Selucius Garfield, who was, in 1849–50, a member of the State Constitutional Convention, and afterward a delegate to Congress from Washington Territory. He was a fine speaker and writer. At that time, he was a Democrat in politics. When, however, he was elected to Congress from Washington Territory, it was as a Republican. He is now residing in Washington City. While in control of the paper, Mr. Garfield secured the services of Samuel Williams, who became a partner in the business. Mr. Williams afterward became the managing editor of the Louisville *Courier*, and is now prominently connected with the press of Kansas City, Mo. He is recognized as one of the best newspaper men in the country. Afterward, the paper was conducted by Judge M. M. Cassidy, now of Mount Sterling, and Judge Burgess, now a Circuit Judge in Missouri. In 1857, Col. William E. Simms and John G. Craddock took charge of the *Flag*, and under their management it was one of the ablest edited papers in the State—Col. Simms being the political editor. Col. Simms afterward, in 1859, was a candidate in this district for Congress, defeating Gen. John M. Harlan, now an Associate Justice on the Supreme Bench. He was afterward a Colonel in the Confederate service, and also one of the Senators from Kentucky in the Confederate Congress. Since the war he has retired entirely from public life, and resides at Mount Airy, his home-place in this city. John G. Craddock and R. W. Clayton conducted the *Flag* in 1858, and were succeeded by W. W. Pike, now of Cincinnati, who published it until the fall of 1861, when the war came on and the paper was suspended.

The Paris *True Kentuckian* was established in February, 1866, by a joint-stock company, with John G. Craddock, as editor and publisher. The *Citizen* was then published by Messrs. Lyle & Walker, but its political principles were not in accord with the views of a majority of the people of the county; the *Kentuckian*, being a Democratic paper, from its first issue received a liberal support; its subscription list rapidly increased, and its columns were soon overcrowded with advertisements. Since that time, its subscription has been steadily increasing until it now has the largest number of subscribers of any county paper in Kentucky, and as a newspaper is the most remarkable success of any journal in the State. It contains a vast amount of local, State and general news. It is, perhaps, only just to say that Col. Craddock has been ably seconded in his efforts to make the *True Kentuckian* a good paper by John W. Hite, one of the best newspaper men in the State, as well as by an efficient corps of reporters.

Within the last few years, a number of papers have been started in Paris. In 1875–76, G. R. Keller, conducted a weekly called the *Saturday Night*. Afterward, the *Sunday Courier* was established, edited by the late Louis S. Howell, and, in July, 1880, Messrs. John Gnadinga and Gus. Fee commenced the publication of a campaign paper, the *Bourbon Republican*. These papers were all short-lived. In October, 1880, G. R. Keller started the *Semi-Weekly Sun*, which was continued until January 1, 1882. A few weeks ago, Bruce Champ commenced the publication of the *Bourbon News*.

Such is a brief sketch of the newspapers of Paris. The *True Kentuckian* is known almost everywhere, whilst the old *Citizen*, after many vicissitudes, has reached its seventy-fifth volume. The men who founded it, like the men who laid the foundations of our little city, have passed away, and it is one of the few old landmarks of the past. In its day it has played no inconspicuous part in the history of the town and county, and whatever may be its future, its past, at least, is secure.

The Rescue Fire Company was organized March 16, 1874. The city furnished the company with a splendid handbrake engine and four-wheeled hose carriage, and afterward purchased of the Ahrens Manufacturing Co. of Cincinnati, Ohio, a No. 4 steam fire engine, which was given the name of R. W. O'Connor, and a two-wheeled hose carriage, calling it O. A. Gilman. Afterward, a hook and ladder truck was bought for the use of the company, which they named the Ever Ready. The company has rendered invaluable services to the people of our city, and is one of the best inland fire organizations in the State. The following-named members are its present officers: R. W. O'Connor, President; Nich. Kreiner, V. P.; A. J. Lovely, Secretary; J. T. Doyle, Treasurer; J. A. Stewart, First Chief; Nich. Kreiner, Assistant Chief; William Mitchell, First Engine Director; W. F. Ficklin, Second Engine Director; C. N. Fithian, First Line Director; E. B. January, Second Line Director; Frank Webb, Third Line Director; W. M. Goodloe, Fourth Line Director; G. F. Smith, First Pipeman; G. W. Nippert, Second Pipeman; J. D. McClintock, Third Pipeman;

Frank Carr, Fourth Pipeman; W. O. Hite, Engineer; John M. Schuman, Assistant Engineer. Standing Committee, J. A. Stewart, William Mitchell, C. N. Fithian, G. F. Smith, A. J. Lovely.

The Paris Gas Company was organized November 24, 1866. S. Salomon was elected President, and Allen Bashford, Secretary, with the following Board of Directors: R. T. Davis, Jacob Spears, W. W. Mitchell, Dr. L. D. Barnes. Capital stock, $28,500. November 23, 1867, R. T. Davis was elected President, and W. W. Mitchell, Secretary; in 1874, B. F. Pullen was elected President, and James Paton, Sr., Secretary, and continued in office until January, 1878, when Dr. Ed. Ingels was elected President. January, 1879, A. Shire was elected President and Secretary. The capital stock was unchanged, remaining at $28,500, and was owned by seventeen stockholders. For a number of years, the company declared no dividend. Since 1879, under the new directory, it has paid an annual dividend of from 6 to 8 per cent, besides accumulating and setting aside a surplus fund of $1,000. Very much of the success of the company is due to the efficient President, Mr. A. Shire, who has managed its affairs with signal ability. The city of Paris has stock in the company amounting to $10,000, which is now yielding a good revenue. The following are the present officers of the company: A. Shire, President and Secretary; J. R. Swiney, Treasurer; Board of Directors, A. Shire, J. R. Swiney, J. K. Ford, W. B. Erringer, J. T. Hinton.—*McChesney.*

CHAPTER XII.

PARIS EDUCATIONAL HISTORY—THE BOURBON ACADEMY—PUBLIC AND PRIVATE CITY SCHOOLS—THE GARTH FUND—A SKETCH OF HIS LIFE—COLORED SCHOOLS AND SOCIETIES—SOME MANUFACTURING AND MISCELLANEOUS NOTICES, ETC., ETC.

AT an early day, the people of Paris enjoyed unusual educational advantages. The Bourbon Academy was founded in 1798, by an act of the Kentucky Legislature, and a donation of 6,000 acres of land appropriated toward its endowment. William Garrard, David Purviance, Augustine Eastin, John Edwards, Andrew Todd, John Allen, William Kelly, Thomas Jones, Sr., Hugh Brent, John Stone, James Brown, Sr., Barton W. Stone, James Matson and James Kenney were the original trustees of the institution. The lands donated by the State were located upon the south side of Green River. They were leased out at first, and finally sold for the benefit of the academy.

In 1799, a committee was appointed to select a suitable location and purchase grounds for the academy. A tract of eight acres of land was purchased on the Maysville road, nearly opposite the residence of Young Moran. The land was purchased of John Henry, the trustees paying him £105. A frame building was erected, thirty feet long and eighteen wide, capable of accommodating from thirty to forty pupils, and in May, 1800, the first session of the Bourbon Academy was begun, with Isaac Tull as teacher. The terms for tuition then were, to say the least, modest: For teaching reading, writing, spelling and common arithmetic, $8 per annum, and for English grammar, Latin and the sciences, $12.50 per annum. He was restricted to teach only thirty scholars, and the subscribers to the endowment fund of the Academy were given the preference to send their children. In January, 1802, Mr. Tull was succeded by James H. Russell, who taught only a short time, William T. Fowler taking charge in October of the same year, and the school continued under his superintendence for some years.

In 1805, the lot on which the public school building now stands was purchased for $110, from Thomas Mitchell, the school property in East Paris having been sold for $500 to Samuel Pyke; and a more commodious school building was erected in 1806–7, to meet the increasing educational wants of the community. The new building was large enough to accommodate a hundred or more pupils. In the year 1807, the Academy was re-opened with the Rev. John Lyle as President, and his brother Joel R. Lyle and James H. Dickey as assistant teachers. In the "Sketches of Paris," it is stated that Mr. Lyle continued in charge of the academy until 1810, when he resigned and established a female seminary. In Collins History of Kentucky, we find the following: "November, 1806.—The first female academy in the West, if not in the United States, established at Paris, Ky., by Rev. John Lyle, with from one hundred and fifty to three hundred pupils." From this it is evident that Mr. Lyle continued as President of the institution but a short time. His brother also resigned, and in 1808–9 became publisher of the *Western Citizen.* David V. Rannalls was elected President of the academy in place of Mr. Lyle, and Willis M. Arnold, assistant. The latter was succeeded in 1811, by Joseph Russell. In the same paper, we find the following: "An examination of the students of Bourbon Academy took place on the 9th inst., attended by several members of the Board of Trustees and citizens of the town, when the improvement of the scholars, under the tuition of Mr. David V. Rannalls, was very pleasingly evinced in the several departments of their studies. The Board of Trustees of the Academy by their committee took occasion to express their approbation of his exertions," etc. The paper is signed by Anthony Thuntin, Jr., James Hickman and Val Peers. In 1813, Mr. Ezra Howe was elected Superintendent, and provided his own assistant teachers. In 1814, Daniel Baldwin was appointed Professor of the Latin and Greek languages. In the "Sketches of Paris," the following reference is made to Mr. Baldwin: "Notwithstanding his superior abilities as a teacher, he retained his position only one year, for it appears that he did not get along as smoothly as possible with the students. He administered a severe chastisement to one of the pupils, which was the cause of his becoming the recipient of similar chastisement from the hands of the parent. The Bourbon Academy, however, is indebted to him to the extent of two shares of bank stock, a private donation made by him for the purpose of encouraging students who displayed the most proficiency in the dead languages, by giving them premiums. We find the following in his bequest: 'It shall be recorded, that this money was recovered by me from Edward Bayse, in a case of assault and battery.'

"Mr. Baldwin was succeeded in 1815 by Alban Stewart, with John Stevenson as assistant. In 1816, Stevenson gave place to Benjamin W. Hayden, who continued to teach until 1826. William E. Gallaudet, in October 1816, was appointed professor of the languages; he taught only a few months. In April, 1817, John Gayle was appointed President, who held the position for two years. At that time there were fifty-nine students in the academy—twenty-seven in the classical department, and thirty-two studying the other branches.

"In 1819, the Rev. James McCord was elected President, with Ebenezer Sharpe as Assistant Professor. Mr. McCord died in 1820, while in office, and the duties fell upon Mr. Sharpe, who discharged them most faithfully for seven years; so much so, that when he resigned, he received the unanimous approval of the Board of Trustees for the ability and skill with which he had managed the institution. In 1821, Charles Lincoln was appointed Assistant Teacher for one year, and the next year David Dunlap was appointed; and, in 1823, the Rev. Guerdon Gates was appointed Professor of the Natural Sciences. In October, 1824, John H. Harney, afterward the distinguished editor of the old Louisville *Democrat*, was employed by Mr. Sharpe as assistant, and in 1826 he was appointed Professor of Natural Sciences in place of Mr. Gates, who was compelled to resign on account of sickness in his family; but in October of the same year, he was recalled and elected Superintendent. He continued in charge till 1829, when John Roche, a former Professor of Languages in Transylvania University, was elected. He resigned in a few months, and the duties again devolved upon Mr. Gates. In 1831, Ebenezer Marston was elected Superintendent, and it remained under his supervision for some years. After this it began to lose its prestige, and the rooms in the building were rented out from time to time to different parties for private residences and for teaching private schools and one of the rooms was for awhile occupied by the Masons as a lodge room.

"The following persons taught school there at different periods: A. L. Mehurin, William Henderson, father of the Rev. H. A. M. Henderson, late Superintendent of Public Instruction; James Riddle, Simeon Smith, A. C. Raymond, Harvey Wood, Rev. A. E. Thoms, Daniel Vaughan, Joseph Raymond and John H. Pratt. About 1850, Mrs. Emily Tubman, a lady of great wealth, and who is renowned for her charitable works, rented a room in this building, and established the 'Tubman Free School,' paying the teacher, Mr. Redmon. Schools were taught in this house by Mrs. Murray, Mrs. Reed, George A. Irvine, Paul Guyser and Messrs. Stone and Colton. It was conducted in this way until 1856, when the Trustees of the Bourbon Academy, by a special act of the Legislature, transferred the property and the management of the institution to the Trustees of the town of Paris, and in this year was erected the City School building, as it now stands, exclusive of the commodious additions of 1875. It was completed in 1857, and was first occupied by Prof. J. B. Anderson and his two daughters, in teaching a high school. He was followed by Revs. George Varden and W. B. Browne, who taught school together until the commencement of the great civil war, and during that period it was occupied by the Federal troops as a hospital. After the war, it was repaired and again occupied for its original purpose, W. E. Clark and Thomas J. Dodd teaching separate and distinct schools.

"The Paris City School was organized in 1865, with Prof. Julius Herrick as Principal. Mr. Herrick held the position to 1867, when he was succeeded by Rev. Dr. George

Varden, from 1867 to 1868 ; Prof. W. H. Lockhart was elected Principal in 1868, and served until 1871 ; W. E. Clark from 1871 to 1873 ; Ben. D. Best from 1873 to 1874. Prof. Puckett was appointed in 1874, and held the position of Principal until June, 1880, when Rev. H. R. Blaisdell, the present incumbent, was appointed. He is assisted by Misses Anna L. Oldson, Mary B. Spears, Nellie Fithian, Mrs. L. Walker and Mrs. Alice Woodward. The attendance is about three hundred. For efficiency, it is claimed that it is not surpassed by any public school in the State. The same School Board is in office under whose supervision the additions were made some years since. This fact is a striking proof of their faithfulness, and of the good sense of the people. In politics, they are equally divided ; while all belong to different churches and politics and religions, bids are not allowed to influence their action. They are elected for a term of three years—two members of the board being elected annually. The following is a list of the members of the board : James M. Thomas, Chairman ; Dr. Joseph Fithian, Secretary ; J. H. Brent, Esq., Henry Spears, H. M. Rucker, W. W. Massie."

Private Schools.—In addition to the City School, Paris has the advantage of several first-class educational institutions. The Garth Female Institute was organized in the summer of 1875 by a joint-stock company, with the late R. T. Davis as President. The institution was named in honor of William Garth, whose name is so prominently associated with the educational interests of the county, and of whom further notice is made in this chapter. Prof. C. E. Young, formerly of Staunton, Va., and a graduate of the University of Virginia was elected Principal, which position he continues to hold. The institution having become involved, was sold publicly in the spring of 1880, and purchased by the Principal, who is now sole owner. The buildings are unsurpassed in beauty, convenience and location by any school building in the State. The course of study is unusually thorough and complete. Every department of study is under the charge of competent instructors. As now organized, the corps of teachers is as follows : C. E. Young, Mathematics and Natural Sciences ; Miss Mary E. E. Johnson, Moral Philosophy and Higher English ; Mrs. E. Muth, German ; Miss Bettie Young, Principal of Primary Department ; Mrs. C. E. Young, Matron and Teacher of Calisthenics ; Prof. E. Amende and Mrs. Minnie Wilson, Music.

Bourbon Female College was founded at the close of the war by Prof. Walker Buckner, who conducted the institution several years. He was succeeded by Mrs. A. E. Randolph, now a missionary in China, who was assisted by Col. George M. Edgar and Miss Kate Edgar. At that time the school was under the patronage of the Presbyterian Church.

In 1874, Prof. J. A. Brown, now President of Harrison Female Academy, at Cynthiana, Ky., purchased the property. He associated with him in the conduct of the school Prof. Wharton S. Jones, now of Memphis, Tenn., and under their joint management the college was eminently successful.

In 1880, Prof. W. S. Jones and Mrs. A. B. Clay took charge of the college. Prof. A. Sanders leased the property in Septembeı 1881. The average attendance during the past year has ›een about seventy-five. The course of study embraces the branches usually taught in first-class female schools. The following persons comprise the faculty : A. Sanders, Principal, Mathematics and History ; Dr. George Varden, Language and Psychology ; Miss Mary B. Dennis, Natural Sciences and Composition ; Mrs. E. M. Avirett, English Literature and Reading ; Miss Alice Daugherty, Music ; Prof. A. M. Gutzeit, Assistant Music ; Miss Emily Halliday, Art.

The Edgar Institute was organized in 1875 by a joint-stock company, with Cassius M. Clay, Jr. as President. Col. George M. Edgar was elected Principal, with Capt. M. H. Crump and Prof. B. B. Ford as Assistants. It at first embraced the department of military instruction, and the pupils were required to be uniformed, but this feature was afterward abandoned. During the principalship of Col. Edgar, he was also assisted by Prof. W. H. Lockhart and Rev. Dr. George Varden. He continued in charge of the institution until the summer of 1879, when the property was purchased by Prof. B. H. Waddell and Col. C. H. Withrow. In July, 1881, Col. Withrow retired, and Prof. Waddell became the sole owner of the school. He continues to be the Principal, and is assisted by his brother, Capt. James Waddell. The school buildings occupy a commanding position, overlooking the city ; the grounds comprise about twenty acres ; the school building is new, and the institution certainly offers advantages of a high order. The property now used as the Institute, formerly was the homestead of the late Hon. Garrett Davis. Judge Matt Turney, in 1876, succeeded Mr. Clay as President of the institution, a position which he now holds.

Miss Maria Tipton has a select school of thirty scholars. She is considered one of the finest teachers in the State, and has recently purchased the late residence of Mr. J. H. Bassett, with a view of opening a boarding school for young ladies. Mrs. Jessie Parrish has charge of the department of music.

Prof. Yerkes has a select school for boys and young men. He stands in the first rank of educators, and within

William Garth

the past year has declined an appointment to a professorship in Center College, at Danville, being unwilling to give up his school in Paris.

For the past ten years. Prof. W. H. Lockhart has taught a select school, and many of his graduates have taken high rank in the educational institutions of the country. He is a thorough and accomplished teacher, and has done much to promote the cause of education in the State. He is Common School Commissioner of Bourbon County, a position which he has filled with marked ability and faithfulness for a number of years. His papers and addresses on educational subjects evidence research, thought and a trained mind.

St. Joseph's Academy, under the charge of the Sisters of the Visitation, is beautifully located on a commanding eminence overlooking Paris. The school was organized in 1870, under the control of the Sisters of Loretto, who remained about five years. They were succeeded by the Benedictine Sisters of Covington, who had charge for about two years. Then the Sisters of Notre Dame, Covington, who kept it only one year. The Sisters of Visitation of Maysville, who have been here three years, have purchased the property, and are building up a successful school. Mother Gonzaga, who is admirably qualified for the position, is the Mother Superior. She is assisted by a full corps of competent instructors.

The parochial school, numbering about one hundred pupils, is also under the management of the Sisters. The Catholic school for boys is taught by Miss Lucy Tully. Rev. Father Barry teaches a night school for young men—tuition free.

[The following sketch of a good man and a zealous friend to education, was written for this work by Mr. William Myall, a beneficiary of the "Garth Fund." He pays a deserved tribute to a deserving man, and we publish it in full in Paris' educational history, together with Mr. Garth's will, as of general interest to the reader.—Ed.]

William Garth, the subject of this sketch and founder of the "Garth Fund," was the son of Thomas Garth, a native of Scott County, Ky. His mother's maiden name was Nancy Thompson. Thomas Garth came to Bourbon County at an early date, and settled on a farm about five miles northwest of Paris, on the Paris & Georgetown road. At this place, William Garth was born on the 29th of March, 1815. He was educated in the schools of Bourbon County, with the exception of a year or two spent in the college at Georgetown, devoted principally to the study of mathematics, for which science he early developed considerable talent. When just out of school and while not yet twenty-one years of age, he was elected County Surveyor for Bourbon County, which office he held until elected Professor of Mathematics in the Georgetown College, when about twenty-four years of age. After filling this chair for eight or ten years he resigned, and retired to his farm in Bourbon County; a part of the farm formerly owned by his father and on which he had been raised. This farm, however, did not come to him by inheritance. When he reached majority his father gave him $5,000, which was all he ever received from his father's estate. With this money and the interest accrued thereon, together with what he had saved in his profession, he bought a portion of the old homestead, when a few years later his father, having become embarrassed, was compelled to dispose of part of his estate. For several years, Mr. Garth carried on this in connection with his professorship at Georgetown, and it is worthy of mention, as showing the industry and energy that marked his life, that he very frequently walked from Georgetown out to his farm on Friday evenings—a distance of about twelve miles—and back again on Sunday evening. While in Georgetown he was married to Mary Bartlett, a Northern lady who was at that time teacher in a female school in Georgetown, but there were never any children by this union.

Having resigned his Professorship and retired to his farm near Paris, he continued to reside there until overtaken by the calamity which resulted in his death. His life was exceedingly quiet and unassuming, but always full of employment. Business prospered in his hands and he soon accumulated a fortune which, at the time of his death, amounted to about $60,000; yet, though always a good business man and an excellent farmer, he was very far from being a man who allowed himself to be engrossed by mere money-making. Indeed he seems to have cared but little for money except as a means of doing good, and his strict habits of business appear to have been more the result of a fixed and conscientious rule of life, than of a desire for pecuniary profit. As an indication of this, both his heart and his hand were always opened freely to whoever appeared to him to need and to deserve assistance, and neither any individual nor any enterprise worthy of help ever applied to his generosity in vain. Indeed, he was more than once heard to say, in his quiet manner, that he did not regard it more his duty to pay his taxes than to contribute to the building of schoolhouses, turnpike roads, churches, or to any other enterprise that was likely to make the people of his native county either better or happier. The educational interests of his county always found in him a zealous supporter and friend, and he at one time made a proposition to become one of five persons who should contribute $20,000 each, for the purpose of endowing a college to be located at

Paris. The proposition failed of its purpose, however, as the other subscribers could not be found, and is therefore only deserving of mention in that it serves to illustrate the large public spirit of the man which constantly showed itself in his life and which was illustrated yet more forcibly after his death, when the generous provisions of his will were made known the public.

As a business man, he was exceedingly prompt, accurate and systematic. His obligations of whatever nature were met with a religious scrupulousness, and so strict was his observance of what he conceived to be the requirements of good faith in business transactions, that he never allowed a piece of his paper to mature without having made provision for its prompt discharge or arrangement.

It is, however, in his private relations that we see most in Mr. Garth to love and esteem. His even temper, never ruffled or excited in the most trying circumstances of life; his calm concentration of nature, overflowing only in deeds of benevolence and love; his strong human sympathies, and the unassuming simplicity of his life and manners could not fail to win the love and respect of all. As a man, he was exceedingly modest and retiring, and shrank from everything that was likely to bring him into any sort of unpleasant publicity. His habits were such as we would expect in such a man—plain and simple to a degree. In his food and drink, he was temperate almost to abstemiousness, never using stimulants of any kind, and abstaining entirely from the use of tobacco. This was no doubt a question of health with him, and the preservation of health was, in his opinion, a moral obligation. Though never a member of any church, his nature was deeply religious. No man ever had a stronger sense of duty; no man ever tried to discharge his duty more faithfully. Throughout life, the idea of the imperativeness of duty, and of the binding force of even the slightest moral obligation was always paramount in his mind. He conceived that his word once given was as binding as his bond. This was most noticeable in his business relations, though it extended equally to the most minute affairs of life. If he made an appointment to be present at any assembly, or to meet any one at a given place or time, he was sure to be there promptly at the appointed hour. These are matters that lay so much on the surface of his life that they could not have escaped the notice of any one who knew him, and it is impossible that a man so scrupulously observant of his slightest promise should not have had the respect and confidence of every one who was permitted to look into his character and his life. The moral influence of such a man cannot easily be estimated. Death came upon him suddenly and unexpectedly in the prime of life, but his influence, so far from being destroyed by his death, was then only for the first time fully felt and recognized.

In the latter part of August, 1860, Mr. Garth, attended by his wife and his two half-sisters, Anna and Amanda Garth, started on a pleasure trip through the Northwest. Before going he called on Mr. John Lucas, who then lived in Harrison County, and who had always been one of his most intimate friends. There had been for several years an agreement between them that in event of the death of either, the other should make a settlement of his estate. The object of Mr. Garth's visit was to inform Mr. Lucas of his intended trip, and to tell him where his valuable papers, including his will, would be found in case he did not return alive.

Having attended to this matter, the party set out on their tour, and reached Chicago the first week in September. About 9 o'clock on the night of September 7, they took passage on the "Lady Elgin" bound from Chicago to Milwaukee. The night was intensely dark and stormy, and the "Lady Elgin" had not proceeded more than twenty miles on her way when she was struck by another boat that ran upon her in the darkness, and so severely injured her that she filled with water in spite of all efforts, and sank in less than an hour. A large number, perhaps as many as one hundred of the passengers, took refuge on the upper deck and the pilot-house, which floated off when the boat went down. Mr. Garth and his party were of this number. The lake was exceedingly rough and wild, and the wind blowing directly landward, drove the wreck among the breakers on the shore, when it was capsized. Only a few of the strongest swimmers, dashed on the shore by the fury of the waves, were able to retain their footing. These escaped, but all the rest, including Mr. Garth and his entire party, were lost. It is very probable that Mr. Garth, who was a very cool and unexcitable man, could have saved himself had he not been encumbered by the presence of his wife and sisters, and no doubt he lost his own life in the effort to preserve theirs.

His body, and that of his sister Amanda, were washed ashore near the point where they were drowned, and were carried to the city of Milwaukee where, not being identified, they were buried, the expenses of the burial being defrayed by money found on his person. The bodies were exhumed a few days afterward, identified by friends who had gone on in search of them, and brought to Paris and buried. The body of his other sister was picked up near Chicago about ten days after the disaster, and that of his wife, after drifting about for nearly three weeks, was carried entirely across the lake and cast out on the opposite shore, still in a good state of preservation. These were also brought home aud interred in the cemetery at Paris.

Mr. Garth's will, which was written with his own hand, on the 22d day of August, 1859, was filed for record in the Bourbon County Court on the 22d of September, 1860, only a few days after the recovery of his body. It was not until now that the people of Bourbon County fully realized how deep was the sympathy which William Garth felt for the struggles and sorrows of the world, how earnestly he desired to ameliorate the condition of mankind, and how truly noble and magnanimous was the quiet, earnest man who had passed his simple and unpretentious life in their midst. We have already noticed his devotion to the cause of education. He looked upon that as one of the great means by which the world was finally to be redeemed, and it was perhaps not less this belief than a generous love for his native county and a broad philanthropy that reached out its arms to all the poor and struggling youth of the generations to come, which led him to insert in his will the following provision which illustrates the character of the man in terms which, though simple and unostentatious as his life, are yet far more eloquent than any eulogy that could be written: "The entire balance of my estate not herein disposed of I wish to be appropriated to the cause of education in the following manner, viz.: So soon as my executor shall have paid off the before-mentioned special legacies, and has ascertained the balance in his hands of my estate, he shall cause to be published in the papers of the county of Bourbon the following proposition: If in one year from this time the citizens of Bourbon County will secure by good subscriptions the sum of $100,000 (to be paid in a reasonable time) to be appropriated to the endowment of a college to be located in Paris, Bourbon Co., Ky., then he will immediately pay over to those who may be appointed Trustees of the college such before-mentioned balance of my estate in his hands (here specify the sum) to be applied by said Trustees to the endowment of a Professorship of Mathematics in said college. If at the expiration of one year from the date of this advertisement the conditions therein are not complied with on the part of the citizens of Bourbon County, then I direct my executor to pay over such before-mentioned balance of my estate in his hands to the Treasurer of the county of Bourbon, to be by the Bourbon County Court, a majority of all the Justices being present, safely invested in such manner as they may deem best, and the interest on such investment they are to apply to the education of such poor, worthy and sprightly young men of Bourbon County as they may think most conducive to the public good, and in the distribution of this interest as above directed the court may pay for tuition, board, books and clothing, any one or all as in their opinion may be deemed best. I further direct, that if any one or more of the beneficiaries of this will should not be living, or any child of such beneficiaries, when it is presented to the court for record, that his, her or their legacies must be appropriated by my executor to the cause of education in exactly the same manner as the before-mentioned balance of my estate was directed to be applied."

Owing to delays arising from litigation and from the confusion of the period of the civil war, the estate was not finally settled until 1866. The advertisement of this provision being then made according to the directions of the will, the citizens of Bourbon County failed to subscribe the required sum, and on the 1st day of April, 1867, the executor, Mr. John Lucas, paid over to the Treasurer of Bourbon County, to be held by the County Court in trust for the purpose set out in the will, the balance of said estate remaining in his hands after payment of all debts and legacies, amounting to the sum of $42,612, and on the 9th day of the same month this whole sum was invested in stock of the Northern Bank of Kentucky, at $125 per share. The first two dividends were also invested in bank stock and added to the principal, as follows: November 9, 1867, $1,610, invested in stock of the Farmer's Bank at $115 per share, and January 13, 1868, $1,443 invested in Northern Bank stock at $120.25. The fund now amounted to $45,665, and on the 6th day of April, 1868, L. K. Elliot, B. F. Rogers and J. M. Hughes were appointed Commissioners for its management, and for the purpose of examining applicants for the benefit thereof and to report to the County Court the names of such youths as they might deem worthy of selection, under the provisions of the will, and the amount to be allowed to each. In the following February the name of Matt Turney, now County Judge, was substituted for that of J. M. Hughes, and these Commissioners continued to serve until the death of B. F. Rogers in the summer of 1871. G. C. Lockhart was appointed to fill the vacancy caused by this death, and in 1876 Franklin Kennedy was substituted for L. K. Elliott, and he together with Judge Turney and G. C. Lockhart constitute the present Board of Commissioners.

The provisions of the will have been faithfully and conscientiously executed, and already many a young man whose lot in life would have stood like a mountain between him and his hopes of knowledge and usefulness, has had reason to bless the memory of William Garth. In the thirteen years in which the fund has been in operation there has been expended in appropriations for the assistance of young men selected by the Board, more than $36,-

000, or an average of nearly $3,000 yearly, the appropriations varying from $300 to about $50, according to the necessities of the case. During these years there has been an average of nineteen young men kept in school by this fund, and nearly one half of this number each year in college, for it was not the intention of Mr. Garth that the recipients of this generous benefaction should be turned away with only the rudiments of an education, but that each one whose tastes led him to desire it, might be enabled by its assistance to avail himself of the most thorough training afforded by our best institutions of learning.

The fund has been established so short a time that its great practical results are perhaps as yet but little manifest, except to those who have shared the blessing of its benefits, and have been enabled by it to prepare themselves for honorable and useful positions in life. It was not so much the object of Mr. Garth to educate the youth of his native county, merely for the help that such education might be to them as individuals, though no doubt this was one of the considerations that led him to make the bequest, as it was "to conduce to the public good" by promoting in the most effectual manner possible the higher education of the people. It is therefore apparent also that the bequest was not meant to be local in its effects, but was intended as a great public benefaction, since it must have been foreseen that a large majority of the young men educated by it would pass from Bourbon County to a broader theater of action. It was, in a word, a touching manifestation of a large and intensely earnest human sympathy, a philanthropy that reaches out its helping hand to the generations yet to come, and sought to lighten the burdens of life by increasing light and knowledge among the poorer and less fortunate classes of his countrymen. The beneficent effects of such a deed can only be seen in the long results of time. Indeed they can never be seen in their fullness for they are never completed. Incapable of exhaustion or of alienation, it stands in our midst a perpetual and ever-acting agency for good, dispensing its blessings without favor, and shedding upon many an anxious and aspiring mind the divine light of truth and knowledge. No other citizen of Bourbon County has left so endnring a monument; no other has deserved to be remembered with greater gratitude by her people; no other has been so great a benefactor to mankind. More than this need not be said—less could not be. In a quiet spot in the little cemetery at Paris his body sleeps the last long sleep of peace, but his name will live forever in the grateful recollections of the thousands who will be blessed by his beneficence and who, in honoring his memory, will feel that they are performing a sacred duty to one who was to them a brother and a friend.

The will alluded to in the foregoing sketch, and from which Mr. Myall makes an extract, is given entire, and is as follows:

Will of William Garth.—I, William Garth, of the county of Bourbon and State of Kentucky, being of sound disposing mind and memory, not knowing at what time, God in His good providence, may call me hence, and desiring to dispose of my estate while in the full possession of my mental powers, do make and publish this writing as my last will and testament.

My executor must pay all my just debts, and in these, include my promises to pay usurious interest.

I give my wife, Mary M. Garth, $15,000. I give to my mother, Lester Nancy Garth, $1,000. I give to my half-sisters, Sarah A. Fisher, Amanda Garth, Anna Garth, Alice Garth and my half-brother, John Garth, each, the sum of $1,000.

I wish the graveyard where my father, Thomas Garth, was buried, to be inclosed with a neat stone fence, and for this purpose, I authorize my executor to use a sum not exceeding $500.

My negro man "Ben" is to be emancipated if he is willing to leave the State of Kentucky. If not, he and my other slaves are to have the privilege of selecting masters for themselves, provided it can be done, at no greater sacrifice than one-fourth of their value.

My said negro man "Ben," is to be paid $140 for his services for the year ending December 31, 1859.

I hereby nominate and appoint John Lucas, of Harrison County, my executor, with full power to qualify and act, without giving security, unless some of the beneficaries of the will should object. And when my executor has settled my estate, that he is to be allowed $5,000 for his services.

The entire balance of my estate not herein disposed of, I wish to be appropriated to the cause of education in the following manner, viz.: So soon as my executor shall have paid off the before-mentioned special legacies, and has ascertained the balance in his hands of my estate, he shall cause to be published in the papers of the county of Bourbon the following proposition: If in one year from this time the citizens of Bourbon County will secure, by good subscriptions, the sum of $100,000 (to be paid in a reasonable time), to be appropriated to the endowment of a college to be located at Paris, Bourbon Co., Ky., then, he will immediately pay over to them who may be appointed Trustees of the college, such before-mentioned balances of my estate in his hands (here specify the sum), to be applied by said Trustee to the endowment of a Professorship of Mathematics in said college.

If at the expiration of one year from the date of this advertisement the conditions therein are not complied with on the part of the citizens of Bourbon County, then I direct my executor to pay over such before-mentioned balance of my estate in his hands to the Treasurer of the Court of Bourbon County, to be by the Bourbon County Court, a majority of all the Justices being present, safely invested in such manner as they may deem best, and the interest on such investment they are to apply to the education of such poor, worthy and sprightly young men of Bourbon County, as they may think most conducive to the public good, and in the distribution of such interest as above divided, the court may pay for tuition, board, books and clothing any one or *all*, as in their opinion may be deemed best.

I further direct, that if any one or more of the beneficiaries of the will should not be living, or any child of such beneficiary, when it is presented to the court for record, that his, her or their legacies must be appropriated by my executor to the cause of education in precisely the same manner as the before-mentioned balance of my estate was directed to be applied.

To enable my executor to carry this, my will, into effect, I authorize him to sell publicly my entire estate, the land in three payments, one, one-third cash, one, one-third in one year, and the balance of the property on six months' time.

In testimony whereof I have hereunto set my hand and seal, this the 22d day of August, 1859.

William Garth [seal.]

Colored Schools.—The colored city school is under the charge of the Board of Education. J. C. Graves is the Principal; Mrs. Lucy Fraser, Assistant. Average attendance about fifty pupils. Rev. James M. Thomas conducts a select school of about thirty pupils in the Baptist Church. Reuben Butler also teaches a select school in the Methodist Church with thirty pupils.

Such are the educational institutions of Paris, which will compare favorably with those of other institutes in the State. They are ample to meet all the educational requirements of the times, and no one who desires an education but can avail himself of its advantages.

Hiram Lodge, No. 5, Masons (colored), organized in 1867. Officers—Thomas Kelly, W. M.; A. N. Smoot, S. W.; J. M. Porter, J. W.; George Watson, Treas.; E. J. Smoot, Sec.; Henry Craig, J. W.; Frank Thompson, Tiler.

Knights Templar (colored), organized in 1878. A. N. Smoot, E. C.∴; Thomas Kelly, G.∴; J. M. Porter, C. G.∴; J. W. Hatton, P.∴; E. J. Smoot, S. W.∴; Richard Kelly, J. W.∴; Henry Craig, W.∴; Frank Jones, S. B.∴; John Spears, S. B.∴; Alfred Bedford, G.∴

United Brothers of Friendship Lodge, No. 36. H. C. Smith, W. M.; Robert Claxton, D. M.; W. G. Smoot, Treas.; James Arnold, Sec.

Knights of Friendship—A. N. Smoot, K. C.; J. M. Porter, S. K.; William Smoot, Treas.; H. C. Smith, Sec.

Bourbon Star Lodge, No. 1,697, I. O. O. F. (colored), organized in 1869—George Wilkes, N. G.; Stephen Conway, V. G.; Morris Forsten, Treas.; Thomas Kelly, Sec.; Harry Hawes, R. S. to N. G.; Alfred Jackson, L. S.; Peter Mason, N. F.; A. N. Smoot, P. N. F.; Henry Howard, P. N. G.; Moses Murphy, W.

The following is the present municipal government of Paris, together with its material resources: A. J. Lovely, Mayor; James Paton, Sr., Clerk City Council; James Mernaugh, City Marshal; Hugh Henry, Deputy Marshal and Collector; W. O. Hite, City Janitor.

Councilmen—First Ward, Henry Turney, Henry Butler, Ben Perry; Second Ward, Mike Dowd, Bush Hart, W. F. Spears; Third Ward, Charles V. Higgins.

The receipts from all sources for the year ending April 10, 1882, are as follows:

From Collector		$10,708 61
Same, for license		249 54
Same, for fines		243 90
From fines		395 00
Same, for license		403 00
From James Paton, Clerk		1,463 89
James M. Thomas, for tuition		12 00
W. H. Lockhart, State School tax		981 12
John T. Hinton, M. & L. Turnpike dividend		120 00
A. Shire, gas dividend		920 00
		$15,497 06
Cash on hand April 7, 1881—		
City Fund	$210 03	
School Fund	506 35	
Gas Fund	314 16	
		$1,030 54
		$16,527 60
Amount transferred from City to School Fund.		1,000 00
Total		$17,527 60
Amounts paid during year ending April 10, 1882—		
From City Fund	$8,995 08	
School Fund	5,094 69	
Gas Fund	1,944 25	
		16,034 02
Balance cash on hand April 10, 1882—		
City Fund	$182 17	
School Fund	879 45	
Gas Fund	431 96	
		$1,493 58
Total		$17,527 60

RESOURCES OF CITY—

	Estimated Value.	Cost.
Real Estate	$10,500	$15,000
Fire engine and apparatus	7,500	12,500
115 shares gas stock	12,650	11,500
Total	$30,650	$39,000

LIABILITIES OF CITY—

Balance of note due Northern Bank	$900 00
Interest on above note	50 00
1 Engine note due January 10, 1883	775 00
1 Engine note due January 10, 1884	725 00
Total	$2,450 00
Less cash in hands of Treasurer	1,493 58
Total debt	$956 42

To show the importance of Paris as a shipping-point, there was shipped during the year 1881 1,200 car-loads of stock.

At an early day, there were a number of manufactories in Paris, which were kept busy supplying the wants of the people—for at that time the cost of wagoning goods was so great that it was cheaper to manufacture them at home than to buy them in distant places and bring them here.

Samuel Pike was a leading manufacturer of the early times. He was a native of England, and came here about 1810. He had but small means, and was himself a practical wool manufacturer. He was the first man who carded wool in Paris. He also made rope, bagging, etc., which he shipped South, and brought back cotton and manufactured it. In 1815, he built a cotton factory or mill where L. Price & Co.'s store is now situated, and continued the business until 1825. Another factory was built by him in 1822–23, on the ground east of the present Christian Church. The factory built in 1815 was merged into this in the fall of 1825, and continued in existence until 1837. It had a capacity of 720 spindles.

Mr. Pike also had a hemp factory at the upper end of Pleasant street, built about 1818, which he carried on until his death in 1837. He was succeeded in the business by Henry T. Duncan. It was run until 1840.

A cotton factory was built on the site of White's distillery about 1830, by Philip Adams & Co.; capacity about seven hundred and twenty spindles. It afterward passed into the hands of Kelly & Wilson, by whom it was run until 1851. A market was found at home for the most of their goods; the surplus was shipped to Louisville.

A cotton mill was built some time between 1820 and 1830, by Charles Ainsworth, of 240 spindles, on the corner above where Mrs. Ogden now lives. About 1835, a factory was built on the site of the Jones Block, on Main street. Its capacity was 240 spindles. It was run for a number of years.

The Paris Flouring Mill, which still exists, antedates all of these. The first flour mill, a frame structure, was built in 1800. It was owned by Thomas Jones. It passed through several hands, and was bought in 1859 by William Shaw, who still owns it. Across from where Mr. Shaw's warehouse stands, Mr. Jones built a fulling-mill, which was successfully carried on until 1854–55. Mr. Shaw's flouring-mill is one of the institutions of Paris. The flour manufactured is known and sought after in all directions. It is even shipped in large quantities to England. The mill is always taxed to its utmost capacity, frequently being run night and day to supply the demands of its customers. Mr. Shaw takes much pride in it, and is always improving and beautifying its surroundings.

The completion of the Kentucky Central Railroad in in 1854, placed Paris in easy connection with Covington, Cincinnati and other manufacturing cities, and the result was that articles which had before that time been manufactured here, could be brought by rail and sold here for less than our manufacturers could make them, and they could not compete with the manufacturers in more favored localities; the market here was not so large; the facilities for manufacturing were not so great; coal was much higher, and so the manufactories were all abandoned, and our people became and still remain dependent upon the manufactories of other cities. And so, from that time to the present no effort has been made to revive manufactures. With high-priced fuel here, there could have been no successful competition with other points. But it is not improbable that the long-expected and long-wished for time, when Paris will become a manufacturing town, will soon dawn. The mountains, rich in mineral resources and timber, are being penetrated with railroads; coal will soon become cheap; and, then, with cheap fuel and fine water-power combined, Paris ought to become an important manufacturing city. Capital in plenty is here. It needs only confidence and enterprise to bring about a result so desirable.

During the present year the Kentucky Central will be extended from this place to Richmond, and soon thereafter direct connection will be made with Knoxville, opening up the trade of the entire South. The building of other roads is also contemplated. The repair-shops of the Kentucky Central are to be located here, and with roads diverging in every direction, Paris will offer advantages as a manufacturing point which cannot fail to attract capital.

The planing-mill of Capt. James M. Thomas, the flouring-mill of William Shaw, and the large distillery of Messrs.

White & Ferguson, constitute now the manufacturing interests of Paris. The time, it is believed, however, is not far distant when other industries will spring into being, and a new life be infused into our community.—*McChesney.*

[NOTE.—The following article on Turnpike Roads, by Frank Kennedy, Esq., is given in conclusion of the history of Paris. Although some of the facts embraced in it are given in the chapter on Internal Improvements in Bourbon County, yet it is of sufficient interest to appear complete.—ED.]

One of the most valuable improvements in Bourbon County is its system of turnpike roads. Every road that leads to its county seat is graded to an elevation of about three degrees, and paved with broken rock, on the Macadam plan, to a depth of twelve to fourteen inches in the center, thinning off to six or eight inches on the sides. The first macadamized road in Kentucky was constructed through Bourbon County in the years from 1830 to 1835, under the charter of the Maysville, Washington, Paris & Lexington Turnpike Road Company. It is also the best road of the sort built in the State. It has the broadest and lowest graded road-bed, few of its elevations exceeding two degrees, while its wooden bridges are monuments to the fidelity and skill of Mr. Wernwag, their builder, whose name—the "Wernwag bridges"—have made historical. In 1847–48 and '49, the roads leading from Paris severally to Georgetown, Winchester, North Middletown and Flat Rock, were granted corporate privileges by the Legislature, and shortly afterward converted into turnpikes. Since then, road after road has been taken in hand and improved until the turnpikes are more than forty in number, and extend 215 miles within the limits of the county. To all of these the county, through its magistrates, subscribed stock, and is by far the largest stockholder in the county. These turnpikes have cost on an average about $2,300 per mile, except the first one, which, as before stated, cost nearly $6,000. More than half a million dollars have been expended in their construction. The county, in its corporate capacity, has paid $190,000, averaging about $900 per mile, while individuals have subscribed and paid more than $300,000.

It is estimated that the yearly expense of repairs on the roads and toll-houses, falls little short of $75 per mile on an average. These are paid out of the tolls collected at the gates from passers over the road.

After defraying expenses, dividends are paid to stockholders, if there be anything left to divide. Very few of them are so successful as to be able to declare dividends, and they necessarily small, except to persons who have purchased depreciated stock at very low rates.

Estimating stock at par value, the roads mentioned beow, since they commenced operations, have paid in dividends as follows:

The Maysville & Lexington, in forty-five years, have paid $82.\frac{65}{100}$ cents on the dollar's worth of stock; that is an average of $1\frac{83}{100}$ per cent per annum.

The Paris & Winchester have returned, in twenty-four years, 60 cents on the dollar, or $2\frac{1}{2}$ per cent per annum.

The Paris & North Middletown have returned, in twenty-four years, 80 cents on the dollar, or $3\frac{1}{3}$ per cent per annum.

The Paris & Georgetown have returned, in twenty-four years, 85 cents on the dollar, or $3\frac{54}{100}$ per cent per annum.

The Paris & Clintonville, in sixteen years, have returned 25 cents on the dollar, or $1\frac{56}{100}$ per cent per annum.

The Millersburg & Indian Creek, in sixteen years, have returned $24\frac{1}{2}$ cents on the dollar, or $1\frac{53}{100}$ per cent per annum.

These are the best returns made by any of the forty-three roads in the county. Of the whole number, less than one-fourth declare dividends.

It is easy to see that, as moneyed investments, they are not generally profitable, but as conveniences—public and private—their value is inestimable. In short, they are indispensable. The farmer who is ten miles away from town, on a good turnpike, is about as near in point of time, as the one who is three miles out; and is nearer in time, convenience and comfort than the man who lives one mile from market on a dirt road.

The half million dollars expended in turnpike roads in the county has added to its general wealth $2,000,000 at a low estimate. If they were suddenly annihilated and mud roads re-adopted, the lands of the county would fall to one-half of the prices they now command. There remain only about a half dozen public roads which are not macadamized, and these have lost their importance as public highways, and are useful only as neighborhood necessities. As the work of improvement is still in active progress, it is almost certain that in ten years more there will not be a public road in the county but will be of easy and secure travel at all seasons, in darkness as well as daylight.

The wisdom and liberality of the fathers who pioneered the system, have been nobly sustained by their sons, except that the latter have fallen into the error of constructing the roads too cheaply. That "the best is the cheapest," is eminently illustrated in the building of turnpike roads. A reduction of one degree would have added comparatively little to the cost of construction, and the saving would be fourfold in cost of repairs.

The county stock is represented by an officer called

"Commissioner of Turnpikes," who is elected by the Magistrates, and whose duty is to attend all meetings of the stockholders, and vote the county stock, supervise the general interests of the roads, give legal advice to their managers, collect dividends on county stock, and report annually to the Court of Claims.

We are indebted to Mr. F. Kennedy, the present Commissioner, for details of facts and figures on this subject:

Mr. Kennedy is an attorney at law in Paris, and has very full and elaborate statistics of the receipts, expenditures and dividends of the roads from their beginning. He has prepared also an index of charters and their various amendments of the roads in the county, the whole work filling a large book and involving a great deal of careful and patient labor, which is both convenient and valuable for reference.

"Fair View" Residence of Thos. H. Wilson, near Paris on the Maysville and Lexington Pike, Bourbon Co. Ky.

CHAPTER XIII.

MILLERSBURG PRECINCT—DESCRIPTIVE AND TOPOGRAPHICAL—SETTLEMENT OF THE WHITES—THEIR HARDSHIPS AND PRIVATIONS—EARLY INDUSTRIES AND PIONEER IMPROVEMENTS—TURNPIKE ROADS AND BRIDGES—CHURCH AND SCHOOL HISTORY CENTER IN THE TOWN.

"History is the essence of immemorable biographies."
—*Carlyle.*

THE little events of every-day life are like the stones in a mosaic, each going to make up the whole picture, and it is often that these trifling occurrences are of far more interest to us than the great events of the time. Doubtless the builders of the Parthenon were more pleased with the goodness of the mid-day meal which their wives brought them than they were with the magnificence of the temple they were erecting. In all probability, Shakespeare thought more of the acting qualities of the ideal characters he created than of the echoes they would send down through the long corridors of time. So, in the annals of a county or a town, our aim is to chronicle, not great events that effect the destiny of a nation, but rather the homely events of every day life, and such as have occurred within the last hundred years. The pioneers who bore the brunt of toil and danger; whose lives were spent, not in studious halls where college lore is conned, but amid "savage scenes and perils of war;" and the youth whose infant cradles were rocked to the music of the hurricane's roar, the scream of the panther and the howl of the wolf; these and kindred incidents are such as embellish every portion of the dark and bloody ground, and as we have said, are of more interest to us than the great questions which shake empires and kingdoms. These scenes and incidents, and those figured in them, deserve perpetuation in history. The original pioneers have passed away—the last of the old guard are gone, and many of their children, too, have followed them to that "bourn whence no traveler returns." It is highly fitting then that a record of the "old times" should be made to stand as a monument to their hardships and dangers.

"We heard it first at the dawn of day,
And it mingled with matin chimes;
But years have distanced the beautiful lay,
And its memory floweth so swiftly away,
That we call it now 'Old Times.'"

Millersburg, the Election Precinct No. 2, of Bourbon County, is small in extent, and is "neither oblong nor square," nor could a Philadelphia lawyer tell just what is its shape. It borders on Nicholas County from near the center of Bourbon, to the north line of the same, and for the remainder of its boundary has Flat Rock, Paris and Ruddel's Mills Precincts and Harrison County. With this lucid description the reader will draw his own conclusions as to its shape and boundaries. It is drained by the Hinkston and its tributaries. Hinkston forms the boundary line between Millersburg and Nicholas County for some distance, then enters the precinct, runs nearly west to the village of Millersburg, and changing its course flows north for about four miles, when it curves abruptly to the west, forms the boundary line for a short distance between Millersburg and Ruddel's Mills, then enters the latter precinct and unites with the Stoner, near Ruddel's Mills Post Office, and together with it forms the South Fork of the Licking River. Steel's Run, in the northwest corner of the precinct, empties into the Hinkston; Miller's Run flows into the Hinkston about two miles north of Millersburg; McClellan's Branch empties into the Hinkston opposite the village. Flat Lick and Walnut Run are small streams in the southeast part of the precinct, and are tributaries of the Hinkston. The surface features of Millersburg are similar to those of Paris Precinct, the land being rolling or undulating, and but little waste land. The timber growth was originally black walnut, hickory, white and blue ash, oak, maple, box elder, and buckeye, most of which has been cut off. A few scattering trees and groves are left, the latter cleared of the underbrush, and are finely set in blue grass. It is a good agricultural district, and farming and stock-raising are carried on extensively. The people are intelligent, well educated, courteous and hospitable.

The first settlers in Millersburg Precinct came from Pennsylvania. In 1778, eighteen men, all heads of families, set out from Sherman's Valley, near Carlisle, in Pennsylvania, for Kentucky. They journeyed on foot through the wilderness, and so far as is known arrived at their destination without encountering any serious adventure. The names of these men could not all be obtained, but among them were Robert Pollock, William McClellan, William Steele, David Marshall, Henry Thompson, William McClintock, John, William and Robert Miller, and John Patton. A pre-emption grant of 400 acres had been furnished to each of them from the Governor of Virginia as an inducement to them to settle in Kentucky. Upon their arrival they proceeded, with their surveyor, a man named Johnson, to lay out and survey their respective claims. Four of this colony located their land within the present limits of Millersburg Precinct, viz., John and William Miller, William McClellan and William Steele. They located their 400 acres, and then proceeded to take up 1,000 acres each, at twenty shillings per hundred acres, upon which they built their cabins and planted a little corn, a precaution that was necessary to enable them to hold their pre-emptions. McClellan built his cabin about one and a fourth miles south of the village of Millersburg, a few hundred yards from the present Maysville pike, on land that is now owned by J. B. Barton, A. Butler and Robert McClellan. Steele settled near Steele's Ford, on the Hinkston, but the exact spot is not known. The land taken by him, however, is now owned by Daniel Thompson, the J. L. Taylor heirs, Thomas McClintock, William Layson and others. John Miller pre-empted the land upon which Millersburg stands, but settled about a mile north of the town, a short distance from the present Millersburg & Cynthiana pike, on land now owned by Z. M. Layson, Abraham Barton, the J. McClintock heirs, Charles Clark, etc. William Miller built a cabin about a mile south of Millersburg and half a mile west of the old Maysville pike, on the farm now owned by John Bedford. Other land taken up by him is now owned by Frank Champ, Dr. Best and others. Each of the Millers built block-houses, where the families collected as a protection against the Indians in times of alarms, which for the first few years of their settlement were numerous and frequent.

After securing lands, erecting cabins and planting a crop of corn, they, in the latter part of the year, returned to Pennsylvania for their families and supplies. In the following year, they came back to Kentucky, making the trip by land to Pittsburgh, and thence down the Ohio on flat-boats. During the voyage they were compelled to keep in the middle of the stream, through fear of the Indians who infested the banks, and were ever ready to attack a small party of whites. Once, in attempting to land, Robert Miller was shot by the Indians, who secured his body. Mr. Miller had upon his person a silver watch, and wore silver knee-buckles and shoe-buckles, which were then fashionable. Some years afterward, a man came to Millersburg wearing these relics of the unfortunate victim, which he had bought from the savages. They were recognized and purchased by John Miller, a brother of the murdered man. Owing to the hostility of the Indians along the Ohio, the party did not land at Limestone (Maysville), as they had intended, but proceeded to the mouth of Beargrass, now Louisville, where there was then a fort and settlement. The unsettled condition of the country arising from the Revolutionary war, then in progress, and the depredations of the Indians, incited to murder and bloodshed by British emissaries, their intended settlement was delayed, and it was not until about 1785–86 that the members of the little colony took possession of their lands. From this period dates the settlement of the section now embraced in the precinct of Millersburg. The early trials and struggles of this band of pioneers would make a volume of itself, if the facts could be obtained. They all died upon the lands embraced in their original claims, leaving posterity living in the surrounding counties. William Steele was shot and severely wounded by the Indians while making his original survey, and he carried the ball to his grave. From the date of these settlements new-comers increased in numbers, and the surrounding country rapidly filled up. The war-whoop of the Indian died away in the distance beyond the Ohio, peace settled down over the country, and prosperity crowned the efforts of the pioneers.

Among the first manufacturing industries were those of mills. The first establishment of this kind was erected by the Millers. John Miller put up a saw and grist-mill so long ago that no one now remembers the date of its erection. It was built of logs, upon the site now occupied by the Foster Mill, in the southern part of Millersburg, on Hinkston Creek. As early as 1808, flour was shipped from this mill to New Orleans, and for years it was a considerable institution in the neighborhood, and was patronized by the people far and near. The mill now standing upon its original site is a frame structure, was built by Jefferson Vimont, and is run by both steam and water—by the latter when the creek furnishes sufficient quantities, and by steam when it does not. A mill was also built by William Miller, just across the creek from that, put up by his brother, and of the same character and capacity, with the exception that a fulling attachment was added, which was probably the first of the kind in the county. The original structure was torn down and a frame building erected in its place, which long did service as a mill. The building is still standing, but is not running at present. Another mill was built in the precinct, some four miles south of Millersburg on the Hinkston. It was a log building, and like the one last mentioned, is not now in operation.

The early manufacturing industries outside of the village consisted chiefly of distilleries. The first one of these was built by John Miller, previous to the war of 1812. It was located about a mile northwest of Millersburg, near the Nicholas County line, and but a short distance from the old John Miller Station and block-house, on land now owned by the widow of James McClure Miller. The "All-healing balsam of life and comfort" turned out from this pioneer establishment was manufactured under the "Old Copper, Sour Mash" system, and what was not consumed by the pioneers for camphor (!), was shipped to New Orleans with other exports. Another distillery was built by Robert McClellan, and another by William Turner. It is said that there have been more than twenty distilleries built in this precinct at different times since its settlement, and it is not a very good section for distilleries either. More schoolhouses and fewer stiil-houses would be an improvement, not only in this section, but throughout Central Kentucky. There are at present three distilleries in Millersburg Precinct, viz.: Joshua Barton's, Joseph Grimes', and Davie's, the two former, of which we believe are not now running. These are more fully noticed in another chapter.

The first road regularly laid out through the precinct was probably what now forms the Maysville & Lexington pike. When this first became a public highway no one can now tell, but it is known to be first road in the State, that was macadamized. Louis Vimont, Sr., was one of the early citizens who took an active interest in the construction of this pioneer road. He was a contractor in the building of it, and not only fulfilled his own contract but completed other sections in different places, where the contractors had failed, using a considerable amount of his own funds in doing so, as the company's exchequer was empty. The next pike built was the Millersburg, Ruddel's Mills & Cynthiana, built about 1853–54. The next was the Millersburg & Cynthiana, begun in 1859, and completed in 1860, and the Millersburg & Cane Ridge, built the same year. Previous to building any of these roads, the old "Buffalo Trace" was the main throughfare. The first bridge in the precinct was built across the Hinkston, by a man named Parker. It was a wooden structure, and was built about 1815 or 1820. The architecture was poor, the bridge "top-heavy," and after standing a few years, it capsized. For many years after, the community was without a bridge, and so remained until the Turnpike Company built one; also of wood. This was burned a few years ago, when a substantial iron bridge replaced it.

The church and educational history of the precinct centers in the village, and will be given in that connection. Millersburg being a college town, the surrounding country has depended on it for education, and hence but little attention has been paid by the precinct to the common schools.—*Perrin.*

CHAPTER XIV.

THE TOWN OF MILLERSBURG—ITS FOUNDER—EARLY GROWTH, PROSPERTY AND MANUFACTURING INTERESTS—CHURCHES AND CHURCH HISTORY—THE CEMETERY—SCHOOLS AND COLLEGES—A SKETCH OF THEIR INFLUENCE, ETC.

THE village of Millersburg was founded by Maj. John Miller, in 1798, who was the original owner of the land upon which it stands, and for whom it was named. He was one of the colony mentioned in the preceding chapter, and came out and pre-empted land in 1775. Maj. Miller laid out his town in the year mentioned above (1798), under an act of the Legislature passed for the government of laying out towns, and had surveyed into lots one hundred acres of land. Seven trustees were appointed, in whom were vested the power of controlling the land which had been devoted to town purposes, and their successors have since exercised a supervising control over it and the affairs of the town. The charter was amended by an act of the Legislature in 1873–74, and again in 1878–79, for the appointment of officers, etc. The following article is from the *Bourbon News*, published in Millersburg and is so applicable to the town, and contains so much good sense, that we give it entire. Under the head of "Our city and her wants," the *News* says:

The signs of the times indicate that the people of Millersburg are not as progressive a people as citizens of other and smaller towns in the State. Our wants are many—so many that we can only speak of those which are absolutely necessary to advance our town to the front rank, where she properly belongs. There may be many impediments of which we have no knowledge, that have heretofore prevented our "city paps" from taking steps toward remedying the evils of which we propose to speak. Be that as it may, if it has been impossible for them to take any action in these things, it is time for the citizens to take into consideration the necessity of improvement in several matters of which we shall make mention. Where shall we begin? Let us notice first the most important want—a fire company with a good engine. We know not at what moment a destructive fire may reduce to ashes our entire city, hence we should be prepared to meet the destructive element with a well-organized fire company. 'Tis true, an engine cannot be had for any small sum of money, but the cost of an engine is not to be compared to the loss that would follow a fire in the business portion of our town. The question of a fire company will be duly considered after the greater portion of our town is in ashes. The next thing in order will be street lamps. Within the recollection of the oldest inhabitant, night pedestrians in our town have been dependent upon moon to guide them along paths of safety. But this should not last forever. Our sister cities no longer depend on the uncertain light of the moon, and why should we? At very little expense, lamps sufficient to light the entire town could be procured. Street lamps would not be such an important factor if it were not for the fact that when a person lifts his foot from the ground he has not the faintest idea where it will land the next step. We undoubtedly have rougher sidewalks and crossings than any other town in the known universe. Why is it so? If the persons owning the property will neither repair nor construct sidewalks, it behooves the city authorities to act. What can the "powers that be" do? Purchase the material, procure the hands, have the work done, and have the same charged to the persons owning the ground. They will cheerfully foot the bill, for it has certainly been neglect on their part that such work has not been done long ago. If any one should refuse to pay for such work, they can be compelled to do so. Why are violators of the law, who are tried and sentenced by the courts of this place, sent to Paris to work out the penalty on her streets when our streets need work so badly? There is one other matter to which we wish to direct special attention, and that is the fence—or the place where it ought to be—around the public square. The square is the property of the town, and the town has turned it out to grass, or, rather, has turned the stray stock in to grass. The place could be made an ornament to the town, and every one who claims to be a resident of this place should make it his duty to see that it is kept in good condition. We only desire to call attention to the above wants, and do not speak of them simply for the sake of having something to grumble about. They are things that are important, and demand immediate attention. Millersburg can be made a most desirable place in which to locate. It now has many advantages over other towns in the State. Persons coming here to seek homes are not favorably impressed with the dilapidated condition of public property. There are no appearances of thrift; on the contrary, appearances are against us, and indicate a lack of that spirit of progress which characterizes other towns. Our educational interests are great inducements to persons seeking a place to locate. Our people are thrifty, in educational interests, but they are overlooking some very important points, which, if attended to, would redound to their interests in the end. There may be circumstances over which our authorities have no control, that have prevented them from taking any steps looking toward the improvement and building-up of our town; if so, it is to be hoped that they will push aside every impediment and open up a new era in the history of this place.

The first store in Millersburg is believed to have been started by a man named Smoot. Henry Savery, a very enterprising Frenchman, opened a store soon after Smoot. These stores were both established between 1800 and 1805. Robert and Joseph Miller, sons of Maj. John Miller, had a store as early as 1808. This was quite a business little place in early times, and sold large quantities or goods. Flour, whisky and pork were shipped on flat-boats to New Orleans, where they were paid for, usually, in silver. The silver was taken by the merchants to Philadelphia and Baltimore, where it was laid out in goods, and the goods hauled across the mountains in wagons or conveyed on pack-horses. The very transportation of the money was a serious undertaking. Just think of carrying several thousand dollars in silver from New Orleans to Philadelphia on horseback—there were no steamboats then, nor railroads. It was easy enough to go to New Orleans on flat-boats, but to come back up the river they were not much of a success. Hence, people traveled in those days principally on foot and horseback. The trade of Millersburg grew rapidly, and it was one of the live and enterprising business places of the country. A post office was established in an early day, and Louis Vimont was the first Postmaster. He held the office for a great many years, and was finally turned out by Gen. Jackson, under the rule that "to the victor belongs the spoils." Vimont would not support Old Hickory for the Presidency, and by the eternal! the old hero kicked him out of the office. Since his day, the following men and women have served as Postmaster General of the little "burg:" Charles Talbott, Aquilla Willetts, —— Bassett, Isaac Parnell, Mrs. Kelley, Mrs. Vimont, and the present incumbent, R. B. Boulden.

The town of Millersburg was, in the old time, quite a manufacturing center. Flour-mills, hemp factories, fulling-mills, cotton factories, carding machines, distilleries, etc., etc., were in operation. As early as 1817, William F. Baker had a fulling-mill in the village. He was a grandson of William Miller. Joseph Miller started a woolen factory in 1818, in a stone building, which is still standing near the Hinkston. Samuel Colvin ran a carding-machine near the same place about 1830. A hemp and rope factory was built on land now owned by Joseph A. Miller, opposite the railroad depot, but by whom the building was originally put up is not known. About the year 1828, Robert Batson commenced the manufacture of spinning-wheels, both large and small sizes. This business he kept up for a number of years, in fact until we became too proud to use them, and too fastidious to wear clothes of home manufacture. A man named James had a large fanning-mill factory here as early as 1810, and in 1844 William Larimore commenced the manufacture of hemp cradles. He did a large business, shipped them to Missouri, and to all parts of Kentucky, and made quite a fortune in the business. But these busy scenes have passed. The railroad, the great revolutionizer of the nineteenth century, has opened up other fields, and carried manufacturing interests to more eligible localities. The very limited railroad facilities of Millersburg has deprived her of her manufactories, and will keep her in that condition until her means of shipping are improved. As it now is, but little is left, except a tradition of former glory, and Davie's distillery—the latter just opened for business, and fully described in a preceding chapter.

Of the early newspapers of Millersburg, we have learned but little. In a copy of the *Bourbon News* before us, we see reference made to A. Dudley Mann, "once the editor of the *Kentucky Intelligencer*, published in Millersburg about 1824, during the Jacksonian candidacy days, at the old Vimont building." Beyond this mere allusion, we learned nothing of the *Intelligencer*. The *Bourbon News*, published by Bruce Champ, Esq., is a large eight-column paper, and was established by Champ & Roby, the first number being issued on the 12th of January, 1881. Shortly after the paper started, Mr. Champ bought out his partner, Roby, and conducted the paper at Millersburg until 1882, when he removed his office to Paris, issuing the first number of the *News* from that city on the 7th of March. The paper started with a cash capital of *eighteen dollars*, and by energy and perseverance the proprietor has worked up a large circulation, and is furnishing to his readers an excellent paper.

The Millersburg Deposit Bank was chartered March, 1870, and went in operation the 1st day of September of that year. Its directors then were: William McClintock, Jr., President, Robert Tarr, William McMiller, John T. Taylor and Thomas McClintock; with Dr. A. G. Stitt, Cashier. Since the first year, its paid-up capital has been $50,000. Its career has been one of the most fortunate and successful known to the history of banking. Although it experienced the financial crisis of 1873, and witnessed the failure of a number of its debtors, yet all their paper had been so securely indorsed that not a loss was sustained! After a term of near seven years had been passed, the cashier was presented with a valuable gold-cased chronometer, by the stockholders, in consideration of his not having sustained the loss of a dollar to that date! And to this period—in the twelfth year of its progress, but a single loss has been met—a small one—and that by a loan recommended by a director, in opposition to the judgment of the cashier.

Its present Directors are: Robert Tarr, President, William McMiller, Sr., James M. Hughes, Thomas McClintock and John A. Miller, Jr., with same cashier as at the beginning. John W. Poynter was clerk for the first year; Willie Elliott, the second year; and George F. Stitt, from that time to the end of 1881, and from then until the present time, March, 1882, Harmon A. Stitt. Hiram Bassett, Teller, from the fall of 1872, to the present.

The Millersburg Cemetery Company was chartered February 28, 1860, and the company regularly organized thereunder on the 28th day of April succeeding, by the election of the following persons, by the stockholders, as Directors—Dr. A. G. Stitt, Dr. G. S. Savage, William McClintock, Jr., Z. M. Layson, Horace R. Miller, James McMiller and Jesse H. Boulden.

A meeting of said Trustees was thereupon immediately held, at the same place—in Dr. Stitt's office, Millersburg—when Jesse H. Boulden was elected President of the Board, Dr. Stitt, Secretary, and William McClintock, Jr., Treasurer. On the 30th of same month, the Trustees met and decided to purchase a portion of land from each, John McClintock and William Bradley, so as to comprise a tract of about thirteen acres, at $200 per acre. The plat has since had about three acres added to it. In June, following, Mr. Benjamin Grove, Topographical Engineer, of Louisville, Ky., was employed to lay out the grounds, at a fee of $250. On the 14th of July, after, Mr Patrick Maney and several others were empolyed and put to work on the grounds, under direction of the engineer, and by Saturday, September 15, 1860, the carriage drives and avenues were graded and the lots all ditched, when, on the afternoon of that day, the stockholders met on the ground, pursuant to a request in the *Kentucky State Flag*, of Paris, and proceeded to draw for lots to which they were entitled, as shareholders of $100 each. They were Harmon D. Ayres, Mrs. E. A. W. Bryan, Jesse H. Boulden, J. H. Forsyth, Z. M. Layson, Alexander S. Miller, William McMiller, James McMiller, Horace R. Miller, John A. Miller, John M. Miller, James A. Miller, Joseph W. Miller, William M. McClintock, Jr., John McClintock, George S. Savage, A. G. Stitt, James Whaley.

The total receipts from all sources, to this date, for sale of lots, digging graves and for products of the grounds, etc., exceeds $15,000; all of which has been expended for inclosing, grading and ornamenting the grounds; for a vault that cost near $1,000, and for a lodge for the superintendent, which cost $2,500, except $1,000 invested in bank stock, and about $5 on hand. At the beginning of the enterprise, lots were sold at 15 cents per square foot, surface measure, and $3 was the price for digging a grave; but the present price for lots is 25 cents per foot, and $5 for a grave. The present Directors are: J. H. Boulden, President; A. G. Stitt, Secretary; Z. M. Layson,

Treasurer; William McMiller, Alexander McClintock. But *one* vacancy has occurred in the Board by death, since its organization, nearly twenty-two years since, viz., William McClintock, Treasurer.

The topography of the grounds is very handsome, and the soil could not be better adapted, as neither clay nor rock has ever been reached in any of the hundreds of graves yet dug!

It contains a great many handsome monuments, of Scotch granite, American and Italian marble, ranging in cost from a few hundred to several thousand dollars. It is said to be the most neat and handsomely kept cemetery in the State; in fact, as a visitor to it remarked, "the lovliness of these grounds robs the grave of half its gloom." Mr. William Bassett, Jr., has been Superintendent for the last two years.

Millersburg is like unto "a city that is set on an hill;" its churches and educational facilities produce a light that "cannot be hid." Its church history dates back beyond the memory of man almost. The first Methodist Church was built in Millersburg in 1827, but the church society was organized long previous to that date, and the "circuit riders" preached at different houses, mostly at Thomas Purnells. The building was a plain brick, 30x40 feet. About the time the church was finished, there was a "great shaking in the dry-bones of the valley," and many of the people were made to "see the error of their ways," and were converted to God. In 1847, under the ministry of Rev. George W. Brush, the present church was built. This church has been a station in the Kentucky Conference for some twenty years. It has had seasons of prosperity and times of adversity, and now numbers about two hundred members, with a good Sunday school. The Presbyterians had a church organization very early in Millersburg, but of its history, either past or present, we have been able to learn nothing, owing to the negligence of its friends. It seems that one of the first churches in Millersburg was the Old Republican Church which stood in the public square, in which all denominations worshiped for a time. A Sunday school, we learn, was established in it by the Presbyterians as early as 1824, and was the first one in Millersburg.

The Baptist Church of Millersburg is supposed to have been organized as early as 1818, and that the following were among the original members: John James, Mathew Denman, Joseph Kethley, Jemima Nicholson, Elizabeth Isham, Susan Denton and others. These were regularly organized into a church, as above mentioned, which, for a time, seems to have been, next to the Presbyterians, the leading denomination in this section of the State. Further particulars of this church, however, could not be obtained, and brief as is the above sketch, we are forced to pass it without further notice.

The Christian Church, a branch of the Baptists who held different views on some points, organized a society about 1831–32. Among their original members were Thomas Eads, William Miller, E. Owens, James Batterton, Joseph McKine, Roger Laughlin, Thankful West, Nancy Miller, Patsey Miller, Anna Adair, Sally Cook, Lucinda Throckmorton, Patsey M. Baker, Dr. A. W. Bills and wife, John Batson, Elizabeth Cress and perhaps others. Rev. Robert M. Batson preached for them until his death in 1833. They held their meetings in the same church with the Baptists, occupying it one-half the time. In 1838, they united with the New-Lights, a branch of "dissenters" from the Presbyterian Church, under the leadership of Barton W. Stone. They continued to worship in the Baptist Church until 1842, when they built their present brick edifice, at a cost of about $3,000. Elder Taylor Sharrard is the present Pastor. The church has a good membership and Sunday school.

This comprises the church history of Millersburg, so far as we are able to obtain it, and, though meager, is the best we can give under the circumstances, and were the editor to express himself frankly, he would say it is better than the churches deserve. They have had ample time, and have been repeatedly urged to furnish their history, but have not done so, and we have been forced to use such facts as we could obtain elsewhere. To sum up, there are four churches in the town—Presbyterians (who have the finest building), Methodists, Baptists and Christians. In addition to these, there are three colored churches, viz.: Baptist, Methodist Episcopal and Christian. These colored churches are in a flourishing condition, and have large memberships. The colored people are very zealous in religious matters, and these churches attest their devotion to the Master's cause. They also have a very flourishing school, which is attended by all the colored children who can afford to indulge in the luxury of education.

The Masonic Order is represented in Millersburg by Amity Lodge, No. 40, F. & A. M., and Millersburg R. A. Chapter, No. 46. Among the records we find "A History of Masonry in Kentucky," in which it is stated that a charter was granted to "Unity Lodge, No. 10, Millersburg, Ky.," September 18, 1805, but we find no record of charter members, or when the charter was surrendered.

Amity Lodge, No. 40, was chartered August 27, 1817, with John H. Sanders, Master; William Bowles, S. W.; and Allen Trigg, J. W.; by the Grand Lodge of Kentucky, at Mason's Hall in Lexington. John Willett, D. G. M. and R. T. Todd, Grand Secretary P. T. A charter was granted

Millersburg Chapter, No. 46, by the Grand Chapter in Louisville, August, 1851; with M.·. E.·. Joseph Grubb, H. P.; E.·. William Nunn, K.; and E.·. Caleb Lettin, Scribe; and rechartered October 20, 1874, with M.·. E.·. H. Bassett, H. P.; E.·. James M. Collier, K.; and E.·. John G. Smedley, S. The present officers (1881) are: M.·. E.·. W. M. Miller, Jr., H. P.; E.·. S. C. Allen, K.; and E.·. E. P. Thomason, S. The present officers of Amity Lodge are: Garrett Mann, W. M.; W. C. Goodman, S. W.; and I. L. Ylursley, J. W.

We find from the records and our own observation, that the membership has always included some of our best citizens, and many donations have been made in a quiet but effectual way to the distressed and needy. Amity Lodge donated at one time $100 to the Masonic Widows' and Orphans' Home, at Louisville. Her membership voted almost unanimously to pay the $1 assessment for each and every member, for five years, to the same, and paid it; and at the last election did the same thing in reference to paying 50 cents for five years on each member to the same charity, and they will pay it.

Halleck Lodge, I. O. O. F., was instituted September 22, 1853, with the following charter members: James Nelson, G. W. Hughes, Malcom McBride, James McGriffin and John S. Elkington. For several years the membership averaged from thirty to forty, but declined during the war, though it never suspended work. It has dwindled down to twelve active members. The hall property, with a comfortable storeroom underneath valued at $2,000, together with about $1,000 in Widows' and Orphans' Fund, $800 in cash and notes constitute the assets of the lodge, with no outstanding liabilities. The present officers are: W. H. Payne, N. G.; G. W. Hervey, V. G.; J. T. Batson, P. G.; W. H. H. Johnson, Treasurer; and Bruce Champ, Secretary.

As to the common schools of Millersburg, there is but little to be said. The place being what is termed a "college town," it is almost needless to say, that the common schools have never flourished to any great degree. Who taught the first school in the place, or where the first schoolhouse stood, is alike unknown at the present day. The early history of its schools is similar to that of other Kentucky towns, and while better than no schools at all, were far inferior to our present system of schools. Without going into an extended sketch of the common schools, we devote a brief space to the colleges and acadamies, which have made Millersburg widely and favorably known throughout the country.

The following sketch of the Millersburg Female College, is written by Dr. Gould, the President, for this work:

What is now known as Millersburg Female College was originally opened as the Millersburg Male and Female Seminary, in September, 1852, by Rev. John Miller, M. D., of the Kentucky Conference, Methodist Episcopal Church South, Col. Johnson had previously conducted in the village a female branch of his military school located at Blue Lick Springs. In 1854, Dr. George S. Savage, of the same church and conference, succeeded Dr. Miller; and in 1856 the name was changed to the Millersburg Male and Female Collegiate Institute. In 1859, the male department was set off as the Kentucky Wesleyan College; and the female, remaining in the old buildings, took the style and designation of Millersburg Female College.

In 1867, Dr. Savage was succeeded by Prof. Hamilton; he, in 1869, by Prof. Brown; he, in 1870, by Prof. W. H. Savage; he, in 1872, by Savage and Gould; they, in 1874, by Savage, Gould and Abbett; they, in 1875, by Gould and Abbett; and they, in 1877, by George T. Gould, who has since remained as sole proprietor and President.

On the night of December 29, 1878, the entire buildings, with their contents of pianos, desks, apparatus, furniture, etc., was destroyed by fire. The President, nothing daunted by such overwhelming loss, rented at once houses, rooms, furniture, everything necessary for continuing the school, and without the loss of a single day, conducted it to the close of the term in June. The community showed its interest by raising a fund of $3,500, as a loan, to aid in the erection of new buildings. These were begun in March, 1879, and in September of the same year, the school moved into the large, handsome and convenient edifice, which it now fills to overflowing.

This building is one of the largest and best arranged for the education of young ladies, to be met with anywhere in the State, and with its large and handsome grounds it is one of the chief ornaments of the county; heated by steam, and with numerous halls, galleries, and ventilating flues, comfort, health and convenience are admirably combined.

The school has shown a steady growth under its present management, until now it is the largest female school in the State, both in faculty and in number of students, and is rapidly spreading the fame of Bourbon County, as an educational center, throughout the South and West.

The course of study is extensive in literature, business, music and art; the corps of teachers, arranged upon the plan of subdivision of labor, is composed of eighteen specialists, able and distinguished in their respective departments; and the teaching is thorough and fully abreast of the times.

Altogether, the school is one of the most widely known and popular of the many schools in the South for the education of young women; and its progressive history in the last few years, gives large hope of even more eminent success in the future.

The following excellent sketch of the Kentucky Wesleyan College was written at our request, by Prof. D. W. Batson, President of the institution, and will be read with interest by all of its friends: The Kentucky Wesleyan College, located at Millersburg is the property of the Methodist Episcopal Church South, and is now under the immediate control of the Kentucky and Western Virginia Annual Conferences of that church.

Previous to the session of the Kentucky Conference in 1858, several friends of education in Millersburg undertook to establish in that town a male and female collegiate institute. The prime mover in the enterprise was Rev. T. P. C. Shellman, but he succeeded soon in interesting several others, and they were but a short time in raising some $10,000 or more. A building committee was appointed at once, consisting of Dr. A. G. Stitt, Mr. Alex S. Miller, and Mr. William Nunn; the grounds were purchased, just without the northern limits of the town, on a commanding eminence, and soon the foundations for a large building for the institute were in process of construction. This much was done in the summer of 1858.

In September of that year, the Kentucky Conference met in session in Millersburg. The members of the Conference catching the spirit of education of the people of Millersburg, resolved during the session to establish a school of high grade in the interest of the church, "for the promotion of literature, science, morality and religion." The grounds purchased for the Male and Female Collegiate Institute, with the incomplete foundations, together with all the subscriptions, were tendered the Conference just at that time by the proper authorities, and the Conference at once accepted, laying the corner-stone of the main building for the new institution they were about to establish, with imposing Masonic ceremonies, on the Saturday of the Conference session, September 11, 1858. Addresses were delivered on the occasion of laying the corner-stone, by Bishop H. H. Kavanaugh, Rev. Jefferson Hamilton, D. D., Judge William T. Moore and Hon. Garrett Davis. The building committee of the first enterprise was continued, and soon the walls of the Kentucky Wesleyan were in process of construction upon the foundations which had been begun for a male and female institute. An agent was appointed also before the adjournment of the Conference to secure subscriptions and donations toward an educational fund for the support of the new institution. By the succeeding fall, the fall of 1859, the sum of $57,000 in cash and in good and reliable notes had been secured, and January 12, 1860, the Board of Education of the Kentucky Annual Conference of the Methodist Episcopal Church South was chartered by the Legislature of Kentucky, with "all the rights and privileges of corporations, aggregate, etc., for the proper conduct and government of said college," subject to the supervision of the Conference, to whom the board was to report their acts and doings annually. The first Board of Education elected by the Conference consisted of the following gentlemen, six ministers and six laymen: Rev. W. C. Dandy, Rev. Daniel Stevenson, Rev. J. H. Linn, Rev. J. W. Cunningham, Rev. J. C. Harrison, Rev. Robert Hiner, David Thornton, Moreau Brown, Hiram Shaw, B. P. Tevis, William Nunn and A. G. Stitt. The members of the board were divided into three sections, consisting of two ministers and two laymen each, one section of four members going out of office each year, and the Conference electing each year four new members.

The outbreak of the civil war prevented the college from being opened at once. The building was used for a high school in charge successively of Prof. A. G. Murphy, Rev. T. J. Dodd and Rev. S. L. Robertson, till 1866. In September of that year, a Faculty of four Professors in the Literary Department and one in the Theological, having been duly elected, the college was opened in regular form Rev. Charles Taylor, A. M., M. D., D. D., was the first President. The Board of Education at that time consisted of Rev. Robert Hiner, Rev. H. P. Walker, Rev. T. N. Ralston, Rev. Seneca H. Hall, Rev. S. L. Robertson, Rev. T. J. Dodd, Dr. Joshua Barnes, Dr. A. G. Stitt, Moreau Brown, David Thornton and W. M. Leathers, with Rev. Robert Hiner, Chairman; Rev. S. L. Robertson, Secretary and Agent; and David Thornton, Esq., Treasurer. The total number of students the first year, the year 1866–67, was ninety; but there were no graduates till 1868, when Benjamin D. Best graduated in the Bachelor of Science course of study. Dr, Taylor continued President of the college till June, 1870, four years only. The last year the students numbered one hundred and forty-four—the largest attendance the institution had yet had. Dr. Taylor, however, felt under the necessity of resigning, and Rev. B. Arbogast, A. M., was elected President. About this time, the Western Virginia Conference was invited by the Kentucky Conference to become part owners of the college, and to give it their patronage. They subscribed a small amount toward erecting a building for students to room in, and have since had two representatives on the Board of Education. In June, 1872, President Arbogast, having become involved in business matters, resigned his position, and Prof. John Darly, A. M., Ph. D., who had been Professor of Natural Sciences in the institution for two years, was elected President. He con-

Jno. Allen Gano Sr.

tinued in the office till June, 1875, when he resigned, and gave up all further work in the school-room, having been actively engaged in teaching in schools of advanced grade for over forty years. He went to spend his remaining days with his daughter in New York City, but died the following year, after a very short illness. After Prof. Darly's resignation, Rev. T. J. Dodd, D. D., was elected President for a term of three years, but after serving the institution one year only, he was elected to a professorship in Vanderbilt University, at Nashville, Tenn., and resigned the presidency of the Kentucky Wesleyan; Rev. W. H. Anderson, D. D., was then elected President. He held the position also only three years, till June, 1879. In July, 1879, Prof. D. W. Batson, A. M., was elected President, with a Faculty consisting mostly of Alumni of the institution. Prof. Batson had been connected with the college himself ever since 1868, entering as a student in September of that year, graduating in June, 1874, and since that time filling the chair of Mathematics. At the time of his election to the presidency, he was the youngest College President in the United States, but being thoroughly interested in the work the board had called him to do, he succeeded in restoring the institution to something like its former prosperity, the attendance being almost doubled within the first two years after his election. He is President of the college at this (1882) writing.

The endowment of the college has never been what it should be, and the mistake was made of securing what endowment it has had, by granting scholarships entitling the holders to keep one student for each scholarship in the institution free of tuition, one year for every $10 contributed to the endowment. Hence, the college has had to labor under many difficulties that money would have removed. There have been several agents appointed at different times, but very little if anything has been added to the endowment since the war, so that now the productive funds of the institution amount to something more than $32,000 only.

The buildings and grounds, however, are well located, costing something near $30,000, and are capable of accommodating 150 to 200 students. A college library has also been begun in addition to two very respectable society libraries, and the institution is well supplied with chemical and philosophical apparatus, maps, charts, etc., and possesses the foundation of an excellent museum. The attendance upon the college for the first fifteen years of its existence, has averaged a little over eighty five students a year, representing some nine or ten different States.

The number of graduates ranging, since 1868, from one to seven each year, up to June, 1881, is fifty-five. Of that number, thirteen have entered the ministry of the church. Eleven have already entered, or are intending to enter, the law. A very respectable part of the number have chosen teaching as their life business, while a few have taken up medicine or pharmacy. The other avocations of life, such as farming, merchandising, banking, etc., are also pretty generally represented among the graduates. Of those who have spent a time at the college, without graduating, many occupy at present prominent places, both in Church and State. The college, therefore, considering the difficulties it has had in its way, has been a large success, and has occupied a worthy place among the institutions of learning throughout the land.—*Perrin.*

CHAPTER XV.

FLAT ROCK PRECINCT—ITS BOUNDARIES, TOPOGRAPHY AND SURFACE FEATURES—EARLY SETTLEMENT—LIFE IN THE WILDERNESS—IMPROVEMENTS AND PIONEER INDUSTRIES—SCHOOLS AND CHURCHES—VILLAGES, ETC.—MASONIC LODGE—SKELETON OF A MASTODON DISCOVERED.

THE division of Bourbon County, to which this chapter is devoted, is known as Flat Rock Precinct, and is No. 3 of the election precincts. It is situated in the eastern or southeastern part of the county, lying a little south of east from Paris. It is bounded north by Nicholas County and Millersburg Precinct, east by Nicholas County, south by Montgomery County, and west by North Middleton Precinct. In the northwestern part of the precinct the land is undulating, and in the southeastern part hilly and somewhat broken. The products are wheat, corn tobacco and grazing, the latter being carried to a considerable extent. Its principal stream is Hinkston Creek, which forms the boundary line between the precinct and Nicholas County, the main tributary of which is Boone's Creek. Rockbridge is a small tributary of Boone's Creek. Brush and Clear Creeks are small streams in the northeast part of the precinct, which flow into Hinkston. These streams afford an excellent system of drainage, and also an abundance of stock water. The original timber growth was oak, ash, hickory, walnut, elm, locust and sugar maple. Before subjected to cultivation, cane grew abundantly in portions of the precinct and there is still some of it to be found on Cane Ridge, so named from the heavy growth of cane there in early time.

Among the early settlers of Flat Rock Precinct, were were William Rodgers, Christopher Skillman, Hamilton Wilson, John Desha, Peter Banta, and others. Rogers and Skillman settled near Cane Ridge in an early day. Wilson was an old soldier of the war of 1812, and died quite recently. John Desha was a brother of Gov. Desha. Banta was an early settler, and an early surveyor in this section.

It is known to few persons, perhaps, in this precinct, that the mortal remains of a brother of the famous Daniel Boone repose within its sacred soil. On the farm of Anson Bryan, formerly the land of Jefferson and Anderson Bryan, on Boone's Creek, two miles from Flat Rock, near a buckeye tree, lie the remains of Boone, a brother of the old pioneer and Kentucky Indian fighter. He was killed on his way to the Blue Licks, being shot by an Indian from a hickory tree that stood near by. This was known as the "Buffalo Trace."

Another incident worthy of note in this chapter is the following: The grandfather of the Bryans, John Noble, was a soldier in the British Army, and was surrendered under Lord Cornwallis, at Yorktown. Dissatisfied with his army life, he determined never to return to the "old country," hence came to Kentucky, and settled in what now forms this precinct, where he remained for the rest of his life, an honorable and respected citizen.

Many others came in and settled in this part of the county, in early times, but they have been lost sight of and forgotten.

Life in the wilderness at an early period of the history of Kentucky, was hard, rough and dangerous. The lurking Indian was always ready to pounce upon his white foe, whenever necessity or imprudence led him away from his friends, or the protecting walls of the block-house or station. And after the power of the savages had been broken and danger from their incursions lessened, wilderness life still had its hardships and privations. Land had to be cleared, more comfortable houses built and crops cultivated. The means of cultivating the soil were meager. The plow was the old "Cary" or "barshear," usually drawn by a yoke of oxen, and other implements were of equally as poor quality. For harvesting the small grain, the reaping-hook and the scythe and cradle were used. Reapers and mowers had not been invented, nor any of the improved agricultural implements of the present day. Each member of the family, both male and female, had to work and perform their part of the labor in supporting life and building up a home in the wilderness. Household furniture was as primitive as the implements used in cultivating the crops. Wooden stools took the place of chairs, pewter plates and tin cups adorned the table, which was usually a rough-hewn slab; bedsteads were of the rudest kind, both in material and in construction, and the beds were often composed of leaves and grass, which honest toil rendered

"Soft as downy pillows are."

But the rich virgin soil amply repaid the husbandman for his toil, and gave forth rich harvests, and as the advancing years brought improvements in the modes of cultivations, and population increased, life became more endurable, until it reached the perfection we find at the present age.

Among the pioneer's early trials was the anxiety arising from the trouble of obtaining bread for his family. Few as were the agricultural implements then in use, the raising of a crop of corn in the rich soil was comparatively a light matter, but the converting of it into meal was a far more serious job. Pounding corn in a mortar and grinding it in the coffee-mill, were means often resorted to. The first mills built in the neighborhood were horse-mills. These were quite an improvement on hand mills and mortars, but would be considered poor makeshifts at the present day. Several horse-mills were built in what is now Flat Rock Precinct in early times, but of them we learned but little beyond the mere fact of their existence. The oldest mill now in the precinct is Ellison's mill, run by water-power. Owing to the fact that the streams are all small in this section, but few mills of any consequence has ever been built in the precinct, and the people have had to do their milling elsewhere.

Like all portions of Bourbon County, Flat Rock Precinct is well supplied with excellent macadamized roads. A pike runs from North Middleton to Plum Lick, known by the name of "Plum Lick Pike." The Cane Ridge & Paris pike leads from Paris to Flat Rock; the Cane Ridge & Jackstown pike connects those two places, which give to the road its name, and the Cane Ridge & North Middleton connects the place which give it its name. These pass in all directions, giving the inhabitants the most thorough means of travel and transportation. The first magistrates of Flat Rock Precinct were John F. Talbott and Stephen Terry. The present Justices are T. M. Squires and James N. Stone.

There are several villages in Flat Rock Precinct, but all of them put together would not make half a town. Flat Rock Village is the largest and most important, and has a white population of fifty, and a colored population of one hundred. It is situated on the Paris & Flat Rock pike, thirteen miles from Paris, and comprises, in business, one store, one drug store, and one blacksmith-shop. Socially, it contains two churches, one school, one Masonic lodge, and a colored church and school. A post office was established in 1840, and "Billy" Payne was Postmaster. In 1878, it was removed to Plum Lick. The Methodist Church was organized previous to 1850. Among the original members were J. R. Cray, F. M. Hinkle, Richard Hinkle and B. W. Soper. The first pastor was Rev. Mr. Brush. A church edifice was erected in 1849 by the Methodists and Christians in partnership, and used in common until 1877, when the Christians sold out to the Methodists, and built one of their own. The present membership of the Methodist Church is fifty, under the pastorate of Rev. J. W. Harris. The Christian Church was erected in 1877 at a cost of $2,000, and is a comely edifice. Previous to the building of it, the Christians worshiped with the Methodists as noted above. The present membership is 200, and their present pastor the Rev. Mr. Jones.

Hope Lodge, No. 246, A., F. & A. M., was organized in 1850. Its original officers were W. P. Bramlette, W. M.; Aquilla Robb, S. W.; James Donall, J. W.; and Edward Payne, Sec. The present officers are James R. Rodgers, W. M.; Edward Rice, S. W.; Richard Hopkins, J. W.; A. Evans, Sec.; and James Hopkins, Treas. There are thirty-one members on the rolls, and the lodge is in good working order, and out of debt.

Plum Lick is situated at the forks of Boone's Creek, five miles from North Middletown, in a northeast direction, and two and a half miles from the Montgomery County line. It has had quite a number of names, and if the world stands long enough, it will probably have a few more. It was first known by the classic, or rather unclassic name of "Pin Hook." This was afterward changed to Levy, but wherefore, deponent saith not. The origin of these names are unknown; upon the subject, history is silent. The next name bestowed upon the romantic little village is Plum Lick, the origin of which is likewise veiled in obscurity. The population of the place is forty souls and as many bodies, and the business is comprised in two stores and a blacksmith-shop. The post office was moved from Flat Rock to this place in 1878, and A. B. Thomason is Postmaster, and has been since its removal. Two mails are received per week. The first store was kept by a man named Nathan LaForgee. Since the adoption of the local option law, the village has been very quiet and orderly. Jackstown, in the northeast part of the precinct near the border, has one store and a blacksmith-shop. It is but a small collection of houses, and has very little business. Cane Ridge Post Office is located ten miles from Paris at Thomas Ashbrook's blacksmith-shop, and near the Cane Ridge Church. The first Postmaster was B. B. Bramlette, the present one is Thomas Ashbrook.

The following incident is of historical interest, and is here given that it may be perpetuated in the county's history. It was communicated to the *Western Citizen*, of August 26, 1853, by Mr. J. Miller, of Millersburg. The spot mentioned is in this precinct, and will be remembered by many of the old citizens, and the article itself is as follows:

In making an excavation a few days since, on the land of Mr. C. C. Rogers, in this county, about ten miles south of Millersburg, and the same distance east of Paris, on the South Fork of Brush Creek, one of the tributaries of Hinkston, the remains of a mastodon were discovered. That the animal or animals to which these belonged were of immense size, will appear from some measurements of the parts preserved, though in a greatly decayed condition.

A section of one of the tusks, consisting of two feet two inches of the anterior, or smallest extremity, measures twenty inches and a half in circumference at the largest end. This tusk was supposed to be over eight feet long when discovered. One of the grinders is eight inches long on the face, four wide, and nineteen in circumference; its weight is about six pounds. About two-thirds, as near as can be ascertained, of the right lower jaw is in a tolerable state of preservation, and has two of the grinders in position. The curved margin of this is three feet one inch in length, and the jaw is eight inches thick. Its depth immediately behind the last molar, and including the remains of the ramus, is about twelve inches. Only one of the vertebræ has as yet been secured (a dorsal); the breadth of this would make the spinal column more than fifteen inches from side to side, and the aperture for the passage of the spinal marrow measures three inches full; the spinous process of this bone must have been nearly two feet long. Diameter from the external margin of one of the condyles of the occipital bone to same margin of the other, ten inches full; diameter of th foramen magnum, three and a half inches. Circumference of the neck of the femur, sixteen and a half inches; circumference of the same below the trochanter minor, seventeen inches scant.

In the present condition of the remains, these of course are more or less imperfect measures, but assuming the basis of calculation adopted by the naturalists in the Newburg, N. Y., specimen discovered in 1845, and believed to be one of the largest of the *Mastodon Maximus* of Cuvier, this animal would be above twelve feet high, nineteen feet long, and weight about nineteen thousand pounds. The parts I have been able to secure are in such a decayed state that no attempt at complete restoration can be successful. There is also very conclusive evidence that the parts obtained belong to two skeletons at least; the angles of three lower maxilaries being now among the fragments discovered and in my possession. Two of these belong to the left, and one to the right side. The teeth in that of the right side, and in the more perfect one of the left do not correspond, and the diameter of the jaws is very different. The Messrs. Rogers intend prosecuting the search for the remainder of the skeletons at a future time. Through the politeness and attention of these gentlemen and Col. Ware, these remains have fortuna'ely been secured. They are now undergoing a process by which they will be rendered hard and durable, and capable of being handled. The skeletons were imbedded in a low, marshy situation, near a fine stream of spring water, surrounded by high undulating land of the very best quality in this or any other State. It was first occupied by the white settlers more than half a century since.

—*Perrin.*

CHAPTER XVI.

NORTH MIDDLETOWN PRECINCT—TOPOGRAPHICAL AND DESCRIPTIVE—PIONEER OCCUPATION—EARLY TRIALS AND TROUBLES—ROADS, BRIDGES, ETC.—INDUSTRIES—VILLAGES—CHURCHES AND PIONEER PREACHERS—SCHOOL AND SCHOOLHOUSES—KENTUCKY CLASSICAL AND BUSINESS COLLEGE.

NORTH MIDDLETOWN, known as Election Precinct No. 4, lies southeast of Paris, and is bounded on the north by Millersburg Precinct, on the east by Flat Rock Precinct and Montgomery County, south by Montgomery and Clark Counties and west by Paris and Clintonville pikes. The surface varies from undulating and rolling, to broken and hilly, in southern and eastern portions, and along the numerous streams. It is separated from Flat Rock Precinct by Cane Ridge, the soil of which, from a greater proportion of clay, is not so easily affected by drought. The principal streams are Stoner Creek and its numerous tributaries. Stoner Creek flows into the precinct from Clark County, traversing it from southeast to northwest, and receiving as tributaries, Donelson Creek, Indian Creek, Scott's Creek and Harrod's Creek, all of which flow northwest. Strode's Creek flows through the western part in a north direction. The soil is very fertile, and most of the precinct is devoted to grazing, no effort being made to raise any more corn or small grain than is needed for home consumption. Sheep and cattle raising is the principal industry. Upon the whole, it is one of the rich and flourishing precincts of the county.

The first settlement in what is now North Middletown Precinct, is supposed to have been made by Peter Houston. He and two brothers, James and Robert, came to Kentucky from North Carolina, with Daniel Boone upon his second trip to the State, the former settling on Cane Ridge, about two miles northeast of North Middletown Village, where he lived for many years. His ancestors came over in the Mayflower, and were among the sufferers of Plymouth Rock. He built a malt-house here ninety-five years ago, and for a long period, furnished all the distilleries in Bourbon County with malt. He was a soldier in the war of 1812. William Davis was an early settler, and squatted near the Clark County line. He died there some years later, and his family moved West. John Lander settled on the place now owned by W. D. Gay, where he run a distillery for more than twenty years. Charles Lander, his father, settled near North Middletown Village in a very early day. Stephen Kines, John and Ephraim Herriott, Patrick and Robert Scott and John Forden, were all early settlers in the vicinity of the village of North Middletown. Many other families there were, who might be mentioned with the early settlement of the precinct, but their names have been forgotten in the lapse of time.

The first decade or two after the settlement of this section by white people, were years of toil and danger and suffering. We, of this day of peace and plenty, can form little idea what our ancestors had to undergo seventy-five and a hundred years ago in the wilds of Kan-tuck-ee. To support their families and guard them from the dangers of wild beasts and savages, often put them to their wits' ends. Not until after the close of the war of 1812, was perfect peace and tranquillity secured to Kentucky. After this the beautiful and rich lands of Central Kentucky was rapidly settled and occupied.

Among the early industries of the precinct were a number of mills and distilleries. Robert Owen, whose father, Thomas Owen, came from Maryland, and settled near the present town of Winchester, built a mill and distillery in 1806. The mill was a horse-power tread-wheel, the first mill of the kind in Bourbon County. He operated the distillery about thirty years. "Those were the days," said an old gentleman, "of honest whisky, when one bushel of meal made two gallons of whisky, which sold at 25 cents per gallon." James Wells had a grist-mill one mile west of North Middletown, where Seamands' mill now stands. About 1820, Maj. Manson Seamands bought Wells out, and attached horse-power, in order to run in dry weather. The mill is now owned and run by Preston J. Seamands, having been in his family for sixty years. The stones used by Wells were native Laurel County rock. The mill has been greatly improved, and now has two run of excellent buhrs, with a capacity of 200 bushels of corn and 100 bushels of wheat per day. It is a commodious three-story building, valued at some $10,000. The dam is made entirely of locust logs. Excellent pikes traverse the precinct in every direction. The Paris & Mount Sterling pike runs east and west through the entire precinct. The Cane Ridge pike runs from North Middletown to the Paris & Flat Rock pike, which bounds the precinct on the north. The Plum Lick pike, from North Middletown to Plum Lick, a distance of five miles; the Bigstown pike, toward Winchester; the North Middletown & Clintonville Pike, and the Seamands' Mill pike, which runs to Stony Point, leave very little dirt road in the precinct. Good substantial bridges span most of the streams where the roads cross them, several of which are covered bridges. A daily stage line pass over the Paris & Mount Sterling pike, between those two cities.

North Middletown Village is situated on Paris & Mount Sterling pike, two miles southeast of Paris, and twelve northwest of Mount Sterling; it has about three hundred and fifty population. The original name of the place was "Swinneytown," in honor of an early settler of the neighborhood. It was incorporated as a town in 1818, and its name changed to North Middletown. The name Middletown was given to it in consequence of its situation between Paris and Mount Sterling, and being midway between Millersburg and Winchester. Afterward the name "North" was added to it to distinguish it from Middletown, in Jefferson County. The first house in North Middletown was built by William Adair, who kept a tavern in it at an early day. The first store was kept by James Cogswell about the year 1815. The post-office is kept by John B. Stivers. The business of the town is comprised in the following: Six stores (three grocery, two dry goods, one drug store), one bank. one saloon, two physicians, one Masonic lodge, one college, one district school, one livery stable, two churches, three blacksmith-shops, three wood-shops, two colored churches and one colored school.

The first church in North Middletown Village was built in 1823, as a union church by four different denominations, viz.: Methodist, Baptist, Presbyterian and "New-Light," or Christian. It was torn down in 1879, and a large brick schoolhouse erected in its place. The town has now two churches.

The Methodist Episcopal Church South, located in the village of North Middletown, is an old church, and was one of the four mentioned above, as building the union church in the village. The present church edifice was built in 1848, and was dedicated by Rev. H. B. Bascom, before he became a bishop. Those prominently connected with the building of it were Jonathan Owen, George W. Owen, John W. Scott, John C. Hall, and Stephen Kimes. Old "Father" James, Frank Philips, Dr. George Savage, T. J. Dodd, George T. Gould, Dr. Charles Taylor, Dr. R. Reed are among the ministers that have filled the pulpit during the last fifty years. The Rev. T. P. C. Shelman held a successful revival many years ago, during which forty persons joined the church. The present pastor is Rev. J. W. Harris. This church has furnished considerable material for forming new churches, and has lost a great many by death and removals, until but forty members are now on the records, and the church is mainly supported by a few families.

The North Middletown Christian Church also worshiped, for a short time, in the old Union Church. The history of this church, which dates back to 1817, is rather interesting, and we give it at some length, from facts furnished us by Elder W. I. Mason. It was originally of the Baptist denomination, and among the first members were James Sims, Enoch Mason and John Rash. They were regular attendants at their church in Montgomery County, but often met in their own neighborhood for worship in private houses. In 1818, James Sims built a very large brick house, one mile east of the village, about 30x25 feet, for the purpose of being used as a place of worship. Mason was in the same year licensed to preach. In 1819, they organized a church, consisting almost entirely of those who had gotten letters from the church at Grassy Lick, in Montgomery County. It is not known how many went into the organization, but among them were James Sims and wife and daughters, John Rash and wife, Enoch Mason and wife, and John Campbell and wife. Elder Mason was their pastor. It is believed that the first persons ever immersed in the neighborhood were Miss Louisa Harris, a young lady, and two aged colored women, named respectively Sally and Elly, mother and daughter. Mr. Mason gives the following sketch of the three men most prominent in the forming of this church, viz.: Sims, Rash and Mason. "James Sims was about fifty years of age and a leading man in the neighborhood. He possessed good business qualities, was wealthy for those times, had a large share of common sense, a good library, the contents of which he read and understood, and was a good conversationalist. He was extensively known, and entertained many strangers with unbounded hospitality. He died, at the age of eighty-seven, in Jefferson County. John Rash was born and raised in Clark County, and was converted at the age of thirteen, under the preaching of Elder Ambrose Dudley. He was conscientious, honest and candid, without guile and transparent as glass. He was firm almost to a fault, and if he had lived in times of religious persecution would have courted the stake if his Master's cause had required it. He died, in 1842, in Nicholas County. Enoch Mason was younger than either Sims or Rash. His moral character was without reproach and he had the confidence of his brethren. He had a well-balanced mind, was warm in his feelings and gifted and enthusiastic as a speaker. He preached extensively in the adjoining counties and had charge of his home church until his death, which occurred in the fall of 1824."

Rev. Jeremiah Vardeman, a minister of great power and eloquence, often visited the church, and Dr. Fishback, of Lexington, and many other noted preachers. In 1821, a large building of hewed logs was put up, of the style of most country churches, and was about twenty feet wide and forty-eight feet long. It has long since disappeared, and the acre of ground donated to it by John Black is now covered over with graves and inclosed by a rude stone wall. In 1823, a spirit of inquiry arose in this church upon some of the views and practices that prevailed among the Baptists. This finally resulted, in 1828, of the church embracing the new doctrine, as it was called, of Alexander Campbell, with one exception—Daniel Bradley, who took out a letter of dismissal. After the death of Elder Mason, Elder William Morton preached three years, and was succeeded by Thomas Parrish, an eminent preacher. Elder John Smith was the next preacher, and proved an excellent pastor. In the fall of 1834, Elder Aylet Raines was called, and was the pastor uninterruptedly for fourteen years. In 1838, Elder John T. Johnson, of Georgetown, held a protracted meeting at this church, during which 184 persons joined the church and were immersed, and, as it was cold weather, ice nearly a foot thick had to be cut to get to the water. Dr. A. Adams was the next pastor, followed by Elder W. R. McChesney. The membership from 1840 to 1850 was about three hundred. Many other able divines followed those mentioned until the pastorate of the present minister. The present church edifice was built in 1842. The membership is now 250 and the pastor is Elder R. Graham. Mrs. Elizabeth Trimble is the only one of the early members now living.

A Masonic lodge was organized in North Middletown in 1824 as Washington Lodge, No. 79, and William Duncan was the first Master; N. L. Lindsay, Senior Warden, and Samuel Thomas, Junior Warden. It was established during the anti-Masonic excitement of Morgan, which reduced the membership down to three, viz.: James Cogswell, Samuel Thomas and N. L. Lindsay. But when the excitement died away, it revived again, and is now in a prosperous condition. Ground was originally donated by Col. Cogswell, on which to erect a building for church, school and Masonic purposes. The present officers are John B. Stivers, Worshipful Master; Charlton Lowe, Senior Warden; John B. Grimes, Junior Warden; Isaac Laughfin, Treasurer; and James Oden, Secretary.

North Middletown Deposit Bank was incorporated in 1869, and commenced business January 1, 1870. The capital stock was $50,000, with the privilege of increasing it to $100,000. The first officers were T. J. Evans, President; A. T. Mitchell, Cashier; and A. L. Bean, James Scott, J. S. Berry, Hy Gaitskill and John Trimble, Directors. The bank has made money and is now controlled by the following board and officers, viz.: J. S. Berry, President; W. W. Hedges, Cashier; and E. K. Thomas, T. J. Evans, Charles Harris, D. H. Bratton and James Scott, Directors.

North Middletown Woolen Mill was built by Reuben Lewis about the year 1830, who operated it with horse-power. Lewis sold out to Joseph Mathews, and he, in company with his brother-in-law, W. P. Schooler, enlarged and put in steam. It did a very successful business during the late war. The mill and machinery were removed to Mount Sterling in 1881.

Kentucky Classical and Business College, located in the village of North Middletown, was established, in 1860, by J. T. Patterson, now of Hamilton College, Lexington. It was originally known as "Patterson Institute," a name given to it in honor of its founder. In 1877, E. V. Zollars succeeded to the management of the institution, a position he still occupies. This school claims to be one of the best in Central Kentucky. Its full course is comprised in a preparatory department, which in every detail is a model school. The collegiate department embraces five distinct courses of study, viz.: English, Classical, Latin Scientific, Business and Normal. In addition to the departments named, there is a musical department, an art department, etc. The institution is capable of keeping a large number of students, and the boarding of the sexes is entirely distinct, all young ladies from abroad being expected to board in the institution.

The buildings of the Kentucky Classical and Business College are large and commodious, and stand in the center of a beautiful lot of seven acres of ground, finely improved and handsomely ornamented with forest trees and evergreens, which affords a most delightful place for outdoor exercise. The rooms are sufficient in number and size to accommodate eighty young ladies, and the entire part of the building is heated by steam. The following appears in the published catalogue of 1880–81: "We are thoroughly equipped to carry on our various departments and courses in detail, giving ample time to every item of work. The numerous practical drills that we have introduced into our school from time to time, will be made more prominent than ever before. We are now able to say with confidence that our students will have the benefit of a good library, selected with special reference to the wants of the school. The health and beauty of our location is not surpassed in the State, our large grounds afford room for ample out-door exercise, and the isolated situation enables our young ladies to enjoy a freedom from restraint, which contributes largely to both their health and happiness. With our sightly grounds, our commodious buildings in thorough repair, heated and ventilated by the best modern methods, our pleasant surroundings in general, we think we can offer young ladies a home in which the *ennui* so common to school life will be almost a stranger."

The first session of the Kentucky Classical and Business College, under the supervision of the present manager, Mr. Zollars, numbered one hundred and fifty pupils, forty of whom were boarders. At the present time (1881) there are sixty-nine boarders in the institution, with a large number of day scholars. The present faculty is as follows: E. V. Zollars, President, and Professor of Chemistry and Mathematics; W. S. Smith, Principal of Normal Department; A. Skidmore, Professor of Ancient Languages, etc., Miss M. Zollars, Teacher of Intermediate Department and German; Miss Carrie Van Dervort, Primary Department and Model School; Miss Jessie Florence, Teacher of Composition and History; Miss Addie E. Thomas, Assistant in Mathematics and Science; A. S. Dabney, Sciences, Ancient Languages, and Teacher of French; Miss Alice Hobbs, Teacher of Music; Miss Annie Gaff, Teacher of Vocal Culture; Miss Emma Thomas, Assistant Teacher in Music; Miss Sallie B. Ireland, Teacher of Drawing, Painting, etc.

The first school ever taught in what is now North Middletown Precinct was in an old log house one mile east of the village, on the farm now owned by John Arnold. James Brown was the first teacher. Education has made considerable progress in the precinct since that period, as evidenced in the fact of the excellent institution at North Middletown Village, already noticed. The people have always evinced their interest in educational and religious matters. This led to religious meetings coeval with the settlement of the precinct. The first regularly established church was one and a half miles east of the village, and was known as "Lower Bethel." It was of the Missionary Baptist denomination, and was organized previous to 1800. The church was built in that year, and many noted preachers administered to the little flock, among whom were Jeremiah Vardeman and Enoch Mason. The latter, together with his wife and daughter, are buried just back of the pulpit.—*Perrin.*

CHAPTER XVII.

CLINTONVILLE PRECINCT—GENERAL DESCRIPTION—PHYSICAL FEATURES—EARLY SETTLEMENT—DIFFICULTIES ENCOUNTERED—PIONEER INDUSTRIES AND IMPROVEMENTS—THE CHURCH HISTORY—SCHOOLS AND VILLAGES—AN OLD MASONIC LODGE.

"I know that there hath been a change."

CLINTONVILLE PRECINCT lies in the southern part of Bourbon County, with Clark and Fayette Counties on the south and southwest, and with Hutchison, Paris and North Middletown Precincts on the west, north and east, and is No. 5 of the election precincts of the county. It is fine blue grass land, gently rolling, and has some of the best stock and grazing farms in this celebrated stock region. The original timber was walnut, ash, hackberry, sugar maple, box elder, buckeye, elm, honey and black locust, with a very little oak. The precinct was covered with cane when first settled, but in 1799 this all suddenly died out. It is drained by Strode's and Green Creeks and their branches. The latter flows in a northeast direction, and is very crooked; Strode's Creek merely touches the southeast corner of the precinct. There are quite a number of small brooks which flow into these streams. No railroads and but few villages mar the beauty of this fine agricultural section.

The settlement of Clintonville Precinct dates back beyond the memory of the living. Among its pioneers we may mention Henry Crose, Alexander McGill, James Dennison, George Renick, Spencer Buchannon, Reuben Clarkson, Avery Grimes, Green Clay, Daniel Thatcher, Maj. Levi Crose, James Bristow, John McKinney, Julius Clarkson, James Jones, Adam Funk, James Runnick, Dennis Leary, Henry Parvin, John Cunningham, John Duncan, William Fisher, Henry Segester, John Hildreth, Thomas Boges, B. S. Mills, Amos Duke, John Harper, the Cutrights and Shropshires, Dr. Clay, James Lampton, James Kendall, Ancil Clarkson, John Dickinson, Jo McConnell, John Hazelrick, the Stipps, Harry Wigington, Samuel Muir, the Hutchcrafts, John Hornback and others. These were all early settlers in what is now Clintonville Precinct, but to say who was the first one of the number to erect a cabin here is to assume quite a responsibility. It is a point we shall not attempt to establish. Most of these men came from Virginia about the close of the Revolutionary war, or soon after, for the purpose of locating farms in the rich Western lands. Many of them still have descendants living in Bourbon County, but they themselves have long since passed to their final account.

Green Clay, who is mentioned as being among them, lived most of his life in Madison County, but owned considerable land in this precinct. He was a man of prominence, a surveyor, and thus obtained large tracts of land for his services. It is told of him that when a mere boy, he was employed as a chain carrier by surveyors, and being very handy with a pen, he would get hold of their books, and make copies of surveys, plats, etc. When he had thus procured as many copies as he wanted, he struck a bee-line for Richmond, Va., and got patents on his lands, and when the surveyors came in for the same purpose, found themselves "just in time to be a little too late." In the war of 1812, he tendered his services to the Government, and was made Brigadier General of the first Kentucky troops that went out. He led 3,000 of his brave Kentuckians to the relief of Fort Meigs, when besieged by the British and Indians, and upon his arrival, cut his way through their lines into the fort. The opinion entertained of the military abilities of Gen. Clay by Gen. Harrison was such that, when he left Fort Meigs, he placed it under the command of Clay. While in command, the fort was invested by 1,500 British and Canadians, and 5,000 Indians under Tecumseh, but so stoutly was it defended, that the enemy soon raised the siege and retired.

John McKinney, another of the early settlers mentioned above, and who died in this precinct, taught the first school ever established in Lexington. He was familiarly known as "Wild Cat" McKinney, from the fact of having a most terrific fight with a wild-cat, which attacked him in his schoolhouse, while teaching this pioneer school at Lexington. The fight was a severe one, and lasted several minutes, when he succeeded in killing the vicious beast, just as several persons, in answer to his cries for help, came to his rescue. So exhausted was he from the encounter that he kept his bed for several days afterward. Levi Crose, another of these early settlers, was a blacksmith, and supposed to be one of the first in this part of the county. He had a gunsmith's shop also, and lived one and a half miles west of Clintonville. Henry Crose was a Revolutionary soldier, and came here very early. He entered about 2,000 acres of land in what is now Clintonville Precinct. This land is mostly owned now by Alex Johnston and Robert Estill. The Cutrights and Shropshires had three sons apiece, all large men. A kind of feud existed between the families, and finally the six young men decided to settle it by a regular fist fight, a la Sullivan and Ryan. Moses Shropshire, one of the boys, was a member of the church, and was brought up before the ecclesiastical tribunal and disciplined for fighting. In his acknowledgments to the church, he said, "Yes, I had a fight and got whipped, but it was through my own awkwardness that I did get whipped," apparently caring for nothing but to excuse himself for getting whipped. Julius Clarkson, another of the number mentioned, was a very early settler, and is believed to have raised the first tobacco ever raised in this precinct. He cultivated tobacco very extensively. James Jones, also an early settler, was one of the first to manufacture tobacco, and used to sell it, after it was manufactured, at *sixpence* per pound. People came long distances to buy it. Jones is said to have been an upright and honest man, and very highly respected. Adam Funk settled very early, and was a man of great physical power, weighing some 250 pounds. He used to boast that he weighed thirty pounds when he was born; he and a man named Palmer once had a fist fight, which created great interest throughout the neighborhood.

The first settlements were made in Clintonville Precinct before the country was safe from Indian depredations, and the people were often in great danger from prowling bands. They were, however, a brave and fearless people, many had participated in the Indian wars of the time, and some in the Revolutionary war, and were used to hardships and dangers. And even after the storm of savage warfare died away beyond the Ohio, other trials and dangers remained and had to be overcome. The wilderness had to be subdued, lands cleared, houses built and roads and mills established. It was only after years of toil that the pioneers were able to enjoy prosperity.

Among the early mills of what now forms Clintonville Precinct were those of Bristow, Pettit and Reed. The latter was the first owner of a mill, which afterward passed into the hands of Mr. Hornback, then to Mr. Thatcher. It was a saw and grist mill, and is now owned by Matt D. Hume. Pettit's was also a saw and grist mill, and was built on Green Creek; the land now is owned by Squire Cunningham. Bristow's Mill was first a horse-power tread-wheel, but afterward water-power; he also had a saw-mill in connection. The mill was discontinued about 1850. Levi Crose had a mill, and had a kind of threshing machine attached to it. It was rather a unique affair. Sev-

Paris Mills, Wm. Shaw, Prop. Paris, Ky.

eral distilleries may be included in the early industries of the precinct. William Tillett and Daniel Thatchel both built distilleries in an early day. The latter was on land now owned by Samuel Clay, and was built as early as 1817; Tillett's was on land now owned by Thomas H. Clay. Henry Segester had a distillery on Green Creek, where John Livar now lives. There was also a distillery on land now owned by Jake Eppisun, but it is not known who built or owned it. Dennison has a distillery at Clintonville previous to 1800. A hemp factory was built by Henry T. Duncan about 1844, on land now owned by Charlton Alexander. It continued in operation until about 1855.

The first roads were laid out where the pikes are now located. Many of the old roads have been constructed into pikes. The precinct is now well supplied with pikes, of which the following may be mentioned: The Winchester pike forms the boundary line between Clintonville and North Middletown Precincts; the Paris & Clintonville pike passes through almost from north to south; Clintonville & Thatcher's Mill pike, east and west through the southern part; Stony Point & Seamands' Mill pike zigzags east and west through the center, while Bethlehem & Paris pike forms the boundary between Clintonville and Hutchison Precincts.

There has been two or three murders committed within the limits of the precinct. About 1806, John Price was killed one night in his own house—by whom was never known. He lived on land now owned by James E. Clay, and the house in which it occurred was ever after believed to be haunted. Several parties who were known to be brave, and had often faced death on the battle-field without quailing, tried to sleep in the house, but agreed afterward with the popular belief, that it was actually inhabited by the supernatural. About 1800, a man named Smith killed a man with a rock, and some years later a man named Scott was found dead in a barn. But such facts as these are better forgotten than perpetuated on the pages of history.

The first tavern in the precinct was kept at what was known as "Cutright's Station," about a mile from where Clintonville now stands, on land owned at present by Alex Johnson. It was kept by a man of the name of Stipp, who was a very large man, and a great fighter, and used to pitch his unruly guests outdoors without ceremony. Levi Crose kept the first blacksmith shop in the precinct, Dr. Clay was the first physician, and Finch Scruggs the first Postmaster.

The only church in the precinct outside of the village of Clintonville, is Stony Creek Church, situated at the crossing of the Stony Point and Seamands' Mill and the Paris and Winchester pikes, on the line between Clintonville and North Middletown Precincts.

Stony Point Regular Baptist Church, of Clintonville Precinct, was organized August 24, 1863. Some of its first members were from Green Creek Church, Middletown Precinct, same county. They left their church, owing to dissensions among its members, and united with the Stony Point people under the direction of Elders Barrows, Dudley, Reding, Eve and Morris and Lewis Corbin was installed as the first pastor, and was active as such until the infirmities of old age compelled a partial relinquishment of his pastoral duties, and on the third Saturday in December, 1829, Elder William Rash was called to his assistance. Elder Corbin presided as Moderator at business meetings of the society, however, besides doing light pastoral work up to within a short time of his death, which occurred about the year 1840, when Elder Rash was duly elected pastor, and continued as such until his death in 1855. Elder E. S. Dudley succeeded Elder Rash, and has, up to the present time, continued in that capacity. The church, during Elders Corbin and Rash's time, was very prosperous and had a large membership, but of late years, owing to the departure of its oldest and most active members, by by death and otherwise, has dwindled to a small company of twelve members, who still worship in the original log building, which has been slightly improved in appearance by an outside dress of clapboards. The building is located on the Middletown and Frankfort Cross Roads. The society first formed at Wigington's Mills, and had a membership of forty persons. The matter of a location for their building was discussed at that time, and also a title. They decided to locate it at a point near the mill, and it being somewhat stony, it was decided to call it Stony Point Church. The society not being able to purchase this location, the present one was donated to them, upon which they immediately built. The generous donor was Capt. Davidson, at that time a wealthy land-owner of Clintonville.

The first school believed to have been in the precinct was taught about two miles west of Clintonville, by a one-legged man named Logwell. The Armenian Baptists worshiped in the same house for a number of years. Another early school was taught one mile east of Clintonville, on the farm of Dennis Leary. This schoolhouse was burned about the year 1825. There are but two public schools in the precinct, one at Jones' Cross Roads, a place consisting of two or three houses, and the other at Clintonville. The people seem alive to the cause of education, but do not take a proper interest in the support of common schools.

The village of Clintonville is situated at the intersection of the Paris & Clintonville, the Chilesburg, and the Clintonville & Thatcher's Mill pikes, about fifteen miles from Paris. It was originally called Stipp's Cross Roads, from the fact that George and John Stipp were the first settlers in the vicinity. Willis Young had the first store; E. H. Parrish afterward had a store. In early times it was the scene of a great deal of horse-racing. The wealthiest men of the neighborhood would often come out to witness the fun barefooted with their breeches rolled up nearly to their knees. In 1858, Stipp's Cross Roads, which had changed its name to Clintonville, doubtless from the Masonic Lodge which had been established there under the name of De Witt Clinton Lodge, was incorporated, and John K. Hildreth was elected Mayor, and John Rutledge, Marshal. The organization lasted about three years, when, at the outbreak of the war it ceased to exist as a municipal town. The place now contains one store kept by William Heathman, who is also Postmaster; one blacksmith shop, two churches, one Masonic Lodge, an excellent school, and a colored church and school.

The Masonic lodge located here is one of the old lodges of the State, and from old records appears to have been organized about 1825–26. It is designated De Witt Clinton Lodge, No. 86, and among its early members were Abner Cunningham, William Price, William P. Hume, Julius C. Bristow, Mathew D. Hume, Benjamin Parvin, Walter Jones, Thomas Parker, A. Lawell, Levi Crose, William Chamblin, John C. W. McKinney, John Cutright, Samuel Leary, Thomas Hughes, Charles S. Clay, Robert Ellis, Cornelius Cutright. An old record-book we were shown, supposed to be the first, the officers were: James Brassfield, W. M.; William Pierce, S. W.; Jesse Cunningham, J. W.; Abner Cunningham, S. D.; and J. C. Bristow, J. D. This lodge was organized in a church, which has long since disappeared, the meetings were afterward held up-stairs in George Stipp's house. After working thus for several years, it was moved to the upper story of the store of C. F. Scruggs, and a few years later, bought a house and three-quarters of an acre of ground for $175, which was used until about 1870. The lodge, then together with the public school, erected an excellent brick building at a cost of $3,260, the lodge occupying the upper, and the school the lower story. It is in a healthy condition, was once very strong in membership, but removals, and the formation of new lodges, has brought the number of its members down to fifteen. The meetings are held on the 2d Saturday of each month, at 2 P. M. in the afternoon.

The Presbyterian Church at Clintonville was organized very early. The church was built on land donated by Henry Cutright, and among the early members were Sidney Clay (who contributed largely toward building it), Squire Menniss, Andrew Scott, and several of his family, William Scott, Isaac Van Meter, William Moxley, wife and daughter, Isaac Cunningham, Jilson Berryman and wife and William Trimble. Rev. Mr. Hall was the first minister. The first trustees were Sidney Clay, William Trimble and Andrew Scott. The membership was never very large—about thirty; the church flourished until the death of Mr. Clay. After his death dissensions arose, and the regular services were at last discontinued. The church building was taken for a schoolhouse, and finally about 1867, was burned. The present edifice was built a few years ago, is a frame, and is of modern style—has a steeple, organ, etc. Rev. Mr. Boggs is the present pastor, and the membership is about sixty. Sunday school is regularly carried on. There is a tradition that the first church here was built of hewed logs previous to 1800, and that Rev. Mr. Lyle was the preacher, and also taught school in the neighborhood; that about 1828–30 the brick was built, which is mentioned above, as being finally taken for a schoolhouse. Of this early history, however, but little is now remembered.

The Reformers or Christians organized a church here early, and erected a brick building at a cost of about $2,000. Among the first ministers were Elder Raines, who preached to them for eleven years. This old church was torn down previous to the war, and a neat frame church built, which also cost some $2,000. About the year 1837, a revival meeting was held here by Elders John A. Gano and John T. Johnson, and over one hundred were converted. This was a union church when first built, and the land was deeded to the church by Jacob Tenebaugh. The present frame church is 45x70 feet, Elder L. H. Reynolds is the pastor, the membership is about 100; Isaac Stipp and William Heathman, Elders; John, William and James Stipp, Deacons. A flourishing Sunday school is maintained.—*Perrin.*

CHAPTER XVIII.

HUTCHINSON PRECINCT — DESCRIPTION AND TOPOGRAPHY — THE COMING OF THE PIONEER — EARLY STRUGGLES WITH DANGERS AND PRIVATIONS—VILLAGES—PIONEER IMPROVEMENTS—MACADAMIZED ROADS—RELIGIOUS AND EDUCATIONAL—HUTCHINSON ACADEMY.

THIS precinct, one of the most interesting, and one of the richest in historical incidents. lies in a southwest direction from Paris, and is bounded on the north by Hume & Bedford pike, south and east by Bethlehem & Paris pike, north and west by Fayette County, and is known as Election Precinct No. 6. The precinct is drained by Houston Creek and its tributaries. The main stream of Houston runs north through the center and empties into Stoner Creek. Among its tributaries are Smith's Creek and Little Houston. These streams water and drain the country well through which they flow, and afford an abundance of free stock water. The surface of Hutchinson Precinct is undulating and beautiful, without hills or bluffs, but sufficiently rolling to avoid monotony. The timber was originally very plentiful, and is still abundant in certain localities, and consists of oak, elm, hickory, sugar-maple, walnut, etc., etc. The people are engaged in farming and stock-raising, it being a fine grazing section. Much attention is given to sheep-raising. In the last few years, a number of farmers have engaged in the cultivation of tobacco. The Kentucky Central Railroad passes through the precinct, and Hutchinson Station affords ample means of shipping the surplus products of the neighborhood.

In the early settlement of Hutchinson Precinct some noted and historic families are included. One of the oldest residents of the precinct now living is Greenup H. De Jarnette, a namesake of Gov. Greenup, who was a near relative of his grandmother De Jarnette. His great-grandmother married first a man named William Hoy, and afterward John Calloway. She was among the first settlers at Boonesboro, and was noted for her prudence and sagacity. When Du Quesne, with his allied force of whites and Indians, made his attack on Boonesboro in August, 1778, and sent into the besieged, a proposition for nine men to come out and treat, she warned them against the treachery of the Indians. When the nine men were seized by the Indians, and were fired upon by the main body, she stood by the gate with a heavy iron panhandle in her hand ready to brain the first savage who attempted to enter. She died a few years ago in Montgomery County, at the great age of 112 years. Mr. De Jarnette's grandfather came from Cumberland County, Va., and settled in Madison County in an early day. His wife was Judith Johnson, a cousin of Hon. R. M. Johnson, Vice President of the United States from 1837 to 1841. His oldest son, and father of Greenup De Jarnett, whose name was John, married a daughter of William Hoy, who was in the fort at Boonesboro. He was one of the first men to volunteer in the war of 1812, and while stationed at Fort Meigs, he was taken sick and died at the age of thirty, leaving a young wife and four children.

James S. Jacoby, living near Hopewell Church, is another of the early settlers in this precinct. The date 1791 is on the chimney of the house in which he has lived all his life. Mr. Jacoby's parents were both German, and their early history has some of the romance of a sensation novel. They became acquainted on board ship, the destination of both being America, and when the ship touched England, they went ashore and were married. Upon their arrival in America they settled in Virginia, and in 1875 emigrated to Kentucky, settling upon the place where Mr. Jacoby now lives. The latter is of the third generation that has occupied this farm. His grandfather settled it originally ; dying in 1787, it was occupied by his widow and her sons, who built the present residence. It was the home of Mr. Jacoby's father all of his life, and at his death it descended to the present owner, now in his sixty-sixth year, who, with the exception of a few years in Georgetown and Maysville, has spent his whole life upon it as did his father before him. His father was drafted in the war of 1812, and his uncles, Ralph and Fred, were both in the battle of the Thames, under Col. R. M. Johnson—Fred was killed in this battle. Mr. Jacoby's father married Mary Stark, a daughter of James Stark, who was among the early settlers of this section. Mr. Stark settled near where Hutchinson Station now stands when the Indians were troublesome. He frequently left his plow at the alarms of approaching danger, and carried the children to the fort at Bryant Station. Upon one occasion he was returning from Lexington, accompanied by a man named Peyton, who was riding a little in advance of him, when he (Peyton) was shot by the Indians. He did not fall from his horse, but rode on until he came to a small stream, now known as Peyton's Run, on the farm of Miss Mary Kleiser, when his horse jumped it, and Peyton fell off. He was discovered soon after by Stark, who carried him to the fort, where he soon after died. His last words were, "The Indians have shot me."

Another pioneer family in this section was that of Joseph Kleiser, who built the house where his daughter, Mary Kleiser, now lives. He was a native of Switzerland, and when grown to manhood, went to London, where he served an apprenticeship at clock-making. In an early day, he came to Virginia, and, in 1785, to Kentucky. He built the house in which his daughter lives, in 1790. He married Elizabeth Lyter before leaving Virginia. She was of German origin, and bore him ten children, none of whom are now living except Mary, and she, although in her seventy-fifth year, is hale and hearty, with but few gray hairs. Zachariah Wheat settled where John Ashurst now lives, about the year 1790. Philip Ament, from Germany, settled on the farm now owned by G. H. Ament, near Bethlehem Church, about the same time. He married a Widow Miller, who had seven children to start with, and whose husband was drowned on the voyage to this country. G. H. Ament has a clock in his possession which was purchased by his father, and is now more than a hundred years old.

Indians were still troublesome when the first white settlements were made in what is now Hutchinson's Precinct, and the danger from their hostile incursions into the State was great, and rendered the situation of the pioneers extremely critical at times. Less resolute men would have abandoned all, but the pioneers of Central Kentucky were made of sterner stuff, and manfully contested the right of the savages to the "dark and bloody ground." Their courage and perseverance succeeded, and finally won for them and their children peaceful and happy homes. After the danger from the savages was over, emigrants flocked in by hundreds, land was cleared and houses built, roads were opened, and mills erected in different sections, until life became somewhat pleasant and easy. The first roads through the precinct were trails and bridle paths. One of the first roads was the Lexington and Paris. It was the first road macadamized in the county, and is one of the best turnpikes in the State. It passes through Hutchinson Precinct from northeast to southwest. The Paris & Clintonville pike bounds the precinct on the east; the Paris & Bethlehem pike passes through the eastern part from Paris to Bethlehem Church—a distance of six miles. The Hutchinson & Bethlehem pike, the Houston pike, and the Antioch pikes are cross pikes connecting the main roads, and leave but little dirt road in the precinct. Good substantial bridges span all the streams where these roads cross them. The Kentucky Central Railroad runs almost parallel with the Lexington & Paris pike through the township. This road has been of considerable benefit to this section of the country in affording means of travel and transportation, and furnishing the best market to the people at their own doors. An early mill in Hutchinson Precinct was built by Greenup De Jarnette. The first blacksmith-shop was kept on the farm of Joseph Kleiser, and the first blacksmith was Aquilla Willett. The first magistrate was Squire Moreland. The Department of Justice is now represented by Squires J. W. Beatty and J. Smith Kenney.

Hutchinson Station is the nearest approach to a village in the precinct. It is on the Kentucky Central Railroad, a short distance south of Paris, and its birth was cotemporaneous with the building of the road. It was named for Martin Hutchison, who built the first house in the place, which is now occupied by Mrs. Hutchison. Mr. Hutchison also built the first storehouse and blacksmith-shop, which were occupied respectively by Milton Berry and Patrick Gartland. A post office was established, of which Mr. Hutchison was Postmaster. Mrs. Hutchison now represents Uncle Sam in this department. The population of the village at this time does not exceed fifty white persons perhaps, and contains one store, one blacksmith-shop, one church and one school.

Hutchinson Academy was established in 1857. The first schoolhouse was a log building, which stood where the present one now stands. Lyman G. Curtis, of New York, taught here for twelve years. The trustees under whom the school was organized were Martin Hutchison, Aaron Smedley and Fletcher Wilmot. The present elegant building was erected under the supervision of Prof. Newman Curtis, a brother to Lyman G., who is now teaching his tenth year, and has an attendance of sixty pupils. The present Trustees are: James S. Jacoby, James McLeod and E. P. Claybrook, all energetic, active and warm friends of education. It is the intention of the Trustees to enlarge the building during the coming summer, employ additional teachers and make a regular graded school of it.

Lowe's Station, name for Solomon Lowe, was originally in this precinct, but in 1879, it was moved over into Fayette County, and the name changed to Muir's Station.

Hutchinson Precinct is pretty well supplied with churches, and her people have no lack of religious facilities. Hopewell Presbyterian Church is one of the oldest in the precinct, and is located at the junction of the Lexington & Maysville, and the Hopewell & Bethlehem pikes, some ten miles from Paris.

Greenwich Methodist Episcopal Church was organized and worshiped originally in the schoolhouse. A church edifice was built in 1833. The church was removed to Huchinson Chapel in 1876, but part of the congregation went to Paris and part to Lexington, uniting with churches at those places. The building is now used by the colored people.

Hutchinson Chapel of the Methodist Episcopal Church South, was built in 1876, at a cost of $1,600 ; the present membership is about fifty. Rev. B. G. Sedwick is pastor. A Sunday school has been held each year, but usually suspending during the winter season, officers and children aggregating about forty.

Moreland Lodge, No. 124, I. O. O. F., was organized March 10, 1855, by A. C. Halleck, D. D. G. M., with the following charter members: W. H. C. Moreland, O. H. Burbridge, G. W. Bain, John W. Bain, James A. Wilson and W. B. Skinner. The first officers were: W. H. C. Moreland, N. G.; O. H. Burbridge, V. G.; J. A. Wilson, Secretary; and John W. Bain, Treasurer. The present officers are: W. B. Skinner, N. G.; I. L. Wilmott, V. G.; Francis Hall, Treasurer; and A. Morrow, Secretary.

The first school in Hutchinson Precinct was Greenwich Academy, which was on the farm of James Jacoby, and the first teacher was a man named Lapham. There are at present two schools in the precinct besides the one at Hutchinson's Station, viz.: one at Bethlehem and one at Jones' School house. They are flourishing schools, but scarcely sufficient to accommodate the wants of the community.—*Perrin.*

CHAPTER XIX.

CENTERVILLE PRECINCT—TOPOGRAPHY AND PHYSICAL FEATURES—SETTLEMENT OF THE WHITES—THE OLDEST MAN IN THE PRECINCT—EARLY TRIALS AND DIFFICULTIES—PIONEER INDUSTRIES AND IMPROVEMENTS—ROADS, CHURCHES, SCHOOLS, DISTILLERIES, POST OFFICES, ETC., ETC.

CENTERVILLE PRECINCT No. 7 lies in the northeast part of Bourbon County, and is bounded on the southwest and on the west and north by Fayette, Scott and Harrison Counties, and on the east and south by Paris Precinct. The surface of the land is gently rolling or undulating; along the streams the absence of steep rock cliffs and bluffs are quite noticeable. The soil is very rich and fertile. The precinct is separated from Fayette and Scott Counties by a high ridge, usually called "Beech Ridge," from the species of timber growing on it. The soil of this region is a trifle thinner than other portions of the county, but not so susceptible to drought, and, if well cultivated, produces good crops; it is superior to the lowlands for grass. Townsend Creek rises about one mile south of Centerville Post Office, and traverses the precinct from south to north, uniting with Mud Lick Creek, and emptying into the Licking River. Silas Creek and Flat Run separate the precinct from Harrison and Scott Counties, and Cooper's Run separates it from Paris Precinct on the east. The timber growth is comprised in the species indigenous to this section. Upon the whole, it is as fine an agricultural and stock-growing regions as there is in Bourbon County.

The first settlement made in what is now Centerville Precinct by white people was about the year 1790. In that year, Capt. Thomas Conn located 2,000 acres of land west of the village of Centerville, upon which he built a strong frame house where William Gaines now lives. Capt. Conn was a native of Ireland, and emigrated to Maryland in an early day, where he married a Miss Maddox, then removed to Virginia, and settled near Front Royal. There he resided until his removal to the county of Kentucky, as stated above. He owned a very remarkable colored man called "Big Ned," who built a house and barn—the latter still standing—the lumber for which he sawed with a whip-saw, and the shingles of which he put on with wooden pegs. Ned lived to an old age, and when he died, was buried in the graveyard on William Gaines' place. Capt Conn died in 1811, at the age of seventy-eight years; his wife died in 1821. They had several children, of whom the oldest son was one of the first Congressmen from Kentucky. The second son, Jack, was a noted Indian fighter, and came to Kentucky about 1780 (before his parents came), built a block-house, where his father afterward built his dwelling, and raised a small crop, but the Indian troubles of the times drove him from the place. He and his brother William, the latter father-in-law of John A. Gano, Sr., who still lives on a part of the old Conn tract of land, were both in the war of 1812, and in many Indian fights of that stirring period. Jack was in the battle of the Thames, and believed, to his dying day, that he himself killed the noted chief Tecumseh. The story is thus told by Mr. Gano: "Jack was a very fine marksman, and at eighty years of age could beat any of the boys of the neighborhood shooting with the rifle. Being a kind of Indian scout, in this battle, he obtained permission from his Captain, who knew his prowess well, to fight the enemy 'on his own hook.' In the engagement he was 'treed' by an Indian while trying to get a shot at a noble looking warrior who stood in full view. By exposing a part of his body, he drew the fire of the one, and then taking deliberate aim at the 'noble-looking warrior,' he fired, and the Indian fell. After the battle, he said to a comrade, 'Come with me and I will show you an Indian I killed.' On the way he described the whole circumstance, where and how he shot him, and upon arriving at the spot, he said, 'there is the Indian I killed.' A British officer who had been taken prisoner, was standing by, and upon hearing the remark, replied, 'then you killed Tecumseh.' So Jack believed to his death that he, and not Col. Johnson, killed the noted Indian chief." William Conn, a brother of Jack, as already mentioned, settled where John A. Gano, Sr., now lives, and built the rear portion of the house now occupied by Mr. Gano, about the year 1804 or 1805. The front portion was built in 1814–15, by Samuel and John Allison. The house is still in an excellent state of preservation, and is one of the best in the neighborhood.

The oldest man now living in Centerville Precinct is Jesse Hall, whose farm is located on the extreme western border, near the Scott County line. His father, James Hall, was a native of Baltimore County, Md., and emigrated to Kentucky in 1796. He bought the place on which Jesse now lives, from a man named Theobald, who afterward moved to Georgetown, where he kept a tavern. Jesse Hall still occupies the place of his father's original settlement, and is now in his ninety-first year. He has always lived here, except from 1858 to 1873, which interval was spent in Missouri, and in Harrison County. He was a carpenter, and worked at the trade for many years—he helped to build the house now occupied by Mrs. Isabella West, near the noted Russell Cave, in Fayette County. When the draft was made for the war of 1812, he volunteered as representative of his class of ten. He afterward hired a substitute who was killed during the war. A pioneer family of the name of Shanks lived near where Jacksonville now stands in early times. They were all murdered by the Indians, except one girl, who was carried off a captive. At the same time, they captured a white boy named George Lail, whom they raised and brought up as one of themselves. Lail married a white woman by whom it is alleged he had *many* children. His parents living here were wealthy. He afterward returned to his native county, and, finding his brother wealthy, wanted a division of the property. His brother refused to accede to his wishes, when he returned to the Indians, saying that they were more honest than the whites. Mr. Hall says that, at the beginning of the century, the settlers' cabins stood thicker than dwelling houses do at the present day, and that about 1812 the county had 2,800 white voters more than there are now, both white and black. This, however, may be easily accounted for by the difference in extent of territory then and now. The winters, Mr. Hall says, were very mild in those early times, with but little snow, and the cattle kept fat in the woods the year round. Favored as the country was by nature, and adapted to the wants of civilized man, the first years of its occupancy were years of incessant toil and danger, and of almost daily struggles with savage foes. After the close of the war of 1812, peace and security settled down, and prosperity crowned the early privations of the pioneers.

The early industries of what is now Centerville Precinct are comprised in a few mills, distilleries and shops. This section was principally an agricultural region, and little attention was devoted to other interests. A man named Bowman built and operated a mill and distillery, on Townsend Creek, about one mile south of Jacksonville, in a very early day. They disappeared more than fifty years ago, and no trace of either now exists. Benjamin Shropshire, John Shropshire and S. B. Clarkson, each had distilleries on Silas Creek from 1815 to 1818. But like Bowmans, they have long since pased away. A few blacksmith shops were kept in different parts of the precinct; one of the earliest remembered was kept where Centerville now stands by one Charles Williams, who purchased twenty acres of land of Capt. Conn.

The first road laid out through this part of Bourbon County, was the road leading from Lexington to Cynthiana. It was laid out as a county road about the year 1796. Charles Williams, mentioned above, kept the first tavern on this road, on the present site of Centerville; the road was a mail and stage route until the building of the Kentucky Central Railroad, when the mail was transferred to that route. The Paris & Georgetown road was also an early stage and mail route, and is still so used, three mails passing each way over it to and from Frankfort per week. The latter road passes through the southern part of the precinct, in an east and west direction, while the Lexington & Cynthiana road runs nearly north and south. Both of these roads have been macadamized, and are now as fine thoroughfares as are in the country. The Gano Hill pike runs north and south through the western part, almost parallel with the Lexington & Cynthiana pike. The Silas pike leads from Jacksonville to Newtown & Leesburg pike, and passes through the north part of the precinct. The Clay & Kiser pike runs from Johnston's Cross Roads to Kiser's Station, and the Hume & Bedford pike partly bounds the precinct on the southern border. It will thus be seen that the precinct is traversed in all directions by excellent pike roads.

The village of Centerville is located on the Lexington & Cynthiana pike, midway between Lexington and Cynthiana, and where the latter road is crossed by the Paris & Georgetown pike, midway between Paris and Georgetown. From this fact it obtains its name of Centerville. The first house in the village was a tavern kept, as already noted, by Charles Williams. He also built and operated a blacksmith shop. The first store was kept by Paterson & Gaines. Before the roads were piked, Centerville was quite a prosperous place, and supported several stores, wood and blacksmith shops, taverns, etc. It was on the direct route from the counties south, to Cincinnati, and as all produce was hauled in wagons, and all the cattle and hogs driven to market on foot, Centerville had a large share of custom from teamsters and drovers. But the building of railroads, and the macadamizing of neighborhood roads, thus giving access to the county seat, with which they were unable to successfully compete, drove it into a decline, until at the present day it is but a mere hamlet, with a white population of 64, and a colored population of about 100. Its business is represented by two stores, two blacksmith shops, one wood shop, an excellent school and one physician. There is also a colored church; the present Postmaster is Dr. Fritz.

Jacksonville is also located on the Lexington & Cynthana pike, four miles north of Centerville, and like the latter place, in early times, enjoyed a large business from drovers and teamsters, being located upon the same popular thoroughfare; but the same causes which curtailed the trade of Centerville, has likewise injured that of Jacksonville. It now has a white population of about 40, one store, and one blacksmith shop. It also has an excellent school. A new schoolhouse was erected in 1879, at a cost of $300, to take the place of the old one which has just been burned. The present teacher is W. A. Allen, and the attendance about thirty pupils. The first house built on the present site of Jacksonville is supposed to have been built by a pioneer preacher named Corbin. The first store was kept by Squire Samuel Allison, and the first blacksmith shop by a man named Duncan.

The first school taught in the precinct was in a house built for the purpose, on the farm of John A. Gano, about the year 1798, and the teacher was Thomas Ford; the next was a man named Smith, then Billy Conn. Mr. Hall went there to school when he was but seven years old. Probably the first preacher in the precinct was Rev. Ambrose Dudley, who figured extensively in this section of the country in religious work in early times, and of whom more will be said anon. The first tavern kept within the present bounds of the precinct, was in 1790, at Johnston's Cross Roads, five miles from Paris, on the Paris & Georgetown pike. The first magistrate in the precinct was Austin Respess, and the first Constable was John Kendrick. The majesty of the law is now represented in the persons of T. J. Barlow and Joseph Hawkins, who are the Justices of the Peace for the precinct. The name Centerville is received from the village of that name.

The Pleasant Green Methodist Church was organized so long ago that little can be learned in regard to its early history. All the old books are lost or have been destroyed, and with them much of its history. The first church edifice was built at an early day, but the exact date cannot be given. The present church was built in 1850. It was once a vigorous church, strong in numbers and noted for able preachers, among whom may be mentioned Revs. William Vaught, John Hughes, John Hiner, Peter Kavanaugh, etc. But death and removals have decreased its membership until at present it has but eighteen active members, and of these only three are males, viz.: Elisha McDaniel, David Allen and Richard Brand.

Silas Creek Baptist Church is located on the extreme north border of the precinct, on Silas Creek, which forms the boundary between Bourbon and Harrison Counties. The church was organized August 30, 1800, with the following members: Benjamin Neale, Charles Smith, Sr., William Kendrick, Benoni Kendrick, Charles Smith, Jr., Ann Porter, Elizabeth Smith, Francis Underwood, Sally Stewart, Francis Kendrick, Joshua Jackson, John McCoy, Benjamin Kendrick, William Arnold, Thomas Porter, Patty Smith, Ann Jackson, Elizabeth H. Smith and Fanny Kendrick. The first regular pastor was Elder George Eve. The first building was erected in 1800, at the time the members mentioned above separated from the church at Cooper's Run, and, assisted by Rev. Ambrose Dudley, formed this church, known far and wide as old "Silas Church." The present brick church was erected about the year 1854, at a cost of $3,000. At the time it was built, Elder James R. Barbee was pastor. About the year 1828, when Elders Stone and Campbell were causing such "a shaking in the dry bones of the valley" with their new dogmas, the excitement reached this church, and caused a split in the membership, as in most of the Baptist Churches of the country. The clerk was one of the new converts, and not only went over to the Reformers, but took his records with him, and for some time refused to surrender his books to the Baptists. A year afterward, however, he returned all the books dating back to the original organization of the church, and these are now in the hands of William Sparks, the present clerk. The present membership of Silas Church is eighty-five, and the present pastor, Elder George Hunt. Services are conducted the second Saturday and Sunday of each month, and a Sunday school regularly maintained.

Elizabeth Baptist Church was organized in 1811 by Rev. Ambrose Dudley, who was the first pastor. It is situated in the southern part of the precinct on the Hume & Bedford pike. It was named for Elizabeth McClanahan, who donated the land upon which it stands. In 1827, Rev. Thomas P. Dudley, of Lexington, was called to assist his father in the pastorate, and although now very old and feeble, the church still retains him as their pastor, and since the death of his father, Rev. Ambrose Dudley, he has been the sole pastor, until very recently, an associate has been called to assist him.—*Perrin.*

CHAPTER XX.

RUDDEL'S MILLS PRECINCT—DESCRIPTION AND TOPOGRAPHY—EARLY SETTLEMENT—THE RUDDELS—PIONEER IMPROVEMENTS AND ACHIEVEMENTS—PRE-HISTORIC REMAINS—RUDDEL'S MILLS—CHURCHES, SCHOOLS, CEMETERIES, ETC., ETC.

"Ha! how the woods give way before the step
Of these new-comers! What a sickening smell
Clings round my cabin, wafted from their town
Ten miles away."—*Daniel Boone.*

RUDDEL'S MILLS PRECINCT lies northeast of Paris, and is No. 8 of the election precincts of Bourbon County. It is bounded on the north by Harrison County, on the east by Millersburg Precinct, on the southeast, south and west, by Paris Precinct, and is one of the richest precincts, historically, in the county. The land is undulating or rolling, with some hills along the bluffs and water-courses. The timber consisted of walnut, sugar maple, buckeye, locust, elm, oak, hickory, etc. The principal streams are the Hinkston and Stoner, which, uniting at Ruddel's Mills, form one of the important branches of the Licking River. A number of small tributaries flow into these streams in the precinct, thus affording the most ample means of natural drainage. The main line of the Kentucky Central Railroad passes through the west part of the precinct, which is beneficial for shipping its surplus products. Shawhan's and Kiser's Stations are the most important shipping-points. The former is located seven miles north of Paris, and within one mile of the northern boundary of the precinct. It is a place of considerable trade, supporting two stores, and containing a white population of about fifty souls. The extensive wholesale liquor warerooms of Gus Pugh & Co. are also located at this point. The site of this station, embracing several acres, was donated to the Kentucky Central Railroad by Daniel Shawhan. When the post office was first established at this place, Mr. Jacob Duncan was appointed Postmaster, which office is at present filled by J. C. Lyter.

Kiser's Station, two miles south of Shawhan's, is an important shipping-point, being the outlet for the produce of the large distillery of Ford & Bowen, located one-half mile above. A neat and substantial suspension foot bridge crosses Stoner Creek at this point.

Perhaps no other precinct of Bourbon County has so much early history connected with it as the one we are writing at present. If it were possible for us to recall a century, and seat ourselves at the fireside of some hardy pioneer, it would be an easy matter to write an accurate account of that early day. Had our forefathers but imagined that that they were daily acting chapters of unwritten history, they, perhaps, would have taken more pains to chronicle the events that we find so difficult to obtain at present.

The first settlement ever made by a representative of the "pale-faced" race within the limits of the territory above described, was that of Isaac Ruddell, sometimes spelled Ruddle, and most commonly pronounced Riddle, giving the primitive sound to the first vowel; but as the first settlers of a country are generally supposed to devote more time to subduing their enemies that to studying philology, we will take it for granted that the latter pronunciation is a popular corruption that is unavoidable in names that will admit of it. He was a Virginian by birth, and built a log cabin near the spring, north of where the brick house, erected by James Coons, now stands. This was as early as 1776. He planted an orchard of apples,

T E Moon

pears and peaches, as well as cultivated a small patch of corn and vegetables. As the Revolutionary war was then in progress, the Indians, incited by the British, were traversing the State in war parties, and committing depredations on all unprotected settlements. In consequence of the insecurity afforded by an isolated settlement of this character, Ruddell and others moved with their families some three miles down the river to an old fort, which had been abandoned by Hinkston in 1776.

In June, 1780, this fort was captured by Col. Byrd, who had command of about one thousand Canadian and Indian troops. As soon as the surrender of the fort was made, the Indians seized upon all the inmates and claimed them as their prisoners. The Indians being the most numerous, Col. Byrd could not protect them. The children who were too young to travel, were killed, either with the tomahawk, by dashing their brains out against a tree, or by throwing them into the fire. Isaac Ruddell's family consisted of his wife, son Steven, aged about twelve years, Abram, six years, and an infant three years old. The babe they threw into the fire, and two Indians stood, tomahawk in hand, over the mother, so that, should she manifest any feeling for the innocent victim, they might take her life.

From Hinkston, Byrd advanced to and captured Martin's Station, after which he retreated to the Ohio River by way of Falmouth, and down main Licking. When they had crossed the Ohio, his Indian allies left him, taking with them their captives, and when the tribes separated, they carried their prisoners to different localities, thus dividing families. They remained in captivity four years, until after the close of the war. Upon his return, Isaac Ruddell cleared out a portion of the land surrounding his cabin. He and his wife both died here about the year 1808 or 1810, and were buried in what is known as the old Presbyterian Graveyard, a tract consisting of some two acres, which he had donated for burial purposes. Here in oblivion they lie, no stone or slab to tell succeeding generations their last resting-place.

, Stephen and Abram Ruddell were both adopted into Indian families, and Stephen married a squaw. He did not return for many years, and in order to induce him to stay here, his father built him a house where the James McIlvain house now is, and supported his Indian relatives a long time, in order to keep him until he was weaned from them. They were frequently visited by considerable numbers of their tribe. Stephen was of a tall, athletic form, straight as an arrow, with coal black hair hanging down the back of his neck. His ears were trimmed long and pendent, in which he wore rings, Indian fashion. He was a Baptist, and after his return, he frequently preached at the Mills. He said he had accompanied the Indians on war expeditions, and had murdered and scalped many white captives, often continuing the use of the tomahawk till his arm would give out from pure exhaustion. His was not a prepossessing appearance, and his manner of speaking of his butcheries created a feeling of aversion to him. He removed to Missouri about the year 1820.

Abram Ruddell, after his return from captivity, settled near the clay bank on Hinkston, where he lived for many years. For several years he owned and operated the log-mill on the north side of Hinkston. He always stated that he had never murdered a captive or white person. He served as a volunteer in the war of 1812, and afterward moved out West.

The formation of Bourbon County was previous to the admission of Kentucky as a State, and when agitating the question of the county seat an effort was made to have it located at Ruddel's Mills, and the effort would probably have been successful had not Mrs. Ruddell strenuously opposed it on the grounds that "the boys living in the country towns were so bad they would rob her orchard."

An Irishman named Mulharen married a daughter of Isaac Ruddell. Mulharen & Ruddell manufactured from pumpkins a species of brandy which possessed the inestimable property of "making drunk come."

Among the oldest families whose name is still preserved among the inhabitants may be mentioned the Shawhans, the Kisers, the Pughs and the Smeltzers. Nicholas Smith settled near Shawhan's Station. Uriah Humble, James Cummins, Henry Mann, Henry David, Rudy Mock and others, were noted as early and prominent settlers of their respective neighborhoods.

At the village of Ruddel's Mills, on the west side of Stoner, near its mouth, may be seen the remains of a circular earthwork of some pre-historic race. It is about seventy-five yards in diameter, and appears to have been thrown up in an embankment, with a ditch some thirty feet wide, leaving a gateway or open space facing the stream on its eastern side. Several works of similar description, but smaller, were on the river above and below the main one and apparently arranged so as to command a view of the surrounding country. (For a more extended account of the pre-historic remains of this section, see general chapter on that subject).

The industries or occupations of any people or community are mainly controlled by surrounding circumstances. In the first settlement of a country, the inhabitants, after fortifying themselves against danger and supplying the immediate wants of their animal natures, turn their attention naturally to accumulating a surplus. The value of that surplus, in our time, is regulated, we say, almost entirely by the great law of supply and demand; but total inaccessibility to any market of importance tended to nullify the action of that law in those days. So beyond the crude implements and machinery necessary for the supplying of the wants of the animal body, the people of that day cannot be said to have had any industries until an outlet was found for their produce. Perhaps one of the earliest industries, as it is now the most extensive, was the distillation of spirits. An old inhabitant informs us that, when he can first remember, nearly every house on Townsend Creek was a "still house," aside from their necessary concomitant—a mill. There were no manufacturing industries till more recent date. The present site of Ford & Bowen's distillery was originally occupied by a large cotton mill of 720 spindles. This was built, in 1828, by Thomas & Hugh Brent, the work having been done by John Shaw, who was their first Superintendent. This was burnt in 1836, and rebuilt by Abram Spears the following year. A woolen mill was attached to this factory, and cotton and wool made together until 1855, when it was turned into a distillery, as noted elsewhere.

The numerous churches of this precinct attest the interest felt in religion. Perhaps the first church in the precinct was what was called "Stoner Mouth Church," which was located at Ruddel's Mills. The old graveyard is still cared for, and contains some monuments of quite ancient date, notably that of Daniel Shawhan, born in December, 1738; died May, 1791.

About the year 1818, the nucleus of the present Mt. Carmel Church was formed. During the revival of Rev. Barton Stone at Cane Ridge, in 1801, five members of the old Stoner Mouth Presbyterian Church attended, for which offense they were denounced from the pulpit by their pastor, Rev. Samuel Reynolds. These five were John Shawhan, William Bodkin, a Mr. Vennerman, John Brown and Nathan Sellers. A camp-meeting was afterward held on the farm of John Shawhan about the year 1818, and from the converts at that camp the present church was organized. They built a church of brick about 1822 or 1823, which was remodeled in 1859, and is now quite a handsome country church, worth about $3,000. Among the early preachers were Barton Stone, David Peroines, Reuben Dooley (of Ohio), Alexander Campbell, John Morrow and his son William, Samuel Rogers, John I. Rogers, John Rogers, Joshua Irvine, John A. Gano, John T. Johnson, the Pinkertons and others. Joseph Frank has charge of the congregation at present, and has a large membership.

The Christian Church at the village of Ruddel's Mills was organized, about the year 1842, by Elder John A. Gano, assisted by Allen Kendrick, John Rogers and John Holton. The building, a commodious frame structure, was erected about 1844, at a cost of $2,700. Among the members who first allied themselves with this church were Dr. Wall, Mrs. Steward, A. Lowry and wife, George Mock and family, Willis D. Collins and family and others. The church roll now contains something over a hundred names, and is administered to by the Rev. J. S. Stafford the first and third Sundays in each month. They also have a good Sabbath school in connection, which meets every Sunday. Among those who have filled the pastoral office in times past were John T. Johnson, John Smith, Hardin Reynolds, A. P. Terrill and others.

The present Methodist Church is a substantial brick structure, and was erected, about 1850, at a cost of $4,000, to take the place of the old brick church, which was torn down. This first church was erected about sixty years ago. The brick work was done by John Stevens and the wood work by Benjamin Bowen. Among the preachers that filled the pulpit of the old church, none, perhaps, was more noted than old Josiah Whittaker, whose peculiar, blunt ways of illustrating Scripture and general truths are still held in remembrance by his hearers. The present church is called Moore's Chapel, mainly built from a fund left for that purpose by Wilmot Moore at his death.

The Presbyterians have a small church at Shawhan's Station. It is a frame structure, neatly built, cost about $600; was first organized by Bishop Forsythe in 1863.

This precinct is supplied with its full quota of common schools, for a history of which the reader is referred to a general chapter on public schools. It may be interesting to note the fact that the first school ever started in the precinct was in a log house on Henry David's place and taught by James Lafferty.*

The first Magistrates under the new constitution of the State were George W. Wyatt and W. B. Smith, with John Howard as Constable. Those offices are at present filled by William Bowen and Daniel S. Talbot, with John Ewalt as Constable.—*E. T. Brown.*

* Much of the history of this precinct is obtained from an article written by Dr. Harper and published in the *Western Citizen*.

SCOTT COUNTY.

CHAPTER I.

EARLY SETTLEMENT BY WHITE PEOPLE—THEIR CONFLICTS WITH THE SAVAGES—VICISSITUDES OF WILDERNESS LIFE—FORMATION OF THE COUNTY AND ITS CIVIL ORGANIZATION—PUBLIC BUILDINGS—CIVIL DIVISIONS—POPULATION—ELECTION, COUNTY OFFICERS, ETC.

"Lo! our land is like an eagle, whose young gaze
Feeds on the noontide beam, whose golden plumes
Float moveless on the storm, and in the blaze
Of sunrise, gleams when earth is wrapped in gloom."

THE geological features of Scott County, together with the pre-historic and Indian history, are mostly given in Chapters II and III, of Part I, of this volume, and, therefore, we begin the history of Scott with its settlement and organization as a county. More than a hundred years have come and gone since the Anglo-Saxon began to exercise dominion over these beautiful blue grass lands—erst the hunting grounds of the red man and his kindred. These years have been full of changes, and the visitor of to-day, ignorant of the past of the country, could scarcely be made to realize it. The tangled wilderness has disappeared before the energy of the husbandman, the wild beasts have given place to domestic animals, and the savages are only remembered in fire-side legends. Indeed the grand transformation is like a tale of enchantment.

It is believed by some, though without just grounds, perhaps, on which to base the supposition, that the first settlement in Kentucky by white people was made within the present limits of Scott County. This supposition, we say, is most probably erroneous; at any rate, it is contrary to all accepted history on the subject. It is, however, pretty generally conceded, and is doubtless true that the first permanent settlement north of the Kentucky River, was made upon the present site of Georgetown. This settlement was made in November, 1775, by John McClelland and his family, and David Perry, Col. Robert Patterson, William McConnell and Stephen Lowry, at the "Royal Spring," one of the finest springs of water to be found in this land of fine springs, and now within the corporate limits of Georgetown, in the history of which city, it is more particularly noticed. This little party came down the river from Pittsburgh, built a cabin at the spring referred to, where they remained until the following April. During the summer of 1776, they built a block house at this cabin, which was fortified in the usual pioneer style, and was known for years after as "McClelland's Station." This was doubtless the first fortified station north of the Kentucky River—that at Lexington not being made until in the spring of 1779. The station was attacked by Indians in December, 1776, which following immediately on the heels of the defeat of the whites under Col. John Todd, near the Lower Blue Licks, when on an expedition to "Limestone" after powder, so terrified the occupants of the station that they abandoned it and retreated to Harrodsburg, where they remained until times became more settled and safe.

Another of the early stations of Scott County was at the "Great Buffalo Crossing," where the buffalo trace crossed the North Elkhorn, and was made during the winter of 1783–84, by Col. Robert Johnson, the father of Hon. R. M. Johnson, Vice President of the United States from 1837 to 1841. Col. Johnson was a native of Virginia, and emigrated to Kentucky while it was still a county of the Old Dominion. He was a high-toned gentleman, of great personal courage, and took an active part in the terrific struggles of the pioneers with the savages. His sons partook of their father's estimable qualities, and filled exalted stations in life with credit to themselves and honor to their country. The Forks of Elkhorn was also a station or early settlement of the county. Among other early settlers additional to those mentioned, are the following, who rank among the pioneers: Alexander and William McClelland, brothers to him of McClelland's Station,

Andrew and Frances McConnell, Charles Lecompt, Charles White, Capt. Edward Worthington, William Plascutt, Capt. William Hubbell and others whose names are not now attainable.

Says Butler in his history of Kentucky, referring to life in the wilderness of Kentucky: "Let us for a moment consider the situation of our pioneers at this period of their history. They were posted in the heart of the most favorite hunting ground of numerous and hostile tribes of Indians, on the north and on the south—a ground endeared to these tribes by its possession of the finest game, subsisting on the luxuriant vegetation of this great natural park, in a fatness not surpassed by the flocks and herds of an agricultural society. It was emphatically the Eden of the red man. Was it then wonderful, that all his fiercest passions, and wildest energies should be aroused in its defense against an enemy whose success was the Indian's downfall? So formidable were these enemies into whose mouths our handful of hunters had thrown themselves, that they occupied the present territory of Tennessee, and the whole northwestern side of the Ohio River, now embracing the States of Ohio, Indiana, Illinois and the Territory of Michigan. These territories were then the stronghold of the most ferocious and warlike tribe of Indians on this continent. They had frequently wasted the frontiers of the Carolinas, Pennsylvania and Virginia, with the tomahawk and with fire. Moreover, the enemy was at this time freely aided by the arts and treasure of Great Britain, furnished by her military officers from Detroit to Kaskaskia. Thus the pioneers of Kentucky were separated by three or four hundred miles of Indian wilderness from the nearest fort of their countrymen at Pittsburgh; and fully six hundred miles from the seat of Government in Virginia, with forests and Indian country between. Under these appalling circumstances, may not the forlorn and perilous situation of our first settlers bear some honorable comparison with the gallant daring of the fathers of our great Republic who led the way across the Atlantic wave, and founded the empire of freedom at Jamestown and at Plymouth?"

The facts contained in the following incident is taken from Collins' History of Kentucky, and affords an excellent illustration of pioneer life. It shows what our ancestors had to contend with, and the dangers to which they were exposed. We condense from Collins as follows:

"Capt. William Hubbell (mentioned above as an early settler of the county), was a Revolutionary soldier, and, after the close of the war, removed to Kentucky, and settled in Scott County. After living here a few years, he went back to the East, and, when ready to return to Kentucky he procured a flat-bottomed boat, on the Monongahela River, on which he embarked, with Daniel Light and William Plascutt and his family, consisting of his wife and eight children. Soon after passing Pittsburgh, on their way down, they discovered signs of Indians along the bank of the river, but they saw no savages until they got below where Gallipolis (Ohio) now stands. Before they reached the mouth of the Great Kanawha, their party had been increased to twenty, and comprised nine men, three women and eight children. The addition of men were John Stoner, three named respectively, Ray, Tucker and Kilpatrick, and a Dutchman and an Irishman. For the better means of defense, the nine men were divided into three watches for the night, each watch to be on the lookout for two hours at a time. Their arms, which were of a very poor quality, were collected and put in order for instant use. Early in the night, after passing Gallipolis, a canoe was dimly seen floating down the river, supposed to contain Indians who were reconnoitering. Other indications were observed of the close proximity of a large body of hostile Indians. In this perilous situation, they continued during the night, and Capt. Hubbell, although he had not slept more than an hour since leaving Pittsburgh, was so strongly impressed with the surrounding danger, as to be unable to do so now.

"At daylight in the morning, they were hailed from the Ohio shore, and asked to land, as there were some white persons who wished to get passage on their boat. Believing it to be an Indian artifice, Capt. Hubbell very flatly declined, and kept on his course, and, as a consequence, the plaintive wail soon changed into a tone of defiance and insult. The sound of paddles was heard, and, in a short time, three Indian canoes were seen through the mist rapidly advancing. With the utmost coolness, Capt. Hubbell proceeded to 'clear his deck for action.' Every man took his position, and was ordered not to fire until the savages had approached so near that the 'flash from their guns would singe their eyebrows.' On the arrival of the canoes, they were found to contain from twenty-five to thirty Indians each, and as soon as they were within musket shot, they poured into the boat a severe fire, which wounded Tucker and Light. The three canoes placed themselves at the bow, side and stern of the boat, so that they had an opportunity of taking in every direction. The fire now commenced from the boat, and had a powerful effect in checking the confidence and fury of the Indians. After firing his own gun, the Captain took one belonging to a wounded man, and was in the act of firing it, when a stray ball took away the lock. Very cooly he turned around, picked up a fire-brand, and, applying it, discharged the piece, with fatal effect to his foes. A constant fire was kept up on both sides for some time, and the little party was fast becoming disabled; but they continued to defend their boat stubbornly. Notwithstanding the disparity of numbers, and the exhausted condition of the defenders, the Indians, finally despaired of success, drew off, and retired to the shore. But the trouble of the whites was not yet over. Their boat drifted near the shore, where a large number of Indians—four or five hundred—were seen rushing down the bank. Ray and Plascutt, the only men who were unhurt (Capt. Hubbell being badly wounded), were placed at the oars, and protected by the sides of the boat from the Indians, while the others were ordered to lie down in the bottom of the boat, as it was but a few yards from the shore. The Indians opened a terrific fire, but did not attempt to board. While thus exposed, nine balls were shot into one oar, and ten in the other, without injuring the rowers. This ordeal lasted some twenty minutes, when the boat drifted out into the middle of the stream, and was carried by the current beyond the reach of the savages. Of the nine men—Tucker and Kilpatrick were killed; Stoner was mortally wounded, and died shortly after. All the rest of the men were more or less injured; Capt. Hubbell was wounded in two places, one in the arm, which bled so profusely, he was obliged to tie his coat sleeve around his arm, in order to retain the blood in it, and thus stop the flow. Of five horses on board, four of them were killed. The women and children were unhurt, except a little son of Mr. Plascutt, who, after the battle was over, came to the Captain, and, with great coolness, requested him to take a bullet out of his head. On examination, it was found that a ball, which had passed through the side of the boat, had penetrated the forehead of this little hero, and remained under the skin. The Captain took it out, when the little fellow remarked, '*That is not all!*' and, raising his arm, showed another severe wound. His mother inquired, 'Why did you not tell me of this?' 'Because,' he cooly replied, 'the Captain directed us to be silent during the action, and I thought you would be likely to make a noise if I told you.'

"The boat arrived at Limestone without further molestation on the next day after the battle. Crowds of people flocked to the shore to see the boat that had been the scene of such heroism and such carnage, and to visit the brave little band by whom it had been so heroically defended. Capt. Hubbell was unable to rise, and had to be carried from the boat to the tavern, where he had his wounds dressed, and remained several days before proceeding to his home in Scott County. An examination of the boat showed that its sides were literally filled with bullets and with bullet holes. There was scarcely a space two feet square in the part above the water, which had not a ball remaining in it, or a hole through which a ball had passed. The holes were counted in the blankets, which had been hung up in the stern of the boat, and, in a space, in one of them, five feet square, there were found 122 bullet holes."

Thus, through such scenes, the pioneers fought their way in the wilderness of Kentucky; with a heroism, like that which prompted Leonidas and his 300 Spartans to defend the pass of Thermopylæ; until the last man went down, Hubbell and his companions defended their boat. And, what is true of Hubbell, is true of all the early settlers of the blue grass country.

A word in this connection is not out of place, of Capt. Daniel Gano, an early settler of the county, and a man who still has many descendants living here. He was a son of Rev. John Gano, a Baptist preacher, who had prominent connection with the early Baptist Church of Kentucky. While attending Brown University—then only in his seventeenth year—Capt. Gano volunteered as Ensign of Artillery. He was in the skirmishes at New York and White Plains; a Lieutenant in 1776, with Montgomery, in the memorable winter march to Quebec, and was near him when he fell. As a Captain of artillery, he distinguished himself in a number of engagements during the Revolutionary war. He came to Kentucky with Gen. James Wilkerson, as a Captain in the regular army, and was among the first settlers of Frankfort, removing to Scott County in 1809, where he died in 1849, at the age of ninety years. He was of the order of Cincinnati, his diploma being signed by Gen. Washington himself. He is represented as the venerable head of a large family, and a remarkable man in his personal and mental vigor.

The increase of settlements and of population required, from time to time, the formation of new counties, for the purpose of strengthening the arm of the law in the protection of the people. Fayette, as we have seen, was one of the original counties, into which the Territory of Kentucky was divided. In 1788, Woodford County was formed from the Territory of Fayette and in 1792, the year that Kentucky was admitted into the Union as a State, Scott was set off from Woodford and became an independent county. It was named for Gen. Charles Scott, who was Governor of the State from 1808 to 1812. He was born in Virginia, and was a soldier—it may almost be said—by birth, breeding and education. He was a Corporal in a company of militia that shared in the defeat of the ill-fated Braddock in 1755. At the commencement of the Revolutionary war, he raised the first company that was recruited south of the James River, and was appointed by Gen. Washington to the command of a regiment in the Continental line. He was with Gen. Wayne at the storming of Stony Point, and was at Charleston, S. C., when it surrendered to Sir Henry Clinton in 1778. When the war was over, he removed to Kentucky, and in 1785 settled in what is now Woodford County. He was with Gen. St. Clair in his disastrous defeat on the 4th of November, 1791, when he beheld 600 of his comrades-in-arms, butchered in one hour by savages. He commanded the Kentucky troops under Gen. Wayne, in his memorable victory over the Indians in 1794. He is described as a man of "strong natural powers, but somewhat illiterate, profane, rough in his manners and very eccentric." Many good anecdotes of him are still extant, of which Collins gives the following as a specimen :

While Gen. Scott was Governor of Kentucky, a fellow with more egotism than brains, in order to attain notoriety for some imaginary or pretended wrong, challenged the Governor to fight a duel. To this challenge, however, the old battle-scarred veteran paid not the slightest notice. Meanwhile the silly braggart having committed himself, by letting the public obtain a full knowledge of the affair, after waiting in vain for an acceptance, and not even receiving an answer, went personally to Gen. Scott to demand an explanation, when the following took place: "Gen. Scott, you received a challenge from me!" "Your challenge was delivered, sir." "But I have received neither an acknowledgment nor an acceptance of it." "I presume not sir, as I have sent neither." "But of course you intend to accept?" "Of course I do not." "What! not accept my challenge? Is it possible that you, Gen. Scott, brought up in the army, decline a combat?" "I do with you, sir." "Then I have no means of satisfaction left, but to post you a coward." "Post *me* a coward? Ha, ha, ha! Post and be ——; but if you do, you will only post yourself a —— liar, and everybody else will say so." And there the matter ended.

But to return to the organization of the county. The next year after its organization (1793), it was called on to contribute to the formation of Harrison, and again, in 1794, it contributed liberally to the formation of Campbell County. Since then it has remained intact, and is now bounded on the north by Owen County; northeast and east by Harrison and Bourbon; south by Fayette and Woodford and west by Franklin. As stated in another chapter, it is drained by tributaries of the Kentucky River, the principal of which are the North Elkhorn, South Elkhorn and Eagle Creeks. The surface is level, or gently rolling, very rich and productive, except in the north and northwest portions, which are somewhat hilly and broken. As small as is its territory, it ranks about the tenth in the State in wealth. It is a fine stock county, and many of the stock farms, for which Kentucky is so justly noted, are located in Scott, and, with the stock interests, will be referred to in another chapter. The following description of the county is by Mr. A. D. Offutt, and is very minute. It is given as of interest to all who live within its limits, and is as follows:

This county is about twenty-five and one half miles long from north to south, with an average width of about seventeen and one-half miles. A ridge, separating the waters of North Elkhorn from those of Eagle Creek, runs entirely across it in a westerly direction. There is about one-third of the county, which is known as "Eagle," on the north of this ridge; it is much more rolling or hilly than that situated south of it. The surface soil is rich, loose and friable, overlying clay, resting upon Lower Silurian limestone, producing blue-grass, clover, timothy, tobacco and the cereals, when first put under cultivation, as abundantly as the best Kentucky blue-grass land. But much of the cleared or arable land has been taxed, year after year, with crops of corn, the consequence of which is, the hillsides are badly washed, and more or less of the surface soil gone. However, it is very susceptible of improvement, and not a few of the farmers have commenced it, and clothed the hillsides with carpets of blue-grass. It is to be hoped the good work will continue, and that this salubrious, picturesque and beautiful part of the county may, erelong, "blossom as the rose." It has been called "the land of the free and home of the brave," a patriotic and sociable people, the young ever ready for a reel or round dance, "a horse swop" or a fox hunt. If "their church doors stand open wide, night and day, like the heavens to which they lead," so also their latch-strings are always out, and the wayfarer meets with a greeting and cordial welcome.

This part of the county, when in a state of nature, was heavily timbered, of which there still remains an abundance. There is a supply of good spring water for all agricultural and grazing purposes, except on the ridges, where ponds are readily made. The value of this land has never been properly appreciated.

The ridge dividing the waters of North Elkhorn from those of Eagle Creek promises to be one of the most valuable fruit belts in Kentucky, and that, as well as all north of it, is most admirably adapted to sheep-husbandry. There is probably no part of the United States that excels it for this purpose. Many gentlemen are already engaged in this pleasant and lucrative occupation, and yearly others are being added to their numbers. There are railroad facilities for transportation to Cincinnati at their back doors for a market. One gentleman on the ridge, Mr. B. Hall, now has 1,100 breeding ewes; they are principally cared for and grazed on Eagle. Others count their flocks by hundreds.

The southern division of the county is noted for its Short-Horn breeding. It adjoins Bourbon and Fayette. A small portion of the northwestern part of this division of the county closely resembles what is known as Eagle. The remaining portion, when viewed by a geologist, appears as if Dame Nature was in a frolicsome mood when, with her canny hand, she fashioned this part of her domain. North Elkhorn, from its entrance into the county until it passes out of it, is almost continuously boxing the compass. Its general course is north-northwest, dividing it in about equal parts. In the county, it has eight tributaries from the north side, and but one from the opposite side. This is Cane Run, the Minnehaha of Kentucky. This may be accounted for when it is known that the ridge between the two streams is always contiguous to North Elkhorn, and at one place, at least, a stone may be thrown from the ridge into its waters. The soil is deep and of unsurpassed fertility, gently undulating, based on Lower Silurian (cavernous) limestone. The under-drainage is perfect. There is no surface rock. It is not uncommon to see springs break out of the side of a depression in the surface, or natural basin, run a longer or shorter distance, according to the size of the basin, and disappear in the bowels of the earth. When these sinks can be successfully closed, valuable ponds are formed for fish culture and stock purposes. Mineral water is found in different parts of the county, in artesian wells at a depth of about one hundred and twenty-eight feet, and sometimes in springs.

The timber is burr-oak, black and white walnut, black and white ash, black and honey locust, sugar maple, buckeye, hackberry, wild cherry, etc. Much of it was originally covered with cane, and particularly the Cane Run Valley. A wash or gully is seldom or never seen.

It is hardly necessary to say, after what has been said, that blue grass grows here most abundantly. It grows every day in the year when the thermometer is above 32° and there is sufficient moisture in the earth.

The first court house of Scott County was erected in 1796, and stood on the public square. The lower story was built of stone, in a very rough manner, and the upper story was of wood. It contained several rooms, which were let out to traders, schools, etc.. to the highest bidders. This building was taken down in 1816, and a new house erected in the following year. It was of brick, was much better than the first one and was finished in plain style. A still better court house was built in 1847, which served as a temple of justice until 1875, when it was destroyed by fire, following right on the heels of the destruction, by fire, of the Paris court house. During the next two years, the present magnificent structure was erected, at a cost of about $40,000, and is said, by knowing ones, to be the best court house in the State for the amount of money it cost. It is all paid for, too, which is the pleasantest part of it. Fuller particulars of the different court houses and jails are given by Dr. Gano, in the history of Georgetown.

The first jail was erected in 1795–96, on the northeast corner of the public square, and was of logs, with grated windows. In 1811, a man by the name of Scott was in jail for stealing. He tried to burn himself out, and came near burning himself up before he was rescued. The second jail was built, in 1820, on Spring Branch, where the present house stands. The third and present jail was built about the year 1847, and is a substantial structure.

The county farm and poor house should be noticed in this connection. Like the same institutions in many other counties of Kentucky, it is not what it ought to be. Many of our poor houses are a shame and reproach to the counties in which they are located and to Kentuckians at large. We should take good care of our poor, for none of us know how soon we may have to

"Go over the hills to the poor house."

The Scott County Poor House and Farm are located in Lytle's Fork Precinct. The house was built in 1867. The first keeper was F. K. Holland. The present one is Asa Southworth. The house now contains about twenty-five inmates. The county furnishes the keeper a farm of 200 acres and gives him $90 each per annum for keeping the paupers.

But little was learned of the organization of the courts of Scott County. They will be more particularly referred to in another chapter. Their organization, however, was the same as in other counties. The names of early officers of the county could not be obtained. Without going into details of the early courts and their organization, we will give the names of some of the later officers of the county. The first Board of Magistrates were Sim Griffith, John Wait, R. T. Branham, E. Allender, G. E. Beadel, Asa Payne, Alexander Carrick, James Fields, John Lindsey, James Johnson, John W. Forbes, James Cannon, John Garth, Robinson Jones, Henry Edmondson and John P. Gano. Willis Dehoney was Sheriff at that time and B. W. Finnell, Judge. The present county officers are James F. Askew, Master Commissioner; George V. Payne, County Judge; H. V. Johnson, County Attorney; Notley Estis, Circuit Clerk; J. Henry Wolfe, County Clerk; Joseph F. Finley, Sheriff; James Pullen, Jailer; B. F. Randal, Coroner; Eddy Butler, Surveyor; Alex. Oder, Assessor; and V. F. Bradley,

School Commissioner. The present Board of Magistrates is already given.

At the time of the formation of Scott County, it was rather large in extent, thinly populated and did not require to be subdivided into precincts or districts. As the population increased, however, for the sake of convenience and to facilitate business, it was laid off into districts, for election and other purposes. With some changes since the time of formation, the county is at present subdivided as follows: Georgetown Precinct, No. 1; White Sulphur Precinct, No. 2; Stamping Ground Precinct, No. 3; Lytle's Fork Precinct, No. 4; Big Eagle Precinct, No. 5; Turkey Foot Precinct, No. 6; Oxford Precinct, No. 7; and Newtown Precinct, No. 8. Each of these precincts have a general polling place at some convenient point, where the sturdy yeomanry meet to exercise the rights of suffrage guaranteed to free-born American citizens, including (of late years) those of African descent. They likewise have two Magistrates and a Constable, who dispense even-handed justice to the people of their respective precincts. These Magstrates form the County Court, and at periodical meetings transact the county business. At present the Board of Magistrates is as follows: Georgetown Precinct—James C. Lemmon and James F. Sconce, and L. M. Peak, Constable; White Sulphur Precinct—W. B. Galloway and John C. Glass, and W. S. Thomason, Constable; Stamping Ground Precinct—John S. Lindsey and Charles Murphy, and V. C. Bradley, Constable; Lytle's Fork Precinct—John W. Ireland and Paschal Wood, and S. Browning, Constable; Big Eagle Precinct—J. K. Marshall and Z. T. Skirvin, and J. A. Guill, Constable; Turkey Foot Precinct—Thomas B. Hiles and J. V. Autle, and A. Wilson, Constable; Oxford Precinct—E. M. Hambrick and W. H. Salyers, and J. H. Barkley, Constable; Newtown Precinct—W. A. Smith and M. H. Kendall. There is no Constable in this precinct.

The official census of Scott County, since its organization as a county, in 1792, is as follows: In 1800, 8,007; in 1810, 12,419; in 1820, 14,219; in 1830, 14,677; in 1840, 13,668; in 1850, 14,946; in 1860, 14,417; in 1870, 11,607; and in 1880, 14,965, of whom 5,002 are colored. The present assessed valuation of the land, according to the Auditor's last report, is $4,024,510 in round numbers, or an average of $22.66 per acre.

A few words might appropriately be said in this connection of the early industries. Although Lexington boasts of having been the great manufacturing center of the West, in early years, yet Georgetown and Scott County were ahead in some things. Of the early manufactories of Scott, we extract from Collins' history, as follows: "The first fulling mill and the first rope walk in Kentucky were each established by the Rev. Elijah Craig, a Baptist preacher, at Georgetown, in 1789. The first paper mill was built at the same place (Georgetown) by the same Baptist preacher, Rev. Elijah Craig, and his partners, Parker & Co. The enterprise was begun in the summer of 1791, but the manufacture of paper successfully was not accomplished until March, 1793. The mill house was 40x60 feet in size, the basement of stone, and the two and a half stories above of wood—a good frame, with not a cut-nail in the building, even the shingles being put on with oak pins. The large volume of clear water from the Royal Spring, running over a limestone bottom, was an attractive sight. The mill dam was erected in 1789. Here was turned out the first sheet of paper in the Great West—made by hand, sheet by sheet. There was no machinery in those days to wind over fifty miles in one beautiful white continuous sheet. The first mill was burnt down in 1837. Some printed sheets of the paper still exist; and one other elegant relic, now in the paper-mill of Mr. Stedman, on Elkhorn, in Franklin County—a powerful iron screw, of finished English make, six inches in diameter, four and a half feet long, and weighing 800 pounds. What enterprise, and at what cost it required at that day of bad roads and poor freighting facilities, to get that screw from England to its place in this mill!"

Georgetown also made the first Bourbon whisky in the State, in 1789, at the fulling mill above referred to. This, however, was a bit of enterprise for which she deserves no thanks whatever, but, on the contrary, would have been entitled to more credit if she had refrained from its manufacture. These facts show that Scott County was once an enterprising and manufacturing section, more so than at the present time.

The first two or three decades after the formation of Scott County, there was little or no party strife, and the citizens generally voted for their favorites, wholly independent of party discipline or party bias. It was not until about 1823–24 that political war was inaugurated under the style of "Relief" and "Anti-Relief" parties, or "New Court" and "Old Court" parties. For three years or more, the most violent struggle ensued, scarcely equaled in the history of the State, except at the close of the late war. These parties—Old and New Court—finally drifted into the Whig and Democrat parties, the latter of which is still one of the great political parties of the time.—*W. H. Perrin.*

SCOTT COUNTY COURT HOUSE, KY.

CHAPTER II.

MORAL IMPROVEMENT AND DEVELOPMENT—EARLY CHURCHES AND CHURCH HISTORY OF SCOTT—PIONEER PREACHERS —REV. GANO AND OTHERS—EDUCATIONAL HISTORY—EARLY SCHOOLS OF KENTUCKY— JOHNSON'S INDIAN SCHOOL—THE PRESS, ETC., ETC.

GO ye into all the world, and preach the Gospel to every creature, was given as a command to the children of men eighteen hundred years ago, by the lowly Nazarene. Nor was it intended alone for the salvation of those nations, who, year after year, brought tribute to Cæsar, but with prophetic vision, the world's great Redeemer gazed on nations then unborn, and heard the cry of those who, in all ages, groaned beneath the yoke of sin. Then for the redemption, He gave to His disciples those commands which in later years have caused His people to widely spread God's glorious truth. When from Atlantic's coast, even from Pymouth Rock, the Star of Empire first renewed her journey westward, and the pioneers of a mighty race descended the western slopes of the Alleghanies, then in the van of the great army, the heralds of salvation bore aloft the Cross of Christ, and planted it firmly in the great valley of the Mississippi, destined to become the home of a mighty nation. The solitary settlers of the dark and bloody ground rejoiced to hear those early messengers proclaim the glad tidings, or wept at the story of Pilate, his pitiless crown of thorns, and the agonies of Golgotha and Calvary. The dark and gloomy forests were pierced by the light that shone from the Star of Bethlehem, and the hymns of praise to God were mingled with the sound of the pioneer's ax, as he exerted his energies in rearing a cabin to shelter his loved ones from the inclement weather and from wild beasts.

These holy men of God, who exposed themselves to all the dangers of wilderness life for the purpose of doing their Master's will, traveled on foot or on horseback, among the early settlers of Scott County, stopping where night overtook them, and receiving the hospitalities of the cabin, without money and without price. Reverently asking the blessing of God upon all they did, their lives were simple and unostentatious, their wants few and easily satisfied; their teachings were plain and unvarnished, touched with no eloquence save that of their daily living, which although not "locusts and wild-honey," yet was seen and known of all men. They were of different religious sects, yet no discord was ever manifested between them, but a united effort was made by them to show men the way to better things by better living, and thus, finally, to reach the best of all—a home in heaven, that

> "The good old paths are good enough, * *
> The fathers walked to heaven in them, and *
> By following meekly where they trod, all reach
> The home they found."

They were not only physicians for the soul's cure, but they sometimes ministered to the body's ailments. They married the living, and buried the dead; they christened the babe, admonished the young and warned the old; they cheered the despondent, rebuked the willful and hurled the vengeance of eternal burnings at the desperately wicked. Wherever they came they were welcome, and notice was sent around to the neighbors and a meeting was held, while all listened with interest to the promises of the Gospel. For years, these pioneer preachers could say literally, as did the Master before them: "The foxes have holes, and the birds of the air have nests, but (we), the sons of men, have not where to lay our heads."

The Baptists are said to have been the pioneers of religion not only in Kentucky but in Scott County. The first church society organized in Kentucky was by Rev. Lewis Craig, a Baptist minister, on South Elkhorn, five miles from Lexington. For forty years, this was one of the most prosperous churches in the State. Elder Craig often preached within the present limits of Scott County. He had been a valiant champion of the Baptist cause in Virginia, and was several times imprisoned in that State for preaching the Gospel contrary to the Church of England, which was then the prevailing religion in the Old Dominion. Among other early preachers of Central Kentucky, belonging to this denomination were Elders John Gano, Ambrose Dudley, John Taylor, William Hickman, Joseph Reding, William E. Waller, Moses Bledsoe, John Rice, Elijah Craig, William Marshall, etc., etc., many of whom preached at intervals in Scott County, and some of whom were residents of the county. Of these, Rev. Elijah Craig lived in Georgetown, and is mentioned elsewhere as a pioneer business man, as well as a pioneer preacher. Rev. John Gano, who has many descendants, both in Scott and Bourbon Counties, settled in Kentucky in 1788, and was one of the most eminent men of his day. He spent many years as an itinerant minister traveling over the United States, from New England to Georgia, and for twenty-five years was pastor of a church in New York City. During the Revolutionary war, he was Chaplain in the patriot army, and by his counsels and prayers greatly encouraged the American soldiery. Many interesting anecdotes are related of him by Benedict, of which the following is a sample: While in the army, he was on his way one morning to pray with the regiment, when he passed by a group of officers, one of whom (who was standing with his back toward him) was uttering his profane expressions in the most rapid manner. The officers, one after another, gave him the usual salutation. "Good morning, Doctor," said the swearing officer. "Good morning, sir," replied the Chaplain; "you pray early this morning." "I beg your pardon, sir." "O, I cannot pardon you; carry your case to your God." Another anecdote is equally as good. One day he was standing near some soldiers who were disputing whose turn it was to cut some wood for the fire. One profanely said, he would be —— if he cut it. But he was soon afterward convinced that the task belonged to him, and took up the ax to perform it. Before he could commence, however, Mr. Gano stepped up asked for the ax. "O! no," said the soldier, "the Chaplain shan't cut wood." "Yes," replied Mr. Gano, "I must." "But why?" asked the soldier. "The reason is," answered Mr. Gano, "I just heard you say that you would be damned if you cut it, and I had much rather take the labor off your hands than that you should be made miserable forever."

The following tribute was paid to him by one who knew him well: As a minister of Christ, he shone like a star of the first magnitude in the American churches and moved in a widely extended field of action. For this office, God had endowed him with a large portion of grace, and with excellent gifts. Having discerned the excellence of Gospel truths, and the importance of eternal realities, he felt their power on his own soul, and accordingly he inculcated and urged them on the minds of his hearers with persuasive eloquence and force. He was not deficient in doctrinal discussion, or what rhetoricians style the demonstrative character of a discourse; but he excelled in the pathetic—in pungent, forcible addresses to the heart and conscience. Like John, the harbinger of our Redeemer, 'he was a burning and a shining light, and many rejoiced in his light.' Resembling the sun, he arose in the church with morning brightness, advanced regularly to his station of meridian splendor, and then gently declined with mild effulgence, till he disappeared, without a cloud to intercept his rays, or obscure his glory."

Rev. John Taylor was another of the pioneer preachers of the Baptist Church, who used to preach in this county at times, when the country was little else than a wilderness. He was long an itinerant minister of Kentucky, and was a preacher of "great Scriptural plainness." The fields of his labors extended from the Kentucky to the Ohio Rivers, and he usually visited six or eight associations each year. Elder John T. Johnson was a native of Scott County, and is still remembered by many of the citizens of Scott. He died in 1856, at Lexington, Mo., in the sixty-eighth year of his age.

The Presbyterians were, perhaps, the next religious sect in Kentucky, followed by the Methodists. These denominations established churches in early times in Scott County, and while it may be the Baptists have predominated, yet other sects have long been well represented in the county. Rev. Barton W. Stone, originally a Presbyterian, but for many years prior to his death a Christian preacher, and one of the best known clergymen of Kentucky in his day, often preached in Georgetown and in Scott County. He is so extensively mentioned elsewhere in this volume, that it would be superfluous to repeat it here.

It is not possible to say when the first church was built in Scott County, or where it stood. It was not for several years, however, after the organization of church societies that an effort was made to put up a church building. But as the country settled up, and the wealth of the people would permit, temples were erected to the Most High, until now, side by side with the schoolhouse, we find in every neighborhood those

> "Steeple towers,
> And spires, whose silent fingers point to Heaven."

In the chapter devoted to the precincts of the county, all information that can be obtained of the individual organization of the different churches in the county and the erection of church buildings will be given, together with all local and historical facts connected with them.

Schools.—It was recently said, that "governments like ours are founded upon the presumption that the people have sufficient intelligence to perceive and sufficient virtue to appreciate the principles by which they should be guided. Republics fall and despotisms arise when virtue departs from the councils of their rulers, and ignorance prevails among their people. The only true policy, therefore, which can be followed by those who are charged with the administration of government, is the encouragement of every measure which tends to raise the standard of mental and moral excellence." Thus only can the stability of the free institutions upon which we pride ourselves so much be assured, and the blessings of republican government transmitted to our posterity. Renown gained in bloody warfare may gild our place in history, but victory upon a thousand battle-fields can furnish us no guaranty of perpetual greatness and security. "The genius of Napoleon could raise his country to the highest rank among the military powers of Europe, but a little earlier in the history of France it could not have checked the fearful revolution engendered by the vices of the nobility and the ignorance of the common people. In this instance, a so-called Republic sprung into existence upon the ruins of a fallen dynasty. It discarded the rule of intelligence, merged in hopeless confusion the ideas of liberty and license, whilst above the gates of its charnel-house was written the fearful legend, 'Death is an eternal sleep.' The existence of a government like this was of necessity brief, but nothing less than the hand of despotic power could reduce its chaotic elements into order, and save the people from the ruin which their own brutality had brought upon them."

So has it ever been. Superstition and barbarism are the sure results of a lack of education, and to those evils are traced the decline of Greece and Rome. "Nations and States are only relatively great as they lend their countenance to virtue and their aid to the broadest and most liberal education. Not merely the education of the favored few who are born to wealth and station; not the instruction of children in the mysteries of a political or religious creed, the logic of the churchman, the intricacies of legal lore or the technicalities of medical science, but an education higher and broader in its scope, which sheds its radiance in the hovel as well as in the palace; which lifts men and women above the dominion of stupidity and superstition, and qualifies them for an intelligent performance of the labors and duties of life." Whether or not we need such education in Kentucky, is a question which will admit of but one answer.

It is a fact much to be regretted that Kentucky does not pay more attention to the common schools. In late years she has made considerable advancement in this direction, but she is still far behind many of her sister States in her common school system. One great drawback to common school education in Kentucky, has always been, that it was looked upon as somewhat degrading, as a kind of scheme inaugurated for the benefit of poor children. The following extract is from the report of the Educational Committee of the State Legislature:

> Public education is no humanitarian movement for the benefit of the *poor* children of the Commonwealth. It is a system intimately associated with, and fundamental to, the social order, and contemplates the improvement of citizenship without reference to the private fortunes of those upon whom it expends its forces. The idea that the common school is a charity institution has been, and is to-day, the most formidable barrier to the maturing of laws for the government of the system, and of securing the means necessary to perfect its usefulness. When viewed simply as an institution for the benefit of paupers, it affords a temptation to legislators to neglect it, and to refuse to it that fostering care which it imperatively requires. Dignify it as a natural and necessary element in the perpetuation of our republican liberties, and it challenges the attention of the statesman as well as the philanthropist, and demands of him the exercise of his most sagacious powers in the solution of the problem which it presents. Knowledge is the universal *right*, as it is the universal *interest*, of men.

The people displayed an early interest in educating their children, and yet when the Legislature passed the free school laws, it raised a great deal of wrath among the masses. This was not only the case in Kentucky, but in all the neighboring States. In the spirit of internal improvement which well nigh wrecked several of the Western States, tax-payers heartily indorsed their Legislators for voting away millions of dollars in internal improvements, but as heartily condemned them for passing laws compelling them to support "*pauper schools*," and the poorer classes were loud in their condemnation because these school laws made "pauper scholars of their children." This, we say was the case, not only in Kentucky but in many other States, and we regret that too much of the same spirit still prevails in Kentucky. With that spirit of pride, and for the sake of appearance, which together have ruined so many, families pinch themselves and scrape together funds to send their children to some third or fourth class academy or college, because "the free schools are only intended for poor folks." When rightly viewed, however, our free school, or common school system, is the very foundation of education, and is the grandest, broadest and most liberal scheme ever adopted by any nation upon the face of the globe—that of educating *all* its children at the public expense.

The schoolhouses of the early period were of the poorest kind, and it is a fact to be regretted that in many portions of Kentucky little improvement has been made in their architecture. A majority of the Kentucky schoolhouses are built of logs, and many of them are wholly unfit for the purposes for which they are intended. No money is more judiciously expended than that used in building comfortable and convenient schoolhouses; it is really "bread cast upon the waters, that will return after many days." Most of our cities and large towns have good public school buildings, but in the country there are very few that even deserve the name of schoolhouses.

Who taught the first school in Scott County is not known at the present day, nor when nor where the first house for school purposes was built. But the settlers of the county were of the better class of citizens, and most of them were blue-blooded Virginians—facts which indicate that schools were established at an early period. Scott County and Georgetown have ever maintained their reputation for excellent schools, which are evidenced in the character of those in Georgetown at the present day, and which will be fully written up in connection with the history of the city of Georgetown. Of the public schools of Scott the following statistics are from the last report of the State Superintendent of Public Instruction :

Amount paid teachers for the year ending October 10, 1881 :

White	$4,755 45
Colored	602 62
Total	$5,358 07
Number of white children in the county of school age	3,752
Number of colored children in the county of school age	1,751

There are in the county thirty-nine school districts, in which are schoolhouses of the usual Kentucky type, and in which schools are taught for the regular terms each year. In addition to these, the county is divided into fourteen districts for the benefit of the colored people. They have schoolhouses in each of these districts, and take considerable interest in educating their children. The following extract is very true of the early schools, and so true, even at the present, of many of the common schools of Kentucky, that we give it as a step looking to their improvement. It should be attentively perused:

" It was our misfortune, in boyhood, to go to a district school. A little, square, pine building, blazing in the sun, stood upon the highway, without a tree for shade or shadow near it ; without bush, yard, fence or circumstance to take off its bare, cold, hard, hateful look. Before the door, in winter, was the pile of wood for fuel ; and there, in summer, were all the chips of the winter's wood.

" In winter we were squeezed into the recess of the furthest corner, among little boys, who seemed to be sent to school merely to fill up the chinks between the bigger boys. Certainly we were never sent for any such absurd purpose as an education. There were the great scholars ; the the school in winter was for *them*, not for us pickaninnies. We were read and spelled twice a day, unless something happened to prevent, which *did* happen about every other day. For the rest of the time we were busy in keeping still. And a time we always had of it. Our shoes always would be scraping on the floor, or knocking the shins of urchins who were also being educated.' All of our little legs together (poor, tired, nervous, restless legs, with nothing to do !) would fill up the corner with such a noise, that every ten or fifteen minutes the master would bring down his two-foot hickory ferule on the desk with a clap that sent shivers through our hearts to think how that would have felt if it had fallen somewhere else ; and then, with a look that swept us all into utter extremity of stillness, he would cry, 'Silence in that corner !' Stillness would last a few minutes ; but little boys' memories are not capacious. Moreover, some of the boys had great gifts of mischief, and some of mirthfulness, and some had both together. The consequence was, that just when we were most afraid to laugh, we saw the most comical things to laugh at. Temptations, which we could have vanquished with a smile out in the free air, were irresistible in our little corner, where a laugh and a stinging slap were very apt to woo each other."

As rapid strides as we have made in education, there is still vast room for improvement in our common schools. Of the colored schools, State Superintendent Henderson said in his annual report of 1880 : " In most of the cities the municipal authorities have supplemented the State bonus by giving to them all the taxes paid by the people of color, and some of them have dedicated other resources beyond the revenue derived by levies on their property. We shall always cherish, as a proud consciousness of courageous duty performed, that we have stood steadfastly for the education of the colored race, and incurred all the criticism and hostility which prejudice and passion have visited upon us, without a cowardly apology, or any disposition of mind or heart to explain away our record. It is gratifying that the representative men of the party that placed us in office have approved our course, and disapproved the antagonisms it has invited from those who adhere to hereditary prejudice instead of rising to the level of an intelligence which respects the issues which the changed relations of this race have introduced into the policies of this State. We shall never lament that we fought for a principle dearer than personal promotion when it was proposed, in the University Bill, to rifle them of all hopes of further assistance by depriving them of all interest in the proceeds of any dedication of the proceeds of the sales of public lands to education by the United States Congress. We have, for prudential reasons affecting our white system, never favored a division of the fund dedicated to it for colored educational purposes."

Johnson's Indian School.—As we have stated, the schools and colleges of Georgetown will be carefully and fully written up in the educational chapter devoted to that flourishing little city. In conclusion of our sketch of general education of the county, a few words of an institution now forgotten by many of the citizens of Scott will be of interest perhaps to our readers. We allude to the Indian school once maintained by Col. "Dick" Johnson. This school was located at White Sulphur Springs. When the general Government bought the lands of the Chickasaw and Choctaw Indians, and located them west of the Mississippi River, the annuities due them were devoted to the education of Indian boys. Col. Dick Johnson, then a Member of Congress, and afterward Vice President of the United States, was appointed Superintendent of this school. He located it at his farm five miles west of Georgetown, at Blue Spring. This was about the year 1822 or 1823; it is known, by citizens still living, to have been in operation in 1825, as La Fayette, in his tour of the country in that year, visited it at Blue Spring, and a great feast was prepared for him by the neighborhood, the ladies making a cheese for the occasion that weighed 500 pounds. In 1831, the school was removed from Blue Spring to White Sulphur Spring, which was also on a farm owned by Col. Johnson. He employed teachers and ran his school as a regular boarding school, receiving so much per week for board and tuition. There were generally from two to three hundred Indian boys in attendance, and it brought a considerable revenue to Col. Johnson's exchequer. Some of the boys afterward filled prominent positions in the country; one is now practicing law in New York, and several others became preachers of the Gospel. In 1833, during the raging of the cholera, it was terribly fatal at the school. There were two physicians residing near, who usually attended the students; but, one day, when the disease was at its worst, Col. Johnson sent to Georgetown for Dr. Ewing, who was a partner of Dr. Gano, and had been the Surgeon of Col. Johnson's regiment in the war of 1812. Dr. Ewing, being unable to leave, Dr. Gano went in his stead, and says that seventeen of the boys died that day. He advised Col. Johnson to change the location of the school, as he thought both the location and the arrangement of the buildings were favorable to the spread of the disease. Col. Johnson rejected the suggestion, however, with scorn, saying, "He would stay there and die with the last one of them. About the year 1836 or 1837, the school was discontinued.

The Press.—This important factor is more fully written in the city of Georgetown; but a few words, in conclusion of this chapter, is not inappropriate. Says Robert Bonner, the great New York *Ledger* man: "The only imperishable memorial is the printed page. No art save that of printing can reproduce the original emanations of genius in unlimited number, and as long as Time shall last. Statues, monuments, paintings, molder and fade, and with them the names of those they were intended to memorialize: but the volume of to-day may be reprinted ten thousand years hence, if the world shall endure so long, and the last copy will be for all practical purposes, as available as the first." This is very true, and no town of any consequence, at the present day, is found without its printing office and newspaper. The city of Georgetown has now two quite flourishing papers—the Georgetown *Times* and the *Every Saturday*. The former was established in 1867, and was the only paper published in the county until 1878, when the latter paper was established. The *Times* is edited and published by Mr. John A. Bell, and the *Every Saturday* by James B. Finnell.—*Perrin.*

CHAPTER III.

INTERNAL IMPROVEMENTS—EARLY LEGISLATION ON ROADS—LAYING OUT ROADS IN KENTUCKY—RAILROADS OF THE COUNTY—AGRICULTURE—SKETCH OF IT BY MR. GANO—STATISTICS—AGRICULTURAL SOCIETIES—DISTILLERIES, ETC.

AS far back as 1748, an act was passed by Virginia, requiring all roads to or from the court house of each county, and all mills and ferries, to be "kept well cleared from weeds, bushes and other obstructions, and all roots to be well grubbed up for thirty feet wide." In 1785, an act was passed by Virginia, which was still in force when Kentucky was admitted into the Union in 1792, and was re-enacted by the Kentucky Legislature in 1797, providing for the opening of new roads, and the alteration of former roads under surveyors appointed by courts. "All male laboring persons, sixteen years old or more, were required to work the roads, except those who were masters of two or more male slaves over said age; or else pay a fine of 7s. 6d. ($1.25) for each day's absence or neglect thus to work." In the absence of bridges, milldams were required to be built at least twelve feet wide for the passage of public roads, with bridges over the pierhead and flood-gates. The surveyors were authorized to impress wagons, and to take timber, stone or earth for building roads, and a mode of paying for same out of county levy was provided.* Among the early acts of the Legislature, was one pertaining to roads—it was passed December 14, 1793. This act "appointed Bennett Pemberton, Nathaniel Sanders and Daniel Weisiger Commissioners to receive subscriptions in money, labor or property, to raise a fund for clearing a wagon-road from Frankfort to Cincinnati," such road being deemed "productive of private convenience and public utility," and the route lying through an unsettled country which could not be cleared in the usual manner by the county courts. This road would pass through Scott County, and was a matter of some interest to the people.

Gov. Desha in his annual message to the Legislature December 4, 1826, took strong ground in favor of a turnpike road from Maysville to Louisville, "passing through the most important towns of Cynthiana, Georgetown and Frankfort." He suggested other important connecting roads, and closed the subject as follows: "The subject of common schools and internal improvements may be made auxiliary to each other. Let the school fund now in the Bank of the Commonwealth ($140,917), the proceeds of the sale of vacant lands, the stock in the banks belonging to the State ($781,238), and all other funds which can be raised by other means than taxes on the people, be vested in the turnpike roads; and the net profits arising from tolls on these roads be forever sacredly devoted to the interests of education." Turnpike roads were an early institution in the blue grass region, and among the first companies incorporated for the building of turnpikes were that for the Lexington & Georgetown Turnpike, Georgetown & Frankfort and Georgetown & Cincinnati—the latter road was incorporated February 8, 1819. Scott County has her share of turnpike roads. Diverging from Georgetown, they traverse the county in all directions, and are unsurpassed by the public highways of any country.

Railroads.—The pioneer railroad of the West, touches a corner of this county, and has one station, Paynes', within the limits of Scott, from which much shipping is done for the southern part of the county. Until the completion of the Cincinnati Southern Railroad, this was Scott's only means of railroad shipping and transportation. The history of this old pioneer road—the Louisville, Cincinnati & Lexington—is fully given in Part I of this work, and will not be repeated here.

The Cincinnati Southern Railroad passes through nearly the center of Scott County, from north to south. The charter for this road was granted by the Legislature of Kentucky in the latter part of January, 1872. The completion of this great trunk line between the North and South, is but the culmination of the project agitated some fifty years ago, viz., the Charleston & Cincinnati Railroad, and covers much of the same ground it was designed to occupy. There are few roads in the United States (none of equal length perhaps), the construction of which involved the outlay of a like sum expended on the Cincinnati Southern—a sum little short of $14,000,000. Its cost has been enormous, and while it must, in time, become a great highway of travel and traffic, yet it will be long before it pays a large per cent upon the sum invested in its construction.

Scott County did not, as a county, take any stock in the road, or vote a tax toward building it. The citizens got up a subscription, sufficient to purchase the right of way through the county to the railroad authorities. In some instances, the right of way was donated by the parties through whose lands the road passes, and the amount subscribed was large enough to purchase it in all other cases. The road was opened for travel in the winter of 1879–80, and has been of great value to the county and convenience to the people.

The Frankfort, Georgetown & Paris Railroad is an enterprise still in the future. It was agitated as early as 1871 under the title of Paris, Frankfort & Big Sandy. The county subscribed $350,000 to it, but after much excitement, wire-pulling, etc., it was buried under the financial crash of 1872–73; the subscription never being called for. The question has been recently revived as the Frankfort, Georgetown & Paris, but does not carry with it the popularity of the old enterprise. The route surveyed for it passes through the southern part of the county, and hence the people at large take little interest in it. The question of issuing bonds failed to pass by a popular vote of the people. The project does not amount to much as a railroad enterprise any way, and if the road is ever built will be of little value except as a means of local travel and traffic. A subscription sufficient to purchase the right of way along the route of the road is, at most, the county's interest in the enterprise, and all that may be expected from it.

Agriculture.—The following excellent article upon the agriculture of the county, was written for this volume by Rev. John Allen Gano, Sr., a man well known, not only in this county, but throughout the surrounding counties, as a stock raiser and breeder, and one who has paid great attention to the science of agriculture. Upon this subject, he says: "The writer can only sketch a brief outline from personal observation since about the fifteenth year of the nineteenth century. Although only a youth, we were quite

*Collins on Internal Improvements.

conversant with farming operations. The farm lands at that remote period, with few exceptions, were almost in their virgin freshness and strength, the soil rich and productive, and although farming implements were fewer and of ruder construction than now, and cultivation less thorough, as a general thing the yield was far more abundant. The amount of land in cultivation was much less, even up to the middle of this century than now. The number of laborers, mostly negroes, was in the excess of the need of the farmers, so that if a farmer wanted to hire help, the price of a good able-bodied negro man was not more than $70, the hirer furnishing him his board and clothing. This latter, was by no means costly, being entirely of home manufacture; the food was plenty of bread, meat and vegetables; and for drink, water or good milk. The negroes then were a happy, contented race—many of them were truly religious. When masters were kind, as it was ever their interest to be, there was but little of 'eye-service,' as they were often stimulated to exertion by rewards of praise.

"There was, in the early period, but little outlet for the products of the farms, and far less of the spirit of speculation than at the present day. The result was that farmers had plenty at home; they handled less money, it is true, but they lived easier. They did not recklessly plunge into debt; they lived more at home, with themselves and with their families, and were far happier. There was, too, much more sociability, neighborly feeling and good cheer generally among them. There was not such a rush after the rapid accumulation of great wealth, and hence fewer failures among farmers. The staple productions were much the same then as now, corn, wheat and oats predominating. Of meadow-grass, timothy was given the preference. Some hemp and tobacco were grown, but not so extensively as in after years. In those days of household manufacture, nearly every farmer had his 'patch' of flax, and the prudent housewife looked carefully to the handling of the flax and wool when prepared to her hand. She not only made them into cloth for family clothing, but often the means of procuring by barter, at the neighborhood store, other needed goods or groceries. Fifty or sixty bushels of corn, and thirty bushels of wheat per acre, were oftener produced then, even with the rude implements of agriculture, than half the amount is now. Since more of the lands have been cleared up, we have more of our world-renowned blue grass, and it is more cultivated and its value more highly appreciated than formerly. It would even now be better for the farmer, if he would be content to cultivate fewer acres of land, and they of the freshest and best, and grass at once all their worn-out and exhausted lands, that scarcely now pay for cultivation.

"As already stated, there was little outlet in the earlier part of this century from Scott County for the products of her soil. Macadamized roads and railroads were then unknown. A few enterprising citizens wagoned over rough roads, at considerable cost, and great labor and inconvenience, to the Ohio River, or at certain stages of water, to the Kentucky River, pork, flour, whisky or cordage, whence by flat-boats, it was transported to the Lower Mississippi River country, and to the then famous mart—New Orleans.

"After many months of absence the voyagers returned, and brought back in barges sugar, coffee, molasses, etc. Other enterprising citizens in that early period bought up droves of stock, horses and mules, and took them to South Carolina, and in addition to these, hogs to Virginia, then the best hog market we had. This business was in few hands, and the returns were but meager as compared with the trade of the present day. The toil, labor and exposure undergone by those resolute drovers and the men in their employ, was very poorly repaid in the small profit realized, and often they experienced serious and discouraging losses.

"The writer vividly remembers the fine, large, flourishing orchards of apples and peaches to be seen in the county sixty years ago. The enemies to orchards and fruit now so numerous and destructive, were then almost or quite unknown, and hence there was an abundance of fine fruit to regale the appetite almost the entire year round. In certain kinds of small fruits the present far surpasses those early times. But strange as it may seem, the apple crop of the present day is greatly inferior, and we have to depend for our best supplies on importations from other States.

"Stock of various kinds in Scott County have been greatly improved since the early settlement. Enterprising citizens brought to the county well-bred horses and cattle, and began early in the present century the improvement of of both of these valuable kinds of stock, while as yet but little attention had been paid to sheep and swine, except, in some rare instances, an infusion of the blood of the China hog among swine, and the Merino among sheep, at considerable cost, was attempted. These efforts ultimately led to the more valuable and admirable crosses we now have, greatly to the benefit of the farmers."

In conclusion of Mr. Gano's sketch, we append the following statistics of Scott County, which is taken from the Georgetown *Times*, and compiled for that paper from the Auditor's report:

WHITE LIST.

Number acres of land	177,509
Value of land	$4,024,510
Average value of land per acre	$22.60
Value of town lots	$450,825
Number of horses and mares	2,957
Value of horses and mares	$144,620
Number of mules	721
Value of mules	$35,690
Number of sheep	15,904
Value of sheep	$69,631
Number of hogs	6,077
Value of hogs	$7,090
Number of cattle	6,877
Value of cattle	$117,186
Number of stores	67
Value of stores	$102,040
Value under equalization law	$422,135
Value of carriages	$26,135
Value of gold and silver watches, plate, etc	$22,320
Total valuation	$5,422,496
Tax at 4½ cents on the $100	$24,672
Number of sheep killed by dogs	90
Value of same	$442
Pounds of tobacco grown	290,900
Pounds of hemp	1,450,228
Tons of hay	7,827
Bushels of corn	609,950
Bushels of wheat	157,506
Bushels of barley	36,045

COLORED LIST.

Total valuation of property	$61,661
Males over twenty years of age	1,172
Children between six and sixteen years of age	735

In point of wealth, Scott ranks tenth in the State, according to the report of the Auditor, which speaks well, when we take into consideration her small extent of territory. And in the matter of enterprise, it is an item to her credit, which may as well be given here as elsewhere, that since June, 1878, she has paid $22,000 toward the building of turnpike roads. As a further step in her enterprise, she would do well to make her turnpikes all free roads.

There was an agricultural society in the county at one time, but it has passed out of existence.

Distilleries.—Like all the blue grass counties, Scott has always been famous for making whisky. Mr. Collins tells us that the first Bourbon whisky made in the State was made at the fulling mill of Rev. Elijah Craig, in Georgetown, in 1789. The blue grass region has kept up its reputation for good whisky, and still makes the best in the world—if the word *good* may be, without violence, applied to the greatest known evil in existence. Whatever may be the views and opinions entertained by a majority of the people at the present day, in regard to the making of whisky, it was considered as honorable a business fifty or a hundred years ago, as any other manufacturing business a man could engage in. Even preachers did not deem it derogatory to their high and holy calling to lend their countenance to its manufacture, engage in it themselves, or drink a little of it occasionally "for the stomach's sake." Whisky, at the present day, is one of the largest commercial interests of Central Kentucky. However, it is not so extensively made in Scott County at the present time, perhaps, as in some of the neighboring counties. As a business, it is more particularly mentioned in the respective precincts where now manufactured.—*Perrin.*

CHAPTER IV.

THE CATTLE INTERESTS OF SCOTT—BREEDING OF SHORT-HORNS AND THE IMPROVEMENT OF CATTLE—THE FIRST BREEDERS AND IMPORTERS—SALES AT "LONG" PRICES—THE DIFFERENT HERDS OF THE COUNTY—FINE SHEEP, ETC., ETC.

THE first emigrants to Kentucky were from Virginia, North and South Carolina, Maryland, Pennsylvania, etc. They brought with them such cattle as they had, and such as their ancestors had brought from beyond the seas. What they were, no one can tell; but a mixed and motley crew. This was the case all over the State. The best of them, when paired together for a succession of years, no two of the produce would be alike, and none of them resemble either parent. This portion of the county was somewhat behind Clark, Bourbon and Fayette in their efforts to improve their herds. While these counties were breeding, grazing and feeding good grade cattle, Scott was raising hemp and corn, breeding and feeding hogs, horses and mules for the Virginia and South Carolina markets, and paying much attention to the rearing of blooded horses. However, the county was not wholly indifferent to her interests in this direction. Previous to 1817, a very few bulls of "Patton Stock," a cross between the unimproved Short and Long Horns, were introduced, and a Long-Horn bull, of the "Swinton importation," was also brought to this county. This is known as Mr. Saunder's importation, although several other gentlemen were associated with him. It was made to Fay-

Col. E. D. Offutt Sr

ette County, and just here we will say that, in our humble opinion, the Short-Horns of this importation were the equals, at least, of any of the later importations. While it may be said that we never saw any of the original animals, we have seen very many of their purely bred descendants in Kentucky, as well as the get of these imported seventeen bulls at Miller's Iron Works, Va., that would have been ornaments to any show yards. They were Short-Horns *that had short-horns*, and every characteristic of the race. But the wand of the magician passed over them, and their value was no more.

It may be out of place here, as well as futile, to make an argument tending toward proving the purity of their blood. We wish only to say, the blood of the "white heifer that traveled" to give Mr. Colling's herd a widespread reputation, was from the same herd as one of the despised seventeens. (We never had any of this blood in our Short-Horn herd, and may be considered an impartial witness in their behalf.)

John C. Talbot, Esq., we believe to have been the first gentleman to introduce a Short-Horn bull into the county. He was of "'17 blood." His grandson, John C. Payne, is now breeding Short-Horns on his old plantation, near Newtown. His father, Remus Payne, Esq., was one of the earliest Short-Horn breeders in the county.

Junius R. Ward, Esq., was the first to introduce Short-Horn cows into this county. They were of J. Hare Powel's importations. These were Carolina, by Pontiac (4734), and Miss Calhoun, by Felix, 501½ American Herd Book. That is, they were descended from Col. Powel's importations to Pennsylvania, from cows left by him with Hon. C. A. Barnitz, of York, to breed "on shares" during Col. Powel's absence in England. Mr. Saunders, the importer of the "seventeens," made his purchase of Mr. Barnitz in 1831. In what year Mr. Ward made his purchase of Col. Saunders we are unable to say. Both of the cows proved to be prolific, and their bulls were used without restraint by all who choose to avail themselves of so good an opportunity to grade up their cattle. A portion of Mr. Ward's Short-Horns are recorded in Vol. II American Herd Book, and a single entry in Vol. III. Although Mr. Ward used in his herd such bulls as 415 Orontes 2d (11877), bred by the Earl of Burlington, and other bulls of equal merit, for want of a herd book record, when his herd was disputed at public auction, about twenty years ago, none of them brought over grade prices.

The next gentleman in the county to breed Short-Horns was Capt. N. Craig. His first bull was Thaddeus 2286, bred by Gen. James Garrard, Bourbon County, Ky., a most excellent animal; of somewhat unfashionable pedigree. However, Capt. Craig had the satisfaction of selling him for $1,000. After this, he bought, at different times, several high-priced cows and bulls. Among the bulls, Wellington 7th 2370, bred by Isaac Vanmeter, Clark County, Ky.; Saladin 2168, imported by R. A. Alexander, and others equally good. Capt. Craig is still breeding; but, for some years, we have seen no public record of his herd.

Mr. James Gaines is the first gentleman that brought to the county an imported Short-Horn cow. He bought her of Mr. John Thorn, of Fayette County. She was imported to Fayette. He had been grading up his herd for a few generations, with Kirkpatrick and other Short-Horn bulls, and owned Meteor 705 alias Milton 713, bred by Fayette Importing Company. After breeding his and her descendants for a time, he could not identify the short-horns from the grades, and as occasion might offer, sold any of them as grades. It may be said with much truth, that no animal on his place ever drew a hungry breath, and that grades and Short-Horns were all superior animals. This gentleman was held up as an example of honesty and fair dealing in all his business transactions. But he thought more of his mules than he did of his Short-Horns. His son, E. P. Gaines, continues to use Short-Horn bulls in this herd; but mules are a specialty with him also, and he is now (March, 1882), feeding three hundred and ninety-seven for market.

The first imported Short-Horn bull ever in the county was 1038, Neptune 743, a red and white bull of good size, quality and much style, imported in 1837, by Henry Clay, Jr., of Fayette County. He was brought to the county the same year by E. P. Johnson, and was second to 2109½ Kirkpatrick, 1744, the same fall at the Franklin County fair.

Mr. James Bagg may also be placed among the earlier breeders of Short-Horns in Scott County; his herd was not large, but a good one. He always wanted the animal to be equal to the pedigree. Mr. Bagg was a native of Yorkshire, England, and had a personal acquaintance with many of the English breeders. After making several importations of Short-Horns to the United States, he settled in Kentucky, and finally in Scott County. While there he exercised much influence in inducing others to engage in the business of breeding Short-Horns. Mr. Bagg and the writer of this article lived on adjoining farms; from him we obtained much information about Yorkshire, and his Short-Horns and character of their breeders. Mr. Bagg still lives at an advanced age in Fayette County.

In 1836, E. S. Washington brought to Fayette County the bull London, and cows Reality by Malcolm (1190), and Snowdrop by Kirkpatrick 1617; at the same he brought Kirkpatrick for A. D. Offutt and himself, and for A. D. Offutt the cow America by Kirkpatrick. These were all Powel-bred

Short-Horns. It would be hardly fair to pass Kirkpatrick by without a remark. We will only say, that at a fat-cattle show at Washington City, two of his bullocks were first and second, and that he won the honors, as an aged bull, on three different show-yards in Kentucky.

In 1837, at the sale of David Sutton, in Fayette County, E. S. Washington, G. Marshall and A. D. Offutt, became the purchasers of 1653, Cyrus 393, by Wellington 1085, out of the most famous cow of her day, Cleopatra by 433 Pilot (496) bred by Mr. R. Booth, England.

In 1838, E. S. Washington and G. Marshall, at the sale of Samuel Smith, deceased, bought Prudence by 129 Imp. Comet (1554), a uterine sister of the renowned 1060 Otley (4632), by 401 Norfolk (2377). Prudence was exhibited at several fairs out of the county, and upon every occasion was deservedly first in her class. We have seldom, if ever, seen her equal from that day to the present.

In 1839, at the sale of Gratz and Cooper, Fayette County, E. S. Washington added to his herd Virginia 2d by 685, Bertram (1716), also Chenoa. Virginia was a cow of great merit. Chenoa proved barren.

Subsequently, A. D. Offutt added to his herd Ruby 2d (bred by Col. Powel) by 685 Imp. Bertram (1716). Col. Powel, while in England, commissioned George Coates, an old breeder, and editor of English Herd Book, to buy him the best bull in England. Bertram was selected, and Mr. Coates certified that, "this bull combines more perfection in form, handling and dairy qualities than any bull I ever saw. I consider him very much superior to old Comet, bred in my neighborhood and sold by public auction for one thousand guineas," etc.

The blood of Bertram was diffused through many of the earlier herds in Kentucky. The herd of E. S. Washington, G. Marshall and A. D. Offutt, may be considered as properly belonging to Fayette County, each of their residences being in that county, but contiguous to the Scott line, and part of each of their lands being in the latter county, and Mr. Offutt removing to Scott, and there again breeding Short-Horns. And besides all this, Kirkpatrick, Cyrus and others of their bulls were sold into this county.

September 15, 1840, a large draft from these herds was sold at public auction, and subsequently a few others. Victoria by Carcase (3285) finally went into the hands of Dr. S. F. Gano, near Georgetown; from her he bred 4236 Redfield 2101 by the Earl of Seaham (10181) the sire of 3244 Camfield 2594 out of Red Rose, by Earl of Seaham (10181), a young bull of as much promise as we ever bred or owned.

Among the early breeders of Short-Horns in Scott County, not referred to, were George W. Johnson, A. D. Offutt, James C. Lemon, Urias M. Offutt, Dr. James S. Offutt, Capt. Willa Viley, M. B. Webb, R. F. Ford, W. D. Crockett, John McMekin, D. H. Coulter, W. A. Smith, J. W. Bradley, John Duncan, Rev. W. G. Craig, James W. Craig, A. J. Viley, Gen. John Pratt, D. J. Flournoy, P. L. Cable, and subsequently James M. Stone, M. Polk, James Suddeth, J. E. Duckworth.

But two only in the above list are breeding at this time in the county, and while they have been at considerable expense in procuring good Short-Horn bulls to use in their herds of Short-Horn cows, have made no public record of their breeding for many years.

In 1853, the Scott County Importing Company made its first importation, Messrs. James Bagg and William D. Crockett, agents; it consisted of four bulls, and seven cows or heifers. The bulls were Pathfinder 805, Capt. Lawson 310, Cunningham 1415, and Baron Fevisham 13,-414. The cows were Yorkshire Rose, Venus, Carnation, Enterprise, Rosamond, Cameo and Casket.

They were sold at the farm of M. B. Webb, Esq., January 10, 1854. The first two of these bulls were retained in the county; the third went to Fayette, but near the Scott line. Yorkshire Rose also remained in the county, in the hands of P. L. Cable; and Venus, with J. C. Lemon, Esq.

The heifer Muffin, red roan, bred by Earl Ducie, by Usurer (9763), imported by the Northern Kentucky Company, and sold at their sale in 1853, was bought by D. H. Coulter and W. A. Smith; brought to this county.

In 1854, this company made a second importation under the style of "The Kentucky Importing Company." Messrs. James Bagg and Wesley Warnock were the agents. Mr. Warnock accompanied Mr. Bagg to England, remained there but a short time, and then went to Spain in quest of jacks.

This importation consisted of six bulls and fifteen cows. The bulls were Emigrant 472, Sirius 4381, McGregor 675, Earl de Grey 2801, Oakum 763, and Strouffer 311. The cows were Irene, Amazon, Bessie Howard, Lizzie, Pine Apple, Ruby, Commerce, Peeress, Winny, Mary, Welcome, Shepherdess, Grace Darling, Downhorn, and Matilda by Villiers (13959), from Matilda descended the world-wide renowned show heifer Fanny Forrester. This second importation was sold at the farm of Mr. C. W. Innis in Fayette County, near the Scott line, in 1854. Emigrant went to Bourbon County; Mr. R. A. Alexander, of Woodford County, became the owner of Sirius; McGregor went to John Hill & Co., Bourbon County; Oakum and Capt. Strouffer to Scott County.

It was some years after these sales before any new

herds were established, but the owners of those already established were bringing many good Short-Horn bulls from other counties to be used in their herds, and these, together with the old bulls already in the county, and such as they were breeding, gave them every facility for breeding the best of Short-Horns, as well as grading up the common stock. We will name a few of these bulls just as they occur to us, all of which we have seen: 2109½ Kirkpatrick, Prince Albert, the second of No. 850, 1653 Cyrus; Cyrus, Jr., 349, 1973 Golden Kirk, 3224 Bruce, 415 Orontes 2d, 1526 Cedric, 2660 Saladin. (We sold 3241* Camfield to George W. Washington, Esq., a breeder of Short-Horns, and an extensive feeder of cattle on the South Branch of the Potomac. He was the equal in style. size, form and quality of any bull we ever bred or owned, Mr. Washington after serving on the awarding committee for breeding cattle at Lexington, saw Camfield in his harem, and before walking around him, bought him. He wanted to place him at the head of his herd, and for a show bull. A few days after his arrival at home, he exhibited him at Winchester, Va., where he was first in his class, and first in sweepstakes); 3244 Camfield, 3243 Camfield Duke, 2362 Muscovite, 5505 Mazeppa, 718 Burnside, 4553 Washington 2d, 3754 Henry Kirk, 3565 13th Duke of Goodness, 3082 Alfonso, 3734 Harbinger, 5011 Duke of Elmwood, 3068 Airdrie Jem, 4505 Union Duke, Junius 606½, 7942 Tempest Duke, Doremus 1451, Milo 2d 3164, Warburton 3538, 10263 Melrose's Duke, and Roan Princeton 8969, the sire of the best bullock, a white, cow bred in the county out of Balmoral.—American Short-Horn Record, Vol. IV, p. 395. Without forcing before he was four years old, his live weight was 2,260 pounds.

Among the most prominent herds in the county is the Elmwood herd of Short-Horns of W. N. Offutt, Esq., of Scott County. This herd was established in 1868. Purchases were made from the herds of Rev. John A. Gano, of Bourbon County; F. P. Kincaid and A. J. Alexander, of Woodford County; B. F. & A. Vanmeter and B. B. Groom, of Clark County, Ky.; A. M. Griswold, of New York, and other distinguished breeders.

The first public sale from this herd was made July 28, 1875, at an average of $450, and were purchased by breeders from Connecticut to Minnesota. Again, on August 13, 1876, there was a draft sold at public sale that averaged $919. (This sale was made with T. J. Megibben.) The cattle were purchased by such breeders as the Bow Park Association, of Canada, A. J. Alexander, and others equally noted.

*The numbers before the name of an animal refer to American Short-Horn Record; plain numbers after the name to American Herd Book, those in parentheses to English Herd Book.

After the sale in 1876, the owner of this herd retained but four cows and two heifers. Since that time, he has made numerous private sales of his bulls and a few females. The families now represented in this herd are Two Wild Eyes, descending from Wild Eyes 8th by Duke of Northumberland, bred by Thomas Bates, of England. There are three Rosamonds, descending from Rosamouth 7th, bred by Walcott & Campbell, New York Mills. This family descended from C. Mason's herd, of England. Four Statiras, descended from Statira 10th, imported by the North Elkhorn Importing Company in 1875. This family descended from the Earl of Carlisle's celebrated herd, England. There is one Victoria, represented by Victoria 7th; she was in the great New York Mills' sale in 1873, and is known as the Mason Victoria. The tenth dam of Victoria 7th was No. 1 in the great Chilton sale. There are also two Mazurkas—their dam Mazurka 27th by Royal Oxford (18774); one of them by 26th Duke of Airdrie, and the other by 6248 Chilton Duke 4th. This is one of the most celebrated families in Kentucky. There is one Vellum, descended from Imp. Vellum by Abraham Parker (9856); this is one of Mr. A. J. Alexander's most popular families. There is one Miss Wiley, represented by Miss Wiley 36th by Barrett (1424½); second dam by 10th Duke of Thorndale. This is from the same family as the London Duchess, sold by Mr. Edwin Bedford at long prices. Mr. Offutt uses a pure Kirkleavingston bull—8802 Kirkleavingston Oxford. There are four handsome bull calves, from five to eight months old, in this herd.

The owner of this herd has a flock of pure South Down sheep, descended from six imported ewes, purchased in 1877–78, and from an imported buck (No. 28), bred by Lord Walsingham, England.

Among the next in prominence is the herd of John C. Payne, of Newtown. In this herd we find eleven Goodnesses, descending from Imp. Goodness by 414 Orontes (11877); four Mazurkas, descending from Imp. Mazurka by 252 Harbinger (10297); two Carnations, descending from Imp. Carnation by 4827 Bridget; two Filagrees, tracing to Imp. Filagree by 9856 Abram Parker. Bulls at head of herd—6273 Constance, Duke of Grassland and 8802 Kirkleavingston Oxford 32983.

Mr. L. T. Thomas, Georgetown, Ky., commenced breeding in 1873. His herd consists of nineteen head—three Marys, nine Mandanes, four Ianthes, two Arabellas, and one Amelia; 4694 Airdrie Prince at head of herd.

Mr. J. M. Hall, Georgetown, Ky., commenced breeding in 1877. His herd numbers seventeen head—four Marys, six Gems and five Carolines; 9054 Oxford Duke (a Victoria) at head of herd.

Mr. J. F. Musselman, Georgetown, Ky., commenced breeding in 1878. His herd numbers fourteen Irenes and Phyllises; 7363 Belle Duke of Cloland at head of herd. The first bull used in this herd was —— Kirkleavingston Lad; the second, Barrett (1424½).

Mr. R. E. Roberts, Georgetown, made the first purchases in view of establishing a Short-Horn herd, in the summer of 1879. They now number seventeen in all. Among his females are Young Marys, Young Phyllis, Rosalinds, Carnations, Goodnesses, etc. The 6th Duke of Barrington is at the head of his herd.

Mr. Elley Blackburn, Great Crossings, has very recently commenced breeding Short-Horns; his herd numbers, in all, four head. Among them are Guynns and Miss Wileys. With those have been used 5659 Proud Duke 2d, and 8969 Mazurka's Treble Duke.

R. C. Prewitt commenced breeding Short-Horns in 1881; his herd consists of four head only. In it we find a young Phillis, an imported Tulip and an imported Donna Maria. Belle Adin at head of herd.

Mr. William H. Graves, Georgetown, commenced breeding in 1869; numerous individuals and large drafts have been sold from this herd. It now consists of three females, tracing to Imp. Cleopatra by Pilot (496). Three to Imp. White Rose by Publicola (1348); two to Carolina by Pontiac (4734); one to Elizabeth by Velocipede (5552), and one to Young Mary by Jupiter (2170). Ten in all.

The herd of A. D. Offutt and A. M. Offutt, Camfield, near Georgetown, consists of sixteen head, twelve of which are descended from the Booth cow, Imp. Cleopatra, by Pilot (496), through Red Mary by Camfield, and Melrose by Camfield Duke. The bulls at head of herd are 10706 Baron Sharon, and 10771 Cambridge, Duke of Sharon.

The herd of Dr. W. T. Risque, Payne's Depot. Checkmate 34743 at head of herd. In the herd are three bull calves, all by Checkmate. One descends from Wild Rose, one from Rose of Sharon and one from Young Mary. Among the cows are one Rosabella, tracing to Imp. Rosabella, by 1242 Velocipede; two to Imp. Wild Rose by Chorister (3378); Two Imp. Young Mary by Jupiter (2170); one to Imp. Rose of Sharon by Belvedera (1706); two to Imp. Maid Marian 2d by Lord John (11728), and one to Imp. Baron Oxford's Beauty by Baron Oxford (23375).

In the herd of Alexander Brown, near Georgetown, there are eight Mandanes, tracing to Imp. Mandane by 470 Richmond; one to Imp. Cleopatra by Pilot (496); one to Imp. Young Mary by 958 Jupiter; one to Imp. Daphne by 2018 Harrold; two to Imp. Goodness by 414 Orontes, and two to Imp. Adileza by 224 Frederick.

In a sale catalogue of Short-Horns belonging to W. H. Murphy, Esq., a year or two since, cows tracing to the following imported cows, were sold: Filigree, by Abram Parker (9856); Alice-Maud, by Grand Duke (10284); Gaily, by Sir Thomas Fairfax (5196); Goodness, by Orontes (4623); Mary, by Jupiter (2170); Valeria, by Hopewell (10332); Peri, by Grand Duke (10284); Imp. Columbine, by Lord of the Harem (16430); Mazurka, by Harbinger (10297); Young Phillis, etc., etc. The most of this herd remained in Scott County.

There are several other breeders of Short-Horns in the county, among them Dr. J. W. Prowel, J. D. Smith, Dr. R. I. Smith and Jo. Evans, but we have had no response from them. There is at this time about two hundred and fifty Short-Horns in the county. The majority of them are red with a little white, some roans, a few red and white, two that are white, and a few that are red.—*Alfred D. Offutt.*

P. S.—There are quite a number of South-Down sheep, of very superior quality, bred in the county. The first established flock is that of Alfred D. Offutt, two miles south of Georgetown.—*A. D. O.*

CHAPTER V.

WAR RECORD—REVOLUTIONARY HEROES—INDIAN TROUBLES—THE WAR OF 1812—COL. JOHNSON'S REGIMENT—DEATH OF TECUMSEH—OUR DIFFERENCE WITH MEXICO—SCOTT COUNTY IN THE LATE CIVIL WAR, ETC.

"Nor war's wild note, nor glory's peal,
Shall thrill with fierce delight."—*O'Hara.*

FROM time immemorial the differences of opinion have been settled by the arbitrament of war. Individuals, dissatisfied with existing relations and circumstances, have invoked the god of battles, and turned the red hand of slaughter against their brethren; others, instigated by passion, ambition or caprice, have, by the powers of will or genius, strewn the earth with human clay, and filled the heavens with awful lamentations. Nations, delighting in conquest, and seemingly in slaughter, have shaken the earth with their elephantine tread, and scattered the hard-earned products of civilization with infinite disregard; others have united in hideous schemes to deluge the world with blood, until the name of civilization has seemed a synonym for unlimited reproach. Enlightened man converts into an art the barbarous plans of human destruction, and establishes institutions of learning wherein are taught the most gigantic and expeditious modes of terminating life.

The world witnesses a strange paradox when man, after thousands of years of intellectual and moral advancement, still resorts to his physical nature to secure subservience to his desires. Might, not right, still rules the world with despotic sway. War, as a result of dissimilar views, necessarily follows from conflicting enlightment in all departments of human thought. So long as minds refuse to see alike, conflicts will occur, storms of war will trouble the earth, and the reign of peace will be clouded. The first war with which Scott County had any connection was the Revolution, which gave to the country liberty and independence. Although at that time but few white people lived within the present limits of the county, yet so many of the settlers who afterward came to the county, were in the struggle for freedom that reference, though brief, must be made to that war.

The causes of the Revolution and the history of our independence are too familiar to be detailed here. The hardest times the country has ever seen, perhaps, were immediately succeeding the establishment of peace. The colonies were no less than bankrupt, and privations and hardships in the most direful degree were willingly borne when victory and peace were secured. The paper money, by means of which the war was carried on, was worthless, and the harvests, of necessity, had been so nearly neglected that starvation stared the colonies in the face. Time alone, and at last, retrieved the havoc of war. When the country had in a measure recovered from the stroke, enterprising people began to push westward. The Government offered extra inducements to settlers, and finally the rush for the West became so great that the settlers began to unlawfully invade the territory of the Western Indians. This brought down upon them numerous and bloody wars with the savages. As soon as Kentucky was admitted as a State, and even before, settlers began to boldly appear, regardless of the rights of their red neighbors. It is probable that two-thirds of the white men who located in the county prior to 1800, had been engaged in the war of the Revolution, and that the most of the other third in the early Indian wars of Kentucky. After this long lapse of time it is impossible to give the names of these old soldiers; many of them, however, will be found in the biographical department of this volume.

In less than a third of a century after the close of our war for independence, another war with Great Britain cast its dark shadow over the land. When it became known west of the Alleghanies that war was inevitable, and had already been declared, the settlers on the frontiers were filled with distrustful forebodings. A coalition between the British and the Indians was anticipated, and, as soon as it became certain that this dreaded alliance had been effected, the pioneers throughout Kentucky made hasty preparations for defense. Block-houses were erected, and the militia in each county and community mustered and equipped themselves with the implements of war. In almost every settlement, particularly in Central Kentucky, companies were organized for a determined resistance against any foe that might appear. These companies were independent of the soldiers sent into the regular service. The first events of this war were such as might have been expected from a nation pacific, mercantile and agricultural. Defeat, disgrace and disaster marked the opening scenes; but the latter events of the contest were a series of splendid achievements. "The war spirit of Kentucky blazed forth with unprecedented vigor. Several thousand volunteers at once offered their services to the Government, and fifteen hundred were on the march for Detroit, when the intelligence of Hull's surrender induced them to halt. This disastrous news was received with a burst of indignation and fury, which no other event ever excited in Kentucky. The military ardor of the men seemed rather increased than diminished by the disaster, and a call of the Governor for 1,500 volunteers to march against the Indian villages of Northern Illinois was answered by more than 2,000 men, who assembled at Louisville under Gen. Hopkins."

Scott County, in the war of 1812, furnished nearly six companies, which formed the larger part of Col. R. M. Johnson's regiment. The respective Captains of these companies were Lynn West, Stephen Richie, Joseph Ready, John Duvall, Jacob Stucker and John W. Ready—the latter a cousin to Joseph Ready. Of these six companies, there is not known to be but three living representatives, viz.: Judge Warren, Mr. Ford and John T. Pratt, the latter of whom communicated to us most of this information. Mr. Pratt was in the battle of the Thames, but being hotly engaged in another part of the field, he did not witness Col. Johnson's charge. In Capt. Stucker's company were nine pairs of brothers from this county, viz.: Conrad and Jesse Wolf, Isaac and Jacob DeHaven, James and Gabriel Long, Edward and Henry Ely, Joel and John Herndon, Zachary and Wyatt Herndon—cousins of Joel and John—James and Edgcomb Suggett, Henry and William Berry, Edward and William Johnson—sons of Col. James Johnson. Other members of that company were Thomas Blackburn, John Pearce, Spencer Peak, Thomas Suggett, Robert Payne, Ben Chambers, John Pratt, etc., etc., etc. Moses

A. Faris and George M. Bower were also in the war of 1812 as Surgeons.

Richard M. Gano, the father of Dr. Gano, of Georgetown, entered the war as Major of Col. Charles Scott's regiment, and succeeded him as its Colonel. He commanded the regiment in the battle of the Thames, and at the close of the war he was made Brigadier General for gallant service during the war. A sketch of Col. R. M. Johnson will not be inappropriate in this connection. His father, Col. Robert Johnson, was a pioneer of Kentucky, and an early settler of Scott County. Col. "Dick" was born in Kentucky in 1781, received his early education in the country schools of the time, and finally entered Transylvania University at Lexington, where he took a regular course and graduated. He commenced the study of law with Col. George Nicholas, one of the most celebrated jurists of his day, but upon his death, which occurred soon after, Mr. Johnson continued his studies with Hon. James Brown, then a distinguished member of the Kentucky Bar. Before he was twenty-one, he was elected to the State Legislature, from Scott County, where he served with considerable honor, and in 1807 (being in his twenty-sixth year) he was elected to Congress, and at once entered upon the theater of national politics. When the war-clouds began to gather in our horizon in 1811–12, and an appeal to arms seemed inevitable, Col. Johnson was among those who believed that no other alternative remained to the American people. Accordingly after supporting all the preparatory measures which the crisis demanded, in June, 1812, he gave his vote for the declaration of war. As soon as Congress adjourned, he hastened home, "raised the standard of his country, and called around him many of the best citizens of his neighborhood, some of whom, schooled in the stormy period of the early settlement of the State, were veteran warriors, well suited for the service for which they were intended."

The service of Col. Johnson and his famous regiment of mounted riflemen in the war of 1812 is so well known that it seems superfluous to go into particulars here. It is very generally believed, that Col. Johnson killed the noted Indian Chief Tecumseh in the battle of the Thames. The fact, it is true, has been disputed by a number of writers on the subject, yet it is hard to shake the general belief, that Johnson was the author of the great chief's death. Says Col. Johnson's biographer: "In October, 1813, the decisive crisis in the operations of the Northwestern army arrived—the battle of the Thames—which led to a termination of hostilities in that quarter, was fought and won. The distinguished services of Col. Johnson, and his brave regiment, in that sanguinary engagement, have scarcely a parallel in the heroic annals of our country. The British and Indians, the former under command of Gen. Proctor, and the latter under that of Tecumseh, the celebrated Indian warrior, had taken an advantageous position, the British in line between the river Thames and a narrow swamp, and the Indians in ambush on their right, and west of the swamp, ready to fall upon the rear of Col. Johnson should he force a retreat of the British. Col. Johnson, under the orders of the Commander-in-chief, divided his regiment into two battalions, one under the command of his gallant brother, James, and the other to be led by himself. Col. Johnson with his battalion passed the swamp and attacked the Indians, at the same moment that his brother James fell upon and routed the British regulars. The contest for awhile between Col. Johnson's battalion and the Indians was obstinate and bloody, the slaughter great, but success complete. The gallant Colonel was in the very midst and thickest of the fight, inspiring, by his presence and courage, the utmost confidence of his brave followers, and though perforated with balls, his bridle arm shattered, and, bleeding profusely, he continued to fight until he encountered and slew an Indian chief, who formed the rallying point of the savages. This chief was supposed to be the famous Tecumseh himself, upon whose fall the Indians raised a yell and retreated. The heroic Colonel, covered with wounds, twenty-five balls having been shot into him, his clothes and his horse, was borne from the battle-ground faint from exertion and loss of blood, and almost lifeless. Never was victory so complete or its achievement so glorious. Fifteen hundred Indians were engaged against the battalion of Col. Johnson, and 800 British regulars against that of his brother. Both the Indians and British were routed, and an end put to the war upon the Northern frontier, distinguished, as it had been, by so many murderous cruelties upon the part of the savage allies of the British."

Col. Johnson continued to serve his constituents in Congress until 1819, when he voluntarily retired and returned home. The people of Scott County at once returned him to the State Legislature, and that body elected him to the United States Senate. After serving out his term, he was almost unanimously re-elected to the same exalted position. In 1836, he was elected Vice President of the United States under Martin Van Buren, and for four years presided over the Senate with great dignity. At the expiration of his term, he retired to his farm in Scott County, where he spent the remainder of his life. He was a member of the State Legislature at the time of his death, which occurred in 1850, in Frankfort. Col. Johnson was one of the able men of Kentucky, and sprung from an able and talented family, most of whom (the male members) were statesmen and soldiers. James Johnson, a brother to Col. Dick, and Lieutenant Colonel of the latter's regiment, was a soldier of promise, and distinguished himself while in the service; also served several sessions in Congress with ability. John T. Johnson, another brother, was for a short time a member of the Appellate Court of Kentucky, subsequently a Member of Congress, but finally became a minister of the Christian Church, a position he filled with great usefulness. The father, Col. Robert Johnson, was himself a soldier and statesman, and served his country well and faithfully. He was the grandfather of Hon. George W. Johnson, who was born near Georgetown in 1811, and who was the Confederate Governor of Kentucky during the late war. He labored earnestly to place Kentucky by the side of the other Southern States in the rebellion, and set on foot the organization of a provisional government, which was effected by the Convention at Russellville, Logan County, November 18–21, 1861. A constitution was adopted, and Mr. Johnson was chosen Provisional Governor, and, December 10, Kentucky was admitted a member of the Confederacy, though the State at large never acknowledged it. He was mortally wounded in the battle of Shiloh, while fighting temporarily as a private in the Fourth Kentucky (Confederate) Infantry. At the time of his death he was fifty-one years of age.

But to return to the war of 1812. Scott County bore her part in it, until "Old Hickory" conquered a peace at New Orleans. Thus a war, that opened with the disgrace of Hull's surrender, closed in a blaze of glory at New Orleans. Croghan's gallant defense of Fort Stephenson; Perry's victory upon Lake Erie; the total defeat by Harrison, of the allied British and Savages, under Procter and Tecumseh, on the Thames, and the great closing triumph of Jackson at New Orleans, are scarcely equaled in the annals of war, and reflected the most brilliant luster on the American arms.

The Mexican war next engaged our attention after the war of 1812, and in it Scott County was well represented, though no organization went from the county. All readers are familiar with the circumstances resulting in this war, which are fully given elsewhere in this work. It was, from the battle of Palo Alto to the capture of the city of Mexico, one grand triumph of the American soldiery. There is, perhaps, no other account on record, of a war between two rival powers of the same magnitude of these, in which every battle was won by the one and the same contestant. It is not known, just how many men went from Scott County into the Mexican war, but as there was a full company made up in Bourbon County, there was doubtless a considerable number from Scott in it.

In the spring of 1861, the great civil war burst upon the country. The part taken by Scott County in the late war, is not easily written; it is a subject, too, that must needs be handled very carefully. Located on the border as we are, it is very natural that our people should see the war, its objects and results in different lights, and from different standpoints. This we say was natural, and we, for one, find no fault with any man for an honest difference of opinion with us. It was never intended that we should all see alike; if it had been, then we would not have had the late war at all, and our Northern neighbors would have been deprived of a great fund of venom against us.

We can give but a brief sketch of the part taken by Scott County in the late unpleasantness; referring the reader to the published works upon the subject for more minute details. The Adjutant General's report of the State, 1861–1865, gives very accurately, and in a plain and comprehensive manner, the Federal side of the question, while the history of the "First Kentucky Brigade," and "Duke's History of Morgan's Men," ventilate the situation from a Southern standpoint. Among the Federal officers from Scott County were John S. Long, Scott H. Robinson, Edmund H. Parrish, Joseph L. Frost, James C. Hunter, Ruben Lancaster, Edward C. Barlow, James H. Robey, and perhaps others. John N. Long commenced raising a company in August, 1862. He had been commissioned Captain by Gov. Robinson, and after enlisting some eighteen or twenty men, he was induced to "change his base," by the approach of Bragg's army upon Louisville. He joined Burbridge's command as a kind of body-guard. They were in the Vicksburg campaign, and after having been in the service about a year, were ordered home and discharged by the Governor.

Scott H. Robinson was made Captain of a company which was recruited partly in Scott and partly in Harrison Counties. He served through the war, and at its close was commissioned as First Lieutenant in the regular army; he was wounded on the Western frontier in a skirmish with the Indians, and died some time after at home.

Edmund H. Parrish was promoted from Sergeant-Major to Captain of Company C, Sixth Veteran Cavalry, February 15, 1865; captured April 1, 1865, and lost on steamer Sultana April 27, 1865, while coming up the Ohio River.

Joseph L. Frost was commissioned Major of the Twenty-sixth Infantry. He was promoted from Adjutant April 10, 1862, and resigned the 5th of May following.

James C. Hunter was appointed Orderly Sergeant February 15, 1865, promoted to First Lieutenant, June 15, and mustered out of the service September 6, 1865, at Louisville, Ky.

Reuben Lancaster was promoted from Sergeant to Captain of Company B, Sixth Veteran Cavalry, and mustered out with the regiment September 6, 1865, at Louisville.

Edward C. Barlow went into the service as Adjutant of the Fortieth Kentucky Infantry. Upon the resignation of Capt. Rice, of Company B, he was promoted to the Captaincy of that company, and mustered out at the end of its term of service, December 30, 1864, at Catlettsburg, Ky. He served some time as Captain of Provost Guard, and was in command of the post at Mount Sterling, Ky., when it was captured by Gen. Morgan. Col. D. Howard Smith, of Morgan's command, was a personal friend of Capt. Barlow's, and secured his parole without any difficulty.

James H. Robey was First Sergeant of Company D, Seventh Volunteer Cavalry, was promoted to Second Lieutenant, July 23, 1862, and was promoted First Lieutenant, but never mustered as such. He was mustered out with the regiment July 10, 1865, at Edgefield, Tenn.

Dr. Stephen Gano was Surgeon of the Seventh District of Kentucky, with headquarters at Lexington; he ranked as Lieutenant Colonel of the private soldiers; there were about one hundred from the county of Scott who went into the Federal service. Their record was that of Kentucky soldiers from the Revolutionary period down to the present time.

Among the students at Georgetown College, when the war broke out, were six Chinese boys (half native), two of whom, James and William Hunter, young men of considerable promise, entered the service in Capt. Long's company, with whose father they were boarding. William served as a private, and James was promoted to engineer in Gen. Burnside's corps.

The Confederate service received a great many more recruits from Scott County than did the Federal cause. The first company raised in the county for the South was recruited by James E. Cantrill, now Lieutenant Governor of the State. He joined Col. Smith's regiment—the Fifth Kentucky—and Gen. Buford's brigade. Press Thompson was Lieutenant Colonel of the Fifth, and Thomas Brent, Major. In Capt. Cantrill's company, Andrew Wilson went out as First Lieutenant; W. S. Offutt as Second Lieutenant, and David Holding as Third Lieutenant. James Davis went out with William H. Webb's squad, and joined the company of W. C. P. Breckinridge. Holding, of Cantrill's company, resigned, and Davis was made Brevet Second Lieutenant. Wilson and Offutt then resigned, and Davis was made First Lieutenant, with W. N. Offutt as Second.

Capt. William H. Webb raised a squad of some twenty-odd men, and after consolidating with James A. Jones' company (who was killed at Glasgow), formed the nucleus of Col. Breckinridge's company. With this squad of Webb's were several prominent Scott County men. Dr. J. A. Lewis, now of Georgetown, went out as a private, and afterward became Adjutant of Col. Breckinridge's regiment—the Ninth Kentucky. F. Gano Hill, of Bourbon County, was also of this squad. He afterward became Captain of the same company (Company A). When Breckinridge's company was organized, it was Company I of the Second Kentucky, but when Gen. Bragg came into Kentucky it was re-organized, and became Company A of the Ninth. Breckinridge was made Major of the Battalion, and William Jones, of Louisville, became Captain of Company A. Breckinridge's battalion was afterward consolidated with Maj. Stoner's battalion, and became the Ninth Kentucky (Confederate) Cavalry, commanded by Col. Breckinridge.

J. Henry Wolf, now County Clerk of Scott County, recruited a company of about one hundred men, of which he was made Captain; Erwin Zeising, First Lieutenant; George Nelson, Second Lieutenant, and Berry Marshall, Third Lieutenant. Zeising left the command in Tennessee, and is now in Missouri. Nelson was wounded and came home. Henry Conn became First Lieutenant in Zeising's place, and I. N. Newton succeeded Nelson as Second Lieutenant, and John Lindsay became Third Lieutenant in place of Marshall. The company participated in Morgan's Mountain Campaign, in which, with 1,200 men, he opposed the Federal Gen. Morgan with an army of 3,500 men, and captured from the latter twenty-four pieces of artillery, forcing him to bury twelve of his heaviest pieces at Cumberland Gap.

George Tilford also raised a large company, mostly in Scott County, of which George Holloway was First Lieutenant; John T. Sinclair, Second Lieutenant, and James Ferguson, Third Lieutenant. Altogether, there is supposed to have been 1,000 or 1,200 men in the Confederate service from Scott County. So far, we have only given the names of commissioned officers, and have mentioned all whom we could obtain. Doubtless many have been omitted. But unlike the National forces, we have no Adjutant General's Report to refer to, giving a correct record of all officers and privates who went into the service. The only record of them is in the minds of men, and in such works (Duke's History, etc.) as we have already mentioned.—*Perrin.*

Asa. H. Owen

CHAPTER VI.

GEORGETOWN PRECINCT — INTRODUCTORY AND DESCRIPTIVE — BOUNDARIES AND TOPOGRAPHY — EARLY SETTLEMENT—HARD TIMES OF THE PIONEERS—INDUSTRIES AND IMPROVEMENTS--SCHOOLS, VILLAGES AND CHURCHES.

"A song for the free and gladsome life,
In those early days we led,
With a teeming soil beneath our feet," etc., etc.
—*Gallagher*.

THE velocity with which the world moves is simply astounding, yet it moved slow enough in the beginning. In the early ages, it took nearly a century for a *boy* to think of leaving the family roof-tree to begin the battle of life on his own account, and three or four times as long to attain the prime and vigor of manhood. Rome was seven hundred years in expanding her power and reaching the zenith of her glory; the temple of Diana at Ephesus saw two and a half centuries from its foundation to its completion, and the architects of Babel and the Pyramids planned work for hundreds of years ahead. But that is not the style of doing business at the present day; we make a fortune and lose it in less time than that. Everything is done with an object and a rush. We live fast; three or four lifetimes are crowded into one.

Speaking of the Olympian festivities and the old Roman triumphs, and the millions expended on them and their accessories, one of our shrewd business men recently remarked, "We've got beyond all that now, and I am glad of it, for such things wouldn't pay." That is it exactly; we have no time for what don't pay. We are economical, and count the cost with the closeness of a Jew. Anything that there is money in catches our attention, no matter what it is. And in everything we do, is the same rush and hurry; we never calculate projects a hundred years ahead but live wholly in the present. Although Central Kentucky lacks much of that energy and enterprise characteristic of the Western States, yet it affords a striking example of the rapidity with which we move. A hundred years ago, Kentucky had but a few hundred inhabitants; now her population is almost equal to that of the thirteen colonies at the time of the Revolutionary war. In this immediate section, behold the change! The finest plantations and princely homes occupy what a few years ago was a wilderness. But this is the fast age of the nineteenth century, and illustrates our fast way of living.

The precinct to which these pages are devoted, known as Georgetown Precinct No. 1, contains but little history of interest outside of the city of Georgetown. All of the most important facts are given in connection with Georgetown, and but a mere glance will be taken at the precinct at large. The land embraced in it is as fine, if not the very finest in the county. It is gently rolling or undulating, and is a rich limestone soil. The Elkhorn and its branches afford excellent drainage, and at the same time water the country through which they flow. The original timber of Georgetown Precinct consisted of oak, hickory, black walnut, elm, honey locust, sugar tree, buckeye, etc., etc., but little of which is now left in its natural state. Much attention is paid to stock-raising, and many of the fine stock farms of the county are located in this precinct. The Cincinnati Southern Railroad, running north and south, passes through, by which the surplus stock and other products are shipped to market.

Settlements were made in the present precinct of Georgetown more than a hundred years ago. Indeed, it has been claimed that the first settlement made in Kentucky was at "Royal Spring," now included in the corporate limits of Georgetown. But, as noted in another chapter, this is hardly correct; it was probably, however, the place of the first settlement north of the Kentucky River. This settlement will be more particularly mentioned by Dr. Gano, in the history of Georgetown. It was made by the McClellands and McConnells about the year 1775–76, and a fort or block-house was built at the spring above mentioned. Robert Johnson and John Suggett were also early settlers. They first stopped at Bryant's Station, and then came to Woodford County, now Scott, and settled on a claim of Patrick Henry, at Great Crossings, in 1790, where a stockade was built.

Near where old North Elkhorn Church stood, on land now owned by E. N. Offutt, Sr., was built the old Flournoy fort. He (Flournoy) was a Virginian of French descent, who came to Kentucky and settled that farm in 1780. He brought his window-glass with him on horseback, and it is said that this was the first house with glass windows in this part of Kentucky. The house, which was inclosed by a stockade, is still standing—a hundred and two years old. The marriage of Gen. William H. Henry to a daughter of

Flournoy took place in this house. Gen. Henry commanded the Kentucky troops under Gen. Shelby in the war of 1812. Mr. Flournoy made several trips across the mountains with pack-horses, and was finally, on one of his trips, murdered by the Indians. A daughter of his was shot by the Indians, while she was going to the spring for water. Her grave, together with several soldiers killed in he fort, are still to be seen near the old house.

The first pre-emption was that of Col. John Floyd's, made in 1779, containing 1,000 acres, and covering lands whereon Georgetown now stands, and including the spring, then called "Floyd's Royal Spring." The same year, Virginia granted to Patrick Henry, for services as Governor of the State, some 5,000 acres of land in this precinct, extending from near Georgetown to Capt. Craig's, at White Sulphur. Christopher Greenup, afterward Governor, Daniel Bradford and others, also had large grants of land here. Gen. John Payne served as County Surveyor of Scott County, from 1790 to 1817, when the conflict of claims became so great that the Legislature at last passed an act giving the land to the party who retained possession twenty years. Under these claim troubles, lands depreciated in value to a very great extent. As an example of such trouble, the same body of land was sometimes claimed by five different parties, thus involving almost unending litigation.

The early years of the pioneers were years of hardships. It took great efforts to procure the necessaries of life, and a sufficiency of clothing to keep them warm. Is was almost useless to bring in sheep for a number of years after settlements were made, owing to the number of wolves and bears, and other ravenous beasts, which would sometimes destroy an entire flock in a single night. Hence, the people had no choice save that of adopting other expedients, or appearing

"In nature's light and airy garb."

So, one of the early crops of the country was flax, grown for domestic purposes. Of this a coarse and substantial linen was made, which was manufactured into clothing for the family. Even after flax was raised in sufficient quantities, and sheep in considerable numbers had been introduced, it was quite an arduous task to spin and weave cloth for the entire wearing apparel of the family. It is, perhaps, not over-drawing the picture to say that the summer wear of the boys until eight or ten years old, was very nearly akin to the Highland costume, inasmuch as it consisted of a long tow shirt—only this and nothing more. The tools and agricultural implements were about on a par with everything else. And the time that has passed since the settlement of the country has witnessed as great improvements in agricultural implements as in any of the other "arts and sciences." Taken together with these primitive outfits were the dangers experienced in the early years from savages, and we find ourselves wondering that the country was ever settled at all.

The preparation of grain for making bread, in a new country, is a matter of no slight importance, for while grain may be produced from the soil as easily in a new country as in an old one, it is not so easy to have the grain converted into meal. The first settlers resorted to many a method for grinding corn, but many of the processes were at once slow and toilsome. The first mill in Georgetown Precinct was a small water-mill at Great Crossings, built previous to 1800, and is at present owned by Mr. Glass. Thompson's mill is a very old one. Joel Scott had a fulling-mill a short distance below Thompson's mill, where he carried on an extensive business; he wove broadcloth and other costly fabrics. Tanneries, distilleries, etc., etc., were among the early industries in addition to mills.

A fine system of turnpike roads traverse Georgetown Precinct in every direction, diverging from the city of Georgetown. The first road was a continuation of Main street to Great Crossings; the next was from Georgetown to Big Bone Lick. Among the roads now intersecting the precinct and centering in Georgetown, are the following: Lexington & Georgetown pike; Covington pike; Payne's Depot pike; Stamping Ground pike; Long Lick pike; Dry Ridge pike; Dry Run pike; Paris pike; Oxford pike, with a number of cross pikes.

There is little to say of the schools outside of Georgetown. When the first school was taught in the precinct, and where the first schoolhouse was erected, are questions that cannot be answered at this distant day. No place is better supplied with educational facilities, perhaps, than Georgetown. These schools and colleges are more fully written up in a succeeding chapter, and of Science Hill Academy we shall speak further on in this chapter.

The village of Great Crossings is a small place, and has but little business, in consequence of its close proximity to Georgetown, being situated only four miles from the latter place, on the Stamping Ground pike. It received the name of Great Crossings by the buffalo trace from the interior of Kentucky to the Ohio River, crossing North Elkhorn Creek at the spot where it is located. A few stores and shops, a church, etc., comprises the present village.

Georgetown Precinct is well represented with churches. The Baptist Church at Great Crossings is one of the oldest churches of Central Kentucky. A history written of it in 1876, by Prof. J. M. Bradley, is of considerable interest to all its members. Its great length only precludes its insertion entire in this volume, but as a matter of interest we give the following extract: "The church was constituted ninety years ago (1885) the '28 and 29' of last May. Its first Pastor, Elijah Craig, was twice imprisoned, in Virginia, for preaching the Gospel—once in Culpepper and once in Orange. After the pastorate of Craig, the church has enjoyed the preaching of Joseph Reding, James Suggett, Silas M. Noel, Thomas Henderson, A. M. Lewis, James D. Black, B. F. Kenny, Y. R. Pitts, William C. Buck, William G. Craig, R. T. Dillard, Howard Malcom, John L. Waller, William F. Broaddus, A. R. Macey, D. R. Campbell, Cad Lewis, S. P. Hogan, J. G. Bow and B. Manly, Jr., an array of preaching talent such as, we will venture to assert, no other church in Kentucky can claim. During this period, about fifteen hundred have made profession of religion, been baptized and afterward received into the fellowship of the church, besides others who have been received by letter and those in the original constitution. There have been in this number white, black and red men. Seven churches have been constituted, chiefly of members leaving this church, viz.: Stamping Ground, Dry Run, Mountain Island, North Elkhorn, Long Lick, Pleasant Green and Midway, four of which—Stamping Ground, Dry Run, Long Lick and Midway—are still in existence, so that the Great Crossings may well be called the "mother of churches." The church has sent out five ordained preachers and licensed six others to exercise their gifts." This venerable church can soon celebrate its own centennial. In 1880, it reported 588 members.

Dry Run Baptist Church was organized in February, 1801, and Rev. Joseph Reding was the first pastor. The first church was built of logs, upon the site where the present church now stands. It was afterward weatherboarded, the members and neighbors contributing to its building in the first place. Among the original members were James Weathers, Nicholas Long, Col. John Miller, Joseph Elgin, Bennett Osborn, etc. Rev. Mr. Trott, an early school teacher, was also an early preacher of this church. Rev. Lucas was afterward pastor. James D. Black was a blacksmith and a powerful preacher. He was pastor for over twenty years. Other pastors were Nealey, Duvall and Hodges. About the close of the war, the present church was built, at a cost of $2,000. The present pastor is Rev. Mr. Skillman.

North Elkhorn Baptist Church is three and a half miles from Georgetown, and was organized, in September, 1801, under the ministerial labors of Rev. Mr. Eaves. He was from Virginia, as were most of the original members. The first church edifice was a frame building, erected by Samuel Cooper, one of the leading members of the congregation. It, at one time, had a large membership, reaching as high as 150. The church was sometimes called Cooper's Run Church. Rev. Joshua Leathers was one of the early ministers and a powerful preacher. In 1835, the church split, and the sections were known respectively as "Particular" and "Regular" Baptists. The latter went to neighboring churches, while the Particular Baptists held the church building and kept up the organization until about the year 1850, when the house was sold by Cooper's heirs and turned into a schoolhouse, known as "Science Hill Academy." This school was taught by Prof. Roach, Prof. Williams and others. For more than twenty years, it was conducted as a school, and was then discontinued, owing to the surrounding land being bought and roads closed up leading to it. The building is still standing, and is now used for a barn.

This comprises a brief sketch of the precinct, outside of Georgetown. As the history usually centers in the county seat, leaving the precinct in which it is situated somewhat barren, we will search no further for historical facts and data, but begin a new chapter with the city of Georgetown.—*Perrin.*

CHAPTER VII.

CITY OF GEORGETOWN — ITS EARLIEST HISTORY — SCHOOL NOTICE — THE TOWN INCORPORATED — ELIJAH CRAIG AND OTHER PIONEERS — PAPER MILL, TANNERIES, ETC. — EARLY BUSINESS — FIRST COURT HOUSE, ETC., ETC.

"A song for the free and gladsome life
In those early days we led."

GEORGETOWN, the county seat of Scott County, is located in the southern part of the county, in the famous Blue Grass Region twelve miles north of Lexington, and some sixty-six miles south of Cincinnati by the Southern Railroad. It is beautifully situated on high, undulating table-land, on the south side of North Elkhorn, a considerable stream; on its western border is the large spring branch bursting from a limestone bluff, with a volume of water capable of turning a flouring-mill a few hundred yards from its source.

In very early times this spring was known as Floyd's Royal Spring, in later times as the Republican, and in more modern times as the Big Spring. It is a great Royal, Republican, Big feature in the make-up of Georgetown; big with blessings to thousands, of coolness, cleanliness and comfort, and free to all, both man and beast. On the bluff above where this stream bursts forth the first settlement or station was made by white men. In October, 1776, Col. Patterson, with the two McClellands, Ben and John, with other persons from the neighboring stations, erected a fort or station called McClelland's Fort.

In 1776, the Indians, enraged at the encroachments upon their favorite hunting-grounds, and urged on by the British, made frequent incursions into Kentucky, and became so troublesome that the weaker stations were abandoned.

The settlers at Hinkson Station took shelter in McClelland's Fort, Simon Kenton accompanying them. Maj. George Rogers Clark having prevailed upon the Virginia Legislature to afford the pioneers some assistance, arrived in company with a lawyer named Jones at the Three Islands late in the winter, with a considerable quantity of powder and lead. They concealed it on the lower island, and proceeded to McClelland's Station in order to obtain a party to bring it off to the settlements. McClelland's Station being too weak to furnish a sufficient escort, Clark, piloted by Kenton, set out for Harrodsburg. Unfortunately, during their absence, Jones prevailed on ten men to accompany him to the place where the ammunition was concealed. They set out, and on Christmas Day, 1776, they were encountered by the Indian chief Pluggey, with his men, and defeated. Jones and William Grayson were killed, and two of the party taken prisoners; the remainder escaped into the station. Clark and Kenton soon afterward arrived with some men from Harrodsburg, having immediately returned on the news of the disaster. On the morning of January 1, 1777, Pluggey and his warriors appeared before the fort. McClelland and his men sallied out, and were repulsed by the Indians. McClelland and two of his men being killed and four wounded, the Indians immediately withdrew. The station was soon afterward abandoned, and the settlers returned to Harrod's Station.

In 1782, Elijah Craig, one of the famous family of that name, emigrated from Virginia after the close of the Revolutionary war, and settled on the lands on which Lebanon Town, afterward Georgetown, was located.

Very early in the history of Georgetown, and while Scott County was yet a part of Fayette, the cause of education was fostered and encouraged. The *Kentucky Gazette*, edited and published by John Bradford and his brother Fielding, the first newspaper published west of the mountains, with the exception of one at Pittsburgh, has the following:

"Education.—Notice is hereby given that on Monday, 28th of January next, a school will be opened by Messrs. Jones and Worley, at the Royal Spring in Lebanon Town, Fayette County, where a commodious house, sufficient to contain fifty or sixty scholars, will be prepared. They will teach the Latin and Greek languages, together with such branches of the sciences as are usually taught in public seminaries, at twenty-five shillings a quarter for each scholar. One-half to be paid in cash, the other half in produce at cash prices. There will be a vacation of a month in the spring, and another in the fall, at the close of each of which it is expected that such payments as are due in cash will be made. For diet, washing and house-room for a year, each scholar pays £3 in cash, or 500 weight of pork on entrance, and £3 cash on the beginning of the third quarter. It is desired that, as many as can, would furnish themselves with beds; such as cannot, may be provided for here, to the number of eight or ten boys, at 35s a year for each bed. ELIJAH CRAIG.

"LEBANON, December 27, 1787."

In 1790, Georgetown was incorporated by the Legislature of Virginia, and named in honor of George Washington. March 10, 1792, the Indians stole ten or twelve horses from near Grant's mill, on North Elkhorn, and on Tuesday night following, they burned a dwelling house, together with all the household furniture, belonging to the proprietors, who had left their house late in the evening. This was about the last incursion of the Indians in the neighborhood of Georgetown.

Elijah Craig, named above as the proprietor and founder of Georgetown, was a Baptist preacher, and one of three brothers—Joseph, Lewis and Elijah—who were made famous in Virginia by religious intolerance and persecution. They all removed to Kentucky, and Elijah settled here. He was a man of decided character, a good speaker, an acceptable preacher, and of very considerable business qualifications, accumulating a large property. He built and owned the upper mill, now DeGarris, the lower mill, known as Grant's mill, and with Mr. Parker, of Lexington, the paper-mill on the Royal Spring branch, where Capt. Lair's mill now stands. This was the first paper-mill, and manufactured nearly all the paper used for printing or wrapping purposes, for Lexington, Louisville, Cincinnati, and the villages around, for many years. This paper-mill was built in 1795, and burnt down in 1832. It was the first paper-mill and the only one for many years west of the mountains.

The house erected by Mr. Craig for his residence stood on the hill, on the west side of "Floyd's Royal Spring Branch," as it was then called. Col. Floyd, a soldier of the Revolution, had a military land warrant for a thousand acres; this survey was on the south side of North Elkhorn, and includes the land on which the town was laid out, and the Spring Branch, and running west, and known as Floyd's survey, and patented in 1779.

One of the first brick houses in the town was erected by Mr. Craig, and in which he resided for many years, was the house owned by the late Col. A. K. Richards and destroyed by fire a few years since. Mr. Craig also erected a factory for the manufacture of hemp, north of his dwelling, and on the opposite side of the road, near the place now occupied by the Desha monument. The first settlements made in the town, were mostly on the bluff, east of the Spring Branch, and were, no doubt, located with a view as much to comfort and convenience as for safety, in supplying themselves with water. The first settlers of the town were largely from Virginia, some from Maryland, Pennsylvania, New York, New Jersey, North Carolina, and Massachusetts. They were enterprising, intelligent, and many of them educated men and women. The town is claimed to have been surveyed and laid out by Fielding Bradford, a very competent surveyor, and afterward Judge of the county, assisted by John Payne, the first County Surveyor, and a Brigadier General in the war of 1812. Elijah Craig erected and owned the framed hotel that stood on the northwest corner of Main and Main Cross streets, on the site of the Georgetown Hotel, recently destroyed by fire. It was first occupied as a hotel by his son-in-law, Capt. Grant, who was killed by the Indians in 1794, on the Ohio River below the mouth of Licking River, he with others having pursued the Indians, who had made an incursion and carried off some horses from the neighborhood of Georgetown. In 1780, the Virginia Legislature granted lands to Kentucky for educational purposes, and the citizens of Georgetown very early availed themselves of the grant, and built what was known as Rittenhouse Academy; the first house erected for that purpose was of hewed logs, and stood on the north side of what is now called College street, not far from the head of the Spring Branch, and is occupied at present as a private residence.

Firearms were a necessary household article in these early times, and in 1784 Mr. Edward West, from Fredericksburg, Va., settled in Georgetown as a gunsmith. He erected a log house near the Spring Branch, where he manufactured rifles chiefly, for which there was great demand. He also invented a mold for casting or molding pewter into plates and basins, then in great request and almost indispensablè to every housekeeper.

Capt. John Hawkins and his brother Martin emigrated from Virginia and settled in Georgetown about the year 1790. They were merchants. Capt. Hawkins erected a brick and frame building which he occupied as a residence on the northeast corner of Main and Hamilton streets, and now occupied by John Mullin as a hotel. Capt. Hawkins was a prominent citizen, and in 1792 was the first Clerk of Scott County Court. He removed to Hopkinsville, Christian County, about the year 1820, and died there at an advanced age.

Mr. Martin Hawkins was a citizen of Georgetown for many years, and a successful merchant; he erected one of the first brick houses in the town. It stood on the south side of Main street, near the site of the building now occupied by Thomas Barkley as a grocery. It was built with the gable to the street, and had an elevator for lifting goods to the second story; this was a wholesale house, and Mr. Hawkins did a large business. His residence, a frame building, stood upon the alley just in the rear of the Fitzgerald drug store, and fronting on Main street. About 1813, he removed to the beautiful blue grass farm south of town, afterward owned by Mr. Thomas Smarr, and at present occupied by Mrs. A. K. Richards. He married Miss Mary Shipp, of Fayette County, about the year 1800. Mr. Hawkins died in 1824 or 1825. Mrs. Hawkins survived him many years, and died in Georgetown. They left five sons and three daughters, all of whom are dead except Mr. Richard Hawkins, who still resides in the town at an advanced age.

Abram Scott was here as early as 1794–95. He lived in a log house very much after the style of a fort, with portholes on all sides, and a projecting roof; it stood on the east side of the Spring Branch. He carried on blacksmithing in a shop that stood near the site now occupied by John Rowland's brick shop. Mr. Scott was a prominent man in the municipal affairs of the town, often elected a member of the Board of Trustees, and on many of its important committees, an industrious and useful citizen.

Capt. Lynn West was born in Virginia in 1775, and came to Georgetown with his Uncle Edward West in 1784, and worked with him in the gunsmith business until 1797, when he returned to Prince William County, Va., and while there married Miss Susan Jackson. Before going to Virginia, he had erected a dwelling on the corner of Hamilton and what is now called Bourbon street. He returned to Georgetown and continued the manufacture of guns and other implements. In 1812, he volunteered as Captain of an independent company, First Battalion, First Regiment of Scott's command. He died in 1836. Capt. West was an energetic, industrious and high-toned man. He was fond of fine-blooded horses, of which he raised and ran a good many. He left a family of nine children. Mrs. Susan West survived her husband many years, and died in 1860, an excellent, devoted and pious lady, a member of the Baptist Church.

Among the earliest settlers of Georgetown and the first professional lawyer was Mr. Samuel Shepard, he was born in Massachusetts, Middlesex County, October 19, 1765, and, with his brother, Zenas Shepard, removed to Kentucky about 1790; he was married to Miss Fannie Barlow, of Scott County, in 1792, and was living in Georgetown in 1795, practicing law and keeping a house of entertainment. The house was a log and framed house, and stood on the east side of Main Cross street, near where the present Catholic Church stands. Some years afterward, he built a large brick house on the lot south of the town, and which now forms a part of the Female Seminary. He practiced law many years, and died in Ohio in 1839. Mrs. Shepard survived him many years. He left four sons, all of whom are dead.

William and Thomas Story emigrated from Pennsylvania, and settled in Georgetown about 1790. They sank and carried on a large tannery; it was in the valley on the east side of Main Cross street, and north of the Pratt property, and now a part of it. They worked a large number of hands, and furnished a great portion of the leather for home manufacture.

The residence of Mr. William Story, where he lived a great many years, is the old frame, the second house north of the Pratt Hotel.

Mr. William Story was a prominent citizen of the town, often a member of the Board of Trustees. He married Miss Eliza, sister of John Bradford, editor of the old *Kentucky Gazette.* She was an intelligent and excellent lady, and died in 1833. Mr. Story survived her a few years.

Capt. Thomas Story conducted the business of tanning for several years. Volunteered in the war of 1812, the First Lieutenant, Capt. West's Company, First Regiment, Scott's Brigade; served out his time of enlistment, and removed to Missouri in 1820.

One of the first physicians who settled in Georgetown was Dr. John Stites, born in New Jersey and educated in New York. He emigrated to Kentucky and settled in Georgetown about 1795. He was an educated man, and eminent in his profession. He was the grandfather of Judge Stites, now of Louisville. He died in Georgetown in 1811.

William B. Warren emigrated from Virginia and settled in Georgetown about 1794. He practiced law for many years, and was successful in his profession. He was Judge of Quarter Sessions Court, a man of fine personal appearance, quiet and retiring. He erected and occupied a frame house on the south side of Main street, on the site now occupied by the Farmers' Bank. He afterward removed to a brick residence that now forms a part of Warrendale, and where he resided at the time of his death. He married Miss Maria Fauntleroy, who survived him several years. He died in 1824. They left two sons and three daughters. Mrs. Margaret Johnson, widow of Col. T. F. Johnson, alone surviving.

Capt. William Theobalds came from Virginia and settled in Georgetown about 1790. He built and occupied a large frame building on the south side of Main street, near the site of the present residence of Mr. William O. Thompson. This was a famous old hotel. Capt. Theobalds was an admirable hotel keeper, and so good was his cheer that many of the farmers of that day, like the boys of the present, after the arduous labors of County Court day were over, got left. Capt. Theobalds married Miss Brown, sister of Judge William O. Brown, of Harrison County. They raised a large family of children. He removed to a farm near the "Stamping Ground" in Scott County about 1820, where he died.

The first court house erected in the town stood on the public square, near the site occupied by the present handsome structure. The lower story was of stone and very rough, and upon this a frame building was erected for the court rooms proper. A flight of steps from the ground to the second story on the south side was the mode of approach to the court room. The lower story was divided into rooms that were rented out for the benefit of the town. Here schools were kept, and various tradesmen occupied these rooms that were rented out annually to the highest bidder. This house was built about 1793 or 1794, and after fulfilling its particular purpose of dispensing justice, it was also used for schools, churches and general meetings. It was pulled down in 1816, the frame-work removed up on the north side of Main street, near the lot occupied by Dr. Craig's late residence, and converted into an oil factory by Mr. Charles Cullen.

Capt. Robert Hunter settled in Georgetown about the year 1794. He removed from Virginia. He owned and occupied the red frame house on the east side of Main Cross street and the first house, north of and adjoining Pratt's Hotel. Capt. Hunter was often a member of the Board of Trustees, and a prominent citizen of the town.

Hezekiah Ford, Alexander McKoy, Thomas Johnston and Adam Johnson were all early settlers from 1790 to 1800. Alex. McKoy was the first Commissioner and Tax Collector for many years of the town; a soldier of the war of 1812. He has one daughter living in the county, the mother of Dr. Ford and the Rev. C. Ford of "Stamping Ground."

Capt. James H. Mahoney removed from Maryland and settled in Georgetown in 1798 or 1799. He erected a frame building on the east side of Main Cross street, on the site now occupied by the "Pratt House;" here he conducted a hotel for many years. About the year 1820, he removed the frame and erected a brick house in its stead that forms the front of the present hotel. He was a popular and successful landlord, fully identified with the prosperity of the town, and one of its prominent citizens. He lived to an advanced age, and died in 183–, leaving two daughters—Mrs. Lewis West and Mrs. Chambers.

Bartlett Collins, the two McClungs, John and David, Bernard Moore, James Bell, John and James Lemon were very early settlers of Georgetown. Bernard Moore, for many years, carried on saddlery and harness-making under the old court house. In 1799, James Garrard, then Governor of the Commonwealth of Kentucky, under an act of the General Assembly of Kentucky, deeded unto Robert Johnson, Bartlett Collins, John Hawkins, John Hunter, Elijah Craig, Toliver Craig, William Henry, John Payne, Samuel Shepard, William Warren and Abraham Buford, Trustees to the Rittenhouse Academy, a certain tract or parcel of land containing 5,900 acres of land, lying and being in the county of Christian and on the Cumberland River, for the purpose of establishing and endowing an academy.—*S. F. Gano.*

CHAPTER VIII.

GEORGETOWN—GROWTH AND DEVELOPMENT—GANO FAMILY—THE STEVENSONS, OFFUTTS AND OTHER PIONEERS—VILLAGE ORGANIZATIONS—TRUSTEES—MANUFACTORIES AND BUSINESS INTERESTS—MISCELLANEOUS SUBJECTS, ETC., ETC.

WE have endeavored to trace the decade of Georgetown from the first insignificant and straggling village of Lebanon, lying along the margin of the stream that glides along its western border, to the more imposing town, with its broad Main and Main Cross streets, with here and there a substantial residence or business house, with a court house and its necessary adjunct, a jail, erected on the public square, conveniently located at the intersection of the above streets, with an endowment of nearly 6,000 acres of land for educational purposes, with schools, the preaching of the Gospel; with an intelligent, enterprising and industrious community of mechanics and business men; with a county territory extending north to the Ohio River, for Cincinnati then (Fort Washington) a village on our border, just across the river, traded with Georgetown. Capt. Daniel Gano, a Captain of artillery in the United States Army, and stationed at Frankfort, with a corps of men had blazed a road from Georgetown to the Ohio River, at the mouth of Licking. This road was along the Dry Ridge, along the way pioneered by the buffalo and Indians—the buffalo in quest of the Big Bone Lick, and the Indians in quest of game and the scalps of their invaders. Georgetown grew rapidly from 1800.

Richard M. Gano settled here in that year; he was born in the city of New York July 7, 1775, and removed to Kentucky with his father, the Rev. John Gano, and settled at Frankfort in 1789; married Miss Elizabeth Ewing, of Bedford County, Va., in 1797, and soon after removed to to this place. He was a merchant for several years; volunteered in the war of 1812 as Major of Scott's regiment, First Bat.; commanded the regiment at the battle of the Thames, and was brevetted a Brigadier General. He built several houses in the town, and sold goods for many years in the house on the southwest corner of Main and Cross streets, now occupied by Kinsea Stone, as a grocery. He removed to the property known now as the Stedman Mill property, soon after the war. He was one of the proprietors of the city of Covington, with his brother Gen. John S. Gano and Maj. D. Carneal, having purchased the Kennedy farm and laid out the town in 1814–15. He died at his home October 22, 1815, in the full vigor of his manhood. His first wife died April 9, 1812, and his second wife, Mrs. D. Goforth, survived him, and afterward was Mrs. Joel Scott, of Frankfort.

Gen. Gano was a man of great energy and will, and of enlarged benevolence, and aided materially in building the first Baptist Church and promoting education in the town. Six children of his first wife survived him, four of whom are still living--Mrs. M. H. Ewing, Mrs. C. V. Henry, Elder John A. Gano and Dr. S. F. Gano, the eldest of whom is eighty-two, and the youngest seventy-five years.

Judge Cary L. Clarke came to Georgetown with his wife, Mrs. Eliza Clarke, about the year 1802; he was a lawyer by profession, a man of culture and intelligence. They removed here from the city of New York. Their residence stood on the southeastern corner of the large lot now being very rapidly built up. The house stood on the site of the building recently owned and erected by Mr. W. S. Elgin, on the corner of Hamilton and Bourbon streets. It was a plain, substantial two-story frame house, with large grounds and comfortable surroundings. It was burned down a few years since. Judge Clarke was a Judge of the Circuit Court and for many years Clerk of the Circuit and County Courts. He was a prominent and influential citizen. He had a nail factory, in connection with Moses L. Miller, for several years after the war of 1812. He died July 23, 1819. His widow survived him many years; she died August 23, 1854, a most excellent and devoted member of the Methodist Episcopal Church. They left five children, one son—Dr. James Clarke, of New Orleans, and four daughters, only two of whom are living—Mrs. Kate Applegate, of Louisville, and Mrs. Charlotte Hollingsworth, of Hannibal, Mo.

Georgetown now became a real, live place and assumed the dignity of an incorporated town, by virtue of an act of the Legislature:

SCOTT COUNTY, SCT.:

FEBRUARY COURT, 1804.

John Mosby and John Thomson, gentlemen, are appointed Judges to superintend the election for Trustees for the town of Georgetown for the present year, and John Hawkins, Clerk pro tem., agreeable to an act of the General Assembly.

A copy. Test: JOHN HAWKINS, *Clerk.*

The said Judges having previously advertised the citizens of Georgetown that an election for their Trustees would be held at the court house on this day, to wit, the 10th day of March, 1804, met agreeable thereto and received the votes, as follows in the poll below:

Persons voted for—John Branham, William Story, R. M. Gano, J. Hawkins, J. Wallace, John Lemon, B. Moore, S. Shepard, William Warren, Lynn West, M. Hawkins, R. Hunter, John McClung, William Theobalds, William Browne.

And the following are the names of the voters: Samuel Shepard, James McClung, John Lemon, Jr., John Green, James Mahoney, James Crawford, Zenas Shepard, Thomas Offutt, James Bell, Alexander Stewart, William Theobalds, John Branham, Lynn West, Henry Hardie, Thomas Story, William Story, William Browne, M. Hawkins, John Stites, Job Stevenson, James Lemon, Jr., Adam Johnson, Heza Ford, James Ewart, B. Moore, John Greenhalgh, Thomas Marntn, William Warren, Joseph Dean, John Dean, William Patterson, Robert Hunter, Lindsey Campbell, Nicholas Bitner, Isaac Ferrell, R. M. Gano, Charles Graham, David McClung, John Hawkins, Fred Warnuck, Alexander McCoy, Jr., John Wallace, John Patterson, Hugh Hart, James Clark.

March 10, 1804.

We being appointed Judges to the above election for Trustees of Georgetown, do proclaim that William Story, Samuel Shepard, John Branham, John Hawkins, R. M. Gano, Lynn West and Robert Hunter are duly elected agreeable to the above poll.

JOHN MOSBY,
JOHN THOMSON.

Test: JOHN HAWKINS, *Clerk pro tem.*

From the above election, it appears, there were forty-six voters, residents of the town. It might be assumed that there were from 250 to 300 citizens in the place.

Job Stevenson was born in Baltimore County, Md., in 1773, and, with his father Thomas Stevenson, removed to Kentucky in 1790. They were conveyed down the Ohio River on flat-boats, to Limestone (now Maysville), thence on their pack-horses to Washington, which was then a fort, defended by Simon Kenton and others.

It was not long after this that Capt. Hubble, descending the Ohio River on a flat-boat with a party of immigrants, was fiercely attacked by a large party of Indians, who, after a desperate fight, were repulsed. Thomas Ste-

H C Kimball

venson, with Kenton and others, met this gallant band at Maysville, aided them in landing and burying their dead. Thomas Stevenson settled on a tract of land near Fort Washington. Job Stevenson labored on his father's farm, until, in his sixteenth year, he learned the saddler's trade in Washington. In 1803 or 1804, he started out on a "tramp" as a "journeyman saddler," and, by the merest accident he reached Georgetown, where he soon found employment, and worked for several years, until he commenced business for himself. He was an industrious and energetic man, working at his bench night and day, rather than disappoint a customer. His business increased so rapidly that he was soon enabled to give employment to as many as twenty-five hands, many of these men of families, who derived their support from his establishment. He manufactured a very large quantity of all kinds of work in the harness and saddlery business. Carrying on a large trade in lumber, salt, iron castings, machinery, stock of all kinds, extending his trading operations, through the mountain regions of Kentucky and to Cincinnati, Ohio. Having two or three farms, and giving employment to large numbers of men in his many departments of business. He accumulated a large property, built houses, etc. The house destroyed by the late fire, owned by A. W. Forward, he occupied as a shop for many years. The house owned and occupied recently by Maj. B. F. Bradley, was built by him for his residence, and many other houses in town. After more than half a century spent in close application to business, and by his industry and attention having amassed a large property, he embarked in politics, representing his county in the Legislature several terms. Neglecting his business or leaving it in the hands of others, he became involved in surety, his mind lost its balance and he took his own life in 1837. He was a Magistrate of the county for many years, and it was proverbial of him that when litigated or troublesome cases came before him, he split the difference, or, like Solomon, divided the child in dispute. In 1807, he married Miss Mary Jones, daughter of Mrs. Tomlinson, a lady of rare excellence and piety, and a school-teacher in Georgetown. Mrs. Tomlinson, formerly Mrs. Jones, was an intelligent lady, a pioneer and leading member of the M. E. Church, and her house was the home of the Methodist preacher for many years. Squire Stevenson married his second wife, Mrs. Honeycutt (*nee* Blair), sister of Hon. Preston Blair, formerly of Frankfort, Ky., in 1835. His first wife left three sons—Rev. Evan Stevenson, Edward and Hiram, only one of the last is living, in Illinois.

In 1806, Joseph S. Norris came from Maryland and settled in Georgetown. He lived on Hamilton, near the residence of Judge Rhoton, and conducted a cabinet-maker's shop, manufacturing furniture, etc. He was often elected a member of the Board of Trustees, and served as County Surveyor for a great many years, and died on his farm, two miles north of Georgetown.

Thomas Offutt, from Maryland, was living in Georgetown in 1807; he was a boot and shoe-maker, and lived on the corner of Main Cross street and Jefferson, on the site now occupied by Judge Payne's residence. He was Overseer of the Streets and Tax Collector of the town, for some time. He died on his place, on the Cincinnati pike some ten miles north of the town, at an advanced age.

James B. Crawford settled in Georgetown in 1807. He was, for a great many years, the jailer of Scott County, while the jail was on the public square his residence was in the house on Main Cross street, west side, now occupied by Mrs. Oliver Gaines; after the new jail was built, he occupied the house of the jailer on the Spring Branch. Mr. Crawford was often a member of the Board of Trustees. He married a daughter of Mrs. Miller, of the county, the first wife of the late Benjamin Osborn, of this county. Mrs. Crawford was a most devoted and pious member of Methodist Church, a highly intelligent and gifted lady.

William Brown came to Georgetown to reside about the year 1806. He carried on the manufacture of hats, fur and wool, on a large scale, employing from eight to ten hands, and trading largely with the neighboring counties. He accumulated quite a large property by his industry and enterprise. He built and owned the two-story brick house on the east side of Main Cross street, now occupied by Mrs. Dr. Grissim; he likewise built and resided in the house just south of the former, now owned by Capt. J. L. Sinclair. His shop stood on the lot occupied by the coal-yard attached to this property. He aided materially in building the first Presbyterian Church. He married Mrs. Adams, of Fayette, before removing to this place.

George Douglass Brown left Ireland in 1807, and came to Georgetown the same year. He worked with his brother, William, several years, and afterward carried on the business alone many years, when he engaged in merchandising. He built and owned the brick house on the north side of Main street, just west of the Corner Hotel, lately destroyed by fire.

John Adams, born in 1777, in Hagerstown, Md., moved to Georgetown about the year 1801, and settled on the hill in the southern part of the town, and occupied the house now owned and occupied by his daughter, Mrs. Priscilla White. He carried on for many years an extensive establishment for the manufacture of fur and wool hats. He employed as many as ten or twelve hands in his business. After supplying the home demand, he had an extensive trade with the neighboring towns and counties. He traded for young mules and other stock, which he reared on his farm near town.

A number employed by him were heads of families, among whom Mr. John Strong, Maj. John Felty, a brave and distinguished soldier of the war of 1812, Mr. Frederick Zimmerman and others. Mr. Adams married Miss Mary Downing, of Fayette County, and raised eleven children, four only of whom are living. He lived to an old age; died March 10, 1837; his wife survived him many years.

Frederick Zimmerman was born in Lancaster, Penn., where he served an apprenticeship to the hatting business, He came to Lexington, where he married Miss Mary Haggard, daughter of Mr. John Haggard, an early settler of that city. He removed to Georgetown in 1806, and settled in the southern part of the town, in a house that stood on the east side of Main Cross street, on the corner occupied by Clark's carriage shop. He worked in the establishment of Mr. John Adam's many years. He died at an advanced age, leaving two sons and two daughters—John F. Zimmerman, a journalist and publisher of Danville, Ky., and David Zimmerman, for many years a merchant in Lexington.

Josiah Pitts came from Virginia to Kentucky, and settled about the year 1806 or 1807. He married Miss Lucy Craig, daughter of Mr. Elijah Craig, and lived on the hill west of the town, in the house lately occupied by A. Keene Richards. Perhaps no citizen of Georgetown contributed more to the material interests of the town and county during his business career than did Josiah Pitts. He embarked largely in trade, purchasing all the tobacco, wheat and flour, hemp bagging cordage, bacon and whisky produced, not only in this county, but in the neighboring regions. This produce he shipped by flat-boats from Frankfort and the mouth of Salt River below Louisville, where it was hauled by wagon, and once in the year, at the proper stage of water, it was carried to Natchez and New Orleans, and exchanged for gold and silver and bills on the East. For many years, Mr. Pitts conducted a very lucrative trade. He employed many of the young and active men of the county, who would conduct this flotilla of boats, dispose of the produce, and pack the specie back on their persons or on Indian ponies. Many young men started in this way, and the farmers received pay for their surplus produce. Tobacco was the staple then. The Old Virginia farmers bringing with them from the old State the tendency to like agricultural pursuits, large quantities of tobacco were raised in the county. Hemp was also raised in very early times; when it was brought to Kentucky, we have been unable to learn. It was not specially a product of Virginia. There were three hemp factories in operation in the town and neighborhood at that early day.

Mr. Pitts contributed largely to the facilities for the trade of the place. He had large means, and he used it for the benefit of others as well as himself. He was fond of fine blood horses, and indulged his Old Virginian fondness for racing.

The depression that followed the war of 1812 overtook him, and greatly reduced his circumstances. He died in 1815, preceded a short time by his wife. They left five children, all of whom are dead.

Applegate & McPhatridge were conducting a tailoring establishment in Georgetown in 1805–6. John Applegate was the son of Mrs. Osborn, by her first husband. William Applegate (killed by the Indians) was born in Scott County; carried on a large tailoring establishment for many years, and died in 1866.

He married Miss Ford, daughter of Hezekiah Ford, one of the first settlers of the place. She was an excellent and pious lady. She died in 1860, and left three children, one daughter, Mrs. C. West, and two sons, William H. Applegate, of Louisville, and J. E. Applegate, of this place. In 1807, Georgetown had quite an accession to her population from the city of New York—Mr. James Betts and wife, who came from England. They settled in Georgetown, in 1807. Mr. Betts was a butcher, and supplied the town for several years; he finally settled on a farm near town, on Elkhorn Creek, now occupied by his daughter, Miss Sarah Betts.

Mr. Betts was the first, and up to his death, remained a Deacon of the Baptist Church.

Three children survive, one daughter, as above, and two sons, James and Sampson, of this place.

William Hewitt and wife were from England, and settled in Georgetown in 1807. They came from the city of New York. He followed the business of tailoring for many years; he was one of the constituent members of the Baptist Church. He lived on the northeast corner of Main and Water streets, near the bridge. He died in 1817, his wife having preceded him some years. His son-in-law, Mr. James Chalk, came to Kentucky with him, and settled in Georgetown. He was a tallow chandler, and furnished light for the good citizens of the place. Mr. Chalk was an excellent man, a Deacon and leading member of the Baptist Church. He owned and occupied the house on the south side of Limestone street, now occupied by Mr. William Offut. His widow survived him several years; one son, James, and three daughters are living, one (Mrs. T. I. Burns) a citizen of this place. William Hutchings and wife, English people, came to Kentucky at the same time with the above, and settled here, but soon after removed to a farm near town.

Dr. William H. Richardson removed to Georgetown from Fayette County, in 1806. He occupied a house that stood on the south side of Main street, on the site of the Farmers' Branch Bank. He practiced his profession successfully up to the war of 1812, when he volunteered and served as surgeon in Col. R. M. Johnson's regiment of mounted men.

After the war, he removed to Lexington.

He was Professor of Obstetrics in the Medical Department of Transylvania University. He practiced his profession successfully many years, and in 1831 removed to a farm in Fayette County.

In 1807, a Masonic Lodge of A. Y. Masons was chartered and established in Georgetown. The following were among the earliest members: Cary L. Clarke, Samuel Shepard, Robert Hunter, R. M. Gano, Dr. John Stites, Dr. William H. Richardson, Col. R. M. Johnson, Joseph Dean, William Warren, John Holroyd, John D. Craig, James Grant, Thomas W. Hawkins, Josiah Pitts, William Sutton, Abraham S. Van De Graff and others, many of whom were initiated previous to the war of 1812.

This was the beginning of old Mt. Vernon, No. 14. She dwelt in many places before she finally settled down in her own temple, where she now holds her regular conclaves. The old lodge has a grand history, of her own, that would make a book full of interest. Many great and good men have gone from her hall to every department of life, to teach a better and higher manhood and a nobler charity.

In 1809, the first market house was built in Georgetown. It was erected on the east side of the public square. It was built by John Shellers and Thomas Fisher and I. Pines, at a cost of $404.43. It was of brick, and well arranged.

In 1807, John McFall, an Englishman, removed from New York to Georgetown, bringing a large stock of dry goods; he purchased the then new brick house on the corner of Main and Cross streets, now occupied by K. Stone. He died within the year, and his widow, after a few years, returned to New York.

Thomas W. Martin, the first Postmaster, died September, 1807. George W. Miller succeeded him as Postmaster, and died in 1814.

Dr. John Holroyd and Theodoric Boulware taught a school in the Rittenhouse Academy; Dr. Holroyd was a graduate of Brown University; they both afterward became Baptist ministers.

In 1809, Mrs. De Charmes and her daughter, Miss Sarah, with her son James, settled in Georgetown. They were an English family, and removed from New York. Mrs. De Charmes established a female school of a high grade, where, in addition to the usual branches, music, drawing, and other accomplishments were added. This school had a fine reputation. Scholars were drawn from Lexington, Frankfort, Louisville, and the teachers were refined and cultivated ladies. The building stood on Water street—the same house erected by Mr. Craig in 1789. When the war came on, the school was suspended, and the ladies removed to Frankfort, where a British officer, a prisoner at Frankfort on parole, captured Miss Sarah, and after the war, carried them back to England.

In 1809, Dr. Alex Montgomery settled for the practice of medicine; he volunteered in the war of 1812, and was killed at the disastrous defeat of River Raisin. He was highly esteemed by all who knew him.

In 1809, Peter Mason kept the Georgetown Hotel. He married Miss Grant, and in a few years removed to the country.

He was succeeded by Capt. Mahoney, who kept this house for a short time. It was here, for the first time in the history of the town, the first manslaughter was committed, and great was the sensation it produced. For years it was the theme of conversation in its terrible particulars. Duly killed Holland in an encounter with knives. A conflict was expected on their meeting—both were prepared. They had been friends—young men from the same neighborhood. They had been trading down the river, quarreled about a settlement; both anticipated the meeting, and although Holland was regarded as the more dangerous of the two men, Duly killed him in the first onset. The excitement was very great. Hon. John Rowan, regarded then as the ablest criminal lawyer in the State, was brought to Georgetown to defend Duly. He was found guilty, and sent to the penitentiary for many years. In the present days of lax laws and loose justice, it might have been called a case of self-defense.

In 1811, the first newspaper, the *Telegraph*, was established in Georgetown; it was published and edited by Shadrach Penn. From its appearance, it was printed on paper manufactured at the paper mill that stood on the Spring Branch. It is well printed and very readable. A publication of the by-laws for the government of Georgetown, signed by John Branham, Chairman, and William Shepard, Clerk, would be very good reading for the present board. John R. Mahan informed the public that he continues the saddling business in all its various branches. Pitts, Cowan & Co., commission merchants, Natchez, Miss., keep every description of Kentucky produce.

J. W. Hawkins wants those who are indebted to him for merchandise to bring in their hemp, and would like to purchase twelve or fifteen thousand gallons of whisky.

Dr. G. C. Berry has commenced the practice of physic and surgery in Georgetown and its vicinity.

S. I. Richardson, counselor and attorney at law, will punctually attend the Fayette, Bourbon and Scott Circuit Court. He resided in Georgetown.

Peter Mason has removed from Georgetown to Mount Sterling, Ky., and has opened a hotel.

Dr. William B. Keen has moved to Georgetown, to the house lately occupied by Dr. John Stites, deceased.

Robert P. Henry will continue to practice law in the Scott Circuit Court. His office is in Mr. Job Stevenson's new brick house.

Mr. Penn's paper is filled with good reading matter. After the paper was discontinued Mr. Penn married Miss M. George, daughter of Mr. Leonard George, who kept the corner hotel on Main and Cross streets.

Mr. Penn soon after removed to Louisville, where he edited the *Advertiser*, a leading Democratic paper in the State. Mr. Penn was an able journalist and ready writer, and George D. Prentice, as editor of the *Journal*, encountered no abler or worthier foe than Shadrach Penn.

Among those who went forth to the field of battle from Georgetown, was Charley Mansfield, a printer in the *Telegraph* office, who never returned to chronicle the brilliant victory of the Thames. He was a volunteer in Capt. West's company, Scott's regiment.

In 1809, Messrs. Wolfe & Henderson removed from Pittsburgh to Georgetown and settled here. They carried on the manufacture of powder. Mr. J. Wolfe removed to the country and Mr. Henderson died a short time afterward. His widow was a useful and important character in the town and county for more than a fourth of a century. She was a most excellent nurse and midwife, and stood well in the community as a true Christian woman. She married for her second husband John Beatty, and was left a widow again in a few years. She was a kind, attentive nurse, and rendered good service in the cholera of 1833. She died about 1854, leaving three daughters—Mary, who married Judge B. T. Thompson; Adeline, who married John Chaham; and Betty Beatty.

Mr. William Tompkins Shepard was born in Georgetown in 1793, perhaps the first child born in the place, oldest son of Samuel Shepard; he was for many years Clerk of the Board of Trustees; studied law with his father; volunteered in the war of 1812; was at the battle of the Thames; returned to Georgetown and died January, 1858.

Mr. Charles Frazier settled in Georgetown in 1811, and practiced medicine for three or four years. He was an excellent physician and very highly esteemed in the community.

Rowland Hannah removed to Georgetown in 1807; he was a widower with two daughters—Sally, afterward Mrs. Greenup Keene, the mother of S. Y. Keene; and Nancy, afterward Mrs. William Emison, still living a widow in the northern part of the county.

Mr. Hannah was an Irishman by birth, and came to Kentucky at an early day. He was a merchant and sold goods many years under the old court house. It was the custom then for merchants to pack their specie on horseback. They would meet at Maysville or some other point from the neighboring towns, and go in a body for mutual protection to Philadelphia. Mr. Hannah rode the same horse nine years in succession across the mountains, carrying his gold and silver for the purchase of goods. He was a successful merchant, and retired in his old age from business in comfortable circumstances. He married a second wife, Miss Mattie Emison, of Scott County, who survived her husband several years, and died in 1854, leaving four daughters—Mrs. James H. Davies, Mrs. Irene Hibbard, Miss Margaret and Miss Lizzie, who still reside in Georgetown.

Capt. Lewis West was born in Georgetown in 1800—the oldest living man born in the town—the son of Lynn West, with whom he worked at the gunsmith's business. He became skillful in the manufacture of rifles and pistols, and, after he embarked in the business for himself, had orders for more than he could furnish, employing several hands in his shop. He built a house on the east side of Hamilton street, corner of Washington, where Mr. Judson Stiffee now lives, and his shop occupied the opposite corner. He lived in this house and conducted the gunsmith business from his boyhood until he was seventy-nine years of age, and is now in fine health at eighty-two. He married Miss Sarah Mahoney, daughter of Capt. James H. Mahoney, in 1823, and, after half a century of married life, she died in 1874, and left five children.

Rev. Joseph Smith Tomlinson, D. D., was born in Georgetown in the year 1802. Received his early education from his mother, Mrs. Sarah Tomlinson. He was apprenticed to his brother-in-law, in his twelfth year, to learn the trade of saddle and harness making. After a few years, he became clerk and manager of the large establishment. All his leisure moments were devoted to the acquisition of knowledge and the improvement of his mind. He united with the Methodist Church while very young, and, in his seventeenth year, he was licensed to exercise his gifts as an exhorter. In 1820 and 1821, he was enabled to attend the Rittenhouse

Academy, then under the care of Mr. Charles O'Hara, a fine scholar and admirable teacher.

Although devoting a portion of his time to the bench and shop, he was so close a student as to keep up with his classes. He acquired a good knowledge of the Latin and Greek languages, and of Mathematics, in which he excelled. His mind was logical.

Having prepared himself for college, he was enabled, by the kind offices of Mr. Clay, to enter Transylvania University as a beneficiary of the Morrisson Fund.

A diligent student, after four years' close application, he graduated in the class of 1825. He was selected to deliver the welcome address to La Fayette, on behalf of the university.

Very soon after, he was elected to a professorship in Augusta College, Kentucky. Dr. Tomlinson was not a man to stand still. He was an indefatigable student, and in a few years he was elected to the presidency of the institution, under the control of the Methodist Denomination, of Kentucky. He remained at the head of this institution until 1849, when the dissensions in the Kentucky Conference, growing out of the slavery question, resulted in the withdrawal of its charter.

He was soon after elected to and accepted a professorship in the Ohio University at Athens, and the year following elected its president, which he declined on account of his failing health.

Dr. Tomlinson was at times the subject of great nervous prostration and mental despondency. His mind had been too long and too heavily taxed, and mental alienation followed. He finished his course amid the bitter lamentations of the whole community. He died at Neville, Ohio, June 4, 1853.

Dr. Tomlinson was married three times. His first wife, Miss Eliza P. C. Light, daughter of Rev. George C. Light, of Lexington, he married in 1825; she was the mother of four children, and died in 1842. His second wife was Mrs. Campbell, daughter of John Armstrong, and his third wife was Mrs. Davis, of Ohio, who is still living.

Dr. Fletcher Tomlinson, brother of the above, was born in Georgetown in 1802, and received his early instruction from his excellent and pious mother; he likewise served an apprenticeship to the saddlery business in Mr. Stevenson's shop. He studied medicine and practiced his profession in Bracken County.

Ben. B. Ford was born in Virginia, son of the Rev. Reuben Ford, a Baptist minister; removed to Kentucky in 1811, and settled in Georgetown. He taught a school in 1812, in the house on the west side of the Spring Branch, where the Desha monument now stands. He was a fine scholar, had a large school, a lawyer by profession; he gave up his school and commenced the practice of the law in 1816. He married Miss C. Flournoy, daughter of David Flournoy, Esq., of Scott County, in 1818; soon after removed to his farm in the county. After a few years, he returned to town, and was Clerk of the County Court from 1827 for many years. In 1837, the Clerk's office on the southwest corner of the public square was burned down, and the records and public papers were burned or badly mutilated. The Circuit Court office was kept in the same building and shared the same fate.

Mr. Ford was an early friend and patron of Georgetown College, a Trustee and Secretary of the Board from its organization until 1850; a prominent member of the Baptist Church, himself and wife having united with the church in 1827. He died on his farm near town in 1858, his wife having preceded him a few years. They left two children, a son and daughter.

John C. Buckner was born in Fredericksburg, Va., and came with his father's family to Kentucky at an early day. In 1811, he removed to Georgetown, and was merchandising with Abner Le Grand, of Lexington. He continued in business alone for several years; he built and occupied the house on Main street, now occupied by Mrs. Jane Miller.

He married Miss Mary E. Gano, daughter of Gen. R. M. Gano, 1813. He removed to Lexington and died in July, 1825.

His widow survived him several years, and died near Covington, Ky., July 11, 1850, leaving three children—Elizabeth G., wife of M. K. Dudley, Esq., of Covington, Ky., and R. M. and William H. Buckner (both of whom are dead).

In 1813, Mr. Harmon Stiffee removed to Georgetown with his family. He was a harness maker, and worked many years in the large establishment of Squire Stevenson. He died at an advanced age, in 1833, during the prevalence of the cholera. His widow lived many years after and died, leaving two sons—George and John—and several daughters. Mr. George G. Stiffee came with his father to Georgetown, and was apprenticed to Job Stevenson in 1813. In 1825, in connection with Henry Clarke, carried on the business of saddle and harness making. After a few years, Mr. Clarke died, and in 1834 Mr. Abner Lyon; they conducted the same business for thirteen years.

He married Mrs. Susan Crockett, daughter of Capt. Lynn West, in 1842; they are both still living. Mr. Stiffee was a member of the Board of Trustees of Georgetown College for many years, and a Deacon of the Baptist Church.—*Gano.*

CHAPTER IX.

GEORGETOWN—RELIGIOUS AND EDUCATIONAL—THE BAPTISTS, METHODISTS, PRESBYTERIANS, ETC.—EARLY MINISTERS —CHRISTIAN CHURCH ORGANIZATION—BARTON W. STONE—OTHER DENOMINATIONS—COLORED CHURCHES, ETC.—GEORGETOWN COLLEGE—BACON COLLEGE—THE MILITARY INSTITUTE—THE FEMALE ACADEMY—OTHER INSTITUTIONS.

THE first Baptist Church was organized at Georgetown in 1811. The Rev. George Biggs presided. It was constituted with the following members, viz.: John Hawkins, John Thomson and wife, William Hewitt and wife, James Betts, James Chalk and wife, William Hutchings and wife, John McFall and wife; Mr. John Thomson, Clerk; William Hewitt and James Betts, as Deacons. They met for preaching in the old court house once a month, under the pastorate of Mr. Biggs. Mrs. Alice Betts was the first person united to the church by baptism, in 1811. Soon afterward, there were added, by letter, John Branham and wife, Dr. John Stites, Charles Cullen and Mrs. Doleman. The Rev. Mr. Biggs continued to preach monthly until 1814, when the Rev. Theodoric Bouldware succeeded to the pastorate. The church prospered, and many were added by baptism and letter.

Two of those who united with the church by letter became preachers, viz., William Spencer and Robert Reed.

"At a meeting of the Commissioners in Georgetown, on Saturday, February 9, 1812, for the purpose of carrying into effect the building of a meeting-house in said town, upon examining the amount of subscription papers, find that upward of $1,000 is already subscribed. All good citizens, who feel themselves interested in the accomplishment of this laudable undertaking, are again called on for their assistance. M. Hawkins, *Clerk.*"

The above advertisement is found in the *Telegraph*, a newspaper published at that date. This effort to build a meeting-house was not accomplished until 1815, when the first brick church was finished and occupied. It stood on the site now occupied by the First Colored Baptist Church, in the northwestern part of the town, near the Spring Branch. In 1818, the Rev. Samuel Trott was pastor; he also taught a classical school in the town. He remained in Kentucky about two years. Rev. John Taylor occasionally supplied the church. In 1821, the church was supplied by two ministers, the Rev. P. S. Fall and Rev. William Spencer as co-pastors. This double pastorate did not prove beneficial to the church.

In 1823, the Rev. Jacob Creth, Sr., succeeded to the pastorate, and under his ministry a number were added to the church. His nephew, the Rev. Jacob Creth, Jr., succeeded him, for two years, preaching monthly. In 1827, the Rev. William C. Buck became the pastor of the church, and during the first year of his ministry a remarkable revival of religion prevailed, and more than one hundred were added to the church. In this year, the first Sabbath-school was established, and has continued to the present time. Mrs. M. H. Ewing was a teacher in that school, and is still living.

The Rev. John Bryce, from Richmond, Va., succeeded to the pastorate in 1829, and during his ministry many were added to the church. In 1832, the Rev. Addison N. Lewis, from Virginia, succeeded to the care of the church. During his pastorate, several were added to its membership The Revs. George and Edmund Waller and Dr. Silas M. Noel and others preached occasionally for the church about this time.

Dr. J. S. Bacon, President of the college, preached as a supply, as did also Dr. B. F. Farnsworth, who succeeded him as President in 1836. The Rev. James Black succeeded to the pastorate in 1836; he was a successful minister and very acceptable preacher. In 1840, Dr. Howard Malcolm, D. D., was elected to the Presidency of Georgetown College, and a few months later to the pastorate of the church. He was successful in both stations; a man of cultivation, great energy and will; he left a strong impress, not only on the church, but also on the community.

During his pastorate, the present commodious house was erected, on Hamilton street, with the efficient assistance of Gabriel B. Long and others. The old house was leased to the colored members of the church. Rev. George C. Sedgwick was pastor of the church in 1842. Dr. Duncan R. Campbell came to Georgetown from Mississippi in 1846, and was soon after called to the pastorate of the church. During a protracted meeting held in January and February of 1847, a large number were added, and the church was greatly strengthened and built up.

In 1850, Rev. J. L. Reynolds, D. D., of South Carolina, elected to the Presidency of the college, succeeded to the pastorate, and served the church with acceptance for two years. He was an eloquent and accomplished minister. He was succeeded by the Rev. J. M. Frost, Sr., in 1852. In the first year of his ministry, more than seventy were added to the church. He was an earnest, zealous, devoted preacher of the Gospel, but his health failed. The Rev. Samuel W. Lynd was elected Professor of Theology in the college, and succeeded to the pastorate of the church in November, 1853. Dr. Lynd was a successful pastor, a preacher of rare excellence.

The Rev. A. W. La Rue succeeded Dr. Lynd as pastor of the church in 1857; many were added under his pastorate. He was a humble, pious and godly man.

The Rev. T. J. Stevenson succeeded to the pastorate of the church in 1859, and during the very trying period of the civil war was an acceptable and useful minister. The Rev. A. C. Graves and the Rev. C. Lewis supplied the church in 1865, and were succeeded by the Rev. J. B. Tharp in 1867.

The Rev. Henry McDonald succeeded to the pastorate of the church in 1869, and quite a number were added during his ministry. He was succeeded by the Rev. R. M. Dudley, in 1877. The Rev. C. G. Skillman succeeded as pastor in November, 1879, and is the present efficient and zealous minister of the church. A number have been added during his pastorate. Its present officers are Prof. D. Thomas, Dr. John M. Lewis, Warren Clayton and George G. Stiffee, Deacons; H. Nannelly, Treas.; Prof. Farnham, Clerk. There is a large and well-ordered Sabbath school under the superintendence of Prof. J. J. Rucker, ten teachers and officers; average attendance, one hundred and twenty.

The first Methodist Church was constituted about 1817, with Mrs. Sarah Tomlinson, Mrs. Cassandra Stevenson, Job Stevenson and wife, Michael Goddard and wife, Phil B. Price and wife, William Shellers, Sr., John Shellers, Joel Peak. For many years, they met in private houses, the court house, and occasionally in the First Baptist Church. They had preaching from the circuit preachers, which was seldom, as the circuit then organized was very large. The Rev. William Burke, H. McDaniel, Jonathan Stamper, John Ray, Harris, Gunn, Edward Stevenson and others who itinerated the circuit. Their first house of worship was erected about the year 1820, and stood on the east side of Mulberry street, south of Main. It was a plain, brick structure, with ample room for the congregation. Here Bishop Crouch, the Rev. Henry Bascom, in his earlier days, Rev. George Light, and the Rev. Joseph S. Tomlinson, the great revivalist Maffitt, and others supplied the pulpit, while numbers were added to the church. In 1847, the present house on Hamilton street was built. The Rev. Evan Stevenson was mainly instrumental in its erection. From time to time many and large additions were made to the church. In 1849, S. S. Deering supplied the church, and in 1850, Rev. Evan Stevenson was the supply; in 1853–61, Rev. W. F. F. Spuell; in 1857–58, Stephen Noland; in 1855–56, Hartwell J. Perry preached for the church; 1867–68, P. L. Henderson and William McD. Abbott, and in 1869–70, S. Noland; 1871, James A. Henderson; 1872, James E. Letton, and in 1873, H. W. Abbott; 1874, Richard Deering; 1875–76, John Reeves; 1877, George D. Turner; in 1878–79, ———.

The Particular Baptist Church was organized in 1827. Those who united in the organization were Mrs. Mary Hawkins, Mrs. Elizabeth Breckenridge, Thomas H. Graves and wife, and James Sullivan and wife. Their first house for worship was erected in 1837, the present house is situated on the northeast corner of Main and Mulberry streets; was built in 1856, and occupies the site of the former house. Elder Thomas P. Dudley was present at the constitution of the church, and from its organization has been its pastor for more than fifty years, having resigned some two years since, on account of his great age and infirmities. He was succeeded by Elder J. T. Moore, a citizen of Georgetown, who was born in Scott County, and educated in Georgetown.

The Christian Church.—In the past history of our native village, Georgetown, a more deeply interesting period will not be found than that embracing the residence as a citizen and the labors as a teacher of the learned and pious Barton W. Stone, who may be justly said to be one of the founders of this large and respectable body of Christians. Mr. Stone was born in Maryland, December 24, 1772. After acquiring in Virginia and North Carolina a good English and classical education, he removed to Kentucky in the winter of 1796–97. He was married to Miss Elizabeth Campbell, daughter of Col. William Campbell, of Millersburg, Ky. He came as a preacher to Georgetown in 1811. The distinctive plea of Mr. Stone and his associates, was for the union of all Christians, "upon the foundation of the prophets and apostles," the word of God the only rule, the name Christian the only patronymic. I went with my father to hear him preach in the old court house. His first wife died in 1809, leaving him four little daughters, and late in 1811 he married his second wife, Miss Celia W. Bowen, near Nashville, Tenn.

In 1816–17, he removed to Georgetown to take charge as Principal of Rittenhouse Academy. It was the good fortune of the writer to be placed in the school of Elder Stone, at Georgetown; under him much time was devoted to the study of the languages. He preserved remarkable order in his school by his kind and dignified demeanor. The school was governed by kindness and love. To the influence of this great and good man, I owe under God, much of the happiness I have realized in life. His residence was a short distance east of the town. Here he very soon organized a small church of six or seven members. Of these, Miss Polly Carey, Mrs. P. Story, wife of William Story, Mrs. M. Henderson, B. W. Stone and wife, and it may be Mrs. Applegate, H. Osborn and John Whitney were in the organization. This church, under his pastoral care and preaching, grew rapidly, and in a short period increased to near three hundred members. Mr. Stone endeared himself to the hearts of all who formed his acquaintance by the purity of his life, his uniform piety, and his great zeal in his Master's cause.

About the year 1818, the church erected a brick house of worship; at first it was located where the present house stands, on ground previously used as a burying-ground, on the south side of what is now College street, between Main Cross street and Hamilton.

In this house he preached for years as the faithful pastor, teaching school through the week. Under his most efficient and benevolent exertions, many well-prepared and useful preachers were given to the church and to the world, who but for him might never have arisen to such usefulness. I allude to such as Harrison Osborn, James Robertson, Marcus Wills, Perseus Harris, John Rogers, Harrison Gray, James Hicklin, Stephen G. Marshall, Leonard J. Fleming and many others.

Elder Stone ever filled with ability and with entire satisfaction his responsible positions as instructor of youth and as the beloved pastor of the church to which he ministered so long. Like his Master (when not engaged in the school room), he was actively engaged "going about doing good." I shall here insert, from Collin's History of Kentucky, page 120, the following: "A Methodist preacher in Jackson, La., once remarked to the writer of this article, in the presence of two Old School Presbyterian clergymen, 'I know Barton W. Stone well, having lived neighbor to him for a considerable time in Tennessee. A lovelier man or a better Christian in my judgment never lived, and he was no more a Unitarian than those brethren there are,' addressing himself at the same time to the two preachers." The person who from a regard to truth and justice bore this honorable testimony, was Mr. Finley, son of Dr. Finley, a former President of the University of Georgia.

During the many years he had the care and oversight of the church, he enjoyed often the co-operation and assistance of those excellent and distinguished ministers in the Christian Church, Francis R. Palmer, Thomas Smith and Thomas M. Allen. The two first often preached in Georgetown and its immediate vicinity with great effect.

In the year 1824, Elder Alexander Campbell, while on a visit to Kentucky, came to Georgetown. He and Elder Stone became acquainted; they soon discovered they were advocating the same great principle, and became convinced ultimately that they and all associated with either of them should be united in the work in which they were engaged. In 1826, Elder Stone commenced in Georgetown the publication of a monthly called the *Christian Messenger*. In 1827, I professed faith in Christ, was immersed and associated with the Christian Church. In 1831, a meeting was held in Georgetown to bring about a union in fact between those who held the views and were united with Mr. Stone, and those who agreed with Elder Campbell. This led the way to a larger assemblage for the same purpose in Lexington in 1832, and resulted in a general union throughout the country. Elder Stone continued the *Christian Messenger* as sole editor until 1832, when John T. Johnson, a citizen of Georgetown, and a prominent lawyer and ex-Congressman, having withdrawn from the *Baptist*, became a co-editor of the *Christian Messenger*, and so continued until Elder Stone removed to Illinois. Elder J. T. Johnson abandoned politics and the law, and gave himself wholly to preaching the word and writing for our periodicals. At the solicitation of the church, through Elder Johnson, I agreed to preach for them monthly, Elder Johnson having the care of the congregation. In 1836, Elder David G. Burnet removed to Georgetown to take the Presidency of Bacon College recently located there. He preached regularly for the church, and it was my pleasure often to co-operate with him.

At a later period, Dr. Absalom Adams located in Georgetown, became an elder in the church, and preached for them.

By the union, we had the co-operation and labors of such able men as Alex. Campbell, Philip S. Fall, John Smith, John T. Johnson, the Jacob Creths, Sr. and Jr., the Morlones—William and John—George W. Elley, Lewis and William Pinkerton, David G. Burns, Curtis J. Smith, Walter Scott and R. C. Rickets, all of whom preached at Georgetown at different times, besides many others, viz.: the Rogers, Irvine, Flemming, Rice, B. F. Hall and William Brown. The church in Georgetown in more recent years had the services of David Henderson, Lard, McGinn, Crutcher, Cave, Wiles, Hobson, J. A. Gano, Sr., R. M.

L. L. Herndon

Gano, Jones, and is at present under the care of Elder Howe. After a lapse of about sixty-five years from its constitution, this church is in a prosperous condition, with a good substantial spacious edifice, in which to worship God, while many who have labored for her welfare have gone to their rest.

The Presbyterian Church of Georgetown was organized June 16, 1828, by a commission of West Lexington Presbytery, the Rev. Eli Smith presiding. The Ruling Elder's name is lost, but these are the names of the ladies who went into the organization: Mrs. Eliza Finnell, Mrs. Sarah Lyle, Mrs. Hannah Henderson, Mrs. Jane Brown, Miss Martha Adams, Mrs. Nancy Eckels, Mrs. Isabella Dickey and Miss Sarah Ann Lyle.

In the spring of 1829, this little band of Christians, encouraged by the substantial assistance of William Brown and Barak Offutt, commenced the erection of a church building, which was not completed for several years, although religious services were held in it.

The congregation at the first were seated on rough boards, while the minister had a covered box for a pulpit. The first sermon in their building was preached by the Rev. Dr. Edgar, of Frankfort. The Rev. Nathan Hall, the Rev. John Blackburn, the Rev. Mr. Harrison and other ministers preached occasionally to this congregation, until 1831 the services of Rev. S. Salisbury were secured for one-half his time. In a sessional minute of March and August of 1831, it is stated that Joseph Phillips was ordained and installed a Ruling Elder, that seven persons were received into the church by profession, and eleven by certificate, of which number Mrs. Lavinia Kenney, Mr. Joseph B. Kenney and Mrs. Mary Buford Duke are still living as active and valuable participators in church work. During the ministry of the Rev. Mr. Salisbury and that of the Rev. William Scott, this covering about four years, this church grew in strength by the addition of other substantial people to its communion, developed in Christian liberality, and added to its efficiency by the election of John Bond, John Wilson, William Herriott and James Anderson as Ruling Elders, and Charles Eckels and Joseph B. Kenney as Deacons.

In 1838, Rev. James K. Burch began his work amongst this people as a stated supply. His Christian zeal and ability were conspicuously exhibited during the three years he labored here; sixteen persons were added to the church, and James H. Daviess and James C. Baker were installed Ruling Elders. September 12, 1841, the Rev. W. R. Preston, of South Carolina, commenced his labors here, dividing his time with the churches at Georgetown and Versailles. He was a successful laborer, adding unto the church twenty-six persons. His successor (the fourth stated supply) was the Rev. E. K. Lynn.

The sessional records give account of his ministerial industry, of the co-operation of the people, and of the accession of twenty-nine members to the fellowship of the church; besides they state that on the 17th day of April, 1846, Joseph B. Kenney, Charles Eckels, Charles Nichols and Thomas H. Lambe were ordained and installed Ruling Elders. In November, 1847, the Rev. Samuel J. Baird was called as pastor, at a salary of $600 per annum; on the 27th day of that month he was installed. The Rev. Stuart Robinson, the Rev. J. H. Brown, the Rev. F. G. Strahan conducting the services by order of the Presbytery.

Then followed another brief but pleasant and profitable pastorate, that of the Rev. H. V. D. Nevins, who, for about four years, beginning April 20, 1850, preached to this people. For the next three years there was stated preaching for only twelve months, and this brief time was divided by the labors of the Rev. W. G. Hand and H. E. Thomas. August 20, 1856, the Rev. Daniel P. Young, a licentiate of West Lexington Presbytery, began his work here. He was ordained and installed pastor, April 13, 1857. This was one of the most pleasant pastorates this church ever had, during which time (a little over eight years) eighty-one were added to the church.

November 1, 1857, Dr. William L. Sutton was ordained Ruling Elder, and September 19, 1863, James H. Kenney and Alfred D. Offutt were installed Deacons.

On the 26th day of September, 1865, the Rev. William R. Brown was installed pastor. He labored here about five years, receiving into the communion of the church thirty-four persons.

It was during this pastorate that the congregation commenced the erection of a new and handsome church building, which was formally dedicated to the worship of the Triune God on the 16th day of June, 1870, just forty-two years to the day, after this church organization was effected. November 19, 1865, Alexander Offutt and Henry Stevenson were installed Ruling Elders, and M. E. Nichols and Charles B. Lewis were set apart to the office of Deacon. William Brown resigned his pastorate February 15, 1870. The present pastor, the Rev. J. G. Hunter, then a licentiate of Ebenezer Presbytery, began his ministry here, October 9, 1870, and on September 14, 1871, he was ordained and installed pastor. October 26, 1873, Alfred D. Offutt, Dr. John A. Hamilton and M. E. Nichols were ordained and installed Ruling Elders, and James H. Moore, William N. Offutt and G. F. Clackner, Deacons. November 4, 1877, J. F. Musselman, E. N. Offutt, Jr., and Elley Blackburn were ordained and installed Deacons, and on the 25th of

November Joel C. Tarlton was set apart to the same office.

During this pastorate (now of a little more than eleven years' duration), there have been gathered into the communion of this church 150 persons, and there have been contributed by the church for its own support, and for general benevolence, through the General Assembly's Committees, nearly $30,000. The present membership is 170, and the contribution for the ecclesiastical year is $3,150.

The officers of the church at present are the Rev. J. G. Hunter, Pastor and Moderator, with Joseph B. Kenney, Alfred D. Offutt, Dr. John A. Hamilton and M. E. Nichols, Ruling Elders; and James H. Kenney, James H. Moore, W. N. Offutt, G. F. Clackner, Elley Blackburn, E. N. Offutt, Jr., J. F. Musselman and Joel C. Tarlton, Deacons.

The Church of the Holy Trinity (Protestant Episcopal), a stone structure in the Gothic style, will seat 350 persons. The building was commenced in September, 1866. The corner-stone was laid by Assistant Bishop (the Rev. George D. Cummins), in November, 1867, and consecrated by him in June, 1870.

The parish was formed, and the articles of association and also the petition for admission into the Diocese of Kentucky, was signed in March, 1864, by John Clark, G. Schultz, Henry Clark, R. A. White, Tyson Beall, William F. Pullen, Elie B. Swearinger, Jr., William H. Fitzgerald, Mrs. Beatrice Clark, Miss Agnes Clark, Mrs. Julia A. Clark, Miss Laura E. Clark, Miss Sarah Beall, Miss Eliza C. Beall, Mrs. Rebecca Beall, Mrs. Cornelia Barkley, Mrs. Maria A. White, Mrs. A. D. Webb, Miss Roberta Webb, Miss Annie E. Webb, Miss Lilly Kearney, Mrs. Mary H. Pullen, Mrs. A. Kearney, Miss Josie Cole, Mrs. Eliza W. Johnston, and admitted the same year. The first Vestry chosen after the Parish was recognized was Henry Clark, Senior Warden; G. Schultz, Junior Warden, and John Clark, Tyson Beall, Hon. A. Duvall, J. Stoddard Johnston, Dr. B. F. Elliott.

The Rev. John W. Venable having been the rector from its formation to the present.

The Catholic Church was established in 1869, by the purchase of the old Presbyterian Church, on the east side of Main Cross street, at a cost of $3,500. Father Bow was the first priest of this diocese. There are about fifty families worshiping with this church. Father Halley is the present officiating priest.

The First Colored Baptist Church was organized in 1869. It occupies a large brick building on the site of the old First Baptist Church, leased for ninety-nine years. They rebuilt the house at a cost of $8,250. They had the services for many years, as pastor, of Rev. Reuben Lee, a man of fair education, pious and discreet, and one who exerted a good influence among his people; during his ministry large numbers were added to the church.

Its present membership is 472. The present pastor is J. L. Dudley; salary, $550. The Deacons are Cliff Prewitt, John Smith, Perry Orr, William Brent, Newt Goodloe, Wash Bland and W. L. Barley. Good Sunday school; regular average attendance, 90; F. C. Nutter, Superintendent; J. M. Burley, Church Clerk; seating capacity of the house, about 500.

Wesley Chapel, the first colored Methodist Episcopal Church, was organized in 1866. It has a good brick house situated on the west side of Mulberry street, north of Main, at a cost of $5,000. The number of its membership is 236; a good Sunday school, average attendance, 69; present pastor, C. J. Nichols.

Georgetown College is situated on a beautiful elevation in the southeastern portion of the town. The buildings consist of: First, main edifice, one hundred feet long by sixty wide, two stories high, and a basement. It contains a handsome chapel, 60x40 feet, spacious halls for library, cabinets, museum, philosophical rooms, laboratory, etc. Second, Preparatory Department (formerly Rittenhouse Academy rebuilt), sixty feet square, two stories high; recitation rooms below, with two fine rooms in the upper story for society rooms, viz., Ciceronian and Tau Theta. Third, Pawling Hall, first named in honor of Issachar Pawling, a citizen of Mercer County, Ky., who left a bequest of some $20,000 for the education of poor young men preparing for the Baptist ministry, and upon which sum, though a small amount, this college had its beginning. This hall has recently been greatly enlarged and improved by the earnest and self-sacrificing labors of several ladies, at an expense of $6,000 or $7,000.

Georgetown College is indebted mainly to the zeal and energy of Mrs. Gov. James F. Robinson and Mrs. Prof. D. Thomas and Mrs. Dr. B. Manly, for this beautiful and commodious improvement. It is capable of furnishing rooms for more than fifty students, besides apartments for the Superintendent and family. Fourth, President's house, a plain and unpretending building situated near the college. The lawn embraces, with the ground attached to the President's house, some twenty acres. The college has a library of several thousand volumes, philosophical and chemical apparatus, cabinet of minerals, etc.

Georgetown College was chartered in 1829. The names of the original corporate members of the Board of Trustees from the charter, approved January 15, 1829, are: Rev. Alva Woods, President of Transylvania, Elder Thomas P. Dudley, Lexington, Ky., and these two are all that survive. Dr. Ryland T. Dillard, Dr. Silas M. Noel, Dr. William H.

Richardson, Jeremiah Vardeman, Rev. John Bryce, David Thurman, ex-Gov. Gabriel Slaughter, Joel Scott, Peter Mason, Peter C. Buck, Jephthah Dudley, Benjamin Taylor, George W. Nuckols, Benj. Davis, William Johnson, Samuel McCay, Thomas L. Smith, C. VanBuskirk, James Ford, Guerdon Gates and Cyrus Wingate.

These are the men in whose hands the small bequest of Pawling was placed to build up in Kentucky a Baptist College, the first west of the mountains. In 1829, the eloquent Dr. William Staughton, the first President elect, did not live to enter upon the duties of his office, but died in Washington City, December 12, 1829, on his way to Kentucky. The Rev. Joel S. Bacon was elected June 21, 1830. The following is a list of the faculty who were present at the opening of the session, April 18, 1831: Rev. J. Smith Bacon, A. M., President; Rev. N. M. Whiting, A. M., Professor of Languages; Th. F. Johnson, Esq., Professor of Mathematics, etc.; Samuel Hatch, M. D., Professor of Chemistry; William Craig, A. M., Tutor College proper; William F. Nelson, A. B., Principal of Preparatory Department; Dr. Bacon resigned in 1833. In 1836, Rev. B. F. Farnsworth occupied the Presidency for a few months, and made a sincere but ineffectual attempt to rescue the college from its embarrassments. In October 13, 1838, Rev. Rockwood Giddings, D. D., then pastor of a Baptist Church at Shelbyville, Ky., was elected President, and succeeded in harmonizing the conflicting elements in the Board of Trustees, that had been threatening the life of the college. Only one year of service was allotted to him, for he died October 29, 1839. During Dr. Giddings's year of labor in the field he secured a very considerable subscription, some $70,000, a large portion of which was paid, but the hope of completing the endowment was cut short by his death before he had finished his noble work.

Dr. Giddings never entered upon the duties of instruction. The college was managed by the rest of the faculty. Profs. J. E. Farnham, Garth and Hawkins, and one year later Prof. D. Thomas, was added to the faculty. A very large part of the subscription obtained by Dr. Giddings was lost by the great financial crash that followed.

The main college building was completed by the funds collected from the Giddings endowment. Previous to this time, there had been no building except the Rittenhouse Academy occupying the site of the present academy building.

In 1840, Dr. Howard Malcolm assumed the Presidency, and with the new buildings, the collections made from the endowment and the general interest on the subject of education, he was successful in bringing the college into a state of considerable efficiency. His personal energy and will were displayed in his whole management, and the institution will bear to its latest day many marks of his activity and energy.

After ten years' service in 1850, Dr. Malcolm retired, in consequence of his difference with the friends and patrons of the college, on the subject of the great compromise or gradual emancipation of slavery. The Rev. Dr. J. L. Reynolds, of South Carolina, was elected as his successor, and for two years conducted the institution.

Rev. Dr. Duncan R. Campbell was elected to succeed to the Presidency in 1853. He was a man of rare ability and efficiency, of strong will and great firmness of purpose, and no name is more worthy of being commemorated in connection with the college than Dr. Campbell's. At his entrance upon the presidency, there was a remnant of the Giddings endowment of about $10,000; the rest had been invested in the buildings and grounds, and much the larger part originally subscribed had never been collected, owing to the circumstances already referred to.

It was evident the college needed an endowment, and to this end Dr. Campbell directed his energies with such zeal and success, that in the course of two years he had obtained a subscription of more than $100,000. To his successful exertions, the larger part of all the funds the college owns is due to-day. In addition to the above, and during his administration, Dr. Campbell raised a sufficient subscription to purchase a large and valuable property for a President's house, at a cost of $6,000 or $7,000.

This property has since become a part of the Female Seminary, and is owned by Georgetown College. The college reached its highest efficiency and greatest prosperity, both in funds and students, under his administration just previous to the war. As the only Baptist College in the west where young men might receive theological as well as classical instruction, students were gathered from all the South and West. The subscriptions to the Campbell endowment were made payable in five years, bearing interest, and an understanding was had with many of the donors that if the interest was paid, the principal might remain in the hands of the donors indefinitely.

When the great calamity of the civil war came, many of these bonds remained unpaid, and it swept away the all of many of the givers. In that deluge, nearly every endowment of every Southern college went down. Of the Campbell endowment more than one-half was collected and safely and judiciously invested. By an act of the Kentucky Legislature in 1857, the Western Baptist Theological Institute at Covington, had its properties divided and one-half of the net proceeds that remained were transferred to Georgetown College, and constitute the fund (some $25,000) upon which the Theological Institute is maintained. The lamented death of Dr. Campbell in 1865, in the very flower and vigor of his age, left a vacancy which was filled by Dr. N. M. Crawford, of Georgia, who presided over the college until 1871, when he resigned in consequence of failing health and died a few months afterward. In 1871, Dr. Basil Manly, formerly Professor in the Southern Baptist Seminary, Greenville, S. C., entered upon the duties of the office as his successor. In his own graphic language, his work and that of Dr. Crawford have been, like Nehemiah and his helpers in repairing the walls of Jerusalem, to remove the rubbish and get down to a solid foundation, and prepare to rebuild and enlarge the work. Dr. Manly resigned in June, 1879, to accept a Professorship in the Southern Baptist Theological Seminary at Louisville, Ky. In 1879, Rev. Richard M. Dudley, pastor of First Baptist Church at Georgetown, and an alumnus of Georgetown College, was elected Chairman of the Faculty of the college, and, in 1880, succeeded to the Presidency. His energy, industry and capacity give assurance of success to the friends of the college.

In 1858, Mr. Alex Macklin, of Franklin County, made a bequest of some $8,000 to the college, for the purpose of aiding poor young men in obtaining an education; and, a few years later, Maj. F. C. McCalla, long a Trustee and Treasurer of the college, made a donation of some $15,000 to the college.

The funds of the college, available and safely invested, amount to about $90,000. The real estate, grounds and buildings, about $75,000. William B. Galloway, Secretary of the Board of Trustees; George V. Payne, Treasurer.

During the fifty years that Georgetown College has been in existence, it has sent forth many scholars in all the professions of life, and many of these are holding high and responsible positions. Its prospects for greater usefulness were never brighter than at present.

In 1836, Bacon College was established under the auspices of the "Christian Denomination." Rev. David Burritt was its President for a few years, with a full corps of teachers. After a brief struggle without any permanent endowment, it was merged in the Western Military Institute.

The Western Military Institute was incorporated by act of the Legislature in 1846 or 1847, and had a full corps of professors: T. F. Johnson, Superintendent; W. F. Hopkins, Professor of Natural Sciences; William S. Martin, Professor of Mathematics; J. J. Wyche, Professor of Languages; R. H. Forester, Professor of Law; James P. Mason and Thomas J. Smith, Preparatory Department. This institution did not long remain here, but was removed to Blue Lick Springs.

Ex-Senator Blaine, since so distinguished in the political history of the nation, was then a young man from Pennsylvania, and taught in this school.

Georgetown Female Seminary. In 1846, J. E. Farnham, Prof. of Natural Science in Georgetown College, organized a Female Seminary. It was first located in the corner building known as the Georgetown Hotel. He had able and accomplished assistants as teachers. In 1847, he erected a large and commodious building in the southeastern part of the town on Hamilton street, on the grounds now occupied by Col. Estill's residence. It was conveniently arranged, and contained from thirty-five to forty rooms, and was capable of accommodating one hundred pupils; it cost $25,000. It was conducted with great success for twenty years, drawing large numbers of pupils from the South and West, besides a very liberal patronage in the neighboring counties. No female school in the west enjoyed a higher reputation, or offered better facilities for acquiring an education of a high grade. It was burnt down in 1865, and Prof. Farnham disposed of the property.

Female Seminary.—After the destruction, by fire, of the seminary building in 1865, that had been successfully conducted by Prof. Farnham for twenty years, a temporary management was made for Prof. J. J. Rucker to take charge of a female school on his own property that soon passed into the hands of Prof. Tharp.

In 1869, a new seminary building was constructed on the grounds of the college, adjoining the President's house, and owned by the college. Prof. Rucker had charge of the same, and has continued to conduct it to the present very successfully and satisfactorily, with the assistance of his most estimable wife.

The Female Collegiate Institute, T. F. Johnson, Esq., Principal, was organized March, 1838. In 1847, the attendance was about one hundred. The assistants were experienced teachers from the best female schools in the United States, and resided at the institute. The collegiate year is divided into two sessions.

The advantages possessed by this school, together with the character of those connected with it, gave it a wide reputation, and made it a success for several years. It was discontinued about 1847–48.—*Gano.*

CHAPTER X.

WHITE SULPHUR PRECINCT—GENERAL DESCRIPTION AND TOGOGRAPHY—SETTLEMENT BY WHITE PEOPLE—THEIR HARDSHIPS IN THE WILDERNESS—PIONEER INDUSTRIES AND IMPROVEMENTS—VILLAGES, CHURCHES AND SCHOOLS—COL. JOHNSON'S INDIAN SCHOOL, ETC.

"I stand alone, like some dim shaft which throws
Its shadows on the desert waste, while they
Who placed it there are gone—or like the tree
Spared by the ax upon the mountain's cliff,
Whose sap is dull, while it still wears the hue
Of life upon its withered limbs."—*The Aged Pioneer.*

THE common experience of old age is a wish to live over again the life that is swiftly drawing to a close. How many mistakes have been made! how many hours have been unprofitably spent! how blind to good advice and influence! The stealthy and inevitable approach of death baffles the desire for a renewal of youth, and fills the heart with bitter remorse at thought of what might have been. Youth is always bright with hope and expectancy; but as the years glide by, the scales falls from the eyes, and the sorrowful experience of earth trace wrinkles of care upon the brow, and bend the once stalwart form toward the grave. No rocking vessel on life's great sea can escape the angry rain that dances upon it, or avoid the bitter winds that check its course. Let us learn then, from the wretched experience of others—learn from the lives that have gone down amid the gales of sorrow that encompass the earth, to shun the shoals and quicksands that beset our course, that the sunset of life may be gilded with the gold of eternal joy.

There is a strange attraction in reviewing the occurrences of past years, and in noting the wonderful improvements that have resulted from the expanding intelligence of man. Within the short space of the last half century, the United States has experienced almost unparalleled growth in all that makes a people great. Inventions in all departments of progress have succeeded one another with great rapidity, until the means of sustaining life are vastly numerous, and within the reach of all. No State in the Union has seen greater change than Kentucky during this period. The forests have disappeared; costly residences have gone up where once stood the log cabin; riding and gang plows have succeeded the old wooden mold-board; harvesters have succeeded the sickle; knowledge has driven ignorance from the land; railroads have usurped the duties of the old stage coach; telegraph lines have bound distant lands together, and telephones neighboring towns; and thousands of other changes have taken place.

In no section are these changes more palpable than in this small division of Scott County. White Sulphur Precinct has changed vastly in the last hundred years. Could some of the noble red men rise from their moldering dust, and come back to these hills and plains, where once they roamed in undisputed sway, they would be as much dazed as Rip Van Winkle when he awoke from his long nap in the Catskill Mountains. The precinct of White Sulphur, which is designated as Election Precinct No. 2, is situated in the southern part of Scott County, and is one of the wealthy precincts. It is of a gently rolling surface, or undulating, and drains well without artificial means. The principal water course is South Elkhorn Creek, which rises in Fayette County, and flows into the Kentucky River. It forms the boundary line between Georgetown and White Sulphur Precincts, and affords ample means of drainage. The original timber growth, but little of which is remaining in its primitive state, was burr-oak, hickory, sugar tree, black walnut, etc., etc. The Cincinnati Southern, and the Louisville, Cincinnati & Lexington Railroads pass near the precinct, affording good shipping facilities to the people.

White Sulphur Precinct was settled previous to the beginning of the present century, but who was the first white settler within its limits is not now known. James Leake settled where Virgil McManus lives, and is supposed to have been among the first in this immediate section. Patrick Vance bought the place in 1795, and it has been in the Vance and McManus families ever since. Mr. McManus and his wife have five grand and great-grandfathers and mothers buried in the St. Pius Cemetery. Patrick Vance was among the very early settlers of White Sulphur Precinct. Three men, named, respectively, Millan, Massee and Ford, were also early settlers. They were from Virginia, and came to Scott County about the year 1800, settling in what is now White Sulphur Precinct, on South Elkhorn Creek—a portion of the farm is now owned by Mr. John Y. Kinkead. They built a mill soon after their settlement. As Indian troubles grew less, and a degree of safety was felt, the precincts as well as other portions of the county, rapidly settled, and the sound of the woodman's ax was heard, where lately the yell of the savage and the crack of his rifle alone broke the stillness.

In the early history of this country, everything among the pioneers was plain, simple, and in conformity with the strictest economy. This was not only true of their dwelling, furniture and provisions, but also of their clothing. For several years, the men wore, almost exclusively, pants and hunting-shirts of buckskin, and caps of coon or fox skin, while both sexes clothed their feet in moccasins. Cotton goods were extremely hard to get in that early day, because they were manufactured mostly in England, and expensive in this country. As a consequence, the pioneers of the West found this one of the hardest demands to meet. Many were the expedients devised by them, especially by the frugal and economical dames; for, ever since that wonderful experiment, devised by mother Eve, of preparing an entire wardrobe from fig-leaves, woman has been greatly gifted in laying plans and adopting expedients in the matter of clothing. But clothing was one of the smallest considerations at that day, beyond a sufficiency to keep one warm, and the supplying of bread and meat were of far more importance, and often puzzled the pioneers to obtain it for their families. This, together with the dangers from Indians, rendered their lots very unenviable.

Among the first industries of the pioneers of White Sulphur were mills, tanneries, etc., and were established at an early day. The first mill in the precinct, perhaps, was that built by Millan, Massee and Ford, on the South Elkhorn. It was built soon after they settled in the country. A large portion of the original mill is still standing, and is at present owned by Patrick Dunn, who is now using it. A gristmill was built on South Elkhorn, near the old village of Sodom, in 1825, by George Ware. It is now owned by a Mr. Fisher. Other mills were built in the early times, but of them we have but little information. David Thompson built a paper-mill very early, and had a flouring-mill attached to it. Mr. Thompson owned the farm now owned by D. B. Galloway, and which was once owned by Col. "Dick" Johnson. A tannery and a cotton and hemp factory were early institutions of the village of "Sodom."

The first road laid out through the precinct was that known as the "Iron Works" road—it runs between Payne's Depot on the Louisville, Cincinnati & Lexington Railroad, and the Georgetown & Frankfort Turnpike. The first road macadamized was the Georgetown & Frankfort pike, and was built about the year 1850. That with the Midway & Georgetown pike, are the only pikes touching the precinct. The first bridge was built on South Elkhorn, where the Midway pike crosses it. It is a wooden, covered bridge and belongs jointly to Scott and Woodford Counties, being on the line between the two. All the bridges of the precinct are covered, and are built of wood. The Justices of the Peace of White Sulphur Precinct are J. C. Glass and J. B. Galloway.

A village, known as Sodom, once existed in this precinct, but has passed away, and is doubtless forgotten by many of the people. In the language of Goldsmith

> "Sweet smiling village, loveliest of the lawn,
> Thy sports all fled, and all thy charms withdrawn."

It was located in the central part of the precinct, and was laid out by James and George Ware, who settled the surrounding land. The village was founded in 1825, and at one time contained 150 inhabitants. The Wares built a cotton and hemp factory on South Elkhorn at that time, which led to the laying-out of a village. A tannery was established by Henry Hardy. There was also a shoe-shop, and a carding machine. A storehouse was built and a store opened by Mr. Alexander Bell, and the place was quite flourishing. But railroads drew the bulk of trade to other localities, and Sodom disappeared as effectually as if it had shared the fate of its namesake of Biblical notoriety. The ruins of Baalbec are in many respects a mystery; Palmyra, at least in vastness, surpasses even Baalbec; Athens, Rome, Jerusalem and other scenes of decay, appeal to our pity, but "it shall be more tolerable for Sodom, etc." It has disappeared from the face of the earth, and many of the citizens of White Sulphur have forgotten its existence; even those who remember it can only, like the Jewish captives of old, "hang their harps upon the willows," and weep at its untimely fate. Not a trace of it is to be seen, except the old mill race.

The village of White Sulphur is situated on the Georgetown & Frankfort pike, about eight miles from Georgetown. The first house in the place, was built in 1831, and was used as a blacksmith's shop, and the first resident, James Hendrickson, a blacksmith. A hotel was built here in 1835 by Col. Dick Johnson, who made the spring a place of fashionable resort. The old foundations are still to be seen. The place now has seven dwelling houses, two storehouses, only one of which is now selling goods two blacksmith shops, only one in operation, and a district schoolhouse. The latter is a large brick of sufficient capacity to hold one hundred and fifty persons, and is used jointly for school and church purposes. The village takes its name from the famous White Sulphur Spring, once the seat of Col. Johnson's Indian School, noticed in another chapter. It contains between fifty and one hundred inhabitants at present. A post office was established at White Sulphur Spring, which is known by the name of White Sulphur, about 1850, and Mark Dehoney was the first Postmaster—the present Postmaster is J. E. Butler, who also keeps the store, and has been in business here since 1875.

The Precinct of White Sulphur has always paid considerable attention to schools. The Greenwood Schoolhouse was the first schoolhouse built in the precinct. It was originated by J. G. Brooks, Asa Branham, James Lair and John H. Thompson; the first teacher was Anthony Martin, who began with twenty-eight pupils. The present teacher is Miss Swihawk, of Lexington. Education in the precinct is in a flourishing state.

As we have said, Col. R. M. Johnson's Indian School, was located in this precinct at one time, which contained some two hundred Indian boys. The principal teachers were McCready and Henderson. But as this school is written up in another chapter, we will not repeat its history here. While the school was in progress, the Spring was a great place of resort, and the Indian students used to give some interesting exhibitions. The spring is on the farm of Mr. A. Thomas, one mile from the Georgetown & Frankfort pike. The water is so strongly impregnated, that stock does not need much salt.

St. Pius Catholic Church, near White Sulphur, was built about 1820. Combs, Tarleton, Goff, Twyman, Greenwell, Harding and Frazier were prominent in building this church. There is a farm in connection with it, for its benefit, and that of the pastor. When the church was built, it had a large membership of some two or three hundred families, but at present there are but twenty or thirty families belonging to it. Death and removals have depleted its numbers. It contains but six members now, that worshiped in it fifty years ago. The first church was a frame; the present one is an imposing brick structure.

Visitation Monastery was opened in 1875, with but six scholars, but now has about fifty. It was built originally for a seminary, but changed hands in 1875, and became the Visitation Monastery, as above noted. It is under the supervision of St. Pius Church, and affords ample means for an education to Catholic girls.

On the farm of John Y. Kinkead were once training-stables and a race-track. Here the noted horses, Gray Eagle and Wagoner, were trained for the turf. The stables are gone—not a trace of them is left to show where they once stood.—*Perrin.*

CHAPTER XI.

STAMPING GROUND PRECINCT—LOCATION AND BOUNDARY—EARLY SETTLEMENT—ORIGIN OF NAMES—EARLY CHURCHES AND VILLAGES—ROADS AND STREAMS—POST OFFICES, SCHOOLS, MILLS, ETC.

"All those things which are now held to be of the greatest antiquity were at one time new, and what we to-day hold up by example will hereafter rank as precedent."—*Tacitus.*

PERHAPS no other division of this county is more replete with historic matter than the one described in this chapter. Stamping Ground, or in common parlance, "The Stamp," is No. 3 of the election precincts, and is bounded on the north by Owen County and No. 4, or Lytle's Fork Precinct, on the east by No. 4, south by No. 1, or Georgetown precinct, and on the west by Franklin County.

The land, except a small portion in the northeast, has a general western slope, and possesses an admirable system of natural drainage in the numerous streams and branches which wind through it in different directions. The principal one of these is North Elkhorn, which passes through the southwest corner, receiving as tributaries McConnell's and Lecompte's Runs, with their numerous branches. These two streams were named respectively for William McConnell and Charles Lecompte, who as early as April, 1875, left the Monongahela country and came down the Ohio River to the mouth of the Kentucky, and up that stream to the Elkhorn region. They explored the country around the neighborhood of the "Big Spring," but made no permanent settlement. The surface of this precinct is hilly and broken in the northern part, and undulating in the southern. The soil partakes of the character of the rest of the county, though varying in fertility in different localities. The usual farm products and stock are raised and exported, and of late considerable attention has been paid to the culture of tobacco, which bids fair to soon become the staple crop.

The timber consists mainly of oak, ash, poplar, walnut, maple and elm.

The first road through this precinct was the Georgetown & Cincinnati road, which was cut out about 1790. At present many of the roads are macadamized, the principal through pike being the one from Georgetown through Stamping Ground, to the Owen County line. There are several cross pikes which serve as good outlets to this main thoroughfare. The streams are bridged at the deepest fords by substantial wooden bridges.

It is not known exactly when the first settlement was made within the limit included in this chapter. Anthony Lindsay, whose family is still represented in the precinct by William O. Calvert, John Lindsay and Mrs. Robert Sprake, all of whom are his grandchildren, built a fort or station near Stamping Ground, about 1790. Mr. W. O. Calvert states that he remembers seeing a few posts of the old fort which were left standing by his mother, who was a daughter of Anthony Lindsay. This fort, being near the great thoroughfare from Georgetown to the Ohio River, was a regular stopping-place for all travelers.

Thomas Herndon and Cornelius Duvall settled on McConnell's Run about the same time (1790). In this immediate neighborhood there sprung up a school quite early, and in 1795 a church was organized near Stamping Ground, by the Baptist denomination. This church, first called McConnell's Church, was organized by Rev. Ambrose Dudley and William Cave. It was rebuilt in 1819, and again in 1858. It is now one of the best country churches in the county. The congregation has lately purchased a parsonage at a cost of $1,500. The church roll now numbers 275 members, with a flourishing Sunday school of 100 pupils. The following are the names of the thirty-five original members: Elijah Craig, Rhodes Smith, John Hawkins, John Payne, Jacob Martin, Thomas Herndon, John Scott, James Key, Richard Seebree, Joseph Wiley, Daniel Baldwin, Benjamin Branham, John Cook, John Brock, Jesse Hambrick, Hannah Scott, Mary Herndon, Vinson Smith, Nelly Branham, Ann Baldwin, Deborah Stewart, Sarah Martin, Susan O'Banner, Lydia Hambrick, Mary Ficklin, Elizabeth Key, Elizabeth Craig, Jane Cook, Ann Threlkeld, Nathaniel Mothershead, Toliver Craig, Thomas Ficklin, E. Seebree, Ruth Mothershead and Sarah Hawkins.

Among the noted preachers who have ministered to the congregation since its organization may be mentioned Elijah Craig, Lewis Craig, William Hickman, Jacob Creath, James Suggetts, Samuel Trott, Theodrick Bolivar, Silas Noel, J. D. Black, George Hunt, John S. Waller, E. D. Isbell, A. C. Graves, R. M. Dudley, T. J. Stevenson and J. A. Booth, the present pastor.

The Christian Church at Stamping Ground was organized by Elder John T. Johnson. They worship in a substantial frame house, and have a large and increasing congregation.

The village of Stamping Ground takes its name from the fact that in the first settlement of the country, the Buffalo used to congregate at the salt springs at this place, and "stamp" the ground as they stood under the shade of the trees. The village being the largest in the precinct, naturally enough gave the name to the precinct itself. It now contains three hundred inhabitants, supports four stores, two blacksmith shops, one school, under the management of W. H. Cooper, and containing some forty-five pupils. One distillery, one hotel, one undertaker, one photographer, four physicians, two churches and one colored church and school, one Masonic Lodge, No. 203, and one woolen factory. The first post office in Stamping Ground was established in 1814, with Alex. Bradford, as Postmaster, an office now filled by J. H. Gatewood.

The distillery, now owned and run by Crigler & Crigler, was first erected for a woolen mill in 1864, by McMillan & Wright. It was turned into a distillery in 1868, by Robert Samuels & Co.

The woolen mill, now owned and run by Wright & Brother, was first erected in 1844, by A. G. Goodman, and used as a college till about 1854, when it was turned into a woolen mill by E. R. Wright, the father of the present owners. Skinnersburg, on the eastern border and Minorsville in the north, are villages of less importance.

There is a flouring mill on the waters of North Elkhorn, owned by I. T. Reynolds & Co. It was built in 1845, by a man named Threlkeld.—*E. T. Brown.*

CHAPTER XII.

LYTLE'S FORK PRECINCT — GENERAL OUTLINE AND TOPOGRAPHY — EARLY SETTLEMENT — PIONEER INDUSTRIES AND IMPROVEMENTS—CHURCHES AND SCHOOLS, SCHOOLHOUSES, ETC.—ROADS, BRIDGES, ETC.

"What's past, and what's to come, is strewed with husks,
The formless ruin of oblivion." —*Shakspeare.*

THE unheeded lapse of time is the greatest enemy of the historian. The events of one moment are so closely crowded by those of the next, and so much occupied are we in performing the duties of the present that, almost unawares, we literally fulfill the Scriptural injunction, "Take no thought for the morrow." History is commonly defined to be a record of past events, but shall we wait till the events must be recalled by defective human memories before we record them ? Then we get no perfect history for no memory is perfect; often he who is most sure is least to be relied upon.

The record of events, however, is simply chronology ; the field of history is wider and more varied, comprehending the effect of daily transactions upon the progress and civilization of the human family.

That division of Scott County known as Precinct No. 4, or Lytle's Fork, as it is most generally called, adjoins the Owen County line on the northwest. The Stamping Ground Precinct touches its southwestern border; Georgetown Precinct on the south, and Turkey Foot on the east, complete the boundary.

Lytle's Fork of Eagle Creek, with its tributaries, Indian Creek, Lake's and Hess' Branch, takes a tortuous northerly course through the center of the precinct. The general slope of the great majority of the land is with the course of this creek, the water-shed between it and the waters of Elkhorn being near the southern border of the precinct.

The surface in the northern part is considerably broken and hilly. In the south the land is still uneven and rolling, but the breadth of the ridges afford arable fields of larger size. The soil, though subject to the usual washing away of a hilly country, is yet fertile in character, being a part the Silurian formation, and is admirably adapted to the culture of tobacco, wheat, corn and other staple products.

The timber growth consists of pine, chestnut, the usual varieties of oak, linn, sycamore, white and black hickory, beech, sugar-tree and persimmon, the last, as its name (Diospyros—fruit of the gods) implies, being much valued for its fruit.

Little is known of the settlement of this precinct prior to the year 1790. Near that time a settlement was made on Little Eagle Creek, by Col. John Stone, on land now owned by William Wigginton. One of Col. Stone's grandchildren, Mr. B. Hall, is still a resident of the county. About the same year (1790), Daniel Gano, settled on the farm now owned by Dr. Emison. On a branch of Little Eagle, and near Salem Meeting-House, may still be seen the remains of his old house. He was the youngest Captain of the Revolutionary war, having command of a company of artillery. He lined many of the guns used in the siege of Quebec. When they were making their assault, he remarked that there was one cannon left loaded. An old drunken Irish soldier, hearing him, said, "Give her one more kick." By its discharge, Gen Richard Montgomery was killed, and so great was the dismay caused in the American ranks by this fatal disaster that the success of the assault was frustrated. Among the early settlers may also be mentioned John Harwood, William Boyce (from Delaware), and Obadiah Ellis (from Baltimore), Paris and William Griffith (from Delaware); all of the above came out and settled here not far from the year 1790.

Perhaps the oldest church in this precinct is Salem. It is the property of the Methodist Society of Christians, and was first organized about 1823. Among those who were present and identified with its organization were William Banks and wife, William Boyce, Obadiah Ellis, Squire John Rollins. Among the pastors who have administered to the congregation from time to time, we give the names of Dr. Rhoton, Josiah Whittaker, S. S. Deering, H. H. Kavanaugh, W. W. Chamberlain, W. W. Spates, W. C. Atmore and others. The building was originally a log structure, 25x30 feet, but to subserve the wants of an increasing membership, this old building was replaced by a frame of nearly double the capacity, and far more pretentious in appearance. There is a good Sunday school in connection with the church, having an average membership of about fifty pupils, under the superintendency of Mr. James Warren. The church roll now contains about ninety names.

Corinth Christian Church, situated near the head-waters

of Lytle's Fork, was organized about 1836 by Robert Whitton. Among the early preachers were Joshua Willhoit, Pleasant Whitton, Hiram Ford, Henry Edmonson and others, whose names we are unable to determine. In 1838, the house was remodeled and enlarged to meet the demands of an increasing congregation. The first schoolhouse was built on Col. Stone's land, of logs, in 1825. Martin Brent was first teacher. There are at present ten well-regulated schools in this precinct, called, respectively, Skinnersburg, Long Lick, Bradley, Harvey Risk, Warnock, Gorham, Griffith, Warren, Robinson and Whitton.

There is one distillery located in this precinct, which was built in 1874 by R. H. Risk. It has a capacity of sixteen bushels of grain per day, and the brand manufactured is noted for its superior qualities.

There is a saw and grist-mill located on Lytle's Fork, known as Beatty's Mill. It was built by George Beatty in 1812, and is now owned by William Rice.

The first road in the precinct was called the Mountain Island road, and runs from the Georgetown & Dry Ridge pike to Mountain Island in Owen County. The first bridge over Lytle's Fork was on the Long Lick road.

The County Poor House, located in this precinct, is mentioned under the general county history.—*Brown.*

CHAPTER XIII.

BIG EAGLE PRECINCT — ITS DESCRIPTION AND TOPOGRAPHY — COMING OF THE WHITE MAN—EARLY DIFFICULTIES — PIONEER IMPROVEMENTS AND INDUSTRIES—RELIGIOUS—THE PARTICULAR BAPTISTS— OTHER DENOMINATIONS—SCHOOLS, VILLAGES, ETC.

THE Election Precinct No. 5, known and designated as Big Eagle Precinct, is bounded on the north by Owen and Grant Counties, on the east by Big Eagle and Licking and the Cincinnati Southern Railroad, on the south by Little Eagle and on the west by Little Eagle and the Owen County line. It is well watered and drained by Big and Little Eagle and their tributaries. Big Eagle has its source near Leesburg, and empties into the Kentucky River at Monterey. Little Eagle rises some seven miles north of Georgetown, and unites with Big Eagle at Wall's Mill, on the Cincinnati pike. A branch of Ray's Fork rises near Hinton's Station and empties into Big Eagle in the vicinity of Mallory's Mill. Another branch of the same stream rises near Corinth and forms the main channel, on the lands of Joseph Burgess. The original timber consisted of black locust, walnut, poplar, blue and black ash, sugar maple, oak, etc. The land is considerably rolling, and in places along the streams quite broken and hilly, but rich and productive. The Cincinnati Southern Railroad is in convenient reach and affords excellent shipping facilities.

Settlements were made by white people in what is now Big Eagle Precinct in an early day, but the precise date is not known. Among the pioneers were Boswell Herrington, Capt. Fontleroy, Peter Jones, Stafford Jones, Reuben Lancaster, Beverly Nelson, Samuel Marshall, Milton Threlkeld, Garnet Wall, John Peck and John Mulberry. Many descendants of the early settlers of this section are still living, and some of them still possess the lands of their ancestry. The story of the early settling of this precinct is that of all Kentucky—one of hardship, danger and privation. The emigrant who goes to the Far West at the present day has the railroad to convey him and his goods to his contemplated settlement, and when he arrives at his new home he settles down without fear of savage beasts or savage men. But it was far different here seventy-five or a hundred years ago. There were no railroads then to bring the emigrants hither, but there were innumerable dangers to be met with upon their arrival, dangers that only strong arms and brave hearts could overcome.

The numerous streams in this precinct furnish excellent water-power for machinery of a light character. This was early utilized by mills, and a number of these useful "institutions" were built by the first settlers: Emison's, Wall's, Merriman's and Jones' were among the first built in this region. They were all "water-mills," and took their names from the parties who built them. Emison's (now owned by Mallory) and Jones' are still in operation. The distillery of T. J. Marshall was built subsequent to the war was run by steam and was quite an extensive establishment, but for several years it has been standing idle.

The State roads between Cincinnati and Lexington, now called the Cincinnati pike, was the first road through the precinct. Toll was then collected upon it from pedestrians, as well as from horsemen, vehicles, etc. The road, known as the "Mulberry road," and which forms the dividing line between the counties of Harrison and Scott, was the next road laid out. The community is now well supplied with these useful thoroughfares. The first pike was that known as the "State pike," and was built in 1843 and 1844. The second was the Green Mill pike, built in 1876; also, the Cynthiana & Big Eagle pike. The first bridge in the precinct was that built at Jones' old mill; one was built soon after, over Big Eagle, at Mallory's Mill. These were both wooden structures. A bridge was also built across Big Eagle, where the State road crosses it, and another where the Cynthiana pike crosses it, near Sadieville.

The church history of the precinct dates back almost to the period of settlement by white people. The first church was known as "Elk Lick Church" and the denomination the "Particular Baptists." It was organized in 1799, and among the early pastors were Elders John Connor, and Ambrose and Thomas P. Dudley. Ray's Fork and Hartwood Churches were organized soon after. The two latter were also Baptist, but of that denomination that were not so "Particular." These two latter churches have been remodeled somewhat, and are all wooden buildings.

Hebron Church was quite an old one, but is long since abandoned, and the new one erected upon its site, is of the Christian denomination, and is called Mount Olivet. At present the membership is large and flourishing, and a very interesting Sunday school, the only one in the precinct, is maintained at this church. It is conducted on the union principle, and attended by all denominations.

It is not known who taught the first school in the neighborhood, nor when nor where it was held. It is not improbable, however, that a school was taught early, as this section was settled very early. We have an account of a church organized in 1799, and schools usually followed close after churches. There are now five schoolhouses in the precinct, in which schools are taught each year for the usual period, only, however, in the primary branches.

Big Eagle Precinct boasts of several villages, under somewhat high-sounding and historical names, but all of them put together would not make much of a town. They are Sadieville, Stonewall and Corinth. The first named (Sadieville) is a station on the Cincinnati Southern Railroad, and dates its birth at the time of building the railroad through the county, about 1876, and was incorporated in 1881. The first Postmaster was James Jones, and the present one ——— Fears. One of the district schools of the precinct is located here, and is, at present, (1882) taught by a Mr. Rollins. The business of the place consists of that usually done at a small railway station. Its population is about seventy-five.

Stonewall is a small village some sixteen miles from Georgetown, on the State road. The first tavern in the precinct was kept by John Hennessy, for the purpose of boarding hands while engaged constructing the State road into a pike. He afterward sold it to T. K. Hollins, who kept it as a public house. Corinth is a small unimportant place, consisting of but a few houses, shops, etc. This comprises a brief sketch of the precinct from its settlement down to the present time.—*Perrin.*

CHAPTER XIV.

TURKEY FOOT PRECINCT—INTRODUCTORY AND DESCRIPTIVE—TOPOGRAPHY, TIMBER, ETC.—SETTLEMENT OF THE PIONEERS—THE NAME OF TURKEY FOOT—EARLY INDUSTRIES AND IMPROVEMENTS—VILLAGE AND POST OFFICE—CHURCHES, SCHOOLS, ETC., ETC.

STANDING as we do down the stream of time, far removed from its source, we must retrace its meanderings with scarce anything to guide save the few moldering relics of the past which lie along the shore, and even these grow fainter and still more faint, and uncertain as we near its fountain, if, indeed, they are not wholly concealed in the debris of years. Written records grow less and less explicit, and finally fail altogether the nearer we approach the beginning of the community, whose life it is our purpose to rescue from the gloom of a fast-receding past. The old pioneers have sunk to rest, after the toils and privations of the border, whither they had come, buoyed up with hope and renewed with vigor, to build, for themselves and loved ones, homes, amid the beautiful scenery, while yet the whoop of the Indian and the howl of the wolf resounded on every side. Here and there a white-haired veteran, bowed with the weight of years and toil, who was born and has been reared upon the soil, remains to tell us of those days "lang syne," and from their lips principally we have received the data from which to weave the fabric of this history.

That portion of Scott County, now known as Turkey Foot or Election Precinct No. 6, lies in the north central part of the county, with Big Eagle Precinct on the north, Harrison County on the east, Oxford Precinct on the south, and Lytle's Fork and Georgetown Precincts on the west. The land is rough and broken, but is quite productive, and well adapted to tobacco raising. The timber was, originally beech, hickory, ash, mulberry, black-walnut, etc., etc. The principal streams are the East and West Forks of Big Eagle, which rise in Oxford Precinct, and flowing northward unite in Turkey Foot Precinct, thus forming Big Eagle Creek. From this circumstance the precinct received its name—the fancied resemblance of the junction of these streams to a turkey's foot.

The settlement of Turkey Foot Precinct dates back to a period more than ninety years gone by. Of the early settlers of the country now embraced in this precinct, we may mention William Vance, Asher Hinton, Benjamin Carr, —— Reed, William Price, Abraham Fields, Benjamin Peck, Edward Burgess, Peter Antle, John Gibson, Patrick Watson, John and P. Hyles, Cornelius Butler, James Sutton, Joshua Murphy, Joseph Leach and others. Mr. Vance settled near Turkey Foot Post Office in 1790, on the farm now owned by his son, Capt. Joe Vance; Mr. Hinton and Mr. Carr also settled about 1790, on farms now owned respectively by their sons. Reed settled near Turkey Foot Post Office about the same time. He has a son, Eben Reed, still living in the precinct; William Price also settled about the same time, on the place now owned by Thomas Hyles. Jacob Price, his son, lives in the precinct. These early settlers, with the others mentioned above, are all dead, but many of them have descendants in the neighborhood, who occupy the lands of their ancestors.

Nothing is more common than to hear the aged, pioneer, when in a loquacious mood, relate the difficulties, hardships and discomforts of his early trials, without it is to hear him tell how free, how cheerful, and how glorious were the days of his early pioneer life, when free, and "wild, as the wild bird, and untaught, with spur and bridle undefiled," they lived, untrammeled by the conventionalities of fashionable life. Both of his pictures are true. What was pleasant and beautiful, was so in excess; and what of life there was that was fraught with danger and deprivations, and obstacles to be surmounted, was bitter indeed. Though there are none of the original settlers now living, there are those who, born here in the pioneer days, remember some of the early scenes, and have so often heard the story from their ancestors as to be as familiar with the hardships of frontier life as though they had personally experienced them. In a country like this, even its wildest state, there was not so much of uncompensated hardship for the hunter and trapper, considered by himself, provided he had good health. But to men with families, weakly women and helpless children, there were seasons when, in behalf of his family, great suspense and anxiety fell to his lot. He could move from danger; he could seek supplies and shelter, but his family could not. It is unnecessary to go very minutely into the details of pioneer family history; it is "an old, old story." The pioneer's battle with danger, privation and poverty; his daily struggle for the necessaries of life, is an oft-repeated tale, and needs no repetition here.

The early industries of Turkey Foot Precinct were comprised in mills, tanneries, distilleries, etc. Among the pioneer mills were those of Holden & Hyles, Steele's, Hinton's and perhaps one or two other small affairs. Holden & Hyles' was situated on a fork of Big Eagle Creek; Steele's also was on the same stream. Hinton's was a horse-power mill, and was in the southern part of the precinct. A tannery was started by William Jackson in 1805; and some years later, one was opened by a man named Brissy. Both have long since ceased operation, and no trace of them now exist. Pemberton's distillery, on a fork of Big Eagle Creek, was the first whisky factory in the precinct. Another distillery was built in 1826, by John Price, in the eastern part of the precinct. There is no trace left of either of these early institutions. A distillery was built by Samuel Greene about 1860, but it is not now in operation.

The first road through Turkey Foot was known as the "Turkey Foot road," and ran from Harrison County through the little hamlet of Turkey Foot to Georgetown, and was laid out about the year 1795. The only pike is the Lexington & Covington pike, formerly known as the Dry Run pike. It is the dividing line between Turkey Foot and Lytle's Fork Precincts.

The village of Turkey Foot is a small collection of houses, and contains a store, a blacksmith shop, church, Masonic lodge, post office, etc. The place was settled about the year 1790, by William Vance, as already noted. The Postmaster of Turkey Foot is Mandeville Hinton.

The Christian Church at Turkey Foot was organized in 1854, and a frame church building put up. Among the ministers that have officiated to its congregations are, Elders Brown, Rogers, Williams, John A. Gano, Sr., and perhaps others. The church has now about one hundred members. Elder Gunn is the present pastor.

A schoolhouse was built on the farm of George Maddox about 1850, and Samuel Greene was the first teacher in it. There is no school there now; house long since torn down. The precinct is somewhat deficient in educational facilities. The only school now in the precinct is taught in the church at Turkey Foot, by Frank Sutton, who has some thirty pupils. Like most of Scott County, the people depend chiefly on private schools and academies for the educating of their children.—*Perrin.*

CHAPTER XV.

OXFORD PRECINCT—TOPOGRAPHICAL AND DESCRIPTIVE FEATURES—TIMBER, ETC.—SETTLEMENT OF THE PIONEERS—THEIR EARLY TRIALS AND TROUBLES—ROADS, MILLS, SCHOOLS—OXFORD VILLAGE—CHURCHES AND SUNDAY SCHOOLS.

OXFORD PRECINCT, known as Election Precinct No. 7 of Scott County, is bounded on the north by Muddy Ford & Dry Run road, on the east by Bourbon & Harrison Counties, on the south by the Cynthiana & Georgetown road and on the west by the Georgetown & Turkey Foot road. Miller's Run is the principal stream, and has its fountain-head within a mile of the village of Oxford; running thence in a southwest direction, it empties into the Elkhorn. There are a few other small streams and brooks in the precinct, thus affording an excellent system of natural drainage. The original timber growth was sugar maple, walnut, blue ash, burr-oak, "shellbark" hickory, etc. The people are engaged chiefly in agriculture and stock-raising, and are intelligent and industrious as a class. The village of Oxford is the only approach to a town in the precinct, and is a place of considerable business.

Oxford Precinct was settled in an early day, but of its pioneers little is now known, beyond the fact that they came here when most of the country around and about them was an unbroken wilderness, swarming with wild beasts and savages. Amid such scenes, they made their homes, lived out their time and died. Among the few names gathered, as ranking among the pioneers of Oxford, was Jesse Browning, who settled one mile northeast of the village; on land now owned by Willis Gunnell. Charles Hamilton was one of the earliest settlers, and located about a quarter of a mile north of the present village of Oxford. He had a family of six children. John Ritchie and James Risk were also early settlers in the same neighborhood. A number of other families, perhaps, are entitled to mention as early settlers, but the long period that has elapsed since they came to the country has veiled their settlement in obscurity and buried their names in oblivion. Such are the ways of human nature.

> "If you or I to-day should die,
> The birds would sing as sweet to-morrow;
> The vernal spring its flowers would bring,
> And few would think of us with sorrow."

The early years of the pioneers were years of privation, toil and danger; privation in building up a home for their families, toil to provide them with the necessaries of life and danger from the Indians and wild beasts that, in early years, infested the country. We, who are enjoying the fruits of their labor, know very little of what they had to encounter in those pioneer days. Born in the midst of abundance and "lapped in luxury," we would shrink and flee from the dangers to which they were daily exposed.

The first roads through the precinct were made upon the early Indian trails through the forest. These were, at first, sufficient for the pioneer's train of pack-horses, but when wagons were introduced these trails were cut out to admit their passage, and thus were made the first roads, which, from time to time, have been improved, until they have reached their present perfected system. The road from Cynthiana to Georgetown bears the name of being the oldest road in or passing through the precinct. The next road was the Oxford and Newtown. The first pike was the Oxford & Georgetown pike, and was commenced in June, 1868. It was completed the next spring, and continued to Leesburg in 1870, except about a mile and a half in Oxford, which gap was finished in 1880, and the road is now known as the Georgetown, Oxford & Leesburg Pike. At the present writing (1882) there is a pike in course of of construction from Kinkead Station, on the Cincinnati Southern Railroad, to Oxford Village. The first bridge built in the precinct was a wooden bridge, built over Miller's Run, on the Oxford and Leesburg road. Taken altogther, Oxford Precinct is well supplied with roads and highways.

The early settlers were forced to get their milling done in other and distant neighborhoods, as we have no account of any mill in what now forms Oxford Precinct, until within a very recent period. The first and the only mill said to have been built in the precinct is owned by D. P. Moore, and has been in operation but a short time. It is a steam grist-mill, and is located on the Muddy Ford & Dry Run road. It does a large business and is of considerable benefit to the community.

Who taught the first school in what is now Oxford Precinct is not known at the present day. Like every portion of Kentucky, there is not sufficient attention paid to the common schools. Too many people depend wholly upon educating their children in the academies, seminaries and colleges located in town, and seem to think it low and disreputable to patronize the common schools. This is a sadly mistaken idea, and until we take more interest in them and spend more money upon their support, we must expect the education of our children to fall far short of what it should be. The very best that can be said of the schools of Oxford Precinct is that they are lamentably deficient.

The village of Oxford, five miles from Georgetown, was laid out and settled by a man named Patterson, who owned the surrounding land. The place was first known as Patterson's Cross Road, and as proprietors changed the name changed also, being successively that of Burkley's Cross Roads, Marion Cross Roads and finally Oxford, the name it now bears. Where and from whence this famous name was received, it being that of one of the most distinguished spots in England, our authority fails to state. Although never as renowned in history as its English namesake, yet, if all reports are true concerning its earlier career, it was once a place of rather widespread notoriety. But within the past few years the beneficial effects of local option has metamorphosed it into a quiet, respectable and prosperous village.

The oldest tavern, and the only one ever in the place, was kept by Hart Boswell. It was a brick structure, and is still standing, a relic of the "by-gones." The first stores were kept respectively by B. P. Anderson, Cary Ward, Glenn Rickerson, Cannon & McDaniel, etc., and were of the class usually kept in small country villages in an early day, and came under the head of general merchandise. A man named Bailey kept a tailor-shop here some twenty years or more. Shoe shops, blacksmith and wood shops were among the early industries of Oxford Village. There are now two stores, viz.: S. S. Moore and C. T. Price, both of a general merchandise character. A blacksmith and wood shop is kept by William Ryles. This comprises the general business of the quiet village at the present time.

The Oxford Christian Church was organized at the Old Sugar Ridge Schoolhouse in July, 1831, and in 1847 a new frame church was built, under the supervision of Elder John A. Gano, Sr., who had in connection with him, in his early ministrations in this pioneer church, Elder John Smith, who was better known throughout this section, perhaps, by the euphonious appellation of "Raccoon" Smith. The original membership of the church was about one hundred. In 1881, the building was handsomely repaired and refitted, under the pastorate of Elder C. T. Forscutt, an Australian by birth, who was largely instrumental in its improvement.

The Oxford Methodist Church was organized about the same year and at the same place of that mentioned above. It retained for many years its original membership, but from natural causes, such as death and removals, it has been greatly depleted in numbers. A new brick church has been built in Oxford Village, where the old congregation now worship.

Providence Presbyterian Church was organized, about the year 1835, by Rev. Mr. Forsythe. Among the original members were Messrs. Gray, Polk, R. W. Barclay and Mr. Hamilton. Some of the pastors have been Revs. Forsythe, Straghn, Umstead and Spears; present pastor, Rev. J. K. Hitner. The church building is brick, and the membership is about thirty-five.

The Oxford Union Sunday School was organized by Rev. John J. Dickey, and has an average attendance of about thirty children.—*Perrin.*

CHAPTER XVI.

NEWTOWN PRECINCT—DESCRIPTIVE AND TOPOGRAPHICAL FEATURES—EARLY SETTLEMENT—PIONEER TRIALS AND HARDSHIPS—MILLS, ROADS, BRIDGES, ETC.—RELIGIOUS—METHODIST AMD OTHER CHURCHES—EARLY SCHOOLS—VILLAGE OF NEWTOWN—ITS BUSINESS, ETC., ETC.

ELECTION PRECINCT No. 8, known and designated as Newtown Precinct, lies in the southeast part of Scott County, and is bounded on the north by the Cynthiana & Georgetown road, on the east by the Bourbon and Fayette County lines, on the west by the Lexington and Newtown pike and the Oxford road, and on the south by the Fayette County line. Its surface is rolling or undulating, and is fine blue grass land. The original timber was walnut, sugar maple, ash, cherry, hickory and oak, principally the latter. The principal streams are Cherry and Boyd's Runs, North Elkhorn and Little Elkhorn, which drain the land well, and afford an abundance of stock water. The principal pursuits are farming and stock raising, and a number of fine farms are located in this section. The people are industrious, honorable and enterprising, and withal educated and intelligent.

Among the early settlers of Newtown Precinct were Nelson and Clifton Smith, James Parks, Samuel Walker, James McCroskey, Austin Bradford, George Hume, Gen. Henry John Wallace, Newton Cannon and David Flournoy. The precise date of their settlement is not known, but as there were settlements made in the county as early as 1775, it is altogether probable that settlements were made in this section within the succeeding decade. The pioneers above mentioned were from Virginia, and came down the river in boats, as was the custom with many of the settlers in this section of the State. They landed at Maysville, then called "Limestone," and from thence journeyed across the country, bringing their goods on packhorses. Wagons were scarce in the settlement for several years after the first white people moved in. But few descendants of this first installment of pioneers are now living in the precinct, and hence not much could be learned of them. Their life was the same as fell to the lot of all the early settlers in Central Kentucky. The first years, were years of toil, privation and danger—a hard and stubborn contest for a foothold in the wilderness. The Indians were plenty, and often troublesome, as will be seen by reference to the chapter on Indian history. They not only plundered the settlements, stole horses and committed other depredations, but they did not hesitate to murder the settlers indiscriminately when occasion presented. Thus the early settlers of the section now embraced in Newtown Precinct lived the first years of their frontier life, not only in danger of their lives from savages, but also from want and from wild beasts. But their efforts prevailed; their perseverance was crowned with success.

The precinct of Newtown, being mostly a stock-raising and agricultural district, the hum of machinery but little disturbs the Short-Horns and South-Downs as they graze upon the blue grass pastures. The first and only mill ever in the precinct was, or is, known as "Lemon's Mill," on the North Elkhorn, and was built by Joshua Leathers. It is still in operation, but since its erection has been changed into a distillery, then converted back into a mill. A tannery was established in a very early day by Joseph Moring, but it has long since passed away with other relics of the "by-gones." In the pioneer times it was the custom for every man to take hides to the tanyard, have them tanned, and have his shoes, and those of his family, made at home; but that, too, has become one of the lost arts.

The first public road through the precinct was the Lexington & Newtown road, and was also the first that was macadamized. The converting of it into a pike was begun in 1849, and the work was completed in 1852. The Paris & Georgetown pike, which passes through the precinct, was also begun in 1849, and finished in 1852. The Leesburg & Newtown pike was built in 1857. The first bridges were built by the turnpike companies, and were wooden structures. It will be seen by these roads that, in the matter of highways, the precinct is well supplied. Good roads add materially to the prosperity of a community, and by this system of improvements its standard of wealth and prosperity is often determined by strangers.

The precinct is well supplied with churches. The Methodist Church was organized about the year 1804 by Anthony Houston and others. The original building was a wooden structure, and was burned in 1849. It was rebuilt in 1852, of brick, at a cost of about $1,600. The present membership is small.

The Presbyterian Church was organized in 1809, as the Cherry Spring Presbyterian Church, and had for its first pastor Rev. John Lyle. The original Elders were John Scroggins, John A. Miller and David Torrence. We have been unable to learn any further particulars of this organization.

The Christian Church at Newtown was organized in 1856 by Elder John A. Gano, who was its first, is its present, and has been its only pastor. The church edifice is of brick, and is a good, comfortable building. Its original membership was about the same as that maintained at present. A flourishing Sunday school is supported, and is the only one in the precinct. The average attendance is about thirty.

Of the early schools of the neighborhood we know but little. The first taught, of which we have any account, was by Nelson Smith, Esq., one of the early settlers, who took up a school for the purpose of teaching his own children. It is said that there was no other person in the immediate settlement at the time competent to take charge of the school, and Mr. Smith, in order to afford his own children an opportunity of "schooling," thus opened a school, and extended its benefits to the other children of the community. The schools and facilities for receiving an education have improved since that day, and the precinct is now better provided, though there is still room for improvement in the public schools, not only of this precinct, but of the whole county.

The village of Newtown is rather venerable, and has been "town" for many years. It is situated near the Fayette County line, at the junction or crossing of the Lexington and of the Leesburg pikes. It originated into a town by the farmers selling lots to mechanics who built shops of the different trades and commenced business. This led to the establishment of a store at the place, which supplied goods to the mechanics and to the surrounding families. The first store was opened by Martin Bates, who kept a general variety of goods. A shoe shop was opened by a man named Johnson, and a blacksmith's shop by Billy Anderson. This latter was of considerable notoriety throughout the country, for a great distance. Anderson was a very fine mechanic, and made edge-tools of different kinds, with which he supplied the people, and the excellent quality of which rendered him very popular. The only store is at present that of S. Ornsparber, general merchandise. There are two shops—one blacksmith and one wood-shop. This comprises the business of the place at the present time. The only school in Newtown Precinct, is located here. It is in a very flourishing condition, and well patronized, with an average attendance of about sixty pupils. It was organized in this village in 1862, and the first teacher was a man named Tompkins. The present teacher is George Williams (1882), and all the primary branches are taught, usually taught in a common school.

Newtown Precinct is a rather quiet, unassuming community, and has no very thrilling history. Its people move on "in the even tenor of their way," attend to their own business, and leave others to do the same. No railroads traverse the precinct, disturbing the people with the screeching of their locomotives and the rumbling of their trains, but everything is done in the good old way of the fathers.
—*Perrin.*

Harrison County Court House.

HARRISON COUNTY.

CHAPTER I.

SETTLEMENT OF THE COUNTY BY WHITE PEOPLE—LIFE IN THE WILDERNESS—ITS HARDSHIPS AND PRIVATIONS—ORGANIZATION OF THE COUNTY, AND ITS MACHINERY SET IN MOTION—THE ERECTION OF PUBLIC BUILDINGS—ELECTION PRECINCTS, POPULATION, ETC.—COUNTY OFFICERS.

"* * * may thy fame be made,
Great People! As the sands shalt thou become;
Thy growth is swift as morn; when night must fade,
The multitudinous earth shall sleep beneath thy shade!"

IT is a curious truth that when two living friends part, they are, as it were, dead to each other until they meet again. Letters may be interchanged, but the *present* of the one is not the *presence* of the other. That was a trite simile of a late writer, "that in this world we are like ships on the ocean—each striving alone amid the war of the elements; and in the far-forward distance shadowed before us are the dim outlines of the land of death. Some reach it soonest, but thither all are bound." No sadder realization of the inscrutable decree that, "Dust thou art, and unto dust shalt thou return," is wanting than collecting the history of a country or people. Here, we look around us for the old landmarks, and find them moldering in the graveyards. The pioneers who braved the perils of "flood and field," to open up this country, have melted away like mists before the morning sun, and, as we said, repose quietly in the graveyard. The pioneers are all gone, and many of their children are now old and tottering toward to grave. Soon they, too, will have disappeared, and fortunate is it for the historian that he has, through them, rescued from oblivion some of the facts pertaining to the settlement of this famed section.

Much of the early history of Harrison County is given in the first part of this volume, under the respective heads of "Geology," "Pre-historic," "Indians," etc., and will not be recapitulated. But its history will be taken up with its settlement by the whites. From the most reliable data at hand, there is but little doubt that the section now embraced in Harrison County was seen by white people as early as 1775, though it is probable that no permanent settlement was made until a year or two later. Collins gives an account, which bears every evidence of being correct, of a company of men, who, in the spring of 1775, made a visit here "in search of lands to improve." This company consisted of John Hinkston, John Haggin, John Martin, John Townsend, James Cooper, Daniel Callahan, Matthew Fenton, George Gray, William Hoskins, William Shields, Thomas Shores, Silas Train, Samuel Wilson and John Wood. "In the neighborhood between Paris and Cynthiana, they improved lands, made small clearings, built a cabin for each member of the company, named after some of them Hinkston and Townsend Creeks, and Cooper's Run, and afterward settled Hinkston and Martin's Stations. Of the settlement of Hinkston Station we gather the following: Col. John Hinkston, the grandfather of Thomas Hinkston, settled Hinkston Station in April, 1775. The station was on the old Buffalo trace or Indian route, from the big spring at Georgetown to the Lower Blue Licks in the present county of Nicholas, and on the farm now owned by John Lair, near Lair's Station. There was quite a fierce engagement here with the Indians shortly after its settlement—Col. Hinkston being in command of the station, and the notorious renegade, Simon Girty, of the Indian forces. The ammunition gave out at the station, and Col. Hinkston was forced to surrender himself to the Indians. This he did under promise that the remainder of his men, and women and children, should be allowed to remain at the station unmolested, and he (Hinkston) to be furnished with Girty's uniform, which would be a guaranty of safety while a prisoner. These conditions were complied with, and he was taken to the "broad ford" on the South Fork of the Licking, which is in the northern portion of this county, and about two miles north of what is now Colemansville. He was there hid and guarded by a large number of Indians, who formed a circle around him, facing to the center, and thus lay down to sleep. When slumber closed upon them, his cords were untied by Mrs. Boyers, who was also a prisoner, and he sprang to his feet, seized a gun and ran to the bank of the river, which was here very deep, plunged in and swam safely to the other side, amid a perfect shower of bullets from the Indians who had been suddenly awakened, and were in hot pursuit. On the following day, he returned to the station, with his clothes torn, and presenting a very unnatural appearance. At first, he was not recognized by his friends at the station, but climbing into a tree he made himself known, when he received a hearty welcome as one who had come back from the jaws of death. The station was abandoned after this for a few years. John Townsend, on Townsend Creek, and John Cooper, on the waters of Hinkston, *raised corn*, in 1775, from which the latter furnished seed to a number of improvers in the same region in 1776."

These improvements were made in conformity with a law of Virginia passed in 1774, donating 400 acres of land in Kentucky, to every person, who made an improvement, built a cabin, cleared a piece of ground and raised a crop of Indian corn. This opportunity of procuring cheap farms brought many adventurous persons to Kentucky in 1775–76, and the company above referred to, was, perhaps, the first visitors to what is now Harrison County, unless those pioneer hunters—Boone and Kenton—had passed through it on hunting excursions. Another company came to Harrison in 1776, among whom were George Bright, William Craig, James McMillen, Thomas Moore, William Nesbit, Col. Benjamin Harrison (the first Sheriff of Bourbon County), James McGraw, Robert Thompson, Joseph Peak, William Huston, Robert Kean and others. Several of these parties made improvements and raised crops during this year. In this way, many of the settlements were made in this part of the State. Men would come in squads, locate lands, make the necessary improvements to entitle them to the 400 acres of land, and then leave them. The Indians were numerous, and opposed, with all the power which desperation infuses, these encroachments of the whites, and sought every means to harass and murder them. Most of the parties mentioned above, were driven from their early improvements through fear of the Indians. Many of the settlements were attacked, the settlers captured, the settlements laid waste, and the whites either murdered or carried away as prisoners. Ruddel's Station shared their fate. Ruddel's was one of the early settlements made within the limits of the county. It was upon the site of the improvements made by Hinkston and others, and who were driven away by the Indians. Some years later, Isaac and James Ruddel, with a few companions, resettled it. Its capture is mentioned in another chapter of this work, among other Indian depredations and barbarities. Thus the first occupation of the country by our ancestors was under difficulties and exposed to many dangers.

Hall's sketches of the West has an extract from a letter written at Boonesboro by Col. Richard Henderson, one of the proprietors of the Transylvania Land Company, under date of June 12, 1775, shows something of the state of affairs here, and the interest manifested in securing the rich lands of Central Kentucky: "We are seated at the mouth of Otter Creek, on the Kentucky River, about 150 miles from the Ohio. To the west, about fifty miles from us, are two settlements within six or seven miles one of the other. There were, some time ago, about one hundred at the two places, though now, perhaps, not more than sixty or seventy—as many of them are gone up the Ohio, etc., and some returned by the way we came to Virginia and elsewhere. These men, in the cause of hunting provisions, lands, etc., are some of them constantly out, and scour the woods from the banks of the river near forty or fifty miles southward. On the opposite side of the Kentucky River, and north from us about forty miles is a settlement on the crown lands of about nineteen persons, and lower down toward the Ohio, on the same side, there are some other settlers, how many, or at what place, I can't exactly learn. There is also a party of about ten or twelve, with a surveyor, who is employed in searching through that country, and laying off officers' lands; they have been for more than three weeks within ten miles of us, and will be for several weeks longer, ranging up and down that country." These last parties referred to were no doubt, the companies, whose settlement we have mentioned above. The surveyor was probably James Douglass, who surveyed much of the lands of what is now Bourbon, Harrison and Nicholas Counties.

An old manuscript written by Thomas Anderson, who came to Kentucky with his father's family in 1783, and when he was but nine years old, in our possession, gives some rather interesting facts of their trip to this country and their settlement. Mr. Anderson was born in Pennsylvania, and when six years old his father removed to North Carolina, and came to Kentucky, as above stated, in 1783, locating in Lincoln County. In 1788, he removed to and settled in Harrison County. Mr. Anderson thus describes the trip to Kentucky and their settlements in Lincoln and Harrison: "The first night after we started into the wilderness on our journey to Kentucky, the Indians surrounded our camps and stole eighteen horses, among them one of my father's, which left us but two. This made it rather hard on them, one of which soon afterward gave out, and we left it on the way. My mother then had to walk and carry her child. We had four cows, and my father gave them for a young horse, which enabled us to bring our stuff through. We heard the Indians on the mountains round our camps when they got our horses. After we crossed the Cumberland River, part of the men went back and followed the Indians, but soon lost the trail, and so we lost our horses. My father settled on land leased from Col. Harrod at Craig's Station. We lived in a tent until we built our cabin, and during the time (while in the tent) a heavy snow fell, and one night a wolf came to the tent, and took a ham of bacon from under my head while I was asleep, and started away with it, but the dog attacked him and he let it fall. We tracked him to a canebrake not far away, but could not catch him.

"Old Mr. Gill had some hogs that had gone wild and lived in the canebrake, and he told my father if he would catch them he might have half of them. So father found where the hogs slept by the side of an old log, and fed them for a few days at their bed. After awhile he built a strong pen around them with a trap door for them to go in. One morning he went there before day and sprung the trap door upon them and fastened them in. He then sent me after Mr. Gill, who came, and they divided the hogs. We tied and hauled them home and killed them. This was the first pork we had ever killed in Kentucky." This was the way the first settlers lived in the Kentucky wilderness. Though this was in Lincoln County, it was but the same that the pioneers underwent in all parts of the State. Mr. Anderson thus describes their removal to and settlement in Harrison County in 1788:

"In 1788, my father removed to Harrison County, and settled on Indian Creek, about four miles east of Cynthiana. There were but few settlers in the neighborhood then. Father came over the year before, and bought fifty acres of land from Frank Mann, for which he paid twenty shillings an acre. He also hired a man to build him a house, and we moved into it in the spring of 1788. I came in the fall of 1787, although but fourteen years old, and worked all winter clearing ground and making rails; I made two thousand rails, cleared about ten acres of land, and during the time boarded with a man named Thomas Butler, who was a great hunter. When we settled here deer and bears were plenty between our house and Cynthiana. About a year after our settlement in Harrison, I was in the woods one day with Jo. Smith, when we heard what we at first thought was a locust, but it 'sung' too long for a locust, and so we concluded it must be a snake. Upon searching for it, I at last spied it—a large rattlesnake stretched out on a log. I got a stick and held it and cut its head off; then attempted to cut its rattles off, when it struck me on the wrist with its bloody neck as vicious as a tiger. Smith said I turned pale; I really thought it had bit me, until I reflected that I had cut its head off." Mr. Anderson tells the following story that is illustrative of frontier life: "A boy about eight years old, was lost in the woods here in the spring of 1787. It was while my father was over here purchasing his land and arranging for having a cabin built, and he turned out as did everybody else in the settlement, to look for the lost lad. He was not found for nine days, and when finally he was discovered, he had to be run down, for he had grown perfectly wild while lost. After they got him, and his excitement had somewhat worn off, he said he had often heard them blowing horns, and hallooing, but was afraid to show himself, lest they might prove to be Indians. He had lived on roots and nuts; had built a hut of sticks and bark, and made him a bed of leaves, and thus was playing Daniel Boone on a small scale." These extracts have been given merely to illustrate the mode of life in the early times, and to show our readers what the pioneers of the beautiful Blue Grass Region had to withstand while subduing its canebrakes and forests. We will give one more short extract from Mr. Anderson's reminiscences of early life:* "Our mode of life when I was a boy was plain, our food was beef, fish, fowl, bread of light loaf and batter cakes; vegetables, Irish potatoes, cabbage, turnips, onions, greens, etc. Wild fruit was plenty, and used in many ways. Our clothing was all home-made. We raised flax and sheep in those days; the men and women all pulled flax together. The first to ripen was pulled first; the young girls and boys would have quite a party after the flax was pulled. The flax was rotted, then broke, swingled—the men would break it and the women would swingle—after which it was made into cloth by the women, and the cloth into clothing. We would shear the sheep about the middle of May; the men would do the shearing and the women washing the wool, and when dry, there would be wool-pickings, at which the young people would have quite a frolic. The wool was carded and spun at home—carded upon hand cards and spun upon the big wheel—and then wove into blankets, jeans, flannel, linsey, etc.; or knit into stockings as necessity required." Such were the pioneer times over which the aged wavering mind loves to linger—times when

> "Fancy yet brings, on her bright golden wings,
> Her beautiful pictures again from the past."

We have seen how, when Bourbon County was formed,

* These reminiscences were written by Mr. Anderson when he was eighty-four years of age, in good health, and as he expressed it, "able to shoot a rifle as well as a boy of twenty."

it was a vast territory of almost boundless dimensions, and how, as settlements increased, Scott County, in 1792, was formed out of the extensive territory of Woodford. So, as the population continued to increase, Harrison, in 1793, was erected from Bourbon's "broad domain," and from Scott—the two contributing liberally to its formation. Like Bourbon, Harrison comprised a large tract of country extending to the Ohio River, and from its original territory several counties have been wholly or in part created, viz.: Campbell in 1794; Pendleton and Boone in 1798; Owen in 1819; Grant in 1820; Kenton in 1840, and Robertson in 1867. Thus, Harrison may be very truly termed a prolific mother. The county is at present bounded on the north by Pendleton County, on the northeast and east by Bracken, Robertson and Nicholas, on the south by Bourbon, and on the west and northwest by Scott and Grant Counties. It is watered and drained by the Licking River and its tributaries; the southern part lies in the Blue Grass Region proper, and partakes of the beautiful rolling surface of that famous land, while the northern part is inclined to be somewhat hilly and broken, but the entire county is rich and productive. Harrison received its name from Col. Benjamin Harrison, an early resident of Bourbon, the first Sheriff of that county, and its representative in the State at the time of the formation of this county. He was a native of Pennsylvania, and removed to Bourbon prior to its formation as a county in 1785, where he held many prominent positions, among them, in addition to those mentioned above, that of the representative of Bourbon in several of the Danville Conventions. He was also a member of the convention that formed the first constitution of Kentucky. Cynthiana, the county-seat, is a beautiful little city, and was laid out in 1793. Its history will be found in subsequent chapters of this volume.

The first court of Harrison County was held in February, 1794. Robert Hinkston was the first Sheriff; Benjamin Harrison, Hugh Miller, Henry Coleman, Samuel McIlvain, Nathan Rawlings and Charles Zachary, Justices of the Peace, all of whom were sworn in February 4, 1794, and formed the first County Court; they elected William Moore, Clerk. They held their first court in the house of Morgan Van Meter; Richard Henderson was the first County Attorney; Daniel Lindsay the first Coroner; Archibald Hutchinson, Thomas Rankin and William Hall qualified as Constables. Henry Coleman was the first Surveyor, with Benjamin Harrison as Deputy; also John Little and Edward Coleman as Deputies. At this session of court, a ferry was granted to Benjamin Harrison across the Licking River; he was also appointed Commissioner of Tax. Among other business done was a tavern license granted to Robert Harrison in Cynthiana, for one year; also one to William Harrison; a ferry to Robert Harrison across South Licking, near the mouth of Gray's Run, where the present bridge is. At the next session of the court held April 1, 1794, called the Court of Quarter Sessions, the tavern rates were fixed as follows: Whisky, half a pint, 6d; breakfast, 1s; dinner, 1s 3d; supper, 1s; bed, 6d; corn and oats, 2d per quart; stable and hay for one horse, twenty-four hours, 1s. The seat of justice was at this court fixed at Cynthiana, on ground laid off for that purpose. The court agreed with Robert Harrison to build a stray pen, "ten panels square, nine rails high, staked and ridered," and for which he was afterward allowed £7 10s. The court also agreed with Thomas Rankin to erect a "pair of stocks" on the public ground in Cynthiana.

Of the building of the first court house, the records give no account. But at the session of court held in October, 1797, an order was passed to repair the court house—it is supposed that one was built about 1794—as at the session of court held in June of that year, it was "ordered that public building for the county be erected." The second court house was built in 1816. The plan was reported by a board of commissioners, comprised of Gresham Forrest, William Brown, William Moore, James Kelley and Thomas Holt, and was as follows: Brick, upon a stone foundation, fifty feet in the clear, with a chimney at each corner. The first story twenty feet high, the second one in proportion, with "hip" roof, and cupola in center. Gallery over court room reached by two flights of stairs from opposite sides; the building entire cost about $12,000. A clerk's office was erected on the square with two apartments, each sixteen feet square, and fire-proof. The plastering of the court house was first given to John Stamp for $750, but he failed to comply with contract, and it was given to Reuben Payne for $850. He did not finish the job—was paid $600 for the work done, and the remaining $200 was afterward (in 1820), appropriated to repair the rod and spire. This house was burned January 24, 1851. It had been insured by the Protective Insurance Company, of Hartford, Conn., and after a great deal of trouble and some litigation, a compromise was effected. A contract for a new court house was made with John Huddleson & Co. They did part of the work and failed, when a new contract was made as follows: with R. M. & W. B. Calhoun for carpenter work at $2,270; J. F. Harrick at $375 for painting and glazing; B. F. Pullen, of Paris, the plastering at 37½ cents per square yard, and $60 extra for plastering the pillars. A copper roof was afterward ordered instead of iron, and $800 appropriated for the difference in cost.

The first jail was built by Thomas Mounts in 1795, who

received therefor £57 10s. A new jail was built in 1803, and, in 1804, Anthony Arnold the Jailer, protested against this jail, as being insufficient to hold prisoners. Another jail was built in 1852, which burned in 1862, and then the present one was built. More particulars are given of these public buildings in Mr. Marshall's history of Cynthiana to be found elsewhere in this volume.

The first division of the county into districts or precincts, of which we have any account, was in 1798, when it was "laid off into thirteen districts for the aid of the Constables." Without going into a description of all the changes, however, that have been made in its civil division, we will give it as districted at present, which is as follows: Cynthiana, No. 1; Sylvan Dell, No. 2; Richland, No. 3; Berry, No. 4; Rutland, No. 5; Unity, No. 6; Leesburg, No. 7, and Claysville, No. 8. In each of these precincts there are two Justices of the Peace and one Constable. These Justices of the Peace form the Board of Magistrates or the County Court, and, in connection with the County Judge, transact all county business. The Board of Magistrates at present is as follows: C. J. Land and R. J. Whittaker in No. 1; Peter Florence and David Ross in No. 2; John B. Jouett and J. N. Whittaker in No. 3; Charles Lail and James McMurtry in No. 4; T. W. Hardy, and W. N. Matthews in No. 5; N. J. Henry and H. M. Levi in No. 6; T. B. Arnett and R. J. Levi in No. 7; and R. G. Taylor and W. T. Asbury in No. 8.

Previous to the adoption of the new State Constitution in 1849–50, all county officers were appointive. When the new constitution went into effect in 1850, the same became elective. The first set of county officers under the new regime was as follows: P. Wherritt, Clerk; William B. Glane, Sheriff; John A. Berry, Deputy Sheriff; W. W. Trimble, County Attorney; H. Coffman, County Judge; Samuel C. Frazer, Coroner, and J. A. Thorp, Surveyor.

The present county officers are H. H. Haviland, County Judge; P. Wherritt, Clerk; William Lafferty, County Attorney; Enoch Craigmyle, Jailer; Aaron Dills, Coroner, and R. M. Collier, Sheriff. The first Board of Magistrates under the new State Constitution were, for No. 1, Samuel Williams and Edward Wait; for No. 2, Daniel Wait and D. H. Raymond; for No. 3, A. M. Cameron and D. Hardin; for No. 4, R. S. Haviland and S. A. Whittaker; for No. 5, J. P. Blair and M. D. Martin; for No. 6, Benj. Robinson and Joseph Miller; for No. 7, George Lemmon and E. D. Cason, and for No. 8, Benjamin Cummins and William English.

The County Poor House and Farm is a regular county institution. The Harrison County Poor House is located in Berry Precinct, and is kept by Mrs. Polly De Jarnette. She has kept it for the past twelve years under a contract with the county. Newton Henry, Esq., is the Commissioner, and Dr. A. B. McGill, the physician in charge. The present buildings were erected in 1866, and consist of a large and commodious brick, and several small frame houses, the whole being sufficient to accommodate some fifty persons. The inmates at present number twenty, for which the keeper is paid $1.70 per head each week.—*W. H. Perrin.*

CHAPTER II.

RELIGIOUS HISTORY OF HARRISON COUNTY—PIONEER CHURCHES AND PREACHERS—CHURCHES OF THE PRESENT DAY—EDUCATION—SCHOOLS OF THE COUNTY—SCHOOLHOUSES—SUPERINTENDENT'S REPORT—COLORED SCHOOLS, ETC.

FOR a century, men have been toiling in this region for the generations that are to come. It was not for themselves; nor were they certain that their children would inherit the results of their labors. In the early day, they saw the wilderness slowly transformed into a garden; then, too, they welcomed the pioneer minister, who, single-handed and alone, came here through many perils, to proclaim messages of divine love. Many sermons that burned with fervor, have been preached in the groves which surrounded their homely cabins. How many souls have been saved, how much good done in the humble sphere of these pioneer soldiers of the Cross, the advance guard of the grand army that followed them, the angels themselves may not know.

The early religious history of Harrison County is somewhat obscured. The most that is known is, that the early settlers were mostly moral and upright people, who had been members of some religious organization before coming to this State, and upon their settlement here, lost no time in gathering up the stray sheep and bringing them back into the fold. Before houses of worship were erected, the worshipers would assemble in the forest, each man with his gun; sentinels would be placed to guard against surprise from the Indians, while the minister with a log or stump for a pulpit would dispense the Word of Life and salvation. It was thus that our ancestors planted the seeds of Christianity in the wilderness of Kentucky.

It is not known when or by whom the first church society in Harrison County was organized. But as settlements were made here over one hundred years ago, and heralds of the Baptists and Methodists were in Kentucky also a hundred years ago, it is probable that churches of these denominations were established previous to 1790. Without going into particulars of the different churches in the different parts of the county, suffice it, there are between twenty and thirty in the county of the several denominations. Collins mentions seven as being in the city of Cynthiana, two in Claysville, one at Havilandsville, one at Antioch Mills, two at Colemansville, two at Leesburg, one at Buena Vista and one at Rutland. In addition to these in the towns and villages, there are a number that stand in the country. In the chapters devoted to the election precincts, all the churches will be fully written up so far as facts and data can be obtained, and hence no particulars will be given here, but we will proceed to the educational history of the county.

The facilities possessed by our Government and country for disseminating the benefits of an education are unsurpassed by any nation on earth, and no other country perhaps does so much to bestow upon its youth a mental, moral and physical education. It has been very truly said that "Education leads into exercise the active powers of man, those which God has endowed and made active for this end." Science enlarges these faculties and gives them scope and vigor. The memory, the understanding, the taste, the power of association are all to be cultivated. They grow by exercise, and only in this way. We premise by saying that the trust conferred upon those having the superintendence of the public schools is a responsibility scarcely less or inferior in importance to that of the administration of the Government. The Government itself in no slight degree depends upon the education of those by whom it is hereafter to be controlled. Amid the various conflicting opinions on moral, political and religious subjects, there is need of charity and forbearance, concession and compromise. Citizenship is of no avail unless we imbibe the liberal spirit of our laws and our institutions. Through the medium of the common schools are the rising generation of all nationalities assimilated readily and thoroughly forming the great American people. The common schools are alike open to the rich and the poor, the citizen and the stranger. It is the duty of those to whom the administration of the schools is confided, to discharge it with magnanimous liberality and Christian kindness. While the law should reign supreme, and obedience to its commands should ever be required, yet in the establishment of the law which is to control, there is no principle of wider application, or of higher wisdom, commending itself to the broad field of legislation or of municipal action, to those who enjoy its benefits and its privileges, and to which all should yield a cheerful obedience, than a precept which is found with nearly verbal identity in the teachings of Confucius and those of Jesus Christ, acknowledged by all and endeared to all by association and education, viz., "All things whatsoever ye would that men should do to you, do ye even so them."

A learned teacher and author, in speaking of the duties of instructors of youth, says their duty is "to take diligent care and exert their best endeavors to impress on the minds of children and youth committed to their care and instruction, the principles of morality and justice, and a sacred regard to truth, love of their country, humanity, and universal benevolence, sobriety, industry and frugality chastity, moderation and temperance, and all other virtues which are the ornaments of society." It will not be insisted that this duty, so beautifully set forth, is other than in conformity with the constitution of our State. Neither will it be claimed that the Bible, in any of its translations, is averse to sound morality, or to those virtues designated as proper to be inculcated. Our Legislature very justly leaves the selection of books to be used in our schools to the directors, teachers and superintendents, who are elected by a majority of the community for which they act, thus reflecting the will of their constituents. There is no compulsory attendance, no religious tests required, no essentials of belief, no property qualifications to entitle a scholar to the benefits of the common schools of this State. The constitution and laws impose no test or other impediment to debar any from the public schools. Although there is no compulsory educational laws, the question has been strongly agitated, and received the sanction of many of our ablest statesmen. Some of our sister States have adopted such laws, and we, for one, favor the same system in our own State. A late writer has these sensible remarks on the subject: There is yet an advance step to be made to complete the system, and that is the adoption of the compulsory feature. Parents who will not voluntarily send their children to school should be made to do so by the mandates of the law; and the time is near at hand when it will be so enacted, and when every child in Kentucky shall have the benefit of at least a rudimentary education. Those who are especially jealous of their rights, oppose compulsory education on account of its interference with their precious liberty, not thinking that the law which compels them to pay taxes, work roads, serve on juries, and do many other disagreeable things, is just as much of an intrenchment upon their liberty to do as they please as it would be to compel them to send their children to school; besides the liberty to bring up children in ignorance and vice is one of those things that ought to be interfered with and prevented if possible. A government that depends upon the intelligence of the people for its existence must use the necessary means to compel the education of the masses, or go to destruction."

The way to carry out the grand idea in the Declaration of Independence—to make all men free and equal—is to do it through universal education. The unlettered man cannot be the equal of the educated man, nor can he have a free and fair race in the pursuit of happiness, handicapped by ignorance.

Another step which is to be a tremendous stride in the direction of universal and cheap education is yet to be made. It is the simplification of the uses of letters in spelling and forming words, so that the English language may be rapidly and cheaply learned by children and those of other tongues. This great reform has long been advocated by wise and thoughtful men, and is now, in many sections, actively inaugurated. There is a class of professional educators who wish to make a monopoly of their profession by making our language so hard to learn that it takes years of labor and mints of money to acquire it; but this class must, in time, give way to wiser and better men. Many of the nonsensical, useless, wicked and fraudulent letters, that have marred our beautiful language and made it a stumbling-block to children and foreigners, have already been dropped out of the places they have wrongfully occupied in hard and crooked words, that cost so much to learn. When the English language becomes purified and made plain and easy to learn, it will become the universal language of the world.

The church, in the past ages, assumed to be the special patron of education, and, as a part of that education, the religious dogmas of the day were engrafted upon the untutored infant mind, the cunning priest well understanding that "just as the twig is bent the tree is inclined." That time has passed by with us, thanks to the liberty-loving intelligence of our people. We have lived to see

"The Church and State, that long had held
Unholy intercourse, now divorced.
She who, on the breast of civil power,
Had long reposed her harlot head
(*The church a harlot when she wedded civil power*),
And drank the blood of martyred saints;
Whose priests were lords;
Whose coffers held the gold of every land;
Who held a cup of all pollution full!"

Harrison County is laid off into thirty-nine districts for school purposes, in many of which are pleasant and commodious schoolhouses, and in all schoolhouses of some description, though some of them scarcely deserve the name. In addition to these, there are also fourteen districts for the colored people, and they have their teachers, schoolhouses and school fund. According to the last report of the Superintendent of Public Instruction, the amount paid teachers of the white schools of Harrison County for the year ending October 10, 1881, was $7,024.06; for teachers of the colored schools, $433.84; total amount paid teachers, $7,457.90.

In addition to the public schools of Harrison County, there are private schools of an excellent character, which are particularly mentioned in connection with the towns and precincts in which they are located. The public schools, too, are also noticed further in the same connection, and all local facts pertaining to them fully given.

The following extracts are from the report of the State Superintendent, and should be carefully considered by teachers and Trustees:

"Trustees are charged with the enforcement of the rules and regulations of the State Board of Education for the government of common schools, and no school is *legally* taught, and entitled to the fund, in which these rules and regulations are not observed. Trustees have no right to annul, amend or disregard these rules, and teachers will always respect them, even though directed to disregard them by the Trustees.

"A pupil can be suspended for a definite time, or expelled for the term, for incorrigibly bad conduct or refusal to obey the rules. Pupils can be suspended or expelled for persistent tardiness or absence. The right of Trustees to make such rules as will enforce regularity of attendance has been several times affirmed by the courts, and notably and recently by the Supreme Court of Iowa.

"Trustees are empowered to provide that children under nine or ten years of age shall not be confined in school more than three or four hours a day—according to age. They may also make exceptions of children of infirm health, when such do not disturb the classification of pupils.

* * * * * * *

"Through the instrumentality of our common school system, 250,000 children of our State are being taught the elements of an English education. The distance between a person who can read and one who cannot is practically infinite. The man who can read may put himself, if he will, into communion with the recorded genius of all past ages; into sympathy with nature as generalized in the sciences; into commerce with the best thoughts of the living present; and form independent opinions upon every question which challenges his curiosity or affects his relations and interests. Besides, many, reported in no single year, have received the partial benefits, or exhausted the capacities to instruct, of the common school system, so that the blessings it confers are much wider than the annual statistics exhibit. It has turned many thousands into the schools for higher education who, but for its recruiting-sergeancy, would never have crossed the portals of academic and collegiate halls. Through its agency, ambition for learning has been excited in thousands of minds, which, without its inspiring agency, would have remained without a yearning for scholastic learning. Parents, seeing the unfolding capacities of their children's minds, and the blossoming of aspirations for knowledge, have been induced to make sacrifices to put them on the road to higher learning, who would have vegetated in indifference but for its quickening and mind-inspiring power. Into thousands of homes it has carried an intelligence absorbed by parents, and has exerted an educational power on those whose benefits have never entered into official exhibits. Tastes have been developed that have improved the quality of domestic happiness, and refinements developed which have hung otherwise barren walls with prints and paintings, and transformed uninviting cottages into vine-clad and embowered homes. Estimate, upon a tuition basis, the costs of primary instruction at $5 to the pupil child for a term of schooling, and it aggregates the surprising amount of $2,000,500, thus demonstrating the economy of a system which puts a school in every neighborhood and knocks at the doors of the lowliest cabins with the tender of an education as free as the mountain air.

"Statisticians have been able to demonstrate the money value of educated labor, and the commonwealth probably receives every year, in the fruits of a productive industry, tri-fold the costs of the system. They have also tabulated its economics in the prevention of crimes and dissipations, which would have entailed grievous burdens upon those who pay the costs of society. It has greatly added to the value of property, and served to content thousands with their native lot; while as an advertisement to emigrants, it has acted as a magnet to draw thousands from abroad to our own borders. Every man with a proper concern for his offspring, when contemplating a change of residence, makes, as a conditioning feature, inquiry into the facilities afforded for the education of his children. The very best outlay for a country inviting immigration is the money put into the agents of education. A tasteful and well-equipped school-house never fails to create local pride; and we have never known a community making a prudent expenditure on an efficient school to regret the enterprise after its advantages had been made manifest.

* * * * * * *

"It is recorded that Burke pronounced 'education the chief defense of nations.' The superiority of the Southern to the Federal soldiery, in the early stages of our civil war, was because the South gave the flower of her culture to the field, who carried with them into the camp and battle that pride of character which is ever the most reliable chivalry when confronting danger."

The following is so sensible that we commend it to the careful perusal of every one of our readers:

"In Kentucky we have devoted much attention to the improvement of our animal stock by breeding, and have reached a degree of excellence in this respect which has given a world-wide reputation to our studs, herds and flocks. Our horses are kings of the turf, our Short-Horns premium at the World's Fair and our Southdowns rival the bucks and ewes of their native English heather. Is it not time we were devoting ourselves to the culture of the human animal, lest our stock should become superior to their proprietor groomsmen, herdsmen and shepherds? Physical culture has turned the wild horse of the desert into the Arabian steed, the Derby courser, or the Percheron draft; the boar of the forest into the Berkshire porker; the "scrub" of the mountains into the big-uddered Durham. It is not to be believed that the most careful breeding of the human stock can produce grander specimens of our race than Bacon, Clay, Breckinridge (J. C.) and the like, but we are justifiable in believing that, by the observance of certain known laws, the general quality of the race can be improved. It is the opinion of a medical expert, recently brought out by the trial of the slayer of Judge Elliott, that a majority of men are, more or less, insane—perfectly balanced minds being the exception instead of the general rule. It seems to have been generally conceded, ever since the dictum *Orandum est, ut sit mens sana in corpore sano*, that the essential conditions of a well-ordered mind are (1) a brain free of all hereditary predispositions to disease, and (2) a normal state of the rest of the physical organs. When it is known that the sins and virtues of parents descend as a heritage to children, all who respect their responsibility will feel a concern for their personal habits and health, which transcends self."

The progress being made among the colored people in matters of learning is very gratifying to all friends of the race and of education. That education can improve the African race it is folly to debate. Every community numbers some intelligent and virtuous and thrifty colored men, who are conspicuous shafts of light rising out of the dark

Born November 9th 1794.

depths in which most of their blood are plunged. Can we point to a solitary instance of thrift and strict rectitude among them without finding associated with it an elevated intelligence and morality? Left to themselves, however, and without education, the negro will deteriorate and become worse and worse year by year.—*Perrin.*

CHAPTER III.

INTERNAL IMPROVEMENT—TURNPIKE ROADS AND BRIDGES—RAILROAD HISTORY OF THE COUNTY—THE MANUFACTURE OF WHISKY—SOME OF THE DISTILLERIES—AGRICULTURE—FAIR ASSOCIATIONS AND OFFICERS—STATISTICS, ETC.

THE turnpike system of Harrison County is scarcely so perfect or so extensive as in some of the neighboring counties. Bourbon, Scott, Woodford and Fayette, for instance, are better supplied with the excellent macadamized roads perhaps, for which the blue grass region is so famous, than is this county, although Harrison has a number of turnpikes passing to points of importance. Among them may be mentioned the Paris & Cynthiana pike, the Leesburg & Newtown pike, the Cynthiana & Falmouth pike, the Cynthiana & Leesburg pike, the Connersville & Scott County pike, the Leesburg & Leeslick pike, the Cynthiana & Shady Nook pike, the Cincinnati, Georgetown & Lexington pike, and others. These are fine macadamized roads, and are the pride of the county, as well as the turnpikes at large are the pride of the blue grass region. Bridges span the streams where these roads cross, thus rendering travel safe and free from high water.

Railroads.—The railroad history of Harrison County is exceedingly brief and is comprised chiefly in the Kentucky Central, which is fully written up in the part of this volume devoted to Bourbon County. All that can be said of it in connection with Harrison County is what is purely local. There was subscribed toward building it something like $125,000 by wealthy citizens of the county, and the right of way generally granted by those through whose land it passes. The subject of issuing bonds by the county was put to a decision of the legal voters and defeated, the county thus refusing to issue bonds.

The county took no action whatever in the project of the Cincinnati Southern Railroad, and, as we have said, the railroad history is given in that of the Kentucky Central.

Whisky.—Harrison County is noted for its distilleries. Collins, in his history of Kentucky, says: "In Harrison County there are thirty distilleries, which manufacture annually about 50,000 barrels of whisky, much of it of quality unsurpassed in the world. The manufacture of and trade in this whisky constitute the greatest business and wealth of Harrison County." One of the very first industries of the county was the distillation of whisky, and whisky seems to have been a pioneer beverage as well as a pioneer industry. John Miller, we learn, had a distillery in what is now Leesburg Precinct, more than seventy-five years ago, and Joseph Woolley operated one in the present precinct of Richland about 1825 or 1830. In what is now Rutland, there was a distillery started as early as 1791–92, by John Kemper, and Samuel Kendall had one on the Middle Fork of Raven nearly as early. Thus the business commenced in an early day, and has grown and kept pace with everything else, and perhaps gone ahead of some things we regret to say. But speaking of the importance of whisky, from a commercial standpoint alone, it certainly is the most valuable business interest of the county.

Among the thirty distilleries (more or less) now in operation in Harrison, we may mention the following, but will not pretend to say whether any of them, like the woman's babies, have gotten away or not:

The Edgewater Distillery is one of the oldest in the county, and was built in 1837 by Shawhan & Brandon, and at that time was the largest in this section of the country, having a capacity of about one hundred bushels per day. It was run about four years by this firm, when Brandon broke up, which proved very disastrous at the time, as it involved several other parties in the wreck. After this catastrophe, the distillery was run by Mr. Shawhan, until it passed through bankruptcy, which was about 1850. It was then bought by John Lail, Sr., and for about three years was operated under the firm name of Lail & Foley, then leased by them to Shawhan, Snell & Megibben, who ran it for some three years, when the lease expired. The junior partner, Thomas J. Megibben, then bought it and has since owned and operated it. Through these different changes of ownership, the capacity of the distillery has been increased until it is now about five hundred bushels per day. Its name has become familiar and favorably known to many wholesale whisky dealers both in the United States and Europe.

L. Vanhook & Co.'s distillery is situated on the Cynthiana & Falmouth pike, just outside of the city, and was built by Peck, Vanhook & Co., in 1868. It was burnt in 1869, and rebuilt in the same year; has a capacity of 300 bushels per day, and produces annually some three thousand barrels; amount now in bond, 6,000 barrels. The size of the distillery is 35x55 feet, three floors, three brick warehouses with a capacity of 7,500 barrels. Ten hands are employed at an average of $1.50 per day wages each. Brand—"L. Vanhook & Co., Pure Bourbon." One hundred and fifty cattle, and 400 hogs are fed; cooper-shop attached, which turns out 4,000 barrels per annum. Shipments are made over the Kentucky Central Railroad from Cynthiana.

Excelsior Distillery, present firm Megibben, Bramble & Co., is located at Lair's Station, three and a half miles south of Cynthiana. It was bought in 1868 by Thomas J. Megibben & Bro., and has a capacity of 700 bushels; uses two engines of ninety horse-power; distillery is 70x40 feet; three floors; two brick and one iron-clad warehouse, with total capacity of 17,500 barrels; annual product, 8,000 barrels; now in bond, 11,300 barrels; brand, "T. J. Megibben & Bro., Excelsior Distillery." A cooper-shop attached with daily capacity of fifty barrels; feed 250 cattle and 500 hogs annually; employ forty hands, on an average of $2 per day; obtain 75 per cent of corn from the county; telephone connection with Cynthiana, five miles distant, by pike. Thomas J. Megibben & Bro. are now (February, 1882), erecting a large flour-mill and distillery at Lair's; capacity of mill fifty barrels of flour per day; of distillery, 150 bushels per day.

Crescent Distillery, located at Cynthiana, present firm C. B. Cook & Co.; it was bought in 1868 by C. B. Cook; William Adams admitted as a partner in 1874; capital invested, $50,000; capacity, 150 bushels per day; annual product, 2,500 barrels; now in bond, 6,000 barrels. Brand —"C. B. Cook, Crescent Distillery;" employ twenty hands at average wages of $2 per day. The distillery is 35x70 feet; three floors; three brick warehouses with storage capacity for 8,000 barrels; feed 800 hogs; cooper-shop attached, with capacity of 3,000 to 4,000 barrels per annum.

Ashbrook Distillery, built in 1840, by Abram Keller, and sold to Cook & Ashbrook, in 1861, afterward to Ashbrook Brothers—the present firm—in 1874; capital invested, $40,000; capacity, 300 bushels daily; annual product, 2,500 barrels; amount in bond, 5,000 barrels. The size of the distillery is 40x60 feet—three floors, with three stone warehouses—capacity, 9,000 barrels; employ ten hands, at average of $1.50 per day. Brand, "A. Keller, Bourbon," and stands very high in New York market. The brand was bought with the distillery—sweet mash—and has the name of being the best sweet mash in this part of the State. The distillery has made more or less whisky every year since 1840; its shipping is done from Keller's Station, on Kentucky Central, one and a half miles from Cynthiana. The water supply is received from an excellent well, 160 feet deep. There is a mill adjoining the distillery, one of the oldest in the county. It was built by Mr. Lamb, who also kept a store and carding factory. Lamb used to grind flour, haul it to Claysville, and ship it thence to New Orleans by flat-boat. The mill is now used for the distillery alone, and both are run exclusively by water-power.

Poindexter Distillery—firm Wiglesworth & Brother—on site of old mill which belonged to Philip Keath more than seventy years ago. John Poindexter rebuilt the mill, and added the distillery about 1850. It was bought by Wiglesworth Brothers, who tore down and rebuilt both mill and distillery in 1880. The capacity is 100 bushels daily; annual product, 1,500 barrels; amount in bond, 2,500 barrels. The size of distillery (iron-clad), is 40x100 feet; three floors, two iron-clad warehouses, with capacity of 6,000 barrels; new brick warehouse in process of erection; employ eight hands, at $1.50 per day. Brands, "Poindexter Bourbon," "Wiglesworth Bros.," sweet mash whisky. Feed some cattle and 250 hogs annually; buy barrels in Cincinnati at $2.50 each; mill and distillery both run by water when sufficient; at other times by steam.

Craig's Distillery, at Berry's Station, was built by John M. January in 1853. It was sold to Davis, who ran it a short time, and sold it to S. B. Cook; he ran it from 1860 to 1867, then sold it to his son, C. B. Cook, who ran it eight months, and sold it to Lair, Redmon & Co.; they ran it to 1871; then Lair & Kern ran it until 1873; John L. Pugh from 1873 to 1874. It then stood idle until 1880, when it was bought by T. G. Craig, and has been run by him since. It has a capacity of 200 bushels per day, and produces 2,500 barrels annually. The building is 32x64 feet; three floors, two warehouses; capacity, 3,500 barrels; now in bond, 1,800 barrels. Brand, "T. G. Craig." Feed 100 cattle and 500 hogs; employ twenty hands at $1.50 per day each; get 60 per cent of grain from the county.

Redmon Distilling Company is proprietor of Distillery No. 15, of the 6th District. It is located on Leesburg pike, a half mile from Cynthiana, on Gray's Run, and was built about 1859 by John Redmon. After passing through several hands, it was bought by the Redmon Distilling Company, in March, 1880, when buildings were fully repaired and rebuilt, and new machinery put in. The present company is composed of five men—Thomas Hinkson, President; L. Vanhook, Treasurer; J. A. Wolford, Secretary, and S. J. Ashbrook and W. A. Cook, Directors. Capital invested, $50,000; capacity, 160 bushels per day; two large brick warehouses, with capacity of 6,000 barrels; 3,000 barrels now in bond. Brand, "Redmon Distilling Co.," "H. C. Ky." Employ eight hands, at average of $1.50 per day; make sweet mash whisky. Feed but few cattle and hogs.

We don't know how many more distilleries there are in the county now in operation. We learned the history of those which are here given, and then became discouraged at the gigantic task before us, and so thought to let the above serve as examples of the business. Enough is given to show the extent and importance of whisky-making as a manufacturing interest. What more is necessary?

Agriculture.—The following article on the agriculture of Harrison County was written especially for this work by H. B. Wilson, Esq., and is worthy of the perusal of every farmer in this region. He says: "An agricultural history necessarily varies from writings usually given for information and preservation. In the past this has been sadly neglected, but the future will develop these resources in such a manner as the theme deserves. No wider field for thought is given to man than the agriculture of the country. It is the base upon which is built the great structure of prosperity, and without, all would be ruin and destruction. Geographically, the county is situated in the blue grass region, and a large portion of its lands are among the very best, and when offered for sale bring as high prices as those of any other county. Many portions of the State were furnished with lumber from its hills and valleys, while its lands were being opened for cultivation.

"By the early settlers, the maple was used for supplying themselves with sugar and molasses, deriving therefrom quite a large revenue. Its sap being very sweet by evaporation becomes sugar. The people depended much upon their success in this department of industry, to supply themselves with means to purchase coffee, tea and salt, together with other necessaries of life not furnished by the farm. The housewife made nearly all the fabrics from which the clothing was manufactured. The present luxuries were unknown to the farmer.

"The soil is exceedingly fertile and rich, and produces all the crops, common to the State, in great abundance. Corn, wheat, rye, oats, hemp and tobacco are grown in all portions of the county. The lands along South Licking are better and more productive than those along Main Licking, the former producing the very best blue grass, grains of all kinds, hemp and tobacco, while the latter the finest quality of tobacco and corn. It has now become one of the largest tobacco producing counties in the United States. Tobacco was grown chiefly in the more hilly portion, but at this date it is fast usurping the staple articles of the very best lands. The finest and most salable article grown upon virgin soil, where the leaf mold of ages has enriched it, giving it a bright appearance, but yielding less pounds per acre than old lands well rested and manured. It is one of the most difficult crops to handle properly, and but few farmers master the science. Often the very best crops are ruined either in housing, stripping, bulking, or in finally preparing it for the market. It furnishes work for the planter at all seasons of the year. If planted more than two or three years upon the same land in succession, it soon shows its exhaustive effect, and other land is sought for its cultivation. Fertilizers have never been used to any great extent other than clover and stable manures.

"No county in the State, perhaps, surpasses the southern portion of Harrison in the yield of corn and wheat per acre. The soil, underlaid for the most part with clay, before reaching rock, and that at a depth of five and ten feet, causes it to successfully resist drought as well as the injurious effects of heavy and long-continued rains. A sufficiency of limestone underlies all the soil and is mingled with it to renew the elements taken from it by the various crops, and to enrich it instead of impoverishing it. Being well watered, it is well adapted to grazing purposes.

"All portions of the county grow the finest grasses, the blue grass furnishing food better adapted to the wants of domestic animals than any other kind. Clover is grown chiefly for the enriching elements it contributes to the soil. In its season, no grass surpasses it in fattening stock. Domestic animals are reared with success, and great improvements have been made in them. The county has always been noted for its beautiful and fleet-footed horses. The early settlers used the saddle and heavy draft horse, but now we have such as are desired in all the markets of the world. The cow, hog and sheep rank with the best of the land. Large herds of Short-Horns are bred and reared in our midst, and the hills and valleys are covered with flocks of the Cotswold, Southdown and other kinds of sheep; hogs are fed upon corn produced on our own soil. The early settlers frequently in the fall months, gathered them together in large droves and traveled on foot with them to the Carolinas and Virginia. To this generation and in this age of steam this would be tedious and slow work.

"The farming implements used by the pioneers were of a very common kind. The plows for breaking the land were made with iron or steel points, and wooden mold-boards. The writer never saw one with iron or steel mold-boards until about the year 1845. The virgin soil was easily turned, but now, while the soil may be as rich and fertile, it is more compact and requires a better implement for breaking than the one of by-gone days. To-day, the plow that is in use has almost reached perfection. All other farming implements and methods of agriculture have undergone a complete change. Wheat, rye and oats were then sown broadcast by hand; now the drill is used by all progressive farmers. Corn was dropped by hand and covered with the hoe, now the work of planting is done by machinery. Harvesting then was done with the old reap-hook, each man cutting and binding about one acre per day. Now the harvester, with twine-binder attached, does the work completely, leaving the grain in bundles, and doing the work of a dozen men. The mowing machine has unsurped the place of the old scythe before it was hung in the tree of the late Daniel Webster. Then the grain was gathered into the barns and at the stack-yard, and the flail in the hands of the farmers threshed out the kernels, or the horse put upon the treading-floor to tread it out, it was winnowed by blankets, the fanning-mill being unknown. Now the shrill whistle of the steam engine, driving the separator and straw-stacker, is heard during the threshing season upon every farm, putting the grain cleaned and measured into the sack ready for market. Thus is progress stamped upon the age, and man calls to his aid powers unknown to those of the latter part of the eighteenth century and the early years of the nineteenth. Change is not always progress, but with the agricultural class of the county it has been a grand improvement.

"To get the products of the farm to market was a problem, requiring considerable talent to solve. The early settlers had to depend upon their own teams to haul their surplus to some shipping point. The waters of Main Licking were utilized as a means of getting to the markets of the world. Claysville, a small town located upon its banks, was the only shipping point for many years. Bacon, flour, tobacco and everything raised, were hauled to this town over dirt roads, loaded on flat-boats, and at "high tide" were taken down stream to the Ohio River, thence to New Orleans. Return trips were made by walking home. Maysville, after the building of Maysville & Lexington turnpike road, became the main shipping point, until the year 1854, when the Covington & Lexington Railroad was completed as far as Cynthiana. Upon its completion, a new impulse was given the farmer, and every available tract of land was called into requisition, and made to grow large and remunerative crops. Wealth began to flow into the farmer's pockets, and every undertaking prospered. Success followed success, until the destroying hand of war swept over the land. The agriculture of the county always assuming a higher standard of excellence. From time to time, all improved implements were introduced and all machinery adapted to the wants of the people, displaced the old and cumbersome methods of cultivation."

The following statistics from the last report of the Auditor will be found of interest to our farmer readers:

Assessed valuation of land..............	$3,347.405 00
Average value per acre....................	17 81
Number of horses and mares, 6,229; value,	219,925 00
Number of mules, 906; value..............	33,070 00
Number of sheep, 21,429; value...........	65,185 00
Number of hogs, 11,849; value............	32,145 00
Number of cattle, 7,891; value............	122,950 00
Total value of taxable property........	4,929,625 00
Number of pounds tobacco produced......	1,841,005
Number of pounds hemp produced.......	12,208
Number of bushels corn produced.......	812.195
Number of bushels wheat produced......	130.065

Agricultural Association.—The first fair association was organized about 1856, with Gen. Lucius Desha as President, and J. A. Kirkpatrick, Secretary. It was kept up without interruption until the organization of new fair in 1875. The present Harrison County Fair Association was incorporated April 19, 1875, by H. E. Shawhan, T. J. Megibben, H. C. Magee, C. R. Kimbrough. Felix Ashbrook, and John K. Lake; capital stock $25,000. The first officers were T. J. Megibben, President; C. R. Kimbrough, S. J. Ashbrook, F. G. Craig, G. R. Sharp, James T. Talbott, H. C. Magee, H. D. Frisbie, W. H. Roberts, R. C. Wherritt, and J. L. Patterson, were elected Directors. G. R. Sharp and H. C. Magee were elected Vice Presidents; R. M. Collier, Secretary; and T. T. Magee, Treasurer. The same officers were retained for several years, except that N. W. Frazier and W. W. Smith were elected directors in place of Sharp and Magee, who were elected Vice Presidents. They leased the present grounds from W. H. Wilson, for ten years, with privilege of fifteen; he to use buildings when not used for fair, and association to have the privilege of removing them at end of lease.

Same officers were elected for 1876, except C. R. Kimbrough and S. J. Ashbrook, who were elected Vice Presidents. The same result was had in 1877; also in 1878. In 1879, W. H. Wilson was elected a Director, being the only change in the board. No other important changes have been made, and for 1882 (the present year) the officers and directors are as follows, viz., T. J. Megibben, President; C. R. Kimbrough and S. J. Ashbrook, Vice Presidents, and R. V. Bishop, Secretary. The Directors are M. S. McKee, C. R. Kimbrough, J. R. Lake, N. S. Frazier, F. G. Craig, Samuel Ashbrook, C. H. West, James Mathews, W. H. Wilson and William Victor.

The President and Directors are elected by the stockholders, who in turn elect their Treasurer and Secretary. The officers and managers of the association are men of intelligence, energy and enterprise, and alive to the importance of such an association, and of the results to be derived from it. The success with which they have managed its affairs is shown by its present flourishing condition.—*Perrin.*

CHAPTER IV.

THE CATTLE INTERESTS — EARLY INTRODUCTION OF FINE STOCK INTO KENTUCKY — DIFFERENT IMPORTATIONS AND IMPORTING COMPANIES—THE '17'S—BREEDING AND QUALITY OF STOCK—PRESENT BREEDERS, THEIR HERDS, ETC., ETC.

ALTHOUGH the breeding and rearing of fine cattle has never assumed such huge proportions in Harrison as in some of her sister counties, yet the excellence of some of her present herds, and the increasing interest that has been engendered of late years, demand more than a passing notice.

In the formation of the "Blue Grass Region," nature has bestowed her gifts with an unsparing hand. A climate mild and salubrious; a soil possessing the mineral elements necessary for the highest development of animal and vegetable life; traversed in every direction by living streams of pure limestone water; an admirable distribution of field and forest, hill and dale; not lacking in meteorological conditions, it is no matter of surprise that such a preponderance of physical conditions should manifest itself in the production of cattle of superior excellence. The peculiar adaptability of the world-renowned "Kentucky Blue Grass" (poa pratensis) to the perfection of beef cattle had won for Kentucky-bred beef an enviable reputation, even before any effort was made to improve the character of the stock fed. This success naturally re-acted on the traders' energy, and efforts were soon made to produce a class of stock which would yield better returns for the amount of feed consumed, and for the time required in rearing them.

The first importation of improved stock into Kentucky was nearly cotemporaneous with her admission as a State, and this was followed by other importations at frequent intervals up to the year 1817. Several different families, among them, notably, Bakewells, Herefords, Long-Horns, etc.; but the Short-Horns or Durhams proved their superiority in so many respects that, at the present day, they have outstripped all competitors for popular favor.

Says Mr. William Warfield, in his chapter in the history of Fayette County, and to whom we are indebted for most of the information relative to the early history of the cattle interest in the State: "The first introduction of improved cattle into Kentucky was due to the enterprise of the sons of Matthew Patton, Sr., a resident of the rich valley of the South Fork of the Potomac. In 1783, Mr. Patton had procured for his use, on his Virginia plantation, a bull imported from England by Mr. Gough, of Baltimore, Md., which was described by Mr. Patton himself as "very large and of the Long-Horn breed."* In 1785, three of Mr. Patton's sons, and his son-in-law, Mr. Gay, brought several of the half-breed heifers, the get of this bull, with them to Kentucky, "near where Nicholasville, in Jessamine County, now stands." In 1790, Matthew Patton himself, emigrated to Kentucky, to Clark County, bringing with him several more half-bloods, the calves of the same Long-Horn bull. These cattle were very large and rangy, fattening slowly and late, but, at maturity, making excellent beef. Some of them were also first-rate milkers. They are described by Mr. B. Harrison, who knew the original animals well, as "large, somewhat coarse and rough, with *very long* horns, wide between the points, turning up considerably." Having seen the benefit wrought by one cross of improved stock, Mr. Patton could not fail to try more. Accordingly we find him as early as 1795 procuring, through his son William, two new animals of the Gough and Miller stock, of Maryland and Virginia. In all the old records a very sharp distinction is drawn between these new animals and the bull used earlier, these being ascribed uniformly to the "milk," and he as uniformly to the "beef" breed, and these breeds being always identified respectively with short and long horns.

Mr. Harrison's description of these new-comers fully bears out these old distinctions.

The bull (subsequently entered in the American Short-Horn Herd Book as Mars, 1850), he says was a deep red, with white face, of good size, of round, full form, with more bone than the popular stock of the present day; his horns somewhat coarse." The heifer (Venus) "was a pure white except her ears, which were red, of fine size, high form,

*See letter of Mr. Benjamin Harrison, grandson of Mr. Patton, in *Franklin Farmer*, of February 9, 1839.

short, crumply horns, turning downward." Here then we see the first seed of Kentucky's Short-Horn interest being sown. The seed, however, did not bear much immediate fruit. Venus produced but two calves—both by Mars, and both bulls—and then died. Nor was Mars much resorted to by the neighboring breeders, the price of service, $2—certainly moderate enough—being considered exorbitant at that early day. One of Venus' calves was carried to Chilicothe, Ohio, by William Patton. The other calf was retained in Jessamine County by Mr. Roger Patton, and Mars remained in Clark County till 1803, when he was carried by Mr. Peoples to Montgomery County, where he died in 1806, being the first Short-Horn bull ever brought to Kentucky. The half-blood bull calves by Mars and his son were in the meantime scattered all over the grazing region of Kentucky, making a marked improvement in the common stock.

In 1803, Messrs. Daniel Harrison, James Patton and James Gay (son and sons-in-law of Matthew Patton), sent back to Mr. Miller's herd in Virginia for another bull of the "milk" Short-Horn breed, and got a two-year old, Pluto 825, certified to be by an imported bull, and out of an imported cow. "He was a dark red or brindle (roan)," says Mr. Harrison, "and when full-grown was the largest bull I ever saw, with an uncommonly small head and neck, and light, short horns, being very heavy fleshed, yet not carrying so much on the desirable points as the fashionable stock of the present day, with small bones for an animal of his weight. The people were now at last awake to the value of these importations, and flocked to Pluto with their cows, although the service price was still at $2. Mr. Patton bred him to the produce of Mars, and the improvement was marked, Mr. Harrison asserting that the produce of this double Short-Horn cross on the half Long-Horn basis, was a class of animals whose superiors "in all the essential qualities of the cow kind" have rarely been seen. In 1812, Pluto went to Ohio, where he soon afterward died. Not, however, before the cross-bred descendants of himself and Mars had become so numerous as to gain a sure footing in Central Kentucky.

The importation in 1810 by Capt. William Smith, of Fayette, of the bull Buzzard, who was himself of mixed blood, and proved of little note; of "Inskip's" brindle in 1813; of the Care stock, imported by Mr. Daniel Harrison from Maryland, in 1814; and of the bull "Shaker," which had come from Mr. Miller's stock through the Ohio Shakers, completed the list of cattle brought to Kentucky previous to the year 1817, and these bulls crossed on the native stock of the country produced the "Patton Stock," a great improvement on the old breeds; but still, owing to the early death of Venus, breeders had no possible chance of securing thoroughbreds from this stock alone.

The superior excellence of the Patton stock over native cattle naturally stimulated the minds of breeders to attempt the possibility of further improvement.

In the autumn of 1816, the attention of Mr. Lewis Sanders, of Fayette County, was called to the prices brought by Short-Horn cattle at the sale of Charles Collings, of Kenton, England—especially the 1,000 guineas that Comet brought, a price hitherto unheard of in Kentucky. He determined to import some of this improved Short-Horn stock, and by the advice of his friend, Capt. William Smith, included in his importation a pair of Long-Horns.

He lodged with the commercial firm of Buchanan, Smith & Co.. of Liverpool, $1,500, with orders to send to Yorkshire and procure a pair of Holderness, and then to the River Tees, in Durham, for a pair of Short-Horn Durhams; then to the County of Westmoreland for a pair of Long-Horns, his final intention evidently being to obtain a pair of each of the three most celebrated classes of stock then in England for the purpose of trial and comparison. It being not long after the great war, prices had fallen much in England, and the purchaser, Mr. Etches, was able to secure two pairs of each breed, making in all twelve head, which were shipped to Baltimore on the steamer Mohawk, as per the following invoice:

Invoice of cattle shipped aboard the Mohawk for Baltimore, consigned to Messrs. Hollins & McBlair, merchants there:

(1) One bull from Mr. Clement Winston, on the River Tees; got by Mr. Constable's bull, brother to Comet.

(2) One bull, Holderness breed of Mr. Scott, out of a cow that gave thirty-four quarts of milk per day; large breed.

(3) One bull, from Mr. Reed, West Holme, of his own breed.

(4) One bull, Holderness breed, from Mr. Humphrey's; got by Mr. Ware's bull of Ingleton.

(5) One bull, Long-Horned, of Mr. Jackson Kendall, out of a cow that won the premium.

(6) One bull, Long-Horned, from Ewartson, Crosby Hall, is of a very fat breed.

(7) One heifer, from Mr. Wilson Standcross, Durham breed.

(8) (9) (10) Three heifers, from Mr. Shipman, his own breed.

(11) (12) Two heifers, Long-Horned breed, from Mr. Ewartson, Crosby Hall, of the Westmoreland breed.

Of the above, No. 1 was afterward named Tecumseh

(5409); No. 2, San Martin (2599), and No. 3 [or 4] Comet 1382; No. 7, the Durham Cow; Nos. 8 and 9, respectively, Mrs. Motte and the Teeswater Cow. Two other animals reached Kentucky from England in 1817. These were the two bulls, John Bull 598½, and Prince Regent 877, and were imported by Mr. James Prentice, of Lexington.

With this notice of this importation of 1817, it seems proper to add a word as to its quality.

Owing to the fact that no register existed in England prior to 1822, it was impossible that any extended pedigrees could be procured. All the evidence taken together is, however, conclusive as to the purity of the stock. Mr. Etches, the great English stock judge, so testifies at length, and indeed the invoice bears it out on its face."* And it is the testimony of some of the oldest and most successful breeders in Harrison County, that the descendants of the old '17 stock are not surpassed in good points by any of the more popular varieties of the present day. With these remarks on the importation of Short-Horns and their early introduction into Kentucky, we will proceed to notice the different herds now represented in the county, with a general sketch of the families which compose them.

As far as we have been able to determine, the pioneer breeders of Short-Horns in Harrison County were Messrs. S. F. and J. J. Tebbs.

The former of these gentleman married a daughter of Dr. Martin, of Clark County, one of the early breeders of Short-Horns in Central Kentucky; the latter, Mr. J. J. Tebbs, is still living in Harrison, near Cynthiana. He commenced breeding in 1837, with some cows of the old 1817 stock, procured from his father, and bred by Hubbard Taylor, of Clark County. Shortly after this, he purchased of Charles Garrard, of Bourbon County, some pure Short-Horns, viz.: Lady Motte and Rose Bud by Garrard's bull Exception. Still later in 1842, he added to his herd some pure Short-Horns, purchased of Dr. Martin, of Clark County, and being a portion of the descendants of the importation of Martin, Taylor & Co. Among the cows represented in this importation were Dorinda, Georgiana, Dulcedorum, Glorietta and Garcia, obtained from Dr. Rodman, of New York, and Leonida, Beauty, Jessy and Sprightly obtained from Mr. Paley, in England. Among the animals brought to Harrison by Mr. Tebbs was the imported bull Bullion, which he used on his herd for several years, and the three cows, Florence, Amana and Gem. Previous to this purchase, however, he had obtained from the same source, the cow Amelia, and the bull Bonningham. Mr. T. was also the owner of the bull Pacific for two years, also at a later date Sir Howard, obtained from Battle & Co., of Clark County. His present herd consisting of about twelve head, is headed by Master Suddeth, purchased from the Vanmeters, of Clark County.

Following closely in the wake of Mr. Tebbs in the Short-Horn interest, was Gen. Lucius Desha, one of the most extensive and successful breeders now represented in the county. He began in 1847, with two cows, May Rose, running back to Imp. White Rose, by Publicola (1348), and Rose Bud, tracing to Imp. Daisy. Previous to this, Gen. Desha had been much interested in fine stock, and had taken much pains to elevate the native stock of the county, but owing to the absence of the American Herd-Book previous to this time, the above two were the first ever registered. Shortly after he added to his herd, Mary Ann, 25th, and Miss Gray, both bred by Mr. R. A. Alexander, of Woodford County, and tracing to Imp. Mary Ann, by Middlesboro (1234). These were followed in succession by Sallie Moore, tracing to Imp. Cleopatra; Verity, tracing to Imp. Rose Bud by Harsley by (2091) Primrose by Belle Duke of Airdrie, 2532, tracing to Imp. Galatia by Frederick (1060), Arabella by Langton 3061, of same strain as Primrose and Imp. Clochette by Duke of Grafton. The above-mentioned cows form the foundation of the present herd which consists of about seventy-five head, in about the ratio of nine females to one male.

Among the bulls which have been used upon his herd may be mentioned in their order:

Reuben 2123, by Garrett Davis 518, tracing to Imp. Beda, by Magnum Bonum (2243).

Paramount 1993, by Pacific 798, tracing to Daisy. Imported in 1832, by Dun & Smith.

Red Gauntlet 3330, by Emigrant 472, tracing to Imp. Daisy.

Favorite 2d 499, out of Imp. Irene by Sheldon (8557).

Renick McAfee 7184½, by Renick 3339, dam Mary Clay Forsythe by Renick 903, tracing to the Durham cow of the importation of 1817.

Cunningham 9711, by Gen. Robert E. Lee 5699, dam Rebel Lady by Duke Albert 5523, tracing to Imp. Fanny by Selim (6454).

Hinkson Duke 10229, by 16th Duke of Airdrie 7880, out of Lady Seaham 7th, she by Victor 7th, tracing to Imp. Ianthe by Barforth (3085).

Lanan 10th's Duke 17601, by 14th Duke of Airdrie 7879, dam Lonan 10th by Imp. Duke of Airdrie (12730).

Gibraltar 17183, by Royal Prince of Fairview 12861, and out of Imp. Clochette by Duke of Grafton (21594).

King of the Oaks 20143, by Imp. Breast-Plate, 11431, and out of Imp. Clochette by Duke of Grafton as above.

*See the testimony in full in *Farmers' Home Journal*, February 6, 1873.

Duke of the Oaks 22939, by 2d Duke of Oneida 9926, and out of Imp. Clochette.

Rosamond's Oxford 33749, by 10th Earl of Oxford 14161, and out of Rosamond 5th, she by 3d Duke of Geneva and tracing to Imp. Rosamond by Onarington (10671).

The bare mention of the above animals, which form the foundation of the General's present herd, is a sufficient indication of the excellence of his stock, and he has always been able to dispose of his surplus at private sale, and at remunerative prices.

In 1850, Dr. G. H. Perrin, now a resident of Cynthiana, and one of the oldest men in the county, engaged in the breeding and rearing of Short-Horn cattle. He purchased from William Alexander, of Woodford, the bull calf Langton, for which he paid $600, it being then only six months old. He also purchased of George Bedford, of Bourbon, the celebrated Belle Duke, of Airdrie, by Duke of Airdrie, and a full brother of Kentucky Duke. His first cow was Valette, obtained from Gen. James Garrard, and the produce of his fine bull Exception. He also purchased another cow, the produce of Dr. Martin's bull Bullion. With these as a start, he engaged in the business for several years, but owing to his advanced age, he has taken but little interest within the past few years.

Succeeding Dr. Perrin in chronological order is Mr. Anselm C. Shropshire, near Leesburg, who first became interested in Short-Horns in 1852, his start being made with the one cow Mary Ann, of Imp. Zelia family. Shortly afterward, he purchased from Silas Corbin, of Bourbon, four cows of the Matilda family, and later, of William Crockett of Scott, two cows tracing to Imp. Mary Ann by Middlesboro. Still later, he added to his herd the cow Diamond by Imp. McGregor 675, he being brought over by the Scott County Importing Company in 1854, through their agents, Wesley Warnock and James Bagg, Esqs. With the addition of some calves of the Amelia strain, the above are representatives of his present herd. These have been served at different times by some of the best bulls of the country.

In 1871, Mr. Shropshire purchased the bull Landable, by Imp. Duke of Airdrie, and out of Imp. Lizzie. Later, he added Johnson Duke of Clarke, bred by Abe Renick, of Clark County, and purchased from William Sandusky, of Illinois, for $500. His herd at present is headed by the Duke of Burlington, of Cleopatra family, and bred by Alfred D. Offutt, of Scott County.

Among the sales made by Mr. Shropshire, always private and principally of his own breeding, may be mentioned Duke of Moscow, sold about 1870, to John Martin, of Ohio, for $1,600.

In 1874, the bull Longfellow to James Bishop, of Randolph, Ill., for $1,000.

The bull John Diamond, in 1874, to S. S. Arnold, of Chariton, Iowa, for $500. And John Diamond 4th, sold to William Dehart, of La Fayette, Ind., for $300.

Among his sales of females were Lady Whiteface, a Matilda, to James Bishop, of Illinois, for $1,000; also to the same party at the same time a suckling Amelia calf for $500.

He sold to James Johnson, of La Fayette, Ind., the Matilda cow, Dora 1st, for $1,000, and an Amelia heifer for $600.

To A. C. Funk, of Illinois, he sold Dora 2d, a Matilda, for $750, and her calf, Matilda Climax, for the same amount. To the same party, he sold the finest cow he ever raised, Matilda Johnson, for $2,000.

Gus Allman, of Illinois, purchased from him Lonan 1st and 2d, paying $1,500 for 1st and $1,000 for 2d.

To an Illinois breeder, William Campbell, he sold Lonan Duchess, tracing to Imp. Mary Ann, by Middlesboro, for which he received $1,200.

Most of the calves of his present herd, consisting of about twenty head, are by the bull Royal Butterfly, of the Ianthe stock.

Mr. James L. Patterson, near Broadwell, began to indulge his taste for fine stock in 1854, at which time he purchased of Joseph Wasson, of Fayette County, three cows and one bull of the Amelia family. In 1865 or 1866, he bought several more females of the same family from Charles Brent, of Bourbon County.

The addition of a Javelin cow, of Matson & Co.'s importation, and some Amelias purchased of John A. Gano, of Bourbon, which was further supplemented, in 1880, by a Desdemona bull, sired by Lanan Duke 19th, and purchased from B. F. Bedford, complete the foundation of his present herd which consists of about forty head.

Among the most successful sales from Mr. Patterson's herd, we mention a bull two years old, sold to Mr. B. B. Groom, of Clark County, for $2,000, to form part of his herd exhibited at the Centennial Exposition at Philadelphia in 1876. Unless the weather is unusually severe, Mr. Patterson generally allows his stock to run at large.

Noah S. Patterson began breeding in 1855, in partnership with his brother Joe. Their first stock consisted of the bull Russian, purchased of James Tebbs, of Harrison, and two Amelia cows obtained from Joseph Wasson, of Fayette. Later they purchased from Bishop Forsythe two cows tracing to the importation of 1817. They bred from these till the war, after which Mr. Noah Patterson secured a Young Mary cow from Bishop Forsythe, which had been

bred by William Warfield, of Fayette; also a Venus cow from Capt. John Hill, of Bourbon. In 1879, he added a Desdemona cow, bred by B. F. Bedford, of Bourbon. The produce of the above cows crossed on Duke, Oxford and Desdemona bulls from his present herd which consists of ten head.

J. Levi Patterson embarked in the Short-Horn interest in 1858, with a cow of the 1817 stock, purchased of John A. Gano, and the bull Huon, obtained from John Wasson, of Fayette. He continued to breed in this family till 1868, when he bought of William Warfield, of Fayette, the heifer Verbena, a Young Mary, and the bull Error, of Cleves family, and from John A. Gano a few of his Minerva strain. In 1869, he procured of Capt. George Moore, of Bourbon, Ianthe, and, in 1876, bought Valley Flower, a Rose of Sharon, of B. F. Bedford. His herd now consists of twenty-two head, and are all Ianthes, Young Marys or Rose of Sharons.

After Error, he purchased of T. J. Megibben Rosa Lad, a Rosamond bull, and he is now breeding to the Desdemona, Duke of Crombia. Among the noted animals raised by Mr. Patterson was the bull Duke of Harrison. He also owned Red Daisy 8th, purchased from T. J. Megibben in 1874, and sold to B. B. Groom in 1875, as a two-year-old, for $2,100, to appear in his centennial herd.

Mr. John M. Berry, at Berry's Station, began breeding in 1865, with the cows Flora 4th, Ruth and Moss Rose 3d, of Young Mary and Phyllis families. These were purchased from Thomas Van Meter, of Clark County, from whom, and Thomas P. Dudley, he has since procured others of Young Mary, Phyllis, Victoria, Elizabeth, Mrs. Motte and Pansy families. He has been the owner of the bulls Lyon (17523), Duke of Fayette, Bramton (7606), London Duke 7th (14801), Rockingham (15361), Belle Airdrie (22116), Cambridge Rose Lad, and others. Among his best sales were Flora 4th to Henry Williams, Cynthiana, for $400, and Strawberry 1st and 2d, to William Hunter, of Hamilton, Ohio, for ——. Mr. Berry's herd at present contains twenty-six head, of the different families mentioned, his favorite strain being the Young Marys.

T. J. Megibben started his herd in 1865, with the three cows, Sallie Ward, 2d and 3d and Elfleda, purchased at the sale of Charles T. Garrard, of Bourbon, and tracing to the importation of 1817, made by Col. Lewis Sanders. He bred to these till 1868, at which time he formed a partnership with Mr. Wesley Warnock, of Bourbon, and they selected for the foundation of their herd several Short-Horns from the different herds of the Blue Grass Region, including Young Marys, Phyllises and Rose of Sharons. They bred to these for four years, and held a sale, at which some of the females brought as high as $2,500. In 1869, they had added to the herd Lonan 10th and 39th, and the bull Financier, all obtained at the sale of Daniel McMillan, Xenia, Ohio. In 1873, September 10, Mr. Megibben attended the sale of Messrs. Walcott & Campbell, near Utica, N. Y., and brought into the county the bull 2d Duke of Oneida 1776, for which he paid $12,000. At the same sale he and E. G. Bedford, of Bourbon, purchased the 4th Duchess of Oneida for $25,000; she only lived a short time, and gave birth to a bull calf, which proved of no value. He purchased at the same time the 3d Maid of Oxford for $1,000, and the heifer, Cherry Constance for $1,750. Shortly after this, he purchased of Col. John B. Taylor, of London, Canada, four heifers of the Craggs family, to which we may add several of the Lady Bates family previously obtained at the New York Mills sale. In 1875, he purchased of William S. King, of Chicago, Wild Eyes of Lyndale for $5,000. To these he added two more of the Wild Eyes tribe, which he purchased from J. D. Carr, of Gabilan, Cal., they having been bred by Hon. M. H. Cochran, of Hillhurst, Canada. In 1872, he purchased of J. W. Wadsworth, Genesee, N. Y., Kirkleavingston 13th. Among the other strains of late purchase were represented the Bates Secrets, Nettle, Princess, Peri, Bloom, Rosamond, Garland, Mazurka, Miss Wiley, or London Duchess, Gwynne and others. Among the bulls used have been 14th Duke of Airdrie, 2d Duke of Oneida, 10th Earl of Oxford, purchased from Cornell Bros. in 1876 for $10,000; 2d Oxford of Vinewood, from B. B. Groom, of Clark County, by 14th Duke of Thorndale, for which Mr. G. paid $17,900.

Among the animals purchased by English parties and returned to that place were two Rose of Sharons for $5,500, and one Princess, purchased by B. B. Groom, for George Fox, of Harefield, Eng. Messrs. Warnock and Megibben purchased in 1868, of Noah Buchanan, Miss Rose Jackson, and her first calf after they bought her, Miss Stonewall Jackson, by 13th Duke of Airdrie, was exported to England, and is now in the herd of Mr. George Fox. In the partnership herd were represented the families Phyllis, Young Mary, Imp. Donna Maria, Imp. White Rose, Imp. Amelia, Imp. Pomona, Craggs, or Duchess, Springwood, etc. The partnership was closed in 1876, the sale netting about $36,000, since which time Mr. Megibben has been engaged without a partner, and his herd, consisting, of over a hundred head, is made up of the descendants of the above families.

Elijah Kirtley, near Cynthiana, began breeding in 1872 with the calf June 3d, of Elkhill, purchased at the sale of Richardson & Hughs, of Fayette, for $300, and the cow, Rosa Linda, from Anselm Shropshire. In 1877, he added to his stock the cow Maggie 5th from Luther Vanhook, and bred by James L. Patterson. These three cows and their descendants, headed by the bull Lord of Springhill, constitute Mr. Kirtley's herd, seven head in all.

F. B. Smith, near Jacksonville, commenced raising Short-Horns in 1872, having purchased an Ianthe cow of John Hill, of Bourbon. Later he obtained of Gen. R. M. Gano the cow Mattie 6th, Vol. IX p. 101, A. H. B. To these he afterward added Minerva 6th of Pattersondale, an Amelia. His present herd of fifteen head consists of the descendants of the above cows. His first bull was Duke Philip 1st, purchased of George M. Bedford, and running to Imp. Phyllis. He was followed by Sterling Duke 2d, of the Rosabella family.

Daisy Duke of Hustendale, bred by James Hall, of Paris, heads his present herd.

S. J. Ashbrook, in 1872, purchased of John A. Gano, of Bourbon, the two heifers, Leona 2d by Indian Chief and Minerva 18th by 16th Duke of Airdrie. The former of these produced for him nine calves, four bulls and five calves, which have produced ten calves of each sex. The second heifer (Minerva 18) has produced three bull calves and six cow calves, which in turn have given birth to twelve females and six males. Mr. A. now has about thirty cows and heifers, the produce of the two original heifers. He has sold his bull calves at good prices, and adds, as his experience, that Short-Horns are the cheapest and most profitable cattle that a farmer can handle.

Mr. Henry Williams, Cynthiana, began breeding in 1868, with the cow Flora 4th, bought of John M. Berry for $400. He kept her till her death in 1880, having sold from her $3,000 worth of produce, one of her calves, London Mary, having been purchased by Baylis T. Gordon, of Clay County, Mo., for $700. He also sold one of her grandcalves to Cyrus Jones, of San Jose, Cal., for $550, who afterward shipped her to Japan.

In 1872, Mr. W. also bought at Hughes & Richardson's sale Indian Princess 2d, a Lady Seaham. He has traded in fine stock considerably, but at present his herd consists of but four head, one cow tracing to Imp. Rosamond by Sir Charles Napier, and the other tracing to Mrs. Motte, together with their two calves.

Mr. John Lair, Lair's Station, became interested in Short-Horns in 1875, owning as the foundation of his herd the three cows, Florence 2d, Lucretia 4th, and Red Rose, and the bull Kelvenside. To these he has added by subsequent purchase, Irene 3d of Elkhill, Verona, Verona 2d, May Fair, May Fair 3d, Rose Wood 4th, Maggie Patterson, from E. Kirtley, Cynthiana, Ky.; 2d Duke of Valley Farm, from T. J. Megibben, 6th Duke of Ashland, from A. H. Bedford. Mr. Lair's herd, at present consists of some twenty head, in which are represented the Rose of Sharons, Young Marys, Daisies and Imp. White Roses. This last family, which runs back to Imp. White Rose by Publicola 1348, Mr. Lair prefers for milk and butter. His experience is, that if Short-Horns are properly and judiciously crossed, they can be made good milkers, and that considering the fact that it takes no more feed to support a Short-Horn than a scrub, they are by far the most profitable for a farmer to handle.

Dr. H. C. Smith, Jacksonville, in 1881 procured of W. H. Current, of Paris, the cow Amelia of the Amelia family. Later in 1882, he added four cows, tracing back to the Teeswater cow, of the importation of 1817. These and their calves, seven head in all, make up his present herd.

J. Willie Kimbrough, son of C. R. Kimbrough, Cynthiana, Ky., purchased at the sale of W. T. Hearne, of Fayette, in 1878, the cow Boston Belle 7th, for $225; from her he has sold two calves for $175, and still has three of her calves and the cow, which represent a value of $750.

With this brief notice of the different herds, we close the chapter of the Short-Horn interest of Harrison County. Besides the thoroughbred class, the stock of the county has been greatly improved by thoroughbred crosses on native grades, and so manifest, to every one who gives it a thought, is the superiority of the thoroughbred over common grades that no doubt the close of the present century, will witness quite a revolution in the cattle interest of the county.—*T. J. Megibben.*

CHAPTER V.

WAR HISTORY OF HARRISON COUNTY — HER PIONEERS IN THE REVOLUTIONARY ARMY — THE WAR OF 1812 — ITS RECRUITS FROM THIS SECTION — OUR WAR WITH MEXICO — THE WAR O THE REBELLION—HARRISON'S BLUE AND GRAY.

"Of all the hearts
That beat with anxious life at sunset there,
How few survive, how few are beating now."—*Shelley.*

MANY of the early settlers of Harrison County had been soldiers in the Revolutionary army, and at its close had received grants of land in the "County of Kentucky" for their services in the war for independence. According to Collins' Kentucky, there were, in 1840, living in Harrison County, the following Revolutionary soldiers who were receiving pensions: James Bean, aged seventy-seven years; Samuel Caswell, seventy-seven; Leonard Eddleman, seventy-nine; Benoni Jameson, seventy-six; William H. Layton, eighty-three; Thomas McCalla, eighty-seven; Jacob Miller, seventy-five; Philip Roberts, seventy-seven; William Sutton, seventy-eight; Louis Wolf, Sr., eighty-nine, and John Wood, ninety years. Also two widows, Mrs. Mears and Ann Whittaker, receiving pensions for their husbands. With this number living in the county in 1840, it is probable there were included in the early settlers several hundred Revolutionary soldiers.

In the war of 1812, Harrison County contained several hundred inhabitants, and most of her able-bodied men subject to military duty served at some period during the continuance of the war. From Dr. Perrin we learn that the county turned out some 400 or 500 men all told. Among them were the following commands: The Sixteenth Regiment of Kentucky Militia, Col. Andrew Porter; Capt. James Coleman commanded a company of cavalry, and as fine a company as was in the Northwestern army. It was in Col. "Dick" Johnson's regiment, and took part in the battle of the Thames. Capt. William Brown's company of volunteers; Capt. M. Forrest commanded a company in which Dr. Perrin went out as a private, but of which he was soon promoted to Quartermaster. Many of the Harrison troops participated in the battle of the River Raisin. Capt. Thomas also commanded a company at the battle of Dudley's defeat. Col. Boswell also commanded a regiment that contained many Harrison County men, and a number of whom participated in the battle of the Thames. Thus Harrison County bore an honorable part in the war, and poured out the blood of her bravest and best in defense of the country. Of all those who went out from the county, there are but two known to be at present living, viz.: Dr. Perrin, of Cynthiana, now eighty-eight years of age; and a Mr. Harris, who is probably about ninety years old.

As a matter of some interest to soldiers of the present day, we give the following abstract from the Quartermaster's Department during the war of 1812: Rations—one and half pounds of beef, three-fourths pound of pork, thirteen ounces of bread or flour, one gill of whisky. At the rate of two quarts of salt, four quarts of vinegar, four pounds of soap, and one and a half pounds of candles to every 100 rations. And from the Paymaster's Department: Colonel, $75 per month, five rations, and $12 for forage; Major, $50 per month and three rations; Captain, $40 per month and three rations; First Lieutenant, $30 and two rations; Second Lieutenant, $20 and two rations; Ensign, $20 and two rations; Sergeant Major, $9; Second Master Sergeant, $9; other Sergeants, $8; Corporals, $7; musicians, $6; and privates, $6 per month. This presents quite a contrast to the long prices paid to officers and soldiers in the late war.

In the war with Mexico, Harrison County fully maintained her good name for courage and patriotism. Nearly an entire company (sixty-eight men), was made up in the county, under command of the following officers: John Shawhan, Captain; William Henry Vanhook, First Lieutenant; George P. Swinford, Second Lieutenant; and Dr. John Kimbrough, Third Lieutenant. The company participated in the battle of Buena Vista, where it lost four men killed, viz.: John S. Jones, Corporal; and privates William McClintock, James Pomeroy and D. P. Rogers. Fifteen men died of disease before the company was mustered out of the service, an event which took place in June, 1847, at New Orleans.

The history of the Mexican war is so familiar to all readers that a sketch of it is unnecessary here. The leading facts are, however, given elsewhere in this volume, and will be found of considerable interest.

The great war between the States next engaged our martial attention, and from 1861 to 1865 raged with a force and energy unparalleled in the history of war. The excitement swept over the country like an epidemic, and although Kentucky designed remaining neutral, the war feeling took possession of many of her patriotic sons, and aroused them to deeds of valor, as the "fiery cross" stirred up Roderic Dhu's "Highland hornet's nest." Under the pretext of self-protection, the militia was enrolled, and these organizations formed the nucleus of many of the companies and regiments which eventually rallied under the "Stars and Stripes" and the "Southern Cross." Our space will not allow an extended sketch of the late war, even were it a safe and pleasant subject to write upon, which it is not. It is of too recent occurrence to admit of a historian treating it without suffering his prejudices to crop out to some extent, and hence we shall confine our remarks less to particulars than to generalities, and leave to some future writer more minute details.

The Twentieth Kentucky Infantry (National service), drew as many men from Harrison County as any other organization formed during the war, perhaps. Among the recruits to this regiment were the following commissioned officers: Cornelius McLeod, Captain of Company I, promoted to Major October 14, 1864, but never mustered as such; was mustered out of the service January 17, 1865; William C. Musselman, promoted from First Lieutenant Company F, to Captain of Company D, January 1, 1863; Henry Kimbrough, First Lieutenant, resigned February 21, 1862; W. Kinney, promoted from Corporal to Sergeant April 2, 1862, to First Lieutenant October 16, 1862, mustered out of the service January 17, 1865; Alonzo Jackson, Quartermaster, died January 15, 1863; William B. Dunn, Captain Company —, dismissed May 6, 1865; William H. Curran, Assistant Surgeon, resigned August 2, 1862; Robert Beckett, Second Lieutenant Company I, resigned January 23, 1863; John C. Northcutt, promoted from Sergeant to Second Lieutenant of Company F, May 21, 1862, to First Lieutenant May 1, 1863, and mustered out January 17, 1865, at Louisville; Dr. P. N. Norton, promoted from Hospital Steward to Assistant Surgeon August 2, 1862, and mustered out January 17, 1865.

The following sketch of the operations of the Twentieth Infantry is from the published report of Gen. Lindsay, as Adjutant General of the State: The Twentieth was formed in the fall and winter of 1861, by Col. Sanders D. Bruce (now editor of the *Turf, Field and Farm*, of New York City). It was mustered into the United States service by Lieut. Col. Chetlain, United States Mustering Officer, on the 6th of January, 1862. When its organization was completed, it proceeded to Nashville, where it was assigned to Gen. Nelson's division. It participated in the battle of Shiloh, and in the engagements which resulted in the capture of Corinth, Miss. It engaged in the pursuit of Bragg's army to Louisville; followed them to Mt. Vernon, Ky.; then returned to Nashville. From this time it was employed in Southern Kentucky and Tennessee, until July 5, 1863, when it was was attacked at Lebanon, Ky., by Gen. Morgan's (Confederate) Cavalry, and, after a severe engagement, was forced to surrender, in order to save the town from destruction. During its entire service, it participated in the following battles, in which loss was sustained: Shiloh, Corinth, Lebanon (Ky.), Kenesaw Mountain, Dallas, Acworth and Atlanta, Ga. It was mustered out of the service at Louisville, January 17, 1865, the recruits and veterans being transferred to the Sixth Veteran Cavalry.

The Sixth Kentucky Cavalry was made up in this section of the State, and drew quite a number of men from this county. Among the commissioned officers of the regiment, Harrison furnished the following: William P. Roper entered the service as Captain, and was promoted to Major of the Sixth, then to Lieutenant Colonel, and mustered out July 14, 1865, at Edgefield, Tenn. Samuel Kimbrough, Second Lieutenant, resigned September 30, 1863; James H. Coffman, promoted to Captain Company B, September 15, 1862, and mustered out at Louisville December 23, 1864; A. P. McLeod, entered the service as Sergeant, promoted to First Lieutenant October 7, 1862, and mustered out December 23, 1864.

The operations of this regiment are given in the war history elsewhere in this volume, and will not be repeated in this. Bourbon County furnished a number of men to the Sixth Cavalry, as well as Harrison, and its second history will be found in that county.

The Seventh Kentucky Cavalry was the next regiment that drew men from Harrison County. Among the commissioned officers were A. J. Jones, who was promoted from Second to First Lieutenant, February 7, 1863, and promoted to Lieutenant Colonel of the One Hundred and Thirty-sixth Colored United States Infantry; William O. Smith was Major of the Seventh, and resigned February 5, 1863; D. P. Watson was promoted from Sergeant Major to Adjutant, November 14, 1864, and mustered out of the service July 10, 1865, at Edgefield, Tenn.; H. McC. Magee entered the service as a private, and transferred, by promotion, from Company C to Second Lieutenant of Company M, January 29, 1863, and mustered out July 10, 1865; Jesse Bryant was promoted to Captain February 7, 1863, and mustered out July 10, 1865, at Edgefield, Tenn.; A. M. Spradling was promoted to Second Lieutenant, but as such was never mustered. The sketch of this regiment is also given in connection with Bourbon County, as many men were from that as well as from this county.

The Eighteenth Kentucky Infantry drew on Harrison County for a part of its force. Among the commissioned officers from this county were the following: B. T. Riggs, James F. Miller and A. G. Roper. Capt. Riggs was promoted from Second to First Lieutenant January 17, 1863, to Captain March 28, 1863, and transferred to Eighteenth Veteran Volunteer Infantry, and mustered out July 10, 1865, at Louisville. Miller entered the service as Sergeant October 16, 1861, was promoted to First Lieutenant January 17, 1863, and resigned June 14, 1863. Roper was promoted from Sergeant Major to First Lieutenant in the Eighteenth Veteran Infantry June 23, 1865, and mustered out with the regiment.

The Eighteenth saw considerable hard service during the war. Its operations were confined principally to Kentucky and Tennessee. The battle of Richmond, Ky., was one of the severest in which it participated during the war. Its loss in this engagement was 52 killed and 115 wounded, and nearly all the remainder of the regiment captured and paroled. Among the killed were Capts. Lewis of Company H, and Culbertson of Company K, and Lieuts. Washburn, Company F, and Dunlap, Company I. Among the wounded and captured were Col. W. A. Warner, Lieut. Col. J. J. Landrum, Capts. M. Mullins and W. P. Fisk, and Lieuts. Patterson and Moss. On the 4th of April, 1865, the non-veterans—only seventy-two in number—were mustered out of the service at Goldsboro, N. C., and the veterans and recruits transferred to the Eighteenth Veteran Volunteers.

The Fourth Kentucky Infantry also received a large number of men from this county, among whom were the following commissioned officers: Charles T. Schable, B. S. Tucker and Robert F. Long. Capt. Long entered the service as Sergeant, was promoted to Second Lieutenant March 23, 1862, and transferred to Company F, promoted to First Lieutenant November 1, 1862, and to Captain March 23, 1864, was mustered out March 19, 1865, at Macon, Ga.; Tucker was promoted from Second to First Lieutenant, Company K, March 23, 1862, and resigned March 6, 1865; Charles T. Schable was promoted from Second Lieutenant Company K, to First Lieutenant Company A, May 8, 1864, to Adjutant September 29, 1864, and honorably discharged May 15, 1865. This regiment also receives further mention elsewhere, as many of its men were from Bourbon County.

The Fortieth Kentucky Infantry drew a few men from Harrison County. Of the number, Thomas R. Rherer and Isaac N. Whittaker were commissioned officers. The former entered the service as Captain June 23, 1863, and resigned July 24, 1864; Whittaker was Second Lieutenant of Company G, and resigned January 31, 1864. This regiment was mounted, and served principally in Kentucky, participating in all the battles in Kentucky against Gen. Morgan and his rebel cavalry.

The Fifty-fifth Kentucky Infantry was also recruited in this section of the State, drawing quite a number of men from Harrison. Among them were the following shoulder-straps: Calvin Griffin, James P. Robinson and Nehemiah Spradling. Griffin was First Lieutenant of Company C, and died August 15, 1865; Robinson was Captain of Company C, and was mustered out with the regiment September 19, 1865, at Louisville; Spradling was Second Lieutenant of Company C, and was mustered out with the regiment. This regiment was organized at Covington, in November, 1864, and served in Kentucky, mostly in guarding the Kentucky Central Railroad until ordered on the Saltville expedition, during which campaign it performed good service. After the return from Virginia it was again assigned to duty in Kentucky until its muster-out in September, 1865, at Louisville.

The Frankfort battalion of State troops also contained a few men from Harrison County, and Capt. James T. Musselman and First Lieut. W. N. Matthews. This battalion served principally in defending the State Capital against the attacks of guerrillas, and rendered important duty while in the service.

The foregoing facts, pertaining to the action of Harrison County in the late war, are taken principally from the Adjutant General's Report of the State, published by Gen. Lindsay, of Frankfort, and may be relied on as substantially correct.

The names of Confederate soldiers and officers from Harrison County are not so easily obtained as those who participated in the unpleasantness on the Federal side. As there are no published reports, we are compelled to rely upon what we can learn through personal inquiry. The following are the names of some from this county, who bore commissions in the Confederate service, but whether it is a complete list or not, we are unable to say. They are: H. McDowell, Lieutenant Colonel Second Kentucky Infantry; O. G. Cameron and John Shawham, Majors in cavalry battalion, and Ben Desha, Major of the Ninth Kentucky Infantry. Jo. Desha was Captain in the First, and afterward in the Fifth, Kentucky; W. T. Beaseman, Captain in the Second Kentucky Infantry; ——— Kennant, Captain in the Ninth Kentucky Infantry; A. J. Beale, Captain in same regiment; James N. Frazier, William White and Joseph Harding, Captains in cavalry regiments. McDowell went out as Captain, but rose to the rank of Lieutenant Colonel; his company, made up mostly in this county, aggregated eighty-nine men, of whom three officers and twelve privates were killed, and three privates died of disease; about sixty-five, of the eighty-nine men, returned home after the conclusion of peace. Ben Desha was promoted from Captain to Major of the Ninth Infantry. Other promotions were—from the ranks to Lieutenant—Phil Murphy, H. M. Carpenter, J. H. Webb, J. M. Carroll and R. M. Wall; and from Lieutenant to Captain, A. J. Beale and Oscar Kennard.

Capt. Shawhan's company was made up principally in this county. The officers were John Shawhan, Captain; William H. Vanhook, First Lieutenant; J. N. Frazier, Second Lieutenant, and Charles Fowler, Third Lieutenant, with about seventy enlisted men. Capt. Shawhan was killed in October, 1862. The company was mustered into the service of the C. S. A. in October, 1861. Another company, largely from this county, was officered as follows: O. G. Cameron, Captain; Joseph Harding, First Lieutenant; William French, Second Lieutenant, and William Burns, Third Lieutenant, with seventy enlisted men. About sixty of each of these companies returned home after the war was over. Company C, of the First Kentucky Infantry, which was also made up mostly in this county, comprised nearly one hundred men, with the following commissioned officers: Jo. Desha, Captain; W. S. Rogers, First Lieutenant; L. M. Thomson, Second Lieutenant, and D. H. Thomson, Third Lieutenant. Lieut. Rogers was promoted to Captain, and was killed at Augusta in the fall of 1862; Lieut. D. H. Thomson was killed at Chickamauga September 20, 1863; and Lieut. L. M. Thomson died of disease during the war.

Our data for this part of the war history of the county is meager, and doubtless imperfect. We have no published reports or lists to draw from, and memory is often treacherous. We have given all the facts we have been able to obtain.—*Perrin.*

CHAPTER VI.

CYNTHIANA PRECINCT—DESCRIPTION AND TOPOGRAPHY—TIMBER GROWTH, ETC.—EARLY SETTLEMENT—"ROUGH HABITS, COARSE FARE AND SEVERE DUTY"—PIONEER INDUSTRIES—CHURCHES AND CHURCH HISTORY—EDUCATIONAL—VILLAGES, ETC., ETC.

"A dirge for the brave old pioneer!
The patriarch of his tribe!
He sleeps, no pompous pile marks where,
No lines his deeds describe;
They raised no stone above him here,
Nor carved his deathless name—
An Empire is his sepulcher,
His epitaph is Fame."—*O'Hara.*

HE who attempts to present, with unvarying accuracy, the annals of a county, or even of a district no larger than a precinct, the authentic history of which reaches back through a period of nearly a century, imposes upon himself a task beset with difficulties on every hand. These difficulties are often augmented by statements widely at variance, furnished by the descendants of early settlers, as data from which to compile a true and faithful record of past events. To claim for a work of this character perfect freedom from error, would be simply to arrogate to one's self that degree of wisdom not possessed by mortal man. In the pages which follow, we incline to those statements supported by the greater weight of testimony. To give facts, and facts only, should be the aim and ambition of every one who professes to deal with the incidents of the past.

The precinct of Cynthiana, which is Election Precinct No. 1, is situated rather in the southeast part of Harrison County, and is bounded on the north by Berry and Richland Precincts, on the northeast and east by Claysville and Sylvan Dell Precints and Nicholas County, on the southwest and west by Leesburg and Unity Precincts, and is mostly fine blue grass land. It is large in extent, comprising nearly a fourth of the county, and lays well, being generally rolling, but not rough or broken, and produces well. It is drained and watered by the Licking River, and its numerous tributaries, among which may be mentioned Townsend Creek, Paddy's Run, Seller's Run, Indian Creek, Sycamore Creek, Gray's Run, etc., etc., with a number of smaller and more insignificant streams. The original timber was oak, black walnut, hickory, elm, sycamore, sugar tree, buckeye, etc., with an undergrowth in places, of cane, which, however, soon disappeared. Corn, oats, wheat, hemp and tobacco are extensively grown; also considerable attention is paid to stock-raising and grazing, and many fine herds of cattle and studs of horses are to be seen in the precinct, as well as some of the noted stock farms of the Blue Grass Region. The country is well supplied with excellent turnpike roads leading into Cynthiana, and the precinct is intersected by the Kentucky Central Railroad, all of which tends to enhance the value of property, and at the same time afford the best means of moving the surplus stock and produce of the farmers.

The settlement of the territory now known as Cynthiana Precinct dates back beyond the memory of anybody living. Even the names of many of the pioneers are forgotten. A few more rolling years, and the last name will sink into oblivion, if not rescued and placed upon the pages of history. Like Cæsar, the pioneer "came, he saw, he conquered," and then sank to rest, and his name passes from the minds of men. Among the early settlers of this section, we may notice briefly Judge James R. Curry, who died last year at an advanced age; Gen. Josephus Perrin, father of Dr. Perrin, of Cynthiana—the latter already has passed his fourscore years; the Newells; Richard Henderson, a lawyer, who lived to a great age; William Lewis; Isaac Miller; —— Shawhan; the Frazer family; George Hamilton; Gavin Morrison; and a host of others now forgotten. Mr. Shawhan was the father of Joseph Shawhan. Mr. Lewis was from Maryland, and died many years ago. Mr. Morrison owned land in the precinct when the county was formed. Of the Frazer family, some of the second generation lived to be over eighty years of age, and are now dead. So the country settled up, and that portion now forming Cynthiana Precinct was occupied at an early date, perhaps nigh onto one hundred years ago.

The carving of a home in the wilderness of Kentucky a century ago was a herculean task, and one from which the most of us would shrink at the present day. Savages had not then relinquished their claim to the "dark and bloody ground," but were clinging to it with death-like tenacity. Bears and wolves and panthers were plenty, and roamed the forests everywhere. Provisions, except game, were scarce. None of the luxuries and but few of the comforts of life were to be had. For years, the pioneer's home was the most miserable of cabins, and his food and raiment were equally poor; and yet the pioneer was happy and enjoyed his wilderness life. The following, from a bard of the pioneer days, tells a pretty true story of pioneer life:

"The old log cabin, with its puncheon floor;
The old log cabin, with its clapboard door.
Shall we ever forget its moss-grown roof?
The old rattling loom, with its warp and woof?
The old stick chimney of 'cat and clay?'
The old hearthstone where we used to play?
No! we'll not forget the old wool wheel,
Nor the hank on the old count-reel.
We'll not forget how we used to eat
The sweet honeycomb with the fat deer meat.
We'll not forget how we used to bake
That best of bread, the old Johnny-cake."

There are doubtless those still living in Harrison County who can appreciate and realize the truth of the above lines, who remember the old log cabin, with its puncheon floor, etc., and the old spinning wheel and the loom. These rough times and these relics of a pioneer age, however, have passed away, and the country, where, a few years ago they reigned supreme, is now the cradle of plenty and the home of education, refinement and wealth.

The pioneer's attention is always directed to the importance of a mill, and one of his first cares is the erection of some kind of a rude institution to provide his family with the staff of life. Mills were built upon the numerous water-courses of this precinct in an early day, but of them we know little at the present time. Distilleries were also an early institution and operated almost as soon as mills, for our pioneer fathers thought they could not subsist without a little bitters for the stomach's sake, an idea that has been handed down through their descendants to the present day with most remarkable accuracy. At the present day there are a number of mills and distilleries in operation in the precinct.

The roads of Cynthiana Precinct are of a quality she may well be proud of. The first roads were but Indian trails and buffalo traces through the thick forests. As the whites came in and settled the lands, roads were made. The trees were chopped out of these trails and traces, so that wagons could pass. These were improved and "worked" from time to time, until finally the Macadam plan of road-making was introduced. The principal roads were macadamized, until at the present day, among the roads passing through the precinct and centering in the town of Cynthiana, are the following macadamized or turnpike roads: The Cynthiana & Oddville pike; Leesburg & Cynthiana pike; Ashbrook Mill pike; Indian Creek pike, Cynthiana & Raven Creek pike, the Millersburg pike, and perhaps others. The inauguration of the turnpike road system was the beginning of a new era in this section. It enabled the people to move their stock and produce with greater facility; made their property, especially their lands, more valuable, and was otherwise beneficial to them. Finally the Kentucky Central Railroad was built through the county—a measure that overflowed their cup of prosperity. But these matters are more particularly mentioned in another chapter.

The Gospel was introduced into the precinct with the pioneers themselves, and long before churches were built, services were held in their cabins, and when the weather permitted, in the groves. When no minister was to be had, some one in the habit of "praying in public," would read a chapter from the Bible—sing one of the "songs of Zion," and then lead in prayer to the Most High, for the preservation of life in the wilderness, and the benefits of health. As their numbers and wealth increased, church buildings were erected in different sections, and ministers employed. Just when or where the first church edifice was erected in Cynthiana Precinct is not now known, unless it was in the town of Cynthiana. As the church history of the precinct centers mostly in the city, it is more than probable that the first edifice intended as a temple of worship was erected there. Most of the church and educational history is given in the chapter devoted to the city.

Mount Hope Chapel (Methodist Episcopal South) is located on the Connersville pike, six miles from Cynthiana and one mile southeast of Connersville. It was organized in 1875 by Rev. S. S. Deering. It has now sixty-five members, a good frame building which cost about $1,800. Services are held every fourth Sunday, and Sunday school services when the weather is good. Mount Zion Church (Methodist Episcopal South), five miles from Cynthiana on the Oddville pike. There is a Presbyterian Church at Broadwell's Cross Roads, which is also five miles from Cynthiana.

Education has always received the hearty support of the people of Cynthiana Precinct, though the public schools have not received that attention their importance demands. Who taught the first school in the precinct, we are not able to say, neither where the first schoolhouse stood. Like the churches, they will be fully and thoroughly written up in the chapters on the town.

There are several hamlets in the precinct, but all put together would not make a small village. Lair's Station is merely a mill, a distillery, two or three houses, and a shipping point. It is on the Kentucky Central Railroad in the southern part of the precinct. Poindexter Post Office is on

Residence of T. J. Megibben Cynthiana, Ky.

the Licking River at the mouth of Sycamore Creek. Oddville Post Office is in the northeast part of the precinct, on the Cynthiana & Oddville pike, about ten miles from Cynthiana.

The history of the surrounding section so thoroughly clusters around the city of Cynthiana, that when the latter place is fully written, there is but little left to say of the precinct, beyond the fact of its mere settlement. We will drop the thread of its history here, to be resumed by Mr. Marshall in a new chapter.—*Perrin.*

CHAPTER VII.

CITY OF CYNTHIANA—LAID OUT AND CHARTERED—CYNTHIA AND ANNA—SOME OLD HOUSES—BRIDGES AND RIVER IMPROVEMENTS—FIRST SALE OF LOTS—COURTS, OFFICERS, ETC.—JUDGE REED'S PRAYER—THE CITY'S WAR EXPERIENCE.

"History is the essence of innumerable biographies."—*Carlyle.*

"Recollection is the only paradise from which we cannot be turned out."—*Richter.*

IN age, Cynthiana is almost venerable. Its charter is dated December 10, 1793, and in eleven years more, the town may celebrate its first centennial.

To appreciate the breadth of this period, we may remember that, in 1793, Isaac Shelby was then first Governor of Kentucky; George Washington was then first President of the United States; the population of the young Republic was then but three millions; George III was still on the throne of England; the first Napoleon had not then been heard of; John Wesley had been dead only two years; Alexander Campbell was then only five years old, and Henry Clay was a youth of sixteen, writing in a law office in Richmond, Va.

In 1793, it is true, ten years had elapsed since the formal close of the Revolutionary war, but Kentucky was not then a land of peace. The Indians yet disputed possession of the soil, and only eleven years before was fought the unfortunate battle of Blue Licks, and only two years before were made the still more disastrous campaigns of Gens. Harmar and St. Clair. Men whose posterity now live around us in ease or luxury participated in all these actions, and in many others of similar character. No steam vessels then traversed the rivers, no railway trains then flew from city to city, no telegraph annihilated distance. Estimated by events, the period since the foundation of our town seems great, for the mind can only appreciate the lapse of time as aided by a knowledge of the progress of affairs, and unless so aided, we do not clearly recognize the difference between one century and twenty centuries. But, on the other hand, when we see around us, as familiar acquaintances, the children, grandchildren, or direct descendants, in however remote degree, of actors in historic deeds, then the great chasm between the past and the present disappears; our forefathers then seem blended with our cotemporaries, and the three generations that have figured on the stage of human life since Kentucky became a State, all seem yet present and proper recipients of our love, our respect or criticism. Then, too, as we make companions of the pioneers of our land, we are enabled to properly estimate the mighty contrast between the two eras. If we now have all that which demonstrates the comforts and advantages of a high state of civilization, we are indebted for it to the men of old. Involuntarily, our thoughts linger in admiration and gratitude over the checkered story of the early life of our State, and when we address ourselves to the specific details of the history of our own neighborhood, we proudly and thankfully remember that the founders of Cynthiana were duly represented in the great affairs of their time. It was an age of action, not of theory; it was an age of deeds, not of words, and the old foresters, our ancestors, were equal to the occasion. Their diet may have been simple and scanty, their privileges, as we now count them, may have been few and insignificant, yet they do not so much deserve our sympathy as they merit undying honor and veneration; for they conquered the wilderness and prostrated forests till timber became a valuable commodity; they chastised the Indians till vengeance was satisfied; they plodded, plowed and planted till the far-famed blue grass region became a smiling reality, destined in the future to be the home of plenty and hospitality, of luxury and refinement; of fine cattle and renowned horses; of fair women and brave men; of orators, jurists and statesmen.

It suited the convenience of a few of these old worthies, in 1793, one year after Kentucky became a State, to establish a county seat on the South Fork of Licking, and they accordingly petitioned the Second General Assembly to give legal sanction to their choice, with the following result:

CHAPTER XXXV, ACTS OF THE SECOND GENERAL ASSEMBLY OF KENTUCKY.

An Act to establish a town on the lands of Robert Harrison, in the County of Bourbon, approved December 10, 1793.

WHEREAS, It is represented to the General Assembly that

one hundred and fifty acres of land lying on the east side of the South Fork of Licking, opposite the mouth of Gray's Run, the property of Robert Harrison, has been already laid off into a town, with convenient streets and alleys, the lots containing half an acre each ; therefore,

Be it enacted by the General Assembly, SECTION 1. That the said town be established by the name of Cynthiana, and the property thereof vested in Benjamin Harrison, Morgan Van Matre, Jeremiah Robinson, John Wall, Sr., and Henry Coleman, Gentlemen Trustees, who, or a majority of them, are, by virtue of this act, directed to sell the residue of lots in said town for the best price that can be had, giving three months' previous notice in the *Kentucky Gazette*, taking bond and sufficient security for the moneys or specialties arising from such sales, which shall be transferable to the said Robert Harrison or his legal representatives, and execute deeds in fee, as well to those who already have purchased lots, as to them who may purchase in future, obliging the purchasers to build on each lot within four years after such purchase, a house eighteen feet long and sixteen feet wide, with a brick or stone chimney thereto.

SEC. 2. *And be it further enacted*, That the said trustees or a majority of them shall have power to settle and determine all disputes concerning the bounds of said lots, and establish such rules for the regular building thereon, as to them shall seem convenient; and in case of death, resignation or other legal disability of any of the said trustees, it shall be lawful for the other trustees to supply such vacancy, and the trustees so elected shall be vested with the same power and authority as those particularly named in this act.

SEC. 3. If the purchaser of any lot shall fail to build thereon within the time before limited, the said trustees, or a majority of them, may, thereupon, enter such lot and sell the same again, and apply the money for the said town.

SEC. 4. *Provided, nevertheless*, The said trustees shall have power to alter the present form, plan or figure of said town, or to enter upon the lots set apart therein for public uses ; *Provided, however*, That nothing herein contained shall be so construed as to impair any contract that may have been entered into between the said Harrison and those who may have purchased lots of him previous to the passage of this act.

SEC. 5. *And be it further enacted*, That nothing herein contained shall prevent any person who may have a more legal or equitable claim to the land so laid off in said town than the said Robert Harrison, from recovering the moneys arising from the sales of said lots, from the said Robert Harrison, his heirs, etc.

SEC. 6. This act shall commence and be in force from the passage thereof.

By act of the same General Assembly, Harrison County was formed of parts of Bourbon and Scott Counties, and named in honor of Benjamin Harrison, Chairman of the first Board of Trustees, and Representative in the Legislature from Bourbon County. By the same authority, and at the same time, Cynthiana was made the county seat, and named in honor of Cynthia and Anna, two daughters of Robert Harrison, who had dedicated the ground now called the public square to the county, and who was the first owner of "one hundred and fifty acres of land opposite the mouth of Gray's Run." Tradition relates that Robert Harrison was a blacksmith, a good workman, a gay, healthy, rollicking son of the wilderness, just the man for the times ; and that his blooming young daughters, not then grown, were the favorites of all their father's customers and neighbors. The name Cynthiana, of course, gave general satisfaction. But Robert Harrison soon sold out his rights to the soil here, for his farm was already, in 1793, "laid off into convenient streets and alleys," and before Cynthia and Anna had reached womanhood, he removed to Portsmouth, Ohio. There he flourished in business, his family grew up, and one of the daughters, we are not informed which, married a successful young merchant of Philadelphia, and became an honored matron in a prosperous family of that city. We should gladly know more of those who gave name to our town, but further tradition, in this regard, is silent.

The new county seat, however, at once assumed its rank and privileges, and proceeded to exercise them. Within six months after its establishment by act of Assembly, the courts were sitting, county offices opened, the proper officers appointed, deed books, record books, minute books, etc., were ready to receive entries. The contents of these old books, yellow with age, are still preserved, and, we trust, will yet be preserved for the information of him who may undertake the part of city historian a hundred years hence. They contain many an item of interest which we have not space to recount.

Several houses had already been erected on the site of our town before 1793, it may be confidently inferred, for provision is made in the charter for the recognition of the validity of any sales of lots made by Robert Harrison, in anticipation of the act of Assembly. But it is not easy to identify many of these early buildings. Careful investigation, however, indicates the log house standing on the low bluff near the river, a few yards above the spring, its gable end looking to the west, built of buckeye timber, to be the very oldest now existing in the town limits. So thought Judge Curry and other citizens qualified to have an opinion. The old hut certainly has the appearance of a lonesome pioneer's lodge whence Indians might be watched.

In 1790, Dr. James McPheters, not a resident till 1795, built the weather-boarded log house standing west of the court house, on the corner of the alley and square. It has been successively, residence, court house, law office, printing office, and, perhaps church. We are assured that in this house Guthrie's once popular old arithmetic was printed by Adam Keenan and Schrawyer, the only text-book on its subject generally used for many years in this part of the State. In this old house also, Henry Clay defended a fellow named House, accused of murder, in 1806. At the close of Clay's brilliant speech, House's wife, anything but a beauty, jumped up and kissed the blushing orator (he was then only twenty-nine), in the presence of the densely packed throng of spectators.

In 1805, William Moore built the brick house on the corner of Pleasant and Main streets, now the residence of William Turtoy.

In 1806, the frame building on Main street, opposite the court house, was built, now the property of Henry Warfield.

In 1807, Gavin Morrison built the brick house on Lot 16 of the old plat, now the residence of Judge Boyd.

In 1809, the large brick building now known as Peck's Flouring-Mill, recently purchased by Musselman & Riggs, on the bank of the river above the bridge, was built for a woolen manufactory. It seems to have been used as such till 1818, when Gen. Josephus Perrin moved his cotton-spinning establishment into it, from the corner of Walnut and Penn streets, the site recently of Aaron Diltz's flouring-mill, and continued the business until about 1825. For many years previous to 1875, it stood unoccupied.

In 1812, Dr. Andrew McMillan built the two-story brick, now called the Faerber House. In 1820, Alexander Downing built the finest residence then in town, on the corner of the square and Market place. It was burned in 1835. About 1820, also, Enoch Worthen built the two-story brick, called now the Whitaker House. Gov. Desha, it is stated by old citizens, bought this property of Worthen, and sold, about 1838, to Jeremiah Bassett. The south end of this building is now occupied by Miss Walter's Select School.

In 1819, the old brick house at the entrance of the bridge was built by Robert Patterson. In this house was born the jolly, good-hearted Bob Rankin, well known a few years ago to the traveling public as the popular "host" of the Rankin House, now the Smith House.

For seventeen years after the act of 1793, the river was crossed by ford or ferry only, the ferry being owned and attended by Thomas and Robert Hogg. The first bridge was built in 1810, by Andrew Porter, grandfather of W. W. Trimble; a second was built in 1817, at the same place; a third, still, at the same point, was built in 1835, or 1837, by Greenup Remington, and this, after forty-seven years' service, bids fair to last an indefinite period longer. About 1820, a bridge was built by John Bruce lower down the river, opposite the Howk plantation, and where Pleasant street intersects the river. This bridge was carried away by high water in 1828; two adventurous young men, William Bruce and William Oder, were on the bridge when it gave way, but were rescued after having received a pretty "close call." The bridge at this point has never been rebuilt.

In 1818, Gen. Josephus Perrin, father of Dr. George H. Perrin, superintended a survey of South Licking, from Cynthiana to the Ohio River, with a view to its navigation by means of lock and dam. Should the navigation have been found practicable, the landing here was expected to be at or near the foot of Pleasant street, for this, it was thought, would be the principal thoroughfare of the town. The pavement of Pleasant street was, therefore, extended toward the river, and a Mrs. McCann, as the name is remembered by an old citizen, was compelled by the Trustees of the town to sell, or permit to be sold, her lot on the corner of Pleasant and Race streets, for taxes to pay for her share of the pavement, the taxes being all she ever received for her lot.

About the same time, and probably looking to the navigation of the Licking as an event in the near future, Judge J. R. Curry built a fine $5,000 mansion on a beautifully situated lot of three acres, on the west side of the river, nearly opposite the foot of Pleasant street. In 1835, Andrew Moore, who had then owned the place for some years, offered it to Robert Jones for $1,500. While Jones was considering this offer, the house was burned. Meanwhile the navigation of the river, even with lock and dam, was found to be impracticable. The expectations of Pleasant street declined, the pavement proceeded no further in the direction of the river, nor was it thought worth while to restore the bridge at its terminus after it was swept away in 1828.

Less than three months after the act of establishment, the first Court of Quarter Sessions was convened on the 4th of March, 1794, at the house of Morgan Van Matre, by the magistrates, Benjamin Harrison, Hugh Miller and John Wall. The first Circuit Court was organized on the 7th of February, 1803, John Allen, Hugh Miller and John Wall, being the Judges, three presiding officers then, and, for years afterward, occupying the bench both in the Court of Quarter Sessions and in the Circuit Court.

William Ardery was the first Sheriff, appointed at the same time, 1794, as the three Magstrates of the Court of Quarter Sessions. At the end of two years, the oldest of the three Magistrates became, as a rule, the Sheriff, but Ardery continued Sheriff for several terms, by what authority does not clearly appear. The High Sheriff, rarely, or never, himself, rode in the execution of the duties of his office. He farmed out his office, that is, he sold at public auction to the highest bidder, at the court house steps, the privilege of collecting the county revenues. This custom continued till the adoption of the new Constitution in 1850.

William Ardery farmed out the office for the first time to James Patton in 1794. At this time, and till the adoption of the new Constitution in 1850, the courts appointed their own Clerks, and William Moore was thus appointed the first Clerk of both courts, that is, of the Court of Quarter Sessions, which may be considered our present County Court, and also Clerk of the Circuit Court. The Clerk was allowed to appoint his sons as his successors, and so the office of County and Circuit Court Clerk was held by William Moore, and by Andrew and Henry Coleman Moore, his sons, till 1832, a period of nearly forty years.

Thomas B. Woodyard succeeded the Moores, and held the office till 1837, Andrew Moore also still holding one of the clerkships. In 1842, Philip Brown was appointed Clerk of the Circuit Court; soon resigned, and was then appointed to hold both offices. James R. Curry succeeded Brown as Circuit Court Clerk, and Perry Wherritt succeeded Brown as County Clerk. J. S. Boyd followed as Circuit Court Clerk, and Charles T. Wilson became County Clerk in 1861, Perry Wherritt having been arrested for political reasons. Then followed James F. Ware, A. J. Beale, and, finally, W. W. Longmoor, the present incumbent in the office of Circuit Court Clerk. Perry Wherritt was re-elected County Clerk in 1866, and still holds that office.

We make room here for a few items of great interest, supplied through the kindness of Judge Boyd, from the records of the Circuit Court Clerk's office:

"Henry Clay, on the 7th day of September, 1801, produced his license to practice law, and took the oath required by law, and was admitted as attorney of the Quarter Sessions Court of Harrison County."

On the 6th day of June, 1806, there is an order in the handwriting of Mr. Clay, entered in the order book of the Circuit Court in said county, in the celebrated case of the Commonwealth of Kentucky *versus* Adam House and Andrew House, indicted for the murder of Thomas Mefford. The Houses were ultimately cleared, though the first trial went against them in spite of the mighty Clay.

"At the Circuit Court of said county, held on the 7th day of February, 1803, being the day on which the said court was organized, Richard Henderson, William Garrard, Thomas Arnold, Jesse Bledsoe, Robert Trimble, James H. McLaughlin and Richard M. Johnson presented their licenses, and took the oath required by law, and were admitted as attorneys at law in said court."

The first recorded deed is dated the 1st day of April, 1794, made by James Lemmon to Alexander Adger, conveying to Adger, "for fifty pounds sterling" (the decimal currency was not yet in much vogue), one hundred acres of land lying "on the waters of Townsend, a branch of the South Fork of Licking." Even as late as 1798, Record Book "A" exhibits the following entry, showing the usual reckoning of accounts to be in sterling money: "Harrison Court of Quarter Sessions: William Moore, Clerk of this court, produced an account on criminal proceedings to the amount of one pound, eighteen shillings and four pence, which, being examined and allowed by the court, is ordered to be certified to the Auditor of Public Accounts."

On the 4th of March, 1795, the original Trustees of the town, Benjamin Harrison, Morgan Van Matre, Jeremiah Robinson, John Wall and Henry Coleman, sold to Hugh Stevenson Lot No. 42 of the "Old Platt," the ground now occupied by Marks McCabe; also, at the same time, Lot No. 15 to Benjamin Harrison, now occupied by William S. Wall; also Lot 29 to Robert McBride, now the residence of William A. Cook; also to John McLaughlin Lot 75, now the site of the Christian Church; also to Lewis Marshall, noted scholar, critic, teacher, and eccentric, then resident in Bourbon County, but never a citizen of Harrison, Lots 69, 83, 84, 85, 86, 99 and 100, now the property of Mrs. Frazer, near the present residence of Henry C. Nebel; also to William Rankin the half-acre Lot 25, now the site of the Faerber House, on Main street.

In 1799, the Trustees sold to William Mountjoy Lots 18 and 19; and in 1806, to Gavin Morrison, Lots 16 and 28; all of the land now forms part of the ground on which Judge Boyd's residence is situated. The residence was built by Gavin Morrison. The Judge's present limits include all of Lots 16 and 20, and about half of 17 and 19, the original purchasers of the whole being William Mountjoy and Gavin Morrison.

In 1796, the Trustees sold to Robert Hinkson Lot 34, now occupied by the residence of William Turtoy.

We are indebted to William Garnett, Sr., for the brief notice of Hugh Newell, one of Harrison County's most highly esteemed and admired public men, and which is as appropriate in this connection as elsewhere. He was a brilliant natural orator:

"Hugh Newell was a citizen of Harrison for eighty years, and in all that time, with the exception of the years from 1861 to 1867, when he lived near Colemansville, he lived on the same place which his father settled.

"The schools in the days of his boyhood were what would not now be tolerated. The teachers were not unfrequently men of no qualifications. The books used were whatever volume the boys could find at home. Some read lessons in the life of Gen. Francis Marion, others in the New Testament, and some in works of biography or romance. The paper used was not ruled until after it was bought and sewed into a copy-book—the boys ruling it themselves with pencils hammered out of bullets into the shape of horse-shoe nails. The schoolhouses were rude log structures, with an open fire-place in one end. The seats were rough benches without backs. The writing-desk was a long board, supported by legs, and fastened against the wall the whole length of one side of the room, while a long window, one pane of glass high, let light in upon it. The schools were taught by the quarter—the teacher boarding around with his patrons—the three winter months being generally the months in which the larger boys and girls attended. Reading, writing and a smattering of arithmetic were the branches taught. Such were the schools that Hugh Newell, for three or perhaps four quarters, attended.

"In those days, the produce of the country often found its market in New Orleans. Flat-boats would be built and loaded on the Licking, and go out in a rise of the river. At New Orleans the boat and cargo would be sold and paid for in silver dollars, which the boatmen would wrap up in their blankets and fetch home on their backs, making the journey from New Orleans to Cynthiana on foot, within from thirty-five to forty days. His father built a boat at Ecklar's Mill, on the South Licking, and loaded it with flour and bacon, which he took to New Orleans, and returned overland through the Chickasaw country, home.

"Hugh Newell was in the war of 1812. He served a six months' campaign in Capt. William Ellis's company of Kentucky Rifles, in Col. John Allen's regiment. The company was raised August 12, 1812, and participated in the battles of the River Raisin, fought January 18 and 22, 1813, in the vicinity of Detroit, Mich. In the battle of the 18th, the British and Indians were beaten. In the battle of the 22d, the Americans were defeated. Col. Allen, and many prominent officers lost their lives in the engagement.

"A deep snow had fallen, making the country around a trackless waste. Hugh Newell attempted to wend his way back to Fort Defiance and escape being captured by the Indians. After wandering, as he thought, in the right direction, he, on the evening of the third day after the battle, found himself at a house near the battle-field, and within sight of the spot where our wounded and prisoners had been massacred. A woman of English birth, who had married a Frenchman, met him at the door. She saw that he was an American, and told him he could not stay there, as the Indians would burn her house and murder her family if he was seen, but urged him to go to the barn near by and she would fetch him food. She offered him her moccasins to wear, so that his tracks to the barn, if seen by the enemy, would excite no suspicion. He found the moccasins too small for his feet, but went to the barn where the woman brought him something to eat. On the eighth day after the defeat, he reached Fort Defiance. In those eight days, he suffered much from cold and hunger. Along the route he found wheat sheaves at deserted settlements and subsisted upon wheat rubbed out in his hands.

"It was in the year 1834 that he became a candidate for a seat in the Lower House of the Legislature. From that time until the year 1867, he was in active political life. He served many years in the Lower House, was four years in the Senate, and was a member of the Constitutional Convention. During the whole course of his political career, he was never but twice defeated. He was always an uncompromising Democrat of the Jeffersonian school. His colleagues at different times, were Whitehead Coleman, Dr. Innis, Clark Perrin, John O. Beasman, Lucius Desha, Joseph Shawhan, and others not now remembered. He served with such men as Thomas F. Marshall, Garrett Davis, John Speed Smith, Richard M. Johnson, Ben Harden and John L. Helm.

"In the deliberative bodies of which he was from time to time a member, he encountered in debate the first minds in the State, and where he failed to win the points at discussion, he was sure to render the victory of his adversary fruitless. His encounter with ex-Gov. Helm on the school question attracted much attention, and gained for him a reputation co-extensive with the State as an original thinker and powerful speaker.

"In the days of his best manhood, he was indeed a most effective speaker. Within the strong grasp of his mind a mass of facts yielded as metal in the crucible. And here was the secret of the wonderful power which he possessed, of solving, by a single bold expression, the most perplexing problems. And while the scholarly adornments of rhetoric were never his, few men excelled him in profound feeling, in clear conception and forcible utterance. Always being first convinced himself, he seldom failed to carry conviction to the breasts of others. His knowledge of men was vastly greater than his knowledge of books, yet his fund of information bearing upon the political issues of the day was both great and astonishing. He was ever a man of progressive sentiments, and had done much even at the sacrifice of his own, for the advancement of the material interests of his county and State."

The first courts were held in private dwellings, as for instance, at the house of Morgan Van Matre, in 1794. It is not easy to fix precisely the date of the erection of the first court house belonging to the county, but it must have been before 1810; and there is reason to believe that, such as it was, the structure must have been of very humble pretensions.

The count house square, as laid out in 1793, extended from Pike to Main streets, this occupying nearly twice its present limits. In 1816, it was determined to sell, if authority could be had, the north part of this fine square, in order to assist in defraying the expense of a new court house. In the acts of the Twenty-Fourth General Assembly, Chapter 334, page 546, we find an "act entitled an act authorizing the county of Harrison to sell a part of their public ground, approved February 3, 1816." In April following, the County Court appointed William Brown, Perry Crosthwait, James Finley, Thomas Holt, James Coleman, Charles Redmon and William K. Wall, Commissioners to "lay off the north end of the public ground" into city lots for sale, and to hold the money received therefor, in trust, for the designated purpose, namely, to assist in paying for a new court house.

These Commissioners accordingly laid off the north end of the square, and about May, 1816, sold to Alexander Downing and William Lamme, Lot 133 for $1,550 ; to David Lamme, Lot 134, for $725 ; to Bela Metcalf, Lot 135 for $690, Lot 137 being reserved by the commissioners till November following, "to prevent sacrifice," when they sold this also to James and Bela Metcalf for $950, the total proceeds amounting to $3,915.

At the same April term, the County Court issued the following mandate, which we copy from Record Book "C," page 140 : "April Court, 1816, ordered that a new court house be erected on the publick ground in Cynthiana, to stand upon the foundation (site) of the present (1816) court house, and such ground as will be adequate to a building ——— feet in front, fronting Main street, and ——— feet in depth westwardly, and also that a convenient Clerk's office be erected on said publick ground, at a suitable place, and that Gresham Forrest, William Brown, William Moore, James Kelley and Thomas Holt, be appointed Commissioners who, or a majority of them, shall consult skillful workmen, and prepare a well-digested plan for said building, having care that the court house be made sufficiently spacious to provide for the growing wealth and population of this county, that the building be projected on a neat and durable plan of architecture without any needless extravagance of ornament, and well contrived for the comfort and convenience of our different courts ; that they also digest a plan for a Clerk's office to contain two apartments, fire-proof, and report the plans and probable expenditure to be made for said buildings to the next term of this court."

The "expenditure" was reported, but only filed, not apparently recorded, and could not readily be found. Indeed, without the kind aid of Judge Boyd, we should not have been able to give this authoritative explanation of the division of the public square, and its contraction to about half its original dimensions. The same court appointed William Brown, William Moore, James Kelley and Thomas Holt a building committee for the intended new court house. At the May term, 1816, this committee reported a plan to build of stone, four feet above the ground, the rest of the wall to be of brick, a chimney at each corner, the first story to be twenty feet high, the second proportional ; covered with hip roof, two flights of stairs to second story, and a clerk's office, also to be built, not worth while to describe here. After some deliberation, a third story was added, and for years used as a church, as a ballroom and assembly-room, still remembered as the scene of the gayety and fashion of the period. The building was surmounted by a lofty spire over the center, had the usual jury rooms, and some say, was a more sightly edifice than the present one. The Clerk's offices, however, were accommodated in separate, small buildings, situated within the inclosure of the court house ground. Here, also, on the same ground, was the log jail which stood in the court house yard, almost within reach of the Judge's voice, till 1844, when it was removed to its present situation on Pike street. The present jail was built of stone, by a Mr. Brannock, and the jailer's residence adjoining was built of brick, by a Mr. Smith. The second court house was burned on the 24th of January, 1851, having caught fire from a stable on Pike street, owned by A. J. West. None of the county books or papers were lost.

The present court house, the third since the establishment of the town, was built by John Huddleston, in 1853, at a cost of about $12,000, $6,000 or $7,000 less, probably, than a similar work would now cost. E. Wyatt Martin, who was accidentally drowned a year or two since, hauled the rock-hewn door sills and lintels from Cincinnati on wagons over dirt roads. It contains in the second story a fine auditorium and two jury rooms, and on the ground floor the Circuit Court Clerk's office, consisting of two large apartments, the office of County Clerk similarly well accommodated, the office of the County Judge, the Sheriff's office, and two law offices, which are rented and always in demand. The building is surmounted by an imposing dome, which is furnished with an eight-day town clock. It faces the four cardinal points, and its bell may be heard a mile distant or more. It was a fine timepiece ten years ago, but of late it has not been so reliable. In 1877, the court house was repaired at an expense of $1,800. In 1881, the Judge's desk was removed from the west side of the auditorium to the north side, at a cost of $150.

In connection with the account of court houses, our readers may be interested and gratified to see the following strange entry which appears on the first page of the Harrison County Common Docket, under date November 27, 1851. It is a prayer, written by the once well-known and favorite Judge Walker Reed, who died a few months after the above date, in Maysville, Ky. His memory will ever be dear to posterity, for he was an upright and most kind-hearted man, a little eccentric, but yet a just and learned Judge:

Judge Reed's Prayer.—"Inasmuch as we had resolved to join this day in prayer with the good people of Harrison, according to the proclamation of our Governor, and our intention has been frustrated by the coming of strangers—lawyers from a distance, who are half through the will case of Redmon, and they have promised to pray as soon as we get through—we will pray as we set, and they argue to jury for the prosperity of the State, for the health of its people, for the good of all the States, and the continuance of the Union; for the spread of the glorious Gospel, and for the conversion of the whole world to its sublime truths; that peace on earth and good will among men may prevail; that our weapons of war may be converted into utensils for husbandry, and that all disputes in future may be settled by Congress of nations, and that we no longer desire war, or learn the art of destroying nations. We pray for our enemies also, and forgive them as we ask forgiveness of our Father in Heaven. And all this in the name of our Lord and Savior Jesus Christ. Amen.

"We pray as we set in court, as speeches are being made to the jury, and all the jury may pray, all the people may, and I have no doubt have prayed, and thus fulfilled the saying, 'Praise the Lord at all times, and give thanks for everything, for the earth is the Lord's and the fulness thereof.' And 'a soldier or private man can pray in the ditch or in the field as sincerely as in a pulpit.'—*Sterne.* Yes, and we should pray in the house and out of it, by the wayside, and in coming and going.

"And the truth is that the *humble* man is never heard for much speaking.

> 'God reads the language of a silent tear
> And sighs are incense from a heart sincere.'

"'God have mercy on me a sinner,' is better said to our Savior than to thank Him that we are better than other men, that we have paid our tithes, etc. Yes, humility is a great Christian virtue, and if found ever in a man celebrated above his fellows for wisdom, renders him more and more worthy even among those who possess it not. I have written more than I intended. I only meant to say that I would have went to church, and united with the people in prayer but for the case under trial, and even then I left it to the jury, and they voted to go on with the trial.

"November 27, 1857."

Cynthiana's War Experience.—Since the early years of the present century, war had been known to our citizens only by hearsay and history. It is true large contingents had been furnished by the town and vicinity for the Indian wars in the Northwest, and in the war of 1812, as also for the Mexican war of 1846–47. Many a citizen-soldier had returned alive and well from these military expeditions, and had always had willing audiences to the story of the battle of the Thames, of Buena Vista, of Cerro Gordo, or of Molino del Rey, till, as matters of history, all were familiar with them. But the scenes of all these were far off, and, therefore, though recent, they shared almost the dimness of the antique. The very monuments, raised in our midst to the memory of the lost, partook rather of the ideal and historic than of the real and present.

But in the late conflict between the States, the realities of war were brought before our people with terrible clearness. Battle and fire raged in the streets. Men, women and children had to take care of themselves as they could, without regard to property, for life was at stake. The loss of life, however, was not great in either of the two battles of Cynthiana, though nearly half the property of the town was destroyed in the second engagement, that of June 11, 1864. The burnt districts have been well rebuilt, even better than before; but some of the losers have never recovered from the destruction of that July, 1864, and seemingly never can, if we may judge from the attitude of Government toward war claims, as indicated by the last report of the Congressional Committee on such matters.

Eye-witnesses of both the battles of Cynthiana say the account of them is so accurate, though not quite complete, in Collins' History of Kentucky, that we copy the entire description from that valuable work. One important correction is made by T. A. Frazer, who remembers that the Confederate Col. Martin, then suffering from a previous wound, accepted the hospitality of his house the night before the action of the 12th of June, 1864. The Colonel stated, on retiring to rest, that battle was impending, and that he should probably be called up before morning. He actually was sent for by his command about 3 o'clock in the following morning, and at once proceeding to his position, the battle began. This proves that the Confederate command was not surprised. No doubt they were "at breakfast," but this does not necessarily imply that they were surprised, for old soldiers will eat in the midst of a fight if they have a chance.

First Battle of Cynthiana.—Says Collins: "On July 17,

1862, the Confederate Gen. John H. Morgan, with a force of 816 strong when he started, nine days before, upon this first Kentucky raid, attacked the Federal forces at Cynthiana, nearly five hundred strong (mainly home guards), under Col. John J. Landram, who, after a brave resistance, were overpowered and defeated, and the town captured. The Federal pickets were surprised and captured, or driven in; and before the commander had time to dispose his force, the Confederates commenced shelling the town, producing a wild consternation among the inhabitants. Capt. William H. Glass, of the Federal Artillery, occupied the public square, from which point he could command most of the roads. Another force took position on the Magee Hill road south of the town, along which the Confederates were approaching. A third detachment was instructed to hold the bridge on the west side of the town, toward which Morgan's main force was pouring. Capt. Glass opened on Morgan's battery, which was planted on an eminence a quarter of a mile distant, between the Leesburg and Fair Ground Turnpikes. The Confederates were now approaching by every road and street, and deployed as skirmishers through every field, completely encircling the Federals. Their battery on the hill having ceased its fire, Capt. Glass, with grape and canister, swept Pike street from one end to the other. By this time, the contestants were engaged at every point. The fighting was terrific. The Federals commenced giving way. The force at the bridge, after a sharp fight, was driven back, and a Confederate cavalry charge made through the streets. A portion of the Federals made a stand at the railroad depot. A charge upon the Confederate battery at the Licking bridge was repulsed, and the Confederates in turn charged upon the force at the depot, while another detachment was pouring deadly fire from the rear, about one hundred and twenty-five yards distant. It was here that Col. Landram was wounded, and Thomas Ware, one of the oldest citizens, Jesse Currant, Thomas Rankin, Capt. Lafe Wilson, and others were killed, besides a number wounded. Unable to stand the concentrated fire, the handful of Federals that were left commenced a precipitate retreat. The Seventh Kentucky Cavalry posted north of the town to hold the Oddville road were soon overpowered, and compelled to surrender. Three-fourths of the Federal force had now been killed, wounded or captured, and the Confederates held undisputed possession. The prisoners were marched into town and lodged in the upper room of the court house, and their paroles made out and signed that night.

"*Second Battle of Cynthiana.*—" On Saturday, June 11, 1864, Gen. Morgan marched a second time upon Cynthiana, defeated and captured the forces under the command of Gen. E. H. Hobson. The first of this series of engagements took place early in the morning, between the One Hundred and Sixty-eighth Ohio Infantry, commanded by Col. Conrad Garis, and Morgan's whole command, about 1,200 strong. The Federals were soon overpowered, and fell back to the depot buildings (where Col. Berry fell, mortally wounded), and thence to Rankin's unfinished hotel; others retreated to the court house. The Confederates, following closely, charged into these several places, causing the utmost consternation among the inhabitants. While the battle was raging, a stable opposite the Rankin Hotel caught or was set on fire, and the terror of the flames added greatly to the alarm. Across the river, west of the town, another battle began between Gen. Hobson, commanding the One Hundred and Seventy-first Ohio, and a detachment of Confederates. This is known as the battle at "Keller's Bridge," one mile north of Cynthiana, which had been destroyed by the Confederates on the Thursday previous, to prevent the sending of troops along the railroad. The trains which had conveyed the One Hundred and Seventy-first Ohio to this point were backed down the road two miles for safety, but were there thrown from the track by the Confederates and burned. Upon being disembarked, the men were supplied with ammunition, and proceeded to eat their breakfast. Suddenly their quiet was disturbed by the rattle of musketry at Cynthiana, telling that hot work was going on there between the One Hundred and Sixty-eighth Ohio and the Confederates, and in a few minutes the fields around themselves were alive with Confederates. A volley of musketry was poured in upon them by a squad of Confederates massed behind the fence of a clover field. Gen. Hobson was now completely surrounded. The Confederates displayed great activity in firing, and considerable skill in keeping under cover from the fire of the Federal troops. The fight continued about five hours, the loss on both sides unusually heavy. Gen. Morgan, who was in Cynthiana when the fight at the bridge commenced, arrived on the field at 9 A. M., with re-enforcements, and with these the line was drawn still closer, and Gen. Hobson was finally compelled to accept the flag of truce and Morgan's conditions of surrender—that the private property of the troops should be respected, and the officers retain their side arms. The Federal forces were drawn up along the pike, their arms stacked and burned, and they were marched through Cynthiana, a mile east, to a grove, where they found the other Federal forces who had been in the fight at Cynthiana, prisoners like themselves. After resting an hour, the prisoners were marched three miles north, on the Oddville pike, where they passed Saturday night. Early on Sunday morning, with the first announcement of the approach of

OLD HOMESTEAD

CATTLE BARN

EDGEWATER DISTILLERY T.J. MEGIBBEN, PROP. NEAR CYNTHIANA, KY.

Burbridge, came an order from Morgan to the guard over the Federal prisoners to start them north, which was done, and that, too, on the double quick, Morgan's main force, pursued by Burbridge, following at a distance of a few miles. This forced march brought them to Claysville, twelve miles northeast of Cynthiana, where they were halted, drawn up in line, paroled, and allowed to depart. While the battles were in progress on Saturday, the fire continued to rage, notwithstanding vigorous efforts to stop it by the citizens. By 12 o'clock, all the business portion of the town was consumed, with most of the contents. The fire, commencing at Rankin's stable, swept on to the West House, burning all the buildings; thence across to Broadwell's corner, and down to Isaac T. Martin's store; thence across to Dr. Broadwell's buildings, to the jail, including that and the adjoining buildings, twenty-seven in all, the most valuable in the place. On Sunday morning, the 12th of June, the day after the two battles above described, Gen. Burbridge, with a strong force, fell upon Morgan's men at Cynthiana, while they were at breakfast. Fatigued as they were by the previous day's operations, which resulted in the defeat and capture of two distinct Federal forces, the Confederates were not in condition to withstand the shock of a fresh body of troops. Burbridge with his cavalry was enabled to flank them, and thus turn their lines; while his infantry in the center advanced steadily, forcing them back on the town. The fighting commenced on the Millersburg pike, about one mile east of Cynthiana. But the Confederates, unable to hold out against the rapid and determined advance of superior numbers of fresh troops, supported by artillery, soon gave way, and by the time they reached Cynthiana were in full retreat, and the retreat a rout. One by one they fell back through the town, crossed the river, and followed the Raven Creek pike. Thus ended the last battle that was fought at Cynthiana in the war for Southern independence."

Lists of the losses of property in this action are subjoined; the arguments supporting the claims of citizens for just and legal compensation by Government, the adverse report of the Committee on War Claims, and finally, the resolution of the Kentucky General Assembly. This resolution is an implied remonstrance against the disregard by Government, of what is felt to be a just and legal claim.

Mr. Carlisle, on leave, introduced in the House of Representatives November 5, 1877, the following bill, which was read twice, referred to the Committee on War Claims, and ordered to be printed:

A Bill for the relief of certain citizens of Cynthiana, Ky., whose property was destroyed by fire on the 11th day of June, 1864.

Be it enacted by the Senate and House of Representatives of the United States of America, in Congress assembled, That out of any money in the treasury, not otherwise appropriated, there is hereby appropriated, and ordered to be paid to the following citizens of Cynthiana, in the State of Kentucky, the following sums for and on account of property destroyed by fire on the 11th day of June, 1864, to wit:

To James J. Parish, the sum of $1,600; Elizabeth Oxley, administratrix of Lawson Oxley (deceased), $16,555; Greenup Remington, $10,000; W. W. Trimble, $2,500; Henry Johnson (colored), $1,100; Charles A. Webster, $18,350; Francis M. Gray, $4,100; James S. Frizell, $12,680; Frank Box, $6,722; Ellen English, administratrix of Thomas English (deceased), $2,000; Thomas A. Frazer and Henry E. Shawhan, $7,000; Susan Tomlinson, $4,000; John L. Magee, $18,000; Greenup Remington, administrator of Eliza Bell (deceased), $3,000; Herman Rohs, $200; David A. Givens, $15,747; Isaac N. Webb, $1,000; James E. Dickey, $713.50; John Quinlan, $120; William L. Northcutt, $21,570.75; John Newton Smith, $5,113; John Newton Smith (guardian), $2,000; Heinrich C. Nebel, $653; John Bruce, $1,372; Mary A. Hall, $420; Eliza T. Rankin, administratrix of T. R. Rankin (deceased), $6,563; Joseph W. McIntosh, $31,730; Robert C. Wherritt, $32,000; F. X. C. Nott, administrator of Adeliza Murphy (deceased), $4,000.

The said payments to be in full satisfaction and discharge of all claims and demands by the said parties, or their heirs or representatives, for, or on account of the loss or destruction of their property, at the time of the attack made upon said city of Cynthiana by the Confederate forces, under the command of Gen. John H. Morgan, on the 11th day of June, 1864, during which the United States forces, under command of Col. Conrad Garis, of the One Hundred and Sixty-eighth Regiment Ohio Volunteer Infantry, took shelter in the houses of said citizens, thereby causing them and their contents to be set on fire and destroyed by the enemy.

The grounds upon which certain citizens of Cynthiana, Ky., whose property was destroyed by fire on the 11th day of June, 1864, claim relief, are as follows:

On said 11th day of June, 1864, Col. Conrad Garis, of the One Hundred and Sixty-eighth Regiment Ohio Infantry Volunteers, took shelter in said city by placing his command in houses to resist an attack of the then approaching enemy, under command of Gen. John H. Morgan, and during the fight which ensued, the city was set on fire by the enemy to dislodge the Federal forces, resulting in the destruction of the houses and merchandise of said claimants, as set forth by the allegations of the petitioners, and clearly sustained by the evidence submitted, which is also corroborated by the affidavit of Col. Conrad Garis and others.

There is no doubt that said property was taken by the officer and absolutely used by him as a shelter or fortification to protect the lives of his men from the bullets of the enemy, and that said taking, use, and occupancy resulted in the destruction of the houses and merchandise.

Now, the question arises, is this a legitimate claim against the Government? I answer that it is. And to sustain my answer, I beg to refer to the judicial authorities, the text writers, the Constitution, and the legislative precedents bearing upon the subject.

In Grant vs. The United States, 1st N. & H. Reports, the court says:

"It may safely be assumed as the settled and fundamental law of Christian and civilized States that governments are bound to make just indemnity to the citizen or subject whenever private property is taken for the public good, convenience or safety."

The Cynthiana property was taken for the public good, convenience and safety, and while thus occupied it was destroyed, and lost by said claimants.

In the case of Mitchell vs. Harmony, reported in 13 How., 115, Chief Justice Taney delivering the opinion of the court, says:

"Private property may be taken by a military commander to prevent it from falling into the hands of the enemy, or for the purpose of converting it to the use of the public; but the danger must be immediate and impending, or the necessity urgent for the public service, such as will not admit of delay, and where the action of the civil authority would be too late in providing the means which the occasion calls for."

And again he says on page 134:

"There are, without doubt, occasions on which private property may lawfully be taken possession of or destroyed to prevent it from falling into the hands of the public enemy, and also where a military officer charged with a particular duty may impress private property into the public service or take it for public use. Unquestionably, in such cases, the Government is bound to make full compensation to the owner."

Again he says, page 135:

"In deciding upon this necessity, however, the state of the facts as they appeared to the officer at the time he acted, must govern the decision; for he must necessarily act upon the information of others, as well as his own observation. And if, with such information as he had a right to rely upon, there is reasonable grounds for believing that the peril is immediate and menacing or the necessity urgent, he is justified in acting upon it; and the discovery afterward that it was false or erroneous will not make him a trespasser."

All the evidence on file points directly to the fact that the city of Cynthiana was taken by Col. Conrad Garis to prevent it from falling into the hands of the public enemy, and that the houses were converted to the use of the public and absolutely used to protect the lives of his men. The danger was immediate and impending, and the necessity was urgent for the public service, and was such as would not have admitted of delay.

This presents a case where private property was impressed into the public service and taken for public use, resulting in its destruction; and under the opinion of the court, as delivered by Chief Justice Taney, the Government is clearly bound to make full compensation to the owners.

The case of Mitchell vs. Harmony was brought up by a writ of error from the Circuit Court of the United States for the Southern District of New York. David D. Mitchell was an officer of the army, and was sued in an action for trespass by Manuel H. Harmony, and the jury found a verdict for plaintiff for $90,806.44, for which, with costs amounting to $5,048.94, the court gave judgment amounting to $95,855.38. The property of the plaintiff was taken by military authority. As a consequence of the taking, the goods fell into the hands of the enemy. The courts held that the taking was unnecessary, and, therefore, required the officer in command to make compensation for the loss of the goods. But Congress held that, inasmuch as the officer acted in good faith, and for what he believed to be the interest of the Government, the Government ought to protect him against the consequences of his misfortune. Congress, therefore, assumed the defense of the officer before the Supreme Court, and, when judgment was finally rendered against him, assumed the payment of said $95,855.38.

This is what I term a legislative precedent, and respectfully ask it to be compared with the Cynthiana claims.

Was the taking, use, and occupancy authorized? The rule which will justify the taking of private property for defense or destruction is well settled, and rests upon the same principle which gives to the individual the right, in the case of aggression to life or limb, to take the life of the aggressor. In either case, it is the necessity, seeming or real, which gives the right and justifies the individual or officer. The engagement so swiftly followed the taking, makes complete the urgent and immediate necessity of the taking, use and occupation of said houses.

Mr. William Whiting, in discussing the subject of war claims with direct reference to the liability of the United States, growing out of the late war, writes with extreme caution, but even he asserts that—

"If the private property of loyal citizens, inhabitants of loyal States, is appropriated by our military forces for the purpose of supplying our armies and to aid in prosecuting hostilities against a public enemy, the Government is bound to give a reasonable compensation therefor to the owner."

Again he says:

"When individuals are called upon to give up what is their own for the advantage of the community, justice requires that they shall be fairly compensated for it; otherwise public burdens would be shared unequally."

The Cynthiana property was taken to aid in prosecuting hostilities against a public enemy. Said claimants were called upon to give up what was their own for the advantage of the community. Their property was actually taken for the use of the army, and used as a shelter to protect the lives of our men, and while occupied by the army it was destroyed. This being the case, the fifth Article of Amendment to the Constitution imperatively requires that the public shall make compensation for it.

On June 1, 1870, Congress passed an act to pay Otis N. Cutler, of Missouri, the sum of $50,000 for 268 bales of cotton, seized by order of Gen. Grant at Lake Providence, Louisiana. The property of said Cutler was used for military purposes in equipping the steamer Tigress for running the blockade of the Mississippi River at Vicksburg on the night of April 22, 1863. This cotton was destroyed by the rebels on the night of April 22, 1863. The boat and cotton were sunk on the trip. If the Government must pay for property taken by its army and then destroyed by the enemy, it seems to me it ought to pay for the property destroyed at Cynthiana, Ky., June 11, 1864, giving proper consideration to the sworn statements of officers on both sides, and especially to the affidavit of Col. Conrad Garis, who took and used it as a shelter to protect the lives of his men while resisting the attack of the enemy; and more especially because these statements are sustained by the corroborative sworn statements of fifty-eight citizens whose characters for truth and veracity are duly certified by the highest authority known to the law, and further sustained by the statements of thirty claimants. The act of taking the cotton above referred to was approved by Gen. Grant, and the papers in the case show that he examined its merits while acting as Secretary of War, and that although he refused to pay the claim, for want of authority, he pronounced it "meritorious," and recommended the claim to Congress.

On January 17, 1871, Congress passed an act making compensation to the Kentucky University for buildings destroyed. The buildings were taken by military authority; they were destroyed by accident; the Government not only paid for the damage and injury to said buildings, but for the damages to the grounds adjacent, and the museum and personal property of said university, and approved by President Grant.

On June 22, 1874, Congress passed an act making compensation to the Kentucky Agricultural and Mechanical Association for damages to their fair grounds, resulting from their occupancy by United States troops during the late war of the rebellion, which payment was recommended by the commission and by the Secretary of War, and approved by President Grant.

On June 22, 1874, Congress passed an act to pay John L. T. Jones, of Montgomery County, Md., for rent of building, and destruction of same by accidental fire while being occupied as quarters by the United States troops under command of Gen. Hubert Ward, in November, 1862.

On April 6, 1876, Senate Bill No. 628 passed the Senate, and afterward the House of Representatives, making compensation to John A. Anderson, surviving co-partner of the firm of Anderson & White, for cotton taken by military authority September 5 and 24, 1862, to make temporary breastworks at Nashville, Tenn., resulting in the cotton being lost and destroyed while thus used for the protection of the army.

One other legislative precedent I deem worthy of notice. It is the message of President Grant of June 1, 1872, returning to the Senate, without his approval, "An act for the relief of J. Milton Best, of Paducah, Ky." It passed the Senate January 5, 1871, by a vote of 28 to 15. It failed to pass the House of Representatives during that Congress. It was again reported to the Senate during the Forty-second Congress (second session), and on the 8th of April, 1872, and passed by a vote of 27 to 12. It was considered in the House of Representatives on the 8th of May, 1872, and passed without a division. The veto message asserts, as a general principle of both international and municipal law, that all property is held subject not only to be taken by the Government for public use (in which case, under the Constitution of the United States, the owner is entitled to just compensation), but also subject to be temporarily occupied, or even actually destroyed in times of great public danger, and when the public safety demands it; and, in this latter case, governments do not admit a legal obligation on their part to compensate the owner. Mr. Howe, from the Committee on Claims, to whom was referred said message, says the committee has not found any such general principle affirmed either in international or municipal law, but has found the very reverse of that to be affirmed by all law, international and municipal.

Among the text writers, Vattel discusses the very question, "Is the State bound to indemnify individuals for the damage they have sustained in war?" "Such damage," he says, "are of two kinds; those done by the State itself, or the sovereign, and those done by the enemy. Of the first kind, some are done deliberately and by way of precaution, as when a field, a house, a garden, belonging to a private person is taken for the purpose of erecting on the spot a town rampart, or any other piece of fortification, or when his standing corn or his storehouses are destroyed to prevent their being of use to the enemy. Such damages are to be made good to the individual, who should bear only his quota of the loss." The same author speaks of damage caused by inevitable necessity, and he instances "the destruction caused by the artillery in re-taking a town from the enemy. These are merely accidents. They are misfortunes which chance deals to the proprietors on whom they happen to fall."

The distinction between the two kinds of damages is clear. One is the result of accident; the other is the result of design.

The sovereign, clothed with the right to make war, has the right to march troops and fire guns. Damages, which are the accidental result of such lawful acts, do not constitute a ground of claim. But whatever property the Government takes from its own obedient subjects, for the more efficient prosecution of the war, should be compensated for, no matter whether it be forage fed to the cavalry horses, powder burned, timber used on fortifications, houses removed to make way for such fortifications or houses destroyed to make them more secure.

Hugh Grotius asserts the same doctrine. He says:

"The king may, in two ways, deprive his subjects of their rights, either by way of punishment, or by virtue of his eminent power. But if he does so in this last way, it must be for some public advantage, and then the subject ought to receive, if possible, a just satisfaction for the loss he suffers out of the common stock."

Again, he says:

"The State has an eminent right of property over the goods of the subject, so that the State, or those that represent it, may make use of them, and even destroy and alienate them, not only in extreme necessity, but for the public benefit; to which we must add that the State is obliged to repair the damages suffered by any subject on that account out of the public stock."

Justice Randolph, in the case of the American Print Works vs. Lawrence, 1 Zabriskie, 248, says:

"In cases where the State, by virtue of its right of eminent domain, reserves the property of a citizen, and appropriates it to the use of the public; or, in prosecuting some great work, such as a canal or railroad, even in its sovereign capacity, or through the power delegated to an incorporated company, finds it necessary, not merely to take the soil and property of the citizen, but to destroy the mill-seat, divert its water-course, or commit other irreparable damage to private rights, in order to effect the great object in view; in such cases, not only must private rights yield to the interest and wishes of the State, but it is a positive evil suffered by an individual for the supposed gain of the whole community, at the will of that community; and, upon every principle of justice, the public should make compensation."

The uniform action of Congress has been in strict accord with the principles adjudicated by the courts, and declared by the commentators. Congress has recognized the principle in a great variety of cases, and, so far as can be discovered, has never denied it.

I deem it proper to refer, just here, to President Grant's message of February 11, 1873, vetoing Senate Bill No. 161, for the relief of those suffering from the destruction of the salt works near Manchester, Ky. In this message, he says:

"This bill does not present a case where private property is taken for public use, in the sense of the Constitution. It was not taken from the owners, but from the enemy; and, it was not then used by the Government, but destroyed."

I call attention to this case to show that President Grant

(assisted by his Cabinet and Constitutional advisers), seemed to base his objection to the passage of said bill upon constitutional grounds; and this is one among the many grounds I take to sustain the Cynthiana claims, as the evidence on file shows, beyond question, that the taking, use and occupancy were precisely as contemplated by the Constitution, where it says:

"No person shall be held to answer for a capital, or otherwise infamous crime, unless on a presentment or indictment of a grand jury, except in cases arising in the land or naval forces, or in the militia, when in actual service in time of war or public danger; nor shall any person be subject for the same offense to be twice put in jeopardy of life or limb; nor shall be compelled in any criminal case to be a witness against himself, nor be deprived of life, liberty, or property, without due process of law; nor shall private property be taken for public use, without just compensation."

To the foregoing precedents a great many might be added. Not a single case has been found in which Congress has denied the liability assumed in the precedents cited. Not a single authority has been found controverting the principles asserted by Grotius, by Vattel, by Whiting, by the Court of Claims, and by the Supreme Court of the United States.

During the war of the Revolution, a number of the colonists who adhered to the Crown, and were known as loyalists, were made to suffer heavily because of their loyalty. The insurgent authorities drove them from their homes, and confiscated their estates. The war terminated in the triumph of the insurgents. The despoiled loyalists at once appealed to Parliament for indemnification for their losses. A commission was appointed to inquire into the extent of such losses. The claimants were required to state, in proper form, every species of loss which they had suffered, and for which they thought they had a right to receive compensation. None of the injuries complained of were inflicted by the Government of Great Britain; they were inflicted by the action of its enemies. In principle, their claims were precisely the same as the claims of our loyal citizens would be if they were to demand compensation of this Government for injuries sustained not through its action, but through the action of its late enemies. Nevertheless, for such claims Parliament undertook to make compensation, and, after a long and careful examination of the claims, appropriated a sum for their settlement amounting to more than $16,000,000.

In September, 1871, immediately upon the close of the Franco-German war, France, although defeated, and subjected to the payment of a fine of 3,000,000,000 of francs to her conquerors, did not ask to avoid the obligation of making compensation to her despoiled subjects. Accordingly, the National Assembly provided not only for the payment of all private damages inflicted by the French authorities, but also provided for the payment of all exactions made upon French subjects in the name of taxes by the German authorities. The same decree appropriated 100,000,000 of francs, to be placed at once in the hands of the Ministers of the Interior and of Finance, to be apportioned between the most necessitous victims of the war; and appropriated a further sum of 6,000,000 of francs, to be distributed by the same ministers among those who suffered the most in the operations attending the attack made by the German Army to gain entrance into Paris.

Hugo Grotius wrote his treatise upon the "Rights of War," amidst the unparalleled barbarities which attended the Thirty Years' War. It is doubtful if war between civilized nations ever before or ever since has been so cruel as that. In the single "Duchy of Wurtemberg, history asserts that 8 towns, 45 villages and 36,000 houses had been laid in ashes, and 70,000 hearth-fires completely extinguished; 7 churches and 444 houses had been burned at Eichsted. Many towns that had escaped destruction, were almost depopulated, 300 houses being empty at Nordheim. More than 200 had been pulled down at Gottingen, merely to serve as fuel. The wealthy city of Augsburg, which contained 80,000 inhabitants before the war, had only 18,000 left when it closed. In 1635, there were not hands enough left at Schweidnitz to bury the dead, and the town of Ohlan had lost its last citizen. Forests sprang up during the contest and covered entire districts which had been in full cultivation before the war, and wolves and other beasts of prey took possession of the deserted haunts of man."

Yet, standing in the midst of such widespread, unsparing devastation, Grotius did not hesitate to affirm, in the language already quoted, the obligation of the State to repair all damages suffered by any subject by the *destruction* of his *property for its use;* and he added this most significant injunction: "Neither shall the State be absolved from this obligation, though for the present not able to satisfy it: But when the State is in a capacity, this suspended obligation shall resume its force."

All claims against the Government must be urged upon one or more of the three grounds: (1.) Either that the claimant has benefited the Government or (2) that he has been damaged by the Government, or (3) that he has been promised money by the Government. But a promise is not of the slightest validity if it be unsupported by a consideration, either of benefit to the promisor or of loss to the promisee. When such conditions do exist, a promise adds nothing to the obligation to pay. The case of the Cynthiana claims is supported by both—by the consideration of loss to the claimants, and of benefit to the Government. The claimants were injured by being deprived of their property; the Government was benefited by the additional security afforded to a weak and imperiled garrison. No promise could add validity to such a claim; hence no claim ever was or could be preferred against the Government resting upon more impregnable grounds. It is sustained by the principles adjudicated by the courts; it is sustained by the commentators; it is sustained by precedents of Congress; and, above all, it is sustained by the Constitution; and, besides, it is sustained by the precedents and usages of all Christian and civilized governments.

If precedents are not to be blindly followed, neither ought they to be wantonly destroyed. They are evidences of truth, and the force of the evidence is in proportion to the integrity and wisdom and patriotism of those who established them.

The question I now call upon you to decide, is not whether you shall establish a new and doubtful precedent, just now proposed and for the first time presented to your consideration, but whether you shall break down and destroy long-established precedents, patiently built up and sustained during a series of years, again and again, by this nation and its highest and most revered authorities.

And are you not bound to deliberately consider the claims of the citizens of Cynthiana, Ky., in the light of former precedents? These claimants have justly supposed that the policy of protecting private property against seizure and destruction for the public good. use, convenience or safety, was fully settled, not by a single act, but by repeated and deliberate acts of the Government, performed at distant and frequent intervals; and now, in full confidence that the policy is firmly and unchangeably fixed, they come before you praying for relief.

As to compensation. Undoubtedly, in every case where private property is rightfully taken by military authority for the public good, use, safety or convenience, resulting in its destruction, the owner is entitled to just compensation from the Government for it.

But what is just compensation? Various definitions have been given. It is stated as meaning a fair equivalent, or being made whole, as far as money is the measure of compensation. Take either of these definitions as the rule of compensation, and the claimants in this case would be entitled to compensation for their property at its marketable value at the time when and the place where taken and destroyed.

The fifth article of the amendment to the Constitution of the United States contemplates that private property shall not be taken for public good, use, safety or convenience without just compensation.

In order that justice may be done to the Government and to the claimants; we ask Congress to pass a bill authorizing and directing the Secretary of War to appoint and send a commission to the city of Cynthiana, in Harrison County, Ky., instructed to ascertain all the circumstances under which said property was taken and lost, and the kind of property lost by each claimant, and its marketable value at the time and place, and report the facts to Congress on or before December 15, 1878, for action.

W. S. Haviland, Attorney.

On March 3, 1879, Mr. Keifer, from the Committee on War Claims, submitted the following report, on the relief of certain citizens of Cynthiana, Ky., which was laid on the table and ordered to be printed:

The Committee on War Claims, to whom was referred the bill (H. R. 1030), and the petitions of certain citizens of Cynthiana, Ky., for and on account of property destroyed by fire on the 11th day of June, A. D. 1864, during the battle between the Union and the so-called Confederate forces, having considered the same, respectfully report:

That the petition alleges that on the said day a fire occurred during a battle at Cynthiana, Ky., in which property was destroyed belonging to certain citizens thereof, and of the value, viz.:

James J. Parish	$ 1,600 00
Elizabeth Oxley	16,555 00
Greenup Remington	10,000 00
W. W. Trimble	2,500 00
Henry Johnson	1,000 00
Charles A. Webster	18,000 00
F. M. Gray	4,100 00
James S. Frizell	12,680 00
Frank Box	6,700 00
Ellen English, administratrix, etc	2,000 00
Frazer & Shawhan	7,000 00
Susan Tomlinson	4,000 00
J. L. Magee	18,000 00
G. Remington, administrator, etc	3,000 00
Herman Rohs	200 00
D. A. Givens	15,747 00
J. N. Webb	1,000 00
J. E. Dickey	700 00
John Quinlan	120 00
W. L. Northcutt	22,570 75
J. N. Smith	5,113 00
J. N. Smith, guardian, etc	2,000 00
H. C. Nebel	653 00
John Bruce	1,372 00
Mary A. Hall	420 00
E. T. Rankin, administratrix, etc	6,563 00
J. W. McIntosh	31,730 00
R. C. Wherritt	32,000 00
F. X. C. Nott, administrator, etc	4,000 00

The aggregate value of the property alleged to have been destroyed is $231,500, which sum it is proposed by said bill to appropriate for the benefit of the sufferers.

It is proper to state that on behalf of the said claimants, it has been proposed to your committee to report a bill authorizing and directing the Secretary of War to appoint a commission for the purpose of investigating the said claims, and to report thereon all the circumstances under which said property was occupied and destroyed, and the nature and value of the same.

Your committee have considered the claims in every aspect in which they have been presented, and have unanimously arrived at a conclusion in relation to the same.

The conclusion arrived at by your committee, renders it unnecessary to consider the question of the value of the property destroyed.

Your committee have considered the petition of claimants as true, and have accepted the language used in the bill as reciting the real circumstances under which claimants' property was destroyed, and the nature of the same.

The concluding part of said bill is as follows:

"The said payments, to be in full satisfaction and discharge of all claims and demands by the said parties, or their heirs or representatives, for, or on account of the loss or destruction of their property, at the time of the attack made upon said city of Cynthiana, by the Confederate forces, under the command of Gen. John H. Morgan, on the 11th day of June, 1864, during which the United States forces, under command of Col. Conrad Garis, of the One Hundred and Sixty-eighth Regiment Ohio Infantry Volunteers, took shelter in the houses of said citizens, thereby causing them and their contents to be set on fire, and destroyed by the enemy."

The claims are all of the same character; all the property of each claimant is alleged to have been destroyed from the same cause, at the same time, and under like circumstances. The property destroyed consisted of houses and their contents. It will be sufficient to give here the circumstances under which the property of one of the sufferers was destroyed.

James J. Parish, who lost a house and its contents, says in his petition:

"Said house and contents was destroyed by fire, and was situated on south side of Pike, between Walnut and Church streets, and adjacent to east side of Kentucky Central Railroad track, and east of the Rankin House, in the city of Cynthiana, in Harrison County, Ky., as set forth by the affidavit of William J. Stone, who set it on fire, and herewith filed. Said loss occurred under the following circumstances, to wit:

"On the 11th day of June, 1864, the Federal forces, under command of Col. Conrad Garis, of the One Hundred and Sixty-eighth Regiment Ohio Infantry Volunteers, took shelter in said city, by placing his men and other citizen soldiers in houses to resist an attack of the enemy under command of Gen. John H. Morgan, when said city was set on fire by said enemy, to dislodge said Federal forces."

The following is the substantive part of the affidavit of William J. Stone, late Speaker of the House of Representatives of the State of Kentucky, and referred to above. He says:

"That his age is thirty-four years, and that his post office address is Eddyville, Lyon Co., Ky., and that he is the identical William J. Stone, who was Lieutenant of Company F, Fifth Regiment Kentucky Cavalry Volunteers, commanded by Col. D. Howard Smith, in Gen. John H. Morgan's command, C. S. A. forces; and, on the 11th day of June, 1864, our said forces marched upon the city of Cynthiana, in Harrison Co., Ky., when and where we attacked a Federal force who had taken shelter in houses in said city, under command of Col. Conrad Garis, of the One Hundred and Sixty-eighth Regiment Ohio Infantry Volunteers, and, in order to dislodge said Federal forces, our said forces set said city on fire. I was ordered, and did set a house on fire, on south side of Pike street, on east side of Rankin House, near the Kentucky Central Railroad, to drive the Federal forces out of said Rankin House."

The affidavit of D. Howard Smith is to the same effect. He says:

"That he is now Auditor of Public Accounts for the State of Kentucky, and that he is the identical D. Howard Smith, who was Colonel in the command of Gen. John H. Morgan, C. S. A. forces; and, on the 11th day of June, 1864, our said command marched upon the city of Cynthiana, in Harrison Co., Ky., when and where we attacked a Federal force, who had taken shelter in houses in said city, under command of Col. Conrad Garis, of the One Hundred and Sixty-eighth Regiment Ohio Infantry Volunteers, and in order to dislodge said Federal forces, in compliance with orders from Gen. John H. Morgan, our said forces did fire said city to drive said Federal forces out of said houses."

Col. Conrad Garis, the Commander of the Union forces at Cynthiana, Ky., at the time of the battle (June 11, 1864), in his affidavit states:

"That his post office address is Washington Court House, Fayette Co., Ohio, and that he is now Treasurer of said county; and that he is the identical Conrad Garis, who was Colonel of the One Hundred and Sixty-eighth Regiment Ohio Infantry Volunteers; and, on the 11th day of June, 1864, he took possession of the city of Cynthiana, in Harrison Co., Ky., by placing his said command in houses to resist an attack of the enemy, under command of Gen. John H. Morgan, when said enemy set said city on fire to dislodge his said command; and, Col. George W. Berry, who was mortally wounded in said battle, assisted in distributing his said command in the different houses, and also gave valued assistance in said engagement."

The most favorable statement of the circumstances, under which said property was destroyed, as presented by and on behalf of claimants, is to the effect, that Col. Garis, in command of the Union troops at Cynthiana, Ky., found a battle with the enemy was imminent, took possession of the place, and distributed his forces in some of the houses of claimants, and perhaps others, with a view to protecting the place from falling into the hands of the enemy, as well as to protect his command in battle; and, while thus held, a battle ensued, in which the Confederate forces, to dislodge the Union soldiers, set fire to the place, and caused the destruction of the houses and property, for which payment is now sought from the United States.

That a great misfortune fell upon certain of the inhabitants of Cynthiana there can be no doubt, and for which they were not responsible.

Your committee assume that all the claimants were loyal. The legal presumption is that they were, as they resided in a loyal or non-seceding State.

The claimants' property was destroyed by the general ravages of war, and for which payment is never made, under the law of nations, or upon any principles of public policy or duty.

Primarily, the destruction was caused by the enemy. Confederate troops fired the buildings; but this fact would not, in the opinion of your committee, change the liability from what it would have been if the Union forces had, when a battle was imminent, or while it raged, set fire to the buildings and caused their destruction. The loss would still have been classed with property destroyed by the misfortunes and casualties of war, for which no compensation is ever made to friend or foe, loyal or disloyal. The petitioners have pressed, with much earnestness, upon your committee, through their counsel and otherwise, the theory that the seizure of the houses, under the circumstances stated there, was an appropriation of the same, to a public use, within the meaning of the Constitution, and its destruction, while thus appropriated, gave the owners the right to a just compensation for the same. They contend that the latter clause of the fifth amendment to the Constitution of the United States secures them this right.

The clause relied on is as follows:

"Nor shall any person * * * be deprived of life, liberty or property, without due process of law; nor shall private property be taken for public use without just compensation."

The error is in assuming that a commanding officer, by occupying, under the exigencies of a battle, by his troops, private buildings, or by shielding himself and his troops behind them during a conflict, within the meaning of the Constitution, appropriates private property to a public use. The temporary occupancy of private property, by the troops of the United States, even where a battle is not imminent or actually raging, has never been held or regarded as an appropriation of the same to a public use. When private property is taken for public use, merely to be held temporarily, no appropriation, in any Constitutional sense, results. Mere possession of private property, by public officers or soldiers of the United States, cannot be construed to be an appropriation of the property to a public use.

It has been expressly held that where a building was burned by accident, where it had been seized by the war power of the General Government for a hospital, or for other use by the United States authorities, that there was no liability resting upon the Government to pay for it. [Lagow's Case, 10 Court of Claims, 266; Green's Case, 10 Court of Claims, 466; Filor's Case, 9 Wall., 45.]

It is said there is a case where the United States were held liable for the appropriation of a mill burned by an officer of the United States to prevent it from falling into the hands of the so-called Government.

This case is known as the Grant Case, and will be found reported in 1st Court of Claims, p. 41. It is only a decision of the Court of Claims, and, as authority, it has been doubted.

Your committee, however, does not think it necessary, for

the proper determination of this case, to deny the authority of the Grant Case.

In that case, there was a complete destruction of the property, by a direct order of an officer of the United States, to prevent its falling into the hands of the Confederates, and being used by them to aid the rebellion. There is no analogy between that case and the cases of the Cynthiana citizens, whose property was destroyed in battle by Confederate soldiers.

In the case of Dr. Best, of Paducah, the commanding officer of the United States, had, by order, destroyed his valuable house to set it out of the range of the guns of the United States Army, and to prevent the possibility of its use, by the enemy, in case a battle took place at that place. A bill was passed through Congress to re mburse Dr. Best for loss of his house ; but President Grant vetoed the bill, on the ground that there was no just liability resting on the Government to make good such loss. His veto was sustained. There may be many reasons why Dr. Best should have been paid ; but, certainly, if he had no valid claim, the Cynthiana claimants have no shadow of right to have their losses reimbursed. It will be a dangerous precedent to recognize or establish the principle, that property destroyed by Confederates, shall be paid for by the United States Government.

Your committee are unanimous in concluding that the several claimants, on the representations set forth in the petitions, and the recitations of the bill, have no valid rights whatever against the United States Government. It would only be doing a vain thing, attended with much expense, to authorize the appointment of the board asked for, as, on the showing of claimants, they have no possible claims for which the United States can be held liable.

Your committee, therefore, report back the said bill, and respectfully ask that it do not pass.

This adverse Report did not deter the Kentucky General Assembly from the following action on the subject:

Resolution of the Kentucky General Assembly, in regard to the war losses by fire at Cynthiana in June, 1864. WHEREAS, on the 11th day of June, 1834, Col. Conrad Garis of the One Hundred and Sixty-eighth Regiment of Ohio Infantry Volunteers, took shelter in the city of Cynthiana, in Harrison County, Ky., by placing his men in houses to resist an attack of the enemy under the command of Gen. John H. Morgan, and, during the fight which ensued, the city was set on fire by the enemy to dislodge said Federal forces, resulting in the destruction of the houses and merchandise of the following persons, viz.: J. J. Parrish, F. M. Gray, Thomas English, W. W. Trimble, John L. Magee, D. A. Givens, John Quinlan, J. Newt Smith, Mrs. Mary A. Hall, Robert C. Wherrift, Lawson Oxley, Henry Johnson, James S. Frizell, T. A. Frazier, H. E. Shawhan, Eliza Bell, Isaac N. Webb, William L. Northcutt, H. C. Nabel, Thomas R. Rankin, Greenup Remington, Charles A. Webster, Frank Box, Harmon Rohs, Susan Tomlinson, J. E. Dickey, I. N. Smith, John Bruce, J. W. McIntosh, and F. X. C. Nott, administrator, etc.

And, WHEREAS, it appears the houses were converted to the use of the Federal soldiers, and absolutely used to protect the men as the danger was imminent and impending, and the necessity was urgent for the public service, and was such as would not have admitted delay, it seems the property was taken possession of by the Union forces whilst resisting the hostilities of the public enemy; and said citizens were called upon, and required to give up their private property for the advantages of the community ; this property having been actually taken for the use of, and used by the army of, the United States as shelter, and while thus occupied, it was destroyed.

These being the facts in the case in the opinion of this General Assembly, the fifth article of amendment of the Constitution of the United States, contemplates that private property shall not be taken for public good, use, safety or convenience, without just compensation therefor, otherwise public burdens would be shared unequally.

Be it, therefore, *Resolved* by this General Assembly of the Commonwealth of Kentucky, That our Senators and Representatives in the Congress of the United States be respectfully requested to urge upon the Government of the United States the speedy settlement and payment of said claims; that the Government take such early and speedy steps as they may deem proper to accomplish this end, by bill or otherwise, in order that justice may be done alike to Government and claimants, we suggest that our Senators and Representatives urge Congress to pass a bill authorizing and directing the Secretary of War to appoint and send a commission to the city of Cynthiana, in Harrison County, Ky., instructed to ascertain all the circumstances under which said property was destroyed, and the kind of property lost by each claimant, and the marketable value at the time, and report all the facts to Congress for consideration and action.

Approved March 6, 1880.

I certify the above to be a true copy of the original which passed by both Houses and signed by the respective Speakers.

(This is a copy of forgoing resolution, signed by)

THOMAS G. POORE, Clerk H. R.

—*L. G. Marshall.*

CHAPTER VIII.

CYNTHIANA—EARLY MILLS AND OTHER MANUFACTORIES—PIONEER MERCHANTS AND MERCANTILE HOUSES—MARRIAGES—POSTMASTERS, ETC.—PHYSICIANS, DISEASES AND EPIDEMICS—LATER INDUSTRIES—BANKS AND BANKING INSTITUTIONS—CITY GOVERNMENT, ETC.

ALEXANDER DOWNING built a flouring-mill in 1818 on the corner of Poplar street and the alley. The mill was worked by inclined plane and horses, and the business was carried on till 1822. Also, in 1818, Callent & Addison established a cotton factory on the now new street east of Main street, not far from the present site of Mrs. I. T. Martin's residence. The business was continued till 1825. About the same time, Josephus Perrin built and carried on a flouring-mill for seven or eight years, on the site afterward occupied by Aaron Diltz's flouring-mill, now the site of Mr. Diltz's new brick residence on Walnut street. This mill was at first set up in the large brick building since known as Peck's flouring-mill. The exact period of its suspension we have not ascertained, but it was not a financial success.

From 1816 to 1825, and, perhaps, for a few years longer, Samuel Patton owned and operated a woolen factory on the site of Mrs. David Wherritt's present residence.

The so-called Peck's Mill building has passed through so many hands, and been the scene of so great a variety of business, that it may be worth while to chronicle more minutely its history.

Isaac Miller was president of the company who built the house, in 1809, for factory use; it had then the largest rooms to be found in town, and as early as 1818, our fellow-citizen, Robert Jones, remembers that Thespian societies held public exhibitions there. It was rather a fashionable resort, Mr. Jones himself bore a part, and played Lady Randolph. After this, Josephus Perrin occupied the place, as stated, for cotton spinning. We cannot trace its course of business without intervals.

But in 1845, the executors of Asbury Broadwell sold the property to John Harmon Frazer, who had his office in or adjoining the building, and kept large quantities of whisky on storage and on speculation there. For years it was only used for such purposes by the various parties into whose possession it came, and while no great show or stir was apparent about the premises, it hardly ever ceased to be the receptacle of large property interests. John Harmon Frazer's assignees sold the place to Gray & Cox. These, again, sold to J. A. Cook & Wolford; these to C. B. Cook, in 1865, who used it for manufacturing purposes for a year or two. C. B. Cook sold to Peck & Van Hook about 1866. This firm received into partnership Ben Potts, who soon sold out his share to J. W. Peck & Co., who, in 1876, established a very successful flouring business in it. The building became then known as Peck's Mill, and its daily product has been since about seventy-five barrels daily, at any rate, while Peck was interested, his connection with it as flour manufacturer lasting six years. It is pronounced by Mr. Peck the most profitable business establishment in the place, excepting only the most prosperous distilleries, and these excepted only in the most favorable years for the liquor trade. During the present year, 1882, Peck sold the old place to Messrs. Riggs & Musselman, who are continuing the same line of business (flour manufacture), with every prospect of financial success.

All these early manufacturing experiments had but a short-lived existence. It has been suggested that these attempts were inspired by the dawning popularity of Henry Clay's Protective System, and that their collapse was hastened by the powerful opposition encountered by Mr. Clay's policy. At any rate, it became evident in a few years, that protection by government to home manufactures, could not be relied on as an assured permanency.

Other manufactories in our city of a more recent date, on a larger scale, and on a different basis, will be noticed in another part of this sketch.

It is proper here to record the name of George Hamilton, as the first merchant who was ever engaged regularly in trade in Cynthiana. His place of business was on the ground now occupied by the jail, on Pike street, though even before George Hamilton, as an old citizen remembers, a store was kept by Isaac Miller, father of our former well known citizen, Maj. Newton Miller, before the establishment in 1793. But Isaac Miller's store, at that time, was on the west side of the river, not far from the site of the present bridge. During the first twenty or thirty years of the town's existence, the tendency of the sale and settlement of town lots was directed toward the vicinity of the river,

Lewis Veatch

as it was then thought the navigation of the stream was, at least, among the possibilities.

Asbury Broadwell began merchandising in 1813, on the site of Dr. Beale's present residence, on Main street. He married the sister of Dr. Andrew McMillin, by which marriage he acquired a handsome property, which he, by his eminent business talents, built up to a fine fortune. He moved his business in 1830, from the first location, to the present site of Dr. Hood's drug store, corner of Pike and Main streets. He died in 1843.

Thomas Ware began as a merchant in 1824, keeping a general stock, as early merchants generally have to do, and continued ten years. His location was the present site of J. W. Peck's extensive grocery. He resided in the South for some years after 1834, and was, at last, killed in the first battle of Cynthiana, in 1862.

John M. January did a heavy mercantile business in various departments from 1832 to 1850; his place of operations was the present site of the Fennell Brothers' clothing store. He broke, and died in 1862. James Finley, and also James Kelley, are remembered as early merchants before, and for some years after the war of 1812. But all the early merchants broke after the war of 1812, sooner or later, except Col. Miller, who had both wealth and business talents.

It is proper to preserve the names of the parties to the first marriages on record in our county, though we have not the means of ascertaining whether they were, or became, citizens of Cynthiana. We mention, therefore, the following as they occur under their respective dates:

1794, May, Samuel Van Hook and Hannah Trousdale; June, Traverse Edwards and Elizabeth Coleman.

1794, June, Ezekiel Laiton Hinton and Martha Caldwell; Thomas Hinkson and Elizabeth Poor; Thomas Ravenscraft and Nancy Langdon; Thomas Martin and Betsey Ellison; Joel Frazer and Peggy Miller.

1795, June, Joseph Kincaid and Jane Martin; John Hamilton and Mary Curry.

1795, July, Richard Ellis and Elizabeth Jones; David Campbell and Frances Norman; Samuel Wilson and Betsey Snodgrass; James Furnace and Asena Furnace; John Wall and Mary Cartwill; July 24, Ebenezer Davidson and Margaret McCandless.

The list might be continued to the present time, as the record is preserved entire. In the earlier record, however, the day of the month is often omitted.

Until 1801, the town seems to have been able to do without a post office; but in that year the series of Postmasters begins, which list we are enabled to supply, with the dates of their appointments, furnished from the Post Office Department at Washington, through the kind attention of Hon John G. Carlisle:

April 2, 1801, James Coleman; July 1, 1802, Caleb Kemper; April 1, 1804, Christian McConnico; January 8, 1805, James Finley; December 23, 1816, James Kelley; December 23, 1818, Hartwell Boswell; June 24, 1820, Armistead Whitehead; January 22, 1825, Asbury Broadwell; December 20, 1833, William A. Withers; January 14, 1841, Asbury Broadwell; May 31, 1841, Jeremiah V. Bassett; September 24, 1845, Perry Wherritt; September 5, 1849, John B. Gruelle; November 16, 1852, Charles H. Anderson; October 17, 1853, John B. Gruelle; July 5, 1854, Charles H. Anderson; February 14, 1855, David A. Gevens; May 26, 1856, Oliver Lucas; September 16, 1856, Alexander Williamson; April 30, 1861, A. J. Morey; June 1, 1861, Benjamin C. Day; November 12, 1861, Luther Van Hook; January 2, 1863, Lewis Coppage; January 4, 1866, Henry M. Magee; December 12, 1878, Mattie D. Todd.

The office became Presidential on the 9th of July, 1870.

Names and the proper dates attached serve to recall or correct many a half-forgotten event of the past. It is with this view of the subject that we present considerably extended lists of the names of citizens engaged in the various avocations of life; yet we have not attempted to make the ensuing catalogue of physicians so complete as to include the name of every one who has practiced the healing art in Cynthiana. Still, it is believed few names of those who became permanent residents as physicians will be missed.

It is proper also to warn the readers that our notice here is not much more specific than a simple catalogue, not intended to be at all biographical, though several of the names are fruitful themes of biography; especially extended accounts of Dr. McPheeters, Dr. Timberlake, Dr. Andrew McMillin, Dr. George H. Perrin, Dr. Joel C. Frazer and Dr. Abram Adams should be furnished, but we are not assured that space and time will be allowed.

At the head of the list we place the name of Dr. James McPheeters, who practiced his profession here as early as 1795. He belonged to a large family of professional men in Rockbridge County, Va. Many of his kinsmen were clergymen and physicians, and all were more or less eminent. A brief sketch of his life, written by his brother, is appended to this article.

Very nearly, if not quite, contemporary with Dr. McPheeters, was Dr. Septimus Taylor, still represented by numerous descendants in our town and county. Also, nearly contemporary was Dr. Reynolds. In 1807, we have Dr. David Holt; in 1808, Dr. Timberlake, who died in 1828. In 1812, we have Dr. Joseph Holt. In 1812, also, we have Dr. Andrew McMillin; in 1817, we have Dr. Joel C. Frazer, of great distinction; in 1820, Dr. Hendershot; in 1816, Dr. Duncan; in 1825, Dr. George H. Perrin began practice here, and is still an honored citizen among us. In 1822, we had Dr. Samuel McMillin; and in 1828, Dr. Abram Adams began here, and practiced a full half century. In 1830, we had Dr. Harmon; and in 1832 Dr. Jack Desha. In 1837, Dr. Lewis Perrin began practice here, and in 1876 returned to his native place, Abbeville, S. C., where he died in 1880. Dr. Lewis Perrin was prominent both in politics and medicine. In 1832, Dr. Thomas Magee began practice, and continued till 1849, when he died of cholera. Dr. John Kimbrough began about the same time, and also died in 1849. In 1850, we had Dr. John A. Kirkpatrick, who died a few years ago; in 1850, also, Dr. William H. Adair; in 1858, Dr. H. McDowell, still in extensive practice among us; in 1859, Dr. A. J. Beale, now for the second time member of the General Assembly; in 1860, Dr. McCloud; in 1865, Dr. Rutherford, who died some years ago; also in 1865, Dr. Augustus Murray; in 1862, Dr. John H. Righter; also, Dr. John H. Smiser, the latter three being the first homeopathic physicians resident in our city; in 1870, Dr. James P. Madison, eclectic; in 1878, Dr. Thackeray M. Hedges; in 1880, Dr. E. W. Martin; also in 1880, Dr. F. Gray, also Dr. W. T. McNees.

Of dentists, we may mention the following as resident in 1849 and the succeeding ten years: Dr. John Childs, Dr. Cazidivant, Dr. Moffat and Dr. Herschfield. In 1868, we had Dr. Ed. Peckover; in 1869, Dr. C. L. Donnelly; in 1877 and in 1879, respectively, we had and still have in our city Dr. S. S. Johnson, and Dr. F. M. Miller.

We place here, by way of eminence, a brief sketch of the first physician who ever practiced medicine in Cynthiana—Dr. James McPheeters. This we are enabled to do in the words of his brother, the Rev. William McPheeters, who left, in manuscript dated 1842, Raleigh, N. C., a very interesting history of the family. We make room only for the notice of one member, though the story is full of the stirring events peculiar to the early settlement of our country. The penmanship of the work is beautiful, legible, systematic, and the arrangement so methodical, the honesty and reliability of the whole so evident, that the reader follows his guide with entire ease and confidence. The family was large; one hundred and seventy-nine are named in their proper places in their respective branches, and Joseph Moore, maternal uncle of Dr. McPheeters, had sixteen children, while the Rev. William, the Doctor's brother, who is the author of the history from which we make this extract, had the goodly number of fourteen children; the latter was married three times, and gives us a carefully written account of his three wives. Many clergymen appear in the family, and all, or nearly all, seem to have been Presbyterians. William McPheeters, father of the Doctor, was born in Pennsylvania in 1729, removed to Rockbridge County, Virginia; married Rachel Moore, of that county, and died in 1807. He had ten children, of whom James was the fourth, and William, the writer from whom we copy, was the ninth. We preserve both the form and paragraphs of the original, as follows:

4. JAMES. Born May 5th, 1765. He acquired a liberal education, commenced the study of medicine in Staunton, Augusta Co., Va., and afterward attended the medical lectures, Philadelphia. Doctor Rush being at that time one of the lecturers.

He married his cousin, Elizabeth Coalter, a daughter of Michael Coalter, May 25, 1791. For ten years he practiced medicine in the town and neighborhood of Fincastle, Botetourt County. Afterward, he removed in the year 1795 to Kentucky, and settled in the town of Cynthiana, Harrison County. [This date must, of course, be correct, being stated on the reliable authority of William McPheeters, but the Doctor may have visited Cynthiana as early as 1790, bought property, and built the house, which united local tradition ascribes to him, on the west side of the court house, on the corner of the alley and the public square.]

In the years 1796 and 1797, he was a *great sufferer*. He lost his eyesight in a great measure, and was otherwise afflicted, being confined to his room and bed for ten weeks, and unable to sit up. He, however, gradually recovered his health, and, to some extent, his eyesight, so as to enable him to resume the practice of medicine; and, for more than two years, he enjoyed comfortable health. But he was again visited with sickness; and departed this life November 9, 1799, aged thirty-four years and six months. He died at the house of a Mr. Borr, a few miles from Lexington, to which town he had probably gone with the view of obtaining medical aid. He was buried in a graveyard near Mr. Borr's, on a road leading from Lexington to Cynthiana.

For many years, he had been a member of the church. His wife, Elizabeth, also was a church member, and esteemed a consistent and exemplary Christian.

After the death of her husband, she removed from Cynthiana to the State of Missouri.

The children of this family were five in number. The three first named were born in Virginia, the other two in Kentucky. 1, Sophronia; 2, Philander; 3, Theophilus; 4, David; 5, James Augustus.

1. Sophronia McPheeters was born January, 1792, and departed this life in the month of September, 1808, in the seventeenth year of her age.

2. Philander McPheeters was born August 2, 1793. He was killed in battle by the Indians at Fort Meigs, May 5, 1813, aged nineteen years and nine months. Col. Boswell was commander in the engagement.

3. Theophilus McPheeters was born November 15, 1794. He now (1842) resides in Mississippi, near to the city of Natchez. [For particulars of his family, see Appendix.]

4. David McPheeters was born August 30, 1797, and died October 10, same year, aged about nine weeks.

5. James Augustus McPheeters was born April 30, 1799. He

studied medicine, and now resides (1842) in the city of Natchez, Miss.

Our author having thus completed his account of Dr. James McPheeters, addresses himself to the history of his sister, Rebecca McPheeters, who married John Gamble in 1785, and had eleven children. He states that John Gamble was born in 1757, and died 1831; that Rebecca was born in 1767, and died in 1833.

A few more such authorities as William McPheeters would enable us to make the history of Cynthiana complete and accurate.

A few lines are here given to diseases and epidemics, rather to celebrate the general absence than presence of violent scourges among us, for the town has not commonly been a sufferer from these causes. But in June, 1833, cholera broke out violently in Cynthiana, carrying off upward of fifty citizens. Mrs. William K. Wall was the first person attacked, the disease soon terminating fatally. Hon. William K. Wall, her husband, was at the time engaged, and in the midst of a speech at the court house, when he was hastily summoned to her aid at his residence, only a few yards distant. But no rescue was possible. The cholera raged about three months, when it ceased as suddenly as it had begun. In July, 1849, there were a few cases of cholera in town, two of the victims being Dr. Thomas Magee and Dr. J. W. Kimbrough; also a considerable number of cases occurred in the vicinity, especially on Raven's Creek.

In 1851, on Saturday, the 14th of September, cholera again suddenly appeared, carrying off Daniel Musser, Thomas Trimnel and David Woodruff, his wife, and three of his five children. Other victims were John Fuller, brick mason; Stephen Shumate, cabinet-maker; and eight or ten negroes. The scourge broke out Saturday night, and ceased the following Tuesday, nor has it prevailed here since. In 1832, just a year before the first cholera visitation, Dr. George H. Perrin remembers that scarlet fever prevailed fearfully in town, attacking young children mostly, and that about the same number died from this malady as from cholera in the following year. Dr. Perrin, to whom we are indebted for numerous and valuable items, also says that during the last sixty years, diseases have changed somewhat in type, and are less inflammatory; that names are occasionally modified, and that the treatment of disease has materially changed in some particulars. There was formerly but one system of medicine of much authority, while there are now several, and, of course, a variety of treatment. Blood-letting was common, but now it is rarely practiced. Of himself, on this point, Dr. Perrin relates that in 1851, he was one day, while in town, annoyed by an itching of the ear; that he tried to relieve the, at first, slight uneasiness by the usual means of touching or rubbing, but the itching continued, and became more and more intense, and at last the ear began to throb violently. He then returned quickly to his residence across the river, now the Howk place, and told his wife that he was going to bleed himself, that he was threatened with a rising in the head, or something serious of that kind. He took a quart of blood from his arm, but the throbbing of the ear continued. He then tried a strong aperient medicine, which was duly attended by its proper specific effect, but still the throbbing remained as violent as before. He then proceeded to bleed himself again, two hours after his first bleeding, and took another quart of blood from his arm before the throbbing ceased. Thus two quarts of blood were taken in two hours, and the Doctor is confident that the blood-letting saved his hearing, if not his life. As it was, even, he was wholly deprived of hearing in the affected ear for two years after the attack.

In 1850, Henry F. Cromwell began the manufacture of carriages, wagons and plows, and for some years worked thirty hands. The business was suspended in 1861, and not resumed till 1871, when Mr. Cromwell, having returned from the South, re-established his manufactory on Pike street, nearly opposite the Smith House. He now employs about a dozen hands, and estimates the business moderately at $5,000 annually.

In 1872, Joseph Fennell invented what he calls his shin, ankle, and speedy cut, a horseboot, patented and now known to horsemen throughout the United States. In 1876, he invented his hoof and speedy cut, also well and favorably known. Both contrivances are intended for the use and benefit of fine stock. The inventer carries on the manufacture under his own roof, and the work is all done under his own eye, in the rear of the Fennell clothing store, which fronts both Main and Pike streets. The business has been estimated as high as $10,000 annually.

V. H. Pate & Co. established in 1873 a carriage manufactory on the corner of Pleasant and Walnut streets. They employ ten hands, and the annual amount of their business is about $10,000. They have turned out some very fine specimens of work.

The large flouring mills, distilleries, etc., are noticed on another page.

The bank of Cynthiana was chartered in 1818, of which William C. Moore was President, and Henry Brown, Cashier. It was a joint-stock bank, of the sort sometimes called the "Owl Creek," having a capital of $25,000. Its office was kept in a house on the McMillin lot, now the Faerber House. We did not trace its existence later than 1820, though according to the recollection of some, it was not finally closed till about 1828. A two-dollar note of this bank was shown to us by C. F. Delling. It bears date 1819, and is ornamented with a vignette, representing pretty fairly the bridge and vicinity. At this period the paper of the bank of the Commonwealth of Kentucky was current throughout the State, but in 1820 or 1821 its paper was at a heavy discount, not less than 50 per cent. In 1822, the General Assembly enacted a law to the effect that any one who refused the Commonwealth's paper for taxes or public dues should wait a year longer for his claim. This measure not being very effective in supporting the depreciated currency, the Assembly next year declared that for refusing the Commonwealth's paper, the offender should wait two years for his money. The Court of Appeals, composed of Judges John Boyle, William Owsley and Benjamin Mills, decided this law unconstitutional. The Legislature removed the Judges in 1824, and appointed William T. Barry, John Trimble and Haggin in their places. The next General Assembly removed the new appointees and restored to their seats the old Judges who had condemned the law, though, in fact, the latter had never recognized the legality of their removal, and had considered themselves and behaved themselves all the time as if still constituting the Court of Appeals. Kentucky, therefore, had two *quasi* Courts of Appeal. The times were excited, party feeling ran high, and it was not easy for banks of moderate power to sustain their credit. The "Owl Creek" bank, of course, went out early, but the old Commonwealth Bank ultimately redeemed its paper, dollar for dollar, not actually and entirely closing out its affairs till 1830. Even then, probably, only the influence of the two branches of the United States Bank, the one at Lexington and the other at Louisville, assured the end of that honorable and honored banking corporation.

From about 1830 till 1857, we hear no more of banks in our town. However, in June, 1857, the Deposit Bank of Cynthiana was established on a capital of $25,000, J. W. Peck, President, and J. S. Withers, Cashier. It paid interest on deposits at the rate of 5 per cent, as we remember, and for five years it paid semi-annual dividends of 5 per cent to the stockholders. When the little bank settled up to make way for another enterprise, it paid to its stockholders a dollar and twenty-five cents for each dollar of their stock—certainly a pretty fair showing of financial management.

In June, 1862, the Deposit Bank was succeeded by a branch of the Commercial Bank of Kentucky, with a capital of $100,000 ; Henry E. Shawhan, President, and J. S. Withers, Cashier. The mother bank was situated at Paducah, and wielded a capital of about $2,000,000. The war between the States having come on, and continuing and increasing in violence and magnitude, the banking business was seriously injured throughout Kentucky. Notwithstanding, the branch at Cynthiana was successful, and made handsome profits on its capital, but these, when shared in common with the mother bank, and with the other less successful branches, were not sufficient to pay to the stockholders more than about 3 per cent semi-annually in dividends, and sometimes not even so much. The Commercial Bank Directors, in 1868, erected the fine marble front bank building in which the present National Bank is accommodated, at a cost of $23,000, the Carpenter Brothers being the contractors and builders. It is situated on the west side of Main street, one door south of public square. In laying the foundations of the building, the brick wall of John Spohn's residence, which closely adjoins, was injured, and the accident cost the bank $600. The plan was furnished by James K. Wilson, an architect of Cincinnati, J. W. Peck and J. S. Withers constituting the building committee. Four rooms above the apartments used by the bank are rented as private offices, and two below, the latter forming the basement.

In 1871, the Commercial Bank sold its banking-house here to its successor, the National Bank, for $15,000, and withdrew its branch from the place, in accordance with the wishes of a large majority of those in the vicinity who had been stockholders.

The new organization of the National Bank, of which Henry E. Shawhan was made President, and J. S. Withers, Cashier, entered upon business with a capital increased to $150,000. This bank, during the last ten or twelve years, has enjoyed an uninterrupted stream of prosperity, the stock always commanding a high premium, the best sale being 40 per cent, and even 50 per cent premium was recently refused. The officers report a surplus fund of $40,047, a pretty good index of strength and commercial thrift. We copy and preserve here on permanent record as an item of general interest, the following latest official statement of the affairs of this bank :

Semi-annual statement to the Stockholders of the National Bank of Cynthiana, December 31, 1881.

RESOURCES :

Loans and Discounts	$286,522 84
U. S. Bonds (par value)	158,700 00
Banking House	15,000 00
Due from Banks and Bankers	84,051 75
Due from Treasurer, U. S.	6,750 00
Cash and Cash Items	44,391 92
	$595,416 51

LIABILITIES:

Capital Stock	$150,000 00
Circulation	135,000 00
Individual Depositors	255,362 36
Due to Banks and Bankers	5,855 27
Dividend No. 20, payable January 5, 1882	7,500 00
Fund to pay Federal and State Taxes	1,316 20
Surplus Fund	32,000 00
Undivided Profits	8,382 68
	$595,416 51

Gross earnings (six months) ending December 31, 1881		$14,468 34
Expense Account and Taxes	$3,957 84	
Dividend, 5 per cent payable January 5, 1882	7,500 00	
Added to Surplus Fund	2,000 00	
Added to Undivided Profits	307 44	
Bad Debts charged off	703 06	-$14,468 34

J. S. WITHERS, *Cashier*.

In 1877, was established the Farmers' Deposit Bank, on a cash capital of $100,000, J. W. Peck, President, and Luther Van Hook, Cashier. This bank has also been a success from the beginning. The stock commands a premium of 8 per cent, and it has already a surplus fund of $6,000. It pays semi-annual dividends of about 4 per cent, the last January dividend, however, having been withheld, as some unusual expenses were to be incurred. In October, 1881, the Farmers' Deposit Bank was transformed into the Farmers' National Bank of Cynthiana, but remaining under the management of the same board of officers and directors. It is situated on the north side of Main street, one door east of the public square, in a two-story brick building formerly owned by D. A. Givens. The house was purchased by the bank in November, 1881 and cost $4,500. The upper rooms are rented as private offices. Quite recently, the directors have had a vault constructed, of admirable design, for the safe-keeping of the books and other valuables of the institution. The plan of the vault is that of Hall's Lock and Safe Company, the most approved, perhaps, in the county. It is built of solid masonry from the bottom of the cellar to the first floor, twelve feet square. On this foundation stands the large safe, surrounded on all sides, top and bottom, by iron walls which stand a few feet from the front and sides of the safe so as to admit access to the door of the safe and make room for some shelving. The iron walls are then surrounded by brick work two feet thick, in contact with the iron, an arch of the same thickness covering the top. Strength, convenience, and perfect security are evidently assured. The masonry and iron alone cost $1,200, not including the safe, which is valued at $2,000. The office has also been beautifully fitted up.

We are furnished the following item of permanent interest relative to the Farmers' National Bank, by Mr. Van Hook, the cashier:

Report of the condition of the Farmers' National Bank, 16th of March, 1882:

RESOURCES.

Real Estate and Fixtures	$ 6,600 00
U. S. Bonds	75,000 00
Premium Account	1,218 75
Redemption Fund	2,250 00
Revenue Account	201 54
Expense	82 15
Loans and Discounts	111,332 62
Due from Banks	2,744 07
Cash in vault	25,076 56
Aggregate	$224,505 69

LIABILITIES.

Capital Stock	$100,000 00
Surplus Fund	4,000 00
Undivided Profits	2,260 03
Circulation	45,000 00
Rent Account	12 75
Discount Account	1,325 85
Exchange	303 66
Due other Banks	1,311 78
Individual Deposits	71,921 13
Aggregate	224,505 69

The new Constitution having been adopted in 1850–51, the County Court was re-organized accordingly, and though principally an affair of the county at large, we include it in our sketch of the town, so far, at least, as to present a list of the presiding officers of that court, and their dates of election. The County Judge keeps his office at the county seat, and is always, during his term of office, a citizen of the place.

The first County Judge under the new organization was Henry Coffman, elected in 1851. These officials then succeeded each other in the order indicated below:

David Snodgrass, 1854; Louis Day, *ad interim;* James R. Curry, 1858; Marc L. Broadwell, 1862; James R. Curry, 1866; C. W. West, 1870; W. W. Cleary, *ad interim;* L. Desha, Jr., 1873, re-elected, 1874; Henry H. Haviland, 1878, and is now in office.

By favor of L. M. Martin, Esq., we have the following catalogue of County Attorneys for the last forty years, nearly, which we present in retrograde order:

W. T. Lafferty, appointed 1882; John F. Morgan, elected 1878; A. Perrin, elected 1870; C. W. West, appointed 1868; J. S. Boyd, elected 1866; J. Q. Ward, elected, 1862; W. W. Cleary, elected 1858; W. W. Cleary, appointed 1857; Thomas A. Curran, elected 1854; W. W. Trimble, elected 1851; the same appointed, 1850; same appointed, 1849 ; McCalla Thompson, appointed 1848 ; W. W. Trimble, appointed 1847, 1846, 1845, 1844.

The charter of the city was approved by the General Assembly on the 2d of March, 1860 ; and for twenty-two years our people have enjoyed the advantages of a city form of government, yet there are citizens who think well of the former management by trustees, a system which had answered the purpose very well for about seventy years.

Under the city charter, from April 12th, 1860, to April, 1861, Samuel F. January held the office of Mayor, and so was the first of the line of Mayors. All city officers are elected in April of each year according to the charter.

Mayors.—Second, M. L. Broadwell, 1861–63 ; third, C. G. Land, 1863–66 ; fourth, George Lemmon, 1866–70 ; fifth, Joseph Fennell, 1870–71 ; sixth, F. G. Ashbrook, 1871–72 ; seventh, Caleb Musser, 1872–74 ; eighth, T. E. Ashbrook, 1874 to October ; ninth, C. B. Cook, October, 1874, to June, 1880 ; tenth, W. S. Wall, June, 1880, to 1883.

City Attorneys.—First, A. H. Ward, April, 1860 ; second, R. M. Kelley, April, 1861 ; third, J. Q. Ward, 1862–63 ; fourth, J. S. Boyd, 1864 ; fifth, James L. Griffith, 1865–66 ; sixth, C. W. West, 1867–68–69 ; seventh, W. W. Cleary, 1870–71–72–73 ; eighth, John K. Lake, 1874 ; ninth, J. W. Elliott, 1875 ; tenth, C. W. West, 1876–77–78–79 ; eleventh, Achilles Perrin, 1880–81–82.

City Marshals.—First, William Smith, April, 1860 ; second, Thomas Flinn, *ad interim ;* third, James H. Coffman, 1861 ; fourth, William T. Magee, *ad interim ;* fifth, J. E. Dickey, 1862 ; sixth, John Bruce, 1863–64–65–66 ; seventh, J. C. Wickliffe, 1867–68 ; eighth, W. B. Glave, 1869 ; ninth, R. M. Hedges, *ad interim* in 1869 and 1870 ; tenth, T. D. Woodward, *ad interim* 1870 ; eleventh, H. M. Keller, 1871–72 ; twelfth, William Turtoy, 1873 ; thirteenth, H. M. Keller, 1874–75–76–77–78–79–80 ; fourteenth, H. T. Hoffman, *ad interim* ; fifteenth, A. J. West, 1881–82.

Until 1879, the city fathers had no better assembly-room than the little 20x30 room on Pleasant, between Main and Walnut streets. They held their meetings in the second story, and all around, and below them in the lower story, were crowded, the fire department and other paraphernalia appertaining to such bodies. In 1878, however, they sold the old place to C. B. Cook and T. A. Frazer for $400, and purchased the eligible situation now occupied near the corner of Pleasant and Walnut streets, of T. A. Frazer, for $700, and erected the present fine Council chamber, ample for all city purposes. Frank M. Curl was engaged as contractor, and in 1879 the building was finished. It is an elegant brick structure, well suited in every respect to its purpose, while it is an ornament to the city. It is distinguished by a handsome square tower, has a prisoner's cell, engine room, Council room, office for miscellaneous purposes, etc.

City Officials, 1882.—W. S. Wall, Mayor ; William Addams, A. J. Morey, James S. Smiser, John Spohn, Thomas Hinkson, J. A. Wolford, John W. Renaker, John G. Montgomery, Councilmen ; A. Perrin, City Attorney ; W. H. Throckmorton, Treasurer ; John S. Miller, Clerk ; A. J. West, Marshal ; H. C. Nebel, Commissioner and Engineer.

By favor of the gentlemanly Clerk, Mr. John S. Miller, we have the following statement in addition to numerous other items of a similar character, from the same source :

COST OF CITY PROPERTY:

Council Chamber and Engine House	$ 5,104 80
Furniture for Council Chamber	150 00
Hook and Ladder Truck	450 00
Engine and Hose	6,480 00
Ten Cisterns (Fire Department)	1,500 00
City Street Lamps	700 00
Aggregate	$14,384 80

The streets of the city are well paved, curbed and macadamized ; only brick buildings are allowed to be erected in the central portion of the town. The steam fire engine is believed to be of the best pattern yet invented. It bears the words, "Ahrens & Kamman ; Pat. Jan. 31, 1871, No. 159. C. Arhrens & Co., Builders, Cincinnati, 1876. A. B. Latta's Patents, June 6, 1859, May 22, 1855, May 2 ; July," etc.

It was selected by C. B. Cook, a good judge of such works. It has repeatedly proved its power, and for the last three or four years a feeling of security against fire heretofore unprecedented among our citizens has prevailed. The town is out of debt.

By favor of a member of the Fire Department, we have the following statement, copied from the first City Record Book.

Maiden City Volunteer Fire Department.—"February 14, 1876. Adjourned meeting of the citizens, held at the court house, with Hon. C. W. West in the chair, for the purpose of organizing a fire department for this city ; the Secretary, W. H. Throckmorton, read the report of committee, which was appointed at a previous meeting, to select names for the company, they having obtained sixty-nine names, and upon motion, said report was received and committee discharged. T. T. Forman then moved that the chair appoint a committee of three to draft a constitution and by-laws for the government of said company. The motion prevailed, and T. T. Forman, C. B. Cook, Sr., and

James S. Withers were appointed in accordance therewith. A motion being made and carried that an election be held to elect officers, the following were elected: H. C. Nebel, Chief; J. L. O'Hearn, First Assistant Chief; J. H. Spohn, Second Assistant Chief; T. T. Forman, Secretary; William Addams, Treasurer; A. O. Robertson, Captain Hose Company; J. A. Eveleth, Lieutenant Hose Company; C. B. Cook, Chief Engineer.

"On motion the meeting adjourned to meet February 26, 1876, C. W. West, Chairman, W. H. Throckmorton, Secretary.

"Since the organization up to the present time, the company has been kept in good shape, and contains now twenty active members, all that are necessary to carry same through. They have done some good work and are the pride of the city, and are now (1882) officered as follows, on the twelfth election in six years: F. A. Barbee, Chief; J. A. Wolford, First Assistant Chief; T. Y. Whitaker, Second Assistant Chief; J. R. Madison, Secretary; J. M. Clary, Captain Hose Company; H. A. Pollmeyer, Lieutenant Hose Company; F. Robitzer, Captain Hook & Ladder Wagon Company; J. A. Wolford, Treasurer."

In the treasury are $240, for the benefit of the disabled or sick. This money was obtained by donations and benefits given for the company. Fortunately none have, thus far, needed any part of this fund.—*Marshall.*

CHAPTER IX.

CYNTHIANA—SECRET AND BENEVOLENT INSTITUTIONS—THE PRESS—BISHOP KAVANAUGH AS A PRINTER—EDUCATIONAL—HARRISON ACADEMY—GRADED SCHOOLS—COLORED EDUCATION—THE MOORE FUND, ETC., ETC.

ON the 4th day of September, 1810, pursuant to a dispensation from the Grand Lodge of Kentucky, Richard Henderson, Master, George W. Timberlake, Senior Warden, and James Finley, Junior Warden, opened a lodge in the first degree in this place. This was the first official meeting of Freemasons in Cynthiana. The original minutes of this meeting, in good preservation, were shown us by Henry Warfield, who has in his possession the Masonic records for the first ten years or more. At the next meeting, three days after the first, Isaac Miller and Edward Coleman petitioned for initiation. They were accepted by "unanimous vote," as the minute has it, on the 7th of September, 1810. They were thus the first of the Ancient Order ever initiated in Cynthiana. Also, at this second meeting, the name, Saint Andrews Lodge, No. 18, was assumed, and has been retained to this day. Petitions now came in rapidly, and the called meetings were frequent, for Freemasonry always flourishes in new settlements.

The charter of Saint Andrews Lodge is dated the 9th of August, 1811, and is signed by Joe Hamilton Daviess, the sixth Grand Master of Kentucky, who was killed at the battle of Tippecanoe one month afterward.

During the first year of their organization, the Masons do not seem to have occupied any lodge room of their own, but in 1817, they purchased the upper story of the Harrison Academy building, now the site of the City School, and had it properly fitted up. Here the lodge met for more than fifty years.

In 1872, the Masons sold out their interest in the second story of Harrison Academy to the City Council for the sum of $2,000, and for a year or two rented the upper room of Eveleth's store. In 1873, Masonic Hall was erected by Samuel O. Eckler, contractor, at an expense of $6,700. It is a fine three-story brick, situated on the west side of Main street, three or four doors south of the National Bank. The lower story is rented by Jost Hoessli, as a stove and hardware store. The second and third stories are occupied by Masonic societies. Saint Andrews Lodge has upheld the time-honored character of Masonry for unostentatious benevolence. It contributed liberally, a few years since, to the Masonic Orphan Asylum at Louisville, also $700 to the South, and is now out of debt. The first Master was Richard Henderson, and the last, at this writing, is John L. Waites. Saint Andrews has given one Grand Master to the State, namely, I. T. Martin, 1866.

The first Chapter of Royal Arch Masons in our city was organized in 1832, and is No. 17 of the State. The first committee on by-laws was composed of Thomas Ware, Joseph Desha and Enoch Worthen. The Chapter still flourishes, and meets regularly. The Council was organized in 1866, but its work has been relegated to the Chapter.

In 1872, a Commandery of Knights Templar, No. 16, was organized, the first officers being Caleb Musser, Commander; A. J. Beale, Generalissimo, and J. M. Poyntz, Captain General. This department of Masonry is here very flourishing, and its numerous public displays have been characterized by the usual medieval splendor. At present the number of members is sixty-eight, the superior officers being Oscar Kennard, Commander; J. T. Hedges, Generalissimo, and James A. Stewart, Captain General.

For about ten years past, Westanna Lodge of the Independent Order of Odd Fellows, successor of the old Harrison Lodge of Odd Fellows, No. 191, has flourished here, and by many a benevolent act has sustained the reputation of Oddfellowship. The number of members, at present, is sixty-five; they meet every Tuesday evening, but have not yet an official habitation of their own. For some years they rented the second story of Masonic Hall, but now they meet in Renaker's Hall. When a member is disabled, he receives $5 a week from the order.

At present the officers are: J. S. Miller, District Deputy; H. M. Keller, Noble Grand; Charles Rieckel, Vice Grand; A. H. Ward, Past Grand; and F. A. Barbee, Secretary.

It is proper to state that the Harrison Lodge, which preceded the present organization, had, for twenty years or more, before the burning of the town in 1862, a prosperous career. In the fire of "'62," however, their lodge room, on the corner of Pike and Main, was burned, together with their books, records and furniture, and also nearly $2,000 in money or its equivalent in claims, which were never recovered.

Cynthiana Lodge, No. 33, of the Ancient Order of United Workmen, was established on the 5th of April, 1874. The first officers were; Samuel H. Williams, P. M. W.; Frank M. Curl, M. W.; Paul King, G. F.; Oscar Kennard, O.; James W. Lacy, Recorder; James F. Keller, Financier; James A. Remington, Receiver; William M. Nourse, Inside Watch.

The officers for 1882, are: Charles Rieckel, P. M. W.; Frank M. Curl, M. W.; James T. Hedges, G. F.; William Addams, Guide; Oscar Kennard, O.; John K. Madison, Recorder; John J. Williams, Financier; James A. Remington, Receiver; William H. Throckmorton, Inside Watch; Hugh M. Keller, Outside Watch.

At present there are twenty-six members in good standing. Their regular meetings are held on the first and third Wednesdays in each month. The order is not a mere assemblage of names, nor are its constituents contented with the mere declaration of principles and theories, but their deeds are practical. Six thousand dollars have been paid by this order, within the last five years, to the families of deceased members of this city alone, distributed as follows: To the family of James H. Toadvine, $2,000; to the family of John S. Lail, $2,000; to the family of Samuel H. Williams, $2,000.

School and Teachers.—By an act of the General Assembly on 22d of December, 1798, Benjamin Harrison, William E. Boswell, Henry Coleman, Hugh Miller, John Wall, Samuel Lamme, Samuel McMillin, Samuel Cook and Robert Hinkson, were appointed trustees of what was to be called Harrison Academy, which institution lasted till 1872, a period of seventy-four years. It still exists in a much modified form, as Cynthiana Graded City School, for the latter occupies the ground and enlarged property of the former, the whole having been transferred by the trustees of the academy to the City Council on specified conditions, ten years ago; the foundation is therefore in its eighty-seventh year.

The Press.—The *Guardian of Liberty,* the first newspaper we hear of in Cynthiana, was published weekly, from January 18, 1817, to March 13, 1819, by John G. Keenan, editor and proprietor. It may have had a longer existence, but the numbers comprised within the above dates are now in the possession of the historian, Richard H. Collins, of Louisville, who kindly offered to submit the file to our inspection; but, as it has been much mutilated by previous item-hunters, it was not examined with reference to this work.

The *Guardian* was printed in the old weather-boarded log building west of the court house, on the corner of the square and the alley, at least, a part of the time. On this paper worked as printers two young type-setters, now gentlemen of national reputation; we mean Bishop H. H. Kavanaugh, now of Louisville, and Hon. A. Dudley Mann, now resident in Chantilly, France. Both were then in their early teens, and both are said to have manifested, even then, predilections for the high spheres of life they afterward reached. When a boy, Mr. Mann used to say he should be a statesman; and we may well imagine that the young Kavanaugh dreamed of his own great career of usefulness. A late note to the Bishop elicited the following reply, which we are allowed to incorporate in this work. It will be read by all with intense interest.

LOUISVILLE, KY., March 23, 1882.

MR. ——— ———, CYNTHIANA, KY.:

Your respectful letter of the 20th ult. was duly received. To your inquiry in regard to the Hon. A. Dudley Mann and myself, I have to say that, in the days of our youth and apprenticeship to the printing business, we did work together for some length of time in the printing office of John Keenan, of Cynthiana, but this at the time was not my proper home. I was learning the business—the art of printing in the book office of the Rev. John Lyle, of Paris, Ky.; but was sent for a time to assist Mr. Keenan in publishing his paper in Cynthiana, and it was during this time that I was associated with Mr. Mann. Though we were but boys, then but recently in our teens, he was so peculiar that he made a lasting impression upon my mind. He was singularly ambitious

"Airy Castle" Residence of G. W. Bowen, Shawhan, Bourbon Co. Ky.

and aspiring. He seemed resolved to be great. As a printer, he looked to Ben Franklin as his model man. The highest position was the glory at which he seemed to aim. I thought he had capacity, if persistent in the means, at least, to reach distinction, and he has done it, and I enjoyed his success. Whether at that time he was putting on airs, or spoke from personal conviction, or only to imitate others, I could not say; but he claimed to be skeptical. I was a boy professor of religion, and hence we debated this question frequently. Where his matured reflections have conducted him, I am not advised, but that he has reached a lofty distinction I am glad to know. He is now regarded as a distinguished American diplomatist, and this implies enlightenment and force.

As it regards the relative position of the printing office to the court house and cardinal points of the compass, I do not so well recollect. It was not far from the bridge, and yet not very near to it, but rather above it on the river. It was a wooden house.

I once met Mr. Mann, to my surprise and pleasure, and, as I recollect, going somewhere East, after he had attained his manhood, but do not remember whether Mr. Clay was on the train; as from such dignitaries I was rather inclined to shrink; but my friend (Mr. Mann) perhaps more wisely would avail himself of such an opportunity to improve his views on the topics of the day. I do remember that some attraction of the kind deprived me of having a longer interview with Mr. Mann than I did have on the occasion.

In regard to the ministers of the Gospel who may have resided at Cynthiana at an early day, I cannot give much information.

Among the earliest of the Methodist ministers known to me, was by marriage an uncle of mine, the Rev. Leroy Cole, who lived about a mile from town on the road to Paris by the way of Ruddel's Mills.

The first Presbyterian preacher known to me was the Rev. Mr. Moreland, a very pathetic, earnest, and powerful revivalist; and what was known as a Secessionist or Covenanter, the Rev. Mr. Rainey; but you can get among the citizens of the place a more extended and accurate account than I can give you.

Wishing you success in your laudable enterprise,

I am respectfully yours, H. H. KAVANAUGH.

The Cynthiana *Advertiser* succeeded the *Guardian of Liberty* about 1821, and continued till at least 1827; a number of that year is shown at the *News* office. The *Advertiser* published the acts of the General Assembly by authority, and must have been an important journal in its day. Gen. Jackson was prospective candidate for the Presidency, and there was apprehension that the will of the people might be thwarted, as some claimed it had been in the election of John Quincy Adams. The *Advertiser* shown us contains a review of Gov. Desha's proposed method of electing the President, but Jackson went into the Presidency on the old plan by too strong a vote to permit question or invite revision of the constitutional election laws. Jackson and the *Advertiser* have now both receded a half century into the past, though the puzzle of the best mode of electing the President still remains. W. F. Birch, editor and proprietor of the *Advertiser* is remembered as a man of talents.

The Cynthiana *Gleaner* was published here from 1830 till 1838, by William and James Campbell. The *Visitor*, a literary paper was also published by the Campbells, editors and proprietors of both papers, during the same interval. A religious paper was published about the same time in Cynthiana, of which we have not obtained exact information.

In 1850, John Atkinson started the Cynthiana *News*. In 1851, it was purchased by A. J. Morey, who, as editor and proprietor, has published the *News* down to the present time, a period of upward of thirty years. He may claim to be the Nestor of newspaper men in our town. The publication was suspended during the troubles of 1861–65, but since the close of the war, the paper has made its regular weekly appearance. The *News* had the entire field to itself until 1869, when the Cynthiana *Democrat* was established, and put under the editorial management of C. W. West, who occupied the position about one year. In 1870, R. W. Musser became editor; in 1872, Caleb Musser; in 1873, Adolphus Musser; in 1874, Green R. Keller; in 1875, A. O. Robertson; in 1877, H. P. Diltz; in 1881, Achilles Perrin; in 1882, W. V. Prather, the present editor aud proprietor. All the Cynthiana papers have been Democratic. Their subscription lists have commonly numbered from one thousand to two thousand five hundred. Both the *News* and *Democrat* are equipped with job offices, which, together with the advertising departments, render the business self-sustaining, if not lucrative.

The Academy was, at first, located on ground which now forms part of the Old Cemetery, in a stone building which long ago disappeared, but is still remembered by old citizens. The Harrison Academy was moved from its first position to the site of the present City School in 1810; but both the old and the new situations were occupied for a few years after the transfer for school purposes. Citizens are still living, who, in their young days, attended school at both places.

Samuel Endicott, a distinguished classical teacher, swayed the scepter in the old cemetery building as early as 1806, and our venerable fellow-citizen, Dr. George H. Perrin, was one of his pupils more than seventy-five years ago. Endicott is described as a severe but most successful instructor. On two or more different occasions, dissatisfaction became so strong that he had to retire and practice his art elsewhere, and twice was he recalled by his old friends, who chose to put up with his harshness for the sake of his thorough and excellent teaching. Thus he taught, not always in peace, but always with high reputation, till 1831. In the following year, he was appointed County Court Clerk, and so ceased to be reckoned among pedagogues, though his son, Thomas, attended to the duties of the clerkship, so that his father, while Clerk, still taught at intervals, but not in the academy. As late as 1834, it is remembered that he held a school in a house occupying the site of the present Masonic Hall. Gen. Lucius Desha was one of his pupils, and bears honorable testimony to the very high educational abilities of his old preceptor. In 1838, he removed to Henderson, Ky., and died there some years after. His daughter, Anna Maria, assisted her father in his schools, and was herself a teacher of distinction, seemingly inheriting her father's special talents. She was still living, a few years ago, in Lexington, Mo. Severe and haughty as he was to evil-doers in school, Endicott was a gentleman of princely bearing and polished manners.

In 1813, Jesse Olds, and his son, Augustus, occupied the academy as principal and assistant, during the absence of Endicott, who was probably then residing in Millersburg, Ky. We are assured that Olds was in charge as late as 1828, but it appears that Olds and Endicott held the position alternately for some years, or that one taught in the academy, while the other, at the same time, occupied some other place in town. James Kelley is also remembered as a teacher of these early times.

Especially is William Garmany, an Irishman, to be mentioned, known as a teacher of languages, who kept his school at intervals in the stone house on the old cemetery ground, from about 1817 till 1830. He came here from the South, and became a classical teacher of reputation, but though of good habits, it is remembered that he saved no money, and about 1838–39 he concluded to return. He resided rather probably as a needy guest at the house of Dr. Joel C. Frazer for some weeks before his departure, and finally left for Georgia in company with William R. Fowler, a noted stock dealer of that time. He, no doubt, made the journey through the kind aid of Dr. Frazer and Fowler. Dr. Perrin cannot recall him to mind as a teacher, but we are assured of his career as such by people who say positively that they attended his school. For instance, Mr. Henry F. Cromwell recollects that he himself and the late Maj. Newt Miller were boys together at Garmany's school; that they used to go out and catch snails, bring them into school, place them on their slates, and set them to running races. The very oddness of the story inspires confidenee in the memory of the narrator.

In 1822–23, Alexander Downing taught a private school in the house now occupied by Mr. Benjamin Day, on the west side of the square.

In 1837, Rev. Charles Crowe, a graduate of Dublin University, Ireland, assisted by a Rev. — Green, held school in the academy building. Rev. — Cowgill occupied the position during the summer of 1837. Mr. Crowe returned to Ireland in 1844, and quite recently was residing at Clonis, in his professional capacity as clergyman.

In 1838, a Mr. Shepherd is remembered in charge of the academy, for about six months, followed by a Mr. Barnes the same year. Messrs. Barnes and J. M. Elliot took charge of Harrison Academy in 1840. The next year, J. M. Elliott and George M. Clarke assumed control of the same institution, which they held for two years. They had the largest school that had ever, up to that time, been taught in our city or county. Elliott was a classical teacher of fine abilities and high reputation. He returned to Ohio whence he came, in 1843. Clarke still resides in Covington, Ky., and is now a prosperous business man.

In September, 1845, Mr. J. W. Peck, now a well-known business man of our town, was appointed Principal of the academy, and held the position one year. He then embarked in successful business operations. Mr. Peck was succeeded by Prof. J. H. Smith, of the University of Cambridge, England, and was, perhaps, the most learned of the long line of Principals who have held the reins in old Harrison. Besides the usual ancient languages, he read Hebrew and Syriac easily, without grammar or lexicon. He returned to Carlisle, Ky., in a year or two, where he had married Miss Nancy West. His connection with the academy lasted only about three years, but he taught a select school for sometime in the Wall schoolhouse, on the corner of Pike street and the public square. He returned from Carlisle in 1861, and bought several town lots, including the present residence of Judge Boyd, to whom he sold the eastern portion of his purchase, now the Judge's place, and built for himself a new frame house, a little further west, fronting the river. Here, for twelve or fifteen years, he lived the life of a retired scholar, engrossed with his books. He died in 1876, at the age of seventy-seven. He was a Swedenborgian in religious faith, and was perfectly familiar with the voluminous Latin works of the great Swedish mystic and seer.

William H. Crutchfield succeeded Prof. Smith in 1847 or 1848; we regret that we are often compelled to speak of dates with uncertainty, for we have not been able to recover the records of the old school board; but Crutchfield retained his position till 1853, and taught the higher branches with distinction and popularity. He was a man of superior intelligence; he had been Librarian of the Congressional Library at Washington. On terminating his engagement here, he moved to Lexington, where he continued his avocation for some years, and died in 1876.

In 1854, Rev. Carter Page began his long career as Principal of the old academy. He was a classical teacher of very high repute. He had talents, tact, and tenacity, for he held his ground longer than any of his predecessors, except the great Endicott, and he rivaled that noted teacher in all his best qualities. He was undoubtedly an instructor of the first order. From 1854 till 1866, he sustained the school, not yielding to the disturbances of the war till he had endured three years of its interruptions. In 1865, or, perhaps, in 1866, he resigned his position here, and moved to Anchorage, Ky., and there became Principal and proprietor of a young ladies' boarding school, which had, for the previous ten years, been conducted by Rev. George Beckett; but he soon went on to Missouri, where he bought property, and by the last advices, was still teaching with his wonted success.

After the retirement of Mr. Page, the academy was graced by the government of two ladies, Misses Alice and Mary Duncanson, in the fall of 1865. The young ladies were from Lexington, and in less troubled times would have had a more favorable field for the display of their educational abilities. But as it was, Principals came and went in rapid succession. In the spring of 1865, we find Rev. — Jeffreys in charge; in 1866, we find Rev. Isaac M. Reese, a kind-hearted, modest gentleman whom everybody loved; in 1867, we find Rev. J. W. Wightman, from South Carolina. He also had the respect and good-will of all parties, but he thought his clerical duties hardly compatible with earnest school employments, and relinquished the situation at the end of one year. In 1868, we find R. W. McCrery, a young classical teacher, just graduated from Georgetown College. He also held the position but one year, though he was an instructor of high attainments, and has, since his residence here, evinced the resources of a genuine educator, at Shelbyville, Ky., where he conducted the new City Public School, under his superintendency, to the summit of prosperity. He now resides in Frankfort, and for some years has been on the State Board of Examiners.

In July, 1869, the writer of these chapters was elected Principal of Harrison Academy, and retained the position for three years under the old regime, and then, from 1872 to the present time, 1882, he has been annually re-elected under the new organization. The last Board of Trustees of Harrison Academy, appointed by the County Court, was composed of Gen. Lucius Desha, President; Dr. N. C. Dille, J. W. Kimbrough, R. C. Wherritt and T. A. Frazer. This board turned over its responsibilities to the curators of the new organization in 1872.

It may be worth while to place the names of the Principals of the old academy, and their respective dates, in the order of their succession, so that they may be seen at glance. Many of them, perhaps most of them, taught private schools in town, either before, or after, their connection with the academy.

Samuel Endicott, at intervals, from 1806 to 1835; Jesse Olds and his son, Augustus, at intervals, from 1813 to 1830; James Kelley, between 1818 and 1825; William Garmany, at intervals, 1817 to 1837; Rev. — Cowgill, 1837; Rev. Charles Crowe, 1838; Rev. — Green (Assistant), 1838; — Barnes, 1839; — Shepherd, 1839; J. M. Elliott and Barnes, 1840; J. M. Elliott and George M. Clarke, 1842; J. W. Peck, 1845; John Henry Smith, 1846; William H. Crutchfield, 1852; Rev. Carter Page, 1854; Misses Alice and Mary Duncanson, 1865; Rev. —— Jeffreys, 1865; Rev. Isaac M. Reese, 1866; Miss Anna Milton, Assistant; Rev. J. W. Wightman, 1867; Miss Anna Milton, Assistant; R. W. McCrery, 1868; Miss Eunice Martin, Assistant; L. G. Marshall, 1869; Misses Rebecca Anderson and Gippie Jackson, Assistants.

We pause here, before completing the story of the old academy, and proceeding with our account of the establishment and progress of the Graded City School on the foundation of the old Harrison, to notice several meritorious private schools of the town which flourished before the troubled times of 1861–65, though we do not claim that our list is quite complete, for the whole field is one in which we have no predecessor to guide us.

Mrs. Johnnie B. Anderson taught a primary school in Cynthiana as early as 1833, and continued till 1852. She was a faithful, industrious teacher, the mother of a family of female teachers who have achieved reputation.

Mrs. Isette taught a school of decided excellence, in the little frame house on the west side of Main street, now the property of J. S. Withers, from 1832 to 1841. She was a lady of superior talents and accomplishments. She owned the house and lot on the north side of Pleasant street, adjoining the railroad, now the property of John J. Williams. She sold her place to J. W. Mackintosh; Mackintosh sold to Benson Roberts; Mrs. Roberts sold the same to John J. Williams. Mrs. Isette moved to Versailles, Ky., about 1842.

Mrs. Louisa A. Delling, formerly Mrs. Louisa A. Ormsby, began teaching in Cynthiana in February, 1851, and continued in that employment till June, 1861. During the first year she occupied the so-called Anderson Schoolhouse, on Main street. The next year she held school in the Wall Schoolhouse, on the corner of Pike and Court streets. For seven years and a half she taught in her own house, on the corner of Pleasant and Walnut streets. She was a teacher of high standing and of more than usual accomplishments. She had, too, some financial abilities, and saved money. In 1861, Mrs. Ormsby married C. T. Delling, Esq., merchant of our city, since which time she has discontinued teaching.

Mr. Charles H. Anderson held a school of respectable character, in the small frame house, named for him the Anderson Schoolhouse, on the east side of Main street, from 1841 till about 1848. He was killed on the Kentucky Central Railroad, near the town, just this side of the Oddville pike crossing, in 1855.

Very early, it does not appear exactly how early, but probably at the beginning, in 1798, the County Court received authority to appoint the Trustees of Harrison Academy ; and under this authority, Dr. George H. Perrin was President of the Board from 1825 till 1864, a period of thirty-nine years, but as we have not been able to consult the records of this body, we cannot present the succession of presiding officers under the old organization. The trustees elected their Principal, allowing him to select his own assistant, if he so desired. It was customary to charge him, at least, in the latter years of the academy, $100 annual rent, which, however, he might expend, if he thought proper, in supplying suitable conveniences about the school building. The Principal furnished his own fuel, janitor, apparatus, and paid his own assistant. The County Court kept the house in repair, such as it was, and the Freemasons defrayed their own expenses in their rooms of the second story, the two lower rooms only being ever used for school purposes. Thus the academy was a highly appreciated benefit to the county, as it always offered a suitable place for the accommodation of a school of rank. Classics and the higher branches were always offered to students attending school in this building, no Principal being ever elected, it seems, who was not able to sustain the dignity of old Harrison in this respect. The very first schoolhouse on the present site, we have no particular account of ; very likely it was some abandoned private residence, but after the measures taken in 1817, to be related presently, a pretty considerable school building was erected and finished in 1820. The ground not being leveled, the building had a high stone basement, entered by a door, not often kept closed, and horses could be, and sometimes were, stabled and fed in the basement. In 1851, this structure was taken down to prevent its falling down, and a much larger one erected and finished in 1853 ; it was of brick, two-story, sixty feet by thirty. This building, to which a south wing was added in 1874, yet stands in good preservation.

The persistent life of the old institution will, perhaps, be made more intelligible by the following extracts from the official records of the County Courts.

HARRISON ACADEMY, March 15, 1817.

Benjamin Warfield and Sarah, his wife, conveyed to Gavin Morrison, William Brown, etc., trustees of Harrison Academy (on its present site), parts of lots 1 and 2 in Hinkson's Addition, town of Cynthiana, for the purpose of erecting a seminary building. Afterward, May 22, 1817, Richard Henderson and Fanny, his wife, conveyed to Gavin Morrison, etc., trustees as aforesaid, the balance of Lot No. 2, in said addition, for the same purpose. Still later, June 18, 1824, William K. Wall and others, then trustees of Harrison Academy, conveyed to Enoch Worthen and others, trustees of the town of Cynthiana, the Old Cemetery lot on which stood a stone structure used and called Harrison Academy, being the same lot which was conveyed by Benjamin Harrison and the original trustees of the town of Cynthiana, to the trustees of Harrison by deed bearing date 1804, now lot forming part of the Old Cemetery in the north part of Cynthiana. The consideration for this last said conveyance being as described in the deed, fifty Spanish milled dollars.

So, substantially, the record furnished by the kindness of Judge Boyd, whose experienced eye quickly discerns what is wanted in an old record book.

Thus the legal transfer from the Old Cemetery lot to the so-called Hinkson's Addition took place in 1817, but tradition has it that the school was transferred and held in some sort of building as early as 1810.

By act of 1816, the trustees were authorized to use so much of the $5,000 for which they sold the seminary lands (an old Congressional grant made when Kentucky consisted of a few large counties, and the benefits of which these large counties monopolized to the exclusion, of course, of most of the smaller counties cut out of these larger ones in after times, and of which fund Harrison County was one of the lucky heirs), as in addition to the fourth of the $5,000 which they were already allowed to use for that purpose, would be sufficient to erect a suitable building. It was this fund, together with the aid furnished by a partnership with the Freemasons in the occupancy of the building and grounds, and some repairs provided for by the County Court, that maintained the establishment as a seat of learning till its recent conveyance to the town.

The Graded City School.—For some time prior to 1872, there had been an increasing desire among our citizens to establish a free city school, open to all resident white children of pupil age, and offering a course of instruction, at least, equal to what had been customary in the old academy.

It may be of interest to present the following extract from page 430 of the first record book of the City Council, as showing the energy and determination of members to put the school on its present basis :

MAY 14, 1872.

Councilman Beale introduced an ordinance to open a public school in the city of Cynthiana, whereupon it was moved to refer the same to the Committee on Propositions and Grievances, to report by Saturday, May 27, 1872. Lost.

Councilman Beale moved that the Rules be suspended, and the ordinance to establish a public school be put upon its passage. Carried.

Councilman Beale also moved that the ordinance be passed—the ordinance being read was adopted by a unanimous vote.

C. MUSSER, *Mayor*.

F. G. ASHBROOK,
A. J. BEALE,
C. B. COOK,
H. D. FRISBIE,
A. W. LYDICK,
R. M. MARTIN,
JOHN T. HOGG,
JOSEPH H. SHAWHAN, } *Councilmen.*

Meanwhile, there had been provided no buildings or grounds for the accommodation of the new city school. It was soon ascertained, however, that the Board of Trustees of the Harrison Academy were willing to transfer their charge to the City Council on the authority of an act of Assembly, which was duly obtained, Saint Andrews Lodge also selling out to the Council its rights to the upper story and its approaches, for $2,000.

The City Council at once proceeded to establish, instead of the academy, a public graded school, provided with a full corps of teachers, and, by the conditions of transfer, a course of instruction not inferior to that of its predecessor. During the first year of the city school, the registered number of pupils was 199. In 1873–74, it was found that the school required larger accommodations, and the south wing of the building was added, which, with desks and other furniture, cost about $4,000, supplying four more fine school rooms. Since 1874, the annual registered number of pupils has been about 300, seven teachers being engaged. The work is distributed into seven grades, two of which constitute the high school. The course of instruction is similar to that of the best schools of the kind in the country, if not even more extensive. Diplomas are conferred, by special act of Assembly, upon those who complete the course. The diplomas are of two grades, the General and the Scientific, but a large majority of those who complete the course take the General Diploma. The number of graduates up to this year, 1882, inclusive, is between forty and fifty.

A considerable library has been accumulated, numbering about fifteen hundred volumes, most of which were contributed by the United States Congress, through the kind offices of W. S. Haviland. These consist of the usual public documents coming from that source. There are, however, five or six hundred volumes of the first order of interest and value, as works of reference. Almost every question that ordinarily arises among advanced students may be answered by consulting these reference books. Some of the best were bought with the money presented to the library by the old Literary Society of Cynthiana, when it quit business a few years ago. George E. Stevens, of Cincinnati, also contributed several of the best and most useful books of reference in the library.

In 1878, the City Council relinquished control, by act of the General Assembly, and the school is now managed by a separate corporate body of eight trustees, acting under legislative authority.

This board, at present, 1882, is composed as follows:

Officers.—Dr. H. McDowell, President; Luther Van Hook, Vice President; L. M. Martin, Clerk; William H. Throckmorton, Treasurer.

Trustees.—L. Van Hook, T. A. Frazer, term expires 1882; W. W. Longmoor, Dr. A. J. Beale, 1883; Charles Rieckel, L. M. Martin, 1884; W. C. Musselman, H. Mc Dowell, 1885.

Our account of Harrison Academy has been unavoidably blended with frequent notices of private enterprises of a similar character, for most of the Principals and teachers of the academy established private schools of their own, either before or after their connection with that institution. This has been a pretty common occurrence ever since 1817, when the academy was moved from the old cemetery lot to the present situation. These private schools not rarely offered educational facilities fully equal, it was claimed, to those at the academy. But they all lacked permanency.

However, in 1872–73, Mr. N. F. Smith founded a private school which has attained character and popularity, and has had a longer duration than any individual enterprise of the kind in our town. The Smith Institute is well situated in the large brick residence, formerly the property of Charles T. Wilson. The course of instruction is extensive, and the educational work is rendered effective and attractive by philosophical and chemical apparatus. The number of pupils has ranged from seventy to about one hundred.

In 1876, Miss Lizzie Corbin opened a select school in the residence of the late Prof. J. H. Smith, on Pike street, fronting the river. The school was well conducted, and had numerous friends. A regular course of instruction was pursued, and the school prospered for two or three years, but the Principal accepted an engagement offered by the Midway Orphan School, and so this enterprise terminated.

In 1878, Mr. J. A. Brown purchased the finely situated

residence of John K. Lake, Esq., formerly the home of the late M. L. Broadwell, on the south side of Pike street, east of the railroad. Here Mr. Brown established the Harrison Female College, under a Board of Directors, with a full course of instruction, corps of teachers, and the usual specialties appertaining to the education of young ladies. The school has enjoyed a very flattering and profitable patronage. Twelve or fifteen graduates have distinguished its annual Commencements.

The notice of schools would not be complete if we should omit to state that there has been a Catholic school in town almost continually since Father Brantz built the first Catholic Church here in 1859. This school has commonly contained forty or fifty pupils, and has always occupied the old church in rear of St. Édward's Church.

A colored school has also been held in town since about the year 1868; it is pleasantly situated on the so-called "Common," in a comfortable house near the river. It has generally been satisfactory to those for whom it was intended.

Here, too, is the proper place to notice some other educational matters, though not all of them are strictly confined to our town.

The Moore Fund.—In 1832, Henry C. Moore died, son of William Moore, first Clerk of the County and Circuit Courts of Harrison County. Henry C. Moore, by his will set apart $15,000, half of his estate, for the education of poor orphans of Harrison County. This disposition of the property was contested by the heirs in the courts till 1838, when the will was sustained. The fund was then loaned to the county at 6 per cent, and the annual income thereon, about $800, distributed semi-annually to pay for the education of poor orphans. The County Court appoints a commissioner to see to the proper disposition of the fund, who receives a small sum, perhaps $15 annually, for his trouble. The teacher is required to state, under oath, the number of days each orphan pupil has received instruction. During the earlier years of the distribution, the teacher was paid 12 or 15 cents for each day, so that twenty orphan pupils would be worth about $3 per day. But for the last four or five years the distribution has been only 6 or 7 cents a day; not that poor orphans have greatly increased in number, but for years many teachers hardly understood the scheme, or, at any rate, neglected to report the instruction of beneficiary pupils and put in their claims. Yet the Henry C. Moore fund has been a great and highly appreciated benevolence in Harrison County, and the name of its founder will ever be remembered with feelings of gratitude and affection.—*Marshall.*

CHAPTER X.

CYNTHIANA—RELIGIOUS HISTORY—SOME EARLY MINISTERS—THE METHODISTS AND PRESBYTERIANS—OTHER CHURCH ORGANIZATIONS—FORMATION OF COLORED CHURCHES—RICHARD HENDERSON AND ISAAC MILLER—SUMMARY, ETC., ETC.

"Ye birds,
That singing up to Heaven-gate ascend,
Bear on your wings and in your notes his praise."
—*Milton.*

IT was twenty-five years after the establishment of the town before any effective steps were taken toward the erection of sacred edifices, but there is ample evidence that almost coincident with the beginning of the place, religious people and religious assemblies were numerous. Bishop Kavanaugh, when a young man in his "early teens," was a resident here about 1815, engaged in the printing office of John Keenan, remembers his uncle, the Rev. Le Roy Cole, a Methodist, who lived about a mile from town on the Paris road; he also recalls Rev. —. Moreland, "a very powerful revivalist;" also Rev. William Rainey, a few years later the "covenanter;" and the Bishop presumes that the names of others may be obtained by consulting long-resident citizens.

But in the earlier years, private dwellings, or the rude public buildings of the time, were open, on all proper occasions, for the accommodation of religious assemblies; for it is quite natural that a majority of the people, descended as they were from church-going stock, should adhere to the habits of their ancestors. Besides, it will be remembered, that in the first quarter of the present century, there was an unprecedented activity in religious affairs, especially in the Western States. Barton W. Stone was often in this vicinity, and sometimes right here in Cynthiana; and a few years after him, Alexander Campbell, then in the glow of early manhood, traversed Kentucky, advocating his peculair views with all the power and attractiveness for which he afterward became so renowned. All orders of Christians were wide-awake, zeal was stimulated, and the liberality of those who had the means to give, responded to the ardent appeals of the

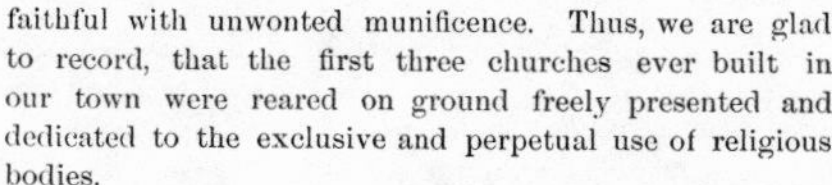

faithful with unwonted munificence. Thus, we are glad to record, that the first three churches ever built in our town were reared on ground freely presented and dedicated to the exclusive and perpetual use of religious bodies.

On the 9th of October, 1818, Richard Henderson, and Fanny, his wife, deeded to the Trustees of the Methodist Church of Cynthiana, namely: Le Roy Cole, Peter Barrett, John Frazer, Joshua Jones, James Finley and Carter Anderson, the lot on which the present Methodist Church stands, on the corner of Church and Pike streets, exclusively for church purposes, as a free gift, subject, however, to this condition: that if ever used for any purpose other than religious worship, the property should revert to the heirs of the original donor.

There must have been, even then, at that early day, a pretty strong and numerous membership, a full account of which would now be of great interest and value; but the actors of those times have mostly passed away, leaving us only tradition, and the unimpaired rights to the ground on which they raised their first house of worship.

The Trustees received their lot from Richard Henderson in 1818, and in 1820 they had finished a large and commodious brick church, which would comfortably seat 500 people. There are still members living who remember with a sort of melancholy pleasure the venerable old house. It burned down in 1844, and in the following year was replaced by a smaller edifice, constructed also of brick, and fronting Church street. This building had a basement in which schools were sometimes held, and the auditorium was reached by a broad stairway up to the entrance, forming an approach a little perilous in icy weather. It was decked with a spire of the olden time, and seated about two hundred and fifty persons. There the last Conference held in Cynthiana was assembled in September, 1869, Bishop Kavanaugh, presiding; but the audiences proving too large for the house, the members accepted an invitation to meet in the Presbyterian Church, which, in turn, being found unequal to the occasion, Conference availed itself of the hospitality of the Christian Church, where the official business of the meeting was concluded. At this Conference, Rev. C. W. Miller, then Presiding Elder of his district, and resident of Covington, but now of Lexington, was assigned to the pastoral charge of the Methodist Church of Cynthiana. The new pastor entered upon his duties with characteristic energy. The gathering shadows of indifference or discouragement which had been for years hovering over his people were soon dissipated before his earnestness, his devotion, tact and talents. The membership of the church was in a few months more than doubled. Early in 1870, steps were taken to erect a more suitable house of worship. Caleb Walton, H. D. Frisbie and Henry Williams were appointed a building committee. The old house fronting on Church street was taken down, and the contractors, Messrs. Humble & Son, of Covington, undertook to set up a new, handsome and very comfortable church edifice fronting on Pike street, according to specifications, all of which they executed with such dispatch that the house was up and finished almost before outsiders had had time to bestow their advice and criticism. The building is provided with a basement where fuel is stored and the furnace located. The audience room is thus raised above Pike street, from which the vestibule is conveniently reached by two or three steps, thence communicating with the interior by two doors. In the south end of the vestibule there is a neat study and library-room, fitted up to accommodate the pastors' reading and writing, for Dr. Miller was devoted to ecclesiastical learning as well as to his specific clerical duties. In the north end of the vestibule there is a corresponding room for miscellaneous articles. The desk, fronted by a balustrade, is situated under the dome of a tastefully arranged bay-window in the rear of the auditorium. The walls and ceilings are handsomely finished in fresco. The arched windows extend from the chair-railing nearly to the ceiling, and are supplied with stained glass of rich and varied colors, and the conventional spire indicates the religious character of the edifice. It will seat three hundred and fifty or perhaps four hundred people. The whole cost of the work was $11,000 nearly, and the church is substantially out of debt, with a membership of about two hundred and fifty.

In November, 1870, the new church was dedicated by the Rev. Dr. E. W. Sehon, of Louisville, prefacing the ceremony of dedication by a captivating discourse, in the style and manner of which he knew so well how to mingle the lofty, the graceful and the pleasing. It was twenty years since he had preached in Cynthiana, he said, and should it be twenty years before he preached here again, we should see him no more. His remark was, indeed, prophetic; he died in Louisville six or seven years after this visit to our town.

Meantime, the church, under the guidance of an able pastor, with its new house of worship, and with its largely increased membership, entered upon a period of prosperity which has continued to the present time. The loss of about half of the original building ground, by decision of the courts in 1872, did not, in any considerable degree, diminish the strength and efficiency of the church, though it was a pretty rude shock to the reverent feelings with which all had learned to view the old gift of Richard Henderson and Fanny, his wife. Until this decision, the church lot extended on Pike street, to J. W. Peck's premises.

As far back as 1828 or 1830, James Chambers, one of the early trustees, had a small claim against the church for stone work and carpenter's work, as appears in recorded affidavits. The claim lay in abeyance till 1842, when Asbury Broadwell, Mrs. Le Roy Cole, James Chambers, Daniel Tebbs and John Walton (father of Caleb Walton), all having claims of some such nature, in the shape of notes, were disposed to urge them ; but finally, all either relinquished or compromised them, so that they were no more heard of, except James Chambers, then steward of the church. His claim, only $81.87, turned out to be in the shape of a mortgage given to him for this claim by the trustees at some time not exactly now known. It was not till 1854 that Chambers, having removed to Illinois, attempted to foreclose this mortgage. Suit was then brought, and judgment having been rendered favorable to Chambers, a minority of the trustees executed a deed conveying to him the hillside lot extending about a hundred feet on Pike street to J. W. Peck's line. The case was carried to the Court of Appeals, and, on the 3d of June, 1872, decision was at last rendered adverse to the validity of the deed, but sustaining the integrity of the mortgage, as being executed by competent parties. So, the lot was lost by the church. On the 23d of December, 1872, the Master Commissioner of the Circuit Court, Achilles Perrin, Esq., sold the much contested ground at public auction, to W. W. Cleary for $174.20, to which amount the original claim of $81.87 had increased by interest and costs. On the 23d of June, 1873, Cleary sold the same to W. A. Cook & Co. for $350, and on the dissolution of that firm a year or two after, W. A. Cook who still holds it, became the owner, at the price of $250. The history of this affair is preserved in the records of the courts, and thus our information about it is even more than we need, while, on the other hand, the early church books having all been consumed in the fire that carried off the first building in 1844, we are forced to remain ignorant of much of what we commonly prize most, namely, the ups and downs of resolute beginners. Completeness and accuracy are therefore beyond our reach.

Dr. Miller remained in charge of the church four consecutive years, from 1869 to 1873, the full time allowed by law of conference. He was assigned to Frankfort, then to Lexington, where he now resides. He was a delegate last year to the Ecumenical Methodist Council, held in London, England.

We name in retrograde order the clergy for the last thirty or forty years :

Rev. Dr. James A. Henderson, 1882 ; Rev. B. F. Sedwick, 1878 ; Rev. W. J. Snively, 1876 ; Rev. John R. Deering, 1875 ; Rev. — Reynolds, 1874 ; Rev. R. Hiner, 1873 ; Rev. Dr. C. W. Miller, 1869 ; Rev. J. W. Wightman, 1866 ; Rev. S. S. Deering, 1864 ; Rev. Samuel Kelley, 1863–64 ; Rev. S. X. Hall, 1862 ; Rev. W. J. Snively, 1861 ; Rev. Samuel Kelley, 1860 ; Rev. B. F. Sedwick, 1858 ; Rev. William H. Winter, 1856 ; Rev. Jacob Ditzler, 1855 ; Rev. — Smith, 1854 ; Rev. W. W. Trainer, 1853 ; Rev. J. W. Minor, 1852 ; Rev. —— Johnson, 1851 ; Rev. James Wells, 1850 ; Rev. Richard Holden, 1849 ; Rev. S. S. Deering, 1847.

Presbyterian Church.—Here we meet again the benevolent Richard Henderson and his wife, Fanny, together with Isaac Miller and his wife, as the donors of the ground on which stood the first Presbyterian Church in Cynthiana ; yet our story is embarrassed by the usual paucity of contemporary documents, and thus a trap all the time stands ready to catch the narrator in some mistake of omission or commission ; and besides this, the writer at first hand is preparing a statement, about whose correctness there are many good judges among his readers, whom he cannot consult before he commits himself to print.

However, on the authority of the County Court records, we are enabled to say that the site of the first church was a free gift, presented by Isaac Miller and the same parties who, two years before, endowed the Methodist Church in a similar manner. For the recovery of this item, and for the collection of most of the following reminiscences of the early times of the Presbyterian Church, we are indebted to Hon. J. Q. Ward.

No reliable information has been obtained as to the precise time when the Presbyterian Church was organized in our town ; but a very early day, some years at least, before the acquisition of a building lot, there were Presbyterian Church organizations in the vicinity, and, presumably, in Cynthiana. At Mount Pleasant, about five miles west of Cynthiana, there was a Presbyterian organization before 1820 ; also at Ruddel's Mills, about eight miles southeast, and another some two miles northeast. But, confining ourselves to the special subject in hand, the history of the church in Cynthiana, we find the following entries in the books of the County Court Clerk's office :

On the 21st day of August, 1820, Richard Henderson and Fanny, his wife, conveyed, as a free gift, to Benjamin Robinson, Alexander Downing and Isaac Miller, trustees of the Cynthiana congregation of Presbyterians, under the jurisdiction of the Synod of Kentucky, a lot of ground for the purpose of having erected thereon a house of worship, and a pound for horses. The lot is described

"FOREST HILL" RESIDENCE OF WILLIAM SKINNER, NEAR SHAWHAN STATION, BOURBON CO. KY.

as follows: "A lot in that part of said town called Hinkson's Addition, being a part of what is termed 'Outlot No. 1,' and bounded as follows, to wit: Beginning on Second Cross (now Pleasant) street, leading to the lower bridge (which was carried off in 1828) across the river, at at a point 198 feet of the northwest corner of said Outlot No. 1, thence with said street 50 feet, thence south 104 feet 4 inches to a stone, thence west 54 feet to a stone, thence north 104 feet 4 inches to the beginning."

Also, on the same day, 21st of August, 1820, Isaac Miller and his wife conveyed, as a free gift, to the same trustees, except to himself (Miller), for the same purpose, an adjoining lot west, of the same size as the above, making a front of 104 feet, and 104 feet in depth.

The church was, at this time, connected with the Ebenezer Presbytery. There is no reference to the church work on the minutes of the General Assembly, until the year, 1830. It is then reported as having a membership of twenty. In 1831, a membership of sixty-three was reported. About 1825, a building for church purposes was erected on the lot presented by Henderson, but there is no extant report of its cost, its builders, or its committeemen. We know, however, from other sources, that it was a brick structure, about 40 by 60 feet.

For the next ten or eleven years we hear little or nothing of the young church. The situation of the building lot, in Hinkson's Addition, seems not to have been satisfactory. It formed part of the now vacant lot on the south side of Pleasant street, in rear of J. W. Peck's residence. It was allowed to revert by suit in law, to the heirs of Isaac Miller, one of the donors.

In 1836–37, William Lamme donated to the church the lot on Main street, where the present church stands, and the building on the first lot described was taken down, and rebuilt on this Main street lot. Lamme purchased the lot of Samuel Moore, and later received the same from his father, William Moore, the first Clerk of the Court of Quarter Sessions of Harrison County, in 1794. The principal parties engaged in this enterprise were William Lamme, Isaac Miller, George Kirkpatrick, William Thompson, Maj. Kimbrough, Hubbard Tebbs, Samuel Williams and Rev. William H. Forsythe.

It seems that Lamme did not own the lot at the time he gave his bond to the church for it; that the title was in Samuel Moore, then residing in Missouri. Lamme had paid large sums for Moore, and thought he could undertake to give away the lot. No trouble was apprehended from this circumstances, nor, indeed, were the facts in the case hardly known to the parties most interested till 1840, when William Thompson, one of the earliest members, had some difficulty, the nature of which does not appear, with his brethren; and was dismissed from or voluntarily severed his connection with his old church. He then made out a bill for work on the building of 1836–37, amounting to $500, and the trustees refusing to pay it, he took possession of the house and kept it for years, but was finally dispossessed by a suit in ejectment. Thompson, while in possession of the church property, had joined the Episcopalians, and, it was thought, made an offer to turn the building over to that denomination, on what precise terms, is not now known. But Maj. James R. Curry says that being at Leesburg one day, he was told by Joseph Wasson that the Episcopalians there were about to trade their Leesburg house to Thompson for the Presbyterian Church in Cynthiana. When Curry heard this report, he at once sent to Samuel Moore, of Missouri, and obtained from him a deed of the church lot to the trustees of the Presbyterian Church. Thompson's plans also required a deed, and he also sent to Moore some time after and, strangely enough, got from him a deed to the same lot for himself. The conflicting claims arising from this *quasi* double ownership, were, at last, adjusted in favor of the church, but only after a long and tedious suit.

The carpenters' work on the first Main street house was done by Samuel Williams; the brick work by William English.

The house was not a costly one, the carpenters' bill of Williams, and the board-bill of English and his hands while laying the brick, amounted to only $124.95¼, yet the church remained for some years uncompleted. Rev. William H. Forsythe tells how he raised the money on a county court day to buy the bill—how the ladies raised the money to pay for the turned work around the pulpit—and, as to front doors, he says: "They were made by Greenup Remington. There were no doors to the house, and James Allen laughed about there being no doors to the house. I spoke to Remington, and told him if I got a good fee for marrying a couple, I would pay for the doors; they were to be made and painted, and I left the money to pay for the doors earned in this way."

The church seems never to have had a resident pastor till 1861. The pulpit was occupied by various clergymen of the vicinity, as suited their convenience or self-sacrificing devotion to the cause. No doubt they were remunerated according to the abilities of the little congregation. But the old records of the church have been lost or destroyed, and tradition has preserved very little of historic interest. In 1861, however, the church entered upon a more pronounced, if not a more prosperous existence. Rev. George Morrison became the regular pastor in 1861 and continued two years. In 1865, Rev. R. H. Kennaird began preaching for the church as stated supply, and officiated one year. From the 28th of May, 1866, to September 9, 1866, the church enjoyed the labors of Rev. J. D. Matthews. On the 1st of July, 1869, Rev. Harvey Glass was called as stated supply, and served as such one year. On the 1st of July, 1870, he was called as pastor, and shortly thereafter was installed, and served the church three years more. Mr. Glass was young, barely in the prime of his manhood, and this church was his first charge. His audiences were then usually small, but he displayed talents of the highest order, not of a cast quite so popular as he has since shown, and he gave unmistakable tokens of the fine mental endowments by which he has since reached great eminence. He had learning and eloquence, sometimes of even Demosthenean power, and yet, he had a certain sweetness of temper, a cheerful disposition, and a kind and sympathetic word for every one needing comfort. Mr. Glass now resides at Richmond, Ky.

In 1873, Rev. B. M. Hobson was elected pastor of the church, and though he never accepted the call, he served the church as pastor elect till the fall of 1878, when he moved to Missouri. He was a man who commanded general respect. Rev. J. E. Triplett succeeded Dr. Hobson in May, 1879, and served the church as stated supply till May, 1881. Rev. J. S. Van Meter succeeded Mr. Triplett, and was installed as pastor in October, 1881, and still retains his charge. Like Mr. Glass, he is a young pastor of superior talents and high promise, a favorite with his people and the public.

Late officers of the church have been Major Kimbrough, elected Elder April 2, 1854; Samuel Williams, April 2, 1854; S. B. Curran, of Claysville, April 3, 1864; D. A. Givens, April 8, 1866; J. Q. Ward, August, 1870; and J. A. McKee, September, 1872; the three latter are still in office. Achilles Perrin and James McKee are the Deacons of the church, elected January 25, 1880. The present membership of the church is eighty, the list going back to 1854 only.

In 1876, the church built in 1836–37 was taken down, and during the three or four years succeeding, the present fine brick edifice was erected. It is the most beautiful house of public worship ever built in Harrison County. It is of the gothic style of architecture, in general, though not strictly of that order, 70x50, with lofty tower at the northeast front corner, high, gothic windows of stained glass, and provided with an ample, well-lighted basement, to which are added the Pastor's study and a committee room. A bay window in the rear accommodates the desk, both in the basement and in the main apartment above. Service is now held in this handsomely finished basement. The main audience room, not yet finished, is reached by two stairways, from the vestibule of the basement, and then is entered by a single broad door from the upper anteroom, which is lighted by front windows of admirable design and beauty.

The plan of the building was furnished by an architect of Cincinnati. The building committee was composed of D. A. Givens, J. Q. Ward and R. C. Wherritt. The work was done by the late J. J. Parish, and is one of the finest specimens of that skilled mechanic's numerous works. No city can show a better brick wall. The expenditure requisite to carry the building to its present state of advancement has been $12,000, and when the great auditorium is completed, the whole cost will have been only $14,000.

The Christian Church of Cynthiana was organized in 1827, when Barton W. Stone was in the zenith of his fame, and Alexander Campbell had just reached assured greatness and undying celebrity.

The adherents of these two great Christian leaders had not then united, for John Rogers says, in his biography of John T. Johnson: "This union did not take place till 1831–32. A meeting of four days was held at Georgetown, embracing the Christmas of 1831, and another at Lexington, of the same length, embracing the New Year's Day of 1832. At these meetings, the principles of our union were fully canvassed. We solemnly pledged ourselves, before God, to abandon all speculations, especially on the Trinity and kindred subjects, and to be content with the plain declarations of Scripture on these topics." Ever since the great Cane Ridge meeting in 1801, Barton W. Stone had been a powerful revivalist and reformer in the land. Inspired, not by him, but, no doubt, by the same general causes, the founders of the Christian Church of Cynthiana framed and signed in 1827 the following compact, which we copy from the original:

> We, whose names are hereunto annexed, do agree to form ourselves into a Church of Jesus Christ, taking the Bible as the only rule of our faith and practice, and the name of Christian as that by which to be called. Done in Cynthiana, Harrison Co., Ky., on the 24th day of July, in the year of our Lord, 1827. Eleven Todd, Rebecca Miller, Patsey Kemp, Eliza Haggerty, Polly Ann Haggerty, Catharine Douglass, Hannah Wall, Margaret Miller, Jemima Todd, Mary Porter, Mary Carmon.

These eleven names ought to form a perpetual church roll of honor.

At the end of 1828, the register shows a membership of 56; at the end of 1829, there are 78; at the end of 1830, 92; at the end of 1831, 113; at the end of 1832, 122; at the end of 1833, 131; at the end of 1834, 133; at the end of 1835, 135; at the end of 1836, 136; at the end of 1837, 136; at the end of 1838, 149; at the end of 1839, 167; at the end of 1840, 273; at the end of 1841, 273; in 1842, there were 11 accessions, and the register is here discontinued for some years, or lost. Deaths and removals are often indicated, but not the dates. We can, therefore, only conjecture the actual membership during any particular year, except for 1840, when we know from a letter of Elder John A. Gano, that the number was 184.

The church met for worship in the court house, or elsewhere as convenience required, for three or four years, but measures were taken in the second year of the organization to procure a lot and erect a house of its own. We again copy with pleasure from the old register and record-book:

At a meeting of the members of the Christian Church in Cynthiana, at Brother John Trimble's, on Monday night, the 22d day of December, in the year of our Lord 1828, Brother Enoch Worthen was called to the Chair. *Resolved,* That additional subscription papers be opened for the building of a meeting house in Cynthiana, to be sent among the brethren at Paris, another at Georgetown, and another at Union neighborhood. *Resolved,* That Brothers Enoch Worthen, Thomas Smith and Andrew Moore, be appointed a building committee, with power to contract for the building of a meeting house in Cynthiana; and that they report at a meeting to be held on the 3d Monday night in January next. *Resolved,* That the meeting adjourn.

A. MOORE, *Clerk.*
E. WORTHEN, *Chairman.*

At a meeting of the members of the Christian Church, held at Brother John Trimble's house, on Monday night, the 19th day of January, in the year of our Lord 1829, Brother Enoch Worthen was chosen Chairman.

The building committee, heretofore chosen, reported that they had purchased a lot of ground to build a meeting house on, for the sum of $100 (the present site), and had likewise contracted for the stone work at $1.37½ per perch, and the sash at 6 pence per light, and that they had not, as yet, progressed any further; and time is granted them to report at some future meeting. Brothers Wesley Roberts and John Bruce, two of the Trustees of the Cynthiana Meeting House, resigned. *Resolved,* That Brothers John Hendricks and Enoch Worthen be chosen Trustees of the Cynthiana Christian Meeting House, in their room and stead. *Resolved,* That the meeting adjourn till the third Monday night in February next.

A. MOORE, *Secretary.*
E. WORTHEN, *Chairman.*

At a meeting of the members of the Christian Church, held at the court house in Cynthiana, on the 2d day of January, 1830, Brother T. M. Allen was chosen Chairman. *Resolved,* That Brothers Wesley Roberts, John Hendricks and Thomas Ware be added to the building committee. *Resolved,* That the meeting adjourn.

Att.:
A. MOORE, *Secretary.*

At a meeting of the members of the Christian Church, held at the house of Brother Eleven Todd, on the 2d day of January, 1830, Brother Thomas Smith was chosen Chairman. *Resolved,* unanimously, that Brother John Cartmell be appointed a Deacon in addition to the other Deacons heretofore appointed. *Resolved,* That the meeting adjourn.

Att.:
A. MOORE, *Secretary.*

Six years later, we have the following (no explanation or sign being given by which we might understand the cause of so great a chasm in the record of proceedings):

At a meeting of the members of the Christian Church, held at the Christian Meeting House in Cynthiana, on Monday, the 7th of November, 1836. *Resolved,* That Brother William S. Patterson and Thomas Oder be chosen Trustees of said meeting-house, in the room of Brother John Hendricks (removed), and Brother Thomas Smith (resigned.) *Resolved,* That the meeting adjourn.

Att.:
A. MOORE, *Secretary.*

And so ends the old record entire; nothing further is told in writing of the first meeting-house, or of the church affairs, except the register of the names of members, up to 1840. Had the record of proceedings been larger, we might have copied less; but, as it is, even the whole is too little to satisfy the friendly interest of the reader, or the wants of the historian. We are permitted, however, to supplement, in some measure, the brief minutes of those early business meetings by the following valuable letter from the venerable Elder, John A. Gano:

CENTERVILLE, KY., February 1, 1882.

DEAR BROTHER NORTHCUTT:

I should have replied to your last sooner; but wished to examine some lengthy memoranda in my diary, and have, for some days, been quite ill. Even now, the amount of information on that portion of the history of the church in Cynthiana, from its organization, in 1828, to the year 1850, is very meager indeed.

After the organization, I was much with the church up to 1831, Brother Allen and I supplying the church alternately once a month, and often going together. He continued his labors occasionally till his removal to Missouri, in 1836. Other preachers, the meanwhile, also preached there, viz., Elders John Rogers, John Smith, Joshua Irwin—the last preached regularly—I cannot say in what years, but with others, more or less, to 1839. In 1840, we had a memorable and successful meeting, attended by Brothers Walter Scott and John T. Johnson. I was with them. At the yearly meeting at Dry Run, in Scott County, the church in Cynthiana represented a membership of 184 in the year 1840. Brother Joshua Irwin preached for the church in 1842, but I cannot say whether all the year or not. I preached regularly once a month during the years 1846–47. Should I be able to gather up any thing more, I will send it.

With kindest regards to all, I am, most truly,

Yours, etc., JOHN ALLEN GANO, SR.

Dr. Perrin remembers to have heard Rev. Thomas Campbell, father of Alexander Campbell, preach in Cynthiana in 1835, and the Doctor commends his abilities.

Elder John A. Gano, as we have seen, "was much with the church after its organization till 1831," and also Elder Thomas M. Allen till 1836, and then Elder Gano again, for the two years, 1846–47. The church in those days was evidently supplied with much preaching, of the highest order, if not with the greatest regularity. The first meeting-house, however, seems not to have been finished till 1840, though meetings had been held in it for some years before, as for instance, the last business meeting of members mentioned in the old record book, in November, 1836. It was built by the irregular voluntary contributions of members. No special contractor is remembered as concerned in the work. The house was of brick, had the usual church spire, a good bell, was a single story high, and Greenup Remington remembers that the gable ends were blown down before the roof was put on, and had to be rebuilt. He himself had, perhaps, the largest single job on the building, that of finishing the interior, at a cost of $400. The whole expenditure, he thinks, must have been about $3,500. The house would seat comfortably 350 people, unless perhaps when the weather was cold, in which case it was warmed by kettles of charcoal placed about on the floor. With some little drawbacks, it was quite a respectable old house, and lasted from 1830 till 1868. It saw the beginnings and early progress of the church which has now become so strong and prosperous. Its walls had re-echoed the voice of Barton W. Stone, of Thomas Campbell, father of Alexander, of Alexander himself, of John T. Johnson, and of many another leader of men. It deserves a more detailed history, but the total absence of any written information about it after 1830, leaves us dependent only on the doubtful recollection of a few citizens who have been absorbed in other business for half a century.

In 1868, the old house was taken down, and the present fine edifice built on the same ground, corner of Main and Mill streets, at an expense of something over $12,000. The work progressed rapidly, though there was no contractor on the building, but Greenup Remington was superintendent of the hands; and early in 1869, or late in 1868, the church was finished and dedicated. It is 70x42 feet, and seats comfortably more than 450 people. The building faces Mill street, and the front is decorated by a massive square tower, of moderate elevation, completed by four spires, one at each corner, the highest points being, perhaps, seventy feet above the pavement. A large, finely-finished bay-window occupies the rear, affording ample space for the desk, chairs, and table for the use of speakers, company and secretaries, if required. Here also is the baptistry, so arranged as to be out of the way, and invisible except when the baptismal rite is to be celebrated. The house is on a rock foundation, and the basement under the rear portion of the building accommodates the Sunday school, the furnace and the fuel. The heating apparatus always works well, and the air in the auditorium is always sweet and agreeable. The high ceiling, the dome of the bay-window, and the walls are all finished in stucco of beautiful design, and light is admitted through stained glass of tasteful hues. The main entrance is approached from the pavement by six or seven broad stone steps leading into the anteroom, which communicates with the great audience-room by three doors—a central, a right, and a left door. The seats are arranged in two ranks, divided by a broad central aisle from front to rear, and separated from the walls by aisles of convenient breadth, thus affording superior facilities for the movements of visitors and attendants. Proper intervals separate the benches, so that the audience can stand or sit without awkwardness or a sense of suffocation, which sometimes attends closely arranged benches.

As the house approached completion, and its plan having become apparent, commended itself to public approbation, several handsome individual contributions were made, the mention of which we preserve with pleasure:

Chandeliers, valued at $250, were furnished by the late Henry E. Shawhan.

The work in fresco was provided for by Hon. T. J. Megibben, and cost $325.

The pulpit was presented by the late C. B. Cook, at an expense of $110.

The seats were all furnished by the late T. V. Ashbrook, and cost $700.

The stained glass was presented by G. W. Taylor, and cost $250.

The whole number of active members at present, as ascertained from the register, is 262. The Sunday school numbers 117. Seventeen new members were received last fall, during the ministrations of Elder Howe.

We are aware that our sketch of the Christian Church in Cynthiana, as in fact of the others, is defective in point of fullness. But more could hardly be done with the means at hand, and the time allowed. We should be glad to preserve the name of every Elder who ever had an engagement, long or short, with the church. The following names and dates are supplied according to the memory of citizens:

Between 1841 and 1850, arranged in the order indicated below, we are advised to place Elders Poole, Weakley, Joshua Irwin, John M. Holton, John A. Gano (1846, 1847), John A. Dearborn, R. H. Forrester and John G. Tompkins.

Between 1850 and 1864, we arrange Elders Samuel Rogers, assisted by his son, Elder John I. Rogers, who preached one Sunday a month in 1861; T. N. Arnold, in 1862; and R. C. Ricketts, in 1863 and 1864.

From 1860, to the present time, 1882, we have exact names and dates, as follows:

The well-known Samuel Rogers began his ministration in Cynthiana in 1852, nor was any formal close of his engagement with the church ever made till June 18, 1877, when death dissolved all his engagements. He died at Carlisle, but was buried in Cynthiana in the old cemetery, in the midst of the people he had loved so well. During the last ten or fifteen years of his life, he was too infirm to keep regular appointments, but the church honored itself by kindy announcing to the venerable Elder that he might consider himself always invited, and that he was to be remunerated accordingly.

We copy a few lines from his autobiography, published in 1880, showing the mutual respect and affection of both church and elder:

"Immediately upon my return to Carlisle, I had a call from the American Christian Missionary Board to evangelize in Hamilton County, Ohio, but, not being willing to leave Kentucky at this time, I accepted a call from the congregation at Cynthiana to preach for them once a month, and to make my home in their midst. I believe it was in the year 1852 that I removed my family to Cynthiana, and have been perfectly contented with my situation ever since. I bought a little home of William Withers, who, for years afterward, was my fast friend and faithful adviser, and whom, if yet living, I would as confidently approach for a favor as any man on earth. He gave me my own terms, and I may say, my own time, in which to pay for my home. I found in and around Cynthiana the most liberal and generous people I have ever known. The aged middle-aged and the young were alike kind and obliging; not for a few days, or months, or years, but during almost a quarter of a century their kindness and generosity have been unabated. I have often thanked God that it was my good fortune to fall in with such a people in the evening of life. Thus far, it has been a blessed and peaceful evening, leaving out of view the late unholy conflict between the North and the South. And even in the midst of the troubles consequent upon that unnatural conflict, my friends did not forsake me, but were always ready to comfort and succor me in times of deepest distress. Happy is the man who is surrounded with such neighbors and brethren as I can boast. In the olden times, I had known the fathers and mothers of many of these people, and in moving into their midst they recognized me as their father and treated me accordingly. If I were not afraid of leaving out some of them, I should like to put them upon the roll of honor. I will make the attempt at any rate: The Witherses, Ashbrooks, Garnetts, Smisers, Pattersons, Shawhans, Wards, Nicholses, Smiths, Millers, Williamses, Remingtons, Walls, Northcutts, Fraziers, Wilsons, Talbotts, Vernons, Ammermans and others.

"I was employed to preach once in each month at Endicott's, and, as I have stated, I preached once in each month at Cynthiana. For the balance of my time, I was employed to preach under the direction of the State Board in the county of Owen. My chief points of operation in the county were Owenton and Liberty, though I distributed my labors over the county generally. I had very marked success at Buck Creek, where I organized a large congregation, which I believe is still flourishing. I reported that year, as the result of my missionary work, about two hundred and fifty additions. It is curious to observe how one, starting out from his native place in early manhood, drifts on and on through the shifting scenes of life, until, by some unaccountable turn of the tide, he finds himself in his declining age, at the very place where he was born, and among the friends and in the midst of the scenes of his early youth. Such has been my fortune. I feel like one who, after long and tedious wanderings up and down the earth, has come home to die. And I thank God that he has cast my lot in such pleasant and familiar places in my declining age. A few hours' travel would carry me to the place where, more than three-quarters of a century ago, my father built his first cabin in the wild forests of Kentucky, while my mother and I were safely housed in Strode's Station. Much nearer is the sacred spot where my dear lamented wife spent her joyous childhood days. And still nearer stood the cabin where we were made husband and wife, and where I was also married to the Lord Jesus Christ. And yet a little nearer, even in the very neighborhood of my present home, I made my first efforts in preaching.

"For a number of years, I preached once a month at Indian Creek, and once a month at Mount Carmel. A nobler people than they never lived. When too old [he died in his eighty-ninth year] to labor for them regularly, these churches adopted a resolution that, whenever it suited me to visit them, I should understand that I was invited; and I rejoice to testify that upon every such visit I was well rewarded for my labor. Grassy Spring, in Woodford county, and other churches were alike kind to me in my old age. Among all these people I felt perfectly at home, and they all deported themselves toward me as dear and dutiful children. With such surroundings, it is not strange that I should be content to spend there my remaining days."

In 1866, Elder J. D. Wilwroth preached two Sundays a month; in 1867, Elders D. W. Case and Allen Broadhurst supplied preaching. From 1868 to 1871, Elder D. W. Case supplied the pulpit three Sundays a month. He was a powerful reasoner and an able defender of his religious principles. In 1871, Elders E. Y. Pinkerton and I. B. Jones supplied the church. In 1872, Elder J. C. Frank began his engagement, and continued four years. In 1876, Elder J. C. Walden assumed charge, and also retained the position four years. Mr. Walden was a man who commanded great respect in this community, both in, and out of the church.

Elder Walden was succeeded in 1880 by Elder William Stanley, who is still with us. He is well read in civil law, as also in theology. He is often brilliant and powerful, a hard student, and a painstaking pastor, devoted to his profession and people.

The doctrines of the Church of England were first promulgated publicly in Cynthiana by Dr. Berkley, of Lexington, in 1846. Dr. Berkley was an accomplished scholar, speaker and churchman. His pleasing address commended his views to the favorable consideration of his hearers, and his learning and uprightness of character commanded their respect. He was then comparatively young, and, many years ago, moved to St. Louis, where he still lives, an honored and revered clergyman.

During the same year, 1846, Rev. —— Moore, Rector of the Episcopal Church of Paris, visited our city in the interests of his order, once a month, perhaps, organized a church of four members and became their pastor. Service was held in the court house; sometimes, by courtesy, in the Methodist Church, and sometimes in the Presbyterian Church. Rector Moore continued his charge only a year or two, removed to Smithland, Ky., and died there in 1850.

After the retirement of Mr. Moore, we find no special pastor in charge for two or three years, till 1852, when Rev. Carter Page was chosen Rector, and held that office till 1865. Mr. Page was an able and popular preacher, and also an eminent teacher of the classics. During this whole period of twelve years, Mr. Page combined successfully the arduous duties of preacher and teacher; he now resides in Missouri, as mentioned in our article on schools, industrious and spirited as ever.

One of the four members who constituted the church at its first organization, was Dr. George H. Perrin, still among us, a most affable, learned and venerable gentleman. He was, and is, fully "up" in the history and learning of his church; and might easily have been a most powerful polemic in the theological field, had he so elected, if we may judge from the luminous and incisive essays which have occasionally appeared from his pen. He is a man, too, of action as well as decided convictions; and in 1852 the church had no house of worship. That same year, a lot on Walnut street, fronting Mill street, was purchased of Henry F. Cromwell for $225, and the building begun. It was to be of stone, the ground plan in the form of a Latin cross, that is, a cross of which the shaft below the transverse bar is longer than that part which rises above the transverse bar. Of this church, the nave is the main shaft, and the transept is the transverse bar, when we look upon the whole structure as a Latin cross. The main shaft, measured externally, is 75x33 feet, the interior forming the nave, which is 65x26 feet; and the transverse bar, measured externally, is 66x26 feet, the interior forming the transept. In the north end of the transept is the vestry room, and in the south end is the music room, not now provided with an organ. The altar and desk are in the east end of the nave, which will seat about three hundred people. A huge square rises about sixty feet, unfinished, on the south side of the western end of the nave, and in this tower is the main door to the audience room or nave. In 1876, a bell, costing $600, was placed in the tower. The tones of the bell are rich and grand, but not fully appreciated, because they are badly muffled by the very narrow gothic windows of the tower. In fact, the whole building is of the strictest gothic order of the fourteenth century, without ornament, however. Its massiveness and air of repose remind the spectator of what he may have read or seen of the old churches in the North of England or Scotland, or the Hebrides. When we enter through the door of the somber tower, the effect of the interior is in keeping with that of the exterior. The high, narrow gothic windows admit a softened light through the stained glass. The antique, the dim, the solemn, and the beautiful seem all combined, whether by accident or design, in the simple architecture.

The building cost only $6,500, and was carried to its present degree of completion in 1854, when it was duly consecrated by Bishop Benjamin Bosworth Smith, of Kentucky. Of the expense, Dr. Perrin supplied $5,500, a fact which we state from motives of justice, though the good Doctor modestly advised us to let the circumstance go unmentioned. William Thompson, who had joined from the Presbyterians, contributed $1,000. In the construction there was no contractor, the stone-work being done by good workmen, under direction of interested members. The wood-work was made and finished, ready to be put up, in Cincinnati; it was then hauled to its destination and put together, as unceremoniously as the stone-work. The seats, however, were made by William Roper. The building stands back about fifty feet from the street pavement. The plan of the church was model, three or four feet broad by as many high, made by Bishop Smith at Frankfort, at the moderate cost of $10, and sent to the church at Cynthiana. This model was exactly imitated in the building. Bishop Smith still lives, and is now the senior Bishop in the Episcopal Church of English-speaking people throughout the world. He was consecrated in 1832, and is thus in the fifty-first year of his episcopate.

After Rev. Carter Page's pastorate of twelve years, Rev. Dr. Totten, of Lexington, supplied the church for two years. In 1869, Rev. Walter Tearne, formerly of Covington, became resident rector. In 1870, Rev. — Stewart officiated as resident rector. In 1871–72, Rev. —Stanbury, of Newport, Ky., supplied the church once a month. In 1873, Rev. G. A. Weeks, of Paris, preached once a month. In the same year, Rev. J. S. Johnston, of Mount Sterling, became rector, and continued with great popularity, till 1879. Many desired Mr. Johnston as a permanent resident among us, but superior inducements took him away to Georgia, where his fine abilities and fine qualities make him as great a favorite as he was here. In 1880, we had Rev. G. A. Weeks again, of Paris. Mr. Weeks is respected as a polished and most highly accomplished clergyman. In 1881, we had Rev. E. S. Cross, as resident rector, a gentleman of genial manners and high attainments. He is still with us, but overtures are made to him from another quarter, which he may think proper to accept. The membership of the Episcopal Church here has never been large; it now numbers thirty-seven.

The Baptists, though always numerous in Kentucky, do not seem to have obtained an early foothold here in their church capacity. No doubt, there were scattering members of that communion in Cynthiana from the beginning, and certainly long before their church establishment here. Having no organization of their own conveniently near, they served to swell the great congregations that used to listen to Barton W. Stone, to Le Roy Cole, to John T. Johnson and to Alexander Campbell; and if they had not the happiness of worshiping in a church of their own, they rejoiced in sympathy with the happiness of those who had.

But in 1867, Rev. Dr. S. L. Helm having delivered a series of powerful discourses here, aided by Rev. J. R. Barbee, a life-long resident of this vicinity, the first Baptist Church of Cynthiana, composed of twelve members, was organized under their care. These two men, who may be regarded as the founders of the church in Cynthiana, have had an extended experience as evangelists and missionaries. Elder Barbee has called together many a little group of Baptists, formed them into a church and conducted them to prosperity. Dr. Helm, also, is eminently successful in building up from small beginnings. He takes at first sight; he captivates all hearts at once; he reminds one of the doughty orators of old, when Kentucky was a wilderness; he is what they call "magnetic." This is a word that has recently crept into use as descriptive of talents whose power is not exactly understood; but it signifies nothing more than a certain goodness, grace and natural adaptation to the work in which it is exhibited. Any one who has a good heart, good looks, common sense and suitable qualifications for his profession is "magnetic." In this way, Dr. Helm is magnetic, and where the field is not greatly pre-occupied he has no difficulty in collecting a following.

The little church, in 1867, proceeded directly on its organization, and held regular services, as usual with houseless churches, in the court house. Rev. Dr. George Varden, of Paris, became the first pastor. He is a scholar, known in the higher circles of learning, both in this country and in Europe.

In 1868, Rev. A. F. Baker was called to the pastorate, and served the church two years, with preaching once a month. He was evidently and sincerely devoted to his calling, and he was justly and greatly respected.

In 1870, Rev. W. W. Williams was elected pastor, and, though he remained perhaps less than a year, he was beloved by all who knew him, for he was a good man and an able preacher.

In 1871, the church called Rev. Dr. Robert Ryland, of Lexington, as pastor, to preach, at first once a month, and, in the second year of his connection, two Sundays a month. He held the position two years, and in his pastorate the first measures were taken and carried almost to completion for the erection of the much desired house of worship. Dr. Ryland had been, for many years, President of Richmond College, Va., and had the bearing of a scholar and monitor. He was devoted to his church and the cause of education, an able advocate of the Baptist doctrines and the author of a successful work on Communion.

In 1873, Rev. A. L. Jourdan, of Newport, Ky., was elected pastor. He had been regularly educated at the Baptist Theological Seminary at Chicago. He was an earnest and enthusiastic preacher, serving the church two years, one Sunday a month part of the time, and, for a while, two Sundays a month.

In 1876, the church called their old friend Dr. Helm, but, to their great regret, he did not accept.

In 1877, Rev. Cleon Keyes, of Lewisburg, Mason Co., Ky., was elected pastor, and has been annually re-elected to the present time, 1882. Goodness, sincerity, and an undeviating adherence to his principles are his eminent qualities. In his appeals he is often powerful, and abounds in apt anecdote; he is well informed in theological lore and its related branches, yet his taste is to present his mission in the simplest and most direct manner. The church has never had a resident pastor.

Until 1873, the Baptists in Cynthiana had no house of worship which they could call their own, and even then only the walls and roof were in position, while the want all the time was keenly felt, especially by the lady members. But the membership was small, and the financial out-go was an important consideration, though there was some wealth in the church; and the liberality of the public could be counted on as something. Yet, finally, all obstacles had to give way, and in August, 1871, a lot, on the east side of Walnut street, between Pike and Pleasant streets, in the center of the city, was purchased of Mrs. Sergeant for $800. John Van Deren, C. G. Land, Samuel O. Eckler and Paul King were appointed a building committee, and the contract for the work was given to Samuel O. Eckler. An actual beginning of the work was not made till the spring of 1872, and in the course of that year the walls and roof were finished, but not till January, 1875, was the house complete, except the spire, intended to rise from the top of the now unfinished tower. The building committee had acted with what energy the circumstances allowed. The work had cost $8,000, and all but $500 of this amount had been paid. In January, 1875, Rev. Henry McDonald, Professor in the Theological Department of Georgetown College, was invited to preach the sermon of dedication. Every foot of room in the house was occupied by the audience, and the good humor and happiness of both Pastor and members on the completion of the long-wished-for building, seemed to communicate itself to the people. They rejoiced with the happy church, and when it was announced that a debt of $500 still remained unpaid, for work and material, it turned out to be an easy matter to raise the money before dismissing the congregation. Elder Jourdan, in announcing the result of the collection, said with gratified countenance, "We wanted $500; well, we got it; we got more than that, good measure, running over, pressed down and shaken together." Kentucky people, and probably all the rest of the world, are always glad to help those who honestly try to help themselves.

Here it is proper, and, in fact, imperative justice, to state that the church had helped itself into the possession of a house of worship, mainly through the unwearied energy and devotion of Miss Georgie A. Richardson. She had begun to agitate the subject, and that effectively, almost from the date of organization, in 1867. In 1869, collections, or promises, had become encouraging to those who were determined not to fail. In 1874, a year before the dedication, we find in the minutes of the Thirty-seventh Anniversary of the General Association of Baptists, in Kentucky, held at Frankfort, on page 14, the following allusion to the building prospects in Cynthiana.

"Through her great love for the cause, and the untiring perseverance of Miss Georgie A. Richardson, money enough was collected to erect a neat, brick house of worship in Cynthiana, and cover it last fall. She hopes, by the blessing of God, to see it finished inside this summer." And again, on page 15: "If one pious female in Cynthiana can collect funds to build a nice house of worship, what should we accomplish if we could get all the Baptist ladies in Kentucky at work?" Probably more than three-fourths of the building expenses of the Cynthiana house, or about $6,000, were obtained by "one pious lady's" appeals to a liberal public.

The church edifice is neither large nor imposing, but none is more comfortably arranged for speaker, hearer, organ and choir. The house is 54x38 feet, the whole length being utilized by the bay-window, which receives the desk. The building is on a stone foundation, raised three or four feet above the ground, and broad, stone steps lead up to the front door of the ante-room, which communicates with the interior by two noiseless doors, right and left. The convenience of aisles, next the walls, had to be sacrificed to sitting room, but yet the auditorium is perfectly neat, cozy and agreeable. It will seat, if crowded and supplemented with chairs, about 300 people.

A few special contributions to the house must be noticed.

Hon. Felix G. Ashbrook presented the very excellent bell, which cost $325.

Mrs. Artie Ashbrook presented the beautiful communion service, which cost $45.

Mrs. Felix Ashbrook provided the carpets.

Miss Georgie A. Richardson, a music teacher of great reputation, presented the fine cabinet organ, which cost, at a much reduced price, $275.

Mrs. Paul King supplied the desk with an elegant quarto Bible and hymn book, $16.

Mrs. John Van Deren and Mrs. W. C. Musselman, provided the handsome chandeliers, which cost $45.

The membership is now about seventy-five.

The Catholic communion in Cynthiana now comprises about one hundred and twenty families, and thus contains about six hundred souls. Those families are principally of German and Irish nationality, not very unequal in number,

Thomas Hinkson

though quite a number of them reside beyond the city limits. Thus, by census, there are at present in town only thirty-five German voters, and twenty-four Irish voters, and the German population is estimated at one hundred and forty-four, the Irish at one hundred and twenty, within the city limits.

By one of their number we are favored with the following statement:

The first Catholic services in Harrison County were held in Broadwell's Meeting-house, on the Ruddel's Mills pike, by Father Kroeger, from Holy Trinity Church, Cincinnati, Ohio, in 1849. After Father Kroeger came Fathers Elkman, Lancaster, McMahon and McGuire. These came as missionaries from 1849 to 1853, once to three times a year. In 1853, Rt. Rev. George A. Carroll, first Bishop of the Diocese of Covington, sent Father Force as Pastor of this congregation, residence in Paris, Ky., he having for his parish, Paris, Cynthiana and Falmouth. Services were held once a month, and every alternate fifth Sunday in a month. After Father Force, there came in succession Fathers Allen, Perry and Brandts, assisted by Fathers Devine, Wright and Quinn; then Fathers Brossart, Major, Cook, Feighery, in succession; and, lastly, came the present (1882) pastor, Father Merschmann, assisted by Father Sang.

From 1853 to 1862, services were held in Wall's Schoolhouse, corner of Pike and Court streets. In 1858, Louis Pollmeyer, Thomas English and Patrick McCaffrey, as Trustees, purchased a lot from William T. Redmon, on Walnut street, running back to the railroad. This lot being rejected by the Bishop, was sold, and, in 1861, Rev. E. H. Brandts purchased of William Roper the lot on which the church now stands for $500. It is situated on the west side of Walnut street, between Pleasant and Mill streets. Father Brandts built a frame church, and a schoolhouse in the rear of it, in 1862, at an expense of $3,000. The work on these buildings was done by John O. Day.

In 1871, the frame church was moved back on the lot, and the foundation of the present structure was built by Thomas Lowery. The corner-stone was laid the same year under the auspices of Rev. E. H. Brandts, by Rt. Rev. A. M. Toebbe, Bishop. In 1873, Rev. F. Brossart, then pastor, had the building put up and placed under roof. The brick work was done by J. J. Parish; the lumber work was done by Mills & Spellmire, of Cincinnati, Ohio; the slate roof was put up by Bierman & Co., also of Cincinnati, Ohio.

In 1875, Father Major, then pastor, having had the floor and the windows put in, the church was dedicated in October of that year. In 1881, Fathers Gadker and Merschmann ceiled and commenced plastering the church; this part of the work will be completed by the 1st of July, 1882. The church, when finished according to the plans of the architect, Mr. Pickett, will cost $30,000. Up to the present time $20,000 have been expended.

From services once or twice a year in 1849 and 1850, there are now services every day in the morning, and three times on Sunday; also, the church has now a resident Pastor, Rev. Father Merschmann. The congregation has a cemetery out Main street, about a mile from town, containing eight acres, well situated.

The first Catholic school in Cynthiana was taught in the Wall Schoolhouse, in 1861–62. In 1863, the school was opened in the back room of the old frame church. Now the school is taught in the old frame church itself, occupying the whole building, and is thus provided with two large school rooms. The school is commonly held ten months in the year.

The first teacher was, in 1861–62, Miss Anna Riley; her successors have been, in 1863, Miss Kate Stapleton; in 1869, Miss Heffle; in 1870, Miss Kate H. Morrow; in 1871–72, Mr. Menzer and Mr. Macauliff; in 1872, Mr. Dennis Archdeacon; in 1873, Misses Copeland and Brown; in 1875, Mr. John D. Connor; in 1881, Sisters of Mercy; and in 1881–82, Father Sang, who still wields the rod.

The church and school building are on the same lot, the latter nearly hidden by the magnitude of the new edifice, which is designated Saint Edwards. This is the most conspicuous building in the place; it is 120 by 50 feet in dimensions, and the vast auditorium is in the clear, 100 feet long by about 45 broad. There are three front entrances to the vestibule, from which two doors lead to the interior, and two stair-ways in this vestibule lead to the gallery across the front of the nave. The large sacristy in the rear permits an effective arrangement of the great altar in the sanctuary, over which extend gothic arches, adjusted according to the rules of perspective. The whole building is, indeed, of gothic architecture, though the laws of that order do not seem to have been strictly observed in all particulars. The tower in front rises to a height of ninety feet, and when finished will ascend thirty-six feet higher. The immense roof is slated with tiles of two colors, gray and dark red, arranged in broad stripes, extending from end to end of the building. In the middle stripe are the Latin initials, familiar to the world, *I. H. S., Jesus Hominum Salvator*, Jesus, Savior of Men. These letters, constructed of tiles differing in color from the surface on which they stand, are legible a mile or more distant. Saint Edwards Church when fully finished will seat comfortably 750 people, occupying gallery and all. Claims, aggregating

$6,000 or $7,000 yet remain unpaid, and remind the curators of the importance of good financial management.

In 1853, the Colored Methodists found themselves able to build a church of their own. At an expense of $1,000 they erected a comfortable frame building for church purposes, on the north side of Pleasant street, east of Main. It was conveniently located, and easily seated about 300 persons. Here the church met for twenty-five years in the enjoyment of their religious privileges; but, in 1878, the trustees sold the old house to the Colored Union Benevolent Society for $300.

The church then bought of W. L. Northcutt, for $700, ground on Pleasant street, a few yards from the river, sufficient for a church lot and parsonage; they there built their new brick house of worship, finishing it in 1871. The building cost fully $6,000, the bell (very good) costing $150, and the parsonage, a small frame dwelling, costing $250. It will easily seat 500 people; it is pleasantly furnished, has windows of stained glass, carpeted aisles, and gives entire satisfaction. Services are held every Sunday, and, indeed, oftener. The brick work was done by the late J. J. Parish, of our city. The Colored Methodists have now a membership of 260.

In 1857, the Colored Baptists of Cynthiana bought of J. J. Parish a lot, on the bank of the river, about four hundred yards above the railroad depot, and thereon built a small brick church, costing less than $700. In a few years, the house was enlarged, at an expense of $2,500, and then would seat 250 people. The brick-work of this building also, and of the enlargement was done by J. J. Parish. The situation, however, was not satisfactory, as the railroad trains passed close to the windows of the house, and in 1880, the property was sold to W. H. Wilson, for $275, certainly a very low price. During the same year, the trustees purchased of Henry Palmer, colored, for $300, a building lot, on the corner of Bridge and Church streets, still not far from the railroad, but in a much better situation than the old one. Last year, 1881, their new brick church was erected on this lot, by Ed. Clarke, colored, of Lexington. It is a large and spacious building, capable of seating, when finished, 500 people. It has a basement which is finished, and in which services are held every Sunday. To the present time the expenditure has been $3,100, and it is estimated that $1,000 more will complete the work on the interior and the unfinished tower. The membership is now 300.

A few words may properly be given to the memory of the first two donors of church building lots in our city.

Richard Henderson was a Scotchman, a lawyer, and in the early years of our town, resided on and owned the fine plantation across the river, known as the Howk place. He built the brick residence now standing there, about 1822. In 1828 or 1829, he sold the farm to Gov. Joseph Desha. He died not many years thereafter, but of his movements after the sale of his estate, we are not informed. He was the donor, it will be remembered, of the Methodist Church building lot in 1818, the first church property ever held in town. He was also equal partner in the similar endowment of the Presbyterian Church in 1820, on Pleasant street.

Col. Isaac Miller, the associate of Richard Henderson in the presentation of church building ground to the Presbyterians, was a man of wealth, a life-long, active business man of our town. His business operations certainly began some years before 1809, for in that year he occupied as a factory, the old brick near the river, now known as Peck's Mill, and recently purchased by W. C. Musselman & Co. He was the second (Hamilton being the first) merchant who ever sold goods in Cynthiana. Col. Miller resided in a fine mansion, on the present site of Mrs. J. A. Cook's splendid residence. He died about 1850.

Summary of church membership and sitting capacity of meeting houses:

	Membership.	Seats.
Methodist Church	250	350
Presbyterian Church	80	400
Christian Church	262	450
Episcopal Church	37	300
Baptist Church	75	300
Catholic Church	600	750
Colored Methodist Church	260	500
Colored Baptist Church	300	500
Aggregate	1,764	3,850

On paper, at least, a pretty good showing of interest in church matters, for a town of 2,100 inhabitants.

Cemeteries and Monuments.—From 1793 to 1868, just three-fourths of a century, the only burial ground for the deceased of Cynthiana, was the old cemetery, on the east side of Main street, in the northern limits of the town. It was reserved for that sacred purpose when the town was laid out by Robert Harrison, in 1793; it contains a little less than four acres, and appears in the first "Platt" of the town, recorded under the date, 1797, on page 268 of the first deed book. Two generations of Cynthiana's good people have there found their last resting-place; and during that considerable period it was capacious enough for its design, besides making room, in one corner, for the old stone building, in which Harrison Academy was first taught In early times, people here were, no doubt, healthy and long-lived; and not a few met violent deaths away from home, among the Indians and in various warlike expeditions.

It is not even yet full, and is still used, though rarely, by preference of some families, whose kindred have made their long home in the old cemetery.

In 1868, however, a more eligible situation, larger area, and more distant from the center of town, was thought desirable. This was found about one mile out, on the south side of the Millersburg road. The new ground contains about forty acres, and, within the last few years the good taste and liberality of the managers have rendered the place one of the most beautiful in the State. The site is commanding, and here was the scene of the last battle of Cynthiana, in 1864; it has been, therefore, appropriately named Battle Grove Cemetery. We copy the act of incorporation, as preserving the names of the founders, and as exhibiting the authority of the rules under which the property is governed:

AN ACT TO INCORPORATE BATTLE GROVE CEMETERY.

Be it enacted by the General Assembly of the Commonwealth of Kentucky, SECTION 1. That Gen. L. Desha, A. H. Ward, John S. Boyd, I. T. Martin, John McKee, R. C. Wherritt, F. G. Ashbrook, Thomas V. Ashbrook, H. Cox, J. S. Withers, T. J. Megibben, S. J. Ashbrook, Hubbard W. Shawhan, John W. Kimbrough, Henry Williams, Charles R. Kimbrough, J. Mac-Kimbrough, C. B. Cook, G. R. Sharpe, J. W. Peck, W. W. Trimble, M. Kimbrough, John H. Dills, James Miller, J. Q. Ward, Andrew Garnett, William Winston, H. M. Keller, J. Levi Patterson, N. C. Dille, J. A. McKee, William H. Roberts, Joseph H. Shawhan, Napoleon B. Wilson, Joseph Howard, Spears M. Smith, Noah S. Patterson, W. H. Forsythe, James N. Snell, George W. Taylor, W. G. Van Deren, J. J. Parrish, D. C. Ferguson, William A. Cook, H. E. Shawhan, John L. Shawhan, J. B. McClintock, James Gray, John C. Wilson, H. C. Eals, Joseph Shawhan, Sr., H. E. McShane, Jacob Reneker, Jr., Amos Ammerman, D. A. Givens, L. Vanhook, W. L. Northcutt, C. C. Carpenter, J. W. Musselman and John S. Day, be and they are hereby made a body politic and corporate in law, under the style and firm of the Battle Grove Cemetery Company, and by that name shall be able and capable in law to have and to use a common seal, to sue and be sued, to plead and be impleaded, and to do all such other things as are incident to a corporation. The said company shall have power to purchase any quantity of land in the county of Harrison, not exceeding one hundred acres, and receive a conveyance of the same, with such covenants of warranty as they may think proper. The land and appurtenances, when conveyed to said corporation, shall be held solely and exclusively for a cemetery and ornamental grounds connected therewith, and shall never be alienated, sold, or used by said corporation for any other purpose than burial lots, as hereinafter prescribed. But the said corporation may permit their superintendent or other officers to use that portion of their grounds and buildings not sold for burial lots, for horticultural purposes, Provided the same is used in a manner not inconsistent with the reverence and respect due the cemetery of the dead. The said grounds, fixtures, shrubbery and everything growing therein shall always be exempt from State revenue, but shall not, after the ground has been fully paid for, be subject to be levied on or sold by judgment, execution or decree, for any other debt or cause whatsoever. No road or passway shall be opened through said grounds, unless by consent of the company. The said company may receive and take by devise or bequest any legacies that may be devised to them, to be appropriated solely and exclusively to the ornament and improvement of said cemetery grounds, and may vest in State stocks or loan out any spare funds that, from time to time, they may have; but they shall never exercise, or attempt to exercise, any banking powers.

SEC. 2. A majority of the aboved-named persons, or of the survivors of them, shall have full power and authority to appoint a board of seven trustees, who shall elect one of their own number as chairman. Said trustees shall remain in office until their successors are qualified, and have power to fill any vacancies that may occur in their body, by death, resignation or removal. The term for which the first board of trustees shall serve, shall be designated and limited by those who appoint them as above. After the first board of trustees have been appointed, as above, and have qualified, they and their successors in office shall exercise all the corporate powers of the corporation. The seven trustees shall afterward be elected once in every five years, by a majority of the shareholders who vote, due notice of the time and place of voting being being first given by publication of four successive weeks in all newspapers published in Cynthiana, and the election shall be conducted by judges appointed by the board then in office. The trustees thus elected shall remain in office five years and until their successors are qualified. If anything should prevent an election within the prescribed time, a majority of the trustees in office shall have the power, and it shall be their duty to call a meeting for, and cause an election of their successors as soon afterward as convenient. The trustees shall at all times have the power to fill any vacancy that may occur in the board by death, resignation or removal. Death or removal from the county of Harrison, or resignation, shall vacate the seat of a trustee. Four trustees shall constitute a quorum for the transaction of business. Each person owning burial lots to the value of $100, shall be regarded as holding a share, and each share shall entitle the holder to one vote in the election of trustees; but no person or body corporate shall be entitled to cast more than ten votes. When a share is vested in several persons, a majority of those present at the time of voting in whom the legal title is to such share, shall be entitled to cast such vote. The trustees shall keep a regular record of their proceedings, and of all sales, transfers and disbursements, and shall always preserve an accurate map and survey of the ground and lots, and have the same recorded in the Clerk's office of the Harrison County Court. Each trustee shall, before he enters on the duties of his office, make oath before some officer competent to administer the same, that he will faithfully and impartially discharge the duties of a trustee according to the best of his abilities, and will not be influenced in his conduct as trustee by sectarian or political partialities.

SEC. 3. As soon as the ground is purchased, and the trustees have qualified, they shall have power to lay out and ornament the same; and from time to time alter, repair, and add such buildings and fixtures as may be necessary for the use or ornament of the cemetery grounds, and for this purpose, and for the purpose of defraying the incidental expenses of the corporation, shall apply the funds belonging to the same. They shall have power to lay off, sell and convey burial lots, either at public or private sale ; to make from time to time by-laws and regulations for the control, management and care of the cemetery grounds and graves, and the mode of ornamenting the same, and regulate the mode in which bodies shall be interred, and make such other by-laws and regulations as may be necessary for the purposes of the corporation. They shall have full power to enter upon and remove any ornaments, fixtures or shrubbery that may be placed on or around the graves, against the by-laws or regulations of the corporation. They shall have the power to appoint, from time to time, such superintendent and other officers as they may think necessary, and take from them such bond as may be required. The proceeds of the sale of lots, and all money that may come to the corporation from any other source shall be applied, first, to reimburse those who have made advancement for the original outlay purchase of the establishment, and shall afterward, in all time to come, be applied to ornament and improve the ground, and defray incidental expenses.

Sec. 4. When a burial lot is purchased, the trustees shall give a certificate thereof, under the seal of the corporation, which shall vest the purchaser with title. This title may be transferred according to such rules and regulations as may be prescribed by the by-laws of the corporation, but in no other manner. If not transferred by the grantee, it shall descend or pass by devise, as other real estate. Such lots shall never be used for any other purposes than burial lots, and if applied to any other use, the title shall revert to the corporation.

Sec. 5. If any person shall forcibly and without lawful authority violate any of the graves of the dead, or deface any of the tombstones, monuments or inclosures, or injure any of the grounds, shrubbery, fixtures or buildings or in any manner damage the grounds of the corporation ; such person or persons so offending—besides being liable to an indictment for a misdemeanor and punishable according to the discretion of a jury—shall be liable to the corporation in an action of trespass, and the damages, when recovered, shall be applied by the corporation to restore as far as possible any injury that has been done.

Sec. 6. This act to take effect from its passage.

Approved January 25, 1868.

PRELIMINARY ORGANIZATION.

The charter was obtained in the winter of 1868, and the preliminary meeting of the incorporators was held May 2, 1868. The meeting was called to order by I. T. Martin, Esq., and on his motion, Gen. Lucius Desha was called to the chair, and C. W. West, Esq., elected Secretary. Committees were appointed to secure a subscription of $13,000 of stock, and to select suitable grounds for the cemetery. On the 23d day of May the committee appointed to raise subscription of stock reported that they had secured the amount desired—that is to say, $13,000—and the committee appointed on grounds reported in favor of a piece of ground east of the town, belonging to Henry Williams, Esq., which the incorporators agreed to purchase at $200 per acre—there being thirty-eight and three-quarter acres in the tract. The incorporators then proceeded to the election of trustees to serve the corporation for five years, which resulted in the election of I. T. Martin, T. J. Megibben, R. C. Wherritt, J. S. Withers, J. A. McKee, D. A. Givens and Noah S. Patterson. The trustees were then duly qualified under the charter, and organized by the election of I. T. Martin as President, C. W. West as Secretary, and James S. Withers as Treasurer. The directors thus organized, employed Benjamin Grove as Topographical Engineer, and began work with a large number of hands, and the work was so far advanced that it was determined to dedicate the grounds on the 4th day of November, 1868, and the Masonic Fraternity were invited to dedicate the grounds, and Rev. J. M. Worrall to deliver the oration. On the day designated, a large number of Masons and citizens assembled and proceeded to the grounds in procession, where the solemn and impressive ceremonies of the order were had ; M.·.E.·.I. T. Martin, Grand High Priest of Kentucky, officiating. The ceremonies of dedication were preceded by a solemn and appropriate prayer by the Rev. J. W. Wightman.

The grounds were then dedicated by the Masonic Fraternity with imposing dignity, a conspicuous part of which was the very touching address of Hon. I. T. Martin, then in declining health, and conscious that he was erelong to be a permanent occupant of the spot he was consecrating. Especially fine and instructive was the concluding oration, by Most Eminent Grand Commander of Sir Knights of Kentucky, Rev. John M. Worrall, of Covington. Space is precious, but we cannot forbear making room for a few lines of his most interesting lecture. After speaking of the burial customs of Egyptians, Greeks, Romans, early Christians and Germans, he proceeds as follows :

The use of rural cemeteries, or places set apart for the burial of the dead, is of later date. The oldest, and in some respects the most renowned and interesting, is Pere la Chaise, near Paris, in France. It is the most crowded with monuments, and contains the remains of some of the most renowned personages of modern history. Yet this, in beauty of arrangement and in rural adornment, is far inferior to several in this country. A late traveler in Europe, distinguished for careful observation and good taste, remarks : "The beauty of this cemetery is an obsolete tradition, handed down from the time when every American graveyard was fearfully repulsive. As compared with our present burial places, it is by no means beautiful. It has nothing rural about it, but is literally a city of the dead."

In Italy, near Naples, there is a cemetery remarkable for the form and material of which it is composed. It is 490 feet long, 170 feet wide, and 60 high, and contains 50 ship-loads of earth brought from Jerusalem, for its construction. England has clung with singular tenacity to the practice of burying in churches and consecrated edifices. To a very limited extent has she begun the work of laying out and adorning rural spots for the dead. It is to the honor of our own country and people, that in this respect we are in advance of all other nations ; yet among us these rural cemeteries were of slow and difficult growth. To the efforts of an eminent citizen of New Haven, Conn., we are indebted for the first public ornamented burying-ground in the United States. In 1796—more than seventy years ago—he purchased ten acres of land just outside of New Haven, and with a few friends obtained a charter, setting forth this as the object, to obtain a place "larger, better arranged for the accommodation of families, and by its situation, better calculated to impress the mind with a solemnity becoming the repository of the dead." Notwithstanding the worthiness of the purpose, and the small size of the grounds attempted to be improved, the enterprise lagged, and few seemed to take interest in it. It was nearly fifty years before it became self-sustaining, and a really beautiful rural cemetery. Now, this New Haven burying-ground—securely inclosed, deeply shaded, and handsomely ornamented, with many thousand dollars in reserve to keep it in perpetual beauty and order—stands first in time of all the ornamental cemeteries of our country. Thirty-five years after, Boston followed in this line of improvement, and laid out the cemetery of Mount Auburn, in Cambridge. Taste and wealth soon lavished their riches upon these grounds, and in a few years, this spot became famous for beauty and elegance in design and ornament. Very soon there arose of these beautiful burial places, Greenwood, near New York; Laurel Hill, at Philadelphia; and then followed Mount Hope, at Rochester; Spring Grove, at Cincinnati; Cave Hill, at Louisville; Forest Lawn, at Buffalo, and many others. So that they are multiplying over the whole land, until soon this high order of beauty, and evidence of Christian civilization, will be found to adorn the neighborhood of every respectable city in the land. In what striking contrast are these places of taste and beauty, to the many neglected and unsightly spots, with nodding tombstones, and rank weeds and grass, where rest the remains of so many loved and distinguished among our forefathers! A rural cemetery, a quiet and beautiful resting-place for our loved ones that have passed away, will soon become, if it is not already, a necessity, a thing demanded for every well organized and right-feeling community.

It is to the setting apart of such a spot for its proper use, that we are assembled here to-day, to dedicate and consecrate this spot, beautiful by nature, to the repose of the dead. Henceforth its trees are sacred from the axman's stroke; its fields no more to be vexed with the plow; its shades a retreat for thoughtful men and women; its sounds to be the music of solemn worship, softening and soothing the mourning accents of sorrow; its hills and valleys consecrated to the rest of the weary pilgrim whose journey on earth is finished.

The locust grove in which Morgan made his last stand against Burbridge has disappeared, except a few scattering trees intentionally spared, but numerous members of the primeval forest remain, and these have been supplemented with various beautiful shrubs and evergreens, tastefully arranged by the hand of reverence and affection. Besides the multitude of paths, a winding drive, broad, smooth and dustless, traverses the ground in all directions. The cemetery forms almost an exact square, the north side being coincident with the Cynthiana & Millersburg road, while the southwest corner touches the Cynthiana & Lair's Station pike, where a gate allows ingress from that quarter; but the north side is considered the front, and there is the principal entrance, close by the cottage of the superintendent. The business affairs of the property have been well managed by the Board of Directors, as may be seen by the last statement just rendered, which we are permitted to copy:

Entire cost of the ground, 38¾ acres, bought of Henry Williams, June 9, 1868	$ 7,753 77
Lots to date, March 1882, have been sold amounting to	36,999 42
Received from quarry	240 90
For opening graves	1,858 15
For vault fees	346 60
For laying foundations for monuments	360 05
Total receipts	$39,805 12

DISBURSEMENTS.

Paid for land	$ 7,753 77
Paid for labor	7,967 50
Paid for general expenses	10,673 61
Paid for engineer	600 00
Paid for trees and shrubbery	823 96
Paid for vault	3,032 19
Paid for fencing	1,578 96
Paid for lodge and gate	2,964 20
Total	$35,394 19

Officers and Board of Directors, 1882.—J. Q. Ward, Pres.; D. A. Givens, Sec.; J. S. Withers, Treas.

Trustees.—J. Q. Ward, T. J. Megibben, J. S. Withers, J. A. McKee, D. A. Givens, Noah S. Patterson.

Monuments.—Three public monuments, all now standing in Battle Grove Cemetery, are to be noticed.

The oldest of the three is the Mexican Monument, erected by the people of Harrison County in memory of their fellow-citizens who lost their lives as volunteer soldiers in the war with Mexico. In 1848, it was placed in the court house yard, where it stood for twenty years, and in 1868, by order of the County Court, it was moved to Battle Grove Cemetery. The pedestal is 6 feet 5 inches square; the base, 6 feet square; the die, 3 feet square, and its whole height is 24 feet.

On the east side it bears the inscription: "In memory of the Harrison County volunteers who fell at Buena Vista, and of those who died of disease while in the service of their country."

On the south side—"Died of disease, Isaac N. Anderson, aged 27 years, at home; Isaiah Miller, aged 17 years, at home; Harvey Humble, aged 23 years, at Puebla; John Loyd, aged 25 years, in Mexico; James Sullivan, aged 21 years, at New Orleans."

On the west side—"Died of disease, Worthen Cummins, aged 23 years, at Memphis; William O. Duncan, aged 21 years, in Texas; Oscar B. Worthen, aged 25 years, at New Orleans; Francis Smith, aged 23 years, at home; Jonathan C. Overly, aged 29 years, in Mexico; James H. Fisher, aged 26 years, in Mexico."

On the north side—"Killed at Buena Vista, John A. Jones, aged 27 years; William A. McClintock, aged 26 years; David P. Rogers, aged 21 years; James Pomeroy, aged 19 years.

Next in order is the Henry C. Moore Monument. We copy from the County Court Record: "It is ordered by the court that a marble monument be erected over the grave of Henry C. Moore, in the cemetery of the town of Cynthiana, at a cost not to exceed $500, which monument is to be of Italian marble; and that Greenup Remington be, and he is, appointed a commissioner to carry said order into full and complete effect. Said order was unanimous. March 12, 1860.

The commissioner acted promptly, and the same year the monument was put up in the Old Cemetery. It is the genuine tribute of a grateful people to a noble benefactor; for Henry C. Moore gave his all for the education of the poor orphans of his county. The monument is a beautiful specimen of work, made at the marble works of W. A. Hill, of Paris. In 1868, it was moved from the Old Cemetery to Battle Grove Cemetery, by order of the County Court.

The monument stands on a limestone base, 4 feet square and 12 inches thick. The first marble base is 38 inches square and 12 inches thick; the die is 30 inches square by 30 inches thick; the cap on the die is 36 inches square and 10 inches high, beveled on top; the base on the cap is 24 inches square and 9 inches thick. The shaft at bottom is 19 inches square, and 7 feet and 2 inches high; the the cap on the shaft is 1 foot 6 inches square and 1 foot high. The whole height of the monument is 15 feet 4 inches.

On the east side of the shaft are sculptured in high relief, two orphans supporting each other; also on each side of the shaft are sculptured two sets of moldings with three stars between each. On the base of the cap are sculptured a square and compass, inclosing the mystic letter "G." On the base of the monument is sculptured in high relief a raised shield bearing this inscription: "Erected by the Harrison County Court to the memory of H. C. Moore, who donated his whole estate (on a contingency which occurred), to be converted into a perpetual fund, and the interest annually applied to the poor orphans of Harrison County."

Both the Mexican monument and the H. C. Moore monument are cenotaphs, that is, they do not mark the grave of any one, but only perpetuate the memory of those to whom they are dedicated. But the Confederate monument, which we now proceed to notice, is surrounded by the actual graves of forty-eight brave soldiers who fell in defense of the "Lost Cause." It is constructed of Italian marble, and was built and furnished in 1869, by Muldoon & Co., of Louisville, at a cost of $2,200. Its base is 4 feet square and 3 feet high; the shaft is 22 feet high, and the whole height is 25 feet. The Confederate flag is beautifully draped over the top and forms a most appropriate ornament. On the base are sculptured in high relief, from below in succession, crossed cannon, muskets and swords. In the same manner are pictured on the shaft, above, a palmetto leaf and an olive leaf crossed. It was paid for by means of public entertainments, such as tournaments, Thespian exhibitions, festivals, and by private liberality on the part of people desiring to testify what respect they could, for brave men who had sacrificed their all to their principles. It was procured and erected under the auspices of a Monumental Association, of which A. J. Beale was President, I. N. Miller and H. W. Shawhan, Vice Presidents, and C. W. West, Secretary.

The Confederate monument bears no lettered inscription; no word tells of its significance; but though silent, it is eloquent, and we offer no comment.

Census of Buildings, Population and Miscellaneous Facts.—Four advanced students of the City School, W. L. Northcutt, William C. Robertson, Daniel Broh and Manville G. Land, who are quite competent for the work, have taken the trouble to count the houses of the town and the business establishments. The census thus made indicates: Number of houses of all kinds, 504; whole number of brick, 204; whole number of frame dwellings, 262; whole number of brick dwellings, 108; number of dry goods houses, 4; grocery, 7; notions, 12; clothing, 5; confectionery, 5; hardware, 2; saloons, 13; hotels, 5; tin shops, 1; livery stables, 5; wholesale whisky, 4; drug stores, 2; butcher shops, 4; banks, 2; saddlery, 3; jewelry, 2; agricultural implements, 1; barber shops, 3; printing offices, 2; schools, 5; colored school, 1; carriage factory, 1; wagon factory, 1; blacksmith shops. 6; lumber yards, 1; flouring mills, 2; distilleries, 1; shoe shops, 4; churches, 10; undertakers, 2; millinery, 2; bakeries, 3; billiards, 2; news depot, 1; ice, 1; wholesale tobacco house, 1; cooper shops, 2; coal merchants, 2; machine shops, 1; photograph galleries, 2; lawyers, 9; resident clergy, 5. In addition we may say, post office, 1; court house, 1; United States Deputy Collector, 1.

Special mention may be made of Æolian Hall, on Pike street, built in 1871 by a joint-stock company, and cost $16,000. The audience room is in the second story, and will seat 500 people comfortably; 800 have occupied the room on occasions of great attraction. It is provided with ample stage and scenery, and is one of the most useful public buildings in the place. The two lower rooms are rented for mercantile purposes.

Renaker's Hall, adjoining Æolian Hall, was built in 1868 at a cost of $8,000. It is three stories high, the two lower being rented for business purposes. The hall itself, in the third story, is 21x60 feet, at present occupied by the Odd Fellows.

In 1879, a very pretty and completely equipped post office building was erected on Pike street, by Miss Mattie D. Todd, at an expense of $3,000. The lot was purchased of C. A. Webster for $600. The brick work was done by the late J. J. Parish. Few towns of 2,000 inhabitants, if any other, are so handsomely supplied, in this regard, as Cynthiana.

The Rankin House, now known as the Smith House, was finished about the close of the late war. It is valued at $18,000, is three stories high, and stands fifteen feet from the railroad, on the south side of Pike street. It will accommodate about one hundred and fifty guests, and on great occasions, twice that number have found entertainment under its roof. The Smith House is well and favorably known throughout the country. At the time of the last battle of Cynthiana, in 1864, it was under cover, and the floors were in position, but otherwise the building was unfinished. The Federals made a stand in the house, occupying each of the three stories, and firing from the windows. The walls still bear many marks of the Confederate shot, not defacing the building, but only reminding the traveler of the late "unpleasantness."

Within the last fifteen years, our town has been adorned by a considerable number of new and beautiful dwelling houses, evincing both the prosperity and good taste of the people. Special mention may be made of the splendid mansion of Mrs. J. A. Cook, delightfully situated on Pike street, cost $45,000. On the same street, J. W. Musselman's fine residence, $9,000; Dr. John O. Hodges', now owned by F. G. Ashbrook, $10,000; Joseph H. Shawhan's, now owned by Lee Whaley, $5,000. On Church street. J. A. Remington's, $5,000; H. F. Cromwell's, $4,500. On Main street, W. W. Longmoor's, $4,500; John G. Montgomery's, $10,000; Paul King's, $4,500. On Penn street, C. B Cook's, $20,000. On Walnut street, Dr. T. W. Hedges' $6,500. These and many others of recent erection, together with those of older date, give our place an air of solidity and commercial strength.

In 1854, the Kentucky Central Railroad was finished, passing through the eastern limits of our city, since which time we have had the convenience of an express office. The first express officer was T. R. Rankin; the second, A. S. Welch, appointed in 1866; D. W. Jewett in 1869, and the same year, the present incumbent, Col. John T. Hogg. The completion of the railroad was celebrated here by a grand picnic, on the 8th of June, 1854, on the ground now the site of Hon. T. J. Megibben's new residence. During the day, summer as it was, the weather turned wintry cold, and all the blankets that could be purchased or borrowed, were put in requisition, and still the light-clad throng suffered intensely.

Many from Covington and other points, who had come attired in summer apparel, concluded to stay in town till a change of weather. Since that period railroad connections have greatly multiplied, till now, a passenger may enter the train at Cynthiana and proceed to the Atlantic Ocean by way of Richmond, Va., without change of cars.

Our town is lighted at night by street lamps, at an annual cost for fluid and attendance of $650.

We are distant from Cincinnati sixty-six miles; from Lexington, thirty-three miles; from Georgetown, twenty-one miles; from Millersburg, twelve miles; from Paris, fifteen miles. The population of Cynthiana in 1810 was 369; in 1830, 978; in 1840, 798; in 1860, 1,237; in 1882, 2,006; the latter number being taken from the census of assessor for the present year, Mr. C. G. Land. According to the same authority, the assessed value of the property of the town for the present year, was $707,000, the actual value, of course, being much greater. Of the population, 2,006, 1,213 were white, and 793 colored; white males over twenty-one, 307; colored males over twenty-one, 163; German voters, 35; Irish voters, 24.

Latitude of Cynthiana, 37° 23′. Longitude west of Washington, 7° 17′.

By way of brief notice, we subjoin the following sketches of some of the prominent men, whose lives have made part and parcel of the history of our city.

MAJ. WILLIAM K. WALL.

The subject of this sketch had an intellect so strong, and his superiority was so pronounced that we naturally inquire who were his progenitors, and under what influences his mind and character were developed?

During the Colonial days, but the exact time is not recollected, three brothers—Nicholas, Garrett and James Wall—emigrated from England to this country, and settled in New Jersey. Garrett Wall, the grandfather of William K. Wall, removed from New Jersey to Virginia, where his son, John Wall, was born, in 1742. John Wall was married twice; his second wife was a widow, and her name was Hannah Cronondike, and her maiden name was Ketchum. She was a native of New Jersey, and was eight years the junior of her husband. She and John Wall were married in 1779, and moved from Virginia to Pennsylvania, where four sons were born to them, Garrett, Samuel, Stephen and the subject of this sketch, who was born in Washington County, in that State, on the 19th of May, 1786.

John Wall came thence with his family to Kentucky, about 1791, sojourning a short time in Mason County. He moved to Harrison County in the early part of 1792, purchased a tract of land situate about one and one-half miles above Cynthiana, on Licking River, and resided there from a short time after its purchase until his death. He represented Harrison County in the Legislature in 1794, and from March, 1794, when the Quarter Sessions Court first met in the county, he was one of its Associate Judges, and continued to be during the existence of the court.

The schools at that day were very indifferent, but imperfect as the means of gaining knowledge were, William K. Wall received a good English education, and became a fair Latin scholar. The ordinary curriculum of the schools is intended for common minds, and not for such minds as his. He triumphed over all obstacles in the way of obtaining an education, and became, in the fullest sense of the word, an educated man. After leaving school, he commenced reading law in the office of Col. Richard M. Johnson, and was licensed to practice law in 1809, by Judges John Allen and William McClung, and located in Cynthiana to engage in the practice of his profession.

He was married twice, his first wife was Miss Priscilla Taylor, daughter of Dr. Septimus and Mary Taylor. His second wife was Mrs. Clementina Machir, her maiden name January. She was a niece of Hon. Humphrey Marshall—one of the historians of the State.

Early in Maj. Walls' professional career his practice became large and lucrative, and so continued until his death, which occurred March 22, 1853. Like many lawyers of distinction, he gave a part of his time to politics. He represented Harrison County in the most popular branch of the Legislature in the years 1814–15–16–17 and 1818, and his district in the Senate from 1846 to 1850. During the session of the Legislature of 1850, he made a speech against the adoption by the people of the present Constitution, which was published on pages eighty-one to ninety, in the *Old Guard*, edited by the Hon. Thomas F. Marshall. It is commended to the readers of that paper by its distinguished editor in these words: "Instead of our leading article, we place the speech of Mr. Wall, of Harrison, at the head of the *Guard* to-day. We need not apologize to our readers for the substitution. We doubt not they will be gratified by the change."

This speech, although not among the best efforts of Maj. Wall, is referred to as a specimen of his style of reasoning.

Maj. Wall was Commonwealth's Attorney from 1820 to 1843, when he resigned the office.

He was among the most effective advocates of his time, which was prolific of great men. There were giants in those days. We cannot better conclude this sketch than by copying one of the resolutions adopted by the Harrison County bar at the time of his death, in the following words:

Resolved, That William K. Wall was a lawyer of massive intellect, of comprehensive judgment, of keen discrimination, of great logical power, and of address, skill and eloquence as an advocate, surpassed by few of his cotemporaries. Reared in youth among the hardy yeomanry of Harrison County, at a period when the opportunities for acquiring education were exceedingly limited, he rose by the force of a superior intellect, to a high rank in his profession. He was one of Nature's noblemen—its patent of nobility stamped upon his mas ive brow—a man who bore in his demeanor the impress of greatness. Guileless and childlike in his nature, benevolent and affable in his disposition, and graced with the modest characteristic of the truly great, he won and enjoyed the esteem and affection of all his associates. He was born in Washington County, Penn., and was brought by his father to Kentucky in early boyhood. He studied law under Col. Richard M. Johnson, and volunteered under that gallant officer in the last war with England, as a private soldier, doing gallant service in that second struggle for the independence of his country. He was Commonwealth's Attorney for this Judicial District for a period of twenty years, in which station his abilities as a criminal lawyer shone pre-eminent. At various periods of his professional life, he represented his county and Senatorial District in the State Legislature. He died at the age of sixty-seven years, in the full maturity and vigor of his powers. The memory of his many personal and social virtues, will long survive in the hearts of his family, and in the mournful recollections of the community in which he lived and died.

COL. WILLIAM BROWN.

During the first third of the present century, the most eminent member of the Cynthiana bar, after William K. Wall, was, no doubt, William Brown. He became a citizen of Cynthiana about 1795, when he married Miss Harriet Warfield, but does not seem to have begun the practice of law till 1807. From this date till his removal to Illinois, near Jacksonville, in 1832, Col. Brown was the recipient of a continuous and very large and lucrative law practice, in this and adjoining counties. He was especially successful in land suits, and accumulated a fine fortune, becoming the possessor of 1,000 acres of land and an extensive slave property. He owned the valuable farm and built the house, now the residence of Joel H. Frazer, half a mile from town. He is described as a benevolent man, a liberal one, and able to be liberal; he joined the Methodist Church a few years before his removal to Illinois. Col. Brown was elected a member of Congress from this district in 1818. In 1826, he was beaten for the State Legislature by John O. Beaseman.

In the vicinity of his new residence in Illinois, he purchased large tracts of land with the ample means obtained by the sale of his extensive property in this State. The rise of value on these new investments soon made him still more wealthy, and enabled him to leave all his children quite independent. He lived only two or three years in his new home, but of his four sons, James, William, Lloyd and

Cane Ridge Meeting House.

Residence of Mrs. Artie Ashbrook, Cynthiana, Ky.

Elisha, William became an eminent Judge in Illinois, and sustained the high reputation of his father. Judge William Brown, the son, however, lived but a few years after his accession to the Illinois bench. His son, James, was Lincoln elector, in the State of Illinois, on the Republican ticket, in 1860. His son, Lloyd, still survives, and is a resident of Booneville, Mo.

Barton S. Wilson, uncle of our fellow-citizen, Charles T. Wilson, and son-in-law of Col. Brown, was for years a prosperous merchant of Cynthiana; he now, or quite recently, resided also in Booneville, Mo.

GAVIN MORRISON.

Gavin Morrison deserves to be remembered as one of the earliest settlers and promoters of business in Cynthiana. He was born in 1750, of Scotch-Irish ancestry, in Washington County, Penn., and educated as an intended clergyman of the Presbyterian Church. It does not appear precisely when he came to Kentucky, but in 1794, he purchased numerous city lots in Cynthiana, among which was the ground now occupied by Judge Boyd's residence, and in 1807 built the brick house still there standing. He also owns several lots on the bank of the river, including the ground now occupied by John Spohn's slaughter house. On this ground, he for many years had a tannery, and carried on an extensive business in the manufacture of leather. He also owned the fine farm, now the residence of Gen. Desha, and in 1801 sold the place, then consisting of 500 acres, to William Ford. In 1803, he bought more lots in Cynthiana, and continued to add to his property of this kind till 1818–19. One of his later purchases being the lot on Pike street, now the site of the Democrat printing office, recently bought by George Williams, where he erected a fine dwelling house, afterward known as the Curry residence. He himself, however, while living in town, always resided in the Boyd House, where he died in 1825; and his widow also continued to reside there till her death in 1846. He was grandfather to the late Mrs. Perry Wherritt.

In 1824, being then seventy-four years old, he made a trip to his native place in Pennsylvania, on horseback, to receive his share of an estate that had fallen to him, amounting to $9,000, which he converted into gold, and brought, securely packed in a stocking, home with him, making his solitary journey both ways on horseback. He was evidently a man of energy and intrepidity. He owned, at the time of his death, three squares of city lots, besides the present Boyd residence, had a good deal of ready money and was known to be possessed of considerable wealth. After his death, however, no money could be found. and much speculation has been indulged in as to the whereabouts of Gavin's money. Some have thought he buried it and never revealed the place, intentionally or unintentionally, for he died suddenly, and some have suggested other explanations, but the subject remains yet a mystery.

DR. ABRAM ADDAMS.

Dr. Abram Addams was born in Adams County, Penn., on the 15th of April, 1800. He was the son of William and Esther Addams, and when two years old, moved with his father to Culpepper County, Va. Here becoming acquainted with Dr. John Esten Cooke, he studied medicine with that distinguished physician, and in due time graduated in the Medical School of Winchester, Va. When Dr. Cooke was called to fill a professional chair in the Medical Department of Transylvania University, at Lexington, Ky., Dr. Addams came with him as a member of his family, and remained for some years, attending medical lectures in Transylvania, acting sometimes as amanuensis for Dr. Cooke, and finally again graduated, receiving his diploma in 1828 from the first great medical school of the West.

During his residence with Dr. Esten Cooke, he wrote in his capacity of amanuensis, the whole of that author's noted work on the "Congestive Theory of Fevers," as also several other works well known to the profession.

From Lexington, Dr. Addams removed to Athens, Ala., in 1828–29, where he began the practice of his profession, and became acquainted with his future wife, Miss May A. Coleman, an accomplished young lady from Harrison County, Ky., then on a visit to Athens, Ala. In 1830, Dr. Addams returned to Kentucky, and to Cynthiana, in whose vicinity resided Miss Coleman, who was the daughter of Capt. James Coleman, well known as the commander of the large Harrison County Company of Mounted Infantry in the war of 1812. The same year, 1830, Dr. Addams married Miss Coleman, by which marriage he had three children, two of whom died of cholera in 1833, and in 1835 his wife and infant child died. In 1836, Dr. Addams married Miss Mary T. Wall, daughter of Maj. William K. Wall. By this marriage, he had ten children, eight of whom still survive. Dr. Addams died in Cynthiana on the 15th of April, 1875; his widow now lives near her son-in-law, Mr. A. S. Welsh, in Colorado. In 1873, Dr. Addams himself visited Colorado, and returned in 1874. His scientific attainments and habits of close observation qualified him to understand and appreciate the wonders of that Western country, and few travelers could tell so well what they had seen.

His professional life in Cynthiana covers a period of forty-five years, during most of which his practice was extensive. He was a surgeon of eminence, and successfully performed numerous major and capital operations in that department of his profession. He was a competent writer on subjects pertaining to his art, and the medical journals were enriched by many a contribution from his pen. Above all, to his honor be it said, he was a man of strict truthfulness; there was not a spark of deceit in his nature. Whenever Dr. Addams said anything, as a matter of fact, the subject was ended by common consent. Of a kind and genial disposition, he was the favorite companion of all; happy with the merry, and as readily sympathizing with the sorrowful. He would not intentionally say a word that would impinge on the feelings of any one; but of so pure a gentleman *we* may be allowed to repeat what has been said by more than one good judge in our hearing, namely, that Dr. Addams was the best physician, take him all in all, that ever resided in Cynthiana.

His grandfather had the second "d" inserted in his name to distinguish it from others of the same name.

Of the Doctor's ten children by the second marriage, the following still survive: Priscilla Esther (wife of A. S. Welsh), Elizabeth, William Wall, Louisa Bell (wife of W. W. Longmoor), Mary Taylor, Tinie, Nannie (wife of Homer Longmoor), Abram.

THOMAS HOGG.

Thomas Hogg was born in 1780, at Hinkson's Station, three miles south of Cynthiana, and died in 1861; he was thus personally acquainted with the very beginnings of the town, and nearly seventy years of its history. His father was Michael Hogg, an emigrant to Kentucky from the vicinity of Pittsburgh, Penn, at a very early period not precisely known. But before the place was thought of as a town, and probably before there was a road on the ground we call Cynthiana, Michael Hogg became the original owner of the land now occupied by David Burke, on the west side of the river, opposite to the town, at the western entrance of the bridge. His family stayed some of the time, for safety, at Hinkson's Station. But finally, he became a permanent occupant of his farm, now the Burke place; and eventually, the town being established in 1793, on Robert Harrison's land, directly across the river from Michael Hogg's place, a ferry became requisite, as a bridge could not then be afforded. Thomas Hogg, therefore, and his brother Robert, sons of Michael Hogg, established a ferry at the present site of the bridge, and for seventeen years after the establishment of the town, this ferry was the only means of crossing the river when it could not be forded. Thomas Hogg inherited his father's landed estate, and in 1832 married Miss Clarissa McCall, a lady from Christian County, Ky., who was in Cynthiana on a visit, and acquaintance resulted in marriage. In 1853, he sold his farm to John Redmon; the latter, some years after, sold to Caleb Musser, and the latter's creditors sold to David Burke. Thomas Hogg, after disposing of his farm, moved into town, where he resided till his death, as stated, in 1861. His son, Col. John T. Hogg, our well-known fellow-citizen, is the express agent of the city, which position he has held for the last fifteen years. Michael Hogg, father of Thomas, married Mrs. Woods, whose first husband had been killed somewhere in Kentucky, by the Indians. She, all her later life, kept a garter which she took from the body of her first husband after he was killed, and this was the only relic she possessed of her first marriage.

Robert Hogg, brother of Thomas, and partner in the ownership of the ferry, removed to Hancock County, Ky., and died there in February, 1857.

WILLIAM MOORE.

The name most familiar in the various records of our county is that of William Moore, the first Clerk of the Court of Quarter Sessions, and also of the Circuit Court. He was born in Virginia about 1760, and we find him a citizen and officer at the establishment of the town of Cynthiana in 1793. He retained his office to the day of his death, by apoplexy, in 1829. He was a man of strict integrity, and a thoroughly competent officer, as evinced by his long retention of a responsible public position, and also by the unbroken tradition of uprightness that hangs about his name. He was an active member of society; in religious faith, a Presbyterian. He accumulated a handsome estate; built, in 1807–09, the house now occupied by William Turtoy, and some years before his death bought and resided on the farm now owned by Capt. Joe Desha, He had a large family, educated his children liberally, and was allowed to appoint two of his sons, Andrew and Henry C., Clerks of the County Court and Circuit Court, respectively. Of his daughters, one became the wife of Elliott Boswell, another the wife of John O. Beaseman, another the wife of William H. Forsythe, and another the wife of Hubbard Tebbs. All his daughters are now dead, as also all his sons, Samuel Moore being the last survivor, who married the daughter of Samuel Lamme; removed to Missouri, thence to San Francisco, Cal., where he died. His widow still lives in San Francisco.

DR. JOEL C. FRAZER.

One of the best-remembered names in Cynthiana and Harrison County is that of Dr. Joel C. Frazer, though he died nearly twenty years ago, in 1863. He was born in 1798, at the William Redmon place, about a mile from town, on the Lair's Mill pike. His father, John Frazer, was the original owner of the farm, and when he moved to Falmouth, Ky., about 1826, he purchased a farm one mile south of that place, and his house became the hospitable home of all the Methodist clergy of the surrounding region. He died in 1835, loved and respected by his neighbors and friends. His farm is now owned by the heirs of Henry Dills, children of his granddaughter.

Young Joel read medicine at an early age with the well-known Dr. Timberlake, who was a leading physician of the place from 1810 to 1828. In 1822, Dr. Frazer married Miss Ruth Warfield, who died two years afterward. The Doctor was still reading and practicing, and having attended medical lectures at Transylvania University, graduated in medicine in 1824. He at once, after graduation, proceeded to St. Charles, Mo., intending to establish himself there. But the place turned out to be distressingly healthy, so much so, in fact, that the Doctor and several other young professional men there found it impossible to pay their hotel expenses, and, as a last resort, they concluded to get into a skiff, without saying "good-bye" to anybody, and float down the river to some more favorable locality. At the last moment, however, the innate manliness of Dr. Frazer revolted at the measure, and he refused to proceed, while his companions actually carried out their intentions, and thus disappeared from St. Charles. With Dr. Frazer, the whole scheme was, no doubt, only a piece of pleasantry, for he was, all his life, the embodiment of wit and merriment. But he soon thought best to return to Cynthiana, where he married in 1826, his second wife, Mrs. Sanders, whose maiden name was Nancy Williams. For a few years his practice seems not to have been great, though he carefully remitted all the dues left unsettled with his St. Charles creditor. To improve his business, he removed to Paris, Ky., in 1833, but returned in about a year to his native place again. All this time his character as a physician was constantly rising, for he was devoted to the science of medicine and fond of the practice. He began now to take rank as a physician of the first order, and entered upon a most successful career of nearly thirty years' duration As to business, he had more than he sometimes wished. He soon found himself able to purchase the fine farm (330 acres) and residence once owned by Col. William Brown, half a mile from town, which place is now in possession of his grandson, Joel H. Frazer; also of James Allen, the noted race-horse dealer, 220 acres, now the property of John K. Lake, Esq. He died at the age of sixty-five, not very old, but he had been eminently successful, both financially and professionally. In addition, he was beloved as a citizen and greatly respected by the profession.

Dr. Frazer had one son, Hubbard Williams, born in 1827, who also became a physician, graduating at Transylvania in 1850, but died before his father, in 1859. He was a young man of splendid mental endowments, but of delicate constitution. He had his father's popular turn of manners, was even more witty and brilliant, scholarly and intelligent. His short career, however, did not admit of great professional achievements.

ALEXANDER DOWNING.

A well-remembered pioneer of Cynthiana is Alexander Downing, granduncle of our present very efficient Postmistress, Miss Mattie D. Todd. He was born in Western Pennsylvania. About 1780, married Miss Mary Bracken, of Pittsburgh, a lady of eminent intellectual endowments and religious virtues. He came to Cynthiana in the first years of the present century, and entered at once into active business. His name appears constantly in the county records of that period, as the purchaser of city lots and in numerous other transactions. He was also a merchant, traded largely in wheat, built the mill near the old tanyard, speculated, met with losses, and failed like all the other merchants, except Isaac Miller, after the war of 1812, though Downing held his own till 1821–22. He then opened a private school in the house on the west side of the square, now the site of Ben Day's residence, and taught successfully for several years, for he was a man of accomplishments. About 1826, he removed to Mississippi, and was soon appointed Surveyor General of that State, for, among his other capabilities, he was an expert land surveyor. In that position, he rapidly acquired property, which, in a few years, became a fortune of, perhaps, $150,000. Twenty years after his failure in Cynthiana, he found himself able to pay his old debts, and did pay them, scrupulously, every dollar of them, taking measures to hunt up every one of his old creditors, and, when they had died or could not be found, he ordered that the heirs of such should be found and their claims made good, principal and interest. He was a man of strict commercial honor.

When Alexander Downing went to Mississippi in 1825–26, his wife had just died, leaving five children, four boys and one daughter; all in early childhood, the daughter being only six months old. These were committed to the care of his brother-in-law, Maj. James R. Curry, who reared the whole family of children to maturity as carefully and kindly as their father could have done, supplying them all with liberal educational facilities, except, perhaps, those of some of the boys, who carried their more advanced studies into collegiate institutions. We regret, a little, to say we cannot learn that Downing ever looked upon this munificent benevolence, on the part of Maj. Curry, as a favor deserving rich remuneration, as it certainly did; and that it was surely a matter of not less sacred obligation than the other debts which he so punctiliously searched out and paid up. But he died suddenly, perhaps tragically; for, when old and infirm, he was returning to his home in the South, on a steamboat on the Mississippi River, he was found one morning dead in his stateroom, not far above Vicksburg. This occurred in 1863–64, during the civil war; it was a time of violence, and law was asleep. He was not murdered, but he was robbed of what he had about him—whether before or after his death, we know not—although he had the kindest of friends and acquaintances as fellow-passengers. He lived long enough to redeem all his business obligations, scattered as they were throughout the country, but apparently not long enough to ascertain his indebtedness to those who had sheltered and educated his young family during the years when Fortune refused to smile.—*Marshall.*

CHAPTER XI.

SYLVAN DELL PRECINCT—BOUNDARIES AND TOPOGRAPHY—SETTLEMENT OF THE WHITES—THEIR EARLY TRIALS AND TROUBLES—PIONEER INDUSTRIES—VILLAGES—CHURCHES AND SCHOOLS.

HISTORY is but an imperfect record of human experience, though, notwithstanding its defects, it is of almost infinite importance to the race, for the probable events of the future can be foreknown only by a knowledge of the past. Men and nations are wise only as they can look into the future, and anticipate coming events which "cast their shadows before," and this can be done only from analogy with what has taken place in the past. "The proper study of mankind is man," and history in its widest sense is such a study. This places the historian in the light of a public benefactor to succeeding generations. His name will become embalmed in song as the cycles of time sweep by, and will become colossal in the hearts of generations yet unborn, a sublime monument to the departed genius of past ages. It is not expected that the simple narrative of these pages will be anything more than a mere record of events that have occurred within the restricted limits of this small division of Harrison County. To sketch the progress and improvement from the coming of the pioneer to the present time is the extent of our aim in this chapter.

Sylvan Dell Precinct, or "Buena Vista," as it was formerly called, which is described as Election Precinct No. 2, lies in the extreme eastern part of the county, and is bounded on the north by Precinct No. 8 and Bracken and Robertson Counties, east by Robertson and Nicholas Counties, south by Nicholas County and Cynthiana Precinct, west by Cynthiana Precinct, and had a population by the census of 1880 of 1,600, of whom only about ten per cent were colored people. The inhabitants are chiefly engaged in farming, and are plain, energetic, prosperous people. The land of the precinct slopes toward the north, as evidenced in the fact that all the streams trend toward the Ohio River. The North Fork of the Licking River forms the north boundary for a distance of five miles; Beaver Creek traverses the central portion of the precinct from southeast to northwest, receiving as tributaries Brushy Fork and James Run from the west; Coleman Creek, in the northeast, is a small tributary of the North Fork of Licking River. The land is hilly and rough, but generally fertile, and admirably adapted to tobacco and corn, which are the chief crops; merely a sufficiency of wheat is raised to supply the home demand. A heavy growth of timber, of which there is still considerable standing, covered the land, chiefly oak, ash, hickory, walnut, elm, etc. Many portions still contains a thick undergrowth, affording an excellent shelter for small game, such as quails, pheasants, rabbits, etc., which abound in great numbers. Larger game was plenty in the early time, and many of the pioneers became famous hunters, making the pursuit of game their chief occupation. Originally this precinct included portions of Nos. 1 and 8, but recent changes have reduced it to its present dimensions.

The date of the first settlement made in what is now Sylvan Dell Precinct is not definitely known. The first white settlers are supposed to have been John Scott and George Low. Scott settled at Scott's Station, a place which he founded and which is now known by the romantic name of "Shady Nook," to distinguish it from Scott Station in Jefferson County. Low settled half a mile from Scott's Station. Clem Satterfield also settled about half a mile from the Station. A family of Popes, of whom Jacob Pope was the oldest, settled near where Sylvan Dell Village now stands. Thomas Harvey and David Evans were also early settlers. Many other families came in now, and the country rapidly settled up.

The early life of the first settlers was rather rough, and it was only by hard work and close economy they managed to live. Money was scarce and hard to get in those early days. There was no market for surplus produce. Cincinnati and Louisville were insignificant villages, with no trade or market. Farming was not a science as it is now. Agricultural implements were few, and they of the crudest kind. The neighboring blacksmith usually made the plows, and some neighbor, with an ax and an auger, would "stock" them. There were no such plows as we have at the present day. But as time passed on, improvements were made until prosperity crowned the efforts of the settlers.

One of the first industries in the precinct was a mill. There were several horse-mills erected in an early day. A man named Caruthers had one of the first remembered. Thomas Moffatt built a mill and a distillery near Scott's

Station very early. David Snodgrass built the first water-power mill in the precinct, near the present village of Sylvan Dell. A Mr. Marsh had one about half a mile below on Beaver Creek. Quite an extensive grist and saw mill and distillery were erected by Freman & Florence in the northeast part of the precinct, but it has lately been abandoned. There are at present no mills or distilleries in operation in the precinct. Samuel Craycroft and H. H. Harding have each a large tobacco packing establishment which works up most of the tobacco crop at home. Evans & Craycroft have a store near the Republican Church, about one mile from Sylvan Dell. L. D. Routt has a store at a place called "Routtsburg" near Salem Church. The first Magistrates were David Snodgrass and John Waits. The department of justice is at present represented by David Ross and Peter Florence, Magistrates, and McCoy, Constable.

The village of Shady Nook, formerly Scott's Station, was laid out, or rather settled, in very early times. It was named for John Scott, its pioneer, but was afterward changed as already noted, to Shady Nook. It is six miles due east of Cynthiana, its nearest shipping-point, and is connected with it by a good turnpike road, which is being extended to intersect the Lexington & Maysville pike six miles north of Millersburg. The first store was kept in the village by John S. Whalley; the first blacksmith was Francis Scott. The place now contains two stores, which do a good business, post office, church, physician, school, etc. It is quite a business place, and has a flourishing trade. The post office was established in 1875, with Joseph Scott as Postmaster, an office he still retains. The mail is received tri-weekly. The school is an excellent one, and has a daily attendance of about sixty pupils. It has been in charge of Prof. J. Florence for about three years, who has brought it to a good state of perfection. The village has a population of forty-five souls and as many bodies. The church is Methodist Episcopal, and was built in 1870. It is a frame building; the first pastor was Rev. John S. Cox; the last one Rev. J. S. Ruggles. There is no regular pastor at present; the congregation is small, the church having but about fifteen members.

Sylvan Dell village is located six miles north of Shady Nook, and six miles northeast of Cynthiana, but has no connection with the latter place by pike. It is a small village, and has only about thirty inhabitants, and one store, two blacksmith-shops, one dentist, one physician, etc. The first store was kept by Richard Whittaker. Lawson Miller is Postmaster; mail is received tri-weekly.

The Salem Christian Church is an old organization, but the date of its formation could not be ascertained. The first church was built in 1850; the present one in 1870. Revs. Mr. Snodgrass and Vanhook Lee were early preachers of this church. It has a flourishing membership at present.

Republican Christian Church was originally organized by Elder Barton W. Stone, about the year 1814–15. A log church was built in 1816 on the ground where Republican Church now stands. The New-Lights, as they were called, met there to worship occasionally until 1835, when the Christian Church proper was organized by Elder John Robards with the following members: Fielding McDuffey and wife, Nicholas White and wife, James Davis and wife, Walter Evans and wife, Thomas McFarland and wife, Thomas Harvey and wife, David Snodgrass and wife, Jonathan Evans and wife, Joshua Evans and wife, John Pope and wife, and several others. A prayer meeting was organized, and John Pope and David Snodgrass from speaking in meeting became ministers, and were pastors of the church for several years. The old log church was burned in 1837, and the same year a frame edifice was built, 24x32 feet, but this being too small to hold the congregations, in 1870 a house was built, 36x50 feet, a frame, at a cost of about $1,800. The membership at present is about two hundred and seventy, of whom Elder Bela Metcalf is pastor. It has always been noted for large congregations, and a handsome little cemetery is adjacent, where sleep many of the early members.

Education received the early attention of the people of the precinct. Schools were taught in the neighborhood almost as soon as there were children enough to start one. The name of the first teacher is lost "'mid the rubbish of forgotten things," but the foundation he laid for education of the youth of the country still lives. The precinct has four good schools, and education is in a flourishing condition.—*Perrin.*

CHAPTER XII.

RICHLAND PRECINCT—TOPOGRAPHY, PHYSICAL FEATURES, ETC.—SETTLEMENT OF THE WHITES—THEIR EARLY LIFE, INDUSTRIES AND PRIVATIONS—ROADS AND OTHER IMPROVEMENTS—CHURCHES, SCHOOLS, VILLAGES.

RICHLAND PRECINCT is situated in the northern part of Harrison County and is Election Precinct No. 3. The land is hilly, rough and broken, with a general slope to the northeast, and is intersected by a number of small streams. Richland and Little Richland unite near Havilandsville, affording excellent drainage to the northern part of the precinct. Little Harrison, a tributary of Harrison, flows through the southeast, and Curry's Run cuts off the southwest corner of the precinct. There are no turnpike roads, but plenty of dirt roads, traversing the country in every direction, which are kept in as good order as the surface of the ground will permit. The people are industrious and prosperous, and are engaged principally in agriculture, their chief crop being tobacco, to which the soil is specially adapted. The tobacco commands a ready sale, and is bought up mostly by speculators, at prices ranging from 6 to 15 cents per pound, the usual average being about 10 cents.

The soil in this rough, broken region, while not comparing in strength and quality, to the more level lands of the blue grass section proper, yet is rich, and produces many crops in abundance. It is as fine a tobacco region, almost, as the State affords, and much better adapted to that crop than the richer lowlands. It also produces wheat and corn well, but these do not receive that attention that is paid to tobacco.

It is not known of a certainty at the present day who was the first white man to settle in what is now Richland Precinct. Robert Scott and William Stuart are supposed to have been among the first, if not the very first. They both planted orchards at a very early day, trees of which are still standing, and are bearing fruit. Scott gave name to the "Scott apple," since called by nurserymen "Milam." It is told of Simon Kenton, the pioneer and great Indian fighter, that he has often helped to make cider in the orchard of William Stuart. It was also visited, when in early bearing, by Daniel Boone. A few trees now are all that are left of these early efforts at fruit-growing.

Micajah Browning, Squire Pollard, Robert Blackburn and the Marsh family are also early settlers in this section. Christopher and James Price, from Maryland, settled in this neighborhood among the pioneers. Many other families might be mentioned in this catalogue, but we failed to learn their names, or any facts relating to their settlement. The early history of the precinct, or the section now comprised in it, is not to be had from the first hands, and hence many facts relating to the pioneers and their hard knocks with the savages are lost to the reader. When the whites first began to people this region, Indians, hostile and barbarous, claimed it for their hunting-grounds, and hotly resented the white man's encroachments upon their cherished domain. These white settlements were bought at the price of blood and life. Many a white man, whose temerity led him beyond the walls of the station or block-house, paid the penalty with his life. A brother of William Stuart was accidently killed by one of his own men, while an Indian scout, near the Lower Blue Licks. The accident cast a shadow over the entire community, far more so than if he had been killed in an Indian fight, for in those cases such accidents were to be expected.

Among the first improvements in a newly-settled community, after the pioneer gets up a cabin to shelter himself and family, is a mill. This is his great source of anxiety, and usually his first object of interest. Mills run by horse-power were the first erected in the present limits of Richland Precinct. William Stuart is believed to have built the first water-mill. It was built on Richland Creek, near where now stands the little village of Havilandsville, but ceased work many years ago. Traces of it, however, may still be seen. A number of distilleries rank among the early industries of the precinct. More than fifty years ago, Joseph Woolery operated a distillery near Antioch Mills, but all trace of it is now gone. There was also a distillery, years ago, near Mount Gilead Church, but it, too, has long since ceased business. Other pioneer industries, such as mills, tanneries, early shops, etc., etc., have likewise vanished with those who operated them. "Decay is written upon every living thing," and man, as well as the works of his hand, molder away and perish beneath the sweep of time.

If the people of Richland Precinct are not a religious people, it is their own fault, for certainly they do not lack church facilities; Curry Chapel, Barlow Chapel, Benson Chapel, Crow Chapel and Mount Gilead Church are among the houses of worship in this section.

Curry Chapel is one of the oldest Methodist churches in the precinct, and built its first edifice about the year 1830. It was torn away and rebuilt in 1840, and is a large frame building. The first pastor was Rev. W. J. Snively—the present one, Rev. A. J. Sawyer. A Sunday School is carried on when the weather is good, and regular weekly class and prayer meetings. The church numbers 203 members, and is in good condition.

Barlow Chapel (Methodist) is located two and a half miles southeast of the little village of Richland. The first house was built in 1873, but was burned before it was dedicated. It was immediately rebuilt, and is now a flourishing church with 178 members. The first pastor was Rev. R. Lancaster, followed by Revs. Demaree and Chamberlain. The present pastor is Rev. A. J. Sawyer. Sunday school, with weekly class and prayer meetings; preaching every second Sunday. Benson Chapel (Methodist) is one and a half miles northwest of the village of Richland, and was built in 1875. It is a large frame building, and will seat about four hundred and fifty people. The church was organized by Rev. B. F. Bristow, who was its first pastor. He was succeeded in the pastorate by Revs. D. G. B. Demaree and W. W. Chamberlain; the present pastor is Rev. A. J. Sawyer. The names of 131 members are on the records. Preaching is had on each third Sunday, with regular weekly class and prayer meeting, and Sunday school when the weather is propitious. Crow Chapel (Methodist) was built in 1849, and is located one and a half miles northeast of Richland Village. It was organized by Rev. James Crow, from whom it received the name of Crow Chapel. Among the pastors since Rev. Crow are Revs. Samuel Veach and Ransom Lancaster. The present pastor is Rev. A. J. Sawyer. The number of members is 119; preaching is had on the first Sunday in each month; Sunday school services, when the weather will admit, and class and prayer meeting once each week.

The Christian Church at Mount Gilead was built in 1868, and is in a thriving condition, having upward of one hundred members.

Education, as well as religious matters, receive the attention of the people of Richland Precinct, and schools were established in an early day. The first school taught was by R. S. Haviland, about the year 1819. There are now four excellent district schools in the precinct. These are maintained for the usual term each year and are well attended. An item in the history of the precinct that speaks well for its morals, and should be written down in letters of gold, is that it has voted the local option law, and the thirsty individual has to go now three miles beyond its limits to get a drink of the "critter." Many other sections would do well to follow the example of Richland. The population of the precinct is 1,300, most of whom are white people, only about one and a half per cent being negroes. The first magistrates in the precinct were W. D. Haviland and S. B. Curran. The present are J. N. Whittaker and J. B. Jouett, and J. M. Strave, Constable.

Richland Precinct is almost as well supplied with villages as it is with churches, and all of them put together would not make a city quite as large as Cincinnati. Havilandsville is perhaps the most pretentious of these embryo cities. It is located in the northeast part of the precinct, about fifteen miles north of Cynthiana, and was named for R. S. Haviland, father of the present Judge of Harrison County. He was one of the most enterprising men ever in the precinct. The first store was kept by him, where the village now stands, as early as 1832–33. He also put up a woolen and cotton factory in 1838, and manufactured jeans and lindseys for the Southern trade, which was transported thither in wagons and raw cotton brought back in return. He manufactured and shipped tobacco to New York, and also operated a large pork-packing establishment, butchering from 800 to 2,000 hogs annually. These were made into bacon, and, together with manufactured goods, were shipped south in flat-boats, the cargoes of which were often worth $60,000. There is still considerable business done in the village. W. B. Arnold operates a large flour mill and wool-carding machine, and W. D. Hickman carries on a store and a tobacco prizing establishment, which does an extensive business. Mr. Hickman is a man of considerable energy, and does a business of about $40,000 per year. Havilandsville has a white population of about fifty; has two stores, one blacksmith shop, a post office, physician and the industries already noticed. The post office was established years ago, and R. S. Haviland was commissioned Postmaster. The present Postmaster is Mr. W. D. Hickman.

Antioch Mills is a small village, situated three miles west of Havilandsville. The first building was erected in 1867, and was a blacksmith shop. The town has been built since 1878. The first store was kept by Thomas Anderson. The general business outlook shows two stores, one undertaker, one milliner, one post office, one physician, one pump-maker, one flour and saw mill, one carpenter shop, a good school and a church, and about fifty population. The flour and saw mill is run by Alvin Sellers, and does a good business. He is also Postmaster. The place ought to be well educated, as four teachers make it their home, and one music

teacher, besides the school that is carried on yearly. The church is of the Christian denomination, and was organized, on the 8th of October, 1848, by Cyrus N. Williams, John McKinney, William Kirkwood and Coleman Clayton. The first church edifice was built of logs, and cost about $300. It was built the same year the church was organized, and, in 1860, it was replaced with a frame building, at a cost of $1,100. The society was organized with fifty-four members and has 156 at present. The first Elders were Thomas J. Baltzell, Washington Simpson, P. F. Whittaker and John A. Thorpe; Deacons, John Gruelle, George Cummins, John Woolery and Joseph Adams. Elder William Kirkwood is the present pastor, and the church is flourishing.—*Perrin.*

CHAPTER XIII.

BERRY PRECINCT—PHYSICAL AND TOPOGRAPHICAL FEATURES—EARLY SETTLEMENT—LIFE IN THE WILDERNESS—MILLS, ROADS, DISTILLERIES, ETC.—CHURCHES AND SCHOOLS—VILLAGES.

BERRY PRECINCT is situated in the north part of the county, and is described as Election Precinct No. 4. For quite a distance on each side of the Licking River the surface is generally level, presenting some fine bottom lands, which for farming purposes are unsurpassed in the county. Aside from this valley, the country is hilly and broken, often rising into rugged bluffs, but where at all susceptible to cultivation, the soil is rich and productive, and the people industrious and prosperous. A number of streams traverse the precinct, among which may be noticed the South Fork of Licking, Mud Lick, Stratton's Run, Snake Lick, Raven's Creek, Long Branch and several smaller brooklets. The South Fork of Licking flows through the precinct from south to north, receiving in its course the waters of Mud Lick, Stratton's Run and Snake Lick from the east, Raven's Creek, with its tributaries of Long Branch and Darby Hollow Branch from the west, while Crooked Creek, a tributary of South Fork of Licking, forms a part of the northern boundary, thus watering and draining the country well through which they flow. The timber growth is similar to that in this section of the country, consisting mainly of oak, walnut, hickory, sugar tree, ash, etc. The chief products are corn, wheat and tobacco, the latter being the principal crop, which, from the close proximity of the Kentucky Central Railroad, the planter is enabled, with advantage to himself, to ship to the best markets. The precinct is bounded north by Pendleton County, east by Richland Precinct, south by Cynthiana Precinct, west by Rutland Precinct, and had a population by the last census (1880) of 2,250, fifteen per cent of whom were colored and two per cent foreigners. A number of villages are located in the precinct which will be more fully noticed further on in this chapter.

Among the early settlers of Berry Precinct, or the scope of country now embraced in it, may be mentioned John Smith, Nathan and John N. Smith, Col. R. W. Porter, William Dickinson, John Burroughs, Jacob Sowders, Haman Million, Abijah De Jarnette, and others not now remembered. John Smith came from Virginia in an early day, but whether he was that John of Pocahontas fame or not, we are not informed. As the name is an uncommon one, it is altogether possible that he was the same man. He bought or patented 1,500 acres of land near where Berry Station now stands, for which he paid 12½ cents an acre, in maple sugar. Nathan and John N. were his sons, and always lived on this place. Thomas W. Smith, a son of Nathan, and a grandson of the original John, still lives on the old place. Burroughs and Sowders were also from Virginia. Dickinson bought a body of land near the present town of Berry, about two or three miles square. Col. Porter settled near by about the same time of Dickinson. Million settled on Raven's Creek, and De Jarnette about half a mile south of Berry's. Of other pioneer settlers, we have been unable to learn anything. In those early days, the people who had sought homes in the great wilderness paid but little attention to preserving historical facts. They had enough to do to preserve their own lives from prowling savages, who were always on the lookout for the unwary whites. For years after the first settlements were made in this section of the country, the pioneers held their lives in their hands, as it were, and when they laid down to sleep at night, it was with a grave uncertainty of ever waking again in this world. But the pale-faces' indomitable energy and perseverance prevailed, and "lo! the poor Indian!" shrank before them and was lost in the shadows of the great West.

The first roads through this section were trails made by the Indians. These were afterward "cut out" and improved by the settlers. The Lexington & Covington State road was the first public highway through the precinct, and passes through the village of Colemansville. Before the era of railroads, it was an important thoroughfare. There are no turnpikes in the precinct, and most of the dirt roads are only accessible to horsemen. A good road tax could be judiciously invested in this part of the county. The Kentucky Central Railroad follows the valley of the Licking River through the entire precinct, and is of great advantage to the people, affording ample means of shipping the large amount of tobacco produced in this region. Several stations, viz., Robertson's, Berry's and Boyd's, are all shipping points of this popular product.

Numerous mills were among the early industries of the settlers of Berry Precinct. The first were horse-mills, which afterward gave place to water-power. The first mill operated by horse-power was erected by John Smith near the present village of Berry. Abijah De Jarnette built a mill and distillery one and a half miles south of Berry, in a very early day. Both have long since disappeared. Spencer Pigg built a mill one mile above Berry, probably the first in the precinct, except Smith's horse-mill. Whitehead and Frank Coleman built one near Colemansville, and Barnett Oder one near Coleman's. These are all, except the Coleman Mill, long since gone. Andrew Boyd started a distillery in 1843 at Boyd's Station. He sold it to B. K. Reynolds, who moved it to Covington in 1873. Other mills and distilleries are mentioned in connection with the villages where they are located.

There are a number of churches in Berry Precinct, showing that the people are religiously inclined. Besides those in the villages, a Presbyterian Church was organized by Rev. Mr. Forsythe, about three and a half miles north of Berry Station, and a church built in 1860. The membership is sma . and at present there is no regular pastor. Fairview Baptist Church is in the extreme east part of the precinct, and was founded in 1877, by Rev. A. L. Jourdan. The church edifice was built in 1878. At present there are fifty-three members under the pastorate of Rev. S. H. Burgess, of Berry. Providence Baptist Church is situated three miles northeast of Berry, and was established about the year 1869. It has a membership of forty, under the pastoral charge of Rev. J. R. Barbee, of Cynthiana. A Methodist Church is about being organized by Rev. A. J. Sawyer. There is one colored church in the precinct, which is largely attended, as the colored race are noted church-goers.

The educational facilities of the precinct are good, and amply supply the wants of the community. Of the first schools taught in this section, we know absolutely nothing, nor could we learn the names of the first teachers. There are at present eight schools in the precinct, all taught by competent teachers. There is also one colored school, which affords educational advantages to the colored children. The first Magistrates of Berry Precinct were Charles Lail and I. N. Ramey. The department of justice is at present represented by Charles Lail and James McMurtry, Justices of the Peace, and E. D. Stone, Constable.

This section of Harrison County seems to be prolific in the matter of villages. Several dot the hills and valleys of Berry Precinct. The oldest one in the neighborhood is Colemansville, situated one and a quarter miles west of Berry's Station, on the old State road leading from Lexington to Covington. It was founded in an early day by Whitehead Coleman, who was an early settler in the vicinity. Before the building of the Kentucky Central Railroad, it was a place of considerable importance, and had an extensive trade. Its location on the old State road made it the trading-point for a large scope of country. But with the building of railroads it lost its prestige, and now but little business is carried on. One store and a few shops comprise its business at the present time. It also has two churches. The Baptist Church here was organized about the year 1846, by Rev. Thomas Waggener, of Pendleton County. The church building was erected in 1865. Among the first members were John C. Johnson, Mrs. Victor, Mrs. Mary L. Gray, Mrs. Webb, etc., etc. The present membership is eighty-five, under the pastoral charge of Rev. Amos Stout.

Berry's Station is the most important village in the precinct, and has a population of about four hundred. It is a live, energetic place, and does a large business. Its laying-out as a village dates back to the building of the railroad through this section. Col. George W. Berry donated land and built the first store, and was the first Postmaster upon the establishing of a post office. The first tavern was built and kept by W. W. Bradley. A steam-mill was built by A. J. McNees, which was burned in 1866. He rebuilt it in 1870 as a water-power mill; it has a capacity of 250 bushels of grain per day. Mr. McNees owns the two tobacco warehouses which are in operation here, and which have an annual capacity of 300,000 pounds. As a sample of the business energy of the little town, one merchant in 1880, alone sold $35,000 worth of goods.

The village was incorporated in 1866, and is governed by a Board of Trustees. The present board is J. H. Swinford, J. B. Crouch, F. G. Craig, J. A. Newberry and W. G. Vanderen. L. D. Huffman is Police Magistrate, and R. M. King, Marshal. The business now comprises two stores, two confectioneries, two millinery stores, one drug store, three blacksmith shops, two wood shops, one distillery, one shoe shop, one tin shop, one hotel, one flouring-mill, two tobacco warehouses and packing establishments, stock-yards, one post office, telegraph and freight offices, one colored church and school, one white school and white church, one Masonic lodge, one lawyer, one resident minister, four doctors, and two undertakers. (No reflection is intended by mentioning the doctors and undertakers in the same connection.)

The church was organized here in November, 1881, in the hall over Renaker's store, by Rev. A. J. Sawyer. No building has yet been erected, but it is the intention to build during the coming year. Rev. Mr. Sawyer administers to the spiritual wants of the little flock. A prosperous union Sunday school is carried on, numbering one hundred and twenty-five pupils, under the superintendence of G. G. Crenshaw.

The Masonic Lodge was organized in 1845, as Taylor Lodge, No. 164, and now has upon the roll thirty members. The present officers are G. B. Durant, Worshipful Master; J. B. Croult, Senior Warden; John Carr, Junior Warden; O. W. Grissom, Treasurer, and S. P. Crouch, Secretary. The school is one of the most flourishing in the county. Two teachers are employed, and the daily attendance is about eighty pupils. Prof. E. O. Ware is Principal, and Miss Alice Kimbrough, assistant teacher. With all the moral influences emanating from these moral institutions—church, Sunday-school, Masonic lodge, and school—the village of Berry must be a model place, and the very pink of human excellence. No people can be very bad surrounded by all these civilizing and refining influences. The present Postmaster of Berry is T. H. Rankin; telegraph operator, James Farley; freight agent, J. C. Blair; hotel-keeper, J. L. Jouett. The post office at this place is the distributing point for some six or eight other post offices in the northeast part of the county. The County Poor House, which is more fully mentioned in another chapter, is located here, and also Craig's distillery, which is likewise mentioned in the chapter devoted to that interest.

Boyd's Station, in the north part of the precinct, is situated on the Kentucky Central Railroad, midway between Cincinnati and Lexington, and is the central water station and coal supply of the railroad. It was named for Andrew Boyd, Sr., who was one of the early settlers in the vicinity. He operated a distillery where the village now stands as early as 1843. Like Berry's Station, the place sprang into existence upon the building of the railroad. It is a small place, with about one hundred inhabitants, and boasts of three stores, a post office, tobacco warehouse, mill, etc. The post office is kept by James Woodbury; the tobacco warehouse does quite a large business, and the mill is in good condition. It has a capacity of 200 bushels of grain per day, and is operated by J. P. Blair. This mill was originally built by Whitehead Coleman about the year 1810, and is the oldest mill in this section of the country. It was formerly known as the "Broad Ford Mill," in consequence of the great width of the river at this point.

Robertson Station is situated on the Kentucky Central Railroad in the southern part of the precinct, nine miles from Cynthiana, and has a population of thirty souls and a like number of bodies. There is one store kept by E. S. Blackford, who is also railroad and express agent, Postmaster, etc. A flour-mill, owned by J. Bowman, does a large business; there is also a saw-mill in connection. A lawyer and physician attend to the legal business, and the pains and aches of the place.

Durbantown is a still smaller place. It is situated three miles northwest of Berry's Station, and has a store, blacksmith shop, and a branch post office, kept by Luke Stone.—*Perrin.*

CHAPTER XIV.

RUTLAND PRECINCT—ITS TOPOGRAPHY AND PHYSICAL FEATURES—COMING OF THE PIONEERS—SETTLEMENT—EARLY INDUSTRIES—ROADS, ETC.—RELIGIOUS AND EDUCATIONAL—VILLAGES.

THE division of Harrison County to which this chapter is devoted is known as Rutland, and described as Election Precinct No. 5. It lies in the west part of the county, and is bounded north by Grant County, east by Berry and Unity Precincts, south by Unity Precinct and Scott County, west by Scott County, and contains a population of 975, of whom 9 per cent are colored. Tobacco raising is the chief product, though corn and wheat are grown to some extent. A number of small streams flow through the precinct, the principal of which are the North, Middle and South Forks of Raven's Creek; these also have a number of small tributaries. The surface is broken and hilly, with a general slope to the northeast. The people are intelligent, energetic, hospitable and alive to the importance of education, which is evinced in the number of schools in the precinct.

The settlement of Rutland Precinct was coeval with that of other portions of Harrison County. To say with positiveness who was the first settler in this immediate vicinity is beyond the power of the historian; the matter must be left in some degree of uncertainty. John Kemper, it is asserted, settled on the South Fork of Raven Creek as early as 1791, about one and a half miles from the present village of Rutland, where he built and operated a distillery. William Kinman, a native of Maryland, also settled on the South Fork of Raven Creek. Jonathan Hedges came from Virginia and settled on the farm now occupied by J. Burgess, three-fourths of a mile above Rutland, where he built a horse-mill. In the year 1791–92, Edmund Dunn settled on the farm now owned by Mr. Burgess above referred to. About the same time, Christopher Musselman settled on the farm now owned by T. W. Hardy. Benjamin Dunn and Thomas Redd settled on the Middle Fork of Raven Creek about the year 1792, where Redd built a mill. Lewis and Samuel Kendall also settled on the Middle Fork of Raven Creek—the latter built a distillery there. Frank Robinson settled on the North Fork of Raven. His house is still standing, and is occupied at present by J. Burgess, Jr. Thomas T. Thompson and Nicholas Miller, from Virginia, settled in the same neighborhood. The Renakers and the Faulkners, also Whitfield Collins, were early settlers of the precinct. Other families there were entitled to mention as early settlers, doubtless, but we have no record of them.

Could the chronicler of our early history draw a correct picture of this country eighty or ninety years ago, the reader would see, first, an almost unbroken forest, filled with skulking savages and wild beasts; and next the rough, unhewn log hut of the pioneer, its crevices filled with clay; the small clearing adjacent so covered with stumps that one could easily have leaped from one to another, and thus have passed over the entire farm. Could he, we repeat, draw such a picture, it would bring before many a reader similar scenes, whose impress has been left in the mind by the oft-repeated stories of the gray-haired grandsire, recounted with many an animated gesture, as he "lived o'er again those olden times." But these early scenes, surrounded by danger, are long since passed, and the waning quarter of the nineteenth century finds peace and plenty and security where its opening period showed nothing but danger and privation.

The first thought of the pioneer, after securing a home in the wilderness, was a mill, where he might obtain bread for his dear ones. The first mill in what is now Rutland Precinct was a horse-mill built by Jonathan Hedges, on a place now owned by Mr. Burgess. Thomas Redd built a mill on the Middle Fork of Raven Creek, somewhere about 1795. It was run by water-power, and relics of it are still to be seen upon the spot where it stood. John Kemper erected a distillery on the South Fork of Raven, one and a half miles from Rutland, about 1791–92. He was one of the first settlers in the precinct, and opened this distillery soon after his settlement, as whisky was deemed as essential then in the wilderness as meat and bread. Samuel Kendall also had a distillery on the Middle Fork of Raven very early. These distilleries presented a ready market for the settlers' surplus grain.

The principal roads through Rutland Precinct are the Cincinnati, Georgetown & Lexington Turnpike, which merely touches the northwest corner; the Mount Zion & Rutland pike, made in 1880, is to be continued to Hinton Station, on the Cincinnati Southern Railroad, which passes along the border of the precinct. Rutland is now connected with Cynthiana by pike, a distance of eleven miles.

Religious training was not neglected by the early settlers of Rutland Precinct. About the year 1800, a church was organized by a minister of the name of Morehead, known as the "Raven's Creek Baptist Church." The building was of hewn logs, and had a gallery all round on the inside for the men, as it would have been considered highly indecorous for the men and women to have occupied the same room during church service. The building, it is said, resembled a large, plain two-story house, with a huge square hole cut in the second floor. Among the first members of this church were the Kinmans, Dunns, Samuel Blair, Nicholas Miller and others of the early settlers of the surrounding country. Elders Thomas P. Dudley, George Marshall and Tobias Willoughby were some of the early preachers who administered to the wants of the congregation. Elder Dudley is still living in Lexington, and is about ninety years old. The church had once a strong membership. The building was finally crushed by a large tree falling on it, and the congregation, which had somewhat decreased in numbers, removed to Twin Creek Baptist Church, otherwise known as "Dutch Chapel." A colored church is situated in the extreme north part of the precinct, where the dusky population meet for Sabbath worship.

Friendship Baptist Church is located in the northern part of Rutland Precinct.

Rogers Chapel (Methodist) is located three miles south of Rutland Village, and was built in 1874. It has eighty members, under the pastorate of Rev. G. W. Lancaster. Services every fourth Sunday.

The first school in the present precinct of Rutland was taught in a small log schoolhouse on the farm of Christopher Musselman. In this rude temple of learning, Willis Whitson applied the lubricating oil to the complicated machinery of the human mind as early as 1815–20. Most of the schools at that early day were taught in private dwellings. Among others of this kind, a man named Billy Duty did his *duty* to the rising generation by teaching a "subscription school" in the cabin of John Burgess. Thus the early educational mills ground on, until the establishing of free schools. At the present time, there are six schools in the precinct, all flourishing and well attended.

The village of Rutland is situated four and a half miles from Hinton Station, on the Cincinnati Southern Railroad, and ten miles from Cynthiana. It has about thirty inhabitants, and was laid out, or settled, in 1848. The first house was built by Meredith Collins, on land given him by Whitfield Collins, and originally owned by William Kinman. Meredith Collins kept the first store in the place, and sold out to F. M. Bailey, who succeeded in getting a post office, of which he was made the Postmaster. Upon application for a post office, he bestowed the name "Rutland" on the village, in honor of Rutland, Vt., his native place. The mail is received from Hinton Station twice each week—on Wednesdays and Saturdays. The first mail route through Rutland Precinct was over the Leesburg & Williamstown State road, and was between Cynthiana and Williamstown. A. B. Bowen is the present Postmaster of Rutland. The village has one general store, one hotel, one blacksmith shop, one woolen factory, one shoemaker, one wagon-maker, one post office, one teacher, one physician, two barbers, one Masonic lodge.

Mullin Lodge, No. 296, A., F. & A. M., was established about the year 1850, mainly through the influence of John Mullin, the merchant and Postmaster of Rutland at that time, and from him it received its name. The present officers are C. H. Stewart, W. M.; Richard McKenney, S. W.; S. W. Collins, J. W.; Carter Redd, Treas.; and James L. Wolf, Sec. The lodge is in a flourishing condition, and has about sixty members, many of whom have taken the higher degrees, being members of the Commandery at Cynthiana.

Raven Creek Lodge, No. 584, A., F. & A. M., is located near Friendship Church, and was organized through the efforts of Thomas W. Hardy, in 1875. The first officers were Thomas W. Hardy, W. M.; Silas Dunn, S. W.; Jesse Hampton, J. W. The present officers are Z. T. Skinner, W. M.; P. S. Brooks, S. W.; Matt. Slattern, J. W. The names of twenty-six members are on the rolls, and "peace and harmony" prevail among them.—*Perrin.*

CHAPTER XV.

UNITY PRECINCT—TOPOGRAPHICAL AND DESCRIPTIVE—EARLY SETTLEMENTS—HARD LIFE OF THE PIONEERS—MILLS ROADS, ETC.—CONNERSVILLE—SCHOOLS AND CHURCHES.

NO sadder realization of the inscrutable decree, that "Dust thou art and unto dust shalt thou return," is wanting than the gathering of the history of a country or a people. For example: In Unity Precinct, we look around us for the pioneers and find them moldering in the graveyard. The first generation are all gone, and the second and the third, and even the fourth are crowding after them and will soon disappear in the shadows of the Dark Valley. This country, once the haunt of the wild beasts and the hunting ground of the red Indian and his kindred, has undergone a wonderful transformation since the palefaced pioneers first made it their home and commenced the subjection of the wilderness they found here in unbroken grandeur. The wild forest has disappeared, and so have the pioneers who reclaimed it, and that period is fast rolling on when no one can say, "I knew them." It is the divine fiat that we fulfill our mission here and then pass away.

Unity Precinct, which is described as Election Precinct No. 6, is located in the southwest part of the county adjoining Scott County, and is rather broken and hilly. It was originally heavily timbered, and in places there is still much of it left standing. It was chiefly oak, walnut, sugar maple, hickory, etc. It is well watered and drained; Mill Creek taking off a small part of the northeast corner, and Twin Creek, a tributary of South Licking, with its two forks, drains the entire precinct from Connersville to the northeast. Tobacco is the main staple, only sufficient grain being produced for home consumption. The people are industrious and intelligent, and upright in their dealings with the world. Although not favored with the wealth, nor with the rich lands of their neighbors but a a short distance to the south of them, yet they are content, and their lands, at all susceptible to cultivation, are productive. The precinct formerly included the most of Berry Precinct within its limits, and the voting-place was at Buck Cason's, which attained for it the name of "Cason's Precinct." But after the division into precincts under the present constitution, this was called "Trickum," then was finally changed to the name it now bears.

In looking back over the past of this section of the country, much difficulty is met with in collecting its history. A cheerful readiness to tell everything known, and to volunteer much information of events of doubtful occurrence, is met with everywhere. The names of many of the early settlers have passed beyond the powers of recollection, and the gloom surrounding many important circumstances is impenetrable to the historian's utmost researches. This applies particularly to this precinct, where none of the first settlers are left, and where much of the early history passed into oblivion with the death of the pioneers. The first settlers in what is now Unity Precinct are supposed to have been Buck Cason and Charles Courtney. They came from Virginia, but the date of their settlement here is not now remembered. Adam Renaker was from Maryland, and settled in the precinct soon after Cason and Courtney. John Conner and Benjamin Conrad were also early settlers. Conner was from Virginia, and was an Old-School Baptist preacher. Conrad had a horse-mill near Connersville. Of other pioneer families in what now forms Unity Precinct, we have no definite information. It was not long, however, after the Indians met their Waterloo from Gen. Wayne in 1794, that much of the available lands in this immediate section were occupied, and began to be more endurable. The early hardships were forgotten, and the homely ways and rude garb gave way to a more refined spirit of civilization. Substantial log houses sprang up in all directions, taking the places of the rude huts and cabins which had been at first erected. The settlers began to surround themselves with something more than the bare necessities of life. Schools, churches, etc., began to appear, and something like pleasure was felt in living in the fast disappearing forests. Progress and improvement continued until the state of prosperity was reached we find here to-day.

The first roads in the precinct were trails made by the Indians in their hunting excursions through the forests. These, upon the settlement of the whites, were cut out for wagons and otherwise improved to their present state. One of the first mills was built by Benjamin Conrad, in the neighborhood of Connersville. Several distilleries, on a small scale, were erected in an early day, where the surplus grain raised by the settlers found a market. But few industries, however, have been carried on in the precinct, outside of farming. To this pursuit, the people are chiefly devoted. One of the first magistrates was George Lemon; the present magistrates are H. M. Levi and Newton Henry.

Connersville, the most important village in the precinct, is located in the extreme southern part, near the line, about seven miles southeast of Cynthiana. The first store was kept by John H. Conner, in 1830, and from him the town took its name. Lewis Conner kept the first tavern, and E. M. Bailey was the first Postmaster. It was through his influence that the town was christened Connersville, in honor of its first merchant. By the last census, the village had 125 inhabitants, and the present showing of business is as follows: Three general stores, one physician, one shoemaker, one undertaker, two hotels, two blacksmith shops, one post office (of which B. M. Tucker is Postmaster) and one cooper-shop. A mill and distillery were erected some years ago by Boyers and Pemberton; the distillery has ceased business, but the mill is still in operation, and does a large amount of custom work.

Unity, formerly called "Trickum," is located in the center of the precinct, seven miles from Cynthiana. It is the voting-place of the precinct, and here, on election day, the honest voters assemble to exercise that "right guaranteed to all freeborn American citizens," that of depositing their unbulldozed ballots. Whence the place received the name of "Trickum;" whether it was a *tricky* place, or because no better name could be found at the time, we are not authorized to say. The population of the place is fifty souls; represented by one store, one hotel, one blacksmith shop, one wood-shop, etc., also one church.

Twin Creek Baptist Church, or "Dutch Chapel," as it is usually called, is situated in the northern part of the precinct. It is the old style, or Particular Baptist, and was organized in 1830, by William Conrad. John Conner was also a Baptist preacher, and used to administer to the faithful in this community. The church now has about thirty members, and Elder J. J. Gilbert is the pastor.

Salem Chapel (Methodist), was the first church established in Unity Precinct. It was organized a number of years before the erection of a building. The first house was built in 1835, and was of white-oak logs. It served the purpose of the congregation until 1854, when it was torn down, and the present frame church building erected upon its site. The present membership is seventy-five, and services are held on the first Sunday in each month; present pastor, Rev. J. R. Lancaster. This church is located about three miles northeast of Connersville, on the road leading from Connersville to Lexington.

Mount Zion Chapel, also a Methodist Church, was established very early. Their first church building was erected about 1830. This was torn down in 1857, and the present building erected. The first pastor of the church was Rev. Josiah Whittaker; the present, Rev. J. R. Lancaster.

Education received the early attention of the people of Unity Precinct. The first schools were those known as subscription schools, and were taught in any empty building at hand, and the early churches used to serve both for religious and school purposes. One of the first schools taught in the precinct was in the neighborhood of Cason's, by Christopher Whitson, some time about 1820. There are at present five schoolhouses in the precinct, in which good schools are maintained for the usual period every year.—*Perrin.*

CHAPTER XVI.

LEESBURG PRECINCT—TOPOGRAPHY AND DESCRIPTION—PIONEER SETTLEMENT—EARLY LIFE ON THE FRONTIER—ROADS, MILLS, DISTILLERIES, FACTORIES, ETC.—CHURCHES AND SCHOOLS—VILLAGES.

LEESBURG PRECINCT, or No. 7 of the election precincts of Harrison County, is situated in the extreme southern part of the county, and is bounded on the north by Unity Precinct, on the east by it and Cynthiana Precinct, on the south by Bourbon County and west by Scott County. The surface of the country in Leesburg is less rough and broken than in the north part of the county, partaking more of the nature of the rolling blue grass lands of Scott and Bourbon Counties. The timber is similar to that described in other precincts of this county. Huskins' Run flows through the southern part of the precinct, emptying into the South Fork of Licking River. Silas Creek flows along the southern border, forming the boundary line between Harrison and Bourbon Counties. Gray's Run and its tributaries drain the central part, while the north part is drained by Mill Creek. All of these small streams are tributaries of the Licking River. They afford an excellent system of natural drainage, and in early times furnished power to numerous mills erected by the pioneers. Chief products are corn, wheat, hemp, tobacco ; grazing is carried on to some extent.

One of the first settlers in what is now Leesburg Precinct was William E. Boswell. He came from Loudoun County, Va., about the year 1790–91, and settled near the present village of Leesburg. He was of a proud, old family, and committed an act of disobedience by marrying against his father's will, for which he was disinherited. This led him to seek a home in the wilderness of Kentucky, where he took an active part in the stirring events of her early history. He was elected to the Legislature in 1793, when scarcely more than twenty-one years of age, and was re-elected every year until 1806. In 1799, he was elected to the convention called for the purpose of revising the State Constitution. He was a Colonel in the war of 1812, and he and Col. Dudley commanded the two regiments forming Gen. Green Clay's brigade. His son, B. T. Boswell, is still living in the neighborhood, and has in his possession a trunk, which his father's old body servant carried at the siege of Fort Meigs, and which still bears the marks of tomahawks received in the battle or siege. The early neighbors of Col. Boswell were Elijah Chinn, John Kinkead, Elkanah Jennings, Billy Lowry, David Dickson, James Ward, William Gray and sons and William Frances. John Craig, Sr., also lived in the neighborhood, and was from North Carolina. He settled here about the year 1790–91. His son James was a soldier in the war of 1812, and was taken prisoner at the battle of the River Raisin, but was exchanged after a short captivity.

An early settler in this vicinity was a man named Lee. His tragic death is still remembered, and is often narrated by the old people of the neighborhood to the curious stranger. He was shot by an Indian while peeping from behind a tree near the present little village of Leeslick. The tree is still pointed out, and stands within twenty feet of the spring which bubbles from the ground in the midst of the village.

The early life and enjoyment of the pioneers were simple and rude in comparison to what they are at the present day. The time of the men was taken up in their farming operations ; all the family supplies were produced by them ; meat, bread and a few vegetables being the main staples in the way of provisions. Whisky was a common beverage ; the surplus grain was made into whisky, and thus put into more convenient shape to handle ; it was almost a legal tender. A great source of enjoyment among the young people was the pioneer quilting-party. These old-time quilting-parties were usually wound up with a dance. A log cabin with puncheon floor was no obstacle to those who wished to "trip the light fantastic toe." The pleasure and enjoyment of those times, if not so refined as now, were of quite as much interest to the young people. The early farmer worked to a great disadvantage ; his teams were oxen, and his plows of the rudest description, made principally of wood by some farmer more handy with tools than his neighbors. Crops were not raised and harvested without the severest manual labor. Those days of toil and privation are over, and the most prosperous farms and happy homes are to be found where erst the pioneer labored.

Leesburg Precinct is well supplied with roads—those

highways of travel which build up the commerce of every country. The Leesburg & Newtown pike was the first built through the precinct, which was about the year 1850. The Cynthiana & Leesburg pike was continued to Oxford, in Scott County, in 1870. Megibben pike forms the east boundary; the Connersville & Scott County pike extends from Connersville into Scott County; Leesburg & Leeslick pike, built about 1860, extends to within one mile of Connersville.

The pioneer improvements and industries in this locality were comprised in mills, distilleries, tan-yards, hemp factories, etc. Proctor Cleveland and John Paul, two early settlers in the vicinity of Leeslick, built horse-mills, which were probably among the first mills in the community. John Craig is supposed to have built the first water-power mill. It was on Mill Creek, near where the Connersville & Cynthiana pike crosses the stream. John Conner used to fish there when a boy, and caught many fine bass; he also caught a pickerel there once which weighed five pounds. Col. Boswell built a mill about the year 1810, and John Miller opened a distillery sixty or seventy years ago, where the surplus corn found a ready market. Benjamin Conrad, an early settler, had a horse-mill near Connersville. Other mills, factories, etc., will be mentioned in connection with the villages.

The first church edifice built in what now forms Leesburg Precinct, was known as the "old Mount Pleasant Church." It was of logs, and was built about the year 1795; Rev. Mr. Lyle was the first preacher. This rude temple of worship satisfied the simple wants of the congregation, until 1840, when it was torn down and a substantial brick erected in its place. Among the ministers who have been in charge are Revs. Phillips, Moreland, Van Meter, etc. The latter is the present pastor. The church was moved to Broadwell in 1860. The Old School Baptists built a church known as the "Mill Creek Baptist Church," in 1810, of which John Conner was the first preacher. It was torn down in 1865, and has not been rebuilt. The first school was taught at old Mount Pleasant Church in 1795, by a man named McCollum. The precinct has no lack of educational facilities at the present day. Good schools are taught for the usual term each year, and are well attended. The first magistrate was William English. The majesty of the law is now represented in the persons of Richard Levi and Thomas Arnett, Magistrates, and John Coppage, Constable.

Leesburg was laid out as a village by Col. Boswell in 1817, who owned the land. It was first called Boswell's Cross Roads, but the name was afterward changed to Leesburg, for the town of that name in Virginia, whence Col. Boswell emigrated. It has a population, at present, of 225, of whom about 175 are white. The first store was kept by William Cogswell, who embarked in the business about the year 1818. He was also the first Postmaster upon the establishment of a post office. The first blacksmith shop where the town now stands was kept by John Hardrick from 1803 to about 1818. A tavern, the first in the place, was opened, in 1821, by Levi P. Scroggins. This was formerly a live, energetic business place, but the era of railroads has done for it what has been done for thousands of others—destroyed its business prospects. Years ago, considerable manufacturing was carried on in Leesburg. A hat factory was established by Jouett & Griffith in 1830, which did quite an extensive business for a time. A hemp factory was established, in 1837, by M. & W. Anderson. This was turned into a cotton factory, the next year, by William Hearn. Another hemp factory was established, in 1842, by Zach Graves. As early as 1819–20, there were two tan-yards in full operation. The first was established by Samuel Kinkead; the second by Hamilton & Cummings. The business outlook now presents the following exhibit: Four general stores, one blacksmith shop, one woodshop, one undertaker, one carding factory operated by W. A. Walker. Socially, morally and intellectually, it shows up as follows: One white church, two colored churches, three white schools, one colored school, one Masonic lodge (recently deceased), and the local option law, since 1875, has been in force.

The first church in the village of Leesburg was built in 1830. It was known as "Republican Church," and is now used by the white public school. The Christian Church was built in 1833, and Elder John A. Gano was the first pastor, as well as the present one, though others have intervened. The present membership is represented to be between 400 and 500. The first member of old Republican Church is said to have been Joseph Wasson, who was baptized in Silas Creek in 1826. The two colored churches are of the Baptist and Methodist denominations. Of the three white schools, one is a public school and the other two are private schools. All are in a prosperous condition and well attended. The colored school is also well attended by the colored children of the village, who are laudably engaged in educating themselves for future Congressmen and policemen.

The Masonic lodge was established in 1820, and known as "Warren Lodge." It flourished for a number of years, then ceased to exist for a time, was revived and continued to "work" until 1880, when it again went into "winter quarters," whence it has not issued at the present writing. *Requiescat in pace.* Leesburg is the vot-

ing-place of the precinct, and here, periodically, assem ble the sturdy yeomanry to exercise their rights of franchise.

Leeslick is a small place of about forty inhabitants, and was named for one Lee, who was shot here by the Indians, when this section was scarcely as safe an abiding-place as it is now. The circumstance has already been alluded to in this chapter. There is a fine spring of white sulphur water, which made it a place of great resort by the Indians, and also by the deer and buffalo, which came here to slake their thirst. The place has now two stores, one blacksmith shop, one school (near by), one saw and grist mill, etc. The first store was opened by John Scott in 1835. A distillery was erected and operated by Thomas Arnett, but has been discontinued. Both the saw and grist mill do a good business.

Broadwell comprises but a small collection of houses, and received its name from Asbury Broadwell, who owned the land upon which it stands. It is situated on the old State road, leading from Lexington to Covington, and before the day of railroads was a thriving place. Broadwell built a storehouse, which was occupied by Cox & Thornton, the first merchants. There is but little business now done in the place. A blacksmith shop and a post office, of which Mary A. Lail is Postmaster, is about all there is in the way of business.—*Perrin.*

CHAPTER XVII.

CLAYSVILLE PRECINCT—SURFACE AND PHYSICAL FEATURES—ADVENT OF THE PIONEERS—THEIR BUFFETS WITH SAVAGE BEASTS AND SAVAGE MEN—PIONEER INDUSTRIES—CHURCHES AND SCHOOLS—VILLAGES, ETC., ETC.

"Time, though old, is swift in flight,
And years went fleetly by—"

CLAYSVILLE PRECINCT, which is No. 8 of the election precincts, though the last in number, is one of the early settled and important sections of the county. The village of Claysville was once an enterprising place, and shipped largely to New Orleans by way of the raging Licking.

The precinct of Claysville lies in the northeast part of the county, and is somewhat broken and hilly. It is bounded on the north and east by Robertson County, on the south by Sylvan Dell, or Precinct No. 2, on the southwest by Cynthiana Precinct, and on the west by Richland, or Precinct No. 3. The land is mostly hilly and broken, but produces well, growing the finest of tobacco, which is the main staple. Corn and wheat are also cultivated to more or less extent. The streams are the East Fork of Licking and Beaver Creek, with their tributaries, of which Harrison and West Creeks are the most important. These streams, with a number of branches, which are nameless on the maps, drain the lands well, and afford the greatest abundance of stock water. The original timber growth was very fine, but the the settler's ax has despoiled much of the finest forests. Hickory, black walnut, sugar tree, wild cherry, oak, hackberry, buckeye, etc., etc., grow in abundance. Little of the natural forest is now left, the timber having been thinned out, even where the land has not been cleared up for cultivation.

The settlement by white people of Claysville Precinct was coeval with the settlement of other portions of Harrison County. Among the pioneers were the families of John Whitehead, Stephen B. Curran, — Dean, Daniel Durbin, the Obey family, etc. Whitehead and Curran settled near Claysville, lived to be very old, and are long dead. Dean died at an advanced age. Durbin was a very early settler. He was the grandfather of the Rev. Mr. Durbin, the celebrated traveler in Palestine and the Holy Land. Obey was an old settler, but died many years ago. These are but a few among the pioneers of Claysville Precinct. Names of others are lost.

"'Mid the rubbish of forgotten things."

The first years of the settlers of Claysville were years of toil and privation. The people had many trials to contend with, not the least of which was the depredations of Indians. Even after the savages ceased to wantonly murder the settlers, they never let an opportunity pass to steal whatever they could lay hands on, on the principle that what they obtained from the pale faces was clear gain. There were many other troubles to be met and overcome. The trouble of procuring bread was sometimes great. The settler's trusty rifle could easily furnish his family with meat, but bread had to be otherwise obtained. This led to the building of mills very early, and the Licking River and Beaver Creek were the scenes of some of the earliest mills built in Kentucky. Distilleries were not far behind mills in the way of pioneer manufacture, and, as a modern industry, they have kept pace with mills, if they have not even passed them, in the onward march. There are still both mills and distilleries in operation in this section.

The roads of Claysville are not to be compared to other and more favored sections of the county. The rough nature of the ground renders turnpiking rather an expensive operation; hence roads of that character are scarce in this precinct. The dirt roads are good—in summer.

The first school in the precinct is somewhat obscure, but is supposed to have been taught in a little log cabin erected for school purposes in the village of Claysville more than fifty years ago. The teacher was a man named Duncan, and was of the old-time style. He believed in the use of the rod, and, it is said, enforced his belief very vigorously. There are at the present day four schoolhouses in Claysville Precinct, including one in the village.

The church history of the precinct compares with that of other portions of the county. But we learned little of the erection of church buildings and the organization of church societies in Claysville Precinct.

The village of Claysville, years ago, was one of the most important business points in Harrison County. As we have already stated, it shipped largely by flat-boats to New Orleans. It is situated on the Main Licking, twelve miles northeast of Cynthiana, and nine miles from Poindexter Station on the Kentucky Central Railroad. It exports tobacco, grain and stock, and has a tri-weekly stage line to Milford and Brownsville. Its business comprises two general stores, one grocery, one physician, one tavern, two blacksmith shops, two carpenters, one teacher and one flour-mill. The building of the Kentucky Central Railroad, some miles distant from Claysville, killed its trade, and from that date its business has greatly declined.

Smithville Post Office is in the southern part of the precinct, and is merely a country post office, with no approach even to a village. This comprises a brief sketch of Claysville Precinct. There may be items of interest over-looked, but the foregoing is the result of our researches.—*Perrin.*

NICHOLAS COUNTY.

CHAPTER I.

SETTLEMENT OF THE WHITES — ROUGH LIFE ON THE FRONTIER — THE DIFFICULTIES MET WITH — THE COUNTY ORGANIZED—THE COURTS AND OFFICERS OF THE COUNTY—THE CENSUS, ELECTION PRECINCTS, ETC., ETC.—PUBLIC BUILDINGS — BLUE LICK SPRINGS — OTHER NOTES AND INCIDENTS.

"We shunn'd not labor ; when 'twas due
We wrought with right good will ;
And for the homes we won for them,
Our children bless us still." —*Gallagher*.

NICHOLAS COUNTY, like the little Republic of San Marino, is small in extent of territory, and nearly as rough and hilly. San Marino is the smallest and one of the most ancient Republics in the world, having stood, amidst the mutations and revolutions of empires and kingdoms for more than seven hundred years. It consists of a craggy mountain, 2,200 feet in height, situated amidst the lesser ranges of the Appennines, and embraces but twenty-one square miles. Its free institutions and government have stood unchanged and undisturbed by the surrounding nations of Europe, and Napoleon, in his Italian campaign, sent a special ambassador to assure its Government that the rights of the Republic should be scrupulously respected, an assurance the great soldier never violated. Nicholas County comes near being the San Marino of Kentucky ; the latter has but 8,000 inhabitants—Nicholas had but about 11,000 at the last census. In point of numbers, area, mountainous surface, and a lofty, chivalrous hospitality, the two sections are very much alike.

The settlement of Nicholas County is cotemporaneous with that of other portions of Central Kentucky, and extend back something like a hundred years. Collins says, that, in 1789, the only station between Maysville, then known as Limestone, and Lexington, was the Lower Blue Licks. It was erected by a man named Lyons, who followed making salt. He entertained travelers and had a family of negro servants, and was doubtless the first white settler within the present limits of Nicholas County. He dealt fairly with the settlers, and is said to have had a large run of custom. The settlers were in the habit of going to the Licks for salt-making, from 1775 down, camping there, but no permanent settlement was made until Lyon's.

Irish Station was another settlement, some five or six miles from Blue Licks, and was settled a few years later. James Parks, Jr., James Stephenson, George M. Bedinger and Samuel Peyton, were early settlers in the county, and have descendants still living. In the chapters devoted to the different towns, cities and election precincts, the names of many other early settlers are given, together with time and place of their settlement. This is sufficient to show the occupation of the country by white people. The pioneers did not have smooth sailing for a good many years after their settlement. "Milk Sickness" was one of the evils they had to contend with, though it made its appearance long after settlements were made. The State Geological Survey attributes the fact to the water, and says: "The water that runs off the slopes of the ridges, about seventy feet above the valleys, over the outcrop of the silicious mudstone, is highly charged with magnesia, and is also milky from suspended particles of clay or else of extremely fine silex. This description of water, if habitually used, acts injuriously on man and stock."

Collins relates the following of an apple-tree, which is of interest as a curiosity at any rate : "An apple-tree, remarkable for size and venerable for age, was, in 1852, still thrifty and healthy, upon a farm then owned by ex-Gov. Thomas Metcalfe, on the road from Samuel Arnett's to Carlisle. One foot above the ground its circumference was ten feet ; at four feet up, eight and a third feet around ; eight feet up, eight feet ; then it had three prongs, five and a third feet, four feet seven inches, and three and three-fourths feet in circumference. When a seedling scion, in

1795, it was found near the "Burned Cabins," a favorite camping-place for emigrants, and transplanted to Samule Peyton's yard, to the very spot it occupied more than fifty-seven years after. It bore abundantly of apples good for cooking and late use."

Among the early settlers of Nicholas County was the Metcalfe family—the father of Gov. Metcalfe, who was a Captain in the Revolutionary army. He moved to Fayette County, Ky., in 1785, and a few years later settled in the present county of Nicholas. Thomas Metcalfe, his eldest son, and afterward Governor of the State, was brought up here, and is still remembered by many of the citizens of the county. His father died when he was but nineteen years old, and from that time on the care of the family devolved on him. He was a stone-mason by trade, and, in after years, when he became a noted politician, the sobriquet of "Old Stone Hammer" clung to him through many an exciting campaign. A more complete biographical sketch of him will be found in connection with Carlisle.

The famous battle of Blue Licks—a battle almost without parallel in the annals of Indian warfare—occurred in this county. The battle of Blue Licks was fought on the 19th of August, 1782,* and proved to the whites a second Braddock's defeat. It took place on the old State road about half a mile north of the Lower Blue Licks. The whites were led by Cols. Todd, Boone and Trigg, while the savages were commanded by the notorious Girty—the white renegade. The summit of Cedar Hill, where this famous battle was fought, is barren and sterile, a fact that has often been a matter of wonder, inasmuch as it is underlaid with the same blue limestone formations that elsewhere afford so fertile a soil. This phenomenon has been imputed by the more superstitious to supernatural agencies arising out of the fact of this battle, and the terrible slaughter of the pale faces by their savage foes. A more sensible explanation of the matter, however, is made from a scientific standpoint. The State Geological Survey (Vol. III, p. 105), says: "This remarkable phenomenon is found in the fact that, at an elevation of one hundred and thirty to one hundred and forty feet above low water in the Licking River, the fossiliferous beds of the blue limestone are here covered up by the barren sand and quartz pebbles strewed over the site of the battle-ground. This sand and gravel lies from seventy to eighty feet above the layers of the blue limestone, exposed not far above the bridge." But to return to the battle of Blue Licks, which like that of Blenheim, was a famous victory—for the Indians. A more complete defeat of the whites never occurred on Kentucky soil, notwithstanding the entire State was for years one vast battle-ground. It was a miniature Blenheim, and a change of a word or two in the following quotation from Southey's highly descriptive poem, fully illustrates Blue Licks:

"They say it was a shocking sight
After the field was won—
For many, many bodies there
Lay rotting in the sun;
But things like that, you know, must be
After a famous victory."

A few days after the battle, Gen. Logan, who was advancing with a strong detachment from Lincoln County to assist in the pursuit and chastisement of the savages, arrived upon the fatal and disastrous field, where the sickening spectacle of bodies "rotting in the sun" met his view, but the enemy were gone. Nothing remained to him but to bury the dead. This he did, and then disbanded his army and returned home. But the battle of Blue Licks is more particularly described in a preceding chapter.

The Blue Lick Springs, which furnish the Blue Lick water, famous the world over, are located in this county. It is highly proper that such historic spots should be perpetuated, and we give place to the following account of these noted springs: The Upper and Lower Blue Lick Springs are among the most valuable in the world, and the water from both of which has an extended sale and use probably not equaled in the United States, if elsewhere in the world. As fashionable watering-places, or resorts for health, recreation and amusement, the accommodations at the Upper Spring have always been limited, and the attendance correspondingly small. At the Lower Spring, which has been much more widely known, the improvements were very greatly extended in 1845. * * * * The large cedar grove which occupies the site of the battle-ground was formerly inclosed and set in blue grass. The water of the two springs does not greatly differ in component properties. It is highly valuable water, and acts as a nervous stimulant, diuretic, etc.

For a hundred years or more these springs have been known to the whites, and for the first forty years of that time furnished much of the salt supply of Middle and Northeast Kentucky. The Upper Blue Lick Salt Works in 1805 were fed by three pumps set in a spring—from which flowed as much water "as would supply 1,000 kettles." At the same time, salt was more extensively manufactured at the Lower Spring. The following analysis, by Dr. Robert Peter, State Chemist to the Geological Survey, of this water is of interest: "The large Lower Spring emitted 678 gallons per hour, equal to 26,272 gallons in the day of twenty-four hours. Supposing the saline matters to constitute but

* While the country is celebrating so many centennials—the battle of Blue Licks should be celebrated on the 19th of August, 1882.

Nicholas County, Court House.

one per cent of the water, the amount brought out in one hour would be more than fifty-eight pounds avoirdupois. But say that fifty pounds an hour is the proportion, the quantity will amount to 438,000 pounds per annum." The original discovery of these springs is said to be as follows: A party of men from Pennsylvania discovered the Upper Blue Licks in 1773. Maj. John Finley, Col. James Perry, James Hamilton and Joshua Archer were of the party. They were engaged in surveying lands, and after surveying several tracts, they, on the 26th of July, 1773, surveyed one which included what they called the "Blue Lick" at the time, and until some of the company found a large lick down the river; then they called it the "Upper Blue Lick," and the other the "Lower Blue Lick." On their return to Pittsburgh, they drew lots, and this tract fell to Finley, who, after the Revolutionary war (in which he was Major of the Eighth Pennsylvania Regiment of Continental troops), came out and settled upon it. At his death, it fell to his son David D. Finley, who occupied it until recently.

Nicholas County was set off and organized into an independent county in 1799, and was the last county formed in Kentucky prior to 1800. Its territory was taken from Bourbon and Mason Counties, and at the time of its formation, its area was much more extensive than now, as it contributed some 25,000 acres toward the formation of Robertson County in 1867. After this huge bite was taken off its northern frontier, it left Nicholas one of the small counties of the State—like the Irishman's horse, "it is little but it is ould," and holds its place among its neighbors with as much dignity as San Marino itself. It is situated a little northeast of the center of the State, and since the last change in geographical limits, is bounded as follows: On the north and northeast by Robertson and Fleming Counties; on the east by Fleming County, on the south and southeast by Bourbon and Bath Counties, and on the west by Harrison County. It is drained by the Licking River and its numerous tributaries, and that portion of the county which lies contiguous to Bourbon and Bath is gently rolling and undulating—the remainder is rough, broken and hilly. The timber consists of walnut, blue ash, poplar, sugar-maple, hickory, several species of oak, beech, elm, etc., etc.—the staple products are corn, wheat, rye, oats, tobacco, etc., etc., with some hemp, cattle, hogs, sheep and whisky, though the latter receives little attention as compared with some of the surrounding counties.

The county being formed, the next step was the organization of the courts, and the putting in motion its civil machinery. This was accomplished with the opening dawn of the present century, by a session of court held at the house of Martin Baker in June, 1800. The act for the formation of the county, which passed the year previous, was produced, bearing the signature of Gov. James Garrard, and appointing as Justices of the Peace Marvin Duvall, Cornelius Hall, Eli Metcalfe, John Collier, David Gray, William Thompson, Thomas Vaughn, Henry Dawson and Martin Baker, Jr., gentlemen, all of whom were present and duly sworn. Nathan G. Standeford presented his commission from the Governor as Sheriff and was qualified; Lewis H. Arnold was appointed first Clerk, giving John Drake, Nathan G. Standeford and Thomas Arnold as security in the sum of £1,000. David Irwin and Thomas Scott produced licenses to practice law; George M. Bedinger was appointed County Surveyor; Thomas Cobrill was appointed Constable; David Irwin, first County Attorney; Philip Kenton the first Coroner and also the first Jailer.

At this meeting of the court the county seat was located on the land of Henry Clay, Jr., on Main Licking, in the bend of the river, below the mouth of Stony Creek, opposite Maj. Bedinger's Mills. Clay agreed to set apart ninety acres of land to be laid out in town lots—the lots to be sold by him on a credit of four years, and two acres to be donated to the county for the public buildings. Bedinger also agreed to set apart thirty acres on the opposite side of the river for town lots; and further agreed "to ferry, free of charge, on court and other public days, all parties of the county attending the court house, and all the inhabitants of the county who should be invited across the river to stay all night with friends." Two acres were set apart on Clay's place for a jail and "stray pen," but there is no record of a court house being built at this place. A jail, however, was built according to the following plan: "Building to be sixteen feet square, foundation of stone three feet thick, and high enough to be raised above the ground, on which is to be a floor of square timbers laid close and one foot in thickness, over these was laid crosswise a floor of three-inch plank pinned with two pins to the square foot. On this floor was built a wall of like timbers, one foot thick, fitting closely; and inside of this another similar wall, leaving a space of one foot between the walls, which was filled with stones not less than two feet in face, and not less than eight inches thick, placed on edge, with the small interstices filled with small stones, lime and sand; at the height of eight feet another floor to be laid similar to the first, and the outer wall continued upward eight more feet, and a third similar floor laid, the whole to be covered by a substantial roof of shingles. Each story contained two windows eighteen inches square, furnished with bars of one inch iron, placed three inches apart. All timber to be of white oak, yellow locust or walnut." According to the report of the Commissioners, the jail was not to cost over £200, and payment was to be made in wheat at 3s, 6d per bushel, or money, at the option of the citizen, or if not paid before 1802, it must be in money.

The court house was not allowed to remain here long in peace and tranquillity. An act was passed by the State Legislature in 1804 to remove the county seat to the farm of James Ellis. The Commissioners met February 11, 1805, and laid off the ground for the public buildings, it being a plat, rectangular in shape, 20x16 poles. A deed to the plat from James Ellis to the Justices of the county was acknowledged in July, 1805. Here was erected a jail and a log court house. A jailer's house was added to the jail in 1805, erected by William McClannahan, at a cost of $403.75, he being the lowest bidder. May 9, 1816, Commissioners Roland T. Parker, of Lewis County; William B. Blackburne, Joseph Morgan, Thompson Ward, of Greenup County; and Anderson Miller, of Franklin County, met to receive propositions for a permanent location of the county seat. At that meeting, a proposition was submitted by John Kincart, donating one and three-fourths acres of land for a public square, setting apart fifty acres to be laid off in town lots, every alternate lot to be sold, and the money derived therefrom to be used in erecting public buildings; he also accompanied his proposal with a subscription of $515.99, from 113 citizens, in sums ranging from 50 cents to $20; he further offered the use of his house till a suitable court house could be erected. Proposals of fifty acres of land were also severally offered by William Holladay, Isham Johnson and Samuel Arnett; Jacob Jones offered one acre; G. M. Bedinger offered the old ground and $1,000; Thomas Jones, of Paris, proposed one and one-third acres of land for a public square and $500—all upon the condition that the county seat was to be located upon their respective places. At the May term of court, 1816, the order passed accepting the proposition of John Kincart. The town was surveyed and laid off in 139 lots by James Thomson, and christened Carlisle. A jail, similar to the one at Ellisville, was built by Robert Hamilton in 1816. The contract for building the first court house was let to different parties; the stone and brick work was done by Thomas Metcalf, Alexander Blair, Thomas West and Samuel Fulton for $1,700. The plastering was taken by Thomas Metcalf and Robert Dykes for $840. The carpenter's and joiner's work was taken by James P. Ashley and William McClannahan for $2,800. The whole was completed in 1818. This building was torn down and the present one erected in 1844, the entire contract being taken by William Secrist and Green Remington for $4,600; the clock was put in in 1847.

The present jail was built by West and Fitch Munger for $6,000, and is a substantial structure.

The county seat was thus finally and permanently located, but so frequently had it been changed and removed from one place to another, that for several years after its present location the county officers were in the habit each morning, of sending out their deputies to ascertain if the capital had again been removed during the night. In another chapter will be found the names of many of the county officers, past and present, and to avoid repetition we will omit all mention here, except of the present incumbents, which are as follows: County Judge, A. J. Banta; Circuit Clerk, T. J. Glenn; County Clerk, John A. Campbell; Sheriff, John Herrin; Jailer, Robert Kincart; Assessor, J. B. Potts; Coroner, William A. Fowle; and School Commissioner, B. H. Robinson.

The Poor House and Farm, as a county institution, should have mention among the public buildings. Of the Nicholas County Poor House, there is but little to say. It is on Fulton Creek, about four miles northeast of Carlisle, and was located here in 1858. The buildings are of logs and are sufficient to accommodate thirty paupers, and the farm attached comprises fifty acres. The house at present is kept by O. P. Brothers; it is under the supervision of the county court, and is supported by a per capita tax.

Previous to the adoption of the present constitution, the county was laid off into but few divisions. In 1850, however, it was divided in a number of districts for election and other purposes, in order to facilitate its business. It is at present divided into six election precincts, which are named and numbered as follows: Lower Blue Licks, No. 1; Headquarters, No. 2; Ellisville, No. 3; Carlisle, No. 4; Union, No. 5; and Upper Blue Licks, or "Buzzard Roost," No. 6. These precincts, as stated elsewhere, are each supplied with two Justices of the Peace and one Constable, who attend to the business of their respective precincts, and the Magistrates, taken together, form the County Court, and transact all general county business.

The census of Nicholas County, from the time of its organization in 1799, is as follows: In 1800, 2,925; in 1810, 4,898; in 1820, 7,973; in 1830, 8,834; in 1840, 8,745; in 1850, 10,361; in 1860, 11,039; in 1870, 9,129; and in 1880, 11,869. The growth in population of the county, it will be seen from the above figures, though somewhat slow, has been steady, almost trebling in eight decades.—*W. H. Perrin.*

CHAPTER II.

MORAL AND INTELLECTUAL DEVELOPMENT—ESTABLISHMENT OF CHURCHES—THE DEERING CAMP-GROUND—ITS GREAT SUCCESS—SCHOOLS AND SCHOOL HISTORY—COLORED SCHOOLS—THE PRESS-WAR HISTORY.

If we work upon marble it will perish; if we work upon brass, time will efface it; if we rear temples, they will crumble into dust, but if we work upon immortal minds, if we imbue them with pure principles, with the just fear of God and love of fellow-men, we engrave on those tablets something which will brighten to all eternity.—*Daniel Webster*.

THE religious and educational history of Nicholas, showing its moral and intellectual development, should not be omitted in a work of this character. The preaching of the Gospel was coeval with the settlement of the county. "In the cool and silent shade they knelt down, and offered prayer and supplication" to the Author of their being, for his protecting care. Mr. Kennedy, in a sketch of the Presbyterian Church of Carlisle, written for this work, says: "The first church of any denomination ever organized in what is now Nicholas County, was organized about 1795-96—at Old Concord, two and a half miles southeast of Carlisle, a point which, by reason of the almost wonderful religious experiences which the church at that point enjoyed, and the singular manifestations there witnessed in the early part of this century, has a historic and pleasing interest, as connected with church history in Kentucky, second to no place in the State. The extraordinarily large crowds of people traveling from afar, and bearing with them 'daily bread' sufficient to sustain them through even long protracted sieges, and waiting before God and upon the Spirit and the word. The inspiration with which the services of sermons, exhortations, prayer and song seemed to fill them, and take so deep hold as to be by some regarded as a sort of frenzy, the unusually large number who daily at these meetings found the peace in believing that passeth understanding—these, we say, were almost marvelously astounding, particularly to those, at least, who not having an indwelling knowledge and consciousness of the power of the Gospel, backed and driven home to the hearts of men by the Holy Spirit, were only prepared to witness such manifestations with and in a spirit of unbelief." A more complete history of this old church will be found in another chapter. An early minister of this church was the Rev. Barton W. Stone, one of the ablest ministers of his day, and of whom a lengthy sketch will be found elsewhere in this volume. He was pastor of this church, and Cane Ridge Church, in Bourbon County, at the same time, and became pastor of them as far back as 1798. He was a Presbyterian in those early days, but finally became a disciple of the new doctrine of Alexander Campbell, and a zealous minister of the Christian Church from that time until his death. The particulars of the organization of churches and their early pastors will be given in their respective towns and precincts, and no further history given here than merely the introduction of Christianity into the Western wilderness, as Kentucky was then known. In conclusion of this preliminary sketch, we will devote a few pages to the famous "camp-meeting grounds" near Carlisle, as being altogether appropriate.

The following extract of the "Deering Camp Ground," is from "*The Camp-Meeting Daily*," August 7, 1878, Vol. I, No. 1, and gives the "Origin of the Deering Camp-Meeting," etc., by Rev. Morris Evans. We reproduce the extract, which is as follows: "Deering Camp-Meeting is held on Parks' Hill, located on the Licking River. This hill is a triangular elevation of some seven or eight acres in size. The top of the hill is about 200 feet above the level of the Licking River, on the north side of the cliff overlooking the river. On the southeast side is the valley of Cassidy Creek, along which runs the Carlisle and Flemingsburg pike; also, on the side of the hill, a branch railroad, connecting the Kentucky Central Railroad with the saw-mill. The southwest side is headed by the Maysville & Lexington branch of the Kentucky Central Railroad; here, too, is a hilly bluff looking down on the railroad. From almost every point, the eye has spread out before it a panorama of beautiful scenery. This hill seven years ago was an isolated spot left to grow up in briers and the rough undergrowth indigenous to these Licking hills. It gave no promise of the beautiful resort, carpeted with our Kentucky blue grass, and shaded by magnificent forest trees, where the refinement and culture of our county can find respite from care, and the repose of a country home, where Dame Nature has doffed her rough attire and smiles in loveliness to welcome all appreciative visitors. The hill is named after Col. T. S. Parks, the efficient and generous President of the Washington Manufacturing & Mining

Company. This company owns the camp-ground, hence the name of the location.

"As a place of religious worship, it is called 'Deering Camp-Ground' in honor of the Rev. S. S. Deering, of the Kentucky Annual Conference, Methodist Episcopal Church South, by whom this enterprise was first conceived, projected, and then brought into existence by his faithful and persistent endeavors. At this time, Mr. Deering was pastor of the Carlisle Circuit, in the bounds of which the grounds are located. Among the many very valuable achievements of his long, laborious, career but few, if any of his enterprises will reflect more credit upon his sound judgment and diligent labor than this. Each succeeding year is showing more and more its capacity for good and exact adaptation as to location and surroundings for the great purpose contemplated. The following letter from him in response to a request for information as to its early history, will be read with interest by all:"

GARRARD COUNTY, KY., July 26, 1878.

BROTHER EVANS—When I lived in Carlisle, seven years ago, I noticed a large element of society which attended church nowhere. In my association with the people, and in traveling over the county on foot and on horseback, I found many families unreached by any Christian agency then in use. These are facts; and I had often noticed them before, and it excited in me the question, What can be done to wake up and interest these people in religion? Is there not some way to call them out and associate them with the better elements of society, and to get their thoughts on God, their duty to Him and to themselves and to their country? I could see that a circus, a picnic, an election, a fair and many other things which excited curiosity and made an idle hour pleasant to them, could and would draw them, and I said to myself, "a woods meeting, that's the thing for them;" it will draw them, and while the novelty is getting them into position, I can preach the Gospel to them and sing to them of "Jesus and His love." Walking to an appointment one day from Myers' Station to Sam. Ishmael's, I passed by Parks' Hill, then a tangled thicket of briers and brush, I thought I saw a good place for a "woods meeting" if I could get the use of it and get it cleared up. But minus money and friends, how was such an end to be reached? I found that the ground belonged to Parks, Dorsey & Co., and to one of the members I went with my accounts. When he and Mr. Jeff Glenn heard me, he said he would have the ground cleared up, and we'd look at it. That was one step. That done, I suggested a camp-ground as you now have it. Mr. Glenn and his friends feared the sentiment of the people was not up to a point which would allow such a thing as to pay your way to worship. I replied that if I had the means to build I'd risk it. Then he said they would build a shed, and if it didn't succeed as a meeting, it would do for a tobacco shed. And thus assured, I went forward for a camp-meeting.

But then a new difficulty crossed me. The church objected, threatening to stop the supplies if I didn't stop the camp-meeting. Some said the people would steal all the melons, fruit, chickens and roasting-ears in the vicinity. Others said it would bring in a tide of debauchery. At one time, violent threats were made in view of my perseverance. Meantime, with fasting, prayers and many tears, the work was pushed. Col. Parks, Mr. Glenn and others, nobly seconded all my efforts; but the strain on my sensitive nerves became too great for me, and Dr. Tilton sent me off to rest awhile.

While the District Conference was in session at Carlisle, I persuaded Mr. Glenn, who was then Superintendent of the rail road, to give all the members a free ride to the camp-ground, and thus by a free ride, get many of them to see what else they could see on the ground. They voted the arrangement a success, and gave it their countenance and commended it to the people.

At this stage Brother Poynter's help was sought and by him was as cordially given, as he always gives it where his judgment approves. He helped me to get the preachers to come, for they, like many others, gave it the cold shoulder, and he encouraged his people in Millersburg to attend. Bishop Kavanaugh also gave his influence to the meeting. A few noble women, may heaven bless them! they will never know in this world how my heart blessed them when I saw their dear faces at the first meeting, giving me words of encouragement.

At length, with a good shed, a few cottages and a meager outfit generally, our first meeting began. Some of the good old-time Methodist people came in promptly, but, as of old, "when the sons of God came to present themselves before the Lord, the devil came also." The weather was hot, the grounds were dusty, the water gave out, and just then, with the mercury at ninety, some good old ladies, in lighting their pipes for a smoke after dinner, dropped a match among the dry rubbish which had been taken from the ground, and in half an hour we were surrounded by a ball of flame, and, for awhile, it looked as if everything on the ground would be burned up. But quiet came, Moses preached, there was a good meeting and the evening train came; but, alas! a rain came up; most of the coaches were open flats; the ground had been worked up to a powder, and, with the rain, the hurrying to and fro there, left the grounds the wettest, muddiest, the most hungry and thirsty, mad crowd of men, women and children that I ever saw.

But withal, we had a good meeting; good was done. The company saw there was good in it, at least enough of them did, to go forward and fix for another meeting the next year. And so, from year to year, they have improved the grounds, and the meetings have become more and more interesting to the public, and the attendance has increased each year with the company's improved accommodations, and the present meeting will no doubt excel any former one in the means of enjoyment afforded to all who may attend. If those having the management could prevent the worldly, pleasure-seeking element of our nature from pressing the occasion into the service of the carnal mind, the camp meeting ought to be a power for good; but the half-skeptical state of the public mind just now will require great diligence on the part of the Christians to keep out the worldly spirit.

S. S. DEERING.

The above extract gives so complete a history of this famous "camp-ground," that further attempt at description would be superfluous. Enough has been said upon this subject, and of the churches at large, to show that the people of Nicholas are a God-fearing people, and pay considerable attention to the claims of the Gospel.

The schools of the county next require a few words at our hands. Like all portions of not only Central Kentucky, but the entire State, there is not the attention paid to the common schools their importance demands. The Northern and Western States are far ahead of us in educational matters. According to the last report of the State Superintendent of Schools, there are in Nicholas County 3,409 white children of school age, and 337 colored children. The amount paid to teachers of white schools for the year ending October 10, 1881, was $5,321.12; amount paid colored teachers, $210.10. The county is laid off into forty-seven districts for the white schools, in which are schoolhouses of a rather inferior quality. There are four colored schools in the county—one in Carlisle, one in Ellisville, or "Shakerag," one in Headquarters, and one in "Buzzard's Roost." The schools are supplied by the county, except the Carlisle School, which is taught by the minister of the Reformed Church.

The white schools are supplied with the best teachers to be had in the vicinity, and are male teachers mostly. The following extract pertaining to country schools is sensible, and deserves a careful perusal: "Country schools are neglected both by those who write for our educational papers, and by institute instructors, unless some eminent educator condescends to devote a portion of time or space to his views of the country teacher's work; but then they are theoretical and not practical, and every country teacher is obliged to apply them with many modifications. Men who have spent years in common schools, and are fresh with experience in successful practice, are the ones whose opinions we are anxious to hear; not some eminent character who has probably taught one or two terms in the country years ago, and then stepped thence into the higher schools, and now goes around lecturing to Teacher's Institutes for $50 per week. Country teachers are not so easily imposed on as this, and it is one reason why so many do not attend the county institutes. Experience has taught many that these instructors are but blind guides when they lecture about country schools. The country teacher is by far the most original." These remarks contain much truth. It is impossible to teach the country schools with the same amount of red tape that is bound around those in cities and large towns. There is a little too much form and ceremony in all the schools for the rapid advancement of the pupils.

The State Superintendent has the following upon compulsory education, a subject now attracting considerable attention in several of the States: "The African race is here and 'will not go.' Shall it remain in ignorance, and entail by the costs of crime a greater expense to the State than their education, besides furnishing the tremendous power of a corrupt constituency to rural demagogues who aspire to feed and fatten at the 'public crib' on the products of intelligence, industry and virtue? Such views as the facts compel our forcing the two questions of compulsory and moral education upon the public attention, as a preventive of crime and waste.

"Can the State leave to the election of ignorant parents, unconscious of the benefits of education, and the shame of ignorance, or to truant children undisciplined by parental authority, the decision of this great interest of education. In times of pestilence, municipalities compel cleanliness and the use of prophylactics. Is not the moral and mental health of the people equal in importance to their physical health? It is well known that even disease of an epidemic character is born in the slums, and bred in the purlieus of of ignorance and vice. * * * * * Our children flock to the same schools, congregate on the village commons, read the same literature, and compete for the prizes, 'etc., etc." Then it is not only essential to educate our children and our neighbor's children, for the sake of dispelling ignorance, but for the sake of cleanliness, which we are told is next to Godliness.

The press is so well written up by Mr. Chappell in the history of Carlisle that we can find nothing to say of it here, but refer the reader to his sketch.

The war history is also written up in other chapters of this volume, and will not be repeated.—*Perrin.*

CHAPTER III.

INTERNAL IMPROVEMENTS—THE OLD MAYSVILLE ROAD—OTHER TURNPIKES—BRIDGES AND RAILROADS—BUILDING OF THE KENTUCKY CENTRAL RAILROAD—DISTILLERIES—AGRICULTURE—ITS RISE, PROGRESS AND GROWTH IN THE COUNTY.

AMONG the internal improvements of Nicholas County are her turnpike and macadamized roads. In quantity and quality, these scarcely compare with some of the surrounding counties, but are, withal, a fine system of roads. That great thoroughfare of travel, the old "Maysville Road," passes through Nicholas County. The following is from a newspaper article written by Mr. Chappell: "In the year 1832, a survey was made through Nicholas of that great highway forming a part of the route from the Capitol City of Washington, passing through Maryland, Virginia, Pennsylvania, Ohio and Kentucky, on to Florence in Alabama. Two routes had been surveyed, one via Carlisle and one via Forest Retreat. At that time, Gen. Metcalfe was in Congress, an ex-Governor and a man of wealth and influence. He was bitterly opposed to the Carlisle route, and used his influence in behalf of the survey by his own farm and homestead which he called Forest Retreat. Notwithstanding the General's opposition, Carlisle could have had the road for about *eight thousand dollars!* But, alas! the warm friends of the road were few, and unable to cope with the General. It would have cost the road all the difference to have made it through Carlisle, for every one knows what a favorable route the road has, following the bed of Stony Creek and its tributaries; still there was a wish that Carlisle might get the road, on the part of the directory, because, as the county seat of a county through which twelve miles of the road had to run, it was felt that in justice the county seat should have it. But the die was cast, and the road was located within two and one-half miles of us, and for nearly fifteen years we floundered in the mud, held in scorn and derision by our neighbors, and compelled to see the trade from our very doors carried off to Millersburg and Mayslick, while even Forest Retreat and Oakland Mills put on airs, built up their great mills and stores and competed with us for the little that was left. In the meantime, the Maysville directory angered at our indifference, stuck a toll-gate right under our very nose, leaving a long unbroken stretch to Millersburg, thus turning the whole tide of our trade from Beaver Creek, Steele's Run, the Lower Brushy Fork and all the circumjacent country right into the lap of Millersburg. And there that toll-gate stands to this day, a standing insult to the town, and yet a memorial of our own folly."

Thus it is, that like the base Judean, "who threw a pearl away, richer than all his tribe," we throw away the golden opportunities that lie before us. It is another example of the superiority of our "hindsight" over our "foresight." Had this road passed through Carlisle instead of a few miles from the town, the advantages would have been large, and far exceeded the insignificant sum of of $8,000. But our ancestors were not alive to enterprise, such as characterize their wide-awake descendants.

The first turnpike in Nicholas County, aside from the Maysville road, was chartered in 1845, and extended from Carlisle to Forest Retreat, a distance of three miles. In 1855, a survey was made for the Carlisle and Sharpsburg pike, but the road was not completed for several years later. At the present time, several turnpike and macadamized roads diverge from Carlisle leading to the most important places in other neighborhoods. Good bridges span many of the larger streams, where the most important roads cross them. An early improvement in the county was a ferry. What is still known as "Parks' Ferry," was established very early across the Licking River, not far from Upper Blue Licks. Other ferries were established where trade and travel most required them.

The railroad history of Nicholas County is soon written. It is comprised in the Maysville Division of the Kentucky Central, and may be briefly told. The Maysville road was chartered as the Lexington & Maysville Railroad, and the project was agitated as early as 1848—about the same time the Lexington & Covington Railroad enterprise was inaugurated. After expending something like $1,500,000 upon it, the enterprise failed—the Lexington & Maysville Railroad went into bankruptcy, Henry Waller, of Maysville, President, at the time. Just after the close of the late war, a new company was organized, with Abner Hord, President. Mason County subscribed $200,000, and Bourbon $200,000. The charter gave the company license to issue $500,000 in bonds, but Nicholas refused, by a vote of her people, a bonded debt. She, however, afterward voted 3 cents on the $100 of taxable property of the county toward the completion of the road. After expending the amount of subscriptions, it was still unfinished, and the bonds were sold in New York for $500,000, with which sum the work was completed in 1871, and the road put in running order. After being in operation for a few years, the company found it could not pay expenses, the road was sold at public auction by the United States Marshal of Kentucky, and bid off to Mr. Henry Bell, of Lexington, for J. B. Alexander, of New York, for $400,000. It was operated for two or three years under this regime, and then sold to the Kentucky Central, and has since been operated as a division of that system.

From the nature of the country through which it passes, it seems somewhat strange that it pays no better than it does. It appears that, like the Indian's gun, which was "more expense than profit," its earnings have never been sufficient to put it in first-class order, or even keep it in good repair. With one terminus at the Ohio River and the other at Lexington, where it has connections with all parts of the State, are facilities that ought to give it an extensive business. The following editorial, however, from the Carlisle *Mercury*, of December 1, 1881, shows something of the estimation in which it is held in the community through which it passes. Speaking of the condition of the road and the numerous accidents, the editor thus humorously pays it his respects:

"For peculiar eccentricities and an odd make-up generally, we will bet a grease spot against 5 cents' worth of wind pudding that there is no railroad in the United States that can hold a burnt chunk, much less a candle, to the old dilapidated, rickety, lop-sided string of twisted iron and rotten logs that stretches its ragged length up the happy valley of the Brushy Fork, under the high-sounding title of the Kentucky Central Railroad. If the concern were to occasionally blow up an engine, run over some one, or jump through a bridge, it would be nothing out of the regular line of railroad catastrophes, but the crazy old thing has a habit of doing so many peculiar acts that we are nervous when in its vicinity, and, at the approach of a train, we feel a disposition to get out of the way, as it is liable at any time to cut a funny caper. We have known a railroad train to jump through a bridge and down a hundred feet into a river, killing seventy-five persons, but we have never heard of any other than a Kentucky Central train that has, while running along through a perfectly level section of country, jumped up in the air and come down slap across the track, and we do not think there is another railroad in the country whose trains get off the track to 'butt' stone walls. Whatever peculiarities may characterize it in the future, we do not think it can surpass its recent rare eccentricities. On last Wednesday evening, while coming up from Maysville, the freight train was suddenly taken with one of its eccentric whims and deliberately got off the track, went over and lay down in a fence corner like a tired hog, where it lay barricading the way and delaying the passenger train until late the next day."

The following appeared in the same paper a few weeks previous to the extract given above: "A. K. C. train jumped the track down at Elizaville the other day, and another train on the same road jumped the track over at Talbott's Station, ditching five freight cars. From these latest freaks it will be seen that the regular jumping-off place has been changed from Millersburg to any where along the line from Maysville to Covington. It would have been better to have kept up the old habit of jumping off at one place, as the passengers would know just when to cling to their seats. While going down to Maysville the other night, a headlight on the train took fire and burned up, and the train had to go to Maysville in the dark. On another occasion, the engine blew out its whistle and has been gliding into the stations without the usual signal. Again while going up the road the other day, the train was suddenly seized with one of its peculiar fits and jumped 'slap dab' up against a stone wall, tearing away a pair of steps, and abruptly shaking up the passengers. What next?"

The manufacture of whisky has received some attention in Nicholas County, though not to that extent that it has in other blue grass counties, which make it one of their main staples. It was an early industry in this county, however, and many of the early settlers indulged in its manufacture. Hence, distilleries and mills were cotemporaneous manufacturing industries of this section. But, in later years, the people have advanced a step above this rather questionable business, devoting their talents and energies to more creditable, if less remunerative, callings, and the distillation of whisky now receives little attention in the county.

The agriculture of the county next claims our attention. The following sketch is written for this work, by Thomas Kennedy, Esq. The article is well and ably written, and we earnestly commend it to our readers. It is as follows:

"The History of the Agriculture of Nicholas County since its formation in 1799, does not differ materially from that of the surrounding counties. The preparation of the land for the plow was a work of the most arduous character. The entire surface of the county was thickly covered with large timber, the growth of centuries. Beneath this large timber, but struggling up in dense masses, was an undergrowth similar in kind to the larger growth, and plentifully interspersed with briers and thorns. To grub and remove such an undergrowth, then to cut down and chop in proper lengths the trees, splitting the smoothest and best of the trunks into rails or firewood, and piling up and burning the remainder of them before the ground could be tilled, was a task that required in its performance the most vigorous muscle and the stoutest heart.

"The pioneers of this county were specially endowed in body and temperament for the accomplishment of this work. The timber was of various kinds, and its quality in this county, as it stood in its native grandeur, was probably unsurpassed. During the first forty years after the foundation of this county, the best of the timber was destroyed as an incumbrance upon the ground and an obstruction to the operations of the farmer. To allow it to decay was too slow a process. It was cut into convenient lengths and piled into heaps—log-heaps as they were then called—and burned. Log-rollings and quiltings were among the chief merry-makings in those days. The farmer who proposed to clear out a 'piece of new ground,' cut down the trees chopped them into the required length, cut and piled the brush so as to have it out of the way, and, having fixed upon a day, invited all his neighbors to the 'log-rolling.' His wife having 'put a quilt into the frames,' invited all the ladies in the neighborhood to the quilting, selecting for the quilting the same day fixed for the log-rolling. The invited guests of both sexes were on hand promptly, soon after the usual breakfast hour, and ready for business.

"Log-rolling consisted not in rolling the logs, except rarely, but in carrying the logs from the places where they lay and piling them together in a heap. For this purpose handspikes were used. These were the bodies of saplings —usually dogwood—selected on account of their toughness, and about six feet in length, and from two and a half to three inches in diameter. A handspike was put under each end of the log, so that the log would rest on the middle of the spike, and if it was very large and heavy, one or more spikes were put under near the middle of the log, and one man grasped each end of the spike, and in that way the log was carried to the heap. Lifting thus at the handspike was the severest test of the physical strength and endurance of a man in raising and carrying a heavy burden. These handspike exercises strained every nerve to its utmost, and happy was the man who possessed sufficient backbone to carry him triumphantly through such an ordeal. If he 'outlifted' every other man on the ground, he was declared the champion of the handspike, while on the other hand, if one 'let down' at the handspike, he was an object of derision, because he lacked physical strength to carry his allotted burden. In these days the politicians, who are the most successful log-rollers, are not noted for an excess of backbone. But our ancestors esteemed chiefly those qualities, the exercise of which was most conducive to their well-being.

"The log-rollings were also occasions for leaping, wrestling, running foot-races and other manly exercises, and occasionally for a fist and skull encounter, the sanguinary consequences of which tended in no small degree to keep alive the memory of the name of the 'dark and bloody ground' which Kentucky has so long borne—a name which at one time was regarded as the synonym of chivalry, but as now applied savors rather of reproach.

"In the house, the women plied their needles with skill and industry, and by the time the last log was put upon the heap the quilt was finished. After supper, the fiddler took his stand, and while he indulged in the usual amount of twanging the strings and drawing the bow across them to ascertain if the fiddle was in proper tune, partners were chosen, and when the music began, 'Merrily danced the Quaker's wife, and merrily danced the Quaker.' The cares and toils of life were all forgotten amid the excitement and joyousness of the dance.

"The farmers in the early days of the county depended very largely upon their maple trees for a supply of sugar and molasses. The season usually opened about the middle of February, and closed from the 1st to the 10th of March. A maple tree grove, or 'sugar camp,' as it was then called, of one hundred trees, would yield ordinarily from one hundred and twenty-five to one hundred and fifty pounds of sugar and fifteen to twenty gallons of molasses in a season. While molasses was delicious to the taste, the sugar was not especially palatable in tea or coffee. The loaf sugar was a luxury that was only indulged in on very rare occasions. The party of tea-drinkers who could sweeten their tea with loaf sugar thought themselves highly favored.

"The waste of timber that has been going on for so many years has almost denuded the country of trees. There are but very few 'sugar camps' left in the country. The making of maple sugar and molasses is no longer a necessity, but to the extent they are now made they are sold and bought at fancy prices, as luxuries.

"The implements of husbandry were few and extremely rude. The 'Cary' plow that was used for breaking up the ground, had an iron bar and a wooden moldboard, and made a furrow about eight inches wide and from two to three inches deep. While the soil was fresh and had depth, the quality of the plowing was not so material. But when the soil began to be exhausted, particularly where

the surface was hilly, the shallow plowing that was done put the soil into a condition most favorable to be washed away by the first hard rain. The process of clearing out a fresh piece of ground was so tedious and involved so much hard labor that the farmer raised the same kind of crop year after year upon the same piece of ground. The result was the soil was exhausted, the land was washed into great gullies, and in that exposed and non-productive condition it was turned out into the commons. In too many instances no effort was made to repair the waste that had been committed, but the old field was relegated to Nature for her to reclaim it by whatever renovating powers she might possess. Many farmers in the early days of the county, as well as at the present time, seem to be possessed with the delusion that their land can only be prepared for the production of grasses by cultivating it in grain until it is completely, or at least well-nigh, exhausted. The consequences of such a course of farming are painfully apparent in many parts of the county.

"Prior to 1840, the Diamond plow was introduced, and was a great improvement. It was a strong, steady-running plow, capable of plowing the ground to any depth, that might be desired. It was manufactured as far back as 1840 by T. J. McCormick, Esq., who now lives at Forest Retreat, but who then lived on the Maysville & Lexington Turnpike, two miles east of Millersburg, but in this county. Neither the house in which he then lived nor the shop in which he worked is standing. Other plows have superseded the Diamond, but it is doubtful if any of them excel it in efficiency. In process of time, the harrow came into use. The principal improvement in the harrow has been to increase its width and the number of its teeth, thus adding to its weight and effectiveness. After the harrow came the roller; its advent among the clods, and its crushing effect upon them, was viewed with the liveliest satisfaction by the unfortunate boy who was too small to plow, but was regarded as just the proper age to hoe the corn. Hoeing corn has almost fallen into disuse, yet as a means of cultivation, one good hoeing is equal to at least two plowings. Farmers are gradually awakening to the folly of allowing their old fields to lie out fallow. A non-producing field is not only dead capital, but it is a sad disfigurement of the face of nature. To reduce fruitful land to a barren condition is a gross abuse of the bounty of a beneficent Creator. It is more deserving of condemnation than the conduct of the wicked and slothful servant, who hid his Lord's money, but preserved at least what had been entrusted to him. At first the sickle was the only implement used in harvesting wheat. The reaper would cut a 'through' about four feet wide, holding the grain with his left hand as he cut it, then dropping it in handfuls on his left. When he reached the end of the 'through,' he placed the sickle on his left shoulder, and thence returning, bound into bundles the grain he had just cut. Each reaper cut about one acre per day. The price ranged from fifty to seventy-five cents per day, and three square meals, but the day was generally from daylight till dark, with a short rest at noon. The fastest reaper was usually selected for the leader for the day, and the reaper who 'gave out,' and had to go to the shade to rest, was the victim of many a rude joke. The sickle has almost gone out of use. Grain cradles were introduced about 1825, and are still in use. On account of the unevenness of the surface of a large part of the county, and the presence of rocks, it is difficult, if not impossible to use advantageously the modern reapers. The cradle is much used, and will continue to be, not more from choice than from necessity. The grain, whether wheat, rye or oats, was separated from the straw by means of a flail which consisted of two sticks of wood fastened together at the ends by means of a cord, and leaving a space of two or three inches between the ends of the sticks. One of the sticks, the one which the flailman took in his hands, was about six or eight feet in length, and the other was about half that length. The bundles were untied and laid upon rails, underneath which was a sheet that received the grain and chaff as they were threshed from the straw. The grain was separated from the chaff by throwing both up into the air, and as the grain fell to the ground the chaff was blown away from the wheat by the wind. Afterward, the grain was trodden out by horses, either upon the floor in the barn or upon the ground in the open air, and the grain and chaff were then separated by the use of the wheat or wind-mill, then called a wheat fan. While the steam or horse power threshers now in use will thresh as much grain in a day as could formerly have been trodden out by four or six horses in a month, the process is not especially economical, and it is very difficult to get pure, clean seed wheat from the thresher because of the rye, cheat and cockle that collect in and are carried by the thresher. The chief products of this county have been corn, wheat, oats, hay, rye and tobacco. Very little barley or hemp has been raised in the county. The soil of Nicholas is well adapted to blue grass, and also to timothy and (red) clover, all of which are raised from seed that is sown. White clover seems to be indigenous to the soil, and is regarded by farmers as excellent for grazing, especially for hogs. Forty years ago it was the custom of farmers to turn their hogs upon (red) clover by the 10th of May, at which time the clover was in full bloom. Of late years, it is rarely in bloom before the 20th of May. The breeding of horses has been extensively followed in this county, but has never been very profitable to the farmer. Mules have been raised to a considerable extent, and fattened and driven to the Southern market principally, and have been a source of considerable income to the county; but, as a general rule, among those who handled mules, the greatest profits were made by the farmer who raised and sold them at weaning time. A majority of the mule traders, that is, those who bought them when fatted and drove them to and sold them in the Southern markets, have failed in business sooner or later. The raising of cattle has been, and is yet, a favorite industry with the farmers of Nicholas, and those who have intelligently devoted their energies to that business have uniformly prospered.

"The existence of slavery in the county did not, so far as can be ascertained, have any decided or even perceptible influence upon the agriculture of the county. At the beginning of the late civil war, the number of slaves in the county was about 2,250, and were owned principally by those living in the western and southern part of the county.

"According to the Auditor's report, the number of acres of land in this county in 1850 was 141,000 acres. In 1877, the county of Robertson was formed in part out of territory belonging to Nicholas County. About 25,000 acres were taken from Nicholas and included in Robertson. The part thus taken was not an average in value with the remainder of the land in this county.

"In 1880, the number of acres was 116,864, valued at $1,893,270, or $16.20 per acre. The increase in the value of real estate during the decades above named has not been as large as could be desired, nor can even that increase be attributed solely to the improvement in the soil as a result of judicious farming. There must be taken into account the general growth and development of the country, the local improvements, such as turnpikes, the railroad, and increased cost of buildings erected, especially in the county seat and in the other towns within the county.

"Hemp has not been cultivated except to a very limited extent. Forty to fifty years ago, Col. John S. Morgan, then a leading citizen of the county, raised hemp for several years on his farm near Carlisle. Also, Nimrod Wood, one of the principal farmers in the western part of the county, cultivated hemp for many years prior to the late civil war, and to some extent during and for a few years succeeding the close of the war. The difficulty of commanding the kind of labor necessary to handle and prepare hemp for market has been the obstacle in the way of raising it more extensively. A considerable area of land in the county was adapted to the growth of hemp. Upon soil that is adapted to the growth of hemp, several crops of hemp may be raised in succession without exhausting the soil. The last crop of hemp raised in the county was raised in 1868, and amounted to 15,000 pounds. The crop in 1867 amounted to 25,000 pounds.

"Tobacco, that is now becoming one of the chief products of the county, was cultivated on a very limited scale in the county for about thirty years before the late war. Its growth was confined to the northern part of the county, and chiefly to that part of the county that was included in Robertson County at its formation. The farmers in the more fertile portions in the county did not cultivate it, because it was regarded as very exhausting upon the soil and also for the reason that its culture necessitated the expense of erecting large barns in which to house it while preparing it for market. Prior to the war, the price of it did not at any time exceed $10 to $12 per hundred pounds, and generally ranged from $6 to $8 per hundred for the quality raised in this county, while eight to ten hundred pounds to the acre was an average crop. The high prices that have been realized during and since the war have greatly stimulated its production. The quality has been much improved and the average yield per acre has been increased thirty per cent. Many farmers now raise 1,200 to 1,500 pounds per acre, and some even exceed the latter figures, and obtain prices ranging from $12 to $20 per hundred pounds, according to the quality of the tobacco when prepared for market. The work of raising it is not very laborious, but requires skill and unremitting care and watchfulness in handling it from the time the plants are set out until the finishing touch is given to it preparatory to starting it to market. Experience has demonstrated that the deteriorating effects upon ground produced by growing tobacco upon it may be not only entirely counteracted but improved by sowing rye upon the ground as soon as the tobacco is cut. When the rye is sown early, so as to be forward in growth, it prevents the land from washing, furnishes excellent grazing for stock, and when turned under in the spring, is one of the very best of fertilizers. During the year 1881, there were shipped 488 carloads of stock from Carlisle, of which number 240 were cattle, 126 hogs, 108 sheep, 6 horses, and 8 mules. Not all of the above stock was raised in this county, but it is estimated that that which was brought from other counties for shipment from this point did not excel that which was driven from the western portion of the county for shipment from Cynthiana. Seven hundred and fifty hogsheads of tobacco were shipped from Carlisle, also eighty carloads of wheat, in 1881.—*Perrin.*

CHAPTER IV.

THE FINE STOCK INTERESTS OF NICHOLAS COUNTY—CATTLE IMPROVEMENTS—IMPORTATION OF SHORT HORNS—SOME OF THE FINE HERDS AND BREEDERS—MERINO SHEEP—OTHER IMPROVED BREEDS—THE IMPROVEMENT IN HORSES—HOGS, ETC.

THE stock-rearing interests of this county are very meagre, compared with the leading interest in some other counties which make up the famous stock-producing region of Kentucky. With a mild atmosphere, it is the most favorable for the production of blue grass and stock. The southern portion of the county is of a lower degree of productiveness, and the northern portion extremely rough, rocky, and not adapted to the production of cereals, grasses or stock. The following article on the improvement of stock was written for this chapter by Col. Parks, of this county, and is as accurate as can now be ascertained. "The first attempt at breeding in the county was due to the enterprise of Mr. Charles Neal, who in the fall of 1847, at a sale made in Paris, Kentucky, by John A. Gano, purchased the cow Cambria, got by 686 Bertram 2d (3144), bred by Col. J. H. Powell. This cow afterward became famous as the 1st dam of all the Jenny Lind family, the posterity of which are found in many of the most popular herds of this and other States. This cow, Cambria, the purchase of Mr. Neal, having been bred by Mr. Gano (see A. H. B., Vol. 3, p. 458), calved upon May 1, 1848, producing Jenny Lind 1st, a roan, got by Locum (11698); 1, dam, Cambria, by Bertram 2d (3144); 2, dam, Virginia 2d, by Bertram (1716); 3, dam, Lucilla by Memnon (1223); 4, dam, Virginia, by General (272); 5, dam, Rosemary by Flash (26?); 6, dam, Red Rose, by Petrarch (433); 7, dam, by Alexander (20); 8, dam, by Traveler (665); 9, dam. by son of Bolingbroke (86). After this issue, the cow Cambria was again bred, this time by Mr. Neal, to a well-bred bull owned by himself, but without a pedigree. After this breeding the cow proved barren, was fattened and beefed; the excellence, however, of the produce of this valuable cow has been manifest in the top herds of Nicholas, and has been sought after by various prominent breeders of this and other States. Mr. Neal not being aware of the value of the animal of which he was the possessor, sold Jenny Lind the 1st, when but a calf, to Mr. J. R. Campbell, deceased, at the top of whose herd she subsequently stood. She was bred to Tombigbee 2298, and produced a roan, calved March 15, 1852, Jenny Lind the 2d (see A. H. B., Vol. 3, p. 458). This cow was sold at the sale of J. R. Campbell, then deceased, September 8, 1857, to Col. T. S. Parks, for $260, at the top of whose herd she stood, and whose produce were numerous and valuable, in various herds of this and adjacent counties.

Jenny Lind the 3d, a light roan, calved August 29th, 1854 (see A. H. B., Vol. 3d, page 458); got by Imp. Javelin (11610); 1 dam, Jenny Lind 1st, by Locum (11698). This excellent animal was sold at the J. R. Campbell sale on the 8th of September, 1857, to Letton and Godman, of Bourbon County, for the sum of $425. Jenny Lind the 4th, red and white, calved December 20, 1854, (see A. H. B., Vol. 3, page 458); got by Imp. Earl of Seaham, 1499; 1, dam, Jenny Lind 2d, by Tombigbee, 2298; 2 dam, Jenny Lind 1st, by Locum (11698); she was sold to John A. Rice, of Bourbon County, for $176, at the J. R. Campbell sale; from her produce, there were also many excellent animals; Jenny Lind the 5th, red and white, calved November, 1855 (see A. H. B., Vol. 3, page 458); got by Imp. Deceiver, 409; 1, dam, Jenny Lind 2d, by Tombigbee, 2298; 2, dam, Jenny Lind 1st, by Locum (11698); this excellent animal was sold at the above-mentioned sale, when twenty-two months old, for $300, to Mr. Robert Chandler, of Mason County, Kentucky. The produce of this valuable heifer were of importance in the stock-raising intersts of Mason County. Jenny Lind the 6th, also a red and white, calved September, 26, 1855; got by Cripple, a bull bred by Isaac Vanmeter, deceased, of Clark County, Kentucky; got by Wellington, 2366; dam Amelia, by Prince Albert 857, 1st dam of Jenny Lind the 6th, was Jenny Lind the 1st, by Locum (11698); this heifer was sold at the sale of Mr. Campbell before she was two years old, to Col. Robert Simms, of Nicholas County, for $151; she was considered one of the finest of the produce of old Jenny Lind, and from her sprang many of the finest animals of this and other counties, and now make up the principal crosses and some of the most valuable animals of the popular herd of James Hall, of Bourbon County; Jenny

Lind 7th and 8th, twins, were calved July 14, 1857; got by Wiley 3d, 2386; 1 dam, Jenny Lind 1st, by Locum (11698); these fine calves were also sold at the J. R. Campbell sale, before they were two months old, to Harvey W. Rice, of Bourbon County, for $230; these he bred, and produced many fine animals, thus adding laurels to the already noted and famous Jenny Lind family of Short-horns. Fashion, another valuable cow, sold at this sale, a roan, calved April 1st, 1852, bred by Isaac Vanmeter, deceased (see A. H. B., Vol. 3d, page 406), got by Renick, 903; 1, dam, Fancy, by Prince Albert 2d, 857; 2, dam, Hannah Moore, by Goldfinder (2066); 3, dam, Young Mary, by Jupiter, etc. (2170); she was bought by Mr. Campbell, and at his sale purchased by Dr. J. Taylor, of Clark County, Ky., for $321, and was considered a noteworthy cow in the breeding of the latter county. Many other valuable cows of the best and most popular breeding were sold at the above-mentioned sale, going to different prominent herds in the region. Many valuable bulls were also sold upon that occasion, such as: Percy, 2016 (3d Vol., A. H. B.), red and white, calved July 7, 1854, bred by R. A. Alexander, got by Orontes 2d, 1966; 1, dam, Phyllis, by Samson (a well bred Kentucky bull, L. F. A.); 2, dam, Juliana, by Tariff, 1023; 3, dam, Lucinda, by Contention (3479), bred by Gen. James Dudley, sold to B. W. Mathers & Co., of Nicholas County, for $520.

Another valuable bull owned by this gentleman was Wiley 3d, 2386 (A. H. B.); was calved September 10, 1855, bred by R. A. Alexander, got by Imp. Sirius (13737); 1, dam, Imp. Alice Wiley, by Rumor (7456); 2, dam, Miss Hudson, by Hermes (8145); 3, dam, Mayoress, by Carcase (3281); 4, dam, Matson, by Tyro (2781); 5, dam, Miss Mason, by Falstaff (1993); 6, dam, by Dr. Syntax (220); 7, dam, by Charles (127); 8, dam, by Henry (301); 9, dam, Lydia, by Favourite (252); 10, dam, Nell, by the White Bull (421); 11, dam, Fortune, by Bolingbroke (86); 12, dam, by Foljambe (263); 13, dam, by Hubback, bred by Mr. Maynard, (319). This popular bull was sold by Mr. Campbell to Rice & Co., of Nicholas County, and was subsequently purchased by Dr. J. Taylor, of Clark County, placed at the top of his herd, and was the producer of many fine animals in various herds of the State. Numerous other valuable bulls, which have been at the top of some of the good herds of the region were sold at that sale. Among them were such as Ashland, 1212, (3d Vol. A. H. B.); Yorkshire, Sinbad, Baron Trenk, Bolivar, Sancho Panza, Duke of Nicholas, Jupiter, Richard III, Bedford, Mike Fink, and Eminence. Mr. Campbell produced many fine animals during his short career as a breeder, and his sale, although made after his death, is said to have been one of the best conducted and most important of that day. He was a breeder of many fine qualities, and his early death after engaging in that interest was a loss heavily felt, but his name will be long remembered in connection with the Short-horn interests of Nicholas County."

Sheep raising has been greatly increased since the late war. "The most improved varieties," says Mr. Kennedy, "are largely sought after and are bred and reared in large numbers, yet the supply is not equal to the demand. The breed of sheep originally in the county, did not differ greatly in quality from what is now known as mountain sheep. About the year 1837, Merino sheep were introduced into the county by Henry Clay, presenting two sheep to Ex-Governor Metcalfe. Afterwards the Southdown and Cotswold were brought in, and since the late war a few Leicester sheep have been imported into the county. During the late twenty years farmers who have raised lambs by crossing mountain sheep with the Southdown or Cotswold have realized handsome profits. The lambs and the wool from the the sheep usually bring about double the sum which the sheep cost."

In an article on the agriculture of the county, Mr. Thomas Kennedy says of hogs: "There has been a marked improvement in the quality of hogs during the last fifty years. The efforts of those who have engaged in raising hogs in order to improve the breed have been so far successful as to substitute for the long-snouted, big-boned, flat-sided hog, that could scarcely be fattened under two years old, and that formerly roamed at large during the winter through the forest, feeding on mast, and during the summer and fall through the fields, feeding at pleasure on the grain, a hog of less bone, more compactly built, which fattens at any age, requires less feed, and whose fattening qualities enable it when matured to attain to a weight at least fifty per cent. greater than did the hog of fifty years ago."

There has probably been less improvement in farm horses than any other species of stock bred in this county. The blooded horses kept here are either racers or trotters, and their cross upon the common "plugs" produces a race that is too light-boned for steady farm work or heavy draft purposes, and yet lacking for speed necessary to be racers or trotters. They are neither well adapted to the plow nor to the dray, nor to the track. Some of them make what is technically called a good "roadster," and are in good demand for

J. S. Parks

that purpose, at prices that are remunerative to the farmer. From the foregoing facts and statistics it will be seen that Nicholas is not quite so famous for her fine stock as some of her neighboring counties. There is, however, a good deal of valuable stock raised in the county each year.—*Perrin.*

CHAPTER V.

CARLISLE PRECINCT—ITS GENERAL DESCRIPTION AND TOPOGRAPHY—EARLY SETTLEMELT—PIONEER LIFE —MANUFACTURING INDUSTRIES AND ENTERPRISES—THE OLD BUFFALO TRACE— ROADS, ETC.—SCHOOLS AND TEACHERS—CHURCHES, ETC., ETC.

"The wind is shaking the old dried leaves
That will not quit their hold."

MANY years have passed since the first white man came to what is now Carlisle Precinct. Its forests, where erst the savage trapped the wolf and hunted the deer, are now fertile fields, dotted here and there with lordly mansions, while the Indian yell has died away forever on this side of the great Father of Waters. The young men have grown old, and the old men are in their graves, who first saw it in its pristine beauty, and joined hands to reduce it from a waste, howling wilderness to its present highly cultivated state.

This precinct, which is election precinct No. 4, is situated almost in the center of the county, and is bounded on the north by Headquarters Precinct, on the east and south by Union and Upper Blue Licks Precincts, and on the West by Ellisville Precinct. The surface is rolling, and even broken in places, rising into bluffs along the water courses. The soil is a strong limestone, red loam, rich and very productive in the southern and western part; the remaining portions are rough, poor and rocky. The best soil produces blue ash, the finest of poplar and black walnut, sugar tree, etc., etc. From the latter, sugar is extensively manufactured. The thin lands produce beech, the different kinds of oak, hackberry, hickory, and many other varieties, common to this section. A heavy growth of cane covered the land originally, but has all long since disappeared. It is drained by the Licking and its tributaries, several of which flow through the precinct, thoroughly draining the country and furnishing an abundance of water for stock and farm purposes.

Settlements were not made in Carlisle Precinct as early as in some other portions of the county. The early settlers are all long since gone, and 'Squire Stephenson and 'Squire Powell are about all there are left of the second generation. The father of 'Squire Stephenson, James Stephenson, came from Westmoreland County, Pennsylvania, to Paris, Kentucky, in 1788, where he remained a short time, and then came to what is now Carlisle Precinct, and settled on the farm owned at present by Henry Parker, four miles from Carlisle, between the two branches of Somerset Creek. He had served three years in the Revolutionary war, and soon after its close he followed the tide of immigration to the Western country. He broke the first land ever cultivated on the waters of Somerset Creek. Here he cleared five acres of ground, and while thus engaged, he lived in camp. His wife was El'zabeth Caldwell, born at Carlisle, Pennsylvania, in 1761, and died in 1848; he was born in 1749 and died in 1810. At the time of his settlement here, his only neighbors were John Blair, on Taylor's Creek, at the mouth of the Concord Spring branch, and a Mr. Bushfield, who died on the farm now owned by Benjamin Gore.

Other early settlers, and neighbors of Mr. Stephenson are all dead and gone, and their names mostly forgotten. The names of many of them are given in connection with the city of Carlisle, where centers the larger portion of the history of the precint. One who might be mentioned however, was James Parks, Sr., from Huntingdon, Pa. and who settled a little north of Carlisle; on land now owned by Rev. John Neal. He had an early mill on Cassidy Creek, which is more particularly mentioned in another chapter.

The young men and women of the present time have no conception of the mode of life among the pioneers of this country, seventy-five or eighty years ago. Indeed one can hardly conceive how such changes could have taken place in so short a period of time. In nothing are the habits and manners of the people in any respect similar to those of a half, three-fourths, or a century ago. The clothing, the dwellings, the diet, social customs—in fact, everything has undergone a total revolution. The camp in the woods, the cabin daubed with mud, the old wooden mold-board plow, and other pioneer relics of the past have given place to the wonderful improvements of the nineteenth century.

Bread, "the staff of life," is an article sometimes difficult to obtain in a new country. When we look around us, at the fine flouring-mills of the present day, it is not easy to realize, that years ago a man sometimes, in this section, had to go a long distance to mill. Mills, however, were built as early as surrounding circumstances would permit. The first water-mill in the precinct is supposed to have been built near where the depot in Carlisle now stands. It was built about 1833–5, by Samuel Kincart. He had a horse-mill previous to this, near the same spot. About 1810, John Hamilton built a mill a little southwest of Carlisle. It was also a horse mill and did an extensive business on account of Mr. Hamilton's reputation as miller. Nathaniel P. Robinson built a cotton factory on the Maysville Pike, a short distance from Carlisle, about 1834, which finally became Oakland Mills, and which was a rather large concern. A distillery, one among the first in this precinct, was built by John Miller, one mile east of Carlisle. Since then several others have been built about and around the town of Carlisle. The early manufacturing interests of the precinct outside of Carlisle amounted to very little. A tannery, currying and saddlery establishment, a few mills, etc.; the saddlery was some two miles north of Carlisle. It was the first in the county, and was carried on by different parties.

The first road through the precinct was the old buffalo trace. It was made by the buffalo in passing from the Lower Blue Licks to the Cane Ridge country in Bourbon County, and was about one hundred feet wide and some two or three feet deep. The Maysville Turnpike followed this trail much of the way through the County, and was the first pike not only in this precinct but in the State. Another trace from the Upper Blue Licks crossed Cassidy Creek at the village of Buzzard Roost, passed through Moorefield, down the forks of Somerset Creek, through the old Adam Fergus farm, along McBride Creek, across Hinkston into Bourbon County. The history of the Maysville Pike is given elsewhere. Several other pikes center in Carlisle and extend out through the precinct, among which are the Carlisle, Sharpsburg and Mt. Sterling Pike; Forest Retreat Pike; Carlisle & Union Pike; Rogers' Mill Pike, Parks' Ferry Pike, etc., etc.; the latter not fully completed.

The early schools of Carlisle were of rather ordinary degree. They have somewhat improved since then, but there is room for still greater improvement. The first school in the precinct, and said to be the first in the county, was taught upon the land now owned by Mrs. Henry Potts, about 1800. It was taught by Thomas Shannon, in a little log building with a puncheon floor. The next school was taught at old Concord Church, a short time later. The school history of the precinct, however, is more closely connected with the town of Carlisle, where it receives further mention.

The first church organized in what is now Nicholas County was in the present precinct of Carlisle—old Concord Church. It stood about two and a half miles southeast of where the town of Carlisle is located, and was organized in or about the year 1795. Rev. B. W. Stone was one of the first if not its first minister. He became pastor of it and old Cane Ridge in Bourbon County in 1798. The first church edifice was built of logs, in which the congregation worshiped until the present building, which is a large, commodious frame, was erected in 1860, at a cost of $2,000. This church is more particularly noticed in another chapter. Some of the early members of this church were: Samuel M. Waugh, James Thompson and Thomas Donnell. Rev. John Lyle was the next pastor after Rev. Stone, and administered to the congregation for several years.

The Poor House, or County Poor Farm, is located in this precinct. This institution, however, is noticed more at length in connection with the county buildings. The Maysville division of the Kentucky Central Railroad runs through Carlisle Precinct, and has been of benefit to the people in more ways than one. It has increased the value of their lands, brought the best markets to their doors, and, while but a poor excuse as a railroad, it is much better than no railroad. Its history is given in the county at large, and in the chapters devoted to the city of Carlisle. Most of the history of the precinct centers in Carlisle, as we have said, and will be found in that connection.—*Perrin.*

CHAPTER VI.

CITY OF CARLISLE—LAYING OUT THE TOWN—FIRST SALE OF LOTS—PUBLIC BUILDINGS, HOTEL, ETC.—BUSINESS ENTERPRISES AND MANUFACTORIES—NAMES OF EARLY SETTLERS AND LOT OWNERS—FIRST COUNTY OFFICERS, ETC.

"Sweet Auburn! loveliest village of the plain."

—*Goldsmith.*

LET us go back to the year 1810. At that time the county seat of Nicholas was at Ellisville; the courts having been held first at Bedinger's Mill, then at the Blue Licks; but no permanent county seat had been made until Ellisville was named as the fortunate locality. The great public road leading from the upper Blue Licks to Millersburg, bisecting the county into two nearly equal parts, connecting the hill country of the East with the blue grass plains of the West, afforded, of course, the most eligible sites for farmers, mechanics, hotel-keepers or others who desired to see the world and turn to the best advantage the labor of their hands.

At a point along this road about twelve miles from Upper Blue Licks and eight miles from Millersburg, lived an honest farmer named Samuel Kincart. This gentleman owned a tract of land skirting along Brushy Fork containing somewhere near 200 acres. In 1810 he built a good, substantial brick house on the north side of the road, and prepared to otherwise improve and adorn his homestead. He had already a fine orchard adjoining the house on the east. But in 1811 he died, and was buried in the northeast corner of the orchard, and his son John succeeded to the farm.

About this time there was manifested by the good people of Nicholas a growing dissatisfaction at the location of the county seat; especially the thrifty farmers of Hinkston and Somerset creeks, who declared that there was neither good sense nor equity in locating the county seat so far from the center of the county, and especially right in among the persimmon and blackhaw bushes—the stealthy retreat of the festive raccoon, the cunning fox and grinning opossum, to say nothing of the occasional visits of the prowling wolf or the inquisitive bear.

These mutterings of discontent grew louder and louder as the years rolled on, until in 1814–15 they reached the ears of the Kentucky Legislature, and that body passed a bill authorizing the removal to a more central point, and appointed commissioners to examine, locate and report the result of their labors when completed.

The commissioners inspected various sites, but soon narrowed down the question between two of the most eligible ones. One of these was a point on the old main dirt road from Maysville to Lexington, afterward known as Forest Retreat; the other was the Kincart farm. In the meantime all Ellisville was in an uproar, and threatening the direst vengeance against all concerned in the removal scheme. But the commissioners were inexorable and the location was duly made at Kincart farm. The legislature confirmed the decree, and a charter for the new site was granted under the name of "Carlisle" —probably in honor of Carlisle, Penn. It is not known positively why the commissioners selected that name, but supposed to be as above, because some of the early settlers were from near that city in Pennsylvania.

On June 15, 1816, fifty acres of the Kincart farm having already been laid off into streets, lanes and alleys, the new town was thrown open for the first regular auction sale of town lots. The following are the names of the original streets—beginning east and running west: Walnut, Second, Main Cross, Elm and Sycamore; beginning north and extending southward: North, Mulberry, Main, Front, South and Water. The lots were all laid off fronting these streets, and averaged about 65x130 feet. The streets were made sixty feet wide, and all alleys or lanes fifteen feet wide. The lots were numbered consecutively, from 1 to 139.

As above stated, these 139 lots were thrown open to public auction on June 15, 1816; but before we go on with our sale, let us go back a few days and note some of the events which were occurring in anticipation of that great event.

On June 5, 1816, the following proceedings of the town council appear recorded in the archives of the town: "At the house of John Kincart, in the town aforesaid, the place fixed by the commissioners as the permanent seat of justice of Nicholas County, a majority of the trustees of said town met according to appointment. Present, James Byres, James Thomson, Andrew S. Hughes and Lewis H. Arnold.

"1st. *Resolved*, that Elijah Mitchell be appointed Clerk of this Board.

"2nd. *Resolved*, that David Byres be appointed President of this Board.

"3rd. *Resolved*, that David Byres be appointed Treasurer of this Board.

"4th. *Resolved*, that James Thomson be appointed Surveyor, for the purpose of laying off the fifty acres of land mentioned in the commissioners' report, appointed to fix the seat of justice for the county aforesaid, and that he return one plat and survey to this Board.

"5th. *Resolved*, that the Clerk of this Board be directed to give notice (by advertisement) to the several subscribers who have subscribed money to aid in the erection of the public buildings in the town of Carlisle, to make payment against the third Monday in June inst., to David Byres."

On the 14th day of June following, a full meeting took place which included Mr. James Ardery in addition to the four councilmen already named. At this meeting plat and report were filed by Surveyor Thomson, which were approved by the Board. At this meeting John Kincart filed a deed for the property to the trustees and selected the odd numbers of the lots upon the plat of the town as a consideration for the purchase of the land. At this meeting also Michael Letton was appointed the town crier for the sale of the lots and to receive two dollars per day as a compensation for the same. The morning of the memorable 15th of June dawned bright and clear, and buyers from all parts of the surrounding country flocked in to attend the sale.

But just here a hitch took place which threatened to knock the future metropolis into smithereens. Thomas Jones, a doughty farmer living near by, a man of great ponderosity, being about the size of Sir John Falstaff, appeared upon the scene and laid claim to the whole fifty acres, and hundreds of acres more of the contiguous territory, from Dan even unto Beersheba. In fact, suit was then pending in the Federal Court at Frankfort, in favor of said Falstaff, or Jones, against the said lands, and so in the name of law, justice, honor and fifty more expletives, seasoned with more fearful maledictions than were ever conceived or uttered by Ancient Pistol, Sir John, or Thomas, forbade the sale! Here was a go, and for a time it seemed as if they were not going to baptize, rantize, circumcise, or otherwise take the new born into the family of county seats at all. Finally a compromise was effected; Kincart, the owner *de facto*, proposed to Sir John, the owner *de jure*, to give him one-half the proceeds of sale of Kincart's lots. This was agreed to, and the sale went on. The public road was taken for Front street, and the town laid off by Kincart's house, though not precisely due east and west. The orchard became the public square, and Kincart's property, lot No. 1. This lot, with the dwelling, was knocked off to Kincart for $2,000. One hundred and thirty-eight lots more were successively sold at prices ranging from fifteen to two hundred and forty dollars. And now began the erection of the public buildings.

The old log court house at Ellisville, was removed here and erected temporarily on the east side of the public square, on lot No. 37, Second street. This was, however, soon succeeded by a new and, for those days, elegant court house built of brick in the center of the public square, and erected under the supervision of Gen. Thomas Metcalfe, who then lived in the suburb s of the town, in the extreme northwest quarter. The first jail was also a log structure, and was removed from Ellisville at the same time as the old court house. But a new brick jail was soon after erected and made historic as being, in after years, the first schoolhouse opened in Carlisle for the colored children after the Emancipation Proclamation of President Lincoln. The old weather-beaten house still stands at this writing (January, 1882). It was (the jail) never remarkable in its day for anything save its admirable adaptedness to aid prisoners to escape. As the jailer's house was nearly a square distant, there were but two *supposed* ways of holding a prisoner. One was to put him in the dungeon heavily ironed, and the other to hire a guard to stand over him with an old, flint lock musket. It not unfrequently haphened, however, that the prisoner went off in the dead of night like Samson with the dungeon doors upon his back or out of the window before the old musket could be got to "go off."

From the very first sale of lots population began to pour in from all quarters, as probably it most always will be the case in any new enterprise. Hotels, stores, offices and dwellings were rapidly and speedily erected, and the town began at once to take rank among the business points of the State. The old brick farm house became a hotel, and was ably kept by Peyton Shumate, Esq., who raised a large family of handsome daughters, several of whom afterward became noted as hotel keepers, especially Mrs. Amanda Tureman, who earned a fine reputation as proprietress of the Goddard House in Maysville, and Mrs. James Dudley, of the Dudley House in

Flemingsburg. "The Old Black Tavern" so called from the logs being painted black, was removed from Ellisville in 1816 and placed upon lot No. 45, situated on the east end of Main street. The hotel was kept by James Ellis, son of James Ellis, Sr., after whom the town of Ellisville had been named. The third hotel of the town was the large frame building upon the corner of Front and Second streets, and now (1882) known as the Saint Cloud Hotel. This house was built by Alexander Blair, Sr., in 1816. It was first leased to Bennett H. Evans, who successfully managed it for several years. The following anecdote of Mr. Evans is related by himself: He was standing in the door of his hotel one day when two countrymen, evidently strangers, rode along the street in front of him. One of them happened to cast his eye upon Evans' sign, bearing in modest letters his name, B. H. Evans. The countryman read it "Be Heavens," and turning to his fellow traveler remarked that it was the last place in the world he would have looked for that name. In 1817 John and Jesse Hughes, twin brothers, kept a hotel in the frame house situated on Front street, lot 33, and the same as now owned by A. McDaniel, Jr., so that it will be seen that as early as 1816–7 we had no less than four hotels.

The first dry goods store kept in Carlisle was by John G. Parks, Esq. He removed the stock of goods owned by him at Parks Ferry here in 1816, and opened out in the Kincart residence. But soon after completing a stone building on Front street, in front of the court house door, he moved into that and continued until his appointment as County Clerk in 1829. Prior to 1816, Mr. Samuel M. Waugh kept a dry goods store in the frame house situated upon the public road about one mile and a half east of town, upon the farm now owned by Silas W. Campbell. In 1817, Mr. Waugh built a small frame building adjoining 'Squire Parks' stone house just referred to, and moved his stock into it. Here he continued to carry on business and to perform the duties of Justice of the Peace for several years. Kincart & Foster, a firm composed of James Kincart (brother of John) and David Foster, opened a dry goods store in 1816, in a frame house upon the corner of Front and Elm streets. These three formed the list of pioneers in the dry goods trade.

Soon after the town was laid off, a nail factory on a small scale was opened by a German citizen, named Peter Schwarzwelder, in a one-story frame which stood upon the corner of Main Cross and Front streets. The first mill ever established in Carlisle was by James Dudley, and was located upon lot 84. The mill was a tramp-wheel power, and ground corn only. Prior to this, before the town was laid out, a water mill with an overshot wheel was erected upon Brushy Fork by Samuel Kincart. He also owned a draft horse mill, and both mills were located south of Water street.

The first woolen mill was owned by Lloyd Rollins, and built on the rear of lot No. 20, the same lot upon which 'Squire Parks built the stone house previously referred to. A carding factory and fulling-mill was afterward built by Samuel Hall, at the east end of North street, on lot No. 78. The third woolen factory was built and owned by James Dudley upon Main Cross street, on lot No. 90. This factory continued under successive ownerships for nearly fifty years, and was finally sold out and torn down by Mr. B. F. Adair, about 1870.

The first tan-yard was owned by Col. Henley Roberts. It was sunk in 1816 upon lots 114 and 115, and continued to turn out a goodly quantity of leather for more than thirty years, until the death of Mr. Asbury Teal, the last owner, about 1850. The second tan-yard was opened by Nathaniel P. Robinson, a former dry goods merchant, of Carlisle, on the east end of Front street, just beyond the town limits, being the same as occupied now (1882) by Archdeacon Bros. as a carriage shop. The third and last tan-yard was constructed by George Robinson, brother of N. P., upon lot No. 31. To show the importance of this branch of business in those days, we will state that all three of these tan-yards were in operation at the same time. At the present day there is scarcely a vestige of either left.

The making of saddles, bridles and harness has always been a considerable item in the business of Carlisle. The first saddle ever made in the place was made by Thomas M. Stephenson, who was then an apprentice of Robert Dykes. Mr. Dykes came to Carlisle in 1816, and carried on the saddlery trade on lot No. 4 on Main-cross street. In 1818, Mr. Stephenson opened a new shop one door below Dykes, both houses being erected upon the same lot. Other shops were opened successively by William and Lawson Smith, on lot No. 31; by George Robinson, Andrew Couchman and others.

The tailoring business was introduced by Isaac Messick. John Camplin also worked at the trade a short time and then went to Sharpsburg. The following persons worked at the business in Carlisle prior to 1820, to-wit: Benjamin Antrobus, Col. George R. Foster, Azariah Conyers and Greenberry Ross. The first billiard table set up in the town was in 1816, by Robert Batson, who, however, remained but a short time and then removed to Millersburg.

The first hatter of the new county seat was Jesse Boulden, who in 1816 had his shop and dwelling on lot No. 62 on Main street, the same as now owned by Mr. F. E. Congleton. In 1819, John Dougherty, the jolliest Irishman who ever lived, came here from Flemingsburg, accompanied by his fast friend, John Hadden. The two friends bought out Boulden, and the latter removed to Millersburg, where he carried on the business for a long period of time. Dougherty and Hadden carried on the hatter's trade quite extensively; their shop was located upon the alley, on the rear of lot No. 19.

Shoes were first made in the new town by Gavin Mathers. His shop and dwelling were located on lot 52, the same where the tall and tapering spire of the Presbyterian Church now stands. John Foland worked as a journeyman in the shop, afterward as partner, and finally succeeded to the business after the removal of Mr. Mathers to the country, about 1830.

The Carlisle bank was established in 1817, and blew up in 1819—a brief and disastrous career, fully exemplifying the evils of an unredeemable paper currency. Dr. John R. Ward was president, Moses Hopkins, cashier, and William Hughes, Samuel M. Waugh and Daniel Bedinger, directors.

A very important branch of business in those days was that of cabinet-maker. All the bedsteads, bureaus, corner cupboards, candle stands, breakfast, dining and kitchen tables, had to be made at home, from lumber sawed in our midst. In 1817, Richard D. Henry, a modest, unassuming young man, came to Carlisle to settle for life. He was a cabinet-maker by trade, and a first class workman at that. He had a turning lathe attached, and turned out rapidly bed posts, chair and table legs, and other articles used in the trade. He was probably the first one who carried on the trade in Carlisle, and for a long time did quite a good business.

During the period from 1816 to 1820, John Davidson settled here, and opened a cabinet shop, doing considerable business for more than twenty years. In 1819, John Rogers, another young cabinet-maker moved in among us to settle for life. He also had a turning lathe; but he did not pursue that calling long, as it was not long before he became a teacher in our schools, and subsequently a minister of the gospel.

Among the legal profession, our first citizens were, R. W. Webber (familiarly called "Dick"), Angus C. McCoy, Thomas P. Tall, Robert C. Hall, Jonathan M. Tanner, and General A. S. Hughes.

Dr. John R. Ward, president of the Carlisle bank, was among the earliest physicians of the new town. As the names of all the first citizens engaged in business from 1816 until 1820, may be of interest to future generations, we will here append them, and close this chapter: Hotel Keepers—Peyton Shumate, James Ellis, John Hughes, Jesse Hughes, John Dudley; Cabinet Makers—Jacob Leer, John Davidson, John Rogers, R. D. Henry; Carpenters—John Dalzell, John Henry, James McGann, Joseph D. Butler, William McClanahan, James P. Ashley, John E. Cotton, Richard Doggett, William Secrest, Jesse Burton, John Ross; Wagon Makers—Isaac Peck, John Matchett; Stone Masons—Thomas Metcalf, Joseph Paxton; Confectioner—John Delaney; Butcher—Samuel Moore; Circuit Clerk—L. H. Arnold; County Clerk—Andrew S. Hughes; Farmer—John Kincart; Merchants—John G. Parks, Morris Morris, James Kincart, David Foster, N. P. Robinson, John Campbell; Grocer—William Porter; Shoemakers—John Chipley, Aaron Smedley, John Rodgers, Gavin Mathers, Lloyd Sheckels, John Foland; Saddlers—T. M. Stephenson, Robert Dykes, Richard McGinnis, Joel Howard, John McMakan, Hugh Nesbet; Tailors—Jonathan Camplin, Benjamin Antrobus, George R. Foster, Azariah Conyers, Greenberry Ross; Citizens—John Morris, William Doty, Nathaniel Selby, Richard Payne, Arthur Doggett, William Hall, William Hughes, William Clayton; Lawyers—Angus C. McCoy, Robert C. Hall, R. W. Webber, Thomas P. Tall, J. M. Tanner, Moses Hopkins; Tinner—John Messick; Brick Mason—John Harris; Brick Maker—A. Smedley; Nail Cutter—Peter Schwartzweiler; Minister—Rev. John Rankin; Doctors—John R. Ward, Hood & Foster; Blacksmiths—Jonathan Johnson, John Doty; Tanners—John Mitchell, Redding Roberts, John Boyd, George Robinson; Hatters—Jerry Shannon, Jesse Boulden, John Dougherty, John Hadden; Wool Carders—James Dudley, Loyd Rollins, Samuel Hall; Trader—Moses Selby. Of these, many moved away long years ago, and nearly all have passed away from earth; the old cemetery at Carlisle holds the ashes of a great number.

"Their bodies have crumbled back to dust,
But their souls are with the blest, we trust."

The first court ever convened in Carlisle to consider questions pertaining to the welfare of the county, assembled at the house of John Kincart (the old farm-house first named), on the 16th day of July, 1816. There were present the following Magistrates: Lute Tarver, Thomas Davidson, Samuel M. Waugh, James H. Thompson, Hugh Wiley, Morris Morris, John Throckmorton, Thomas S. Jenkins, John Baker and A. Marshall; Clerk, Andrew S. Hughes. The first session of the Circuit Court was held

September 1, 1816; Judge John Trimble, of Harrison County, presiding; Lewis H. Arnold, clerk. Judge Trimble presided as Judge several years, and afterward practiced law in Nicholas Circuit Court. He was a straightforward, plodding business-like lawyer, a great admirer of the British Code of practice, and always carried a big green bag in his hand, in accordance with the custom of English barristers. The first suit on docket was *Sir Thomas Jones* v. *Samuel Irvin & Co.*, chancery. This, and kindred suits of Jones to recover certain tracts of land under some old land titles, went on for ten years or more, and greatly exasperated the people against him. Jones at that time lived in the house just beyond Dorsiana, and which, for a long period of years, belonged to Col. John S. Morgan and heirs. Sir Thomas kept a number of sheep, and in order to protect himself from the hungry town dogs, invented a trap, the like of which never has been seen before or since. It was made of a stout hickory sapling, one end planted firmly in the ground, the other end bent down and fastened by a trigger to the ground. From the end of the pole was suspended a leather noose, and a piece of raw meat made fast to the trigger; the whole so contrived that, when a prowling cur came along and made a grab for the meat, he sprung the trap; the noose made a grab for the dog, and the pole flying back toward a perpendicular, suspended his dogship by the neck high in the air, greatly to his astonishment and decidedly against his ideas of the fitness of things. It may be added that the more the dog kicked the tighter the noose clasped, until—well, that's the end of our first dog story.

In the period we are now considering, there stood on the ground where the great brick block now stands, occupied by Adair & Brewington, a continuous row of houses, one story in height, as follows: Two frame rooms on the corner, then a brick of one room, and lastly a one-story log kitchen. In the front of this row Peter Schwarzweiler lived, and carried on the business of a nail-cutter. Uncle Peter was a sober, industrious, public-spirited citizen, who always attended to his own business, and allowed everybody to do the same.

About the year 1820, under a contract with the town trustees, he built a spacious market-house on the northeast corner of the public square. When completed, however, the trustees refused to pay in full, in consequence of an alleged failure to comply with the contract. Uncle Peter sued the trustees, and was beaten in the suit, which so enraged him that one morning about daylight he seized an ax, and, proceeded to demolish as much of it as he thought had not been paid for.

The market-house built by Uncle Peter became one of the most popular resorts of our town, especially during our three days August election. Here booths for the sale of all kinds of edibles were set up; drinks, too, were sold, such as cider, ginger pop and blackberry cordial—the latter generally compounded of ten gallons of bust-head whisky to one quart of blackberries and one pound of sugar. Regular dinner was set, and roast beef, pig, mutton, bread, pies, cakes and coffee, were served for twenty-five cents. Music and dancing were also kept up during the day and often far into the night. Jack Briggles was the champion singer and barefoot dancer, while "old Uncle Kit" was the best jig and comic dancer. This was in the days of slavery, and the booths were kept by colored people altogether, it being always understood that the first and last days of the election were holidays. Ah! these were glorious days for our town boys, the memory of which, along with the big ginger cakes and watermelons we used to eat, will last "as long as memory holds her seat."

Uncle Peter never got over his anger against the town about the market-house job, and after he left here, and was gone some time, he came back again with the intention of renewing his suit against the trustees. He got as far as Uncle Billy Mathers (father of Barton W.), where he took sick and died, and was buried in the old cemetery.

The following anecdote, although happening long after Uncle Peter died, will nevertheless show how strong a hold he had in the minds of our citizens. In 1840, during the great contest for the Presidency, Colonel Henry Roberts, a well known farmer then living on Somerset, was making a Democratic speech in the old court house. At that time, Melville Metcalfe (son of the General), whose eccentricities are well known to all—although a Whig in politics, turned a political somersault and landed in the Democratic camp. On the occasion referred to, the court house was crowded to hear the great issues of the day discussed. It was decided Colonel Roberts was to make a speech and Melville was to sit behind him and prompt him in case he went wrong. The Colonel opened out and proceeded vigorously to defend the administration, especially against the attacks made by the Whigs upon Van Buren, on account of the heavy defalcation of one Samuel Swartwout, when the following ludicrous incident occurred.

Colonel R. (continuing): "And not content with these attacks upon Mr. Van Buren, fellow citizens, they (the Whigs) have the audacity to charge upon him the defalcation of this Mr. Swartzweiler"—

METCALFE (from behind, in a low tone, jerking the Colonel's coat-tail): "Swartwout, Colonel."

COLONEL R. (resuming): "As I was saying, they have the impudence to charge upon us the rascally doings of this man, Swartzweiler"—

METCALFE (exitedly): "Swartwout, I say."

COLONEL R. (confused): "As I said before, not content with their other falsehoods, they have the meanness to charge upon the administration the stealings of this man, Swartzweiler"—

METCALFE (angrily): "Swartwout, g—d d—d you, I'll leave the party. You haven't a bit of sense in the whole d—n concern."

The deep well upon the public square, which belongs to the county, from which such a vast quantity of pure limpid water has been obtained, as also an immense cargo of old boot-legs, pots, kettles, buckets, chains, ropes and dippers, as well as a vast army of dead rodents and felines was dug in 1816. Hans Huddleson, father of our present esteemed "Captain" "Colonel" or "Major" Huddleson, and William Bird, a stout double-fisted fellow, aided in the work. One day while down in the well, a heavy stone fell in, striking Bird on the head, well nigh making a dead *duck* of him. But Bird was *game* to the last, and afterwards moving out to Indiana, it is said *feathered* his nest handsomely and became quite wealthy.

At a meeting of the Board of Trustees, held at the court house, September 15, 1818, Dick Webber, a prominent lawyer, was elected clerk of the board, and held the office several years at an annual salary of ten dollars. At the same meeting proposals were advertised for the building of a bridge over the branch, junction of Front and Walnut streets. On the 21st of September following a contract was closed with Jarmon Hukill for the bridge, to be completed in seventy days from the date of contract. It was a wooden bridge, with two stone abutments, six feet high, fifteen feet span, sleepers of white oak, and flooring two inch oak, and cost when completed, $198.50.

In those days Carlisle had it in her power to have secured at trifling cost, property which to-day would give her a glory and renown beyond any town in the State. The hill range skirting along our southern boundary was then a dense forest; trees of every kind and size, from the juicy hawthorn to the giant oak; wild grapevines with their long graceful tendrils, hung like a bridal-veil over the bushy hawthorns, or boldly clambered up the sides of the giant oak, and hung their tempting clusters far beyond the reach of the cunningest fox of them all. Now let us suppose to-day the town owned twenty acres of this hill in its primeval state, with its grand old trees and rustic arbors; its cool sequestered shade from summer's ardent heat; its gorgeous tinted hues for autumn's pensive hours; its solemn gloom and grandeur 'mid winter's stormy reign—what price could be put upon it which our citizens would not promptly reject? Yet it is what we once had, and might have had for aye, for a mere song.

Another grand opportunity thrown away by our village, was the nucleus of what might have been to-day a fine Seminary of learning. One of the first acts of good will upon the part of the county towards the town was the building of a brick seminary, to be forever dedicated to the education of the youth both of the town and county. The building is still standing, being the property of the late Elijah West, Esq. In bygone days two separate schools have been taught in the house at the same time. It was in the old brick Seminary that many of the first youths of Carlisle received the rudiments of an English education. We say rudiments, because in those days reading, writing, grammar and arithmetic constituted the four cardinal accomplishments necessary for any young lady or gentleman to shine in any society; correct spelling was considered of vital importance. Every Friday afternoon was set apart for the spelling-match, and these spelling matches generally brought a crowded house of parents and other deeply interested spectators. Generally the school-master appointed two captains, who in turn chose out the spellers until an equal number were drawn upon, on opposite sides. It was not uncommon for rival schools to challenge each other in this friendly war of words.

In connection with the Seminary we must not omit to mention "The Village Green," two whole squares—from Main street to North street, and from Elm to Sycamore—although the lots had all been sold, were yet for many years left vacant, and these two squares became the village play-ground. It was here during the hours of recess at the Seminary that the youth of both sexes met to play. The most popular game was "prisoners' base;" in this game the girls often proved themselves as fleet of foot as the boys. We may here state that "pinbacks" were then unknown. Three garments at that time constituted the average costume of our school girls, with occasionally the addition of shoes and stockings, and may be a calico apron. We forget, however, that each had a calico sun bonnet, which she generally carried in her hands. "Complexions spoiled?" Lord bless you, no!

it was worth a twenty miles ride to see those rosy-cheeked, bright-eyed girls—" The Hill, The Seminary, The Village Green!"

"These were thy charms, sweet village, sports like these,
With sweet succession, taught e'en to it to please,
These round thy bowers their cheerful influence shed,
These were thy charms! but all these charms are fled."

On the 16th day of April, 1822, an order was issued by the trustees for the first paved sidewalks. How our citizens ever got along in the winter time, and especially how the ladies ever did their shopping, is a mystery beyond any explanation. On the 12th day of May, 1823, William McClanahan returned the first list of taxable property of the town, which we have on record, amounting to $107,215. At the same time it was ordered that a tax of nine cents on the hundred dollars be levied for the benefit of the town. The revenue of the town, for that year, therefore, was about ninety-six dollars and fifty cents. Beg pardon, we forget—the wax figures yielded five dollars more.

Jacob Leer, " Uncle Jake," was the first jailer of the county, and was a cabinet-maker by profession, but devoted his time mainly in the manufacture of wheat fans. He was also a good officer, stern in the discharge of his duty, but kind and attentive to the wants of his prisoners. He was a German by birth ; spoke English fluently, but did his " cussin' " in Dutch. He took the first German newspaper which ever came to Carlisle. Uncle Jake and his frau lived upon lot No. 17, and his shop stood upon the corner of the same, thus being fully one square distant from the jail. He was a good citizen, harmless, peaceable and industrious. Like all good people, however, he had his trials and crosses to bear ; his wife was a shrew, a termagant, as homely as she was cross. Uncle Jake smoked his pipe and bore it all with becoming fortitude. Only sometimes, when the storm was raging loudest, like Rip Van Winkle, he would take his pipe from his mouth, and in a subdued deprecating tone, say " dond schole." After the death of his frau, about 1831, to show his respect for her memory, he with his own hands chiseled the rough stone which was to mark her last resting place. About the year 1840 he opened the first baker shop in the place. The cakes, pies, bread and ginger pop were made for him by Peter Rentz, a German from Cincinnati, whom Uncle Jake imported for that purpose. Uncle Jake died about ten years after his wife and was buried by her side in the old cemetery.

General Andrew S. Hughes was the first County Clerk of the new county seat. He was Clerk at Ellisville, and his residence there was the favorite resort of the elite of society. He came along with the records of his office and served several years. In 1814 he was married to Rhoda Hughes, a sister of General Thomas Metcalfe. In 1821 he was appointed by President Monroe Indian agent for the Northwest, through the influence of his brother-in-law, General Metcalfe, who was then a member of Congress from this district. General Hughes entered at once upon the discharge of his duties, and was stationed at Saint Louis, in the then new state of Missouri, leaving his family still in Carlisle. But within a year he sent for them, and thereafter became a citizen of that great commonwealth. General Hughes was a lawyer by profession, well versed in legal lore as well as the current politics of the day, and a man of considerable ability.

Mrs. Rhoda Hughes, wife of the general, was one of the most accomplished and intelligent ladies who ever lived in Carlisle. Educated a Protestant, soon after her removal to Missouri, to the surprise of her friends, she embraced the Catholic religion, and became a warm supporter of the Roman Church until her death.

Their son, Bela Metcalfe Hughes, is still living in Denver city, Col. Like his father, in many respects (he too has the title of General), is an able and distinguished lawyer, and a man of great force and dignity of character. In 1876, he ran upon the Democratic ticket as a candidate for Governor of the State, but owing to too much money against him, he was defeated. General Hughes is also a devout Catholic.

Lewis H. Arnold, Esq., was clerk of the Circuit Court at Ellisville, and like General Hughes, came along with the records of his office to make this his future home. Mr. Arnold married a sister of Jack Throckmorton, one of the first families of the State. In the minute and careful attention he gave to the duties of his office, his courteous and dignified bearing, the unsullied reputation of his private life, his public spirit and devotion to the cause of morality and religion, Mr. Arnold won the respect and esteem of the whole county. Mr. Arnold was the first contractor upon the Carlisle and Forest Retreat Turnpike road. The first section, passing through Carlisle, included a heavy cut and fill at Menifee's hill, as also and expensive cut clear through the whole length of Front street. Being wholly unacquainted with the nature and expense of such work, there was a considerable loss entailed upon Mr. Arnold; but such was his stern devotion to honor and right that he would not consent to any abatement of the contract, or of the loss by any slighting of the work, or by any sharp practices, such as are too common at the present day. About the year 1839, Mr. Arnold admitted his son, James L. Arnold, into the office as deputy clerk, for which position the son had been for some years qualifying himself; and upon the death of his father, about 1849, James L. succeeded to the office, which position he held until during the war of the Rebellion. Lewis H. Arnold sleeps the sleep of the just in the old cemetery, where so many of our village fathers have been gathered.

At the regular election, in August, 1824, the following board of trustees were elected: James G. Leech, Jacob Leer, John Dougherty, Aaron Smedley and Greenberry Ross. At the first meeting of the board James G. Leech was elected President, and Greenberry Ross Treasurer. At the same meeting the following order was made:

"On motion of Aaron Smedley, seconded by John Dougherty, it is ordered that tickets be procured to the amount of two hundred dollars, with blanks to be filled up by the trustees for change, agreeable to such order as they may hereafter make. And on motion it was further ordered that John Dougherty procure said tickets, to be paid for out of any funds belonging to the trustees."

And just here, we see the wonderful progress being made by this wonderful corporation: such is the expanding nature of her commerce, such the giant strides of her manufactures, that she is compelled to resort to the expansion of the currency. How John Sherman, had he lived in that day, would have held up his hands in holy horror! Tickets, forsooth—a sort of infant greenback; aye, and to the fearful amount of two hundred dollars! Ah, Uncle Jake, how could you have ever so far departed from the sound principles of finance.

November 20, 1824, it was "ordered that Aaron Smedley, Sen., be appointed market master for the present year." At the same time it was also "ordered that there shall be regular market days appointed for the convenience of the citizens of this county, and that those days be every Wednesday and Saturday in each week; and that the time of market in those days shall be from sunrise till 10 o'clock A. M.; and that no article of marketing shall be bought or sold at any place in said town, only at the market house. But this order shall not prohibit any person marketing through town after 10 o'clock on the regular market days."

At a meeting of the board of trustees, held March 28, 1825, it was "ordered, that Jacob Leer be appointed to procure a scraper for the use of said town." It does not appear exactly what the scraper was for, but we have no doubt Uncle Jake would have gladly used it to scrape the backs of Jones, Smith and Brown, the recalcitrant citizens who had defied him in his ordinance against piling wood in the streets. April 19, 1825, the second valuation of town property was returned, and amounted to $120,000. This was again since the first assessment (1823) of about $12,000. A list of those liable to taxation was returned a short time before, and amounted to seventy-one; assuming this to be one-sixth of the whole number, would give a total white population of 426; add to this probably 125 slaves, and the total population of the town in 1825, was about 550.

In June, 1825, the first regular caravan of living animals made its grand entree through the streets of Carlisle. The trustees imposed a tax of two dollars per day on the managers for exhibiting it. It was customary then to travel the elephants by night, as they were regarded as too big a curiosity to be seen without pay. The elephant on this occasion was ushered in after midnight and safely housed in the stable which then stood where the new "Dew Drop" saloon now stands. By daylight next morning, streams of people began pouring in to see the show; and when the grand entree was made with the band of music at the head, the excitement rose to fever heat, and more than a thousand people rushed pell-mell after the caravan, each anxious to secure the first ticket of admission.—*J. A. Chappell.*

CHAPTER VII.

CARLISLE—AMUSEMENTS—ENTERTAINMENTS AND MANUFACTURING INDUSTRIES—ANECDOTE OF COLONEL RUSSELL—THE MAYSVILLE PIKE—THE CHOLERA IN CARLISLE—INTERNAL IMPROVEMENTS—A REBEL RAID—BANKS, NEWSPAPERS, ETC.—ODDS AND ENDS.

THE winter of 1828-29 was one of the most brilliant seasons ever witnessed in our history. There were a large number of fine looking young men and a score or two of the prettiest and liveliest girls ever seen in any town of equal size. We may say that in those days our young men were possessed with a goodly ambition to be somebody and to do something. It was during this winter that our first Thespian Society was organized. The place selected for the rendition of the plays was the suite of rooms on the west side, up-stairs, in the old court house. In those days none of our young ladies had the courage to take part in the performance. Hence, the characters, both male and female, had to be assumed by the young men. The following gentlemen composed the regular or stock company: E. F. Chappell, William Norvell, D. R. Atchison, T. S. Parks, J. P. Campbell, Elijah Deskins, Thomas Porter, Jr., Hugh Ryan, W. H. Russell, James M. Hughes and E. H. Parks. In addition to these, occasionally, William R. Campbell, Mr. Massie, and others not remembered. Among the plays selected, were Goldsmith's "Good Natured Man" and "She Stoops to Conquer;" "Pizarro," a historical drama, scene laid in Peru, South America, and others not now remembered. Two plays were generally given in one evening. Some good drama, comedy, or melo-drama, winding up with some roaring farce, such as "High Life Below Stairs."

In this last piece the acting of Atchison and Ryan would have stamped them as stars in any theater of the present day. Considering the limited space the actors had, their plays were well represented with scenery and all the accessories necessary to render the performances pleasing and attractive. The gentlemen who represented female characters had doubtless the more difficult *role* to sustain, since they had to undergo a complete transformation in dress, and also to change their voices, gestures and gait to suit the most refind and delicate touches of the female character. Their was one advantage in their being all of the sterner sex, which was that one dressing room sufficed for all. Not the least curious sight of all, perhaps, would have been the "green room," where petticoats and breeches, stockings and boots were mingled together in startling coincidence and bewidering confusion. From the proceeds of the performers the bell which hangs in the court house steeple to-day was purchased and presented by the Society to the town and county, and though fifty years have passed away, and nearly all of them sleep the sleep that knows no waking, the clear ringing tones of the old bell still speaks to us of the cultivated tastes and liberal public spirit of the members of the first Carlisle Thespian Society.

In the year 1828 Samuel S. Smith started the first Sunday-school in Carlisle. Though organized as a Presbyterian school, in was in fact a Union school, as—for a time at least—all denominations attended it. Mr. Smith was Superintendent, and a teacher also. His mother-in-law, Mrs. Hockady, and his wife, Mrs. Serena Smith, were also teachers. The school was held in the old court house, as up to that time there was not a solitary church building in the town. This school was continued on through all the succeeding years as a Union Sunday-school by the Baptist and Presbyterian churches until 1879, a period of half a century.

Of the wool-carding mills, there have been three in our village. One of these was built and owned by James Dudley, for a number of years a citizen of Carlisle, and afterward proprietor of the "Dudley House," in Flemingsburg. As before stated, Mr. Dudley was married in Carlisle in 1822, to Eliza Shumate, and several of their children were born here. Peyton Shumate Dudley, the present dry goods merchant of Flemingsburg, his brother William, and if we mistake not, his sister Mary. On removing from Carlisle, the wool factory passed into the hands of James Robinson, and he was succeeded by William Metcalfe, from Flemingsburg. The second mill was built by Samuel S. Hall, and stood on lot No. 78, being just south of James Kenneally. He built it about the year 1824, and carried on the factory here until he left Carlisle, in 1834. He combined the business of a fuller with that of carder, and made fulled cloth, blankets, &c., of a very excellent quality. The heavy iron plate used by him for pressing cloths, is still doing good service in the fire-place of the back room of Judge Holladay's present residence, and weighs fully 400 pounds. 'Squire Stephenson paid Mr. Hall $1 for it when he (Hall) was selling out to move away;—the plate cost Hall about $30.

We now advance to our fourth period of time, from 1830 to 1835. We have seen the steady growth of our village from the time it was first laid out in 1816, with its old log jail and court house, its motley assemblage of old frame and log dwellings, and its scattering population of less than 100 souls, to the year 1830, with its brick jail, clerk's offices, and elegant court house; its bagging factory, three tan-yards, two hatter shops, three cabinet shops, three tailor shops, three hotels, two carding factories, three saddle shops, three smith shops, two shoemaker shops and twelve or fifteen stores and groceries, and a thrifty and industrious population of over 600. Our "city fathers" had—as many of their successors in office down to the present day have had—many a conflict with the people to bring them up to that standard of high moral excellence, good taste and refinement which was the sole aim and study of those two truly good men, Jacob Leer ("Wouter Van Twiller") and Peter Schwartzweiler ("Hard Koppig Piet.")

We have now to record the advent of another distinguished citizen, who, in point of fact, has been entitled to notice at an earlier period. This was Colonel William Henry Russell. It is not known what year precisely he came to Carlisle, but it was probably as early as 1826. He bought the farm either of General Metcalfe or Mrs. Lucy Ogden, where Mrs. Rogers now owns, in the northwest quarter of the town. Colonel Russell was a lawyer by profession, a patrician by blood, tastes and habits. Besides the profession of the law, the Colonel was a sort of amateur farmer, and carried on his farming in quite a handsome way. Like Horace Greeley, he had some very advanced ideas of agriculture, as the following anecdote will show. During one of the years he lived on the farm, he had raised a fine crop of wheat and other small [illegible], and as in those days everybody had a number of slaves employed, so, too, had the Colonel. After his harvest had been cut and all safely stacked—seeing that his servants would be likely to have a good leisure time—he called them together and remarked that it would now be a good time for them to *tap their trees and go to making sugar!*

In 1830 he was elected to the Kentucky Legislature from Nicholas. It was at that session that a United States Senator was to be elected. It was charged against the Colonel that he had promised the leading Democrats of the county to vote for their nominee, in case he was elected, although in politics the Colonel himself was a Whig. Be this as it may, when the election came on, the Colonel voted for the nominee of the Whig party. In 1832 or thereabouts, he moved to the State of Missouri. Many reports since then have reached us of the active part taken by him both in Missouri politics and in business speculations. Soon after his removal to Missouri, he was riding along one night, and his route lay along an unfrequented road, partly through a dense forest. Upon this occasion the loneliness of the ride and the cool night air together, suggested the propriety of fortifying the outward man by the application of a stimulating cordial to the inner man. Like Burns in his "Death and Doctor Hombook:"

> "The village ale had made him canty,
> He was na' full, but just had plenty."

And so, riding cheerily along, he thought of the good old days when he lived in Carlisle, and "hornswoggled" the Democrats of Nicholas out of their Representative. His pathway lay, as we have said, through a lonely forest; he had just passed an open space and was entering a point of deeper gloom, when suddenly a big mountain owl from the top of a lofty tree near by, called out in deep sepulchral tones—"Who-hoo, who-hoo, who-hoo." At this sudden and peremptory challenge, the Colonel pulled up his horse so suddenly, that the beast falling back upon his haunches had well nigh unseated his rider. "Who-hoo, who-hoo, who-hoo," again came from the mysterious sentinel of the upper air. "Colonel William Russell, late Representative from Nicholas County, Kentucky, be gawd sar—who the devil are you?"

In 1828, Samuel S. Smith and John B. McIlvaine erected the hemp, bagging and bale rope factory mentioned in former chapter. In 1829, it was in successful operation. The number of hands employed were about thirty, all of whom were slaves. The hire paid was from six to twelve dollars per month and board and clothing. [illegible]ks occupied two-thirds of the square south of the [illegible] west of Metcalfe's new mill. The spinners walk extended the whole length of the square, 138 feet deep. On Christmas day, 1829, the first annual parade of the hands took place. It was a sort of military dress parade; each one was dressed out in his best Sunday suit. In addition each wore a pair of epaulettes, a white sash with big tassels at the end, and a waving plume in each hat—all being made of the finest hackled hemp. At the head of the column marched the standard-bearer (the flag being also of hemp); next came the musicians; one whom we remember as "Uncle Dick," who beat the kettle-drum, and one named Nelson, who played the fife. Nelson was one of the most ingenious fife-players ever known, and were he living at the present day would be regarded as a genuine curiosity. He may truly be said to have been born a natural fife-player. Not a sign of an instrument had he, but the sound was made by simply blowing or whistling through his closed teeth. These two, with a big bass drum, formed the band, and more enlivening military strains have never been heard in the streets of Carlisle. The column moved about 10 o'clock a.m., and marched, countermarched and marched again through every street of the town, followed by a rabble of men, boys and dogs. The holiday exercise generally wound up about 2 o'clock p.m., with a big dinner and a dance, lasting until the "wee sma' hours" of the next morning.

This was truly the military age, an age which produced a most plentiful crop of "carpet Knights," Captains, Colonels, Majors and Generals. It is true, no war with any power, great or small, was impending; the treaty of Ghent had long since been ratified and the "flag of the free" floated in proud defiance in every quarter of the civilized world. But the martial spirit engendered by the wars of the Revolution and the still later conflict with the mother country in 1812–15 still burned brightly in the bosoms of our patriot sires. The old militia law of the State was still in full force, and no day was so highly esteemed in our town as "muster day," whether it were

LAMAR HOUSE, CARLISLE, KY.
G. CHEATHAM, PROP'R.

"company," "battalion," or regimental." The day appointed by the officers for such review were generally set apart as festive occasions. Even the slaves were often allowed a holiday, and many of them came to town and set up booths for the sale of ginger cake, cider, cordial, &c., to which the weary soldiers were full often fain to resort to quench their raging thirst or satiate their ravenous appetites. Such occasions were the glory and pride of the officers, from General down to the humblest Corporal. Dressed out in a full suit of regimentals, and mounted upon "fiery, untamed steeds," they dashed furiously about the streets, and gave command in tones of thunder, which could only have been excelled by Wellington at the battle of Waterloo, or Bernadotte at the dreadful carnage of Leipsic.

Among the many names conspicuous in 1829 for their military skill and ardor, we may mention Major A. B. Crawford, Colonel Wm. H. Russell, General G. W. Ruddell, Colonel G. R. Foster, Captain Edward F. Chappell, Colonel Wm. Norvell, Colonel John S. Morgan, Colonel T. S. Parks, General Thomas Metcalfe, General Thomas Alexander, Colonel Wm. Hamilton, Captain John Harris, Colonel Matt. Arnold, and many others whose names can not now be recalled.

Warned by the occurrence of some minor fires, the trustees, on the 31st of January, 1828, ordered that John Dougherty be appointed a commissioner to let out to the lowest bidder the making of two long ladders and two short ones, also fire hooks, for the use and benefit of said town.

It was some time in the fall of 1830 that Mr. Pinney, agent for the "American Hydraulic Company," visited Carlisle, at the request of the Trustees and citizens, bringing with him a small but powerful engine much in use in that day, but now entirely obsolete. A conference was held with the representatives of both town and county, the result of which was that if Mr. Pinney could throw a stream of water from his new engine to the top of the court house spire, a distance of ninety-five feet, the County Court would give him four hundred dollars and the town Trustees a like sum, making eight hundred dollars for his engine. The contract was agreed to, the hour of trial fixed, and the owner hired eight of the biggest, stoutest negro men in town to aid him. A large crowd assembled, the engine made fast in her wooden shoes, and the reservoir filled to the brim from the public well. Mr. Pinney mounted on top and directing the nozzle skyward, gave the signal to the swarthy sons of toil to do their level best. In an instant sixteen brawny arms whirled the iron handles with such tremendous force that they fairly bent beneath the strain. The aqueous fluid, drawn suddenly into the fearful vacuum, rushed with lightning speed through hose and nozzle, till its crystal drops sparkled far above the topmost point of the tapering shaft, then fell down in a shower upon the eight dusky backs below, amid the loud huzzas from the assembled crowd. 'Twas enough; Carlisle had her fire engine, and could now afford to laugh at her less fortunate sister towns.

It was not long before the boys had a chance to try the engine. In June, 1832, a terrific fire broke out in the extensive bagging and bale rope factory of Samuel S. Smith & Co. As intimated in a previous chapter, these works covered more than half the square bounded by Second Cross, Water, Front and Walnut streets. The spinning walk extended the whole length of the lot from North to South; the hackling department up-stairs over the north end of the spinning walk; the weaving house next east, then the quilling mill, and lastly the hemp magazine, all fronting on South street—the street fronting the railroad. In addition there was a large two-story boarding house situated in the center of the hollow square. All these buildings were wooden ones save the magazine, which was brick. It was 10 o'clock at night when the fire was discovered and the alarm given. In ten minutes the engine came thundering down the street—*a la* city style—and our hardy firemen, thoroughly equipped with buckets, axes, fire hooks and engine, prepared to take in the situation and put out the fire, no matter how big it was. But alas! owing to the great headway it had obtained, and the perishable nature of the buildings and their contents, nothing could be done to arrest the fire in its stronghold. Accordingly all efforts were directed to saving the adjacent buildings. The residence of Rev. John Rogers was in extreme danger, being but a few feet from the burning magazine, and but for our fire engine would have been destroyed. The next house nearest was that of E. F. Chappell, which was saved by tearing up the carpets and spreading them, together with old quilts and blankets, on the roof and kept well saturated with water.

The burning of the factory was a great loss to the town, as it cut off our largest business enterprise and lost us a population of fully fifty souls—all producers. On the 7th of January, 1831, the trustees appropriated fifteen dollars towards paying for the engine, the citizens raising the balance of their four hundred by private subscription.

At a meeting of the board of trustees held at the office of William Norvell, July 25, 1832, present, R. D. Henry,

Joseph F. Tureman, Elijah West, John S. Smith, "Ordered that twenty-five dollars in silver be appropriated toward the payment of the balance due on the fire engine, and that the treasurer pay the same when called for." At the same meeting it was "Ordered that Joseph F. Tureman, N. P. Robinson and John Davidson, be appointed Commissioners to have an engine house built upon the public square, the front forming part of the fence around the public square."

It was about the year 1831, that N. P. Robinson, one of our most active merchants and business men, erected a cotton factory upon lot No. 124, at the west end of Front street, the first and last enterprise of the kind ever attempted in Carlisle.

The cotton-mill was an indifferent success, and after the removal of Mr. Robinson to Oakland Mills, about 1834, the machinery was suffered to perish by neglect, and a good deal of it carried off by the town boys.

The destruction of the bagging factory already referred to, cast a gloom over the business of the town from which it did not soon recover.

General Samuel Fulton was not a citizen of Carlisle, but lived on the farm next east of the late A. S. Waugh. he served several terms in both houses of the Kentucky Legislature; was a good, well-meaning man, and in some things a man of shrewdness and intelligence. We mention his name here because of his opposition to bringing the Maysville Pike through Carlisle. To do the General justice, he was really in favor of no pike at all. He was in the Senate, we believe, when the bill came up chartering the road. One argument used by the General and others opposed to the bill, was, that big, heavy wagons would be put on the road that would haul great cargoes of goods, and that an injury thereby would be done to those who had already capital invested in small wagons! It is reported of the General that in a speech once made by him in the Senate, referring to a Senator who had made a very powerful speech, he used the following very emphatic figure of speech:

"MR. SPEAKER: I would rather have a he cat drawn tail foremost down my naked back, than to have the gentleman after me with one of his *sarsasms!*"

But the turnpike was finished, and sure enough, there were the great broad-tread wagons, drawn by their six powerful horses, hauling great loads of merchandise to Lexington, Cynthiana, Paris, Georgetown, Richmond, Winchester, Lancaster and Danville. Two daily stage lines, carrying from thirty to forty to each coach; carriages, hacks, buggies and rockaways, carrying the very *elite* and wealth of the State; the merchandise of all lands poured along the great highway, while we poor benighted denizens of Carlisle sat in silence and solitude:

> "Far from the madding crowd's ignoble strife
> Our sober wishes never learned to stray,
> Along the cool, sequestered vale of life
> We kept the noiseless tenor of our way."

William Shakspeare said: "There is a tide in the affairs of men which, if taken at the flood, etc." That was the time we had our golden opportunity. We missed it —that was all.

Wood & Lowry, one of the strongest and most successful firms which ever did business in Carlisle, was composed of Mr. Garrett Wood and Dr. George G. Lowry. A partnership in the dry goods business between these two gentlemen had been formed at Helena, in Mason County, where they for a time carried on business. They came to Carlisle—that is, Mr. Wood did—with a stock of goods about 1831 or 32. The old stone house owned by John G. Parks then, was rented, and Enos Burns was employed as clerk. It is doubtful if there ever was anywhere outside of Paris, France, any proprietor and clerk who excelled Wood and Burns in politeness and suavity of manners. The house did business here only about two years, but they made money during the time beyond question. The firm being afterward dissolved, Mr. Wood went to Missouri, where he continued a successful business up to the time of his death.

Dr. Lowry visited Carlisle again in 1842 with a view to locate here. He bargained with Mr. Joseph F. Tureman for his private residence, store-room and stock of goods. The price was agreed on, terms fixed and all, but somehow the contract was never carried out. The Doctor, perhaps very wisely, concluded that he would stick to his farm and the practice of his profession. In these he was thoroughly proficient. About 1850, he bought the fine farm then owned by Henry Bruce, Jr. On this tract he built a spacious brick residence, and the farm afterward became widely known as the model farm of the State. Dr. Lowry died some twenty years since, leaving quite a large family well provided for.

Our onward march with our history now brings us down to the year of 1833, the year made memorable throughout the United States as the period of the first appearance of the Asiatic cholera. We in Carlisle, in common with all the towns and cities of our country, were awaiting its arrival in our midst in terror and trepidation. We had tracked its course from the time it appeared in Moscow, with almost a grim certainty of its presence among us at no distant day. There were no telegraphs or steamships in those days, and we had to bide the slow and tedious passage of the sailing vessels requiring generally from twenty-five to thirty days before we could hear any tidings of the whereabouts of the terrible scourge. In June, 1832, it first made its appearance on this side of the Atlantic, at Quebec, and June 10 at Montreal. On the 21st of June it appeared at New York; at Philadelphia, Albany and Rochester in July; Boston, Baltimore and Washington in August and in October; from Cincinnati it leaped to New Orleans.

In the meantime our citizens were not idle in preparing to meet the apprehended danger. Several families hastily packed up and fled from their homes and spent the whole summer in log huts and cabins remote from the town, some finding an asylum among relatives and friends. The writer remembers of one farmhouse where four whole families were quartered. It was the same now owned by Henry C. Reed and mother, to-wit: Mr. and Mrs. Jeremiah Clark and three boys, Mr. and Mrs. E. F. Chappell and three children, Mr. and Mrs. Joseph Clark and four children, and a black family of seven or eight. It was not until June 17, 1833, that the first case occurred in Carlisle. This was a black man named George, belonging to N. P. Robinson. He lived but a few hours, and was soon followed by Dr. Milton G. Thurman, an estimable young physician boarding with N. P. Robinson, a nephew of Solomon G. Ward. A black man and wife living at Dr. Menifee's, name now forgotten; a black man and woman living at Dr. Leech's; Christopher Goodwin and wife, Caroline, living with Thomas Arnold; Miss Sallie Harris, a daughter of Captain John Harris, then living where Mrs. Mary Mathers now lives; a married daughter of Thomas Jones living near town; Thomas Hadden, partner of John Dougherty, hatters on Front street; a black man owned by Hadden; Thos. Caldwell, a large, fleshy man, living in the two-story where A. McDaniel, Jr., now lives; Mrs. Smedley, first wife of Aaron Smedley, who lived where John M. Chevis now lives—in all, fourteen persons, six white and eight black—and all on Front street.

During the months of June, July and August, nearly all kinds of business were suspended in Carlisle. Mr. Joseph F. Tureman relates that none of the business houses were kept open. All that he did was to open his store of a morning, and stay a few hours, waiting for any one who might come and call for some article of medicine. As for all kinds of dry goods, no thought was taken of them, or of accumulating the goods of this world. For a time it seemed that all were only interested in laying up treasures in Heaven, "where moth and rust doth not corrupt and where thieves do not break through and steal." At old Concord, religious services were held nearly every Sunday. On one occasion Rev. William Vaughn, the faithful servant of God, preached there to a large audience, who were moved to tears by the fervid eloquence of the preacher and the apparently near approach of death.

On the 17th day of June (the day the first case of cholera appeared) the Board of Trustees met; present: Joseph F. Tureman, John S. Morgan and Matthew Reed. It was "ordered that Gavin Mathers be employed to haul a load of lime and to place it upon the public square in Carlisle, for the use and benefit of the citizens, who are requested to use the same for the purpose of checking the cholera."

"Ordered, That William Secrest, James Scott and William Stewart, be appointed a committee to examine the cellars, back premises and alleys, etc., and see that the same be clear of filth, etc.; and if not, they are to employ help to put them in good order, for which the trustees will pay, and that they enter forthwith upon the duty of their office." Signed,

M. Reed, President.

William Norvell, Clerk.

It is honorable to record, that while many fled from the visitations of death, there were a noble few who were always prompt at the cry for aid, going from house to house, doing all in their power to relieve the sufferers, and closing their eyes and preparing their bodies for interment when the last struggle with death had ended. Among those whose names deserve to be remembered for their self-sacrificing heroism, are those of Colonel William Norvell, James Robinson, Edward Parks and others, who are now dead.

In November, 1833, that most sublime but terrifying celestial phenomenon occurred, called at that time "the falling stars," but now generally recognized as a "meteoric shower." It was about three o'clock in the morning when the whole heavens, ablaze with these flying messengers of light, attracted the attention of some one who was sitting up with a sick person. He had just stepped out of the door to go for a doctor, when the grand and awful scene bursting upon his vision caused his

> "———two eyes like stars to start from their spheres,
> His knotted and combined locks to part,
> And each particular hair to stand on end
> Like quills of the fretful porcupine."

The alarm was instantly given, and spread with rapidity throughout the town. The cry from house to house, and street to street, was, "Get up! get up! the world is coming to an end!" For awhile a fearful consternation prevailed; knees smote, teeth chattered, and loud outcries of mortal terror gave a faint idea indeed of the apocalyptic vision when the dead, small and great, shall stand before the presence of God. Bibles were gotten out which had long laid away covered with dust; knees were bowed in prayer, and every token in truth, of a peril as dread as it was mysterious. Well does the writer remember that scene; it is pictured upon memory's tablet in form and color so distinct that it can never fade away—no, not until that great day itself shall come, and the feeble outlines of the ante-type be swallowed up in the far grander sublimity of that "eternal blazon." Oh! happy will he be if he can stand in that dread presence with as little fear of that awful scene, as he stood under the blazing heavens, in the street hard-by his humble cottage home in Carlisle, in November, 1833. Still, no sound of the archangel's trump broke upon the expectant ear; nor did "the sheeted dead squeak and gibber in our streets." But still the sublime spectacle went on. Myriads of stars shot athwart the heavens, coursing like fiery steeds across each other's path, leaving behind them monster trains of light, which lingered long after the star itself had disappeared. And yet the cool November air caught no breath of heat from the flashing meteoric blaze. The fixed stars smiled as serenely as ever before upon the mortal terrors of their sister earth. Gradually terror gave way to confidence, fear to admiration, and our people stood spell bound, gazing still in awe, but no longer in fear, upon the grandest spectacle it has ever been the lot of man to behold, until the light of the "bad revolting stars" was lost in the brighter effulgence of the morning sun.

The source whence the meteors came was traced to that quarter in the heavens occupied by the Leonis Majoris, and independent of the earth's rotation and exterior to our atmosphere. As computed by astronomers at the time, it could not have been less than 2,238 miles distant from the earth.

To give some faint idea of the amount of light thrown upon the earth's surface, we would say that one could have easily picked up a pin anywhere in the streets of Carlisle. There is no wonder that people were fearfully alarmed at the appearance of the "falling stars." Only three months had elapsed since the Asiatic cholera had made such sad havoc among the human race; and putting the two occurrences together, it was well calculated to create the impression that the "crack of doom" was at hand.

It may not be uninteresting to know that the first body ever buried in the old graveyard, which lies alongside the new cemetery, was that of a little boy. In 1821, Willie Smedley, son of Aaron Smedley, pulled a coffee pot full of boiling coffee over onto his head and face. The hot fluid entered his ear, causing his death in a few hours. He was at the time just across the street at his grandfather's, who lived in the old frame house torn down some eight years ago to make way for the handsome gothic cottage built by Police Judge Mann. His father lived where Squire J. M. Chevis now owns. At this time General Thomas Metcalfe lived where Mrs. Rogers formerly lived. The General owned all the land clear down to the public road then leading to Forest Retreat. So far no burial ground had been established in Carlisle. People who lost friends generally went to Old Concord, or some old family burying-ground in the neighborhood. Mr. Smedley, however, not wishing to bury his little boy so far from home, got the consent of General Metcalfe to bury in the corner of his farm just where the Millersburg and Forest Retreat roads diverged from the town limits. And thus we have the origin of the Carlisle Cemetery. The second person buried was old Mr. George Robinson, father of N. P. and George Robinson, mentioned in our former chapters. He was a member of the Masonic fraternity, and it was the first Masonic burial of Carlisle. This was about the year 1822. There was a great concourse of people assembled from far and near to witness it. The great lights in Masonry were carried in procession by a venerable brother, and there being then no hearse to convey bodies to the grave, the coffin was carried by four stout brothers acting as pall-bearers. And so, by permission of the General, persons continued to bury there until about 1827, when the General sold the farm to his sister, Mrs. Lucy Ogden. From Mrs. Ogden a purchase was made by the town, and set apart for the sole purpose of a burying-ground. There were no lots held or sold by any one—any and everybody, black and white, had a right to enter and dig wherever they chose.

Due north from Carlisle, on the old dirt road to Maysville, and within one mile of town there are two hills. Over this hilly road from 1816 to 1848, a period of 32 years, all the freight from Maysville to Carlisle was hauled in wagons, the price per hundred pounds varying from fifty cents to $1.50, according to the condition of the roads. The longest of these hills approaching town is known as "The Steam Mill Hill," and about the year 1830, a Mr. N. G. Baldoc built a steam mill at the foot of the hill near A. S. Waugh's. In the winter time the mud on the long hill was generally so deep that it was sometimes supposed to have no bottom. Teamsters

hauling goods from Maysville, generally unloaded fully one-half their cargo at Arnett's old "Indian Queen Hotel." On reaching the hill alluded to the wagoner would dismount and commence the heavy task of reaching the summit. By the time he had gained one-third the elevation, one-third more of his cargo had to be discharged, and along with it a volley of oaths, such as might have shamed our army in Flanders. At two-thirds of the way toward the top another lot of freight and another discharge of infernal artillery; and fortunate was the poor wagoner if he gained the summit with one W box of dry goods and a kit of mackerel. But he had his revenge by unloading "cuss words" enough to fill a dictionary; and looking back over the muddy way along which was strewn his boxes, bales and barrels he caught sight of the smoke of the steam mill at the base, and all of them by common consent dubbed it that "d—d steam mill hill."

This side of the point above named there is a smaller elevation, but steeper at one point than any one on the long hill. It has been avoided now by the grading of the Park's Ferry Turnpike. This hill sloped downward toward the town, and the only trouble our friend, the wagoner, had about it was that, in descending, his wagon and team seemed like they were standing on their heads, and he had, in the summer time, to put on all the brakes to keep his wagon from rolling out his horses into pancakes. But to the origin of the name. Since the laying out of our town in 1816, we have had four public executions of persons condemned to die. Of these four, three of them were black men, and all three of them hung on the hill last named. The sentence of death pronounced upon them was, that "in one-half mile from the court-house" the penalty of their several crimes was to be executed upon them by a public hanging. The first man ever hung here was Burris, a black man belonging to Erasmus Riggs, somewhere about 1820. The place selected by the sheriff was the summit of the hill named, and which, therefore, became known as "Gallows Hill." Our next hanging was Bill, an old black man, seventy years old, who also met his fate on Gallows Hill. The third and last of the series was Thomas Fulton, a free, mulatto, colored man, in 1838. Tom lived on the waters of Beaver Creek, and owned a small piece of ground with a cabin on it. An order had been made by the County Court to survey a new road through that neighborhood. It so happened that the proposed line lay through Tom's land. He had been heard to make his threats that no road should be surveyed through his premises. When the day arrived for the survey, sure enough there was Tom with his loaded gun, his "soul in arms and eager for the fray." He ordered the men off; a fierce quarrel ensued, and Tom banged away with his gun, killing outright one of the surveyors. He was tried, found guilty and condemned to die.

From the time our town was laid out, until 1835, our market was always bountifully supplied with fish caught in our own Kentucky streams. Licking River, which washes our northeastern boundary, and Hinkston upon our southwestern, were literally filled with the finest specimens of the piscatorial tribe which one could desire to see or eat. Pike, bass, channel cat, red horse, new-lights and perch, all were found in a liberal supply and of the finest quality. The price paid was generally five cents per pound. But we had also a source of supply right at our very doors. All that part of Brushy Fork which flows through Dorsiana, was as good a place to fish as there was in Kentucky. And following the stream all the way down to where it empties into Hinkston, just above Millersburg, there were noted places to fish, where fine perch, cat-fish, and not unfrequently bass, were caught which would weigh from half a pound to a pound each. About eighty yards below where the Dorseyville bridge crosses the creek, there stood, in 1834, an old walnut tree which grew upon the bank of the stream on the hither side; sitting under the shade of this tree many a fine string of fish has been taken by the boys of Carlisle, as late as the year 1839–40. The same locality was used for a great many years as a baptizing pool. In some of the great revivals of 1830 to '40, no less than fifty or sixty have been immersed there on a single occasion. Looking at the stream in its present reduced and shallow state, we might well ask: What has become of all the water? It has been ascribed to the destruction of timber, and almost universal cultivation of the soil along its banks. The loose soil, being washed out by the rains, has settled in the bottom of the creek, and so reduced and narrowed its bed, that there is no basin to hold the water, and so it flows right off toward the rivers, leaving no sufficient depth for the fish to dwell in, as in "ye good olden times."

The subject of a fire department continued to agitate the bosom of our town guardians from year to year. There was hardly a meeting of the Board of Trustees held that some project for the purchase of some sort of fire apparatus was not discussed. And so the trustees resolved to do many great and mighty works of public improvement. Saint James says that "faith without works is dead." In the case of our city fathers it was works—on paper—without any faith in their ever being performed. The order to purchase, or have made, a lot of fire hooks and ladders had been made out and passed as early as 1829, but it was not until 1838 that the work began to assume a tangible shape. On the 2d day of April of that year, the board met at the store of Smedley & Dougherty. "On motion, it was unanimously resolved that a competent number of fire-hooks be procured for the benefit of the town of Carlisle, and that the same be paid for out of any money in the hands of the trustees." In order to carry out this resolution, John Dougherty and Henry Fritts were appointed a committee to procure such fire-hooks on the most reasonable terms. Still the committee failed to act. On the 29th of March, 1839, it was "ordered that William Stewart and B. M. Teal be appointed a committee to purchase fire-hooks in place of Messrs. Dougherty and Fritts, who have declined to act." This time they found the right man. Uncle Billy Stewart concluded he would "take the bull by the horns" and have the hooks and ladders made, let come what might. And so the fire-hooks were made and safely laid away alongside the old market-house ready to be brought into active use in case of any sudden invasion of the fire fiend. An opportunity soon presented itself for testing the merits of the fire-hooks. Some time in 1840 a fire broke out in the large livery stable attached to the hotel kept by A. Summers, Esq., now the St. Cloud Hotel. The stable stood on the south side of the alley on Second street, where Sam Berry's ice house now stands. On the upper or north side of the alley stood the granary, a one-story frame, where all the corn, oats, etc., were stored for use at the stable. These two buildings were erected at the same time the old hotel was erected, about the year 1817.

Although it was early in the night when the fire broke out—soon after 8 o'clock—it would have been impossible to have put it out, even with a first-class engine and fire department. The stable being built wholly of frame, well seasoned at that, and filled with hay and straw, of course burned with fearful rapidity. The flames very soon overleaped the alley and fastened upon the granary.

The distance from the granary to the hotel was so short as to greatly endanger the latter, which in turn would have threatened the whole block on Front street, fronting the court house. "Pull down the granary!" was the cry from lip to lip as the roaring flames leaped high in the air, and swayed menacingly toward the densely built portion of the town. Then it was that our hardy firemen bethought them of their fire-hooks which had so recently been prepared for the salvation of the town against fire.

"The fire-hooks! the fire-hooks!" shouted the crowd as they rushed past the hotel where feather-beds, chairs, boot-jacks, mattresses, quilts, bed-comforts, looking glasses, etc., were flying into the street below from the open windows above. Soon the fire-hook procession came upon the scene, each ponderous machine borne upon the shoulders of a score of stalwart men. But here a new and unexpected difficulty arose: how to get the fire-hooks raised to the top of the burning building. A jockey once describing his horse, said that the horse had but two faults in the world. "What are they?" asked an inquisitive bystander. "One is, that he is hard to catch, and the other is, that he is no account when he is caught."

These two points covered the whole ground with regard to the Carlisle fire-hooks. There was not muscular power enough in Carlisle, Sharpsburg and Millersburg combined, to have raised one of them to an angle of forty-five degrees—particularly when the farther end had to be pointed at a burning building, with the thermometer at an altitude of 300° Fahrenheit. There was a great deal of heaving and setting, puffing and blowing and whooping and shouting, ending by a still greater torrent of cursing and swearing, and a throwing down of "the fire-hooks" prone to the earth, in the most contemptuous scorn and indignation. Fortunately the night was calm, and the frames of the burning houses fell in before the badly scorched walls of the hotel took fire, and the old hotel escaped by the skin of its teeth. But the fire cooked the goose of the Carlisle fire-hooks, the Alpha and Omega of that species of property in our town. The irons were taken off and sold to the blacksmiths, and the trees of which they had been made converted into fire-wood.

In 1835 there were three families living in Carlisle, whose history deserves a special notice. These were John Boyd, and William and Lawson Smith. Mr. Boyd then lived in the brick house just across the east end of the culvert, where Jesse McDaniel now lives. Wm. Smith lived next door east of Boyd, where Jno. A. Campbell, Esq. now lives. Lawson Smith's house was just at the opposite side of the culvert, where Mrs. George now owns. John Boyd kept a grocery in the one-story frame now occupied by Frey & Harris, in front of the court house door. The Smith Bros. carried on a tanning and saddlery business upon the same lot occupied by Lawson.

On the last day of the election, Aug., 1835, in a quarrel between Boyd and Smith, the parties came to blows, and before any one was aware, Wm. Boyd, son of John Boyd, ran in and stabbed Smith to the heart. Boyd was sometime after arrested and tried for the murder, but broke jail before the trial was concluded, and ran away. He was himself shot to death by some unknown person in Illinois about thirty years after, while sitting in his chamber at night.

About the year 1834, a co-partnership in the dry goods business was formed between Aaron Smedley and John Dougherty. The business was carried on by them in the old frame building which stood on the lot now covered by the three-story brick owned by The Farmers' Bank, and Mathers & Saunders. The partnership was a very harmonious one, the partners generally taking it time about going to Philadelphia for their semi-annual supplies. If Wood & Lowry was a firm of exceeding politeness, Smedley and Dougherty exceeded in jollity. Both of them were pretty good on telling jokes and hard yarns. Their store was a favorite resort for all who desired to "laugh and grow fat." Mr. Smedley was the chief salesman with the ladies—a faculty which his son, John, of Hughes & Smedley at Millersburg, retains to this day—a sort of family distinction as it were. Mr. Smedley's wife died with the cholera in 1833, and it was during the time of his widowerhood that he was in business with Boss Dougherty. About 1838 or '39 he married Miss Catharine Hughes, daughter of Jesse Hughes, Esq., perhaps the prettiest girl ever raised in Carlisle. About this time the partnership was dissolved; Mr. Smedley bought a farm near Moreland, in Bourbon County, to which he immediately removed.

Soon after Wood & Lowry moved away a new competitor came upon the stage in the dry goods business. This was John McMahan. He was a citizen of the town, and continued to reside here until 1840. On the 18th of August, 1830, he was appointed collector to collect the town tax for the years 1829 and '30, and also the delinquent taxes for 1828. About 1836 he opened a small dry goods store in the old stone house where Wood & Lowry had been located. James E. Secrest was employed as clerk by him. In 1837 he bought the property where 'Squire John McKee now lives, which then included the ground whereon Tureman & Howell's drug store now stands. Here he fitted a little, narrow room with a little, frame bedroom in the rear, and moved his stock into it. During the years 1837, '38 and '39, Mr. McMahan's sales scarcely reached beyond $5,000 per annum. December 1, 1837, James E. Secrest left the store and was succeeded by Jas. A. Chappell. In 1839, Mr. McMahan was the largest taxpayer in Carlisle, he being assessed at $14,000, while Mr. Tureman was placed at $13,000. But alas! Mr. McMahan's was but the shadow and show of wealth. It was all on a credit. Nor is it probable that he was ever at any time really worth to exceed $4,000. In 1840, he was compelled to succumb to the pressure of the times. He failed in business and moved away during that year to the State of Ohio, where he lived several years, and afterwards went to Illinois.

It was, we believe, in 1837 that the shinplaster epidemic broke out all over the land. This grew out of the scarcity of change. The banks having suspended throughout the whole land, there was, of course, no silver money, either large or small, paid out, and as the banks did not issue bills below the denomination of one dollar, there grew such a scarcity of small change as to become a serious inconvenience, and to create a popular clamor for relief. To remedy the evil, prominent business firms in almost every city or town of any size had printed small bills of the denomination of 6¼ cents, 12½ cents, 25 cents, 40 cents, and some even 75 cents. These were to be redeemable at any time, at the option of the holder, when presented in amounts of five dollars or upwards, in current bank notes. Some of these tickets were printed on very poor paper, and after being worn some time, looked greasy and dirty, and these, together with their small size, obtained for them the soubriquet of "shinplasters." The shinplaster was freely taken at home by everybody, but were often refused when they got beyond their own limits. Mr. A. Broadwell, of Cynthiana, issued by far the largest amount in this section, and his "plasters" were pretty freely taken—sometimes fifty miles from home. The amount issued by Mr. Dougherty and endorsed by Mr. Tureman did not reach beyond $400. Mr. Broadwell's shinplaster bank, we think, ran up to $3,000. Mr. Hazelrigg, of Mt. Sterling, also issued a goodly quantity of them.

Among the dry goods firms in Carlisle between 1830 and 1840 was that of Morgan & Bruce. This firm was composed of Col. John S. Morgan and his brother-in-law, Henry Bruce, Jr., of Fleming County. Their place of business was in the old frame house now owned by Colonel Parks, and occupied by Thomas Sammons & Bro. in the year 1832 or 33, and continued until about 1835. After Mr. Bruce retired from the business in Carlisle, he settled upon the farm adjoining the Bruce homestead. About 1846 he sold that place to Dr. Lowry and purchased the the fine farm on the Maysville Turnpike near Mayslick. After a stay of several years upon the farm he sold it to Captain John F. Piper of this county. He moved to the city of Covington and purchased a fine old brick mansion upon Sanford street, near the bank of Licking river. At this time he was worth fully sixty thousand dollars. At the breaking-out of the war Mr. Bruce took strong ground in favor of the South. So sanguine was he of success that he bought fifteen or twenty likely young slaves, three of whom he sent to Carlisle for safe keeping. But Mr. Lincoln's Proclamation, a year or two after, of course wiped out that much capital with a stroke of the pen. He was put under surveillance by the Federal authorities and not allowed to reside in Kentucky; accordingly he moved to the city of New York. He is now in Kansas City, where he is located as lessee of a splendid hotel in that flourishing city, doing well and enjoying life as only one of his happy disposition can enjoy it.

On lot No. 83, there was as early as 1820 an old grist-mill. This was built by a man named George Peck. Peck was an ingenious fellow, and employed his leisure hours (that is, when not taking toll) in making combs out of horn. One of these combs fell into the hands of Mrs. Martha Ross, mother of Judge Ross, who kept it as a curiosity for a good many years after. The mill-stones were so hewn that one worked within the other, more like an old-fashioned coffee-mill. As late as 1845, these old stones and part of an old cog-wheel were still lying on the spot, but the mill-house had disappeared, and to-day not a vestige is left of the first grist-mill in Carlisle.

The year 1840 was a gloomy period in the history of the town, the suspension of the banks in 1837, followed in the State by the issue of Commonwealth Paper, the loss of confidence, and the fearful stagnation in business, culminated in 1840 by pinching hard times. Constables after levying upon property to satisfy executions, found no buyers to attend their sales; and so had to postpone them from time to time, and oftentimes the creditor would attend and bid in property enough to satisfy his claim, at ruinous prices. It was during this year that there were but two dry goods stores in Carlisle. These were Jas. F. Tureman and John Dougherty. Such was the dullness of the times that Mr. Tureman's sales amounted to but little over seven thousand dollars. But the recuperative power of the country soon began to tell upon business, and new firms were organized, new plans projected, and 1841–42–43 and '44, each showed a scale of progression in the interests of trade. Thus far the town had no turnpike communication with the outer world; but in 1845, a charter was obtained for a turnpike from Carlisle to Forest Retreat, a distance of about three miles. About nine thousand dollars were subscribed by the citizens, and in the spring of 1846, the work was begun. It was in 1848 before it was completed, and in the month of November of that year, E. P. Johnson & Co., of whom Jack Hughes was a member, began a line of stages, semi-daily, between Maysville and Carlisle. Our townsman, J. A. Chappell, was the first passenger entered upon the way-bill.

The completion of this long and much needed improvement gave a new impetus to the trade and business of the town. In the meantime our old court house as early as 1840 began to show signs of decay; the circular wall on the east gave way and threatened to jeopardize the lives of judge, jury and bar; and so our circuit judge in 1843 ordered its removal. In 1844, the lofty spire of the old house succumbed to the force of circumstances. The present new court house was completed in 1845, at a cost of about $8,000, including the old material. At the same time the present new clerk's offices were completed. In 1855, a survey was made of the route of the Carlisle and Sharpsburg Turnpike. At that time the Maysville and Lexington Railroad was also being surveyed, and the same corps of engineers employed on the railroad were hired to make the survey of the turnpike. The railroad was then considered a fixed fact, and our citizens were now looking round for turnpike connections. Although the county of Nicholas had by a decisive vote refused a bond subscription of $100,000 to the railroad, our town citizens, and many also from the county, united in a liberal cash subscription, and thereby secured the location through Carlisle. The history of the railroad will, no doubt, more fully appear in the Bourbon County or Paris City Department. As before indicated, the survey of the Carlisle and Sharpsburg Turnpike was made in 1855, but it was not until some five years after, that a subscription was made to the capital stock of the road sufficient to put the road under contract.

From 1856 to 1860 was a period of extraordinary prosperity; in the three years of 1857–8–9, one prominent dry goods and grocery firm cleared $6,000 each year, or $18,000 for the three years, upon a purely legitimate business. The opening of the Carlisle and Sharpsburg Turnpike was a great advantage to the place, and has continued ever since to be a main feeder to the trade and business of the town. In 1861, Messrs. Chappell, Bruce and McIntyre erected a large brick building on the corner of Front and Main Cross streets. In the second story of the building they constructed a town hall, 73x38 feet. This hall, for about twelve years, was much used for exhibitions, entertainments, etc. Many noted suppers, for the benefit of the several churches, were given there. At one of these suppers, given by the Christian Church, there were more than 400 persons present, and the receipts amounted to over $600. It was in the month of June, 1862, that a supper was given by the

ladies of the Baptist and Presbyterian Churches. Never was such a tempting display of viands seen in Carlisle. It was during the strawberry season, and the ladies spared no pains nor expense to make their entertainment a grand success. It was about noon, the very day the supper was to come off, when they were all up in the Masonic hall, which was in the third story of the building, immediately above the town hall. Here they had their tables set, while the town hall below was to be used as a grand reception and promenade room.

In the midst of their busy preparation for the great event, the whole community were thrown into the wildest excitement by the cry of "The rebels! the rebels are coming!" And in fact some Union scouts attached to the Home Guards, came flying pell mell through the streets and gave the general alarm. Then indeed there was mounting in hot haste. Those who were known as warm Unionists quickly mounted their horses and rode away. It was only a few moments before a squad of rebel cavalry about 60 strong, commanded by Capt. Pete Everett, dashed into the town, and having picketed all the streets, proceeded leisurely to dismount on the public square and to help themselves to a number of horses. In the meantime the gallant Captain heard of the elegant supper which the ladies had set out in the Masonic Hall, and so he dispatched his orderly to wait on the ladies and notify them that he and his company of bold soldier boys would do them the honor to dine with them. The announcement brought tears to the eyes of the fair ladies, and as our history must be veracious, we are compelled to state that they were not tears of joy. A delegation of "Southrons," that is, those who were supposed to be in sympathy with the South in the great contest then impending—headed by Mrs. E. M. Bruce, whose husband was at the time a member of the Confederate Congress—was hurriedly sent to Capt. Everett, to respectfully decline the honor, and as Dogberry would say, to most humbly give the Captain and his cavalrymen leave to depart. But the Captain's stomach and conscience being both at that time of the day in accord with a good dinner, could not be moved from his purpose. He however agreed that if the ladies would wait on the table right nicely and give his boys a good hearty dinner, he on his part would guarantee perfect security to all and singular of the property held in fee simple by the ladies, including all their silver ware, table cloths and napkins, all their roast duck, cold ham, chicken-salad, cakes, pies, ices and strawberries, except so much of the edibles as might be necessary to satisfy the appetites of the aforesaid hungry squad of cavalry. This compromise was accepted by the ladies with the best grace they could, and the soldiers were marched at once to the tables, stacking their arms at the door. After thoroughly satisfying their appetites, the Captain and his men quietly mounted and rode away towards Mount Sterling. The ladies soon cleared away their tables and the supper went on, realizing the handsome sum of five hundred dollars. It was believed that but for the raid of Captain Everett's troops two hundred dollars more would have been realized.

It has always been the misfortune of Carlisle that no manufactories of any kind to amount to anything have ever been established here since the burning of the hemp factory in 1832. In 1864, Mr. Weaver moved a few looms here and made a few yards of a very fair article of heavy jeans, but the enterprise soon died out for the want of capital to sustain it. Some years ago an effort was made to establish a shoe factory on a moderate scale; after passing through several hands with indifferent success, the enterprise fell into the hands of Chappell, Bruce & McIntyre, and in 1862 they made up over $7,000 worth of custom work. But it was found impossible to compete with Eastern manufactories and the work was abandoned. About 1870, Mr. R. C. King obtained a patent for a blue grass seed-stripper, both for hand and horse power. For the hand machine he has had a good demand, and there is no doubt but that he could have had a large export demand for both machines if he had put more capital and enterprise, into the business. About the same time Archdeacon and Brother opened a carriage manufactory on a limited scale. These gentlemen have succeded very well in their business, and have built up a very fair paying trade. For a long period of years Carlisle was entirely without a flouring-mill: but about 1853 the citizens raised a subscription of about two thousand dollars, and tendered to John McConahay, who put in operation a steam mill, located below Water street, just at the foot of Second street. About two years after Mr. Elbridge Waller succeeded to the mill, and in connection with it, established the first and last distillery ever erected in the town limits.

In the year 1863, Daniel S. Talbert, Esq., from Bourbon County, moved to Carlisle and purchased the property from Mr. Waller; but in June, 1864, the mill, distillery and all, took fire and burned to the ground. There was another Rip Van Winkle sleep took place, until eight years after, Messrs. Piercy & Saunders built a steam mill in the suburbs of the east end. Before completion, however, it was purchased by Henry C. Metcalfe. Mr. M. V. Bostain, a popular young gentleman from Sherburne, in partnership with Mr. Metcalfe, completed the mill, and put it in successful operation, under the firm name of Metcalfe & Bostain. Not satisfied with this mill, however, in 1877, Mr. Metcalfe projected a new one, to be supplied with all the modern improvements, to produce flour by the new patent process. In this last project Mr. Metcalfe was associated with Mr. Thomas Johnson. In 1878, the property was sold to Capt. S. G. Rogers and Mr. Bostain. It was during this year that the tubular boilers of the mill exploded, killing Mr. James Summers, the engineer. Since then the mill has been enlarged and improved, and is to-day, for its capacity, one of the finest mills in the State. On the 5th day of October, 1871, the first rail of the Maysville & Lexington Railroad was laid into town. Quite a large number of our citizens were present, and, as the track was laid across the town limits, many of them stepped upon the car, and thus became the first railroad passengers ever to enter the town. The completion of this long-desired and long-deferred improvement gave new life and enterprise to the place. In order to aid in securing the completion of the road, the town, in its corporate capacity, in 1868, voted a subscription of fifteen thousand dollars to the capital stock. For this purpose bonds were issued, bearing six per cent. interest, and having twenty years to run. In 1873, the town sold the certificates of stock to some Maysville parties at twelve and one-half cents on the dollar. This sum was set apart as a sinking fund, to be further increased by annual taxation, to be used in the extinguishment of the debt. Since then, some six thousand dollars of the bonds have been purchased by the Town Treasurer, Mr. F. E. Congleton. To this gentleman's able management may, no doubt, be largely attributed the final extinguishment of the debt, principal and interest.

Reference has been made in another chapter to the Carlisle Bank, chartered in 1817 and suspended in 1819. From that time on for thirty years there was no bank in Carlisle. In 1850 Mr. John Dougherty opened a deposit bank on Front St. in the new three-story building erected by him. Mr. Isaac H. Howell was his clerk. Mr. Dougherty kept an account with Braisted and Dougherty, Merchant Tailors 299½ Broadway, New York, upon whom most all of his eastern drafts were drawn. In 1859, Messrs. Chappell, Bruce and McIntyre opened a private bank of deposit in the building on the old Tureman corner. Their New York house was the Metropolitan Bank. Soon after this, and after the death of Mr. Dougherty, a deposit bank was opened by Mr. Henry Edsall and Wm. P. Ross, Esq. These gentlemen in 1865 were succeeded by the present Deposit Bank. This last is a regularly chartered bank, having a capital of about $85,000. The present officers are W. P. Ross, President, F. E Congleton, Cashier, Wm. W. Howard, Clerk, and Horace M. Taylor, Correspondent. During the present session of the Legislature, a charter has been granted for the Farmers' Bank of Carlisle, with a capital of $50,000. The following constitute the present board of directors: Capt. S. G. Rogers, W. T. Buckler, Judge J. M. Kenney, Henry Pickrell, and Thomas Pickrell. These gentlemen have purchased the original Dougherty bank building, and have fitted it up in handsome style. They have a splendid new fire and burglar proof safe, built by the Hall's Safe and Lock Company, with a patent time-lock. The financial strength and business qualities of the stockholders will no doubt ensure the Farmers' Bank a sure footing among the sound institutions of a similar character in the State.

It was in the year 1853 that the first newspaper was ever printed and published in Carlisle. This was the *Carlisle Ledger*. Col. Sam. J. Hill, brought an old style hand-press, and a limited outfit for a small county paper here from Maysville. He obtained a subscription of about 350 names, and this with a small advertising patronage, and some job work, enabled him to put the paper under way. Mr. Hill's wife, and a son and daughter, were all type-setters. In his employ there was also a very large, fleshy colored woman, named Jane; or as she was generally called, "Big 6." Hill did the press work and Jane inked the rollers. The *Ledger* was never very "well posted," and hence it is not surprising that it "got out of balance," and at the close of 1854, was found to be plus on the wrong side. In the spring of 1855, the Native American party secured the control of the paper, and changed the name to the *Carlisle American*. The *Ledger* had been neutral in politics, but with a Democratic leaning. The *American* was placed under the editorial charge of the writer of these chapters, and the subscription raised to four hundred. It was published as a campaign paper at one dollar for six months. It was during the memorable year of the rise and fall of the "Know Nothing" party. Hon. Charles A. Moorehead, was elected Governor of Kentucky, and Hon. A. K. Marshall, defeated Hon. Wm. E. Simms, for Congress from the Ashland District. In the county, Dr. G. C. Faris was elected on the same ticket to the Legislature. The decisive battle between the hitherto ubiquitous and victorious Sam and the Democratic party, was fought in Virginia in her gubernatorial election the same year, and resulted in the complete overthrow of the "natives." Hon. Henry A. Wise, the successful candidate, was in the

City of Baltimore on the night when the election returns came in, and was called out by an immense mob of enthusiastic Democrats upon the balcony of Barnum's Hotel. After the prolonged cheers of the people had subsided, he addressed them in the following memorable words: "Fellow citizens, we have met the black knight with his vizor down, and his shield and his lance are in the dust." With the Virginia defeat came the overthrow of "Sam," and the *Carlisle American* shared in the general wreck. It was not long after that Colonel Hill packed his kit and tramped to a more inviting field. In 1860 Messrs. Chappell, Bruce & McIntyre published a monthly paper, called the "*Nicholas Advocate*"; it was printed at the *Gazette* office, Cincinnati; subscription price, 50 cents per annum. The edition was 500 copies, about 300 bona-fide subscribers, the remainder were distributed gratis among the patrons of the firm. During the same year a humorous little sheet was published here by Walter W. Tureman, called the *Rat Terrier*.' This was printed by W. W. Pike in Paris. The motto of the *Terrier* was "Rats, to your holes."

In the year 1867, the present Carlisle *Mercury* was founded, by Dr. Preston Lindsay and W. R. Anno. In 1868, Mr. Anno retired and Dr. Lindsay continued until 1869, when he sold out to Capt. T. F. Hargis and Joseph Norvell. These gentlemen only ran the paper a few months, and turned it over to C. W. Munger. In the year 1870, Mr. John B. Scudder and Calvin W. Darnall purchased the paper, press, fixtures, subscription list and good will, entire. Under this last management the *Mercury* rapidly rose in popular favor, and at once took rank among the most influential county papers in the State. On the morning of the 5th of January, 1873, the *Mercury* office was completely destroyed by fire; nothing was saved but the subscription list. Never was public sympathy more thoroughly aroused. The Kentucky Press Association hastily responded by a liberal contribution. New subscribers by the score came flocking in, offering to pay one and even two years' subscription in advance. In the mean time, Thomas A. Davis, of the Maysville *Republican*, nobly came to the rescue, by placing his office at the disposal of the unfortunates, and at once a half sheet was issued, announcing that only a temporary suspension would occur. In a few days after, a new power press and a complete outfit were purchased in Lexington, and the *Mercury*, Phœnix-like, rose from the ashes to enter upon a new career of prosperity. This continued until the death of John B. Scudder, in 1876. At that time the edition of the paper reached nearly 1400 copies. The death of Mr. Scudder was a sad loss to the paper as well as to the whole community. Mr. Darnall continued the paper until 1878, when he sold out to Prof. T. C. H. Vance and W. J. Kehoe. Prof. Vance continued his connection but a year, and was succeeded by the present owners, the Kehoe Brothers, William J., Henry C. and Thomas, under whose management it still flourishes.

For sixty-four years after its incorporation, the town, or village government was vested in a board of trustees. These trustees were elected annually, and were vested with power to levy a tax, to pave the sidewalks, improve the streets, abate nuisances, control licenses and regulate the markets. In 1870, or about that time, the legislature granted the corporation the right to elect a police judge and town marshal, to whom were confided the preservation of the public peace, the enforcement of fines, also jurisdiction co-equal with the magistrates and constables of the county. In the year 1880 the village form was changed, and a city government established. The city was laid off into three wards—called the east, west, and middle wards, with two councilmen each from the east and west wards, and three from the middle ward. The other officers are mayor, marshal, treasurer, and city attorney. Mr. Chas. W. Munger was the first Mayor elected under the new government. During its history, Carlisle has suffered considerably from fires. In 1832 the large hemp factory and rope-walk of Samuel Smith and Co. was burned; in 1838, the dwelling of D. O. H. Stout; in 1840, the stables and granary attached to Maj. Summers' hotel. On Sunday morning, January 5, 1873, a terrible fire destroyed the large three-story brick building known as Masonic Hall. Southward the fire spread to the alley in the rear. Westward it consumed the row of frame buildings, and was only arrested by pulling down a one story frame, which alone saved the county jail and the residence of Jno. M. Chevis Northward the fire crossed the street, and the entire row of brick buildings extending westward fell a victim to the devouring flames. In this fire no less than fifteen firms were thrown out of business for the time being. Prominent among these were the *Mercury* office, three dry goods stores, one boot and shoe store, one millinery store, a restaurant, etc., etc. On the morning of the 28th of May, a fire broke out in the large three-story frame building owned by Parks, Dorsey & Co., situated upon the railroad, at the corner of South and Second streets. This large structure was completely destroyed, and the fire crossed the street and reduced to ashes a row of three or four other frame houses. Of the firms burned out at this fire the following had been burned out 3d of January previous, making twice burned out inside of five months, to-wit: F. M. Peale & Co., Charles Pendleton, Thomas George and John Brown (colored). Our last great fire occurred on the night of the 14th of March, 1875, It originated in the small one-story frame house, situated on Front street, at the east end, and used as a ten-pin alley. There was a tremendous high wind blowing at the time from the west, and one after another, two livery stables, a tin-ware shop, a carpenter shop, and a blacksmith shop, were swept away in the twinkling of an eye. In fact, the fire was only stayed in its destructive march, because there was nothing more left in its path to feed upon. During the past twelve years the growth of the town has been steady and healthy, and at this writing shows signs of further progress in population and business. The present population of Carlisle, including the suburbs not yet incorporated, is about one thousand three hundred.—*Chappell.*

CHAPTER VIII.

CARLISLE—ITS RELIGIOUS HISTORY—THE PRESBYTERIAN CHURCH; REV. MR. RANKIN ITS FIRST PASTOR—ORGANIZATION OF OTHER CHURCHES—ELDER ROGERS—THE MASONIC FRATERNITY, ETC.

"Blessed are the pure in heart, for they shall see God."—*Matthew V: 8.*

THE Church history of Carlisle forms an interesting part of the history of the town, and we devote considerable space to its notice. The following sketch of the Presbyterian Church was written, at our request, by one who is thoroughly conversant with its history, and should be read with interest by all its members:

It is to be regretted that a great part of the official history of the Presbyterian Church of Carlisle has been lost or mislaid, especially as the volume or volumes of the record of its sessional and congregational proceedings thus not at hand, cover the period embracing the organization of the church and the next twenty-five years of its existence. In the preparation of this article, recourse has been had, in a large measure, to the testimony of living witnesses, and a sort of tradition (the latter, especially, coming from different sources), not always voicing in exact harmony.

The first church of any denomination ever organized in what is now Nicholas County, was organized about 1795–6, at old Concord, two and a half miles southeast of Carlisle. It had upon its rolls a great many as pure men and women, as sincere and devoted Christians as the good Lord ever blessed any community with. Carlisle, as is elsewhere stated in this volume, was laid out and its naked town lots sold in June, 1816. At that time Rev. John Rankin was, or became within a year after, the pastor of the Concord Church, which for several years next before, had been supplied by Rev. John Lyle (familiarly and lovingly called Father Lyle), he being the immediate successor of Mr. Stone. Mr. Rankin was also Pastor, at the same time, of the Somerset Church (now, if not then, in Montgomery County); and as early as 1817 Carlisle became a preaching point, a sort of missionary field, and Mr. Rankin held, if not statedly, as time and opportunity would allow, occasional meetings in the court house, until sometime in the latter part of 1820, or early in 1821, when the Presbyterian Church, of Carlisle (made up mostly of persons bearing letters from Concord), was organized. How appropriate and pleasant it would be to rescue from near oblivion, the names of the founders of the church; those zealous, earnest, godly men and women, the fathers and mothers of the church, whose hands laid the foundations, and who invoked with their warm, glowing-hearted benedictions, the blessings of God upon it. But this is denied us, and as the names of all or any considerable number cannot, with any sort of reliable accuracy, be given, we must content ourself with brief notices of the first office-bearers of the church.

The first Pastor of the church, Rev. John Rankin, was born February 4, 1793, near Dandridge, Tennessee, and united with the church at that place. He received his education at Washington College, Tenn., and was licensed to preach the gospel by Abingdon Presbytery. He was ordained by West Lexington Presbytery, and installed over Concord congregation, his first charge, and was pastor of it four years, ending in 1821; during all of which time he preached at Carlisle, and after its organization, as Pastor of the Carlisle Church. From Carlisle, he removed to Ripley, Ohio, in the fall of 1821, and for forty-four (44) consecutive years, served in his ministerial capacity, the Presbyterian Church at that place. Imme-

J. A. Chappell

ately after this long service, he became pastor or supply to the New Richmond Church, where he remained two years.

He next took charge of the church at Granville, Illinois, where he remained two years, concluding a continuous ministerial relation to the church of fifty-two years duration. That he should have served one congregation, going in and out before them and breaking to them the bread of life for forty-four years, as he did at Ripley, stamps him as a man of positive qualities and characteristics, and is a circumstance, with due recognition of God's overruling providence, authorizing him to feel some degree of pride. He is still living, and had, what must have been to him a great pleasure, the opportunity, the physical and mental power, as well as the faithful inclination, on Sabbaths, the 11th and 18th days of September, 1881, to preach to a Presbyterian congregation at Kingston, Indiana, a congregation which was then, and had been for twenty years, under the pastoral charge of his son, Rev. Arthur R. Rankin, and a church made up in good part of the descendents of those to whom he had preached as pastor sixty years before, in Kentucky. Of the fifty persons enrolled at the organization of the Kingston Church, nearly all of them had letters rom Concord, Carlisle and Somerset churches in Kentucky. He preached those two Sabbaths at Kingston to crowded audiences, and though bordering on the ripe old age of eighty-nine years, with wonderful vigor holding the close attention of all, even the children. He was always a man of strong, outspoken convictions, fearless and zealous, even to what might be regarded as the confines of fanaticism, in the maintenance of them, and in the prosecution of his life work. His attainments were highly scholarly, and he was blessed with strong, natural mental ability.

As to those who constituted the first ruling elders of the Carlisle Church, there is some doubt; all however agree that Samuel M. Waugh, who had served in Conco d church in the same capacity, was one of them; and we can find no one who can suggest who the others were; save that Mr. Rankin's recollection as stated in a letter from his son already mentioned, is that Nathan Nesbitt and Samuel Fulton were also of that bench of elders. Others think that Mr. R. is in this, possibly in error. Be this as it may, these two men were so prominent in their relation to the early church, and so conspicuous in every good word and work, as to have deserved such distinction at the hands of the congregation, and to have their names and memories emblazoned on the page of the history of the church of which they were so early, so consistent, and so valuable members. Nathan Nesbitt survived the organization of the Church but a short time, and being called to the participancy of the joys of the church triumphant, left on earth the sweet odor of a pure and spotless reputation; a heritage to his descendants, richer than worldly goods—a heritage of joy and comfort forever.

Samuel M. Waugh was one of the earliest settlers of Nicholas County; he was a farmer (as were also the other two who have been mentioned in connection with the ruling eldership of the church at its organization), "was a stalwart of the stalwarts," so to speak, in moral and Christian solidity and integrity. He lived to a very advanced age, having filled with conscienciou s fidelity, and with intelligence and acceptance to the people, at least two civil offices. He left quite a number of children and descendents, upon whose minds and hearts he impressed by precept and example, his own rigidly correct characteristics. One of his sons, Archer S. Waugh, was for a long time, and up to his death, a ruling elder in the church of his father, was instant in season and out of season, in all things looking to the welfare of the church and its cause, and the spread of the gospel. His sincere, earnest, and unremitting exertions in the line of Christian duty, and fidelity to the Master were proverbial.

Samuel Fulton, though his early opportunities for storing and disciplining his mind were quite meager, having however a strong native intellect, was at the meridian of his life a man of very considerable intelligence and force of character, and possessed moral and Christian principles of a high order—this is attested by evidences of enduring character. We find, from the civil records of the county, that he represented the people of his district in the Senate of Kentucky one term, and was elected three times by the people to the House of Representatives. We say these things are indications of moral as well as intellectual fitness. Whether the people of this generation are governed in matters of that kind by such considerations, they were in his day and generation, as the records, so far as this county is concerned, almost, if not quite universally, proclaim. A man's advancement to political prominence did not at that day depend upon the amount of money he had, nor the party work he had performed, of either a high or low degree. We have no access to a list of the ministers who have presided in the desk of the church and have ministered at the baptismal font, the marriage altar, the sick bed, and the grave, pointing its membership to the Lamb of God, in whom, and in whose shed blood, is all true happiness in this life, all consolation and solace in sickness, and, at the trying hour of death, the only hope of indescribable, unending joys beyond the grave. It is doubtless a long list. We give the names of such of them as we are sure have been pastor, or supply, to the church since Mr. Rankin's pastorate:

Rev. Solomon G. Ward, dead; Rev. John T. Hendrick, D. D., now of Paducah; Rev. Mr. McConaahay, Rev. W. Y. Allen, still living; Rev. James Matthews, still living; Rev. James P. Hendrick, now of Flemingsburg; Rev. G. M. Hair, now of Pennsylvania; Rev. Mr. Carson, Rev. John Rule, still living; and Rev. Henry M. Scudder, the present pastor of the church, who at the beginning of this year (1882) entered upon the tenth year of his ministerial services with it. We have said that during the early years of the church it held its meetings in the court house. This continued to be the case until 1839, when the Presbyterian and their Baptist brethren of the town and vicinity, jointly built a plain substantial house of worship, which they occupied alternately until 1879, when, the house being no longer fit or safe to use, the Presbyterians bought out the Baptists, and remodeled the old structure, indeed almost replaced it, with a new building of rare taste and beauty, at a total cost of about $7,500. This pleasing consummation is due in large measure to the indefatigable energy and labors of the present pastor, Mr. Scudder, to whom the people of his charge owe a debt of gratitude, not only on this account, but because of his able, efficient and successful labors in every department of the duty which has devolved upon him.

The membership of the church has increased considerably in numbers (numbering now 120) during his connection with it, and the church is in a healthy, vigorous, spiritual condition. Following is a brief extract from the *Carlisle Mercury* of September 2, 1880, giving a description of the new church building, which was dedicated on the 5th day of September, 1880, the pastor being assisted on the occasion by Rev. R. Douglass, of Woodford County, who preached the dedicatory sermon, and by Rev. Dickson, then of Millersburg, but now of Pine Bluff, Arkansas:

"The building has a seating capacity of 340; ceiling, 20 feet high; the windows are Gothic, beautifully filled with various colored glass; the walls and ceiling are finished in the highest architectural style of fresco art; the casings and wainscoting are splendidly grained in walnut; the floor in the three aisles, and the area about the pulpit and door, are covered with scarlet and damask ingrain carpet; the pulpit is after a *recherche* design, richly finished with mahogany veneering; the pews are models of comfort and elegance, while the chandeliers, three in number of six burners each, are crystal, and are as novel, and pretty as anything we have seen in that line. In short, the entire internal arrangements and appointments are highly pleasing to the eye; rich in conception and, at the same time, such as will minister in a high degree to the comfort of an audience.

"The external front view of the building is grand and commanding. The tower (brick) rises to a height of 40 feet, and is surmounted by a spire 76 feet high, making a total height from the ground of 116 feet."

The following sketch of the Baptist Church was written by W. H. Fritts:

The Baptist Church at Carlisle, Ky., was organized February 25th, 1819, with a membership of seventeen. Walter Warder, a name familiar in every Baptist household in this section of the State, was the only minister present, and his signature appears upon the certificate of organization. The articles of faith, rules of decorum, etc., appear in his handwriting, which is a sufficient guaranty of their orthodoxy, could no other be had. He was chosen the first pastor and served the church in that capacity until March 1823, a period of four years, during which time there were forty-five additions.

In April, 1819, Henly Roberts was chosen clerk, which office he held for a period of twenty-five years with an interim of two years. In May of the same year, Henly Roberts and Thomas Champ were chosen and ordained as deacons. In November, 1821, a committee was appointed to select a site for a church building, and in June, 1822, a similar committee was appointed to superintend the erection of the house. The walls were raised a few feet above the ground, but were never completed.

Elder John Smith, afterward a well-known minister in the movement inaugurated by Alexander Campbell, accepted the care of the church in July, 1823, and served it one year. The association met with the church in 1824, at which meeting Walter Warder presided as moderator, and preached the introductory sermon, but no mention of the meeting appears in the records of the church. In 1825, and in 1826 and 1827, John Smith appears again as pastor. In September, 1827, Walter Warder accepted the pastorate a second time. During this year, under his ministrations, the church enjoyed a gracious refreshing from on high, there being twenty additions by baptism in three months, although there appears to have been no protracted effort. William Vaughn accepted the pastorate in February, 1829, and continued for two years. It was in the year 1830, that the strife in the Baptist Churches of Kentucky, engendered by the faction of Alexander Campbell, culminated. Franklin Association had taken decided grounds against the party of Campbell; Elkhorn, in a stormy session at Silas Church, Bourbon County, had taken a similar position; Tate's Creek had withdrawn all fellowship from church and association that favored Campbellism, while the North district had been split in twain, and later in the year the contest came up in our own Bracken. Splits had actually occurred in the Mayslick and Bethel Churches. Millersburg had narrowly escaped, but the church at Carlisle passed the ordeal without trouble, which fact is undoubtedly to be attributed to the influence of her pastor, William Vaughn.

Brother Vaughn was succeeded by James Duvall in 1831. From August, 1832, no business was transacted until February, when Dr. Vaughn again accepted the care of the church, and remained its pastor until June, 1836. Elder John Holladay succeeded Dr. Vaughn in 1836, and continued until the fall of 1840. He was ordained at Millersburg, Ky., in January, 1830, Walter Warder and William Vaughn being present. Perhaps no man ever enjoyed more fully than he the confidence and esteem of all who knew him.

During the pastorate of Brother Holladay, in the year 1846, sixteen members, Henly Roberts being one of them, were dismissed by letter and constituted the church now known as Locust Grove. E. D. Isbell, D. D., of Missouri, served the church most acceptably from 1848 until 1850, during which time valuable additions were made.

The cholera prevailed in 1849, and August 1st was observed by the church as a day of humiliation and prayer. Clark King officiated as pastor from 1851 until 1855. In 1853 the pastor was assisted in a meeting of seventeen days' duration by Dr. W. W. Gardner, which resulted in thirteen additions by baptism and two by letter. Elder John James succeeded Clark King as pastor in 1855, for one year. He was succeeded by J. W. Bullock, in April, 1857, who resigned, the following December, to take charge of Mayslick church. The church remained without a pastor for two years following, but was visited during the time by Rev. C. Keyes, who labored zealously for a number of days, the result of which was the addition of fourteen valuable members.

Having previously been called, Rev. J. W. Brown began his labors with the church in January, 1860, and continued them for a period of ten years. Brother Brown, who recently died in Texas, was highly esteemed by the church, and during his pastorate there were thirty-six additions to the church.

Elder J. Pike Powers succeeded to the care of the church in the fall of 1870, but resigned after a pastorate of less than two years, to take charge of the church at Mt. Sterling, an interest which he had been mainly instrumental in establishing. He was the first resident pastor the church ever had. His ministrations were most acceptable to the congregation, and the church parted with him with much regret.

The venerable Robert Ryland, D. D., succeeded Brother Powers in a short pastorate of less than two years, and he in turn was succeeded by Rev. C. Keyes, in February, 1874. Brother Keyes had endeared himself very much to the church by his earnest and efficient preaching in several protracted meetings. His labors continued about two years, when he resigned, that the church might secure a resident pastor.

Rev. A. N. White, a native of Mississippi and a graduate of Crozier Seminary, succeeded Brother Keyes, and ministered to the church for three years. The pastorate of Brother White forms an era in the history of the church not soon to be forgotten ; for, greatly through his efficient labor, a beautiful house of worship was successfully erected and dedicated to the worship of Almighty God. The church from its organization had worshipped in private houses and in the court house, until the year 1838 or 1839, when they built a house jointly with the Presbyterians. The two churches had sustained amicable relations with each other for long years, worshiping together as one people, yet each sustaining its own organization and ordinances, but latterly little animosities had arisen, and it seemed as though Providence was indicating that the time had come for a dissolution of the partnership. The church, accordingly, in July, 1876, appointed a committee to confer with a similar committee appointed by the Presbyterian Church, with reference to a dissolution by some amicable method. This action resulted in the sale of the Baptist interest for the sum of thirteen hundred dollars. With this sum as a nucleus for a building fund, the church, with a determination that almost astonished themselves, went heartily to work, and, in 1878, erected the beautiful house which they now occupy, one of the handsomest for its size in this section of the State, costing the sum of $5,000. The house was dedicated Sunday, October 26, 1879, Rev. T. C. Stackhouse, of Lexington, Ky., officiating, assisted by Rev. A. N. White, the former pastor. The house was filled to overflowing, and over $600 was raised to assist in paying the debt. It was a joyful day to the Baptists of Carlisle, and many thanksgivings from grateful hearts to the Giver of all good.

Rev. W. G. Riggan, of Virginia, a student of the seminary at Louisville, after having served the church as pastor for a term of fifteen months, in May, 1881, offered his resignation, to take effect in June, for the purpose of accepting a position in the seminary at Louisville. Brother Riggan, during his short pastorate, had greatly endeared himself to the whole church, as well by his genial, Christian conduct, as by his earnest, able and zealous ministrations in the sacred desk. The church, with saddened heart, accepted his resignation, assured that only a sense of duty had been the prompting cause of it.

We are glad to be able to state that the church extended a call to Rev. R. B. Garrett, another of Virginia's favorite sons, and that he accepted and began his labors about the middle of September, 1881. The church has never been numerically strong, the highest number ever attained being that reported last year, seventy-eight. She has, however, manifested a willingness to assist in every good work, always a friend to missions, thoroughly Baptistic in principle and practice.

The Christian Church of Carlisle is of more recent organization. In the year 1790, the house known as the old Concord Church was built. This proved to be the nucleus of the Carlisle Church. In the year 1792, Barton W. Stone was pastor of this church and of the Cambridge Church jointly. When Carlisle was founded in 1816, this was still the nearest meeting-house, nor was there any other until the first Christian Church edifice was built about the year 1830. In the meantime, up to that time the church was known as the Carlisle and Concord Church. After 1830 the church in Carlisle became a separate and distinct organization. The history of the body from that time forward until 1867 was only a part of the history of her first pastor, Rev. John Rogers.

The early fathers of the church were godly men, men of sincere Christian piety. It is indeed doubtful if ever any body of Christians had a more devoted band of followers than the early Christian Church of Carlisle. Among them were such men as Henry Dinsmore, Robert Ardery, William Mathers, Robert McCune, John Byers, Gavin Mathers and Thomas M. Stephenson.

The peculiar tenets of the church, ignoring as they did all human creeds and confessions of faith, and crystallizing in them all the anti-Calvanistic sentiment of the community, were well calculated to take deep hold upon the minds of men who were deeply imbued with the spirit of civil and religious liberty—men with whom any form of dictation, whether in civil or religious matters, would be likely to arouse a sentiment of dissent and opposition. If there were those who sincerely believed in the doctrines of saving grace by faith of election, foreordination, and final preservation, as set forth in their respective creeds and rules of faith, the Christian fathers were equally sincere to reject them all, and, to use their own language, cling to "the Bible, and the Bible alone, as the only rule of faith and practice." Certain it is, they built up a large and influential church, numbering now, and for many years past, more than three hundred members. Much of this prosperity was no doubt due, under God, to the faithful labors of their first pastor. From 1816 to 1830, all denominations preached in the old court house. The Christian Church in Carlisle was the first one to have a house of their own. This, as already stated, was built about 1830. In 1862, or thirty-two years after, the present large and commodious house was built. Rev. John Rogers continued to fill the pulpit until his death, in 1867. Since that time several ministers have served the church, among whom were Elders Willoughby, Briney, Yancey, Stover, Myers, Jones, and, lastly, the present efficient pastor and thorough Christian gentleman, Elder L. H. Reynolds.

The name of Rev. John Rogers deserves to be embalmed in the memory of all who knew him, and is justly entitled to a conspicuous place in the memory of the town. He was born in Clark County, Kentucky, Dec. 6, 1800. He there learned the trade of a cabinet-maker; came to Carlisle in 1819. Though then but nineteen years of age, he became deeply interested in the subject of religion, and as early as 1820 actually began preaching. He was a pupil of the venerable Barton W. Stone, under whose ministrations, we believe, he first embraced religion. He worked at his trade for the first few years, occasionally teaching a school, and nearly every Sabbath preaching at some church or school house. In 1829 he taught a school at the school house which then stood on the Pettus farm near Thomas Kennedy's. He then lived in the brick house Patrick Shay now owns.

After 1830, Mr. Rogers gave up all other pursuits to engage in the active work of the ministry. There has never been scarcely anywhere a man more devoted to his profession or of more untiring energy. It was about 1829–30 that the first old brick church for his congregation was built. The site selected was lot No. 108, which had been bought by David Nicholson, June, 1816, for $86. It was, in 1829, purchased by the trustees of the Christian Church, and the house built by subscription. In this Mr. Rogers continued to preach at least once a month, until the new church was completed in 1862. In the meantime he became an evangelist, and visited all parts of the surrounding country, extending his visits even to sister States.

For forty-seven years, Mr. Rogers sustained the rela-

tion of pastor to the Christian Church in Carlisle. The annals of time furnish but few instances, indeed, of such a relationship continuing so long, continuous and unbroken. It was while attending a protracted meeting at Dover, Mason County, Kentucky, on the 1st of January, 1867, that he preached his last discourse. It was at night; the house was crowded; fired by the theme which filled his whole being, and the evident sympathy of his audience, he made, it is said, the finest effort of his life. The effect was signal and marked. A deep and solemn feeling pervaded the assembly, while numbers came forward with penitential tears, to seek an interest in the atoning sacrifice of Jesus, the "Lamb of God that taketh away the sin of the world." Ah! little did that solemn audience think it was the last time they should ever hear that faithful voice! that no more in life should those kindly hands be stretched over them in heavenly benediction! On the way home to the house of a friend, with whom he was stopping, he took sudden and violent cold; going out of a heated church into the cold night air, he neglected the precaution of his overcoat, and the sudden change brought on an attack of pneumonia. His family were promptly notified, and his daughter, Julia, was immediately dispatched to his bedside. All that devoted affection and neighborly attention, aided by the best medical skill, could do, were unavailing. Calmly and peacefully he died, on the 5th day of January, bequeathing to his family his tenderest blessing, and a name upon which not a single act of reproach or dishonor had ever cast a stain. His death took place at the home of Mr. Bennett, in Dover, with whom he had been stopping during the meeting.

In the meantime, years before, when his son Richard died, he had selected a lot for family burial, in the new cemetery. This the citizens of Carlisle offered him as a free gift, thinking it was no more than due to one who had done so much for the town. But this Mr. Rogers, with characteristic modesty, refused to accept in full, but agreed to accept one-half, he preferring to pay the other half cash. Here, on the 8th day of January, 1867, he was buried; in sight of the town which for nearly half a century had been his home.

The foregoing brief outlines of the life of Rev. John Rogers were published in the *Carlisle Mercury* some three years ago. Since that time we have been furnished with some memoirs of his life, written by himself; these memoirs were written in the years 1855 to '63, and proceed only from his birth to the year 1834. It was no doubt his intention to have brought them down to the close of his life, and have them published by some friendly hand after his death. The writer rejoices, that to him has fallen the honor of giving even this humble token of his regard for his old preceptor and friend. In this autobiography, many interesting facts pertaining to the early history of the town are brought to light, and it is to be regretted that the whole work has not been completed and given to the world. In the year 1819, Mr. Rogers records an interview with John P. Durbin, then a young Methodist divine, upon his first circuit. The two young men were well acquainted; both had served an apprenticeship in the cabinet-making business; Durbin in Paris, and Rogers in Millersburg. Young Durbin in that interview, "spoke in raptures of the great lights of Methodism, especially of Dr. Adam Clarke. He seemed to have him before his mind as a model; he spoke of the great number of languages the learned Doctor had acquired by his own industry, and seemed resolved to imitate his example." It is only necessary to state, that young Durbin afterward became the great and learned Doctor of Divinity, who preached so long and successfully in the Fourth street Methodist Church, in Philadelphia; who afterward traveled through Europe and Asia visited the Holy Land, and upon his return, wrote an interesting book of his travels; and, like his model, Dr. Adam Clarke, many valuable aids to the study of the Bible.

In the year 1824, Mr. Rogers purchased the brick house and lot, No. 139, on South street, being the same as it stands to-day, for which he paid two hundred and fifty dollars.

In 1825 Mr. Rogers visited Missouri, on a preaching tour. He rode horseback 1,700 miles, preached one hundred sermons, and was back home inside of three months. He made successively, trips to Virginia and Ohio, traveling all the time on horseback. During these missionary tours, it is safe to say that he rode on horseback more than eight thousand miles, or one-third the distance around the globe. Such in brief was the life of this earnest, devoted man of God. Who can estimate the amount of good accomplished in that forty years of active, ceaseless, untiring labor? "They that turn many to righteousness shall shine like the stars forever and ever."

Not having access to the record of the Methodist Church, the date of its organization can not be distinctly stated. It was doubtless at an early day, probably as early as 1821. Like all other denominations they preached in the old Court House. No effort was made by that body to build them a house of worship, until the advent of Rev. Geo. W. Brush, about 1844. That gentleman had been installed but a short time, before he set about the work of building. Popular as a minister and man, a genial whole-souled, earnest Christian, all denominations took pleasure in contributing to the fund. In the summer of 1846, the house was completed, and formally dedicated to the worship of Almighty God. The sermon was preached by Bishop Bascom, from the text which contains King Solomon's sublime prayer at the dedication of the Temple. It is needless to say that it was a grand discourse, full of eloquence and power. After the sermon, the pastor made an earnest appeal to his audience for aid to pay off the church debt. It was a successful call, as very nearly enough was raised to liquidate the debt. Among those present and contributing on that occasion, were Ex-Gov. Metcalfe, and Dr. John F. McMillan. Rev. G. W. Brush continued to stay as long as the Bishop would allow him. Since that time the pulpit has been filled by some of the ablest men of the denomination—Trainer, Bruce, Buckner, Shelman, Snively, Chamberlain, Deering, Kelly, and others whose names can not now be recalled. The old Church in 1876—or thirty years after its erection—began to look dingy and dilapidated. And so measures were taken by Pastor Kelly to build a new one. Accordingly the present handsome edifice was completed and dedicated in 1878. Revs. Morris Evans, Newton and Nugent, have served as pastors since that time. The Methodist Church at this time numbers about one hundred and twenty members. This year of grace, 1882, will be made memorable by the denomination, as the year of the first session of the Kentucky Conference with the Church in Carlisle. It was chiefly through the influence of Pastor Deering, and the members of the Carlisle Methodist Church, that the Deering camp ground at Parks Hill, was opened some eight or ten years ago.

From the very start almost of our town history, the principles of Free Masonry struck deep root and found a congenial soil not only in the limits of the town but throughout the county. In 1819 a dispensation was granted to certain of the brethren to open and hold a lodge of Master Masons in Carlisle. The following minutes, taken from the records of the Grand Lodge, have been kindly furnished by Grand Secretary Hiram Bassett.

"August 20th, 1820: Robert M. Elliott took his seat as Representative from Nicholas Lodge No. 65 U. D." In the afternoon of the same day, "the committee to examine the working of Lodge 65 made a further report which was concurred in as follows:

"* * * They have examined the working of Nicholas Lodge U. D. at Carlisle, County of Nicholas and State of Kentucky. They find their work regular, dues paid, dispensation returned, charter prayed and deemed reasonable. They recommend that a charter be issued to them under the name, style and designation of Nicholas Lodge No. 65; and that Brother Robert M. Elliott be the first Master, James Hughes Senior Warden, and James B. Clark Junior Warden."

At the same meeting of the Grand Lodge, Most Worshipful Henry Clay was elected Grand Master and signed the charter. At the same meeting Covington Lodge No. 64 was chartered and their charter was also signed by Grand Master Clay.

To have been honored as one of the few holding charters under so illustrious a signature, has always been the boast of Lodge 65. Upon the return home of Worshipful Master Elliott, the Lodge was called and the officers installed by proxy of the Grand Master. Their first meetings were held in the up-stairs room of the old stone house on Main Cross street. At that time a flight of steps on the outside of the building southwardly afforded access to the lodge room. In those days, too, the "old stone" was looked upon with feelings of mingled awe and dread. Fearful reports of what had been seen and heard up-stairs — the clanking of chains, the fearful noises and rappings, the groans of the tortured, the baleful lights that flashed from the windows—all combined to foster the popular belief that the brethren of the mystic tie held nightly levees with the devil; insomuch that at night little boys hurried by with bated breath, and even in the daytime looked up to the windows with nervous trepidation.

Robert M. Elliott, our first Master, was a farmer, and then lived near the old Baptist Meeting House, on Brushy Fork; he married the widow McIntyre, mother of Mrs. Melville Metcalfe; some years after this, Mr. Elliott moved from Nicholas and settled in some of the eastern counties. James Hughes, our first Senior Warden, bought lot No. 139—the same as afterward owned by Elder John Rogers—at public sale, on the 26th day of January, for forty-six dollars, on three months time. He and his brother William built the stone house (where the Lodge was held) in 1817; they there opened a dry goods store, and continued in business until succeeded by Thomas Porter, Esq., of Flemingsburg, about 1823.

James B. Clarke, our first Junior Warden, was a lawyer of Carlisle in 1820; his mother married Jonathan M. Tanner, Esq., also one of the first lawyers.

The first petition presented for membership in the new Lodge, bore the signatures of John Dougherty, Joel Howard, and R. C. Hall.

About the year 1835 the Lodge suspended its meetings. Through mistake the jewels of the Lodge were carried off to Missouri, by Joseph Clark, a citizen of the town, who had kept a tailor's shop in the old lodge-room. The Grand Lodge suspended the charter, and the old Lodge for a number of years, lay in a dormant state, to be afterward revived to a career of greater prosperity. In 1842 John Dougherty, Joel Howard, R. C. Hall, and other brethren, applied for a rehabilitation from the Grand Lodge, and their old charter name and number were restored by that body.

In the year 1844, while Mr. Dougherty was absent in England and Ireland, the members of Nicholas Lodge held a meeting, and resolved to change the name of the lodge to Dougherty Lodge, in compliment to that gentleman, a distinguished honor which he ever after held in the highest regard.

On the 19th day of October, 1848, Nicholas Chapter Royal Arch Masons was organized, and opened for work by M∴ E∴ Isaac Cunningan, of North Middletown Chapter, proxy of Grand High Priest, assisted by Judge Samuels, of the same Chapter, as Principal Sojourner. The following officers of Nicholas Chapter were duly elected and installed at the first regular election, to wit: John Dougherty, H. P.; Joel Howard, K.; William Norvell, S.; J. F. McMillan, C. H.; Samuel Rogers, P. S.; A. M. Clark, R. A. C.; J. B. Emmons, G. M. 1st V.; R. C. Hall, G. M. 2d V.; John M. Chevis, G. M. 3d V.; F. Munger, Sec.; Willis Sims, Treas. The following three Companions were the first trio exalted to the sublime degrees: Fitch Munger, J. A. Chappell and J. M. Chevis. There are but few Chapters in the State which has exalted as many Companions as Nicholas Chapter No. 41.

It was some time in the year 1853 that a Council of Royal and Select Master Masons was organized in Carlisle under proxies of the Grand Council of Kentucky. A. H. Jameson, T. J. G. M., and L. D. Croninger, C. G., both of Covington Council, under the name of Adoniram Council No. 31. About fifteen petitions for the degrees were presented the first night. The first presiding officer was J. A. Chappell, who had previously taken the degrees in Covington Council. About four years ago the Grand Council of Kentucky by compact with the Grand Chapter, merged the Cryptic degrees into the Chapter, and Adoniram Council, with all her sister Councils, and with all her pleasant memories and associations of the past, sleeps the sleep of eternal oblivion. During the great fire in Carlisle on the 5th of January, 1873, the records of Adoniram Council were destroyed, and what is worse—a loss irreparable—the old Charter of Nicholas Lodge No. 65, signed by Henry Clay, also perished in the roaring flames.

On the 23d of April, 1875, a Commandery of Knights Templar was organized at Masonic Hall by Right Eminent Grand Commander Sir H. T. Bassett, assisted by past Eminent Grand Commander Sir M. H. Smith, Maysville Commandery, with 25 Knights, headed by Hencks' brass band, visited Carlisle upon the occasion and assisted very greatly in the imposing ceremonies. The following were the first officers elected by Carlisle Commandery No. 18: Sir G. T. Gould, E. C.; J. A. Chappell Gen.; J. A. Mathers, C. G.; W. P. Ross, Prel.; T. J. Glenn, S. W.; H. C. Metcalfe, J. W.; W. O. Saunders, Tr.; W. W. Howard, Rec.; James Collier, St. B.; A. C. Brewington, S. W. B.; H. C. Reed, Warder; Lucien Mann, C. G. In April, 1877, the Grand Commandery of Kentucky held its Annual Conclave with Commandery No. 18.—*Chappel*

CHAPTER IX.

CARLISLE—A CHAPTER OF BIOGRAPHIES—GOV. METCALFE—HIS LONG AND USEFUL LIFE.—OTHER BUSINESS MEN AND PIONEERS OF THE TOWN—SOME OF THEIR PECULIARITIES AND ECCENTRICITIES.

"There is a history in all men's lives."

THOMAS M. STEPHENSON is the only one now living in town who lived here prior to 1820—if we except Joseph D. Butler and John McClannahan, the only ones living anywhere, who were citizens then. Thomas M. Stephenson was born June 14, 1797, upon a farm about four miles east of Carlisle; he came here an apprentice to Robert Dykes, on the 18th of December, 1816; he married Elizabeth McCormick, and settled in the lower two-story frame house, now owned by Judge Holladay, where they lived for twenty-three years.

No family probably in Carlisle ever entertained company so liberally and hospitably as this. Mr. Stephenson was, and still is, a prominent member of, and an elder in the Christian or Reform Church, and it used to be said that every Sunday he issued a sort of *carte blanche* to the entire membership to dine with him. His wife and Mrs. John Davidson carried on the first millinery business of Carlisle. In their days the huge leghorn and Dunstable bonnets were in fashion. We have no artist to draw cuts in our midst, or we would embellish this chapter with a picture of one of them; suffice it to say that the crown was about as big as an ordinary water bucket, and the brim was from one foot to twenty inches broad, and stood out from the crown at an angle of about forty-five degrees. The principal business of the milliner was to "do them up;" that is, bleach them and change the shape to suit the caprices of fashion. One of them once bought, lasted for years, sometimes becoming almost an heirloom in the family. General Metcalfe, it is said, once gave his entire wheat crop for one of them, for his sister Sally.

Mrs. Stephenson died December 8, 1855. After the death of his wife, Mr. Stephenson went to Missouri, April, 1858; returned August, 1863; went back to Missouri, September, 1865, staid seven years more, and finally returned to Carlisle, June 22, 1872. There is no one, living or dead, whose name has been so long connected with our town history; he was town trustee in 1822–23–26 and 1834–35, was also a justice of the peace during several years; it is through him, mainly, that we are now indebted for an effort to rescue our history from oblivion.

Nathaniel Perrine Robinson, in 1816, commenced business in Carlisle, building a double log cabin on the corner where Archdeacon's carriage shop now stands, and also sinking the second tan-yard of the town on the same lot. From the very start he carried on an active and profitable business. Combining the making of saddles with his tannery, he found a home market for all the leather he could turn out. But his ambition went further. In 1824 he built the brick block on the S. E. corner of Front and Main Cross streets. Here he opened out with a stock of dry goods, groceries, etc., still maintaining his tannery and saddlery business. He also kept the post office several years in the same building. Not content with this, about 1831 he built a brick cotton factory (the present old photograph gallery), and sent to Paris for James Robinson to superintend it. The power was a tramp wheel of four-horse power, and the goods turned out were cotton yarns and cotton batting. A few years later, however, he conceived the project of building a great steam mill upon the Maysville Pike, which had just been completed, and thus became the founder of the present village of Oakland Mills.

Captain John Harris belongs, indeed, to our first period, having been a citizen prior to 1820. He was one of our very first brick masons, and burnt the brick for a large number of the houses now standing in Carlisle. Captain Harris' wife bore him five children. She died many years since, and he afterward married a widow living near the Blue Licks. He, himself, died at a good old age, and was buried in our town cemetery.

A history of Carlisle would be incomplete without some mention of Uncle Drury Jones. He was never a citizen of the town, but moved here as early as 1806, from Virginia, bringing a wife, one step-daughter and twenty slaves. It was his boast to the day of his death, that he once had, right on the very site of our town, "a tobacco patch." He rented the land from Samuel Kincart, and it is said of Uncle Drury that he never owned a foot of land in Kentucky, notwithstanding his large number of slaves. His wife died soon after he came to Nicholas, and his step-daughter married Simeon Glenn, who lived and died (by his own hand) at his home on McBride's Run, the next house below Dr. Henry Reed's. Uncle Drury kept a horse mill for a long period of years at the old Hamilton place, now Mrs. Parks', on McBride. Some of the old mill house is standing to this day.

General Thomas Metcalfe belongs rather to the county than to the town. But his name is given in chapter VII as a citizen of the town, and although his residence was in the suburbs, he carried on his trade in town and was to all intents and purposes a citizen. General Metcalfe was born in Fauquier County, Virginia, March 20, 1780, and when a child his parents moved to Fayette (now Robertson) County, Kentucky. The father dying soon after left the care of the whole family upon the eldest son, Thomas—a sacred trust promptly accepted and nobly sustained. He attended school a while in Fayette County, and was apprenticed to a stone mason. About 1802 he married Nancy Mason, and in 1809, when war was threatened between England and the United States, he boldly advocated war, and was afterward chosen a captain of infantry and served with much distinction under General Harrison at the siege and battle of Fort Meigs. At the close of the war he removed to Carlisle and built our first brick court house, and labored at his trade more or less for several years. He served four years in the Kentucky Legislature, and in 1819 was elected to Congress, and served by successive re-election till 1828, when he was nominated for Governor against William T. Barry, and elected by a good majority. Prior to this (1820) he had bought a farm, and, with his own hands laid the foundation of the old family mansion, which he called "Forest Retreat." After serving his time out as Governor, he devoted himself to the cultivation of his farm. He owned a large number of

slaves, three of whom were plasterers by trade, and made a good deal of money for the General.

In 1834 General Metcalfe was elected to the State Senate; in 1840 he became President of the Kentucky Board of Internal Improvements. When General Harrison was nominated for the Presidency in 1840, Metcalfe went to Ohio and tendered his services to his old comrade in arms in the mighty political battle (or revolution) then raging throughout the Union. Dressed in the old costume—a gaily fringed hunting shirt and slouch hat—his clarion voice ofttimes rang out in tones of fearful denunciation of Van Buren's administration. It was at one of these immense outpourings of the people (at Chillicothe, we believe), that Metcalfe was presented by the citizens of the town with a beautiful polished steel stone hammer with an ebony handle. This he regarded as the highest honor ever paid him, and during the rest of the campaign always carried it swung at his belt. From this time on he gained the sobriquet of "Old Stone Hammer."

He was the intimate friend and companion of Henry Clay and John J. Crittenden, and these three and Aris Throckmorton, of Louisville, made up many a game of whist at the Blue Lick Springs. In June, 1848, Crittenden having resigned his seat in the United States Senate to run for Governor, to aid in the election of General Taylor, Governor Owsley appointed General Metcalfe to the vacant Senatorship. He was afterward confirmed by the Legislature for the balance of the term, which expired March, 1849. The following letter from the General to Dr. John F. McMillan, then a State Senator from Nicholas and Mason, may not be uninteresting:

"WASHINGTON CITY, January 6, 1849.

"DEAR DOCTOR: I thank you for the telegraphic information received yesterday morning in regard to the election of United States Senator. As soon as I may receive an official account of the matter, and the credentials, I will endeavor to make the proper acknowledgments to my friends.

"The information, as first received, was incorrect, and to me it seemed a puzzle. George Metcalfe, instead of Governor, as I supposed. The vote stood for Metcalfe forty-four, for Howell (not Powell), thirty-eight. Believing in some mistake, I hastened to the telegraph office to ascertain whether it could not be corrected. The conductors of machine took my account which they had sent to me, and promised to have the error corrected, if any there was, in course of an hour or less. I passed on to the Navy Department on some business, and as I returned calling again at the office, they furnished me with the anticipated correction. The vote, as given in this dispatch, was for Metcalfe eighty-eight, for Powell thirty-eight.

"On yesterday we had in the Senate an earnest debate in which I took part, and regret that the whole debate in reference to that atrocious nomination for Minister to Rome can not be published. If not induced from some good reason not at present occurring to me to abandon it, I will make an effort before the adjournment to take off the injunction of secrecy — though I doubt my success."

After his term of office expired, General Metcalfe retired once more to his farm at Forest Retreat. His wife died a year or two first, and on the 18th of August, 1855, the General himself fell a victim to that dreadful scourge, cholera. Upon the highest point of his farm, now owned by T. J. McCormick, just in the edge of the orchard, to-day may be seen the grave of the patriot statesman, the most distinguished of all the citizens of our town, one whom the people both of town and county always delighted to honor!

Eldridge W. Burden, with his brother Robert, came to Carlisle about 1826. Eldridge was a young lawyer then reading in the office of E. F. Chappell, Esq. Bob was a plasterer by trade, and in the year 1828, they were both boarding at Chappell's.

The Burdens were both popular young men; steady, peaceable and attentive to business. In the winter of 1828–9 Eldridge was a member of the first theatrical club which was ever formed in Carlisle. Eldridge held his position as clerk of the Board, until the 5th of June,1832, when he resigned, and Col. Norvell was elected in his stead. It was, perhaps, about 1828 to 1831 that Eldridge and Major William Wall, of Cynthiana, practiced law in Carlisle together as Wall & Burden. Their office was in the one-story frame which then stood where the parlor of the St. Cloud Hotel now stands. In the fall of that year, he and his brother Bob bade farewell to Carlisle, and moved to the State of Missouri, where, we believe, they are living to this day.

Horace Metcalfe, son of Eli F. Metcalfe, and half-nephew of General Thomas Metcalfe, entered the office of General Hughes, at Ellisville, in 1814, as Deputy Clerk. Horace came to Carlisle as our first Deputy County Clerk, and succeeded to the office when General Hughes accepted the post of Indian Agent, under President Monroe. He built the well-known brick residence now owned by Dr. Tilton, about 1822, and here he continued to reside until his untimely death—March, 1829.

Solomon G. Ward came to Carlisle as early as 1820.

He, however, lived upon a farm near town, being the same as now owned by Mr. James Clay. Mr. Ward was first educated for the legal profession, but afterward became a minister. He was at the battle of Bladensburg, Aug. 24, 1814, which preceded the capture of Washington by the British, under Admirals Cockburn and Ross. He was also at Baltimore during the unsuccessful effort to storm Fort McHenry, by the British fleet, during the same year. Mr. Ward was at one time pastor of the Carlisle Presbyterian Church. He was a patrician by birth and education, an old-school gentleman, a deep thinker and a philosopher. For some years prior to his death he was engaged in the preparation of a "Universal History," but after his death his sons, somehow, failed to give the world the benefit of their father's labors.

Captain James P. Ashley who followed the county seat through all its mutations, captain of the night patrol at Bedinger's mill, Blue Licks, and Ellisville, came along with the balance of the town of Ellisville and settled for life. He was born in Culpepper County, Virginia, about the year 1780; came to Kentucky about 1800; stopped for a time at Paris; then went to Mason County and engaged work as a carpenter with a Mr. Robin Clark, at stocking plows. He then built a boat on the Ohio River, loaded it with plows, and in partnership with Matthew Throckmorton, started for the Southern market. Landing at New Orleans, and finding the market extremely dull, they shipped their valuable cargo to San Domingo, the largest well-known Island of the Bahamas, lying about fifty miles to the southeast of Cuba. Throckmorton went with the cargo and died on the Island, a victim of yellow fever. No return was ever made for the cargo, and as there were no steamboats in those days, Ashley and the rest of the crew were compelled to return the long and tedious journey by land. Arriving at home, he went directly to Clark, whom he owed for the plows, and worked for him by the day's work until the whole debt of fifteen hundred dollars was paid! After this he came to the Blue Licks and built several mills for old Major Bedinger.

Captain Ashley was an eccentric character, we might say an oddity. He drove no less than sixteen droves of hogs to Virginia, the last of which severely crippled his finances. Often when he had returned from his trips, if any one asked him if he made money, he would reply, "No; about come out even—but I had a d——d sight of fun." That he was a man of high principle and punctilious sense of honor, let his great plow speculation prove. How many of those who are in these last days squandering the hard-earned money of too-confiding friends, will go to those whom they justly owe and make such full and ample restitution as he did? Captain Ashley lives among the countless dead in the old cemetery. Sleep on, brave heart, and above thy green and grassy grave "may violets spring!"

As already intimated, the mechanics of Carlisle, from 1816 to 1820, were men of decided skill and enterprise. Among this class of citizens none were more highly esteemed than Joseph D. Butler, house carpenter and builder. He was a soldier in the war of 1812, in the Northwest campaign, under General Harrison. He married a Hayden, an own aunt of J. Addison and Lot D. Young. In 1822 he built the house where Henry Stewart now lives. There are many others, also, both in town and county, built under his direction—all giving evidence of a high order of mechanical skill. Mr. Butler visited us about twenty-two years ago, and is probably still living in Macon County, Missouri.

Robert Dykes carried on the first saddler shop in Carlisle, his shop and dwelling being the same as now occupied by Judge Holliday. The shop was in the front room, while the family lived in the L and the upstairs rooms. About 1826, John Dudley, who succeeded Bennet H. Evans, left the hotel (now St. Cloud), and Dykes became his successor, removing there, and, we believe, soon after abandoning the saddlery business altogether. In the days of Evans, Dudley and Dykes, the St. Cloud hotel was a constant scene of gayety, fashion and enjoyment. Balls, hops, *soiree* and social parties, were almost of nightly occurrence.

As early as 1814, Samuel M. Waugh kept a small dry-goods store in the house standing on the public road first referred to, being the same location as now owned by Silas W. Campbell. In 1817 he moved his stock to the one-story frame of two rooms, which once stood adjoining the old stone house (now R. E. Mann's grocery). Here he kept also his magistrate's office, and after Gen. Metcalfe, was the next magistrate which Carlisle had. Samuel M. Waugh was a good man, a good citizen, an Elder in the Presbyterian Church, and a good example to follow in all the walks of life. He raised a family of four daughters and four sons, the descendants of whom are scattered more or less in the West and South.

John Campbell was another one of our prominent first citizens, and carried on the mercantile business as early as 1818. In 1823 he built the brick store room and dwelling recently purchased and remodeled by B. F. Adair. To this Mr. Campbell removed, carrying on business below, and living in the rear and upstairs rooms until his death, about 1830. He was a good merchant, a man of very strict sense of honor, and a public-spirited

citizen. He did not always, however, have the patience of Job, as our modern retail merchants are supposed to have. On one occasion he had been very much worried with an old lady, who bought a set of cups and saucers, and wanted him to "dash in the thread" with them. After a long time parleying, the old lady bought a skillet with the handle broken off, but could not carry it home with her. She, however, kept cautioning him not to sell it. This she repeated so often that the old gentleman's patience became completely exhausted, when he at last replied, "Burn the danger, madam! There is not another woman in Nicholas County would have it, but you."

Having given brief memoirs of a number of our first citizens, our history would be incomplete without some mention of another old time resident. This is William Porter. If we mistake not, he was the first grocery keeper of the town; settled here prior to 1820. About 1826–7 he succeeded Peyton Shumate in the old hotel, the old Kincart house, named in opening chapter. Here he continued some few years, and afterward kept a family grocery on the corner of Front and Main Cross—now Adair & Brewington's. He married a sister of Edmund Martin, a well-known farmer of the county. The Porters raised a family of seven children—five boys and two girls.

Another old citizen of our second period, was James Perry. He was a citizen here from about 1820 to 1828, was a carpenter by trade, and in 1827, helped build the brick store-room first occupied by J. F. Tureman—now City Store; in 1818, built on the lot 59, the two-story frame which H. M. Stitt, in 1874, tried to move, and which fell to pieces in the attempt.

The young folks of Carlisle may be a little credulous, but it is a fact, that in 1820, there were two fine large ponds in town, upon which, in the winter time, when frozen over, all our Carlisle young men and maidens, old men and women, boys and girls, met to skate. One of these stood right where Joseph F. Tureman's fine brick residence now stands, covering the whole of lot No. 60, and parts of 54 and 59, and was called Perry's pond. The other pond stretched across the whole of lots 137 and 138, between Patrick Shay and Samuel Berry. Perry's pond was a very useful sheet of water. In the spring-time all the town ducks congregated upon its bosom, built their nests under Perry's and adjacent houses, laid their eggs therein, which the town boys carried off about as fast as laid. In the winter it became the skating pond, while at all seasons it afforded a convenient place to duck old drunkards found in a state of "how-come-you-so" on the streets after dark. Miss Nancy Perry, a maiden sister of Perry's—an excellent good woman by the way—was the second wife of Henry Chevis, father of John M. Chevis, Esq. Another sister married James Hughes.

About the year, 1821, Doctor James G. Leach, or, as he was more generally called, Parson Leach, together with his son-in-law, Matthew Reed, came to Carlisle, to cast their lots in a community of which they had heard many glowing accounts. Dr. Leach, was at first a Methodist preacher; but his daughter having married a physician, he studied medicine after he came to Carlisle, and in company with his son-in-law, Reed, afterward became a regular practitioner. In 1824 he was elected a member of the Board of Trustees, and was President of the Board till August, 1825. Dr. Leach was a fine specimen of the old school gentleman. Polite as a Frenchman, pompous as an Englishman, he was yet the most genial and generally useful citizen Carlisle ever had. It made no difference who was going to preach, Baptist, Presbyterian, Christian or Methodist, if they failed to be on time, the doctor was always ready to fill their place.

Was a doctor sent for under whip and spur and none to be found? Doctor Leach was always ready to go to the bedside of the sick and the dying, prompt to administer physic for the body or soul. Doctor Leach was very scrupulous in his dress, and always wore the very finest shirts, with linen cambric ruffles both in bosom and cuffs. He always carried a very fine ivory-headed cane, and also a handsome snuff-box filled with the best Rappee or Maccaboy snuff. He was very genial in disposition, and fond of society. When not engaged in his professional labors, he never failed to call around at the various business houses, where his polite manners and fine conversational powers always insured him a ready welcome. For many years the family lived in the old Kincart brick dwelling. About the year 1839 they moved to Jefferson County, nine miles from Louisville, where the Doctor continued to reside until his death, which occurred about fifteen years after his removal.

Edward Franklin Chappell was born in Richmond, Berkshire County, Massachusetts, November 20, 1795. His father's family moved to Pompey, Onondaga County, New York, in January, 1809. Here Frank, as he was called in New York, took a thorough course of study and graduated at the Academy in Pompey. Like great numbers of the young men of the Eastern States, he conceived a great desire to go West in search of a location less hampered by the close competition of the older States. Accordingly, after a short sojourn in Canada, he came to Kentucky, in the fall of 1820. His first stopping point was Millersburg. Here he contemplated practicing law, having already qualified himself for the profession. Being compelled, however, to resort to other pursuits to enable him to purchase books, and to get a start in the world, we next find him in the Letton neighborhood, about six miles from Millersburg, teaching school. At that time Cane Ridge was the greatest point in Kentucky for big meetings. It was here that Stone, Johnson, Smith, and not unfrequently the great Alexander Campbell himself, preached, attracting great crowds not only from Bourbon, but the adjoining counties. It was at one of these meetings that he first met one of those sweet modest, unassuming young maidens whose presence once seen and felt can never be forgotten. This was Mary Holt Oden, then in her twentieth year, the only daughter of Mrs. Sallie Clark, by her first husband, and was at that time living with the family of her stepfather, on the farm now owned by Dr. Henry C. Reed. An acquaintance sprang up—a courtship—and the young Kentucky girl became the affianced of the handsome, spruce young lawyer of Yankee-land. In February, 1882, Chappell settled in Carlisle, and the following fall (7th of November, 1822), Mary H. Oden became his wife. He began the practice of the law at once, receiving a fair share of the business at the Nicholas bar, and occasionally at Owingsville and Flemingsburg. On the 11th of September, 1823, their oldest child, James Augustus Chappell, was born, whose long connection with the history of the town is tolerably well known. The second child, William Oden Chappell, was born December 14, 1825. When the call was made for volunteers in the Mexican War (1846), William promptly volunteered and was a Corporal in Captain James H. Holladay's company. He entered the city of Mexico along with the legions of the victorious Scott, and returned home with the rest of the company in 1847. January, 1849, he was married to his second cousin, Lucy Mary Stewart. When the war broke out between the South and the North he was in St. Joseph, Missouri; there he volunteered and entered the Confederate service. He was promoted to the rank of Major for his personal bravery, and was killed at the taking of Independence, September, 1861. In the meantime two children had been born, the first dying in infancy. The second, little Mollie, and also the deeply afflicted and universally beloved wife, both died at the home of her father, in Carlisle, in the year 1862. Eliza Helen, the third and last child of Mary H. and Edward F. Chappell, was born August 7, 1828. February, 1849, she was married to Thomas G. Taylor, then a young lawyer of Carlisle. They moved at once to the State of Illinois, where they are still living—now at Jacksonville. In 1825 Mr. Chappell was elected member of the Board of Trustees, and was President of the Board during the ensuing year. For a period of years the family were in straightened circumstances, and, to add to their trials and sorrows, a shadow was creeping slowly upon them—a shadow but too surely marking the stealthy approach of the Angel of Death! About 1829 the beloved wife and idolized mother was taken with a hemorrhage of the lungs. A physician was summoned, and remedies applied. She recovered, but from that hour it was apparent she must henceforth battle with that dread disease, consumption. Bravely, calmly and patiently she bore up under all the trials of life.

On the morning of the 9th of March, 1845, the enfranchised spirit, freed from its tenement of clay, was borne by angel bands to the eternal paradise of God.

David R. Atchison was born in Frogtown, Fayette County, on the 11th of August, 1807. He was the son of a wealthy farmer, and educated for the practice of law. It was late in 1827, or early in 1828, that he moved to Carlisle. The old sign board used by him in Carlisle was preserved sound and in good condition as late as 1846; sixteen years after he left here. From Carlisle he removed to Missouri in the month of April, 1830. He was never married. A man of convivial and fine social habits, he became very popular with the early settlers of Missouri. He was elected to the State Legislature in 1834, and again in 1838. In February, 1841, he was appointed Circuit Judge of Platte County. In the fall of that year he was appointed United States Senator by Governor Reynolds to fill the vacancy occasioned by the death of Senator Linn.

Hon. David R. Atchison was once President of the United States for one day. At the time that General Taylor was elected President of the United States, Mr. Atchison was Speaker of the Senate. The 4th of March fell upon Sunday; and as Mr. Polk's term of office expired at noon, March 4, and as March 4 was Sunday, General Taylor was not inaugurated or sworn in until Monday, March 5, at noon. Consequently, Mr. Atchison, who was President of the Senate, was President of the United States for one day. Some of his friends afterwards jocosely asked him how he felt and conducted himself in his exalted position. To which Mr. Atchison good-humoredly replied that he hardly knew, for he had been so worn out with his labors in the Senate, that he "had slept through nearly the whole of his term." He was re-elected for two terms, the last of which expired

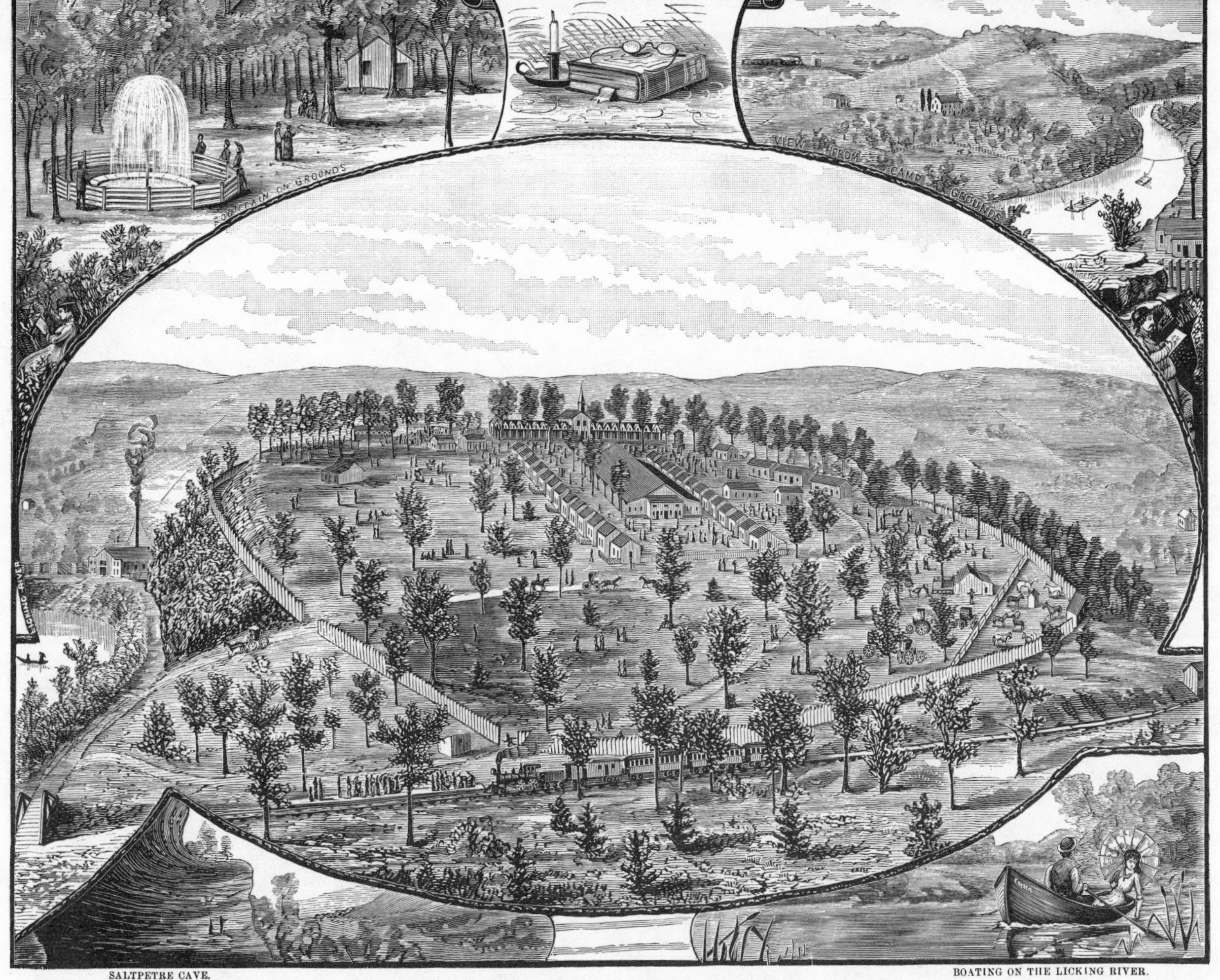

SALTPETRE CAVE.

BOATING ON THE LICKING RIVER.

DEERING CAMP GROUNDS, PARKS' HILL, NICHOLAS CO., KY.

March 4, 1855. He was one of the Senators who drew up the bill to organize the territory of Oregon. He took a prominent part in the repeal of the Missouri Compromise, and actually originated the bill for its repeal. Mr. Atchison, we believe, is still living in Clinton County, Missouri. Those of our citizens still living who remember him, would no doubt be glad to have him visit us again, and see the great improvements made in our midst since he went out from us in 1830.

In 1829 a man from Fayette County by the name of Ooten had a suit in the Circuit Court of Carlisle. His own testimony had been taken, and the opposing counsel in the case, finding the witness' testimony a little hard to get round, had Mr. Atchison summoned to prove something about Ooten's character at home, when the following scene occurred :

COUNSEL—" Mr. Atchison, state, if you please, to the court, what is the character of the witness at home in his own county where he lives ?"

ATCHISON—" Well, sir, that is a pretty hard question to ask one old neighbor about another. "

COUNSEL—"Very likely, Mr. Atchison; but you are lawyer enough to know that it is sometimes necessary to perform even an unpleasant task."

ATCHISON—" Certainly, sir, but then you see that in this case you ought to, and I hope you will excuse me."

COUNSEL—" We can not excuse you, Mr. Atchison ; you will therefore tell the court what you know about the character, be it good or bad, of the witness, Ooten."

ATCHISON—"Oh, no, sir; indeed, I can not think of such a thing, and again I ask the court to excuse me. "

JUDGE—"Mr. Atchison, you have been called by counsel to testify in the case, and the court decides that you must do so. "

ATCHISON—"Very well, Judge, just as you say. Well, sir (to counsel) all that I know about the witness is that he—is a d——d old rascal !"

In conclusion we would say that Mr. Atchison, like all other public men, has had a goodly number of babies named for him in Missouri. Atchison, Kansas, one of the largest and most flourishing cities of that State, was named for him; and also Atchison County, in the State of Missouri.

Among the business men of Carlisle, none have ever occupied a more honorable position than Joseph F. Tureman. He was born in Franklin County, Kentucky, about two and one-half miles from Frankfort, July 7, 1798. The following year his father, William Tureman, moved to Washington, then a flourishing town, and the county seat of Mason County, and opened a hotel. Not long after he commenced merchandising, and, at an early age, his son Joseph entered the store as clerk. In 1813, the family moved to Maysville, and continued merchandising. In 1819, Joseph F. became a partner, but, prior to this (1817), he made his first trip to Philadelphia, being then in his nineteenth year, and still a clerk. Arriving at Baltimore, he embarked on board a steamer, crossed the Chesapeake Bay and landed at Frenchtown, in the State of Delaware. From thence he took stage again, traversing the whole width of that great State to Newcastle, upon the Delaware river—the vast distance of sixteen miles ! Again embarking upon a steamer, he was safely landed at Philadelphia, having been absent from home about twenty-one days. Buying his stock, it was loaded upon wagons and transported by land over the Alleghany Mountains to Pittsburg, a distance of nearly 400 miles. The rates paid at that time were from eight dollars and fifty cents to nine dollars per hundred, and the time required was twenty-five days. At Pittsburg the goods were transferred to keel boats. If a good stage of water, ten or twelve days' time was required to Maysville ; if the water was low, from fifteen to twenty-five days, and the rate per hundred, from seventy-five cents to one dollar and fifty cents. The time required to go East, buy goods and get them home, therefore, was about two months.

In 1822, he opened a separate business house in his own name. In March, 1825, hearing many favorable reports of the then thriving capital of Nicholas, he concluded to pay us a visit, and with a view to a removal here if he liked the prospect. He came, and was so well pleased that he rented a house at once, returned home, and began his preparation to move. On the 18th of April, 1825, two wagons, laden with the furniture, goods, etc., arrived in front of the brick house on the southeast corner of Second and Front streets—now the Kimbrough House. Here Mr. Tureman took possession, at a rental of sixty dollars per annum, for the whole building—dwelling, store room and all.

For three years Mr. Tureman continued to occupy the premises named, but, in 1828—having bought the brick store room partly built by John Rice—he finished and moved into it the same year. This became afterward known as " Tureman's corner." During this year he also commenced building his present commodious and handsome private residence. The lot is No. 60, on the town plat, and although it was then called " Perry's pond," it is undoubtedly the finest location in Carlisle.

Having referred incidentally to Dr. J. N. Menifee in the last chapter, it will not be amiss to give a more extended reminiscence of the Menifee family. Dr. Menifee first moved into the house situated next adjoining the one in which Mrs. Hughes, and her daughter, Jane Stokes, then lived. The doctor hung out his shingle in Carlisle as a disciple of the Thompsonian School of Medicine. Hahnemann invented, as is well known, the Homeopathic system, or as he termed it, "the *law* of cure." This principle he set forth under the Latin motto of "*Similia similibus curantur*"—like cures like. Dr. Thompson's system, on the contrary, set forth the principle that disease, having its seat in the internal or vital parts of the human system, all you had to do was to coax it out through the pores of the skin. This was, at least, the system as expounded by Dr. Menifee. And hence, whenever called to the bedside of a patient, the first thing was to begin on him or her with a line of hot teas. We say *line*, because no general ever drew a line of circumvallation against an enemy's fortifications with more rigid purpose or unswerving precision than did the doctor with his "bitter yarb" decoctions and steaming family fomentations. In order to do this, it was necessary to press into the service all the available crockery of which might be seized or possessed, so that a stranger on entering the room would hardly know whether a man was sick or having his china wedding. Although a good many smiled at the doctor's sweating mania, and others openly ridiculed it, he met with a good degree of success, and obtained a fair show of the public patronage. About the year 1820, he purchased what is undoubtedly the most eligible and desirable location for a residence in Carlisle. This was the property now owned by W. T. Henry, Esq., and which for many years was known as "Menifee's Hill." Here the doctor built a good, old-style brick residence and a small brick medical office, about 100 feet east and north of the dwelling.

Mrs. Menifee was a fine scholar, of an ardent poetic temperament, very aristocratic in her tastes and proud of her lineage. She was probably a descendant of the French Huguenots, and pretty well versed in the French language. As an evidence of Mrs. Menifee's partiality for the land of the Huguenots, she called her first-born child and son Grosjean, equivalent to "Big John" in our English. He was born in Carlisle, on the 28th of March, 1822. Gushon—as he was called here—left home when he was quite young; he was of rather an indolent, roving disposition, often staying away several years at a time. He died of cholera in the year 1849, being then but twenty-seven years of age. When the lobelia mania broke out, a good many years ago, Dr. Menifee became a warm advocate and believer in the virtues of that powerful drug. It was thought in those days that all you had to do to cure any one of any illness, was just to puke him heavily with lobelia. On one occasion Dr. Meniffee was called in to see Esq. T. M. Stephenson. The patient informed the doctor that he was hard to move with an emetic, no matter how powerful might be the medicine. Taking him at his word, the doctor gave him a whopping big drink of lobelia tea, which took such awful and tremendous hold upon the 'Squire's stomach that he nearly puked himself to death.

The doctor owned a farm about three miles northeast of town, which, together with the home tract of fifty acres, kept his time pretty well employed. He was a great admirer of fine stock, and was the first citizen of Carlisle who had a race track for the training of fast horses. At the first and only fair of the Nicholas County Agricultural Association, he took the first premium on an old flea-bitten grey mare, and also one on a fine merino buck. He, by his industry and energy, had secured a comfortable independence for his declining years, and need no longer detract from his enjoyment by any concern for future wants. He was very fond of flowers, and always kept a large pit well filled with the choicest selections from the floral kingdom. He had also a fine orchard, and always kept a good stock of fresh cider to offer his friends and visitors. He died at his home on the 13th of September, 1866, in his seventy-ninth year, and was buried in the new cemetery.

John Dougherty, in 1811, came to the United States, from Ireland. The ship was outward bound about forty days, during which time young Dougherty became proficient as a sailor, and acquired quite a taste for nautical life. Landing at Baltimore he journeyed through Philadelphia, Trenton, and other New Jersey towns to Newark, then a thriving manufacturing city on the Passaic river, nine miles from the city of New York. Here he joined his father, James Dougherty, Sr., who had emigrated to America several years before, leaving the motherless boy in charge of a good Presbyterian family by the name of Blair. Mr. Dougherty, Sr., being a hatter, his son was taken in the shop to learn the trade. In the same shop there was a young Jerseyman by the name of Thomas Hadden, between whom and young Dougherty there sprang up a friendship which lasted as long as life. Applying themselves assiduously to their trade, they soon acquired a thorough knowledge of the business, and both becoming of age in 1817, they determined to seek their fortune in the far West. Together they journeyed, and hearing many rumors of the wonderful fertility of the soil and healthiness of the climate of Kentucky—the "dark and bloody ground," around which the adventures of Boone, Kenton, and other daring backwoodsmen had thrown a glamour of romance highly captivating to young men in search of fame and fortune—hither they bent their way. Landing at Maysville, the travelers were recommended to Flemingsburg. Here (in 1817) Dougherty obtained employment, but Hadden went on to Lexington. Dougherty worked at the trade in Flemingsburg awhile; in 1819, came to Carlisle, and being well pleased with the prospect, he at once opened a shop on his own account.

In the meantime (in 1819), Thomas Hadden had been recalled from Lexington, and a partnership between the two friends was formed, under the name of Dougherty & Hadden. Mr. Dougherty at once became an active business man, and took a prominent part in all that concerned the welfare of his adopted home. On Monday, the 2d day of August, 1824, he was first elected a member of the Board of Trustees. At intervals, subsequently, he was elected trustee fully ten different years. In 1823, he began trading up and down the Licking and Ohio rivers, always buying a small trading boat for the purpose, and, finally, selling boat and cargo. One great object in this was to find a market for the surplus hats. Hadden was one of those quiet, unobtrusive men who kept steadily at his occupation, rarely raising his head from the vat to speak, unless spoken to. As the "boss" was equally industrious, and they always employed several journeymen, it may be readily inferred that more hats were made than could be sold at home. It was the business of the "boss" to distribute the surplus stock. In the time we are writing of, a large trade was carried on by flat-boats down the Licking; cargoes of tan-bark, flour, bacon and miscellaneous products, were shipped from all points as far up as West Liberty, but Parks' Ferry was one of the chief points. The large flouring mill of 'Squire James Parks, Sr., on Cassidy (near the mouth), still partly standing, furnished an immense amount of flour for shipment.

In 1826, Mr. Dougherty shipped a load of flour, hats, etc., from Parks Ferry, via the Licking, Ohio and Mississippi rivers, to New Orleans. At Cincinnati they took on a few barrels of whisky, and some bacon. Arriving at New Orleans, and selling boat and cargo, the boss took passage on a schooner bound for New York, touching at Havana, and other points. This voyage he enjoyed greatly, as it revived all his boyish recollections of a "life on the ocean wave." Landing at New York, he visited his old home at Newark, and returned to Carlisle to enter upon his labor with renewed zest. In 1833, Thomas Hadden, the friend of nearly twenty years fell a victim to the dreadful scourge, Asiatic cholera, and was buried in the old cemetery. A partnership was formed between Aaron Smedley and John Dougherty as Smedley & Dougherty, in the general dry goods business, and continued until 1838. Mr. Dougherty was next in business alone until after the dissolution of the firm of Edwards and Berry in 1840, when Mr. Dougherty and Mr. Edwards were associated together a short time. A nephew of Mr. Hadden, whom he kept as a salesman in his store for a long period of years, was our well-known citizen of late years, Isaac Hadden Howell. Though Mr. Dougherty had become thoroughly Americanized, yet, toward his own green native isle, his thoughts would often turn. Accordingly, in April, 1843, he made his will, bade good-bye to Aunt "Becky" (his wife) and in company with William McDonald, a Scotchman by birth, and a shoemaker by trade, he set out on the long-proposed journey. Dougherty and McDonald landed first at Liverpool; from thence they went to London; after which they each visited the home of their childhood, and after an absence of three months returned safely home again. During Mr. Dougherty's absence, "Nicholas" Lodge, No. 65, Free and Accepted Masons, did him the honor to change its name to "Dougherty" Lodge. This was a graceful compliment done in a graceful manner, and one highly appreciated by him. In 1849, he conceived the idea of building a banking house for himself, and also a store room on the first floor, a couple of offices in the second story, and a Masonic hall in the third story. This design was carried out, and the building completed in 1850. Building a heavy brick and stone vault in the east room, he opened out the first "Deposit Bank" of Carlisle.

We have now followed the young Irish boy down the stream of time to the last act in the drama of life. In the year 1860, he was attacked with calculus and a complication of the urinary organs, and died on the 5th day of August. He was buried by the Masonic fraternity in the new cemetery on the 7th. His funeral was one of the largest and most imposing ever witnessed in Carlisle, there being two bands of music and nearly 200 Royal Arch and Master Masons in the line. After his death his widow had the remains of Thomas Hadden taken up from the old cemetery and placed side by side with her husband. A plain marble obelisk, with the Masonic emblems in relief, marks the last resting place of the two friends. Upon the western face of the obelisk is the following inscription:

> "Here, side by side, repose the remains
> of two who in life were friends, partners in
> business and companions in social life.
> In death they are not divided."

In March, 1823, Thomas Porter came to Carlisle with a stock of goods from Flemingsburg. He had, in 1820, married Lucy Bruce, second daughter of Henry Bruce, Sr., of Fleming County; opened a store in the old stone house now owned by Mr. Pickrell. The family began housekeeping in the frame (two-story) where Musgrove's school was afterward taught. Mr. George S. Bruce, his brother-in-law, a young man, then in his twentieth year, came along with them, and entered the store as clerk. Mr. Bruce remained only about four months. The firm, as first organized here, was Porter & Johnson —Thomas Porter and Elijah Johnson, of Fleming County. About 1827, Mr. Porter bought out the interest of his partner, and continued in his own name. He left Carlisle about 1828, and returned to Flemingsburg, where he continued business for several years longer; then removed to Covington, where, in 1874, he died.

John B. McIlvaine came to Carlisle in 1824, with a stock of goods, remained only a short time, and moved his store to Paris. On the 23d day of June, 1825, he was married to Miss Charlotte Vimont, daughter of Louis Vimont, Sr., of Millersburg. In March, 1822, Mr. McIlvaine came back to Carlisle, along with Samuel Smith, another gentleman who will cut some figure in our history. In 1828, the firm of McIlvaine & Smith built an extensive hemp, bagging and bale rope factory. The bagging factory occupied two-thirds of the whole square, bounded by Sycamore, South, Water and Second Cross streets. The spinning walk took up the whole length of the lot; the weaving was done in the second story, on the corner of South street, the hackling and quilling next east of that, and the brick magazine east of that again, where James George now lives. The large rope or cordage was spun in a shed extending the whole square on Water street, from Main Cross to Second Cross. The hands were boarded in a large two-story frame, within the inclosure between South and Water. The warehouse for the storage and sale of the manufactured goods was the old stone house now belonging to Mr. H. Pickrell. Mr. Smith lived where John McKee, Esq., now lives, and Mr. McIlvaine where 'Squire J. M. Chevis owns. In 1832, Mr. McIlvaine moved to Maysville, where for twenty years he was identified with the wholesale grocery and commission business of that city. On the first day of November, 1852, he left Maysville with his family, and settled finally in the city of Louisville. For a number of years he has been engaged in the wholesale liquor business, and although suffering heavily by loss from fire in 1875, he is still in business, at No. 13 Second street.

Colonel William Norvell came to Carlisle as early as 1826. He was born in Garrard County, Ky., in November, 1803. He was educated for the bar, read law in Lexington, and began practicing immediately on his coming to Carlisle. He was then (1829) about twenty-four years of age, polished and polite in his manners, well read in the current literature of the day, with a thorough knowledge of the usages of polite society; he took high rank at once as a leader in the *beau monde*. He introduced into our social hops (which were almost of weekly occurrence) all the new and popular dances. Himself an adept in the pleasing art, he instructed and prompted in all the difficult parts, until there was not a town in Kentucky more noted for the skill and grace of her dancers. Let it be borne in mind that in those days dancing was considered at once a refinement and accomplishment. The courtly bearing and dignity of the gentlemen, the grace and refinement of the ladies, lent a charm to the scene extremely fascinating. Through the misty glass of fifty years we look back to those brilliant *soirees* at the old hotel (now the St. Cloud) in the days of Bennet Evans, John Dudley and Robert Dykes, and glancing our eyes down the flight of years, we mark in contrast, the maudlin routs and bacchanalian revelries of the present day; the absence of all refinement, gallantry and dignity; the utter want of respect for female character; and, above all, when we see that one-half of our young men attend with a pistol in one pocket and a pint bottle in the other, is it a wonder that the glory of the dance has departed and her evil genius, like Poe's Raven, sits above her chamber doors croaking, "Nevermore!"

In 1835, Colonel Norvell was elected to the Legislature from Nicholas. He was often afterward solicited to run for office by his party, but he steadily declined, preferring to continue in the private walks of life, in the practice of his profession. In politics, Colonel Norvell was an unflinching Democrat. Taking sides with the Jackson party in 1824—when Clay cast his vote in the House for John Quincy Adams—the Colonel followed Old Hickory through all his successive triumphs, and never cast any other than a Democratic vote in his life.

Among the leading mechanics of Carlisle from 1830 to '37, was Joseph Clark. He was a tailor, and kept his shop upstairs in the old stone house, at present occupied by our young townsman, Thomas Pickrell and wife. His dwelling was a two-story frame, and stood right on Main street, just in front of where Mrs. Pickett Taylor now resides. Mr. Clark was, we believe, originally from Clark County. About the year 1836, he moved from

Carlisle and went to Missouri, where some of the family are still living to this day. Mr. Clark had a journeyman who lived with him a long time named Azariah Conyers. Mr. Conyers was very lame, one leg being much shorter than the other. He was a first-class journeyman, and worked at his trade as steady as a clock.

Jesse E. Peyton was, we believe, born in this county about the year 1818. His father lived at the old farm at Forest Retreat, where Jas. McIlvaine now lives. Years after, when his father died, the remains were buried upon the hill back of the house, and his son Jesse had the grave inclosed by a paling, which can be seen to this day.

When Joseph Clark moved to Missouri, Mr. Peyton went to Flat Rock, and in 1840–41 was employed in the store of Garrett, Rogers & Co. In 1842, or thereabouts, Mr. Thomas J. Garrett sent him to the city of Philadelphia to obtain a situation in a mercantile house. Mr. Peyton attached himself to the wholesale dry goods house of Wolf & Boswell, on Market street, between Second and Third. Within the next two years, however, the partners disagreeing in business, the firm was dissolved, and Mr. Boswell opened a new house, under the firm name of James J. Boswell & Co., while Mr. Wolf, associating Mr. Peyton with him, continued the old house as Wolf & Peyton.

James Pettus was born near Paris and raised near Carlisle. His father was a farmer, and lived on the place now owned by Thomas Kennedy, Esq. He learned the tailor's trade, as before stated, with Joseph Clark; and worked there at the same time with Jesse Peyton. He was afterward, in 1840, a partner in the business here with 'Squire John McKee. About 1841 he went to St. Louis, Mo., where he entered as a "jour" in a fashionable merchant tailoring house. Mr. Pettus rose rapidly to distinction in his profession, and made money. Becoming ambitious of a wider field of usefulness, he removed to the city of New York about twenty years ago. He opened a house upon the great thoroughfare of the city, Broadway. His first shop was, we believe, not far from City Hall Park. As his trade moved up town, so did he. His next place of business was corner of Spring street and Broadway. At present he is located still further up town, under the St. Denis Hotel, on Broadway, corner of Eleventh street.

Among the many distinguished men who have figured in our early history, none deserve a higher honor than Colonel John Sanderson Morgan. His father, Jared Morgan, was a native of Virginia, and his mother, Sarah Sanderson, of South Carolina. They emigrated to Kentucky about 1797, and settled in Nicholas, then Bourbon County, near the Blue Lick Springs, where he was born January 6, 1799. In 1812, his father died, leaving him, with his mother and a large family, upon a small and poor farm. Upon this he struggled heroically, laboring both late and early to secure an education for himself, and to aid in the support of the family. In this respect, his history corresponds precisely with that of General Thomas Metcalfe. In 1824, he was elected to the Legislature from Nicholas by the suffrages of the "old Court" party. Soon after this, he came to Carlisle and opened a dry-goods store in partnership with William C. Rainey. In May, 1828, he was married to Eleanor Bruce, of Fleming County. The newly married couple began housekeeping where Henry Stewart now lives, and the store of Morgan & Rainey was held in the frame house on Front street, now Sammons & Brother. Mr. Rainey retiring soon after 1828, Mr. Morgan went on in business with James Squires. Not long after, Mr. Squires retired, and was succeeded by Robert P. Hughes. Colonel Morgan was elected a member of the Board of Trustees four years successively, to-wit: August, 1829, 1830, 1831 and 1832. In 1833, he was elected for the second time to the Kentucky Legislature. In March, 1834, having bought out Thomas Jones, he moved to the country, sold out all his interest in town property, and devoted his whole time to the cultivation of the farm. As a farmer, he was eminently successful, and from his annual earnings continued to add to his landed estate, until he owned near twelve hundred acres, extending on both sides of the road from the town suburbs to Old Concord. In 1838 and 1844, Colonel Morgan was elected a member of the Kentucky Senate from Nicholas and Bourbon—the last time, over Mr. Jacob Hutzell, of Bourbon, after a heated contest upon the subject of relief, or anti-relief. In the great National contests of 1840 and '44, Colonel Morgan took an active part as a stump-speaker. He was, indeed, for years the leader of the Whig party in Nicholas. His plain, straightforward style of presenting facts, his evident sincerity and well-known integrity of purpose, always insured him a warm reception at all public meetings.

In October, 1847, he packed up and took leave of Carlisle for his new home in Covington. He bought a handsome piece of property in the suburbs of the city, and of this he at once took possession. It was about the year 1849, that the building of both the Kentucky Central and the Maysville and Lexington Railroads was projected. Colonel Morgan showed his public spirit by subscribing liberally to both. He gave the Maysville road the right-of-way through his farm, and also a subscription of two thousand dollars. In 1850, he was elected President of the Covington and Lexington road. To the completion of this great work he now bent his whole time and energies, not forgetting often to likewise send words of cheer to the Directors of the Maysville road.

In 1852, Colonel Morgan was appointed Presidential Elector for the Tenth District by the Whig party of Kentucky, in the great Presidential struggle between General Winfield Scott, and General Franklin Pierce.

Another good citizen of Carlisle, whose name deserves special mention, was Doctor Oliver Hazard Perry Stout. This gentleman, then a student of medicine, came here from Flemingsburg, in the fall of 1828. He was born in Mercer County, near Harrodsburg, about the year 1802. At what time he went to Flemingsburg is not now remembered. Coming to Carlisle he bought out Dr. John R. Ward, who then owned the property opposite where Judge Ross now lives, and where Musgrove kept school. Dr. Stout boarded with Ward with a view to become introduced into Ward's practice, of which Stout was to become the successor. Some time after moving here, Dr. Stout bought the large two-story frame property situated on the corner of North street and Second Cross, being lot No. 82, and the same now owned by Mrs. Mary C. Chappell. About 1840 he moved from Carlisle to Moorefield, remaining there a short time only. He next located at Sherburne, in Fleming County. Nor did he long stay there, but removed to Thorntown, then a rising village in the neighboring State of Indiana.

At the sale of town lots held in June, 1816, John Hughes bought lot No. 33, paying for it $180.00. Here the brothers, John and Jesse, built a two-story log house—the lot being the same so long afterward owned by Judge Norvell, at present by A. McDaniel, jr. Here they kept hotel for two or three years. About 1820 they dissolved and moved to the country, and so for a time were lost sight of in the town history. About the year 1831 he returned and succeeded Jerry O'Rear in the hotel (now Kimbrough House). This he continued to keep for five or six years. It was probably about 1840, when the whole family moved to Missouri. A favorite expression of Mr. Hughes was "By gracious !" and by this name a good many of our townsmen once well knew him. He and his wife have both been dead several years.

Jesse Hughes was partner in the hotel, as before stated, in 1817 to '20, with his brother Jack. He afterwards lived in the country at different places—for a number of years at the Robinson farm, now owned by the heirs of Fitch Munger. He kept the St. Cloud Hotel a short time, also. He afterwards lived where Mr. Congleton now lives. After this he moved to Lewis County, staid there awhile, then returned and bought the John Tarr (now Scobee) farm. Here he lived two or three years, then sold the farm and moved to town, bought the Ashley House, and there died in 1858.

In the year 1790 James Parks, Sr., emigrated to Kentucky from the old town of Huntingdon, county of the same name, in Pennsylvania. His family then consisted of his wife and their first-born, John Galbreath Parks, then about two years old, and born in Huntingdon. The family settled first near Steele's Ford, on Hinkston, and the church known as Brick Temple, in Bourbon County. Here they remained a short time, when a purchase was made of the farm nearly north of Carlisle, now owned by Rev. John Neal. This place, a few years later, was traded for the farm at Parks' Ferry, now owned by Thompson S. Parks. It was after Mr. Parks, Sr., removed to this farm, that the first regular ferry-boat was established at that point on Licking river—hence the name, "Parks' Ferry." Here a family of fourteen children was raised to manhood and womanhood. In consequence of the extensive enterprises undertaken by his father—such as the building and running of flour-mills and saw-mills, and transporting by flat boats to New Orleans, flour, bacon, and other products,—young John had but little leisure, even if opportunity had offered, to attend school. When he was about grown, and before the town of Carlisle was laid off, whilst hauling timbers from the hill overlooking Fleming creek, near its mouth on the west, to a site for a projected mill, with a yoke of oxen, he received a serious injury, which so impaired his physical organization as to incapacitate him for manual labor. Representing his father, as soon as he recovered, about the time Carlisle was laid off, he came here and had erected the stone house (now occupied by R. E. Mann, who married his grand-niece), and opened a stock of goods. He continued merchandising till the death of his brother-in-law, Horace Metcalfe, in 1829, who was then clerk of the Nicholas County Court. Mr. Parks was appointed to fill the vacancy, and continued to hold the office to the entire satisfaction of the people till 1854. At the time of his appointment to the clerkship (1829), he was an acting Justice of the Peace, having been commissioned by Governor Adair in 1823. Although 'Squire Parks had no early advantages from schools, he was nevertheless well educated—he educated himself. In 1850, the first election for county offices by the people, under the new Constitution was had. 'Squire Parks had now held the office by appointment for twenty-one years. It was natural, therefore, that he should desire the first term as an indorsement of his official acts. This was accorded him by a decisive majority. It has been the good fortune of the people of Nicholas to have always had in the office a faithful and efficient clerk. During 'Squire Parks' long administration of the office he was more like a father to the people. All came to him for counsel and advice, and we doubt not many a lawsuit has been avoided by heeding his sound and wholesome advice. About 1856 he had the misfortune to be kicked by a young horse, while out on his farm two miles from town, fracturing the femur or thigh bone. This laid him up a cripple for a long time ; in fact, he never fully recovered from the accident. In social life he neither sought nor avoided company, but when approached, no one was more kind, gentle or affable. In dress he was rather eccentric, caring more for comfort than fashion. His hair was always worn long, falling down to his shoulders. In his latter years, when he turned gray, his long hair gave him a venerable and patriarchal appearance. No love sentiment perhaps ever disturbed his soul—he lived and died a bachelor. He died on the 30th day of May, 1862, in the seventy-fourth year of his age.

Eli F. Metcalfe, was born in Fleming County in 1810. In 1826, being then in his sixteenth year, he came to Carlisle, and entered the County Clerk's office with his brother, Horace Metcalfe. He remained there until the death of his brother, in 1829. He then entered the dry goods store of N. P. Robinson. How long he lived with Mr. Robinson before he conceived the project of stealing one of his employer's daughters we do not know, but on the 28th of January, 1834, he was married to Ann E., second daughter of Mr. Robinson. In the spring of 1835, upon the completion of the Maysville and Lexington turnpike, he left Carlisle and moved to Oakland Mills. In August of the same year he sold the mill property and removed with Mr. Robinson's family to Maysville. Here he opened a wholesale and retail grocery under the firm name of E. F. Metcalfe & Co. Shortly afterward, the firm was changed to Ranson & Metcalfe ; and still later, from Ranson & Metcalfe to Artus & Metcalfe. On the 28th of May, 1845, Mr. Metcalfe, having lost his first wife some time previous by death, was married to Miss H. E. Artus, of Maysville, daughter of his partner. In the year 1849, John Preston Campbell, of this county, together with Mr. Metcalfe and his former partner, Mr. Ranson, opened a wholesale grocery and commission house in Cincinnati, as Campbell, Metcalfe & Co. The firm did a large business, but, becoming involved by heavy advances to a large distillery in Higginsport, Ohio, the business was abandoned, and Mr. Metcalfe returned to Maysville, and resumed business with Mr. Simeon Drake, a wealthy farmer of Mason County, under the firm name of Metcalfe & Drake. Upon the reopening of the Southern ports, in 1865, to the commerce of the world, he was sent to Savannah, Georgia, by Eli M. Bruce to open a large cotton warehouse. After the death of Mr. Bruce, Mr. Metcalfe removed once more and finally to Maysville, in 1869, where he will probably spend the rest of his days.

Archibald Summers was born in the year 1777. In 1800, he was married to Margaret Payne. The family came to Carlisle in 1829, and for about four years lived on the premises, on the south side of Front street, just below Elm. In the fall of 1833, Mr. Summers became the owner of the old hotel, having bought out and succeeded Robert Dykes. He was also town magistrate for several years. He was a very popular citizen, a man with a well stored mind, very fond of reading, especially poetry and history. His two favorite books were Ossian's poems and Dante's Inferno. About 1850, Mr. Summers sold the hotel to Robert Carter, Esq., and finally retired from the active business of life, being then nearly seventy-five years old.

David M. Spurgin was born in Mount Sterling, Kentucky, May 7, 1814. When he was fifteen years old he left home to work at the silversmith's trade, with Samuel Hensley. At the expiration of his apprenticeship, he worked as a journeyman in Winchester, in the employ of Mr. Smith Jeffries. In the spring of 1833 he bought out the stock of Hensley, in Mount Sterling, the 14th day of June, packing up all his worldly goods, and placing them in his father's old wagon, accompanied by a faithful old family servant, he set out for Carlisle, his future home. He landed here the same day, and the old colored driver returned the same night as far as Sharpsburg. Mr. Spurgin opened out in the front room of the Dykes property, the same now owned by Judge Holladay. Soon after his marriage, Mr. Spurgin purchased the property now owned by the family of the late James Robinson. His shop was also transferred to the small one-story brick which then stood upon the ground now occupied by the Deposit Bank. Mr. Spurgin was an industrious and skillful mechanic, and there is no doubt many sets of his solid silver spoons, made by his own hands, are still in use throughout the county. His wife was equally energetic and industrious. There never was a finer housekepeer in Carlisle than she. Their garden was always far ahead of anybody else, and the amount of early vegetables turned out by the thrifty housewife was amazing. Mr. Spurgin was always religious, a very enthusiastic Methodist, and on the 16th day of December, 1857, he united with that church in Carlisle. No one, perhaps, read the Bible and Pedo-Baptist authors more closely. Mr. Spurgin was decidedly controversial, and would lay down his hammer at any time to hammer infant baptism into the head of a skeptic. Some years before he joined the church he induced Parson Whittaker, the eccentric old Methodist minister, to come to Carlisle and give the Reformers and Baptists hail Columbia on baptism in general. Whittaker came, and a good audience assembled in the Presbyterian Church to hear him. The preacher took for his text the passage, "Stand still, that I may reason with you before the Lord." He began his sermon at 10:30 A. M., and preached on until half-past 12. At that time, some becoming impatient, began to leave the house. Every time any one started for the door Whittaker would repeat the text, "Stand still, that I may reason with you before the Lord." In his argument against immersion, the preacher used the following forcible and laughable argument: "Stand still, that I may reason with you in the Lord. Immersion is not only unscriptural and unwarranted; it is difficult and inconvenient. Now, there is my friend Spurgin; how could any one baptize such a great big fellow as he is? The only way it could be done, would be to set him down in a chair and then hoist him up and down with a derrick or a big well-sweep." It is needless to add that the preacher made a good sweep upon the feeling of his audience; a large number of them were so overcome with laughter that they shed tears. Parson Whittaker finished his sermon at half-past 3 o'clock in the afternoon, making a continuous sermon of five hours, during which time many of his auditors went home and got their dinners and then returned to hear it out.

Mr. Spurgin left Carlisle in the spring of 1847, and went to Winchester, Kentucky, where he remained until the fall of 1852, when he moved permanently to the flourishing city of Greencastle, Indiana. There the family are spending the evening of their days in the enjoyment of domestic ease and comfort, in the calm satisfaction of a life well spent, and in the hope of eternal life beyond the river.

Robert P. Hughes for a number of years kept a dry goods store in Carlisle, in partnership with John S. Morgan. He was also, we think, at one time a partner of James Squires. After Robert sold out his interest in the dry goods business, he was for a time employed as a salesman by Joseph F. Tureman. About the year 1848, he started to Missouri, in company with Mrs. Robert Bowen, taking his two little boys with him. He got as far as Colonel Morgan's, his old friend and partner, in the city of Covington. While there he was taken violently ill, and after a short but decisive struggle with death, calmly yielded up his life. His remains were brought back to Carlisle, and deposited by the side of his two wives.

Elijah West, with his family, moved into Carlisle about 1832. His first home was in the frame house on Main street, next east of Mr. J. F. Tureman. It was about 1841 he bought from the trustees the old brick seminary and an acre of ground, for $400. Here he lived until about 1865, when he built a new residence on his farm one mile south of town. He was elected magistrate several times and served also several years as member of the Board of Town Trustees. In 1862, he was elected County Judge of Nicholas. Judge West was a good, upright citizen and enjoyed the confidence and good will of the community. Some several years ago—having lost his first wife, he was married to Mrs. Rosanna Hughes, widow of Jesse Hughes, Esq. But, in 1877, the Judge died at the good, ripe age of eighty years. His son, William, is the owner of the homestead near town.

Joel Howard may be classed among our earliest citizens. About 1822, we first hear of him as a boarder at the hotel, then kept by William Porter, and working at his trade (that of saddler) with N. P. Robinson. As in a great many similar cases, Mr. Howard wound up by marrying the daughter of his landlord, Margaret Porter. Should every young man be as fortunate as Joel Howard, it would be wise for every young man in the State to go and do likewise. Not long after, Mr. Howard became the owner of the property on Front street, next west of the corner of Front and Main Cross. In 1832, Mr. Howard was appointed postmaster under General Jackson, a position he continued to hold until 1848, after the election of General Taylor. Mr. Howard held the office also of town trustee several terms.

About the year 1837, there came to Carlisle a new married man and his bride. The gentleman was a lawyer, was from the neighborhood of Ruddel's Mills, and had studied law in Paris under the lead of such men as Garrett Davis, Tom Elliott and others. This was Lyford Marston. The young couple first moved into the brick house formerly occupied by Aunt Kitty Hughes and her daughter, Jane Stokes. Mr. Marston practiced law in the courts of Nicholas and Bourbon, in partnership with the Hon. Garrett Davis, the firm being "Davis & Marston." On the 26th of March, 1839, he was elected Clerk of the Board of Trustees, which office he continued to fill until 1841, when he was succeeded by James P. Metcalfe. Mr. Marston was an original thinker, a close, subtle reasoner and oftentimes sharp, pungent and witty in repartee. During the winter of 1841-42 a debating society was held weekly at the cabinet-shop of John Davidson. The following prominent citizens of the town and county were members and took part in all the debates, to wit: John Davidson, Hugh B. Todd, John F. McMillan, John Hamilton, Moses Hopkins, Granville Edwards, Rev. John Rogers, B. F. Edwards, Col. George R. Foster, Fitch Munger, Lyford Marston, Thomas E. Quisenbury and John W. Finnell. These debates sometimes waxed hot, especially when any deep question in ethics, morals or religion was under discussion. In all such encounters Marston was generally upon the side of the free thinkers, and by his bold and daring utterances created in the minds of a good many the fear that he was drifting into open skepticism, if not downright atheism. Especially was this the fear of Parson Rogers and Professor Todd, both of whom regarded him as already a child of perdition. About the year 1842 or '43 Mr. Marston moved from Carlisle to Bourbon County, where, after remaining some years, he moved to the State of Illinois. Last summer he and his good wife paid a visit to their old home near Ruddel's Mills. While there he concluded he would run over to Carlisle and see how matters looked in this his first home after marriage. While here we jokingly reminded him of the old village debating club, and the fears that brethren Todd and Rogers had, lest he should turn skeptic. His eyes filled with tears as he replied, "I and my wife found the straight and narrow way that leads to eternal life, and both of us have long since been devoted members of the Methodist Church." About four months ago the loved companion, his wife, was summoned home by the shining ones whom Christian saw in his vision just beyond the river of death.

In the history of our town from 1835 to 1840, two distinguished Frenchmen appeared upon the scene, each one of whom spent a summer in Carlisle. It was before the Blue Licks had acquired any great celebrity as a watering place, which, nevertheless, always came in for numerous visits from our townfolks during the season. It was, perhaps, in 1837 that M. Bernard came to Carlisle, simply as a *voyageur*, seeking some place to spend a few months in the quiet seclusion of country life. Though reared and educated in that gayest of all gay cities, Paris, the capital of the French empire, he turned his feet aside from the great cities of America, preparing to study life under a new and hitherto unknown phase. Attached to the Republican party in France, he became a refugee from his native land after the suppression of the insurrection at Strasburg, in favor of the Bonapartists, in 1836. M. Bernard was not a very skillful horseman, although very fond of horseback exercise. On one occasion, he borrowed a horse of Mr. B. W. Mathers to ride a short distance. Mr. Mathers cautioned him to be careful of the horse as he was not very gentle. Bernard had scarcely made the circuit of the public square before the horse ran away and threw him. He was picked up and carried into the old hotel, then kept where Mann & Kennedy's store now stands. A doctor was summoned at once, and when he came, he asked Bernard how he felt: "Oh, Mon Dieu, doctor," he replied, "I pelieve I vill go tead!"

It was in the spring of 1840 that Monsieur Felix Courmont came to our town. He was a brave soldier, a ripe scholar, and a polished gentleman. Like Bernard, Monsieur Courmont was also a refugee, or rather a political exile, from France. He was a warm Bonapartist, and bitterly opposed to the reigning sovereign of France —Louis Phillippe. He was, if we remember correctly, engaged in several conspiracies against the King; was in the insurrection of Grenoble and Paris in 1834, and had a horse shot under him. The horse fell upon Courmont, breaking his leg, and he lay all night in this condition. From the effect of this fall he was lamed for life. He always carried a cane and slightly limped in his walk. The writer, then only sixteen years of age, was well acquainted with Monsieur Courmont, and on one or two occasions bore a jocose love-message from that gentleman to Miss Eliza Rogers, and from the lady to him in return. Monsieur Courmont was boarding at the hotel of Mr. A. Summers, when the hotel stable was burned in 1840, and was greatly distressed at the threatened danger of his landlord. Monsieur Courmont remained in Carlisle only about a year. We heard subsequently to his departure, that he had returned to France under a general amnesty to all political offenders.

Benjamin and Asbury Teal, brothers, were citizens of Carlisle for a number of years. Benjamin was a saddler by trade, and carried on business here about twenty years. He was twice married; his second wife was a Bruce, an own cousin of Mr. George I. Bruce, of this place. The family moved to Illinois nearly 30 years ago, and settled near Bloomington.

Asbury Teal carried on a tannery here for many

years. He owned the property at the West end of Main street, now owned by A. R. Fisher.

Another prominent family in the history of Carlisle, is that of Greenberry Ross, who was born in the year 1791. As early as 1820 he became a citizen of the town. He was a tailor by trade, and carried on a good business until 1839. Mr. Ross was an intelligent workman, and kept in the foreground in regard to all the new fashions and systems of cutting. When a gentleman went to him for a fit, the first thing was to place the customer under the standard and measure his height. Hence, in those days every man knew just how tall he was in feet and inches. Nowadays scarcely one man in ten knows how long he is for this world, and this state of ignorance may be traced directly to the door of the tailors of the present age, who have quietly ignored this good old standard of truth. The attitude of the customer being attained, the next thing was to place an instrument to his spinal column, which contained an ingenious set of wooden screws, one screw for each articulation of the vertebræ. By moving these screws in or out, it was easy to determine whether the subject was sway-backed, hump-backed or straight-backed—points very essential to know in order to secure a perfect fit. In truth, the gent's coat of half a century ago was a marvel of mechanical ingenuity. The sleeves were cut to fit tight as the skin; the coat-tails were narrow, tapering to a point, and were rightly called "swallow tail." But the collar—ah! the collar was the crowning glory of the structure. It was as big as the largest sized horse collar, standing as high as one's head behind, and quilted as stiff and hard as buckram and padding could make it. The Ross family lived for a number of years in the two-story log house, moved from Ellisville in 1817. The property was situated on lot No. 36, and was bought by John E. Cotton, for $91, at the first sale of lots in 1816. Mr. Ross' tailor shop stood exactly on the spot now occupied by Dr. R. J. R. Tilton's medical office.

Another prominent citizen of fifty years' standing, was Mr. William Stewart. He was born in Bourbon County, on the 9th of November, 1800. Married Miss Olivia Ogden, of Bracken County, on the 15th of November, 1825. He removed, along with the Ogden family, to Carlisle, in May, 1830. A blacksmith by profession, Mr. Stewart opened his first smith shop on Elm street, on the south half of lot No. 123. In 1833, Mr. Stewart bought the property then owned and just vacated by Col. John S. Morgan, being lot No. 36, on Second street, and the same as now owned by his son, Henry. Several years after this, he purchased the lot adjoining, and moved his shop thereon. Henry Stewart, the second child, was born October 30, 1830; married to Mrs. Sarah Robinson, *née* McCormack, in 1868. This family, with their three children, Minnie, Robert and Berry, are still living at the Stewart homestead above named. Henry was succeeded by Rhoda and Sallie, both of whom died in early womanhood. About 1860, Mr. Stewart connected himself with the Presbyterian Church in Carlisle, and has ever continued a faithful member of the same. At this time he is living upon his farm near town, in his eighty-second year, and enjoys the satisfaction of having been true and faithful in all the relations of life. No old citizen of the county more fully receives or deserves the confidence of his fellow-citizens.

In the history of the medical profession, none have stood as high in the annals of Carlisle as Dr. John F. McMillan. He was born in Madison County, about 1815. In 1836 (probably) he was married to Miss Phœbe A. Taylor, of Clark County, and the young couple came to Carlisle in 1837, and took lodgings at the hotel of A. Summers, Esq. Here they continued to board until about 1840, when they purchased the property on the corner of Main and Second streets, the same as now owned by Judge Ross. It is to the Doctor's credit that he did more to alleviate human suffering, and at less compensation than was ever done before or since in our town history. The McMillans, both husband and wife, were possessed of more than ordinary intelligence; both were keen, smart and pungent in a witticism or repartee; and upon no one did they exercise these faculties with greater relish than upon one another. In 1861 Dr. McMillan was elected a State Senator from his district, and in 1865 he was elected a Representative from Nicholas to the Lower House. No children were born unto them. In 1862, or thereabouts, Mrs. McMillan died, and her remains were taken to the old family burying-ground in Clark County, for interment. The Doctor himself died in 1870, and was buried in the Carlisle cemetery. For some time there was strong talk of raising funds to erect a suitable monument to his memory, but the project failed for want of prompt action upon the part of his friends.

During the first year of the cholera (1832), James H. Holladay came to Carlisle, then quite a young boy. He read law in the office of Hon. D. K. Weis, and began the practice of law about 1844. At the first call for volunteers in the Mexican War in 1846, he volunteered and was elected Lieutenant in Captain John W. Finnell's company. The boys got as far as Frankfort, but as the quota assigned to Kentucky was already full, they had to disband and return home. In the year 1847, the second call came for troops, and Holladay again enlisted, this time under Captain Leonidas Metcalfe, and was again elected Lieutenant. This time the Nicholas boys were fortunate enough to reach "the halls of the Montezumas," but not till after the victorious legions of Scott had fought the decisive battles of Churubusco, and Molino del Rey, and had marched into the city. Here our boys were stationed for some time as part of the army of occupation. We must not forget to state that, owing to the illness of Captain Metcalfe, Lieutenant Holladay assumed command of the company. and Harlan Berry was promoted to the rank of First Lieutenant. In July, 1848, the company was mustered out. In the meantime, before he had returned home, his Whig friends had nominated him as their candidate for the Legislature, and the Democrats had nominated John Kincart, the pioneer of Carlisle, and then a private soldier under Holladay, as the Democratic standard-bearer. At that time the actual Democratic majority in the county was about one hundred, and it required a man of great popularity with the masses to succeed upon the Whig ticket. The contest was close, hot and fiercely contested, but Holladay pulled through by the skin of his teeth, having some eight or nine of a majority. In the year 1851, he was elected Circuit Clerk, and in 1856 re-elected to the same office. In 1866, he was elected County Judge of Nicholas, and hence his title of "Judge." Judge Holladay has always stood high in the esteem of all citizens, both of town and county.

Among the many worthy citizens of Carlisle, none deserve a more prominent notice than Fitch Munger. He was a native of New York. In 1840, he came to Carlisle, a stranger without means—with nothing, in fact, save an indomitable will, and energy and determination to succeed. We first hear of him, after his arrival, boarding at 'Squire John W. Sharpe's, and teaching school at the Baker schoolhouse. With the proceeds of this teaching he purchased a few law books, and entered the office of Colonel William Norvell to study law. It was not long before he procured a license, and a partnership was formed with his preceptor, as Norvell & Munger. This partnership continued for some five or six years. But about 1850 the partnership was dissolved, and each partner continued the law business singly and alone. Mr. Munger was an earnest, painstaking attorney, and believed in the maxim, "Keep your office and your office will keep you" and surely never was any maxim more thoroughly vindicated than this was in his case. He was, beyond all question, the most thoroughly successful business man who ever lived in Carlisle. Mr. Munger was elected, and served as Clerk of the Board of Town Trustees, for many years. He was also elected a member of the Board of Trustees at different times. He was elected State Senator from the district composed of the counties of Mason and Nicholas, and served with distinction to himself and constituents. In politics, Mr. Munger was a Henry Clay Whig; after the rise of the native American party, he became attached to their brief fortunes, and finally gave in his allegiance to the Democratic party. He was never a violent partisan, but was held in esteem by all parties. For a number of years the family lived in the property on the corner of Second and Main streets, but about 1857 Mr. Munger bought the suburban home formerly owned by G. Ross, Esq. A man of fine physique, of florid complexion, prudent and temperate habits, there was every indication in his case of a long and useful life. But, notwithstanding all these favorable indications, he fell sick and died at his home in 186–. Mr. Munger left a fine estate, valued at over $60,000, to his family, the result of untiring industry and prudent management.

The year 1840–41 was noted in Carlisle history as the advent of three remarkable young men. It is not often that three as promising, business-like and successful young men enter any village in the same profession, who afterward achieve as much distinction in life, and who, during all the years of professional competition, manifest and maintain such cordial and sincere relations of friendship one toward the other. These were Fitch Munger, Thomas E. Quisenberry and John W. Finnell. Mr. Quisenberry was born in Virginia about 1818, and was therefore scarcely more than of age when he came to Carlisle. He studied law under John A. McClung, Esq., of Mason County, and began the practice in 1842. He bought the property then owned by the heirs of Louis H. Arnold, and began housekeeping there about 1849. His office was for many years in the one-story brick which then stood upon the site now occupied by the Deposit Bank. Mr. Quisenberry was fortunate in his financial affairs; he received a handsome estate from a deceased brother, and also a further help through his wife. These sums he prudently managed, all the time adding to them by his lucrative practice and by making some good investments in Western lands. In the year 1862, the whole family moved to the city of Danville, much to the regret of all our citizens. And there, some seven years after, Mr. Quisenberry died, and was buried in the Danville City cemetery.

William P. Ross was born in Carlisle, August 11th, 1825; received a good education for that period, going to school to such men as Elder John Rogers, E. F. Chappell, Mr. Musgrove, Professor Smith, and others. As early as 1843, he began the study of law, under Fitch Munger, Esq.; began practicing in 1847; was elected magistrate in 1848; County Judge in 1851. He was a member of the old County Court at the time of that body's dissolution. It is not exactly the purpose of these sketches to pronounce eulogies upon the living, and certainly in the case of Judge Ross it would be peculiarly unnecessary. To a mind well stocked with legal lore, he has added much general information of men and things, of current history, and of all questions, political and religious, which agitate the public mind at the present day. Humanly speaking, the Judge has had one serious fault, and that is an excess of modesty. But for this, he might have filled many an office of trust and honor in the gift of the people. His name has more than once been mentioned in connection with the highest judicial honors of the State, but to these and all similar suggestions he has ever turned an indifferent ear, preferring the sweets of domestic life in the bosom of his family, where he is loved and honored, to the empty honors of the world. For a number of years Judge Ross has been an Elder in and prominent member of the Presbyterian Church. With him, religion has been paramount; it is this that has shaped his life and given tone and tenor to all his actions.

Another successful business man of Carlisle was J. M. Dallas. He came from Maysville in 1840, a saddler by trade, and began work for Joel Howard. About 1844 he was married to Miss Cynthia A. Gardner, a young lady milliner of the town at that time. Both being industrious, prudent and economical, they soon began to rise in the world. It was not long before they bought them a home, the same as now occupied by Mrs. Jno. B. Scudder. Mr. Dallas was an enterprising workman, a good mechanic, and did much toward establishing a reputation for Carlisle manufactures. He died in the very prime of life, about ten years ago, leaving an estate of nearly fifty thousand dollars to his wife and children. His son, Leonidas, succeeded to the business of his father.

Doctor W. W. Fritts was born in Clark County, Kentucky, in 1816. His father, Henry Fritts, moved to Carlisle in 1835, and William followed in 1836. The father and son were hatters by trade, and purchased the interest of Jesse Massie, a popular citizen of that period. One year after his location here W. W. Fritts was married to Miss Sallie Hamilton, daughter of a well known farmer living near town. Soon after the new married pair moved to Clay County, Missouri, but remained only a short time. On their return here in 1843, Mr. J. F. Tureman and Mr. Fritts opened a drug store—the first one probably ever opened in the place. Not long after Mr. Fritts conceived the idea of studying the healing art, and during a period of years at his leisure, read the leading standards in allopathy. In the year 1853, he graduated at the Louisville Medical College, and as a student under, and partner of, Dr. McMillan, began the practice of medicine and surgery. This he continued until about 1872, when in partnership with his son, Henry, he opened a new drug and book store, as W. W. Fritts & Son.

James Mann was raised a farmer, and lived at the old homestead of his childhood until the year 1865, when he moved to Carlisle. The year previous, he and his son, Al. Boyd, bought out the dry-goods store of Henry Pickrell, and commenced the mercantile business as Mann & Boyd. This partnership continued until 1873, when Mr. Boyd died. In the meantime, in 1872, Mr. William Kennedy, another farmer, moved to town and purchased Mr. Boyd's interest, when the firm became Mann & Kennedy. In 1880, Mr. Kennedy retired from the firm, and opened a new house, taking with him his son-in-law, Mr. John Beck. Mr. Mann continued until the close of 1881, when he sold out to Smith & Veach, and retired, probably finally, from businsss. Mr. Mann has two sons engaged in active business in Carlisle; the eldest, Leonidas F., having some years since embarked in the livery and sale business; he also held for about three years the office of Police Judge. The other son, Reuben E. Mann, is engaged in the grocery business on a large scale, having oftentimes as many as five branch stores under his control. Mr. James Mann is an enthusiastic Methodist, and, what is still more and better, an earnest, conscientious, Christian gentleman; he is, we might say, a licentiate in the ministry, and preaches quite often throughout the county. Mr. Mann is in his sixty-third year, and bids fair to enjoy many years more of a useful and honorable life.—*Chappell.*

CHAPTER X.

LOWER BLUE LICKS PRECINCT—GENERAL OUTLINE AND TOPOGRAPHY—EARLY SETTLEMENT—LIFE ON THE FRONTIER—THE SALT MAKERS—BLUE LICK SPRINGS—THE BATTLE WITH THE INDIANS—CHURCHES, SCHOOLS AND VILLAGES.

"The ultimate tendency of civilization is toward barbarism."—*Hare.*

TO be able to do justice to a territory so famous in the annals of Nicholas County, as that to which this chapter is devoted, one should have lived a century ago. Perhaps no part of the "dark and bloody ground" was in early times more celebrated than this, both in the annals of war and in the arts of peace.

Its soil has been dyed with the hearts' blood of some of Kentucky's bravest sons, and now, after the lapse of one hundred years, it seems proper that the State pay some tribute to their memory.

This precinct, which is Election Precinct No. 1, of Nicholas County, is bounded on the north by Harrison County, on the east by Robertson County, south by the Upper Blue Licks, and west by Ellisville and Headquarters Precincts; Licking River flows through the northern part of the precinct, receiving as its principal tributary, Stony Creek, which has its source near the town of Carlisle, and empties near the Blue Lick Springs. Buchanan Creek rises in Fleming County and empties into Licking River, near Pleasant Valley.

The surface is broken and hilly, much of it being too steep for cultivation.

In the bottoms the soil is rich, being a limestone underlaid with yellow clay, which renders it susceptible of enduring a continued drought. The timber for the most part is composed of oak, ash, elm, cedar, etc.

The early settlement of this precinct is cotemporaneous with the settlement at the Blue Lick Springs. This Spring was discovered by a surveying party from Westmoreland County, Virginia, in 1773. In the division of the different tracts, this one fell to the lot of John Finley, who came and settled on it after the Revolutionary War, in which he was Major of the 8th Pennsylvania Regiment of Continental Troops; at his death it descended to his son, David D. Finley, who continued to live on it for many years.*

No permanent settlement seems to have been made here till about the year 1789, when a station was built by a man named Lyons, who carried on salt making. He had a family of negro servants and entertained travelers; he did a good business in the salt trade, gaining quite a reputation for fair dealing among his customers. It is supposed that the Tanners had a station at the Springs several years before Lyons, but it is not certainly known. Previous to 1789 the Spring went by the various names, "Salt Spring," "The Salt Spring on Licking," "The Lower Salt Spring," "The Salt Lick," etc., and were resorted to by the early settlers for obtaining their supply of salt, they generally going in a body for that purpose. The saline contents were accurately analyzed and weighed by Dr. Robert Peter, of the Kentucky Geological Survey, and from deductions made by him, taking the salt as one per cent. of the weight of water, it seems that the Spring would yield an annual product of nearly half a million pounds. Besides the chloride of sodium, an analysis of the water also gives about twenty per cent. of free carbonic acid gas, about three per cent. of sulphuretted hydrogen, bromide and iodide of magnesium, sulphate of lime and potash, alumina, phosphate of lime, oxide of iron, and silicic acid, with traces of oxide of manganese and cremic and apocremic acids. It is a valuable water, and acts as a nervous stimulant, diuretic, diaphoretic and emmenagogue.*

"On the 1st day January, 1778, Daniel Boone and a party of thirty men, collected from the garrisons of the different stations, came to the Lower Blue Licks to make salt. After they had been at work for about a month, three of the men having been sent home in the meantime with salt, Boone was captured, while out hunting to procure provisions for the party, by a band of 102 Indians and two Frenchmen. He made favorable terms of surrender for the remaining twenty-seven, and they were all taken off to Old Chillicothe, the principal Shawnee town on the Little Miami, near the present site of Xenia, Ohio. Boone was employed by the Indians in making salt, and obtained considerable freedom. On the 16th

*Coll ns' History, page 655.

*Dr. Peter.

day of June, he effected his escape from his captors, having gained information that an attack of considerable magnitude was premeditated against Boonesborough. He traveled the entire distance, one hundred and sixty-miles, in four days, during which he had but one meal, taken at the end of the third day at the forks of the three branches of the Flat Fork of Johnston's Fork of Licking River."*

The manufacture of salt was abandoned to a great extent about 1820, and in later years the place became celebrated as a summer resort for recreation and health. In 1845, the improvements at the Lower Blue Licks were greatly extended, a magnificent hotel was erected, and during the season frequently entertained from 400 to 600 guests. This building was destroyed by fire April 7, 1862, and has not since been rebuilt. A hotel of more moderate dimensions was erected in 1870, by the Bedinger heirs, and is now under the management of John Larue. A third hotel was erected in 1877, by W. T. Overby, and is now owned and managed by Daniel Turney, of Paris, Kentucky. The water of the Springs, known as "Blue Lick Water" is justly celebrated, and has an extensive sale throughout the United States and Europe. With this digression upon the Springs, we return to the early settlement of the precinct. William Bartlett was one of the pioneers, and formerly owned the farm now in possession of J. Hammond. He was engaged at an early day in the manufacture of salt, and at one time owned the Springs. He died in 1842, and some of his descendants still reside in the neighborhood.

Aquila Standiford came from Maryland in 1797, and settled on Licking river, near the Springs. A portion of his original tract is still in the hands of the surviving members of his family. Simon and Mark Kenton were also among the early settlers ; the Kenton homestead being now in the possession of Daniel Day. The land near the Kenton settlement was originally owned by Edwin Collins, and a portion of this is still in the hands of his son, the Collins homestead being owned by Dr. Wells.

One of the most noted characters in the history of this precinct was Major George Michael Bedinger, a brief sketch of whom we take from Collins' History of Kentucky. He was born near Shepherdstown, Va., in 1755, and early in 1779, when 24 years of age, emigrated to Kentucky at Boonesborough. He was one of a company of 10, nearly all from Shepherdstown (among them the late Joseph Doniphan, of Mason County, Captain John Holden and Thomas Swearingen), engaged in improving lands for themselves on Muddy Creek, in what is now Madison County, and "over on the waters of Licking." In May, 1779, he acted as adjutant in the unfortunate expedition of Colonel John Bowman, against the Indian town of old Chillicothe, and was a Major at the fatal battle of Blue Licks, August 19, 1782, each occasion proving him a brave, prompt and efficient officer. In 1792, he was chosen from Bourbon County—which then included his new home near the Lower Blue Licks, now in Nicholas County—a member of the House of Representatives of the first Legislature of Kentucky, at Lexington. He was a representative in Congress for four years, 1803–7. He died December 7, 1843.

*Collins.

Philip G. Ross was also an early settler of this precinct, and located on land now owned by Jeremiah Prather. Elizabeth Harrington settled on the place where she now lives, among the early pioneers of this section. The first store at the Blue Licks was built in 1816, by Major Bedinger. The first hotel was built by a Mr. Biddemore, in 1824, of which S. Moore was landlord; he also was the first Postmaster in the place. The first saw-mill was built by Joseph Bedinger, which was eventually destroyed and replaced by E. Waller, in 1853. Waller sold to P. G. Allison, who ran it till 1869, when it was purchased by L. Abner, the present owner, and by whom the present saw-mill was built in 1875. A. R. Hildreth also runs a steam saw-mill near Abner's, which he built in 1875.

In early times a ferry was owned at the Lower Blue Licks by Daniel Bedinger. A bridge took its place in 1835, a wooden structure, erected by Lewis Wernwag. This was burned during the war, and the present wood and iron suspension bridge erected in its place in 1865 by the Maysville and Lexington Turnpike Company.

For a description of the battle of Blue Licks see general county history.

The only church in this precinct is located on Licking river near the Forest Retreat Pike, and was built in 1855. It is a frame building, and was erected by the Methodist denomination, at a cost of about $600. Union Church, near the Licks, formerly in this precinct, but now inside the Robertson County line, was built in 1861.

There are five schoolhouses in the precinct, ranging in value from $100 to $300: One located at Blue Licks, built in 1861; one known as the Rafferty schoolhouse, on the Maysville and Lexington Pike, built in 1880; the Liberty schoolhouse, a log building, erected in 1855; Sugar Creek schoolhouse, built in 1880. A log school house was built in 1854, near Pleasant Hill, at which the first teacher was James Shockey.—*E. T. Brown.*

CHAPTER XI.

HEADQUARTERS PRECINCT—TOPOGRAPHY AND BOUNDARY—EARLY HISTORY—SETTLEMENT OF THE WHITES —VILLAGES—TURNPIKES AND OTHER IMPROVEMENTS—CHURCHES—SCHOOLS—SECRET SOCIETIES, ETC.

"It is ten o'clock,
Thus may we see how the world wags,
'Tis but an hour since it was nine,
And in another hour it will be eleven,
And so from hour to hour we ripe and ripe,
And then from hour to hour we rot and rot,
And thereby hangs a tale."—*Shakespeare.*

HEADQUARTERS Precinct, which is No. 2 of the election precincts of Nicholas County, lies in the extreme northern section of the county, and is touched on its northern border by the Harrison County line. Ellisville and Blue Licks Precinct bound it on the east, Carlisle Precinct on the south, and Bourbon County on the west make up the complete boundary.

In the south and west the surface is gently rolling, and presents some farming land unsurpassed in point of beauty and fertility by any of the blue grass region. As we approach the northwestern part, the surface becomes more broken, and the soil correspondingly diminishes in fertility, owing, not so much to a change of character as to the fact that so much of the richer portion has been carried away by continued rains. The interior of this precinct forms a watershed between the waters of the two branches of Licking river, Steele's Run taking a southwesterly course into Hinkston, thence into South Licking and Willmore's Run, a tributary of Brushy Fork, itself a tributary of Beaver Creek, which rises in this precinct, and, flowing north-easterly through Harrison County, ultimately reaches Main Licking at Claysville.

The settlement of this part of the county dates as far back as 1795, when George Mann made the first inroad upon the hitherto undisturbed forest. Close in his wake followed Henry Thompson, who took up an original survey of 1,000 acres and divided it with John McClintock. Both of these men were natives of Virginia and left valuable estates, a portion of which is still in the possession of their descendants. Prominent among the early settlers may likewise be mentioned, Major John Collier, George Summit, Peter Snapp, John Conway, Joseph and Hugh McClintock, James McKee and Samuel Kimbrough.

The educational facilities of this precinct were early developed. A log schoolhouse was built on Brushy Fork as early as 1802, and there a Mr. Grosvenor trained the minds and curbed the wills of Kentucky's second generation. Zachary Clayburn taught a school in a house near Hooktown ; this building, erected in 1814, was also a log structure, and was the second one in the precinct. The third school was begun in 1820, by Mrs. Marston, in a log house that had previously been used as a distillery. In matters educational, this precinct has always kept pace with its neighbors. There are at present, five well-regulated schools in the precinct, located as follows : The Baker schoolhouse, near Headquarters, built 1867, at a cost of $200, and used by all denominations for religious purposes. A frame house near Irvinsville, built in 1848, and also used as a meeting house for several years ; the school here was first taught by Nathan Ogden. A log schoolhouse formerly stood near Mt. Carmel Church, on the site occupied by the present frame building ; this school was first taught by Maria, daughter of Colonel Mann. The schoolhouse at Headquarters and the one near Walnut Grove Church complete the number.

Scarcely less interesting than the schools is the church history, which, owing to the care with which the records have been preserved, we are able to give with minuteness. The Mt. Carmel Church, which antedates all others in this locality, was first erected in 1820. The original log building was replaced in 1852 by the present commodious frame at a cost of $1,300. The property is owned by the Methodist Society. Among those connected with its reorganization in 1852, were John Mitcheltree and wife, Daniel Earlwine and wife, James Hillock and wife, Daniel Evans, Ann Hillock, Sally Kennedy, James Kennedy, Elizabeth Kennedy, William Kennedy, Caroline Kennedy, Zachariah Brooks, Anderson Brooks and wife, Arris Evans and wife, Gilead Evans and wife, Milton Geoghegan and wife, Elizabeth Parchall, Robert Cattingham, R. D. Hall, Mary Hall, Frances Brooks and others. Several of the above were also members of the original church in 1820. The church was dedicated by Rev. Mr. Brush, and the pastoral office is at present filled by W. O. Godby.

The Methodist Church at Headquarters was built in 1868, and dedicated by Rev. E. Stevenson and Rev. Mr. Harrison, who became the first regular pastor. At present the church is administered to by Rev. John Ebright.

Walnut Grove Church, in the southwestern part of the precinct was built in 1878, as a Union Chapel, being used as a house of religious worship by the different denominations. It cost about $500, and was dedicated by Rev. J. W. Dixon.

There is also a Methodist chapel in the northwestern part of the precinct, near the Licking river, erected at a cost of $500.

The village of Headquarters, from which the precinct was named, is said to have received its cognomen from a Mr. W. J. Stitt, a soldier of the Mexican war, who christened it upon the location of the post office at that place. Mr. Stitt was also the first settler of the town, having built a store there in 1840 ; he was also the first postmaster. The town is located upon the Headquarters and Steele's Run pike, and contains one store, one shoe shop, one blacksmith shop, one tobacco warehouse, one apothecary shop, church, school, and about fifteen dwellings.

Centerville is a small town, three miles west of Headquarters, on the same pike, and contains a store, blacksmith shop and a few dwellings. The first house was built by Martin B. Cook, in 1812: Richard Cheatham erected the first store in 1860. In 1845, a post office was established, in the house of W. A. Griffith, with J. W. Sharp, postmaster. The office was discontinued six years later. The first mail was carried to this office and Headquarters, from Carlisle, by a Mr. Hackley. The original name of Centerville was Hooktown, which was given to it on account of a robbery which was perpetrated soon after the store was built.

Irvinsville, a small village in the northeastern part of the precinct, and near the Harrison County line, supports one church, school, blacksmith shop, saw mill, and contains about a dozen dwellings. Elias Scott, Joab Yates and Joshua Irvin were the early settlers—after the last of whom the town was named. The post-office was located here in 1847, and the name of Morning Glory given to it, which name it still retains in some localities. Tom Raymond was the first postmaster, and this office is now filled by Forest Peterson. Raymond built the first store in 1847, and, in a few years, sold to N. Rankin. In 1860, the Baptist Church was organized at this place, the meetings being first held in the schoolhouse. John Holliday was the first pastor, and served the church with success for ten years. The members have just completed a frame building, at a cost of $1,000, and have chosen Elder S. H. Burgess for their Pastor. Nathan Ogden taught the first school at this place, in 1848.

Barterville, near the line between this precinct and Ellisville, contains about a half-dozen residences, two stores, one blacksmith shop, one physician, one tobacco warehouse, postoffice, etc. It was first settled by Jacob Myers in 1820. Isaac Feeback was the first postmaster, and J. A. Porter, the present one. The schoolhouse at this place is used by all denominations as a place of religious worship.

The first county road in this precinct was laid out in 1809, running from Steele's Ford, following a buffalo trace to Lower Blue Licks.

The Headquarters and Steele's Run Pike was built in 1867, and is about six and three-fourths miles in length.

The Forest Retreat and Panther Creek Pike, built in 1881–82, extends from the Maysville and Lexington Pike nearly ten miles in a northerly direction.

Irvinsville and Salt Well Pike, also built in 1881–82, extends for five and a quarter miles in the northwestern part of the precinct. There is but one secret society in this precinct, and that is located at Headquarters. It is called Orient Lodge, No. 500, A. F. and A. M. The charter was granted October 19, 1871, and commenced operations under the following board of officers: John G. Burns, W. M. ; Thomas M. Sharp, J. W.; W. J. Kennedy, S.W.; John R. Taylor, S. D.; John S. Hillock, J. D.; E. D. Foster, Sec.; William S. Smith, Treas.; B. W. S. Lowe, S. & T. The present list of officers is : James R. Long, W. M.; Nathaniel Collier, S. W.; H. D. Peterson, J.W.; James A. Smith, Treas.; M. D. L. Burns, Sec.; F. M. Long, S. D.; W. J. Peterson, J. D.; James W. Gaffin, S. & T. At present their roll contains twenty-nine members.—*Brown.*

CHAPTER XII.

ELLISVILLE PRECINCT—ITS BROKEN SURFACE—GENERAL TOPOGRAPHY—EARLY SETTLEMENT—PIONEER INDUSTRIES AND IMPROVEMENTS—ELLISVILLE AS THE COUNTY SEAT—EDUCATIONAL AND RELIGIOUS HISTORY.

"In the mountain scenery yet,
All we adore of nature in her wild
And frolic hour of infancy is met;
And never has a summer's morning smiled
Upon a scene * * * * * *
O'er crags that proudly tower * * *
And knows that sense of danger which sublimes
The breathless moment—when his daring step
Is on the verge of the cliff." etc., etc.—*Halleck.*

THIS division of Nicholas County, which is known as Ellisville, or precinct No. 3, is rough and broken. Indeed, it may almost be called mountainous. Upon the brakes, and hills and bluffs, rising from the Licking River, originally grew giant trees, which for centuries had defied the fury of the tempest.

"The century-living crow,
Whose birth was in their tops, grew old and died
Among their branches,"

and still they had flourished in all their glory for years and ages. Giant oaks, towering walnuts and waving sycamores grew here in almost endless profusion. Such was the aspect of the section of country to which this chapter is devoted, when the pale-face, with all his bustling enterprise, came, and proceeded, literally, to turn things up-side-down.

Ellisville Precinct lies in the northern part of Nicholas County, and is bounded on the east by Blue Licks Precinct, on the south and southeast by Carlisle and Buzzard Roost Precincts, Harrison County on the north, and Headquarters Precinct on the west. The soil, notwithstanding the roughness of the country, is rich and fertile, and is well adapted to tobacco raising, which is the principal crop of the farmers. The timber was that common to this section of the country. The precinct is drained by the Licking River and its tributaries.

This precinct is noted as once having contained the county seat of Nicholas. Prouder than Rome upon her seven hills, "Ellisville," the metropolis of this great county(!) sat majestically upon the Licking Bluffs. In 1804, an act was passed to move the county seat from its original location, to the farm of James Ellis, who had settled some seven miles from the present town of Carlisle. In 1805, the commissioners laid off the ground for the public buildings, 16x20 poles, rectangular in shape—a deed for the same, from James Ellis to the Justices of the County Court, was acknowledged in July, 1805. Here was a courthouse, and also a jail—both built of logs. A jailer's house was also added to the jail the same year. Stores were opened and shops built, and Ellisville became quite a place. It remained the county seat until 1816, when it was again removed, and located where it has ever since remained, and the glory of Ellisville departed forever. It had been laid out with much care upon an eligible site, but the removal of the county seat and county offices to Carlisle killed it. Its decayed buildings have long since shown the "ivy clinging to their moldering towers," or "hoary lichen springing from the disjointed stones." Mocked by its own desolation,

"The bat, shrill shrieking, woos its flickering mate,
The serpent hisses, and the wild birds scream."

Settlements were made in Ellisville Precinct at an early day, though the exact date of the appearance of the first installment of pale-faces cannot be definitely given. Even the names of the first are a little uncertain. But among the pioneers of Ellisville, perhaps, may be mentioned the names of Gilbert and Jacob Feeback, Richard and James Ellis, Charles McClanahan, Esau Richey, Israel Chadwick, etc., etc. They are all long since gone, but descendants of them are still living in the County. After the war of 1812, the country round about this section settled up rapidly.

The first years of the whites in this county were years of toil and hardship, and danger. The journey hither in the first place was long and toilsome, and when they arrived, they had an unremitting struggle with poverty for long years, until the surplus products of the country enabled them to live more easily and comfortably. Upon the land of James Ellis, one of the early settlers of the precinct, as we have already seen, the county seat was established in 1804. From him the place received the name of Ellisville, and when the County was divided into election precincts under the new constitution of the State, this became Ellisville, in honor of the old county seat.

The early industries of the precinct consisted chiefly of mills, with a tannery or two and a distillery, in the early times; also several blacksmith and wood shops. But of these early institutions of pioneer energy and industry we know but little. There is at present a mill at the classic village of "Shakerag."

The first road through the precinct was made on the Buffalo trace, and was long known as the "Trace Road." The Maysville and Lexington Pike passes through Ellisville, and was not only the first pike in Nicholas County, but in Kentucky, and was built in 1833. The Cynthiana and Ellisville Pike was an early road in the precinct. A pike, called the "Forest Retreat and Painter Creek Pike," passes through the precinct. A bridge on the Maysville Pike, at the village of Shakerag, was built in 1833, by Thomas and Lewis Wernwag. It was burned during the war (1863), and rebuilt in 1865, by William Percy.

This precinct has two villages, viz.: Shakerag and Oakland Mills, and both of these put together would not make a respectable-sized town. George W. Seibert was one of the first to settle at Shakerag. Its high-sounding and classical name was given by William C. Craig, a prominent citizen of the place. The town comprises sixteen dwellings, a blacksmith shop, shoe shop, wagon shop, and cooper shop, the latter carried on by George W. Seibert. There are two stores, one kept by Henry Porter and the other by Eli Vaughn. A very fine store, carried on by W. C. Craig, was burned in the year 1881. A schoolhouse and church, combined, was built in 1874. The leading men in its construction were John McClanahan, Geo. W. Seibert and James and William McClanahan. The voting place of the precinct is at this schoolhouse. Shakerag is supposed to be what is left of Ellisville, the former capital. Disgusted at losing the metropolis, the town hid its humiliation and chagrin under a new name—the poetical and euphonious name of Shakerag.

Oakland Mills is a small village, comprising ten dwelling houses, a blacksmith shop, one store, carried on by R. T. Endicott, who also keeps the post office, having held the position about three years. Josiah Parrish is the oldest resident of the place, having been born and raised there. A distillery was built there about 1867, by G. Cheatham, but it is not now running. The Ingle Bros. own the town principally, and carry on a large tobacco warehouse. They handle tobacco very extensively, and do a large and flourishing business.

There is a Methodist Church on Bald Hill, which was built in 1868. It is on the old Buffalo Trace Road. The first preacher was Rev. Mr. Johns. Four denominations worship in that church, though it really is known as a Methodist Church. This, with the Union Church at Shakerag, comprise the church facilities, with preaching occasionally at other schoolhouses.

It is not known who taught the first school in the precinct. The common schools, like many other portions of Central Kentucky, do not receive the attention they deserve. The very most that can be said, is that they are sadly deficient. There is a school at Bald Hill, and one at Shakerag, which constitute the schools of the precinct.—*Perrin.*

CHAPTER XIII.

UNION PRECINCT—ITS DESCRIPTION AND TOPOGRAPHY—INCIDENT OF SOMERSET CREEK—SETTLEMENT OF THE PIONEERS—EARLY IMPROVEMENTS AND INDUSTRIES—MILLS AND ROADS—CHURCHES OF THE PRECINCT—SCHOOLS AND VILLAGES.

"An absolute historian
Should be in fear of none; neither should he
Write anything more than truth for friendship."

UNION Precinct, which is No. 5 of the election precincts of Nicholas County, lies in the southern part, and is bounded on the north by Upper Blue Licks Precinct, on the east by Bath County, on the south by the Bourbon County line, which is Hinkston Creek, and on the west by Carlisle Precinct. The land is rolling in the north part of the precinct and is very rich and productive; the southern part is more hilly and broken, and not so susceptible to cultivation, yet, where a level spot can be found large enough to grow a tobacco plant, it produces of that "weed" an excellent quality. The original timber was blue ash, walnut, maple, beech, hickory, some oak, buckeye, butternut, elm, yellow locust, sycamore, etc., etc., together with a heavy growth of cane, which died out about the year 1798. The main water courses of the precinct are three creeks, all known by the name of "Somerset." The source of one branch is in Bath County, of another in Carlisle Precinct, and of the other in this; all unite in this precinct, and within half a mile's distance. They attained their name from the fact that three brothers named Somers were killed here by the Indians in an early day, one of the brothers on each of these branches, near the junction. These streams, together with the Hinkston, which flows along the boundary, drain the precinct thoroughly, and furnish an abundance of stock water.

The date of the first settlement in Union Precinct could not be ascertained. Among its pioneers were James Brown, Daniel Cassidy, David Gray, Robert Caldwell, James Sanders, T. Davidson, James Hall, William Potts, etc. Brown settled the place now owned by Mrs. Adams; Cassidy settled where Mrs. Potts now lives; and David Gray on the place now owned by Mr. James Duncan; Caldwell settled where B. W. Graves now lives; Sanders where Soaper lives; and Davidson and Hall on the lands now owned by J. Thomas, Esq.; and Potts on the land owned by the Potts heirs. It is believed that most of these early settlers were from Virginia, though it is not known of a certainty at this late day. And as we have said, the date of their settlement here is not known, but it was at least a decade previous to 1800. Their first years, were years of hardship, and often were they hard pushed to furnish their families with the actual necessaries of life. To obtain bread was a difficult task. The forest contained plenty of meat for the expert hunters, but bread was more difficult to procure. This led to all sorts of experiments for converting the corn into meal, such as pounding it in a mortar, grinding it on a hand mill, etc., and to the building of rude mills.

The first mill in the precinct was built about 1795, by a Mr. Stevenson. It was located northwest of East Union Village, on a branch of Somerset Creek, and was both saw and grist mill. In 1797, Adam Kears built and ran a small distillery near the farm now owned by D. H. Dalzell. In 1814, J. H. Hahn and John Sears built a saw and grist mill, on the east branch of Somerset Creek, near the old buffalo trace. These mills were operated for a number of years, and then allowed to go to decay. A "tread mill" was built by Mr. Powell, the father of Nathan Powell, of Carlisle, in 1814. After running it for three or four years, he sold it to a man who moved it out of the county. The roads of Union Precinct are similar to those in the adjoining precincts; two or three pikes passing through it.

The churches of Union Precinct, have an extended history. The first one built in this vicinity, was of logs, and was called Shiloh. There is nothing now left to mark the spot where it stood, save a graveyard. The following with their wives, were the original members of this church: Elder Samuel Robertson, Alexander Adams, Hugh, Samuel and Robert Wiley, Richard and James Campbell, David Jolly, Joseph, Robert and James Stevenson, Joseph Wood, David Gray, Samuel M. Waugh, John Carter, John Riley, Sr., John Burns, Alexander Blair, Alexander Blair, Jr., William Stevenson, John Leeper, David, John and James Robertson, James Parks, Samuel Vogan, Hugh Cowen, John Hopkins, John Mann, etc., etc.

The next church was built by the Methodists, the forerunners of Christianity in the West, as John was the forerunner of the Saviour. It was built on Mount Pisgah—not that from which Moses caught a glimpse of the Promised Land—but a little hill in Nicholas County. It was of logs, and was built in 1814, and some years since, it was torn down and a frame building erected in its stead, at a cost of some $2,000. There are churches in the villages which will be mentioned in that connection.

The educational history of the precinct dates back to 1815, when a school was taught in a log hut, near Mount Pisgah Church, by Joseph Hopkins, which is supposed to have been the first school in this section. There was also a log cabin for school purposes, built near Shiloh church, very early, in which A. Ramsay was the first teacher. There are now but three schoolhouses in the precinct, two of these are frame and one of logs, situated as follows: Frame school buildings at Moorefield and East Union, and log building near Mount Pisgah Church. Scholars average from twenty to forty in each school.

Moorefield is a small village situated on the Carlisle and Sharpsburg Pike, in the northwest part of Union Precinct. It contains two general stores; two blacksmith shops, two tobacco warehouses, one church, one schoolhouse, and a few dwellings. The church here is of the Presbyterian denomination. and was built originally of logs in 1823. It was called "New Concord," and was organized under the ministrations of Rev. William K. Burch. The old log building has been replaced by a substantial frame, which still serves the congregation. The first settler of Moorefield was Benjamin Hall, who located where the village stands, in 1796. His two sons, Samuel and Nathaniel, opened a woolen factory in a frame building erected for that purpose, in 1815, but which is long since discontinued. The first store was opened by Alexander Blair & Son, about 1818; their clerk, James Clark, was appointed postmaster. Mrs. Hall, wife of Benjamin Hall, suggested that the post-office be called Moorefield, after a town near where she was born, a suggestion that was adopted without controversy. In 1819, Blair & Son moved their stock of goods to Carlisle; Samuel Hall succeeded Mr. Clark as postmaster, and bought his brother's interest in the woolen factory, which a few years later was turned into a store room and filled with goods, by Samuel Thompson. He remained about a year, and sold out to a son of Nathaniel Hall. The present stores are owned by W. B. Ratcliff and W. H. Howe, the latter of whom is the postmaster of the place.

East Union is located at the southwest part of the precinct, on the Moorefield and East Union Pike. It has one store owned and operated by Henry Bramlette, one blacksmith shop, a church and schoolhouse, one Masonic Lodge, with a few dwellings. The church is of the Christian denomination; it is a frame building, and cost about $2,500, and has a large and flourishing congregation. The Dunkards had a church here in early times composed of three families who came from the Carolinas, named Hahn, Shultz, and Accerman—Peter Hahn officiating as pastor, and under whose ministrations the church prospered—having at one time about four hundred members. They built a log church, which has moldered into decay, and stood near where now stands the Christian Church.

B. F. Reynolds, Lodge No. 443, A. F. & A. M., located at East Union, was chartered October 24, 1867; the first officers under the charter were elected November 9, 1867, and were as follows: B. F. Reynolds, W. M., G. W. Bramlette, S. W.; J. P. Stevenson, J. W.; B. E. Rice, Treasurer; J. W. Elington, Secretary, and H. W. Call, Tiler. The present officers (1882) are Henry C. Wells, Master; George W. Wilson, Senior Warden; G. W. Kookendoffer, Junior Warden; James A. Duncan, Treasurer; John N. Reed. Secretary; A. G. Shrout, Senior Deacon; Isaac E. Wills, Junior Deacon, and John N. Dalzell, Tiler. There are at present nineteen members.—*Perrin.*

CHAPTER XIV.

UPPER BLUE LICKS PRECINCT—NAME OF BUZZARD ROOST—DESCRIPTIVE AND TOPOGRAPHICAL FEATURES—EARLY SETTLEMENT—HARD LIFE OF THE PIONEERS—IMPROVEMENTS AND INDUSTRIES—CHURCHES—DEERING CAMP GROUND—SCHOOLS, VILLAGES, ETC.

Buzzard Roost! What's in a name? Shakespeare tells us that "a rose by any other name would smell as sweet," and the unpoetical name of "Buzzard Roost," which still clings to Upper Blue Licks Precinct, doubtless exhales no unpleasant odor over the classic hills and dales of this region. The name originated in the following manner: When the little village, which bears the name, was founded, whisky was sold out by the gallon, and that quantity being more than any single individual generally required, several parties would club together, procure that amount, retire to a log on one of the neighboring hills, and proceed to dispose of it by drinking it up. Upon a certain occasion this "happy family" had procured their accustomed quota, and were seated as usual upon their log enjoying themselves hugely, when a traveler—a stranger—happening along, asked the name of the place, and was told that it had no special name. Surveying the group of half-drunken men perched upon the log for a moment, he replied, "Then I will name it Buzzard Roost," and it has borne the name ever since. So much for Buzzard Roost.

Upper Blue Licks Precinct, formerly known as Buzzard Roost, is election precinct No. 6, and is bounded north by Lower Blue Licks Precinct and Fleming County, from which it is separated by the Licking river; east by Fleming County; south by Union Precinct, and west by Carlisle Precinct. The surface in the west part of the precinct is hilly, with several tillable ridges or table-lands; in the north and east parts of the land—as we were informed—is "set up edgewise and covered with large, flat rocks." Near the Upper Blue Licks the soil of the surrounding hills has been so tramped by the buffalo that about three feet of the top earth, more or less, has been washed away. All the streams and water-courses flow toward the Licking river. The two largest are Fleming and Cassidy Creeks. Fleming empties into the Licking at the old Parks mill; Cassidy rises in the southern part of the precinct and empties into main Licking at Parks' Ferry. The soil, notwithstanding the broken nature of the country, is fertile, being similar to that of Bourbon and Harrison Counties, and is underlaid by a deep stratum of yellow clay, and that by limestone. The

timber growth is principally oak, elm, walnut, hickory, hackberry, etc., etc. Besides the usual farm crops, fine crops of tobacco are raised. A number of mounds, and other relics of the mound builders, are found in this precinct. These, however, are mentioned in the chapter on the pre-historic races and Indians, elsewhere in this volume. The Maysville division of the Kentucky Central Railroad passess through the northwestern part of this precinct, crossing the Licking River over a good bridge, about one mile below Parks' Ferry, and the station (Myers') affords good shipping facilities for this section.

There is not much history connected with the early occupation of this precinct. Owing to the rough nature of the larger portion of it, settlements were not made at as early a date as in the more level sections. Among the pioneers, however, may be mentioned Philip Stoops, Andrew Shanklin, Isaac West, and a man named Gouries, all of whom settled on Cassidy Creek. James Parks, more particularly mentioned in connection with the mill interests, was an early settler of the precinct. A man named Hawkins kept a whisky shop at Buzzard Roost, and was the first settler at that place, which in early times was famous, as already stated, for being a place of considerable dissipation. But after 1800 the country rapidly settled up, emigrants came in by scores, and civilization spread over the country.

The hardships of the early settlers are but a repetition of those in other portions of the county, with the exception, perhaps, that they were not quite so severe, owing to settlements being made elsewhere a little earlier. But the life in this locality was hard enough. Until mills were built, the means of procuring bread often brought the people to their wits' end. The fine water-power of Licking and its tributaries soon, however, obviated these difficulties.

The first mill in the precinct was built on the Licking by James Hall, at the mouth of Fishbasket Creek. It was known as "Myers' Old Mill," and was destroyed when the dams were taken out of the river. The next mill was that known as the "Fleming Creek Mill," which was one of the old mills of the country, and is quite historical in its character. It was built in 1808–9 by James Parks, and was located at the mouth of Fleming Creek. The site of the mill was long since obliterated, and the original bed of the creek reclaimed by Colonel Parks, the present owner of the land. The creek, like the Mississippi River, had several mouths, forming a delta, and by damming the upper mouth and turning the water of the creek into the lower, during high water the Licking would back up into the upper mouth, and receding would leave a deposit sometimes a foot in depth. By this process, Colonel Parks has reclaimed some twenty or thirty acres of land, which before was rough and untillable, but now extremely rich and productive, having been cultivated in corn every year since 1853. But this mill, in its palmy days, was one of the best in the country. The stone work was built by Thomas Metcalfe (old "Stone Hammer"), a resident of the county, and afterward Governor of the State. The mill had two run of buhrs, one of which was Laurel Hill rock, and the other Red River stone. The capacity was about forty barrels of flour per day, most of which was shipped to New Orleans by flat boats out of the Licking River. In connection with these shipments, are the following account of sales, invoice and letter, which we give in full, and which are illustrative of the business done by this pioneer mill. They are on a double sheet of paper, three pages of which are occupied in the order following:

Mr. James Parks in acct. with Maunsel, White & Co.

1816			Dr.		Cr.	
Oct.	29	By proceeds 76 Bbls. of flour......			516	81
Nov.	2	To Cash paid M. T. Gleason.......	250			
Dec.	11	By proceeds 300 bbls. of flour, per accts. of this date..............			2,330	68
1817 Jan.	10	By proceeds 100 bbls. Flour, per acct. annexed..................			859	97
"	"	To postage........................	1	25		
"	22	" our draft on Robinson & Rhinelander, New York, @ 60 ds., in your favor...............	3,456	21		
			$3,707	46	3,707	46

Errors Excepted.
New Orleans, Jan. 22, 1817.
MAUNSEL, WHITE & CO.

The above occupies the first page of the sheet; on the second page is the following:

Account of sales of 100 Bbls. Flour rec'd per flat-boat Wm. Newsam, Master, on acct. and risk of James Parks.

Date. 1817	Purchasers.	When Due	No. Bbls.	Price.	Amount.
Jan. 8	Cash,		1	$10.50	$10.50
" 9	Boudorgue,		1	10.50	10.50
" 11	M. Laronde,		1	10.00	10.00
" "	S. Blackwell,		3	11.00	33.00
" 14	Cash.		4	11.00	44.00
" 16	N. Boudorgue.		6	10.50	63.00
" "	E. Trepagny,		2	10.50	21.00
" 17	Cash.		4	10.50	42.00
" 18	"		4	10.50	42.00
" 20	"		4	10.50	42.00
" "	Philippon,		2	11.00	22.00
" "	J. Brandt & Co.	Feb. 22.	68	10.50	714.00
Total,			100		$1,053.50

CHARGES.

Inspection, $4.00; Freight, @ $1½, $150.00....	$154.00	
Storages, @ 6¼c., $6.25; Cartage, $4.70; Labor, $2	12.95	
Cooperage, 25c.; Commission, @ 2½ per cent., $26.33	26.58	193.53
Net proceeds when collected		$859.97

Errors Excepted.
New Orleans, Jan. 20, 1817.
MAUNSEL, WHITE & CO.

The third page is taken up with the following letter:

NEW ORLEANS, Jan. 22, 1817.

JAMES PARKS, ESQUIRE,

DEAR SIR: Since we had this pleasure on 27th Decr. last we received per Wm. Newsam on your account one hundred barrels of Flour, sales of which you will find hereto annexed. And of proceeds $859 97/100. You will see some of it is sold on a short credit. We also send you your account current, amount now due you in conformity thereto when all debts are collected $3,456 84/100 for which sum we send you our dft. drawn in your favor on Messrs. Robinson & Rhinelander, New York at 60 days sight, which we hope will prove satisfactory, and is much better than bills on Philadelphia, and will be easier paper off with you. We understand they are selling at Lexington for six per cent premium. The Banks are doing nothing and altho' it does not appear that there is any further alarm about failures, yet the confidence is not entirely restored. Flour continues to be in great demand and best quality for bakery would bring $11 and 11½ per Bbl. Good superfine fit for shipping is from $10 -$10½ in demand. We sincerely regret that your two first parcels were not as fresh as we could wish, it delayed in some measure the sales as well as prevented our getting so good a price. We recommend to you strongly to send on flour as fast as you can. We send you second of exchange by this mail, and by next you will received the first. Yours sincerely

MAUNSEL, WHITE & CO.

This sheet is folded letter size, sent without cover, and is directed as follows:

25

JAMES PARKS ESQUIRE

Mouth Flmeing near

ELLISVILLE

KENTUCKY.

MAIL

There was a saw-mill in connection with this old mill which did as large a business in its time as the flour-mill. Both were carried away by a freshet about 1840, and were never rebuilt.

Cassidy Creek mill was also built by James Parks. It was about half a mile above the mouth of the Cassidy Creek, and was built between 1816 and 1819, and considered one of the best mills in the State. It had three run of buhrs, of the Red River stone, and had a capacity of sixty barrels a day. In addition to custom work, it averaged from forty to forty-five barrels a day for export, which were shipped to New Orleans. Mr. Parks had a contract to furnish the army at New Orleans during the war of 1812, which flour was ground on his Fleming Creek mills, the same mentioned above as being washed away in 1840. During the height of prosperity of these mills, Mr. Parks packed pork extensively, which was also shipped to New Orleans, and dry goods, groceries, etc., brought back for the trade in this section.

The Upper Blue Licks mill was built about 1862, and is both saw and grist mill. It was built by Richard Spencer, and run afterward for four or five years by Short, Hopkins & Co., when, in 1880, it was purchased by Vaughn, Mitchell & Humphreys, and moved from the Upper Blue Licks to its present site, about half a mile further up the river. A boom was built and arrangements made for drawing logs out of the river by steam. They get all their supplies from the raftsmen of the Licking River, and cut from 200,000 to 300,000 feet of lumber annually, selling to the surrounding country.

The Parks' Ferry Mill is owned and operated by the Washington Manufacturing and Mining Company. This company was chartered in 1869, and owns some thirty acres of ground, about half of which is occupied by the "Deering Camp Ground," a full history of which is found elsewhere in this volume, in the church history of the county. The original stockholders of the company were T. S. Parks, President; T. J. Glenn, M. A. Glenn, R. M. Parks and Benjamin Adair, the latter of whom sold his interest to Thomas Dorsey, before any active steps were taken by the firm. In 1862, a half interest was sold to Collier & Wood. The main business interest of this company at present, is the saw-mill located at Parks' Ferry, and connected by a railway, owned by the Company, with the Kentucky Central Railroads' Maysville branch. They make all kinds of rough, dressed and matched lumber, scroll work, laths, staves, pickets, etc. Their capacity with a 30 horse-power engine, has been about a million and a half feet per annum. In the early part of 1882, a 90 horse-power engine was put in, which increased their capacity to three million feet annually. They have a branch lumber yard in Paris, and also keep about half a million feet in stock at the mill. They work about twenty hands, at an average of $1.25 per day wages.

The Moorefield and Upper Blue Licks Turnpike connects those two places, distance six and one-third miles from each other. This road was the first laid out in the precinct, and is the "old Buffalo Trace," from the Boonesborough country to the Upper Blue Licks, and afterward became the State road. In 1866 a company was formed, and five miles of it was piked, leaving one and a third miles, part at each end, which was not piked until 1879. The Parks' Ferry Turnpike was from Parks' Ferry to within one and one-half miles of Carlisle. It was surveyed and graded the entire distance, but has not yet been entirely finished. The road from Parks' Ferry to Bethel was the first north and south road in the precinct, and there is at the present time (1882), considerable talk of piking it. The roads generally follow the water-courses or ridges, it being impossible to run them across the hills without scaling ladders.

There are two ferries in the precinct; one at the Upper Blue Licks, owned by Samuel Clay, of Bourbon County, and Parks' Ferry, six miles below, owned by Colonel T. S. Parks. The boats at both ferries are propelled across the stream by the force of the current, this peculiar style of boating being the invention of James Parks, the Colonel's brother.

The precinct of Upper Blue Licks is well supplied with churches, and, if the people are not good Christians, it is probably their own fault. Besides several good, comfortable church buildings, there is the Deering Camp Ground, which is famous as a place of holding camp-meetings of the Methodist Church. The first church built in the precinct was, probably, Mount Zion Church, located in the eastern part. It was first built of logs, by the Dunkards, about the year 1830. The present frame structure was built by the Christian denomination in 1850. The first pastor was Peter How. It has now about one hundred and fifty members. Among the early preachers were Reverends Reynolds, Renlen, Samuel McCormick and Morrison. The present pastor is Melom Metcalfe.

Pleasant Valley Christian Church is located in the valley of the same name, was built in 1876, and dedicated by Elder George Kimberly, and, at present, has one hundred and twenty-five members. Its pastors have been Elders Joseph Graves and William Hull. There is at present no pastor. The building is a frame, and cost $800. Sunday-school in good weather.

Parrish's Chapel (Methodist Episcopal South) is located on Cassidy's Creek, about two miles above its mouth. The present edifice was built in 1859, and cost $2,000; was dedicated by Rev. Samuel Robertson; has one hundred members, under the pastorate of Rev. William T. Godby. The original church building was burned about 1830; a log building was then put up and stood until the building of the present edifice. Among the members forty years ago were William and James Stoops, John W. Shanklin, Adam West, and Billy Linn and family. Among the noted preachers that have served it as pastors, may be mentioned Revs. Snively, Cunningham, Savage, Chamberlain, Hobbs, Brush, Kavanaugh, Evans, Kelley, etc., etc. It was originally a Republican church, and under that *regime* the following were among its pastors, viz: Revs. Isbell and Helm.

Murphy's Chapel (Methodist Episcopal), located on Cassidy's Creek, three miles above its mouth, is a frame building, and cost $800. It was organized in 1870, by John S. Cox, at White's schoolhouse. Its first pastor was Rev. M. D. Murphy, after whom it was named. The society now numbers forty-five members, and the present pastor is Rev. H. W. Bailey. Other pastors have been Revs. J. F. Harrison, Tilman Kennedy, S. G. Pollard and B. F. Whitman. The church meets every second Saturday and Sunday; Sunday-school regularly in good weather. As we have said, a sketch of the Deering Camp Ground appears elsewhere in this work.

The first schools of the precinct did not amount to much, nor is it known of a certainty who taught the first one. But one of the first remembered was taught by one John Vaughn on Big Branch. The schools of the present day, are much better than are to be found in many parts of Kentucky, but even in these there is still considerable room for improvement. The common schools are the most perfect means of educating the masses for useful positions in life, and should be earnestly supported. There are four district schools in the precinct, which are usually well patronized.

The Upper Blue Lick Springs, on Licking River, and from which this precinct derives its name, is an historical spot. Salt was found here more than seventy-five years ago, by one McClanahan; five hundred gallons of water made a bushel of salt, which was worth $4.50 per bushel. David Finlay had a mill here very early, and also kept tavern. A more extended notice appears in a preceding chapter, however, and will not be repeated here. The village known as Upper Blue Licks is situated at these springs, and contains one store and post office. The name of the postoffice is "Davidson," after the first, present and only postmaster it has ever had—W. R. Davidson. There is a cooper shop at the village, where casks are made for transporting the Blue Lick water, which is now shipped to all parts of the United States. The village consists of but a very small collection of houses, and is a place of but little general business. Blackhawk is the name of the post office at Myers' Station, on the Maysville branch of the Kentucky Central Railway, near Parks' Ferry. There are several blacksmith shops located at different points in the precinct; three, are at Cassidy's Creek, one at Myers' Station and one on the north side of Licking River, in what is called Pleasant Valley.

Buzzard Roost village is the voting place of the precinct, and as stated in the opening of this chapter, the precinct long went by the same name, but was finally changed to Upper Blue Licks. It is situated on the Moorefield and Upper Blue Licks Pike, about half way between the two places, at the crossing of the Parks' Ferry and Bethel road. It contains one store, and one blacksmith and wood shop. The origin of its name is given elsewhere.

Fitch Munger Lodge, No.——A. F. and A. M., is located at Willow Valley, about one mile south of the Upper Blue Licks. It was founded in 1871, at Buzzard Roost, and named in honor of Fitch Munger. In 1879, it was moved to Willow Valley, and is in good working order. It owns its hall, and has twenty-three members. The first officers were: W. B. Hopkins, Master; W. J. Myers, Senior Warden; Alvin Branch, Junior Warden; W. R. Potts, and H. B. Myers, Deacons; and G. C. Faris, Steward and Tiler. The present officers are as follows: N. C. Crouch, Master; T. Kearn, Senior Warden; T. M. Tant, Junior Warden; T. W. Vaughn, Treasurer; C. T. Neal, Secretary; and Charles McVey, Steward and Tiler.

Pleasant Valley is a portion of the precinct comprising about half a dozen farms, lying on the north side of the Licking River. The land lies well and is very fertile. The first store in the precinct was kept by James Parks. The village called Pleasant Valley, contains about a dozen families, and one merchant flouring mill, owned by W. S. Tant, of Flemingsburg; one blacksmith and wood shop; one church, the history of which has already been given; one physician, and one Masonic Lodge. The latter is known as W. S. Tant Lodge, and was organized in 1876. It has about fifty members, and William Barton was the first Master. The present officers are: Abner McIntire, Master; Cornelius Garey and George Moore, Wardens; William Garey, Treasurer; Charles Shanklin, Secretary; and James Gray, Tiler.—*Perrin.*

APPENDIX.

THOROUGHBRED HORSES OF BOURBON, SCOTT AND HARRISON COUNTIES.

KENTUCKY is noted, not only in this country, but in Europe, and indeed throughout the civilized world, almost, for its fine stock, and particularly its thoroughbred horses. Wherever the American horse is known (and in what country is he not known ?) the Kentucky horse is known, and appreciated as well. The celebrity of the Kentucky horse has been attained principally, perhaps wholly, by the blooded horses bred and reared in the central part of the State, of which Bourbon, Scott and Harrison form a most important part. "There is no region of America," says a writer upon the subject, "so highly favored for the breeding of fine horses as the Blue Grass Region of Kentucky. This is to be attributed in a large degree to the nature of the soil in which he is reared. There is no doubt that animals which are fed upon grass and grain, and drink water impregnated with lime, have larger and stronger bones than those reared upon clay and sandy soils. The best sections of the country to breed and rear fine stock will be found, as a rule, to follow the limestone formations of America. The Blue Grass Region of Kentucky, and that portion of Tennessee with a tier of counties surrounding Nashville, are strong limestone regions, which accounts for the celebrity and superiority acquired by the horses of these sections over less favored portions of America. The high, rolling land, the limestone water, the quantity and quality of the herbage, is the cause, doubtless, of the success of Kentucky and Tennessee breeders. The climate is suitable to the constitution of the horse, and the land grows that description of provender so well calculated for his sustenance and development."

An article upon thoroughbred horses, written recently by Ben G. Bruce, Esq., the able editor of the *Live Stock Record*, contains the following, which will be found of much interest, doubtless, to our readers. It says: "It is a well known fact that horses bred on low, wet and marshy lands, are coarse and heavy in their shoulders; their legs are fleshy, and wanting in that fine, wiry development of sinew necessary for the performance of hard labor; their feet being continually exposed to moisture, become flat, spongy and weak, and, when called upon to undergo severe work, soon become the victim of disease. The sole and frog, being rendered soft by too much moisture, subjects the extremely delicate internal structure to frequent bruises, which, by inflammation produced, so completely deform the parts as to create lameness of an incurable character. Not only are the feet affected by wet and marshy situations, but the whole animal frame. Succulent herbage tends to the production of fat, with loose, flaccid muscles, and sinews of a similar texture, the very reverse of that which is requisite for the thoroughbred horse, or, indeed, for the animal that is to be qualified for speedy or continued exertions; whereas, in the Blue Grass Region, the land is dry and sound, somewhat elevated and rolling, conducing to a clean, wiry and muscular animal.

* * * * * * * * * *

"There is a remarkable difference observable in horses raised from different breeds and on different soils. These differences are most noticeable in regard to the form of the head, ears, muzzle, legs, tendons, muscular fiber, hoofs, skin and hair. The horses bred, for instance, in Pennsylvania, differ as much from the Kentucky thoroughbred horse, as the oak or hickory of the same species in these States. The weight, measure and texture are different. In the Kentucky-bred horse the bones are more solid, the tendons stronger and much better defined, the muscles are more firm and elastic. The Pennsylvania-bred horse's bones are very soft and spongy, light and large. A square inch of bone from a thoroughbred Kentucky horse is much heavier than a square inch from a Pennsylvania draft-horse, the latter being more porous and chalky, resembling pumice stone, while the former is solid, partaking more of the close-grained nature of ivory. The muscular fiber in the one is coarser and more lax, although strong, and bears the same relation to that of the other as cotton to silk. In the

Pennsylvania horses, the arteries are larger and the veins somewhat smaller and more deeply buried, the tendency to take on adipose matter much greater.

"If you take Kentucky horses or cattle to Pennsylvania and the Eastern States, their posterity begins to undergo a change in the first generation; and in the second it is still greater; and in the tenth or twelfth remove they are not the same breed of animals. This change is produced by difference in climate and food. The climate is nearly in the same latitude, and the great change must be caused by the difference in soil, and consequently in the vegetation. Animal formation is modified by the vegetable formations of which it is the result, and the vegetable formations are modified by the elements of the soil from which they derive their nourishment. Not only the forms of animals, but their physical systems, their secretions and excretions are affected by the difference of geological formations from which they derive, through its vegetation, the elements of their organization.

"It is well known that certain localities, from the nature of the soil, produce better grapes, which impart a peculiar flavor and bouquet to the wine made from them. It is also well known that certain sections of Kentucky and Tennessee produce whiskies of peculiar flavor, aroma and excellence; that they cannot be made elsewhere in the same perfection, without the peculiar water and grain to be found in those localities. We cannot grow to perfection the peculiar tobacco of Cuba, which furnishes the high-flavored cigars of that beautiful island. We cannot find a locality in which we can grow the tobacco that portions of Connecticut furnish for cigar wrappers. Why is all this, if the soil, and the peculiar constituents that go to form it, have nothing to do in the formation of animal life? The effect produced in the rose by difference in climate and soil is well known. Its delightful aroma is much less concentrated when it grows in a cold than in a warm climate; its colors are not so varied, nor its texture so delicate. We see marked differences in the influence of soil and climate in the human family. The race of men in a limestone region are larger, as a rule, than those in the sandy or freestone sections of the country. The great stock-producing county of England is Yorkshire, situated on limestone. The nature of the soil and its vegetable productions is the cause of these remarkable differences of form, texture, aroma, etc. If not, why is it that not only certain plants, but certain animals, are never found except in climates indigenous to them, if soils and vegetable products play no part with them? We know that lime, silex and phosphates are taken up by the vital organs of plants, giving them size, strength and firmness. If plants take them up, why should not the vital organs of animals take them from the food raised on such soils? We think that this will go far to show why the dry, rolling lands of Central Kentucky, with her temperate climate, limestone soils and water has proven such a great region for the production of the thoroughbred and highest grades of stock.

"Kentucky is chiefly indebted to her mother, Virginia, for the material upon which her present stock is founded. Virginia has long been regarded, and justly, too, as the race-horse region of America. Her ascendency upon the turf for many years was very decided, but it is probable that racing and breeding commenced simultaneously, or nearly so, in the States of Virginia and Maryland. These two States were principally the homes of men of birth attached to the Cavalier party; race-horses were bred and trained, and many celebrated English sires were imported in the early part of the eighteenth century, prior to the outbreak of the old French war. Bulle Rock, foaled in 1708, by the Darley Arabian, dam by the Byerley Turk, was imported into Virginia before the Revolution, in 1730. Dabster, foaled in 1736, by Hobgoblin, dam by Spanker, was imported into Virginia, in 1742 or 1743. In the New England States, the settlers of which were for the most part attached to the Puritan party, and therefore opposed to all amusements and pastimes as frivolous, at the least, and unprofitable and to horse-racing more especially, as profane and positively wicked, very few horses of thoroughbred blood were imported, or stood in that section of the country.

"Racing was kept up in Virginia for many years, with unabated interest, and to Virginia is the country chiefly indebted for the large number of imported stallions and mares. All her great men were fond of this and kindred sports. Gen. Washington was particularly fond of deer and fox hunting, and he and Thomas Jefferson both ran horses at Alexandria, Va., about 1790. Racing was carried on in Maryland many years previous to Braddock's defeat in 1753, and Gov. Ogle was presented with the celebrated imported stallion, Spark, by Lord Baltimore, who received him as a present from his Royal Highness, Frederick, Prince of Wales, father of King George III. After the Revolutionary war, the country was chiefly indebted to Col. John Tayloe, of Mount Airy, Va., and Col. John Hoomes, of Bowling Green, Va., for the importation of the best thoroughbred horses; but, after 1803 or 1804, for many years importations languished. To Col. John Tayloe we are indebted for imported Chance, Dungannon, Gabriel, Mufti, O'Kelly, Robin Redbreast, Sir Peter Teazle, Volunteer and others. To Col. John Hoomes the country is indebted for the importations Archduke, Bedford, Buzzard, Cormorant, Dare Devil, Dashington, Diomed, Dion, Dragon, Druid, Escape, Herod,

Manfred, Play or Pay, and Sterling. From these horses most of the stock in Kentucky have, in a great degree, descended, especially from Diomed, from whom more distinguished horses have descended than from any other ever imported to America. Indeed, he may be called the American Godolphin, Sir Archy, Timoleon, Boston and Lexington coming in lineal descent from this distinguished horse. After Kentucky and Tennessee were admitted as States, they soon took rank as the great breeding and racing points, and may be said to have far outstripped their noble mother, old Virginia. Kentucky and Tennessee were principally settled by Virginians; and inheriting the tastes of their fathers, racing was commenced while in a territorial state. The material upon which to build up an account of the breeding and racing in Central Kentucky, in its infancy, are meager, and but little effort will be made in this article to look up their earliest history, and introduction."

From all published accounts and data at hand, we find that the sports of the turf was the first amusement the early settlers indulged in, aside from the house-raising, log-rolling and quilting parties. In the old *Kentucky Gazette*, of August, 1789, we find the following notice. "A purse race will take place at Lexington on the second Thursday in October next, free for any horse, mare or gelding; weight for age agreeable to the rules of New Market (three-mile heats), best two in three, each subscriber to pay one guinea, including his subscription, the horses to be entered the day before running, with Mr. John Fowler, who will attend at Mr. Collins' tavern on that day. Subscriptions taken by Nicholas Lafou, Lexington." Capt. John Fowler was one of the very first men in Kentucky who devoted special attention to racing, and to matters pertaining to the turf. He was a Captain in the Revolutionary war, the first Representative in Congress from this district, and for many years was Postmaster at Lexington. He took considerable interest in fine horses, and in racing matters generally.

The following incident is illustrative of the early history of the turf, as its sports were practiced in Central Kentucky by the pioneers. It occurred in what is now Nicholas County, but was then (1795) Bourbon: "About the year 1795, there came there from Virginia a proud young man, mounted upon a very fine thoroughbred horse. He was rather boastful, and assumed airs which highly irritated the wild boys of the Licking Hills, and the native sons of the soil generally. Confident of the fleetness of his horse, he bantered the neighbors for a race. It was known to a few, that a couple of the best racers in the country had been repeatedly run against each other, and were of about the same speed. A poor boy of the neighborhood had, for the amusement of the owners, run them against one another—he riding both the horses at the same time, *a la* circus. The young Virginian was notified that if he would ride himself, they would *run two* (2) horses at the same time against his, and would bet on their success what they could afford, which was mostly the skins of various wild animals, against anything of equal value. The challenge was accepted, and a meadow in the creek bottom near by selected for a half-mile race. The day arrived; the three horses were brought forward. For the rider of the two, appeared this same poor boy,* about half-grown, barefooted, bareheaded, dressed in a tow-linen shirt, with pantaloons of the same material. The dress was not assumed for the occasion, but was the best he could afford, although neither neat nor gaudy. He was endowed with a well-formed head, a keen, penetrating eye, a fearless, benevolent and cheerful countenance; and was animated with a noble zeal for the occasion, believing the honor of Kentucky was at stake. The riders mounted, the boy having one foot on each horse. The signal was given; away went the racers at full speed, and for about two hundred yards, it could not have been decided which was ahead. The boy in endeavoring to run near a stump three feet high, did not guide exactly as he intended; the stump was leaped by one of the horses, which greatly disturbed the equilibrium of the rider, but did not throw him. The Virginian's horse dashed ahead. The other two ran with great fleetness, and at six hundred yards it was neck and neck. At the end of the race, the pair of horses were a full length ahead, amid the huzzas and shouts of the multitude. The young Virginian paid his losses without a murmur. A big treat was proposed by those in luck, and accepted by the crowd. The successful rider was looked for, but could not be found; unaccustomed to applause, he had disappeared. The Virginian, however, avenged himself on two subsequent occasions, by beating each horse singly, they having a different rider. But he was again mortified by being beat by the boy riding at the same time both horses." Thus was the sport of racing introduced into Central Kentucky. This unique race, it will be observed, took place in 1795, almost ninety years ago, and about three years after Kentucky became a State.

In proof of the interest taken in horse-flesh by our fathers, we find as early as 1788, some half dozen or more thoroughbred stallions advertised in the old *Kentucky Gazette*, published by John Bradford at Lexington, and the first newspaper established west of the Alleghany Mountains. Among these were Nero, Flimnap, Mogul, Pilgarlick,

*Thomas Metcalfe, afterward Governor of the State, and U. S. Senator from Kentucky.

Red Bird, Darius, etc., and they were advertised to stand for service for so many pounds of tobacco, or bushels of corn, etc., etc. Among the thoroughbred stallions, which gained some notoriety in the blue grass section, up to the beginning of the present century, additional to those noticed above, are Imported Lath and Tippoo Saib, his son, Slider, Dolphin, Don Carlos, Ferguson Gray, Laburnum, Union and others. These horses, though the best of their day, and conspicuous as breeders in the early history of the thoroughbred horse interest in this section, played no particular or important part in the stock as represented here at the present time, as few, if any, of the noted horses now bred trace their genealogy back to them.

Lexington has always been the grand center of racing, not only of the Blue Grass Region, but for the entire State of Kentucky. For almost a hundred years, racing has been pretty regularly kept up there, and from the first establishment of the *Kentucky Gazette* up to 1800, we find frequent advertisements of meetings to come off, but it was not until November 12, 1795, that the *Gazette* gives its readers a report of races run. It says: "The first day, four-mile heats were won by Col. Simeon Buford's Mogul distancing the field. The first heat, three started. Second day, three-mile heats, five started; won by Abraham Buford's Weazel in two heats."

On January, 26, 1796, a banter was made through the columns of the *Gazette*, by Leonard Claiborne, to run a match with his horse Bumpard for £500 (a pound being $3.33 in our currency), against Col. Simeon Buford's Mogul. Col. Buford accepted the challenge, and the race was doubtless run, though the files of the *Gazette* furnish no report of it. The newspapers, however, of that period did not give the amount of local news found in the press at the present day. It is a matter of some surprise that so little news of a local character did find its way in the early newspapers, for it seems to us that common sense would have dictated to the editor its interest over their usual "Foreign Intelligence," and other State matters to which they gave room each week. It may be of some interest to the young sports of the turf at the present day to read the following notice published in the *Gazette* in 1796: "The following list of weights allowed to be carried: 7 years old, 10 stone; 6 years old, 9 stone; 5 years old, 8 stone; 4 years old, 7 stone; and 3 years old, a feather."* The rules of the turf were quite different then from what they are now, but just as efficient perhaps as those by which we are governed at the present day.

The following list of stallions figured in Central Kentucky from 1797 to 1804, some of whom produced progeny that have proved themselves among the best racers of Kentucky. The list embraces the following: American Godolphin, Scipio, Pantaloon, Flag of Truce, Medley, Lamplighter, Albert Shelley, Postmaster, Hudibras, Republican, Flimnap, Bacchus,* Thompson's Medley, Olympus, and the imported horses, Spread Eagle, Paymaster, Tup and Forrester. "With the exception," says a writer, "of Imp. Spread Eagle, none of these horses left any descendants of note." Among his progeny, may be mentioned the following: Nancy Taylor, who produced Lady Jackson, by Sumpter, and from the latter descended Barbara Allen, Theatriss, Miss Riddle, Uncle Jeff and others well known in their day. Purity came from Imp. Spread Eagle, and also Maid of the Oaks. From these descended Jim, Josh, Anna, Patsey, Mary Belle, Young Maid of the Oaks, Katy Ann, Medoc, Cora, Gypsy, etc., etc. From these, as we have said, some of the best racers in Kentucky have descended, and among which may be mentioned Nannie and Sallie Lewis, My Lady, Aldebaran, John Morgan, Hunter's Lexington, Lotta, Glen Rose, Susan Beane, Acrobat, Glidelia, Susquehanna, Sensation, Onondaga, Glenmore, Liz Morgan, Hunter's Glencoe, Morgan Scout, Ratan, Cuba, Blue Belle, Julia Mattingly, Belle of Nelson and a great many others.

In illustration of the fact that racing, and the sports of the turf took an early hold upon the people, and that Lexington has always been the great center of attraction of the racing interest, we find that a Jockey Club was formed in 1797, and at a meeting, held at Postlethwaite's Tavern, (now the Phœnix) on the 17th of October, of that year, the following resolutions were adopted:

Resolved, That there be a purse race run over the Lexington course, on the second Wednesday, and the two following days in November next; the first day, four-mile heats; second day, three-mile heats; and the third day, for four-year-olds, two-mile heats; aged horses carrying 130 pounds; six years old, 120 pounds; five years old, 100 pounds; and three years old, a feather.

Resolved, That Samuel Downing, A. Holmes, G. Anderson, R. W. Downing and J. B. January be a committee to admit persons wishing to become members of the club.

Resolved, That the next meeting of this club be at this house, on this day week, at 6 o'clock, P. M.

C. Banks, *Secretary.*

From this period on, the races continued pretty regularly, and among those who took an active part we find the names of Maj. Streshly, J. M. Garrard, Col. A. Buford, J. M. Gatewood, Capt. W. Allen, Shelley, Maj. Willis, Mr. Morris, Col. S. Buford and others.

Thus was introduced into Central Kentucky, and into Bourbon, Scott and Harrison Counties, the breeding and rearing of blooded horses, and the training of them for the turf. As a commercial interest alone, the rearing of thor-

*A stone is fourteen pounds, and a feather is five stone, or seventy pounds.

oughbred horses in the blue grass section has contributed more to Kentucky's high reputation abroad than any other of her natural resources and industries. When we consider the high prices which the best thoroughbred horses of this region have brought in the markets, their commercial value is no longer a matter of wonder. The following sales are illustrative of the fact: Mambrino Bertie, $10,000; Steinway, $13,000; Lady Stout, $15,000; Maud S., $21,000; Jewett, $15,000; Alcantara, $18,000; Lady Thorn, $30,000; Blackwood, $25,000; Santa Claus, $25,000; Monroe Chief, $25,000; Van Arnim, $10,000; So-so, $10,000; Mambrino Pilot, $10,000; Nutwood, $15,000; Mambrino Kate, $10,000; Trinket, $12,000; Darby, $16,000; Lulu, $25,000; Dick Jamison, $10,000; Maud Macey, $10,000; Director, $10,000; Grafton, $15,000, etc., etc. Many other high-priced horses could be mentioned, who have contributed toward giving Central Kentucky its great reputation for thoroughbreds, but those given are sufficient, though but a few of the many.

As much interest as is taken in racing and turf-matters by the breeders of fast horses in Bourbon, Scott and Harrison Counties, the facilities for racing have never been such in any of these counties as to at all compare with those of Lexington and Fayette County; and hence, that has always been, as we have said, the great racing center, not only of Central Kentucky, but of the entire State. There, turfmen gather at the fall and spring meetings of the Running Association, together with the most noted horses the country can produce.

One of the finest importations of horses ever made into Kentucky was in the year 1860, by the Kentucky Importing Company. The company was formed in 1859, but did not make its first importation until the next year, when a purchase was made in England of some twenty-five head of fillies and one colt, which were shipped to this country, and to Central Kentucky; one or two of these died on shipboard, and the others were sold at public sale in November, 1860. The war coming on, this importation proved less valuable than it otherwise would have done. Among these fillies were Britannia Fourth, Cairn Gorme, Coral, Cecily Jopson, Clifton Lass, Elltham Lass, King Tom Filly, Filigree, L'Auglaise, Loup Garon Filly, Maud, Rosalind and a number of others. Some of these were stolen during the war, and consequently nothing is known of their produce. From the others descended some of the best racers that have ever been bred in Kentucky. But we have neither time nor space to give particulars of the part played by their descendants on the turf, not only of Kentucky, but the country at large.

The breeding and training of trotting horses has grown to be a large business interest of the Blue Grass Region of Kentucky, equalling, if not even excelling in interest, running exercises upon the turf. Training horses for this species of speed, commenced in this section about the year 1843.

Says Dr. Herr, of Fayette County, "When I located in Bourbon County in 1842, nothing was said about fast trotters, either of breeding or training horses for speed. There was at that time a little interest manifested in fast-pacing horses, and pacing stallions were shown at fairs and spring stallion shows. There being no regular trotting or pacing tracks at that day, the horses were exhibited and paced on the Commons."

Among the pacing stallions that figured in Bourbon and the surrounding counties in the early days of fine horses, may be mentioned Tom Teemer, Tecumseh, Brown Pilot, Black Indian, The Copper Bottoms, Davy Crockett (the best of his day), Tom Crowder, Faro, Captain Walker, etc., etc. Old Davy Crockett was owned by Mr. Blackburn, the father of Hon. Joe Blackburn, Representative in Congress, and was a Canadian horse. Tom Crowder was owned by William Skinner, and between these two stallions (Davy Crockett and Tom Crowder) the greatest rivalry existed, each claiming to be the fastest pacer. Great interest was taken by the public in these two horses, and at the earnest solicitation of friends, the owners brought them together at the stallion show in Cynthiana, to test their speed. Dr. Herr relates the following of this meeting of the celebrated rivals: "Jink Goodman, of Paris, went to Woodford County and contracted with 'Uncle Ned' Blackburn to farm Davy Crockett, and make a season with him in Bourbon County. He (Blackburn) agreed upon the grounds only that I should fit and ride him against old Tom Crowder, at the pending stallion shows of the community, which I readily agreed to do. When it became known that Crowder and Crockett, the famous rivals, would pace at the stallion show in Cynthiana on court day, the greatest excitement was created, for both horses had many friends. According to arrangement, when the appointed day arrived, William Skinner appeared upon the show grounds, mounted on Tom Crowder, full of confidence; while I had charge of Davy Crockett. A great crowd was present. There being no track, we paced on the river bottom flat, or commons as it was called, a distance of 350 yards. We got ready, and made an even start, but at the finish Crockett was so far in the lead that the crowd got across the track, and shut Crowder off. Mr. Skinner was a splendid rider and horseman, and asked for another trial, which was readily granted, and in which Crowder was again beaten as easily as before. Old Davy Crockett could get away out of a stand stillquicker than any horse I ever rode, or have ever seen."

Pacing horses were more fashionable in Kentucky then than trotters, and there were some good ones in Bourbon, and the adjoining counties. Among the stock of Davy Crockett and Tom Crowder were many fine trotters, and even to this day it is considered valuable stock in trotting pedigrees. From pacing matches the sport gradually dropped into trotting matches, but for a number of years, pacing was almost of as much interest as trotting is now. Says our informant: "Occasionally, we made and paced matches on the Lexington Running Track, there being no trotting-tracks in the State. One of these matches was made between Yankee Boy and a horse by Tom Crowder. It was over the Lexington Running Track, and was paced in deep mud. Yankee Boy was beaten, but another match was instantly made for the same horses, to be paced upon a dry track, in which Yankee Boy easily won. Another match was paced over the Lexington track soon after, between a son of Davy Crockett and the Todhunter and Draper Mare, in which the Crockett horse was victorious." Many other small matches were paced here and elsewhere in that early period, between the noted horses then in the full career of their glory.

No interest was taken, as we have said, in breeding and training the trotter, prior to 1842, and one of the first, if not the first, man in Bourbon and her sister counties to embark in this branch of the fine horse interest, was Dr. L. Herr, a resident then of Bourbon County, but now a noted breeder of Fayette. He commenced the business on a limited scale about the year 1843, but according to his own account of it, he could only farm a few mares, and breed them to his stallions. He went to Montreal, Canada, in 1843, and bought two large Canadian horses—Cœur de Lion and Canada Chief, which he brought to this county. The latter horse was sold shortly after to a man in Tennessee, but Cœur de Lion was kept here, and from him descended some of the noted horses of the time. He was a three-minute trotter, while Canada Chief was both a pacer and a trotter, and fast at both gaits. Mr. Herr opened a track specially for trotting, and took great pains in improving the speed of his horses in that gait. The next noted trotting stallion in the neighborhood was Bellfounder, which stood at the unprecedented high price (then for a trotting stallion) of $10, but notwithstanding this, got all the mares he could serve. Other noted trotters of the early period of the trotting horse interest were Tough Sam, Berry Horse, Joe Lancaster, Tom Red, Henry, etc., etc. Neddy O'Blennis was one of the first trotters ever sold in Kentucky for as much as $2,000. He was trained and owned by Herr, and after winning the races at Cincinnati and Louisville, and up to four-mile heats, beating Pilot, Jr., Stranger from New York, and Murdock, he sold him for $2,000. Such a sale naturally opened people's eyes as to the value of trotting horses. Hitherto, fine coach, farm and saddle horses and thoroughbreds, had received all the attention of breeders, but a new era in horse-breeding began now. As soon as it was discovered that breeding the trotter was valuable, many wealthy gentlemen of the Blue Grass Region of Kentucky embarked in the business, among whom may be mentioned: R. A. Alexander, Mr. Dorsey, Col. Richard West, James Miller, Mr. Veech, Capt. M. M. Clay, the Messrs. Simmons, W. H. Wilson, Col. Stoner, Thomas Coons, Joel Berry, Henry Buford, John Stout, Robert Strader, Gen. Withers, B. J. Treacy, Isaac Smith, A. G. Peters, James Cromwell, Robert Prewitt, J. H. Bryant, James Carlisle, Andrew Steele, Dr. Miller, Hunt Bros., the Bowmans, William Bradley, William Buckner, J. W. Shawhan, Robert Pepper, J. S. McCann, Dr. Talbert, Cecil Brothers, Mr. Todhunter, etc., etc. These names are familiar to all who have paid any attention to the trotting horse interest in Kentucky. Many of them were, and are still, residents of these counties, and in later years, other breeders in Bourbon, Scott, etc., have been added to the list, until what is termed the northern belt of the Blue Grass Region may be considered as productive of fine horses as any spot in Kentucky or elsewhere.

In conclusion of this hastily-prepared sketch, which is intended merely as a brief history of the breeding of thoroughbred horses as a commercial interest of the country, the introduction of racing, trotting, etc., and not as an advertising puff of present horse and turf men, we will say, that among the prominent breeders of fine horses at the present day are James Miller, Col. Stoner, Col. Clay, Capt. Moore, the Messrs. Kerr, and others, of Bourbon County; James Cromwell, W. H. Wilson, and a number of others, in Harrison County; while Keene Richards, S. Y. Keene and Col. West* for years, until recently, have been among the most prominent breeders of Scott County. Many others, however, in each of these counties, devote more or less attention to the breeding of horses, but those mentioned are, perhaps, the largest breeders.

*Now resides in Fayette County.

PART II.

BIOGRAPHICAL SKETCHES.

BOURBON COUNTY.

PARIS CITY AND PRECINCT.

JOHN C. BRENT, banker; P. O. Paris; born Feb. 5, 1836; son of Charles S. Brent, who was born in this place, Jan. 28, 1811. The mother of John C., was Matilda Chambers, daughter of Gov. John Chambers. The grandfather of John C., was Hugh Brent, a native of Prena, Williams Co., Virginia; he was born Jany. 18, 1773. In 1799, he married Elizabeth Langhorne, who was born 1782, in Lynchburg, a daughter of Maurice Langhorne. Hugh Brent came to Kentucky in the fall of 1789, with his brother-in-law, Capt. Thomas Young, locating in Lexington, until 1792, when he became a citizen of Paris, and engaged in business up to 1824; he was a successful business man, and by his uniform courtesy and kindness, he won the love and the esteem of all those who had any business relations with him; one of his prominent traits of character, was his love for peace and its promotion. He had four sons and two daughters, viz: Jack, Thomas Y., Hugh I., Charles S., Sarah B. and Betsey. Charles S. Brent was thrice married: first to Susan Taylor; she died, leaving one son, Hugh, now of Covington, Ky. His second wife was Matilda Chambers, who was born March 17, 1815; they were married in 1835; she died Aug. 28, 1866, having borne him twelve children, nine of whom are living. His last wife was Mrs. Martha Ford, born in Pennsylvania, daughter of Benjamin J. Page. Mr. Brent died Feb. 16, 1881; he was raised a farmer, lived near Paris, on the farm; came to town in 1849, and engaged in banking until the war began, then engaged in the commission business in 1862, and in 1869 resumed banking; was president of the same up to the time of his death. He was a member of the Presbyterian Church since 1833, and was twelve years Elder of the same; and in 1839 and '40, he represented his county in the Legislature; he was a man whom the people esteemed as a valued citizen of the Commonwealth. His successor, John C., was educated here in Paris and graduated at Frankfort, under B. B. Sayre. August, 1862, he was commissioned as First Lieut. of Co. B., 9th Kentucky Cavalry, afterwards promoted to Major, was in active service some time, afterwards served on Court Martial, as Senior Major. Upon his return home he engaged in business with his father, as partner in the commission business. In 1869, he was appointed cashier of the Citizen's Bank, which position he yet fills. In 1866 he married Nicolie, daughter of Nicholas and Martha (Page) Ford; he was a native of this place; she of Pittsburg. Mr. Brent and wife are members of the Episcopal Church. Of the brothers and sisters living, are Elizabeth, who resides in Covington, wife of John Marshall; Sprigg J., Charles S., Thomas I., Kelly and Matilda, in Paris; also Belle, wife of Charlton Alexander; Henry C., resides in Kansas City, Mo., attorney at law.

LITTLEBERRY BEDFORD, Surveyor; P. O. Paris; is the grandson of Littleberry Bedford, the pioneer and hunter of Bourbon County. The parents of our subject were Littleberry and Cicely (Rollins) Bedford. Littleberry was born on the Patsey Clay farm July, 30, 1798; his wife Cicely, Jan'y 30 the same year (1798.) The father of our subject after his marriage, settled on the land now owned by the Buckner heirs, near Cane Ridge. He remained here several years, and finally located on a portion of the old homestead, where he remained until his death, Jan. 23, 1880; his wife died in 1843. Upon this old homestead our subject first saw the light of day, February, 1821; he had six brothers and sisters, viz: Elizabeth, who married Smith Lindsey, of Clintonville; Mary, Mrs. James C. Garrard, of Pendleton County; Caroline, wife of Samuel Pryor of this precinct. Thomas F., located in Missouri; Wm. P. and Webster

C., are teachers. Our subject at the age of twenty-one, began teaching, continuing regularly for about ten years, having taught in all about sixteen years. In 1861 he began the vocation of Surveyor, and has since been engaged in this business, and is one of the best in the country. Dec. 24, 1873, he married Miss Fannie Horton, a native of Lexington, Miss. She was a daughter af Memuca and Claramond (Harvey) Horton, who were natives of Georgia. To Mr. and and Mrs. Horton were born five children: Martha, who married Judge Montgomery, of Lexington, Miss. Next in order was Mrs. Bedford; William and George, were killed in the Southern army; Willis B., the youngest, graduated with honors at Edinburg College in Scotland; he now resides in Tucson, Arizona Territory. Since March, 1874, Mr. Bedford has resided on the Jackstown pike, where he has a snug home. He has no children. As relics, he possesses his grandfather's guns; and other articles once in his possession, which are rare and interesting.

JOHN C. BEDFORD, farmer; P. O. Paris; born in Clintonville Precinct, Jan. 20, 1843, the third child and fourth son born to Archibald M. and Elizabeth (Hawes) Bedford. After the marriage of Archibald Bedford and wife, they located in Clintonville, where the family were born, whose names were Aylette, Ellen E., Thomas A., John C. and Archibald W. The eldest child died in infancy; Ellen married William Bedford, and resides in Boone County, Mo.; Thomas A. died in the Southern army, being a member of the 1st Kentucky Battalion of Mounted Infantry. In the spring of 1846 Archibald M. Bedford located on the Stoner, near his brother George, where he remained until his death, Sept. 17, 1860; after his death, John C. lived with his uncle George until he entered the army, joining John Morgan's Standard, he and his brother Archie, and fought manfully and did well their duty until the close of the war. In 1865 J. C. moved to Sangamon County, Ills., and purchased a farm, residing here until 1869, when he returned to this county; in 1870 he purchased the farm he now owns, situated on the Flat Rock Pike; August 18, 1865, married Louisa Huffstetter, a native of Nicholas County, daughter of James and Alvira (Sparks) Huffstetter; both were natives of Virginia; J. C. has six children: Frank, Mary, Mattie, Maggie, Elvira and James; his brother, Archibald W., was born 1845, Jan. 14; Nov. 1, 1865, he married Henrietta Goff, born in Clark County, daughter of John and Martha (Prewitt) Goff; he has three children: John, Mattie and Caswell, twins; Archie resides in this county.

LITTLEBERRY M. BEDFORD, farmer and stock-trader; P. O. Paris. Among the prominent farmers of Bourbon County is the above gentleman, who was born in Paris Precinct, near where Henry Clay now resides; he first saw the light of day July 26, 1823; son of John and Sallie (King) Bedford; he died Dec. 8, 1871; his wife, Sallie, died the year following. Littleberry Mosely was reared to farming pursuits, to which he turned his attention when he arrived to manhood's years. January 12, 1848, he married Mary A. Smith, who was born in this Precinct May 16, 1823, daughter of George A. and Elizabeth M. (Edwards) Smith. The paternal grandfather of Mrs. Bedford was Withers Smith, a native of Virginia, and emigrated to this county quite early, locating on the farm where Mr. Bedford now resides; he had a family of seven children, three daughters and four sons, viz: Charles, George A., Hardridge, James, Margaret, Susan and Lydia. George A., the father of Mrs. Bedford's father, was born in Virginia May 16, 1788; his wife, Oct. 20, 1795; they were married Feb. 20, 1814; twelve children were born to them, who were: Amanda, Sophia, Susan, Elizabeth, Mary, James, Emeline, George, Sarah, Henry, Frank and Margaret. George A. Smith was a farmer, which vocation he followed until his death; he served in the war of 1812; his death occurred April 19, 1854; his wife died Feb. 26, 1859. Mr. Bedford located on the farm he now owns in 1860; seven years later he built his residence, which commands a splendid view of the Stoner river and surroundings below; for several years Mr. Bedford has been engaged in the shipping business, buying largely for the New York market, and is also engaged in his farming interests, which is successfully carried on, having over 1,000 acres of land; he has but one child, Sallie B., now wife of Joseph O. Hodges, son of Samuel Hodges. He has two children: L. Mosely and Mary R. Hodges, grandchildren of Mr. Bedford.

GEORGE M. BEDFORD, farmer and stock raiser; P. O. Paris. The Bedford family are of English origin; they trace their ancestry to one Thomas Bedford, of Charlotte County, in the Old Dominion; he was a large landholder, and of the families who ranked high in social position; he was twice married; first to Mary Coleman, by whom he had three children: Charles, Margaret and Jane, all of whom remained in Virginia; his second marriage was to Miss Spencer, who bore him six sons and five daughters; the sons were Thomas, Benjamin, John, Stephen, Littleberry and Archie; the daughters were: Nancy, who married a Mosely; Patsey, a man by the name of Fuquia; Susan, a Walk; Patsey, a Crenshaw; Mary, a Hamlet; the first one of the Bedford name who came to Kentucky was Benjamin, who was born Dec.

23, 1762, and emigrated first to Madison County about 1787, and raised one crop; came to this county in 1789, and located in the southern part of Paris Precinct; his wife was Tabitha Clay, born Nov. 15, 1761; the father of the above was Littleberry Bedford, who was born in Charlotte County, Va., Jan. 1, 1769; he married Mattie Clay, born in Virginia Sept. 8, 1772; she bore thirteen children; the eldest was Thomas, who was born Oct. 25, 1790, and was killed in the war of 1812; the others in order of birth are: Henry, born Oct. 26, 1792, and married Patsey Dawson; Elizabeth, born Dec. 7, 1794; she married Capt. Wash. Kennedy; William was born Dec. 7, 1796; Littleberry, born July 30, 1798; he married Sicily Rollins; Capt. John was born July 26, 1800, and married Sallie King; Augustin Volney, born Aug. 18, 1802, and Franklin P., born May 14, 1805; he married Henrietta Clay; Benjamin C., born Aug. 17, 1807, and married Caro'ine Moran, afterwards Ann M. Garrard; Patsy, born Nov. 26, 1809, who was the wife of William Green Clay; Archibald M., born Feb. 25, 1812, and married Elizabeth H. Bedford; Edwin G., born Aug. 27, 1814, who married first to Margaret Gerrard, then Lucy Degraftenreed; George M., whose name heads this page, is the youngest of the number; he was born May 19, 1817; who at the age of sixteen started in life upon his own account, having nothing to begin with, save his hands and a willing heart; Nov. 4, 1840, he married Mary A. Bedford, who was born in this precinct Sept. 22, 1824, daughter of Benjamin F., who was a son of Benjamin, the pioneer; after Mr. Bedford's (George M.) marriage, he farmed on rented land; in the fall of 1845, he located on the farm he now owns, where he has since (except two years), spent in Paris; has been among the prominent breeders of short-horn cattle and Cotswold sheep; he has 1,400 acres of land, all self acquired; his father died Aug. 7, 1829; mother, March 2, 1864, in her ninety-second year; religiously, Mr. Bedford is not a member of any sect or denomination; he has five children: Mary E., Julia K., Maria V., George M., Jr., and Benjamin F., Jr.

ALEXANDER HAWES BEDFORD, farmer and stock raiser; P. O. Paris; was born in this precinct March 1, 1838, and is the youngest member of the family, born to Benjamin F. Bedford, Sr., and Ellen G. Buckner, his wife. Benjamin F., Sr., was born May 1799, on the farm now owned by Mrs. Sallie Cunningham, on the Winchester Pike. He was a son of Benjamin, a native of Virginia, who came to Kentucky about the year 1787. Ellen G. Buckner was born Nov. 2, 1799. The old family Bible, now in the possession of A. H., tells the following tale: Elizabeth H., born Nov. 12, 1819; Benjamin T., March 19, 1821; John C., Nov. 17, 1822; Mary A., Sept. 22, 1824; Henry P., April 10, 1826; Stephen, Jan. 17, 1829; Sarah E., Nov. 5, 1830; Franklin, Aug. 29, 1833; Hillory, Aug. 15, 1835; Alexander Hawes, March 1, 1838. A. H. was brought up a farmer, in which business he has since been engaged. He has a farm of 285 acres, which is stocked with Cotswold sheep and short-horn cattle. Nov. 29, 1869, he married Ida R., daughter of Samson D. and Sarah (Stemmons) Talbott, both natives of Kentucky. He was born in this county in 1809, son of Demoval Talbott, of Virginia. Sarah D. was a daughter of Martin and Charlotte (Glasscock) Stemmons. Mr. Bedford removed from the homestead to the place he now owns, after his marriage. He has one child, Dousie P. He and wife are members of the Christian Church.

BENJAMIN F. BEDFORD, farmer and stock raiser; P. O. Paris; the proprietor of "Sweet Valley" farm; was born August 23d, 1830, in this precinct, on the farm now owned by John T. Woodford. The father of our subject was Benjamin Colman Bedford; he married Caroline B. Moran, daughter of Edward B. and Letitia (Clay) Moran, both natives of Bourbon County. The father of our subject was born Aug. 17th, 1807, on the farm now owned by Mrs. Patsey Clay, which was first settled by Littleberry Bedford, the grandfather of Benjamin F. Two children were born to Benjamin C. Bedford and wife, of whom Benjamin F. is the eldest; Edward L., the younger brother, died in his 19th year. Benjamin C. was twice married; his second wife was Ann M. Garrard, born in this precinct, daughter of Gen. James Garrard. This union was crowned with four sons and two daughters, viz: Jephthah T., James, Thomas, Alpheus L., Nancy and Margaret; of the above, Jephthah and Thomas reside in Missouri; Alpheus located in Texas; James died, aged nineteen; both the girls reside in Illinois, Macon County; Margaret married J. H. Pickrell, a prominent farmer and short-horn man; Nancy resides in Harristown, wife of Dr. J. L. Conelly. After the marriage of Benjamin C. Bedford, he located on the farm adjoining the homestead, where he remained but a short time, when he removed near Paris on the Houston, to a place settled by Johnnie Hamilton. Here he lived until 1865, when he located in Monroe County, Mo., but remained there but two years, then moved to Harristown, Ill., where he spent the remainder of his days, passing to his rest in 1877, having for many years been a consistent member of the Christian Church; was received into the church by Elder John A. Gano; and a member of the Masonic Order. He was for many years engaged in raising blooded stock, and encouraged by example and precept the growth and propagation of short-horn cattle. In 1833, by the death of his mother, Benjamin F. was left motherless at an early age. At the age of nineteen he embarked in business upon his own account; several of his boyhood years being spent with G. M. Moran, afterwards making his home at his father's. Sept. 6th, 1859, he formed a matrimonial alliance with Bettie Evans, born in Athens Precinct, Fayette County, daughter of Silas and Parmelia (Quisenberry), both natives of Kentucky. Silas was a son of Richard and Sarah (Pullum). Ten children were born to Silas Evans, of whom eight grew to maturity. Silas Evans was born Sept. 4th, 1820, and died 1878, April 11th; his wife was born 1819, died Sept. 28th, 1858; both were members of the Baptist Church. Since 1859 Mr. Bedford has been a resident of the farm he now owns, consisting of 392 acres; original settler was Washington Kennedy. Mr. Bedford, since 1860, has been engaged in the breeding and growth of short-horns, of which he has a large herd. Has four children, Carrie M., Silas E., Richard E. and Benjamin F.

ASA COLMAN BEDFORD, deceased, was born in Bourbon County, son of Archie Bedford, whose wife was a Miss Clay. Asa Colman was thrice married; first to Susan Burns, second time to Lucinda Hedges; his third wife was Mrs. Hawkins. The only child by his second wife was Mary Kate, now the wife of Felix Lowry of this precinct. She was born in Middletown Precinct in 1847, her mother died young; she was reared by her stepmother. July 14, 1870, she married Mr. Lowry, son of Dr. George G. and Nancy (Bruce) Lowry, of Fleming County, formerly of Virginia. After the marriage of Mr. and Mrs. Lowry, they resided about two years in Fleming, afterwards removed to this county, where they have about 200 acres of land, removing on the same in December, 1875. They have two children, Lucy and Kate.

J. D. BUTLER, farmer; P. O. Paris; was born May 18, 1827, in Hutchinson Precinct; son of Frank and Rachel (Wheat) Butler; Frank Butler emigrated to this State, with his father, from Maryland, and located in this county; he settled on the land now owned by J. W. Ferguson, in this Precinct. There were three sons: Frank, Dudley and Moses. Dudley settled in Ralls County, Mo.; Moses in Hutchinson Precinct. Rachel Wheat was a daughter of Zachariah Wheat. The parents of J. D. died as follows: father, 1838; his mother survived him until 1876; they had three children who came to maturity: J. D., Thomas Z. and Henry; Thomas Z. resides in Texas; the others in this Precinct. At the death of his father, he being the eldest of the family, the care of the family devolved upon him and his mother, and from that time he was thrown upon his own resources; he worked out and made the best use of his time and his limited opportunities; April, 1851, he married Miss Margaret Johnson, daughter of John and Helen (Kenney) Johnson; he was born in 1800, his wife four years later; eleven children were born to them, eight of whom grew to maturity; John Johnson died Oct., 1853, at Calhoun's Mills, in the State of Carolina, while absent with a drove of mules. Mr. Butler located on the farm he now owns, in 1851; during the war he was engaged in purchasing mules for the government; he has 565 acres of land; he is engaged in farming and raising short-horns, which are called the "Willow Dale herd," of good strains of blood, also pure Cotswold sheep. Young stock for sale. Correspondence solicited. He has been successful in his business from the commencement; he is a member of the Reformed Church, and elder of the same; he has six children: James H., Charles E., Birdie, Minnie M., Landon V. and Archie L.

O. H. BUCK, M. D; P. O. Paris; Residence Paris; was born in Monticello, Wisconsin, where he received his literary education. He is son of T. Z. Buck. In 1872 he began the study of medicine, which he pursued until graduation at the Ohio Medical College, at Cincinnati. In March same year he came to Paris and began the practice of his profession, and continued until Oct. 1880, when on account of his wife's health, he removed to Middletown, Ohio, where he remained until February, 1882, and returned to Paris and resumed practice. The Homeopathic School has many friends in Bourbon County, and the physicians that have advocated that system in this locality have met with marked success, which has attended Dr. Buck's efforts since his *first* advent to Paris. In June, 1881, he married Miss Eva Price, daughter of Dr. Price, of Clark Co., and a member of the Presbyterian Church South. He is a member of the A. F. and A. M., and Royal Arch.

H. A. BUTLER, farmer; P. O. Paris; is among the self-made men of this county. He was born in March, 1826, in Hutchinson Precinct; the eldest child born to Francis M. Butler and Rachel Wheat. By the death of his father he was left in care of his mother, who was unable to provide for her three children left upon her hands without any visible means of support. When a youth of twelve, he embarked for himself, working out by the month at very low wages. His school advantages were very limited indeed. Upon his attaining the years of manhood, he was employed to drive and handle stock for other parties; during this time he made fifty trips to New Orleans and forty to New York, eleven of which were performed on foot, the trips occupying seventy days each. In 1863 he purchased 150 acres in Menard County, Ill., for eighteen dollars per acre; two years and a half after he sold it and realized thirty-six dollars per acre; he then purchased 170 acres in Fayette County, which he kept a short time, then purchased 140 acres in Clintonville Precinct. In 1876 he purchased 220 acres, where he now resides, situated on the Flat Rock Pike, which farm he now owns. During the war he was engaged in the mule trade, in a small way on his own account, also was engaged in the hog trade, buying and shipping, which business he followed for several years and proved successful. May, 1868, he married Sarah Kennedy, born in Flat Rock, daughter of Thomas and Nancy (Goodwin) Kennedy. She (Nancy) was a daughter of "Tige" (Enoch) Goodwin, who was one of the early settlers in Flat Rock Precinct. Thomas and Nancy Kennedy had four children: John W., Mrs. Butler, Polly Ann and Mary E.; both sisters married Smith brothers. Mary, wife of J. T.; Polly, of George Smith. Mr. Butler has three children: Nannie R., Jephthah D., and Thomas H. Mrs. Butler is a member of the Reformed Church.

W. S. BUCKNER, farmer and fine horse breeder; P. O. Paris; the proprietor of Cane Ridge Stock Farm; is among the largest breeders of fine and thoroughbred trotting horses in the county; he was born on the farm adjoining, being the second child and son of William and Sallie T. (Woodford) Buckner. Mr. Buckner, though a young man and starting in the business in 1876, is one of the successful breeders in his line, and is destined to become one of the most prominent in his region; he has accumulated a large lot of animals of the best and most approved breeds, and will soon announce annual sales of the same; he has already sold some valuable animals, among whom was Steinway, who sold for $13,000, in 1879; some of his breeds are the Hambletonian, Banner Chief, Membrino Pilot, and others. His farm, composed of 656 acres, situated on the Flat Rock road, six miles from Paris, is admirably suited to the business in which he is engaged. Feb. 26th, 1873, he married Rosa Lindsey, born in this precinct, daughter of Richard and Olivia (Bedinger) Lindsey, both of whom were natives of this county. Mr. Buckner has three children: Olivia, William E. and Sallie Woodford.

W. T. BUCKNER, farmer; P. O. Paris. The Buckner family were from Virginia, in Caroline County. They trace their ancestry to one Thomas Buckner, born May 13, 1728; who married Mary Cocke, and by her had three sons: George, William and Richard, and from them have descended a numerous progeny. The subject of these lines was born in Caroline County, Va., Feb. 9, 1813; he was the only son of William T. Buckner and Mary Monroe.—(His second wife was Sallie Clay). The grandsire of our subject on the paternal side, was Thomas Buckner, who was born Aug. 31, 1755; he married Elizabeth Hawes. He was a son of Thomas and Mary (Cocke) Buckner. Thomas was born, as above stated, May 13, 1728. The father of W. T. was married Nov. 29, 1807, to Mary Monroe; by this marriage, William T. is their only son. He came to this State when a lad; his father located south of Paris, on the Stoner, on lands now owned by Cassius M. Clay, where he lived until his removal to Middletown Precinct, this County; William T., who resides in this precinct, remained at home until he became of age. In 1857, he married Lucy Woodford, daughter of William and grand-daughter of Colonel John Woodford, of Clark County, this State. About the year 1841, William T. located on the farm he now owns; purchased of Henry Towles, where he has since remained. He has a farm of nearly 2,000 acres, which is well situated, and of the best quality. Mr. Buckner has but one son, W. T., who married Clay Wornall, and by her had three children, but one living: Thomas Moore, born Sept. 16, 1881. Clay Wornall was a daughter of James R. Wornall, who was born in Clark County, Ky., Feb. 29, 1811; he was a son of Thomas Wornall, from Virginia. Thomas Wornall married Ann E. Moore, born in Winchester, Scott County, daughter of Thomas Moore, of Virginia.

HARRY BEDFORD, farmer; P. O. Shawhan. Soon after the settlement of Lexington and Boonesborough, a family came to this county from Caroline County, Va., by the name of Bedford, the head of which was Benjamin, his wife's maiden name being Tabitha Clay; they settled in the then wild country and reared a large family; one of the sons being named Benjamin F., born in December, 1799, who received a very fine education, especially in mathematics and surveying. Benjamin F., like his father, gave his whole attention to the development of his farm; he married Miss Eleanor Buckner, who came with her parents from Virginia; she died about 1836, leaving a family of ten children; he married the second time and died in his seventy-fifth year. Harry, the subject of this sketch, was born April 10, 1826; in his 20th year he began clerking, but the Mexican war being inaugurated, he enlisted in the service, and served throughout that struggle, when he returned to Bourbon County and clerked in a store in Paris five years; he then engaged in the grocery business until 1856, when he was elected Sheriff, and after serving his term in that position, commenced farming, at which he has continued since; when the late war broke out, he espoused the cause of the South, first being in the secret service, and afterward Captain of Co. C., Fifth Cavalry, being in the service three years. He was married in March, 1853, to Miss Mary Ewalt, daughter of Samuel Ewalt, of Bourbon, and has nine children: Elizabeth W., Thomas, Ewalt, Anna Pagh, Harry, Wm. B., Benjamin, Mary H. and Eleanor B.; he is a Mason and a Democrat.

BRUCE CHAMP, Editor; P. O. Paris; was born near Millersburg, and spent his early life upon the farm. Upon the 9th of July, 1861, he enlisted in the 2d Ky. Infantry, Company F, Capt. Harvey McDowell, and Colonel Roger Hanson. He was captured at Fort Donelson, at the surrender of the garrison and sent to Camp Morton, and escaped after a short confinement; returning to the service, he attached himself temporarily to Gen'l Morgan's command; two days later he was in the engagement at Hartsville, Tenn., in which his Infantry Reg. took part. After the battle he joined his old command, and with that took part in the battles of Stone River, Jackson, Miss., Chickamauga, Mission Ridge, Buzzard's Roost Gap, Resaca, and at Dallas, Ga., where he was captured in May, 1864, and sent to Rock Island, where he remained until the close of the war, when he returned home and engaged in farming. He was married Feb. 17, 1866, to Miss Jennie E. Miller, daughter of John A. Miller; by her he has had four children, two of whom died in infancy. Those living are Walter T., born Sept. 6, 1868, and W. Swift, Nov. 22d, 1876. In 1870 Mr. Champ left the farm and went to Millersburg, where he engaged in mercantile pursuits, in which he was unfortunate after a continuance of about four years. He then engaged in job printing until the organization of the firm of Champ & Roby, early in 1881, as editors and proprietors of the *Bourbon News*. Soon after it fell into the hands of Mr. Champ. He continued this publication until early in March, 1882, when he moved his office to Paris, and began the publication of a semi-weekly.

JOHN CALDWELL, auctioneer and salesman; P. O. Paris; is a grandson of William Caldwell, the "pioneer." He was a native of the North of Ireland, and emigrated to America prior to the Revolutionary War, in which he participated, and was wounded at the battle of Brandywine. He was among the hardy pioneers who came to Kentucky when the buffalo and other wild game were plentiful. He located on the Houston, one mile West of the Court House. Some of the land he then purchased is now occupied by the Cemetery and Fair Grounds. He was one among the first merchants in Paris, and finally he removed to the place above described, and engaged in farming and distilling; lands he then purchased for a mere trifle will now command hundreds of dollars per acre. He died about the year 1829, aged seventy-five years; he had but one son, Samuel J., who was the father of John; his daughters were: Ann E., wife of Dr. Joseph Holt, who was well known as a physician and politician; as a stump speaker he was also well known; Sallie married Benjamin Warfield; Betsey, Samuel Hall; Lucretia, wife of Luther Smith, who was the founder of Houston Seminary. Samuel Caldwell, father of John, was raised in Paris and clerked in a store; upon coming to maturity he went to Cynthiana, Harrison County, where he married Sophia, daughter of Littleton Roberson, a native of Virginia and an early settler in Harrison County, Ky. Samuel Caldwell served two terms under Capt. Garrard, in the war of 1812; his death occurred in 1831, at the age of forty. He had but two children born to him: William and John; the former went to California, and there died in 1850. John was born March 15, 1817, in Cynthiana, and came to Bourbon County when a young man, and has since been well known in the county as an auctioneer, being one of the oldest auctioneers in the county, having no superior as a salesman.

WALTER CLARK, livery; was born 1859 in Centerville Precinct; son of Edwin and Patsey (Simpson) Clark; he is a native of Virginia; born in 1807 and died 1878; she was born in the county, daughter of John and Susan Simpson; Walter was raised to farming pursuits. April 27th, 1881, he married Mattie Edwards, daughter of Oscar and Patsey (Kennedy) Edwards; Oct. 6th, 1881, he engaged in the livery business, in partnership with his brother-in-law, Oscar Edwards; the stable, situated on Main street opposite the post office, is well located for trade and is doing a large business, having accomodation for 100 horses, and facilities for dispensing *hors*pitality to all who favor them with their patronage, and at the lowest possible rates. Mr. Clark is a member of the Baptist Church; his wife of the Reformed.

SAMUEL CLAY, farmer and stockraiser; P. O. Paris. This gentleman is the largest land owner, and one of the most successful agriculturists in Bourbon County. He was born in this Precinct April 8, 1815, son of Colonel Henry Clay, a native of Virginia (his wife's maiden name was Helm), who emigrated to this county from the Old Dominion about the year 1785. He came here with his father, Samuel Clay, when a lad of eight years. He was a successful farmer. To Henry Clay, jr., was born twelve children; eleven grew to maturity. The eldest was Henry; then in order of birth were John, Sallie, Joseph, Letitia, Henrietta, Elizabeth, Samuel, Mary, Frank, and Matt M., all of whom settled in this county. Sallie married Wm. Buckner; Letitia became the wife of Dan'l Bedinger. Henrietta married three times; first to Mr. Bedford, by whom she had one son, Frank. Her second husband was Robert Scott, by whom she had one child. Her third husband was E. S. Dudley. Elizabeth married Douglas P. Lewis. Mary married E. S. Dudley, the husband of Henreitta. In 1836 our subject married Nancy T. Wornall, who was born January 16, 1816, in Clark County. She was a daughter of Thomas and Sallie (Ryan) Wornall. Thomas was the son of Roby and Edie Wornall, who was a native of Virginia. At the time Mr. Clay started in business for himself, his father gave him 440 acres of land. From this start he has added to it until he now owns over 7,000 in this county, and several thousand in counties adjoining. Mr. Clay is a tireless worker, and believes in the adage that it is better to wear out than rust out, and his career has been one of unusual success. He has had four children: Thomas H., Susan E., wife of Cassius Clay. She died in 1879, leaving four children. James E. resides on farm adjoining.

CAPT. H. M. CARPENTER, farmer; P. O. Paris; the owner and proprietor of "Prospect Hill" was born in Carlisle, Nicholas County, March 9, 1842; son of Dr. J. H. Carpenter and Mary Martin. Our subject remained at home until the outbreak of the war, when he donned the "gray" and enlisted in the 2nd Ky. Infantry, Co. F, July, 1861, and served until the close, coming out with the rank of Captain, having passed through the different grades of rank until he was placed in command of his company; he participated in all the battles in which his regiment was engaged, and was thrice wounded, and at Fort Donelson was taken prisoner and confined in Federal prison for eight months, and upon his release joined his command and did effective service as an officer, and manifested his allegiance to the cause he espoused by four years of active service; upon his return home from the war he resumed agricultural pursuits, and was married the following year, Jan., 1866, to Mary Osborne, daughter of Charles and Melvina (Walton) Osborne; he was born 1808, in Charlotte County, Va.; she, 1810, in Mason County, Ky.; the parents of Charles were Daniel and Martha (Morgan) Osborne; the parents of Melvina were John and Susan (Anderson) Walton; shortly after the marriage of Mr. Carpenter, he moved to Mason County, this State, and engaged in farming; remaining here until March, 1881, when he located on the Douglass Lewis farm, which he now owns, consisting of 230 acres of choice land; his residence for location is one of the finest in the country; of seven children born to him, five are living, viz: Ida M., Melvina, Judith R., Maude and John Walton; the father of H. M. was born Sept. 24, 1815, in Fleming County, Ky.; son of William, who married a Miss Wilson. William Carpenter was a native of New York, and of English descent; the mother of our subject, Mary Martin, was born March 10, 1821, in Nicholas County; daughter of Edmond and Rebecca (Stitt) Martin; eight children were born to William Carpenter, viz: William, Sallie, John, Amanda, Julia, J. H., Flemming and Jane; Flemming settled in Nodaway County, Mo., all others in Nicholas County; J. H. continued a constant resident in Nicholas County until October 1881, when he located in Lafayette County, Mo., and is engaged in farming, and in the occasional practice of his profession; ten children were born to him, viz: James A., William, Laura, James, Edmond, Ella, Sanford, Mattie, Beauregard and H. M.; Mattie married to Conway; William and James reside in Mason County; Sanford, in Nicholas; Edmond, in Florida; H. M. in Bourbon County; the others are deceased; Mr. and Mrs. Carpenter are members of the Christian Church; Mrs. Carpenter's father was an Elder of that organization for forty years.

COL. E. F. CLAY, farmer and stock-raiser; P. O. Paris. The proprietor of Runneymede, was born on the old homestead, Dec. 1, 1841, youngest child of Brutus J. and Amelia Field Clay. He was raised upon the homestead and began a thorough education, being a student for sometime, under B. B. Sayre; also attended school at Harrisburg, with a view to graduation, when the war broke out; he cast his lot with the 1st Kentucky Mounted Riflemen, entering the ranks as private, afterwards chosen Captain, and rose to Lieutenant Colonel, and had command of his regiment, and remained with his command until the close of the war; and in justice to Col. Clay, it can be truthfully said, that no truer or more valiant soldier entered the Confederate service than he. He was nine months prisoner on Johnson's Island. Lost his right eye in an engagement, otherwise came out unscathed. The year following the close of the war, he married Mary L. Woodford, daughter of John T. Woodford, of this precinct; the year of his marriage located on the farm he now owns, which contains 425 acres, best known as the Garrard Place, situated on the Paris Townsend Pike. In 1867, he commenced the breeding of short-horns, which he continued until 1875. Since that time has been quite prominently engaged in the breeding of thoroughbred race-horses, having a track and stables upon the grounds upon his premises, for their use and training. Colonel Clay is fond of the chase, and with his dogs and gun, and in company with boon companions, he makes frequent trips to hunting and fishing resorts. In his business relations is attentive and looks well to his interests, and in all matters of public interest is ever ready to do his part. Has five children: Ezekiel, Woodford, Brutus J., Buckner and Amelia.

MRS. PATSY P. CLAY, farming; P. O. Paris; is the relict of Wm. Green Clay, who was born in this county Jan. 1, 1810; son of Samuel Clay and Nancy Winn. The grandfather of Green Clay was Henry, who was a native of Virginia, and from him have descended a numerous progeny. The above was born on the farm she now owns, Nov. 26, 1809; she is the second daughter of Littleberry and Mattie Clay Bedford, October 6, 1829, was the date of the marriage of Wm. Green Clay to Patsey P. Bedford. They first located near Paris, where they lived years. After which they located in Paris, remaining there about eight years. In March, 1846, they located on the Bedford homestead, where Mrs. Clay has since resided. Mr. Clay departed this life April 17, 1855, since which time she has borne his name, and conducted the farm in conjuction with her sons' assistance. Of the children born to Mr. and Mrs. Clay are Thomas, Maria E., George L., William G., Virginia, Sidney B. and Mattie V. Thomas E. and Sidney remain on the homestead with their mother. Maria E. became the wife of William R. Colcord, and resides in Kansas, having three sons and one daughter, viz: Charles, William, Harry and Maria L. Mattie V. married Francis H. Donaldson, who is now railroad official in Cambridge, Indiana. They have three children, viz: Anna M., Francis H. and Elizabeth G. William G. was among the number who went out to battle for his principles, and died in the defense of the same, June 7, 1862, in Tazewell Co. Va., while wearing the "gray." He was a youth of much promise, and bid fair to attain for himself a bright and promising career had he been spared. Mrs. Clay, in company with her sons, occupy the homestead where she is spending the remainder of her days in comfort and happiness, with her books and papers, of which she is a great reader.

J. R. COULTHARD, milling; P. O. Paris; is the proprietor of one of the oldest mills in Bourbon County. He was born March, 1840, in Fleming County, this State; son of William Coulthard, who was born in England, 1808, son of Robert Coulthard, who emigrated to Canada with his family in 1817. He was a miller by occupation. Emigrated to Fleming County, Ky., in 1839, and his son William married Mary Ann Williams, who bore him two sons and one daughter. She was born in Mason County, this State, December, 1813, daughter of Joseph Williams, who was a native of Culpepper County, Va., and came to Kentucky in 1797, and settled in Mason County, afterwards removed to Fleming County. Our subject came to this county with his father in 1853, and the following year purchased the property known now as the Coulthard mill, and remained here until his death, which occurred 1877. His wife yet survives him. Our subject remained with his father until twenty-four years of age, learning milling of him. December, 1864, he married Margaret E. Hall, a native of this county, daughter of Henry and Nancy (Sanders) Hall, of this precinct. Mr. Coulthard has four children living: William H., Mary E., Nannie and Sidney. His father and mother were both members of the Reformed Church. Mr. Coulthard is at present running the mill in company with his partner, Mr. Honey, Mr. C. being the miller and principal business man of the firm.

HON. BRUTUS J. CLAY, farmer and stockraiser, deceased; P. O. Paris; was one of the prominent representatives of Bourbon County, and one of its honored citizens. He belongs to a numerous family, who trace their ancestry from England to the Old Dominion, thence to Kentucky, where the younger members of the family have became identified. According to an account carefully written by Green Clay, the father of the above, Sept. 12, 1784, is gleaned the following: The family trace their name to one John Clay, a native of England, who came to America as a British Grenadier, during Bacon's Rebellion; from him have descended all the different members of the Clay family. In direct line from the above was John, who was born in Virginia, where he married, and was the father of four sons, one of whom went North, one South, the others lived and died in Virginia, to-wit: Henry and Charles Clay, of Amelia County, Va. In direct line comes Henry, who married Mary Mitchell; by her had four sons and several daughters; the sons were William, Henry, Charles and John, who was the grandfather of Henry Clay, of Ashland. Next in order comes Charles, who was born Jan. 31, 1716. He married Martha Green, who bore him eleven children: Mrs. Mary Locket, Eliza, Charles, Henry, Thomas (who was the grandfather of Senator Thomas T. McCreery), Eliza (Murray), Lucy (Thaxton), Matt (Congressman from Tennessee), Green Priscilla, Mary (Lewis). Green Clay, next in order of descent, was born Aug. 14,

John Cunningham

1757; he married Sallie Lewis; by her had six children, viz: Sidney, Brutus J., Cassius M., Betsey (Smith), Pauline, Rodes and Sallie Johnson. Brutus J. Clay, who is next in descent, was born July 1, 1808, in Madison County, Ky.; he graduated at Center College, and in 1837 settled in Bourbon County, where he engaged quite extensively in stock-raising, being at one time one of the most extensive fine stockraisers in Central Kentucky; 1840, was elected to the State Legislature, and about the same time was elected President of the Bourbon County Agricultural Society, and in 1853 was elected President of the State Agricultural Society, and was honored with a re-election, serving in this capacity eight years in all, declining to serve longer. In 1860, was elected to the Legislature; was elected to the Thirty-eighth Congress, serving as Chairman on the Committee of Agriculture, and as a member of the Convention on Revolutionary Pensions. He was a successful farmer, his farm being one of the best improved in the county. His wife was Anna M. Field, whose offspring was Cassius M., the present incumbent of the homestead. He was born March 26, 1846; he married Sue E. Clay, daughter of Samuel Clay; she died, leaving him four children: Junius B., Samuel H., Annie L. and Sue E. Cassius M. represented his county in the Legislature in 1872, and was re-elected, and like his father, is a model farmer.

ROBERT CLARK, farmer; P. O. Paris; first saw the light of day Jan. 5, 1819, on the farm he now owns; son of Robert Clark, who was born 1780, in Virginia. His parents were Robert and Elizabeth (Gay) Clark, which couple emigrated to Kentucky 1784, locating on the farm now owned by his grandson, Robert; here he remained until his death; his son Robert succeeded him, and married Elizabeth Walls, by whom he had three children: Lucinda, John and Robert. The father of our subject died 1857, on the homestead farm upon which his successor was raised. His education was such as the common schools afforded. His time was taken up in the farm duties when not at school. Dec. 1, 1840, he married Sarah R. Ward, a native of this county, daughter of James Ward and Martha Wright—she a daughter of James Wright, of Virginia. Mrs. Clark died Jan. 17, 1871, leaving three children to mourn her departure. Martha E. married R. P. Barrett, of this precinct. Feb. 21, 1872, Mr. Clark married Mrs. Elvira Stout, relict of Jacob Stout, whose father was Thomas. Jacob Stout died 1866, leaving one child, Cora J. Mrs. Clark's maiden name was Morrison, daughter of Hial A. and Mary A. Morrison. To Robert Clark, the grandfather of the above, was born ten children, who grew up, of whom were John and William, who were soldiers in the war of 1812, both losing their lives in that struggle. Mr. Clark is not a member of any church organization, but a member of the Masonic Order, being a Master Mason and Royal Arch. His farm consists of 600 acres; his home is called "Springdale," situated on Clark's Branch. While Mr. Clark has not made a specialty of thorough bred stock, yet keeps nothing but thoroughbred males, and thus raises a high grade of stock.

M. C. CHAPLINE, dairyman; P. O. Paris; was born in Ohio County, W. Va., Nov. 2, 1828, son of Samuel H., brother of Gen. Moses Chapline. The Chapline family are cotemporaneous with the early history of Wheeling, as was also Noah Zane, who married in the Chapline family. The subject of these lines was left fatherless at an early age; upon his arriving at manhood, he engaged in a cotton manufactory at Wheeling; he was one of the proprietors of the Franklin Cotton Mill, where he was engaged until 1854, when he went to Philadelphia, where he engaged in business, and remained there until 1877, when he came to this county, and engaged in the whisky business. In 1879, he purchased the Lysle farm, just outside of the limits of Paris, at the Junction of the Humes and the Lexington and Paris Pike, where he now resides. His farm cost him $155 per acre. He is engaged in farming and is running the dairy business, having about thirty-five cows. In January, 1865, he married Margaret Lewis, daughter of Douglas Lewis and Elizabeth Clay. Douglas Lewis was born Aug. 4, 1804, in this State. Dec. 23, 1830, he married Elizabeth Payne Clay, daughter of Colonel Henry Clay, of this county. Douglas Lewis, was among the prominent citizens of Bourbon County, and was a Representative in the Legislature. He died Oct. 26, 1867, having been a man that was well known throughout the county where he had been a constant resident. He had several children born him, which are scattered about in the different parts of the country. Douglas resides in Covington; Stephen in Arkansas; Thomas died in 1881; Asa resides at Blue Springs, in Nicholas County; Frank in this county; Howard also in this county. Elizabeth, wife of Mr. Howard, of Montgomery County, and Margaret Helm, wife of Mr. Chapline, and Mary E., wife of Frank Armstrong, of this county. Mr. Chapline is a member of the Knights of Honor.

GEN. JOHN T. CROXTON, deceased; lawyer and soldier; P. O. Paris. Among the citizens of Bourbon County who are worthy of an honorable mention, is the above named gentleman, who was born near Paris in 1829; son of Henry and Ann K. (Redmon) Croxton; Henry was a native of Virginia, and, upon his migration to this State, located at Houston Dale, on the farm now owned by James Hall; his son, John T., was educated at Yale College, graduating with honors in 1857; afterwards began the study of law under James Robinson; after his license was granted he went South, where he engaged in teaching in Mississippi for a short time, when he returned to Paris, and in 1859 began the practice of his profession; upon the outbreak of the war he raised a regiment of men, known as the 4th Kentucky Infantry, which he commanded; he continued in service until the close of the war, serving with distinction, and rose from one rank to another until he was brevetted Major-General. After the close of the war he went South and was made Provincial Governor. He afterwards engaged in the culture of cotton; upon his return to Bourbon County he engaged in the practice of his profession and carried on farming; he practiced in the Federal Courts, and was a successful lawyer; the confinement of his office and his close application to his profession conduced to impair his health, and in order to recuperate, he accepted the position as Minister to Bolivia, and removed his family there in 1872, and died the following year. He was a staunch Republican, and stood firmly by its principles, and was one of the pillars of the party in Kentucky, and worthy of any honor within the gift of the Republican Commonwealth, he being possessed of all the qualifications that pertain to a truly first-class gentleman, and a member of the Masonic fraternity of high order. In April, 1860, he married Carrie R. Rogers, daughter of Nathaniel and Nancy (Moran) Rogers. Mrs. Croxton resides on her farm near Paris; by Mr. Croxton she had two children: Henry Rogers and Annie Barres Deguerra.

CAPT. M. M. CLAY, farmer and stockraiser; P. O., Paris; is the twelfth child born to Col. Henry Clay and Peggie Helm. Col. Henry Clay was one of the leading and representative men in Bourbon County in his time, having been associated with the county since its first organization, he having come to this part of the country with his father, Henry Clay, when a lad of tender years, and for some time lived in a stockade which was situated in the south part of this precinct; he served in the war of 1812, and was one of the staunch and enterprising men of the county, and possessed noble qualities of mind and heart. He died in 1863, in the 84th year of his age. Three of his sons are yet residents of the county, viz: Henry Samuel, Francis P., and M. M.; Sallie married William Buckner; Elizabeth, Douglass P. Lewis. The subject of these lines was raised upon the homestead, in his precinct, and has since (with the exception of three years spent in Arkansas) been a resident of the county. In 1843 he married Mary, daughter of Judge Asa K. Lewis, of Clark County, this State; his wife died June, 1879, leaving no issue. In the fall of 1861, Mr. Clay raised Company C., and went forth with it and joined the 21st Ky. Infantry; he now owns the Scott farm, adjacent to Paris, which is beautiful for situation. Mr. Clay in years past was interested in short horns; more recently in trotting horses. He is one of the public spirited men of the county.

WM. P. CHAMBERS, merchant; P. O. Paris; was born June 13, 1842, in Louisville, Ky., and since 1859 has been identified with the business interests of this place. In December, 1865, he married Kate, daughter of James and Mary C. (Williams) Duncan. James was a son of Major Jerry Duncan, a farmer who was an old resident of the County of Bourbon. Mary Williams was a daughter of Major George W. Williams, a lawyer and a man of prominence in his profession. W. P. and Kate Chambers have one son, James D., born Oct. 23, 1881. W. P. is a son of J. Sprigg Chambers, born in Mason County, Ky., Oct. 30, 1810; his wife was Martha Phillips, born Dec. 21, 1816; they were married Feb. 6, 1834, at Maysville; she (Martha), was a daughter of W. B. Phillips, a merchant and prominent business man of Mason County, Ky. The paternal grandsire of W. P. was Hon. John Chambers, who was born Oct. 6, 1780, in New Jersey. In 1794 he was brought to Kentucky, and for several years lived in Washington, Mason Co. He received a thorough education, completing the same at Transylvania University, at Lexington. From 1797 to 1800 was a Deputy in the Court. He begun the practice of his profession in 1800. In 1812 he served in that war as Major, and Aide to General Harrison at the battle of the Thames; was elected to the Legislature in 1812, and re-elected several times. Was for some time Commonwealth Attorney; served in Congress from 1828 to 1829, and from 1835 to 1839; was offered a seat in the Court of Appeals in 1832; in 1835 he accepted an appointment of Associate Judge of the Court from the Governor, but resigned on account of ill health. From 1841 to 1845 he served as Governor of the Territory of Iowa. Gov. Chambers died in Paris, Ky., Sept. 21, 1852.

GARRETT DAVIS. Among the list of the illustrious dead of Kentucky, no name has passed into history, bearing with it greater honors as a statesman, a patriot, and an honest and faithful servant of the cause of liberty, the Union and his State, than the lamented Garrett Davis. Living, as he did, from the early morn until the eventide of the nineteenth century, at a time when the nation most needed men of stalwart principle and sterling integrity, Garrett Davis filled the busy years of his faithful life full of noble deeds and heroic, unfaltering labor for the nation's good, and that of his native State, and fearlessly battled for what, in his unprejudiced mind, seemed right. The following brief statement of facts concerning his useful and eventful life, are gleaned from a published volume of Memorial Addresses on his Life and Character, delivered in the Senate and House of Representatives of the Forty-second Congress of the United States, Dec. 18, 1872, upon which occasion eulogies were delivered by Senators Stevenson of Kentucky, Cameron of Pennsylvania, Thurman of Ohio, Sumner of Massachusetts, Bayard of Delaware, Trumbull of Illinois, and many other noted statesmen. Garrett Davis was a native of Kentucky; he was born at Mount Sterling, Sept. 10, 1801. His father and mother emigrated from Montgomery Co., Maryland, to the county of the same name in Kentucky. His mother was a Miss Garrett—a family widely known in Maryland, and it was from her family that he derived his baptismal name. His father was a man of marked character; to energy and industry he added strong will and great personal popularity. He was for many years the Sheriff of his adopted county, and several times represented his district in the lower branches of the General Assembly of Kentucky. Garrett Davis was one of three brothers. The brilliant talents of two of them, also long since departed this life, are still remembered in Kentucky. Garrett enjoyed the advantages of what is known in Kentucky as a common school education. His early years were, however, fraught with a constant study of books, and he thus acquired a good English education, and a practical knowledge of the Latin and Greek languages; at an early age he determined to study law, and with a view of gaining practical knowledge, he sought and obtained employment as a deputy in the Circuit Court Clerk's office of Montgomery County. In 1823, he removed to Bourbon County, where he continued to prosecute his legal studies, and where he occupied a clerical position similar to that held in Montgomery County. About the year 1824, he commenced the practice of his profession in Paris, and to it he consecrated the earlier years of his life with enthusiastic devotion. His first wife was the daughter of Robert Trimble, a distinguished Jurist, who became subsequently a Judge of the Supreme Court of the United States. His second wife was a Mrs. Elliott, widow of a prominent lawyer, also of Paris. Mr. Davis was an assiduous law student, and his industry received its reward. His business rapidly increased, and he soon rose to a high position at a bar which then numbered some of the most eminent lawyers of the Commonwealth. He regarded the law as the noblest science of intellectual triumph, and loved the administration of justice. All who have encountered him as an opponent in the trial of an important cause, will bear willing testimony to his high qualities as an able and strong lawyer. His last argument but one, in the Supreme Court of the United States, in the reported case of Missouri *vs.* Kentucky, is a lasting memorial of his legal learning and professional power. Mr. Davis always took an active and prominent part in the political contests of Kentucky, from his earliest manhood—always an ardent Whig, and frequently the selected standard-bearer of his party. In its most excited struggles, his clarion voice rang throughout this Commonwealth in defense of the principles of that patriotic and gallant organization. He was the trusted and true friend of Henry Clay, and enjoyed to a pre-eminent degree his confidence and regard. He represented Bourbon County in the lower branch of the General Assembly of Kentucky for many years. Always conservative in his views, he took a prominent and successful part in shaping the legislation of the State. For eight consecutive years he was chosen over able and distinguished competitors by the electors of the Ashland district, their Representative to the House of Representatives of the United States, and then voluntarily retired. The debates of that body during that period attests his power and strength as a ready and skillful debater. He was nominated as Lieutenant Governor on the Gubernatorial ticket with John J. Crittenden, but at his earnest request was excused by the convention. In 1861, amid perils and dangers of a revolutionary struggle, he was elected as an old line Union Whig, to succeed John C. Breckinridge in the United States Senate. He was the strongest opponent of secession, and at the period of his election, an earnest advocate of the rigid prosecution of the war to restore the Union. The result of the war, so far as it resulted in the overthrow of the rebellion, was as agreeable to him as to any other union man. But the changes in the form of government, the constitutional amendments, the acts of reconstruction, and other governmental acts which, by the dominant party, were deemed necessary in order to make the Government conform to the altered condition of things, were very repulsive to him, and he opposed them bravely and earnestly, though sustained by a hopeless minority. In 1867, he was re-elected to the United States Senate, a proud tribute to his fidelity and zeal in upholding the honor and guarding the interest of his State. For twelve years he occupied his seat in the Senate. Constitutional questions, novel and startling in their character, were during his time discussed and adopted, and Garrett Davis was never silent when duty prompted him to speak, and he was never known to quail before the power of an overwhelming political majority, and amid the bitterest party contests of the past, his honesty was never impeached or his spotless purity of character ever questioned. With him as a Representative, the conscientious discharge of his duty was paramount to every other consideration. His actions were prompted by conviction, and his convictions were the creations of a well-ordered mind, greatly strengthened by a pure and manly spirit, and throughout life he maintained the same elevated standard. In the death of this truly great and good man, Kentucky lost one of its most illustrious sons, his country, one of its purest and ablest statesmen. Such a man was Garrett Davis, and what higher praise could human statesmanship deserve? He died at his home in Paris, upon the 22d of September, 1872, and all that was mortal of the beloved Kentucky statesman rests beneath the blue grass sod of Bourbon County, in the Paris cemetery.

C. F. DIDLAKE; P. O. Paris; superintendent of Paris distillery; was born Oct. 16, 1842, in Clark County, this State; son of Edmond H. and Mildred (Woodford) Didlake. Edmond Didlake, the father of C. F., was a native of Virginia, and emigrated to Kentucky, locating in Clark County at an early day, where he lived for many years, and was Sheriff of the county, and prominently connected with its business interests. In 1851 he removed to McLean County, Illinois, and engaged in farming and commission business, where he died in 1873. He was a Mason, and a member of the Reformed Church. His wife survived him until 1876. Our subject removed with his parents to Illinois when a lad. At the age of eighteen he entered the Confederate Army as a member of the 1st Battallion of Kentucky Mounted Rifles. While in Tennessee, after the battle of Chickamauga, he was captured and remained a prisoner at Fort Delaware until June, 1865. After his release he went to Arkansas, and for three years had charge of his father's plantation. In February, 1869, he came to Paris, and since that time has been in charge of Paris distillery. November, 1872, he married Sarah Goodman, daughter of W. C. Goodman, one of the pioneers of Bourbon County. He has a snug home on the outskirts of the city, just inside its limits.

GEORGE W. DAVIS, furniture and undertaking; P. O. Paris; is the oldest furniture dealer in the place; he was born in this city, Feb. 6, 1827; second son of George M. Davis, who was born in Berkeley County, Va., son of Thomas Davis, who settled at Ruddel's Mills Precinct in this county at an early time. The mother of our subject was Mary, daughter of James McClintock, a native of the Emerald Isle. In 1843, our subject began learning the cabinetmaker's trade with J. P. Kern, and continued until he had completed his trade. In 1848, he began business in this town, in the furniture and undertaking line, and has since continued. June 22, 1851, he formed a matrimonial alliance with Helena, daughter of Jacob and Julia (Young) Miller, and by her had eight children, five living: James K., Nellie, George M., Owen L. and Rudolph. Mr. Davis is a member of the Presbyterian Church and Elder of same. Thomas Davis, the grandfather of our subject, lived for sometime at Ruddel's Fort, upon his first coming to Kentucky, he married Sarah Ruddel, who died at the age of ninety-seven, in Pike County, Mo., where he removed in 1825; eight children were born to him, of whom was George M., the father of our subject. George M. served in the war of 1812, after which he came to Paris, and engaged as a gunsmith and remained until his death, which occured in 1833, of cholera; of the children born to him were: Sallie, who died, aged nineteen; Margaret, wife of W. W. Mitchell; James T. and George M., of Paris; Mary, wife of James Ingels, and Andrew, who died, aged twenty-five.

JOHN H. DEAVER, farmer; P. O. Paris; born March 27, 1822, in Frankfort, this State; son of Richard and Rachael (Taylor) Deaver; she was a daughter of Joseph Taylor, of Frankfort; the paternal grandsire of John H. was James Deaver, a Welchman, a ship-builder by occupation; he, while in Wales, was a member of the Highland Whig party, which was overcome by its adversaries, and he was compelled to flee for safety to America; he settled in Baltimore, prior to the Revolution, and established a ship yard, and for several years was ship owner and builder, until hostilities were begun by the British, when he was burned out; he then moved to Harford County and engaged in farming, where he remained until his death; he had six children, viz: George, Joshua, Aquilla, William, Polly and Richard; about the close of the war of 1812, Richard and some of his brothers started to seek their home in the West, his brothers accompanying him as far as the Blue Licks, where they became disheartened and returned; Richard pursued his steps until he reached Frankfort; his financial circumstances had become straightened, in consequence of the depreciation of the Continental money, and he had to begin anew; while here, he engaged in various kinds of business: carried on merchant tailoring, and ran a saw-mill;

in 1825, he moved to this county, locating in Clintonville, where he carried on his merchant tailoring until 1837, when he removed to Monroe County, Mo., and died there in 1874; he was twice married; his first wife, Rachel Taylor, who bore four children: Joseph, Francis, John H. and Rachel; his second wife was a Mrs. Jones, who bore him six children; our subject remained with his father until 1841, when he left Monroe County, Mo., and came to this county, and for several years was employed as an overseer; in 1852, he purchased sixty acres of land, where he now resides, and locating on the same, has since lived; has added to the same, until he now has 100 acres which cost him from $55 to $75 per acre; Nov. 10, 1849, he married Mary Ann Carter, who was born on the farm she now lives, in 1831; her parents were Arthur and Ann (Shores) Carter; he was born near Hagerstown, Md., Feb. 15, 1787; Ann Shores was born in Fayette County, July 6, 1790; Mr. Carter came to this county when small, being about the year 1795 or '6, locating in this precinct with his parents; to him were born eleven children; Mr. Carter died Sept. 21, 1872; his wife, Ann, June 17, 1869; the parents of Arthur were John Carter and Rachel Smith, both natives of Maryland; of nine children born Mr. Deaver, six are living, viz: Fannie, wife of Capt. Langston; John H., Carrie, James W., Joseph L. and Aquila Bedford; Mr. and Mrs. Deavers are members of the Reformed or Christian Church.

DAVID M. DODGE, farmer; P. O. Paris; born Aug. 1, 1832, in North Middletown Precinct, this county. His parents were Edwin M. and Elizabeth Seamands, (generally pronounced Simmonds.) The Dodge family trace their ancestry to one Tristram Dodge, an Englishman, who came to America and settled Block Island in 1661, and whose grandsons were the earliest settlers at Cow Neck, Long Island. The great-grandfather of our subject was David; according to the best authority given, he was a son of Jeremiah, who was a great-grandson of Tristram. The maternal grandfather of our subject, was Manson Seamands, who was a major during the war of 1812; he died 1856 aged seventy-five years. His wife was a Newton, prior to her marriage, and was a native of Virginia, as was the Seamands also. David Dodge the grandfather of the above, married Dorcas Mills, who bore him twelve children, Edwin M. being among the younger children. David Dodge removed from Pennsylvania to Clark County, this State, and there settled; here Edwin M. was born, about the year 1811, and afterwards located in North Middletown Precinct when a young man, and there married Miss Seamands. His death occurred about the year 1856. His widow afterwards married Kinzea Stone, and by him had seven children. She is yet living and a widow. David M. was raised by his step-father, with whom he lived until twenty years old. February, 1852, he married Miss Adeline, daughter of Pascal and Maria (Hildreth) Fretwell, both of whom were old Virginia families. Mrs. Dodge died 1860, having borne four children, of whom William P. and Bettie are living. Mr. Dodge married his present wife in May, 1861; her maiden name was Rebecca, born in this precinct, daughter of Victor M. and Catharine (Rodgers) Kenney, Victor being a son of James Kenney, who was one of the first settlers. Catharine was a daughter of Thomas and Rebecca (Spahr) Rodgers. The Rodgers family also being among the first settlers in this precinct. Mr. Dodge located on this farm in 1856, and has since been engaged in farming and stock raising, giving some attention to short horns, good horses, and the best of Cotswold sheep. His farm consists of 291 acres; his residence is called "Hill Side." The place was settled by Zeph Robinette, one part of the house having been built nearly a century. Mr. Dodge is a member of S. G. A. Presbyterian Church. Edwin M., died Dec. 31, 1881; he was a son by his first wife. The children of his second wife are Mattie V., David M., James L. and Victor K.

WILLIAM DAVIE, distiller; P. O. Paris; is a native of St. Louis, Mo., where he was born June, 1838; son of James Davie, who was born in Scotland about 1793, and came to this country and located in St. Louis in 1832, and remained here until his death, which occurred in 1869. The mother of our subject was Ellen Shields, who was born in Scotland, daughter of James Shields, who located in St. Louis in 1834; she is yet living. Mr. Davie is a self-made man; his father was poor and had nothing in the way of worldly goods to bequeath to his son, who began upon his own resources, and for five years engaged in the retail drug business, which he finally merged into the wholesale trade, continuing in the same for fifteen years in the city, and did a large and lucrative business. In January, 1867, he married Kittie Ford, a native of Newport, Kentucky, daughter of Thomas D. Ford and Matilda T. Helm, the latter being a daughter of Major Francis T. Helm, of Newport. Mr. Davie came to this county in 1871, and located in Paris, where he has since resided; during this time he has been engaged in the wholesale whisky trade. In May, 1881, he began the erection of his large distillery at Millersburg, which was completed in February, 1882, and which has a capacity of five hundred bushels and is built with all the modern improvements for the manufacture of sour-mash whisky at the lowest possible cost. James Marshall was a great uncle of Mr. Davie, who came to Lexington, Ky., in 1798, and settled there, and for several years was engaged in farming and distilling, sending the product of his distillery by flat boat to New Orleans, and upon one occasion sent a large consignment in this manner in charge of a man, who was never seen or heard of afterwards by Mr. Marshall, who became disheartened and sold his interests there and removed to Beardstown, Ills., on the Illinois River, where he spent the remainder of his days. Mr. Davie has three children: Kittie F., William F. and James A.

ROBERT P. DOW, grocer; P. O. Paris. Among the enterprising young business men of this city, who are doing a thriving business, the result of their own industry and close application to business, is Mr. Dow, who was born in 1843, in the Parish of Cathcart, Lancastershire, Scotland; son of Andrew Dow, whose wife was Jane Pollock, a relative of Pollock, the poet. Early in life Robert was thrown upon his own resources, and earned money to enable him to embark for this country, which he did when a lad of fifteen, landing in New York city, where he worked some time at one dollar per week, in a cigar shop; afterwards hired to a farmer at $5 per month; then was engaged in a printing office some time; subsequently he removed to Greene County, Ind., where he remained one year and a half, working on a farm; afterwards went to Cincinnati, where he worked one year in the plumbing business. At the outbreak of the war he volunteered his services; enlisted May, 1861, in the 5th O. V. I., Co. D., and during his term of service was engaged in the following battles, viz: Winchester, Kernstown, Port Republic, Cedar Mountain, 2nd Battle of Bull Run, Antietam, Chancellorsville, South Mountain, Gettysburg and Wahatchie Valley. Came West with the 12th Army Corps and participated at Lookout Mountain, Mission Ridge, Buzzard's Roost, Resaca and Dallas, where he was shot in the arm, which resulted in the loss of the same, and was discharged in August, 1864; he subsequently graduated at the Commercial College at Cincinnati. In the spring of 1865, he came to Paris, and in June of the same year, set up in the grocery line in a small way, and continued thirteen years in the same building; in 1878, he removed to the store adjoining, where he has since continued and has a thriving and prosperous trade. In 1868 he married Susan H. Rion, daughter of Stockley T. and Martha U. (Rucker) Rion. He has three children, viz: Robert, Rion and Ellsworth. Is a member of the Presbyterian Church.

WILLIAM P. EWALT, farmer; P. O. Paris. The Ewalt family are among the early settlers in Bourbon county. The grandfather of the above was Henry Ewalt, who was the pioneer of the name. He was a native of Germany, and emigrated to America at the time of Bacon's Rebellion, and located on Cooper's Run in this precinct several years prior to 1800, where he purchased land at $1.66 per acre. He married Elizabeth Fry, and by her raised a family of children, among whom was Samuel Ewalt, the father of the above (Samuel), who was born August 12th, 1792, on the farm his father settled. He married Cynthia Pugh, who was born in this precinct March 30th, 1795, daughter of Joseph and Elizabeth (Hunt) Pugh. He was born June 28th, 1753; she, Jan. 1st, 1763, near Strode's Station. Samuel Ewalt served in the war of 1812. He was twice married —first to Miss Pugh, who bore him six children, viz: John H., Wm. P., Elizabeth, Joseph, Mary S. and Sallie S. His second wife was Eliza Smith, by whom he had three children: Ann S., Samuel B., and Cynthia P. Samuel Ewalt, the father of Wm. P., remained on the farm where he was born until his death, which occurred Aug. 16, 1878; his wife, 1833. He was a successful business man, and in all his transactions with his fellowman, acted the part of an honorable gentleman; not a professed Christian, yet lived a moral life, was an energetic business man and generous in his bequests to benevolent enterprises, and had many friends, and but few or no enemies. Of his children who married, were: John H., who married Sarah Snell; by her had four children; Joseph, also settled on the homestead; he married Sophia Spears; his second wife was Henrietta Hedges; Elizabeth married Perry Wornall; Mary S married Harry Bedford; Sallie married Dr. J. J. Adair, now of Harrison county; Ann S. married John T. Wornall, of same County; Samuel B. married Nancy Keller, afterwards Rachel Halleck; Cynthia P. became the wife of William T. Woodford, of Davis County; Will P. was born on the homestead Jan. 24th, 1824. He began farming in 1850, he and Joseph H., which partnership lasted until his death, July 16th, 1877; Wm. P. has never married; he has 190 acres of land, and engaged in farming.

JAMES FEE, grocer; P. O. Paris; represents one of the self-made business men of Paris, whose first stock in trade was fifteen dollars when he began in business here, and from this modest beginning has arrived at his present surroundings. He was born 1825 on Erin's Green Isle, in County Galway, son of James and Hannah (Davenport) Fee. His father was a farmer and coast seaman, navigating the waters on the coast of Ireland. In 1846, when he came to the years of manhood, he longed to cast his fortunes with those of his countrymen who had preceded him. He set sail in Autumn of that year and after a voyage of six weeks and over, he arrived at the land of his destination. The first six years he spent in Maryland and Pennsylvania, and in 1852, came to Kentucky, having nothing but his wife, whom he married in Maryland; her maiden name was Bridget Carlos, born in County Roscommon, Ireland, daughter of John and Peggy Laughlin. When Mr. Fee first came to Kentucky, he lived in Fayette County some time, and worked land for Mr. Beck, now Senator. Afterwards he spent two years and better in Iowa. Afterwards came to this county, and for nine years he worked hard for Samuel Clay in this Precinct. In November, 1861, he was one among the first who volunteered to defend the stars and stripes, enlisting in Co. C, 21st Regiment, Capt. M. M. Clay's command, where he served for sixteen months, when he was discharged on account of disability. Upon his return home, be began in selling goods in a small way through the country, "peddling." Subsequently, he opened up a small store on Walker Hill, where he staid until 1871, when he purchased where he now does business; having in the meantime built up a prosperous business, and is the owner of his home and business house. He has one son, Augustus J., now a partner in the business, born 1858, married May, 1881, to Mary Kraut, daughter of John Kraut, of Indiana; is a member of the Catholic Church.

JAMES KEITH FORD, hardware and distillery; P. O. Paris; represents one of the old pioneer families of the Blue Grass Region. He was born Oct. 23, 1844, in this county, being the third son and fourth child to Nicholas W. Ford, who was a son of William Ford, who was once Sheriff of Fayette County; he was a son of Edward, a native of Fairfax County, Va. Nicholas Ford, the father of James K., married Martha H. Page, March 11, 1834; she bore him six children. Nicholas W. died Oct. 23, 1844, when James K. was very young. He was raised to manhood under the care of his mother. When a young man he began clerking in Paris. In 1863, he went in the employ of the government, continuing nearly three years, after which he engaged in business with Mr. W. Taylor, under firm name of Ford & Taylor, after which he associated with Mr. Bowen. Prior to this he was for a time engaged in business with H. C. Clay & Co., in the whisky trade. Since he associated with Mr. Bowen, they have not only carried on their store, but have more recently embarked in the manufacture of Bourbon County Whisky, brand, "Peacock," at their distillery in Ruddell's Mills Precinct. Dec. 5, 1865, he married Winifred, second daughter of James S. and Mary (Williams) Duncan, Mary being a daughter of Maj. Geo. W. Williams.

WM. H. FISHER, farmer; born Nov. 12, 1829, in Ruddel's Mills Precient; eldest child of Samuel and Lucinda (Talbott) Fisher. Samuel Fisher was born in Lexington, Fayette Co., in 1809; son of William; a native of Delaware, and came to Kentucky about the year 1800, locating in Fayette; afterwards locating in Ruddel's Mills Precinct about the year 1810, and established a woolen factory; he afterwards engaged in farming, which he followed until his death, which occurred in 1835. Eight children were born to him, who grew up: James, Margaret, Samuel, Mrs. Bowman, John, Amanda, Hannah and Maddox. James and Samuel settled in Bourbon; Margaret married a Sutton and moved to Indiana; John settled in Missouri; Amanda, Maddox and Hannah died young; Mrs. Bowman settled in Harrison County; Samuel, the father of our subject, engaged in farming; he succeeded his father in the distillery business, which he run until 1843, when he located in Paris Precinct, on the farm owned by William, his son, situated on the Flat Rock Pike; the farm is called the McClure place; he died here March 18, 1848—death occasioned by the kick of a mule; he was a member of the Reformed Church; his wife, Lucinda Talbott, was a daughter of Hugh and Elizabeth (Carter) Talbott; Henry Talbott, the father of Hugh, emigrated from Hanover County, Va., to Bourbon County, about the year 1789; Hugh was for several years a merchant at Ruddel's Mills; he died in 1832. To Samuel Fisher and wife were born two children: William H., and Susan, who married Charles Nolcini; she died February, 1860, leaving one child, William; Wm. H. was raised a farmer; Dec. 13, 1866, he married Emily Peck, who was born in Fleming County, Ky., daughter of William and Louisa (Stevens) Peck; Louisa was born Sept. 7, 1813, in Fleming County, on Locust Creek; daughter of Joseph and Elizabeth (Weaver) Stevens; he was born December, 1767, in Loudon County, Va.; his wife 1769, and were married, 1788, and removed to Fayette County, where they settled; William was a son of William Peck, of Mason County, Ky.; the former died Dec. 10, 1875. The religion of the Stevens was old Baptist; and the Pecks were Methodists; both families were Whigs. Mr. Fisher has 220 acres of land—the farm called Wood Brook; he has two children: Wm. Peck and Nebilla; he raises short horns; is a member of the Presbyterian Church G. S. A.

JAMES W. FERGUSON, farmer and stockraiser. Prominent among the large land-holders and successful business men of Bourbon County is Mr. Ferguson, who was born Aug. 25, 1830, in Winchester, Clark County; his parents were Abraham and Mary K. (Matson) Ferguson; he was born in Fayette County, Sept. 27, 1803, and died Aug. 1, 1854; he was a son of Abraham Ferguson, a native of Fauquier County, Va.; his father, John, was a native of Scotland, and emigrated to Virginia; his son Abraham served in the war of the Revolution and in the war of 1812. The grandfather of our subject emigrated to Kentucky, locating in what is now Fayette County, upon lands that he obtained from the government by virtue of his services in the war of the Revolution, upon which he settled; Indians were plentiful; while working upon his land his gun was his constant companion for self-protection. This land is now in the possession of the family name, in Brier Hill Precinct. Mary K. was born Feb. 9, 1810, in this county; she died Aug. 2, 1878; she was a daughter of Thomas and Rebecca (Spears) Matson, both families from Virginia. To Abraham Ferguson and wife were born eight children, five sons and three daughters; of those living are Robert M., a resident of Lexington, Ky.; Mary E., wife of James Brownell; Lucy E., wife of James H. Campbell, and James W., who remained with his father until he was twenty-six years of age. In 1840 he moved with his parents to Brier Hill Precinct, in Fayette County; Aug. 5, 1856, he married Martha A. Hume, who was born in Clintonville Precinct, May 7, 1830, daughter of Wm. P., son of John Hume, of Fauquier County, Va.; March, 1857, after marriage, he moved to this county on the farm adjoining where he now resides, upon which he lived until 1875, when he located where he now resides. Mr. Ferguson is engaged in farming and stock raising, and is a large dealer in stock, having been for several years a large shipper, since 1860; he has over 4,000 acres of land, the greater portion self-acquired; his children are William, P. H., Abram L., Maggie B., Robert H., Lucy E., Volney W., Matilda R., and James W.; P. H. resides on the home farm in Brier Hill, Fayette County.

I. N. FRY, farmer ; P. O. Paris ; the Fry family came from Virginia and settled in Bourbon County prior to 1800. The parents of the above were Abram and Nancy (Snell) Fry; both were natives of Kentucky. The maternal grandfather of I. N. was Lewis Snell, who was an early settler in Harrison County. Abram Fry settled on the farm now owned by his son, I. N., at an early time, and run a small distillery for several years on his farm. He died in 1843; his wife survived him until 1863, having borne six children, viz: Minerva, Elizabeth, James, Abram, Lewis and I. N., who was born May 15th, 1824, on the farm he now owns, where he has since remained. In July, 1852, he married Enfield Talbott, daughter of Daniel Talbott; has three children, John, James, and M. T. His farm consists of 240 acres.

JOSEPH FITHIAN, physician; P. O. Paris. The Fithian family trace their ancestry to one William Fithian, a native of England, whose will bears date Dec. 11, 1678. According to a family tradition, they came to America, and were among the little band of refugees who fled from the religious persecution at that time, and landed in South Hampton, Long Island, where they subsequently settled some time prior to the war of the Revolution; nearly all the members of the family that were eligible, served in that struggle; one Phillips was in command of a body of men who were participants in the "tea party" in Boston harbor. The first after William was Samuel, who married Priscilla Burnett. She had several children, among whom was Josiah, born May 6, 1685; his wife was Sarah Dennis. From them in direct line came Joseph, born Aug. 12, 1724 ; he married Hannah Vickers, who bore him Amos, Oct. 11, 1759, who married Rachel Leake; from this couple descended Joel Fithian, who was born May 10, 1797, at Cedarville, New Jersey. He is the father of Dr. Joe Fithian, whose name heads this page, who was born in Philadelphia, Pa., October, 1830. His mother's maiden name was Sarah Sinnockson, born Sept. 14, 1801, in Salem, New Jersey; she was a daughter of Andrew, who was born March 2, 1749, and died July 20, 1819. He served first as Captain, and afterwards promoted to Colonel in the Colonial war. He was a son of Andrew, whose father was likewise of same name; his brother Thomas was a member of the first Continental Congress, and served as Judge for twenty-two years. The Sinnockson family were originally from Sweden. The father of our subject was likewise a physician, and carried on the drug business in Philadelphia. His children were as follows, viz: Elizabeth, Mrs. John M. Peck, of Cincinnati; Dr. Washington, Dr. Joseph and Fannie; but two now living. Drs. Joseph and Washington both of Paris, Joseph graduated in Philadelphia in 1854, soon after came to Kentucky and engaged in the practice of his profession. During the entire war he served as surgeon in the Eighteenth Kentucky; after his time had expired he reurned. For several years past he has been associated with his brother, Washington Fithian, in Paris, in the practice of his profession. He was married to Miss Emma Owen, a native of this county. Three children have crowned this union, viz : Frank, a medical student, Nettie and Georgia. The Doctor is an elder of the Presbyterian Church.

"DEER LODGE" RESIDENCE OF WM. TARR FIVE MILES EAST OF PARIS, BOURBON CO., KY.

JOHN GRIFFITH, hotel-keeper; P. O. Paris; the owner and proprietor of the Thurston House. Mr. Griffith was born in Scott County, this State, in the year 1812, son of Benfield and Aquilla Truitt Griffith. The father of our subject was a native of Delaware, and settled in Scott County in the early part of the present century; he was a farmer by occupation, to which vocation our subject was raised, but left home at the age of seventeen and took to driving stage; being a lover of horses, and staging having a peculiar charm for him, he pursued this exciting and (to him) enjoyable business for many years. There was sharp competition in those days among the various lines, and trusty and fearless drivers were in demand. Mr. Griffith being a man of muscle, and withal a careful and efficient horseman, he was in demand, and continued as knight of the "ribbons" until he was thirty-nine years of age. After he abandoned the stage, he engaged in the livery business, which he run a short time, and since the year 1850 he has been in the hotel business at this place, and has been connected with the Thurston House. Mr. Griffiths keeps a good hotel, and is kind and obliging to his guests. He has about twenty-four rooms for the use of his patrons, besides good sample rooms; also barber shop and bar attached to the same. Free 'bus runs to all trains. Upon the whole travelers will find Mr. Griffith a good man to patronize. February, 1851, he married Mary Reid, daughter of William Reid.

O. A. GILMAN, merchant, farmer and trader; P. O. Paris; is a native of New Hampshire; son of Oscar and Belinda (Fox) Gilman, and a descendant of him who signed the Declaration of Independence. Our subject was raised to agricultural pursuits, and received excellent school advantages. In the Spring of 1863 he entered the U. S. Service, joining the 11th Massachusetts Battery, and participated in all the battles of the Army of the Potomac, and, with the exception of a slight wound received at Spottsylvania, he came through the entire struggle unscathed. He came to Kentucky in 1866, locating in Bourbon County, where he has since been identified with its business interests; is carrying on farming and stock raising, being interested in the breeding of fine stock—horses and cattle, trotting and running stock. In 1869 he married Belle A. Todd, a native of Buffalo, N. Y. Mr. Gilman is a resident of Paris, and is a large dealer in grass seed, wool, grain, salt and poultry. He is a member of the Episcopal Church, and of the several Masonic organizations, A., F. & A. M., R. A. M., and Webb Commandery, at Lexington, Ky.

M. M. GASS, farmer; P. O. Paris; whose portrait appears in this work, was born on the Stoner River in this precinct, May 29, 1806, son of John Gass and Anna Anderson. The paternal grandsire of Morris M. was David Gass, of Scotch-Irish descent, and emigrated from Virginia to Kentucky at an early time, and for some time sought protection in the fort at Boonesboro. He had two daughters that were captured by the Indians. He afterwards settled in Madison County, where he died. John Gass was born in the year 1765, and was with his father in the fort. He grew to manhood, and turned his attention to farming pursuits, and became prominently identified with the interests of Madison County. and served as Sheriff. He removed to Bourbon County in 1793, locating on the Stoner, upon lands now owned by Geo. M. Bedford, and engaged in farming pursuits, and remained here until his death, which took place Dec. 24, 1855. He was a man that was esteemed for his virtues, and was a respected member of the community, a member of the Presbyterian Church and an Elder in the same. The subject of these lines was raised upon the farm where he was born, and has always been engaged in farming pursuits. March 27, 1834, he married Mary A. Goodman, born June 18, 1808, in Albemarle County, Va. She was a daughter of Nathan and Mildred (Clarkston) Goodman, who emigrated to this county in 1817. Mr. Gass located on the farm he now owns in 1872. Said farm was settled by Nat. Davis. Mrs. Gass died. He has four children living, viz: Nannie, wife of John Wood, of Audrain County, Mo.; Mildred married Larken Towles, also of Missouri; Miss Bettie at home; and Sue, who resides in the Precinct, wife of W. P. Hume. Mr. Hume had three brothers and four sisters: James, David, John, Sallie, Betsy, Jane and Polly—Morris now being the sole survivor of the family. Mr. Gass is not a member of any church or society, yet is not an enemy to religion or the bonds of socialism.

W. C. GOODMAN, retired farmer; P. O. Paris; among the time-honored citizens and pioneer business men of this precinct, is Willis C. Goodman, who was born in Albemarle County, Va, Feb. 2, 1799, and emigrated to this county in the year 1817, Nov. 10, with his father, Nathan Goodman, who settled near Paris. He was born in same county and State, in the year 1768. His wife was Mildred Clarkson, daughter of Manoah Clarkson. The grandfather of W. C. was Charles Woodman, a native of Hanover Co., Virginia; his ancestors came from England, as did the Clarkson's, making their first settlement on the eastern shore of Virginia. To Nathan Woodman were born ten children, eight sons and two daughters: Roland H.,

Willis C., Alexander G., Feilden F., Ansalem, Virginia, Mary, Nathan, William and Manoah, all of whom, except Roland, came to Kentucky—he remained in Virginia. At the time Nathan Goodman came to this precinct he purchased a small farm; his "property" was mostly in negroes, of which he brought with him quite a number. He died of cancer in 1838. W. C., early in life, turned his attention to stock trading, which he followed for several years, dealing in mules, horses, cattle and hogs; his operations being confined not alone to this locality, but extended through several of the adjoining States. In the early part of his trading career, he made his father's house his home, until February, 1835, when he wedded Sarah A. Garth, daughter of Jesse and Betsey (Brown) Garth, both of whom were natives of Albemarle Co. Virginia. In 1831, Mr. Goodman purchased the farm he now owns, locating on the same the following year, and that since made this his constant residence. In his business relations Mr. Goodman has been successful. His farm of 600 acres he has since divided, having now 300 acres. Is now nearly eighty-two years of age, and is in the enjoyment of his quiet home, having a good residence on a beautiful site. Six children have honored his marriage, of whom are Elizabeth M., who married Green Clay; Willis, Mary, wife of Judge Matt. Turney; Lewis G., John C. and Sarah. Mr. Goodman's brothers nearly all settled in Missouri, except Feilden, who located in Fleming county, Virginia; married Joseph Watkins and located in same State with her brother. Mary became the wife of Morris M. Gass, and located in Bourbon County; Manoah was killed in Paris.

DOUGLAS HOWARD, physician; P. O. Paris. Among the rising practitioners of Materia Medica in Bourbon County, is Dr. Howard, who was born in Mount Sterling, this State. He was educated at Louisville, and received his medical training in that city, graduating Feb. 28, 1876, and served one year in the hospital, after his graduation, in active practice. In June, 1877, he came to Paris, and engaged in the practice of his profession, where he has since remained, and been successful, having a liberal share of the public patronage. His father was Henry C. Howard, a farmer and merchant, a native of Mount Sterling; he was a son of George Howard, one of the first settlers in that locality when Cincinnati was not in existence. The mother of Dr. Howard, was Bettie P. Lewis, born in the county, daughter of Douglas P. Lewis, who married Elizabeth Clay, sister of Samuel Clay, sr., of Paris Precinct. The Howard family were Whigs, and later were Republicans; his father was commissioned Colonel, under Federal rule, during the late war. Was an Episcopalian and had the following children: George C., Douglas, Anna M., Henry C. and Mary B. The doctor is a member of I. O. O. F.

JOSEPH A. HILDRETH, farmer; P. O. Paris. This gentleman is a descendant of one of the early families who settled in Bourbon County; he was born May 25, 1826. The parents of the above were John and Mary (Findley) Hildreth. The Hildreths were from Wythe County, Va. The Hildreth family came to this precinct in the early part of the present century, locating here, and have since remained. The elder members of the family have since passed away, yet several of the descendants still remain, among whom are: J. A., Mrs. C. M. Rogers; Evaline, Mrs. Nat. Rogers; and Mrs. Caroline Rosebury. In 1854 Joseph A. was united by marriage to Sallie, daughter of George A. and Elizabeth (Edwards) Smith; both families from Virginia. To the above were born six children, now living, viz.: George W., Mariamne, John, Smith, Caroline B. and Ida. Mr. Hildreth has 465 acres of land, and is engaged in farming pursuits.

JAMES HALL, farmer and stock raiser; P. O. Paris; is the owner and proprietor of "Huston Dale" stock farm. He is a native of the Blue Grass region, and identified with its interests since his birth. He first saw the light of day June 11, 1820, in Cynthiana, Harrison County. Mr. Hall has been a constant resident of this county since 1854, and during this time has been prominent in advancing the interests that pertain to short horn cattle, of which he is a breeder and dealer. His farm is located on the Houston, one and a half miles from Paris, it being one among the first settled and well known farms in Bourbon County. January 1, 1850, he was united by marriage to Nancy A. Huston, a native of Fayette County, this State; she was a daughter of John and Elizabeth (Holliday) Huston. The former, native of Virginia; she of Clark Co., this State. The first year of Mr. Hall's marriage he located in this county, afterwards removed to Fayette County, where he remained until 1854, when he returned to this county, locating on the farm he now owns, where he has been engaged in agricultural pursuits. He has but one child, Elizabeth H., now the wife of Irwin Taylor, who practiced law successfully several years at the bar in this county; now a resident of Topeka, Kansas, in the practice of his profession. Mr. Taylor has six children: Huston, Joseph I., Mary B., James H., Elizabeth C. and Lucy. Mr. Hall has been a lifelong Republican, and is a member of the Presbyterian Church North. The father of the above was Samuel Hall, born July 14, 1787, in the Old Dominion, and emigrated to this country, locating in Harrison County, where he died in 1835. His wife was Eliza, born Jan. 29, 1795, in this county, daughter of William and Ann (Southerland) Caldwell. William Caldwell was a native of Ireland, and emigrated to Pennsylvania at an early day, and joined the Colonial Army, where he was wounded, and died afterwards in consequence of injuries received in that struggle. He emigrated to Kentucky, arriving about the time the battle of the Blue Licks was fought, and located near Paris, on the farm now owned by Mr. Wilcox, near the cemetery. He had a family of one son and five daughters: Samuel, Elizabeth, Mrs. S. Hall; Margaret, wife of W. C. Lysle; Lucretia, wife of Luther Smith; Sallie, Mrs. Ben. Warfield; Jane, Mrs. Dr. Joseph Holt.

FRANCIS HALL, farmer and stock raiser; P. O. Paris. Born in Hutchinson Precinct, Jan. 21st, 1828; son of Joseph Hall, who was a native of Yorkshire, England. He and two brothers came to Virginia, and there settled. The mother of our subject was Nancy Hughes, a native of the Old Dominion. She bore her husband eleven children, but five of the number living at the present writing, viz.: Joseph, John, David, Francis, and Mary, and are located as follows: David resides in Missouri, John in Nicholas county, Joseph and Francis in Bourbon; Mary, wife of William Hamilton. Francis was but nine years of age when his father died. He was then placed under the guardianship of another party, with whom he remained until 19, when in 1847, he went to Mexico, and enlisted in the Mexican war, being a member of Company "H," 3d Regiment of Kentucky Volunteer Infantry. Upon his return from the war he came back to this county, where he has since remained. Jan. 27th, 1865, he married Lou Wheat, daughter of William, whose wife was Rebecca Wright, who was a daughter of Thomas Wright, son of Peter Wright. Mrs. Hall died, leaving but one child, Willie Wright. Early in life Mr. Hall learned the saddlery trade, which he followed but a short time. All he realized of his father's estate was $15. For several years he was engaged in driving stock for other parties. Later in life began farming, making his first purchase of land in Hutchinson Precinct, afterwards sold same, and purchased the farm he now owns. The place contains 214 acres called Fair View Stock Farm, situated on the Maysville and Lexington Pike, where he has engaged in farming and stock raising; short horns has recently occupied his attention. He is a Republican in politics; during the late war he was in command of a Company of State Militia. He was for several years a Director of the Agricultural Bank; is a member of Moreland Lodge, No. 124, I. O. O. F., and an officer of the same; and member of the Antioch Church, which is of the order after Alexander Campbell.

W. P. HUME, farmer; P. O. Paris; born in Centerville Precinct, Jan. 4, 1851; son of David J. Hume and Mary Talbott; he was brought up on a farm and raised to farming pursuits; April 18, 1873, he married Sallie Bacon, born near Paris, Nov. 2, 1853, daughter of W. A. Bacon and Belle Talbott; wife died 1878, leaving two children: David P. and Sallie L.; March 17, 1880, he married Sue Gass, born in this precinct, daughter of Morris Gass and Marry Goodman; 1873, he located on his farm, consisting of 243 acres, which he farms; raising good stock; is a member of the A. F. A. M.

D. J. HUME, farmer and stock raiser; P. O. Paris; born Oct. 11, 1824, near Clintonville, this county; son of W. P. Hume, who was born in this county, April 7, 1792; he was a son of John Hume, of Fauquier County, Va., who married Esther Patten, who was also a Virginian. The great-grandfather of D. J. was Andrew Hume, a native of Scotland; some of the family subsequently settled in Ireland. John Hume, son of Andrew, emigrated to this locality about the year 1787, settling on Strode's Creek, and followed the life of a farmer. To him six children were born, viz., Wm. P., Matthew D., Robert, Sallie (Mrs. Richie), Betsey (Mrs. Hughes), Julia (who married a McGaughey), of this number Wm. P., the father of D. J., settled in Bourbon County; Nathan D., in Clark; Sallie, in Mercer; Julia, in Christian County. W. P. married Eliza Hutchcraft, daughter of Thomas, a native of Virginia. After Mr. Hume's marriage, he located in Clintonville, where he lived until 1828, when he removed to the precinct, locating on the farm now owned by J. W. Ferguson, upon which he remained until his death, which occurred March 18, 1875; his wife five years previous, January, 1870. But two children were born to W. P. Hume: D. J. and Mary F. Mr. Hume's second wife was Matilda Renick, Mrs. J. W. Ferguson being the daughter of this marriage. David J. was educated at the common schools, remained with his father until his marriage, which occurred December, 1848, to Martha A. Talbott, born May 1828, in Fayette County, daughter of Benjamin and Mary (Grimes) Talbott, Mary being a daughter of Charles Grimes, of Virginia. Since his marriage D. J. has been an owner and occupant of the farm he now owns, called "Inwood." Mr. Humes has about 2,000 acres of land. He has been engaged in the breeding of short horns since his location on this farm. His father and grandfather both were breeders of fine stock. Mr. Hume has four sons: Wm. P., Ben T., Orlando V. and Samuel C. John S., now deceased, was drowned at the age of fourteen.

H. F. HIBLER, farmer; P. O. Paris; is a grandson of Joseph Hibler, a native of New Jersey, and one of the early settlers in Bourbon County. He settled in this precinct on the farm now owned by H. M. Roseberry. His wife was Jane Jacoby, who bore him two children, Adam S. and Emily. Adam S. Hibler, the father of H. F. was born on this farm in the year 1807, and at the death of his father succeeded him. His wife was Lucy Finch, who bore him ten children, among whom was H. F., whose birth occurred in 1830. Adam S. remained on this farm until 1854, when he removed to Midway, in Woodford County, this State. His death occurred at the above place, 1878. Our subject, during several years of his early manhood, was engaged as a drover, in charge of stock en route for the Eastern market. Jan. 25, 1855, he married Mary E. Brindley, who was born in Ruddel's Mills Precinct, daughter of Nicholas and Lucinda (Stivers) Brindley. Mr. Brindley was a native of Maryland, born Sept. 8, 1802, and married May 28, 1832. When he came to this county he was a poor man, but arose from a small beginning until he became a wealthy man; he was successful in all his business associations, which were uniformly crowned with pleasing results. He was upright and honest in his dealings, and died a Christian, being a member and Elder in the Christian Church. His death occurred 1846, Sept. 17; his wife's May 30, 1849. They had three children who came to maturity: Benjamin F., who resides in Baltimore, a capitalist; Lucy G., who married E. B. Bishop, and located in New Haven, Conn. She died 1874, leaving three children. Of the ten children, born to Adam S. Hibler, Henry F. was the eldest; in order of birth were Emily, Cynthia, Sallie, Joseph, Thomas, Lovenia, Mary E., James, Harry and Lucy, all of whom grew up. Lucy resides in Midway, wife of Richard Starks, a druggist; Cynthia married David Robb, of Versailles; Lovenia married Mr. Richard Richetts; Emma, Amos Parker; Sallie, ex-Sheriff, ex-Mayor, B. F. Pullen. Mr. and Mrs. Hibler located on the farm they now own in March, 1855, and have since improved the home surroundings to their present beauty; the farm consists of 328 acres. They have five sons: William F., James H., Bishop, Edward and Henry.

R. B. HUTCHCRAFT, P. O. Paris; dealer in hemp, wool, blue grass, and grain; was born in Clintonville Precinct; son of Reuben Hutchcraft and Fannie Hedges; Reuben was born in Culpepper County, Va.; son of Thomas, who married a Miss Apperson; Thomas Hutchcraft served seven years in the Revolutionary war, after which he settled in Virginia; he afterwards emigrated to this State, locating in this county, where he remained until his death; he had five children: John, Reuben, James, Nimrod and Mrs. W. P. Hume, all of whom were always identified with this county and its interests; Reuben, the father of R. B., died in 1865; ten children were born to him that lived to be grown: John H. Thomas, Lou., Silas, Mary E. William, Clay, Ella, Reuben Brent, and Nannie; mother died in 1867; was a member of the Baptist Church; he was not a member of any church; was an old line Whig; an upright man, and one that was highly esteemed by his friends and acquaintances; our subject received good educational advantages; was raised upon the farm; in 1873, he came to Paris, and has since been engaged in business, being one of the largest dealers in his line in the city; he is treasurer of the contemplated K. U. R. Road.

W. M. HINTON, jeweler; P. O. Paris; is the oldest jeweller in Paris, where he was born, Sept. 25, 1830, being the eldest son and third child born to Richard Hinton, a well known resident of this county. In 1844, he began his trade with B. B. Marsh, of this place, and continued under his instruction for three years, after which he, worked seven years in Shelbyville, this State, and in 1854, set up in Paris, where he has since continued, and by strict attention to business built up an excellent trade, and accumulated a good home, and a competence by his own perserverance and industry. He has been thrice married, first time, Oct. 1, 1857, to S. A. Jones, daughter of Richard Jones, of Millersburg; she died Dec. 20, 1860, leaving one child, Anna S. His second wife was Maggie, sister of first wife, who died about one year afterwards, leaving one child, since dead. His present wife was Bettie G., daughter of Gen. John M. Millier, of Richmond, Ky., by her has four children; W. M., Charles O., Bertha G., and Robert R. Mr. Hinton is a member of the Baptist Church, and trustee of the same.

JAMES HINTON, farmer and horticulturist; P. O. Paris; born Oct. 18, 1818, in Baltimore, Md.; son of John Abijah Hinton, a native of England, who was educated for the Episcopal Ministry, but afterwards went abroad upon the high seas and became a sea captain; but little of him was known afterwards, as he was lost when our subject was but a babe; consequently but little of the early history of his ancestry is known by the above. The mother of James was Jane Kennedy, a native of the Emerald Isle; she bore her husband two children, Isabella and James; Isabella married Harvey Nash, of New York; she died 1861, leaving four daughters and three sons. Mr. Hinton emigrated to this State with his mother, about the year 1820, and located in Paris, where she died of cholera in 1833. Our subject learned the carpenter's trade, which he followed continuously until 1873, as builder and contractor. Sept. 17, 1846, he married Sarah E. Wheat, daughter of William and Rebecca (Wright) Wheat; his wife died in January, 1861, leaving three children: Rebecca B., William W., and James H. Rebecca B. was first married to Dr. R. T. Weldon, by whom she had one son, William McLeod; she now resides in Cincinnati, wife of Thomas Baldwin. William W. resides in Kansas City, Mo., and James H., in Cincinnati. May 1, 1862, he married Mary A. Sisson, born in Augusta, Bracken Co. Ky., daughter of Lawson and Matilda (Weldon) Sisson; he was a native of Fauquier County, Va.; she, of Bracken County, Ky. Since 1859, Mr. Hinton has been a resident of the farm he now owns, and since 1874 he has given his attention to the culture of fruits and flowers, and nursery stock, making more of a specialty of flowers, and has been successful in his business undertakings. Since 1837 he has been a member of the Baptist Church at Paris. A view of his place will be found in this work.

SILAS HEDGES, deceased. The Hedges' family trace their ancestry to Sir Charles Hedges, an English politician, who graduated at Oxford in 1675 and died in 1714; he had four daughters and one son, whose name was Joseph, who emigrated to America at an early day, locating in Prince William's County, Md.; to him were born nine children, whose names were: Solomon, Charles, Joshua, Jonas, Joseph, Samuel, Catharine, Dorcas, and Ruth; Solomon died in West Virginia in 1797; his family consisted of six children: Rebecca, Joseph, Catharine, Silas, Joshua, and Rachel; Joseph, mentioned above, emigrated to Kentucky about 1789, locating at Stoney Point, in Bourbon County; his children were: John, Samuel, James, Jonas, Charles and three daughters; John was the father of Silas, whose name heads this page; John married Kate Troutman, and by her had the following children, viz: Peter, Silas, James, Nanny, Fannie, Lucinda, Mary, and Scytha; all lived to be grown, and settled in this county; Silas was twice married, first to Frances Branham, who died leaving one son, Willis W., now living in this county; in 1839 he married Elizabeth J. Ewalt, born Jan. 1, 1824, in Paris Precinct, Bourbon County, daughter of Richard and Maria (Stamps) Ewalt. Mr. Hedges engaged in farming and was successful; he was a member of the Christian Church, and a valued citizen; his death occurred June 30, 1880; he had two children: Richard and Mollie; the former died, aged seventeen; the latter married William S. Grimes, born August, 1837, in Clintonville Precinct, this county, son of John S. and Katie (Scott) Grimes; John S., was a son of Sylvester Grimes; Wm. S. Grimes died May 3, 1881, leaving two daughters: Lizzie E. and Sallie S.; Mrs. Grimes resides with her mother in Paris, where they have a handsome residence and several hundred acres of land in this county.

CHARLES V. HIGGINS, retired; P. O Paris; was born Sept. 17, 1807, in Montgomery County, this State; only son born to James and Mary (Williams) Higgins. The Higgins family are of Scotch-Irish descent, of whom William Higgins was the first of whom there is any definite account, he being the great-grandsire of our subject; he removed from Ireland to the Old Dominion, and settled prior to the Revolution, and raised a family of seven sons and one daughter; the sons were: William, Moses, Aaron, Capt. James, John, Joel and Jesse; of the number Moses was the grandfather of Chas. V.; James served in the war of the Revolution, commanding a company. Aaron Higgins was the first one of the name that came to Kentucky about 1780, and entered 3,000 acres of land in what is now Montgomery County; upon this land all of his brothers (above mentioned) settled; Aaron was killed by the Indians at Sinclair's defeat. Moses Higgins married Jane Jeter, by whom he had: James, William, Betsey, Katie, Matilda, Nancy and America; of this number, James was the father of our subject; he was born in 1781 in Virginia, and married Mary Williams, born in 1784, likewise of Virginia birth; she was a daughter of Raleigh Williams, of English descent. Of the Higgins brothers above mentioned, William T. was a physician, and settled in Mississippi, and was drowned while crossing a river. James Higgins was a farmer and brick-mason; he built many of the houses yet standing in Mt. Sterling, Ky.; he had five children born to him; all died before they grew up except Chas. V., who left home and learned the tan and currier's trade, at Boonesborough and Winchester; Nov. 18, 1828, he married Judith Y. Stone, who was born in Bourbon County March 8, 1812; she was a daughter of John and Judith (Parrott) Stone, both natives of Albemarle County, Va., and came here to Bourbon County in 1811. Mr. Stone died March 8, 1821; his wife in 1859; to them were born six children: Elizabeth, Thomas, John, William, Judith and James M., who resides in Texas; he and Mrs. Higgins alone survive. After Mr. and Mrs.

Higgins were married they moved to North Middletown, where he engaged in the tan and currier business, remaining here until 1834; then sold out and moved to Montgomery County, remaining there until 1837, when he returned to Middletown; since that time he has been a constant resident of the county; for several years has been a resident of Paris, where he now resides. Notwithstanding he began with nothing, he has by successful management, amassed a good fortune, having a large amount of land and much valuable town property in this city. He has been connected with the Deposit Bank in this place since its commencement, first as Director, and since 1867 as President. He has but one child, Charles V., present Treasurer of the county. Mr. Higgins is not a member of any church or society, but not opposed to them or the principles they espouse.

R. W. HUTCHCRAFT, U. S. store-keeper; P. O. Paris; born in North Middletown Precinct, July 4, 1832; was the second child and eldest son of his parents, who were James and Eliza (Williams) Hutchcraft. James Hutchcraft was born January, 1800, in Bourbon County, in North Middletown, and died 1863; son of Thomas Hutchcraft, a native of Fauquier County, Va. He came to Kentucky about the year 1798. The mother of our subject was born 1812, in Montgomery County, Ky., daughter of Gen. Samuel L. Williams and Fannie Clark, both families from Virginia. R. W. had but common school advantages; was raised a farmer. Jan. 13, 1807, he married in this county, Susan Croxton, daughter of Henry Croxton and Ann Redmon; shortly after his marriage, he removed to Lee County, Iowa, and engaged in farming. At the outbreak of the war, he "donned the blue," and enlisted July, 1861, in Co. E, 15th Iowa Infantry, and was wounded in the battle of Shiloh. After one year of active service, he was assigned to the Quartermaster's department, where he remained until the close of the war; after which he returned to his family in Bourbon County. In 1867, he moved to Fleming County, this State, remaining there three years, in Government employ as Gauger. Upon his return to this county, he engaged in farming. Since 1878, he has been in Government employ—now Storekeeper. His wife died 1863; by her had four children, viz: Annie, James P., Harry and Davis. 1867, he married Margaret, daughter of Thomas Fleming. By last wife has one child, Emma. Mr. Hutchcraft has a snug home, in this precinct; is a warm friend to education, and a member of the M. E. Church, of which his parents were true followers.

J. W. HARMON, farmer; P. O. Paris. Of the self-made men that have come up from small beginnings is Mr. Harmon; he is a native of the Buckeye State; born November, 1831, in Ashtabula County; son of Norman and Sallie Weldon Harmon, both natives of Connecticut; he died 1873; she, four years later. J. W. is the youngest of a family of five children. He was reared to farming pursuits, but his mind and tastes running in a different direction, he gave his attention to handling machinery and running steam engines. In 1848, he left Ohio and went to New York. In 1854, he came to Kentucky, and has since been identified, first in Clark County, remaining a short time, coming here the following year. For about seven years he was engaged in running a mill, having learned the miller's art, five years in Paris Precinct, on Samuel Clay's farm, and two years in Lexington. From 1863 to June, 1865, he served in the U. S. service in the Quartermaster's department, being located in the meantime in Arkansas. After abandoning his milling enterprise he began renting land, and in 1877 he purchased a portion of the Penn farm, consisting of 270 acres, where he has since resided. June 22, 1859, he married Jeanie H., born in Cayuga County, N. Y., daughter of Archibald and Catharine (Hamilton) Burns, both natives of Scotland, to whom eight children were born, Mrs. Harmon being the seventh; her father died 1865; mother, 1874. Mr. Harmon has but one child, Florence May, born September, 1870. Mrs. Harmon is a member of the Presbyterian Church. Of Mr. Harmon's brothers and sisters are as follows: Miles is a merchant in Ashtabula, Ohio; Lucius, a master mechanic in Ballston Springs, Saratoga, N. Y.; Catharine, wife of John Pelham, in Rockford, Minnesota; Elizabeth resides in Cleveland, wife of Mr. Williams.

JAMES W. INGELS, retired; P. O. Paris. In the year 1782, James Ingels, the grandfather of the above, left Pennsylvania, and, with his family, bent his steps toward Kentucky; the country, then, as the reader can well imagine, was anything but promising or inviting, but the wayfaring man was seeking a home for himself and family, and was prepared to meet hardships; in passing through Maysville, having no gun, he contracted with a gunsmith there to make him one and take his pay in bacon when it could be procured; Mr. Ingels came on with his family, locating at Grant's Station, near Bryant's Station; Mr. Ingels finally raised the necessary amount of bacon and sent a hired boy with it to Maysville to make the exchange; strange to say, the boy, horse and cart, bacon and gun were never heard from until several years after, when Mr. Ingels received a letter from the boy, then a grown-up man, saying that he had wandered off into Ohio instead of going to Maysville; had bought him a home and was doing well, and if he (Mr. Ingels) would come there he would pay him for his bacon, horse and cart, &c.; Mr. Ingels never went. This old pioneer died on the place he settled in 1803; he had five sons and four daughters born to him; Joseph, the eldest, married Mrs. Bryant, a niece of Daniel Boone; James settled on the homestead; Thomas and John settled in Indiana; Edith married Welson Hunt, and located in Missouri; Nellie became the wife of Mr. Victor, and settled in Nicholas County; Boone Ingels, the father of our subject, was born at Grant's Station, 1784, and raised a farmer until seventeen, when his father died; in 1808 he came to Paris, where he carried on the hatter's trade until his death in 1837, when 53 years of age; he raised a family of nine children, eight sons and one daughter. Our subject was raised to the business his father prosecuted, after going for him to St. Louis to buy furs; in 1832 he went to Jacksonville, Ills., where he spent two years in business with Forsythe & Butler; he returned in 1834; the year following he married Amanda Crose, a native of this county, daughter of Levi Crose. Mrs. Ingels died 1855, having borne him nine children; Benjamin, Wilson, Boone, Ella, Belle and George were the number raised. In 1857, Mr. Ingels married Mary Davis, a native of this place, daughter of George and Mary (McClintock) Davis, both natives of Virginia; he born 1794, she, two years later. Mr. and Mrs. Ingels have one daughter, Lizzie. Mr. Ingels has been a successful man in business; he owned 4,000 acres of land at one time, which he sold at a large advance; for twenty-five years he had charge of the paupers in this county; Mr. Ingels has been retired from business several years, and is living in retirement, and enjoying the fruits of his labor in quiet and happiness; has been a member of the Christian Church over forty years.

EDWARD INGELS, retired physician; P. O. Paris; was born in this city in 1821, and was the seventh son of Boone and Elizabeth (Reed) Ingels. Edward was raised in this place and was educated in Lexington, at the Transylvania University, graduating there in 1841. Soon after he graduated he began the practice of his profession in his native town, and continued without intermission until 1871, since that time he has retired from active practice, only prescribing and visiting some of his most intimate friends, who insist upon his still serving them. In 1853 he was united in wedlock to Bettie Massie, daughter of Jonathan Massie; Mrs. Ingels died in 1868, leaving one son, Edward. In 1876 he married Ella (Chew) Pinkerton, daughter of Dr. William and Helen (Ware) Chew. Dr. Chew was a regular graduate in Materia Medica; he was born in Fredericksburg, Va., 1816; son of Joseph Chew. The wife of Dr. Chew was born in Frankfort, this State; she was a daughter of James Ware. Dr. Chew practiced his profession several years in Midway, until 1868, when he removed to Texas where he now resides. To him were born a family of four daughters and three sons. Mrs. Ingel's maiden name, as above stated, was Ella Chew, but at the time of her marriage she was the relict of W. W. Pinkerton, a lawyer by profession, a native of Ohio, and son of L. L. Pinkerton. Boone Ingels, the father of our subject, was a Whig, and at one time represented his county in the Legislature.

THOMAS ISGRIG, farmer; P. O. Paris; is a descendant of one of the early pioneers who came to this county in 1791, at a time when the ground resounded to the tread of the red-man, and the forests echoed to the cries of the panther and other denizens of the wildwood. The subject of these lines was born in 1824, in the edge of Harrison County, four miles from Cynthiana, being the third son, and fourth child in order of birth, born to Daniel and Mary (Current) Isgrig. The grandfather of our subject was Daniel, who was named for his father, Lord Isgrig, who was a native of England, and emigrated to Baltimore County, Md., where the grandfather of Thomas was born, Dec. 26th, 1756. The maternal grandmother of Thomas was Margaret Cole, born on the sea coming from Scotland, 1751. By this marriage six children were born, whose names were William, Margaret, Daniel, Michael, Nancy and Hannah; of this number, Daniel and Michael came to Kentucky, and here lived and died; William, Margaret and Hannah located in Fayette County, Ind.; Daniel, above mentioned, was born in Baltimore County, Md., on the eastern shore, April 3, 1786; his wife, on the opposite shore, the same month, 26th day, one year later. Daniel, Jr., removed with his parents to what is now Harrison County, in 1791. Daniel, Sr., purchased land soon after, for which he paid two dollars per acre; a portion of said land (252) acres, Thomas his grandson, our subject, purchased in 1870, paying therefor one hundred and twenty dollars ($120) per acre. The children born to Daniel Isgrig, Jr., were William, Catharine, Daniel, Thomas, Margaret and Mary; William resides in Ruddel's Mills Precinct; Catharine resides in Edgar County, Ill.; Daniel in Saline County, Mo.; Margaret married J. W. Vanhook of this County; Mary died, aged sixteen. The parents of our subject died Feb. 11, 1877, and Feb. 11, 1852, respectively. They were members of the M. E. Church, as were their ancestors before them. Politically he was a Whig, but voted for Andrew Jackson. Thomas remained with his father until thirty-five years of age; since that time he has been a resident of this county. Sept. 24, 1868, he married Ella Saunders, born December, 1835, in Cadiz, Ohio, daughter of Henry W. Saunders, a native of the Emerald Isle. Mr. Isgrig has one son who bears the name of his grandparents on the Isgrig side. Mr. Isgrig has 252 acres in this precinct, which he rents, and resides in the city limits. He has twenty-two acres situated on the east side of the river, which is beautifully located; he tills the same as market gardner. Since 1879 he has served as Justice of the Peace in this precinct.

WILLIAM ISGRIG, Jr., farmer ; P. O. Paris ; was born in this precinct, June 13, 1843, the eldest of three sons. His parents were William and Letitia (Reid) Isgrig ; he was born June 2, 1819, son of Daniel and Mary (Current) Isgrig; she was born in this precinct, and a daughter of Thomas Current, who were one of the early settlers ; he built a still-house near the place where William Isgrig, jr. now lives. The above was raised in this precinct, and to farming pursuits. Nov. 5, 1868, he married Lou C. Reid, a native of this county; she was a daughter of Greenberry and Amanda (Lancaster) Reid. Mrs. Isgrig died April 25, 1873. Two children were born to her, but one now living, Emma Ray. Oct. 17, 1876, he married Carrie Childriss ; born at Hutchinson Station, daughter of P. G. and Amanda (Wheatley) Childriss; he was born in Pendleton County, Ky., son of John Childriss, of Virginia. Amanda being a daughter of Daniel Wheatley, of the "Old Dominion." Mr. Isgrig located where he now resides, in 1873. He has 200 acres.

THOMAS JONES, retired farmer; P. O. Paris; one among the oldest ditizens now living in Bourbon County; is Uncle Thomas Jones, who has lived under every administration; from Washington down to the present ; he was born Jan. 19, 1792, on Baughman's Creek, near Athens, in Fayette County, this State; his father was James Jones, who was born about the year 1758, in Spottsylvanina County, Va., son of Thomas Jones, a Virginian; James Jones was a Revolutionary soldier, also his brother, William, who was present at the surrender of Cornwallis ; he emigrated to Kentucky, locating in Fayette County, in 1789 ; his wife was Sallie Schooler, also a native of the Old Dominion ; she had three brothers, who served in the Continental army, viz : Horton, Benjamin and William ; the father of our subject was a farmer, and raised a family of ten children—eleven being born ; the educational advantages afforded the family were very poor indeed ; Thomas remained with his father until his majority, after which he hired to his father for a time, then volunteered as a soldier in the war of 1812, and was a member of Colonel Johnson's regiment of cavalry, and was at the battle of Thames, after which he was discharged and returned home ; Jan. 22, 1814, he was married in North Middletown, to Patsey Ashurst, who was born in 1787, in that precinct ; she was a daughter of Josiah and Rebecca (Kennedy) Ashurst ; he was a native of Georgia ; Mr. Jones came to Bourbon County with his father in 1800 ; after the marriage of our subject, he located upon a piece of land, which he had leased near Thomas Station, in Clintonville Precinct ; he had but little to commence with, his entire property amounting to about $300 ; he began with his naked hands in the woods to make his start, and from this small beginning, he after years of hard toil, accumulated about 1100 acres of choice land ; being a man of iron constitution, of indomitable persevernce and a tireless worker, he made a success at last, and accumulated a handsome property ; he gave his attention strictly to farming pursuits ; in 1833, he began raising some thoroughbred cattle, of the short horn class, which he continued in a moderate way, until he abandoned farming and retired, and removed to Paris during the war, where he has since resided; his wife died, leaving him six children, viz: Josiah A., John I., Rebecca K., Sarah D., Thomas D., and Perlina A.—but three now living: Rebecca, now Mrs. Hildreth; Thomas D., and John I.; Thomas resides in Tennessee; his present wife was Lucy A. Monday, a native of Madison County, a daughter of Edmond and Mollie Monday, both natives of Kentucky ; he of Madison, she of Clark county; by last wife has one child, Lillie; he has been a member of the church over sixty years; in 1819, joined the Old Baptist Church; later he joined the Reformed, and now stands like a shock of corn, fully ripe and fit for his Master's use.

J. K. JAMESON, farmer; P. O. Paris; born Nov. 3, 1807, in Harrison County, son of James Jameson, a native of Virginia, and emigrated to Harrison County, Ky., prior to 1800; his father a native of Ireland. His wife's maiden name was Elizabeth Snell, daughter of Lewis and Mollie Snell, whom were natives of Virginia. Ten children were born to James Jameson, but five of the number came to maturity, of whom James was one; he remained with his father until he was married, which was in March 25, 1832, to Mary L. Hutchison. She was a daughter of James Hutchison and Elizabeth Edwards. Mr. Jameson located on the farm he now owns in 1832, and since has

James. S. Jacoby

been a constant resident; he has 333 acres of land. His wife died June 19, 1879, having borne him eleven children; but three are living, viz: John W., Louisa J. and Mary. She (Mrs. Jameson) was a member of the Christian Church, of which Mr. Jameson is also a disciple. Two of his children now deceased lived to be grown, viz: Belle, who married William Davis; by him had one daughter, Sallie B., who married Lee Champ; Nannie, the other grown daughter, married Joseph McClintock, of Harrison County.

NATHAN KENNEDY, farmer; P. O. Paris; was born in Bourbon County, May 20, 1793, the youngest child of his father's family; his father was Joseph, who died in 1797; his wife was Christina Akers, a daughter of Joseph Akers, who died aged 104 years. Joseph Kennedy's ancestors were of Scotch-Irish stock; Joseph Kennedy was one of the earliest settlers in this county. The red man had not given up his hunting grounds here, but was slowly wasting away at the approach of the enterprising white settler. Joseph had six children, four sons and two daughters. The subject of these lines located on the farm he now owns in 1817, situated on the Maysville and Lexington Pike, and has since remained; he purchased his land at $20 per acre of Garret Jones. Mr. Little was the first settler. Mrs. Kennedy died in 1849; Mr. Kennedy has two sons in Missouri, Jacob in Monroe County, Zadock at Pleasant Hill, Cass County. Catharine is the wife of Robert Layson; and David who resides in this precinct, was born 1832, and is the youngest child of the family. At the age of twenty he left home to do for himself; for several years he was employed in stock driving, having in charge mules for the distant markets. In September, 1862, he married Anna Myall, a native of England, who emigrated to this country when two years of age; her parents were Edward and Rachel (Lawrence) Myall, who came to Maysville in 1842; Mr. Myall removed to California in 1877; his wife died in 1864; they had a family of nine children. Mr. Kennedy located on the farm he now owns in 1866; is engaged in farming, and gives some attention to raising fine horses; he has three children: Samuel J., Owen D., and Edward B. He is a member of the Presbyterian Church.

J. B. KENNEDY, farmer and stock raiser; P. O. Paris; is a descendant of one of the first settlers in Bourbon County. Our subject was born Dec. 1, 1824, on the farm now owned by B. F. Bedford. His father was Captain Washington Kennedy, who was born June 25, 1779, and commanded Company in 1812; was son of John Kennedy, a revolutionary soldier, and native of Virginia, and emigrated here and settled on Kennedy's Creek, in 1779. For a further account of the family the reader is referred to the history of Bourbon County, in this volume. The mother of John B. was Elizabeth Bedford, who was born in this precinct, Dec. 7, 1794, on he farm now owned by Patsey Clay; she was a daughter of Littleberry Bedford, the "Pioneer." She died July 18, 1834. Washington died Aug. 14, 1832, leaving John B. an orphan at an early age. He went to live with uncle John Bedford, with whom he lived until he attained his manhood. November, 1845, he was married to Mary M. Kennedy, daughter of Jesse and Polly (Waugh) Kennedy; he was born in this precinct, Aug. 11, 1787, and died April 3, 1863; she born May 11, 1788, and died June 27, 1837. After marriage Mr. Kennedy purchased the farm he now owns, called the "Elm Spring Farm," where he has since resided, and been engaged in agricultural pursuits since 1850; has been engaged in raising short horns, and for several years past been engaged in trading in stock and shipping to the Eastern markets. Mrs. Kennedy died Feb. 2, 1871, leaving two children, Sidney B. and Mary J. Mr. Kennedy's present wife was Mrs. Alice Redmon, daughter of Greenberry Dorsey, of New Orleans. John Kennedy, the grandfather of J. B., entered land upon Kennedy's Creek, which bears his name; he never came to Kentucky to live. He had two sons Eli and Washington, who located on the land. Washington finally purchased his brother s interest, and finally located on the farm now owned by B. F. Bedford.

JOHN LUCAS, farmer; P. O. Paris; born Jan. 18, 1810, at Lucasville, Sciota County, Ohio, son of Samuel Lucas, of Jefferson County, Va.; he was a son of William Lucas, who left Virginia at an early day, and settled in Sciota County, and the place was named in honor of him and the family. He had a son, Robert, who became Governor of the State. The mother of our subject was Sarah Carter, a native of Jefferson County, Va., a daughter of Robert and Elizabeth (Griggs) Carter. Robert Carter located in Fayette County, Ky., about the year 1805. To Samuel Lucas and wife were born five children, viz: William, John, Joseph, Joanna and Alice. Our subject was raised a farmer; his education was limited to that of common school. His father died in 1813, and he came to Fayette County with his grandfather, who brought the family from Ohio. February, 1840, he married Letitia Hardin, a native of Bourbon County, born 1820, daughter of Stull Hardin, of Green River Country. Our subject after his marriage, came to this county; remained about one year; then removed to Harrison County, where he lived until 1842, since then he has been a constant resident of this county; he has a farm of 301 acres, situated in Paris Precinct. Wife died in February, 1864, having borne him three children: William, Hardin and Mary. In 1865, he married Mrs. Sophia Moore, born 1830; by her he has one son, John M. Her maiden name was Morin, daughter of Joseph and Sophia (Edwards) Morin. Mr. Lucas has been a resident of the farm he now owns, since 1868; he is the only remaining child of his father's family. His brother William taught school and moved to Harrison County, and engaged in merchandising there, died in 1840; Joseph settled in the same county; was a farmer; he died 1839; Joanna married Thomas Garth, of this County; she died 1880; Alice married Henry Calmes, of Clark County. Mr. Lucas for twelve years was one of the Directors of the Deposit Bank; he was appointed executor of the William Garth estate, who had left his will in care of Mr. Lucas, prior to his starting on that fated trip. Mr. Lucas is a Democrat, and a member of the Christian Church.

ROBERT LANGSTON, Sr., deceased; is a descendant of one of the oldest settlers in the County This gentleman was born November 19, 1807, in this precinct, on the farm owned by Robert Clark. His parents were Abraham and Isabella (Clark) Langston. Jacob, the grandfather of Robert was a Virginian; he emigrated with his family to Kentucky, about 1790, locating on the farm now owned by John B. Kennedy. Jacob had six children, viz: Abraham, Isaac, Jacob, Obadiah, Kate and Mary. All of the boys, save Abraham, went South and settled in Georgia. The children of Abraham were eleven in number, five daughters and six sons, viz: William, Jacob, Elizabeth, Mary, Robert, John, Polly A., Amanda, Isaac, Abe and Jane. William was born in this precinct, about the year 1797, and resides in Missouri. Jacob is also a native of Missouri, in Boone County, and there died. Elizabeth married John Tate, and settled in Clark County, Ky.; Mary married John D. Bratton and settled in Calloway County, Mo. John died a young man. Polly married Johnson Robertson, she resides in Mo., Lafayette Co.; Amanda married Granberry Reid. Isaac settled in Clay County, Mo.; Abe, in Clark Co. Jane died young. Mr. Robert Langston married Sarah Parish, a native of Pendleton Co., Ky, She died leaving three children, Eliza, Martha and Robert L. Mr. Langston has been engaged in farming for several years; run a distillery and a mill, which was one of the first built in the country; he now is retired from active life, and resides with his son Robert L., who was born Jan. 20, 1846. March 27, 1873, he married Fannie Deavers, daughter of John Dearers of this precinct. Robert L. has four daughters: Sarah M., Lizzie, Alice and Elvira. He is engaged in farming, and walnut lumber trade. Rob't Langston died at the residence of his son, Jan. 24, 1882, of short illness; a man highly respected in the community.

PROF. W. H. LOCKHART, A. M., was born June 10, 1846, at Lexington, Ky. Henry Lockhart, his father, was a native of the north of Ireland, near Londonderry; came to America in 1807, with his father's family, and located at Newburg, New York, in 1826; he settled in Fayette County, and lived there as a farmer and trader until 1866, when he moved to Bourbon, where he has since resided. His mother, Sarah (Richardson) Lockhart, was a native of Fayette County, and daughter of Capt. Marquis Richardson and his wife, Henrietta Catlett, originally Virginians. His mother died Feb. 4, 1860, aged seventy-six years. He was raised in Lexington, attending the best schools of the place, and, finally completing his education in Transylvania University. In 1861, he was elected a Professor in Transylvania University, and continued to teach until 1867, when he was elected Principal of the Paris public school, and was re-elected for three years. He then opened the Paris "Classical Institute," of which he has been Principal and is successfully conducting at the present time. He has been closely identified with the educational interests of Bourbon County for fifteen years, having been elected School Commissioner in 1867, and re-elected since at the expiration of each term. He is at the present time serving as School Commissioner, his term expiring on November of this year. He has also been active in the educational work of the State, having served as Vice President and Secretary of the State Teachers' Association for a number of years, and selected by the committee on programme to prepare papers and deliver addresses on different educational subjects.

J. McMILLAN, dentist; P. O. Paris; the oldest established dentist in Paris, is the above, who was born in this precinct Oct. 12, 1845, son of Robert McMillan. His mother was Armilda, daughter of Thomas Stark, a native of Virginia, who emigrated to Kentucky, locating near Cane Ridge, this county. He was educated at Clay Seminary, at North Middletown. In 1862 he began the study of his profession, graduating in 1865, at the Ohio Medical College, after which he located here in Paris in the practice of his profession, where he has since remained. He is also interested in breeding and handling trotting horses, also farming to some extent, having about 100 acres, part of which is within the cor-

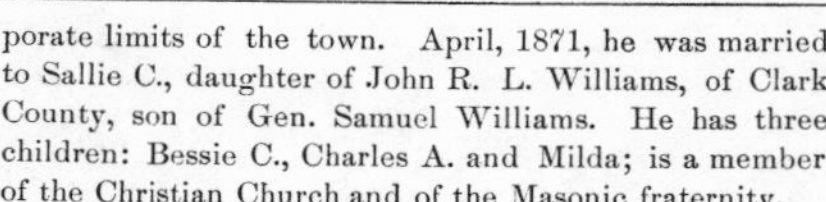

porate limits of the town. April, 1871, he was married to Sallie C., daughter of John R. L. Williams, of Clark County, son of Gen. Samuel Williams. He has three children: Bessie C., Charles A. and Milda; is a member of the Christian Church and of the Masonic fraternity.

JOSEPH MITCHELL, farmer and stockraiser; P. O. Paris; was born in Paris, May 24, 1822. He is a grandson of William and Mary Wilcox Mitchell, who were natives of Pennsylvania, and emigrated to this State, locating near what is now Paris, shortly after the battle of Blue Licks. He was a tanner by trade, and it is supposed that he worked one of the first tanneries in the county. The Mitchell family emigrated first from Scotland to the north of Ireland, from which place they emigrated to America. They belonged to the Old Scotch Church, what is now demominated as Scotch-Presbyterian, and were very strict in regard to their religious ideas of worship. To William Mitchell and wife were born four children; the eldest was William, who settled in Mason County; Thomas was the father of our subject, who located in Paris; James settled in Indiana; Jane was the only daughter. She married James Graham, and settled in Indiana also. William Mitchell lived an honorable and upright life, and died a christian, which life he lived for many years. Thomas Mitchell, the father of Joseph, was born in this county, and early in life learned the blacksmith's trade, but did not follow this vocation long, but learned the saddler's trade, which business he followed for many years. He, too, like his father, lived agreeable to his profession, being a member of the same church. His death occurred in 1836. His companion in life survived him until 1849. Their union was blessed with four children, William being the eldest; Joseph, Mary and Thomas. Of the above, William settled in Paris, and engaged in the grocery business, where he lived until removed by death in Dec., 1867. He left a family of seven children. Mary married George Irvine, and first settled in Indiana, but finally removed to Kansas, and there died, leaving three children. Thomas settled in Lexington, where he now resides. He is cashier in the First National Bank of that place. Joseph, our subject, was raised in Paris, and at the age of twelve, he entered the store of N. B. Ryan as clerk; at the age of twenty-three he became a partner with his employer, in 1845, under the firm name of Ryan & Mitchell, which association lasted until 1861. In 1865 he removed to the farm he now owns, consisting of 430 acres, situated on Winchester Pike, near Paris, where he has since been engaged in farming and stockraising, making a specialty of short-horns and Cotswold sheep. The farm Mr. Mitchell owns was settled by the Breckinridges. Since 1865, Mr. Mitchell has been President of the Northern Bank of Paris, and for many years a member of the Presbyterian Church. He has been twice married; first, in 1847, to Sarah M. Ryan, who was born in Paris, daughter of Newton B. and Ann Griffing. Her family (the Ryans) were natives of Virginia. Mrs. Mitchell died in 1857, leaving two children: Newton, and Sarah M., who married James L. Gay, of Woodford County. His second marriage was consummated Oct. 1867, to Elizabeth J. Brooks, who was born in Clark County, daughter of Samuel and Polly (Gass) Brooks; both were early and representative families of this county. One daughter by last marriage, named Mary.

J. N. MARSH, farmer; P. O. Paris; born in this precinct March 26, 1845, the eldest son of Benedict Beal Marsh, born in this precinct 1808, who was the youngest son of Beal Marsh and Eleanor Corbin, who were natives of Maryland. This ancient couple settled here in Bourbon County, in the latter part of the last century. His settlement was near Paris, on the farm now owned by his grandson, B. B. Six children were born to Benedict B., the eldest was Dryden, who was born 1798; then Abram C., Nicholas C., Thomas K., Rachel and Benedict B.; all lived to be grown. The parents of the above died as follows: Beal, Nov. 5, 1835, his wife Eleanor, May 19, 1810. The father of Nicholas, our subject, was raised on the farm, but this not being satisfactory to him as a business, he went to Philadelphia, where he learned the trade of silversmith, which he followed several years at Flemingsburg; then went to Richmond, this State; afterwards removed to Paris, where he associated with his brother, Thomas K., in the same business, which continued for several years; he finally located on the homestead owned and settled by his father. He then engaged in farming, and continued until his retirement from business. His death occurred 1875, his wife, four years later. Four children were born them, viz: J. Nicholas, Beal G., Thomas K. and Benedict B., also one daughter, who died aged fifteen. Nicholas, whose name heads this page, was married May 22, 1866, to Anna Steele, born in St. Louis, Mo., daughter of Dr. William Steele; a native of Bourbon County. Soon after the marriage he removed to the farm he now owns, which is located on the Maysville Pike. His farm consists of 384 acres, and well improved, having excellent buildings thereon. He is engaged in the breeding and raising of short horn cattle and Cotswold sheep. Six children have been born to him, whose names are, Eleanor R., Thomas K., Martha D., Benedict B., William C., Anna F.

JOSEPH W. McCARNEY, jailor; P. O. Paris; was born 1841 in Harrison County, this State; son of Thomas McCarney, a native of Pennsylvania, who came to Kentucky in 1832, and in 1833 married Sally A. Glenn, a native of Pendleton County, daughter of James Glenn, formerly Sheriff of that County. Our subject came to this County in 1851; he is the eldest of a family of four children, viz: James, Ambrose, and Ella, who is the wife of James Menaugh. Thomas M. Carney died in Paris, May, 1876; his wife survived him four years. Since Sept. 9, 1874, our subject has been jailor of Bourbon County, and served in this capacity with credit to himself and to the satisfaction of the County. In 1876 he married Martha Horton, daughter of James Horton; by this marriage he has two children, Iva and John Current. Mr. McCarney is a member of the I. O. O. F. and Knights of Pythias.

WM. G. MORRIS, deceased, born May 2, 1824, in Ruddel's Mills Precinct; son of Caleb Morris, a native of Virginia, and emigrated to Kentucky, when a young man, and was a participant in the war of 1812; he died in 1870; his wife in 1826. Caleb Morris married Eliza Northcutt, daughter of Nancy (Hutchinson) Northcutt; she bore him two children: William G. and an infant child who died young. William G. was married to Elizabeth Tucker, March 5, 1846, a native of Harrison County; born Feb. 25, 1827; daughter of John B. and Mary (Day) Tucker; he was a native of Maryland, May 9, 1786; she Feb. 7, 1793. After Mr. Morris was married, he located in this precinct; having 308 acres, he followed farming and stock raising, and remained on his farm until his death, Sept. 30, 1881; he was a member of the M. E. Church, and highly respected for his virtues, being a kind husband and indulgent father, and upright in his dealings and business associations with his fellow men. His wife and eight children survive him; the children are: Mary E., Belie, John C., W. F., Carrie, Walter T., K. J. and Ettie; Mary resides in Cincinnati, wife of W. H. Ashbrook; John C. resides on the Tucker farm in Harrison County. John B. Tucker died August 10, 1838; his wife, June 10, 1850, both in Harrison County. They raised a family of eight children: Maria, she became the wife of Nelson Dills, of Harrison County; the other children are Wm. G., Samuel, Elizabeth, Caroline, Mary, Frank B., and Joseph, who resides in this county; Frank B. resides in Boston, Mass.; Mary in Cynthiana, wife of Dr. Beal. Mrs. Morris remains on the farm, which she carries on, assisted by her sons.

YOUNG W. MORAN, retired farmer; P. O. Paris; born in this precinct April 17, 1823, son of Edward B. and Letitia (Clay) Moran, who were born March 18, 1786, and Dec. 10, 1792, respectively. The grand parents of the above were William and Rebecca Barbour Moran, both natives of Virginia; the former born Nov. 23, 1748; she February 22, 1748. Edward B. Moran and wife were married May 10, 1810, which union was blessed with the following children, who were born and married as follows, viz: Caroline B., was born Feb. 29, 1812, and married Benjamin C. Bedford. Nancy Ann was born Oct. 1, 1813, and married Nathaniel Rogers. Rebecca B. Aug. 26, 1815, married Samuel Hedges; Elizabeth J., Feb. 24, 1819, married Harvey A. Rogers; Letitia, Feb. 26, 1821; she died young. Next in order came Young W., as above. Henrietta was born March 28, 1832, but died before coming to maturity. The parents of the above died as follows: Edward B., Feb. 5, 1845; Letitia his wife, Oct. 9, 1857. Our subject was born on the farm his father located, which was situated on the Stoner; the land is now owned by Geo. M. Bedford. He was married July 6, 1853, to Susan King Bedford, who was born May 3, 1831, near Clintonville, daughter of John and Sallie G. (King) Bedford. She was born Oct. 17, 1803, in Nelson Co., Ky., daughter of William and Nancy (Ramey) King, to whom were born Sallie and Susan; the latter is the wife of Dr. Hillory, of Bloomfield, this State. Mr. Moran has been a resident of this county all his life, and has been engaged in farming pursuits; he and Mrs. Moran have about 1,000 acres of land in the county, which they have farmed; since 1872 have been residents of East Paris. Of six children born to them two are living, Edward B. and Sallie King.

JAMES MILLER, farmer and stock-raiser; P. O. Paris; born May 5, 1817, in Harrison County, this State, son of Hugh, whose father was likewise named Hugh Miller, who was a native of Virginia, and emigrated to this State when the country was new and unsettled, locating in Harrison County, and was one of the early Judges in that county. Hugh, his son, was born Nov. 12, 1774. In 1807, April 6, he married Mary Ewalt, who was born Aug. 28, 1785, in Bourbon County, daughter of Henry Ewalt, one of the early settlers in this County. To Hugh Miller, Jr,. were born seven children; of this number Hugh was the elder, born 1808; Henry, 1809; William H., 1812; Polly, 1814; James, 1817; Elizabeth, 1819; Margaret J., 1822. The sons were never married, except James, our subject; he was left fatherless at an early age; his father was killed by a horse. James was raised by his mother. Jan. 12, 1841, he married Annie F. Boyd, a native of Harrison County, daughter of Joseph and

"NEW FOREST" RESIDENCE OF HORACE MILLER, NEAR PARIS, KY.

Alice (Withers) Boyd; he was a son of John Boyd and Katie Montgomery. John Boyd was a native of the British Isles, and emigrated first to Virginia. Alice was born in Fauquier County, Va., daughter of Benjamin and Ann (Markham) Withers ; Benjamin was a soldier in the Revolution; Joseph, his son, participated in the war of 1812. Mr. Miller remained on the home farm until 1872, when he removed to this County, locating on the farm he now owns, called "Sunnyside," which contains about 331 acres ; this farm was settled and improved by Benjamin Rogers. Since 1858, Mr. Miller has been interested in breeding and raising thoroughbred and trotting horses; his stock are well and favorably known in this and adjoining counties. He purchased and brought to this State, Alexander's Abdallah, which has become famous among lovers of fine horses in Kentucky. Three children have been born to Mr. Miller, but one now living, Mary E., wife of J. Quincy Ward, of Cynthiana. Alice died Nov. 23, 1853, aged six years ; Fannie died Jan., 1878; she was the wife of Sidney B. Kennedy. Mr. Miller has two granchildren : Anna C. and Jay Quincy, who are the children of Mary E. Mr. Miller's sisters married and settled as follows, viz : Polly, married Abe Keller, and settled in Harrison County; Elizabeth E., H. Cromwell ; Margaret J., James Patterson, are settled in Harrison County.

HORACE MILLER, farmer and stock raiser; P. O. Paris; the owner and proprietor of "New Forest," of which this volume contains a sketch ; is a descendant of one of the early pioneer families of this county—the only son of Horace Miller—who died of cholera in 1833. The mother of our subject was Caroline, who was a daughter of Benjamin and Anna (Turney) Forsythe. Benjamin Forsythe emigrated to Kentucky from Virginia at an early day, locating in Bourbon County, where he purchased large tracts of land in this, and in Kenton and Champaign Counties, Ohio. Mr. Forsythe's half-sister, Miss Timberlake, became the wife of Judge Trimble, of the Supreme Court of the United States; one of his daughters, married Hon. Garrett Davis; the others married worthy citizens of this State. Mr. Forsythe at his death left one son and three daughters: his son, Newton, was for several years an active business man in this county, and finally located in Jacksonville, Ill. He had a son named Benjamin, who graduated at West Point with distinguished honor; he died at the commencement of the late war, with the rank of Captain, in the regular army. This branch of the family have become extinct, except the wife of Newton, and a grandchild, now residing in Chicago. His daughter, Susan, married Gov. James Clark, by whom she had several children, among whom was Judith, who became the wife of General Bright, of Fayetteville, Tenn. He was for several years member of Congress, before and since the late war. His son, Robert Clark, is now District Judge in California. Gov. Clark married the second time; his step-daughter, Miss Thornton, is the wife of Senator James Beck. His daughter, Mrs. Charlotte (Forsythe) Buckner, now a resident of Winchester, Ky., is the mother of Benjamin Forsythe Buckner. The remaining members of that family, are Dr. Garrett Davis Buckner, of Lexington, and David Turney Buckner, of Winchester. Horace Miller, whose name heads this sketch, was the only son of his parents; he was born Oct. 17, 1831, in Millersburg Precinct; his paternal grandfather was Robert E. Miller, an early settler in this county, and a large land and slave owner; our subject was educated at Bethany College, under the tutorship of Alexander Campbell; Jan. 8, 1852, he married Miss Susan Bonaparte Dorsey, a native of New Orleans; since the age of twelve he has been identified with the Christian Church, of which he is one of the official members; in politics, democratic, and is one of the Curators of the University at Lexington; since 1863 he has been a resident of Paris Precinct, and engaged in farming and stock-raising, dealing in short-horn cattle and Cotswold sheep; for several years he dealt quite largely in mules, his operations extending through this and several of the adjoining States; his residence is called "New Forest;" its location is 2½ miles from Paris, on the Maysville and Lexington Pike. The Maysville and Lexington R. R. runs within 200 yards of his yard gate, where there is a station named "New Forest," in honor of the farm, which contains 610 acres of choice land, handsomely located, and nearly in a square, in plain sight of Paris, and two railroads entering the same. The farm is watered by ponds and never failing springs, has plenty of timber of the best quality; there are two orchards on the farm; both contain the best varieties of fruit, cherries, plums, apricots, etc., also a fine vineyard. The residence is a large two-story brick, with basement of nine rooms; above contains eight large rooms, besides halls, attics, and double porches on the rear; has a double parlor with folding doors; the wood work is of solid cherry, all of which was grown on the farm; the yard contains about ten acres, filled with evergreen and forest trees of all kinds; its long winding avenues and drives are lined with trees and shrubs, forming a compact arbor overhead, giving the place a picturesque and romantic appearance.

L. P. MUIR, auctioneer and fine stock raiser ; P. O.

Paris; this well-known gentleman, whose fame as a successful salesman and judge of fine stock, is as wide as the "Blue Grass Region" itself, was born at Hutchinson Station, this county, in the year 1844; son of Col. Samuel and Sena (Dawson) Muir, to whom were born nine children, six of whom came to the years of maturity—three sons and three daughters; of the sons, L. P. is the eldest; John W., James V. are next in order; the daughters are Mary, who married Milton G. Barlow, of Toledo, Ohio; Alice, married V. Dickerson, of Franklin County; Sena became the wife of Ralph Nelson, and resides in this county. The father of our subject was a son of Samuel Muir, who was a native of Scotland. Samuel, Jr., was in command of the militia for several years, and thus gained the title of colonel. He died 1854; his wife, six years later. Since attaining his manhood's years, he has been engaged in the breeding and growing of fine stock, his partiality being in the direction of short-horns, of which he is an excellent judge and thoroughly understands the short-horn family, and is now the proprietor and publisher of the "Short-Horn Record," which office he took charge of in 1880, and since 1872 he has been engaged as salesman and auctioneer, having a wide reputation and a lucrative business in the line of his profession. In 1879, he married Alice Clark, by whom he has one child: Lewis C. Mr. Muir is a member of the I. O. O. F., and of the A. F. & A. M., also of the Royal Arch Chapter.

W. W. MASSIE, retired merchant; P. O. Paris. As one of the decendants of Bourboun County's early settlers he is the eldest living child of Jonathan and Mary McCormick Massie, natives of Virginia. The paternal grandsire was Thomas Massie, whose ancestors came from the old country, as did the McCormicks. Jonathan Massie emigrated to Kentucky from Virginia when young, riding behind his elder brother on horseback, and located first in Montgomery County. He afterwards moved to Bourbon County, where he married, and engaged in tanning—conducting several tanneries, manufacturing, also, boots and shoes. He owned and operated on Stoner, six miles from Paris, the flour mill known as Massie's mill. He was a successful business man, and having accumulated a competency, retired from business in early life. He was a man highly respected in social life, of regular and simple habits, never extravagant in his tastes, taking no special interest in politics, being eminently a peaceful man and opposed to strife in any form, social, political or religious, but was a substantial member of the Commonwealth. In 1828 he united with the Baptist Church, under the preaching of Jeremiah Vardeman, but subsequently connected himself with the Reformed Christian Church, remaining a member of the same until the time of his death. Eight children were born to him; of this number five reached maturity: two sons and three daughters. William, whose name heads this page, on reaching manhood went to Philadelphia, where he learned the dry-goods business. In 1846 he returned to Paris, engaged in merchandising, which he made a success; in 1871 he retired from active business, having acquired a handsome competence, and having an elegant and tasteful home, he lives in comparative retirement at Hidaway, using a portion of his capital in commercial pursuits as a means of investment. In 1857 he married Miss Anna E. Dougherty, who was born in Bath County, in this State, daughter of Thomas and Elizabeth (Jones) Dougherty. Mr. Massie has had two sons born to him: Wallace and William Charlton. Wallace died Feb. 5, 1879, at Fawkhill Place, Poughkeepsie, N. Y., while attending Commercial College. He was a bright and promising youth; educated at Michigan University, but death marked him for his own, leaving a grievous wound from which they cannot recover. Franklin Massie, the second son, married Lizzie Kenney, only daughter of Silas Kenney, of Fayette, and granddaughter of Robert Clark, of Bourbon. He settled in Paris, and was for several years associated with his brother William in business; after a successful career he moved to a farm near Paris; he made other changes, and finally died at a farm near Muir's Station, in 1878. He left two sons: Robert the elder, now in business in Rich Hill, Mo.; William, the younger, a student at Center College, both being fine young men of bright promise. Eliza, the eldest daughter, married Benjamin Ogden, a nephew of Governor Metcalfe, who was known as the old "Sledge Hammer." Mrs. Ogden has three sons and two daughters: Virgil, Frank, Harry, Belle and Bettie. Virgil, the elder son, married Miss Ella Offutt, of Bourbon County, and lives at present near Marietta, Ga. Bettie, the second daughter, married to William Donney, son of Major Donney, former Prosecuting Attorney for this district. Bettie Massie, the second daughter, married Dr. Edward Ingels, of Paris, who died, leaving one son: Edward Hodge, now a merchant clerk in Cincinnati. Mary Gates Massie, youngest daughter of the family, married B. F. Williams, son of Major G. W. Williams, she also being dead, leaving two sons: Roger and George, young men of fine business and social traits, living now in Lexington, Ky.

PHIL. NIPPERT, baker and confectioner; P. O. Paris. The ancestors of Mr. Nippert came from the south of France, at an early time, and their descendants finally removed northward to what is now, Alsace, where our subject was born, Aug. 21, 1832; he was named for his father, who was a son of Henry Nippert; his mother was Elizabeth Herman, who gave birth to eight children, but two of the number ever came to America. The first adventurer was George M., who came in 1839, and is now a practicing physician in New Brighton, Penn., of the Homeopathic school; Philip left the "father-land" in 1850, when a lad of eighteen; came first to Pennsylvania, where he learned his trade at Pittsburg and New Brighton; in 1853, he came to Cincinnati, where he remained until 1860, when he cast his lot with the people of Paris, and has since remained; he first set up in business opposite the postoffice, next door to the livery stable West, where he continued until 1868, when he located where he now resides and carries on his bakery, confectionery and ice business; he having been the first to inaugurate the ice trade in the town, which he has conducted since 1867; in 1854, he married Sarah Gallagher, by whom he has had six children, viz: George, Lizzie (she died aged sixteen), Henry, Charles E., Philip and May; three of the above in railroad employ—Henry, Charles and Philip.

JONATHAN OWEN, retired farmer; P. O. Paris; whose portrait appears in this work, is one of the descendants of the earliest and among the most respected families in Bourbon County. The subject of these lines first saw the light of day, in North Middletown Precinct, April 27, 1811; son of Robert and Nancy (Foster) Owen. His paternal grandsire was Thomas Owen, a native of Maryland, of Welch descent, and in the year 1786, he emigrated to Clark County, this State, where he died. He raised a family of seven children; the eldest was Robert, who was born in 1776, and was but ten years of age when he came to Kentucky, where he was reared to farming pursuits, and came to Bourbon County in 1798, locating in North Middletown Precinct, and engaged in business as a farmer and distiller, and was a valued member of the community up to his death, which occurred in 1856; his wife preceded him four years. Jonathan remained on the farm where he was born until twenty-five years of age; Dec. 27, 1836, he married Cynthia Scott, who was also a native of Middletown Precinct, daughter of William and Sallie (Hedges) Scott; after his marriage, he engaged in farming, which he continued very successfully until 1875, when he removed to Paris. His wife died in 1868, having borne him three children; the eldest was Sarah, now the wife of Edwin P. Bean, who died, leaving ten children; Nancy, the second child, married Watson M. Gay; the youngest child was Robert both of whom are residents of this county. All of the above Mr. Owens settled upon farms that he had purchased and improved, each in turn taking the homestead as they married and settled down. Mr. Owen, at his father's death, received a small patrimony, yet he succeeded by hard labor and great diligence in acquiring about 2,000 acres of land, besides losing a good deal through misplaced confidence in others; while he labored to save, yet he gave liberally of his means for the erection and establishment of Churches, as well as to encouraging public improvements, which would tend to be of benefit to the community and the commonwealth; he never courted the publicity of office, but preferred to live a quiet and retired life; since 1842, he has been a consistent member of the M. E. Church, and endeavored to live a life in harmony with his profession. He now resides in the suburban part of Paris, where he lives in comparative retirement in the enjoyment of his pleasant home. In 1870, he married Miss Mary Hutchcraft, who was a daughter of John and Margaret (McIlvain) Hutchcraft, He was born Sept. 22, 1791, in Culpepper County, Va.; son of Thomas, who married Ellen Apperson; he died in 1825, aged 66 years. He came to Kentucky in 1802, locating in Bourbon County with his father, Thomas. John Hutchcraft was a good farmer and much interested in blooded horses, and was the first owner of the celebrated horse Bertram; he died as he lived—an upright man, and Mason, June 6, 1868, in Middletown Precinct, where he settled. His wife, Margaret Long McIlvain, was born in Virginia, Dec. 7, 1798, and died May 26, 1842; she was a daughter of Hugh and Mary (Brent) McIlvain; he was born in Scotland, Aug. 26, 1767, and came to Kentucky in 1793, and was a merchant; he died April 18, 1818, near Paris; his wife, Mary Brent, was born June 28, the same year as her husband. Hugh McIlvain had four sons and two daughters. John B. resides in Louisville, and is now the only member of the family living. When Thomas Hutchcraft died, he left the following children: John, Reuben, James, Richard, Nimrod and Eliza H. He willed that John, James and Reuben should live for twenty-one years together, or adjoining, having everything in common, which wish was carried out to the letter, as they during the time lived in perfect harmony, which good feeling ever pervaded the family afterwards. Thomas Owen raised a family of seven children, viz: Robert, John, Jonathan, Samuel, Hester, Margaret and Elizabeth. Jonathan and Samuel removed in early life to Indiana; John in after life removed to Madison County, and there died; Hester married Thomas Farmer, and finally located in Missouri; Margaret became the wife of Richard Hukel, and settled in Clark

County; Rachel settled in same county; she married John Farmer, brother of Thomas. Jonathan, our subject, is of a family of eight children; but two are now living, our subject, and Mrs. G. H. De Jarnett.

HON. CHARLES OFFUTT, lawyer; P. O. Paris; was born Oct. 6, 1856, in Scott County, this State; eldest son of C. L. Offutt and Agnes Jarvis. The subject of these lines was raised to agricultural pursuits, but his tastes not leading in that direction, he received a good education, graduating at Georgetown College in 1876, with the degree of Bachelor of Arts. The year previous to his graduation he began the study of law, graduating in 1877, and immediately began the practice of his profession, locating in Paris. March 26, 1881, he received the nomination as representative of Bourbon County, and was elected August, the same year, and is the youngest man ever elected to the office in the county. He has a good practice, and has before him a bright and promising future. He is a member of the A. F. & A. M., Paris, Lodge, R. A. Chapter, and Webb Commandery, of Lexington, Ky. C. L. Offutt, the father of our subject, was born in Harrison County, this State, in 1830; son of N. E. Offutt and Rebecca Sutfin; the former was born in Maryland Nov. 9, 1803; son of Archibald and Jane Offutt, both natives of Maryland. The Offutt famly are of Welch descent, and came to the United States about the middle of the eighteenth century. Agnes Jarvis was born in Scott County; daughter of Lewis Jarvis, who commanded a company in the war of 1812; his wife was Alissa Baldwin, both natives of Kentucky. The grandmother of our subject, Rebecca Sutfin, was a daughter of Lou and Sallie (Hamilton) Sutfin, natives of Kentucky. Archibald Offutt came to Scott County, Ky., with his family, in 1812; there were nine children, all of whom came to the years of maturity; their names were: Nathaniel E., Sabert, Lewis, Lemuel, Jane, Clarissa, Louisa A., Polly and Mrs. Thompson. To Nathaniel Offutt and wife were born ten children; five of the number came to manhood and womanhood, viz: Richard H., William, C. L., Albert M. and Lou Ann. C. L., the father of our subject, was raised to farming, and has since been engaged in agricultural pursuits in Scott County, where he now resides; in 1854, he was married, and buried his wife 1870, who bore him four children, viz: Charles, John L., Willie, now the wife of John Wilmot, of Clark County, this State; Albert L. is the youngest child.

R. W. O'CONNOR, government store-keeper; P. O. Paris; first saw the light of day Jan., 1846, in Roscommon County, Ireland, son of John O'Connor and Mary Kenney. When two years of age, he emigrated to America, his father locating in Dryden, Tompkins County, N. Y., where our subject attained his manhood, having received the advantages of the village school; he, though young, had some experience as a teacher. He came to Kentucky, and arrived in Paris in the spring of 1866, an entire stranger. He engaged as a clerk for Mr. Nippert, and remained in his employ for thirteen years, losing no time, working seven days in the week. He has been three times elected Councilman, and in 1874, while yet a clerk, was elected Mayor of Paris, serving four years with credit to himself, and to the satisfaction of the citizens. His firmness and decision, as well as his impartiality in the discharge of his duties, made him a popular officer. Since 1879 he has been in Government employ, as store keeper. By his industry and economy he has acquired considerable property, which yields him a reasonable income. He is a member of the Catholic Church; in politics Republican; is a member of the fire company, which mainly through his instrumentality, has been brought to its present excellent condition.

SAMUEL L. PATTERSON, farmer and stock-raiser; P. O. Paris. The proprietor and owner of "Patterson Dale Farm," was born Aug. 1, 1819, in Leesburg Precinct, in Harrison County, son of Joseph, who was born July, 1783, in Augusta County, Va.; he married Susan Smith, a native of Woodford County, this State, she was born about the year 1793, a daughter of Elijah and Hannah (Todd) Smith, both families were natives of Virginia. The paternal grandfather of our subject was Joseph Patterson, who married a Laird, and emigrated to Fayette County about 1794, he died 1829, a farmer by occupation. The subject of these lines was of a family of twelve children, ten of whom came to maturity. He had but common school advantages, having never attended high school or college; he was raised to farming pursuits, his father being a large farmer and successful business man, and was for many years prominently associated with Harrison County, both in a business and legislative manner; he began public life about the year 1822, and for five terms represented his county in the Legislature, and in the Senate four years, and was a prominent member of the church of which he was elder for years, and was a liberal man in all his relations with the church and society, and its demands generally. Samuel L. remained with his father on the home farm, until he was thirty years of age, his father having about 1000 acres of land, which they farmed in common. Jan. 18, 1849, he married Penelope Stamps Ewalt, who was born May 3, 1829, on Cooper's Run; she was a daughter of Richard and Maria (Stamps)

Ewalt, Maria was a daughter of William Stamps and Jane Shores. After Mr. Patterson's marriage, he remained on the land set off to him from his father's estate, to which he added more by purchase from lands adjoining; here he remained until 1866, when he and his brother Eli dissolved partnership and removed to this county; he located on the farm he now owns, consisting of 206 acres, for which he paid $140 per acre. Mr. Patterson is one of the thorough-going and scientific farmers in the county. Since 1852, has been engaged in breeding short-horns, trotting horses and Cotswold sheep. He is a member and deacon of the Christian Church, and in politics is Democratic. Has no children.

IRA J. PENN, farmer, is descended from one Joseph Penn who was born in Maryland, a descendant of William Penn, of Pennsylvania. He emigrated to Bourbon County, Ky., was twice married and had two sets of children; six by the first wife and eight by the last wife. His occupation was farming, and he lived to be very old, and died in Bourbon County, Ky. David Penn, a son by the last wife, was born in Bourbon County, Ky., March 22, 1798; his mother's maiden name was Charlotte Aker; was twice married. On the 11th of March, 1819, he was married to Polly Lyon, daughter of John and Abigail Lyon; they had seven children, four sons and three daughters; three are dead, viz.: David, William and Ann Elizabeth. The names of the others are, Joseph, Jacob, Charlotte, Mary Ellen. Jacob, the oldest son, married a Miss Rogers, and lives in Scott County, near Midway; Joseph married Miss Elizabeth Webb, of Bourbon County, Ky., and is a farmer, living near Crawfordsville, Ind.; William died Oct. 20, 1852; David Penn, Jr., married Catharine Russell, of Montgomery County, Ky. They had several children, only one of whom is now living, Ira J. Penn, a farmer, now 24 years of age, and a resident of Bourbon County. Charlotte, first daughter of David and Polly Penn, was married to Oliver McLeod, who is a farmer in Montgomery County, and who lives near Browns Valley, Ind. Mary Ellen, second daughter, was married Sept. 3, 1845, to Dr. J. P. Russell, of Montgomery County, near Mt. Sterling. They emigrated to Waveland, Ind., soon after their marriage, and still reside there. The doctor has raised a large family of children, two of whom are married. Leonora, the oldest daughter, married Aquilla Groves, of Park County, Ind., and now resides near Crawfordsville. Bessie C., third daughter, married Ira J. Penn, of Bourbon County, Ky. Polly Penn, wife of David Penn, Sen., died July 7, 1856. Some years after her death David was married to Mrs. Paulina Jones, and removed to Harrison County, in the Precinct of Cynthiana, where he now resides. The death of his second wife, Paulina, occurred in the Fall of 1873. Although 84 years of age, David Penn is yet an active old man and is engaged in farming.

B. F. PULLEN, court officer; P. O. Paris. Among the old and highly respected residents of this city, who have served as sheriff and mayor several terms, is the above mentioned gentleman, who was born in this precinct, May 22, 1825; his parents were James and Agnes (McClanahan) Pullen, both of whom were natives of Culpepper County, Va.; James was a son of Zedekiah Pullen, a Virginian by birth, but of Scotch ancestry; Agnes, the mother of our subject, was a daughter of William McClanahan; James Pullen emigrated to this State from the Old Dominion a short time prior to the war of 1812, in which he was a participant; in 1837, he located in Boone County, remaining there until his death, which occurred about the year 1864; eleven children were born to James Pullen; among whom were: William, Elizabeth (who became the wife of Edward Prentice), James, died in New Orleans of yellow fever; Agnes, married James Norman. The subject of these lines during his early manhood, learned the trade of plasterer, which vocation he followed for several years. He has served the county as deputy sheriff several terms, and was twice elected sheriff; in 1864, he was elected mayor of the city, and served twelve consecutive terms; he is a member of the Independent Order of Odd Fellows; in 1877-78, he was Grand Master of the State of Kentucky; as a Free Mason, he has passed through the various degrees pertaining to the Blue Lodge, the Chapter, and taken the orders of Knighthood, being a member of Webb Commandery, at Lexington; in religious matters, Mr. Pullen has always taken an active part, both as lay and official member of the Christian Church of his place; in temporal matters he has been successful, and at one time possessed considerable property, but through his unbounded liberality and his kindness to his friends, and his inability to say no, he has been deprived of the larger portion of his acquired property; yet his honor and integrity as a business man and christian gentleman have never been questioned; in 1846, he formed a matrimonial alliance with Elizabeth, daughter of French Abbott and Elizabeth Prichard, both of representative families in this county; Mrs. Pullen died in 1874, having borne him eleven children; in 1876, Mr. Pullen married Mrs. Sarah (Hibbler) Abbott, daughter of Styrus Hibbler; no children by last marriage.

H. M. RUCKER, banker; P. O. Paris. This gentleman was born in 1820, in Scott County, Ky., son of Lewis D. and Margaret (Goddard) Rucker, both natives of Kentucky. The grandsire on his father's side, came from Virginia, locating in what is now Woodford County, about the year 1775. The Goddard family are among the early settlers in Kentucky. Michael Goddard, the maternal grandsire of Mr. Rucker, was born in the State as early as 1782, and was from that time forward identified with the interests of this State; Lewis D. Rucker removed to Scott County shortly after his return from the war of 1812, remaining there until his death, which occurred in 1867. His wife preceded him in 1836; but three children were born them, who came to maturity: H. M., Margaret, and Catharine, who married William J. Rusk, and settled in Louisiana. The subject of these lines was early in life placed upon his own resources; while a lad of thirteen he began making provision for himself. By economy and perseverance he saved enough means to enable him to enter Georgetown College, graduating there ere he became of age. Soon after his graduation, he taught four years as Professor of Mathematics, at Bowling Green, this State, after which he returned to Georgetowh, where he subsequently engaged in teaching and merchandising, making this his home until he came to Paris, in July, 1854, when he entered the Deposit Bank of Paris as clerk, in which capacity he served until 1857; since has been cashier of the same. He has been successful in his business relations, having secured a competency for himself and family, and withal has been liberal in his contributions to all benevolent enterprises. Since twelve years of age he has been a member of the M. E. Church, of which his father was for many years identified. In 1849 Mr. Rucker was married to Frances S. Scott, of Jessamine County, daughter of Thomas B. and Frances (Sappington) Scott. Mr. Scott's father was a surgeon in the war of the Revolution. Thomas Scott's mother's maiden name was Durbin, prior to her marriage. Mr. Rucker has two sons, Henry and William. The former resides in Coffey County, Kan., attorney-at-law; William at home with his parents.

Dr. JOHN D. RAY, physician; P. O. Paris. One of the prominent physicians of this city, is John D. Ray, who was born in this county, Aug. 27, 1824, eldest son of Dr. L. G. Ray, who was one of the ablest physicians of his time in the county. He was born in Edgecombe County, N. C., Feb. 14, 1799; son of Rev. John Ray, a prominent minister of the M. E. Church; his ancestors were of Scotch-Irish descent. The wife of Dr. L. G. Ray was Elizabeth Stone; while the wife of Rev. John, the grandfather of our subject, was Elizabeth Lewis. Dr. L. G. Ray came to this county in 1823, and began the practice of his profession, and ranked high as a practitioner, and died suddenly of heart disease in 1864, at Goshen, while on the cars at the time the train was robbed. To him were born five children, who came to the years of maturity, of whom John D. was the eldest; the second was William, who was Adjutant under General Price, and died at Corinth; the third is Dr. Edward, now practicing medicine in Paris; Charles resides in Chicago; Arabella is dead. All the children of the grandfather Ray were ministers, except L. G. In 1846 John D. began reading medicine, graduating at the University, at New York; after which he began the practice of his profession in Paris, and has been a constant resident since that time. In 1853 he married Mary E. Hutchcraft, who was born in this county; daughter of Reuben and Fannie (Hedges) Hutchcraft. Mrs. Ray died in 1861, leaving one child, Warren Sweeney. In 1863 he married Mary E. Ricketts, of Warrenton, Va., daughter of John and Margaret (Suddeth) Ricketts. He has one child: Charles A. The Doctor enjoys a lucrative practice, and is highly esteemed for his virtues as a citizen and a healer.

CAPT. GREENBERRY REID, farmer; P. O. Paris; born March 1, 1816, on the banks of the Stoner; son of William S. Reid, who was born in Virginia, 1779; a farmer by occupation, and emigrated to Kentucky in 1804, and the year following he became the husband of Jemima Hedges, who bore him eleven children, of whom our subject was the sixth in order of birth. Mr. Reid died Aug. 21, 1839. Jemima was born in Maryland, 1790, daughter of Joseph Hedges and Sarah Biggs, who emigrated to this country in 1792, locating at Stony Point, and raised a family of nine children, Jemima being the eighth. Joseph Hedges was a captain in the war of 1812, and was a good citizen of the commonwealth. Greenberry Reid was brought up to farming, remaining at home until his majority. Aug. 15, 1837, he married Amanda Langston, who was born May 16, 1815, on the farm now owned by John B. Kennedy. Her parents were Abraham and Isabella (Clark) Langston. Mr. Langston was born about 1779, and emigrated to Kentucky in 1796, and located near where J. B. Kennedy now lives. He died in 1865—his wife in 1836. They raised a family of ten children. For four years after Mr. Reid's marriage he was engaged as Overseer. In 1842 he purchased land near Paris, upon which he resided until 1856, when he moved to Pleasant View, two miles north of Paris, having a farm of 108 acres, where he has since lived. He has two children: George W. and Amanda. Geo. W. married Mary E. Robison, daughter of Johnson and Polly (Langston) Robison; he has one daughter, Ruth Clark. Amanda is the wife of Frank Isgrig. Religiously, Mr. Reid is not a member of any church—but a member of the Masonic Fraternity, Blue Lodge and Chapter. Has always been Republican in principle. In November, 1861, he was commissioned U. S. Deputy Marshall, in which capacity he served until 1863, when he recruited a company of 80 men, Co. H, 40th Reg. Mounted Infantry, and was mustered into service Sept. 28, 1863, and served until Dec. 30, 1864; was in several different engagements. The following year, in April, he raised a company of State troops, Co. "A," and was mustered out in December, same year. Mrs. Reid died of pneumonia, February 6, 1882.

DANIEL ROCHE, grocer; P. O. Paris. Among the enterprising young business men of Paris, who contribute by their business industry to the commercial interest of Bourbon County, and though commencing less than a score of years past, and upon his own resources, yet he has outstripped and surpassed many of the old pioneer business men of the place that were doing business years before he was born. The above was born Nov. 26, 1852, in Millersburg Precinct; the eldest son of a family of four children; his parents were Florence and Mary (Stack) Roche, both natives of Kerry County, Ireland, and emigrated to Kentucky about the year 1848. Florence Roche was a stone cutter by occupation, and plied his vocation in this and adjoining counties up to the time of his death, which was about the year 1858; the children born to him were: Daniel, Thomas, Bettie and Maggie. At the age of fourteen our subject came to Paris and engaged as a clerk, in 1865, for Messrs. Hickey & Dow, remaining with them two years, at which time Mr. Dow purchased his partner's interest, and he continued in Mr. Dow's employ for eleven consecutive years; during this time, by economy he saved enough money to enable him to embark in business for himself, making his commencement November, 1878, and has since continued. He keeps a full line of groceries, queensware, liquors, etc., and has built up a thriving and prosperous trade. April 26, 1881, he married Mollie Parker, from Frankfort, Ky., daughter of Michael and Mary (Flynn) Parker, both natives of the Emerald Isle. He is a member of the Catholic Church.

HON. WILLIAM E. SIMMS, farmer and general business; P. O. Paris; lawyer, soldier, Congressman, and Kentucky Senator to the Confederate Congress during the Civil War; was born in Harrison County, Ky. His father, William M. Simms, was a native of Henry County, Va., came to Kentucky about the year 1809, first settled in Harrison County, removed to Bourbon County in 1828. He was a soldier in the war of 1812; served in Capt. Duvall's C [illegible] 'ort Meigs;
was engaged in [illegible] is life, and
died at his home [illegible] gnatius M.
Simms, a Virgi [illegible] the war
of the Revoluti [illegible] he "Old
Dominion." Th [illegible] notice,
Julia (Shropshire [illegible] County,
Ky., and a daug [illegible] r farmer of that county [illegible] wenty-
first year of her [illegible] d and
William, who co [illegible] ather.
They received a [illegible] f the
county, and at the [illegible] prepared to enter upon [illegible] In
1840, Edward, the [illegible] ied, and William, the subject of this sketch, took his brother's place in the management of their father's business, who was then in very feeble health. After his father's death, in 1844, he commenced reading law with Judge Aaron K. Wooley, of Lexington, Ky.; entered Transylvania University in 1845, in the law department, and graduated with distinguished honor in his class of 1846. He then commenced the practice of law in Paris, Ky., where he now resides. In 1847, he raised a company for the Third Kentucky Regiment of Infantry, to serve for and during the war with Mexico; was elected Captain, and served with his command under Gen. Winfield Scott, in Mexico, until the war closed. Returning home, he brought with him, at his own expense, the remains of those of his company who had died while in the service of their country. In 1849, he was elected to represent Bourbon County in the State Legislature, and served one term. In 1850, he resumed the practice of his profession with success, and for some years devoted to his professional duties his best energies and ability. In 1857, he was editor of the *Kentucky State Flag*, a Democratic newspaper, and advocated with ability the election of Hon. James B. Clay to Congress. In 1859, he was nominated by the Democratic Congressional Convention to succeed Hon. James B. Clay. In this race he was elected over his opponent, Hon. John Harlan. It was during this contest that the personal difficulty occurred between him and the Hon. Garrett Davis, which was, however, honorably adjusted. In 1861, at the expiration of his term in Congress, he was renominated by his party, but in this race was defeated by Hon. John J. Crittenden, upon the Union issue. The civil war being now inaugurated, and believing the South to be in the right, he entered the Confederate army as a Colonel, and served under Gen. Humphrey Marshall, until February, 1862. In the latter part of the year 1861, he

was chosen Senator to the Confederate Congress, by the Provisional Legislature in session at Bowling Green, with Hon. H. C. Burnett his colleague. In 1865, after the cause was lost and the armies disbanded, he, with other eminent Kentuckians, resided for some months near Charlottesville, Virginia. Subsequently, he removed to Canada, but in January, 1866, returned to his home in Paris, and has since mainly given his attention to agricultural pursuits. Col. Simms has filled many positions of the highest public trust and honor in the gift of the people of his State. He served with distinction in both the Confederate and Federal Congress ; was a gallant soldier, an able lawyer, a public speaker of rare ability and power, and possesses in an eminent degree those traits of character that would make him, at all times, prominent in any great social or political emergency. In manner and address, he is plain and unpretending with warm and earnest friendships. He now resides near Paris, in the midst of his family and friends, engaged in those duties and cultivating those virtues which add grace and dignity to a life eventful and historic. He was married Sept. 27, 1866, to Miss Lucy Blythe, daughter of James Blythe, of Madison County, Ky. The issue of this marriage are three children, a daughter and two sons. Col. Simms is a member of the Christian Church at Paris.

REV. J. S. SWEENEY, minister; P. O. Paris. Elder John S. Sweeney is a native of Kentucky, born of a family of preachers, and the great-grandson of Moses Sweeney, who emigrated from Ireland to this State, shortly after the advent of Daniel Boone, and settled in what is now Lincoln County, Kentucky. He was a farmer, but for several years was engaged in salt manufacture. He raised a family of seven children, six sons and one daughter. Job, one of his sons, was the grandfather of our subject; he married Sallie Edwards, who bore him nine children, among whom was Guirn, the father of the above, who was one of the pioneer ministers of the Reformed, or Christian Church; he was born in Lincoln Co. in 1807, and proclaimed the doctrine embraced by the church, almost a score of years before Alexander Campbell joined its standard. Guirn Sweeney married Talitha Campbell, daughter of John, who came from Scotland. Nine children crowned this union, four of whom are ministers of the same church as their father. William G. is a minister in Dubuque, Iowa; George W., pastor at Terre Haute, Indiana; Zach. T. has charge of a church in Augusta, Georgia. The Sweeney family are strong and robust in constitution, and long-lived, some of whom closely verged upon centenarians. John S. early in life had a desire to attain a knowledge of the law, and commenced reading at eighteen years, which he pursued some length of time. At the age of twenty-two he entered the ministry, and began his labors in Greene County, Ills., laboring in that State about fourteen years; five years he was pastor of the First Christian Church, on Wabash Avenue, in Chicago. In 1870 he came to this place and had charge of the church at this place since that period. Elder Sweeney is well known as one of the ablest divines and worthy exponents of the doctrines of his church, in the North or South, having very ably and most successfully measured lances on the forum and elsewhere, with the best talent that could be arrayed against him. He was first married in 1860 to Mary Coons, daughter of James and Mary (Cheatham) Coons. Mrs. Sweeney died 1873, leaving two daughters, Alla and Daisey. His present wife was Alice Monin, by whom he has three sons: John M., William E. and babe.

CAPT. E. F. SPEARS, milling; was born 1840 in Paris, the third son of Abram Spears and Rebecca Ford. At the age of thirteen he began to do for himself, being early in life trained to provide for his own necessities. At the outbreak of the war, he espoused the cause of the South, and in June volunteered his services in the Second Kentucky Infantry as private, he was, however, soon after elected First Lieutenant in Co. "G," and for effective service rendered, he was promoted to a captaincy and led his company until the close of the war. During this time he participated in all the heavy battles in which his command was engaged, except Shiloh, he was three times wounded, and once taken prisoner, yet through all, he acquitted himself as a true and gallant soldier; upon his return to Paris, at the termination to the war, he engaged in the grocery trade for about two years with his brother Henry; in 1867, he engaged in company with others in the distillery and mill business, under the firm name of Woodford, Spears & Clay, which association lasted about nine years, at which time the firm dissolved, Mr. Spears purchasing the mill-site, and the warehouse near by, and engaged in milling exclusively in 1876; his mill is situated in the southern part of the precinct, on the Stoner River; under his management the mill is doing an excellent business; the mill has five run of stone, and the arrangement of the manufacturing portion was with a view to make the "New Process" flour. The mill runs regularly, having steam power attached when the water is low, and with his grading appliances for his wheat, he is enabled to make a straight and regular grade of flour, which is in demand in the market, from the regularity of the brand; in 1866, he married Sallie Wood ford, eldest daughter of John T. Woodford, one of the prominent farmers of the precinct. To Mr. Spears have been born five children, whose names are: Mary, John W., Lizzie, Catesby, and Keith Young.

WILLIAM SHAW, Sr., P. O. Paris; the enterprising miller of Paris, was born February 6, 1814, in Lancastershire, England. His parents were John Shaw and Hannah Cox. The paternal grand-parent of our subject was James Shaw, whose wife's maiden name was Lofton, all of English birth and parentage. Our subject emigrated from England to Kentucky with his parents, in 1821, locating in Paris. His father was thoroughly versed in the manufacture of cotton and woolen goods, and understood well the management of all the details necessary to the successful running of the same. Immediately upon his arrival he took charge of the factory run by Samuel Pike; afterwards went to Maysville where he took charge of a mill for three years; returning then to Paris, he resumed the superintendence of the factory for his former employer, remaining with him until the close of 1828, when he built a lot of cotton machinery for Thomas and Hugh I. Brent, and took charge of same for five years, when the firm changed hands, he still running the same for its successors until 1836. He then became a part owner. His death occurred in August, 1843. He was a man highly esteemed for his virtues; not a member of any orthodox church, but a temperance man and a zealous admirer of Mr. Clay, and a member of the Whig party. To him were born eleven children, nine of whom grew to manhood and womanhood, viz: William, Mary, Elizabeth, Julia, Joseph, Benjamin, John, James and Louisa. The subject of these lines was the eldest of the family of children. He learned the business of his father. In February, 1837, he took charge of the cotton department, which he run until the close of 1846, at which time the care and management of both departments devolved upon him, conducting the same until the close of 1851. He then embarked in the milling business at Ruddel's Mills, where he built two saw-mills and carried on a custom mill also. In 1859, he returned to Paris and purchased the mill property of Daniel Isgrig, where he has since remained. Mr. Shaw has since rebuilt and made several important additions to his mills, and is doing a thriving and prosperous business, with a capacity of one hundred barrels per day, which is mainly absorbed by home consumption. Mr. Shaw deferred his marriage far into bachelorhood. March, 1867, was wedded to Mrs. Catharine Dimmitt, daughter of George Dimmitt, formerly a native of Maryland. Has always been a Republican.

W. H. SPEAKES, farmer; P. O. Paris; born July 31, 1831, in this county; son of Hezekiah and Ann (Garrett) Speakes. The grandfather of the above was named Hezekiah also; he was a native of Virginia, and emigrated to this county with Old Man Kiser, and located in this county at an early day, at a place since called Kiser Station. Hezekiah built a still-house here, which was among the first enterprises of the kind in the county, and remained here until his death, which occurred in 1835; he married Ellen Tucker, and by her had three children: John, Hezekiah, and William—called "Jack," "Hez," and "Will." But one of these survived—"Hez," the father of our subject, who married Ann Garrett, and by her had also three children, named Jack, Hez, and Will. The great-grandfather of W. H. was named Hezekiah; he had three sons, whom he named "Jack," "Hez," and "Will." The one named Hezekiah was the grandfather of W. H.; who had three sons, whom he named "Jack," "Hez," and "Will." Four generations named Hezekiah, each having three sons, each set having the same names, with this difference—the first Hezekiah down to the third had but three sons, but raised but one of them, Hezekiah being the surviving one; W. Hezekiah, our subject, being the fourth in regular descent, but had twelve born, but carried the family name down, naming three of them "Jack," "Hez," and "Will"; but in his case, "Hez" did not survive. Our subject was left fatherless at the age of two years; his father dying of cholera, in 1833. Our subject began life upon his own resources in his early manhood, learned the mysteries of distilling, and for seventeen years had charge of a distillery, and became proficient in the art. Feb. 10, 1857, he married Nancy Palmer; born Oct. 27, 1838; daughter of Thomas Palmer and Judith Collins. The Palmer family are descendants of one Joseph Palmer, a Revolutionary soldier of seven years service; his son, Robert, was born in Bryant's Station, in 1793, who was the grandfather of Mrs. Speakes. Mr. Speakes has 300 acres of land. Children living are: John, Lou, Ellen, William, Lucy, George, Joseph, Blanton, Odella, and Ora.

JOHN K. SPEARS, deceased; born Dec. 15, 1812, in this precinct; son of Solomon, who was born March 1, 1790, in this county; he was a son son of Jacob Spears, a native of Pennsylvania, and emigrated to Kentucky, and settled in this precinct at a very early day, locating on the farm now owned by W. H. Thomas, and built one of the first still-houses in that part of the county; Solomon Spears married, Dec. 12, 1811, Margaret Kerfoot, who was born Sept. 20, 1796, in Virginia, daughter of George and Kittie (Sours) Kerfoot; Solomon Spears died Aug. 21, 1830; his wife, June 30, 1833; he died on the farm his father settled, having succeeded him in the distillery and farming pursuits; his children were, John K., Jacob, Noah, Elizabeth, Lydia A., and Mary E., John K. was married, Jan. 21, 1836, to Emily Morin, born June 1, 1820, in Harrison County, Ky., daughter of Joseph, who was born November 1787, in this precinct, and married Sophia Edwards, a native of Virginia; born, July 25, 1793, in Prince William Co.; Sophia was a daughter of George Edwards, who was a son of Hayden Edwards, a native of Wales, and emigrated from there to Prince William Co. at an early day; George Edwards married Betsey Monroe, daughter of James Monroe; he located in this precinct in 1794, on the farm he lived and died; Joseph Morin was a son of James, who was likewise one of the early settlers in this county; he located on the farm owned by Mrs. Silas Hedges; John K., remained on the farm where born, until 1844, when he moved to the farm now occupied by his widow; his death occurred April 11, 1854, leaving at the time of his death 380 acres of land and the following children: Margaret, Sophia, Solomon, Joseph, Jacob, Noah, Emily, and Catharine K.; Margaret resides in Harrison Co., wife of W. K. Griffith; Solomon, resides in Kansas City; Joseph, on the homestead; Emily, wife of W. H. Clay, of Centerville Precinct; Catharine K., wife of Thomas Wornall, of this precinct; Sophia, married Joseph Ewalt, and died, leaving no issue; Jacob, died young; Noah, married Georgia Childs—he died October 10, leaving three children.

JOSEPH W. STIVERS, deceased; was born in Hutchinson Precinct, Oct. 23, 1830, son of Rozelle P. Stivers, born in March, 1779, who was a son of Reuben. Rozelle married Nancy Barger, who was born 1795, in Culpepper, Va. To them were born the following children: James, John, Elizabeth, Joseph, Sarah, Samuel, Lou, Rebecca and George. Mr. Stivers was married Feb. 27, 1861, in Middletown, Ky., to Mary Settles, who was born Sept. 21, 1840. She was a daughter of John and Polly (Swader) Settles. She died March, 1882. John Settles was born Jan. 28, 1806; his wife, Polly, Jan. 4, 1807, and were married Jan. 4, 1828. Polly was a daughter of Tobias Swader and Nancy De Hayden. To John Settles and wife were born seven children, viz: William H., Benjamin, Elizabeth, Joseph, Franklin, John T. and Mary, who is the wife of the subject of these lines. John Settles died April 22, 1842. After the marriage of Mr. and Mrs. Stivers, they located on Strode's Creek, in Middletown, and engaged in farming pursuits. In 1873 he removed to this precinct, locating on the farm now occupied and owned by his family. To him nine children were born, viz: Joseph Hooker, Harvey S., Ella G., James R., Rebecca L., Lillie S., Rufus P., Eva and Lizzie. Mr. Stivers is the inventor and patentee of the noted Blue Grass Stripper, which is now coming into general use, patented June 21, 1870. He died January 30, 1881. He was a soldier in the Mexican war; went at the age of sixteen as drummer boy, and served over three years in the late war as a field officer in the 14th Ky. Cavalry.

MAJOR JOHN SHAWHAN, deceased. The subject of this sketch was born Oct. 2, 1811, in Harrison County, Ky.; was a son of Joseph Shawhan and Miss Ewalt; Joseph being a son of Daniel Shawhan. The Shawhans came here from Maryland about the year 1795, and settled near the Harrison and Bourbon County line. To Daniel Shawhan were born eight children. Joseph and John settled in this county and were large landholders; Joseph served in the war of 1812; he died in 1872, in his ninety-third year; he was a farmer and breeder of thoroughbred horses; his children are as follows: Betsey, Henry, Daniel, John, Margaret, Rebecca and William. Betsey, now Mrs. Lail, of Harrison County; Margaret, Mrs. Pugh Miller, also of Harrison County. Rebecca married Wesley Hoggins, of Bourbon County, Ky. All his sons settled in this State; Henry, in Cynthiana, Harrison County; Daniel, in Bourbon County; John, in Harrison County; was a farmer, and served as Captain of Company D, in the Mexican war; was sheriff of this county, and represented both houses in the Legislature; run a distillery near Cynthiana; during the late war, in September, 1861, he raised a company of men and was promoted to Major of 1st Ky. Battalion; remained until Oct. 2, 1862; was killed by bushwhackers, in Morgan County, Ky.; his wife, Talitha, daughter of George and Sallie (Anderson) Ruch, Tennessee. To John Shawhan and wife were eight children who arrived at maturity: Sarah, Joseph, Maggie, George H. Helena, John, Daniel, Anna R.; and Joseph, deceased. Sarah and George H. reside in this county. George H. married Maggie Redmon, daughter of John T. and Nancy (Speakes) Redmon; is also a resident of Bourbon County.

A. SHIRE, jeweler; P. O. Paris; is a native to Germany, born in 1842, in Stadt-Langsfeldt, Saxony. He emigrated to this country when a lad, coming to Cincinnati, where he was educated and began learning his trade at the age of thirteen, continuing until sixteen, at the completion of which he started in business for himself, at Cincinnati, and continued there until 1862, when he moved to Western Virginia, and engaged in business about two years; the war being in progress, the country in confusion, Mr. Shire resolved to come to Kentucky, and arrived in March, 1865, and set up business, first on "Bank Row," where he remained until 1869, when he located on the South side, where L. Frank now is; remained here until 1877, when he moved to his present place of business, where he is doing an excellent business, keeping everything in his line at prices reasonable. He is a self-made man, having begun with nothing in the commencement of his business. March 4, 1873, he married Carrie Price, daughter of John S. Price, and Mary Ann Cohn; has four children: William, Nettie, Julius and Samuel. He is a member of the A. F. and A. M. and of the R. A. Chapter, and Secretary of each since 1876; also President and Secretary of the Gas Company.

JOHN J. SHAW, hardware and house furnishing; P. O. Paris; represents one of the oldest business houses in his line in Paris, having been permanently engaged in this line since 1864, making him the oldest established hardware house of those now doing business here. He is a native of Bourbon County; was born July 2, 1833, in Ruddel's Mills Precinct; the fourth son who came to maturity born to John Shaw and Hannah Cox. He came to Paris in 1849, and began learning his trade with H. Wilkins, remaining with him four years and a half; in 1854 he returned to Ruddel's Mills, where he engaged in milling and merchandising, remaining here until October, 1864, when he came to this place and engaged in his present business. May 26, 1864, he married Mary E. January, of Cynthiana; daughter of Ephraim and Mary (Thompson) January; she was a daughter of William Thompson, one of the early settlers in Harrison County. Mr. Shaw is doing an excellent business, having a large patronage. Has three children: William S., Mary L. and John R.

JOHN T. SPEAKES, livery; P. O. Paris; is the senior proprietor of Speakes' Livery, Feed & Sale Stable, which he took charge of April 7, 1880, in company with his brother W. E. The stable is one of the best in town, extends from Main to Pleasant street, and is built of brick and covered with a tin roof. They have accommodation for about 125 horses. They are doing a thriving business in their line, boarding horses by the day, week and month, at reasonable rates, and making a specialty of breaking young horses to harness. They also buy and sell horses and mules on commission. John T. was married, Oct. 13, 1881, to Ada Dawson, daughter of L. B. and Hannah (Hildreth) Dawson. He was born February 6, 1854, in this precinct; son of William Speakes, of this county.

J. L. TRUNDLE, farmer; P. O. Paris. The Trundle family are among the early families who settled in Bourbon County. J. L. was born in Ruddel's Mills Precinct, 1832; son of Daniel and Elizabeth (Amos) Trundle, whose parents, on both sides, were the early pioneers of the Blue Grass Region. Daniel Trundle was born July 9, 1792; his wife, Elizabeth, was born February 27, 1798, in Ruddel's Mills Precinct; her father was Nicholas Amos, a native of Virginia; his wife was Nancy Jones, who also came of one of the early settlers of this country. Daniel Trundle, the father of the above, was one of the thrifty and energetic class of men who made the best of his opportunities and improved his time and his talents for business, and did his part manfully towards developing the interests of the country and securing at the same time a competence for his family. He not only carried on farming, but was engaged in manufacturing his own grain, by means of the small copper stills which were prevalent at that time. He lived a busy life, and in all his business transactions maintained the character of an honorable and upright man and Christian gentleman. He located on the farm now owned by John L., in 1846, where he lived until called home to the Better Land, July 31, 1846. Eight children were left to mourn him. The eldest was Nicholas, who settled in Jackson County, Mo.; Rachel Ann, married W. H. Crosthwait, of this county; Nancy married James Allen; Thomas, William, John L.; Eliza, married Esquire Taylor, of Dekalb Co., Ill.; and Sarah, who married H. C. Jackson, of Moniteau County, Mo. William is a resident of Kansas City, Mo. In 1861, May 7th, Mr. Trundle became the husband of Mary Duncan, a native of Bracken County, this State, daughter of Thornton Duncan and Mary Routt; both were natives of Virginia, near Culpepper C. H. Both the Routts and Duncans were early settlers in Kentucky, and among the first families in their social relations. Thornton Duncan was born August 4, 1800; Mary, his wife, in 1802. Mr. Duncan died in 1872. Six children were born to them, viz: John, Elias, Joseph, Willis, Mary and Tabitha. Mr. Trundle has about 250 acres of land, and is a well-to-do farmer; is a member of the M. E. Church, of which his father was a long time an adherent. Mr. Trundle has been a resident of this farm since 1843, and during this time, in connection with his farming, was for several years engaged in the mule trade, buying for the Southern market; has three children: Bettie, Mary E. and Laura B.

J. L. TAYLOR, merchant; P. O. Paris; was born April 27, 1829, in Cynthiana, Harrison Co.; son of John M. Taylor, a native of Prince William County, Va.; born Jan. 17, 1778, son of William Taylor, a native of

Maryland, who afterwards removed to Virginia. John M. received a collegiate education in Richmond, Va., and in 1808, he came to Fayette County, Ky., and contracted for 1,000 acres of land, and returned to Virginia to receive his inheritance, but his guardian had squandered it, and he was left penniless. He returned to Kentucky, and engaged in teaching in Fayette County; afterwards came to Bourbon County, where he taught several years very successfully. In 1840, he was appointed to take the census of the county; he located at Centerville, where he engaged in selling goods, and was Postmaster at that place. In 1844 he removed to Millersburg, and while there was elected County Assessor, being twice re-elected. In 1855 he removed to Woodford County, to live with his son, E. W. Taylor, where he died the year following. He was a man highly respected in the community, wherever known, and will be long remembered for his many virtues and sterling qualities. In 1808 he was married in Virginia to Elizabeth Webb, who was born 1785, daughter of Foster Webb, Prince William County, Va.; she survived her husband four years; to them were born five sons and one daughter, viz: Richard, Edward W., F. B., John M., J. L., and Emily. Richard, F. B., E. W., and J. L. became merchants; John M., a farmer. Joseph L. at the age of fourteen, engaged as a clerk for his brothers at Millersburg, and afterwards associated with them in business for a time. June 29, 1853, he married Miss Batterton, who was born in Millersburg, in 1836; daughter of James Batterton and Laura Varnon; she died October, 1868; she bore him two children, Oscar R. and Mollie, wife of J. G. Weatherby, of Paris; Oscar R., now of Cincinnati, in commercial life. After merchandising four years in Millersburg, Mr. Taylor removed to Versailles, where he engaged in business, remaining there until 1868, when he afterwards removed to Harrison County, and engaged in farming for a time; afterwards he removed to Covington, Ky., in 1871, and was engaged in business at Cincinnati, where he remained until April, 1880, when he came to Paris, and has since remained engaged in merchandising, under firm name of J. L. Taylor & Co., and carries the largest stock of ready-made clothing in Paris. In March, 1870, he married Mrs. Margaret Shawhan, of Harrison County. Mr. Taylor has been a member of the Christian Church since 1849, his father being a convert under the preaching of Rev. Barton Stone.

WILLIAM H. THOMAS, farmer and distiller; P. O. Paris; born in Middletown precinct, Jan. 20, 1818; son of George Thomas, who was born Aug. 7, 1798, in Bourbon County; he was a son of Moses and Elizabeth (Whaley) Thomas, both of Virginia, to whom were born: James, Mary, Annie, George, Elizabeth, Robert, Harry and Sallie, all of wnom lived to be grown. The mother of W. H. was Susan Strode, born in Middletown, daughter of James Strode. W. H. was the eldest of his father's children; James, Elizabeth, Alfred B. were next in order; James resides in Saline County, Mo.; is a farmer; Elizabeth resides in Missouri, wife of F. M. Hutchinson; Alfred B. married Mattie Talbot, and resides in this county; George W. is a farmer, and resides in Oregon; W. H. was brought up a farmer; on Dec. 1, 1838, he married Nancy Keller, born March 5, 1821, in this precinct; she is a daughter of Captain Abram Keller, who commanded a company in the war of 1812; he married Margaret Anderson, daughter of William, who married a daughter of Colonel Hinkson. Abram Keller was born 1777, in Pennsylvania, son of Solomon, the Indian fighter. In 1844, Mr. Thomas settled on the James Talbot farm, where he remained until 1849, when he located on the farm he now owns, called the Jacob Spear's farm. Mr. Thomas began on nothing; his wife had twenty-five acres of land; he now owns 700 acres and a distillery, which he has been running since 1851. The house Mr. Thomas resides in, was built by Thomas Metcalf, who after became Governor of the State. The father of W. H. died March 22, 1852; he was a race-horse man, and carried on farming; he at one time owned two of the fastest horses in Kentucky; "Brown Kitty," was one of the most celebrated. Mr. Thomas has four children living, viz: Keller, Doniphan, Ida G. and George. Margaret died 1858; she was the wife of John B. Talbott; she left one daughter, Nannie, who married John C. Morris; Anna deceased, she married T. W. Anderson; Clay died at twenty-four years of age, in 1878.

JAMES H. TALBOT, farmer; P. O. Shawhan Station; born May 5, 1830, in Ruddel's Mills Precinct; eldest child of Henry Talbot, who was born in Fairfax County, Va. The grandfather of our subject was Henry Talbot; his wife was Barbara Whaley prior to her marriage, who bore him the following children, viz.: Daniel, Reason, George, Polly Whaley, Nancy McShane, Kittie Whaley, Henry and Charles, all of whom lived to be grown, and raised families and lived to advanced years. Henry Talbott, the grandfather of James H., came to this State about 1792, locating in Ruddel's Mills Precinct, remaining here until his death. The maternal grandfather of our subject was James Frazer, whose wife's maiden name was Catharine Hendricks; to them were born Mary, who

L. Gano Hill

was the mother of James H. The Frazer family came first to Harrison County, emigrating from Virginia about the year the Talbots came. Henry Talbot, the father of James H., succeeded his father on the homestead, remaining here until his death in 1840. His wife survived him until 1868. Amanda was the eldest daughter. She married Henry Eals. Then came Charles, who was Justice of the Peace and at one time Sheriff of the county. Catharine married William Urmston; Mattie, A. B. Thomas; James remained at home until he was twenty-five years of age; was married in 1855 to Mary Smith, daughter of Michael Smith and Mary Howe, both natives of Virginia. In 1856 Mr. Talbot located on the farm he now owns, having 160 acres, which was first settled by one Tucker, who built a powder mill on the premises at an early day. Mr. Talbot has given some attention to breeding short-horns and trotting horses. Has two children: Harry and Charles S., and is a member of the Christian Church, of which his ancestors on the Frazer side were affiliated; on the Talbot side they were Baptists. His grandmother, Barbara Talbot, was blind for many years prior to her death; had an excellent memory. Of twenty grandchildren, she could name one from the other by the sense of feeling.

DANIEL TURNEY, general business; P. O. Paris. This gentleman is a native of this county, and is the second son of Amos and Lucinda McIntyre; he was reared to farming pursuits; soon after the outbreak of the war, he entered the Confederate army, enlisting as a private in Company G., 2d Kentucky Cavalry, and served until the close of the same, being promoted at different times, until he rose to the rank of captain, and with the exception of a wound received at Dallas, he escaped unharmed to the last; upon his return to civil life, he came to Paris, and engaged in the dry goods business for three years and a half; he then engaged in the stock trade, which business he has since followed during this time, he has been engaged in the livery and hotel business, being connected with the Bourbon House for several years; he is yet engaged in stock trading and the livery business; he is the owner and proprietor of "The Arlington," at Blue Lick Springs, in Nicholas County, of which a full description is given elsewhere in this work, to which the reader is referred. Mr. Turney is among the most successful business men in the county, and has amassed a handsome property for himself and family; in January, 1867, he married Miss Mollie Mitchell, daughter of Wm. W. Mitchell, who was one of the highly respected residents of Bourbon County; he died December, 1867, a man whose memory will be long cherished in the minds of his friends and acquaintances, for his many virtues. To Mr. Turney have been born five children, but three living: Maggie, Lucille, and Nellie; two sons who died in infancy. Mr. Turney is a member of the Knights of Honor.

JOHN W. VANHOOK, farmer; P. O. Paris; was born Oct. 6, 1818, in Harrison County, in Cynthiana Precinct, the fourth child born to his parents, who were Abner and Freelove (Hull) Vanhook. The grandfather of J. W. was a native of Virginia, and emigrated to Kentucky when Indians were plentiful and the settlements were few and far between, he having to remain at the station for sometime for protection. He was among the first white men who came down the Licking river in a boat. Abner, the father of our subject, began in the world with nothing, having to make his own commencement in life, having nothing; he died March, 1852; his wife survived him two years after. Their children were: William, Samuel, Archie, Henry, J. W. and Amanda. J. W. started for himself at his majority. For several years he hired out by the month. In November, 1844, he married Margaret Isgrig, daughter of Daniel Isgrig, who was an early settler. Mr. Vanhook moved to the farm he now owns, in 1852; has a good farm and pleasant location near Paris; the farm consists of 191½ acres. Their house was destroyed by fire, but has since been replaced by a large and more modern structure, built of brick, in 1867. Mr. Vanhook is engaged in farming and stock-raising. Has four children: Mary E., wife of Joseph Honey; Lawrence M., Maggie C., wife of Robert Turner, and John T., who resides in Saline County, Mo.

DR. J. T. VANSANT, physician; P. O. Paris; was born in Fleming County, this State; son of John K. and Nancy (Markwell) Vansant, both natives of Kentucky. The subject of these lines was raised on a farm until seventeen, after which he received a collegiate course at Danville, Ky., and his medical education at New York City, graduating in 1877, at the Medical College, and engaged in the practice of his profession in the city where he graduated, remaining here until failing health induced him to seek another latitude, locating in Mt. Sterling, where he continued practicing until October, 1880, when he came to Paris and succeeded Dr. O. H. Buck, a homeopathic physician, who had an excellent practice. The Doctor has followed in his wake, and has been very successful in the healing art, and made many friends, having established a lucrative practice; is a member of the 1st Presbyterian Church, and February, 1882, finds him a bachelor!

PERRY WORNALL, farmer; P. O. Paris. Perry Wornall, one of the representative farmers of Bourbon County, residing six miles north-west of Paris, was born in Clark County, this State, Oct. 12, 1819, son of Col. Thomas Wornall and Sarah Ryan. Our subject resided in Clark County until the fall of 1845, when he removed to Bourbon County, bought a farm on Townsend Creek, where he lived until 1852, when he exchanged his farm for the one he now owns. Feb. 25, 1845, he married Elizabeth, daughter of Samuel Ewalt, Sen., and Cynthia Pugh. The fruit of this marriage was two sons: Samuel E., born March 27, 1845, and Thomas P., born Dec. 13, 1847. Samuel E. resides near Kansas City, Mo.; was married in Louisville, Ky., Oct. 25, 1877, to Alice Wakefield, daughter of Dr. Joseph R. and Ann Rowan Buchanan. They have one child, Rowan B. Thos. P., who lives on the home farm, married Kate K., youngest child of John K. and Emily (Moran) Spears, Oct. 27, 1877; they have one son, William P., born March 2, 1879. Col. Thomas Wornall, the father of our subject, was born of English parents—Roby and Edith Wornall, Dec. 13, 1775; and married Sallie, daughter of John B. and Susan Ryan, in Loudoun County, Va., Jan. 24, 1797. Shortly afterwards he came to Clark County, Ky., and settled between Winchester and the Kentucky river, but soon changed his location to one six miles north-east of Winchester, one of the most productive spots in all the Blue Grass region; on this farm he lived until his death, which occurred Nov. 3, 1838. In 1809–10 he represented his county in the Kentucky Legislature, and during the war of 1812, commanded a company of Cavalry; after his return he was made a Colonel in the Kentucky Militia. He was clerk of his Church, the Regular Baptist, at Stony Point, in Bourbon County, for many years, and served in the same capacity for the Licking Association of Baptists from 1828 to 1834. For many years previous to his death he officiated as Sheriff, County Surveyor, and Master Commissioner of Clark County. He was evidently a man for peace, a man to whom his neighbors and friends could and did go for advice in settlement of personal and financial difficulties. Susan Ryan, his wife, died at F. P. Clay's, in Bourbon County, Sept. 23, 1854. They had ten children born to them: John and Keturah died in infancy; Richard settled in Missouri; had one son, John B., who was elected to the Legislature and Senate in Missouri; Thomas settled in Harrison County, Ky.; Alfred in Bourbon County, Ky.; Mary married Samuel Clay, of this county; Susan married Frank P. Clay, brother of Samuel; Eliza married George Anderson, and resides in Clark County; Jas R. died in 1879; Perry resides in Paris Precinct, and is the subject of this sketch.

JOHN T. WOODFORD, farmer and stock raiser; P. O. Paris. The Woodford family trace their genealogy to one William Woodford, a native of England; he was a merchant, and moved to Caroline Co., Virginia, at an early day. His estate was called Windsor; he was thrice married. First to a Mrs. Whitaker, daughter of an East India merchant; his second wife was widow Bataile, both of whom died childless. Sept 2, 1732, he married Ann, daughter of John Coche, Secretary of State, under the Colonial Government. Her mother's name was Catesby, sister of Marsh Catesby, a writer on Natural History. The eldest son of William and Ann Woodford was William, who was born October 6, 1734; he was an officer under the Colonial Government, with the rank of Brigadier-General. He married Mary, daughter of John and Mildred Thornton. Mildred was a Miss Gregory, daughter of Mildred Washington, sister of Augustine Washington, which relation made General George W. her nephew. Thomas was the second son of William and Ann; he was educated in Cambridge for the ministry, but afterwards became a sea Captain, and died childless. Henry also died a sea Captain. The third generation is John Thornton Woodford (eldest son of William and Mary Thornton Woodford); who was born at Windsor, July 29, 1763. In 1786, he married Mary Turner Taliaferro, who was born March 13, 1772. The fourth generation was William, who was born March 25, 1787; he married Ann Maria Archer, Dec. 1809. She died 1831; he, May 18, 1840. They had the following children: John T., born August, 1812; Samuel B. A., born 1815, he married Martha Holliday; William T., born 1817, he married Mary Halleck; Lucy, born 1821, married W. T. Buckner; Thomas, born 1823; Sallie T., born 1826, married William Buckner. The fifth generation comes John T., who was born August 12, 1812, he married Elizabeth H. Buckner, in Caroline Co., Va., August, 1812, and emigrated to Kentucky, locating in Clark County, 1825, and to Bourbon County, North Middletown, in 1834, where he remained until 1843, when he came to Paris Precinct, and purchased land, where he now resides, and has since remained. He has over 800 acres of land, situated in the extreme south part of the precinct; he has been engaged in farming and stock raising—raising short horn cattle and Cotswold sheep. In February, 1840, he married Miss Buckner, daughter of William Buckner. This union has been crowned with a family of nine children, viz: Sallie, wife of Capt. E. F. Spears, Mary L., wife of Col. E. F. Clay, Buckner, now of Blue Lick, in Fleming County; John T. Jr., near Mount Sterling; Henry, Attorney at Law at Mt. Sterling; Benjamin and Catesby of this County, and Maria.

WILLIAM WRIGHT, farmer ; P. O. Paris ; was born Feb. 25, 1822, on the farm he now owns ; he is a son of Colonel William Wright, who was born in Botetourt County, Va., Dec. 15, 1783. The family traces their name to one Adam Wright, a native of the New England States ; his son Peter emigrated to Botetourt County, Va. at an early period, and married Jane Hughard and settled on Jackson River. To them were born thirteen children, among whom was James, who married Martha Hamilton, and settled on Pott's creek. He and brother Thomas emigrated to Kentucky, locating on the Pike, where Robert Langston lives. James purchased a large tract of land in 1794, upon which he remained all his life. To James Wright was born ten children, of whom William, the father of the above, was one of the number. He married Ann Jackson, and by her had six children, among this number was William, whose name heads this page, who is a great-great-grandson of Adam Wright, of the New England States. James Wright and Martha Hamilton were married Feb. 29, 1776; their children were Sarah, Jane, Andrew, William, Mary, John, Isaac, Rebecca and James R. To William and Ann (Jackson) Wright were born six children, viz : Edwin, Rebecca, Martha J., William, Martha and Mary, but two are living, William and Edwin, who reside in Coles County, Ill. Martha Hamilton was born in Virginia, Sept. 25, 1787, she was a daughter of Andrew Hamilton and Isabella Kinkead, both moved from Virginia and settled in Woodford County, Ky., in 1794. Andrew was a native of Ireland, and emigrated to Augusta County, Va.; he had eight children, among whom was John, who was killed by the Indians. Col. William, the father of our subject, was but eight years of age when he came to this county, he remained here until his death, June 11, 1880, in his ninety-seventh year. His wife, Eliza Jackson, was born in Maryland, daughter of Dr. John Jackson, a native of Ireland, but but was educated in Edinburg, Scotland, and afterward grated to Pennsylvania, where he married Ann Davis, thence to Bourbon County, Ky. Col. William Wright was a man of more than ordinary ability, he acquired a good education and for several years taught school, he was out in the war of 1812, and commanded a regiment from Kentucky. In 1854, he represented his County in the Legislature ; he never sought office; he moved to the place now owned by his son William, in 1814, the year of his marriage, and remained on the same up to his death. He was a member of the Presbyterian Church, and elder of the same, and always sustained the character of an upright man, and Christian gentleman. His son William now succeeds him; he was married Nov. 4, 1857, to Georgia A. Rion, daughter of Newton B. Rion. Mr. Wright has but one child, Anna M.

ANDREW W. WRIGHT, farmer; P. O. Paris; is a native of this precinct; born on the farm he now owns, Feb. 18, 1814, being the second son and third child of John Wright, born in Virginia, March 26, 1786, son of James, son of Peter, who was a son of Adam Wright, of Virginia. John Wright, the father of Andrew W., was born in this precinct, on the farm now owned by Robert Langston. The mother of Andrew W. was Martha Kelly, daughter of James Kelly, of Scotch descent. To John Wright and wife were born the following children, viz.: Amanda J., now of Shelby County, Ky., wife of Morris Thomas; James W. and Andrew W., in this precinct; Isaac resides in Missouri; Mary A. and Martha H. both died young; John N. died after arriving at manhood; also Nancy R. Sarah R. married James Robinett, now of Alabama. Andrew W. was raised to farming; he had but the advantages afforded at the common schools, working at home and assisting his father in clearing the land during the summer, and attending school during the winter. April 25, 1849, he married Naomi Ruth Ward, who was born in Harrison County Nov. 27, 1830. Her parents were John D. and Maria (Hearne) Ward. He was born May 18, 1808, in Harrison County. Maria was a daughter of Clement H. and Keziah Cannon, of Maryland. Mr. Wright remained with his father until he attained his majority, when he began working out by the month; afterwards he purchased land and began farming on his own account. After his marriage he located on the farm he now owns, which was settled by his father. He has a farm of 300 acres; has four children, viz.: Maria Belle, wife of S. S. Gaines, and resides in Centerville ; John, also of Centerville; Sallie, wife of T. K. Marsh, of Harrison County; and William B., at home. For forty-five years Mr. Wright has been a member of the Presbyterian Church G. S. A., and is one of the Elders of same.

JOHN P. WILSON, physician and farmer; P. O. Paris; born Sept. the 4th, 1827, in Paris; is the fourth son and sixth child of a family of nine children. His parents were Henry F. Wilson and Henrietta Parker. The paternal grandsire was named Henry Wilson, who was born March 1, 1754, in Fairfax County, Va., and married Frankie Falkner in February, 1782; she bore him seven sons and five daughters. Henry Wilson emigrated to this county and settled in Flat Rock Precinct, in 1778, and remained there until his death, which was in 1848, in his ninety-fourth year. His children were: John C., William, Burr, Lewis, Henry, Joseph, Barton, Betsey, Frankie, Annie, Mrs. Owens and ———. Henry F., the father of our subject, was born in Flat Rock Precinct; his marriage with Henrietta Parker in —— was blessed with the following children: Hiram P., Mary J., Maria, Henry and Edwin (twins), Henrietta, John P., Georgia A. and Charles T. All of the above settled in this county, who lived, except Henry and Edwin, who settled and now remain in Boone County, Mo. Henry F. spent his early boyhood on the farm where he was born. Upon attaining his manhood's years he engaged in selling goods, running a store on his own account near Flat Rock, afterwards removing to Paris, where he continued merchandizing for several years. He was a member of the Reformed Church, as well as his wife; both of them were pioneer members of the church in Paris. The Doctor was raised in Paris; at the age of nineteen he began the study of medicine, and in 1848 he removed to West Liberty, in Morgan Co., Ky., and engaged in the practice of his profession, returning to this county in 1851, and was married in July, the same year, to Fannie A. Thomas, who was born in Flat Rock Precinct, the youngest and only daughter of David and Lavinia (Simms) Thomas. In March, 1857, the Doctor located on the farm he now occupies, where he has been engaged in farming and in the practice of his profession; has ten children, viz.: David T., Henry C., Anna M., Mary B., Hiram P., James Simms, Henrietta L., John O., Alice S., and Caroline R.

W. T. WOODFORD, farmer and stock raiser; P. O. Paris; is among the staunch and reliable agriculturists in Paris Precinct. He was born in Caroline County, Va., Feb. 17, 1817; is the third son and fourth child born to William and Ann M. (Archer) Woodford. Our subject came to Kentucky with his parents when he was eight years of age, and located with them in Clark County. December, 1839, he came to this county, making his first location in North Middletown, where he engaged as clerk for Samuel H. Crane, remaining with him until 1846, when he came to Paris, and engaged in the dry-goods trade, continuing until 1852, when he decided to abandon merchandising, and engaged in agricultural pursuits, and with this view purchased 620 acres in the south part of the precinct, where he has since lived. This farm was first settled by Thomas C. Woodford, one of the pioneers of this part of the precinct. Since 1856 he has been interested in raising short horn cattle, and made a specialty of Cotswold sheep, having one of the largest and best flocks in the county. As a horseman he encourages the raising of the best breeds; the Diomede and Valentine being his choice. In his farming operations he has been successful. In 1846 he married Mary Halleck, daughter of Jacoby and Lucinda (Dill) Halleck, both families being early representatives in the county as settlers. The Hallecks emigrated from Virginia, and the latter from Maryland. Of the family born to Mr. Woodford are the following, viz.: William B., Lucinda H., Anna M., Halleck, Mary H. and Clara.

JAMES WILSON WRIGHT, farmer; P. O. Paris; was born in this precinct, Feb. 12, 1812, being the eldest son, and second child born to John A. and Martha (Kelly) Wright. Our subject has always been a resident of this neighborhood, in which he was born, and is one of the substantial members of the Commonwealth; he was raised on the homestead, to farming pursuits; soon after leaving the parental roof, and while a single man, he was for several years engaged in selling goods at Moreland, now Hutchinson Precinct; he has been twice married; Feb. 11, 1846, to Harriet Thomas, daughter of Lindsey and Dorcas (Hinton) Thomas; she was born Jan. 30, 1827, in Shelby County, this State; she died May 15, 1866; having borne three children, who came to maturity, viz.: Laura, now wife of Nathan Bayless, of this county, and Isaac K., and William L., both residing in Scott County; Dec. 21, 1871, Mr. Wright was married to Cynthia Jones, who was born in Hutchinson Precinct, daughter of John I. Jones and Mary Swartzwelder, both natives of Bourbon County; Mary was a daughter of Samuel Swartzwelder, a native of Pennsylvania, and emigrated to this county at an early day; Mr. Wright settled on the farm he now owns; March 1, 1847, he put all the substantial improvements on the place that appears to-day; the farm was purchased of his uncle, Andrew Wright; the farm having been in the name of the family since its first settlement; he has 500 acres in one body, and has settled his two sons in Scott County; by his last wife he has three children: Martha Wilson, James W. jr., and Clarence Jones.

BENJAMIN WOODFORD, farmer; P. O. Paris; is the seventh child and fifth son born to John T. and E. H. Woodford; he was born on the homestead farm, Oct. 24, 1856, and was raised to farming pursuits; he received the advantages of common school, and that afforded by the schools at Paris. Oct. 29, 1879, he married Alice Brooks, born in this precinct, daughter of Samuel and Elvira (Scott) Brooks. The following year he moved to Flemming County where he purchased a farm, but he has since sold out and located in this county on the Harrod's Creek Turnpike, where he purchased a farm, and since 1832 has there resided. Has one child, Elizabeth H.

MILLERSBURG PRECINCT.

JULIAN G. ALLEN, merchant; P. O. Millersburg; was born Sept. 21, 1843, to Sanford and Susan (Schumate) Allen, she a daughter of Payton and Mary (Adair) Schumate; Sanford Allen, a native of Bourbon, was a son of Granville and Jane Brannum, also natives of Bourbon; the former was a brother to Julian Grosjean, who died Oct. 17, 1881, having lived a widow since the year 1879; she was the wife of Dr. John C. Grosjean, who died at twenty-seven years of age, after one year of married life; he was young, but a man of great promise and prominence. Sterling Allen, Esq., was a brother; also Francis J. Allen, Esq., a very wealthy man of Cape Girardeau, Mo., noted for his eccentricities and travel in .livery ; and Tandy Allen, a statesman, a leader and a man of prominence in the State of Illinois. The father of Granville Allen was the first Judge of Bourbon County; he had 12 children. The subject of this sketch is the oldest of seven sons now living. Three daughters are also living. Three sons and a daughter, deceased. The family are: Mary, now a Mrs. Dr. Richart, of Sharpsburg, Bath County, Ky.; a Mrs. Chesterfield Cracraft, a merchant at Bethel, Bath County; John Waller, married a Miss Dize Alexander, he a merchant of Sharpsburg; Eliza D., a Mrs. Rev. J. K. Nunnelley, a Baptist minister at Sharpsburg; Frank S., married Miss Imogene Stoner, he cashier of the Exchange Bank at Sharpsburg; Charles P. married Miss Bradshaw, daughter of Capt. Bradshaw, of Paris, Ky., he a merchant at Sharpsburg; Sanford C., with our subject, Henry T., a cadet at West Point; Thomas J., in the dry goods business with J. W. Allen, at Sharpsburg. The father of these was a very prominent man at Sharpsburg, where he carried on the dry-goods business for 39 years, and for 15 years before his death he owned and carried on the Exchange Bank of that place. He started a poor boy, working at 25c. per day, finally, accumulating $500, he engaged in the mercantile business with a Mr. Payne; this they carried on a few years, then started a branch store at Sharpsburg, which, in a subsequent dissolution of the partnership, fell to Mr. Allen; he was enterprising and energetic, and soon proved himself powerful in business circles. He was an extensive slave-holder, an ardent advocate of the Democratic party, and a member of the Baptist Church. Our subject received a business education, beginning in 1853 with his father, and there remaining until in 1865, when he began business at his present place, continuing until the death of his father, when he sold out and returned to Sharpsburg, where he acted as President of the Bank until in September, 18:9, when he again located at Millersburg, where he is doing an extensive business. He was married Feb. 4, 1868, to Miss Mattie E. Miller, who was born Feb. 20, 1849, to Mitchell and Mary (McClelland) Miller; both of whom were related to the first settlers of Millersburg. By this marriage there are four children: Mary, born March 3, 1869; I. D. Aug. 12, 1872; Sanford M., Sept. 22, 1875; Susie Lee, Sept. 19, 1877. He and his brother, J. W., were executors of his father's estate; he is a man of fine business qualifications and diligence in all matters of duty; he is a member of the Masonic Order, and with his family hold a membership in the Baptist Church.

WILLIAM ARDERY, farmer; P. O. Millersburg; son of James H. and Jane (McClure) Ardery, she a daughter of John McClure and Betsey (McDaniel) McClure, James H., son of Alexander and Sarah Moore Ardery, she a daughter of John Moore and Mary (Black) Moore, natives of Virginia, but came to Kentucky, where they purchased a large tract of land at two dollars per acre, in sight of the home of the subject of this sketch, and endured great privation and suffering among the Indians; having at one time made the offer of a pound of silver for a pound of bread or corn. Alexander Ardery was a son of John Ardery, who, with his brother, were linen drapers. in "Auld Ireland;" emigrated to this country at an early day and were among the first to settle in Bourbon County. James H. was born in Harrison County, in Sept. 8, 1809, where he resided until seven years of age, when his father settled upon the farm where subject now lives. His father was born March 21, 1782, his mother in 1785 or 6; the father died in 1838, the mother in 1848. He was the second of a family of ten children, two sons only now living. James H. received about two months schooling in his life, but with the Irish tact and aptness he has acquired an education, business and social position equal to that of many who had greatly superior advantages. He has followed a life of agriculture and stock raising; has been twice married; first, in 1837, to Jane McClure, by whom he had two children: James D., born Oct. 27, 1838; enlisted in July, 1861, under Captain Hope, Second Regiment, commanded by Colonel Roger

Hanson, in which he served gallantly until his sickness and death at Columbus, Miss., in June, 1862. William, the second son, born March 26, 1841, lived with his father, receiving a common school education, and assisting with the farm-work and trading in mules through the South after the war. He was married Feb. 22, 1881, to Emma Davis; born Sept. 28, 1854, to Mrs. Mary (Leeper) Davis, of Harrison County; her father, William Davis, a son of James Davis and Lizzie Matthews; she was kidnapped and brought from London, Eng., to this country when fourteen years of age and sold for five pounds sterling; she was subsequently married in Stafford County, Va.

GEORGE W. BRYAN, lawyer and Police Judge of Millersburg; P. O. Millersburg. The Bryan family, as settlers of Bryan's Station, and from their close connection by marriage with Daniel Boone, bore no unimportant part in the early history of Kentucky. Daniel Boone, in 1755, when about twenty years of age, married Rebecca Bryan, whose family, as well as Boone's, were living at that time near Wilkesboro, N. C. On Sept. 25, 1774, Boone with his family emigrated to the country which he had previously (in 1769) explored as far as the Kentucky River, and thither Morgan, James, William and Joseph Bryan, brothers of Boone's wife, shortly followed with their families. They shared with the other adventurous spirits all the dangers and hardships to which they were subject. In 1779, with emigrants principally from North Carolina, these four brothers settled the Bryan Station neighborhood, and built the fort that is now historic. It would require much space to recount the narrow escapes of these families from the murderous tomahawks of the lurking, skulking savages, or the personal deeds of prowess and heroism and the struggles and privations of those brave men and women. From Joseph Bryan are descended the family now residing in Fayette County. This branch spell their name with a "t," and in this way Bryan's Station has been and is improperly called Bryant's Station. From Morgan Bryan are the Bourbon County family; he was born May 20, 1729, and married Mary Forbes. From this marriage sprang George Bryan, sr., who fought in the Revolutionary war, and at the surrender of Cornwallis at Yorktown. He emigrated with his father from North Carolina, and was married in the fort at Bryan's Station to Elizabeth Neal Rogers, in May, 1780, being the first marriage solemnized in the State of Kentucky. Roasted corn was handed around to the wedding guests in lieu of cake, and mush and milk took the place of ices on this and similar occasions. He was married a second time fifty years later, to Mrs. Cassandra Miller, and died upon the 22d day of November, 1845, in Springfield, Ill. A singular incident concerning Mr. Bryan's life, is the fact that he suffered from a severe attack of whooping cough when over eighty years of age. To his wife, Mary, was born William S., March 17, 1785, at Bryan's Station. He was one of the first settlers of the City of Paris, where he spent the greater part of his life. He was by occupation a saddler and harness-maker, and amassed quite a fortune by strict attention to business. "Uncle Billy," as he was familiarly called by his acquaintances, was always ready to assist a friend in need, and at his death the majority of his estate had gone to pay surety debts. He married Judith Field, Jan. 25, 1811, and to them were born three sons: William H., Geo. W. and Robt. T., and a daughter, Eliza; Wm. H., the eldest son, married a Miss Bartlett, of Louisville, Ky.; by her he had two daughters—Blanche and Florence. He was a merchant in New York, Millersburg, Louisville and Chicago, where he now resides with his family; Eliza became the wife of Frank Tucker, of Bourbon County, and died without issue shortly after marriage; Robt. T., the youngest son, graduated in the classical department of Bethany College, Va., in 1844, and in the medical department of the University of New York in 1848. He married a Miss Kenney, of Bourbon County, in 1849; by her he had one son, Robt. K., a dentist by profession, in Georgetown; he married a second time in 1853, to a Miss Mary E. Offutt, of Fayette County; by her he had three children: Frank, who is associated with his father in the practice of medicine at Georgetown, Ky.; George and Ella, who married Wm. S. Rogers, of Fayette County; George W. Bryan, the second son of Wm. S. Bryan, was born Aug. 23, 1815, and married Elizabeth A. W. Miller, Jan. 15, 1839; he was a merchant in New York and Millersburg, principally in the latter place; he identified himself and his interests with the house of his adoption, and after a useful and an honorable career, died of Asiatic cholera on the 8th of Aug., 1849. He had three children; the two older died young; Geo. W., the youngest, was born July 19, 1848: he graduated in the classical department of the Kentucky Wesleyan College, in 1869, and the law department of Columbia College, New York, in 1872; he is a lawyer by profession; has been elected Police Judge of his native town (Millersburg) three consecutive terms. He has twice traveled over the European countries. He and family are the only representatives of their branch of the Bryan family in Bourbon County. He was married to Miss Mary E. Owens, daughter of Charles and Eliza J. Owens, on the 13th day of October, 1868.

JESSE H. BOULDEN, farmer and trader; P. O. Millersburg; one of the best financiers and business men of Bourbon County; was born, Aug. 2, 1825, to Ephraim Boulden. Our subject, the only child by his first wife, who was a Miss Talbott (for Boulden history see sketch of Rezin Boulden). Jesse H. resided with his grandfather, his mother having died when he was about eight years of age, and at fourteen years of age was placed by him in the dry goods store of Whaley & McClure, where he remained for about seven years. Upon Aug. 13, 1846, he was married to Virrilla Moore, daughter of Abraham Moore (see F. J. Barbee's hist.); by her he had nine children, seven are now living, one died in infancy, and Henry M. was killed at eighteen years of age; those living are: Lizzie, now the wife of J. G. Smedley, whose history appears in this work; Nannie, wife of a Mr. Wolfolk, a fruit grower, near Welaka, S. Fa.; Fannie, wife of Dr. Hurst, whose history also appears in this work; Carrie, wife of John C. Crutchfield, of the firm of Myers & Crutchfield, prominent dry goods merchants, of Lexington; Charlie M. married a Miss Poor, from near Camp Nelson, where he now resides, engaged in farming and trading; Samuel M. and Dick Gano, residing with their parents. During the first two years of married life Mr. Boulden was engaged in the dry goods business with Dr. Noah S. Moore, at the expiration of which time he sold his interest in the business to his partner, and engaged in farming and trading, in which he has since been engaged. During the late rebellion he espoused the Union cause, and rendered valuable service to the Federal Government, in large purchases of horses and mules for their armies. He was a general favorite with the armies of both Governments, on account of his uprightness and truthfulness, and many times was called upon to render service to both sides; the many kindnesses to the "Gray Coats," being reciprocated in raiding upon him, and entailing upon him heavy losses. The courage of his noble wife during those trying times was also remarkable, remaining at home alone and unprotected with a large family of small children; she faced danger unflinchingly, and in numerous instances averted devastation by her fortitude and unwavering determination. Mr. Boulden is a man of great energy and business qualifications, having by his diligence and industry accumulated a large fortune, notwithstanding numerous reverses. He, without security, at one time in business transactions, overdrew his account at the Northern Bank of Paris to the extent of $96,000, which was certainly a display of confidence in his honor. He and family are members of the Christian Church, in which he has found a home for more than forty years, and since 1854 has been a member of the I. O. O. F's.

JOHN W. BOULDEN, grocer; P. O. Millersburg; of the firm of Boulden & Bedford. Thomas Boulden visited Kentucky early in the present century, returned to the State of Delaware, removed his family to Kentucky, and settled in Bourbon County, south of Paris; he subsequently died, as did his wife, in Millersburg. His wife, Sally Boulden, was his cousin and native of Pennsylvania; their children were John, Jesse, Ephriam, James, George, Nathan, Sally, Polly and Cassandra; Sally, eldest daughter married John West, and died of cholera in 1832, at the residence of James Nicholas, below Cynthiana, as she was returning on horseback from Cincinnati; Polly died young; Cassandra married P. Hagan, whose brother, Dr. Hagan, an editor of a paper, at Natchez, was killed in a duel, resulting from some article published in his paper. Hagan removed to St. Charles, Mo., and was drowned from a steamboat while on a trip with horses to Kentucky. His widow returned to Kentucky and afterward married John K. Ashurst, of Bourbon. Three of Thomas Boulden's sons were in the war of 1812: John, Jesse and Ephraim; after their return home, John went to Indiana, married, raised a family and there died; Jesse had two children, a son and daughter; James died a bachelor; George married Julia Lee, and had one son who lived to the age of 22 years; Nathan married Betsey Young, by whom he had two children, William. T. and Mattie A. William, commonly called Billy, was a prominent union man during the rebellion, and was several times the Republican candidate for Sheriff of Bourbon County, and polled next to Grant, the heaviest Republican vote ever cast in the county. The Bouldens are related to many of the most prominent families of Bourbon County, and are also decendants Powhatan as Col. Thomas Boulden, came to this country with John Smith, settled at Jamestown, and married a sister to Pocahontas, (see Emma Willard's history of U. S.) The father of our subject was apprenticed to Boone Ingels, of Paris, where he learned the hatter's trade, and engaged in business for himself at Millersburg; he was twice married, first to Nancy, daughter of Reason Talbott, of Bourbon; by her he had one son, Jesse (see history); the mother died of cholera in 1833, and in 1837 he married Mary, daughter of Maj. John Baker, of Mason County, Ky., by whom he had four children, viz: Rezin B., John W., Nannie J., and Holman T. Our subject was born in the house in which he now lives, on Aug. 21, 1841; he attended school until his fourteenth year, when he began clerking in the dry goods store of J. L. Taylor ; in the capacity of clerk he continued until Sept. 10, 1862, when he enlisted under Capt. Lawson, Col. W. C. P. Breckinridge, and afterward the 9th Ky. Cavalry, with which he served faithfully for three years; was taken prisoner near Bowling Green, Ky., in October; and exchanged in November, 1862, in time to take part in the "Christmas Raid," he afterward continued with the Army of the West; was paroled at Washington, Ga., and returned home broken down in health, on account of which he was unable to engage in business for a few months ; he lived at Catlettsburg and Maysville about a year and a half, when he returned to Millersburg, and engaged in mercantile business, where he has since resided. He was married March 28, 1872, to Mattie, daughter of A. T. Evans (deceased) a business man of Millersburg. He and wife are members of the M. E. Church South. He is running the insurance business in connection with his mercantile pursuits, is Deputy Clerk of the County, and a member of the Royal Arch Masons.

I. L. BECRAFT, farmer; P. O. Millersburg; proprietor of Cedar Hill farm; is a son of Aquilla Becraft, who is a native of Montgomery County, Md., July 22, 1797, to Peter Becraft, born Nov. 5, 1740; his mother, Mary Nixon, born May 25, 1750, in Staffordshire, England; she a daughter of Jonathan and Mary (Bently) Nixon, natives of Yorkshire; emigrated to America at a very early date, settling in the State of Maryland, near Washington City; Peter Becraft died in Maryland, upon his birthday, in 1806, having held a high position as a physician in that county; he is a son of Benjamin, a native of Maryland, where he died; Aquilla came to Millersburg Precinct in 1817, where, on the 4th of September of the same year, he was married to Ann Maria Letton, and returned to his native county, where he remained until 1821, when he again came to Millersburg, bringing his [illegible] sister, Mary, who afterwards married Samuel Hitt, of Bourbon County. Mr. Becraft lived a prominent life in Bourbon County, adding to his possessions, until in 1833, when he removed to Diamond Grove farm, Morgan County, Ill., where he has since resided, and held a high social and official position among the citizens of that State. He was elected as County Judge for a term of four years, and was appointed by the Legislature a Trustee of the State Insane Asylum. His first wife died in 1822, leaving two daughters and a son; Mary, the eldest daughter, now deceased, married John Goltra; left three children in Jacksonville, Ill.: Israel L., born Sept. 1, 1818, the only one now living, and subject of this sketch, returned to the old homestead, where he now resides, in 1841, from Illinois, whither he had gone with his parents; he was married Feb. 16, 1843. Priscilla Parker, daughter of Samuel and Lovina (Hill) Parker, who came from the Eastern Shore of Maryland to Bourbon County, in 1805; by this marriage, there were seven children : Mary, the eldest, now deceased, became the wife of Nicholas Wood, left a family; a son died in young manhood. Those living are : James, married Prudence Letton, daughter of John W. Letton, now residing in Millersburg Precinct ; William, married Sarah, a daughter of Ralph Reynolds, of Jacksonville, he now residing in Champaign County, Ill. ; Maria, wife of William B. Smith, a lumber merchant of Paris ; Charles and Walker, at home. The mother of this family died May 25, 1869. The father was re-married Oct. 17, 1877, o Mahala R. Heathman, a daughter of Eli Heathman. Mr. Becraft is one of the substantial men of Bourbon County, was Magistrate for a term of four years, and with his family are members of church. His father's second marriage was to Nancy Hitt, daughter of Jackey Hitt ; she died March 31, 1880, after a married life of fifty-six years. Their children reside in Minnesota, Missouri and Illinois. Mr. Becraft is still a vigorous, bright and very intelligent old gentleman of eighty-five years, and a general favorite with all who come within the sphere of his acquaintance.

FIELDING JOSEPH BARBEE, farmer and stock raiser; P. O. Paris; proprietor of Glen Echo farm, was born in Scott County, Sept. 4, 1832, to Nathaniel and Catharine (Bradford) Barbee ; she a daughter of Judge Fielding Bradford, who was Judge of the Court of that county, and one of the first settlers of the same; from Virginia; the family is also prominent in the history of Kentucky. Nathaniel was a son of Joseph Barbee, who came from Virginia; among the first settlers of Scott County; he was an industrious and thorough agriculturist; he arose to a considerable degree of prominence in the early history, and at one time represented the county in the State Legislature. The subject of this sketch received a liberal education, attending for a while the Western Military Institute, which was under the supervision of Thornton F. Johnson as President, with a corps of assistants, such as Profs. Forbes, Nevius, Burchard, Johnson, James G. Blaine and others. The children of Nathaniel were: Charles M., engaged in farming in Missouri; Julius, engaged in farming near Nashville, Tenn.; Emma, now deceased, became the wife of Dr. Barbee; Geo. L., farming in Fayette County; Sophia C., married Joshua Arnold, farming near Eminence, Henry County, Ky.; Alexander died in young manhood of yellow fever

"Woodland Villa" Residence of E. G. Bedford, Maysville & and Lexington Pike, Boubon Co. Ky.

in New Orleans while on a visit; Sidney B., residing in Fulton County, Mo., farming; F. J.; Wm. H., farming at Georgetown, Ky. Our subject was married, April 25, 1861, to Miss Susan E. Moore, daughter of Abraham and Mrs. Elizabeth (Jameson) (Allen) Moore. Abraham Moore was a prominent man as a large land-holder, and well known throughout the South as a trader. The fruits of the marriage was one child, John Fielding, born Jan. 29, 1862; attending college at Millersburg. Mr. Barbee is extensively engaged in breeding fancy stock of all kinds; one fancy team of horses he sold to the Japanese Minister, Jiro Ogura, to go to Japan; Cotswold sheep, descendants of imported stock; registered Jersey cattle, and the most popular strains of short-horns, such as the Flora, Branch of Rose of Sharon, Craggs, Young Phyllis, Young Mary's, Imp. Jessamine, London Duchess 15, for which he paid $4,000; Imp. Josephine, Imp. Amelia, and other popular families. Mr. Barbee is one of the most important breeders of the "Region;" his sales, both public and private, have been very large in numbers, and have aggregated very many thousand dollars. He was at one time one of the Directors of the Bourbon County Agricultural Society; from 1855 to 1860 was engaged in the dry goods business in Lexington with Elliott & Co., and during the war was extensively engaged in shipping mules to the South.

JOSHUA BARTON, farmer and distiller; P. O. Millersburg; was born at Black's Cross Roads, March 4, 1835, to Abraham and Catharine (Cumbers) Barton, both of whom are still living, and were born in 1804. Abraham is a son of Joshua; a Marylander; Abraham's family consisted of nine children, four of whom died in infancy. Nancy C. (deceased) was the wife of William P. Knight, by whom she left one child, Mollie H., who resides with the subject of this sketch. Those living are: Mary, the eldest, widow of John W. Bowen, a resident of Nicholas County; Joshua; Emerine, wife of Thomas Fisher, of Bourbon County, and Sue, the wife of Esquire Amos Jameson, near Millersburg. Mr. Barton assisted his father in farming and the manufacture of whisky until his twenty-ninth year, having in the meantime received a common school education. In 1862, Nov. 4, he was married to Miss Jessie V. Paul, of Bourbon County, and daughter of Daniel and Adeline (Morgan) Paul, of Mason County; the ancestry of the former from Virginia; the latter from Maryland. By this marriage there are five children: William F., born Aug. 23, 1863; Albert S., Sept. 5, 1865; Orra F., Dec. 22, 1867; Ida B., Jan. 12, 1872, and Virgil L., Sept. 1, 1873. Mr. Barton is now extensively engaged in agriculture, distilling and thoroughbred stock-raising. His horses of the Hambletonian family, principally colts, having been engaged in that branch of stock culture but a short time. He has a short-horn herd of about sixty head, at the present time, having sold in the year 1881, about forty head of the most popular strains, among them the 5th Lord of Oxford. The principal families making up his present herd, are of the Barringtons, Wattertons, Hilpas, Knightlys, Peris, Princesses, and many others of the most popular blooded stock. Mr. Barton has long been one of the foremost short-horn breeders of the Blue Grass region. He is a member of the Masonic order, and a prominent business man.

JOHN W. BEDFORD, farmer; P. O. Millersburg; born near Clintonville, Bourbon County, June 30, 1827, to John and Sally G. (King) Bedford, she a daughter of William King and Nancy (Reamy) King, who after his death married Redmon Thomas, the latter's ancestors, natives of Nelson County; John, the father of our subject, was son of old uncle Barry Bedford, who came from Virginia, settling in Paris Precinct at a very early date; built the house where Mrs. Patsey Clay now lives; he going to Lexington to have the nails wrought for use in the building. John W. received a good education for the early times, and rendered his father assistance in the business transactions and labor of the farm. There were Ann (deceased), became the wife of Mr. Fish Scruggs; six children were the fruits of this marriage; have settled throughout the country. L. B. Mosby, living in Paris Precinct; J. W.; Washington K., who died in young manhood; Susan R., now a Mrs. Young; W. Moran, also in Paris Precinct, and Mattie, who died in young womanhood. Mr. Bedford was married Oct. 20, 1853, to Victoria Emeline (Shier), daughter of Charles P. and Mary S. (Wiggins) Shier, natives of South Carolina, he a leading business man of Charleston. The fruits of this union are ten children: Charles, now one of the leading business men of Millersburg, of the firm of Bedford & Hedges, Clothiers. Mary, Susan, John, also engaged in business in Millersburg, of the firm of Boulden & Bedford; William, Sally, Mattie, George (deceased), Barry and Edwin. Mr. Bedford, after marriage, engaged in business for a time with his father-in-law in Charleston, then went to Florida, locating on a large cotton plantation, near the famous "Silver Springs," where he was very successful; disposed of his plantation and returned to Charleston again, engaging in business. In 1859 he came to Fayette County, where he resided until in 1871, when he purchased the beautiful home, where he now resides. He has lived a varied life, meeting with success in each branch. Upon his farm, is the location of the William Miller Fort, where lived one of the first settlers of the Blue Grass region.

ALEXANDER BUTLER, farmer; P. O. Millersburg; one of the prominent farmers and stock raisers of Millersburg Precinct; is a native of Jessamine County, and the youngest of five sons and four daughters; was doubly orphaned at about two years of age by the death of both parents. Those of the family now living are: James, the eldest, in his seventy-first year; for many years a prominent merchant at Lexington, where he now resides. William married a Miss Sarah Hubbard (deceased); is now engaged in farming in Randolph County, Mo.; Eva, wife of W. R. Hervey, who is in the Government employ at Louisville; Sarah, wife of William Ernst, Prest. of the National Bank of Kentucky, at Covington; William, the second son, died in 1870; was a farmer in Jessamine County; his wife, Mary A. Settle; Elizabeth, Catharine and Thomas died young; their parents were Thomas and Catharine (Catlett) Butler, who came from Virginia to Kentucky about 1820. The subject of this sketch received a common school education until about fifteen years of age, when he left his native county and went to Lexington, where he engaged with J. C. Butler & Co., afterward Parish & Butler, hardware merchants, with whom he continued twelve years. He was born Jan. 26, 1832, and after having passed his twenty-seventh year, he was united in marriage upon the 12th of April, 1859, to Miss A. J. Miller, youngest child of Alexander Miller; by this union there have been three children born: James A., Feb. 12, 1860; William Ernst, Nov. 17, 1861, and Mattie H., May 31, 1863. Mr. Butler is engaged in general agriculture, and a man of good business qualifications. In 1875, he was elected to the office of magistrate, the duties of which he performed two terms, receiving the hearty support of the people of his community for his honor and integrity. He and family are members of the Presbyterian Church, in which he is an Elder and energetic member, giving liberally of his means to the support of churches and missionary work.

ISAAC R. BEST, physician; P. O. Millersburg; son of Abner O. and Louisa (Reynolds) Best; she, a daughter of Isaac Reynolds, who was born Jan. 1, 1792, and at an early day one of the most prominent shippers by flat boat from Augusta, Ky., to New Orleans, the return trip being made on foot. Abner O. was a son of James and Sally (Overfield) Best, who were among the earliest and most prominent families of Mason County; they had five sons and one daughter, who is the wife of Joseph A. Miller (see sketch); the sons were Thomas L., a farmer and tobacco merchant, of Mason County, the subject of this sketch; Benj. Desha, a merchant, resides at Covington; George R. and William H., farmers, in Mason County. Dr. Best was born Jan. 15, 1840; received a classical education, graduating from Center College, with high honors, in 1860; was, while there, a member of Epsilon Chapter, Beta Theta Phi fraternity. Soon after receiving his literary education, he entered the Medical Department of the University of Pennsylvania, graduating therefrom in 1865, when he immediately engaged in the practice of his profession, at Augusta, Ky., thence to Washington, where he remained until July, 1870, when he sought his present location, where he has built up a large and lucrative practice by his diligence and ability in the profession. He was married to Sally Barbee, daughter of Thomas and Nancy (Fry) Barbee; she a native of Danville, Ky., and sister to Gen. Fry, who was prominent in military circles during the late war. Thomas Barbee, Sr., was an officer in the Revolutionary war. By this marriage there were five sons—Thomas R., Arthur S., Spencer B., Isaac D., and Harry M. The Doctor is a member of the Masonic Order, and, with his wife, connected with the Church.

R. B. BOULDEN, P. M. and Jeweler; P. O. Millersburg; eldest son of Ephraim and his second wife Mary, daughter of Major John Baker, of Mason County, was born May 7, 1838. He began life as a teacher in Dist. No. 1, in his native county,and afterwards in Bourbon County, for several years. He went upon the river as clerk of a steamboat, where he remained for several years, the prncipal part of the time during the war; he was in the Government employ, in the transportation of troops and munitions of war, having for a considerable time charge of his boat. After the war he engaged for several years as clerk in a general store in the country; was for five months U. S. storekeeper at Clay and Pierce's Distillery, No. 80, and afterward traveled for that firm in the State of Mo. He returned to Ky. and engaged in mercantile business at Cynthiana and Claysville, Harrison Co.; failing in that business he returned to the river life, and acted as clerk on a boat plying from Memphis, Tenn., to Jacksonport, Ark., where he remained until he received his license as Captain of a boat plying in the Western rivers; he subsequently returned to Ky. and engaged as traveling salesman for the wholesale firm of H. C. Clay & Co.; this position he held until receiving the appointment of P. M. of Millersburg, Ky., Oct, 24, 1876; by a series of blunders he did not receive his commission until Jan. 25, 1877. He was married Nov. 20, 1878, to Carrie, eldest daughter of James W.

and Lovina Conway, of Bourbon County; she a granddaughter of James H. Johnson, of Nicholas County. Mr. Boulden is a cripple, but a man of fine personal, social and business habits, and a man commanding the highest respect of the citizens of his community.

CHARLES CLARKE, farmer; P. O. Millersburg; proprietor of Forest Grove; was born April 27, 1840. His father was Charles Clarke, born Oct. 9, 1808, in Mason County, where he was a prominent farmer, and held the office of Sheriff for eight years. He was a son of Septimus D. Clarke, a native of Northumberland County, Va.; born Sept. 10, 1781, and died Dec. 29, 1833; his wife was born in 1783, and died in the fifty-sixth year of her age. They had seven children: Charles, Oliver P., Hiram, Leroy and James; two daughters died unmarried. All the sons left families in Mason County, except Leroy, whose posterity are in Missouri. Dr. Hiram Clarke, formerly of Cincinnati, left an only child; he is now in Chicago. Charles Clarke, Sr., was married in 1834, to Miss Eliza Hord. They had six children: John, born in 1836, a prominent farmer in Mason County; Anna J. became the wife of E. E. Pearce, a banker in Flemingsburg; she died Oct. 4, 1878, leaving four children: Charles, the subject of this sketch; Helen died at eleven years; Septimus at two years; Septimus, the yougest child, born in 1846, engaged in mercantile business at Mayslick. The first four were born in April, two years elapsing between each birth; they are respectively, the 17th, 7th, 27th and 11th. Mr. Clark received an academical education, and engaged in farming. He was married Nov. 20, 1861, to America J. Nunn, whose birth occurred March 23, 1844, a daughter of Judge William Nunn (deceased), who was born in Millersburg on the 22d of February, 1808; was a son of Ilai Nunn, born Oct. 1, 1758; was twice married: first, to Jennie Scott, May 27, 1779; second, to Mrs. Jemima Watson, in 1805. Ilai Nunn came from the State of Georgia at a very early date, settling on Cane Ridge. It was at his cabin that the great camp-meeting of that day was held. Mr. Clarke, by this marriage, had six children, two of whom died in infancy; those living are: Fannie, born July 15, 1864; William N., Oct. 11, 1869; Lida, March 27, 1871; Charles, April 19, 1873. Mr. Clarke has traded extensively through the South, and has built up a reputation as being one of the best farmers in Bourbon County. He and family are members of church. William Nunn was a man of prominence in the early history of Millersburg. He was four times married; all his children died young, except the wife of our subject, who was the only child by his third wife, who was Frances, a daughter of William Miller, he of Major John Miller. Mr. Nunn was a man of great liberality, eminent in the support of Methodism, and took an active interest in education. His house was lavishly furnished, and before the advent of railroads, was the resting place of the great Henry Clay, on his way to and from Maysville to Lexington, and numerous others of the most highly educated and prominent men of the day. A number of people who have gone out into the world and held positions of prominence, were educated by Mr. Nunn, who, as an officer and Christian gentleman, held the highest position in the hearts of his fellow citizens. He sought out opportunities to help others, and did good in whatever channel an opportunity was made manifest. Howard Henderson, late Superintendent of Public Instruction, received a highly finished education through him, graduating from the Cincinnati Law School, and from the O. W. U., at Delaware, O.; he entered the ministry, and traveled through the South with Bishop Cavanaugh, preaching, and became one of the most prominent divines in the Conference; he is now located at Hannibal, Mo.

MRS. LIZZIE M. CLAY, farmer; P. O. Millersburg; widow of Greene Clay, who was a son of Sidney P. Clay, he of General Greene Clay, (see hist.) Deceased went to Texas very early in life, where he run a large plantation, raising cotton and stock on the San Antonio river. He returned to Bourbon County, in 1857, where he was married, June 1, of that year to Miss Lizzie Goodman, daughter of W. C. Goodman (see hist). After marriage they returned to their Texan home, where their two sons were born: Sidney P., on the 11th of June, 1858; Greene, upon the 20th of May, 1860, the father dying upon 24th of same month. The widow returned to her father's house, where she resided for eighteen years, when she purchased a part of the old Dick Taylor farm, where she now resides. Mr. Clay was a man of superior excellence, scrupulously exact in all his business relations, honorable in all his impulses, kind in all his feelings—he was the embodiment of every excellence in man; devoted to his family, he was in return the recipient of their undivided affections; brave and chivalrous as a Bayard, loyal to his attachments, benevolent in his actions, regardful of the opinions of those whose opinions were entitled to respect, and indulgent to the failings of his fellow men, he endeared himself to all who came intimately within the sphere of his influence. As a good citizen, he upheld and vindicated the laws—an honest man, he ever "rendered unto Cæsar the things that were Cæsar's;" a firm friend, he would serve to the death all who had won and who deserved his esteem and confidence; young, wealthy, intelligent and brave, with hopes high, and the prospect of a bright future all before him; thus ended the life of a great and good man, and one of the brightest alumni of Center College.

WILL. F. COLLINS, farmer ; P. O. Cynthiana ; son of B. F. and Sally (Turney) Collins, who were married Dec. 12, 1844 ; they had eight children, viz : Peter T., born Feb. 8, 1846 ; Lucinda J., July 7, 1847, Crittenden T., May 18, 1849 ; William F., July 17, 1852 ; Judith A. Oct. 17, 1854 ; George F., April 11, 1858 ; Lucretia E., Feb. 8, 1860 ; Fannie L., Jan. 6, 1863. Deaths : Peter T., Sept. 2, 1862 ; B. F., the father, March 13, 1867 ; Lucretia E., May 26, 1879. Marriages : Lucinda J. to J. T. Talbott, May 17, 1866 ; Judith A. to Willis Boston, Dec. 5, 1877 ; Lucretia E. to Sidney Dills, Aug. 21, 1878; C. T. to Frankie Hamilton, Oct. 24, 1878. The parents of Mrs. Sally Collins were Peter Turney, born July 7, 1781, to Daniel and Susan Turney. Peter was married Jan. 7, 1808, to Judith, born Jan. 16, 1784, to William and Martha Collins ; their children were William, born Sept. 25, 1808 ; Whitfield, May 4, 1810 ; Felix G., March 23, 1812; B. Franklin, July 1, 1814 ; Susan, Dec. 19, 1815 ; Lucretia, Nov. 30, 1817 ; Julia Ann, May 5, 1820 ; Sarah, the mother of our subject, May 16, 1822 ; and Daniel, March 3, 1825. The parents died—he, June 4, 1835, she, Nov. 8, 1853.

GEO. T. GOULD, A. M., D. D., Pres. Millersburg Female College. This gentleman was born in the little sea-coast town of Beaufort, N. C., Dec. 17, 1842; his education was begun in Raleigh, N. C., under that distinguished teacher of boys, Jefferson Lovejoy, Esq. It was continued in Louisville, Ky., in the best public and private schools of the city; and was concluded in Harrodsburg, Ky., at the Kentucky University, then located at that place. In April, 1861, he was licensed to preach by the Quarterly Conference of the Harrodsburg Methodist Church, and filled the pulpit of that station for his father, till the following September. From this time till the early part of Sept., 1862, he filled likewise for his father, the pulpit of the Simpsonville Circuit, Shelby County, Ky. The same month he joined the Kentucky Conference, then assembled in Flemingsburg, and held various appointments of increasing importance, till in Maysville in 1872, his throat completely gave down, and he was compelled to retire from the active work of the ministry. Then it was he became connected with the Millersburg Female College, as joint proprietor and principal, which position he still holds, with the exception of now having undivided control. In 1877, the degree of D. D. was conferred upon him by the Kentucky Military Institute, Col. R. A. Allen, Principal. On his father's side Dr. Gould is related to the large family of the same name that originally settled in New York, and thence have spread into almost every other State of the Union. His mother was an Oliver, a granddaughter of the North Carolina Marshalls—the family from which Gen. Braxton Bragg was directly descended, and which no doubt was a branch collateral to the Virginia Marshalls, and consequently to those of Kentucky. Dr. Gould, though somewhat known as a controversial writer, a reviewer and a platform speaker, has thus far led too active and busy a life in the ministry, and more especially in the school room, to produce any thing of a permanent and extended character. His greatest distinction is having under adverse circumstances, built up the Millersburg Female College, from a mere local school with four or five teachers, and some twenty boarding pupils, to one of the largest and most celebrated Institutions in the South and West, presenting a faculty of 18 able and experienced teachers, and a boarding department of 110 pupils. Dr. Gould is small of statute, but fleshy, weighing 160 pounds, though less than five feet, six inches in height. His complexion is dark, hair thin, speech quick, movements nervous, and manners pleasant. Vim, enterprise, determination, self-reliance, untiring energy, rapidly formed conclusions, and willingnesss to assume risks from which the more timid or less reliant shrink, seem to be the main ingredients in his character. Having not yet reached his fortieth birthday, he is scarcely in his prime, and may reasonably be expected to accomplish even greater things in his chosen field of enterprise.

JOSEPH A. GRIMES, farmer and distiller ; P. O. Millersburg ; a native of Stewart County, Ga., about forty miles from Columbus, where he was born, Nov. 15, 1844, to John and Eliza (Grimes) Grimes ; she died in 1860, aged about fifty years ; he in 1862, aged fifty-four years ; they were natives of North Carolina, settled in Georgia at an early date ; they had three sons and one daughter—John W., who was assassinated in his own dooryard, in 1865, cause supposed to have grown out of war troubles ; Julia A., wife of Henry G. Feagin, a member of one of the wealthy and prominent families of Alabama, near Midway; he has held the office of Sheriff of Stewart County two terms, and is extensively engaged in mercantile and agricultural pursuits ; Robert J. Grimes, engaged largely in agriculture and milling interests in his native county ; served during the war in the Virginia Army, under Gen. Longstreet ; Joseph A. received a liberal education, and assisted his father, who was one of the foremost planters in the county ; he enlisted in 1862, in Captain

Ball's Company, 55th Georgia Regiment, under Colonel Haskill, commanded by General Kirby Smith, with whom he served until the capture of the command at Cumberland Gap., when they were sent to Camp Douglas, at Chicago, where they were held as prisoners until the close of the war ; he then returned to his native county, where he engaged in agriculture until his removal to Bourbon County, in 1867. He was clerk and proprietor of the Bourbon House at Paris for a time, before removing to his present home ; since which time he has been engaged in agriculture and stock raising, also the manufacture of whisky, upon the old copper distilled plan. He was married May 30, 1871, to Sue C. Mackey, daughter of John A. and Lucinda (Conner) Mackey, the latter a native of Nelson County, the former a native of Louisiana, came to Nelson county when a young man, and engaged in agriculture and trading ; they now reside in Warren County, Ky. Mr. Grimes has by this marriage five children, viz. : John R., born April 26, 1872 ; Emma L., March 22, 1874 ; Mary T., June 28, 1876 ; William C., July 29, 1878 ; Joseph A., April 13, 1880.

EDWIN P. GAMBLE, farmer and stock breeder; P. O. Millersburg; was born Dec. 28, 1852, in Cincinnati, to James and Elizabeth (Norris) Gamble, both of whom were of Irish descent; his paternal ancestry were of the nobility of Scotland, originating from Lord Eglinton, of Ayrshire. They left Scotland for conscience sake, when James the Sixth by fraud, craft and corruption, thrust prelacy upon the church of Scotland. This family was not, like many others, induced to return, by false promises of King Charles, but remained in Ireland. Josias Gamble is the first of whom any record is known; his eldest son was David Gamble, of Graan, near Inniskillen, born in 1682; his successor (or second son,) was David, of Ratonagh, Ireland; his eldest son was George, of Graan, near Inniskillen, born in 1772, came to America with his family about 1819; his eldest son was James, the father of our subject, born in 1803 in Graan, Ireland; came to this country with his father, landing in Cincinnati in November of that year, 1819; he is now of the firm of Proctor & Gamble, extensive manufacturers of that city. Edwin P. is his seventh son; he received a liberal education at Kenyon College, Gambier, Ohio; and at Cornell University; subsequently engaging in agricultural pursuits and the breeding of blooded stock, such as short horn cattle, of the most popular strains, Cotswold sheep, and Poland-China hogs. He came to Bourbon County in the Spring of 1876, purchasing the beautiful home, Sunning Hill Farm, where he now resides, taking possession of the same Jan. 1, 1877. He was married April 22, 1880, to Miss Lilly Lawder, daughter of Launcelot Lawder, a resident in the neighborhood of Westwood, a suburban village of Cincinnati; he also a native of Ireland. Mr. Gamble is a young man of refinement, culture, possessing Christain graces, and with his estimable wife, connected with the Methodist Church, at Paris. He is one of the few Republicans of Bourbon County, voting with that party from a conscientious motive.

SILAS W. HURST, physician; P. O. Millersburg; is a son of William and Susan J. (Evans) Hurst, both of whom are now living; she a daughter of Jesse and Hannah (Pitts) Evans; she of William B. Pitts, and his wife a Miss Goddard, who was a native of England, emigrated to Virginia. The Pitts family settled near Poplar Plains, Fleming County, about fifty years ago. William Hurst was a son of Fielding J. Hurst, who died with cholera in 1833, in Fleming County, his wife was a Miss Hickerson; both were natives of Virginia; settled in Fleming County at an early date. The subject of this sketch was born Oct. 28, 1849, received from his parents a liberal education, attended the University of Louisville, from which he graduated in March, 1872, subsequently locating in Charleston, Miss., where he remained a few months, then came to Millersburg, where he has since resided and built up a remunerative practice in his profession. He possesses natural business tact, which he utilizes in speculations, which return him a considerable emolument. He was married Oct. 30, 1873, to Miss Fannie G. Boulden (see Jesse Boulden hist.), by which marriage two sons have been born: Edgar, May 1, 1876, Jesse Henry, Aug. 5, 1877. Dr. Hurst has been honored by the people in the various village offices, a Democrat politically, a highly respected and esteemed citizen, a member of both the Odd Fellows and Masonic Orders, and with his family connected with the Baptist Church, in which he holds the office of Deacon.

HERVEY W. LETTON, farmer; P. O. Millersburg; a resident of Pine Grove farm, was born in the house in which he now lives, May 6, 1809; a son of Caleb, born Dec. 5, 1768, in Montgomery County, Md., he of Michael Letton, and a Miss Willett, both of whom died in Maryland. Caleb was married to Mary Wilcoxon, Nov. 30, 1790, she was born to John Wilcoxon, May 24, 1772. They came to Bourbon County in 1795, with the two oldest children of the family: Martha, born in 1792, Fielder, 1794; the others were born at the home where Mr. Letton now lives; they were Caleb, born in 1796; Anna M., 1798; Verlinder, 1800; Michael, 1802; John W., 1804; James E., 1807; our subject; Mary N., 1811; Melicent C. A., 1814; all lived to maturity, but died in the prime of life; the second of the family living to be the oldest, died at sixty-two years of age; Mr. Letton was married Feb. 28, 1828, to Nancy J. Parker, daughter of Lemuel Parker; she died March 28, 1870; second marriage, March 3, 1874, to Mrs. Mary J. (Kincart) Reed, widow of Dr. George Reed, of Nicholas County; by his first wife, he had twelve children: Samuel P., born Feb. 23, 1829, married and farming in Bates County, Mo.; Caleb E., Oct. 11, 1831, died in his twenty-first year; Julian, died in infancy; Sarah A. M., born June 13, 1835, married a Mr. Hall and died in 1856; Mary E., born Oct. 13, 1837, married Dick Robinson, and died in 1879; John William, born Sept. 26, 1839, living at home; Brice, born June 10, 1842, married to Sarah J. Owen, residing in Millersburg Precinct; Lovina P., born Feb. 5, 1844, wife of Jeff. M. Vincent; Henry S., born Sept. 4, 1846; James H., Nov. 20, 1848, married Lucy Daniels, of Texas, farming in this precinct; Reuben S., born Dec. 8, 1850, died in 1871; Nancy J., wife of Benjaman Patton, of Paris. Mr. Letton has devoted his life to agricultural pursuits and stock trading in the South; has been a member of the Masonic Order for more than forty years, was a Whig during Clay's time, afterward a Democrat, espousing the cause of the Confederacy and giving three sons to service in the cause; Brice, under General Marshall, who after about two years service, returned home on account of ill health; John, under General Morgan, was captured and imprisoned at Camp Chase, but through the influence of a friend—a Confederate General, was released; Henry S., enlisted at sixteen years of age, in Company C., 4th Ky. Cavalry, under General Morgan, was in the advance guard in their raid to the North, and was captured with a few others, was finally landed in prison at Fort Delaware, where he was confined until the close of the war.

JOHN WILL LETTON, farmer; P. O. Millersburg; proprietor of Pleasant Hill farm, was born in Montgomery County, Md., May 22, 1821, to Brice Letton, who was born in 1780, and the youngest son of Michael Montgomery (see history). His mother was Harrietta E. Moore, also a native of Montgomery County, Md., and sister to "Old Zed Moore," who is supposed to have built the first brick house in Paris, where he kept hotel, afterward built the Bourbon House, later he went to the Blue Licks, where he kept the noted summer resort, and died after many years of service. The children born to Brice Letton were eleven, seven sons and four daughters, two sons and two daughters deceased. Those living are: Michael H. in Paris Precinct; Ning W. at Lexington, Mo.; Reuben P. in Silver City, Col.; John Will, Brice S., at Paris, Ky.; Harrietta, widow of Dr. James McClannahan, of Anderson, Ind.; Ann Maria, wife of J. W. Dooley, of Montgomery County, Md. The father of this family was a captain at an early date in the *terrible* contest at Bladensburg. He received an injury in Washington, D. C., when on his way to Kentucky in his old age, from which he never recovered. Our subject lived with his father until he was twenty-one years of age, when he came to Bourbon County, where, in Feb. 6, 1847, he was married to Mary B. Sandusky, daughter of Jacob and Monan (Bowler) Sandusky. (For further knowledge of Sandusky ancestry, see Turner history.) The issue of this union was eleven children, ten of whom are living, viz: Ann M., born Jan. 28, 1848, wife of Louis Gooch, of Jessamine County; Prudence H., born April 17, 1849, now wife of James Becraft; Harriet E., born April 8, 1851, wife of Thomas Redmon; Mary D., born Sept. 27, 1853; Jacob B., July 2, 1855; Sandusky, Aug. 22, 1857, died at seventeen years of age; Laura S., Feb. 8, 1860, wife of Charles Geffinger, at Millersburg; Martha, born Feb. 19, 1862; John W., May 3, 1864; Sally C., Jan. 11, 1867; Rueben E., Jan. 24, 1869. Mr. Letton, after about a year of married life, removed with his family to Decatur County, Ind., where he engaged in stock-raising until in 1862, when he returned to Kentucky and purchased the house which he now occupies, engaging in a general agriculture and stock, shipping to the different parts of the country. He is a member of the Masonic Order at Millersburg.

WILLIAM M. LAYSON, Jr., farmer; P. O. Millersburg; son of Zed M., born May 11, 1811, in Bourbon County, to Isaac and Mary (Moore) Layson; she of John Moore and a Miss Black, natives, the former of Delaware, the latter of Maryland; came to Fayette County about 1788. Isaac Layson, son of John and Margaret (Martin) Layson, located near where Paris now stands, before the first house was built at that place. Isaac had eight children: Wm., Zed M., Margaret A. Moore, John M., Robert W., America (Moore), Ardery and Isaac Z.; the four oldest are still living. The grandparents of our subject were natives of Bourbon County. The father of our subject was twice married; first to Margaret H. Miller, daughter of William Miller, he a son of Major John; by this marriage there were two sons; one of them, Wm. M., born May 6, 1844; his first wife died Dec. 18, 1851. In 1854, he married Sarah W. Varnon, daughter of Benjamin and Sally Varnon; by this marriage there were five children, all living: Margaret H., Edward V., Laura R., Martha M. and Eugenia B.; second wife deceased in 1877. On the 27th day of April, the subject of this sketch left home for the

Confederacy, determined to join the Southern army; afterward joined a party of twenty men, camped on the night of the 5th near Hazel Green; on the following morning, his eighteenth birthday, they were attacked by a party of home guards; finally reached Marshall's command in Virginia, where all of the company enlisted except William and two companions who went to Corinth, Miss., intending to enlist there, but by the advice of friends went to Chattanooga, Tenn., where they joined Morgan's Command, serving two years, engaging in many hard-fought battles, some of which were: Gallatin, Snowhill, Woodbury, Greasy Creek, Green River Bridge, and Augusta; was taken prisoner by the Federals, sent to Louisville, where he remained until Nov. 8, 1863, when, taking the oath was released and returned home, engaging in farming and stock trading in the South. Jan. 25, 1870, was married to Mrs. Maggie (Orr) Morehead, daughter of B. G. Orr, a prominent officer of Nicholas County, where he died; she a granddaughter of John Orr, who served in the war of 1812 under Col. Johnson. They have had four children, two of whom died in one night of scarlet fever; those living are Charles B., born March 31, 1871; Zed Clark, Dec. 29, 1875. They are members of the Presbyterian Church.

ROBERT MILLER McCLELLAND, farmer; P. O. Millersburg; proprietor of Silver Spring Farm; was born Sept. 6, 1822. His father was William McClelland, born Jan. 1, 1800; died June 26, 1864; was the eldest son of Robert McClelland, who was a son of William McClelland, one of the original settlers of Millersburg. Robert was brought when a child to Kentucky; married his cousin, Louisa Miller, daughter of Robert Miller, the eldest child of John Miller, the founder of of Millersburg. Robert Miller, born in 1780, is said to be the first male child born in the State. Mr. McClelland is the eldest of a large family; his father also, the first of a large family, by Robert McClelland. He received a very limited education, being started out by his father at thirteen years of age in the business of trading, which he followed for eighteen years, driving stock of all kinds to South Carolina and Georgia. May 22, 1849, he was married to Miss Frances Suggett, a native of Scott County, and daughter of Louis and Frances (Cason) Suggett, who were from Virginia, but among the earliest and most prominent families of Scott County. By this marriage he had two children, both of whom died in infancy; the mother died June 9, 1859, in Missouri, where he had moved in the fall of 1858. In August, after the death of his wife, he returned to Kentucky, and Nov. 5, 1861, was married to Fanny Taylor, daughter of Stark and Elizabeth (McClane) Taylor, the parents of whom were among the early settlers of Fayette County, from Virginia. Mr. McClelland, by this marriage, had nine children, eight of whom are living; they are: Fatie, born Sept. 18, 1862; Claude, Jan. 28, 1864; Alice, Feb. 8, 1866; Julia, Dec. 22, 1867; Elisha, Dec. 20, 1868; Fannie, Feb. 11, 1871; Robert, Sept. 1, 1872, died March 10, 1874; Beautie, June 5, 1875; infant, July 15, 1880. Mr. McClelland is engaged in a general agriculture and stock raising; is a member of the Baptist Church, in which he has held the office of Church Clerk for twenty years; is a liberal giver of his means to the support of schools and churches, meriting the respect which he has of the people of his community.

JOSEPH W. MILLER, magistrate in Millersburg; P. O. Millersburg; was born Dec. 26, 1835, to Joseph Miller; who was born Jan. 17, 1788, and was the third son of Major John Miller, the founder of Millersburg; he born Sep. 21, 1752, died Sept. 5, 1815; he was born in Carlisle, Pa., and emigrated to Kentucky and located the land on which Millersburg now stands; soon after he returned to Cumberland County, Pa., and married Ann McClintock, and returned with his wife to Kentucky. Beneath the monument in the beautiful cemetery at Millersburg, repose the remains of both. Joseph Miller was married Dec. 28, 1809, to Polly McKee; she a daughter of Paddy McKee, one of the first merchants of Millersburg, and died Dec. 18, 1810, without issue. His second marriage was upon May 22, 1814, to Patsey O. E. McClelland, who was born Nov. 17, 1792; she a daughter of Col. James McClelland (born in 1775, died July 7, 1833; was six times married, and died a Judge upon the bench, in Boone County, Mo.); son of William McClelland, who was a native probably of Virginia, and came to Kentucky in 1776, landing at Limestone, now Maysville, soon after coming down the "Old Buffalo Trace" to the Irish Station. He had eight children, viz: Elizabeth (see Bryan hist.), James A., Martha Jane, John M., Mary, Hunt, and Joseph Woodson, who died in infancy, and Joseph W., the subject of this sketch. Only the oldest and youngest are now living, and with John M., who has two daughters residing at Caanan, O., are the only ones who have heirs. Joseph W. in his earlier life engaged in merchantile business with his father, who was one of the most energetic and prominent men of the Blue Grass region at that date, and spent about thirty-two years of his life in active business; he died in 1853, at the age of sixty-six years; his sons, John M. and Joseph W. took the stock and continued the business until the year 1860, when the latter disposed of his interest in the concern, and the death of his brother James, who was a bachelor and owner of what is now the White Distillery, at Paris, occurring about that time, he was made administrator of the estate, and was compelled to make numerous trips through the South in the interest of his brother's estate, during the hottest times of the Rebellion. He subsequently engaged in farming, and later in merchandising, until the year 1870, since which time he has kept a hotel at Maysville, and acted as agent for the Maysville and Lexington Rail Road, before the sale of the same to the Kentucky Central Company. He has been twice elected to a magistracy, which position he now holds. He is a member of the Masonic Order. He had five children; three died in infancy; they are William, James A., Lizzie B., Mattie, and Elisha.

R. P. MILAM, farmer; Millersburg; son of W. P. and Charlotte (Cothran) Milam, both natives of South Carolina, now residents of Cartersville, Ga.; was an extensive cotton planter, and trader in the north before the war; he was a son of William Milam, an extensive planter in South Carolina at an early date; both the Milam and Cothran ancestry were from Ireland. W. P. by his marriage with Charlotte Cothran, had two children, Rosa, born Aug. 19, 1840, now the wife of Dr. W. L. Kirkpatrick, of Cartersville, Ga.; and R. P., born Dec. 2, 1844; the mother died in the fall of 1864, after which the father was married to Miss Sally Newel, of Harrison County, Ky., in 1866, having by her the following children: Hugh N., Willie G., Ruby and Pearl twin daughters. The subject of this sketch entered the State University at Athens, Ga., in 1859, where he remained until in the fall of 1860, when he enlisted in Company K, 14th Ga. Reg. of Infantry, under Capt. T. F. Jones, Col. C. V. Brunby commanding; here he served for a considerable time. In the spring of 1864 was transferred to the 16th Ga. Reg. Cavalry, Col. S. J. Winn, of Lawrenceville, Ga., under Gens. Lee and Jackson, engaging in numerous contests in Virginia; was wounded at Malvern Hill, after the recovery of which he was transferred; engaging in active duty as Quartermaster of his regiment. At the close of the war he began publishing the Cartersville *Express* at that place, adopting the name of the paper published there before the war by S. H. Smith, who became the partner of Mr. Milam. In 1867, Mr. Milam disposed of his interest in the paper to his partner and came to Bourbon County, where he married, Nov. 29, of that year, to Sally E. McClintock, who died the following July. Was married Feb. 16, 1875, to Mattie A. Miller, daughter of James McClure Miller. They have two children, Lucille, born March 12, 1876; John McClintock, Jan. 27, 1881. They are members of the M. E. Church, South.

ROBERT A. MILLER, farmer; P. O. Millersburg; was born Oct. 27, 1827, and is the fifth child of Alexander Miller, (see history of Joseph A. Miller). He was married Sept. 2, 1853, to Adela Malone Raymond, born May 7, 1837, in Liverpool, England, to Malone and Catharine (Holdaway) Raymond; she, the only child of Edward aud Ann (Arnold) Holdaway; Malone Raymond was a Solicitor, taking upon himself that honor, at the death of his father, being the oldest son. The Raymond family were of the nobility of Ireland. Malone (Raymond), the latter name, taken by the father of our subject's wife, properly Richard Malone, was a cousin to Lord Sunderland, also a cousin to Edwin Malone, a noted writer, Shakespearian critic, and English publisher of Shakespeare's works. Richard Malone was a nephew of the Right Honorable Anthony Malone, Chancellor of Ireland. Elliott Warberton, the noted writer, was a cousin to Richard Malone; Admiral Hamilton, of the English Navy, a cousin also, and his niece married a great-grandson of the celebrated Earl of Rodney, who was raised to the peerage in 1782, on account of his distinguished feats as an Admiral. Malone Raymond and Catharine (Holdaway) had a family of five daughters, the wife of our subject being the youngest; all are married and reside in this county. The mother-in-law of Mr. Miller, from whom this sketch was obtained, came with her husband to this country in 1849; she is a lady of the highest culture, and remarkably bright for one of her extreme age. Mr. Miller has had by this marriage six children; two died in infancy. Those living are Catharine R., born March 24, 1864; Martha H., Jan. 6, 1867; Clarence A., March 24, 1868; Robert W., July 22, 1869. He and family are members of the Presbyterian Church. Mrs. Miller is instructress in the Art Department at the K. F. C. at Millersburg, and is a lady of very high social as well as artistic culture.

JOSEPH A. MILLER, grocer; P. O. Millersburg; was born Feb. 19, 1831; he is the youngest son of Alexander Miller, who was the youngest child of Major John Miller, the founder of Millersburg; Alexander was the father of the following children: John, died in the South in his young manhood; Wm. McClelland, James McClure, Mary McClure, died in young womanhood; Robert A., Joseph A., Ann, also died in young womanhood; Martha Harris, now a Mrs. Judge Wm. H. Savage, residing at Shackelford, Texas; and America J., now a Mrs. Alexander Butler. Our subject, in his youth, received all the advantages of education of his day, attending the Transylvania

M. M. Gay

University two years, and one year at the Kentucky Military Institute. In the Fall of 1861 he enlisted in the 9th Ky. Cavalry, under Gen. Morgan, serving until the surrender. He was very enthusiastic in the Southern cause, and took upon himself the perilous duty of furnishing supplies and clothing for their troops, until a reward of $500 was offered for his body dead or alive; at the time they made the search for him he enlisted in the service, and for a feat of bravery upon the field, in rescuing a fallen comrade, he received a furlough home. He was married Dec. 14, 1871, to Miss Sally M. Best, of Mason County (see hist. of Dr. Best). They have no children, are members of the M. E. Church South, and he one of the town trustees, and a prominent merchant of the village, and a highly esteemed gentleman. His father was born in 1796, and died at 74 years of age; he was twice married, the second time to Ann C. Pelham, an aunt of Major Pelham's, who was distinguished in military circles.

JOHN I. MOORE, farmer; P. O. Millersburg; son of James B. and America (Layson) Moore, (see Layson hist.); James B. a son of John and Polly (Wilmoth) Moore. John I. was the only child of this family; he was born upon the farm where he now lives, March 15, 1844, and received a limited education; on account of the death of his father, in 1855, so that at a very early age he entered a practical business life, with the care and attention of large farming interests left by his father, devolving upon him. By close attention, and a practical application of business principles, he has become one of the prominent stock dealers and farmers of the county. He was married Oct. 18, 1871, to Miss Jennie Pollock, born May 26, 1846, to Robert and Amanda (Bailey) Pollock; he is now residing near Jacksonville, Ill., engaged in farming. The wife of our subject was left an orphan at a tender age, by the death of her mother; she was then taken by her uncle, Squire W. A. Moore, of Woodford Co.; she is also a niece of Judge S. M. Moore, of Chicago. By this marriage there were five children: Wm. A., born Oct. 30, 1872; Mary W., May 22, 1876; America, Oct. 25, 1878; a son and daughter, on Aug. 7, 1880, when the wife died, the children living but a few months. The mother of our subject died March 22, 1881, in her 66th year.

JOHN G. SMEDLEY, merchant; P. O. Millersburg; was born Feb. 20, 1836, to Aaron and Catharine (Hughs) Smedley, she was a daughter of Jesse and Priscilla (Parker) Hughs, both of whom died in Carlisle, the former in 1863, the latter in 1856; Aaron Smedley was born in Paris, Ky., July 25, 1794; died Sept. 7, 1863; he was a son of Aaron, who was born in Pennsylvania, April 4, 1764; died June 31, 1836; his wife was Rebecca Leer; born Dec. 15, 1765, died July 16, 1828; he built the first shingle-roof house in Paris. The subject of this sketch is the oldest of Aaron Smedley, Jr.'s children, who were: John G., Wm., who was twice married; first to a Miss Howell, of New York City, afterward to a Miss Burns, of Leavenworth, Kan., now deceased; he resides in Salt Lake City, engaged in mining and the insurance business; Joseph (deceased), married a Miss Jamison, of Paris, and left two daughters: Broadus, residing with his mother, near Hutchinson Station; Elizabeth died in childhood; Aaron, Jr., engaged in mercantile business in St. Louis; Catharine was a Mrs. Harry Forrester, who is a merchant in Chicago; John G. remained upon the farm with his parents until fifteen years of age, when he entered the store of G. B. & A. Hale, of Lexington, where he continued until the years 1854–5, when he attended the Baptist College at Georgetown, during the years 1857–8; he was engaged in the mercantile business with Upstill, Pierson & Co., of St. Louis; in February, 1859, he came to Millersburg and entered into partnership in the mercantile business with Mr. J. M. Hughs, County Clerk of Bourbon; this firm still continues, doing the largest business in the village. Mr. Smedley was married Oct. 28, 1862, to Miss Mattie Boulden, daughter of Nathan Boulden; by this marriage there was a son, who died in infacy, and a daughter, Maud S., born Oct. 14, 1867; the mother of these died Nov. 22, 1872; he was remarried March 14, 1877, to Mrs. Lizzie Rains, widow of Dr. Rains, of Millersburg; this marriage took place at Jacksonville, Fla., and after traveling through the South, he returned to his business; by this marriage there are two children, viz: Mary, born Dec. 21, 1877; Graham, born Nov. 10, 1879; the mother is a daughter of Jesse Boulden (see history). He is a member of the Baptist Church, she of the Christian; he is a member of the Knights Templar, an enterprising, energetic, and prominent man in business circles.

HAMLET C. SHARP, gauger; P. O. Millersburg; was born in Nicholas County, Ky., Dec. 31, 1858, to John W. and Charity C. (Baskett) Sharp, (see hist.) Hamlet began his education in the common schools of Nicholas County, and completed with a three-year's course in the Wesleyan College at Millersburg. He was appointed Government storekeeper Jan. 1, 1879, and gauger in March, 1881, which position he still retains. He was married in Bourbon County, April 20, 1881, to Miss Belle G. Greene, who was born June 6, 1862, to Robt. P. and Molly E. (Current) Greene, both natives of Bourbon

County, the former born in 1837, the latter in 1847. On Dec. 1, 1881, Mr. Sharp entered into partnership with Jas. M. Collier, at Millersburg, and in addition to attending to the duties of gauger, is now engaged in selling lumber, coal, salt and lime. Owing to his abilities as a business man he has assisted in building up a large and steadily increasing business. He is a very energetic and enterprising business man, and well worthy of the high esteem in which he is held by the community. In politics he is a Republican.

WALLACE SHANNON, farmer; P. O. Millersburg; an enterprising and highly respected young farmer and stock shipper; resides with his mother at their beautiful home, about two miles above Millersburg, on the Cynthiana and Indian Creek Pike. The early ancestry of the family were among the old pioneers of the country, and highly esteemed for their industry and probity.

JAMES H. THOMPSON, farmer ; P. O. Millersburg; was born in Nicholas County, Nov. 21, 1822, about three and a half miles from Millersburg, where he now resides, to Henry and Mary (Wilson) Thompson ; she born in Lexington about 1790, to James Wilson and a Miss Clark, who were very early settlers at that place ; Henry Thompson, Jr., was born in the Sherman Valley, Pa.,near Carlisle, in May, 1782, died in February, 1852 ; he was brought by his parents, Henry and Mary (McClintock) Thompson, to the farm now owned in part by the subject of this sketch. Henry Thompson, Sr., was one of the party of eighteen who settled in the vicinity of Millersburg in 1778, his tract of 1200 acres lying in the edge of Nicholas County. He it seems remained upon his land the principal part of the time after making the first settlement, in a rude cabin in the howling wilderness, being the only settler between Maysville and Lexington, and during the most troublesome time with the Indians, and the great massacre at the Blue Licks. In 1783 he brought his family and remained upon the old homestead until his death. During his lonely life the Indians several times drove him off his land, and drove away his stock, and after bringing his family, his noble wife would stand guard while he plowed their little patch of corn, and did other necessary work. They had five children, three of whom are living: Daniel, Robert and James H., who are the only members of the third generation in this part of the country. John, the oldest son, died in 1860, leaving children in Nicholas County ; Mary married a Mr. McClintock, and died in 1859, leaving two daughters ; James H. received his education upon the farm, and in the limited district school of his boyhood days and remained with his parents until their death, which occurred on the same day of the month, Feb. 15, he in 1852, she in 1860. He remained unmarried until Feb. 11, 1862, when he was married to Miss Marilda Cheatham ; born Jan. 13, 1846, to Forman and Louisa (Bradshaw) Cheatham, residents of Montgomery County, near Mount Sterling. By this marriage there have been seven children, three of whom died in early childhood. Those living are: Brownie, born March 24, 1864; Robert, May 12, 1871 ; Jimmie, Aug. 29, 1875 ; and Elmo, May 2, 1881. Mr. Thompson is a highly respected farmer and member of the democratic party.

CHARLES R. TURNER, farmer; P. O. Millersburg; born July 15, 1842, to William and Susan A. (Sandusky) Turner; she, born Dec. 16, 1820, to Andrew and Betsey (Culver) Sandusky; she, born in 1783, died in 1846, daughter of Charles and Ellen (Shanks) Culver; he died in Maryland; his widow came to Bourbon County with two children, at an early date. Andrew Sandusky was born Dec. 5, 1781, to James and Mary (Brown) Sandusky; were among the very early settlers of Bourbon County. William Turner was born Feb. 17, 1792, in Lexington, in the fort; his father was William, born Nov. 6, 1752, in Md. The wife of the latter was Martha Ricards, born Aug. 19, 1762; William, Jr., was the seventh child of four sons and seven daughters, the eldest born in 1779, the youngest in 1803; two only are now living, Charles, the youngest, a resident of Bourbon County, and Stacy, a Mrs. Ishmel Daily, residing in Adams County, Ill. William Turner, the father of our subject, was three times married; first to a Miss Ricards, who died without issue; second, to Sally Sandusky, who died in 1835; by her there were three children: Martha, a Mrs. Joseph McClelland; Mary Ellen died in childhood; Wm. A., now residing near Kansas City, Mo. By the third marriage there were also three children, by Susan A. Sandusky, a sister to second wife. The children were: Elizabeth, who became the wife of Isaac Bowen, and died in 1855; Sally Lee married Harmon Ayres, who is a prominent stock-dealer and farmer in Saline County, Mo., and the subject of this sketch, the youngest child of Wm., Jr., who died April 13, 1878, and willing the old homestead to his youngest son, who was married Sept. 10, 1861, to Sally A. Redmon, daughter of Thomas Jefferson and Amanda (Redmon) Redmon, residents of Paris Precinct; they have no children. Mr. Turner remained with his parents engaging in agriculture and mule trading, also paying some attention to short-horns. His paternal ancestry were among the very earliest settlers in the county, large land-holders, and stood among the leading men at that early day. His father was one of the first distillers in the county, and sold of his first manufacture at 12½ cts. per gallon. They have occupied the same farm since 1792, and at an early date built a house, putting on a shingle roof, which it is supposed, was the first of that style in the county.

ROBT. TARR, farmer; P. O. Millersburg; was born near Carlisle, May 2, 1828, where his parents removed, a short time before his birth, from Bourbon County, returning in 1838, and settling the farm on which Mr. Tarr now lives. His father was John B. Tarr, a native of Nicholas, born March 4, 1801; he of Charles Tarr, born upon the Eastern Shore of Maryland. The wife of Charles was Miss Bishop, who, soon after being united in marriage, came to the western part of Nicholas County, on Hinkston, which was soon after the year 1790, and became one of the prominent men of the county at that early day. In about 1831 he moved to Adams County, Ill., with all his family except a daughter, who married Richard Adair, "The Tanner," of Nicholas County, and John B., the father of our subject, who remained in the Blue Grass region, where he engaged in farming and raised a family by Milly Turner. (See hist.) The result of this union was five sons and two daughters: Wm., born June 22, 1825. He began life a poor boy; his first enterprise was that of raising watermelons, afterward engaged in farming upon rented land with his brother Robert, when, after a few years, their labors having been crowned with success, they dissolved partnership, each beginning business for himself; Wm. subsequently engaged in distilling, trading and real estate speculation, through which he has become one of the money kings of the Blue Grass region; the second of the family was Charles, born Sept. 15, 1826, died a young man; the subject of this sketch, who devoted his life to agriculture and stock raising; he was for a number of years a director in the Millersburg Bank, and at the death of the first president he was elected to that position; Martha, born Jan. 5, 1830, married Tice Hutzell, and, after his death, married a Mr. Penn, who is also deceased; James, born Jan. 21, 1832, married a Miss Piper and moved to Pettis County, Mo., where he died; his wife is now a Mrs. Porter, of Millersburg; John, a resident of Flat Rock (see hist.); Mary E., born Aug. 30, 1841, became the wife of Col. Sampson D. Archer, of Keokuk, Iowa, where he died and where his family now reside. The subject of this sketch was married Sept. 5, 1861, to America Layson, daughter of Robt. Layson (deceased) and Catharine Kennedy. They have three children—Anna Lee, wife of Jas. L. Shackelford, of Maysville, Robt. L. and John Bishop.

J. T. TALBOTT, farmer; P. O. Millersburg; born Aug. 13, 1822, to George and Unity (Smith) Talbott; she a daughter of Daniel and Nancy (Baker) Smith, who were natives, the former of Delaware, the latter of Eastern Shore of Maryland; came early to Bourbon County; Geo. Talbott was a son of Harry (supposed to have come from England when a youth to Fredericksburg, Va.,) and Barbara (Whaley) Talbott; George raised a family of nine children to maturity, viz.: Daniel, residing at Carlisle; Mrs. William Parker, in Nicholas; Preston W., in Ruddel's Mills; J. T., George H., at Cynthiana; Charles L., in Ruddels Mills; Nancy, married John Parker, she died, leaving heirs at Carlisle; Rezin, married a Miss Elizabeth A. Bell (he deceased), family in Nicholas; J. T. lived with his father (receiving a very limited education) until his marriage, Aug. 27, 1849, to Elizabeth A. Conway, daughter of Nathaniel S. and Annie C. (Baker) Conway; Nathaniel S. born May 28, 1798, died Jan. 6, 1879, was a son of John and Annie (Sutton) Conway, natives of Virginia; came to Nicholas at an early date; Annie C. Baker, was born July 7, 1805, died May 3, 1853, was a daughter of William and Elizabeth (Kimbrough) Baker, natives of Nicholas. Mr. Talbott by this marriage had ten children: Annie B., born Oct. 22, 1850, widow of Hon. Henry C. Dills, of Falmouth; Mary E., born Dec. 25, 1851, wife of Wm. Durham, a farmer of Nicholas County; Jennie U., born March 13, 1854, wife of John R. Madison, of Cynthiana; Fannie G., born July 23, 1856; Willie W., born July 26, 1858, is in mercantile business at Millersburg; Nannie P., born July 22, 1860, wife of Willie McKee, a farmer in Harrison County; Charles M., born July 3, 1862; John C., born March 17, 1865; Arthur, born April 30, 1867, and Stanley, born Aug. 24, 1869; he and family are members of the Christian Church at Indian Creek; a genial wholesouled gentleman, highly respected and esteemed by his neighbors.

DANIEL THOMPSON, farmer; P. O. Millersburg; was born January 24, 1824 (see James H. Thompson's history for history of his people), and spent his early life on the farm with his father until twenty-six years of age, having in the meantime received some knowledge of books under the old select school system, in an old log building with clapboard roof, puncheon floor and split logs for seats, which constituted the seat of learning at that day. In 1850, he was married to Elizabeth J. McClintock, having by her three children, who, with the mother, are now dead. His second marriage occurred Oct. 4, 1859, to Elizabeth Moore, who was born Dec. 1, 1840, to James McClure and Margaret (Layson) Moore. By this marriage there have been nine children born unto them: Mary A., June 26, 1860; Jas. Mc., Jan. 14, 1862; Margaret E., March 6, 1864; John W., Feb. 11, 1866; Saml. D., March 28, 1868; infant daughter, dead; French Moore, Nov. 1, 1873; Robert Presley, Oct. 23, 1876; Harry W., July 28, 1879. Mr. Thompson is quite extensively engaged in raising thoroughbred short horns of the principal families, all his stock having registered pedigrees. He is also superintending large farming interests. In the summer of 1877 he suffered the loss of about $8,000 worth of property in the accidental burning of his dwelling and its effects. He and his family are members of the Associate Reformed Presbyterian Church on Hinkston.

WM. TARR, farmer, speculator and distiller; P. O., Paris; proprietor of Park Place (see Robt. Tarr's hist.); has been twice married: first, to Sarah F. Fisher, daughter of W. W. and Sarah (Garth) Fisher (see Fisher hist.) She died in March, 1873, leaving two children, Thompson H., born Oct. 4, 1866, and Fisher, Aug. 11, 1870. His second marriage was to Miss Mary Fisher, a sister to his first wife. They were married Jan. 25, 1876, the result of the union being three children: James B., born Dec. 24, 1877; Wm. Orr, March 19, 1878, and Mary Best, March 9, 1880. Mr. Tarr has one of the most beautiful homes in Bourbon County, having provided it with all the modern conveniences and tasteful designs, and a large and commodious park well stocked with deer. He is a man of great business tact and ability, his large and increasing business interests extending throughout the country.

THE VIMONT FAMILY. In the year 1776, in or near Paris, France, was born Louis Vimont, Sr., who when he had arrived at the age of twelve years, started with his father and a Mr. John Savary to America, being driven from their sunny land on account of their religious tenets. After landing in Philadelphia the father of Louis was stricken down with yellow fever, from which he soon died, leaving his young orphan son in the care of his companion, Mr. Savary. They were then two strangers in a broad and wild land. They however soon made their way to Gallipolis, O., where they stopped with the French settlers of that section, who were holding a land grant from that Government, about twelve miles from Portsmouth, O. There they resided for some time, thence came to Washington, Ky., and probably before 1795, they settled in Millersburg, where Mr. Savary engaged in mercantile pursuits as one of the very first merchants of Bourbon County, assisted by Mr. Vimont, who was married to Rosanna Rowland, June 1, 1798; she a native of North Carolina, and daughter of John Rowland, who afterwards resided in Harrison County for many years. By this marriage there were four sons and three daughters, all of whom were married, and still living, except one son and one daughter. They were—John Savary, born June 10, 1799; Jefferson T., Sept. 18, 1801; Franklin B., Dec. 4, 1803 (deceased); Charlotte, April 7, 1808, married John B. McIlvain, of Louisville, by whom she has five children: Verger, born Nov. 1, 1810, married William Swift, of Lexington, by whom she had eight children; both are now deceased; Mary E., born Jan. 5, 1819, widow of Dr. Samuel Trotter, of Lexington, had four children: Louis C., born May 2, 1823. Mr. Vimont after living in this country for a time sent for his only sister, Felicity, who settled in Maysville, and in 1848 became the wife of M. Girova, by whom she had one child, a daughter. Mr. Vimont was for many years the leading merchant in the village of Millersburg; also a heavy shipper of produce to the South, and a contractor, in which business his sons superseded him. John Savary Vimont was a merchant in Millersburg, where he was born, until about four years ago. He is still a leading man in the improvement of the village and all the leading enterprises. He was married Sept. 19, 1826, to Ann Russell Throckmorton, daughter of Thomas and Susan (Morton) Throckmorton, who resided at the junction of the Johnson and Licking rivers. By this union there were seven children; Thomas T., Louis B., Joseph D.; Susan, now a Mrs. Sandusky, of Lexington; Rosanna, now a Mrs. Dr. Kenney, of Paris; Cecil J., married a Mr. Batterton; infant daughter (deceased). Three sons and three daughters grew to be men and women, and married (except Louis B.), leaving heirs in the vicinity of Millersburg; except Joseph D., only one is now living, Mrs. Sandusky, of Lexington. The wife of Mr. Vimont died Aug. 21, 1846. The Vimonts are Republican in political sentiment. The oldest son of John S. went into the Federal Army as Captain, afterwards promoted to Lieut-Colonel; was shot in cold blood by an officer in the same command. Louis B. was in the same command with his brother, and died at Chatanooga. The Vimont family are highly respected citizens of Millersburg and the community. Jefferson T. Vimont, second son, received a liberal education, and assisted his father in mercantile business until his marriage, which occurred Sept. 18, 1823, to Elizabeth Mantelle, daughter of William Mantelle, who was for many years a banker at Lexington. After his marriage he built the flouring mill, known as the Elizabeth Mill, which he run for a number of years; then engaged in merchandising in Millersburg, and through his son at St. Joe, Mo., which he continued for a number of years; then engaged in real estate business throughout the West, until the breaking-out of the Civil War, in 1861. At the death of his father he was made executor of the large estate left by him. He had seven children. Louis died in Chillicothe, on his return trip from Washington, D. C., where he had held a position as one of the first clerks in the Treasury Department for a number of years; was married to a Miss Kennair ; left two children ; she is now residing with her son in Lexington. Charlotte unmarried, living with her father. Mary, now a Mrs. Dr. Scearce of Chillicothe ; John, married, and a merchant in St. Louis, Mo.; Thomas married also in St. Louis; Elizabeth, unmarried, at home ; Malcom M., died in young manhood. Mr. Vimont lost his wife a number of years ago; he and family are members of the Presybterian Church; Louis C. Vimont was married Nov. 21, 1844, to Mary W. Nesbit, born May 10, 1827, daughter of Joseph and Mary (Ammons) Nesbit, natives of Cobumbia, Boone County, Mo.; he a Baptist minister at an early date; Mr. Vimont, is related by marriage to Dr. Graham, of Louisville, father-in-law of Joseph Blackburn, at present one of the most prominent men of Kentucky. They had seven daughters and four sons; one of the former died in infancy; ten are now living : Joseph N., married to Alice Graham (deceased, Dec. 7, 1868, after less than a year of wedded life); he was located at San Francisco as a member of the S oc : Exchange at that place; now mining at Tombstone, Arizona; Anna, wife of O. W. Brady, of Nicholas County, married Nov. 28, 1876; Henry S., Thomas A., Belle W., Nancy M., Minnie, Virginia B., Susan and Banks M. Mr. Vimont lived with his father until his marriage, when he engaged in mercantile business for about ten years, after which, for about the same length of time he run the Tower Mills; since the Kentucky Central company has had charge of the railroad through Millersburg, he has acted as General Station Agent at the above named place; also agent for all main lines upon coupon tickets; he is a member of the I. O. O. F., and a prominent citizen; Jefferson M. Vimont, son of Franklin B. (deceased), who at eighteen years of age left his father, Louis, and went to the mouth of Johnson, where he was extensively engaged in farming, distilling and mercantile business, sending his merchandise by flatboat to New Orleans, at an early day; here he continued until in 1864, when he removed to the place where his youngest son now lives, and engaged in farming until his death, which occurred Aug. 14, 1877; he was married Nov. 25, 1824, to Susan W., daughter of Thomas and Susan (Morton) Throckmorton; Thomas Throckmorton, Sr., a native of Richmond, Va., came to Kentucky about 1800, settling on the Licking river, about nine miles below the Blue Licks; the sons of this gentleman became quite prominent in the history of Kentucky; also a son-in-law of Lewis Arnold, an active worker in the political field in Nicholas County; Mr. Vimont by this marriage, had nine children : John S., died at twenty-seven years of age; Mary, now the wife of W. T. Ingels, of Nicholas County ; A. T., died at twenty-nine years of age ; Anna R. died young; Bettie, a maiden lady of high social culture and fine business qualifications, residing in Millersburg, superintending her agricultural affairs and household duties; Sue, wife of J. F. Miller, a farmer in Nicholas County; Louis T., with a twin brother, who died in infancy; he married a Miss Whitehead, daughter of John R. Whitehead, of Harrison County, by whom he has eight children: Charles W., Frank, Claude, Mattie, Fannie, Florence, John, and Louis; Jefferson M., the youngest, born Oct. 27, 1844, and married Oct. 25, 1866, to Miss Lovina Letton (see Letton hist.); they have had six children, three of whom died in infancy; those living are : Nannie L., A. T. and F. Letton. Mr. Vimont is engaged in agriculture and raising of thoroughbred Cotswold sheep and short horn cattle; his sheep are of the finest in the Blue Grass region, and in demand in a number of the different States throughout the union.

JAMES WHALEY, farmer; P. O. Millersburg; son of Leland and Polly (Talbott) Whaley; she a daughter of Henry and Barbara (Whaley) Talbott, who came from Loudoun County, Va., to Fayette County, Ky., in 1792, where they resided two years, then came to Ruddel's Mills Precinct, settling on Hinkston, where they died at advanced ages. Leland was a son of John Whaley, of Loudoun County, Va., where he died about 1787; his wife was Barbara Reamy, who came to Ruddel's Mills in 1795. The father of our subject being the youngest of a large family, was born in 1782, and died in 1873. He remained with his mother until arriving at the age of maturity, when he took charge of the farm, she remaining with him until her death, which occurred in 1827, having passed her ninetieth year. He was twice married: first, to Polly Talbott in 1805, having by her five children: Harriett, born in 1806, married to Benedict Whaley, and died in Missouri in 1863; Evelina, born in 1809, married to Franklin Van Hook, residing in Clinton County Mo.; James, born in 1811; Angeline in 1814, married Henry Talbott; died in 1862; Wm. B., a resident of Paris Precinct. The mother died in 1818. His second marriage was to Catharine, sister of his first wife; by her he had six children: Charles H., born in 1820, residing in Ruddel's Mills Precinct; Mary, born in 1823, and Sarah, in 1825, both of whom died maidens; B. F., born in 1828, residing in Cynthiana; L.W., in 1830, also in Cynthiana; Elizabeth, born in 1833, married to Winfield Hayden, now residing in Marion County, Mo. James, the subject of this sketch, received a limited common school education, and has devoted his life to agriculture and stock raising, with the exception of about five years, dating from 1835, when he was one of the prominent merchants of Millersburg. He was four times married: first, to Tabitha Jameson, in 1837, she dying in 1840; second, in 1842 to Mary Ann Hedges, daughter of John Hedges; by her he had three children: Tabitha, deceased, wife of John Jameson; Martha (deceased); Fannie, wife of John H. Shropshire, farmer, near Georgetown, Scott County, Ky.; his second wife died in 1849; third marriage to Betsey Bowles, in 1850; died in 1875; fourth marriage to Mrs. Elizabeth Redmon, in 1878. He is a member of the Christian church and a respected citizen.

FLAT ROCK PRECINCT.

JUDA A. BANTA; P. O. Cane Ridge; was born Sept. 1, 1799; widow of Peter Banta, who was born Oct. 25, 1791, in Bourbon County; he was a soldier in the war of 1812, under Capt. Thomas Morris, of Bourbon; his father was Henry Banta, born Jan. 22, 1762, and his wife, Sally Shook, born Oct. 27, 1761, in Pennsylvania, where they were married, but came early in life to Kentucky, living for some time in the forts at Bryant's and Harrod's Stations; finally settled upon the old Desha farm now owned by Robt. Hopkins, where they lived for a few years, then moved to the farm which is now occupied by the widow of Peter Banta. He by the help of his sons built the brick house which still stands; he also had every piece of furniture made to order; an old fashioned clock still ticking away has stood in one corner of the room now occupied by Mrs. Banta for more than seventy years. Henry Banta had six daughters and four sons; all are now dead but Abram who resides in Nicholas. (See history.) The eldest, Polly, born March 3, 1785, married a George Develly; Henry born, Nov. 20, 1786, married a Miss Jennie Fulton; Margaret, born ——, ——, was the wife of Gen. Sam Fulton; Andrew, born Jan. 9, 1790, married Betsy Hayden; Peter, married Juda A. Zachry, July 26, 1818; she a daughter of Nathan and Mary (Hughs) Zachry; she a daughter of John Hughs and Sally Phelps, all of whom were natives of Virginia. The Zachry family came to Bourbon County in 1806. In later years he moved to Tennessee, where the father died and where our subject was married. Rachael, sixth child, was born Oct. 9, 1793, married James Bryan; Sally, born April 5, 1796, married Wm. Boardman; Betsy, born in 1798, married Peter Vanice; Anna, born 1802, Aug. 4, married Reason Brace; and Abram, above mentioned. The subject of this sketch raised nine children to be men and women grown; only two of that number are now living: Judge Andrew Banta,of Carlisle, (see hist) and Sally S., born Sept. 14, 1821, widow of Joseph Gibson. She has five children: Mary, a Mrs. D. L. Robbins; Joseph P. in Mo.; William, at home; James; Isabelle J., wife of Lucius Stone, City Marshal of Nevada, Mo. Mr. Gibson was engaged in the mercantile business in Flat Rock; he was a good business man and citizen. While making collections through the country preparatory to purchasing a new stock of goods, his body was found in the Hinkston river after a re-search; supposed to have been drowned, but with indications of foul play. Henry P., the eldest son of our subject, was married to Elizabeth Fulton, and resided in Nicholas County, where he was engaged in milling, and died from accidental injuries received in the machinery; Dewitt Clinton, after marriage, went to Missouri, where he was killed in felling trees for the construction of a house; Wm. B. and Peter J. were both killed in the Confederate army; Margaret C. married Spencer Boyd, of Bath County; left three sons and three daughters; Leonidas, after extensive travelling in Texas and California, having contracted consumption, went to Honolulu, Sandwich Islands, where he died at the house of a missionary at that place; Mary A. became the wife of Henry McClannahan, a merchant in Nashville, Tenn., where she went and soon after died of cholera. Mr. Banta was one of the most prominent and respectable citizens of Bourbon County; was a surveyor and school teacher in connection with his farm life; he was for many years Deputy Clerk, and held other positions of trust. He accumulated a large fortune, but on account of his liberality and willingness to help others, he gave his name upon paper which proved disastrous to his fortune in the loss of several thousand dollars. He was a consistent Christian gentleman, holding the office of deacon for many years in the Christian Church, with which his family were also connected. He was a great and good man, and many were the lamentations at his death, which occurred when he was in his 83d year.

MAJOR NATHAN BROWN, P. O. Cane Ridge; who resides with his sons at Elm Grove farm, was born in Montgomery County, Md., Dec. 27, 1797, to John and Sarah (Holland) Brown ; she was a daughter of William Holland, who was of English descent and probably from that country. Maj. Brown is the eldest of three sons and one daughter ; his education was limited, as he began learning the saddler's trade at fourteen years of age, in the county seat of his native county. In 1818, he was united in marriage to Miss Elizabeth Letton Leach, daughter of Jesse and Polly (Letton) Leach ; by this marriage he had four sons and four daughters ; two of the former and one of the latter died without issue, the eldest living is Sarah Ann, widow of Cincinnatus Henry, resides at Sharpsburg; T. E. and C. L., single and owners of the above-mentioned farm ; Harriet, widow of E. A.

Horton, and Louisa L., formerly a Mrs. Fowl, now a Mrs. William H. Reed. Maj. Brown settled in Flat Rock in the year 1818, soon after marriage, he and wife rode on horseback, bringing all their earthly possessions in that manner from their native home to the latter place, soon after their arrival in Flat Rock one horse died, the other went blind and was sold for but a few dollars, he then traded the side saddle for a cow, which also died. Notwithstanding all the adversity which befell him, he reared his family to appreciate honor and integrity, and prospered in life. His wife shared his trials until in August, 1879, when she in her eightieth year calmly and peacefully went to the rest which she so richly deserved. The sons with whom he resides, started out in life a few years ago, going in debt for a large farm, which by their industry and frugal habits have cleared up and now rank among the best farmers of the precinct. They are engaged in the rearing of thoroughbred Cotswold sheep, and stand among the first of the county. They are members of the Christian Church, and are highly esteemed citizens of the community in which they live.

LOT BANTA, farmer; P. O. Plum Lick; born Jan. 19, 1825, to Andrew and Elizabeth (Hayden), daughter of Lot and Mary (Bryan) Hayden; the former natives of Nicholas, the latter of Bourbon County. Andrew Banta was a son of Henry and Mary (Shook) Banta, natives of Virginia, and were engaged in farming, stockraising and improving the country. He raised a family of nine children; seven are still living, three sons and four daughters, in Bourbon County, except Sallie Ann, a Mrs. Henry Arnold, and Eliza Ellen, a Mrs. Barton Graves, who reside in Indiana. The subject of this sketch spent his early life with his father in the improvement of the farm, the raising of products and stock, receiving but limited educational advantages. He was married Jan. 29, 1852, to Mary Jane Wilson, daughter of Uriah and Elizabeth (House) Wilson, who were among the pioneers of the Blue Grass region; by this union there were five children: Andrew C. married Dora Hughes, now residing in Saline County, Mo.; Elizabeth M., now a Mrs. Jonas Sparks, residents of Nicholas County; Lot B., Mary Eliza, a Mrs. William Young, residents of Nicholas, and James William; they are engaged in a general agriculture.

HENRY BOARDMAN, farmer; P. O. Plum Lick; was born Jan. 14, 1831, to Wm. Boardman, born Nov. 22, 1797, died May 16, 1880; he a son of Benj. and Keziah (Rice) Boardman; he a son of Joseph. The early ancestry of our subject came to Kentucky at an early date, where they engaged in clearing and tilling the soil. The mother of Henry was Sally Banta, born April 5, 1796, died June 21, 1860; she a sister to Peter Banta (see hist.) Mr. Boardman is the only son of the family now living; one son died in youth, one daughter died a maiden, five were married: Mrs. Shelton Utterback, who moved with her husband to Indiana, where she died; Rachel, a Mrs. Wm. Harvy; Sally, a Mrs. Jos. T. Booth; Elizabeth, a Mrs. Henry Soper; Keziah, a Mrs. W. W. Northcutt, a resident of Missouri. The subject of this sketch has always resided in the vicinity of his present home, where he was born. He was married Oct. 27, 1857, to Minerva J. Wilson, daughter of Uriah and Mary (Gillespie) Wilson; she a daughter of Simon and Elizabeth (Simpson) Gillespie, natives of Virginia. They had seven children: Wm. M., born July 28, 1858; John N., May 20, 1860; Richard H., Sept. 9, 1863; John W., Dec. 29, 1865; Jos. E., April 10, 1868; Mary E., Oct. 1, 1870; Minnie Olive, July 12, 1873. All are at home except William, who is engaged in teaching school in Douglas County, Ill. The family are members of the Christian Church at Union, Nicholas County.

WM. F. BRYAN, farmer; P. O. Plum Lick; the youngest of three living children born to Jas. H. and Amanda (Johnson) Bryan; she a daughter of one of the earliest settlers on Boone's Creek, and for a number of years dead; James H., one of the wealthiest farmers of the county, still living. The early ancestry of this enterprising young man came from Virginia, among the first settlers of this part of Kentucky, locating in the wilderness with the wild beast and red man, doing their part toward the civilization and improvement of this great country. The subject of this sketch received a very limited education, but possessing a high degree of native ability, tact and energy, he has become one of the prominent and rising young men of the vicinity in which he lives. He was born Sept. 3, 1854, and married Oct. 26, 1880, to Miss Florence Talbott, daughter of Charles and Emma (Rice) Talbott, who were among the early settlers in the vicinity of North Middletown. By this marriage there is one child, Emma, born Aug. 13, 1881.

ANSON P. BRYAN, farmer; P. O. Plum Lick; son of James C. and Mary (Noble) Bryan, who were natives of Nicholas County. Mr. Bryan is the second son and seventh of a family of eight children, three sons and five daughters, two of whom only, are now living. He was born on the farm now owned by his younger brother, Jeff, Aug. 23, 1832, he was brought up on the farm and received such an education as could be acquired at that date; he remained with his father until after his death, which occured in 1852, subsequently a division of the homestead

WOODBRIDGE STOCK FARM, W. H. KERR & BRO. PROP'S. NORTH MIDDLETOWN, KY.

of 230 acres occurred, when the two sons, Anson and Jeff, purchased from the other heirs their interests in the old homestead upon which they lived and did business together until 1877, when they dissolved partnership, our subject becoming the possessor of a new and elegant home, and 270 acres of choice land at Plum Lick, where he now resides in bachelorhood.

B. F. CROUCH, farmer; P. O. Plum Lick. The early Crouch ancestry of our subject were of English-Welsh descent; came to this country at a very early date, and were among the prominent families near Richmond, Va. His great-grandfather, John Crouch, with his son, John, and his wife, Sarah (Nelson), she a daughter of Jacob Nelson of German descent, came to Bryant's Station, in Fayette County, in 1787, soon afterwards moving to Nicholas County, on Hinkston. He raised a family of seven sons and four daughters, Ambrose, the father of B. F. Crouch, being one of that number, and was early in life united in marriage to Linchie (Branch), daughter of Pleasant and Jennie (Hall) Branch. They raised a family of eight children—four sons and four daughters—all of whom are living, the subject of this sketch being the second child and born Nov. 4, 1825; the others are Ambrose D., Thomas Jefferson, Julianna, and Polly, now a Mrs. Isaac Clinkinbeard, residents of Nicholas County; Sallie, a Mrs. John Clinkinbeard, residing at Danville, Ill.; William B.; Jane, a Mrs. Jack Sharp; and B. F., residents of Flat Rock Precinct. Mr. Crouch received limited educational advantages in his youth, but by the aid of an energetic and enterprising disposition, he overreached others of his companions who had had superior advantages, and has won for himself a place among the substantial agriculturists of Bourbon County. He was married Aug. 1, 1847, to Mary Sharp, daughter of Vincent Sharp. The fruits of this marriage were five children—three sons, and two daughters now deceased; the sons are Thomas D., who married a Miss Sarah J. Booth, and resides in Nicholas County; John William and Robert, residing at home. Mr. Crouch is extensively engaged in stock raising and shipping the latter, aggregating about $50,000 annually. He and family are members of the Christian Church at Flat Rock.

WILLIAM B. CROUCH, farmer; near Plum Lick P. O.; is a son of John H. Crouch, the second son of William and Mary (Stokes) Crouch, she a daughter of John Stokes and Ann (Logan), natives of Maryland. John H. Crouch was one of the substantial farmers of Flat Rock Precinct, who married a Mrs. Cynthia (Hedges) Kennedy, who had one son, J. N. Kennedy; by this marriage there were seven children, two of whom died in infancy. Those living are Isaac T., partner in agriculture of the enterprising young man the subject of this sketch; James C.; Mary L., now a Mrs. J. C. Talbott; William B., and Margaret J.

WILLIAM CLARK, farmer; P. O. Plum Lick; was born March 3, 1821; his father was Thompson Clark, born Dec. 2, 1792, in Montgomery County, Ky.; he of William Clark, who was a native of Halifax County, Va., but came to the State of Kentucky when a young man and married in what is now Bourbon County, then Fayette, to a Miss Winifred Nichols; William Clark was accompained to this State by a brother—Joseph, who died in Montgomery County, and Thompson Clark, who settled in Fayette County, where he lived and died, having served in the Revolutionary war;. Thompson Clark was a soldier in the war of 1812, holding the position of orderly-sergeant under Captain Crawford; regimental commander, Colonel Samuel Williams; William Clark's mother was Deborah Wilson, daughter of Nathaniel and Mary (Jacks) Wilson, who were natives of Kentucky; the early Wilsons coming from New Jersey; Thompson Clark had two sons—William, and John eleven years younger, who resides in Montgomery County, Ky.; William Clark received his early education in a log school house, under the instruction of a Mr. Samuel Nicholson, a Pennsylvanian; among his schoolmates, were Colonel Thomas Johnson and Colonel John S. Williams, now United States Senator; he afterward recived instructions from various sources until about eighteen years of age; he subsequently engaged in teaching and farm work until his marriage, which occurred Nov. 22, 1849, to Eliza Ann Bradley, of Montgomery County, she a daughter of William and Susan (Mark) Bradley, who were natives of Montgomery County and among the early and prominent families of this county; John Bradley, was the father of William Bradley, and Susan Mark was a daughter of Robert Mark, a prominent character of Montgomery County; the result of the marriage of William Clark, were children as follows: Susan Alice, now Mrs. Calvin Gillispie, Jr.; Annie B., Mollie B., now Mrs. David T. Wilson; James B., Emma, now Mrs. James Gillispie, of Nicholas County; Willa, Frankie, Ida D., Maggie L., Eliza E. and Mattie Clyde. He is of a conservative character, paying but little attention to affairs not pertaining to his business, but living a life of devotion to his family and business; he and family are members of the Christian Church at Flat Rock, and living lives of devotion to their christian faith.

FRANK P. COLCORD, farmer; P. O. Cane Ridge. This interesting and gentlemanly proprietor of Burr Oak farm, is a son of C. B. Colcord and Louisa Metcalf, who was a niece of the honored George Metcalf. The father of our subject settled in 1813, at Middletown, this county, from the State of New Hampshire, he being then about twenty-seven years of age, and soon after engaged in business at that place with an older brother who accompanied him to his new settlement. Their spirit of business adventure, however, was not to be satisfied in a village traffic, but they engaged in extensive speculations which proved remunerative, C. B. Colcord being the first man who ever took a drove of mules to New Orleans by land from Bourbon County; he was married to Miss Metcalf in 1824, and by that union were born six children, only two of whom grew to maturity, viz: William R., born Nov. 26, 1827; married in the vicinity of Middletown; now residing in Wachita, Ka., where he is extensively engaged in the stock business. Our subject was born Sept. 17, 1829; received a liberal education, attending the Western Military Institute in 1849 and '50, then located at Middletown; one of his preceptors and intimate friends being the Honorable James G. Blaine, Secretary of State. Mr. Colcord is an enterprising, thrifty farmer, with 432 acres of choice land, about eight miles from Paris, which he has well stocked, and conducts in a successful manner. He was never married, but enjoys an independent life with his pleasant surroundings.

JESSE FISHBACK, farmer; P. O. Plum Lick; born Aug. 15, 1813, in Bourbon County, to Jesse and Jane (Turley) Fishback, who were natives of Virginia, but came to Kentucky in 1812 or '13. The father was in the six months' service in 1813, enlisting from Bourbon County; he was discharged and on his return home was taken sick and died upon the journey, the same day that our subject was born. The early Fishback ancestry were from Germany, some of whom attained to a considerable degree of notoriety at the bar. The later generations have, however, been principally engaged in agriculture. The subject of this sketch was the youngest of four sons and one daughter, two only of whom are now living; Josiah the second son residing near his brother. Mr. Fishback received his education in a log school house, a long distance from his cabin-home in Nicholas County. He adopted the avocation of a farmer's life; remained unmarried and acted the part of a dutiful son to his widowed mother, who died at an advanced age twenty-four years ago. His home is now presided over by a widowed half-sister, Mrs. Sarah Hughs.

THE HORTON FAMILY. Of this well-known family a representative member is William F. Horton, farmer; who was born Dec. 12, 1824; he is the eldest of six living and five deceased children, by Edward Wakeman and Matilda (Henry) Horton, who were natives of Bourbon County; she a daughter of James and Nancy (Ward) Henry, one of the early families of Bourbon; he a son of William and Sally (Fisher) Horton, who were married Dec. 1, 1785, and came from Virginia, down the river from Wheeling to Maysville, Bourbon County, in 1790, settling near North Middletown. Their children were: Elizabeth, born Dec. 17, 1787, who married James Lindsley; both died, leaving two children; James moved to Indiana, and Lucinda married Davis Mason, and left two daughters: Sally, who married a Mr. Hall, residing in Illinois, and Fanny, who married Erasmus Jones, of Henry County, Ky.; Susanna, born Aug. 28, 1789; married John Clay; left one son, William; Milled, born Jan. 3, on Monday, 1796, married Hamilton Wilson; Mary, born March 7, 1792, died young; Edward Wakeman, born April 18, 1793; Gabriel, born Oct. 16, 1794; William, born March 8, 1796; James, May 10, 1798; married a Miss Luckey, daughter of Joseph Luckey; left four children: William D., Joseph L., Sally and Martha; Hiram, born Oct. 24, 1799, married Susan Payne, moved to Tennessee, and left two daughters: Sarah and Ann; Sarah, born July 8, 1801, married Abner Huston, and moved to Lafayette County, Mo.; Edward, born May 15, 1803, married Mary Luckey, and moved to Marion County, Mo.; left one heir: Hiram, who married a Miss Mason, and left heirs: Washington, born Jan. 26, 1806; Cynthia, born Sept. 7, 1807, married John Gibson, and moved to Marion County, Mo.; Cassandra, born Feb. 24, 1809, married Fielding Calmes, and moved to Colusa County, Cal.; Alexander, born April 8, 1811. The brothers and sisters of our subject are Washington and Jackson, twins; Jefferson, Isabel and Hiram; none are married, and all live in Flat Rock precinct, except Hiram, who resides in Johnson County, Mo. The family received limited educational advantages, but all have acquired a fair knowledge. Two of the family, Washington and Hiram, were in the Confederate service, the former under General Marshall served out his time and returned home, taking the oath of allegiance; the latter under General John Morgan, was captured at Buffington Island, remained at Camp Douglas, where he remained until near the close of the war, when he was exchanged by General Lee at the final close. The subject of this sketch resides in a log house built by Hamilton Wilson, who married Milled Horton. Mr. Wilson was born and lived upon the farm eighty-four years, when he became involved, sold out and moved to Covington, thence to Newport, where he died May 4, 1880, in the ninetieth year of his age. Thomas Jefferson

Horton, a surveyor and general farmer; he purchased the farm upon which he and his sister now live in 1863. T. J. and William F. are enterprising farmers and stock-raisers, highly esteemed citizens and prominent men of the county.

FRANCIS M. HENKLE, farmer ; P. O. Plum Lick; was born March 22, 1831, to William and Amelia (Highland) Henkle, who were married Dec. 14, 1826 ; Wm. Henkle was born Oct. 29, 1801, and died Sep. 14, 1876 ; he was a son of Joseph and Jane (Everman) Henkle, natives of Virginia, but came to Bourbon County, 1803; he was a surveyor and after having lived in Kentucky a short time, started to his native land on business and was drowned ; his body was never recovered, but papers were found establishing the fact. Amelia Highland, born Dec. 15, 1801, is still living, and her parents were Denman and Amelia (Johnson) Highland, who were natives of Maryland, but came to Flat Rock precinct about the year 1794. A spring which was located within a few yards of the cabin, was not found for several months, on account of the density of the cane, as they had to cut their way through to every point which they desired to reach. The boys and girls of that neighborhood in their attendance upon church, would walk six miles bare-footed, or until they were within a few yards of the church, when they would stop at a "branch" and put on their shoes which they had carried with them ; the carefulness with which they used them, was because of the limit to one pair annually. The father of our subject by his marriage had four sons and six daughters, all of whom grew to maturity ; five are now living: Marinda J., a Mrs. John H. McGinnis, residing in Piatt County, Ill. ; they have eight sons and two daughters. W. D., a resident of Bourbon, married Mary F. Shannon, and has three sons and a daughter; Armilda P., a Mrs. David Herron, of Mason County ; has four sons and two daughters ; Nancy M., a Mrs. John Black, of Nicholas ; has four daughters ; Margaret, who died Oct. 3, 1876, on her forty-fourth birthday, was the wife of Thomas Shannon, and left six children. Sarah N., was the wife of James Alexander Arnold ; both are deceased, leaving four children. Francis M., never had children, but has raised several to maturity. William E. Arnold, his nephew, he is educating at the Millersburg College. He was married Jan. 2, 1850, to Cassandra Forgy, the daughter of John and Lavinia (Arrowsmith) Forgy. Hugh Forgy, the grandfather, came to America from Ireland about 100 years ago. Mr. Henkle received a very limited education ; being one of the older members of the family he was compelled to assist in clearing up the land, and raising crops for their sustenance. He remained with his father until after marriage, when he came to his present home. He is a man of great natural ability, of the highest honor and integrity, and a liberal giver to the cause of religion, the support of missions, churches, and schools. He has for many years acted as steward of the church, making up the deficiencies, which in many cases were the largest part. He is a thorough christian gentleman, and one of the most worthy members of the M. E. Church South, at Flat Rock, and a man highly esteemed by his neighbors and friends.

JAMES HEDGES, farmer ; P. O. North Middletown; son of Joseph and Margaret (Goulden) Hedges. He was a native of Maryland, and related to Joseph Hedges, who emigrated from England at a very early date ; she a native of the Blue Grass region ; born May 20, 1778, died Aug. 10, 1871 ; James was born Dec. 5, 1819, in the house in which he now lives, and is the next youngest of a family of seven sons and two daughters, eight of whom are now living, an elder brother having died when a young man. The remainder of the family reside in adjacent counties. James Hedges received a very poor education, only attending school about two months during his life ; but, being possessed of a great deal of energy and perseverance, he acquired in leisure moments, under great disadvantages, a practical business education, which has borne him successfully through all of his business transactions. He was married Dec. 30, 1875, to Fannie Higgins, daughter of Thomas and Elizabeth (House) Higgins, both of whom were natives of Bourbon County. Only one of their three children now survives—James Oscar, born Dec. 7, 1879. He is one of the near descendants of the Maryland branch of the Hedges family, to whom is left an estate of great value in London, England. The formation of his farm is of a singular nature, and one of the most beautiful in the county. The soil is very fertile, and from some of the highest points a view can be had of six counties, extending to the furthermost point of observation by the naked eye. A part of his dwelling is one hundred years old, in which he has lived since his birth, and he is now the oldest native of Flat Rock Precinct.

MAJOR JAS. MADISON MENG, farmer; P. O. Cane Ridge; was born in Prince William County, Va., Feb. 22, 1812, to Capt. Chas. and Victoria (Tebbs) Meng; she a daughter of Captain Wm. Tebbs and a Miss Harslip. A singular incident relating to the birth of Major Meng, is the fact that he was born upon the same day of the month upon which the birth of Geo. Washington occurred, and that his father, Chas. Meng, and Capt. Wm. Tebbs, his grandfather, were both Captains under that illustrious General. Captain Chas. Meng, a son of Chas., Sr., who came from Holland to this country at an early date, settled in Virginia. The father of our subject, being born in Winchester, where he lived until fifteen years of age, when they moved to Woodstock, where in later years he became a merchant of wealth and prominence. Inheriting a great amount of property from his wife, he moved to Prince William County, the land of her nativity, where he engaged in farming, and raised a family of eleven children, five sons and six daughters. Major Meng is the only one of the sons now living; Charles, two years older than he, the only one of the deceased sons who left issue, became an attorney of some note in Louisville, where he resided for a number of years, subsequently removing to Christian County, Ky. Two only of the six daughters are living: the widow Swing and the widow of Jos. Kennedy, of Washington, D. C. Major Meng came to Nicholas County in Jan., 1833, where he engaged in teaching school, in which capacity he was engaged for some time in Bourbon and Nicholas Counties; subsequently learned the moulder's trade and the business of making plows at Maysville, which he engaged in at St. Louis, but afterward took up his old occupation of teaching in the vicinity of his present home. He was married in Bourbon County to Amanda Malvina Fitzallen Hall, daughter of Henry and Fannie (Talbott) Hall, who were among the early settlers of Bourbon County. They had two sons, Charles and James, the mother of whom died on the 15th of April, 1874. The Meng ancestry were a long lived people, the father of our subject sitting as an active magistrate at eighty-two years of age, having held the position of High Sheriff, having come into that position as being the oldest magistrate in the county.

WILLIAM T. PARKER, farmer; P. O. Carlisle; was born near Carlisle in Nicholas County, Feb. 18, 1850, to Robert and Eliza (Donnell) Parker (see Donnell history). Robert Parker was a native of Nicholas County; died Jan. 11, 1879, in his seventy-first year, he was a son of Charles Parker, a native of Maryland; came to Kentucky at an early date; he a son of Thomas. The mother of Robert was Tabitha Johnson; his step-mother was Hannah Collins. The subject of this sketch received the limited advantages of a country school, and remained on the farm with his father assisting in the farm work, until about twenty-four years of age, when he purchased the Fielding Letton farm of 123 acres, where he now resides, and which he has under a high state of cultivation. He was married July 20, 1871, to Miss Jennie Smith, daughter of B. W. Smith, whose sketch appears in this work; by this marriage there have been two children born unto them, Sarah Lovina, June 15, 1873; and Robert Luther, April 23, 1877. Mr. Parker is an enterprising young man, doing well whatever he undertakes, and manifesting an interest in the improvment of stock and farm products.

D. L. ROBBINS, farmer; P. O. Cane Ridge; was born June 14, 1837, to Laban L. and Nancy (Piper) Robbins; she a daughter of Samuel and Betsey (Million) Piper, who were among the early settlers of Kentucky. Laban L. is a son of John and Millison (Litton) Robbins; she, a daughter of John Litton. The father of our subject is a native of Flat Rock village; was born Oct. 15, 1820, and married in 1844; he had six children, three of whom died in infancy, and Nancy N. in her seventeenth year, and Millison J., who became the wife of a Mr. Louderback, died in 1868, in her thirty-first year. Our subject is the only surviving member of the family; he was married Sept. 4, 1879, to Mary C. Gibson, a granddaughter of Peter Banta (see history). They have one child, Nancy Belle, born July 5, 1880; he resides with his father, with whom he is engaged in general agriculture and stock-raising; they are members of the Christian Church at Flat Rock, and held in high esteem by the people of the community in which they live.

BARTON WARREN SMITH, farmer; P. O. Carlisle; a namesake of the great reformer, B. W. Stone, who, when he came to Bourbon County, resided in the house in which our subject now lives. Mr. Smith was born on Cane Ridge, Feb. 7, 1818, to John B. and Sally (Hand) Smith; she a daughter of Wm. Hand, who was one of the first settlers of Bourbon, on Hinkston, and with Barton Stone one of first organizers of the "Old Cane Ridge Church," and an energetic and prominent man at an early date; he subsequently moved to Indiana, where he died soon after. John B., born in Virginia, in 1792, was a son of Jacob and Hannah Smith, who moved to Cane Ridge in 1809, settling on the waters of Brush Creek; John B. was married in 1813, and was blessed with three sons and three daughters, all of whom grew to maturity; only B. W. and a sister, Mrs. John M. Prather, residing in Clay County, Mo., have had children. Mr. Smith learned the carpenters' trade, at which he worked for 18 years. He subsequently purchased property at Jackstown, where he run a grocery, and a blacksmith and wood shop for eight years, when he sold out and purchased his present home, in the year 1875. He was married in 1845, Dec. 30, to Sarah St.

Clair, daughter of James and Lovina (Ruarch) St. Clair, of Fayette County. The result of this union was fourteen children: George, Nancy, Sarah, Thomas, Rebecca, Walter, Martha, Matilda, Ellen, John and James, twins; Amanda, and a pair of twins who died at birth; also the mother at the same time. The above are children of James St. Clair. Mr. Smith, by his marriage, had ten children: John, Thomas, Geo. W., James T., Amanda L., Nancy, Jane, Walter, Frank and Clay. Two youngest died in infancy. Clay and John T. are also deceased. Those living are all married; three sons and one daughter reside in Bourbon County. The eldest daughter, Mrs. H. C. Parker, resides in Indianapolis; and Walter at Mt. Sterling. Mr. Smith in early life received but meagre educational advantages, attending the country schools less than six months, but by his studious and industrious habits he has laid up a store of knowledge which makes him one of the interesting and intelligent gentlemen of his neighborhood. He added to the support of his mother who lived with him until her death, at 86 years; also supporting an aged sister, and taking upon himself the support of the family after his father's death. He started in life without the advantages of fortune, but by diligence he has accumulated a comfortable home, and homes for his children around him.

BENJ. FRANKLIN SOPER, farmer; P. O. Cane Ridge; was born Nov. 5, 1828, upon the farm which he now owns, and upon which his father was also born. His mother was Luraner H. Prather, a native of Montgomery County, Md., and daughter of Walter Prathers and Ann Higgins, who came to Bourbon County, Ky., from Maryland, in 1806, with a large family of children, 14 in number, the mother of our subject being then 3 years of age. Charles Soper, the grandfather of our subject, was a native of Montgomery County, Md., but migrated to Bourbon County about 1800. The Sopers and Prathers and Crawfords were from the same neighborhood in Maryland, and after coming to Kentucky settled upon adjacent farms, the land now being owned in part by the subject of this sketch, whose ancestry were all very enterprising, energetic farmers and stock men and raised large families. B. F. Soper received but a meager education, being left an orphan at two years of age by the death of his father. However, by strict energy and native ability he acquired sufficient education to enable him to teach school, which he followed for some time, subsequently engaging in farming and stock raising, in which he was very successful. He was married June 20, 1853, to Miss Dorcas H. Crawford, a member of the pioneer Crawford family mentioned above. They had three children, all of whom are now living, viz: James C., who is connected with the M. K. & T. R. R. was married Oct. 6, 1881, to a Miss Christy, a native of Clay County, Mo., near Liberty, and two daughters, Mary Ellen and Sally Belle, who are living at home. Mr. Soper has been quite extensively engaged in stock traffic, but is now principally engaged in farming and stock-raising. Has been a life-long democrat, a man honored and esteemed by the community in which he lives. He and family are members of the M. E. Church South, in which he has held all the important offices from a sense of duty which he is always ready to perform.

JOHN W. SKILLMAN, farmer; P. O. North Middletown; proprietor of Willow Valley farm, was born Aug. 10, 1811, in Bedford County, Va.; he is the next youngest of a family of seven children, three sons and four daughters, by Isaac and Nancy (Whitely) Skillman; all were natives of Virginia; Isaac came to Bourbon County and settled near North Middletown, in the fall of 1816; where he purchased 216 acres of land (partly cleared) on the line of Bourbon and Clark Counties; his cabin; a double log one, was one-half in each county; all of his children grew to maturity, but two sons and two daughters are now living. Christopher, the youngest of the family, now resides in Platte County, Mo.; Catharine, a Mrs. (Allen) Shropshire, residing in Scott County; Harriette, a Mrs. Wilmott, of Bourbon; Isaac, died in 1856, in his eighty-fourth year, his wife in 1831, in her fifty-fifth year. Our subject received such an education as could be obtained in the log school house of his youth, and assisted in the farm work; upon Feb. 2, 1832, he was married to Adaline Henderson, a resident of Scott County; by her he had seven children, viz: one died in infancy; Isaac, married Cynthia Hayes and resides in Humbolt County, Neb.; A. J., whose sketch appears in this work; John W., married Susan Mark, of Montgomery County, she died in June 1879; Amanda J., now a Mrs. John T. McCauley, residing in Harrison County; Nannie A., a Mrs. George W. Cunningham, who died March 30, 1881, leaving four children, he resides in Ellis County, Texas; Charles C., married to Miss Olivia Price, and resides at Eufaula, Ala.; the wife of Mr. Skillman died in 1848, and he subsequently married Lydia Chambers, a native of Scott County, born Feb. 17, 1817, and a daughter of James and Kittie (Johnson) Chambers, who were natives of Virginia; by her he had three sons: William G., who married Miss Dee Rice, and resides in Clark County; Richard C., and Benjamin F., at home. Mr. Skillman has devoted his life to farming, stock driving to the extreme South, and of late years has paid some attention to the raising of thoroughbred Cotswold sheep; he is a conservative Democrat, and with his family holds a membership in the Christian Church.

JOHN SOPER, farmer; P. O. Cane Ridge; born Feb. 26, 1822, to Lawrence Soper, who was born Sep. 10, 1800; died in Nov., 1877, having raised a family of seven sons by Luraner Soper, his cousin, our subject being the first born. The Sopers were originally from London, England, Cornelius Soper coming to this country and settling in Maryland long before the Revolutionary war. He had seven sons, six of whom espoused the cause of the British, while the remaining son fought for the rights which we to-day enjoy, and at the close of the war settled in the South, and from whom the subject of this sketch derives his ancestral lineage. The other sons all lived to see the close of the war, and settled in the North. Our subject received rather poor educational advantages, but by his great love for books, he mastered the common branches and the Latin language, subsequently engaging in teaching, having received an injury to one of his limbs, which disabled him. He married Oct. 6, 1853, a Mrs. Mary Jane Champ, *neé* Collins, daughter of William Collins, he of Foster Collins, who was a prominent man in the early history of the county, having held for several terms the office of Sheriff of the county. By this marriage there have been born unto them six children, three of whom died in infancy; those living are Eugene B., born Jan. 24, 1857, married to a Miss Rachael Melton Sept. 1, 1880; L. A., born April 6, 1862, attending college at North Middleton; and John, March 30, 1873. In the spring of 1854 he engaged in farming and stockraising upon 100 acres of land which he purchased, going in debt for a considerable sum, but by perseverance and energy he has cleared up the debt and added to his possessions, so that he now has a beautiful home of 250 acres, with all the modern improvements. He now holds the position of Deputy Clerk of Flat Rock Precinct, under J. M. Hughs. He and family are members of the Christian Church.

THORNTON SEE; P. O. Plum Lick; a son of Geo. See, he of Jacob, who was born on the south branch of the Potomac, in Virginia. He came to Lexington about 1780, where his son George was born in 1784; died in his 57th year. Jacob See came to the farm now owned by Wm. See in about 1786, the farm continuing in that name until the present time. The mother of Thornton was a Miss Margaret Thornton, daughter of Thomas Thornton, who came from near Dublin, Ireland, having ran away from that country when a boy; and upon his arrival in America joined the British army, but before the war closed united his lot with the Americans. His wife was Betsey Robinson, a native of South Carolina, where they were married, thence came to Flat Rock precinct. Geo. See had a family of six sons and three daughters. The subject of this sketch was married Feb. 28, 1856, to Mary N. Watkins, daughter of Wm. and Frankie (Frost) Watkins; she a daughter of Joshua Frost and a Miss Phillips, natives of Virginia. By this marriage there have been eight children: the first a son, died in infancy; the eldest now living, Preston S., born May 17, 1858; Geo. D., Nov. 3, 1860; Fanny T., Feb. 3, 1863; Benj. L., Nov. 19, 1865; Margaret E., Jan. 24, 1869; Mary B. April 24, 1872; Tilden, Feb. 10, 1876.

A. J. SKILLMAN, farmer; P. O. Cane Ridge; proprietor of Walnut Grove Farm; is a son of John W. Skillman (whose sketch appears in this work); born Nov. 24, 1834, on Cane Ridge, where he has since resided, coming to his present home in February, 1858. He received a limited education, then engaged in farm work with his father, and spent a short time near Decatur, Ill., returning home in July, and on the following Sep. 26, 1856, he was married to Miss Julia Allen, of Harrison County, and daughter of David and Ellen (Berry) Allen; he a native of Bourbon County, where he spent his early manhood, then moved to Harrison, where he afterwards became a prominent farmer and stock raiser of that county. By this marriage there have been ten children; a son and daughter died in infancy. Those living are: John A., born July 17, 1857; David Clay, Dec. 8, 1858; Harvey A., Jan. 22, 1860; Charles M., April 22, 1864; Benjamin F., Feb. 15, 1866; I. B., Jan. 7, 1871; Wm. F., July 1, 1873; Hattie S., July 4, 1879. Mr. Skillman is an industrious and enterprising farmer. A conservative-democrat politically, and with his wife a member of the Cane Ridge Church.

JOHN TARR, farmer; P. O. Cane Ridge; born in Nicholas County, Ky., June 18, 1834, to John B. and Milly (Turner) Tarr (see Robert Tarr's history). John, the youngest son, received a limited education, but by his own energy and personal effort, he has acquired a general knowledge superior to that of the ordinary farmer. His ability and energy since attaining to his majority has been turned in the agricultural channel, in which his efforts have been crowned with success. He was not married until he had passed his forty-third year, when upon Nov. 1, 1877, he was united in marriage to Miss Sarah Earlywine, a native of Bourbon County, and daughter of Lewis and Dulcenia (Cannady) Earlywine, natives of Nicholas County. They have no children. He is a solid Democrat of the conservative order.

HENRY TODD WILSON, farmer; P. O. Cane Ridge; proprietor of Snow Hill farm; is a son of Joseph, he of Henry Wilson, who came at a very early date from near Culpepper Court House, Va., to Boonesborough, where he took an active part in the building of that place. Was also one of the company who built the block-house and established the fort at "Bryant's Station." At an early age he married a Miss Faulkner, who was a daughter of one of the first settlers at Bryant's Station, and afterwards one of the most prominent and wealthy families of Fayette County. Soon after marriage he removed to the neighborhood of Flat Rock, where he subsequently purchased a 5,000 acre tract of land which (to induce a settlement), he gave to numerous families. Being impressed by a strong belief that a salt well could be secured upon his farm, he determined to make the effort, which required a great amount of time, labor, and the exhausting of all his means. His efforts, however (to the surprise of all the settlers), were crowned with success, which made him the first proprietor of a salt well in Kentucky. The only salt manufactured in the State before that at his works, was by Daniel Boone, at the Blue Licks. Joseph Wilson was the seventh child of a family of eleven children—four sons and two daughters older than himself. He was born in the year 1800, near Flat Rock, when the country was yet in its infancy. He received a limited education, engaging, at an early age, in the capacity of drover, taking to the eastern markets numerous herds of all kinds of stock, and after the advent of railroads continued in the business as an extensive shipper. At twenty-seven years of age he was married to Nancy McCoy, daughter of Thomas McCoy, who resided near Chillicothe, Ohio, by whom he had five sons and three daughters, the subject of this sketch being the second son. The Wilson family have been noted as a long-lived people, of Scotch-Irish descent, the great-grandfather coming with his parents, when an infant, to the city of Philadelphia, in which, without relatives, he was, at the age of seven years, left an orphan by the death of both parents. The subject of this sketch attended school at Flat Rock, becoming quite proficient in the common branches and the Latin language, under the instruction of Prof. Milligan. After eighteen years of age he engaged in the stock business with his father. He was married on the 15th of May, 1855 (at twenty-seven years of age), to Miss A. E. Young, daughter of Johnson A. Young, a prominent stock dealer and farmer near Mt. Sterling, Montgomery County. By this marriage there are four children: William, a law student at Mt. Sterling; Sallie H., Lizzie B. and Mary M. Mr. Wilson spent eight years in Congress lobbying upon bills for the remuneration of his neighbors and himself for the loss of stock during the war. He is a man of honor and integrity and business ability, and, with his family, belong to the Christian church.

BENJ. F. WALLS, farmer; P. O. Cane Ridge; proprietor of Maple Grove Farm, was born Aug. 12, 1840, to Zachariah and Tempa (Osbourn) Walls; she a daughter of William and Keziah Osbourn, who emigrated from Germany to Clark County, Kentucky, settling on Red River, where he raised a large family by two wives. Zachariah was a son of Thos. Walls, who removed with his family from Richmond, Va., to Bath County, Ky., at an early date, he being the youngest of two sons and four daughters; was born in Kentucky. Thos. Walls was a soldier, and was badly wounded in the Revolutionary War. The parents of our subject had ten sons and seven daughters, viz.: Olmstead, died in the Mexican war; Betsy Ann, a Mrs. Myers, died in Illinois, whither she had gone; William married Eliza Alexander and resides in Bates County, Mo.; Reuben, also in Missouri; Isaac married Mary Simms, and died in Bates County, Mo., where his widow now resides; Thomas married Sally Fulton, and resides in Bates County, Mo.; James married Sarah Markwell and resides in Illinois; Kittie A., now a Mrs. Anderson, residing in Cass County, Mo.; Benjamin F., George, deceased; John, married first, Mary Sharp; second, Annie Fletcher, and resides in Bates County, Mo.; Malvina, now a Mrs. Mark Kimes, also in Bates County, Mo.; Violina, a Mrs. Cummins Kilbe, living in Fleming County, Ky.; Tempa, a Mrs. William Williams, residing in the State of Illinois; Keziah, a Mrs. Johnson, in Colorado, and Edgar in Missouri; Malvina and Violina and Keziah and deceased infant were twins. The parents of our subject both died while he was yet young, and being thrown upon his own resources at eighteen years of age, he came to Bourbon County and worked on a farm one year at $15 per month; then went to Richmond, Va., where he engaged in the mule trade for Green & Walker, at $25 per month, continuing for about two years; he then came to the farm which is now his present home, where he worked for his mother-in-law at $15 per month until his marriage, Aug. 21, 1862, to Maria L. Wasson, daughter of Samuel and Sarah (Martin) Wasson; he a native of Pennsylvania, she of North Carolina. Maria L. is the youngest of seven children, two only of whom are now living, the above and Mrs. Elizabeth Summers, of Nicholas. By this marriage Mr. Walls had three children: a son, died in infancy;

Carrie Martin, born June 19, 1866; and Charles Robert, April 25, 1870. He is engaged in farming stock-raising and trading. He started in life a poor boy, but by persistent energy he has accumulated property, and has been liberal in the improvement and education of his children, who are his highest pride.

THOMAS WOODFORD, farmer; P. O. Cane Ridge; was born in Virginia, Oct. 3, 1823, to Wm. and Maria (Archer) Woodford; she a daughter of Dr. Sam. Archer and a Miss Rotherk, all of whom were natives of Caroline County, Va. William Woodford came to Clark County, Ky., with his wife and six children : Mary (deceased), John, Samuel, William, Lucy, and Thomas. after their arrival in Kentucky two others were born, Sally and Madison. All reside in Bourbon County except Samuel, a prominent farmer of Clark County, and Madison, a prominent physician of Harrison. The two daughters were married to cousins, William T. and William Buckner. The father of our subject was a son of John T. and Mary (Tolliver) Woodford, who came to Clark County, Ky., in the fall of 1819, where he engaged in agriculture until his death. The early Woodford ancestry were quite noted in military affairs, the great-grandfather a General in the revolutionary war, and the grandfather a Colonel in the war of 1812. The subject of this sketch received a poor education in the pioneer schools of the day. At the early age of 9 years he was left an orphan by the death of his father; he remained at home until sixteen years of age, when he began working by the month and year, continuing in that capacity until the year 1855,when he rented a farm; living as a rentor until 1861, when he purchased a 300 acre tract, to which he has added, being now in possession of several hundred acres of excellent blue grass land, well stocked, which makes him a handsome fortune. He is an example of industry and frugality, starting out in life a poor boy, but with a determined effort to succeed, he has gained a position among the wealthiest and most prominent agriculturists and stock-raisers of the county; but without a " better half " as a sharer of his wealth, " joys and sorrows," having always lived a bachelor life.

WILLIAM C. WILKERSON, physician ; P. O. Cane Ridge; was born Feb. 8, 1854, to Thomas J. and Anna (Grigsby) Wilkerson, who were natives of Montgomery County, Ky. The grand-parents were N. A. Wilkerson, probably a native of Virginia, his wife formerly a Miss Wells. Thomas J. Wilkerson graduated at the Transylvania University at Lexington, in the year 1848, and immediately began the practice of medicine in Madison County, Ky., where he remained about two years, when he removed to his present home at Kiddville, Clark County, Ky., where he is a member of the County Medical Society, has a very large practice and is a man of popularity in the community. They have five children: William C., Anna M., now a Mrs. E. C. Fox; Emma, now a Mrs. A. A. Clay, who is a prominent man of Clark County; Ivan Ora and Mary Eliza at home. The subject of this sketch received a good education, graduating at the Commercial College at Louisville, also received a diploma from the University of Louisville, on the 25th day of Feb., 1881, when he began the practice of his profession at Flat Rock, having prior to his graduation practiced with his father for about eighteen months. He was married May 12, 1881, to Olive Robbins, daughter of Alonzo Robbins, who was for several years a minister of considerable note in the Christian Church; died about the close of the war. Dr. Wilkerson is a young man of ability and affable manners, by which he has already built up an extensive practice.

James S Moore

NORTH MIDDLETOWN PRECINCT.

JOEL S. BERRY, farmer and breeder of Short-horns, etc.; P. O. North Middletown; is a native of Bourbon County, and was born Feb. 24, 1830. His great-grand parents were of English birth. His grandfather Bazil Berry, and his son Benjamin, emigrated from Maryland, their native state, about the year 1790, and settled in Bourbon County, Ky. Benjamin was born at Hagerstown, Maryland, in 1772, and was first married, shortly after his arrival in Kentucky, to Miss Bowen, a sister of Benjamin Bowen who is well known in the northern part of this County. By this marriage there were ten children. He next married Elizabeth Gault, of Chambersburg, Penn.; the result of this union was two children, one daughter Amanda, who is now the wife of Dr. N. Cannon, of Scott County, Ky., and one son, Joel S. who is the subject of our sketch. He remained at the homestead and assisted his father in the duties of the farm until his father's death, which occurred on the 3rd of April, 1847. Joel was educated at the country schools in his immediate neighborhood, and on the 6th of January 1853, was married to S. Kate, daughter of John Butler, a native of Virginia. This union was blessed with nine children, two dying in infancy. There are living two sons, Walter G., and James Patterson, and five daughters, Alice M., who is now the wife of C. W. Cannon of Missouri, L. Florence, Carrie W., Sallie K., and Annie L. On Sept. 10, 1878, Mr. Berry lost his wife, and on Feb. 1, 1881, was again married, to Miss Mary K. Ware, who was born in South Carolina, but raised in Atlanta, Ga., by an uncle. She was one of the ladies that were sent from that city by Gen. Sherman in 1864, under his general order, that all the women and children should leave the city, that were able to do so. Mr. Berry has been speculating in short-horns for twenty-five years, and for the past few years has been a successful breeder of the same. He has also been a breeder of trotting and saddle horses and Cotswold sheep for the past twenty-eight years. Mr. Berry owns 380 acres of land, is one of the representative farmers of his county; has always been a very active and energetic man and ever alive to the progress and advancement of his end of the county. He was instrumental in building the North Middletown and Winchester, and North Middletown and Owingsville Pikes; was for fifteen years, President of the first named road, and for two years President of the other. Mr. Berry was also one of the principal laborers in getting up the stock, and effecting the organization of the North Middletown Deposit Bank, in 1869; he has been a director of the same since its first organization, and in January, 1881, was elected President of that institution, a position he still occupies. He has been a prominent member of the I. O. O. F., and was one of the charter members of Williams Lodge, No. 113, at North Middletown, and was the first member to pass through all its chairs. Mr. and Mrs. Berry and his five eldest children, are all members of the Christian Church, in which he has filled the office of Deacon for many years. Politically he belongs to the dominant party of his State, and is ever ready, at State or national elections to cast his ballot with the Democratic party.

GEORGE T. BRADLEY, farmer; P. O. North Middletown; son of William and Mahala (Kirkpatrick) Bradley, and was born Aug. 29, 1845; his grandfather, Thomas Bradley, was a native of Virginia, and was born March 5, 1761; when quite young he emigrated to Kentucky, and was married in Lexington, March 5, 1788, to Philadelphia Ficklin; she was born Dec. 15, 1768. By this marriage there were seven sons, viz: Robert, William, Henry, James, John, Jephtha, and Joseph, and two daughters, Margaret and Mary. The second son, William Bradley, was born Feb. 24, 1793, and died Aug. 8, 1861. He was first married in 1818, to Sallie Jenkins; she died May 25, 1819, leaving one son, Robert. William was next married on the 18th of Feb., 1826, to Mahala Kirkpatrick. They had born to them two sons, James W., and George T. (subject), and seven daughters, viz: Sarah M., Eliza J., Amanda F., Mary A., Nancy K., Miranda K., and Mahala F. The mother, Mahala Bradley, died Oct. 28, 1875. The subject of this sketch enlisted in the Confederate army, in June, 1862, under General Morgan. He was in several warm engagements; was wounded three times, once pretty severely; the evidences of which he carries to this day; he served till the close of hostilities, and then returned to Bourbon County, Ky., where he was married on the 25th day of June, 1867, to Susie T., daughter of George L. Redmon. This union has been blessed with two daughters, viz: Mary M., born April 28, 1868, and Lutie T., born Sept. 19, 1870. In 1866, George T. engaged in the grocery business at Dover, Mason County,

Ky., and continued there successfully for two and a half years. He next went to Paris, Ky., and again engaged in the mercantile business. After remaining there about three years, he concluded to remove to the country and engage in agricultural pursuits, a vocation he still adheres to. Mr. Bradley and wife are members of the Christian Church, and he is a Democrat in politics.

S. WESTBERRY COLLINS, farmer; P. O. North Middletown; son of Foster and Elizabeth (Matheney) Collins, and was born in Bourbon County, Feb. 12th, 1817. Foster Collins emigrated from Orange County, Va., in the year 1797, and settled temporarily on the Maysville road in Bourbon County, between Paris and Millersburg; he afterward bought a farm on Cane Ridge, at a point about equidistant from the two towns above mentioned, where he located permanently; he married Elizabeth Matheney, a native of Maryland, who emigrated with her father to this State, during the pioneer period of its history; the result of this marriage was ten children reared to maturity, five sons and five daughters; The third son, S. Westberry, who is the subject of our sketch, was married on the 12th of Sept., 1839, to Elizabeth H., daughter of Wm. Hansford, of Bourbon; this union was blessed with one child, Mary E., who is now the wife of Robt. W. Owen, near North Middletown; on Sept. 12th, 1840, just one year from the date of his marriage, Mr. Collins buried his wife, and from that time to the present, a space of forty-one years, he has lived a single life, centering his heart and affections upon his only child, with whom he now lives in his old days; he has retired from an active life and is enjoying some of the fruits of his past labors. He is a Democrat in politics.

WILLIAM A. CLINKINBEARD, farmer; P. O. North Middletown; was born June 24, 1820, and is a son of John and Sallie (Strode) Clinkinbeard; his grandfather, William Clinkinbeard, emigrated from Maryland, and was one of the first settlers of Strode's Station, in Clark County. He raised two sons and three daughters. The second son, John Clinkinbeard, was born about the year 1795, and was married in 1819 to Sallie, daughter of John Strode, whose father was the first settler of Strode's Station. By this marriage there were only seventeen children, and fifteen of them were raised to maturity. The oldest son, William A., who is the subject of our sketch, was married Sept. 2, 1847, to Harriet B., daughter of James W. Rice, spoken of elsewhere in this work. Our subject and Harvey W. Rice were the first importers of Cotswold sheep to this State; they purchased them of Col. Ware, near Winchester, Va., and was the first stock ever shipped over the Baltimore & Ohio railroad. These sheep cost them an average of $75 per head. Mr. Clinkinbeard and wife are members of the Christian Church.

HENSON DAVIS, farmer; P. O. North Middletown; a native of Montgomery County, and was born Jan. 24, 1817; his grandfather, John Davis, was of Virginia birth, where he married and raised a family of ten children, two sons and eight daughters. He subsequently emigrated to Ohio, and still later to Missouri, where he died. He was a soldier in the Revolutionary army, on account of which he was drawing a pension at the time of his death. The oldest son, James Davis, came to Kentucky about the year 1800, and in 1806 was married to Margaret Moore, of Bourbon County. After living at various places in this State and Ohio, he finally settled permanently on Aaron's Run, in Montgomery County, Ky., where he spent the remainder of his life. He was a soldier in the war of 1812, where he served with credit to himself and his friends. He raised a family of seven children, three sons and four daughters. He came to a premature death by being thrown from a young horse, in Houston Creek, near Paris, about the year 1821, and was drowned. The third son, Henson Davis, who is the subject of this sketch, was married Sept. 15, 1839, to Catharine, daughter of John Laughlin, of Bourbon County. By this marriage there were five children, two sons, viz: John Lucky, who married Ella Staten, of Illinois, where he now resides, and Thomas I., who married Pauline Campbell, of Nicholas County, near Carlisle. Thomas still lives at the homestead with his father. There were three daughters, Margaret A., wife of George W. Sparks; Martha E., wife of Daniel W. Bayless, and Mary Alice, who married Tilford Caywood. She died in 1877, leaving one son, Henry Stanton. Mr. Davis inherited by his wife 100 acres of land in Bourbon County, where he settled, and by industry and economy he has added to it from time to time, till he now owns 576 acres, three miles east of North Middletown; notwithstanding he has had his residence with nearly all of its contents twice destroyed by fire, during his married life, and each time caught him without any insurance. He is not a man that forfeits much of his valuable time on account of politics, yet he always votes with the Democratic party.

WATSON M. GAY, farmer and horse dealer; P. O. North Middletown; son of John D. and Catharine (Gardner) Gay, of Clark County, and was born on the 2nd of January, 1836; his grandfather, James Gay, was a native of Virginia, and was among the early emigrants to Kentucky, and settled on the waters of Stoner Creek, in Clark County, near Sydner's Mill; he raised six sons and one daughter. John D. Gay, the youngest son, was born in 1802, and in 1825 was married to Catharine, daughter of John Gardner, also of Clark County; by this marriage there were four sons and three daughters. Watson M., the youngest son, who is the subject of this sketch, remained with his father on the homestead and assisted in the duties of the farm until January the 22nd, 1857, on which day he was united in matrimony with Nancy, daughter of Johnathan Owen, of Bourbon County; soon after his marriage he moved on a farm five miles north of Paris, near Ewalt's X roads; after remaining here for six years, he purchased a nice farm of 440 acres lying two miles south of North Middletown on Winchester Pike, where he immediately moved and still resides. Mr. Gay has six children, one son, James Hodge, and five daughters, viz: Mary, wife of Jephtha Haggard, of Clark; Bettie, wife of John Sudduth, of Clark; Cinnie, Katie Hood, and Callie. Mary and Bettie are both graduates of Sayre Female Institute at Lexington, Ky. Mr. Gay is one of the representative farmers of the county; makes a specialty of fine horses, both single and matched teams; is a prominent exhibitor at most of the fairs throughout the State, and those that have been his rivals in many of these exhibitions pronounce him quite a formidable competitor; he well merits the enviable reputation he bears of being one of the best and most successful horsemen in central Kentucky; he is a man of very firm convictions, and is a descendant of a family long noted for their remarkable unanimity in religious beliefs; himself and every member of his family, that is old enough, are members of the Methodist Church, and as far back as their ancestry can be traced, without a single exception, they were all members of this religious denomination. Politically, he is an avowed Democrat.

THOMAS J. GOFF, farmer and breeder of short horns; P. O. North Middletown; is the son of Elisha and Nancy (Hedges) Goff, and was born May 9, 1821; his grandfather, Thomas J. Goff, was a native of Virginia, and emigrated to this State in 1790, and settled on Strodes' Creek, in Clark County; his grandfather on his mother's side was John Hedges, a native of Maryland, and came to Kentucky in 1792, and settled in Bourbon County. Elisha Goff, father of our subject, was born in Clark in 1795, and was married Dec. 25, 1817, to Nancy Hedges; she was born Nov. 17, 1799. The result of this union was two sons: John H. and Thomas J., and three daughters, viz.: Margaret P., Mary Ann, and Catharine T. Thomas J. remained with his father until his (father's) death, which occurred March 22, 1831. After this, our subject, in connection with his brother, continued farming in Clark County till 1857, at which time he came to Bourbon and bought his grandfather Hedges' farm, where he followed his favorite pursuit of farming, stock raising, etc., until 1861. About this time, becoming a little restless, and desiring a change of business, he removed to New York City, and engaged in the cattle broker business, where he remained till 1870. At this period he again returned to Kentucky, and settled on a farm near North Middletown, where he still resides. Mr. Goff was married Jan. 28, 1859, to Mary E. Stone, of Bourbon; this union was blessed with three children; two sons, viz.: John S. and May, and one daughter, Allie. In June, 1881, May Goff graduated at the K. C. & B. College, being then only seventeen years of age. His sister Allie is now a student of the same institution. Mr. and Mrs. Goff now own a nice little home of 140 acres, and he rents and controls about 1250 acres more. He is a non-partisan in politics.

THE HOUSTON FAMILY.—Peter and James Houston were early settlers in Bourbon County. Their father, Samuel Houston, was Scotch-Irish, and was born in Dublin, Ireland, in 1731; he emigrated to America in 1751, and located in Shenandoah County, Va., where he married a Miss Hamilton. In 1763 he emigrated to Iredell County, N. C., and when war was declared against the mother country, he enlisted as a soldier, and served to the end, receiving many wounds, but was never a prisoner. He lived to be ninety-nine years old, and died leaving four sons and three daughters, viz: Peter, James, Robert, Samuel, Prudence, Sarah and Jane. The two last named daughters, married Clarks, and lived and died in their native State, leaving children. The other, Prudence, married a Brown, had two sons and died in her native county, but her sons, Franklin and Houston Brown, emigrated to Ohio, where they still live. Samuel married an Alexander, and remained and died at his father's homestead, aged eighty-eight years; he left two sons, Franklin and Samuel, who emigrated to Georgia, in 1852, and located in Hickory Flat, in Cherokee County. The latter was a Colonel in the Confederate army, and after the close of the war, was a delegate to the convention that framed the new constitution of the State. Robert emigrated to Missouri and was a farmer; he was killed by the fall of a tree, leaving several children; some of his sons have distinguished themselves as breeders of Durham cattle, in that State and Illinois. The two remaining brothers of the old family, Peter and James, emigrated to Bourbon County, Ky., in the spring of 1786, and located on Cane Ridge in the North Middletown Precinct; here they battled against canebrakes, forests and the privations of life, which distinguished the lives of all the pioneers in this famous part of nature's wilderness, and were identified with all the hardships and privations to which the pioneers of new countries are always subjected. Peter married Mary Lucky, whose parents, and her two brothers, Joseph and Robert, and a sister who married And. Ireland, from Virginia, had come from Shenandoah County, Va. The same year, the Houstons came from "the old North State" and bought land adjoining them. James returned to his native State, and married Nancy Alexander, and brought her on horseback, through the howling wilderness, to his adopted home. They raised four sons, viz: James, Levy, Abner and Samuel. The first married Rachel Alexander, moved to Lawrence County, Ind., lived a successful farmer until he was eighty-five years of age, and died, leaving a large family of children in his adopted county. The second son married Abbie Kenney, sister of the late Victor Kenney of Bourbon; he was for many years, a Magistrate of Bourbon, lived a successful farmer and merchant, at Ruddel's Mills, and died at eighty years of age, leaving no children. The third married Sallie Horton, of Bourbon, emigrated to Cass County, Mo.; was a well-to-do farmer, died in his eighty-fifth year, leaving two living children; Arbell and James. The fourth and last, married Mary Foster, lived on Cane Ridge, until his sixty-sixth year, a prosperous farmer, and died childless. Peter Houston, the other pioneer, was a remarkable man. He was born Nov. 15, 1765; and although yet in his teens, he joined his father in the Revolutionary war, and did good service during the two last years of that fearful conflict. He was tall and commanding in person, was highly endowed and liberally educated. And after his location in Bourbon, he devoted all his spare time to reading and research, especially in matters of religion, being as was his brother James a devoted Presbyterian. And so close was his application, and so vast was his memory, that at forty years of age he could repeat from memory almost the entire Bible. And in 1801, when the Reformer, Barton Warren Stone, began his great revival at Cane Ridge he was one of the first to accept the new doctrine; he renounced Presbyterianism, and was immersed by Stone, as was his brother James. Thence, from house to house, he visited and exhorted his fellow-men to join in the reformation, and thus greatly swelled the ranks of the reformers; he was also instrumental in building the meeting-house, still standing, and called "Old Cane Ridge," on the spot where the Reformer held his great revival meeting. He helped to cut, hew, haul and build the logs used in that far-famed edifice. In politics he was a Whig, and an uncompromising emancipationist, freeing his own servants, and refusing to receive several that came to him by inheritance. And when Kentucky declared in favor of her second constitution, he canvassed the county urging the citizens to instruct their delegates to abolish slavery in their new constitution, and made hundreds of converts to his policy. But it failed in the convention. After a long and useful life, he and his wife died in their ninety-first year; he never wore spectacles, and, at his death had lost but one tooth, and that was kicked out when a boy, by firing a musket at a wild turkey. At his death he left six children, all sons, viz: John, Carey, Richard, Harvey, Alford, and Samuel. John emigrated to Tennessee, married, was a prosperous farmer, and died in his eightieth year, leaving several children; Carey married Jane Campbell, emigrated to Monroe County, Ind., lived the life of a farmer, died at seventy-five and left several children; Richard married Rachel Smith, located in Bloomington, Ind., was a mechanic, and died at seventy-four, leaving children; Harvey married Ibba Hamilton, located in Monroe County, Ind., was a successful farmer, and died at seventy-two years of age leaving three children; Alford married Jane Smith, was a farmer in Monroe County, Ind., died at seventy-two, leaving several children; Samuel alone, of the six brothers, remained in Bourbon. He was a remarkable man and widely known. He was born in 1781, March 5; he was tall and dignified, was talented and well educated, and had a wonderful memory, he could read a page or hear a speech and repeat, either, from memory almost *verbatim*. His father educated him for the ministry, and then placed him under the care and tutorage of the Reformer Barton Stone. But one year of application convinced him, as well as his tutor, that his tact was not theological. He possessed wonderful pantomime and mimic qualities, and his descriptive powers were grand. These qualities inclined him to the stage, and he was prevented from adopting the dramatic profession with the greatest difficulty by his father. He then married Morning Adams, daughter of John Adams; who was an immigrant from Maryland, and claimed to be a near relative of John Adams, the president, for whom he was named. After his marriage, his father placed him on a small farm, that he might try his hand in agriculture. At this he labored during cropping seasons, and devoted the remainder of his time in executing any and all jobs he could engage from his neighbors; and so apt was he in architecture that he learned to complete a house in all its parts, stone work, carpentering, plastering and painting, and did so complete many; he helped to build the old Paris jail, and the bridge there across the Stoner. Like his father, he was a Whig and emancipationist, and a member of the Christian Church. When the war of 1812 came on, he volunteered his services, but the day before his company was to march, a messenger came informing him that his oldest child was very ill, when he was permitted to substitute Jerry Terry in his place, and reached home just in time to see his child die. In 1827, he sold his farm, with a view to going West, but having ruptured a blood vessel in his lungs, he remained on rented land, hoping to recover, but finally died at the age of forty-seven, leaving nine children ; five sons, and four daughters, viz: Joanna, Irena, Pattie, Mary, Washington, John Q. A., Jefferson P., Clinton M., and Franklin W. The two first died single, the third married Delany Yourk, of Indiana, who is a wealthy farmer in Monroe County of that State ; Mary married Harrison Parks of Indiana, who is a farmer in LaSalle County, Ills.; Washington, married Nancy Parker, of Bourbon ; and John Q. A., married Rachel Taylor, of Indiana ; and both these brothers died ministers of the Christian Church in Illinois ; Jefferson P., married Sarah A. Holtzman, of Bloomington, Ind., and is now a farmer and a breeder of short-horn cattle, in Livingston County, Ills.; and Franklin W., married Fannie L. Simpson, whose father, Levi Simpson, and whose mother Nancy Priest, that was come to Bourbon from Shenandoah County, Va., in 1780. He still remains the only Houston in Bourbon of the old families. Franklin W. was born in 1818, Sept. 22 ; completed his education at Indiana State University, in 1840, and studied law with a view to its practice, but his health having failed, he was advised by his physician to abandon the law and engage in agriculture, which advice he heeded. And by cultivating the soil and trading largely in mules and cattle, he succeeded in securing a comfortable home upon which he now lives, near the homestead of his grandfather, the old pioneer. And still, at the age of sixty-three years, he is devoted to his farm, and is a breeder of Durham cattle and Cotswold sheep. He has always been, and still is, with all his family, a member of the Christian Church, and was for many years, previous to the war, a regular lecturer to the congregation of North Middletown. He was eight years one of the magistrates of the county, and has ever been a devoted friend of common schools and colleges, and has done much, and given much, to advance educational interests. He is also an advocate of internal improvement, and was chiefly instrumental in having inaugurated the Bourbon plan of macadamizing public roads, and contributed liberally for that purpose; he has also written considerably for the press, both political and religious, and on a variety of topics, and in all respects has ever been identified with the interests of his county and State. Thrice was he nominated by the Republican party as a candidate for the State Legislature, and twice made the race, but the Democratic party being largely in the majority he was defeated. Mr. H. has eight children, viz.: Nannie M., who married Daniel Boone, a farmer of Bedford, Ind., and a near relative of the renowned pioneer; French W., who married Fannie Wofford, of Tennessee, and now lives in Lonoke, Ark., trading in cattle and hogs to Little Rock; Laura E., who married Dr. Albert G. Craig, of Ghent, Ky., now a physician in Vevay, Ind.; Fannie L., who married Henry C. Stone, of Bourbon, a farmer in the Flat Rock Precinct; Richard M., who married Ella Young, of Platte City, Mo., and is a merchant in Humboldt, Kas.; Jefferson who is single and is with his father; Quene, who married Joseph Rion, of Paris, Ky., and lives with her parents; and last is Joseph Daniel, who is single, and is practicing law in Winfield, Kan. This is a promising young man; he was educated at Kentucky University and the Law College of Cincinnati; he is talented and educated, commanding in person and impressive in manner, and his friends predict for him a bright future. Already, though but twenty-three years of age, he has won a wide notoriety by his eloquent, pointed and successful advocacy in several important cases at the bar. All of W. H.'s children are educated, and members of the Christian Church. In conclusion, Peter Houston is authority for saying that the name Houston was originally spelled House-son, and later Houseton, and still later Houston, and that some branches of the family had, in his day, still further abridged it to Huston; that other names had been similarly changed, resulting in some instances in forfeiture of estates, legatees being unable to reconcile the spelling of their names with that of the legators. Such changes should not be made without acts of legislation, to which posterity can appeal.

JOHN W. JEWELL, farmer; P. O. North Middletown; is a native of Bourbon County, and was born on the 12th of August, 1830. His father, Ewell Jewell, was born on Bull Run Creek, in Virginia, on the 1st day of March, 1790, and died the 22nd of February, 1862. He came to Kentucky in the fall of 1805 and settled at Winchester. He was a soldier in the war of 1812 and served eighteen months. Was married first to Elizabeth Couchman, by whom he raised four children, three sons : Leslie, Frederick, and Benjamin, and one daughter, Cassie. About the year 1822 he lost his wife, and again married, Augus the 1st, 1829, to Lucinda Boggs, whose father and mother were natives of Ireland. By this marriage there were seven children, four sons: John W., Wm. Allen, Peter Mason and Ewell, and three daughters, Mary E., Sarah M., and Armilda. John W., the eldest son by the last wife who is the subject of this sketch, was married, August the 12th, 1852, to Amanda White, of Clark County. This union resulted in nine children, four sons: Peter L., James W., David E. and Sherman, and five daughters, Lucinda, Jane, Frances C., Armilda and Amanda. Mr. Jewell enlisted, Oct. 2, 1862, in the Federal Army, 26th Kentucky Reg., Co. A., and served till June the 30th, 1865, at which time he was mustered out at Salisbury, N. C. He then returned to Kentucky and took his wife and family and moved to Powell County. From there he removed to Bourbon County, where he still resides. Mr. and Mrs. Jewell and one daughter, Frances C., are members of the Missionary Baptist Church. He is a Democrat in politics.

JOSIAH A. JONES, farmer; P. O. North Middletown; is a native of Bourbon County, and was born March the 16th, 1826. His grandfather, James Jones, was a native of Virginia, and emigrated at an early day to Kentucky, and settled near Clintonville. William S., his second son, was born in 1784 and died in 1844. Was married about the year 1818 to Nancy Ashurst, of Bourbon County, by whom he raised four children, one daughter, Nancy R., who is now the widow of Charles Howerton, and three sons: John W., Benjamin and Josiah A., the latter of whom is the subject of this sketch. He was married April the 15th, 1847, to Leoma Talbott, of Bourbon, who was born August the 7th, 1830. This union was blessed with four children, two sons: Wm. Mason and Allen Gano, and two daughters, Susan A., wife of Alex. K. Young, and Mary L., wife of John G. Redmon. Mr. Jones owns 210 acres of land northwest of North Middletown, Ky. He and wife, also his two daughters, are members of the Christian Church. He is a Democrat in politics.

WILLIAM H. KERR, farmer and breeder of fancy horses; P. O. North Middletown; was born Feb. 18, 1853, and is a son of John W. and Elizabeth A. (Seamands) Kerr, who were married on the 23d of July, 1846. The result of this marriage was two sons, viz.: John A., who died when eight years of age, and William H. (the subject of this sketch), born at his grandfather's, Preston J. Seamands, who is mentioned elsewhere in this work. His (subject's) father, died when he was but eight months old, and he lived with his mother at her father's until the age of six years, when, on May 16, 1859, his mother was again married to J. C. Long, a merchant of New York City. Four years afterwards, subject, with his mother and her husband, to whom he was greatly attached settled in Brooklyn, where he (subject) was a student at the Polytechnic Institute for about three years; he then returned to his native State and entered the Kentucky University at Lexington, living in the family of Prof. Robert Graham for about one year; he then returned and finished his education at Brooklyn, after which he was connected with the Brooklyn Gas Company for about one year; then in the *Tribune* office for a short time. But his natural love for the farm, and his interest in fine horses, brought him back to the home of his childhood, and in 1870 he came back to Kentucky, bringing with him his half-brother, E. C. Long, then only ten years of age, and his mother, who was again a widow, followed in a few months, and has made her home here ever since. With that natural love for the horse characteristic of the true Kentuckian, Mr. Kerr at once embarked in the business of breeding and rearing fine horses; his first venture was the purchase of "Blue Bird," a roan mare by Kerr's Black Hawk, and out of a mare by Kerr's Copper Bottom; he paid $200 for this mare at a three-year old, and when six years old he could have sold her for $2,500. This noted mare competed at the Paris Fair, in 1874, with eight other speed mares—the best in the State—for the prize (silver pitcher and goblets) offered by the *Kentucky Live Stock Record*, and was the honored victor, bearing off the palm in the hotly contested ring. Mr. Kerr next bought the noted trotting stallion "Driftwood," for which he paid $1,000; he raised and sold a large number of his colts, besides buying and handling all his colts raised by other parties that he could get hold of. In 1880 Mr. Kerr took in his brother, E. C. Long, as his partner, the style of the firm being W. H. Kerr & Bro.; the firm now has a fine stable, 47x100 feet, finished off in the most approved style, with all modern conveniences, and own seventy head of horses, one of the most noted of which is "Ed. Clark," a black stallion, by "Driftwood;" dam by "Mambrino Medley;" this horse took the premium at the Sharpsburg and Paris Fairs, when only four years old, against more aged horses; "Woodbridge Girl" and "Woodbridge Boy" are both promising young trotters; either of them can show better records than 2.30. Mr. Kerr owns 315 acres of fine blue grass land, and controls 750 acres more. Upon his own farm he has a handsome residence, built at his special orders, and after his own plans and designs, and which is furnished and fitted up with most excellent taste. He was married, Jan. 12, 1875, to Miss Fannie L., daughter of William Skinner, of this county.

She was educated at the schools of the neighborhood, and at Hocker Female College, Lexington. They have three children, viz.: Clarence, born Dec. 25, 1875, and Fred S., and William G. (twins), born Aug. 1, 1877. Mr. Kerr is an enterprising young man; liberal in every movement for the good and progress of his neighborhood, and a Republican in politics.

ED. C. LONG, farmer and horse dealer; P. O. North Middletown; son of James C. and Elizabeth (Seamands) Long, and was born Oct. 7, 1861. His father was a Virginian by birth, and came to Kentucky when quite young with his parents, and settled near Danville, Boyle County, where he remained till he was eighteen years of age; he was educated at Center College, Danville, and was a classmate of Gen. John C. Breckinridge. Shortly after Mr. Long finished his education, we find him in Baltimore, engaged as salesman in the mercantile business with his cousin, Ellis B. Long, who was at that time one of the most prominent and successful merchants of that city. After he had become thoroughly conversant with that branch of business upon which he had embarked, and being full of ambition, we next find him in the great city of New York, as junior partner with Lee, Case & Co., merchants of that city. James C. was married on the 16th of May, 1859, to Elizabeth A., widow of John W. Kerr, of Bourbon County, Ky.; the result of this marriage was four children, three daughters, viz : Mary Bell, who died in infancy; Fannie L., who died at the age of eleven years, and Bessie A., born Sept. 2, 1870, and is now a student at the K. C. and B. College at North Middletown, and one son, Ed. C., who is the subject of this sketch. Our subject was born at his grandfather Seamond's, in Bourbon County, Ky., and at the age of two years was taken by his parents to New York City, where he remained about ten years, and then returned to Kentucky, accompanied by his half-brother, William H. Kerr, with whom he has since associated himself as partner, the style of the firm now being William H. Kerr & Bro., horse dealers. For a more extended notice of this firm, see biography of William H. Kerr in this work. Our subject, Ed. C., who is yet quite young, being only twenty years of age, has been a student of the K. C. & B. College for a year, after which, through the influence of Prof. L. M. Sniff, ex-Professor of the above school, he was induced to enter Northwestern Ohio Normal School, in which institution Prof. Sniff is very prominently connected, and Ed. C. at this time one of his favorite pupils. Being a young man of more than ordinary intelligence, excellent moral character, of indomitable energy and the importance of business indelibly stamped in him, from his earliest recollections up to the present time, we can but predict for him a bright and successful future.

PRESTON J. LINDSAY, farmer; P. O. North Middletown; son of Reuben Lindsay, who was born in Virginia, and emigrated to this State at an early day and married Nancy Wells; by this marriage there were three children: William H., who married Lucy Lockland in the year 1839; Greenberry, who died at the age of thirty-three; and Preston J., who is the subject of this sketch and was born July the 5th, 1817; when only three years of age he was left an orphan and was taken by his grandmother Wells, by whom he was reared and educated; he received a very liberal education in the old pioneer school houses of his neighborhood; his favorite study was mathematics, and in this valuable branch of education he had but few equals. After he arrived at the age of maturity and was thrown upon his own resources for a livelihood, he turned his attention to agricultural pursuits, and to the present time is a tiller of the soil and enjoying single blessedness. Mr. Lindsay has been prominently connected with the Masonic order since 1839. For three years he enjoyed the enviable position of High Priest of Washington Chapter, No. 26, and has been a Knight Templar and member of Lex. Commandery, No. 2, since 1870; he is also a straight Democrat in politics.

LEAH LAMME, farmer; P. O. North Middletown; Mrs. Lamme is a daughter of James Wells, a native of Maryland who emigrated to Kentucky at a very early day and married Katie Owens, a Virginian by birth, and whose father first settled and named the town of Owingsville, in Bath Co., Ky. Mr. Wells died at the age of 82 years, and his wife at the age of 89. Mrs. Wells was the mother of twelve children, five of whom are now living. Leah, the oldest daughter now alive, and who is the subject of this sketch, was born on the 10th of December, 1797, and was married in 1833 to James Lamme, who was killed with a knife on the 7th of July, 1839, by Peter Hedges. Mr. Lamme left a farm of 298 acres, where his widow still lives. She is now 84 years old, and is a member of the Dunkard Church.

JAMES S. MOORE, farmer; P. O. North Middletown; son of Elisha and Elizabeth (Money) Moore, and was born Sept. 20th, 1820, in Montgomery Co. His grandfather was a native of Scotland, and emigrated to Virginia prior to the struggle for independence. He was killed in the revolutionary army under General Washington. His (subject) grandmother was of English birth. His father, Elisha Moore, was born in Virginia and came to Kentucky about 1809. He married Elizabeth Money, of

Fairfax County, Va., by whom he had seven sons, and three daughters. The fourth son, James S., who is the subject of our sketch, was married Feb. 10, 1842, to Martha A. Bibb of Montgomery. By this marriage there are six living children. Three sons, viz: George A., who is a graduate of the Kentucky University at Lexington, and was honored with the valedictory address on that occasion. He is now a popular teacher at Clintonville. James M., the second son, was obliged to leave the above University, before graduating, on account of failing health. He subsequently regained his health and married Maggie Frazier, and is now one of the enterprising farmers of Clark County. The third son, W. L., married Annie King, of Clark, where he has also engaged in agricultural pursuits. There were also three daughters, viz: Matilda F., wife of J. G. Salmons; Mary E., wife of Thomas Hall, and Martha A., wife of Wm. Rion, of Paris. Martha A. Moore died Aug. 24, 1854. Mr. Moore was next married to Martha A. Crouch of Bath County, the 28th of Aug., 1855. This union is blessed with five living children, two daughters, viz: Minnie J., who is a graduate of the K. C. & B. College, at North Middletown, and now controls one of the best disciplined schools in Montgomery County, and Rosa E. who is a student at her sister's school. The eldest son, Sherman B., is now in the Bible Department of Kentucky University, where he will probably graduate this year; after which, he expects to make a preacher of the Gospel. Allie R. and Clarence E., the two youngest sons, are now students of the K. C. & B. College. Mr. Moore, through the whole course of his life, has been a very active and industrious man, and always placed a very high estimate on education as the above record will testify. He began life in moderate circumstances, reared and educated a large family, has contributed liberally to all charitable institutions that were presented to him, and now owns a nice little farm of 166 acres. He and his entire family are members of the Christian Church, and he is a Democrat in politics.

JOHN V. MOORE, farmer and trader; P. O. North Middletown; was born on Plum Lick, near the Bourbon and Montgomery line, on the 14th of February, 1822. His grandfather was a native of Ireland, and emigrated to the United States about the year 1770 and settled in Virginia, where he remained about eighteen years. He next came to Kentucky and settled near North Middletown, in Bourbon County, where he spent the greater portion of his after life. He was a prominent member of the Masonic Order in his day, and organized the first Masonic Lodge at the above town. He raised three sons and two daughters, and died at the age of eighty-four years. His second son, John Moore, was married about 1808 to Mrs. Mollie (Race) Fulton. The result of this union was seven children—two sons and five daughters. John Moore was a volunteer in the war of 1812, in Capt. Combs' Company, Col. Dick Johnson's regiment. Participated in the memorable battle of the Thames. Saw and examined the body of Tecumseh after he was killed. Immediately after the war he returned to his Kentucky home, where he passed the remainder of his life with his family. He was a man, being born in an honest period of our country's history, was scrupulously exact in all his dealings and assiduous in the discharge of every duty devolving upon him. He attached himself to the Christian Church when about the age of forty-five years, under the preaching of John T. Johnson. He was a man of firm convictions, an avowed Democrat through life, and died at the age of eighty-four. His second son, John V., who is the subject of this sketch, was married January 2, 1844, to Phebe A. Combs, by whom he raised three sons: Richard F., who was killed in the Morgan charge at Lebanon, Ky., on the 5th of August, 1863; Fulton R., who died at Camden, Mississippi, in 1870, and Kelly P., who married Mattie E., daughter of Elder John B. McGinn, on the December 22d, 1880, and who still resides with his father at the homestead. Mr. Moore and family are all members of the Christian Church, and are Democrats in politics.

KELLY MOORE, farmer; P. O. North Middletown; is the son of John Moore, and was born in Bourbon County, Jan. 13, 1827. His father was of Irish descent, but was born, reared and educated in Kentucky, and was first married in 1808 to Mrs. Mollie (Race) Fulton, by whom he raised seven children; his second marriage was to the widow Shryock; by this marriage there were three children—two sons and one daughter. The youngest son, Kelly Moore, who is the subject of this sketch, enlisted in the Confederate Army, in September, 1862, in the Eighth Kentucky Cavalry, under Col. Cluke; he was captured on the Ohio raid with Gen. John Morgan, July 26, 1863, taken to Camp Chase, where he was kept for a month, then removed to Camp Douglas, and was confined in prison till February, 1865; he was then released and permitted to return to his Kentucky home, where he again resumed his agricultural pursuits, and to this day he adheres to this, his favorite vocation. On June 5, 1865, Mr. Moore was united in marriage to Fannie, daughter of Moses S. Thomas, of Scott county; this union has been blessed with one child: Richard F., born July 5, 1867; he is now a student of the K. C. & B. College. Mr. Moore and family are members of the

Christian Church. He has a nice home of 170 acres called "Clover Dale."

☞See sketch of John V. Moore for the early history of this family.

JOHN B. MITCHELL, farmer; P. O. North Middletown; is a native of Bourbon County, and was born April 11, 1853; his grandfather, William Mitchell was a native of Virginia, and moved to Kentucky at a very early day, and settled in Montgomery County, where he raised a family of seven children—six sons: William, Hawkins, Thomas J., Strother, James, and Frank, and one daughter, Margaret who married John J. Anderson; she and her mother were killed by a terrific storm that passed over that country about the year 1848; the house that was occupied by the family at the time of the catastrophe was completely demolished. It is remarkable that seven other members, who were also in the house, miraculously escaped without the slightest injury. Thomas J. Mitchell, the third son, above spoken of, was first married to Miss Gaitskill, of Montgomery County; she only lived about twelve months afer her marriage. He next married Malinda Thomas, of Bourbon County, about the year 1849, and moved immediately to that county; this union was blessed by two children: John B., who is the subject of this sketch, and Alice, who is now the wife of Thomas Gaitskill, of North Middletown. John B. remained at the homestead and assisted in the duties of the farm up to the time of his father's death, which occurred April 16, 1862. At the death of his father, John B. inherited all of the home place, containing 300 acres, except his mother's dower, which he subsequently purchased. His sister Alice inherited 187 acres of the Warren Rogers place, known as the "Castle," which was purchased by her guardian about one year after her father's death; the remainder of the Rogers farm containing 133 acres, was given to their mother, Mrs. Mitchell. John B. is now one of the representative farmers of his county, and is also engaged in breeding and raising short horn cattle and Cotswold sheep. He is a member of the Christian Church at North Middletown, and a Democrat politically.

JOHN W. McCLURE, farmer and trader; P. O. North Middletown; is a native of Montgomery County, son of John and Mahala (Stofer) McClure and was born January 17, 1842. His great grandfather was a native of Ireland, and emigrated at an early day to the United States and stopped for a while in Virginia, and afterward came to Kentucky, where he died. His grandfather, Andrew McClure, settled in Montgomery County where he reared six sons and six daughters. The second son, John McClure, married Mahala Stofer, and settled in his native County, where he, like his father, raised six sons and six daughters. The second son, John W., our subject, after remaining on the homestead till the age of maturity, began business for himself, and on the 27th of March, 1877, was married to Mary C. Mark, of Montgomery. This union is blessed with one child, John Mark. In March, 1880, Mr. McClure moved to Bourbon County, where he now resides. He is an enterprising young man, and owns 135 acres of land, where he farms and handles stock. Mr. McClure and wife are both members of the Christian Church. He is a Democrat in politics.

MRS. BETTIE OWEN, farmer; P. O. North Middletown. Robert Owens was born in Maryland, and emigrated to Kentucky in 1784, and temporarily settled in Clark County; he married when twepty-two years of age and moved to Bourbon, where he reared a family of three sons and five daughters. Geo. W., the youngest son, was born on the 4th of April, 1813, and was married Feb. 13, 1839, to our subject, Miss Bettie, daughter of William Scott, of this county; by this marriage there were fourteen children, nine daughters, viz: Emma, wife of Dr. Joe Fithian, of Paris, Ky.; Nancy S., wife of Marcus Evans, of Clark County; Fannie, who married Wm. Boston, of this county, and died in April, 1881; Sallie, who died in 1867; Bettie, Cinnie, Mary Lou, Carrie and Dixie, and five sons: Joseph, who married Alice Scarce, of this county, and now resides in Ohio; Wm. R., who married the widow Peoples, of Bates County, Mo., where he now lives; Thomas, who is telegraphing in Chicago; George and John Ed, who are still at the old homestead with their widowed mother. Nancy S. graduated at Winchester Female College; Sallie graduated at Oxford, Ohio; Fannie at the Bourbon Female College; Carrie at the Millersburg Female College; Dixie and John Ed are now studen s of the K. C. & B. College. This family are nearly all Methodists; the sons are Democrats. Mrs. Owen has 230 acres of land.

JOHN R. OWEN, dealer in wines and liquors; P. O. North Middletown; is a native of Tennessee, and was born near Rogersville on the 14th of Feb., 1849; his father, W. A. Owen, was also of Tennessee birth, and was married in 1830 to Ellen Moore, by whom he raised ten children, three sons and seven daughters. The second son, who is the subject of our sketch, at the age of thirteen years, like many other boys of his age, became very patriotic, and enlisted in Co. D., Bradford's regiment, Vaughn's Brigade; his father was Captain of the above company; John R., after serving two years in the army, came to Kentucky and settled in Bourbon County, where he has since resided. He was married the 16th of June, 1877, to Nannie Walters, of this county; by this marriage there are two children, Jasper and Fannie E. Mr. Owen is now a resident of North Middletown; he is a Democrat in politics.

J. W. PRESCOTT, farmer and short-horn breeder; P. O. North Middletown. Subject is a native of Louisiana; was born in that State in 1833, where he spent the early part of his life. In 1875, he married Mrs. Mary E. (Bayless) Grimes, of Bourbon County, Ky., where he has since settled, and is engaged in agricultural pursuits. For the past two years he has been engaged, on a small scale, in the short-horn business. Has on hand at the present time, a small herd, selected with great care from the best familes this country affords. Col. Prescott is a gentleman of rare judgment and good business ability, and is likely to become a prominent short-horn breeder in the near future. His wife is a daughter of Nathan Bayless, who emigrated from Virginia at an early day, and settled in Bourbon County, where he raised a family of five children, one son and four daughters. Mary, the second daughter of whom we are now writing, was born in 1831; was educated at North Middletown, Ky., and in 1846 was married to John S. Grimes, of Clintonville. He died in 1865. Mrs. Grimes, after remaining a widow about ten years, was next married to Col. Prescott. She now owns a nice farm, containing about 675 acres of choice land. Her father, Mr. Bayless, when he first came to North Middletown, was without any means whatever, and began in the tailoring business. After getting a little money ahead, he bought a small piece of land, and began dealing in mules. Being a good judge of stock and careful in his purchases, good feeder and an excellent salesman, he soon found himself possessed of sufficient means to own one of the best farms in his county. At the time of his death he owned 1000 acres of fine Bourbon land.

C. H. RICE, farmer and breeder of short-horns; P. O. North Middletown; was born in Bourbon County, July 17, 1843, and is a son of James W. and Patsy (Boyle) Rice; his grandfather, John Rice, emigrated from Virginia to this State at an early day, and settled in Bourbon County, where he raised a family of seven children, three sons and four daughters. The second son, James W., was born Feb. 22, 1804, and was married Dec. 5, 1822, to Patsy C. Boyle, and died on the 11th of May, 1847. James W. ranked among the most prominent men in the county in his day, as was clearly demonstrated by his being twice sent to represent same in the State Legislature. This important position he filled to the entire satisfaction of his constituency, and with honor and credit to himself and family. He raised a family of eleven children, ten of whom survived him, four sons and six daughters, the third son living, C. H., who is our subject, remained on the homestead till the war broke out between the sections, and in 1862 he enlisted in the Confederate Army, under Col. Cluke; was captured with Gen. Morgan in Ohio on the 26th of July, 1863; was first taken to Camp Chase, and afterwards to Camp Douglass, where he remained a prisoner till the close of the war; in 1865 he returned to his Kentucky home, and on the 30th of April, 1867, he was married to Sarah E. Sydner, of Platte County, Mo.; by this marriage there were three sons, two of whom are living, James W., and John I. The youngest son, Henry S., was killed by lightning on the 9th of July, 1879. Mr. Rice owns a nice little farm of 65 acres, and rents 200 more, where he breeds and handles short-horns, of which he has now about thirty head. Mr. and Mrs. Rice and one son are members of the Christian Church; politically he is a Democrat.

RICHARD M. RICE, farmer; P.O. North Middletown; son of James W. Rice, and was born near North Middletown, Bourbon County, on the 28th of February, 1839. (For further notice of his parents, see sketch of C. H Rice in this work.) He received a good English education at North Middletown, where he could have graduated in another term. He began life as a farmer, an occupation he has never had cause to abandon. On the 21st of October, 1858, he was married in Nicholas County, to Jennie E., daughter of Col. I. H. Piper. Jennie E. was born at Jackstown, Bourbon County, on the 29th of March, 1838. Her father, Colonel Piper, was a native of Nicholas, born near Carlisle in 1810, and now lives in that beautiful little city, where he has retired from business. His wife, Parmelia J. Porter, was born in Fleming County, in 1812. Our subject, Mr. Rice, made the race in 1880 for the Democratic nomination for Sheriff of Bourbon County, but was defeated by a small majority. Mr. and Mrs. Rice have four children, two sons, Charlton E. and William P., and two daughters, Ida May and Kate Pearl. Charlton graduates this term at the K. C. & B. College. Ida May was also educated at this school. Subject and wife, and their two eldest children, are members of the Christian Church. Mr. Rice has always lived a quiet life. He is a temperate man in all his habits, and endeavors to live a consistent Christian. He has the reputation of being sober and industrious, scrupulously exact in all his dealings, and commands the respect and confidence of the community in which he resides.

F. C. RIDDELL, farmer and architect; P. O. North Middletown; is a son of Nathan Riddell, of Fayette County, and after remaining with his father till seventeen years of age, he went to New Orleans and engaged in stock trading, a business he followed for five years; he then returned to Kentucky and settled in Bourbon County, where he remained till the war broke out between the sections; he espoused the Southern cause and was among the first men who volunteered from this county in the Confederate Army; he was captured by the Federals on the 26th of July, 1863, with Gen. John Morgan on his Ohio raid; was taken to Camp Chase and confined for two months, thence to Johnson's Island on Lake Erie, where he remained a prisoner till the close of the war. Mr. Riddell then returned to Kentucky and engaged in farming in connection with his trade, which pursuit he still follows. He was married on the 30th of June, 1859, to Miss Lavina W. Stewart, of this county; he has superintended the building of many of the handsome residences and fine stock barns in the vicinity where he lives. He is a member of the Christian Church, and a straight Democrat in politics.

H. C. SMITH, farmer and short-horn breeder; P. O. North Middletown; was born in Bourbon County on the 16th of June, 1848. His grandfather, Weathers Smith, emigrated from Fairfax C. H., Va., to this State about the beginning of the present century, and settled on what is now known as the Duncan Land, which is now owned by Cassius M. Clay. He married Lydia, sister of Geo. A. Smith. She died in 1818, leaving an only son, Algernon Sidney Smith, who was born May the 16th, 1809. Algernon S., after his father's death, which occurred in 1828, came into possession of 779 acres of land on Paris and Winchester Pike, near Thatcher's Mill. He was married Oct. 1, 1846, to Amanda F. Thomas. The result of this union was two sons. Mr. and Mrs. Smith both died with cholera in 1852, within a few days of each other. The younger son, Algernon Sidney, who was named for his father, died at the age of twenty-two years, leaving a childless widow, who now lives with her father, John W. Thomas. The elder son, Henry C. Smith, who is the subject of our sketch, and also his younger brother above spoken of, were taken; after the sudden death of their parents, by their uncle, Owen B. Thomas, and raised to maturity. Mr. Thomas now lives in Boone County, Missouri, having moved there in 1878. Our subject attended school at Stony Point till he was seventeen years of age. He then entered Kentucky University at Lexington, where he was a student for three years, but on account of his health failing, he was compelled to leave the University without graduating. He was married on the 21st of October, 1869, to Nannie C., daughter of Harvey W. Rice, whose father was one of the first settlers here. This couple are blessed with two children, Allie Dee, who was born Jan. 26, 1873, and Henry Stanley, born Sept. 14, 1878. Henry C. bought his first short horns in 1870, and continued in that business till October, 1876, at which time he consolidated his herd of twenty-five head with a herd of seventy head owned by Ed. K. Thomas, which is spoken of in another part of this work. This consolidation, now known as the "Glenwood Herd," and owned by Thomas and Smith, numbers at present 120 head, and is considered one of the best herds in the State. Mr. Smith is one of the representative farmers of his county, owns 250 acres of land three miles south of North Middletown, and for the past four years has been one of the board of directors of the Bourbon County Agricultural Society.

PRESTON J. SEAMANDS, farmer; P. O. North Middletown; is a native of Bourbon County, and was born Aug. 7, 1809; his father, Major Seamands, was born in Albemarle County, Va., and emigrated to Kentucky about the year 1800, and settled in Bourbon County. Major Seamand's commanded a company in the war of 1812, and served with honor and credit to himself, and after the termination of the war he returned to Kentucky, and in a short time afterwards bought what is now known as Seamands' Mill, on Stoner Creek, with about 100 acres of land attached. He was married in Virginia in 1797 to Elizabeth Newton; she died at the old mill place in 1822. By this marriage there were seven children, five of whom were raised to maturity, and four of them are still living—three daughters: Malinda, widow of James Lindsay, of Bourbon County; Elizabeth, widow of Kinzea Stone, also of Bourbon, and Marilda, widow of John G. Sims, of Jessamine County, and one son, Preston J., who is the subject of this sketch. Major Seamands died July 7, 1856, leaving an estate of 650 acres of land, which he divided among his children by his last will and testament. Preston J. assisted his father about the homestead till about twenty years of age, at which time his father put him in charge of the mill and farm; he was married April 27, 1830, to Mary Ann Skinner, who was born in Virginia, but had moved to Kentucky with her father about the year 1816. This union was blessed with four children—two sons: William H., who died in infancy, and James M., who died when only five years old, and two daughters, Elizabeth A., who was born July 24, 1831, and was married July 23,

1846, to John W. Kerr, and Mary F., who was born April 6, 1843, and was married to Dr. W. R. Davis April 6, 1868. Preston J., in 1861, at an expense of several thousand, put his mill in first-class repair, which rendered it in every way worthy of the reputation it had of being the best mill in the county. He has been very successful in farming also, and now owns 500 acres of land besides his mill, town residence, etc.; he has recently moved to North Middletown, rented out his farm, and proposes to retire from active work, and enjoy some of the fruits of his labor. He and wife, and their two children, and also two grandchildren, are members of the Christian Church. He is a Republican in politics.

WILLIAM H. SETTLES, farmer and carriage builder; P. O. North Middletown; was born on the 11th of July, 1829, in Bourbon County; his grandfather, Joseph Settles, was a native Virginian, and moved to Kentucky at an early day and settled in Bourbon, where he remained till about the year 1843, at which time he emigrated to the State of Missouri, where he spent the remainder of his days. He was a man of remarkable constitution, and lived almost an entire century, being ninety-eight years of age at the time of his death. He raised five sons and two daughters; his eldest son, John T., was born in Kentucky in 1806, and married, in 1827, Mary Shrader, who was a second cousin to the old Kentucky pioneer, Daniel Boone. This union was also blessed with five sons and two daughters: William H., the eldest son, is the subject of this sketch. When he was but twelve years of age his father died, leaving the responsibility of his mother and six younger children principally upon his hands. He succeeded, by the assistance of his mother, in giving the rest of the children a fair education, and to this day provides for his aged parent, who is now seventy-five years old. He was married on the 9th of May, 1854, to Lucinda Gardner, of Bourbon; the result of this marriage is seven children, five sons: Benjamin F., Edward P., Owen T., William H., and Robert, and two daughters, Elizabeth, who is the wife of Robert Wright, and Mary Lou. Mr. Settles owns a small farm of 150 acres, besides his town property, which consists of a carriage factory, blacksmith shop, etc. He enjoys the reputation of being one of the best mechanics in the county. He is a member of the Good Templar order; he and wife and married daughter are members of the Christian Church; in politics he acts with the Democratic party.

JOHN B. STIVERS, Postmaster; P. O. North Middletown; is a native of Clay County, and was born June 10, 1821; his great-great-grandfather was a native of Germany; his great-grandfather was also born in Germany, and emigrated at an early day to the United States, and settled in the city of New York; his grandfather was born in that city on the 5th of May, 1759, and at the early age of fourteen he engaged as drummer boy in the Revolutionary Army, and served till the close of that war. He married and emigrated to Kentucky about the year 1784, and settled near Lexington, Fayette County, where R. P. Stivers was born on the 17th of March, 1799. In the year 1819, R. P. was married to Nancy Barger, a native of Virginia. They raised to maturity nine children; the second son, John B., who is the subject of this sketch, was brought by his parents when only six months old, to Bourbon County, where he has ever since claimed as his home. He volunteered in the Mexican war in 1847, in the 3rd Reg't of the K. V. I.; he also participated in the late war between the sections on the Federal side; was a Lieutenant in the Seventh Regiment of the Kentucky Volunteers. Lieutenant Stivers was in several hot engagements, among them were Arkansas Post, Champion Hill, and the Siege at Vicksburg; was wounded eleven times; twice very severely. After the cessation of hostilities, he returned to his native State, where he was married on the 5th of September, 1866, to Miss Fannie Judy. This union resulted in one child, Maud Vernon, who was born on the 3rd of July, 1867; she is now a student of the K. C. and B. College, at North Middletown. Her mother died Aug. 23, 1868. Mr. Stivers was married again on the 17th of May, 1875, to Miss B. J. Peters. He has been a member of the Masonic order for more than thirty years, and is a Republican in politics.

MRS. REBECCA L. SCOTT, farmer and breeder of short-horns; P. O. North Middletown, daughter of Henry and Margaret (Allen) Lander. Her grandfather, Charles Lander, was a native of Germany, and emigrated to the United States at an early day, and settled in Bourbon County, Ky., where he raised a family of seven children, three sons and four daughters. Mr. Lander was quite a prominent man in his day, was a Methodist preacher and farmer, and was elected by a large majority to represent his county in the Legislature. He and his wife both died with cholera in 1833. His second son, Henry Lander, married Margaret Allen, a native of Virginia, by whom he raised a family consisting of eight children, four of whom are still living. One son, Franklin, who lives in Fleming County, and three daughters, viz: Lavinia, wife of Joseph P. Kenney; Fannie, widow of Isaac Skinner, of Clark County; and Rebecca L., who is the subject of this sketch. She was born July 27, 1827, and on the 6th day of January, 1848, was married to William Scott, of Bourbon. He was born in 1827, and died on the 27th of April, 1878. By this marriage there are nine living children, five daughters, viz: Sarah M., Kate, Alice, Bettie, and Lutie, and four sons, Joseph F., who married Miss Thomas, of this county, and now lives in Missouri, Charles F., Robert Lee, and Isaac S. One daughter, Fannie, died when only eighteen months old. Mrs. Scott now owns 248 acres of land on Cane Ridge Pike, one and a quarter miles north of North Middletown. Her son, Charles, superintends the farm and short-horns, of which they have a nice herd at this time. The family are Democratic politically, and Mrs. S. and two daughters are members of the Methodist Church.

JOSEPH C. SCOTT, farmer; P. O. North Middletown; son of Wm. and Eliza (Sparr) Scott, and was born Sept. 22, 1838; his grandfather, Wm. Scott, was a native of Virginia, but emigrated to Kentucky at an early day and settled near Clintonville, where he died with cholera in 1833. His second son, William, married Eliza Sparr, of Clark County; by this marriage there were four sons and three daughters. The third son, Joseph C., who is the subject of our sketch, enlisted, in 1862, in the Confederate Army under Col. Cluke; in the winter of 1862–3 he was captured and taken to Camp Butler in Illinois, where he was held a prisoner for two months and then exchanged; was again captured on the 26th of July, 1863, with Gen. Morgan on his Ohio raid, and taken to Camp Chase and confined for a month, then removed to Camp Douglas, where he remained a prisoner for seventeen months and was again exchanged; after the cessation of hostilities he returned from Virginia to his native State. Joseph C. was married Oct. 27, 1870, to Miss G. A. Yates; the result of this union is two children, Roy Cluke and Bernice Bell. Mr. Scott owns a small farm and is an enthusiastic Democrat.

JAMES SCOTT, farmer; P. O. North Middletown; is a native of Bourbon County, and was born Dec. 17, 1802, on the premises where he now resides; his grandfather and family, together with twelve other families, came down the Ohio River from Pennsylvania in the year 1778, and settled on what was afterward known as Corn Island, opposite Shippingsport, Ky., (now a part of Louisville); he built the third cabin in that place in the fall of that year (1778), but the families composing the little colony were all driven away by the Indians, and Mr. Scott and family found refuge in the fort at Harrodsburg; he afterward located 1,000 acres of land on Flat Creek, in what is now Bath County, but settled in Bourbon County; he raised four children, three sons and one daughter, and died about the year 1804. His eldest son, Robert Scott, settled on a part of his father's place in Bourbon County, built a cabin and afterward married Miss Ann Galloway, by whom he had eight children, five boys and three girls. His second son, James Scott, who is the subject of this sketch, lived upon the old homestead until 1853, when, on the 23d of September of that year, he was married to Emeline P. Offutt; this union was blessed with five children, three of whom are living: Nannie, Emma P., and William Robert. Mr. Scott has about 570 acres of land well improved; he is a Democrat. His mother-in-law, Mrs. Offut, lives with him, is ninety-two years old and remarkably sprightly for one of her years.

EDWIN K. THOMAS, farmer and breeder of short horn cattle, Cotswold sheep and saddle horses; P. O. North Middletown; a native of Bourbon County and son of John W. Thomas, whose sketch appears in another part of this work. Ed. K. was born August 24, 1840, and on September 13, following, he was left motherless. Was then taken to his grandfather, John Thomas, by whom he was raised. He was educated at the Patterson Institute at North Middletown. On Sept. 3, 1861, Ed. K. was married to Caroline S., daughter of Milton Jameson of Montgomery County. Caroline, after receiving a very liberal education in her native county, was, at the age of fifteen, sent to Daughter's College at Harrodsburg, where she finished her education. This union was blessed with three children, one daughter, Eliza Kerr, who died when only five years of age, and two sons, Claude M., who was born Feb. 5, 1863, and is now a student of Princeton College, New Jersey, and Edwin K., Jr., who was born Dec. 14, 1864, and is now at Central University, Richmond, Ky. Mr. Thomas owns 300 acres of land, upon which he has erected one of the most handsome residences in the county, of modern architecture, and named the place Glenwood. This is in the same yard where once stood the house in which it is said that the grandfather of President Lincoln lived. Mr. Thomas bought his first short horns in 1872, and from that time has been a successful breeder. Among the prominent animals bred by him was Airdrie Thorndale, 6100, and Ellen Challenger the Fourth, both of his Young Mary family. These two noted animals won the champion prizes for three years in succession at the great fairs at Paris and Lexington, Ky., an honor that has never been awarded to any other bull or cow in the United States. He also bred the celebrated saddle horse "Montrose," who was the recipient of like honors at the Paris fair. His short horn herd now numbers 120 head, and for the past five years it has won the aged herd prizes at Paris and Lexington, and four out of five of the young herd prizes at each of the above places. Mr. and Mrs. Thomas are both members of the Christian Church, and he is a Democrat in politics.

JOHN W. THOMAS, farmer; P. O. North Middletown; is a native of Bourbon County, and still resides on the old homestead, where he was born. His grandfather, William Thomas, was a native of Virginia, and emigrated to Kentucky in 1796, and settled in Bourbon County. His father, John Thomas, was born in Virginia in 1786, and came to Kentucky when only ten years old. John Thomas married Susan Thomas, a cousin of his, by whom he raised eight children; his eldest son, John W., who is the subject of this sketch, was married in 1839 to Eliza Jane, daughter of Harvey Kerr, of Bourbon; she died Sept. 13, 1840, leaving one son, Edwin K., who was then only about two weeks old. John W. was again married in 1842 to Margaret P. Kerr, a cousin of his first wife. The result of this union was seven children—two sons: Douglas and William, and five daughters: Mary E., Emma, Candace, Nannie, and Alma. They are all married except the youngest daughter. Mr. Thomas owns 350 acres of land, and is a successful farmer; he bred and raised the noted trotting horse Kentucky Prince, who showed the wonderful gait of 2.32 at a three-year old. As there was no colt of his age that had ever beaten that time in the State, he was tempted by the handsome offer of $10,800 for him, a proposition he very reluctantly accepted, Mr. Backman, of New York, being the fortunate purchaser. Mr. Backman has since refused $25,000 for him. Mr. Thomas' family are all members of the Christian Church. He is a Democrat in politics.

LUNCEFORD TALBOTT, farmer; P. O. North Middletown, son of Mason and Susan (Leach) Talbott, and was born August 29th, 1824. His father, Mason Talbott, was born in Loudoun County, Va., on November 13, 1790, and was brought to Kentucky when about two years old, by his father, with whom he settled near Stony Point, Bourbon County. In 1811, he was married to Susan Leach, who was also a native of Virginia. She was born January 1, 1789, and died on the 28th of April, 1857. By this marriage there were three sons, viz: John F., Sanford, and Lunceford (subject), and four daughters, Lena, Mary C., Louise and Leoma. All now living, and the youngest fifty years of age. Mason Talbott died on the 26th of April, 1876, in his eighty-sixth year. His third son, Lunceford, who is the subject of this sketch, was married on the 5th of December, 1855, to Mary C., daugh-of T. P. Young, of Bath County. She was born July 28, 1834. This union is blessed with three sons, John Sanford, Toliver C., and Mason G. The two younger sons are at home, assisting their father in the duties of the farm, while the eldest son is actively engaged in the life insurance business. Mr. Talbott owns 300 acres of land. He and his wife are members of the Christian Church. Politically, Democratic.

HENRY O. THOMAS, farmer; P. O. North Middeltown; is the son of John Thomas, who is spoken of in another part of this work. Henry O. is a native of this county, and was born March 22, 1829, and was married Jan. 20, 1852, to Annie F. Gaitskill; the result of this union was eight children, all daughters: Mary H., who was educated at Warrendale, Patterson Institute and Daughters' Collge; Emma S., who was educated at the first two schools mentioned above; Willie A., Addie E., Lillie B., L. G. F., Maggie C., and Allie R., who received their education at the K. C. & B. College, at North Middletown, an intistution in which Emma S. Thomas is now music teacher; Addie E. is also engaged in teaching near Hutchinson Station, in this county. Mr. Thomas owns a very nice farm of 190 acres three miles south of North Middletown, on the Thatcher's Mill Pike, with good comfortable improvements, variety of ornamental trees, etc., and very appropriately named "Woodland." He is a member of the Masonic order, and a Democrat in politics.

CLINTONVILLE PRECINCT.

A. B. BRECKENRIDGE, farmer; P. O. Paris; is a scion of the old Breckenridge family, which has been prominent in the affairs of Kentucky ever since its admission to the Federal Union. His grandfather, Alex. Breckenridge, came from Virginia at quite an early period and located where "Greybeard," Samuel Clay, now lives. His son, John Breckenridge, was six years old when the family came to Kentucky. He married Ann, daughter of Alex. Brooks, and reared several children, among whom was Abijah B. Breckenridge, to whom this notice is paid. He was born Feb. 1, 1839, and was married in 1857 to Miss Amanda Boone, daughter of James Boone, who has borne him three children, viz.: Jas. B., born July 24, 1864; George A., born Aug. 19, 1870; and Abijah, born Dec. 24, 1873. Mr. Breckenridge owns 140 acres of land, upon which he raises the usual variety of crops; he also pays considerable attention to handling stock. Mr. Breckenridge was originally a Whig, but upon the general "break-up" of parties on the eve of the war, voted the Bell and Everett ticket, since which time he has been an ardent Democrat. Himself and wife accept the tenets of the Christian Church as the rule of their religious practice.

JOHN BUCHANAN, farmer; P. O. Clintonville; was born the 7th of February, 1854, the year of the remarkable drought in Kentucky. He is a son of Noah Buchanan, a native of Bourbon County, still living. His mother was Eliza Rennick, daughter of John Rennick. Mr. Buchanan is a young farmer, owns 103 acres of land and raises a general variety of crops, and breeds a corresponding variety of stock. He has resided in Bourbon County all his life, and as yet is unmarried. His political views are in accord with a majority of Kentuckians, being a professor of the Democratic faith.

JOHN CUNNINGHAM, farmer; P. O. Paris. John Cunningham is of Irish descent. His great-grandfather came from the Emerald Isle and settled in Virginia some time in the early part of the last century. He had a son Robert, who, impressed with the advantages to be found in a new and rapidly developing country, determined to try his fortunes in Kentucky, toward which the tide of emigration was rapidly flowing. Accordingly taking passage on a flat boat at Wheeling, he set out for "the dark and bloody ground" for the mastery of which civilization and savage fury was yet contending. The voyage was a perlious one. Simon Girty, with his Indian warriors kept watch from either bank of the Ohio, and whenever their frail craft drifted near the shore the sharp report of a rifle was sure to break in upon the scene. This necessitated keeping in the middle of the stream. Finally, after many adventures the boat arrived at Limestone, as Maysville was then called. From Maysville he went to Clark County and settled. Here in 1795 was born to him a son, John Cunningham, who was destined to act a prominent part in the early days of Bourbon County. He served for many years as Magistrate, and in 1833 was elected to the Legislature, and served until 1840—a period of seven years. He represented his district in the State Senate one term, 1851–55. He was a noted turfman, and owned among other horses the celebrated Woodpecker, who will be recalled in connection with the great race with Grey Eagle. He married Mary Bean, daughter of John Bean, of Clark County, who still lives in vigorous mind and health at the green old age of eighty-six years, and sits at the head of the table (beneath the same roof) where she began house-keeping more than sixty years ago. She is the mother of six living children: Robert John, James, Louis, William, George and Naomi. John Cunningham inherited many of the qualities which made his father distinguished. He is a man of strong common sense, keen discrimination and unswerving honesty. He has served on the Board of Magistrates for twenty years, and by his vigilant care of the public money has earned the *soubriquet* of the "Watch Dog of the Treasury." He was born the 15th of August, 1820, and resides with his aged mother in the house where he was born. He owns 140 acres of land and gives his attention to farming and breeding short-horn cattle. His herd which was founded in 1851, now contains about thirty-five animals at the head of which is the Second Roan Duke of Oneida; it contains representatives of most of the popular families. In politics Mr. Cunningham is a staunch Democrat of the Jackson type.

JOHN CUNNINGHAM, deceased, whose portrait appears in this work, may be truthfully said to have been one of the representative men of Bourbon County. He was born June 15, 1795, in Hardy County, Virginia. His parents were Robert and Mary Robinson Cunningham, both of whom were natives of the Old Dominion. Robert was born September 15, 1775. Robert was a son of

John Cunningham, a native of Ireland, who emigrated to Virginia prior to the Revolution. Robert was a participant in the Whisky Rebellion of 1794, and served as Major; his sword is yet in the hands of grand children here in Clintonville. He came to Kentucky in 1796, embarking at Wheeling in a flat boat, and settled on Strode's Creek, in Clark County. To him were born John, Belinda, Jesse, Abner, Lucinda, Isaac, Jemima, Maria and Mary. John and Abner settled in Bourbon County; Jesse, Isaac and Maria settled in Clark County; Maria became the wife of Matthew Hume; Elizabeth, wife of John Flournoy, of Scott County; Mary, of George Carlysle, of Woodford County; Isaac became the father of twenty-three children; but one of the number came to maturity, Rebecca, who married Isaac Vanmeter, of Clark County. John Cunningham, the subject of these lines, was married December 27, 1817, to Mary Bean, a native of this State. She was born Sept. 22, 1796, on Strode's Creek, in Clark County. She is the daughter of John Bean, and Eva, daughter of Dr. Peter Sensine, a native of Ireland. Mr. Cunningham removed to Bourbon County in 1818, where he spent the greater portion of his life. He was truly a representative man of his time. His early advantages for acquiring an education were very meagre, but he made the best of his advantages and studied, and read much. Being a close and steady thinker, a liberal patron of good books, and the public journals, he became at length a well-informed man of the locality. He engaged successfully in farming; was a large land-holder at the time of his death; was very methodical and exact in his farming operations, building fence of the most durable character, stone being his choice, of which he has left many monuments in this line. He did much to encourage the breeding and growth of fine stock—horses seemed his favorite class. He gave especial attention to them, and owned the noted horse "Woodpecker." He served as a soldier in the war of 1812, and was a warm and ardent admirer of Henry Clay. From 1833 to 1850 he served as Justice of the Peace; in 1853 he began handling short horns, and continued in this interest up to the time of his death. In 1833 he was chosen to represent his County in the legislature, re-elected in 1839, and to the Senate in 1851, '2, '3 and '4. In all matters that pertained to the good of the Commonwealth, John Cunningham ever bore a prominent part; he largely encouraged the building of railroads and pikes; he was free-hearted and unselfish in his aims and purposes, and labored for the good of his county and country generally, and at his death he was mourned as one beloved by all; he passed away peacefully, Aug. 17, 1864. His wife yet survives him on the homestead, upon which lives John and Naomi; Robert and Lewis on farms adjoining.

MRS. I. M. CUNNINGHAM, farming; P. O. Clintonville; born, December, 1818, in Sandersville Precinct, in Fayette County; daughter of James W. Henderson, son of Thomas, who came from Pennsylvania to Kentucky in the early part of Fayette County's history. The mother of our subject was Betsey, daughter of James and Margaret (McCollough) Hill; both are families of Scotch-Irish descent. Mrs. Cunningham is now the sole surviving member of seven children: John, James, Samuel, William, Daniel, Sallie and Isabella M. John died when he attained his manhood; William became a physician and settled in Covington; Samuel removed to Clark County; the others settled in Fayette County. The parents of the above were staunch members of the Presbyterian Church, of old "secular" stock. January 4th, 1837, she married Thomas L. Cunningham, who was born, 1810, in Clark County, this State. After marriage, located in Fayette County, where they remained until 1842, and engaged in farming and stock raising—he died in April, 1862; was member and Elder of the Presbyterian Church. She has six children: Mary, who is the wife of H. C. Hutchcraft; Margaret married W. O. Shropshire; Amelia, wife of Wm. Haley, of Fayette; boys are: Isaac, James and Thomas L. Mrs. Cunningham and all her family are members of the same church as Mr. Cunningham. Her farm consists of 330 acres, which she still carries on with the assistance of her sons.

LOUIS CUNNINGHAM, farmer; P. O. Paris; another son of John Cunningham; was born Christmas day, 1831; he is a farmer by occupation; owns 141 acres of land called "Sulphur Well," from a well of black sulphur 147 feet deep, recently bored on the place; he formerly made the handling of short-horn cattle a specialty, but has now abandoned the business, and turned his attention to breeding saddle-horses and jack stock; he owns a fine specimen of the Kentucky saddle stallion—Jewell—which he prizes greatly on account of his excellent finish and his direct descent from Washington Denmark, the progenitor of one of the best family of saddle-horses in America; he also owns a fine jack, for which he paid $800. Mr. Cunningham is unmarried; he is and always has been a Democrat.

ROBERT CUNNINGHAM, farmer; P. O. Stony Point; is another son of John Cunningham, a sketch of whose family appears in the biography of the younger John Cunningham in this work. He was born Jan. 13th, 1819. On the 31st of Aug., 1841, he was united in marriage to Miss Maria Louisa Cutright, daughter of Henry Cutright, and granddaughter of Maj. Samuel Cutright, who settled Cutright Station, near Clintonville, in 1779. Their union has produced four children, viz: Henry, who is married and resides in Shelby County, Mo.; Rebecca, who married William C. Stipp; Sallie, who married Ben. Stipp; and Ray, who is unmarried and lives with his parents. Mr. and Mrs. Cunningham are both members of the Christian Church, the former having made his profession of religion in 1840. He is also a Mason, and a member of the Mt. Sterling Commandery of Knights Templar. He owns 123 acres of land, and has been a successful breeder of short-horn cattle. He was a Whig before the war, and his views are now in accord with the Democracy.

HENRY CLAY, farmer; P. O. Clintonville; traces the genealogy of his family back to his grandparents, Henry Clay and wife, who emigrated from Virginia to Kentucky at an early day, spending the first year after their arrival in Bourbon County in a fort located about five miles above Paris, on the Stoner. Capt. James Smith of Indian notoriety, was stationed in the fort at the time. They were married when their united ages did not exceed thirty years, and lived together as man and wife for sixty-seven years. Nine daughters and three sons were born to them ; the father of our subject, Col. Henry Clay, was one of the youngest of these sons. He was born in 1779, and subsequently married Miss Peggy Helm, the daughter of Joseph Helm, of Lincoln County, Ky. Twelve children were born to them, six sons and six daughters. Our subject was born June 4, 1798, and was married at the age of twenty-three years to Miss Olivia, daughter of George M. and Henrietta Bedinger, of Nicholas County, Ky. One child was born to them, and in 1823 both mother and child died. In 1826 Mr. Clay was married to Miss Elizabeth, daughter of Samuel and Elizabeth Scott of Bourbon County. Five children were born of this union, three of whom are living, viz: Samuel Scott Clay; Maggie H., married a Mr. Kelly, and now resides in Philadelphia; and Joseph H. Clay. In 1835 Mr. Clay was again a widower by the death of his second wife. In 1837 he married Miss Mary, daughter of George and Ellis Chadwell, of Jessamine County, Ky. Six children were born of this union, three now living: George, Letitia and John W. In 1859 his third wife died, since which time Mr. Clay has remained unmarried. He is a fine old gentleman, past eighty-three years of age; has spent his life in agricultural pursuits, and bears the reputation of an honest, upright citizen.

THOMAS HENRY CLAY, farmer ; P. O. Clintonville; is a member of that branch of the Clay family which is descended from Henry Clay, who came from Virginia in early times, when Indians still roamed the trackless wastes of Kentucky, and settled in Bourbon County. His father is "Greybeard" Samuel Clay, so called to distinguish him from several other well known gentlemen of the same name in the County. Our subject was born July 28th, 1840, and was married in July, 1864, to Miss Fanny Conn Williams, daughter of Maj. George W. Williams, who in conjunction with Hon. Garrett Davis, represented Bourbon County in the convention which framed the present Constitution of Kentucky. The couple have four children, viz: Alfred, George W., Thomas H., Jr., and Nannie. Mr. Clay owns 3,000 acres of land, and his place is known as "The Heights." He possesses the confidence of his neighbors, and is noted for his energy and thrift.

WM. H. CLARK, farmer; P. O. Clintonville; is a son of Robert Clark, jr., a prosperous farmer of Bourbon County, and a grandson of Robert Clark, Sr., who came from Virginia. His mother was Sarah Ruth Ward, a woman endowed with many excellent qualities, which fitted her for the delicate task of rearing a son, and training his feet to pursue the path which leads to virtue and happiness. She died in 1870. Wm. H. Clark was born Oct. 11, 1853, in Bourbon County, where he received his education. On the 9th of September, 1873, he was united in marriage to Miss Lulie B. Weathers. Their union has been blessed with five children: Hattie P., John F., Lutie R. (died Sept. 5, 1879), Robert J., and Lulie B. He is a farmer in a general way, and owns 152 acres of land called "Pine Valley." In religion, himself and wife are both members of the Baptist Church. Like most of the young men of Kentucky, Mr. Clark is a Democrat in politics.

R. M. HARRIS, farmer; P. O. Stony Point; was born April 14, 1840, in North Middletown. His family is of Virginia descent, Elictious Harris, his grandfather, emigrated from that State and settled in Montgomery County. B. F. Harris, his son, engaged in merchandising in North Middletown for many years. Served for a number of years as Magistrate, and is now located in Paris, in the United States revenue service. His wife, and the mother of our subject, was Elizabeth Herriott. R. M. Harris was joined in marriage with Miss Eliza A. daughter of Reuben Hutchcraft, of Bourbon County, on the 17th of Nov., 1866. The couple are members of the Methodist Church. Mr. Harris is a farmer, and owns 272 acres of good land. Of late years he has paid considerable attention to raising Short Horn cattle. He has an excellent herd of about fifty animals, at the head of which is Sharon Duke 3d. The herd contains representatives of some of the best and most popular families. In politics Mr. Harris followed in the footsteps of his father and is a pronounced Republican.

WILLIAM L. HUTCHCRAFT, farmer; P. O. Stony Point; is a son of Reuben Hutchcraft, and a grandson of Thomas Hutchcraft, who emigrated from Virginia at an early period and settled in Bourbon County; his mother's maiden name was Fanny Hedges; he was born in 1836, and in 1864 was married to Miss Kate Wells, a daughter of Joshua Wells. The couple have nine children: Reuben, Ella, Hallie, Fanny, Ida, Effie and Nettie (twins) and Kate Harris. Mr. Hutchcraft is a farmer, and owns 137 acres of land, upon which he raises the usual variety of Kentucky crops; he served in the 21st Kentucky Federal Infantry during the late war, Colonel, afterwards Gen. S. W. Price, being the commander; he is a Democrat in his political affiliations.

JACOB LIVAR, farmer; P. O. Clintonville. In 1843, John W. Livar, an orphan boy, without friends or education, came from Hardy County, Va., and began to work for Isaac Van Meter, of Clark County. By industry and perseverance he obtained a start in life, and with the continued exercise of those good qualities, he has amassed a large fortune. Mr. Livar's first wife was a Tevaugh, and from that union sprung Jacob Livar, who was born February 5th, 1846. Receiving a common English education, he began life as a farmer and stock-trader, which he has followed with varied success ever since. He now owns 150 acres of land within a mile of Clintonville. He was married Dec. 20th, 1870, to Miss Lizzie Guthrie, of Sumner County, Tenn. They have five children: John G., Anna May, Kate C., Ada C., and Nettie. Mrs. Livar is a member of the distinguished Guthrie family, and is an accomplished lady. She belongs to the Presbyterian communion. Mr. Livar is a Democrat in politics.

A. P. LARY, farmer; P. O. Clintonville; is a son of J. C. Lary, and a grandson of Dennis Lary, who emigrated from the Old Dominion at an early day. J. C. Lary married Mary A., the daughter of Gen. E. Pendleton, of Clark County, who served in the war of 1812, under Gov. Isaac Shelby. Capt. V. M. Pendleton, of Co. D, 8th Ky. Confederate Cavalry, who was killed at Mt. Sterling, was an uncle of our subject. A. P. Lary was born Aug. 17th, 1856, in Bourbon County; he was married April 27th, 1881, to Miss Jennie H. Henderson. Mrs. Lary is a member of the Christian Church. Mr. Lary owns 175 acres of land near Clintonville, where he engages in farming and raising short-horn cattle; his home is known as "Glencoe," where he lives in the enjoyment of the confidence and esteem of his neighbors.

GEO. W. MORROW, farmer; P. O. Clintonville; was born March 14, 1843, in Bourbon County, his parents being James and Louisa (Rennick) Morrow, the daughter of John Rennick. The Rennicks are of Virginia descent. Mr. Morrow was married Dec. 7, 1870, to Miss Sallie Parvin, of Bourbon County. Their union has been productive of five children, viz.: Anza, Louisa, Lillie B. and Mazie. He is a farmer and short-horn breeder, owning 250 acres of land called Grove Hill. Has served four years as Director of the Bourbon County Fair Association, and is at present one of the Magistrates of the Clintonville Precinct. When the late Civil war broke out, he espoused the cause of the South, enlisting in Capt. Pendleton's Company of Col. Cluke's 8th Ky. Cavalry, he followed the fortunes of the stars and bars for three years. He was wounded at Horse Shoe Bend, on the Cumberland River. Mr. Morrow has always been a Democrat in politics.

J. WALKER MUIR, salesman; P. O. Paris; born Dec. 11th, 1848, in Hutchinson; son of Col. Samuel and Lena S.(Dawson) Muir. He was reared to farming pursuits; while yet in his teens he entered a store as clerk, and since 1864 has been employed as salesman in Lexington and in Paris. August, 1871, he married Nannie W. Turner, daughter of E. P. Turner and Sallie Bryant. He has no children; his farm consists of 163 acres; is a member of the Christian Church.

JAMES M. RUSSELL, farmer; P. O. Paris; was born Dec. 29, 1847, in Bourbon County, near where he now resides. He is a son of Robert N. Russell, who was raised near Russell's Cave, in Fayette County. He was a farmer; served as Sheriff of the county, and died in 1852, with cholera. His grandfather was Thomas Russell, a native of Virginia, who came to Kentucky quite early and settled near the cave which has derived its name from him. He mingled freely in political life, and was a prominent man of his time. The mother of our subject was Eliza Matson, daughter of Jas. S. Matson, of Bourbon. Mr. Russell graduated from Yale College, in the class of 1870, and soon after went in company with Prof. Marsh, and others, on a geological and scientific tour on the plains. He also visited Sitka, Alaska, and returning through Mexico, was captured by banditti, who did him and his companions no other injury than depriving them of their pistols and horses. He returned via. Cuba to Kentucky, where he settled down to farming. In 1874 he made the tour of Europe. He is a farmer, owns 612 acres of fine land, upon which he raises the usual crops, and gives attention to the breeding and rearing of short horn cattle, Prince Pace, 2d; a Bates bull is at the head, which contains representatives from most of the popular families. Mr. Russell is a member of the Christian church, and is highly esteemed by his neighbors and friends.

JOHN STIPP, farmer; P. O. Clintonville. The ancestors of Mr. Stipp, like those of many others of this section of Kentucky, were Virginians. His grandfather was Michael Stipp; his father was Frederick Stipp, who emigrated from Virginia and settled near Strode's Station, in Clark County, at quite an early day, where he married Mary, the daughter of William Clinkinbeard. On April 22, 1817, their son John was born. Receiving the rudiments of a common education, he began life as a farmer, which pursuit he still follows with gratifying sucess. He now owns 104 acres of good land, having given to each of his children 70 acres. Mr. Stipp was united in marriage with Miss Martha Schooler, daughter of Benj. Schooler, of Clark, in 1834, by whom he has had four children: Wm. C., Isaac, Benjamin, and Mary C., now the wife of H. C. Weathers. He is a Deacon and leading member of the Clintonville Christian Church. In politics he affiliates with the Democrats.

ISAAC V. STIPP, farmer; P. O. Clintonville; born March 24, 1846, in this precinct, upon the farm he now owns; son of John Stipp, a native of this county; born April, 1817; son of Frederick, a native of Virginia, whose father was Michael Stipp. The Stipp family are among the pioneer families that came to settle in Kentucky at an early day, their first arrival to the State being about the year 1789. The subject of these lines was brought up to farming, it being the vocation of his progenitors. In 1854 he removed, with his parents, to Clark County, where he remained until 1876, when he came to Bourbon, where he has since remained. Feb. 4th, 1880, he married Rebecca Ella, daughter of Robert A. Hopkins, of this county; has one child, Lida, born Nov. 15, 1881. His farm consists of 148 acres. His church membership is with the Reformed Church at Clintonville.

W. C. STIPP, farmer; P. O. Clintonville. This gentleman was born in the Precinct where he resides, Feb. 21, 1841, being the eldest son born to his parents, viz.: John and Martha (Schroder) Stipp; to whom were born William C., Isaac V., Benjamin F. and Mrs. Mary Clay Weathers. Lenora died upon arriving at womanhood. With the exception of the years spent in Clark County he has been a resident of this precinct. April 22, 1868, he was wedded to Rebecca, born 1848, daughter of Robert and Louisa (Curtright) Cunningham. Four children have crowned this union: Rebecca, Sallie, Henry and Ray. He has a small farm upon which he resides, engaged in farming. Is a member of the Christian Church at Clintonville.

ROBERT M. TERRELL, farmer; P. O. Clintonville; comes of the Union of two good Kentucky families, in the persons of John H. Terrell, and Ethe McGill, daughter of Robert McGill, of Bourbon County. The senior Terrell was born in Virginia, but followed the tide of emigration; came to Kentucky, where, by the exercise of his manly qualities, amassed a large fortune, and died respected by the entire community. His son, Robert M., was born Dec. 3, 1850, and was married, in 1868, to Miss Alice Weighert. They have three chidren: Sallie, Edward and Willie. Mrs. Terrell is a member of the Christian Church. Mr. Terrell is a farmer; owns 300 acres of good land, upon which he raises the usual variety of Kentucky crops, and pays some attention to stock; he is a Turnpike Director, and a staunch Democrat.

S. LETCHER WEATHERS, farmer; P. O. Clintonville; is a son of Granville C. and Jane (Scott) Weathers, daughter of Thomas Scott, of Bourbon County. Granville C. Weathers, before his removal to Missouri in 1880, was a prominent citizen of Fayette County, having been the nominee of the Republican party for State Senator, against his successful opponent, Maj. P. P. Johnston. Letcher, his son, was born in Fayette, Oct. 1st, 1857. After attending the common schools of the county, he entered Georgetown College, and would have graduated in five more months, had not sickness interfered and forced him to relinquish his studies. He was married April 4, 1881, to Miss Elizabeth Weathers. He owns 257 acres of land called "Prospect Hill," and devotes his time and energies to farming and breeding short horns. He hopes soon to have a fine herd. In politics, Mr. Weathers clings to the traditions of his fathers, and is an ardent Republican. Himself and wife, like most of the family, are communicants of the Baptist Church.

ED. P. WEATHERS, farmer; P. O. Clintonville; one of the most industrious and thrifty young farmers of the Clintonville precinct, was born July 15, 1851, in Bourbon County. His father, J. T. Weathers, was born in Fayette County, July 4, 1814; the mother of our subject was Bettie, the daughter of Ed. Parrish. On the 21st of Nov., 1877, Mr. Weathers led to the altar Miss Lizzie Parrish, daughter of John Parrish, by whom he has two children: Anna, born January 6, 1879, and Thomas J., born May 25, 1880. He owns a magnificent farm of

410 acres; is a member of the Baptist Church, like most of the Weathers' family; he is a director in the Thatcher's Mill Turnpike Co., and a Democrat in politics.

H. C. WEATHERS, farmer; P. O. Clintonville; is a son of Granville C. Weathers, of Fayette County, a sketch of whom appears in the notice of S. Letcher Weathers, a brother of the above named gentleman; he was born Aug. 10, 1856, received most of his education at the common schools of the community, and took a finishing course under Dr. Hitchcock, at Lexington. In 1877. Mr. Weathers was united in marriage with Miss Filey Stipp, daughter of John Stipp, Esq.; their union has produced two children: Claude, born Aug. 20, 1879, and a girl, born July 24, 1881; his occupation is farming; he owns seventy acres of good land; in politics and religion Mr. Weathers has followed in the parental footsteps, being both a Republican and a Baptist.

HUTCHINSON PRECINCT.

LLOYD ASHURST, farmer; P. O. Paris; was born July 13, 1840, in Bourbon County, and is the son of William and Isabella (Petty) Ashurst; he was a farmer, as was his father and grandfather, the former a native of Bourbon County, and the son of Josiah Ashurst, who was born in Virginia. Our subject was married in 1863 to Miss Nannie E. Penn, daughter of Joseph Penn, of Bourbon County. They are the parents of eight children, viz: Anna Bell, Lulu, Willie, Lottie Maude, Geo. M., Tice and Charles. Mr. Ashurst is the owner of 175 acres of finely improved land, which he farms in a general way, besides devoting some of his time to fine short horn cattle. Politically, he is a Democrat, never having voted any other ticket. He is an Elder in the Christian Church of which he is a member, and is a friend to all educational and religious enterprises.

O. H. BURBRIDGE, farmer; P. O. Hutchinson; was born May 9, 1821, in Scott County, Kentucky, and is the son of Capt. Robert Burbridge, a soldier in the war of 1812, and grandson of Capt. George Burbridge, a soldier in the war of the Revolution. The Blue Grass region of Kentucky boasts of many old and honored families, and of the list there are none, perhaps, more worthy of mention in a history sacred to their memory, than the Burbridge family, all men of broad views, active minds and fine intelligence; they have figured for many years in the public affairs of the State, and have left upon record a career worth of emulation. The old Revolutionary soldier removed to Kentucky during her early history, bringing a family with him, whom he reared to honorable man and womanhood. The father of our subject at that time was but a young boy; he early took an active interest in the stirring events of the times; became a soldier in the war of 1812, and rose to the rank of captain. He married Miss Eliza Ann, daughter of Jno. A. Barnes, of Port Gibson, Mississippi. The three sons born to them have all been active men. Gen. Stephen G. Burbridge, well known to Kentuckians, Thomas B., killed in Russellville in 1867, by guerillas, and our subject, who has also had an active public career. In 1862, he was Colonel of the 24th Ky. Militia, enrolled for the defense of the State, receiving his commission from Gov. Bramlette. In 1859–60, he represented Bourbon County in the State legislature, defeating Chas. C. Lair; he was nominated and elected by the old Whig or Union party; during 1865–6, he was supervising special agent for the treasury department for the District of Louisiana, Arkansas and Texas; he also held the position of Quartermaster Agent, investigating claims in Tennessee; retiring from public life, he devoted his time to his own private business and to the establishing and collecting of claims; he is largely interested in real estate; his home in Bourbon County consists of 235 acres of fine land, besides, which he has over 1600 acres in Texas, eight acres in the suburban town of Englewood, Chicago, and a fine property in Superior City, Wisconsin. He has been for some time interested in the breeding of fine cattle and sheep, and has recently become interested in the breeding of fine trotting stock. Politically, he is a Republican, and he and family are members of the Christian Church. He was married January 8, 1846, to Miss Rebecca S., daughter of James S. Matson. They are the parents of eight children, living, viz: Eliza A., James M., Robert O., Henry (dead), Lucy M., Mary Louisa, Hattie W., Russell C. and Stephen G.

E. G. BEDFORD, farmer, P. O. Paris. Prominent among the beautiful country homes in Bourbon County, is "Woodland Villa," comprised of 675 acres of fine Blue Grass land, and the home and pride of its owner, Mr. E. G. Bedford, who was born August 24, 1814, in Bourbon County, and is the son of Littleberry and Mattie Clay Bedford, and grandson of Thomas Bedford, who was born and died in Charlotte County, Virginia; Littleberry Bedford being a native of the same county, but came to Bourbon County when it still contained a fair population of Indians. Mr. Bedford has been twice married, the alliance both times being with families equal in prominence and reputation. His first marriage was in 1836, to Miss Margaret T. Garrard, daughter of General James Garrard, and grand-daughter of Governor Garrard. His second marriage was to Miss Lucy D. Reid, on the 13th of Sept. 1870. They have but one child living, born of their union on Dec. 10, 1873. For many years Mr. Bedford was counted among the most prominent and extensive breeders of fine short-horns, but on Oct. 28, 1874, he sold at public sale most of his herd, which brought him almost unequaled prices. His best sale while n the business was a bull at $7,000. For twenty-five or thirty years he was one of the Directors of the Bourbon County Fair and Agricultural Association. He was formerly a Whig in politics, but now claims to be an Independent Democrat. Mrs. Bedford is a member of the Christian Church, and a lady well worthy the position she maintains, as the wife of one of Bourbon county's leading citizens.

JAMES BAGG, Sr., farmer ; P. O. Hutchinson ; was born in Somersetshire, England, Nov. 17, 1799 ; son of Thomas and Elizabeth (Harding) Bagg, who came to America in 1820, and resided in New York until 1840, when they moved to Kentucky. James, our subject, did not come to America until 1835, however, when he was engaged in importing stock. He brought the first Cotswold and Southdown sheep ever brought to Kentucky and New York. In 1836 he married Miss Flora Wait, a native of Somersetshire, England, and daughter of Samuel Wait. The young lady when a child, had come over with the family of Mr. Thomas Bagg, and she has borne her husband the following children : Mary Emma, born in New York ; Elizabeth, died in 1874 ; James R.; Hester Wait, now Mrs. Penn ; Anna F., and Samuel. Mr. Bagg has made fifteen trips across the Atlantic in the interest of the stock business, having been engaged largely in the importation of fine stock. He owns 166 acres of land, and his place is called " Hidden Home." He and wife are members of the Episcopal Church ; he is a Democrat.

JOSEPH M. CASE, farmer ; P. O. Hutchinson; traces the genealogy of his family back to his grandfather, Joseph Case, a native of Maryland, and who was one of the old pioneers of Bourbon County, J. M. now living upon and owning the farm where he settled. The old gentleman was born July 11, 1757, and died Aug. 30, 1809 ; his wife Delia was born Dec. 25, 1776, and died June 28, 1833. The parents of our subject were Joseph and Nancy (Tucker) Case, the daughter of Jonathan Case. He was born on the farm now owned by Mr. Case ; spent his life in the quiet pursuits of farming, and died March 23, 1870, surviving his wife but a short time, her death occurring Feb. 14, 1870. Mr. Case has been twice married. His first wife was Miss Pamelia Conner, of Boone County, Ky. Her death occurred Nov. 4, 1871. Three children were born of this marriage, viz : John W., Nannie T., and May Eliza (deceased). His second wife was Miss May Carpenter, to whom he was married in 1877. Mr. Case is proud of the old farm, so long in the hands of his ancestors. It consists of 200 acres of fine land, well improved. He raises a general variety of crops, and pays some attention to the breeding of fine stock. He is a Democrat, and his wife and children members of then Christian Church.

MRS. RACHEL CORBIN, P. O. Hutchinson ; was born in September, 1806, in Bourbon County, Ky., daughter of Beal and Ella (Corbin) Marsh, natives of Maryland. They were married in Baltimore, and came to Kentucky at a very early period. Our subject was married in 1828, to Joshua Corbin, of Nicholas County. He died in 1869, leaving six children : Abram F., Beal, Nathan M., Joshua M., Sarah Chaney, and Martha Dryden. Nathan is a farmer in Saline County, Mo., Beal lives at home, and Joshua M. is County Surveyor of Fayette. Mrs. Corbin owns 118 acres of excellent land, eight miles from Paris, which she rents, but resides in her house upon the farm. She is a member of the Presbyterian Church.

E. S. DUDLEY, minister; P. O. Hutchinson; was born Jan. 28, 1811, in Fayette County, Ky.; son of Gen. James Dudley, who was made a captain in the war of 1812, but peace was declared before he reached the front. He came from Virginia with his father when nine years of age, and settled near Bryant's Station. The father of our subject was the third born of fourteen children, the date of which event was May 12, 1777; he died June 16, 1870; the grandfather, about 1826. The mother of our subject was a daughter of Abraham Ferguson, of Fayette; she died May 22, 1823. Mr. Dudley received his education in the common schools of the county, farmed considerable, and was noted as a mule dealer; he at present owns about three hundred and fifty acres of land, his place being known as "Orchard Grove;" he is a member of the Regular Baptist Church, as was his father and grandfather; he is a minister; was licensed 25 years ago, and is at present Pastor of Stony Point Church; he was married, first to Mary Ann Clay, daughter of Henry Clay, and one child was the result of the union—Mrs. Mary E. Cunningham. His wife dying, he married Mrs. Henrietta (Clay) Scott, sister of his first wife, by whom he had three children—Nancy, wife of J. B. McClintock, of Harrison; Rebecca; J. Ambrose, married and living in the neighborhood. The second wife dying, he married Hattie Bassett, of Nicholas County, Ky. He is a Republican.

J. AMBROSE DUDLEY, farmer ; P. O. Hutchinson ; was born Nov. 18, 1847, in Bourbon County ; is a son of Elder E. S. and Henrietta (Clay) Dudley. He was married in 1865 to Miss Lizzie Kenney, daughter of W. B. Kenney, of Paris, and has two children : E. S., Jr., and Willie Kenney—E. S. being born March 5, 1876, and W. K., Oct. 12, 1878. Mr. Dudley owns 100 acres of excellent land nine miles from Paris, which he farms successfully, and is a Republican in politics.

MRS. AMANDA R. HUTCHINSON, P. O. Hutchinson; was born in Bourbon County, Ky., May 4, 1818; daughter of Jacob S. Hitt and Matilda Jacobs, a native of Maryland. The grandfather of Mrs. Hutchinson was Jesse Hitt, who came from Virginia when her father was but eighteen years of age. She was married in 1835 to Martin Hutchinson, after whose family Hutchinson Station was named, and had twelve children, four of whom are living: Matilda E., (Mrs. Ashurst); Mary W. (Mrs. Morrow); Joseph B.; Hattie K. (Mrs. Harris). Mrs. Hutchinson is the owner of 115 acres of good land, which she rents, and is a member of the M. E. Church. Her husband, Martin Hutchinson, died May 11, 1869.

JAMES H. INGELS, farmer and stock raiser; P. O. Hutchinson; was born July 8, 1825, in Bourbon County, Ky., in the house where he now lives; son of James and Polly (Field) Ingels; she, a daughter of John Field, who came from Culpepper County, Va. The grandfather of our subject, James Ingels, came from Pennsylvania in 1788, settled and built a stone house near where James H. now resides; his mother died in 1854, and his father in 1857. Mr. Ingels owns 345 acres of good land, which he farms, in addition to raising fine stock; he handles short-horns and has a fine young herd: 2nd Bourbon Prince (34627); 4th Ardrie (647); Rose of Sharons; Princes; Daisies; Carolines (Golden Drops); Ianthes; Boston Belles; Floras; Isabellas; Marys; Fielis —42 in his herd. Mr. Ingels is a Democrat.

JAS. S. JACOBY, farmer; P. O. Hutchinson; was born Aug. 25, 1815, in the house where he now resides, and is the son of Jacob and Mary (Stark) Jacoby. The grandfather of our subject, Francis Jacoby, was born in Germany, and started for America in 1764, and upon the same vessel was a maiden named Frederina Lotspirg, also of German birth. The young emigrants falling in love, were married in England, where their vessel touched, and they then proceeded on their journey to the colonies, settling in Virginia, remaining there till 1785, when they moved to Kentucky, with their family, including a son, Jacob, the father of our subject, who was born in 1779. They lived for awhile in a cabin in the then wilderness of Kentucky, and in 1791 built the house in which James S. now lives. The grandfather left a family of twelve children, Jacob being the youngest save two, and only eight years old at the time of his father's death, which occurred in 1789. Jacob died Jan. 28, 1843, his wife having passed away March 24, 1829. Mr. Jacoby, our subject, has resided where he now does, with the exception of short periods at Georgetown and Maysville, his entire life. He was married Jan. 7, 1836, to Miss Mary Headington, of Lexington, who died without leaving issue, when he married Oct. 11, 1849, Miss Agnes M. Kenney, by whom he has had the following children: W. B., born Aug. 27, 1850, died July 11, 1876; Jacob W., born March 16, 1853; James L., born Nov. 11, 1854; John, born Jan. 15, 1857; Ann Mary, born Feb. 6, 1859; M. R., born Feb. 28, 1861. Mr. Jacoby owns 358 acres of land five and one-half miles from Paris, and has served for many years as a Justice of the Peace; also, as School Trustee for about twelve years. Is a member of the M. E. Church South, of Lexington, and has served as Stewart of the same for many years.

JACOB JACOBY, farmer; P. O. Hutchinson; was born Oct. 20, 1817, in Bourbon County, Ky., which has since been his home. His life is an example of the steady, sober industry to be found in many instances in the Blue Grass country, which is now being occupied by the second and third generation of descendants of the old pioneers. Six miles from Paris, on the Paris and Georgetown Pike, he has a nice farm of 157 acres, where his life has been spent; he has taken an active interest in church affairs, and has been a liberal giver in promoting the cause of religion, having been since 1833 a member of the M. E. Church, and an officer in the same since 1864; he is also Superintendent of the Sabbath School supported by hi Church. For eight years he also held the office of Magistrate. In June, 1844, he was married to Miss Elizabeth S. Kerr, who bore him four children before her death, viz: Amanda, born Feb. 25, 1845; Nannie, born June 3, 1847; Mary, Sept. 26, 1849, and James, born March 8, 1852 His second marriage was to Miss Charity E. Haynes, of Fayette County, on March 3, 1857. The children born of this marriage are, Jacob S., born Dec. 15, 1857; Jennie, born May 9, 1859; George, born Jan. 14, 1861; Samuel, born Jan. 13, 1863; Lyle, born Aug. 7, 1864; Charles, Dec. 12, 1866; Benjamin, born June 20, 1869, and Joseph, born Feb. 22, 1876.

B. F. JONES, farmer; P. O. Hutchinson; was born June 24, 1824, in Bourbon County, Ky.; son of W. S. and Nancy (Ashurst) Jones; she is a daughter of Josiah Ashurst, of Bourbon County. The grandfather of our subject came from Virginia and settled at Jones' Cross Roads, near Clintonville. Mr. Jones was married in 1850 to Miss Amanda Roberts, daughter of Joseph Roberts, of Bourbon County, which union has resulted in the following children: Belle, Luty, Lillie, John, Ida, Rosa, Joe, and Frank. He is the owner of

129 acres of excellent farming land, and has resided in the county his entire life. He and his wife are members of the Christian Church. He was a Whig before the war, and has been a Democrat since.

J. SMITH KENNEY, farmer; P. O. Paris; traces the genealogy of his family back to his great grandfather, Robert Kenney, who was a native of Ireland, and emigrated to the United States and settled first in Pennsylvania, but subsequently removed to Virginia, where his descendants remained until Matthew Kenney, grandfather of J. S., in 1796, removed with his family to Fayette County, Ky. Wm. M. Kenney, then about two years old, was of that family. He was born in 1794 in Augusta County, Virginia, and died in Fayette County in 1852. He was a leading member of the community and a prosperous and respected citizen. His wife, the mother of J. S., was Miss Anna Caldwell Smith, daughter of John Smith, of Rockingham, and who was a Captain in the Revolutionary war; she died Jan. 28, 1869. J. Smith Kenney was born in Bourbon County, April 5, 1825. His earlier years were spent in acquiring an education and in assisting his father. His first marriage was to Miss Priscilla Wilmott, daughter of Jno. F. Wilmott. Three children were born to them. Mrs. Kenney died on Feb. 12, 1872. On Dec. 18, 1878, he married Miss Kate Wilmott, sister of his first wife. Three children also have been born of this union. Mr. Kenney ranks among the better class of farmers of Bourbon County, where his life has been spent, excepting from 1848 till 1853, when he lived in Scott County. For many years he was a breeder of fine short horns, but in 1881 sold his herd. His farm consists of 290 acres of fine land, known as "Stock Place." Both Mr. and Mrs. Kenney are members of the Methodist church, and for many years he has held the office of Magistrate. He is a Democrat in politics, and well known as an honorable, enterprising and respectable member of the community.

M. A. KENNEY, farmer; P. O. Paris; was born March 31, 1836, in Bourbon County, Ky., and is one of the substantial, well respected farmers of the county. He was educated in his native county, and brought up a farmer. He now owns a fine farm of 375 acres, known as "Locust Grove." He is not a specialist, but grows a general variety of crops. Politically he is a Democrat, but has never sought political preferment, choosing rather to devote his time and attention to improving and beautifying his home, of which he has every reason to be proud. July 3, 1867, he was married to Miss Jennie Brooks, daughter of Dr. John Brooks. They are the parents of four children. In church and school affairs Mr. Kenney is a liberal supporter, he and his family being members of the Presbyterian Church.

MISS MARY KLEISER; P. O. Hutchinson; is the daughter of Joseph Kleiser, who was born in Switzerland, and came to America after serving an apprenticeship at clock making, settling in Virginia, where he married Elizabeth Lyter. They came from Virginia to Kentucky and settled at an early day, and Miss Kleiser resides in the house where she was born. She owns about 100 acres of fine land, calling her place "Elm Spring." She had managed her farm herself for some years, but at present rents it. She is a member of the Presbyterian Church.

JAMES McLEOD, farmer; P. O. Hutchinson; was born Oct. 20, 1819, near where he now lives, in Bourbon County; son of George and Catharine (Miller) McLeod. The great-grandfather of our subject came from the Highlands of Scotland to America during the Revolutionary War, and settled in Falmouth County, Va., opposite Fredericksburg, where the father of James was born Jan. 12, 1793, and who came to Lexington, Ky., when he was eight years of age. He afterward settled in Bourbon County, and died Aug. 31, 1870. Mr. McLeod owns 400 acres of land, which he has under the best state of cultivation, at the same time handling stock. He was married in 1859 to Miss Mary G. Penn, daughter of Joseph Penn, of Bourbon County, by whom he has six children: Delilah, Katie, Emma, John, George, and James, all unmarried and living at home. Mr. McLeod is a School Trustee.

THOS. J. NICHOLS, farmer; P. O. Paris; was born Dec. 25, 1837, in Fayette County, Ky., and is the son of Abram and Mary (Christian) Nichols, the former a native of Fayette County, and by trade a blacksmith, resided in that county till his death. The latter was born in Prince Edward County, Virginia, and died in Dec., 1880. T. J. was educated in Fayette County, and embarked in business for himself as a farmer. He was Deputy Sheriff under C. S. Bodley, and appointed to fill the vacancy upon the resignation of that gentleman. In 1864, he was a candidate for the office of Sheriff of Fayette County, and was defeated by but twenty-two votes, by W. W. Dowden. He removed from Fayette to Jessamine County, Ky., where he was subsequently married to Miss Juliette, daughter of John Hughes, of that county. They are the parents of five children, viz: Thomas B., John H., Kenney, Susie and William. In 1871, Mr. Nichols removed to Bourbon County, where he owns a fine farm of 300 acres of blue grass land. He is known throughout Bourbon County as a breeder of fine short

horn cattle and thoroughbred horses. He is a friend to educational and religious interests, and is at present Trustee of the school of his district. Mrs. Nichols is a consistent member of the Christian church. He is a Democrat, and was with Gen. W. R. Terrell when he was killed at Perryville. He began life a poor boy, dependent upon his own resources. By industry and good financiering he has acquired an honorable position among the leading citizen of Bourbon County.

JOHN J. PIPER, farmer; P. O. Hutchinson. The Piper family were identified with the early history of Nicholas County, being among the early families that located there during the early part of the present century. The subject of these lines was born in Nicholas County, Feb. 17, 1834; son of Samuel C. Piper and Eliza Smith. Samuel was born on the Hinkston, near Millersburg; son of Samuel Piper. Eliza Smith was born in this county; daughter of Alexander Smith. John J. was raised a farmer, which vocation he has followed since he came to manhood's years. In 1863 he came to this county, locating in Hutchinson Precinct, where he purchased a farm, and has since resided thereon. In 1863 he married Frances, daughter of Armstrong Dawson; by her has two children: William H., and Margaret. His father and mother were members of the Presbyterian Church.

WEBB ROSS, farmer; P. O. Hutchinson; was born in Harrison County, Va., March 28, 1807; son of John Ross, who was born and raised in Pennsylvania, and served in the Revolutionary war for a short time. The land owned by him was deeded to him in 1790. The mother of our subject was Ziporah (Webb) Ross, who married John in Robertson's Fort, in Virginia, in 1785. She was a daughter of Jonas Webb. Mr. Webb Ross married in 1836, Miss Shropshire, daughter of Col. E. N. Shropshire, of Bourbon County, and they have four children: Gabriella, Augusta Georgia, John Hancock, and Robert Wickliffe. He owns 380 acres of land and his family belong to the Christian Church; was a Whig before the war; a Democrat since.

WILLIAM L. SPEARS, farmer; P. O. Muir, K. C. R.; among the brave and adventurous spirits who, defying the privations of the wilderness and the savage vengeance of the red men, left their homes and followed in the wake of Boone and Kenton, to lay low the wilderness and make smooth the road for the advancing tide of civilization into Kentucky, was John L. Spears, of Virginia. Arriving at the infant settlements, he offered his services as a surveyor and school teacher, and they were eagerly accepted, for few men with such attainments had as yet visited the dark and bloody ground. He entered land in the southern part of Fayette County, where he settled, reared a family, and after attaining the green old age of ninety-four years, peacefully died. His son, Lee W. Spears, born in 1804, took possession of the old homestead, married Miss Frances W. Tapp, and raised a family of children, consisting of Charles L., George W., Luther, Riley F., Sarah (Land), Mildred (Davis), Randa (Bronaugh), John L., William L., and Chris. The latter was a private in Co. B, 8th Ky. Cavalry, C. S. A., and died a prisoner in Camp Douglas. William L. Spears was born May 22, 1855; received a common school education, and at the age of nineteen began life for himself. He removed to Bourbon County in 1878, where he is regarded as one of the most industrious and thrifty young farmers in the county. He was married Oct. 5, 1876, to Miss Lyda J. Phelps, daughter of William C. Phelps, of Jessamine County. They have two children, Claude Wilmore, born Oct. 2, 1877, and Randie Lou, born March 22, 1881. Mr. Spears and wife are both members of the Christian Church. In politics his affiliations are with the Democracy.

DANIEL STUART, farmer and stockraiser; P. O. Muir's Station; was born May 6, 1845, in Fleming County, Ky.; son of James and Sallie (Ficklin) Stuart; she is a daughter of Daniel and Delilah (Leonard) Ficklin, who came from Virginia at an early day. The paternal grandfather of our subject was William Stuart, who was of Scotch descent, and came to Kentucky in 1800, settling in Fleming County. The father of Daniel, who died in 1851, had ten children, our subject being the youngest. April 15, 1868, Mr. Stuart married Miss Nannie G. Hutchcraft, daughter of Reuben Hutchcraft, of Bourbon County, and the youngest of ten children born to that gentleman. They have five children: Mary Lou, born July 17, 1870; Sallie, born June 15, 1872; Ella, born May 8, 1874; Benjamin, born June 24, 1878; Fanny, born Aug. 14, 1881. Mr. Stuart owns 385 acres of land, and in addition to running his farm, handles short horn cattle, having a herd of 40, having at the head 10th Boston Duke, and 4th Ardrie. He and wife are members of the Christian Church, and Mr. Stuart is a Turnpike Director and a Republican.

DR. WILLIAM STEELE, retired physician; P. O., Hutchinson; was born Oct. 5, 1808, in Bourbon County, near Steele's Ford; son of John and Jane (Cunningham) Steele; she being a daughter of Capt. Cunningham. The father of this subject was born in Rockbridge County, Va., in 1772, and was a minister in the Reformed Church; he died in 1832. The grandfather of Dr. Steele was a native of Ireland, and came to Kentucky in 1778, dying in 1828. Dr. Steele was married Nov. 17, 1846, to Miss Julia F. Wood, daughter of Nimrod Wood, of Nicholas County, Ky., by which union there have been born six children: Anna J. (Mrs. Marsh); Ida (Mrs. Piper); Ella (Mrs. Norvill); John, Julia F., and Maggie W. The doctor practiced his profession in his early years in Springfield, Ohio, but retired from active practice 30 years ago. He owns 172 acres of land, his place being known as "Warblers's Glen," and himself, wife and family, with one exception, are Presbyterians.

JOHN P. TALBOTT, physician; P. O. Hutchinson; the grandfather of our subject, Aquila Talbott, came to Kentucky at an early day, and located in Paris, where he carried on carpentering and building, during which time he built the court house there, the cupola of which was a piece of architecture greatly admired, even by foreigners. His son, August Talbott, was born in Paris, and has been a farmer all his life. He at present resides in Franklin County. The mother of Dr. Talbott, and wife of August, was Fanny Pryor, daughter of Dr. John Pryor, of this county. Our subject was born June 8, 1836, in Bourbon County, where he received his early education; he attended Transylvania University, where he took a course in medicine, graduating from that institution in 1858. He spent a year additional at Jefferson Medical College, Philadelphia, after which he began practice at Blue Licks, Nicholas County, where he remained until the war, when he entered the Confederate service as Surgeon of the First Kentucky Mounted Riflemen, and remained four years; returning at the close of the war he located at Hutchinson, where he has a fine practice, and is highly respected.

THOS. H. WILSON, farmer; P. O. Paris; is descended from an old and honored English family, and traces his genealogy back to his grandfather, Isaac Wilson, a native of England. The courtesy and chivalry of a Southerner and the honest pride of an Englishman are still to be traced in his descendants. Thos. H., the subject of this sketch, was born in Fayette County, Ky., Aug. 13, 1823, and is the son of Samuel and Rebecca (Layton) Wilson, daughter of Thos. Layton. The earlier years of his life were spent in acquiring an education and in assisting his father. Being possessed of a high sense of honor, and natural financiering ability, he rapidly acquired a financial standing in the community. He now owns 580 acres of fine blue grass land, on which he has resided for many years. He has given much attention to the growing of hemp, in which all his theories put in practice have proved a success. He has handled and bred some fine short horns, though not classed among the extensive breeders. He was formerly a member of the old Whig party, but since the war he has been a Democrat. He was married in 1849 to Miss Margaret, daughter of Geo. McLeod, of Bourbon County; they have four children—Fyette, now wife of Dr. Wm. Warren, of Versailles, Delia, Anna and Kate. He is almost sixty years old. Mr. Wilson is still a man of vigorous mind and clear judgment.

I. FRANK WILLMOTT, farmer; P. O. Hutchinson; was born Sept. 20, 1834, in Bourbon County, Ky.; son of Fletcher and Harriett (Skillman) Willmott, daughter of Isaac Skillman, of Bourbon County, but formerly of Virginia. The grandfather of our subject was Robert Willmott, who was Colonel of Artillery during the Revolutionary war, having been born Dec. 25, 1757, in Maryland, and coming to Kentucky in 1792, settling in Bourbon, which county he represented in the General Assembly of the State seven years, and being one of the framers of the second constitution of Kentucky; dying Aug. 5, 1839. The father of Mr. Willmott was born Jan. 13, 1806, and died Aug. 11, 1855. Mr. I. Frank Willmott was married in September, 1855, to Miss Nancy J. Tanner, daughter of William Tanner, of Bourbon County, she dying in 1870, leaving two children: J. Smith, born April 29, 1858, and William T., born March 19, 1861. Jan. 25, 1872, he married Miss Eliza A. Boone, daughter of Noah Boone, by whom he has had four children: Kate E., born June 7, 1873; Noah Boone, born May 28, 1875; Ashby Carlisle, born April 16, 1877; Laura E., Aug. 31, 1879. He owns a farm of 200 acres of good land, is a member of the Christian Church, as well as his wife, and an Odd Fellow and a Democrat.

CARLTON WILLETT; P. O. Hutchinson; was born Jan. 20, 1801, in Maryland; son of Edward and Ellen (Fisher) Willett; she a daughter of Martin Fisher, of Virginia, and grand-daughter of one of the Shackelfords, of the Old Dominion. The parents of our subject came to Kentucky, by way of the Ohio river on a flat, and settled first at Maysville, then bought a place near Millersburg in Bourbon County, where the father died in 1842, and the mother in 1848. Mr. Willett was married in 1829 to Miss Nancy Coons, daughter of James Coons, of Bourbon County, which union has been blessed with thirteen children, three of whom are dead; those living are—Mary (Mrs. Larvell), Aquila, John, Ninian, Electa V. (Mrs. Craig), W. H. Harrison, A. Hamilton, Horatio Fisher, Scott, Josephine (Mrs. Bagg). Mr. Willett owns 185 acres of land ten miles from Paris, which he rents. He and wife are members of the Christian Church; he is a Democrat.

CENTERVILLE PRECINCT.

JAMES N. ALLEN, farmer; P. O. Centerville; was born Aug. 9, 1822, in Bourbon County, Ky., and is the son of Adoniram Allen and Polly (Cail) Allen, daughter of Jacob Cail, who came from Virginia; Adoniram Allen was a native of Georgia, and came to Kentucky with his father, his mother being dead, and located at Visalia, on the K. C. R. R., where he owned and operated a mill; he subsequently removed to Bourbon County and engaged in farming. Mr. Allen was reared to agricultural pursuits, and now owns a farm of 154 acres, and has also given some attention to the stock business; politically he is a Democrat, and for fifty years has been a member of the Baptist Church. June 17, 1858, he was married to Miss May Tyler, daughter of Wm. Tyler, of Harrison County; she died Oct. 17, 1880; there are four children, the issue of this marriage, living, and two dead: Wm. A., Welburn B. (dead), Albert L., Carrie L., Hugh W. (dead), and Cora G.

J. T. BARLOW, farmer; P. O. Centerville; was born Jan. 31, 1834, in Boone County, Mo., but has lived in Kentucky since 1846, and is the son of Martin B. and Fanny A. (Cantrill) Barlow. Martin was born in Scott County, Ky., from where he moved to Missouri, but died in Illinois in 1875; his wife was born on the farm where J. T., her son, now lives, and died in 1846; she was a daughter of Joseph Cantrill, Sr. The grandfather of our subject came to Kentucky about 1780, and located in Scott County, entering land and developing the same. Mr. Barlow was married in 1855 to Miss Annie R. Lydick, daughter of Jacob Lydick, of Fayette County, and has five children: Lelia, married to J. B. Ammerman, of Texas; Mollie, married to J. T. Hill, of Bourbon County, now of Texas; Bettie, married to John Stamps, of Bourbon County, now of Texas; Ella and Frankie. Our subject resided in Missouri from 1855 to 1862, since which time he has lived in Kentucky, for a short time in Fayette, afterward in Bourbon; he owns 95 acres of good land, farms in a general way and raises stock; has served as Justice of the Peace seven years in the Centerville Precinct, and is a Democrat. Mrs. Barlow is a member of the Old Union Christian Church, of Fayette County.

MARY J. BATTERTON, farming; P. O. Paris; is a representative of one of the old families of Bourbon County. She was born March 1, 1823, and is the daughter of Alfred and Elizabeth (Chowning) George, and the granddaughter of Gabriel George. In 1849 she was married to Benjamin A. Batterton, who died in 1863. Three children were born to them: Elizabeth, now wife of T. J. Shepherd, formerly of Georgetown, Ky., but now a resident of Chattanooga, Tenn.; B. Alfred and Mary S., both unmarried, and residing with their mother. The daughters are members of the Christian Church, and the sons' political views are Democratic. Mrs. Batterton has resided on her present farm since 1849, which consists of 140 acres of fine land, which by her judicious management and the aid of her son, has been and is a comfortable, pleasant and well kept home, as well as a valuable piece of property.

F. P. CLAY, farmer. The Clay family form so important a part of the history of Bourbon County, and the name is found interwoven in the history of so many important events chronicled in this book, that the following brief biography is confined to the subject only. He was born Oct. 26, 1819, in Bourbon, and is the son of Henry and Margaret (Helm) Clay. He was educated in his native county, and reared a farmer. In October of 1842 he married Miss Susan R. Wornall, daughter of Thomas Wornall, of Clark County, Ky. They have a family of four children: William H., Frances P., now Mrs. N. Buckner, Olive and Perry. Mr. Clay has a fine farm of 629 acres, known as "Castle Comfort," and does a general farm business. He and Mrs. Clay are members of the Baptist Church. Previous to the war he was a member of the Whig party, but since that event he has been a Democrat. He is a fine representative of so notable a family, and after having spent over three-score years in his native county, his name and reputation stands above reproach.

JOHN N. CRENSHAW, farmer; P. O. Leesburg; was born July 12, 1824, in Scott County, Ky.; his father, Joel Crenshaw, was a native of Virginia, and came to Kentucky during the early settlement of Scott County, where he located; he engaged in farming, in which he remained interested until his death, which occurred in 1838. In 1846 John N. was married to Miss Fanny Crenshaw, daughter of John Crenshaw, of Harrison County, Ky., of which he became a resident, and resided there until 1864, when he removed to his present fine farm of 280 acres. Politically, Mr. Crenshaw is a Democrat; he is an active and respected member of the community in which he lives, and has taken a deep interest in religious affairs, he and his family being members of the Christian Church. Their family consists of five children: Joel H., at home; Mary A., wife of James H. Shropshire, of Harrison County Ky.; John W., married Miss Fannie K. Thomas, and now resides in Scott County; Bettie and Lulie, both at home. Mr. Crenshaw is a deacon in the Leesburg Church, of which he is a member.

MRS. A. CLAY; P. O. Paris; was born June 14, 1810, in Bourbon County, daughter of Samuel D. and Elizabeth (Cunningham) Scott; he coming at an early day from Dinwiddie County, Va., and dying in 1813, leaving ten children, his wife having died sometime previously. Our subject was married in January, 1832, to Joseph Helm Clay, by whom she had nine children, only one of whom is now living, Isaac C. Clay, who was married June 1, 1870, to Miss Lizzie A. Forman, daughter of Thomas M. Forman, and who has borne him three children; Mary W., Sadie M., and Joseph. Mrs. Clay and her son own 307 acres of land, their place being called "Rosedale." Mrs. Clay is a member of the Baptist Church; Isaac a member of the Christian Church and a Democrat; he resided for two years in Texas.

HUBBELL C. CHINN, farmer; P. O. Leesburg; was born Aug. 16, 1842, in Missouri, his parents, Christopher C. and Nancy (Shropshire) Chinn, having removed to that State from Kentucky in 1831, but afterward returned to Bourbon County. The father died in 1872, but the mother is still living; the grandfather of our subject, Joseph Chinn, came from Virginia at an early day, and was one of those brave and hardy pioneers who helped turn the then wilderness of Kentucky into the blooming land it now is. Our subject married, July 9, 1863, Mrs. Lucy Kendall, and they have one child, Harry Hawkins, born March 29, 1868; Mr. Chinn owns 170 acres of excellent land, and handles short-horns in a moderate way; himself and wife are members of the Christian Church, and he is a Democrat.

W. A. FORMAN, farmer; P. O. Leesburg; traces the genealogy of his family back to his grandfather, William Forman, who was a Methodist minister, and settled in an early day in the history of Bourbon County near North Middletown, where he entered a tract of government land, which he improved and developed, and where he resided until his death, which occurred in 1814. His son, James Forman, and father of our subject, married Miss Elizabeth Allen, daughter of David Allen, who came to Bourbon County from Virginia, of which State James Forman was a native, and was brought to Kentucky by his parents during his childhood. Wm. A. was one of a family of seven children, and was born Oct. 17, 1814; he was reared on his father's farm, and has during his life been interested and engaged in agricultural pursuits and at stock raising. Dec. 12, 1839, he was married to Miss Sarah, daughter of George Chinn, of Harrison County, Ky. Politically, Mr. Forman's views are Democratic, and in religious belief he and family, with one exception, are members of the Christian Church; he owns a fine farm of 280 acres, located about ten miles from Paris; seven children have been born to them: Nancy and George, deceased; James, at home; Sarah, now Mrs. Nichols—Miriam, now wife of George Clark; and William, married Miss Lizzie Sudduth, and resides near the old home.

J. W. FRITTS, M. D.; P. O. Centerville; was born July 6, 1841, in Carlisle, Ky., son of Dr. W. W. and Sarah (Hamilton) Fritts; he, the father, having been born and raised in Clark County, Ky., whilst the grandfather of our subject, Henry Fritts, was a native of, and came from Pennsylvania to Kentucky in 1801, dying in 1879. Dr. W. W. Fritts is and has been for the past forty years a practicing physician in Carlisle. Our subject was married in 1867 to Miss Alice Stapleton, daughter of George W. Stapleton, of Clark County, and has seven children: Frank, Maud, Lizzie, Laura, Willie, May, and Walter. Dr. Fritts received his literary education in Georgetown, where he graduated in 1860, afterward in 1873, receiving his medical education in Louisville, where he was graduated, and received his diploma, settling down to practice in Winchester, where he remained till two years ago, when he came to Centreville, and opened practice, carrying on the grocery business. Dr. Fritts and wife are members of the Christian Church. He served in the Hospitals of the Federal army during the war. He is a Democrat.

REV. JOHN ALLEN GANO, Sr., minister and farmer; P. O. Centerville; whose portrait appears in this work; was born in Georgetown, Scott Co., Ky., July 14, 1805; his father, Richard M. Gano, was then a merchant in that place; his grandfather, John Gano, was a Baptist Minister who served under Gen. Washington as Chaplain in the Revolution; he was lineally descended from a French Huguenot of some prominence, who escaped to the Isle of Guernsey, and sailed to America at the time of the massacre of St. Bartholomew. The mother of John A. was formerly Elizabeth Ewing, from Bedford County, Va., where her parents resided and died; he was the fifth child and first son of his parents, who only raised another son, Dr. Stephen F. Gano, still living near Georgetown; he received a tolerable liberal English and classical education and studied and commenced the practice of law; becoming a convert to the Christian faith, he resolved with the help and blessing of God to preach the Gospel of Christ. The 2nd of Oct., 1827, he married Miss Catharine Conn, the only child and daughter of Capt. Wm. Conn, of Bourbon County, Ky., who resided near the village of Centerville, and gave them the farm near his own, where his father, Thos. Conn, settled in about 1787, where he lived, and died in 1811; he came from Culpepper County, Va., and owned a landed estate around him here of two thousand acres of land. His son, John M. Conn, came to Kentucky before the family, and with servants to assist him, prepared the ground and raised a crop, before the removal of his father's family; this was a very hazardous undertaking as the Indians were about, one had to watch with his trusty rifle, while the others plowed. He removed to the old homestead in 1828 late in the year. Capt. John M. Conn then was living on Townsend Creek on a fine farm, a portion of his father's original survey, where he had long lived and raised a large and interesting family. The father-in-law of John A. had a good farm, a part of the same survey extending up to the village; he had recently purchased the farm of his brother James, who inherited the old homestead, and removed to and is now living in Nicholas County. Col. Thompson Ware, who married Sally Conn, lived on a good farm immediately south of Capt. Wm. Conn and on the Lexington road; Mr. David Stonnoy, who married Miss Cassandra Conn, owned lands immediately west of Col. Ware, all portions of the same survey, on the headwaters of Townsend. Old Mr. John Hall lived at the time on a small farm adjoining, and northwest of them, a part of the Conn survey. The first child born to them, a son, Wm. Conn Gano, born at his grandfather's, Sept. 23, 1828; the second, Richard M. Gano, was born at Springdale, June 18, 1830; Fanny Conn, March 24, 1832; Robert Ewing, June 1, 1834; Stephen F., April 25, 1836; Franklin M., Dec. 11, 1839, Eliza G., Oct. 19, 1841; John Allen, Jr., July 21, 1845; and Mary Eliza, June 10, 1848; all of whom were born at Springdale; Robt., Stephen and Eliza died in early infancy; Mrs. Fanny Conn Spears died at Springdale, Feb. 4, 1850; Wm. Conn Gano died at Rural Glen, July, 1863; Capt. Wm. Conn died at Bellevue, Aug. 7, 1872, the day he was 88 years old; Mrs. Mary Eliza Buckner died at Bellevue, Aug. 4, 1877, leaving four children; and Franklin M. died near Taylor, in Texas, February, 1881, and left three children; his son, Gen. R. M. Gano, is now living at Dallas City, Texas, and his youngest son, John. Allen, Jr., is residing near Taylor, Williamson County, Texas. The father of our subject died in October, 1815, and his mother died in April, 1812, leaving six children.

WILL A. GAINES, farmer; P. O. Centerville; is a representative of one of the old and prominent families of the Blue Grass region; he was born August 9, 1840, in Fayette County, and is the son of O. W. Gaines and Amelia (Smith) Gaines, daughter of John Smith, of Clark County. O. W. Gaines was born in Fayette County, Jan. 28, 1816, and died Jan. 1, 1847; his wife subsequently married W. O. Thompson, of Georgetown. The grandfather of Will A., F. S. Gaines, was born in Shenandoah County, Va., May 31, 1781, and removed to Kentucky in 1802, settling in Fayette County. Will A. owns a fine farm of 180 acres, and is quite an extensive breeder of short horns, Poland-China hogs and Southdown sheep; his herd of short horn cattle consists of twenty-two females, at the head of which is "Young Mary." In politics, Mr. Gaines is a Democrat, and during the war he served in the Ninth Kentucky Cavalry as Sergeant Major, with Col. W. C. P. Breckinridge and Capt. F. Gano Hill. During his service, Mr. Gaines was wounded once, and twice taken prisoner. Dec. 21, 1865, he married Miss Bettie Hill, daughter of John Hill, of Bourbon County. Mr. Gaines has had quite a varied experience in life, but is now giving his entire attention to his farm and stock breeding, of which in the latter he already occupies quite a prominent place in the county.

JOHN T. GARTH, farmer; P. O. Paris; was born Oct. 22, 1843, in Bourbon County, and is the son of Thomas and Joanna (Lucas) Garth. Thomas Garth came to Bourbon County when a boy, and during his life engaged in farming. He died on the farm, where John T. now lives. Mrs. Garth survived her husband for many years; her death occurred Jan. 17, 1881. Mr. Garth is the owner of one of Bourbon County's fine farms of 340 acres, and known as "Greenwood." He does a general farming business, his principal production being grains. He is a Democrat in politics, and a member of the Christian Church. Though still a comparatively young man, he is an active member of the community, and by his honorable and consistent adherence to the principles of right and justice, he is a respected and valuable citizen.

F. GANO HILL, farmer and stock breeder; P. O. Centerville; well known to the citizens of Bourbon and adjoining counties as an extensive breeder and dealer in fine stock; was born July 1, 1842, in Bourbon County. The old home now owned by him being his birth-place. He is the son of John and Mary (Edwards) Hill; she the daughter of Major Geo. Edwards, of Bourbon County.

John Hill was also a native of Bourbon County, and his father was a native of Scotland, but came from Virginia to Kentucky, settling in Bourbon County during its pioneer days. F. Gano finished his education at Kentucky University, of Danville, in 1861. He then entered the 9th Kentucky Cavalry, Col. W. C. P. Breckinridge commanding. He entered the service as a private, and was promoted to the rank of Captain, commanding Co. A. By the request of Gen. John S. Williams he was assigned to his staff, and was subsequently made Inspector-General. While in battle near Columbia, South Carolina, he was wounded and sent to the hospital, but was finally taken in an ambulance, and while in this condition he remained in the service until Gen. Lee's surrender of the Confederate army. He then came back to Kentucky and engaged in the breeding of stock, for which his farm of 360 acres, known as "Hillburn," is peculiarly adapted. His attention has been given in this line to the purest breed, imported Cotswold sheep, and to short horn cattle, though he has also bred some fine trotting horses, and at one time owned May Queen, whose record was 2.20. He is one of the directors of the Bourbon County Fair Association, and is also identified with the Georgetown Pike in the same capacity. He also built what is known as the Gano Hill Pike. In politics he is a Democrat, and for the legislative session of the fall of 1881 he entered the campaign as a candidate for the nomination, but was defeated by Mr. Charles Offutt by but twenty-three votes.

JOSEPH H. HAWKINS, farmer; P. O. Centerville; was born April 14, 1831, in Bourbon County, Ky.; son of Harry and Sarah (Chinn) Hawkins. He, the father of Joseph, was born in Maryland, in 1767, and came to Kentucky when a mere lad, with the McMillans, a surveying party, and settled in Pendleton County, where he married a Miss Fugit, but that lady dying, he moved to Bourbon County, where he married the daughter of Joseph Chinn, from which union resulted three children: Mary Catharine, wife of Hubbell Chinn; Joseph H., and Margaret, wife of William T. Herne, of Fayette County. The old gentleman died in 1842, after a long and eventful life. Our subject was married in 1854, to Miss Nancy Sparks, daughter of Wesley Sparks, which union was blessed with one child, J. Wesley. Mrs. Hawkins dying, Mr. H. took as a second wife Miss Lizzie E. Kendall, daughter of Alfred Kendall, and from which marriage have been born six children: Allie K., Joseph L., Marietta, William, Harry, and Sallie. Mr. Hawkins owns 800 acres of land ten miles from Paris, and his mother, who is eighty-one years of age, lives with him, on the farm upon which she was born. He farms and handles stock, paying some attention to short-horns, with the "Fourth Duke of Ash Glen" at the head. He has about forty animals, Daisies and Maries being the principal families represented. Mr. Hawkins has served two terms as Magistrate of Centerville Precinct; was a Whig before the war, but is now a Democrat; he and wife are members of the Christian Church.

R. A. MOORE, physician; P. O. Centerville; is the oldest of a family of five children born to James and Sallie (Allen) Moore, both natives of Scott County, Ky.; his grandfather, James Moore, was a native of Virginia, and was among the early pioneers of Scott County, Ky. James, the Doctor's father, was a resident of Scott County during his life, and died there, Oct. 4, 1857, his mother, who was the daughter of Robert Allen, dying some time previous to this date. The Doctor received his education at Georgetown, and then took up the study of medicine, subsequently graduating from the medical department of Transylvania University of Lexington, and also received a degree of M. D. from a medical college of Louisville, which he attended; he located first in Trimble County, Ky., where he practiced for five years; he then removed from there to Scott County, Ky., from whence he removed to Jacksonville, Bourbon Co., in 1859; he owns a nice farm of 91 acres, which he has rented. This place, near Jacksonville, is known as "Alta Monte." The Doctor is a Democrat, and by his energy and industry has accumulated a competency, and is still a live, energetic business man, of middle age, having been born on Oct. 4, 1830. Sept. 25, 1856, he was married to Miss Sallie Simms, sister of Col. Simms, of Paris; two daughters were the fruits of this union: Blanche, and Lulie. In 1867, several years subsequent to the death of his first wife, the Doctor married Mrs. Sallie Garrard; six children have been born to them: Duke, Robbie, Maude, Captain, Colonel, and D. Lary.

AUGUSTUS SHROPSHIRE, farmer; P. O. Centerville; was born July 20, 1836, in Bourbon County, and is the son of Col. Ben Shropshire of Harrison County. He was educated at the common country schools, and was reared a farmer. He now owns a body of 203 acres of as fine land, and as finely improved, as can be found in Centerville Precinct, and is called "Spring Hill" on account of a fine spring on the farm. Besides doing a general farming business, he has given much attention to the breeding of fine horses and short-horn cattle, and at present has a fine herd of twenty-five in number, representing most of the popular families, Duke of Ashland being at the head of his herd. Politically, Mr. Shropshire is a Democrat, and in all affairs pertaining to the general welfare of the community he has taken an active part. For the past seven years he has held the office of school trustee. He is a member of the Christian Church, as is also his wife, to whom he was married in February, 1864, and whose maiden name was Fanny Forrester and daughter of R. H. Forrester of Chicago, Ill. They are the parents of seven children ; Ida, Robert, Benjamin, Pink, Palmer, Garrett and Fanny.

B. T. SHROPSHIRE, farmer; P. O. Leesburg; was born April 29, 1825, in Bourbon County, Ky.; he is the son of Col. B. N. and Nancy M. (Parrish) Shropshire. The Shropshire family are of English descent. Our subject was married Nov. 22, 1846, to Miss Elizabeth Jane, daughter of George A. Smith, Esq., and from which union have been born four children: Benjamin F., born Oct. 11, 1847; he married Miss Mary T. Bryant, and died Dec. 2, 1873, leaving one son, W. B.; George S., born Aug. 20, 1849; Gabie S., born March 17, 1852; she married David R. Saunders, now of Texas, and has one child, Benjamin E.; Thomas J., born July 8, 1855; he married Miss Maggie Lonny, of Woodford County. Mr. Shropshire is a general farmer, and owns 250 acres of land, his place being known as "Maple Grove;" himself, wife, and all his children, with one exception, are members of the Christian Church; he was a Whig before the war, but a Democrat since.

JOHN SIMPSON, minister; P. O. Centerville; was born April 7, 1841, in Prince Edward's Island, Dominion of Canada, and is the son of Henry and Jeannette (Stevenson) Simpson. Our subject came to Kentucky in 1867, to attend the Bible College of the Kentucky University. In November, 1873, he was married to Miss Annie Hull, and by which union they have had one child: Robert N. H. Simpson, born Jan. 10, 1875. Mr. Simpson is a minister of the Christian Church, and owns 360 acres of land, 160 of which are in this county.

CHAS. TURNER, farmer ; P. O. Centerville; was born Nov. 16, 1803, in Bourbon County, Ky.; son of William and Patsey (Richards) Turner, both of whom were born in Maryland, and came to Kentucky nearly one hundred years ago; they came down the river to where Louisville now stands, but before that city was founded, and from thence to Lexington, which at that time only contained a few cabins, and remained there several years. They then bought land two miles from Millersburg. The old pioneer died Feb. 1, 1835, at the age of eighty-five years, and his wife followed him eight or ten years later, at the same age as her husband. While at Lexington, William was one of the hunters for the settlement inside the fort, and contributed to the sustenance of the brave little garrison, while the savages roamed around. He was in Bryant's Station when it was besieged by Simon Girty and his barbarous allies, and his wife, Patsey, was present and recollected the famous colloquy between Van Swearengen and Girty. She was also one of the party who went out of the fort for water, when five hundred Indians were so near that she could see the eyes of the red devils. Our subject was married in March, 1827, to Miss Mary Ward, of this County, and has two children : John W., and Lucinda. Lucinda married J. J. Ireland, and has three children : Mary, John, and Frank. Mr. Turner owns 600 acres of excellent land, six miles from Paris, and he and wife are members of the Methodist Church. In politics Mr. T. was a Whig before the war, but since then he has been a Democrat.

RUDDEL'S MILLS PRECINCT

H. C. BOWEN, farmer and distiller ; P. O. Ruddel's Mills. Among the early settlers of Bourbon County was the Bowen family, which came here from near Baltimore, Md., and settled upon wild land, following farming. One of the sons of the first Bowen, Benjamin by name, was born Oct. 8, 1794, whose father dying, was bound out to the carpenter's trade in Lexington; but the war of 1812 coming on he enlisted in the service; but, in consequence of Kentucky's quoto being complete, he was not mustered in. He afterward became a contractor, during which time he erected many buildings, including three churches in Ruddel's Mills. He also farmed and kept a hotel; he was also engaged in distilling. He married Miss Mary Current, of this County, by whom he had six children, H. C., our subject, being next to the youngest of these children. Benjamin died Oct. 7, 1881, having held the office of Constable for many years. Our subject was born Feb. 11, 1842, and since the age of fifteen years has "paddled his own canoe," having by industry and perseverance placed himself in independent circumstances. May 16, 1865, he was married to Anna E., only child of Benjamin F. and Minerva H. Howard, of Bourbon County. She was born April 30, 1849, and died July 31, 1878, leaving five children : Lida, Benjamin, Joseph W., Nannie K. and Hattie. Mr. Bowen has been engaged in distilling and farming since he arrived at manhood, and owns a farm of 364 acres, and a copper distillery. He is a Democrat.

WILLIS D. COLLINS, farmer; P. O. Ruddel's Mills; was born in Bourbon County, Ky., March 13, 1810; son of Foster and Elizabeth (Matheny) Collins ; he being a son of William Collins, and a native of Virginia ; she a daughter of David Matheny, of Bourbon County, and after whom the Matheny Church is named. Foster Collins came to Kentucky in 1797, with his mother and three sisters ; being a farmer, but a man of more than ordinary ability, serving as Constable for ten years, as Magistrate for several years, and as Sheriff two years. He died Feb. 22, 1847 ; his wife, June 27, 1835. They raised ten children. Our subject was married Oct. 2, 1834, to Sally Ann, daughter of Robert and Nancy (Fretwell) Palmer, old settlers of this county, which union has been blessed with three children: Wm. L. and Elizabeth living, and Lucinda, dead. Mr. Collins and wife are members of the Christian church ; he has held several offices, being Deputy Sheriff under his father, a Constable for ten years, and a Magistrate for twelve years; he was at one time guardian for twenty-one children, with all of whom he has settled fully and honorably except four, who are not yet of age ; has settled thirty-three different estates, and done more business of that character than any man in the county. He is and has been a Republican since the formation of that party.

JOHN CURRENT, farmer and distiller; P. O. Ruddel's Mills ; was born in Bourbon County, Ky., in 1838, son of Jesse Current, who raised a family of nine children, five sons and four daughters, John being the second son. Four of these brothers entered the service of the Confederate States, and served under General Morgan. John, our subject, was reared on his father's farm, and has through life been engaged in the same business as his father—farming and distilling—paying special attention to the latter business, and making nothing but the straightest copper-distilled goods, the demand for which he has been scarcely able to supply. Feb. 5, 1861, he was married to Miss Mary Catharine, daughter of Thos. McCarney, of Bourbon County. She died Oct 24, 1875, leaving three children : Anna Lee, Lizzie T., and John McIlvain. Mr. Current was again married, Nov. 26, 1878, to Miss Betty Turney, daughter of Amos Turney, of this County. He owns 184 acres of land, is a member of the ancient and honorable fraternity of Freemasons, and is a Democrat.

DARWIN D. EADS, physician, Ruddel's Mills; was born in Harrison County, Ky., May 11, 1836, son of John and Ellen (McMillan) Eads; he is a native of Spottsylvania County, Va., coming to Kentucky about 1810, but having been married in Virginia, and his wife dying previous to his leaving that State. Mr. John Eads was a farmer, and passed the best part of his life in Harrison County, where he died in 1836, his wife surviving him and marrying, in 1842, Wm. W. Bowman, of Bourbon County, afterward moving to Illinois, where she is still residing. Our subject remained on the farm until sixteen years of age, when he entered the Ohio Weslyan University, at Delaware, Ohio, which he left while in his junior year. In the fall of 1857 he entered Jefferson Medical College, Philadelphia, from which institution he graduated in 1859, and located at Ruddel's Mills, where he has since had a lucrative practice. Dr. Eads was first married in

1862, to Miss Jennie, daughter of Thomas Isgrig, of Harrison County; she died, and Dr. Eads married his second wife Miss Anna, daughter of Frank Adair, of this County, who died in 1876, leaving one child, Benjamin Brindly Eads, now eleven years old. For his third wife, Dr. Eads married Miss Avonia Matheny, daughter of Dr. Matheny of Louisville. Mr. and Mrs. Eads are members of the M. E. Church, and he is a Mason and an Odd Fellow; also a Democrat, but taking no part in politics

H. C. EALES, farmer; P. O. Ruddel's Mills; was born in this County, April 9, 1818; son of James and Lucy (Wyatt) Eales. James was born in Virginia in 1789, and came to Kentucky with his parents, who settled in Fleming Co., Ky., in 1795. He learned the trade of blacksmithing in Bourbon County, at which he worked until he got a start in life, when he commenced farming, which he followed the rest of his life, acquiring a handsome property, owning about 1,000 acres of land. His wife came from Virginia with her parents, who settled in Montgomery County. James died in 1853 and his wife in 1855, leaving a family of six children; H. C. being the fourth, who is a farmer; H. C. married in 1849, Miss Amanda Talbott, of this County, who bore her husband nine children: Harry, Charles, Frazer, Lucy, Kate, Ashby, Amanda, Thomas, and Sidney. Mr. and Mrs. Eales both belong to the Christian Church.

THOMAS M. FISHER, farmer; P. O. Ruddel's Mills; was born May 3, 1827, in Bourbon County, Ky., son of James H. and Sarah J. (Howard) Fisher, and grandson of William L., whose father came from Germany. William L. was originally a brickmason, but was afterward a farmer, and lived to an advanced age, having been the father of nine children; his son, James H., died at the age of thirty-six, having been a farmer, and leaving two children, Thomas M. being the oldest. Mrs. Fisher was afterward married to John Dimitt, of Bourbon County, and is still living. Our subject, during ten years of his early life, worked at carpentering, but since that time has been engaged in farming; he was married July 29, 1861, to Miss Emma Barton, of this county, daughter of Abraham and Catharine (Cumber) Barton, and has five children living: Nannie B., Maude E., James H., Adella and Edna M., and Lida Lee, dead; he owns 131 acres of land, and is a Democrat.

JOHN W. FISHER, farmer; P. O. Ruddel's Mills; was born upon the farm where he now lives, in Bourbon County, May 16, 1830; son of James H. Fisher. Our subject commenced for himself when eighteen years of age, and for some time was engaged at farming; then he taught school one winter, after which he worked at carpentering six years, since which time he has followed farming, owning his father's old homestead, a farm of 115 acres. Mr. Fisher was married Dec. 11, 1855, to Miss Louisa Jett, of Harrison County, Ky., which union has been blessed with seven children, all of whom are living: Cora, S. Anna, Darwin E., Mollie Lou, John R., Claude E., and Fred H. He is a member of the I. O. O. F., and a Democrat.

ELI HOWARD, farmer; P. O. Ruddel's Mills. About the close of the Revolutionary war, among the emigrants from Maryland to Kentucky, was James Howard, who with his family, consisting of wife, three sons, Elijah, Paris and Matthew, and one daughter, Hannah, settled on the Maysville road, between Millersburg and Paris, in Bourbon County, at a point about three miles from the last named place, and now owned we believe by Mrs. Clay. At this place James Howard departed this life at quite an advanced age, but the exact date of his death we have been unable to obtain. The second son, Paris Howard, was born on the eastern shore of Maryland, Feb. 5, 1777; was brought to Kentucky when quite young, and after remaining with his father at the above place till he arrived at the age of maturity, he ventured out upon his own resources, and about the year 1800 was married to Catharine Current, who was also a native of Maryland, and was born April 11, 1782. Paris settled near Ruddel's Mills, where he secured and developed a large tract of land, something near 700 acres. The fruits of this marriage were nine children, six sons and three daughters. This family has since become noted in the history of Kentucky for their remarkable height, weight and longevity. Believing it to be appropriate that a brief but accurate statement of this noted family should be embodied in this work, we submit the following:

MALES.	HEIGHT.	WEIGHT.
Father (Paris Howard),	6 ft., 4 ins.	200 lbs.
Thomas C.,	6 " 4 "	230 "
James,	6 " 6½ "	216 "
John C. (deceased),	6 " 11½ "	266 "
Elijah,	6 " 3 "	210 "
Matthew,	6 " 6½ "	220 "
Eli,	6 " 4¾ "	198 "
7 males.	45 4¼	1,540 lbs.

Average height males, 6 ft., 5¾ ins. Av. weight, 220 lbs.

FEMALES.	HEIGHT.	WEIGHT.
Mother (Catharine Howard),	6 ft., ½ in.	285 lbs.

FEMALES.	HEIGHT.	WEIGHT.
Sarah,	6 " 2 "	165 "
Mary (deceased),	6 " 3 "	160 "
Margaret,	6 " 3 "	215 "
4 females.	24 8½	825 lbs.

Average height females, 6 ft. $2\frac{1}{8}$ in.; average weight, $206\frac{1}{4}$ lbs. Aggregate height of this family of eleven persons is seventy feet and three-quarters inch; weight, 2,365 pounds. At this date (1882) the writer is personally acquainted with quite a number of the grand-children, males and females, that range from six feet to six feet six and one-half inches in height, and are probably still growing. The father, Paris Howard, died on the home place, near Ruddel's Mills, on 27th of July, 1862, in his eighty-sixth year; his wife following him July 14, 1870, in her eighty-ninth year. At this date there has been but two deaths in this large family of children, seven still survive, five sons and two daughters, the youngest child being now in her sixty-first year. Taking into consideration the number of persons composing this family, their height, weight, strength and longevity, they are perhaps without a parallel in the world. The youngest son, Eli Howard, was born March 2d, 1819, near Ruddel's Mills, where he was reared and educated. On the 3d of November, 1842, he was married to Hannah P., daughter of Michael Isgri, of Harrison County. Her grandfather, Daniel Isgri, was a native of Maryland, where he married on the 6th of January, 1777, to Margaret Cole. He subsequently emigrated to Kentucky and settled in what is now Harrison County, where he reared three sons and four daughters. The youngest son, Michael, was born March 27, 1792; married May 19, 1816, to Margaret Current, who was born near Paris, Feb. 15, 1795. "Uncle Mike," as he was familiarly called, was of a lively, jocular disposition, and will doubtless be remembered by many of the readers of this sketch. He died Sept. 24, 1860, in his sixty-ninth year; his wife, on Dec. the 19th, 1875, in her eighty-second year. He left a family of one son and two daughters, one daughter having died several years previous to his death. Our subject, Eli Howard, in a short time after his marriage, settled on a small farm adjoining the old homestead, built a small house in the woods and began clearing around him. Being industrious and economizing through the early part of his life, he now owns a nice farm of 200 acres, well fenced and stocked, and upon which he is endeavoring to retire from active work, and enjoy some of the fruits of his past labors. The result of his marriage was three children: one son, James Alex., born April 24, 1845, and died on the 19th of April, 1867; and two daughters, Mary C., born Nov. 13, 1846, and was married Nov. 26, 1863, to Wm. J. Bowman, of Harrison. This union was blessed with one child, Jennie Lee, who was born Jan. 20, 1865. Mr. Bowman died Dec. 29, 1865; his little girl followed him Jan. 29. 1866, and his wife Feb. 3, 1866. The youngest daughter, Maggie Frances Howard, was born Jan. 25, 1856, and was married on the 10th of Oct., 1872 to F. E. Baird, a native of Harrison but a resident of Bourbon at the time of his marriage, and still resides in the county. Mr. Howard and family are all members of the Methodist Church. He has never held any political office in his life, never sought any, but at all times and under all circumstances he supports the nominee of the Democratic party. Besides his general routine of business on the farm, he has endeavored to make a specialty of raising a few trotting colts; among the most noted of which we might mention, is Lumber, bay gelding, who as a six-year old competed in the speed ring at Cynthiana with several of the fastest trotters of his class in the State for the $100 premium, a prize he won with apparent ease. After being honored with some other smaller prizes at this fair, Mr. Howard sold him for $1,000 cash to the Hon. T. J. Megibben, of Harrison County. He has raised some other promising colts that he sold untrained at fair prices. Mr. Howard has been prominently connected with the Masonic Order for many years, serving as Master of his lodge at Ruddel's Mills for several consecutive terms, and from his first admission into the institution, has been one of its most zealous workers and supporters.

ALLEN M. KISER, farmer; P. O. Ruddel's Mills. Among the emigrants from Germany to America during the latter part of the seventeenth century, was John Kiser, who settled in Maryland, and there reared a family of two sons and three daughters, viz: Jacob, Polly, Elizabeth, Nancy, and John. In 1870, the family moved to Kentucky, and located for one year in Fayette County. They then removed to Bourbon County, where they settled permanently. They, with the help of a number of other pioneer families, erected a fort on the farm now owned by James P. Kiser; there for a time they resided for mutual protection, though the head of each family soon entered a tract of Government land and began preparing a home. The Kisers secured a large tract of land, and their interests being mutual, they soon developed a fine property. John, the youngest son of the family mentioned, was here married to Miss Ursula, daughter of John Rout, who with his family came from Virginia to the new settlement; he became the possessor of a farm, and subsequently of a mill (both grist and saw), and also later he became interested in a distillery, for the purpose of converting the surplus grain of the community into a more marketable form, by reason of its being less bulky. There were born to John and Ursula a family of twelve children, of whom Allen was the oldest; he was born Sept. 6, 1806, and has spent his life in Ruddel's Mills Precinct; farming has been his principal occupation, though he was also in connection with his sons interested in distilling, in which they failed. Allen was married Jan. 29, 1834, to Susan, daughter of Elias and Catharine (McLair) Livingstone, who is a native of Maryland, and formerly resided in Bracken County, Ky. Six children were born to them, four of whom grew to maturity, viz: Elizabeth, wife of W. A. Brannock, of Cass County, Mo.; Mary, who married Thomas McDonald, and dying left one child, named Raymond; Josie, now Mrs. Hamilton, of Cynthiana, and Allen M., whose name appears at head of this sketch. He was born Dec. 26, 1845, and passed his early life on his father's farm; in September of 1862, he enlisted in Co. C, 5th Kentucky Cavalry, under Captain Bedford. He remained in the service until the close of the war, during which time he spent some time under the famous Gen. John A. Morgan, and while with him in Ohio, he was captured and held a prisoner for eight months at Camp Douglass, Chicago; returning to Bourbon County, Ky., at the cessation of hostilities, he married, on June 10, 1867, Miss Minerva, daughter of Saloma Keller. She died Oct. 25, 1876, leaving three children: Laura, Elizabeth, and Shelby. Dec. 10, 1879, Mr. Kiser married Miss Ella Current, daughter of Thomas J. Current, one of Gen. Morgan's lieutenants, and who was killed at Green River Bridge. Politically, both Mr. Kiser and his father are Democrats.

JOHN A. KISER, R. R. Agent, P. O. Shawhan, is the son of John R. Kiser, now a retired farmer, who was born March 7, 1810; and is the son of John Kiser, who came from Maryland to Bourbon County at the date of its earlier history. He was a farmer, millwright and distiller, and remained a resident of Bourbon County until his death. John R. has passed his life in his native county, and spent his early life in helping his father at his various duties. He was the first agent for the K. C. R. R. at that point, and discharged the duties of the office for many years. Recently, however, he has become so far disabled as to have allowed the position to be transferred to his son, whose name heads this sketch. He was married to a lady by the name of Ann Rebecca Dimitt of Bourbon County. Two children were born to them; Nannie, and John A. The latter was born March 1, 1860. He received but a common school education, but having spent many years in the office with his father in the discharge of the duties as R. R. agent, when devolving upon him, were not difficult. April 12, 1881, he was married to Miss Carrie E. Goodman, daughter of Mathew and Mollie Goodman of Bourbon County. Though one of the youngest agents on the line of the K. C. road, his work is always promptly and accurately done, and should he desire a change, his ability has already fitted him for a more responsible position.

W. J. KISER, farmer; P. O. Shawhan; is a descendent of one of Bourbon County's early pioneers; his father, James P. Kiser, is the son of John Kiser. James P. was born March 18, 1828, and now owns and resides on the farm of 283 acres, owned by his father and grandfather; much of his attention has been devoted to the breeding of fine stock, of which he makes thoroughbred Southdown sheep a specialty. June 5, 1852, he married Miss Lucetta, daughter of Jesse and Ingbaur Current, of Bourbon County; six children have been born to them, of whom W. J. is the oldest. Mr. Kiser is a member of the order of A. F. & A. M., and a Democrat; his son, W. J., whose name heads this sketch, was married April 11, 1878, to Miss Nannie K. Remington, daughter of B. F. Remington, of Paris, Ky.; two children have been born to them: Frank P. and William S. The Kisers are well known and respected in Bourbon County as an enterprising, industrious, and intelligent people; and although W. J. is still a young man, he has already made the most of his opportunities, and is a worthy representative of his ancestors.

DR. A. H. KELLER; P. O. Ruddel's Mills; was born at Beaver Dam Springs, Tenn., Aug. 23, 1858; son of Dr. Thomas Fairfax Keller, who was a native of Alabama, and studied law, and after practicing three years, studied medicine, graduating from Bellevue College, New York, in 1847. He practiced the rest of his life in the states of Tennessee, Alabama and Arkansas, moving to North Middletown, Bourbon county, Ky., in 1868, and dying there the following year. He married Miss Susan Warren, who was born in Dublin, Ireland, but who came to this country when nine years of age; she died in 1866, having given birth to seven children, three only of whom are now living: Arthur H., Alexander M., and Leila F. The eldest son, Arthur H., our subject, received a classical education, graduating from Centre College, Danville, Ky., in June, 1879; then entered the Louisville Medical College, from which he graduated Feb. 25, 1881, and commenced practice at Shawhan, but a few months later bought the office of Dr. D. D. Eads, at Ruddel's Mills, where he has already secured a fine practice. He was married April 20, 1881, to Ida G. Bowen, born Jan. 2, 1862, daughter of Geo. W. Bowen of this County. The Doctor is a member of the Episcopal Church, and his wife of the Christian Church. He is an Odd Fellow and a Democrat.

JACOB C. KELLER, farmer; P. O. Ruddel's Mills; traces the geneology of his family back to the early pioneers of Bourbon County; his grandfather, Abraham Keller, came from Maryland to Kentucky in an early day, and settled in Bourbon County; his son Solomon, and father of our subject, was born in 1803 in Ruddel's Mills Precinct; he followed the business of his father, that of farming and distilling. Jan. 7, 1840, he was married to Miss Elizabeth, daughter of John Kiser, of Bourbon County. Mrs. Keller was born March 8, 1809, and has during her life been a resident of Bourbon County; previous to this marriage, however, Mr. Keller had been married, and had a number of children, three of the sons being in the Confederate army during the late Civil war; Jackson S. was killed, George A. returned wounded, Solomon A. was shot down in cold bloo l after his return from the war, he being at that time but a boy of sixteen years. By his last marriage Mr. Keller had a family of twelve children, only four of whom are living, viz.: Isaac, Mattie B., Jacob C., whose name heads this sketch, and Rebecca A. Mrs. Keller, the mother of Jacob C., has a fine farm of 300 acres, which is attended by her sons. Jacob C. is an enterprising, industrious young man, who has made the most of his opportunities for self improvement, and is a worthy representative of so hardy a race of pioneers as were his ancestors.

GRIFFIN KELLY, farmer; P. O. Shawhan; was born in Clark County, Ky., Jan. 15, 1815; son of Griffin and Sarah (Sutton) Kelly, both of whom were from near Culpepper Court House, Va.; he, the father, was a stonemason by trade, and when the war of 1812 broke out enlisted in the service of his country and served gallantly till the end of the struggle, when he removed to Kentucky, where he passed the rest of his life in farming, raising a family of six children, only one of whom is now living, Griffin, the youngest, the subject of this sketch, who at the age of seventeen began doing for himself, raising hemp on his father's farm, and who has continued farming ever since; Nov. 24, 1836, he was married to Miss Mary Cummins, born April 18, 1819, daughter of Nathaniel and Delilah (Hays) Cummins, of Bourbon County; the Cummins' family being natives of Virginia and the Hays of Maryland. Mrs. Hays' father was an old Revolutionary soldier, and one of the early settlers of Kentucky. Mr. Kelly has six children living: Sarah, Washington, Silas, William, Elizabeth and Gano; he lost one son, James N., in the late war, a member of Captain Bedford's Co., 5th Kentucky Cav. Mr. Kelly owns over 100 acres of good land, upon which he has fine buildings, and he and wife are members of the Christian Church at Mt. Carmel.

CAPTAIN THOS. E. MOORE, farmer and stockraiser ; P. O. Shawhan ; was born in Pendleton County, Ky., Feb. 15, 1831, son of Wm. and Margaret S. (Braun) Moore, both of whom were natives of Bourbon County, but whose parents were natives of Virginia. William Moore held the office of Justice of the Peace, and served in the war of 1812. He died in 1833, of cholera. When 16 years old, the subject of this sketch began the battle of life for himself, he being the youngest of six children. He first worked at farming, then clerked in a store, after whieh he attended Bartlett's Commercial College at Cincinnati, from which he graduated; served as Deputy Sheriff under his brother, and was then elected County Clerk of Pendleton County, which position he held four years ; was married Sept. 29, 1859, to Miss Sarah J. Shawhan, daughter of Col. John Shawhan, of Harrison County, Ky., who served in the Mexican war under General Taylor, and was wounded at the battle of Buena Vista, and who served in the late war, but was shot by a guerilla whom he had parolled, whilst on his way to Kentucky to raise a regiment. Capt. Moore entered the Confederate service in 1862, as Captain of Co. D., 4th Kentucky Cavalry, H. L. Giltner, Colonel, and remained through the struggle, being wounded in two places whilst near Nashville. At the close of the war he engaged in merchandising, and was then elected Sheriff, serving two terms. He was also engaged in distilling, and has paid considerable attention to the raising of fine and trotting stock, short horn cattle, and Cotswold and Southdown sheep. He has nine children: Tabitha, Sterling P., John S., Sallie, Minnie, Thomas E., William, Annie S., and George. He owns 300 acres of fine land. On his farm is the ancient fort, mentioned in Collins' history, at the junction of the two streams forming the Stoner.

WILLIAM MILLER, farmer, P. O. Ruddel's Mills; was born in Harrison County, Ky., Oct 13, 1843, son of Pugh and Margaret (Shawhan) Miller; he, born April 13, 1810, and she Aug. 12, 1812, and were married April 10, 1834. Pugh was the son of James and Elizabeth (Pugh) Miller, and Margaret was the daughter of Joseph and Sally (Ewalt) Shawhan. Both the Miller and the Shawhan families were originally from Pennsylvania. James, the grandfather of our subject, moved to Missouri about 1829, where he passed the rest of his days, dying there in 1835; he took his son Pugh along with him to Missouri, but the son not liking it there, returned to his native State where he married and settled down, but died in 1878. He reared one son to maturity, William the subject of this sketch, who has devoted himself to farming. At the commencement of the late war, William, entered the Confederate service, under Capt. Jo. Desha, 1st Ky. Inf., and served as Sergeant one year, when he was transferred to Capt. Jo. Hardin's Co., Maj. Shawhan's Cav. Battalion; was taken prisoner Oct. 7, 1863, and after enjoying the sweets of prison life at Camp Morton, Indianapolis, for over a year, returned home in 1864. Was married Feb. 8, 1866, to Miss Sarah Rule, of Bourbon County, who has borne the following children: James R., born Dec. 21, 1866; Annie L., Sept. 4, 1869; Willie Pugh, Nov. 26, 1871; Mattie Bettie, Jan. 26, 1874; Joseph D., born Aug. 11, 1876. He owns 195 acres of land, is an Odd Fellow, and a Democrat.

JOHN W. McILVAIN, farmer, and short-horn breeder; P. O. Ruddel's Mills; was born July 9, 1849; son of Moses H. McIlvain, a farmer of Bourbon County, Ky., whose father, William, came from Virginia at an early day, and followed farming and distilling, dying in 1853, his wife following him in 1854. Moses H., born in 1825, the father of our subject, died May 3, 1864, in the prime of life, leaving only one child; his widow afterward married J. C. Flowers, but died July 13, 1876. Mr. McIlvain is a farmer, and devotes a great deal of his time to the breeding and handling of short-horn cattle, in which he has been quite successful; he owns a farm containing 425 acres of land, on which he resides. He was married April 16, 1869, to Miss Mattie E., daughter of James Rule, deceased. She died Nov. 6, 1880, leaving three children: Hattie May, William James, and Richard Miller. Mr. McIlvain is a member of the A. F. and A. M., and I. O. O. F.; also a Democrat.

CHARLES REDMON, farmer and trader; P. O. Paris; son of George and Sallie (Hayes) Redmon, and was born on Flat Run, in Bourbon County, Sept. 13, 1816. His father, George Redmon, was born in Pennsylvania in 1781, and when only five years of age he came down the Ohio River, accompanied by his father, and settled on Flat Run, Bourbon County, where he was reared and educated. He began life as a farmer, an occupation he followed as long as he lived. In 1806 he was married to Sallie Hayes, a native of Maryland, who was born in 1786, and when quite young was brought to Kentucky by her parents. George Redmon died on his farm Aug. 1844, and his wife followed him in 1851. The old place is now owned and occupied by Washington Redmon. This couple had born to them a family of eleven children, seven sons, viz: Thomas Jefferson, William T., George L., Charles, John W., Washington, and Solomon S.; and four daughters, viz: Mary Ann, who married Edmund Nunn; Elizabeth, who married John K. Ashurst; Margaret, who married Thomas M. Smith; and Sallie, who married John W. Jones. Of this large family only three are now living, viz: Charles, who is our subject, Washington, and Mrs. Sallie Jones. Charles, like many other boys raised at that date of our country's history, was denied the advantages of a collegiate education, but was sufficiently fortunate to procure at least a respectable knowledge of such branches as were then taught in our common country schools; he was married on Feb. 9th, 1845, to Catharine, daughter of Samuel Talbott, of Bourbon; she was born July 12, 1822, and died Nov. 23, 1853. Mr. Redmon was next married Feb. 5, 1856, to Elizabeth H., daughter of Robert and Susan (Triplett) Trimble, of Fleming County, Ky. Elizabeth was born ————; her father, Robt. Trimble, was a native of North Carolina, and was born in 1788, and when only one year old he was taken by his parents to Tennessee, where he remained five years, at which time he came to Kentucky, where he spent his after life; his wife, Susan Triplett, was born in Virginia in 1806, married there in 1828, and moved immediately to Kentucky, where she died in 1869. Our subject, when he began business for himself, embarked in agricultural pursuits, and from that period to the present has been a successful tiller of the soil; by his first wife, he had born to him three children, two of whom are now living: John W. and Annie, who is now the wife of Harry James, of Paris. George died in 1852, at three years of age; by his second marriage there were also three children, two sons: Charles R. and Castleman N., and one daughter, Stella, who is now a student at the Garth Female Institute, at Paris, Kentucky. Mr. Redmon began life in moderate circumstances, and by industry, economy and close attention to business, has acquired handsome property; he has made it a rule through life to keep his surplus invested in land, thus adding year by year to his beautiful home, known as "Cedar Grove;" his first purchase of land was in 1845, of 106 acres at $40 per acre; in 1849, he bought fifty acres more, at a cost of $50 per acre; in 1852, he added 114 acres more, at an expense of sixty-five dollars per acre; the following year he increased his farm ten acres, at $90.05 per acre; the next tract he bought in

1864, containing fifty-two acres; cost him $111.25 per acre, and in 1866, he added forty-two and one-half acres more, at $115 an acre; the next he bought was a small tract of ten acres in 1871, which cost him the enormous price of $166.60 per acre; his last purchase was in 1879, of thirty acres, at $70 per acre; in 1853, to accommodate his brother, George L., he sold him twenty acres, at $75 per acre; he inherited from his mother's estate twenty-six acres; altogether, he now owns 420 acres lying six miles north of Paris, on what is known as the Redmon Pike. Mr. Redmon has made a specialty of handling mules and rearing and handling fine horses; besides, he has kept good grade cattle, sheep, hogs, etc., in fact all such stock as we find on our model farms of this blue grass region; he has attained considerable notoriety as a horseman, generally bearing off his pro rata of the premiums at all the fairs where he has exhibited; he has never been troubled with any political aspirations, and consequently never held an office in his life, but in all political contests we find him very prompt to deposit his ballot in favor of the Democratic champion.

G. W. RIGHTER, physician and surgeon; P. O. Ruddel's Mills; was born in Harrison County, Ky., March 16, 1844; son of John B. and Rebecca (Smith) Righter; he is a native of Clarksburg, Harrison County, Va.; she of Harrison County, Ky. John came to Kentucky about 1830, and was a farmer and trader in negroes; he died May 16, 1881, and his wife is still living, having raised six children, all of whom are still living. Dr. Righter is the third in the family and received a collegiate education, after which he farmed for a while, but in 1869 yielded to the inclinations of his early life and studied medicine; he entered the Cleveland Homeopathic Medical College in 1869 and graduated in the spring of 1873; practiced two years and then took a course in the Pulte Medical College of Cincinnati, after which he located at Ruddel's Mills, where he has a large and growing practice; he was married Nov. 13, 1873, to Miss Mary Miller, of Harrison County, Ky., daughter of James Miller, and has two children, T. J. and Bettie T. Dr. Righter entered the Confederate service in 1862 and served till the close of the war, having been a member of Capt. Frazer's Co., Breckinridge's Regiment, 2nd Brigade, Morgan's Division, and participated in over thirty engagements; the doctor and wife are members of the Christian Church, and he is a Mason and a Democrat.

JOHN REYNOLDS, farmer; P. O. Ruddel's Mills; was born May 24, 1827; son of Patrick Reynolds, of County Roscommon, Ireland, and came to the United States in 1847, first settling in New York for a short time; thence to Cincinnati, where he lived four years, and from there to Fayette County; then to Bourbon. Mr. Reynolds has been engaged in various work, as contractor, etc., until two years ago, at which time he was appointed Keeper of the Alms House; he was married Feb. 5, 1855, to Mary Gannon, who also came from Ireland; they have six children: Terrence, Bridget, Joseph, Mary A., Elizabeth, and Kate. Mr. Reynolds and family are all members of the Catholic Church.

WILLIAM SKINNER, farmer; P. O. Ruddel's Mills; among those who took an active part in the war for Independence, and who was an intimate friend and neighbor of General Washington, was Nathaniel Skinner, who served through that struggle as Quartermaster, settling after the war on the now historic Bull Run, in Loudoun County, where he passed the remainder of his life, and raising a family, one of whose sons was James, who served as Captain in the war of 1812, and was the father of William, our subject, who was born Nov. 1, 1813. In 1815, James moved to Bourbon County, Ky., with his wife and two infant children, and settled upon a farm, at the same time working at his trade of wagonmaker and blacksmith; he died in Harrison County in his sixty-eighth year, his wife having preceded him several years; they had eight children, William being the oldest. Mr. Skinner has been an energetic business man, and for a number of years traded largely in mules, his market being Richmond, Va.; also dealt in cattle and hogs. He was married, Dec. 6, 1853, to Mrs. Lucy J. Fry, whose maiden name was Eales, and by which union there are two children: Fanny L., wife of W. H. Kerr, and James W. Mr. and Mrs. S. are members of the Christian Church. Mr. Skinner has been identified with the unpopular party in Kentucky, but he has many warm friends, and his integrity as a man is undoubted, he having polled the largest vote ever given to a Republican in Bourbon County, in 1881, when he made the canvass for the Legislature; he owns 356 acres of land, and has an elegant home known as "Forest Hill."

WES. B. SMITH, farmer; P. O. Cynthiana; was born in Harrison County, Ky., Dec. 24, 1824; son of Robert and Mary (Snodgrass) Smith. Robert was born in Nicholas County, Ky., in 1795; Mrs. Smith in Bourbon County, in 1795, she being the daughter of Robert and Mary Snodgrass, who came to Kentucky from Culpepper County, Va. Robert Smith was reared to farming, which occupation he followed through life, with the exception of about nine years, when he was engaged in distilling in Harrison County, Ky., where he lived during the active part of his life. He was married Sept. 26, 1820, and died Sept. 6, 1877; she died Oct. 14, 1871. They reared the following family: Wes. B., William, Robert, Columbus, and Martha. Wes. B., our subject, was the eldest son, and was raised a farmer, but has paid considerable attention to the breeding of short-horn cattle and trotting horses: "Minnie," with a record of 2:22½, was reared by him. He moved to Bourbon County in 1874, where he owns 100 acres of land. He was married March 21, 1849, to Miss Maria Ishmael, daughter of James and Mary Ishmael. Her parents died when she was an infant, and was raised by a cousin, Mrs. Trigg. She gave birth to seven children: Ezekiel R., James W., Columbus Holton, Eugene W., Lewis L., John Charles, and Mattie Cordelia, Mr. and Mrs. Smith reared from infancy and educated John F. Morgan, a lawyer of Cynthiana. Mr. Smith volunteered in the Mexican war, but was discharged on account of sickness; he is serving as Magistrate of Ruddel's Mills Precinct. Mr. S. and wife are members of the Christian Church, and he is a Mason and a Democrat.

T. T. THORNTON, bookkeeper; P. O. Ruddel's Mills. Among the early settlers of Kentucky was a family by the name of Thornton, who came to Bourbon County from Virginia; the head of the family was Anthony Thornton, a farmer, who reared a large family, but there are few representatives of the family now living; one of the sons, however, John Thornton, practiced medicine and graduated from Transylvania University, and practiced his profession at Ruddel's Mills. He was married to Miss Ellen Fisher, of Millersburg, and died in 1874; she died Oct. 3, 1881, having borne two children: T. T., the subject of this sketch, who was born Dec. 11, 1846, and Mary, who died in infancy. Mr. T. T. Thornton received a common school education, and then entered the Miami University, where he spent two years, after which he completed a classical course at Millersburg, and in addition to which he attended and graduated from a Commercial College in Cincinnati; since which time he has followed the occupation of book-keeper, being at present with H. C. Bowen, at Ruddel's Mills; he was married Jan. 10, 1871, to Miss Mattie Stoker, daughter of John Stoker, of Paris; she died March 4, 1880, having borne four children: Maggie, deceased, Lucy W., Eads B. and Mattie. Mr. Thornton is a Mason and an Odd Fellow.

JACKSON THOMAS, farmer; P. O. Shawhan; was born in Montgomery County, Ky., March 19, 1816, son of Robert and Sarah Thomas, both of whom were natives of Virginia, who came to Kentucky in their childhood. Robert was a farmer, and also a trader, operating with flat-boats down the Mississippi River, and dealing chiefly in flour, whisky and tobacco; he died in New Orleans in 1818, leaving a wife and four children: Eveline, Moses, Jackson and Robert. Mrs. Thomas removed with her family to Bourbon County, where she died in 1862. Our subject, being orphaned by the death of his father, began life on his own account as soon as he was able to work, and has ever since been engaged in farming, at present owning 125 acres of good land, upon which he has a pleasant and attractive home; he was married March 6, 1839, to Miss Elizabeth, daughter of Abraham and Nancy Fry, whose parents were among the early settlers of Kentucky. Mr. Thomas has been blessed with six children, three of whom are living: Eveline, Minerva and Eliza, all being married. Mrs. Thomas and daughters are members of the Christian Church, and he is a Mason and a Democrat.

CHARLES TALBOTT, farmer; P. O. Ruddel's Mills; traces the genealogy of his family back to his grandfather, Henry Talbott, who was a native of Loudoun County, Va., but migrated to Bourbon County, Ky., as early as 1795; his wife was a Miss Barbara Whaley, also a native of Virginia. Prior to his removing to Bourbon County, he had purchased a tract of forest land, on which he located and began to improve; he had a family of five sons and three daughters, viz: Daniel, Reason, George, Harry, Charles, Mary, Nancy, and Catharine. Mr. Talbott died about 1819, and his wife some years later; he left a fine property, and a respected and enterprising family of children; of these children Harry, the father of our subject, secured the old homestead by the purchase of the other heirships; he was born Feb. 27, 1789, and was married in October, of 1828, to Miss Mary Frazer, who was the daughter of James Frazer and his wife, whose maiden name was Hendricks; they were of Harrison County, Ky.; the Frazers formerly of Maryland, and of Scotch descent, and the Hendricks from South Carolina. Securing the old homestead, Harry Talbott lived but a few years to enjoy it. He died Oct. 2, 1840, leaving a family of five children to the care and guidance of their mother. They were named James H., Amanda F., Charles, Mary C., and Martha H., all of whom are still living but Mary C. Mrs. Talbott was born Jan. 22, 1802, and died Nov. 29, 1867. Charles, who was the youngest of the sons, born Sept. 12, 1834, remained with his mother; and as the other heirs married and moved away, he, like his father, purchased their interests until he eventually owned the farm, that was redeemed from the forest by his grandfather; he cared for his aged mother until her death, in partial payment for her tender care during his childhood; in August, 1876, he was elected Sheriff of Bourbon County, and re-elected to the same office. He has but recently returned to his farm. June 13, 1878, he was married to Miss Fanny Glenn, daughter of John M. Glenn, a prominent citizen of Bourbon County. Two children have been born to them: Mary, born June 1, 1879, and Anna Lee, born April 11, 1881. Mr. Talbott is a member of the order of A. F. and A. M., and is a gentleman who, though having gone through two political campaigns, still maintained the honorable course of a gentleman, and now has the respect and confidence of the most prominent citizens of his native county.

CHAS. L. TALBOTT, farmer and stock dealer, P. O. Cynthiana; was born in Bourbon County, Ky., on the farm he now owns, Dec. 4, 1831; son of George and Unity (Smith) Talbott. George came with his parents from Virginia when a youth, and followed farming in Bourbon County till his death, which occurred when he was sixty-seven years of age; his companion survived him several years. He acquired a handsome property and reared a family of nine children, six of whom are living, the subject of this sketch being the youngest, who commenced upon his own responsibility when he was twenty years of age, and who has been engaged ever since in farming and dealing in stock, shipping very largly. He owns about 250 acres of good land, besides city property. He was married in March, 1863, to Susan A. Potts, daughter of John and Almira Potts, of Nicholas County, Ky., by whom he has one child, Orville Lee. Mr. and Mrs. Talbot are members of the Christian Church, at Indian Creek Meeting House. He is a Director in the Farmers' National Bank, at Cynthiana, and a Democrat.

JOHN T. TALBOTT, farmer; P. O. Cynthiana; the name of Talbott is perhaps as familiar to the citizens of Bourbon County as that of the posterity of any of the old pioneers. A tracement of the genealogy of the ancestors of John F. being found in the biography of Chas. Talbott, this sketch is confined more particularly to the former. Reason Talbott married Miss Jane Whaley, who was born in the old fort at Maysville, her people being formerly from Loudoun County, Va.; he died in the spring of 1862, and his wife in 1870; they reared a family of four children: Benjamin, Nancy, Emily, and Henry H., the latter being the father of our subject; he was reared to farming, and married Miss Angelina, daughter of Lee and Mary Whaley; he died March 5, 1878, and she about the year 1860; there were born to them three children: John T., Charles L., and Mary C., now wife of F. M. Myers, of Bourbon County. John T. was born in the precinct where he now lives, May 17, 1866; he married Miss Lucinda Collins, daughter of B. F. and Sally (Turney) Collins, of Bourbon County. The ancestors of Mr. Talbott have been an agricultural people, his early life having been spent on his father's farm; he also has engaged in the same business. The Talbott is an extensive family in the county, and John T. is a worthy representative of so hardy a pioneer as Henry Talbott.

B C Glass

SCOTT COUNTY.

GEORGETOWN CITY AND PRECINCT.

WILLIAM WRIGHT ALLEN, P. O. Georgetown; was born in Bourbon County, Ky., October, 1824; his father, Joseph Allen, was born in Loudoun County, Va., in 1792; in 1812, he removed to Bourbon County, settling five miles east of Paris; he was a very successful farmer, and had accumulated about 300 acres of land in Scott County at the time of his death; he was quite an extensive stock raiser; in 1824 he removed to Scott County, Oxford Precinct, where he remained until his decease in 1846; he participated in the war of 1812; the grandfather of our subject was David Allen, who was also born in Loudoun County, Va.; he came to Bourbon County with his wife, five sons and three daughters; the mother of our subject was Catharine Skillman, daughter of Isaac Skillman; they were natives of Virginia; she was born in 1800; came to Bourbon County, in 1816, and married in 1818; she is now living in Oxford Precinct, Scott Couty; she had eight children, the third of whom was our subject who was brought by his parents to Scott County when but three months old; he attended the common schools of Scott County; in 1849, he commenced business for himself, engaging in farming, for which purpose he removed to Fayette County, where he remained only one year, then returned to Scott County, where he has since followed farming; on Feb. 12, 1848, he married Miss Frances Skillman, of Fayette County; she was born in 1832, and died in August, 1849; in 1851, he married Keziah Brand, born in 1828, in Bourbon County; she was a daughter of Richard Brand, the son of Dr. Brand, of Paris, Ky.; Frances Brand was born in 1798, near Stanton, Va.; she was married there and came to Bourbon County, Ky., in 1827; by his first marriage he has one daughter, Frances Wright, who is married, and now lives in Scott County; by his last marriage he has three daughters: Mattie C., Anna L., Josie S., living, and one son dead; the son was James William, who was attending school, and was accidentlly killed by one of his playmates and school friends with a gun; he was hunting birds while enjoying recess at school. During his life-time Mr. Allen has accumulated 350 acres of choice land, situated on the Oxford Pike; he calls his farm "Maple Grove."

R. C. ADAMS, farmer; P. O. Georgetown; was born in Scott County, Ky., to Jerry and Patsey (Scott) Adams, Nov. 25, 1818. He was of Scotch descent; born in Maryland, July 27, 1764, where he learned the trade of a carpenter; he emigrated to Kentucky in about 1780; during his life worked at his trade, and also followed the occupation of farming; he died in 1852. She was of Irish descent, born in Harrison County, Sept. 25, 1783, and died in 1874; she was the mother of twelve children, R. C. Adams being the eighth child and seventh son. He received his education from the common schools of Scott County; at the age of twenty-three, left home with only two dollars and fifty cents in his pocket; with that he made his start in life. He commenced by trading in stock in New Orleans—making three trips a year, and continuing the same for six years; in 1849 he settled down at farming in Scott County, at which he still continues upon his handsome farm of 150 acres of well improved land, most of the improvements having been made by himself. In 1849 he was married to Miss Mary J. Moore, who was born in Scott County and died in May, 1879, aged fifty-one years. Mr. Adams has had four children: Sarah, Alice, married and living in Lexington; Eliza and Bunnie C., at home; Medine, who died in 1861. Mr. Adams is a man of good habits and has the esteem of all who know him. He is a member of the A., F. & A. M., and with his family unites with the Christian Church. In politics, he was an old Line Whig, but now is identified with the Democratic party.

JOHN ANDERSON, P. O. Georgetown; was born in the County of Meath, in the town of Athboy, Ireland, in June, 1827. He left his native home in 1846, having received there a good common school education, and having learned the requisites of a good farmer. He arrived at New York City in April, 1847, where he enlisted in General Worth's regiment, Company K., Div. Eighth Infantry of the Regular Army, and fought in the battles of Cerro Gordo an d Chapultepec and others. In 1848 he came to Kentucky, locating in Scott County, where he worked at stone masonry for five years, when he engaged in gardening and horticulturing, for which he had formed a taste in his school days, having then in Ireland received some instructions in forestry. In the fall of 1862 he enlisted in General Buford's Brigade, Sixth Kentucky Infantry, and fought until the battle of Murfreesboro when he was taken sick and returned home. By the war he lost all he had accumulated, and since 1863 he has had charge of the Cemetery, doing all the landscape gardening in a manner calling forth the admiration of all. He is engaged in the culture of flowers which abound in great variety at the Cemetery for decorative purposes.

ELLY BLACKBURN, farmer and stock raiser; P. O. Great Crossings; was born in Scott County, Ky., in 1842; he is a son of Dr. Churchill J. Blackburn. He spent a time in Georgetown College, but finished his education in the school of B. B. Sayre, at Frankfort. He enlisted in the 13th Arkansas Infantry in 1862, but was transferred the following year to the 9th Kentucky Cavalry, Col. W. C. P. Breckinridge's regiment; while in the Infantry he was at Perryville, Ky., and Murfreesboro, Tennessee; he was a member of Wheeler's Corps, and participated in the numerous engagements of the army of the Tennessee; at Jug Tavern near Athens, Georgia, he was captured, but soon made his escape; he served until the close of the war. In 1866 he married Miss Virginia, daughter of Alexander D. Offutt, of this county, and since their union he has engaged in farming. He has paid considerable attention to the rearing of short-horn cattle. His present place of 371 acres, situated on North Elkhorn, is appropriately named "Elkwood." The father of our subject was born near White Sulphur, this county, in 1803; was educated in the schools of the county, and at a private school in Jefferson County, Ky.; he studied medicine with his father, Dr. C. J. Blackburn, of Versailles, Ky., whose name he bears, and attended lectures at the Transylvania University, at Lexington, in President Holly's time; he located for practice near White Sulphur in about 1830, and practiced for twenty years, with success, when he gave it up for farming, at which also he was very successful, amassing an estate of 500 acres; he was three times married; successively, first, to Miss Keene, of Lexington, who bore him one child; his second wife was Miss Elly, of Scott County, who bore him the subject of this sketch, and a third wife was Mrs. Branham, of Woodford County; his grandfather was Julius Blackburn a native of Virginia, who fought five years in the Revolutionary war, and came to Kentucky in 1790, first living in Woodford County, but afterwards moving to this county.

DR. WILLIAM H. BARLOW; Georgetown; was born in Scott County, Ky., Sept. 13, 1809. He is of Virginia parentage. His father, Thomas H. Barlow, was a substantial farmer. Susannah (Isbel) Barlow was his mother. His father was a particular Baptist; his death occurred in 1825. The subject of this sketch was educated in the Rittenhouse Academy, which afterwards became the Georgetown College. He began the study of medicine at the age of sixteen, with Dr. Alexander C. Keene, of Georgetown, continuing three years. In 1827 he began the practice of his profession in Georgetown, where he has since practiced, in all forty-five years. During the years 1829–30 he was located at Florence, Ky., and from 1832 to 1836 was in Williamstown, Ky. Dr. Barlow is a vegetarian, not having tasted a particle of animal food for thirty-seven years, to which fact he attributes his good health, never having had a headache in his life, and having been confined but five days in his life-time. He has practiced fifty-four years in regular practice, being busy night and day. He never refused to go on account of poverty of both black and white, and to the poor gave his medicine. He has been in attendance at *four thousand* births. In 1881 he retired, feeling that he had done enough actual labor for one lifetime. Dr. Henry Craig was a fellow student of his at college, and in the office of Dr. Keene; he was his contemporary in practice. Dr. Barlow has made a study of literature, being familiar with French; he has a large collection of medical works in that language. He has collected a large library of several hundred standard works, with which he is perfectly familiar. In 1827 he married Miss Louisa Allgaier, of Cincinnati, Ohio. They raised nine children, three of whom are still living, viz: Feresa V., wife of Frank A. Lyon, of Lexington, Capt. E. C. Barlow, and Ouida, now Mrs. Harry S. Orr, of Georgetown. Dr. Barlow's father brought the first racehorse to the county; it was Lamplighter. He kept a stallion and bred blooded horses, but was never on the turf.

CAPT. EDWARD C. BARLOW, jeweler, Georgetown; was born in Cincinnati, Ohio, in 1829, and was but four years old when his parents returned to Georgetown, Ky., where they had formerly resided; he was educated in the Georgetown College and the Western Military Institute, where he was a pupil of James G. Blaine, then a teacher for Col. Thornton Johnson. Our subject left school in 1849 to learn the jeweler's trade with T. J. Shepard, and in 1851 engaged in the jewelry business; he married in 1851 Miss Sarah Rawlins, daughter of Dr. James Rawlins, of this county. Mr. Barlow pursued his calling at Georgetown until 1863, when he enlisted in the 40th Ky. Mounted Infantry, in which he first served as Adjutant, but was promoted to the Captaincy of Co. "B," in 1864.

He served in the Department of Kentucky, and participated in several engagements with Gen. Morgan and Adam Johnson. He was mustered out and honorably discharged Dec. 31, 1864; on his return Capt. Barlow engaged in the pursuits of civil life, with little interruption except three disastrous fires which occurred respectively, in 1869, 1875 and 1876, destroying his business blocks, and entailing an aggregate loss of $20,000. In 1875, he built his present business block in which is located Barlow's Hall, at a cost of $15,000. It is the only public hall in the city, and has a seating capacity of 600. Capt. Barlow has been a member of the City Council since 1862, except two years. He is the active friend of public improvements, and a zealous advocate of common schools. His son, James W., is an active member of the firm of Barlow & Son, which does an extensive business in jewelry, silverware, books and wall-paper.

DUDLEY COOK, farmer; P. O. Dry Run; was born in Fayette County, Ky., to John and Elizabeth (Dingle) Cook, Oct. 11, 1825; he was a farmer, and died in 1862; she was a native of Maryland; came to Fayette County when quite young, and died in 1864; was the mother of nine children, four daughters and five boys, our subject being the youngest. He was compelled to receive his education from the common schools, such as his country afforded in that day. In 1846 he began farming and trading in stock on his own account; in 1857 removed to Boone County, and in 1865 removed to his present residence, where he has since remained, engaged in farming. He is the owner of 363 acres of well improved land, situated on the Cincinnati Pike, five miles from Georgetown. He commenced life a poor boy, and by his close economy and hard work, succeeded in gaining a good property. In March, 1857, he was married to Miss Eliza Cook, a native of Scott County, born in 1836. Mr. and Mrs. Cook have had five children, three of whom are now living, viz: Oscar, Charley and Warren. Mr. Cook is a gentleman commanding the respect of all the people of his community. He has always acted independent of sects or denominations, yet always favored anything knowr to be right, and is not in sympathy with any scheme or enterprise that will not augment the interests of the people at large. He is no partisan, but a firm and solid Democrat.

ROBERT COOK, Junior; P. O. Georgetown. The father of our subject was Robert Cook, Senior; he was born in Port Royal, Va., on March 10, 1782, and was a small boy when he came here with his widowed mother; her husband, who was a native of England and a carpenter by trade, having died in Virginia. His mother settled within two and a half miles of Georgetown, and, as she was poor, he worked hard and purchased a tract of land consisting of one hundred acres, of one Asa Stone, an old Indian hunter; this tract was situated on McConnell's Run. He married on Sept. 15, 1810, to Miss Sarah Curry, a neighbor, who was born Oct. 17, 1791. She bore him twelve children, ten of whom grew up to maturity. He died in 1873, being in his ninety-second year; she followed four years later; both were members of the Christian Church. The subject of this sketch was born in September, 1820, in Scott County, Ky.; he was educated in the schools of the neighborhood, and when grown followed farming, the pursuit his father also had chosen. He dealt extensively in mules for a period of twenty years. While his parents lived he lived with them and cared for them.

HON. WILLIAM S. DARNABY, lawyer; Georgetown; was born Dec. 20, 1821, in Fayette County, Ky.; his father James Darnaby, was surveyor of Fayette County for thirty years; was for a time Deputy Sheriff; a Kentuckian by birth, of Virginia parents; his mother was Ellen Sharp, daughter of Richard Sharp, of Fayette County. William Sharp Darnaby received a good education in the best private schools of the country; served eight years as Deputy Surveyor of Fayette County; at the age of twenty-two, commenced the study of law with Samuel R. Bullock, of Lexington; attended two courses of law lectures at Transylvania University; graduated in 1846; in the following year entered upon the practice of his profession, at Georgetown, where he has since resided; was County Attorney of Scott County for twelve years, serving two terms before, and one after, the war; was elected to the State Senate, in 1857; was, from the first, a strong sympathizer with the cause of the South; accompanied Bragg's Army; was appointed aid to Provisional-Governor Harris, with the rank of Colonel; and, at the close of the war, returned to Georgetown, and resumed the practice of his profession, in which he has taken a leading rank in central Kentucky. In politics he is a Democrat, of the States Rights School. Col. Darnaby was married in 1859, to Miss Fannie H. Lindsay, daughter of James M. Lindsay, of Scott County. In 1872, he was again married, to Miss Lizzie Wheeler, of Hampton, Virginia.

HON. SAMUEL M. DAVIS, State Senator; Georgetown; is the son of Theophilus Davis, who was a prominent farmer of his native county of Shelby, and died in 1845, leaving four sons and three daughters. Of this number, the oldest brother, Col. John F. Davis, served in the Confederate army, on the staff of Gen. John C.

Breckinridge, and during the last year of the war, commanded an Alabama regiment, and was elected Clerk of the Shelby County Court, being also a prominent candidate for the Clerk of the Kentucky Court of Appeals, in the race of 1882. Our subject, Samuel M. Davis, was born in Shelby County, Ky., Aug. 2, 1836. He laid the foundations for his future usefulness in a good English education, obtained in the common schools and Shelby College. On attaining manhood he engaged in farming and trading in his native county, until 1866, when he removed to Georgetown, and purchased a farm near its limits, and continued farm operations with increased success, dealing largely in stock of all kinds, until 1878. In September, 1878, he formed a partnership with J. Webb and conducted a large and successful business in dry goods in Georgetown, until 1882. In politics, Mr. Davis has always been a staunch Democrat, and was first elected to the Georgetown Board of Trustees in 1871, and served in that body seven years, the last three as its Chairman. He was elected Chairman of the County Democratic Committee in 1879, and discharged its duties with ability during the campaigns of 1880 and '81. He was nominated in July, 1880, to fill the unexpired term of Jas. Blackburn, in the State Senate, from the 22nd Senatorial District, and elected to the office without opposition. Mr. Davis is Chairman of the Senate Committee on Sinking Fund, and member of the following committees: Penitentiary, Bank, and Insurance, Morals of Religion, and Propositions and Grievances. He was married in 1865, to Miss Alice, daughter of Joseph B. Kenney, of Georgetown, and has two children living.

NOTLEY ESTES, Circuit Clerk; Georgetown; was born in Scott County, Ky., Feb. 19, 1826; his father, Thomas Estes, was born in Spottsylvania County, Va., in 1785; came to Kentucky when a mere boy with his parents, who first settled in Fayette County; he married a Miss Truitt in 1810, settling in Scott County, where he lived for half a century; of his first marriage there are six children; he was married a second time to a Mrs. Spencer who bore him one child; he followed the occupation of farmer with moderate success, and died in Owen County, in 1862. Our subject is the youngest living son of Thomas Estes by the first marriage, and was raised on the farm where he was denied all except the meager training which the early schools of his neighborhood afforded; he began selling goods in 1853, at Eagle Post Office, and followed it for a time in connection with his farm; from 1854 to 1874 Mr. Estes dealt in live stock, driving to the Covington and Louisville markets; he acted for about twenty years as Deputy Clerk for the northern part of Scott County; at the August election of 1880, Mr. Estes was elected Clerk of the Circuit Court by the Democrats of Scott County, the duties of which he is now discharging; he was married in 1853 to Miss A. R. Offutt, daughter of Thomas Offutt, of Scott County.

PROF. JONATHAN EVERETT FARNHAM; Georgetown; is the eldest son of Roger Farnham, a native of Massachusetts, whose father settled in Connecticut prior to the Revolutionary War, and was born Aug. 12, 1809; his father died in 1817; but, leaving the family in comfortable circumstances, Prof. Farnham was enabled to acquire a good education. He first attended the common schools, pursued his preparatory studies in the New Hampshire Classical Institute, in New Hampshire, and then entered Colby University, under the presidency of Dr. Chaplin. In 1833, he graduated, with the degree of A. B., and for two years was engaged as tutor in the institute. He then studied law at Providence, R. I., for three years, and afterwards at Cincinnati. In 1838, he was appointed Professor of Physical Science, at Georgetown College, which chair he is now filling. During this period of time, he controlled the Georgetown Female Seminary, the property of which he owned. This was one of the most flourishing institutions of the West, receiving, as it did, a very large patronage from the Southern and Western States; in 1865, he disposed of his interest. He is a member of the Baptist Church, and contributed freely toward its support and advancement. In 1838, he was married to Miss E. Butler, daughter of Rev. John Butler, of Winthrop, Maine, and is the father of three children, all of whom are still living and married. He is a man of great force of character, sociable in disposition, and agreeable in manners. His success as a teacher has been eminent.

JAMES L. GRIFFITH, farmer; P. O. Payne's Depot. The subject of this sketch dates his ancestry to William Griffith, who was born in the year 1760, in the State of Virginia, and his parents emigrated to that State from Wales in England, but the exact date is not certainly known. He came to Kentucky from Greenbrier County, now West Virginia, and landed at Louisville on flat boats, in the year 1787. A considerable company of emigrants accompanied him, the most of whom found their way with him to Steele's Run, in Nicholas County, where they settled and where their descendants live to this day. Among the leading families that accompanied him, and whose descendants are to be found there, were those of William and Hamlet Collier, Martin and William Baker, from whom Baker's school house on said stream was named; William, John, and Nathaniel Conway; the father of the present John Hardy, and perhaps others. The land where they settled was then a part of Bourbon County, but was afterwards made a part of Nicholas County. William Griffith received a grant of land from the State of Virginia, a part of which is in the hands of his descendants to this day, having first passed to his son, Martin Griffith, and from him to the late William A. Griffith, and is now held by his children. In person William Griffith was tall and commanding, his body was strong, vigorous and athletic, and the strength and manliness of his intellect was fully in keeping with the vigor of his body. He was active in all the duties that pertained to the infant settlement, and his great energy and force of character suited him for the age in which he lived. He had considerable knowledge of the civil and common law, and was well versed in the politics of the day, and the people were not long in recognizing his worth, and usefulness. He was first elected one of the Justices of the Peace of Bourbon County. He was also a member of the Kentucky House of Representatives for the session of 1799. For some years previous to the said session of the Legislature, the people had been agitating the questions relating to a new Constitution for the State of Kentucky, in all of which he took an active interest and a leading part, and when it was determined to frame a new Constitution, William Griffith was chosen one of the three delegates from Bourbon County to frame the Constitution of 1799. His political knowledge and wisdom was well understood, and his energy greatly facilitated the formation of that instrument. His colleagues from Bourbon County in that work were Nathaniel Rogers und James Dnncan. After the Constitution had been framed and ratified by the people, William Griffith was taken sick with a fever, and died during the year 1800, at the age of forty, at the very beginning of his usefulness, greatly beloved and respected. He was buried on his own land, in a family graveyard, laid out by himself, he being the first to occupy it. Before leaving Virginia, William Griffith had married Sally Baker, a sister of Martin and William Baker, who proved to be more than an ordinary woman, and whose early life seemed to be a necessity to the early settlers. At that time doctors were few and lived a great way apart. After coming to Kentucky she studied medecine and soon mastered the knowledge of herbs, and before civilization had cast its mantle over the county, her practice had extended far and near. She died in the year 1835, after having spent a life of great usefulness. For some years after the settlement was first made, Indians made frequent raids through the country. On one occasion they captured and carried off two horses belonging to William Griffith, and at another time they captured and carried off a negro slave belonging to him, who had gone fishing at Steele's Ford, on Hinkston. The negro was never afterwards heard from. The children had sometimes to be hid in the cane brakes, and the men had sometimes to follow the raiding Indians. William Griffith left several sons and daughters whose descendants are now scattered over Kentucky and the West. The oldest son of William Griffith was Major William Griffith, who settled in Harrison County, between Cynthiana and Leesburg, Ky. He showed marked ability as a financier, and left a handsome estate as the reward of his industry. He made several successful trips to New Orleans upon flat boats, to take out the products of Kentucky's virgin soil before steam boats had become in use on the Mississippi, and brought his money home in saddle pockets on horseback. He was a Major in the State Militia, and was held in high esteem by all who knew him. He was born in Virginia on the 5th day of November, 1782, and died July 7, 1843. His grandson, Wm. K. Griffith, now owns the farm where he lived and died. The second son of William Griffith was Martin Griffith. He was born in Greenbriar County, Va., in 1784, and came to Kentucky when three years old. He lived fifty-one years on the land that had been owned by his father; he then moved to Calloway County, Mo., where he lived for thirty-three years, and died on the 6th of January, 1868, at the age of eighty-seven years. He was a successful farmer, an active Mason, an Elder in the Presbyterian Church and a charitable and useful citizen. He left sons and daughters, all of whom settled in Missouri except the late William A. Griffith, who died upon the old homestead, June 28, 1879. Samuel Griffith was the third son of William Griffith. He lived at Scott's Station, in Harrison County, Ky. He served the people of Harrison County one term in the lower branch of the Kentucky Legislature. He was a faithful Representative, a useful man and a popular citizen. Thomas Griffith was the fourth son of William Griffith. He was a soldier of the war of 1812 and acquitted himself honorably in that war; he afterwards moved to Missouri, where his descendants now live. John Griffith was the fifth son of William Griffith ; he lived and died near Millersburg, Ky. He was an excellent citizen; kind and hospitable and charitable to a fault; he left no children to inherit his excellent traits of character. The descendants of William Griffith are now quite numerous, and many of them have proved themselves useful, successful and honored citizens. William A. Griffith, whose death is recorded above, was born Feb. 29,

1808; his wife, Cynthia Mathers, was born in 1801, and died in 1841; she was the mother of four children, of whom James L., the subject of this sketch, was the oldest; he graduated at the College of Danville, in 1856, after which he engaged in a merchandising and milling business at Pleasant Valley, where he remained until 1861, when he obtained a license to practice law and entered upon the practice of that profession in 1862, at Cynthiana. He filled the offices of City Attorney and City Assessor in connection with his other professional duties; he remained at Cynthiana until 1873, when he moved to Scott County, and purchased a farm and turned his attention to farming; his farm is situated on the Lexington, Bethel and Moore's Run Pike,and contains 165 acres of choice farm land, which he has placed in a high state of cultivation, and he is now engaged in growing the usual farm crops and handling high-grade stock. During the first year of his farm life he built a fine frame residence, which was destroyed by fire in the fall of 1879, and has been replaced by a fine brick edifice, which is an honor to himself, and is spoken of as one of the finest residences in the county. He was married near where he now lives, June 14, 1870, to Miss Adrienne Graves, who was born May 13, 1846; she has borne to him seven children, viz.: James, born Jan. 17, 1873; Mary E., born Oct. 18, 1875; her twin died in infancy; James W., born Oct. 2, 1877, and died the following year; William D., born April 5, 1879; Warren H., born Oct. 15, 1880. Mrs. Griffith was a daughter of Jefferson and Mary (Dunn) Graves; he born Aug. 6, 1803, died March 30, 1880; she died in 1847. Mr. Griffith is a true gentleman and a thorough business man, and in him are embodied all the noble qualities for which his ancestors were noted. Religiously himself and wife are connected with the Presbyterian Church. Politically he is Democratic.

HARVEY C. GRAVES, retired; P. O. Georgetown; was born in Fayette County, Ky., Feb. 19, 1804. The Graves family claim a French origin, and, although the time of their arrival in America is a matter of conjecture, long before the Revolutionary war they were residents of Virginia. His father, John Graves, was born in Virginia, and while quite a young man came to Kentucky, locating in what was then Fayette County. He afterwards returned to Virginia, married, and brought his young wife to his new home in the wilderness, and, in all the conflicts with the Indians, and the trials and sufferings of the early settlements, he took an active part. During the war of 1812, he was appointed commander of a Company of militia, and, in various ways, was an influential and valuable man in the early history of that part of the State. Harvey C. Graves was the fourth in a family of seven children, and, although his father had acquired some means, and was the owner of a fine tract of land in the best part of the State, he grew to manhood on his father's farm without opportunities for more than ordinary education. He early took an active interest in public affairs, and being a man of fine natural ability and superior judgment, he became of great service to his county, especially in building up of the various interests of Georgetown, where his counsels have been felt throughout a long life. He was one of the movers in the establishment of the Georgetown College, and not only made a donation for that purpose, but gave his influence toward building it up, and served as one of its trustees for several years. He was one of the projectors of the "Farmer's Bank" of Georgetown, and has been a member of its directory since its organization. At the organization of the Warrendale Female Seminary, he was elected one of the Board of Trustees, and has since held that position. He has been an extensive farmer and stock raiser of Scott County, and was for many years the largest hemp grower in his part of the country. In politics, he was a member of the Whig party, and stood by the Union throughout the dark days of the rebellion. Lately, he has been identified with the Democratic party. For many years he has been an elder in the Christian Church, and has, during his entire life, been one of the most active and valuable men in his community, and, by an active, successful, public-spirited, unselfish life, he has made the world better for his having lived in it. Mr. Graves was married in 1829, to Miss Lucinda Garth, daughter of John Garth, of Scott County; and after her death, was married again in 1837, to Miss Martha R. Crockett, daughter of N. Crockett, of Fayette County. They have two children, Elenora, wife of James H. Kenney, of Georgetown; and Isadora, wife of John W. Berkley, of Lexington.

JOHN S. GAINES; P. O. Georgetown; was born in Fayette County, near the Scott County line, on March 28, 1844; he attended Georgetown College, leaving in 1861; in 1862, he enlisted in Colonel W. C. P. Breckinridge's regiment, which, under General Morgan, became the 9th Kentucky Cavalry. He participated in the operations of Kentucky and Tennessee; he was captured at Glasgow, Kentucky, where a horse was shot under him; he was sick in prison at Louisville, and Mumfordsville, Ky., until April, 1863, when he was released on oath; he was but seventeen when he enlisted, and received a certificate from his superior officers previous to his capture; in 1863, he returned to Fayette County, and the following year went to Missouri, where he remained until the close of the war; in the fall of 1869, he came to Georgetown, and engaged in the livery business until 1872, when he entered the grocery business, at which he has since continued, his present grocery being situated on the north side of Main street; he employs three clerks; he occupies four stories of the building, No. 14; it is connected with the elevator, and does a volume of business, reaching to $50,000 per annum; his father, O. W. Gaines, born in Fayette County, Ky., was a farmer, and died in 1847; he was a son of F. Strother Gaines, who came from Culpepper County, Va., and settled near Little Elkhorn, Fayette County, in 1803, and who died in 1860, aged eighty-three years; his father and grandfather were members of the Baptist Church.

PROF. R. L. GARRISON; Georgetown; was born in Boone County, Ky., in 1846, and when a boy moved to Owen County; he attended Georgetown College four years, reached the senior year, and left in 1875, to take charge of the Georgetown Public Schools, since which time he has retained the office of Principal, being an earnest and efficient worker. The schools were in a deplorable condition when he took them in charge, but he commenced at the foundation and renovated the entire system, making and carrying out a good and thorough course of study; he has three departments and six grades. When he began he had about sixty pupils, and now enrolls 128. His work deserves special commendation, both as to education and discipline.

JOHN DeGARIS, miller and farmer; P. O. Georgetown; was born Dec. 24, 1807, on the Island of Guernsey. He received a good education in French, and at sixteen was apprenticed to learn the carpenter's trade, at which he worked on his native Island, until 1831, when he came to America, locating on Cape Breton Island, on the Gulf of Canso, working at carpentering on the cabins of vessels for two years, when he removed to Philadelphia, Penn., where he worked in an organ factory for over two and a half years. Going back to his native home, he remained something over a year. In 1839, he came to Lexington, Ky., where he became a contractor and builder, remaining about sixteen years. In 1854, he bought the present mill of Henry Prewitt, and since has run it, giving some attention to farming in connection therewith. His mill has two run of buhrs, and does a custom and merchant business. In 1854, he married Miss Mary E. Cannon, daughter of Alexander Cannon, of Georgetown.

L. L. HERNDON, farmer; P. O. Great Crossings, whose portrait appears in this work, was born to John and Elizabeth Herndon, on March 29, 1811, his birthplace being three miles from Georgetown, Scott County, Ky. His parents were married in 1810, and his mother was a daughter of Major Rodes Thompson, of Scott County. His father was born in Orange County, Va., in 1780, and came to Kentucky about 1809; being an invalid, and coming with a few servants and but limited means, it was due alone to his great energy and perseverance that he achieved pecuniary success from farming and the manufacture of hemp, which he began near Georgetown as early as 1835, being one of the first manufacturers. At the time of his death, which occurred in 1849, he owned several large factories. His wife bore him eight children, four sons and four daughters. Like him, she was a consistent member of the Christian Church; she died in 1832. Three of the sons are residents of Scott county, and one lives in Henry county. His father was again married, the lady being Mrs. Prewitt, of Woodford County; she bore him two daughters. L. L. Herndon was educated in the schools of this county; at twenty-one he began farming. In 1837 he went to Arkansas, where for a period of two years he was engaged in cotton raising. In his early life he, like his father, raised a few thorough-bred horses, but was never a turfman in the modern sense. He moved to his present place at the Crossings in 1850; this formerly was owned by Col. James Johnson. One day recently, while remodeling a building, a Georgetown newspaper, published in 1810, was found between the wall and the fire place mantel, and he sealed it up with others of later dates, returning them to the same place. Mr. Herndon has been extensively engaged in buying and selling real estate, at which he has been very successful, his operations proving lucrative. His present large estate has been acquired largely by his own sturdy efforts. Under the old constitution he was sheriff of the county two terms. In 1859, Mr. Herndon made a tour of continental Europe, in company with A. Keene Richards and L. L. Johnson, making the trip for pleasure, and the profit gained by observation.

REV. WM. J. H. HOWE; Georgetown; was born in Clinton County, Ohio, near Wilmington, in 1843; he received a thorough academic education at Wilmington, and attended Butler University, Indiana (then "North Western"). At the age of fifteen he began speaking in public on various special subjects. He took an active part in the Fremont campaign, speaking at mass-meetings at that early age; in the campaign of 1860, for Lincoln and Hamlin, he took an active interest. He began the study of law at seventeen, and pursued it for several years, but never entered regular practice. In

1872 he withdrew from the Republican party, and was identified with the rise and organization of the National Greenback party, being a delegate to the Toledo Convention from the 5th Indiana District in 1875, which organized that party; in 1878 he withdrew from politics. He united with the Christian Church at the age of nineteen, and in 1865 he began preaching; he was made State Evangelist under the missionary organization of the State, and traveled continually for one year. He then located with the church at Centreville, Ind., of which for one year he was pastor; then he accepted a call to the pastorate of the Christian Church at Corry, Penn., serving a year, when he accepted a call to the First Christian Church of New York City, serving a year. Business matters requiring his attention and presence in the West, he severed his connection with the New York church and located in Wayne Co., Ind. He then evangelized for four years in different parts of the State. In 1873 he went to Union City, Indiana, and filled the pulpit of the Christian Church a year. In 1874 he was called to the First Christian Church of Chicago, Ill., but resigned in a short time on account of ill health in his family. He returned to Wayne Co., Ind., where he evangelized until the close of 1878. In January, 1879, he began his labors as pastor of the Christian Church of Georgetown, Ky., and has since continued. During his ministry over 4,000 persons have been added to the church. He refused the nomination of the National and Democratic parties for Congress for the Fifth Indiana Dist., because he felt that his duty lay in following the ministry; this nomination was equal to an election. The Christian Church of Georgetown is the mother of the reformation. In 1868 he married Miss Mary Scott, of Wayne Co., Ind.

JESSE HAMBRICK, farmer; P. O. Georgetown; was born in Scott County, Ky., July 15, 1803, to Jesse and Liddie (Martin) Hambrick, natives of Virginia, and among the first to enter upon pioneer life in Kentucky. He died in 1862; she in 1803. Owing to the limited school privileges, Jesse, our subject, received only such an education as could be obtained in the common schools at that early day. He entered upon the battle of life as a farmer, and has by his energy and industry accumulated 300 acres of choice farm land, which "as a practical farmer" he keeps in a high state of cultivation. He has always been an extensive dealer and trader in stock, which he has carried on in nearly all States. His farm is situated on the Dry Run road, and the house in which he lives was built of brick, by Waller Roads, in 1774, and was one of the first brick residences built in Scott County. Mr. Hambrick was married in Scott County, Jan. 14, 1827, to Delilah Parker, who was born to Hutchinson and Sarah (Price) Parker, natives of Maryland, July 11, 1805. She is the mother of six children, viz: Santford, Wilford, Jesse, Parker, Eliza Jane and Evermont. Mr. Hambrick is a man of thorough business principles, and has always enjoyed the highest esteem of the entire community. Religiously, himself and wife are connected with the Baptist denomination at Dry Run. Politically, his sympathies are with the Democratic party.

J. A. HAMILTON, M. D., Georgetown; was born Nov. 16, 1833, in West Union, Adams Co., Ohio. The Hamiltons came from Virginia, and settled in Kentucky at an early day, his father being the only member of his branch of the family who settled in Ohio; his father married Miss Matilda G. Armstrong, and reared two children; his parents dying when he was ten years old, his early education was conducted under the care of his relatives at Midway, Kentucky; he subsequently entered the Ohio Wesleyan University, where he completed his literary education, and in 1857 began the study of medicine in Woodford County, under Dr. John Sutton, graduating from the medical department of the University of Louisville, in 1861; entered on the practice of his profession at White Sulphur Springs, in Scott County, in 1870, located at Georgetown, in that county, where he has since resided, closely, actively, and successfully engaged in the medical practice, associated with Dr. John A. Lewis; he has written a number of valuable papers for the medical journals, and although devoting himself mainly to the duties of his profession, he has given a share of his attention to public interests, having been chairman of the School Board—several years a member of that board; President of the Georgetown Gas Company, and actively connected with other local organization, standing deservedly high among the most useful men of his community, as well as occupying a prominent position in the medical profession; he is Elder in the Presbyterian Church; is Superintendent of its Sunday school; is identified with every movement looking to the spiritual and temporal welfare of the town, and is a man of exemplary and upright life. Dr. Hamilton was married in 1862, to Miss Virginia W. Hamilton, daughter of Alexander and Sarah Hamilton, of Woodford County, Ky.; they have six living children.

REV. JOHN G. HUNTER, Georgetown; has been pastor of the Presbyterian Church of Georgetown, for eleven years, during which time there have been added to his church one hundred and fifty persons, and have been contributed by his church about $30,000. Mr.

Hunter was born in Maysville, Mason County, Ky., Nov. 13, 1840. His father, Mr. N. D. Hunter, now of Louisville, is of a family who are the descendants of Sir Robert Hunter, of Scotland, the second son of Hunter of Hunterston, who served in the English army under the great Duke of Marlborough, was knighted for gallantry, and rose to the rank of Major-General; he was afterwards appointed Governor-General of New York and New Jersey, when those States were under the British crown. Some of these Hunters married into the family of Sir Francis Drake of the English Navy, and some into the family connected with Sir William Wallace's family of Scotland. The father and mother of N. D. Hunter, John Hunter, and Jeanie Wallace, lived in West Chester County, New York, on the Hudson, and by blood and marriage were connected with the distinguished Dickinson family of New York and New Jersey; with the Edwards and Burrs, Presidents of Princeton College; with the Garnisses and Chases, both the Bishop and Chief Justice of the United States Supreme Court. The mother of J. G. Hunter was the daughter of Mr. George Herbst, a wealthy banker of Maysville, the son of a German nobleman, a burgomaster of Cassel, in Germany. In 1861, the Rev. J. G. Hunter was graduated from Center College, Danville, Kentucky, and began the study of law, but gave up the profession to enter the service in the Confederate States Army, and near the close of the war he was commissioned a Captain while on furlough at Richmond, by Secretary of War Selden. In 1867 he was matriculated at Union Theological Seminary, Hampden Sidney, Virginia, and after a three years' course of study he was licensed to preach the gospel, and entered upon his life work at Georgetown, where he has achieved a successful ministry. In 1871 he married Miss Catharine Breckinridge Waller, daughter of Henry Waller, formerly of Mason County, Ky. By this marriage he is connected with the Breckinridges, Paynes, Langhornes, amongst the most distinguished families in the State.

DR. HENRY C. HERNDON, farmer; P.O. Great Crossing; was born in Scott County, Ky., Jan. 2, 1815, and educated in Georgetown College, graduating in 1833. He began the study of medicine with Drs. Ewing and Gano. He spent two sessions in the Transylvania University. In 1836, he went to Chicot County, Ark., to practice his profession, remaining eighteen months, when he left on account of ill health; he had secured a large practice. He then located in the northern part of Scott County, where he practiced three years, when he located three miles from Georgetown; here he engaged in farming, giving up his practice; remaining five years, he left and came to his present place, where he has since resided, his pursuit being farming. He owns a tract of 275 acres, one half being in grazing, and the rest in cultivatable land. He was married in 1837, to Miss Mary E. Blackburn, daughter of Thomas Blackburn, of this County. She died in 1854, leaving two sons and two daughters, one son having died since.

M. C. HALL, farmer; P. O. Georgetown; was born in Bourbon County, Sept. 2, 1815, to Theophilus and Mary A. (Heathman) Hall; he was a native of England, and emigrated to America with his father, John Hall, and settled where now is the city of Louisville, Ky.; he died in 1850, aged eighty-four years; she was born in Maryland, and died in Woodford County, Ky., in March, 1865, aged eighty-four years; they were the parents of eleven children, M. C. Hall being the seventh child. His common school education was received in Bourbon County, and at the age of twenty-one attended the Bacon College, Georgetown; he began business for himself by farming and trading in the South, the former he still continues. He is one of the largest land owners of Scott County, having 1,700 acres of land, 1,400 of which border Georgetown. Upon his farm he has a fine residence erected by his own design, situated in sight of Georgetown on the Lemon's Mill Pike; upon his farm he makes the breeding and raising of "Almont" horses and short-horns a specialty. He has been twice married; in Woodford County, Aug 10, 1842, he married Mary Ann Sellers, who died in 1845; in Bourbon County, in 1858, he married a second time, Hannah E. Harris; she died in 1879. By his first marriage they had two children, both of whom are dead; and by his second marriage five children, Joseph M., Mary A., Susie W., John T., and Charley. Mr. Hall is a man of good moral character, and bears a name and reputation which is beyond reproach. He is a member of the order of A. F. & A. M.

T. HOLDING, miller; P. O. Georgetown; son of Benjamin and Sarah (Barnett) Holding, was born in Scott County, Ky., on Jan. 31, 1831; his parents were natives of Virginia, and came to Kentucky in 1805; his father was a farmer; both parents were Methodists, and with their son, James, were principal contributors to the building of the brick church at the head waters of Eagle Creek; the church was called Mt. Gilead, but more generally known as Holding's Church. His father died in 1855, in this county, and his mother died in Missouri, in 1879, aged eighty-three. The subject of this sketch was raised on Eagle Creek, and at the age of eighteen began to learn mill wrighting, with Thompson & Curry, who worked successively in Harrison, Scott and Bourbon counties. He continued with that firm about five years. In January, 1855, he became a partner with S. R. Thompson, in the present mill, which they ran three years, when Mr. Holding removed to Livingston County, Mo., and there worked at carpentering and other pursuits, until 1863, when he returned and again became the partner of S. R. Thompson, continuing four years, when he bought the mill at the Crossings, rebuilt and improved, and owned it five years. In 1875, he went to Missouri, and in 1880, for the third time, came into the Thompson mill, as lessee. In the fall of 1881, he introduced the new process of making flour. There are three run of buhrs, with a capacity of thirty-five barrels of flour per day. The mill employs three persons, and does a custom and merchant business. The water-power is sufficient for nine months of the year, and steam is used for the remaining three months. They make three brands of choice flour, which is shipped to various markets. Mr. Holding has had an experience of thirty-two years in milling business. The mill consists of two stories, the lower of stone, the upper, frame. In addition there are an engine room, wareroom, and other buildings.

DR. JOHN R. HALL, Georgetown, was born in Washington County, Ky., and when two years old was brought to Fayette County, where he grew up and was educated in Transylvania University, being a pupil of the renowned Dr. B. W. Dudley; he graduated in medicine in the spring of 1842, when he went to Vandalia, Ill., two years later locating at Georgetown, Ky., where he became the partner of Dr. John Randolph Desha, continuing until 1847, having had a large practice. He moved to Saline County, Mo., in 1855, nine years later coming back to Scott County, Ky., and has since practiced here. He suggested the formation of the Scott County Medical Society, and at his office in 1864 that organization was formed; he is president of the society, an office he has held for a number of years. In 1843 he married Miss Sarah Anna, daughter of Isaac Van Meter, of Clark County; she died in 1844. In 1847 he married Miss Julia M. Snell, daughter of Col. R. P. Snell, of this county; they have a son and daughter: William E., and Mrs. Jesse, of Georgetown. Dr. Hall was raised near Lexington, and was the personal friend of John C. Breckinridge; he has always been a Democrat.

GEORGE L. HAVEN, Georgetown, was born in Kenton County, Ky., in April 1853; his father, Augustus Haven, was born in Pittsburgh, Pa., in February, 1823, and came to Ohio when a child. He was raised in Cincinnati, and became a stockholder and director in Royer's Wheel Company in that city. He married Miss Ellen Longmoor, of Kenton County, Ky. He is the oldest child of his parents, there being four others living. He graduated from Chickering Institute in 1871. In January 1872, he began business with Howell, Gano & Co., as clerk in their wholesale hardware house, and continued four years; in 1876 he became traveling salesman, and until October, 1881, traveled in Kentucky and Tennessee; then he and his father bought the hardware house of R. E. Roberts, and now conduct a hardware, stoves, and queensware establishment on Main Street, under the firm name of A. Haven & Son.

HON. GEORGE W. JOHNSON, deceased, was born May 27, 1811, near Georgetown, Ky., and was the son of Wm. Johnson and grandson of Col. Robert Johnson. He obtained a fine literary education, graduating at Transylvania University. He studied law and practiced that profession for some time, but finally turned his attention to agricultural pursuits; and, besides his farming interests in Kentucky, conducted cotton planting quite extensively in Arkansas. In 1838 he was elected to the Legislature from Scott County; was always a Democrat; represented his party on several important occasions; made the race for Presidential Elector in 1852 and 1860; declined repeatedly to be a candidate for Congress; acquired great power in his party; was a thorough student of political science. At the very outbreak of the civil war, although not a combatant by reason of an injured arm, he cast his lot with the South, and used every exertion to induce Kentucky to follow the seceded States; left his home with Breckinridge and others in September, 1861; made his way to Virginia, and thence to Tennessee and to Bowling Green, in his own State; set afoot and was largely instrumental in organizing a provisional government for the State, and at the convention assembled at Russellville for that purpose, Nov. 18, 1861, he saw his desires carried into effect. A constitution for the State was adopted, under which Kentucky was admitted under the Confederacy, and he was chosen Provisional Governor. When the rapid events of the war compelled the Confederates to retire from the southern part of the State, he accompanied the army; was a part of the military family of the commander, Gen. A. S. Johnston; participated in the councils resulting in the movement from Corinth to Shiloh; went into that great battle as aid to Gen. Breckinridge; was afterwards aid to Col. Trabue, when the Kentucky brigade was separated from Gen. Breckinridge; his horse was shot from under him; he then entered the ranks of Capt. Monroe's company, and fought during the rest of the day. That night he took the oath of a private, and enrolled himself in Company E, Fourth Kentucky Infantry. On the following day went into battle and early fell, mortally wounded; lay on the field until the afternoon of the 8th, when he was discovered by Gen. McCook and removed to a U. S. hospital boat, where, receiving every possible care, he died on the following morning, April 9, 1862. His remains were sent to Louisville by Gen. John M. Harlan and other Federal officers, and were from thence conveyed to his home in Scott County, where amidst a great display of sympathy and popular regard his body was interred. He was a brave, generous, noble hearted man, and was greatly honored and respected in his community and State. He left a wife and seven children.

HENRY V. JOHNSON, County Attorney; Georgetown; son of George W. Johnson, was born in Scott County, Ky., in 1852. He was educated at Georgetown College, graduating in 1871. He read law with Johnson & Brown, of Lexington, and graduated from the Law Department of Kentucky University, in January, 1873. He then went to Louisville, where he read with General John M. Harlan and Ben. H. Bristow, for a period of eighteen months, and was admitted to the bar in the Spring of 1873. He located permanently for practice in Georgetown in the fall of 1874, in that year becoming the partner of W. S. Darnaby, until he was elected to fill the unexpired term of Mr. Owens, in 1877. In August, 1878, he was re-elected County Attorney for fours years, which office he fills in an acceptable manner.

JOSEPH B. KENNEY. At the close of the Revolutionary War James Kenney, who held the office of Captain in the army, removed from Virginia, his native State, and settled on a farm about three miles from what is now known as Paris, Bourbon County, Ky. He was a successful farmer, raising large crops of hemp, then a comparatively new staple in the State; he was twice married, the first wife was a Miss Frame, of Virginia, and the second wife was Miss Margret Johnson, of Nicholas County, Ky. He had sixteen children. The twelfth child was Joseph B. Kenney, the subject of our sketch, who was born Jan. 19, 1806. On his father's farm he remained till he reached his majority, when, on March 8, 1827, he married Miss Lavinia Lander, and with her removed to the adjoining county of Scott; purchasing about 360 acres in the Dry Run neighborhood, where the Burchs, Burbridges and other influential families were living; to these acres he added others, from time to time, till he possessed 1400 acres, which were all under his personal successful management; besides this land he owned a number of slaves, about forty of whom were set free by Lincoln's famous Proclamation. Together with the special farming business, Mr. Kenney engaged largely in buying and selling hogs, and for about twenty years he packed hogs with the Messrs. S. Davis & Co., of Cincinnati. In 1858 Mr. Kenney gave up his home in the country and the occupations, which for near half a century had interested him, to move into Georgetown, in order to co-operate with the Pastor of the Presbyterian Church and others in the establishment of a female Seminary in that city; but this undertaking, by reason of circumstances beyond his control, was not permanently successful; the Seminary, after doing some good work, ceased to be one of the Institutions of the place; still Mr. Kenney remained in town (where he now resides) identified with other public interests; he has been a Director of the Farmer's Bank, of Ky., President of the Lexington & Covington Turnpike Company, Magistrate of the county, and Trustee of the town, usefully and honorably discharging the duties belonging to these several positions. In no department of activity has Mr. Kenney's life been more conspicuous than in that connected with the Church; for fifty years he has been a communicant in the Presbyterian Church; for over forty-five years he has held office in this church, and for many years he has been an efficient Ruling Elder; his liberality to the cause, his fidelity to his church, his zeal for its welfare, none, who knew Mr. Kenney, could for one moment question; he is truly a pillar in the church; strong, even though the weight of years is upon him. Mr. Kenney has had ten children, six of whom are now living; they have married into other good families of the State, making the family connection a large one. James H. Kenney, the oldest son, married Miss Elenora W. Graves; Margaret married B. C. Glass, Esq.; Sallie F. married Joseph Force, Esq.; Joseph F. married Miss Mollie Thomas; Napoleon B. married Miss Lizzie Rankin; Charles V. married Miss Mollie Grissim; Alice married Hon. S. M. Davis, and Victor M. married Miss Agnes Warren. Greatly blessed and a blessing, Mr. and Mrs. Joseph B. Kenney are enjoying a green old age.

SAMUEL Y. KEENE, farmer and breeder of thoroughbred horses; P. O., Georgetown; was born in Scott County, Ky., in 1817. He received his education in the schools of his native county, and at the age of fifteen went to Lexington to become a clerk in the store of T. C. O. Rear; here he continued for one year and then went to Frankfort, Ky., where he remained about ten years, the last five of which he was superintendent of the inside department of the penitentiary, under his uncle, who was warden at that time. He returned to

Georgetown, Ky., in 1849, and engaged in the grocery business until 1869, when his premises and stock were destroyed by fire. Subsequent to this he associated himself with the late Keene Richards, and did a large business in the rearing of horses and mules for the southern markets, for three years. He was breeding in connection with Mr. Richards until 1876, when he separated from him, taking a fine lot of thoroughbred mares, and the stallion "Bullion" by "War Dance"; he has bred since 1876 from eight to ten colts annually, which are sold at annual sales. "War Dance" was considered the best bred son of Lexington. Mr. Keene is the oldest son of the family. His father, Greenup Keene, was born in Scott County, Ky., in 1791; his ancestors were from England, and settled originally in Maryland. His great-grandfather, John Keene, came to this county about 1790; he was an Episcopal minister, and died here; his son, S. Y. Keene, was a physician and farmer, and very fond of horses; his wife died here, and he went back to Maryland about the close of the last century and married a Miss Goldsborough, remaining there till his death; left here two daughters and one son, Greenup Keene, father of our subject, who died in 1875. He was a merchant early in life and also engaged in farming. For many years he lived with our subject, his son. He married Miss Sallie Hanna, daughter of Roland Hanna, one of the earliest settlers of Georgetown, and a very successful merchant, of Irish birth.

THOMAS C. KELLY, Georgetown; was born in Fauquier County, Va., on Christmas Day, 1799; he was educated in private schools of Virginia; in the spring of 1822, he came to Kentucky and stopped in the vicinity of Georgetown; he was accompanied by his brother, George P., and a classmate; they came on horse-back, the journey lasting fourteen days. It was not his intention to remain here, but the loveliness of the country induced him to do so; he taught two years in Franklin, and in 1825 married a Miss Kelly; then he returned to Virginia, and after a year's stay, came back to Georgetown, where he taught school one year. In 1829, he started to Texas, but his wife took sick at New Orleans and he returned to Franklin County, Ky., where he farmed and taught school until 1833, when he moved to Georgetown and closed up the estate of his father-in-law and bought a farm. In 1844 he settled in Georgetown and conducted the County Clerk's office for John T. Johnson until 1852, when he went to New Orleans and formed a partnership with Preston Thompson in the cotton business, continuing until 1854, in the spring of which year he went to Covington, Ky., where he conducted the office of Circuit Clerk for Major Bartlett until 1863. He was a Union man. His great-grandfather came to Virginia about the time of the settlement of Jamestown, and he and the subject's grandfather were in the Revolutionary war under General Washington, at the taking of Cornwallis; his father was a Lieutenant and his grandfather a Captain in the same war. Mr. Kelly's health being impaired, he is not now engaged in any active pursuit; his wife died in 1840 and left one child, James Y. Kelly, present cashier of the Deposit Bank, of Georgetown.

JAMES LONG, breeder of trotting horses; P. O. Georgetown; was born Nov. 12, 1827, on the place where he now lives. He was educated in the neighborhood schools. He and his brother for years had the management of the homestead, and he at last bought it. About 1870, he began the rearing of trotting horses, from the sires, "Almont," "Mambrino," "Patchen," and "George Miles." He bred, reared and trained Katie Jackson, whose public record was 2:21½ at four years, and whose record at private trial was as low as 2:17. She was sold in 1878 for $6,300. She was from George Wilkes and Petoskey. He also reared Gracie Goodwin, who has a record of 2:30. In addition he raised a goodly number of trotters which sold young. He has a private three-quarter mile track on his farm, for the development of trotters, of which he now has several. When twenty years old, he began dealing in coach and carriage horses, and has had singular success. He continues at this occupation. His breeding farm, called "Carview," consists of 220 acres, equally divided between grazing land and cultivation. In June, 1861, he married Miss Susie M. Peak, daughter of Dudley Peak, of this county. His father, James Long, was born in this county in 1783. He was a farmer and served in Col. R. M. Johnson's regiment in the war of 1812. He was also a dealer in fine horses, and bought the present place in about 1819, it being then wild land. He married a Miss Bradford, of South Carolina, whom he met while on a trading tour in that State. The subject's grandfather, Nicholas Long, was born in Virginia, and settled in this county about 1783. His father owned over 400 acres of land on which he lived for over half a century.

A. K. LAIR, Georgetown; was born in Harrison County, Kentucky, in April, 1833, and was educated there. He was a farmer and merchant before the war. In 1861 he enlisted in Col. Hanson's 2d Kentucky Infantry, and participated in all the battles of the 1st Kentucky Brigade, except Pittsburg Landing and Mission Ridge; he served until the close of the war; after his return in 1866 he bought a mill at Lair's Station, Harrison County, Kentucky, and for four years conducted it with fair success; he was then engaged in merchandizing at the same point; in October, 1877, he came to Georgetown and leased the Georgetown Mills, which he has conducted ever since; in July, 1880, he bought the mill and property; he employs five hands, and does a custom and merchant business; there are four run of buhrs, and the capacity is sixteen bushels of wheat per hour, patent process; he makes two brands, the "Pure Gold" and "Silver Dust;" the products of the mill are consumed largely by local demands; he built a stone addition for the storage of grain, at a cost of $4,000, and overhauled the entire mill, putting in the patent process in 1881; the new addition is 35x55 feet, and three stories high; the mill is run by water and steam, the engine being eighty-horse power.

JOHN A. MULLEN, proprietor of Central Hotel; Georgetown; was born in Switzerland, Ind., Jan. 4, 1841; his father is an old-school Methodist preacher, now living at Florence, Ind.; he was born in Pennsylvania, Feb. 22, 1814; his wife, Elizabeth Smith, was born in Indiana, June 15, 1812; she was the mother of eight children, of whom, John, the subject of this sketch was the third; his parents moved to Kentucky when he was six months old, and his school days were passed in the common schools of that State; he entered upon his career in life as a carpenter and joiner; in 1862, he moved to Indiana, and located at Vevay, where he remained sixteen years, and assisted in the erection of many of the prominent business blocks and dwelling houses of that places; he was the originator of the Charter of Vevay, and formed one of the City Council for a long time; he was also a prominent member of the I. O. O. F., of that place for a number of years; he united with the Methodists when he was but seventeen years of age, and has filled the positions of Class Leader and Sunday School Superintendent several years; at present himself and wife are connected with the Methodist Church of Georgetown, where he moved in the year 1878, and followed his trade for several years, being engaged in erecting some of the finest blocks in the city; in October, 1881, he opened the Central Hotel, where he is still in business and performs the duties of "mine host" with courteousness, alacrity and ability; he was married march 2, 1865, to Louisa Kincaid, who was born in Virginia, July 13, 1842; she has borne him six children, viz.: Margaret, Sally, Jennie, Eva, James, and Emma, the two latter of whom died in infancy. Mrs. Mullen was a daughter of William and Margaret (Scott) Kincaid, natives of Ireland. He born in 1792, she in 1802, now living in Vevay, Ind. Mr. Mullen is an energetic and enterprising man, and possesses the qualifications necessary in gaining the good will of all; politically he is a Democrat.

JUDGE JOHN G. MORRISON, coal-dealer; Georgetown; was born near West Union, in Adams County, Ohio, October 23, 1810. He was left an orphan at a very early age, and lived for a time with an uncle, David Morrison, at Washington, Kentucky; he came to Kentucky at the age of eight years. He moved to Maysville in 1822, and thence to Lexington in 1824, with another uncle, Richieson Morrison, a merchant; he was in that city when Lafayette made his visit there, and remembers well the man whose name is prominent in history. He lived in Lexington, acting as clerk in his uncle's dry-goods store until 1830, when he moved to Frankfort and there opened a like store of his own, which continued two years. In 1832 he went to Philadelphia, Pennsylvania, and was salesman in a wholesale dry-goods house for two years, when he returned to Lexington again, doing business for himself. In 1836, at Great Crossings, Scott County, Ky., he married Miss Nancy B., daughter of Gen. William Johnson, and the following year went to Phillips County, Ark., to plant cotton, but was not successful in this new adventure, owing to the overflow at that time. He returned to Kentucky, living at Great Crossings from 1841 to 1857; from 1842 to 1846 he rode as deputy sheriff of Scott County; he followed the occupation of farming and rope-spinning from 1847 to 18[illegible]6; in 1857 he moved to Georgetown and has since that year resided in the house he first made his home. In 1862 he was elected county judge of Scott County, and served four years, his election being made by the Union Party and without opposition. In 1868 he was appointed United States Gauger for the 7th District of Kentucky, and for three years served in that capacity, since which time he has engaged in the lumber and coal business, his yard being located on Hamilton street. He is a man who can adapt himself to many kinds of business, and as a citizen is much esteemed. He has four children living and two deceased. He is a Free Mason, and in politics was a Whig and later a Republican. He has one brother and two sisters living. His father was born in Ireland, and was a farmer; he died about 1818.

JAMES F. MUSSELMAN, farmer; P. O. Dry Run; was born in Harrison County, Ky., Dec. 5, 1828, to William and Martha (White) Musselman, natives of Kentucky; he born in Harrison County, Nov. 14, 1797; was a farmer by occupation, and died Feb. 2, 1853; she born in Daviess County, Nov. 28, 1801; died July 30, 1854. They were married Oct. 10, 1821, in Daviess County. Their union resulted in three children, who grew to maturity, viz: Mary Ann, born Oct. 3, 1822, wife of Samuel Crust, of Pleasant Hill, Mo.; John W., born Oct. 2, 1838, now living in Cynthiana, Ky.; and James F., the subject of our sketch. The grandfather of our subject was Christopher Musselman, who was born in Lancaster County, Pa. He served in the Revolutionary war, and settled near Bryant's Station, Ky., at an early day, and later moved to Harrison County, and raised a family of four girls and five boys. He died Jan. 29, 1846, at the age of 90 years. James F., our subject, was married May 22, 1856, in Scott County, to Letha J. Hall, who was born to William and Malinda (Stone) Hall, of Scott County, April 19, 1832, and died May 1, 1860. She was the mother of one child, William S., who died in infancy. Mr. Musselman's second marriage occurred in Scott County, Dec. 6, 1870, to Nippie Burgess, who was born in Scott County, March 12, 1847. They have three children, viz: Myra V., born Nov. 27, 1871; Nannie H., born Oct. 30, 1873, and Joseph F., born Feb. 4, 1878. Mrs. Musselman was a daughter of Joseph and Maranda (Penn) Burgess. He born Feb. 4, 1809, and still living. She died in 1858. Mr. Musselman is one of the most prominent farmers in the precinct, and socially ranks very high in the esteem of the community at large. He has passed several years of his life on the plains of Montana and at Salt Lake. He has always been a farmer and has accumulated a large amount of worldly goods. He has a farm of 470 acres of choice farm lands, which as a practical farmer he keeps in a high state of cultivation. He also owns 160 acres of western land, and town property at Cynthiana. In addition to growing the usual farm crops, he is engaged in raising and handling pedigreed stock of the Irene, Phyllis and Bates families. He served one year in the service with Capt. Renick, in the regiment commanded by Col. Walton. He was originally a Whig, but at present his political sympathies are with the Democratic party. He has been a member of the Masonic order for a number of years. Religiously he is a member of the Presbyterian Church, and his wife is connected with the Baptist denomination.

J. TAYLOR MOORE, merchant and clergyman; Georgetown; fourth son of Robert and Ann E. (Pratt) Moore, was born and raised within four miles of Georgetown, Scott County, Ky.; his father was a native of Scott County, where he grew to manhood; he was a farmer and died in 1838, leaving five sons; J. Taylor Moore was born in 1835; he was educated in the county schools; he started in life as a farmer, and at the age of twenty-one, in 1856, he married Miss Melvina Muir, of Fayette County, Ky.; twelve years later she died, leaving four children, two of whom are living; he married Sophia Lewis, of Clark County, in 1876, up to which date he had followed farming at his homestead, in this county; he moved to Georgetown, and in 1878, formed the partnership of Moore & Lemon, since which time he has conducted a grocery business; at the age of twenty-two years, he united with the Missionary Baptist Church, of which he remained a member twelve years; in 1871, he joined the Particular Baptist Church, at Georgetown, was licensed to preach in 1872, and ordained to the ministry in 1875, in which year he became assistant pastor of the church at Georgetown; he is now the pastor of four churches, viz.: Bryant's Station Church, in Fayette County; Elizabeth Church, in Bourbon County; Sardis Church, in Boone County, and that of Georgetown. Beloved by his pastorate, and recognized by all as a Christian gentleman, is the subject of these lines.

P. McCULLOUGH, Georgetown, was born in County Tyrone, North Ireland, on March 15, 1851. He was educated in his native country, and came to the United States when he was but fifteen years of age; he located in New York City and was apprenticed in an omnibus factory in 1866 to learn carriage making. He served three years at wood work, then came to Kentucky and worked as journeyman at Lexington and Versailles, coming to Georgetown in 1874, where he worked at journey work for D. H. Hickey for about two years, and for T. I. Burns one year. In 1877 he bought the shop of Mr. Burns, which burned in 1879 with total loss of building, stock, and tools; there was no insurance. In 1880 he leased the present building of B. D. Best, and has continued the manufacture of vehicles of all kinds, employing from ten to fifteen hands, all departments being represented by skilled workmen in wood work, painting, smithing, and trimming. He turns out about forty finished jobs per year, and has a full assortment of attractive styles in his ware-room, which is connected with the factory. In 1877 he married Miss Jennie O'Neill, of Georgetown.

JOHN C. MILLER, deceased; was born in Scott County, Ky., Feb. 7, 1800. His youth was passed on the farm and in private schools, being the pupil of a man named Laughlin. He chose the profession of law, and became a distinguished practitioner of the Georgetown bar, being often pitted against Governor J. F. Robinson, whose contemporary he was. After some years of successful practice, Mr. Miller retired from its labors and went to Mississippi, where he purchased a tract of over 2,000 acres of cotton lands, which he converted into plantations and owned and worked from 600 to 800 slaves upon it. For many years Mr. Miller and his family passed the winter season in the "Sunny South" and the summer in Georgetown, Ky. He was a Democrat in politics, and died May 5, 1840. He was married Dec. 20, 1821, to Miss Jane Holmes, of Fayette County, who is still living. She was born in Lexington, Ky., in 1802, and was educated in her native city. Her parents moved to Scott County when she was a girl. Mrs. Miller spent eleven winters in Mississippi, performing the journey on the keel and flat boats of a half-century ago, so that at one time she knew every crook and turn of the Ohio and Mississippi rivers. Their marriage bore the fruit of three sons and two daughters, all deceased except one daughter, Mrs. Warren. Robert H. died of cholera in 1833; James and John C. died in 1832. Agnes married John F. Warren, of this County. He became a successful planter and died in Mississippi, in 1863, leaving no children. She is still living with her aged mother. Laura Miller, married Thomas P. Johnson, a son of Euclid and Maria (Warren) Johnson. His father, Euclid Johnson is a brother of Major M. C. Johnson, of Lexingington, and like his brother, a distinguished lawyer; he died at Little Rock, Arkansas. Thomas P. Johnson was born in Scott County, Ky., in 1829, and finished his education in the Military Institute, and went to California in 1849, and spent some years in the mines, and on his return became a Southern planter. He died at Georgetown, April 12, 1862, leaving four children. There are but two sons living, now residents of Georgetown, Ky. His widow, Laura (Miller) Johnson, was afterward married to Dr. Paul Rankin, of Georgetown, but died in 1868.

JOHN E. MOORE, deceased, was born in Scott County. He was quite young when his parents died; he was educated in the common schools of Midway, and in Georgetown College, after which he took a trip to Texas to see the country and get an insight into business; after a stay of nine months, returning to Scott County. He taught school in "Turkey Foot Precinct" for six months; having inherited a farm, he engaged in tilling the ground, reaping successful harvests; he was quite an extensive stock-raiser, dealing mostly in horses and mules; his parents were also of Scott County. In 1859, in Midway, he married; his death occurred in the Spring of 1870, aged thirty-five years; his wife was Miss Mary Harper, a native of Woodford County; she was a daughter of William Harper, a native of the same county, and Anna (Whitley) Harper, a native of Lincoln County; her grandfather, Col. William Whitley, was in the war of 1812, being a volunteer; he was killed in the same battle as Tecumseh, and it is claimed that he is the one who killed the Chief; her grandfather, Adam Harper was a native of Virginia, and at an early day emigrated to Woodford County; he bought 1,000 acres of land, it then being worth but a dollar an acre; it has so grown in value as now to be worth one hundred dollars per acre. Her brother, Frank Harper, is the owner of the prize horses "Tenbroek" and "Longfellow," which were raised by her uncle, John Harper; "Tenbroek" ran against time at Louisville in 1878, winning a silver cup valued at a thousand dollars. Mr. Moore, during his life, accumulated 178 acres of land. Mrs. Moore has six children living, two sons and four daughters; the family worship with the Christian Church; she owns about 600 acres of land from the old Harper estate.

WM. S. NEALE, retired farmer; P. O. Dry Run; was born in Scott County, Dec. 20, 1806, to Daniel and Sally (Shortridge) Neale; his father was born in Fairfax County, Va., in 1758, and emigrated to Scott County and settled at the Great Crossings in about the year 1785, being among the early settlers of Scott County; during his life he followed the occupation of farming; he died in 1813. His wife was born in Virginia in 1770; emigrated with her parents to Boonsborough in about the year 1779, and died in 1875. Wm. S. Neale received his education from the common schools of his native county, and before he was of age began farming on his own account, which he has since continued in connection with trading in the South. In 1872 he retired from farming and all active labor, with the exception of several trading expeditions South. Mr. Neal is a man possessed with good common sense, and enjoys the esteem of the citizens of the community in which he lives. He is a Republican.

COL. E. N. OFFUTT, Sr., retired farmer; P. O. Georgetown; whose portrait appears in this history, was born in Montgomery County, Md., Dec. 28, 1806, and was the seventh child of a family of five sons and three daughters, born to his parents, who were Alexander and Ann (Clegett) Offutt, the former also a native of Montgomery County, Md. He was born Feb. 18, 1767, and was the son of William Offutt, a native of Maryland, and born Oct. 6, 1721; the latter was a native of Maryland; born in 1768, and died in 1833, surviving her husband ten years, he having died Oct. 21, 1823. Miss Ann Clegett was the daughter of William Clegett, who died while a soldier in the Revolutionary war. When our subject was about three years old his parents moved to Scott County, where they arrived in March, 1810. The tract of land on which stands the old homestead, still occupied by the Colonel, was selected as a home, and there the worthy couple reared a family, and built for themselves an honorable name and reputation. By the time he had arrived at man's estate, he had acquired a fair education and a thorough and practical knowledge of farming and stock-raising. Making the breeding of fine stock a specialty, he stood for many years among the leading stock men of the county; he was a shrewd financier, and an excellent business manager, at one time owning 800 acres of land; he has, however, disposed of a part of his real estate, having now but 330 acres. Politically, Mr. Offutt is a man of firm convictions; though never an aspirant for office, he many times having refused to become a candidate for positions of prominence when his election would have been a certainty, choosing rather to remain with his family, and add to the pleasures and comforts of a home. In March, 1881, the Colonel rented his farm and gave up the active management and details of farming. The kitchen portion of Mr. Offutt's residence is one of the most interesting of pioneer landmarks; it was built in 1782, by one Mathew Flournoy, and was the first residence in which window glass was used in that part of Kentucky, east of the Kentucky River. Gen. William Henry, commander of the Kentucky volunteer troops for the war of 1812, was married in this residence. Col. Offutt was married in Scott County in 1836, to Miss Elizabeth A. Lemon, who was born in Lexington, Ky., July 20, 1818; she is the daughter of Joseph I. Lemon, who was born in Georgetown, July 15, 1793, and died June 17, 1836. He was the son of James Lemon, a native of Ireland, whose family consisted of nine sons and one daughter; all of the former were soldiers in the Revolutionary war. The wife of Joseph I., and mother of Mrs. Offutt, was Miss Margaret Leathers, a native of Madison County, Virginia; she was born March 23, 1792, and died Nov. 29, 1868. Eight children have been born to Mr. and Mrs. Offutt, three only of whom are living: Margaret A., wife of Col. Mark Munday, of Louisville; Laura V., wife of William Munday, of Louisville; and Edmonia, wife of Dr. O. H. Witherspoon, of Lawrenceburg; Mr. and Mrs. Offutt are both members of the Presbyterian Church, he joining in 1833, and she in 1839. They are a worthy couple, and held in high esteem by all those who know them. Their lives spent in honest effort to acquire a competency and rear their family honorably, they now enjoy the fruits of their early industry and economy.

WILLIAM N. OFFUTT, farmer and short-horn breeder; P. O. Georgetown; was born in Scott County, in August, 1841. His father, Alexander Offutt, was a native of Maryland; born Oct. 10, 1803; emigrated to Scott County with his parents in about 1810; during his life followed the occupation of a farmer, and died in 1873. His mother was Emeline Smith, born in Scott County in 1824, and died in 1853; she was the mother of five children, William N. Offutt being the oldest child. He attended the Georgetown College to the opening of the war, when he enlisted in the Confederate Army, and served under Morgan to the close of the war; when he began farming in his native county, at which he still continues. In 1868 he began breeding and raising short-horn cattle, and is at the present time making it a specialty. In 1868, in Scott County, he married Miss Sue W. Ford, a native of Scott County; born to Reuben and Mary (Webb) Ford in 1850; he was born in Scott County in June, 1819, attended the school at Oxford, Ohio, and graduated at the Center College when but sixteen years of age. He attended the Transylvania Law School at Lexington, where he graduated with high honors; in 1839 was admitted to the bar, and began the practice of his profession, continuing the same until 1845, when he gave up his profession and began farming, which he continued to the time of his death, which occurred in September, 1856. He was married in Scott County in 1843, to Miss Mary Webb, a native of Scott County, born at her present residence to Mitchum and Susan (Holmes) Webb. Mr. and Mrs. Offutt have had five children, three of whom are living: Reuben F., William N., Jr., and M. Webb. They have the well improved farm of 900 acres, called "Elmwood."

LEWIS B. OFFUTT, auctioneer; Georgetown; was born near Georgetown, Scott Co., Ky., in the year 1817; he received a common-school education and removed with his parents in 1828 to Harrison County Ky., where he resided until 1851. In 1841 Mr. Offutt began his career as auctioneer, first selling stock and farm implements; he soon won a reputation that brought under his hammer a large business in both lands and negroes. About 1855 Mr. Offutt became the principal auctioneer for the whole northeastern counties of the "Blue Grass Region," his services commanding as high as $250 per day. He returned to Scott County in 1851, and since 1864 has been a resident of Georgetown. In politics Mr. Offutt is a Democrat, and during the late war was twice taken by the Federal soldiers and escaped, and was exiled from his home and family for two months, although he had committed no offense. Mr. Offutt is

"GLASTON" RESIDENCE OF V. K. GLASS, NEAR GEORGETOWN, KY.

perhaps the oldest auctioneer in the county and still does a good business as auctioneer and real-estate agent. He has been married three times: first, to Miss Davis in 1837, and of this marriage there is one son, Capt. Nathaniel S. Offutt, of Georgetown, one of the most successful auctioneers in the county; his second wife was Miss Lucy A. George, of Bourbon County, who died in less than a year after marriage; he married for his third wife Mrs. Causey, daughter of John Masterson, one of the pioneers of this county. After years of hard work Mr. Offutt secured a competence for his declining years, and this was largely swept away to the debts of so-called friends for whom he had become surety, yet he cheerfully gave up and paid every dollar even after he was legally released. His father, Archibald Offutt, was born in Maryland, about 1766, and came to Scott County, Ky., in 1816; he died in Harrison County in the cholera epidemic of 1833; he was the father of nine children, five of whom are still living.

B. M. OSBORN, farmer; P. O. Georgetown; is a native of Scott County, and the son of John and Nancy (Miller) Osborn; he was born near his present residence, 1816; his father was a native of Abbeville District, South Carolina, born Sept. 7, 1788; he emigrated to Scott County in about 1812; during his life was a farmer; he died Nov. 7, 1822; his wife, mother of our subject, was born in Pensylvania, in 1794, and died in Scott County, Oct. 27, 1878; she was the mother of three children, two daughters and one son, B. M. Osborn, being the oldest child; his early education was limited to such as the neighborhood schools of Scott County afford; at the death of his parents he lived with his Uncle Benjamin Osborn, and assisted him in all of his business operations until he arrived at the age of twenty-seven years; when he made several trading expeditions in the South with stock; in 1846, he bought a small farm in his native county and began farming and stock raising, at which he still continues, and now being one of the largest land owners of Scott County, having 1,500 acres of land, which is somewhat hilly, and particularly adapted to the raising of sheep, upon which he now has nearly 1,000 of choice breeds. Mr. Osborn is a man of great force of character, sociable in disposition, and agreeable in manner, is a very temperate man, having never tasted intoxicating liquor in over forty-five years; he has always been a hard-working man, and now in the later years of his life is surrounded with those comforts, and enjoying those pleasures that are ever the result of honesty, industry and economy; he was married in Scott County, in 1868, to Mrs. Agatha Osborn, a native of Scott County; he is a Republican.

HUGH O'NEILL, Georgetown; was born in County Derry, Ireland, on New Years' Day, 1846. When he was seven months old, his parents came to the United States, locating at Lexington, where they lived until 1854, and then moved to Scott County, locating on a farm three miles from Georgetown. The subject of this sketch attended the county schools of his neighborhood, until he attained the age of sixteen years, when he learned the trade of horse-shoeing, with John Jackson, and Dougherty Bros., of Lexington, serving five years apprenticeship. In 1866, he located in Georgetown, opening a business for himself, which he followed until 1881. He was shoer for Colonel R. West for five years. Among his customers were Dr. Hurst, of Woodford County; H. C. McDowell, of Franklin County; Keene Richards, who owned race stables, and James Miller, of Bourbon County, who owned trotting stables. He has been a general dealer in horses for fifteen years. In the fall of 1875, he went into the livery business in Georgetown, in the present stables which he owns. He carried on a successful business there until 1881, except during a part of 1878, when he was engaged in the same business in Lexington. In 1881, he leased the stable to Mr. Ayres, and established sale stables in Georgetown, doing a lucrative business in sale and commission. In 1870, he married Miss Tee Pullen, daughter of James Pullen, of Georgetown.

HON. WILLIAM C. OWENS, lawyer; Georgetown; was born in Scott County, Ky., on October 17, 1849. He was educated in Transylvania University, and at Millersburg, and graduated from the Columbia law school in the spring of 1872 and began to practice in Georgetown, being admitted to the bar here in March, 1873. The following year he was elected County Attorney but resigned, and was elected to the Legislature in August, 1877; he was re-elected in 1879 without opposition. In 1881 he was again re-nominated without opposition, and in November, 1881, at the assembling of the House, he was elected Speaker, there being four opponents, viz.; Gov. Merriweather, C. U. McElroy, Jacob Rice, and J. M. Hendricks. His father, Charles Owens, born in Scott county in 1805, was a farmer and a thorough business man. He had one son and daughter by his wife who was a Miss Tucker of Grant County.

GEORGE E. PREWITT, lawyer; Georgetown, Ky.; born in Scott County, Ky., April 14, 1827, near to what is now Kinkead Station, C. S. R.; is the fourth son of Robert C. and Elizabeth S. Prewitt, who, in the year 1835, emigrated to Lincoln County, Mo., where the subject of our sketch resided until he was twenty-two, receiving his education principally in a private school taught by Rev. Wilson Cunningham, a Presbyterian minister of great worth and learning. His father, Robert C. Prewitt, was born in Fayette County, Ky., on a farm, in 1795, and his mother, whose maiden name was Elgin, in Maryland, in 1793, who, with her parents, emigrated to, and settled in Scott County, Ky., when she was a child seven years old, and who is still living in Missouri in the ninetieth year of her age. His said father, before he had attained his eighteenth year, in the Fall of 1812, joined Capt. John Edmondson's Company of Kentucky volunteers, and was present and took part in the disastrous battle of the River Raisin (or Frenchtown) and was there taken prisoner by the British and Indians, and suffered many hardships and indignities before he was exchanged. He was married in 1818, and died in 1850. In 1849 George E. Prewitt returned to Kentucky, and in 1851 began the study of law with Richard Apperson, Sr., of Mt. Sterling, but married and returned to Missouri before completing his legal studies, and was admitted to the bar in that State in 1852; he came to Georgetown in 1854, and was the same year admitted to practice in all the courts of this State, to which he has since devoted his time and talents; he served in the capacity of City Judge of Georgetown for one term, and as Master Commissioner of the Scott Circuit Court from 1856 to 1862.

H. S. PARKS, farmer; P. O. Georgetown; is a native of Scott County, and the son of Ebenezer and Elizabeth (Woodgate) Parks. He was born in 1823. His father was also a native of Scott County, born in 1797; during his life he followed the occupation of a cabinet-maker. He died in 1824. He was the son of James Parks, a native of Rockbridge County, Va., who emigrated to Scott County, and settled in about two-and-a-half miles of Newtown, in about the year 1790. He died in 1837. Elizabeth Parks, the mother of our subject, was born in Fayette County in 1800, and is now living in Scott County. She is the daughter of Jonathan Woodgate, a soldier in the war of 1812. Mr. Parks received his education from the common schools of his native county, and in 1841 he began teaching school, following the same until 1844, when he embarked in the mercantile business at Newtown; retiring from the same in 1847, and again resumed teaching for several years, and during the time traveled through twenty States of the Union, trading in stock. In 1854 he commenced farming and stock-raising in Scott County, which he still continues upon his well-improved farm of 181 acres. Upon his farm he has some Short-horns. In politics he was formerly a Whig, but now is identified with the Democratic party. In 1858 he was elected County Surveyor, and served eight years. He is a member of the A., F. & A. M.

JOHN G. PARRISH, farmer; P. O. Georgetown; was born in Bourbon County, Ky., Oct. 12, 1826; his father, Henry Parrish, was a native of Virginia, and one of the early settlers of Bourbon County; he was a farmer by occupation, and his death occurred in Missouri, in 1834, at the age of about forty-five years; his wife, Sally Bush, was born in Clark County, and died in 1832, aged about forty years; she was the mother of five children, of whom John G., the subject of these lines, was the fourth. He was left an orphan at the age of seven years, when he was cared for by his oldest brother until he was thirteen years old, and then went to live with his uncle, E. H. Parrish; his education was limited to such as could be obtained in the common schools of Bourbon and Clark counties; he entered upon his career in life as a farmer, and trading in stock. In the Spring of 1848, he moved to Fayette County, where he remained until the Spring of 1856, when he removed to Scott County, where he has since remained engaged in farming and dealing in stock, trading principally in mules. He has been thrice married, his last marriage occurred in 1866, to Miss Patty M. Peak, who was born in Scott County, Feb. 25, 1847, to George P. and America (Suggett) Peak; he was born March 23, 1823, died March 1, 1865; she was born Dec. 1, 1820, now living in Scott County. By his second wife Mr. Parrish has one daughter living, viz.: Elizabeth, wife of E. P. Withers. Mr. Parrish holds a prominent position among the practical farmers of the county, as an energetic and enterprising man. Religiously, himself and wife are connected with the Baptist Church.

GEORGE V. PAYNE, Lawyer, Georgetown; was born in Howard county, Mo., December 12, 1843, and at the age of twenty entered Georgetown College, graduating in the class of 1866. He began the study of law here, and gaduated from the Louisville law school in the class of 1867-68. He was admitted to the bar in 1868, since which time he has been in active practice. In August, 1870, he was elected County Judge, and re-elected in 1874, also in 1878, now serving his third term. By the Democratic party he was re-nominated for a fourth term, in 1882. He is a descendant of the old Payne families of Fayette and Scott Counties.

HON. JAMES FISHER ROBINSON, lawyer and farmer and ex-Governor of Kentucky, was born in Scott County, Kentucky, October 4, 1800. His father, Jonathan Robinson, was a native of Pennsylvania, and there married a daughter of Capt. John Black, and began his married life as a farmer in Cumberland County, of that State, on a tract of land given him by his father and father-in-law, in the vicinity of their own residence. Shortly afterward the war of the Revolution commenced, and during its first year he volunteered; was commissioned Captain and served until the restoration of peace. In 1785 he visited Kentucky and bought a farm of six hundred acres in Scott County, upon which he erected cabins for his residence, and, having returned to Pennsylvania in the following spring, removed with his family to his new home in Kentucky, where he continued to reside as one of the substantial and influential citizens until his death, in the eighty-sixth year of his age. Gov. Robinson came of English and Scotch ancestors; his great-grandfather, being a Dissenter, located in Ireland, and there his grandfather, George Robinson, was born, and married a Scotch lady. The entire family moved to America and settled in Pennsylvania, about the middle of the seventeenth century. His grandfather, many years after his father, settled in Kentucky, also removed to this State, where he passed his life on an adjoining farm in Scott County, and there died at the age of eighty-seven. He was an ardent Whig during the Revolution, and served some time as a volunteer during that war. Gov. Robinson's education was commenced under a private teacher at his father's house, was continued under the Rev. Robt. Marshall, one of the most scholarly among the early Presbyterian ministers of Kentucky, and his academic education was completed at Forest Hill Academy, under the celebrated Samuel Wilson. He subsequently entered Transylvania University, where he graduated in 1818. He immediately began the study of law at Lexington, under Hon. William T. Barry, one of the ablest men who ever flourished in Kentucky. A few years afterwards he obtained license and began the law practice at Georgetown, in his native county, and there has continued actively engaged in his profession until the present time, excepting short intervals of political life. In 1851 he was elected, without opposition, to the Senate of Kentucky, to represent the district composed of Scott and Fayette Counties, and served one term. In August, 1861, after a warmly contested canvass, he was again elected from the same senatorial district, defeating Hon. James B. Beck. This canvass was made when the clouds of civil war were gathering over the country, and the great subjects of vital importance to the people were discussed: such as the right of secession, the impending rebellion, the value of the Union, and the proper place to be occupied by Kentucky in the inevitable conflict. In 1862 Gov. Magoffin, the Governor of Kentucky, resigned the office of chief executive, and, there being no Lieutenant Governor, he being a member of the Senate, was immediately elected Speaker, thereby becoming acting Governor of the State, and as such at once qualified, and entered upon his duties, serving as Governor until the end of the term. The period of his administration was filled with troubles, difficulties and perils known to no other, before or since. His conduct was in accord with the administration of the National Government, and his unflinching devotion to the Union, and his strong, manly guardianship of the affairs of the State, brought the best possible good out of the evils of the times. Doubtless but few men in the State were better suited to control its affairs at such a time, reared as he had been, in his school of patriots, and from early life having espoused the Whig principles of National Government, possessing eminently the firm, unexplosive and temperate elements of character and withal being greatly attached to the best interests of his native State. He has been a farmer as well as a lawyer for the last twenty-five years, and now resides at "Cardome" (from cara domus); his fine farm consisting of 300 acres, and joining Georgetown, in a part of that most beautiful region called "Blue Grass," he has been without political ambition, having lived too busy a life to give his attention to the higher aims of the statesman, and being unwilling to become a mere politician; although importuned to accept public office at different times, he has usually declined, preferring to devote himself to his professional and agricultural interests; as a lawyer, he has taken a place among the most learned and able in Kentucky. He has been concerned in many of the great law cases of the State, and so thoroughly did he become identified with the interests of his clients, that his business grew to great proportions, and gave him little time to devote to politics, had he possessed the inclination. Had he given himself to public affairs with that earnestness, learning and wisdom, which characterized his professional life, he would have taken rank among the first statesmen of his day. He possesses in a high degree, many broad and noble traits, which not only gave him strength and dignity in the court and before the jury, but, during his difficult term of office as Chief Executive of the State, enabled him to administer its affairs with great impartiality and justice; firmly suppressing wrong, and protecting the people, regardless of their peculiar sympathies, in their just demands as citizens. He is a man of commanding person and noble presence, and probably no man of the old school is now living in Kentucky, who would have been able at any time to add mere dignity and honor to any position in the gift of the people. Gov. Robinson is now living with his third wife, and has eight living children.

JAMES JEFFERSON RUCKER, Professor of Mathematics in the College and Principal of the Female Seminary at Georgetown, Kentucky; was born Jan. 27, 1828, in Randolph County, Mo. He is the son of Rev. Thornton Rucker, and his wife, Martha, both natives of Virginia, and married in that State. His father was a Baptist clergyman, and among the earliest preachers of that denomination in Missouri. His mother, a sister of William Snyder, a citizen of prominence in Boone Co., Ky., comes from a family having its lineal representatives in this State, Missouri, and Orange County, Va., whence it originally sprung. Remotely this family were by occupation millers, and the Rucker family farmers. About the year 1820 the parents and grandparents of Prof. Rucker emigrated from Virginia to Missouri, settling respectively in Howard and Monroe Counties. In these and Saline and Randolph Counties, Prof. Rucker passed his childhood and youth, mostly in assisting his father on the farm. During this period he received but meager schooling, and at the age of nineteen found himself possessed of but the merest rudiments of an English education. Feeling the absolute necessity for a knowledge of arithmetic for ordinary business purposes, in the fall of 1847 he entered a county school with a view to attain this knowledge. In this school he continued about a year. It proved the occasion of determining his whole future course of life. His teacher, observing that his abilities were of more than usual character, urged upon him the pursuit of a routine of studies especially calculated to fit him for a professional career. Adopting these friendly suggestions, in the fall of 1848 he commenced teaching a country school, employing his leisure hours in self-culture. In the winter of 1849-50 he entered Howard High-school, at Fayette, Missouri, remaining, as pupil and assistant teacher, until June, 1851; in the fall of that year he recommenced the duties of a country school teacher; in the spring of 1852, through the advice, influence, and financial aid of his friend, E. D. Sappington, of that county, a gentleman for whom he has ever since cherished the highest esteem, he came to Kentucky and entered Georgetown College to pursue and complete his studies; here he remained a student, teaching at intervals a school in Bourbon County, Ky., until June, 1854, when, with the honors of his class, he graduated as an A. B.; after graduating he kept up his school in Bourbon County until the fall of 1855, at which time he entered upon the discharge of the duties of principal of the academy attached to the Georgetown College, to which position he had been appointed during the summer of that year. He, however, had scarcely assumed the discharge of these duties when, a vacancy occurring in the chair of mathematics in the Georgetown College, he was temporarily appointed to the place in the capacity of a substitute. He took the chair on the 21st of Nov., 1855, and gave such signal proofs of ability that when the board of trustees met in the following June they at once invested him permanently with the office, which he has ever since continued to fill with honor to himself and profit to the community. Among his pupils in mathematics may be especially mentioned Dr. J. F. Cook, President of LaGrange College, Missouri; Dr. Varden, of Paris; and W. H. Felix, of Covington, Ky. At the close of the war, in 1865, the building at Georgetown, which for twenty years had been occupied by Prof. Farnham as a female seminary, having burned down, a void in that department of education was thereby created, which for a time was keenly felt by the people, who put forth many efforts to remedy the evil, but all unavailingly until Prof. Rucker came to their relief, taking charge of the school and appropriating to its use his own private property until better and more commodious premises could be obtained. Perceiving, however, after a time, through the indications of failing health, that he had undertaken too much by assuming the additional duties of Principal of the Seminary, he sold out property and school to Rev. J. B. Thorp, who continued its management for two years, when the school was transferred to other quarters and re-organized. During the summer of 1868, the citizens of Georgetown projecting a new building for Seminary purposes, Prof. Rucker became the agent of its Board of Trustees to solicit funds and to superintend its construction, devoting much time thereto; and when in the fall of 1869 it was completed, again became its Principal, which he yet remains. This institution now occupies a front rank among all similar ones throughout the State. In 1874 he conceived the idea of aiding Georgetown College financially by having a chair endowed with a fund raised from its former students. The work of canvassing among them was done by himself during vacations. With some assistance from Rev. R. M. Dudley, he succeeded in raising sixteen thousand dollars. This sum being insufficient for the purpose, he applied to the Legislature for an act of incorporation for an association, granting them power to take charge of the fund and increase it. The charter was obtained during the session of 1875-76, the title of the corporation being "The Students' Association of

Georgetown College." Thus provided for, the sum has since become an assured fact. It is now slowly but steadily increasing, with every prospect of ultimately attaining an amount sufficient to meet fully the design of its institution. It is managed and controlled by a board chosen from the members of the association, of which at the present time he is the chairman. About the close of the war, desirous of advancing the moral and religious good of the people, he called a meeting of Sunday school workers for the purpose of uniting their efforts in such a way as to render their labors in the cause of Christianity and Bible truth more efficient. The meeting turned out a success, and resulted in the formation and establishment of the "Baptist Sunday School Convention of Elk Horn Association," an organization which was the first of its kind in Kentucky, of which there are many in the State. For a number of years Prof. Rucker was the chairman of the "Sunday School Board of the Baptist General Association of Kentucky," retiring therefrom only when duties otherwise pressing and ill health constrained him so to do; he has been a consistent member of the Baptist Church since his early youth, having imbibed his religious principles from his father, who was a constant living exemplification of Christian character. To his father he attributes much of his success in life, having drawn from him all those habits of correct training and thought which are so conspicuous in his own daily walk, conversation and manners, and which have been the true foundation of his many years of usefulness; besides all these various occupations heretofore recited, which have engaged his time and attention, he has been an active member of the Board of Trustees of Georgetown nearly the whole period of his residence there, taking a genuine interest in all its municipal affairs, and conserving the public good in every legitimate way possible, to the best of his ability; this he did without the hope of fee or reward, the service being of that class of work which brings no compensation save that of an approving conscience ; to such men the community really never knows how much they are indebted, until they have passed from the business stage of life. Professor Rucker is a man of great public spirit, enlarged views, sound practical knowledge, indefatigable purpose, untiring energy, and withal, of a very conscientious, kind and impressible nature; in manners is courteous, unassuming, modest, and prepossessing. His school, which numbers over one hundred young ladies, is a model of order, refinement, good government, and regularity. On Sept. 10, 1855, he was married to Miss Mary M. Allison, of Bourbon County, Ky.; after marriage they made Georgetown their home, where they have ever since resided; they have four children—a daughter and three sons. In his marriage, Professor Rucker has been extremely fortunate, he having obtained for a life companion a lady of most exemplary character, pleasing address, fine sensibilities, and rare good judgment, and one, withal, of whom it may be truly said, she knows her every duty, and how best to fulfill it.

HOMER S. RHOTON, Georgetown, and Mrs. George, of Clay County, Mo., are the only living children of Benjamin W. Rhoton, who was born in Surrey County, North Carolina, in 1790, and who came to Kentucky in 1811. He studied medicine and graduated from Transylvania University; he was the leading physician of Woodford County, and for many years, the superintending physician in the Eastern Kentucky Lunatic Asylum, being succeeded by Dr. William Chipley. He was Fellow of the Royal Medical Society. As minister of the gospel, he presided over the Southern Methodist Episcopal Church. He resided in Danville, Lancaster, Versailles, Lexington, and Georgetown, coming to the last named place in 1850; here he died in February, 1863. He was twice married, his first wife being Miss Jeffries, and his second, Mrs. Margaret E. Peters, daughter of Frank P. Gaines, and widow of Aleck Peters, a portrait painter of Woodford County. On June 17, 1840, in Lexington, Ky., was born Homer S. Rhoton, the subject of this sketch. Ten years later, he came to Georgetown, and attended the Georgetown College, continuing until he reached the senior year. In 1860 he began as teacher in the city schools, and was Principal of the male department four years. In 1866 he was elected School Commissioner of Scott County, by a unanimous vote, serving ten years. In 1874 he was elected Police Judge of Georgetown, and re-elected in 1878. In 1879 he was elected Treasurer of Scott County, which office he still holds. He is a member of the Students' Association. In 1866 he began reading law with M. Polk and Lieutenant Gov. Jas. E. Cantwell, and was admitted to the Bar in March, 1868, at Frankfort, Ky.

THOMAS H. ROBERTS, farmer ; P. O. Payne's Depot ; was born in Scott County, Ky., Oct. 5, 1843 ; his father, Hillery Roberts, was born Dec. 5, 1798, and died April 25, 1874, and was a son of William Roberts, a native of Maryland, who came to Kentucky in 1790, and settled on the place now owned by T. H. Payne. The mother of our subject, was Lemira Waggoner, a native of Scott County, born Oct. 7, 1807, and died May 8, 1874 ; she was the mother of two boys, viz : Henry P., born July 10, 1837, died Oct. 20, 1857 ; and Thomas

H., the subject of this sketch, who was educated at the Bethel School House at Payne's Depot, and entered upon his career in life by taking upon himself the duties of a farm life, which occupation he still follows, and has by his energy and industry, accumulated about 260 acres of choice farm land, situated near Payne's Depot. Mr. Roberts is a thorough business man and a practical farmer, and keeps his land in a high state of cultivation, and stocked with high-grade cattle. He was married Oct. 13, 1864, to Virginia, daughter of William and Mary (Carr) Payne, natives of Scott County; she was born Dec. 31, 1842, and has borne to him six children, viz.: Henry P., born Oct. 26, 1865 ; William P., born Feb. 1, 1868 ; Mary C., born July 7, 1869 ; Lemira, born May 2, 1871 ; Hillery, born March 26, 1873 ; and Thomas, born Oct. 18, 1875. Religiously, Mr. and Mrs. Roberts are connected with the Baptist Church at Mount Vernon. Politically, Mr. Roberts is identified with the Democratic party.

B. F. RANDOL, Georgetown ; was born in Scott County, on Eagle Creek, in 1838, and was raised on a farm ; at eighteen years of age he went to Winchester, Kentucky, where he clerked two years in a hardware and grocery store. In 1857, he went to Chillicothe, Missouri, where he worked at the carpenter's trade ; he became City Marshall of Chillicothe. In June, 1861, he enlisted in General Price's army, Colonel Slack's regiment, Company G., in the State service ; he participated in the battle of Lexington, Mo. ; at the expiration of one year he was honorably discharged from Price's army ; he then came to Kentucky, and run a flouring mill for S. R. Thomson, in this county, near Georgetown, as partner of T. Holding, for four years ; he was next clerk for C. B. Lewis, agent of Adams Express Company, and afterward for Col. R. Snell ; he again run the flouring mill for two years with T. Holding ; from 1874 to 1876 he sold liquors. In 1876 he entered the furniture and undertaking business, and has since done a large business in that line ; in 1878 he was elected Coroner of Scott County, by the Democrats ; he has always been a Democrat. In 1868 he married Miss Alice Soward, of this county.

JUDGE MILTON STEVENSON, Attorney at Law; Georgetown; is the son of Reuben Stevenson, a native of Maryland, who was born in 1787, and died at Georgetown, Ky., in 1823; he was a saddler by trade; during the war of 1812 he served in Matson's Company of Col. Johnson's regiment. The subject of this sketch was born in Germantown, Bracken Co., Ky., Aug. 17, 1814, and when but three months old, came with his parents to Georgetown, Scott Co., Ky., where he has since resided; he was educated in the Rittenhouse Academy, which afterwards became the preparatory department of Georgetown College. At thirteen years of age he left school, and learned the saddling trade with his uncle, Job Stevenson, who carried on an extensive business, employing over twenty workmen. At his uncle's old stand he carried on business, working twelve hands. At this occupation he continued from 1834 to 1853, after which he engaged in the dry goods business for about five years; he was elected Police Judge of Georgetown in 1851, serving four years during which period he studied law, and in 1858, was admitted to the bar at Georgetown, where he has since continued to practice; before the war he was Assessor of the county, and afterward was Assistant Revenue Assessor; he was a Henry Clay Whig, and was a member of the Emancipation Party, which held a convention at Frankfort, in 1848, and he canvassed the county as candidate for the Legislature on that isuse in 1848 and 1849. When the war came on he was a Union man, and is now a consistent Republican; during the war he was School Commissioner of Scott County, and acted as County Attorney from 1861 to 1865; he earned for himself his possessions, and has ever been an energetic, earnest worker in whatever occupation he has engaged in. He married Miss Griffith, Scott County, in 1849, and his family embraces three sons and one daughter.

NOA SPEARS, banker; Georgetown, Ky.; was born in Bourbon County, Ky., on the 7th of March, 1829. He is the son of Solomon Spears, for many years a farmer in that county, a native of Kentucky, descendants of Virginians. His mother, Margaret Kerfoot, was a native of the Shenandoah Valley, Virginia, and the mother of six children, of whom he was the youngest. He received his early education in the Bourbon County schools, and finished his literary course at Bethany College, Virginia, where he graduated in 1848. He then embarked in mercantile pursuits at Paris, Ky., before he had attained his majority; after four years he retired from business, and engaged in farming, in Bourbon County, which he continued for several years, when, in 1853, he again established himself in business, opening a store in Georgetown, for the sale of dry goods, boots and shoes, etc., which he carried on successfully for some time. In 1860 he was appointed clerk in the Farmer's Bank, at Georgetown, and in 1868, he was elected cashier; which position he still fills. During the war he felt that it was his duty to support the Union, but, nevertheless, his sympathies were strongly Southern. Being unable to resist the natural current of events, however, he took no active part in the struggle, but was afterwards arrested, owing to an overstrained interpretation of a Federal order, and lodged in prison; but after a short time, was released upon the interference and solicitations of friends, who were both numerous and warm. Mr. Spears is a member of the Christian Church, and takes a strong and active interest in all religious matters, doing much by his efforts and sympathies toward the spread of the Gospel. He was married to Fannie C. Gano, of Bourbon County, in 1849, who died soon after, leaving him a childless widower; in 1851, he married his second wife, in the person of Georgia A. Crockett, of Georgetown, and became the father of two children; and in 1864, he was again united in marriage, this time to Mary C. Steffee, also of Georgetown, which union was blessed with two children. His four children are still living. Mr. Spears is a man of many fine traits of character, and is of a genial nature; has an integrity that is unquestioned; fond of innocent amusements; obliging and courteous in his manners and domestic in habits.

PROF. THOMAS SMITH, Georgetown; was born in King and Queen County, Va., in 1835; here he remained until he was thirty years of age; he was educated in the University of Virginia, from which he graduated in an elective course in 1859; in 1855 he began teaching. He enlisted in the army of Northern Virginia, in Stonewall Jackson's Corps, and was afterwards with Gen. A. P. Hill's Corps, engaging in over forty battles; he was wounded in the second battle of Manassas, and a second time before Petersburg, when the Weldon R. R. was taken by the Federals; the first time by shell in the ankle, and the second time a section of six inches of the ulna of the fore-arm was taken out; he served as Adjutant of a regiment in the twenty-second Virginia battalion of infantry; in later years he was Adjutant General of the well known Field's Brigade, which afterwards, was known as Walker's Brigade; he was home on a leave of absence, from the effects of his wounds, when Lee surrendered, and was paroled in the spring of 1865; Prof. Smith taught in Virginia a year after the war; he went to Texas in the fall of 1866, and taught six months in a private school when he was made Professor of Latin in Austin College, at Huntsville, Texas; he was there but a short time when he was taken with yellow fever, being confined seven months by the disease and its effects. In January, 1868, he returned to Virginia, and in November of the same year, came to Kentucky, taking charge of the Central Academy, in Fayette County, where he taught four years; at the end of that period establishing the Winchester High School, where he taught seven years, in the meantime building up a large school. In June, 1879, he was elected Professor of Latin in Georgetown College, a position he still retains to the satisfaction of all.

J. NEWTON STONE, grocer; Georgetown; was born in Bourbon County, Ky., in 1837; reared on the farm, he tilled the soil of his native county until 1875, and devoted his attention to stock raising. In March, 1875, he removed to Georgetown, Ky., and accepted for a time a clerkship in the store of W. N. Atkins, whom he succeeded in business; in 1876 he formed a partnership with his brother, K. Stone, and for three years conducted a large grocery business; he was next clerk in the Georgetown Hotel for a year, and subsequently dealt in mules which he drove South. January, 1881, Mr. Stone formed a partnership with L. McConnell, and again embarked in the grocery trade, where he is at present conducting a handsome business, at the corner of Main and Court streets, in groceries, tobaccos and liquors; he also formed a partnership with Mr. Pierce, a practical tobacconist, for the manufacture of plug and twist tobaccos, and established Tobacco Factory Number 6, in the 7th District of Kentucky; it is located on north side of Main Cross, Georgetown. Mr. Stone was twice married, first time to Miss Drusilla, daughter of John Smith, of Clark County, Ky., in November, 1860; she died in June, 1866; he married a second time, Dec. 20, 1870, to Miss Eliza, daughter of John Hill, of Bourbon County; she died Aug. 1, 1874, and left one living son, John Hill Stone. Of Mr. Stone's ancestry we know that Kinzea Stone, his grandfather, was born in Virginia, where he married a Miss Watts, and emigrated to Kentucky in 1808, settling in Bourbon County, where he resided until his death which occurred about 1848. He was a successful farmer, an old line Whig and raised ten children, two of whom are living. Among his sons, who were all farmers, was Kinzea Stone, the father of our subject, and born in Bourbon County, Ky., in 1813; he lived in Bourbon all his life, and was a successful and systematic farmer, and accumulated a handsome estate of 520 acres; he married Elizabeth A., daughter of Manson Seamands, of Bourbon County; she was the widow of the late Edwin Dodge, and has one son of her first marriage, and of the last marriage there are three sons and four daughters living. Both father and grandfather were members of the Particular Baptist Church, and the former, who died Dec. 24, 1879, was for many years an Elder in the church.

SAMUEL S. SHEPARD; jeweler; Georgetown; is a grandson of Samuel Shepard, who was born in New

Middlesex County, Mass., in 1765. He emigrated to Kentucky before she became a State, riding, it is said, through on horseback. He settled at Georgetown when there were only a half dozen houses in the place, building the first tavern ever erected in the place, which was headquarters and a rendezous for the pioneer hunters of territorial times. He married Miss Frankey Barlow, March 27, 1792, at Georgetown. She was born in 1765 and this is one of the earliest marriages of which we have any record. Samuel Shepard was a pioneer lawyer and surveyor. He was chairman of the Georgetown Board of Trustees, and represented Scott County in the State Legislature in 1804. He had four sons and one daughter. William Tompkins, born March, 1793; Alpheus Xavier Francis, born October, 1795; Thomas Jefferson, born Jan. 15, 1801; James Madison, born September, 1802; and one daughter born in 1807, but died when twelve years old. James M. Shepard never married and was elected to the State Senate from the Counties of Scott and Fayette. Thomas Jefferson Shepard, the father of our subject, was born in Georgetown. He was self-educated, having spent only three months in school, yet he became a good scribe and an extensive reader. At the age of 16 he entered as apprentice in a jewelry house of his older brother to learn the trade. They manufactured the early brass wall clocks, which sold at from $120 to $130, and it is said that the first clock he ever made is now int he possession of a Georgetown lady. He worked here until 1828, when he went to Louisville, Ky., and worked there for Beard & Ayres. He returned to Georgetown in 1831, and bought out the jewelry establishment of his brother, and conducted the business for forty years. He died in February, 1875. He was married the first time to Miss Amanda Smith, of this County, in November, 1830, and raised three children, of which there is but one son living, Clifton R. Shepard, a planter at Laconia, Arkansas. His second marriage was in 1852, to Mrs. Eliza Morford, whose maiden name was Woodruff. There were two sons born of this marriage, viz.: Thomas J. Shepard, jeweler, at Chattanooga, Tenn., and Samuel S., the subject of this sketch, born in Georgetown; started in the jewelry business in 1871, as the business partner of his brother and conducted business under the firm name of Shepard Bros. until 1880, when S. S. became the sole proprietor of a prosperous business.

ROBERT SOPER, merchant, Georgetown; was born in Bourbon County, Ky., in 1834. He was educated at Sharpsburg Academy and Georgetown College, which he left in 1854, and taught a country school until in 1855, and then entered upon a clerkship at Flat Rock, Bourbon County, which he continued two years. In 1857 he opened a general store at Centreville, Bourbon County, continuing nine years, after which he spent a year in Paris, Ky., and in 1867 he came to Georgetown, where he opened a dry goods store, buying the business of F. A. Lyon. In 1874, he moved to his present site, where he made many improvements, and conducted the business until the fall of 1876, when the building and part of the stock burned. In June, 1877, he completed his present three-story iron front building (108x32), which is fire proof. He occupies the entire building, with his residence, first floor sales room, and basement carpet room. He employs in all five gentlemen and one lady, and conducts a most flourishing business in dry goods, furnishing goods and carpets, having also a merchant tailoring department. His business reaches to $75,000 per year. His business rooms are not surpassed by any in the county, being replete with all modern conveniences, and as a business manager he has no superior. His father, Lawrence Soper, was born in Maryland, in 1800, and came with his parents to Bourbon County in about 1803, settling on Cane Ridge, where he followed farming until his death, which occurred in 1879. He left six sons, all but the subject of these lines being farmers.

KINZEA STONE; Georgetown; proprietor of the Maud S. Tobacco Factory; was born in Bourbon County, Ky., near Paris, in 1851, and was raised on a farm, being educated in the neighboring country schools. In 1875, he entered the grocery business in Lexington, and continued but one year, when he came to Georgetown and opened a grocery in his present business house, formerly occupied by R. P. Snell. Here he has conducted a large and lucrative business, dealing in groceries, liquors, seeds and wool. In June, 1880, he opened a tobacco factory, Maud S., in No. 37. District. He employs twelve hands, and sells his manufactured goods, consisting of six or eight good varieties, to the leading wholesale houses in Cincinnati, Louisville, Charleston, West Virginia, and Lexington. His salesroom is located at the corner of Main street and Main Cross, and four men are employed there. He is now serving his third term as Trustee of Georgetown. On Jan. 22, 1878, he married Miss Sallie B., daughter of F. A. Hoover, of Jessamine County, Ky.

JOHN T. SINCLAIR, coal dealer; Georgetown; was born in Scott County, Ky., in the village of Stamping Ground, Jan. 24, 1839. He was educated at Georgetown College; leaving at the age of seventeen; he began life as a farmer, afterwards becoming a merchant, conducting business in his native village, until the war broke out, when he enlisted in Morgan's command, Colonel D.

Howard Smith's regiment, Company B., 5th Kentucky Cavalry, of which he was elected second lieutenant. He commanded Company B. on raids in Kentucky, Tennessee, Ohio, and Indiana, being captured at Buffington, Ohio; he was held twenty-three months at Johnson's Island, Alleghany City Penitentiary, Point Look-out, and Fort Delaware, as a prisoner of war. At the close of the war he was paroled, when he returned to his farm in Scott County. He engaged in merchandising at his native home for a brief period, and served for two years as Constable of Stamping Ground. In January, 1871, he was elected Deputy Sheriff with S. T. Connellee, and served four years. In 1875 he was elected Sheriff of Scott County, and served four years; since which time he has been a representative of prominent Fire and Life Insurance Companies. In 1881, under the firm name of Thompson & Sinclair, he established a coal and lumber yard on Main Street. His parents were natives of this county. His father, Benjamin W. Sinclair, was a physician, and practiced at Stamping Ground, until his death, in January, 1846; he married Elizabeth M. Burbridge, daughter of Thomas Burbridge of this county. The great-grandparents of our subject were from Virginia, and settled in this county in very early times. His grandfather, George Burbridge, was a noted race-horse man.

GREENUP STUCKER, retired; P. O. Georgetown; was born and raised in Scott County, Ky. His father, Jacob Stucker, was a native of Pennsylvania, born Aug. 11, 1764, and died June 11, 1820. When about eighteen years old he came with his mother, two brothers and one sister, to this State, which was not then clear of Indians. They were so plentiful at that time, and so vicious, that oftentimes on his going to the spring for water they would shoot at him, sometimes shooting into the fence so near to him that the splinters struck him. He was in the fort which stood in sight of the residence of his son, our subject, on land now owned by Mr. John Osborn. He became a great Indian hunter, and was the associate of Vallandingham. He and his son James were in the war of 1812, in Colonel R. M. Johnson's regiment. He was Captain of a company and in all the campaigns. He married Miss Betsey Rogers, of this County, in about 1788; she bore him eleven children, all of whom are now deceased, except our subject. He accumulated an estate of three hundred acres, and was a successful farmer. Greenup Stucker was born Sept. 30, 1808, and was raised and educated in pioneer manner. At the age of fifteen years he learned blacksmithing with his brother William. He worked as journeyman a number of years, almost abolishing the pursuit of his trade since the war. He has never married.

PROF. D. THOMAS, Georgetown; Professor of languages in Georgetown College; was born Sept. 20, 1817, in Winthrop, Maine. The family is of English origin; his grandfather was a clergyman in Maine, and his father, William Thomas, was a mechanic in comfortable circumstances. He enjoyed excellent educational advantages, taking his preparatory course for college at Kents Hill Seminary, and at Waterville, Maine; in his seventeenth year he entered Colby University, at Waterville, graduating in 1838 with the degree of A. B. Among the teachers of that time were Prof. Patterson and Prof. Keeley (both since deceased) and Prof. Loomis, now of Lewisburg University, Pennsylvania; and one of his classmates was the notorious Gen. Benjamin Butler. In 1839 he was appointed tutor in Colby College, and a year after was called to the position he now occupies, that of Senior Professor of Ancient Languages and Literature at Georgetown College, Georgetown, Ky., his specialty being ancient languages, but he also teaches the German classes. In 1876 he received from Colby University the honorary degree of LL. D., having previously received from his Alma Mater the degree of A. M. He united with the Baptist Church at the age of fourteen; is an active and consistent member, and is an earnest, indefatigable worker in the Sabbath-schools and foreign-mission interests of his church; is liberal in his donations to the church; prompt and exact in business relations; is genial and hospitable, and entertains his friends elegantly. He has long been chairman of the Baptist Sabbath-school Board for Kentucky. Prof. Thomas is also a farmer, and devotes his leisure time with great success to his agricultural interests. He was married in 1840 to Mrs. Sarah Waller Smith (*née* Burch), sister to the wife of the late John C. Breckinridge. Of their four children two are now living.

DR. JOHN C. THOMASSON, Georgetown, was born in Pendleton County, Ky., April 15, 1857, and was educated in a private school at Butler, Ky. He began the study of medicine with Dr. W. H. Yelton, of Fairview, Ky., in 1879. He attended the Pulte Medical College at Cincinnati, Ohio, during two sessions, and graduated in March, 1881, at once locating in Georgetown, where he has an active practice, being the only practitioner of the homeopathic school at present in the county. His father, Julius V. Thomasson, is of Scotch descent, born March 24,1800, in the State of Kentucky. He follows the occupation of farming, in Pendleton County, Ky.

W. Z. THOMSON, Georgetown; was born in Fayette County, Ky., in 1848, and lived there until 1874; he was educated in Georgetown College, and at eighteen left school to engage in farming in Fayette County. In 1873 he joined the Grange, and was elected secretary of the Lodge. In 1874 he entered the employ of J. Eugene Barnes, of Georgetown, and became an active assistant in the State Secretary's office. The Kentucky Grangers' Mutual Benefit Society was organized in November, 1874, the plans for mutual protection having been prepared by James H. Moore, of Georgetown, and Mr. Thomson, then in Fayette County. They presented the matter to the Kentucky State Grange at Louisville, in 1874, and their plans received a hearty endorsement. The charter was obtained by special act, and an election of officers took place in December of 1874. Dr. B. Manly was elected president, W. B. Galloway, vice-president, W. Z. Thomson, secretary, and Dr. S. F. Gano, medical director, James H. Moore being general agent. The officers remain the same, except those of president and vice-president, Mr. W. B. Galloway being instead of Mr. Manly, who resigned in 1876, and Mr. Wm. H. Warren is general agent. The society has received recommendations at each annual meeting of the State Grange. The membership raised the first year was 280; in 1876 it was 1,100; in 1877, 1,800; in 1878, 2,300; in 1879, 2,500; in 1880, 2,150; in 1881, 2,350. The association has a reserve fund of about $25,000; has had 135 deaths and has paid about $275,000 in benefits. There are eleven directors, representing different parts of the State. Mr. Thomson was married in 1870 to Miss Nannie, daughter of E. P. Gaines, of Scott county.

LEO T. THOMAS, farmer and breeder of short-horn cattle; P.O. Georgetown; was born on the homestead, Oct. 7, 1842. He was educated in this county; he inherited a portion of the homestead, and bought the shares of the other heirs. In 1873 he began the rearing of short-horns, and has now a herd of nineteen. His stock farm comprises 200 acres, about one-third in cultivation, the remainder in grazing lands. Dec. 14, 1880, he married Miss Angie B. Sanders of Gallatin County, Ky. His father, Preston Thomas, was born in Bourbon County, Ky., on Oct. 7, 1807; he was of Virginia parentage; he was educated in Bourbon County, going to Paris (ten miles) to school on horse-back. He married a lady of the same name in 1832, and farmed four years in Bourbon County, when he settled on his present place; he bought 280 acres, and devoted himself to farming with success, and was aided by a goodly number of servants. He died April 4, 1875. He was a member of the Christian Church. He raised three children, all of whom are residents of this county, viz: John W., Annie, now Mrs. J. Harvey Moore, and our subject.

COL. PRESTON THOMSON, retired; Georgetown; was born in Scott County, Ky., in 1815; he is the grandson of Rodes Thomson, a Virginian, who came to Kentucky very early. His only son, the father of our subject, was born at Marysville, then Limestone, Kentucky, in the year 1788, and shortly after this event the family removed to this County and settled where Rodes Thomson had entered a large tract of land, on Cane Run; the old man had a keen sense of the ridiculous, and played many practical jokes on the early settlers and his servants. His son served in the war of 1812, in Capt. Jacob Stucker's Company and Col. R. M. Johnson's Regiment. He was captured at the battle of the River Raisin and taken as a prisoner of war to Canada. About 1812, he married Miss Sallie, daughter of Gen. John and Betsey (Johnson) Payne. Her mother was a sister of Col. R. M. Johnson, and as a brave girl, molded bullets for the soldiers in fort at Bryant's Station. After his marriage to Miss Payne, settled near Georgetown where he lived and run the Thomson mill, which was built and moved there by a man named Pitts. He died in 1852, leaving two sons and one daughter, as follows: Sidney R., who was born in 1813, and died in 1879, and was a successful farmer and miller; Mrs. E. P. Worthington, of Mississippi, and our subject, Col. Preston Thomson, who entered Georgetown College at its opening, and graduated in 1833, in the second class sent out. He was appointed County Clerk by Judge A. K. Wooley, in 1839, and served with distinction in that office until 1856, and was once elected by popular vote. He enlisted in 1862, in Gen. Buford's Brigade where he held the rank of Lieutenant Colonel.

G. B. TUCKER, farmer; P. O. Georgetown; was born in Bourbon County, Ky., in 1809, to Alexander and Ellen (Berry) Tucker; he was a native of Dinwiddie County, Va.; emigrated to Bourbon County about the year 1780; during his life followed farming, and died in 1812, aged sixty years; she was also a native of Dinwiddie County, Va., and died in 1851, aged sixty-five years; G. B. Tucker was their only child; he came to Scott County in 1817, where he received such an education as the common schools of that day afforded. In 1829, he began business for himself by merchandizing, following the same until 1842, when he retired from business, and has since given his attention principally to farming; he has a well improved farm of 500 acres, situated on the Lemon's Mill Pike; upon his farm he has some fine short-horns; in Scott County, in 1854, he married Miss Mattie Morris, a native of Scott County; she died in 1856, aged twenty-four years. Mr. Tucker is a prominent citizen of Georgetown Precinct, bearing a name and reputation which is beyond reproach. His only child, Fanny, is now at home. He is a Democrat.

ELIJAH THORNBERRY, Georgetown; was born in Mason County Ky., April 7, 1805; when a boy he came with his parents to Scott County, where he received a good common school education, and learned the blacksmith trade with William Stucker, at Great Crossings. April 7, 1825, he married Miss Eliza Jones, daughter of William Jones, one of the early settlers of the county. After his marriage he rented and located on a farm near "Dry Run" Baptist Church; here he built a shop and plied his trade until after the war. In about 1866, he moved to Georgetown, where he retired from active labor until his death, in May of 1877. He had six children, four of whom are living. In politics he was a Whig. He and his wife were members of the Missionary Baptist Church, as were their children, excepting one son.

GEORGE W. VILEY, farmer; P. O. Georgetown; is a grandson of George Viley, a native of the eastern shore of Maryland, who came, accompanied by his servants, to Kentucky, during the latter part of the eighteenth century, and purchased a tract of wild land, where he lived until his death in 1814, his wife dying in middle life, in 1832; she was a Miss Martha James, also a native of Maryland, and became his wife in 1785. She bore him ten children, two of their sons being in the war of 1812, viz., Warren and Willa. They were in Col. R. M. Johnson's regiment; Warren died from exposure incurred during the war, soon after his return. Their son, Samuel Viley, the father of our subject, was born in Maryland in 1790, and was a small boy when his parents brought him to Kentucky. He received a common school education, and was a farmer near the old homestead during his life. He was a successful farmer and stock raiser; he was particularly fond of fine horses, and in his later life owned a few thoroughbreds, but was never a turfman. He married Miss Mary Suggett, daughter of John Suggett, of this county; she bore him two sons and daughters, one daughter dying in infancy. He died in 1859. The oldest child is our subject, who was born in this county in 1818, and now resides on the place where his grandfather settled. His education was obtained in the schools of this county, and in Georgetown College; at the age of twenty-one, he began to read law in the office of J. H. Davis of Georgetown; he next attended the Transylvania Law School, from which he graduated in the session of 1844–5, and was then admitted to the bar at Georgetown, but soon relinquished practice on account of failing health. Since 1848, he has devoted himself to farming. In 1877 he married Miss Williena Green, of Owen County, Ky.

JOHN M. VILEY, physician and farmer; Georgetown; was born on the place where he now lives, and which was the homestead of his father, in the year 1823. He attended the schools of this vicinity and Georgetown College, at the age of sixteen, taking charge of the old homestead. At the age of twenty-three he married, and the farm then became his own. He began in 1838 the study of medicine, and without direction, pursued it for two years, and in 1840 began practicing, continuing until 1858 with excellent success, when he gave it up for twenty years, resuming again some three years since. In 1846, he married Miss Susan A. Long, whose mother, aged ninety, still lives; her birth-place was Sumpter District, South Carolina, and she came to this State in 1819; she was a Miss Bradford, and married James Long in 1819, he being a Kentuckian; they settled in Scott County, Ky.; he died in 1859. Dr. Viley's farm was called "Cedar Grove" by his father, because of the avenues of cedars in front of the residence. The Dr. has eight children living. A stream passing through the Viley estate is called McClellan's Run, in honor to the man who made one of the pre-emption rights in Scott County, and held about 6,000 acres here in a solid body. In 1869, Dr. Viley built his present distillery, known as Wilson's Springs Distillery; this has been in operation ever since, barring a few brief periods. It is located on McClellan's Run, and has a capacity of three barrels per day, employing from three to five hands.

JUDGE JUNE WARD WILLIAMS; farmer; Glasgow, Howard Co., Mo. The grandfather of our subject, Charles Williams, came from Culpepper county, Va., and was among the first settlers of Kentucky. He located near the Great Crossings; he raised a large family of children, four daughters and five sons, who were among the most wealthy and prominent citizens of the county; one daughter is living, the grandmother of G. V. Payne; one son, Merritt Williams, the father of our subject, was born in Scott County, Ky., in about the year 1789. He was a farmer and trader, owning about 600 acres in this county; he was an earnest Democrat, but never would accept an office. He married a Miss Eliza Smith, who was a granddaughter of the Gold Mine "Billy Smith." He died in 1855; he raised four boys and two girls: Ann E., deceased, was the wife of Charles G. McHatton; Arch P. is a resident of Frankfort; Barnett died in Louisiana; Sarah was the wife of Dr. Henry Craig, of Georgetown and died in December, 1881; Granville is deceased. June Ward was born in Scott County, near Georgetown, in December, 1833; he was educated in the Western Military Institute, then under Thornton Johnston, and was a pupil of James G. Blaine; he went to Missouri in 1854, and settled in Howard County, where he engaged in farming: here he married Miss Martha Rucker, who was born in Orange County, Va., in 1834; she was a niece of Sterling Price. They have nine living children, four sons and five daughters. Judge Williams is a Justice of the Peace of Howard County, Mo.

CAPT. J. HENRY WOLFE, county clerk; Georgetown; was born in the free city of Bremen, Germany, and was there educated in the common schools, after which he spent two years in a military institute, where he learned surveying and civil engineering. At the age of sixteen years he came to the United States, and spent about eight months in Florida, where he was sent for the purpose of making a survey from St. Augustine to Fernandino. In May, 1840, he came to Kentucky, locating at Georgetown, where he has since remained. Here he engaged in the grocery business until the war broke out, when he enlisted in General John H. Morgan's command, in July, 1862; in September of the same year he returned and raised a company, which went out with General Kirby Smith; of this company he was elected captain. His command became Company D., and was assigned to the 3rd Kentucky Cavalry, under Colonel Gano. He served in the Ohio and Indiana raids, and was captured at Middleport, Ohio, four days after the main army was taken; he was held seven months, when he was exchanged, at which time he had recovered from a wound received at Buffington, Ohio. About one week after his exchange he reported to his old command, under General Duke, after which he was sent to North Carolina to capture deserters. At that time he had charge of the cavalry horses for the winter. The surrender came in April, after which he returned to Georgetown, and was there elected Clerk of Scott County, in 1866; that position he has held ever since, having been four times re-elected, with almost no opposition. His son assists him, and the manner in which they execute their work deserves special commendation. Both father and son excel in penmanship, and all writings included in their work, are remarkable for the beauty and system that are embodied in them.

WHITE SULPHUR PRECINCT.

J. E. BUTLER, merchant; P. O. White Sulphur; is a native of this county and was born in 1852; he is a son of Daniel and Mary M. (Mefford) Butler, both natives of Scott County; his father was born about the year 1807; was a wagon-maker by trade, and died about 1875; his mother was born about 1829. Subject was educated in the common schools of White Sulphur Precinct, and after leaving school in 1871, commenced teaching, which vocation he followed until 1874, when he engaged in merchandising, a business he still follows; he was married April 21st, 1880, in White Sulphur, to Miss Lizzie Glass, a daughter of J. C. and Ann E. Glass; he was born in Owen County in 1817, and she in Scott County about 1832; he (subject) is County Surveyor, since 1879, and is at present a candidate for re-election; he is a Democrat politically; he is a prosperous merchant of White Sulpher, and the only one in the place; keeps a large stock of goods, and is an enterprising business man.

WM. H. BRANHAM, farmer; P. O. Midway; was born in this County, Dec. 6, 1829, and is a son of John and Susan (Quinn) Branham, both natives of Scott County; he was born in 1797 and died in 1868; she was born in 1804. The subject is the fifth of a family of seven children, and was educated in the schools of the neighborhood; he began life as a farmer, and his place is one of the oldest settled in the County; he purchased it in 1858; it is situated on the Midway and Scott County Pike, six miles from Georgetown. He was married in Shelby County to Miss Anna Myles, a native of that county; he is a member of the Baptist Church, and belongs to the Odd Fellows.

A. J. GANO, physician and farmer; P. O. Georgetown; is a son of Capt. Daniel Gano, one of the pioneer settlers of Scott County, and who is frequently and appropriately mentioned elsewhere in this volume. Dr. Gano, the subject, was born in this County, Feb. 26, 1828, and received his education in the schools and colleges of Georgetown. His mother's maiden name was Jemima Robinson; she was born in Maryland, and came to Kentucky with her family in early youth. The result of her marriage with Capt. Gano was eleven children, of whom the subject is the youngest, and of whom there are but four now living. Upon starting out in life, Dr. Gano spent seven years in the drug business, in the meantime studying medicine, and in 1852, he attended the Louisville Medical College, from which he graduated in 1854, locating afterward in the lower part of Scott County; he remained there about one year, then removed to White Sulphur, where he practiced his profession until 1874, when he removed to Midway, in Woodford County, remaining there until 1878, when he located upon his present place, on the Georgetown and Frankfort Pike, five miles from Georgetown. He has a beautiful location and an excellent farm, and is now making extensive improvements, with the view of engaging in sheep raising on a large scale. He is a member of the Christian Church, and of the Masonic Fraternity since 1849, and is a Democrat. Dr. Gano was married in May, 1854, to Miss Ophelia Lee, a daughter of Robert and Martha (Powell) Lee. He was a native of Virginia, where he was born in 1794, came to Kentucky in an early day, and died in 1879; his wife was born in Woodford County, in 1804. They had five children, two boys and three girls.

D. B. GALLOWAY, farmer; P. O. Georgetown; is a native of Scott County, and was educated at Georgetown. When he was about eighteen months old his father moved to Missouri, and his grandfather stole him from his father, and brought him up in his own family. He (the subject) has always lived on a farm, and owns a good farm on the Branham Mill Pike, about three-fourths of a mile from the Georgetown and Frankfort Pike. It once belonged to Hon. R. M. Johnson; afterwards to David Thompson, and was purchased by Mr. Galloway in 1842. He is a member of the Baptist Church, and of the Masonic brotherhood; he is a Democrat, a Granger, and a strong temperance man; he was elected Magistrate in 1845, an office he still holds. So far he has disregarded the Biblical injunction, that it "is not well for man to be alone," for he is still unmarried.

JOHN Y. KINKEAD, farmer; P. O. Midway; a native of Woodford County, Ky.; and a son of James and Betsey (White) Kinkead, was born March 1, 1818. His parents were natives of Fredericksburg, Va., and came to Kentucky in early times; the father was born in 1792, and died in 1833; the mother was born in 1802, and died in 1840. The subject was educated in the common schools of Woodford County, and commenced business as a shoemaker in 1840, but afterwards went into the drug business at Stamping Ground, in which he continued until 1850, when he was married to a young lady of Shelby County, Ky., who lived only four months and in 1854, he was again married, to Miss Mary Nelson, and removed to Missouri, where she died in 1862; she was a daughter of Joseph Nelson, a native of Scott County, Ky.; and who was born about the year 1800. In 1861, Mr Kinkead enlisted under Gen. Price, and served as Quartermaster until the close of the war in 1865, when he returned to Kentucky, and was married a third time, to Mrs. Lousia St Clair. They have only one child, Bettie, who is attending school at Midway, Woodford County. Mr. Kinkead is a member of the Christian Church, and a Democrat in politics. He is now engaged in farming and rearing of fine stock, making specialties of sheep and trotting horses. He owns 225 acres of excellent land and finely improved. It is located on the Georgetown and Midway Pike, about two miles from Midway. It was formerly owned by George Tarleton, who had a fine race-track on it, upon which Gray Eagle and Wagner were trained, the training stables of these noted horses are all gone to decay.

A. M. LYON, farmer; P. O. Midway; is a native of Scott County, and a son of Nathaniel and Abigail (Merriman) Lyon, both natives of Connecticut, and early settlers in this County; both died in Georgetown; the former in 1823, and the latter in 1858; they had four children, two of whom are dead. The subject had few opportunities for receiving an education, as the death of his father necessitated his doing something for himself at an early age; at fourteen he was apprenticed to the saddler's trade, and after serving his time, worked for his late master for $12 per month and boarded himself; in 1832 he went to Indiana, where he remained a few months, then returned to Kentucky, and in 1833 to Georgetown; he went into the saddlery business for himself in 1835, continuing until 1856, when he engaged in merchandising, remaining in that business until 1861; he then bought a farm near Georgetown, on Georgetown and Midway Pike, upon which he has ever since resided; he was married to Miss Mary Fenwick in February, 1843; she died in 1848, and he then married Miss Frances Branham, Oct. 15, 1850, who died in 1857; they had seven children, three of whom are living. He is a member of the Baptist Church, and a Democrat in politics; he has recently divided his farm between his two sons, Henry and John, two worthy, industrious and honorable young men.

B. J. LAUGHLIN, farmer; P. O. White Sulphur; was born in Ireland and came to this country in 1838, and settled in Scott County on his present place in 1869, which is situated about half a mile from the Georgetown and Frankfort Pike, and in sight of White Sulphur Village; it is a beautiful place, consisting of 247 acres, well improved and in a fine state of cultivation; has a handsome brick residence on it, and all out-buildings of like excellent character. Mr. L. is an enterprising, industrious man, and a successful farmer and stock-raiser. He married Miss Mary Lee, a daughter of Robert Lee, who was born in Virginia in 1790, and removed to Scott County in 1805; of this union eight children have been born, and are being educated at Visitation Monastery.

VIRGIL McMANUS, farmer; P. O. White Sulphur; was born in Scott County, June 10, 1833, and is a son of John and Susan (Powell) McManus; the former born in Ireland, Aug. 16, 1789, and died Dec. 5, 1878, and was a farmer and distiller; the latter was born in Franklin County, Ky., Feb. 14, 1806, and died Jan. 7, 1855. They had six children, of whom the subject was the fifth, and all of whom received their education in this County. Subject began life as a farmer, a pursuit he still follows; he was married Feb. 5, 1861, to Miss Josephine Dougherty, a native of Scott County, and born June 14, 1845. The result of this marriage is seven children, all except one living. Mrs. McManus is a daughter of John and Elizabeth (Vance) Dougherty; the former a native of Bourbon County, and died July 11, 1879; the latter a native of Fayette County, and died Nov. 10, 1854. Subject owns 120 acres of very fine land, which is referred to in the history of this precinct as one of the pioneer settlements. He is a Democrat in politics, and an energetic, upright, and enterprising citizen; he and his wife have five grand and great grandfathers and mothers buried in the cemetery of St. Pius, in this precinct.

GARRETT POWELL, farmer and breeder of fine horses; P. O. White Sulphur; is a son of Hon. Urias Powell, a native of Culpepper County, Va., and a soldier of the war of 1812, and afterward a citizen of Scott County. He was a carpenter, but finally bought a farm upon which he lived. He was twice married, first to Miss Minnie Powell, a native of Virginia, and after her death married a lady of Scott County. Subject was born of the last marriage, in 1829; his early life was spent on a farm, and Dec. 22, 1865, he was married to Miss Kenney, a daughter of Richard Kenney, of Owen County; her mother was a native of Scott County. The place now owned by Mr. Powell was originally settled by a man named Wood, about the year 1800, and was at one time owned by Hon. Dick Johnson;

it was bought by Mr. Powell in 1863, and by additions made to it since he purchased it, now comprises 320 acres; it is well improved, and lies on both sides of the Georgetown and Frankfort Pike. Mr. Powell pays considerable attention to fine horses, and has bred some very noted ones, among which is "Monroe Chief," whose time has been 2:18¾; he was sold by Mr. Powell at two years old for $1,500, and has since sold for $17,000; and "D. Monroe" sold for $23,000 in 1874. He sold the dam for $400 at nineteen years of age. He now has two very fine fillies, two and three years old. He started into the business as manager, but by economy and industry, soon accumulated enough to buy a horse, and has kept on adding to and improving his stock, until he has attained a good reputation as a horse breeder.

REV. B. T. QUINN, farmer; P. O. Georgetown; is a son of Richard and Cynthia (Nall) Quinn, and was born in Scott County, Sept. 15, 1825; his father was born in Spottsylvania County, Va., Aug. 8, 1787, and was a school teacher of the early times, but became a farmer afterward, and died Mar. 17, 1870. His wife was born in Franklin County, Ky., March 10, 1804, and died in 1837. The subject was educated in the schools of the time, and in Georgetown College, which he entered in 1842, and remained until 1844; he then began teaching, and also preaching; he had charge of several churches—one at Big Spring, Woodford Co. Mr. Quinn has been married three times; his first wife, Miss Sallie A. French, was born in Franklin County, Ky., and was a daughter of William French, a native of Virginia; after her death he married Miss Cerella Stapp, of Madison County, Ind., and she dying, he married Miss Wingate, a daughter of Isaac Wingate, of Franklin County, Ky., who was a native of Delaware, and was born April 7, 1791; his wife, Jane Snead, was born in Virginia, near Richmond, April 15, 1798, and died Dec. 13, 1875. Mr. Quinn is a member of the Baptist Church; he is a Democrat and a Granger; he has two children; he has not preached for several years on account of asthma, but is engaged in farming; owns 200 acres of good land on Iron Works Road, about five miles from Georgetown.

ALEXANDER THOMAS, farmer; P. O. White Sulphur; is the fifth of a family of seven children, and was born in Bourbon County, April 10, 1812; his parents were natives of Virginia, and came to Kentucky among the pioneers; he was educated in Bourbon County, and began life as a farmer, an avocation he has always followed, with the exception of a period during the late war; he removed to Scott County in 1839, and settled on the Georgetown and Frankfort Pike. He was married to Miss Eliza D. Lewis in 1838, a daughter of Hiram Lewis, of Harrison County, Ky. In 1862 he enlisted in the Fifth Regiment of Cavalry, under General Morgan, and was Quartermaster and Commissary; he was with Morgan on his ill-fated raid through Indiana and Ohio, and was taken prisoner at Buffington; he was at Johnson's Island for a few days; he was then removed to Columbus, O., where he remained for eight months, when he was transferred to Fort Delaware, and after twelve months was exchanged. Mr. Thomas' place was settled by a man named Cason; was purchased afterwards by Col. Dick Johnson, and remained in the Johnson family until Mr. Thomas bought it. Mr. T. is a Mason, a Democrat, and a prominent farmer and stock-raiser.

JOHN F. WAITS, farmer; P. O. Midway; was born in Harrison County, Ky., May 18, 1839, and is a son of Edward and Elizabeth (Parker) Waits; the former was also born in Harrison County, where he lived until 1860, when he moved to Woodford County, and is still a resident of that County, and follows farming. His father came from Virginia in an early day. Mrs. Waits (the mother of subject) was born in Bourbon County about the year 1820, and died in 1871. Our subject was educated in the common schools of Harrison County, and is the third in a family of nine children. He commenced business for himself as a farmer and stock raiser in Illinois in 1862, which business he followed for about one year, when he returned to his father's in Woodford County, remaining there one year, then went to merchandizing, which business he continued until 1871, when he removed to Scott County, and has been engaged in farming ever since. He was married Sept. 19, 1865, to Miss Sallie McConnell, in Midway, Woodford County. Her father was born in Woodford County, Nov. 10, 1801; her mother, Charlotte (Calvert) McConnell, was born in Fayette County, Dec. 15, 1812. They have three children; viz: Jesse C., Charlotte E., and Mattie R. Mr. Waits is a Democrat politically, and both he and his wife are members of the Christian Church. He and his father and brother own a good farm near the Georgetown and Frankfort Pike.

STAMPING GROUND PRECINCT.

THOS. ATKINS, farmer ; P. O. Skinnersburg ; Thos. B., the father of our subject was born in Culpepper County, Va., in 1879, emigrated to Bath County, Ky., in about 1814; in 1837 removed to Nicholas County, and in 1838 removed to Scott County, where he died in 1859. His wife, the mother of our subject, was previous to her marriage Miss Nancy Shackleford; she was born in Culpepper County, Va., in 1806, and died in Lexington, Ky., Jan. 12, 1866. They were the parents of thirteen children, of whom was Thomas, our subject ; he was born in Bath County, Ky., Feb. 3, 1820; his education was limited on account of his having weak eyes ; was unable to obtain even such an education as the common schools of his day afforded. He commenced life a poor man, thrown upon his own resources at the age of fifteen years ; at the age of seventeen he removed to Scott County, where he has since remained engaged in tilling the soil. In 1844 in Scott County, he married Miss Maria Lucas, a native of Scott County, and the daughter of Elijah and Margaret (Moore) Lucas; she was born Jan. 19, 1820. By this marriage they have had seven children, six of whom are now living, viz.: Lois, William, Elijah L., Napoleon, Catharine B., and Robert H. He is a Democrat, and with his wife are members of the Baptist Church. Mr. Atkins is a kind hearted and industrious man; he and his faithful wife have won the esteem of all the citizens of the community of which he is a part.

JOHN L. COTRELL, farmer ; P. O. Minorsville. Thomas, the father of this gentleman, was born in Virginia, where he received his education; in 1801 he emigrated to Greene County, Ohio, and soon afterwards removed to Miami County, where he remained engaged in the milling business to the time of his death, which occurred in 1840, being sixty years of age. His wife, the mother of our subject, was born in Culpepper County, Va., and removed to Greene County, Ohio, about 1800, where she was married; she died in Miami County in 1835, aged 35 years. They were the parents of five children, our subject being the second child. He was born in Greene County, Ohio, April 3, 1815, where he remained, receiving such an education as the common schools of that county afforded. In 1835 he removed to Marion County, Ind., and in 1840 removed to Scott County, Ky., his present residence. He has during his life been a hard-working and industrious farmer, and by his honesty, industry and economy has succeeded in accumulating a good property; he is the owner of 350 acres of land. He is now one of Scott County's magistrates, having held the office for eight years, to the entire satisfaction of all. In 1839, in Scott County, he married Mrs. Sarah E. Nelson, a native of Fayette County, and the daughter of John and Lucy (Sinclair) Reding; she was born in 1822. They have been blessed with fifteen children, thirteen of whom are now living, viz. : Zerilda, James, Maria, Thomas, Benjamin F., Alvin, Alice, John S., Joseph, Stephen D., Willis, Millie A. and Sally. Mr. Cotrell and family are members of the Christian Church.

JOHN CALVERT; farmer; P. O. Stamping Ground; the father of this gentleman, John Calvert, was of English descent; born in Prince William County, Va., March 25, 1774; emigrated to Scott County, Ky., about the year 1790, and died Oct. 10, 1853. His wife was Miss Sarah Johnson; born in Fayette County, Ky., Nov. 6, 1775; she was one of the first two children born in Fayette county, west of the mountains. They were the parents of nine children, six sons and three daughters, of whom was John, our subject, who was born in Scott County, April 10, 1809. He received his education from the common schools of his native county. In 1831 he engaged in the hotel business in Owen County, where he remained until 1834, when he returned to his parental home; remained there about six months, when he removed to Indiana and engaged in the merchandising business, with his brother. In 1841, in Indiana, he married Miss Eliza Jane Sharp, who was a native of Ohio; she died April 6, 1844, aged 23 years. After his wife's death, Mr. Calvert returned home, and remained with his parents until 1859, when he removed to his present residence. He married, a second time, Miss Elvessa Cannon, who was born in Georgetown, Scott County, Ky; Feb. 2, 1831; she is the daughter of Wm. B. and Betsey (Cannon) Cannon. By his second marriage he has had seven children: John W., Edward B., Obed, Martha, Jesse Lee, Elizabeth C., and James Monroe. Mr. Calvert is the owner of 250 acres of land. Himself and family are members of the Baptist Church. He is a member of the A., F. & A. M., Scott Lodge 203, at Stamping Ground, and in politics is a Democrat.

WILLIAM O. CALVERT, farmer ; P. O. Stamping Ground. Obediah, the father of this gentleman, was

born in Scott County, March 6, 1799; during his life he followed the occupation of farming, and died in 1875. The mother of our subject, Elizabeth (Lindsey) Calvert, was the daughter of Anthony Lindsey, the first settler of Lindsey Station and the third settler of the Stamping Ground Precinct. She was born in Scott County in 1806 and died in 1878. They were the parents of thirteen children, of whom was William O., our subject. He was born in Scott County, March 28, 1845. His early days were spent in receiving an education from the common schools of his native county, and assisting in tilling the soil of his father's farm. In Scott County on December 14, 1866, he married Miss Anna Robinson, a native of Scott County, born July 26, 1846, and the daughter of Sanford and Elizabeth Johnson. Mr. Calvert is the owner of 110 acres of land. Himself and wife are members of the Baptist Church. They have been blessed with seven children, six of whom are now living, viz: Ben. S., Quincy A., Amelia F., Oniska, Lindsey, and an infant unnamed.

COL. W. P. DUVALL, retired; P. O. Stamping Ground. Col. John Duvall, the father of this gentleman, was born in Culpepper County, Va., March 14, 1783; in 1791 emigrated to Fayette County, and in 1792 removed to Scott County, being among the first settlers of Stamping Ground precinct. He died Sept. 8, 1859. Jane (Branham) Duvall, his wife, was born in Scott County, Nov. 6, 1785, and died Dec. 12, 1854. Of the ten children born to them, W. P. Duvall, our subject, was the fifth child and fourth son. He was born in Scott County, Jan. 6, 1815; his early life was spent in receiving an education and assisting in tilling the soil of his father's farm, remaining with his father to the time of his death. In 1848 he was elected to the Legislature for one term; in 1865, was re-elected; in 1867 was elected door-keeper of the Senate, and in 1871, was elected to the Senate to represent the counties Scott, Harrison and Robinson. October 4, 1855, in Scott County, he married Miss Caroline Robinson, who was born June 21, 1827. They are the parents of two children, one of whom is now living—George E. He was born Aug. 31, 1856, and in September, 1877, was married to Miss Lillie Wright. He is at the present time carrying on a mercantile business at the "Stamp." Col. John Duvall, the father of our subject, was a captain in the war of 1812, under Col. Boswell.

DUDLEY H. DAVIS, farmer; P. O. Skinnersburg. His father, Elijah Davis, was born in Fairfax County, Va., January, 1777; emigrated to Clark County in 1821, and removed to Scott County in 1823, where he died Oct. 9, 1854. He was a farmer, and a soldier in the war of 1812. His wife, Margaret (Riley) Davis, the mother of our subject, was born in Fairfax County, Va., in 1775; came to Scott County with her husband, and died in 1850. They were the parents of nine children. Dudley H. Davis was born in Clark County Ky., June 24, 1821, and in 1844, in Harrison County, he married Miss Mary E. Brockman; she was born in Harrison County, May 24, 1827. They are the parents of six children, three of whom are now living, viz: Mandeville, Wm. T. and Josephine. Mr. Davis commenced life a poor man, and the first piece of land he owned was only 39 acres. By his perseverance and hard work he has accumulated 900 acres of land. He and wife are members of the Christian Church. He is a Democrat.

SAMUEL ESTES, farmer; P. O. Stamping Ground; is a native of Scott County, and the son of William and Mary (Hockensmith) Estes. William was born in Virginia, emigrated to Scott County, where he followed the occupation of farming, and died in 1855. Mary, the mother of our subject, was born in Scott County, and died in October, 1865. They were the parents of thirteen children, twelve of whom are still living, of whom is our subject, who was born Sept. 30, 1830. He received his education from the common schools of his native county, and on June 21, 1855, in Franklin County, he married Miss Letitia Owens, who was born in Franklin County, April 5, 1836. She is the daughter of William and Elizabeth (Trout) Owens, who are natives of Kentucky. Mr. Estes has during his life followed the occupation of farming, and is now the owner of 135 acres of land. By his marriage he has had eleven children, eight of whom are now living, viz: John W., Thomas H., Laura, William D., Catharine, Betsey, Kate and Addie. Himself and family are members of the Baptist Church. He is a member of the A., F. and A. M., Scott Lodge No. 203, at Stamping Ground. He is a Democrat.

JNO. R. FERGUSON, retired farmer; P. O. Stamping Ground; is a native of Scott County, and the son of James and Lydia (Thompson) Ferguson; he was born April 1, 1798; his father was born in Virginia, in 1770, emigrated to Scott County in about 1782; was married in 1796 and died in June, 1822. The mother of our subject was born in Virginia, March 10, 1773; she came to Kentucky in about the year 1790, and died Oct. 13, 1849. There were born to them five children, our subject being the oldest child. He received his education from the neighborhood school; arriving at manhood he began trading in the South, following the same for four years; since has given his entire attention to farming; in 1825, on Nov. 5th, in Franklin County, he married Miss Maria

Macklin, who was a native of Franklin County, born April 21, 1801, and died Oct. 5, 1841; she was the daughter of Hugh Macklin, a native of Ireland. There were born to Mr. and Mrs. Ferguson nine children, only two of whom are now living, viz.: Alexander and Martha E. Mr. Ferguson is a member of the Baptist Church. A remarkable feature in Mr. Ferguson, is being eighty-four years old and never used a pair of spectacles; he has been a hard-working man, and by his studied economy and business habits succeeded in gaining a good property; he is now the owner of about 300 acres of well improved land. There is no flaw in Mr. Ferguson's character; it is sterling throughout and sound to the very core; his business integrity and purity of his private life have always been above suspicion.

JOHN A. FLUKE, farmer; P. O. Long Lick; Jacob Fluke, the father of this gentleman, was born in Maryland, Oct. 13, 1800, and was brought to Montgomery County, Ohio, by his parents in 1805. He received his education in Montgomery County from the common schools. In 1827 he removed to Scott County, Ky., where he has since remained, engaged in tilling the soil. His wife, the mother of our subject, was a widow, Mrs. Nancy Owens; she was born in Scott County, March 23, 1793, and died Oct. 17, 1878. They were the parents of five children, of whom was John A., our subject. He was born in Georgetown, Scott County, Jan. 25, 1828. He received his education from the common schools of his native county, and arriving at manhood began in agricultural pursuits, which he has since continued to follow. In Franklin County, on May 4, 1854, he married Miss Harriet Harvey, who was born in Franklin County, July 23, 1832, and died in Scott County, Feb. 3, 1864. In July, 1876, he married a second time Mrs. Sally F. Roberts, a sister to his first wife. By his first marriage he had four children, two of whom are living: Arthur B. and Harriet; and by his second marriage one child, Nancy Russell. He is the owner of 330 acres of land. He is a member of the Christian Church. Mr. Fluke, as a farmer, is practical and prosperous; as a citizen he is enterprising and progressive, and, together with his estimable wife, are intelligent and esteemed citizens. He is a Republican.

JOHN H. FORD, retired farmer; P. O. Minorsville; was born in Mason County, Ky., Jan. 28, 1795. He has during his life followed the trade of bricklayer and also that of farming. His wife, Elizabeth McCoy, was a native of Georgetown, Ky.; she was born in 1801, and died in 1880. Mr. Ford is now living with his son, and enjoying good health for a man of his age. He was in the war of 1812, under Col. Richard Johnson. His son, Rev. Hiram Ford, was born in Scott County, Dec. 25, 1830; and in Casey County, Ky., Dec. 15, 1856, he married Miss Elizabeth Conner, a native of Franklin County; born in 1842; they are the parents of two children: John F. and James M. He organized the "Pleasant Hill" (Christian Church) at Minorsville, in 1854, with only fifteen members, and at the present time there are 300 members at the same church; he also organized a church in Owen County. Mr. Ford has been the pastor of six churches for four years, including the two he organized. He is a member of the A., F. & A. M., Scott Lodge, No. 203, at Stamping Ground. He and his father are worthy citizens of their precinct, and most respected by those who best know them.

CHURCHILL B. GLASS, farmer; P. O. Georgetown; His father, James S. Glass, was born in Scott County, Sept. 12, 1812; during his life followed the occupation of farming, and died Jan. 26, 1865; his father, William Glass, and grandfather of our subject, was born in Virginia, in 1776, and emigrated to Scott County in 1796; he was a soldier in the Revolutionary War. Sally A. Sinclair, the mother of our subject, was born in Scott County, April 6, 1815, and now resides with her son, our subject; her father was Armstead Sinclair, born in Scott County, Feb. 25, 1785, and died Jan. 3, 1824; his father was Robert Sinclair, a native of Virginia. Churchill B., our subject, was the oldest of six boys; he was born in Scott County, Nov. 17, 1838; attended the common schools of his native county, and finished his education at Georgetown College, in 1860. During the years of 1861–62 he taught school, and since that time has been engaged in agricultural pursuits. In Scott County, Dec. 19, 1867, he married Miss Mary A. Glinn, a native of Scott County, and the daughter of William and Elizabeth (Moore) Glinn, both natives of Scott County; she was born in December, 1847. They are the parents of two children, one of whom is now living: Anna E. Himself and wife are members of the Baptist Church, and in politics has followed the example of his forefathers by uniting with the Democratic party. He is the owner of 131 acres of land. Mr. Glass is an enterprising man, industrious and frugal in his habits, pleasing and courteous in his manner, and highly esteemed by the people of the community in which he lives.

THOMAS HOOK, farmer; P. O. Stamping Ground. William Hook, the father of this gentleman, was born in Nicholas County in 1800; during his life followed the occupation of farming and blacksmithing; he died in 1869; his father, Thomas Hook, was born in Maryland,

and emigrated to Nicholas County, being among the early settlers. The mother of our subject, Susan Ellis, was a native of Nicholas County, and the daughter of James Ellis, the founder of Ellisville, Ky.; she was born in 1800, and died in 1832. They were the parents of three children, of whom was our subject Thomas; he was born in Nicholas County, Dec. 17, 1827; he attended the common schools of his native county until he was fifteen years of age, at that time he was thrown on his own resources. In 1847, he removed to Scott County; in 1868, he removed to Fayette County; during this period of his life he was engaged in farming, working mostly as a hired hand; in 1871, he removed to Frankfort, Kentucky, where he engaged in the livery business, following the same until 1878, when he returned to Scott County, where he has since remained, engaged in agricultural pursuits. He was married in Scott County, in 1867, to Miss Angeline Triplett, a native of Scott County, born in September, 1840; her father, Mr. S. Triplett, was born in Mason County, 1792, and died in October, 1843; her mother, Sallie (Thomason) Triplett, was born in Scott County, in 1810, and now resides with our subject. Mr. and Mrs. Hook have been blessed with two children: Katie, born Oct. 7, 1874, and Andrew J., born Jan. 7, 1877. Mr. Hook has, during his life, accumulated a good property, and is now the owner of 250 acres of land in Stamping Ground Precinct. He is a popular and deserving citizen, with progressive business habits.

BARTON W. HOUSE, farmer; P. O. Stamping Ground; is a native of Bourbon County, and the son of John and Nancy (Bramlette) House. The father of this gentleman was born in Bourbon County, Ky., in March, 1791, and died in 1875. His father was Andrew House, who was born in Pennsylvania, and emigrated to Bourbon County, Ky., in about 1789; he died in Scott County, at the advanced age of ninety-four years. The mother of our subject was born in Bourbon County, Jan. 24, 1799, and died in 1846; she was the daughter of Parker and Nancy Bramlette, who were natives of Virginia, and emigrated to Bourbon County in a very early day. Of the eight children born to them, Barton W., our subject, was the first son. He was born Nov. 22, 1819, and with his parents in 1830, removed to Scott County, where he has since remained, engaged in the occupation of farming. In Scott County, in 1841, he married Miss Catharine Bramlette, who was born in Owen County, Kentucky, March 8, 1822, and died in December, 1867; she was the daughter of Marvin and Permelia (Estes) Bramlette, who were natives of Virginia. In 1872, in Lexington, he married a second time Miss Helen S. Rynes, who was born in Lexington, Jan. 1, 1838. She is the daughter of Ladson and Eleanor Rynes. He was a native of New-York city, and she of Fayette County, Ky. By his first marriage he had two children, one of whom is living, Hugh B.; and by his second, three, viz.: Ira, and Eva and Florence, who were twins. Mr. House is the owner of 210 acres of land, situated on the Lecompte's Run Pike, near Stamping Ground. Himself and family are members of the Baptist Church, and during his life he has united with the Democratic party.

JAMES. W. HAMILTON, Farmer; P. O. Minorsville; a native of Scott County, and the son of Alexander and Harriet (Davis) Hamilton. His father was born in Harrison County, Ky., in 1808; removed to Scott County in 1833, and died in 1874; he was a farmer. His wife, the mother of our subject, was born in Virginia in 1812, emigrated to Scott County in 1820 and died in August, 1880. They were the parents of ten children: James W. Hamilton was born Sept. 8, 1848. His early days were spent in receiving an education and assisting in tilling the soil of his father's farm. In Scott County, in 1867, he married Miss Frances A. Murphy, who was born in Scott County in Dec. 1850. They are the parents of six children, four of whom are now living, viz: John M., Harriet A., Walter P., and Alonzo. He has, during his life, followed the occupation of farming, and is now the owner of ninety acres of land. At the time of the war he enlisted as a private soldier in 5th K. V., in the company of Capt. Tilford. Himself and wife are members of the Christian Church. In politics, he unites with the Democrat party.

ALBERT HOCKENSMITH, farmer; P. O. Stamping Ground. John S., the father of this gentleman, was born in Franklin County, Ky., Dec. 14, 1799; he was a farmer, and died Sept. 1, 1880; his father, Henry Hockensmith, was a native of Maryland, and emigrated to Kentucky in about the year 1790. The mother of our subject, Julia Gaines, was born in Franklin County, Ky., in 1824, and died in 1850; she was the daughter of James Gaines, a native of Kentucky. Albert Hockensmith was born in Franklin County, Jan. 12, 1847; he attended the common schools of his native county, and began life as a farmer; at the age of twenty-one he removed to Scott County, where he has since remained, engaged in tilling the soil. In 1879, Jan. 14, he married Miss Bettie Holton, a native of Franklin County, who was born March 18, 1853; her father, Mr. L. Holton, was born in Franklin County, Nov. 30, 1822; her mother, Fannie (Holton), was also born in Franklin County. Mr. Hockensmith is the owner of 204 acres of well improved land, upon which he makes the raising of stock a specialty; he is a

Democrat, and, with his wife, are members of the Baptist Church. They have one child, Daisy, born Dec. 15, 1880.

LEONIDAS L. JOHNSON, farmer; P. O. Georgetown. Robert Johnson, his grandfather, was born in Orange County, Va., in 1759; in 1779, with his youngest brother, Cave Johnson, and Wm. Tomlinson, set out upon horseback to make the perilous journey through the wilderness to Kentucky; after a few days traveling alone they overtook, at the Cumberland river, a family of Bryants, with whom they continued to travel till they came to North Elkhorn; here they chartered and secured land from surveys made by John Floyd; leaving his brother, Cave Johnson, and Wm. Tomlinson, Robert returned to Virginia, and in the fall of the same year started with his family in boats to make the journey by water; but the river became so low, finally froze up, and he could go no further than a place now known as Boonsborough, where he with his family passed the winter. In the spring, with renewed courage, he started out again, continuing down the Ohio river, finally came to the falls and landed there; he made a settlement on Beargrass for the summer; during this time Gen. Clark got up an expedition against the Indians in the Miami, Robert Johnson accompanying him. The life of these pioneers was one of incessant toil, watchfulness and danger, the country being filled with marauding parties of Indians; many incidents of their bravery and endurance might be told if space permitted. In 1780 he moved from Beargrass to Bryant's Station, where he lived until 1783; while there he went with Gen. Clark upon another expedition against the Indians; in 1782 was elected a member of the General Assembly, and went to Richmond; when he returned he took command of a company from Bryant's Station, and made another expedition with Gen. Clark to the Miami country against the Indians; in 1783 he moved his family to the Great Crossings on Elkhorn; here he continued to live the rest of his life, rearing a large family; his sons were, William, James, Richard M., Henry, Joel, John and Benjamin, all of them becoming prominent and distinguished men. Richard M. served in his State's Legislature many years, was elected to Congress and Senate of the United States, and also Vice President. James and John T. were elected to Congress. John T. was a popular and successful politician, but in the midst of his career was converted to the Christian religion, as advocated by Alexander Campbell, and spent the remainder of his days in the service of God, distinguished for his piety, zeal and faithfulness. James occupied the home at Great Crossings during his life, leaving a large family of sons and daughters; the sons, William, Edward, James, Richard, Dannie and Leonidas inheriting the force of character and strength of mind from their father and grandfather, all became prominent men in their community; all of these brothers became identified with the South; there is but one of them now living; Leonidas, our subject; he was born Jan. 27, 1818; has during his life principally followed the occupation of farming; he is one of the most prominent and leading citizens of Scott County; he is a man of great public spirit, enlarged views, sound practical knowledge, indefatigable purpose, untiring energy, and withal, of a very conscientious, kind and impressible nature; in manners is courteous, unassuming, modest and prepossessing. In October, 1843, he married Miss Irene Elley, a native of Scott County, and of a family who were of great prominence in Kentucky, and were among the early pioneers. Mr. and Mrs. Johnson have four children. They have one of the handsomest farms in Scott County, situated on the Stamping Ground Pike, six miles from Georgetown, and the fine residence erected by the design of Mr. J. is spoken of as one of the finest farm residences of the county; it is appropriately named, "Clifton."

JAMES B. KELLEY, farmer; P. O. Stamping Ground. James Kelley, the father of our subject, was born in Pennsylvania in 1780, and with his parents emigrated to Lexington, Ky., in 1784. He afterwards removed to Scott County, where he died in 1851. During his early days he followed blacksmithing, and previous to his death gave his attention entirely to farming. He was the son of John and Eliza Kelley, who were natives of Pennsylvania. The mother of our subject was Ann Officer, who was born in Scott County in 1800, and died in 1863. She was the daughter of James and Jane Officer, both natives of Sherman's Valley, Pa. He was a soldier in the Revolutionary war. James B. Kelley was born in Scott County, April 21, 1829. His boyhood days were spent in receiving an education from the common schools of his native county, and in tilling the soil of his father's farm. In 1856, in Scott County, he married Miss Mallie Ferguson, who was born in Scott County, Sept. 12, 1837, and died June 23, 1868. In 1870 he married a second time, Miss Mattie Ferguson, sister to his first wife. She was born Sept. 16, 1851. In 1851 Mr. Kelley commenced farming, which he has since continued, making the raising of stock a specialty. By his first wife he had one child, Mattie, and by his second wife one child, J. Alexander. He is a member of the order A. F. and A. M., Scott Lodge No. 203, at Stamping Ground; is a Democrat, and with his wife are members of the Baptist Church.

WILLIAM NEWMAN, farmer; P. O. Stamping Ground; John, the father of this gentleman, was born in Maryland, in 1762, and emigrated to Fayette County in about the year 1783; at that time there were only two small cabins where the city of Lexington now stands. In 1785 he removed to Scott County, and settled at the Blue Springs, where he remained only about one year, when he removed to Stamping Ground Precinct, and settled on McConnel's Run, he being among the first settlers of that Precinct. Soon after he settled in Stamping Ground Precinct, he, together with Thomas Herndon, built a fort at McConnel's Run, which was afterwards known as Herndon's Station. He died in 1822. Peggy, his wife, and mother of our subject, was born in Culpepper County, Va., in 1765, and with her parents emigrated to Scott County in about the year 1786. Of the seven children born to John and Peggy (Smith) Newman, William was the youngest child. He was born in Scott County, April 5, 1811, and in 1832 was married. His wife has now been dead several years. In 1877 he married a second time, Sally Dixon, who was born in Fayette County, Feb. 15, 1838. John Dixon, her father, was born in Fayette County, in 1812, and is now residing in Scott County. Sally (Wallace) Dixon, her mother, was born in Fayette County in 1809, and died in 1864. Mr. Newman has always during his life followed the occupation of farming, and has by his studied economy and business habits succeeded in gathering together a farm of 170 acres. Himself and wife are members of the Baptist Church. They are the parents of two children, one of whom is now living, Cora. In politics he was formerly a Whig, but now unites with the Democratic party.

ASA H. OWEN, farmer, P. O. Skinnersburg, whose portrait appears in this work, was born in Scott County, August 21, 1812, in the same house he now lives in. His father, Thos. Owen, was a farmer by occupation. He was born in Virginia, Aug. 6, 1768; he emigrated to Covington, Kentucky, in the year 1800; in 1801 removed to Franklin County, and in 1805 removed to Scott County, and settled on the same farm and in the same house occupied by our subject, where he died June 7, 1849. His wife, Jane (Nelson), and mother of our subject, was born in Scott County, May 12, 1787, and died Feb. 5, 1860. Of the three children born to them, Asa H., our subject, was the youngest child. His education was limited to such as the common schools of his native county afforded in his day. He first began merchandising at Skinnersburg, successor to his deceased brother; he followed the same until 1837, when he, with his only brother, managed the farm of their father, and with his brother accumulated over 600 acres of land; but since his brother's death, has been selling at different times parts of his large tract of land, until now he has left, only 141 acres; it being his desire to retire from active labor, and enjoy the fruits of his hard work. Mr. Owen has always been a man of industrious habits, and prospered in all his business undertakings; he has taken an active part in whatever was calculated to advance the interests of the people at large; has been a substantial member of the community, and liberal in his contributions to charitable and educational purposes. He has devoted his life to agricultural pursuits; never sought office, but acted independent of sect or denomination, yet has favored everything known to be right, and opposed to wrong; honestly and openly laboring to promote good morals and advance the common interests of all good citizens.

H. CLAY PREWITT, farmer; P. O. Stamping Ground. Levi Prewitt, the father of our subject, was born in Fayette County, Ky., Sept. 19, 1799; his earlier days were spent in acquiring an education and writing in the Clerk's office at Georgetown. In 1818, with his parents, he removed to Georgetown, where he remained until 1826, when he married Miss Margaret Boyce, who was born in Fayette County, Jan. 10, 1806. By this union they had ten children. At the time of his marriage he removed to Montgomery County, where he engaged in agricultural pursuits, remaining there until 1829, when he returned to Scott County. H. Clay Prewitt, our subject, was born in Georgetown, Jan. 10, 1844; he received his education principally from the Baptist College at Georgetown and the Reform College at Eminence. In 1865, on April 5, in Scott County, he married Miss Sally Stone, a native of Montgomery County. She was born June 27, 1844; she is the daughter of James M., born in Bourborn County in 1816, and Nancy (Hearne) Stone, born in Harrison County in 1825. Mr. Prewitt first commenced farming with his father, and in 1870 bought a farm in White Sulphur Precinct, where he remained until 1880, when he sold his farm and removed to Stamping Ground, having now 165 acres of land. In connection with his farming in 1875 and the two years following, he handled many fine trotting horses, which he afterwards sold at a large profit. He and his wife have been blessed with six children, four of whom are now living, viz.: Mattison, Charley, Lizzie and Carrie. Himself and wife are members of the Reform Church, and in politics he is a Democrat.

PHILEMON PLUMMER, farmer; P. O. Stamping Ground; was born in Scott County, Sept. 13, 1807. He is the son of Wm. Plummer, who was a native of Maryland; born Jan. 17, 1769, and died March 17, 1855. He came to Scott County in about the year 1790. He was the son of Philemon Plummer, a native of Ireland. Rachel (Hobbs) Plummer, the wife of Wm. Plummer, was a native of Maryland, and died in 1833. Philemon Plummer (our subject), has followed the occupation of his forefathers in his native county, that of farming. He has been twice married. In 1828, he married Miss Malinda Chambers, a native of Scott County. She died Sept. 7, 1843. In 1844, he married a second time, Martha L. Mayhall, a native of Franklin County, Ky., born in April, 1807, and died July 24, 1879. By his first wife he had ten children, six of whom are living; and by his second wife, three children, all of whom are living. Mr. Plummer has fifty grand-children, and three great-grandchildren. He is the owner of 200 acres of land. His son, P. M. Plummer, was born in Scott County, Oct. 30, 1845, and married, Nov. 14, 1871, Miss Bettie F. Cox, a native of Franklin County. She was born Sept. 10, 1850. There were born to them five children, four of whom are living. He is a farmer; he and his wife are members of the Christian Church. Wayland Plummer was born in Scott County, Jan. 16, 1850, and in Owen County, in 1871, he married Miss Sarah E. Harsy, a native of Scott County, born Nov., 1851, they are the parents of five children, all of whom are living. He has during his life, followed the occupation of farming. He and wife are members of the Christian Church.

J. T. REYNOLDS, merchant; Stamping Ground; was born in Jefferson County, Ky., Nov. 6, 1840; his father, W. W. Reynolds, was born in Orange County, Va., 1817; emigrated to Jefferson County, Ky., in 1835, and is now residing near Louisville, Kentucky, being engaged in an agricultural works as finisher. Mary A. Cardin, his wife, and mother of our subject, was born in Jefferson County, Ky., in 1820, and died in September, 1873; she was the daughter of John Cardin, a native of Virginia. J. T. Reynolds, our subject, received his education from the common schools of Shelby County, Ky., and also attended the Transylvania College, at Lexington. In 1861, he commenced clerking in a store; in 1867, he commenced merchandizing on his own account at Minorsville, his present residence; he sold out his business in 1880, and is now the proprietor and successful manager of a large store at Stamping Ground, giving employment to two clerks; he was married in Scott County, Ky., in 1851, to Miss Elizabeth F. Ferrell, a native of Jessamine County; she was born in 1851, and is the daughter of Andrew and Susan (Blakeman) Ferrell, who were natives of Virginia. Mr. Reynolds is the owner of 300 acres of land, which he principally rents. He is a member of the Baptist Church; his wife is a member of the Christian Church. Their children are: Herman, Henry G., Susan E., Mary J. and William.

JAMES TAYLOR, farmer; P. O. Skinnersburg; was born in Scott County, May 15, 1818. John Taylor, his father was born in Culpepper County, Va., in 1783, and died in 1823; he was a farmer, and first settled in Scott County in 1805; Fanny (Stanton) Taylor was born in Culpepper County, Va., in 1786; came to Scott County with her husband, where she died in 1826. They were the parents of seven children, our subject being the youngest child. He was thrown upon his own resources at the age of eight years by the death of his parents; at ten years of age he apprenticed himself at the shoemaker's trade for five years; at the expiration of that time he hired out as a farm hand; from his small earnings he succeeded in saving a little sum of money, with which he bought a small piece of land—and by his studied economy and business has succeeded in adding to it, and is now the owner of 213 acres. At the time of the war he was taken prisoner by the federal army as a citizen; after being confined for six months, and being removed several times to different prisons, was released and allowed to return home; he has been twice married—the first time in Scott County, in 1837, to Miss Margaret Stockdell, who was born in Scott County, Sept. 26, 1814, and died March 23, 1855; by this marriage he had eight children, two of whom are now living, viz.: John M. and Milton M. In 1858 he married a second time, Mrs. Burrows, a native of Bath County, born May 30, 1814; she is the daughter of Robert and Mary (Odell) Whitton, who are natives of Virginia. Mr. Taylor is united with the Democratic party, and with his wife, are members of the Christian Church.

ELIJAH THRELKELD, farmer; P. O. Stamping Ground; is a native of Scott County, and the son of Moses and Elizabeth (Thomason) Threlkeld. Moses was born in Scott County, June 4, 1799; during his life he followed the occupation of farmer and miller, being the owner of the large flouring mill known as the "Old Threlkeld Mill"; he died Nov. 3, 1863; his parents were natives of Virginia, and came to Scott County in a very early day, being among the first settlers. Elizabeth, our subject's mother, was born in Scott County, July 13, 1810, and died Jan. 25, 1874. Of the five children born to them, one was our subject, who was born July 29,

1829. His early days were spent in receiving an education and assisting in tilling the soil of his father's farm. At the time of the breaking out of the war he enlisted in the Confederate Army, serving under Geo. Stilford, of Company B., and was engaged in the battle at Snow Hill. During his life he has given his attention to farming, and is now the owner of 200 acres of well-improved land. He is a member of the Baptist Church; he is a Democrat in his political views, and is a quiet, unassuming gentleman, having the good will and friendship of a large circle of acquaintances.

JOHN H. WASH, farmer; P. O. Stamping Ground; is a native of Scott County, and the son of Lucius and Betsey (Casy) Wash. His father was a carpenter by trade; was born in Virginia in 1786; emigrated to Scott County in or about the year 1805, and died in 1857. His mother was born in Franklin County, Ky., in 1802, and died April 15, 1856; she was the daughter of Josiah Casy, a native of Culpepper County, Va. John H. Wash, our subject, was born Sept. 4, 1821; his education was very limited, and in fact received the greater part of it after he became of age. At the age of twelve years he was bound out as a farm hand, where he remained until he was twenty-one years of age. At that time he became an apprentice at the carpenter's trade, working at the same but one year, when he became the manager of farms for different men, which he followed until 1854. By his hard work up to this time, he had saved from his small earnings about $2,000, with which he bought a farm and made a home for his parents, taking care of them to the time of their death. In 1854, in Scott County, he married Miss Mary J. Johnson; who was born in 1831, and died March 26, 1876. At the time of his marriage he began farming on his own account, which he has since continued, now having 120 acres of well improved land. By his marriage he had three children, two of whom are now living, viz.: John and Ely. He is a member of the Baptist Church; a Democrat, and a member of the Scott Lodge, No. 203, A., F. & A. M., at Stamping Ground. By his industry and economy, he has arisen from poverty to ease and comfort; a self-made man, respected and enterprising citizen.

JOSEPH J. YATES, farmer; P. O. Stamping Ground; is a native of Shelby County, Ky., and son of Franklin T. and Louisa (Mitchell) Yates. Franklin T. Yates was born in Scott County, in 1805; during his life worked at his trade of tailor. He died Nov. 4, 1879. Joseph, his father and grandfather of our subject, was born in Washington County, Md., July 16, 1763, and emigrated to Woodford County, Ky., in about 1790. Louisa, the mother of our subject, is a native of Shelby County, Ky., and the daughter of Livingston Mitchell, who was also a native of Kentucky. She was born in 1815, and now resides in Ray County, Mo. Of the eight children born to them is Joseph J., our subject, who was born Nov. 4, 1843, at Shelbyville. He attended the common schools of Scott County, where he received his education, and at the age of nineteen removed to Missouri, where he remained until January, 1872, when he returned to Scott County, where he has since remained engaged in agricultural pursuits. In Ray County, Mo., on Oct. 7, 1869, he married Miss Oniska Spurlock, who was born in Ray County, Mo., Aug. 1, 1859. Her father, M. M. Spurlock, was born in Virginia, in 1822, and now resides in Ray County. Her mother, Mary (Bates) Spurlock, was born in Hart County, in 1822, and died July 30, 1855. Mr. Yates and his wife are members of the Baptist Church. They are the parents of four children, three of whom are now living, viz.: George, born Nov. 29, 1872; Ella, born July 26, 1876; and Walter, born Aug. 27, 1880. Mr. Yates has accumulated a good property and is now the owner of 224 acres of improved land. He is a man of liberal views, but of strict honesty and integrity in all business transactions, and having the confidence of the people who know him.

LYTLE'S FORK PRECINCT.

WILLIAM FISH, farmer; P. O. Sadieville. His father, Frances Fish, was born in Maryland in 1791; emigrated to Scott County, in 1802, with his parents; in 1809, removed to Hamilton County, O., where he was married; in 1826, returned to Scott County, where he died, in June, 1845. He was by trade a shoemaker, and worked at the same during his younger days, but for a number of years previous to his death, followed the occupation of farming. He was a soldier in the war of 1812. His wife, Amy (Decker) Fish, and mother of our subject, was born in Cincinnati, Ohio, in 1800, and died in Scott County, in 1864. There were born to them nine children, of whom was William Fish, our subject. He was born in Hamilton County, O., Nov., 17, 1821; he received his education in his native county; in 1843 commenced business on his own account, by trading in the South. In 1853 he began merchandising in Lytle's Fork Precinct, and continued the same until 1850, when he bought the farm upon which he now resides, and continues the management of the same. In 1850, in Scott County, he married Miss Elizabeth Griffith, a native of Scott County, and the daughter of Thomas and Nancy (Rollins) Griffith. Her father was born in Scott County, in 1801, and died in 1877. Her mother was born in Delaware, in 1808, and died in 1877. Mr. Fish has been a very successful farmer, and is now the owner of a well improved farm of 190 acres. He is a member of the order of A. F. and A. M. West Union Lodge, No. 165; he is a Democrat in politics, and was elected constable in 1881. They have had three children, two of whom are living: Theodore and Thomas F. Whatever Mr. Fish has attained has been the result of indomitable will and energy, having taken his beginning in life in very moderate circumstances. He is one whose progress is sure, and who strictly adheres to principles of honesty as the best policy.

DAVID K. GORHAM, farmer; P. O. Long Lick. John A. Gorham, the father of this gentleman, was born in Fayette County Ky., September, 1787, and died in 1853; the first part of his life was spent in the merchandizing business, and previous to his death was a farmer; in 1813 he was married to Caroline Kerr, a native of Scott County; born in 1797, and died in the same house she was born in, 1877; they were the parents of ten children: David K. Gorham, being the fourth child, and the only one now living in Kentucky; he was born in Georgetown, Ky., April 19, 1822; his early life was spent in receiving an education and assisting in tilling the soil of his father's farm; in 1844, he began farming on his own account, which he has since continued in connection with school teaching, which he has done for the last forty years, principally in the winter season; in 1842 he married Miss Martha A. Thompson, a native of Scott County, born in August, 1825; she is the daughter of John K, and Louisiana (Parish) Thompson, who were natives of Kentucky; at the time of the war, our subject enlisted in the Confiederate Army, Co. D., 3d K. V.; he was in the battle of Chickamauga; in 1866, he was elected to serve as Constable in his native county, which office he held for four years; he is the owner of 300 acres of land in Lytle's Fork Precinct; his children are George H., David L., Mary H., Katie P., Robert W., James W., Cornelia J., Sorenseur, and Virginia; in politics he unites with the Democratic party.

CHAS. HOLDCRAFT; farmer; P. O. Porter; is a native of Indiana, and the son of Seely and Betsy (Steele) Holdcraft. He was born Nov. 8, 1815. His father was of Dutch descent, born in Pennsylvania in 1776 and died in 1859. He was a farmer and a miller. His wife, our subject's mother, was of Irish descent, born in Scott County, in 1791 and died in 1877. They had five children—Charles, our subject, being the third child. His early education was very limited, yet at the present time his education is above the average, having received it principally after doing a day's work in the field. He has spent his life at farming in his native county, with the exception of four years, when he was in Ohio. He was married in Scott County, in 1842, to Miss Sallie Ann Parker, a native of Scott County, born Jan. 11, 1820. Her father, Samuel Parker, was born in Maryland, Dec. 17, 1792, and died in 1879. Her mother Matilda (Boyce) Parker was born in Philadelphia, April 7. 1798, and is now living in Illinois. Mr. Holdcraft is one of the best read men of his precinct, a man of excellent memory, generous and benevolent; he is a true gentlemen, and enjoys the confidence of the community in which he now lives.

MILTON PENN; farmer; P. O. Porter; is a native of Scott County and the son of Samuel and Lotta (Cannon) Penn. He was born Jan. 30, 1814. His father was

born in Maryland in 1782; emigrated with his parents to Scott County in about the year 1792. He was a farmer, and died in 1854. His wife, the mother of our subject, was born in Delaware, in 1785, came to Scott County with her parents in about the year 1795. She died in 1817. There was born to them eleven children, of whom was Milton, our subject, he being the third child. His boyhood days were spent at home, receiving an education and assisting in tilling the soil of his father's farm. In 1836 began farming on his own account, which he has since continued, being now the owner of 215 acres of land. In 1862 he was afflicted with rheumatism, and since that time has been unable to do much hard work. He was married in 1836 to Miss Elizabeth Alsop, a native of Scott County, born in 1836. She is the daughter of Wm. and Anna (Scott) Alsop. Mr. and Messrs. Penn are members of the Methodist Church. Their children are Wm. N., Samuel M., Lourtoutus, Jennie and Maranda.

S. PENN, farmer; P. O. Porter, Ky.; is a native of Scott County, and the son of Samuel and Lotta (Cannon) Penn. He was born Dec. 20, 1816. His boyhood days were spent in receiving an education and assisting in tilling the soil of his father's farm. In 1835 he began farming on his own account, which he still continues, having procured by hard work and studied economy, a good farm of 120 acres. In 1841, in Scott County, he married Miss Elizabeth Sinclair, a native of Scott County, and the daughter of Benjamin and Priscilla Sinclair. She was born Dec. 5, 1821. Mr. and Mrs. Penn have had ten children, seven of whom are now living, viz: Seth T., John M., Sarah E., Mary E., Alexander F., Martha B. and Lucinda G. He is a member of the Baptist Church; his wife is a member of the Methodist Church. He is a member of the order of A. F. and A. M., at Oxford. In politics he unites with the Republican party.

R. H. RISK, farmer and distiller; P. O. Long Lick; is a native of Scott County, and is the son of J. and D. (Ewing) Risk. The father of this gentleman was born in Scott County, in 1801; during his life followed the occupation of farming, and died in 1874. His wife, the mother of our subject, was also born in Scott County, in 1801, and is now living in Oxford Precinct. Of the nine children born to them, was R. H. Risk, our subject. He was born May 12, 1831. His early days were spent in receiving an education and assisting in tilling the soil of his father's farm. In 1855, in Harrisburg, he married Miss Maria E. Hinton, a a native of Scott County, and the daughter of James and Olla (Wash) Hinton. In 1856 Mr. Risk removed to Missouri, where he bought a farm, remaining on the same until 1859, when he returned to his native county, and again engaged in agricultural pursuits; and also in connection with his farming in Scott County, he commenced distilling in Owen County, continuing the same until 1869, when he sold his distillery, and commenced distilling at his present residence, where he has since continued, being a very successful man in each branch of his business. It may be said, to the credit of Mr. Risk, that he was the builder of the new pike running through his precinct; not finding support enough, he took the expense of the contract upon himself and built it, being completed in December, 1881. He is the owner of 800 acres of land, which is principally in blue grass. Mr. Risk is one of the substantial men of the precinct; he has by diligence and economy acquired for himself a home and a sufficient competence, he is a very active and energetic man. Himself and wife have been blessed with ten children, nine of whom are now living, viz.: Leander, Virginia, Reverda, Amanda B., Thomas, Harvey, Mary, Robert and Alexander.

JAMES J. RALSTON, farmer; P. O. Rock Dale, Owen Co.; is a native of Harrison County, Ky., and the son of David and Sarah (Adkinson) Ralston. He was born in August, 1812. His father was born in Fayette County, Ky., in 1793; was removed to Harrison County, Ky., by his parents in 1796, where he remained engaged in agricultural pursuits until 1868, when he died en route to see his daughter in Nicholas County. His wife, the mother of our subject, was born in Bath County, Ky., in 1787, and died in 1860. Of the six children born to them, James J. was the oldest child. He remained with his parents in Harrison County, receiving an education and assisting his father at farming until 1834, when he went to Georgetown, Ky., and worked at the carpenters' trade for five years. In 1839 he returned to his native county and began farming; following the same until 1854, when he removed to Scott County, where he has since remained and followed the occupation of a farmer. He was married in Georgetown in 1838 to Miss Pernilla Redmon, a native of Spencer County, who died in 1855. By this marriage he had three children, two of whom are living, viz: David and Sarah L. In 1857 he married a second time, Miss Nancy Brewer, a native of Hancock County, Tenn.; she was born Nov. 13, 1842. By this marriage he had eight children, seven of whom are living, viz: Mary, James, Jefferson, Lilla B., Rosa, George and Edward. Mr. Ralston has been a very successful farmer; he is now the owner of 215 acres of land.

JAMES M. WARRING, farmer; P. O. Porter; Edward Warring, the father of this gentleman, was born in Sussex County, Del., April 29, 1794; in August, 1811, removed to Baltimore, Md., where he worked at shoemaking. Sept 3, 1812, he removed to Lexington, Ky., and in 1832 removed to Scott County, where he has since remained, and been principally engaged in farming; he has now retired on account of his old age, and is now enjoying the fruits his hard work in the comfortable home of his son, our subject; he was in the war of 1812, and there saw Tecumseh, after he was killed; in 1818, he married Miss Nancy Rollins, a native of Sussex County, Del.; she was born in 1797, and died in 1860; they are the parents of seven children; James M., our subject being the fifth child; he was born in Fayette County, Oct. 27, 1828, and in Scott County, Sept. 24, 1856; married Miss Sarah A. Alsop, a native of Scott County, born in 1837; she is the daughter of William and Corrilla (Hardy) Alsop, who are natives of Scott County; Mr. Warring has during his life followed the occupation of farming, and is now the owner of a farm of 281 acres; he and family are members of the M. E. Church South; he is a Democrat, and a member of the order A. F. & A. M. West Union Lodge, No. 165.

CARLISLE WARNOCK, farmer; P. O. Josephine, Ky.; is a native of Greenup County, Ky., and the son of George J. and Elizabeth (Foster) Warnock. He was born in April, 1814; his father was born in Greenup County, Ky. During his life he was a hunter and trapper, and previous to his death, was a farmer. He died in 1833, aged 45 years. His wife, and mother of our subject, was born in Ireland, and died in 1833, the same year and on the same day of her husband, aged 43 years. They were the parents of nine children, Carlisle Warnock being the oldest child. He was apprenticed at the gunsmith's trade, in Ohio, where he remained one year, and returned to his native county, where he finished his trade. In 1836, he removed to Owen County, and worked at his trade until 1850, when he removed to Scott County, and has since been farming and blacksmithing. In 1836, he married Miss Polly Glass; she was borne in Owen County in 1820. By his marriage he has had ten children, five of whom are living, viz.: William, Robert M., Garrett D., Sarah C. and Martha. He and family are members of the Baptist Church. He is a member of the order A. F. and A. M.

BEN. F. WRIGHT; farmer; P. O. Porter; is a native of Scott County, and the oldest of fifteen children born to James and Lucinda (Carr) Wright. He was born Feb. 1, 1837; his father was born in Scott County, Jan. 24, 1812, and died Feb. 16, 1875. He was a farmer. His wife, the mother of our subject, was born in Scott County in 1814 and is now residing in the county near Stonewall. Benj. F. Wright was educated in the common schools of his native county, and in 1858 began farming on his own account, and is still engaged in the same occupation, having procured by his hard work and studied economy a good farm of 153 acres. In Harrison County, in 1858, he married Miss Sarah J. Michael, a native of Harrison County. He and wife are members of the Christian church; they have two children, James F. and Millie F.

OXFORD PRECINCT.

WILLIAM N. ATKINS, farmer; P. O. Oxford; was born on Dry Run, Scott County, Ky., Sept. 16, 1832; son of Nash and Nancy (Glass) Atkins; he, born in Scott County, May 4, 1807; a farmer and wagon maker by trade; she was born in Owen County, July 5, 1808; they had four children. After receiving an ordinary education our subject began life farming. In 1875 he ran a distillery and engaged in the grocery trade; at present he is engaged on his farm, one and a half miles from West Oxford, and he has his property finely improved, raising fine stock thereon. Mr. Atkins has been married three times: first, Dec. 10, 1850; second, October 17, 1871; third, Jan. 22, 1874; he has the following children: Nash, Lucille, James C., Nannie F., Allie, Lounsford H., Willie, Blanche and Elizabeth. He is a Knight Templar, and a Democrat.

F. M. CANNON, physician; Oxford; was born in Scott County, May 20, 1832; his fathor was John J. Cannon, born in Scott County, June 25, 1792, who was a hatter for many years; then became a farmer, which occupation he followed until death, which was April 20, 1867. His mother's maiden name was Hester Ford, who was born in Scott County, November, 1798, died March 23, 1874; his parents had fourteen children, nine sons and five daughters. He was educated in Scott County, at Stamping Ground Academy; began life as a school teacher, which occupation he followed for four years, then began the study of medicine in the office of Dr. W. B. Paxton, with whom he remained two years, then went to Louisville, and was a student under Dr. Seaton for two years, and finally graduated at the Kentucky School of Medicine in that city. He was married in Fayette County, Nov. 12, 1868, the maiden name of his wife being Mary A. Sidener, who was born in Fayette County, Feb. 21, 1847; wife's father was Jacob Sidener; her mother, Mary Agnes Wilson; he was born in Fayette and she in Bourbon County, (dates not given.) Been engaged in the practice of medicine for thirteen years; then, in farming and practicing also. He has two children, Alonzo, and Mary Frances; religion, that of the Christian Church. He is also a member of the Masonic order. Dr. Cannon occupies a prominent position in his profession, and has been remarkably successful, and is among the leading men of his section; is a man of remarkable physique; is the tallest man of the precinct, being six feet and six inches in height, and weighs two hundred and twenty-five pounds.

AMBROSE DUDLEY HAMON, farmer; P. O. Oxford; was born in Woodford County, Ky., in 1818; son of Ezra and Hannah (Farra) Hamon; he, born in Pennsylvania, March 14, 1774, and came to Kentucky about 1795; a farmer and stone mason, dying in 1863; she, born in Jessamine County, and dying in 1842. They had twelve children, nine boys and three girls. Our subject received his education at the schools of his native county, and began life as a wagon-maker, carrying on that business and blacksmithing, for about twenty years. He was married in Fayette County, in 1848, to Eliza Jane Hardesty, born in Fayette County, Jan. 17, 1825; daughter of Henry and Sarah (Dikes) Hardesty, by which union there have been born five children, four of whom are living: Hannah Lucy, Sally Henry, Fanny Lee, Mary and Ducker. Although advanced in years, Mr. Hamon is one of the most energetic of men, and he has by industry and economy surrounded himself with the comforts of life, having reared a family of highly cultivated children. They are members of the Baptist Church, and he is a Democrat.

JAMES KIMBROUGH, farmer; P. O., Oxford; was born in Harrison County in 1842; the son of Robert Kimbrough who was born in the same county, and whose occupation was that of a farmer. The maiden name of his mother was Elizabeth Frazier, a native of the county of Harrison. His parents had seven children, five of whom are living. James Kimbrough was educated in Harrison county, and began life in the capacity of a farmer. He was married in Georgetown, Dec. 22, 1870, to Fannie W. Allen, the daughter of W. Wright Allen. Her father having been born in Bourbon County in 1824, and her mother, Frances Skillman, was born in Fayette County in 1833. James has, from his early manhood, been engaged in the business of farming. He enlisted in Capt. Van Hook's Battalion of Cavalry, C. S. A., for one year, at the expiration of which, he re-enlisted in Co. K, 9th Kentucky Cavalry, Col. Breckinridge's regiment. His affiliation in politics, has always been with the Democratic party. He is a member of the Masonic fraternity.

NEWTOWN PRECINCT.

J. J. R. FLOURNOY, farmer; P. O. Oxford; was born at Falmouth, in Pendleton County, Ky., Dec. 17, 1801. His father's name was Francis Flournoy, who was born in Culpepper County, Va., Jan. 18, 1773; was a farmer by occupation, and died Jan. 29, 1835. Maiden name of his mother was Sallie C. Goodwin, born in Virginia Feb. 28, 1785; died June 20, 1858; his parents had thirteen children. He was educated at Georgetown under Burton Stone; began life in the capacity of a school teacher; was engaged in the business of farming, and had for many years the position of magistrate in his precinct. He was a zealous member of the Christian religion, and an ardent and enthusiastic Democrat. Mr. F. was one of the early settlers of this section, a man of fine intellectual attainments, an exceedingly charitable man; although having no family of his own, yet he adopted, raised and educated some of the brightest of Kentucky's fair daughters.

M. H. KENDALL, farmer; P. O. Newtown; was born in Bourbon County in 1835; his father's name was Jas. Kendall, and he was born in the county of Harrison June 10, 1797, and was an agriculturist by occupation; he died in 1865; the maiden name of his mother was Mary Hutsell, who was born in Bourbon County in 1802, and died in 1867; his parents had seven children; he was educated at Bethany College, in Virginia, and began life as a farmer; was married in Bourbon County, March 10, 1859; the maiden name of his wife was Eliza Lary; she was born in Louisiana in 1841, the father of whom was Dr. Henry B. Lary, born in Bourbon County, 1812; her mother, Harriet Boote, was born in Louisiana in 1817; he has been engaged in farming, trading and merchandizing; is now holding the position of Magistrate; has nine children, eight of whom are living, viz.: Russell B., William S., George H., John Milton, Amos J., L. Q. Lamar, H. D. L. and Chas. T. (Mary R. dead); politics, Democrat; is a Knight Templar.

DANIEL LARY, farmer; P. O. Newtown; was born in Bourbon County, Jan. 13, 1806; his father was Dennis Lary, who was born in Hardy County, Va., in 1773, and was by occupation a farmer, and died in Bourbon County in 1824; the maiden name of his mother was Sarah Curtwright, who was born in Hardy County, Va., in 1777; came to Kentucky in 1783; died in 1839. His parents had thirteen children; he was educated in Bourbon County, and began life as a farmer; was married in Hancock County, Ga., June, 1835; maiden name of his wife was Sarah A. Thomas, born in 1815; his wife's father was Fred'k G. Thomas, born in Edgecomb County, N. C., her mother being Rebecca Eskridge, born in Edgefield District, S. C. He has been engaged in the business of farming and trading; had two children, both of whom are dead, named as follows: Theresa and Sophia. Politics, Democratic; member of Grangers' Mutual Benfit Association. Mr. Lary is a man of fine intellectual attainments, an enterprising citizen, and has been quite an active man in politics, having filled the position of Representative, from his county, in the Legislature with considerable credit to himself and constituency, in 1875 and 1876.

PAYNE McCONNELL, farmer; P. O. Newtown; was born in Woodford County, in 1857; was the son of James F. McConnell, who was born in Woodford County, in 1828, and whose occupation was that of a farmer, and who died in Scott County, in 1868. The maiden name of his mother was Catharine Payne, born in Scott County, in 1838; his parents having had two children, he was educated in the primary schools of Scott County, and began life as a farmer; was married in Scott County, in 1880; his wife was Rebecca Harp, who was born in the County of Bourbon, in 1861, the father of whom was J. H. Harp, who was born in Fayette County, in 1837; her mother was Isabella Harp, born in Fayette County, in 1839. He has been engaged in the business of farming and trading; he has one child whose name is Henry Lewis; his religion being that of the Christian Church, and his politics Democratic.

SAMUEL MADDOX, farmer; P. O. Newtown; was born in St. Mary's County, Md., June 1st, 1817; his father, Edward Maddox, a farmer by occupation, was born in Maryland in 1776, and died in 1825. His mother was Mary Calliss, born in Charles County, Md., about 1780, and died in 1823. His parents had five children. He was educated in Maryland at St. Mary's College, afterwards called Charlotte Hall, and began life in the avocation of farming; was married in Scott County; his wife's maiden name was Sarah A. Keene, who was born in Scott County, in 1818. His wife's father was Vachel Keene, born in Maryland about 1775; that of her mother being Sarah Y. Fontleroy, born in Maryland about 1785.

Has been engaged in the business of farming. Has two children; one living, whose name is Eleanora James; Edward being dead; is an Episcopalian and a Democrat.

JOHN T. NUTTER, farmer; P. O. Georgetown; was born in Fayette County in 1830. His father's name was James Nutter, whose occupation was that of a farmer; born in Fayette County in 1798, and died in 1866. The maiden name of his mother was Mary Hurst, who was born in Fayette County in 1801, and died in 1851. His parents had seven children. He was educated in the primary schools of Fayette County, and began life as a farmer; was married in Bourbon in 1857, the maiden name of his wife being Agnes Pritchell; born in Bourbon in 1838, and whose father was William Pritchell, born in Virginia; her mother, Lydia Wilson, born in Fayette County. He has always been engaged in farming; has ten children, named as follows: Dora, Bettie, Emma, Susie, Leah, Maggie, Nannie, Keene, Waller and James; politics, Democratic.

J. WELLINGTON PROWELL, farmer; P. O. Newtown; was born in Pennsylvania, May 2, 1818; his father's name was Samuel, who was born in Pennsylvania in 1780, and was a farmer, and died in 1863; the maiden name of his mother was Phœbe Brown, who was of French extraction, and died in 1828; his parents had fifteen children. He was educated in Pennsylvania. Through his own exertions he began life in the capacity of a farmer, and was married in Scott County, Nov. 24, 1868. The maiden name of his wife was Catharine (Lewis) Payne, who was born in Scott County in 1836; her father was Colonel Remus Payne, who was born in Fayette County in 1811; the maiden name of her mother was Mary S. Talbott, born in 1815. He has been engaged in the practice of medicine, and that of a breeder of fine stock, and of a general farming interest. He was in the capacity of Assistant-Surgeon, 5th Company, Washington Artillery, C. S. A., Captain Slocum. He has four children, one girl and three boys, as follows: Early Wellington, Homer Marion, Wade Hampton, and Rosa Belle. He has always been a zealous Democrat; and is a member of the Masonic fraternity. Dr. Prowell is a man possessing extraordinary energy and fine intellectual attainments; is an exceedingly liberal man in his views, and is ever ready to aid in the co-operation of any enterprise developing the interest of his county or State, and is among the leading agriculturists of his county.

JOHN C. PAYNE, farmer; P. O. Newtown; was born in Scott County in June, 1837; his father was Col. Remus Payne, who was born in Fayette County in 1811, was a farmer by occupation, and died in 1880 in Florida; the maiden name of his mother was Mary Smith Talbott, born in Woodford County, May 11, 1815, and died Sept. 4, 1843; his parents had seven children, four boys and three girls. He was educated at Georgetown College, and began life as a farmer. He was married first in Fayette County in 1859; second in 1868; the father of his first wife was Jacob L. Embrey, who was born in Madison County, the maiden name of her mother being Caroline Grimes, born in Fayette County; the father of his second wife was Isaiah Offutt, born in Maryland in 1808; her mother, Rebecca Offutt, born in Scott County in 1820. He has been engaged in the breeding of shorthorns, Southdown sheep, fine horses, and that of a farming interest in general. He had five children, one living and four dead (Mary Smith Payne living). He is a member of the Christian Church, and is a Democrat. Mr. Payne is a prosperous farmer, a very prudent and circumspect man, a prominent breeder of fine stock; he is a remarkably liberal man in his views, and is ranked among the prominent men of his county.

JOSEPH SHROPSHIRE, farmer; P. O. Leesburg; was born in Bourbon County, March 4th, 1811; his father was Joseph Shropshire, who was born in Virginia about 1770; was by occupation a farmer and trader; died in 1844. The maiden name of his mother was Susan W. Neal; born in Bourbon County; died in 1836. His parents had twelve children, five boys and seven girls; he was educated in Bourbon County; education of a primary cast; he began life in the business of farming; was married in Bourbon county in 1839; the maiden name of his wife was Elizabeth Ann Hawkins; born in Bourbon county in 1822. The name of his wife's father was John Hawkins; born in Harrison county in 1798, whose wife was Mary Harcourt, born in Bourbon county in 1799; has been engaged in the business of farming; had eight children, five of whom are living, as follows: Mary Susan, Ellen, Ann Frances, Amelia, Elizabeth Dandridge, Elisa Margaretta, James Hubbell, Sarah Bowman. He was a Baptist and a Democrat.

WALTER SHROPSHIRE, farmer; P. O. Oxford; was born in Bourbon County, Dec. 27, 1843. His father was James H. Shropshire; born Aug. 25, 1808; occupation, a farmer; maiden name of his mother was Maria L. Harcourt; born in Bourbon county April 27, 1815; died Dec. 30, 1852; parents had nine children, eight of whom are living; was educated in Bourbon county, and began life in the business of farming; was married in Scott county, Nov. 21, 1871; maiden name of his wife was Rebecca F. Sutphin, born in Baton Rouge, La., March 13, 1851. Her father was John T. Sutphin, born in Kentucky in 1820, in Scott county; her mother, Ann L. Flournoy, was born in Fayette County, Feb. 26, 1826. He has been in the business of farming and breeding fine cattle and horses. He enlisted in Co. A, Breckinridge's 9th Kentucky Cavalry, commanded by Capt. Lawrence Jones, C. S. A.; has three children: J. J. R. Earl, Flournoy, and Walter H.; is member of the Christian Church and a Democrat.

WILLIAM A. SMITH, farmer; P. O. Newtown; was born in Scott County, Feb. 4, 1815. His father was Nelson Smith, born in Virginia, Sept. 1781; occupation, a farmer; died July 1, 1841. Maiden name of his mother was Sarah Kerr, born in Virginia Nov. 21, 1785, and died in 1853. His parents had ten children, seven sons and three daughters; he was educated in country schools and at Georgetown College; began life in the practice of medicine; was married in Scott County, Oct. 25, 1836. The maiden name of his wife was Julia A. Coulter, born in Clark County, Feb. 1, 1818; her father being Joseph Coulter, was born in Delaware in 1778; her mother, Elizabeth Harris, was born in Clark County. He has been engaged principally in farming, and also in the practice of medicine. He has seven children, four of whom are dead, the names of the living being: James D., Jos. C. and N. Rhodes; dead—Sarah E., Anna A., Emma H. and Mary C. Religion, Presbyterian; politics, Democratic; society, Masonic; also a Knight Templar.

NELSON SMITH, farmer; P. O. Georgetown; was born in Virginia, in 1781; came to Fayette, near Bryant's Station; his father was Wm. Smith, born in Virginia, and was by occupation a farmer; died in 1824. The maiden name of his mother was Mary Rodes, born in Virginia; died in 1828; his parents had nine children, five sons and four daughters; he was educated in Virginia and began life with farming; was married in Scott County, in 1803; the maiden name of his wife was Sarah Kerr, born in Virginia, in 1785; her father was David Kerr, born in Virginia, in 1757; her mother being Dorothy Rodes, born in Virginia. He was engaged in the business of farming; had ten children, as follows: Garland K., Sidney R., David W., William A., James N., Clifton R., D. Howard, Mary A., Elizabeth D., and Emeline; is a Baptist and a Whig.

EDWIN WARD, farmer; P. O. Newtown; was born in Scott County, in 1847; is the son of Carey A. Ward, whose avocation was that of a farmer, and who was born in Harrison County, in 1806, and died in 1861; maiden name of his mother being Eliza Jane Risk, born in Woodford County, in 1809, and died in 1867; his parents having had six children, three by first marriage and three by the second; he was educated at Georgetown College and began life as a farmer, and was married in the County of Fayette, in 1871; the maiden name of his wife was Elizabeth Wallis, who was born in Fayette County, in 1849. The father of his wife was Thomas M. Wallis, born in Culpepper County, Va., in 1797; her mother being Susan T. Dudley, who was born in Fayette County, in 1828; he has been engaged in the business of farming; has three children whose names are: Luella Vachti, Sue Eliza and Edwin Carey. Religion that of Presbyterian; politics, Democratic.

HARRISON COUNTY.

CYNTHIANA CITY AND PRECINCT.

THOMAS V. ASHBROOK, deceased; was a farmer and distiller; born in Harrison County, Ky., Aug. 22, 1828, and died Sep. 30, 1874, son of Aaron and Sallie (Veach) Ashbrook, who were the parents of seven children. Thomas V., our subject, was educated in the district schools of his native county, and was reared to farming, in which occupation he continued, with the addition of distilling. He was elected Mayor of Cynthiana several terms, and was serving in that capacity at the time of his death. Sept. 3, 1857, he married Artemesia Belles; born in Indianapolis, Feb. 10, 1832; daughter of John J. Belles and Dorcas Saunders, of Pendleton County, Ky.; and by which union there were born five children: Felix S. and T. Earl, sons, and Sallie V., Dorcas S., and Mary E., daughters. Dorcas Saunders' mother was a Grant, and her mother was a sister of Daniel Boone, the old Kentucky pioneer. James Saunders, brother of Dorcas, was killed at the battle of River Raisin. Mr. Ashbrook was an officer in the Christian Church for several years before his death; his widow and oldest children are also members of the same church. He was a Democrat.

FELIX G. ASHBROOK, distiller; P. O. Cynthiana; was born near Cynthiana, April 1, 1824; son of Aaron and Sallie (Veach) Ashbrook. He a native of Virginia, born in 1794; was a farmer and came with his father to Kentucky at an early day, dying in 1855; she, born in Harrison County, Ky., in 1796, and dying in 1848. They had seven children, three sons and four daughters, Felix G. being the oldest son. Aaron, the father of subject, began life in moderate circumstances, but by industry and economy acquired a handsome property. He gave to his children before his death about 450 acres, and divided by will 486 more, in addition to another farm of 230 acres which was to be sold and proceeds divided among the children. Mr. Ashbrook, our subject, began life as a farmer, and has continued that honorable occupation ever since. In 1871 he was elected Mayor of Cynthiana, which position he filled acceptably to his fellow citizens. Dec. 26, 1848, he married Elizabeth Warden King, born in Harrison, May 16, 1830, daughter of George and Sarah B. (Garnett) King. Mr. Ashbrook and wife are members of the Baptist Church (Missionary), and he is an A., F. & A. M., a Knight Templar, and a Democrat.

WESLEY AMMERMAN, (deceased); was born in Bourbon County, Nov. 18, 1825, and died April 8, 1877. He was a son of Joseph Ammerman, who was born in Virginia, and Rebecca (Reed), who was born in the same State. He was one of a large family of twelve children. He received his education at the country schools of Harrison County, and began life with agriculture, which pursuit he followed through life. He was married in Harrison County, in 1849, to Louisa Bassett, who was born in Harrison County in 1827, and was the daughter of Jonathan Bassett, who was born in Bracken County in 1801, and Elizabeth Disher, who was also born in Bracken County in 1802. Mr. Ammerman was the father of eight children, five of whom survive him, viz.: Joe B., John R., Edward W., Augustus and Lizzie J. Mrs. Ammerman and family are members of the Christian Church at Cynthiana, and Mr. Ammerman, during his life, was a Democrat, and at one time a Granger. Dying, he left his widow a fine estate of 250 acres, called "Elmwood," four miles from Cynthiana, on Connersville Turnpike.

RICHARD H. AMMERMAN, farmer; P. O. Cynthiana; was born in Harrison County, Dec. 9, 1850; his father, William, was born in Bourbon County, Dec. 6, 1820. He is now farming and living in Harrison County. His mother was Martha H. Brand, who was born in Harrison County in 1825, and is still living, and from this union there are nine children. Our subject received his education in Harrison County, and began life with farming, which he has continued since. He was married in Harrison County, Oct. 17, 1878. His wife was Louella Jameson, who was born in Harrison County, July 26, 1854, and was the daughter of Richard Jameson, who was born in Harrison County in 1821; He died Sept. 19, 1863. Her mother was Margaret Givens, who was born in Bourbon County Jan. 2, 1823. Mr. Ammerman was for some time Supervisor of one of the county roads, and is the father of two children, viz: William Sidney and James C. His wife is a member of the Christian Church at Cynthiana, and Mr. A's political affiliations are with the

Democracy, and he is a member of the Grangers' Lodge at Cynthiana, No. 154, and is the owner of 160 acres of fine land called "Woodland."

WILLIAM ADDAMS, miller and distiller; P. O. Cynthiana; is a son of John and Lucy (Logan) Addams, daughter of Abner Logan, of Fleming County. John Addams was born in Culpepper County, Va., in 1820; he came to Kentucky and pursued his vocation as a teacher with marked success; he died in 1861, and was followed to the grave in a few months by his devoted wife. Thus Wm. Addams was left an orphan at an early age, and had to struggle for his prominence in commercial and social circles. After receiving a meagre education in the common schools he took a position with C. B. Cook & Co., and when that firm sold out to Peck and Van Hook he continued in that relation until 1864, when he became a partner with C. B. Cook in milling and distilling. He was married Oct. 8, 1872, to Miss Cora V. Cook, daughter of his partner. The couple now have four children, viz: Rilla, Lizzie, Cora and Cyrus. Mr. Addams is a member of the Christian Church, but his wife is a communicant of the Episcopal denomination. Mr. Addams was born Sept. 6, 1850, and is consequently just 31 years of age. He has been honored by the people of Cynthiana with a seat in the City Council for the last six years, and is recognized as a safe and reliable business man, a high-toned and affable gentleman, and a useful citizen in every relation both public and private. He is a Democrat.

W. T. BEASEMAM, Ex-Sheriff; P. O. Cynthiana. W. T. Beaseman, son of John O. and Jane (Moore) Beaseman, was born in Harrison County, March 15, 1826. His grandfather, John Beaseman, was a native of Maryland, and emigrated to Kentucky about 1790, and settled in Bourbon County, where he married a Miss Owings, after which family the town of Owingsville was named; he died in 1792. John O. Beaseman was born about three months after his father's death (1792.) His educational advantages were quite limited and before he arrived at maturity, he removed to Harrison County. From there he went to the war of 1812, participated in the battle of the River Raisin, and after the close of hostilities he returned to Harrison County to make it his future home. He represented Harrison County in the House of Representatives in its sessions of 1827, '28, '29, '34, '35, '37, '42, and was in the Senate in 1830 '34. Although he was a man destitute of even an ordinary English education, yet he possessed an originality of thought and peculiarity of expression, equal to any of his cotemporaries. He was elected by the people of Harrison County to the offices above named, by greater majorities and for a longer time, (in the aggregate,) than any other man who ever had a competitor for office in the county in his time, or perhaps since. This popularity was not based on acquired knowledge, nor was it the result of family influence, as his father-in-law, William Moore, called "Clerk Moore," was a Whig, and his sons were also Whigs, while Beaseman was an Andrew Jackson Democrat. His popularity was the result of his own peculiar natural powers. The people loved him and had great confidence in his honesty as a legislator, and his great ambition seems to have been either to occupy a prominent place, or to please the people, for surely no man ever realized less pecuniary reward for public services. In 1820, he married Miss Jane Moore, daughter of William Moore, who was the first Clerk of the Harrison County Court, an office he held during his life-time. Mr. Beaseman raised three sons and seven daughters to maturity; one son, W. T., our subject, and five daughters now living. John O. died at his home in Harrison County in 1848 of paralysis, in his fifty-sixth year, his widow following him in 1860, in her fifty-eighth year. W. T. Beaseman was brought up on his father's farm, receiving a good liberal education in the common schools of his native county. In 1850 he went to California, gold hunting, where he engaged in mining till 1853, with fair success. He subsequently returned to Harrison County, and again resumed his agricultural pursuits. In 1860 he was elected Deputy Sheriff of his county, also served in the capacity in 1871, '72 and again in '75, '6, '7, '8. He was nominated for Sheriff in 1871, but on account of his having held an office in the Confederacy, the committee thought it might cause some disturbance as to his eligibility and they accordingly changed him to Deputy. He served a year in the Mexican War in McKee's Reg. 2nd Ky., in Capt. Cutter's Co. Participated in the battle of Buena Vista. In 1861, he, as 1st Lieut. and Capt. McDowell, organized a company of Harrison boys and joined the Confederate army. In 1863, subject was promoted to Captain of his Company, McDowell being promoted to Major. He was captured at Fort Donelson on Feb. 22, 1862, and was sent to Johnson's Island, where he was exchanged the following September, and served till the close of the war. He is now engaged in settling up his old Sheriff business. He was married in Harrison County, Dec. 20, 1881, to Miss Martha T. Kendall, who was born in 1842. Her father, William Kendall, Sr., was born in Fayette County, Dec. 23, 1794, and died at his home in this county, on Dec. 14, 1875. He was a farmer by occupation. His entire life was strictly moral. It is said that he was

John White

never heard to utter an oath, to speak a falsehood, or to use language unbecoming a Christian gentleman. He was not a communicant in the church, but always defended the Christian religion, and avowed himself a believer in the same. On his deathbed, he not only expressed perfect confidence as to his future happiness, but admonished his family and friends to meet him in heaven. Our subject, Mr. Beaseman, is favorable to the Methodist Church, although not a member of any. His wife is a Presbyterian. He has been prominently connected with the Masonic fraternity for many years, having taken all the degrees from E. A. to K. T.

PROF. JAMES A. BROWN, teacher; P. O. Cynthiana, was born near Millersburg, Bourbon County, Ky., Dec. 9, 1843, and is the youngest of four children, born to Abel and Elizabeth (Pollock) Brown; the former was born March 2, 1801; the latter March 24, 1825 and died Oct. 14, 1847. Mr. Brown removed with his family to Jacksonville, Ill., in 1851, and there successfully pursued the avocation of farming for many years. Being an advocate of thorough education, he sent his sons to Illinois State College from which James, (the subject), was graduated with honors, in the class of '65. Soon after graduating he was elected Principal of the High School at Havana, Ill., which position he satisfactorily filled for four years; having in the meantime studied law, he was admitted to the bar, and practiced for one year, but being elected Principal of the High School at White Hall, Ill., he gave up his practice and again entered upon his duties of teaching. He was married July 29, 1869, to Miss Lizzie Smith, only daughter of William and Jane (Evans) Smith, of Millersburg, Ky. The former was born in Bourbon County, April 2, 1810, and died March 2, 1858; the latter was born Feb. 18, 1810, in Maryland, and is still living. The subject, on the day following his marriage, was tendered the Presidency of Millersburg Female College, then owned and controlled by the Kentucky Conference; he accepted the position and remained in it until the Conference disposed of it to Judge William Savage. Professor Brown now removed with his family to Paris, Ky., and purchased the buildings, which he afterwards chartered as the "Bourbon Female College." He and his wife opened this college the week after purchasing it, with only eleven pupils, having assumed a debt of over $5,000 at ten per cent. interest; but believing that success would crown their efforts, they toiled on in their noble profession, until they built up a school of over one hundred and twenty young ladies, and in three years had paid off the debt. He remained in that college seven years, or until 1878, when he disposed of it to Prof. W. S. Jones, expecting to go to Mexico, Mo., where he had been offered the position of Principal of the High School. But the citizens of Cynthiana, Ky., offered to advance him $2,400 if he would come there and start a female college, a proposition he accepted. He purchased the beautiful place known as the "Broadwell property," in August, 1878, and in September following opened what is known as the "Harrison Female College." Professor Brown has proven to be one of the most successful teachers in Kentucky. He began life with nothing but an education, and now has a fair competency for his old age. He and his accomplished wife enjoy the confidence of the people of Kentucky, and are but fair samples of what can be done with an education. They have a son Willie A., born May 28, 1870, and a daughter, Jennie Russell, born Feb. 27, 1876. They have kept their mother, Mrs. Smith, ever since their marriage, and within the last three years have given a home to their father, Abel Brown, both of whom are now quite stricken in years.

MARCUS L. BROADWELL, deceased; was born in Cynthiana, Feb. 22, 1829, and died July 4, 1870. His father, Asbury Broadwell, was a native of Harrison County, and was born May 29, 1791, and died Dec. 11, 1843. Asbury began merchandising in Cynthiana when a young man; being started in business by a gentleman of Lexington, Ky., with the understanding that as soon as he made enough in his business, he should refund the money advanced by his friend. Mr. Broadwell, by attending closely to his store, soon built up a good trade, and consequently found himself in a short time possessed of sufficient surplus to repay his benefactor, without detriment to his then thriving business. As time run on his business continued to grow until he became one of the leading merchants of Central Kentucky. While he grew immensely rich for a man in this country, yet he was a charitable man; was ever ready to help anyone that was willing to help themselves, but was not the friend of an idler at any time. Asbury Broadwell married Mary E. McMillen, who was a native of Harrison County, and was born March 14, 1802, and died in June 1874. They raised a family of three sons and one daughter, Marcus L., our subject, being the second son. He was educated at the old Transylvania University at Lexington, Ky, where he graduated with honors. He was first married at Georgetown, Ky., in September, 1848, to Sallie Fennell; she died in November, 1849. His second marriage was on Oct. 9, 1852, to Katie E. Dinsmore, who was born at Warrensburg, E. Tenn., on May 25, 1835; her father, William Dinsmore, was born near Carlisle, Ky., and in 1835 was accidentally shot by his brother-in-law in Tennessee, while out hunting, from the effects of which he afterwards died. He was considered one of the handsomest men in his county. Mr. Dinsmore married Martha E. Scruggs, who was born in East Tennessee, in 1814. She is now the wife of C. A. Webster, of Cynthiana, and is remarkably sprightly for one of her age—nearing her three score and ten. Our subject, "Mark" Broadwell, was County Judge and County Commissioner for six years. He never joined the army during the late unpleasantness, but was forced into the first battle at Cynthiana by the Federal troops. He left a family of three sons, William, Ewing, and Fred; and four daughters, Mary, wife of Jack Desha; Mattie, wife of John K. Lake; Bessie and Katie. The family are all Methodists except the two oldest sons. They are Democrats in politics. Fred the youngest son is now proprietor of the leading livery stable in Cynthiana, is courteous and polite to all, deservingly popular, and is every way worthy of the liberal patronage he has secured in his line of business.

DR. JOHN D. BATSON; P. O. Oddville; was born in Millersburg, Bourbon County, Ky., Aug. 5, 1824; son of John A. and Rachel (Drummond) Batson. He, born in Fauquier County, Va., in January, 1787; a farmer, and son of Mordecai and Elizabeth Batson, who were natives of Virginia. She, born in Virginia Nov. 22, 1793; daughter of Amos and Rebecca Drummond, of Virginia. John A. died in Kentucky in 1851, his wife having preceded him to the Land of Shadows in 1839, leaving seven children, our subject being the sixth son. Dr. Batson received his primary education principally in Bourbon and Harrison Counties, and then took a course at the Medical College at Cincinnati, graduating from that institution in 1845, when he commenced the practice of his profession, at which he has continued ever since. Jan. 2, 1853, he married, in Harrison County, Miss Susan C. Crow, born in Harrison County, in October, 1834; daughter of Rev. J. C. and Nancy W. Crow, from which union has resulted three children: David W., James R., and John B. The first named is President of the Kentucky Wesleyan College, the second is a physician, and the third a farmer. The Doctor and his family are members of the Methodist Church, and he is an A., F. & A. M., and a Democrat.

GEORGE W. BUZZARD, Sr., farmer; P. O. Cynthiana. Daniel Buzzard, father of this gentleman, was born in Germany, in 1786; he was the son of Jacob and Anna Buzzard, both natives of Germany; Daniel emigrated to Harrison County, Ky., where he followed the occupation of farming to the time of his death, which occurred in 1843. His wife was Miss Anna Marshall, a native of Harrison County, and daughter of Ralph Marshall, a native of Virginia. She was born in 1793, and died in 1829. They were the parents of five children, one of whom was our subject, George W., who was born May 10, 1818, in Harrison County. He spent his earlier days with his parents in receiving an education and assisting in tilling the soil, of his father's farm. He began life by tilling the soil, which he has since followed, now having 230 acres of well improved land. He is a Democrat and an enterprising, public spirited citizen.

E. W. BRAMBLE, distiller; P. O. Lair's Station; was born in Hamilton County, Ohio, Sept. 6, 1842, to A. L. and Deborah (Stiles) Bramble. His father was born in Pennsylvania, and floated down the Ohio River in a flat boat to Hamilton County, O., with his parents, in 1806. He remained with his parents to the age of twenty-one, when he married, bought a farm of his own, and with a bare supply of the simplest articles of household furniture known to early settlers, all of which did not make a two-horse wagon load, he drove from his paternal home to a little cabin near where now stands the fine residence and homestead of our subject. His faithful wife and he entered upon their new life with that loving courage which could only contemplate a life of unwearying industry. In looking forward to the success that, on such occasions, hope alone promises, they could not dream of the result they afterwards saw and experienced. There was apparently nothing but work ahead, and at it they went with a loving faith and earnest will which became their fixed habit of life, and from which they never rested. Their earlier labors were in the rude forms of farming peculiar to that day. The varied products of their farm found their places in markets in the city, regularly, on the leading market days. While this part of the work continued so systematically, it did not by any means take all of Mr. Bramble's time or talents. From the earliest settlement of the Miami valley the famous yield of its corn found most steady absorption in hogs, and commerce in pork was a necessary sequence. In this Mr. Bramble embarked as soon as the trade opened. He became not only a great feeder of hogs and other stock, but also among the earliest of drovers, slaughterers, packers and dealers. Not confining his business to local operations, he was constantly handling stock at other points, buying in and shipping from most of the great grazing and feeding centers of Ohio, Kentucky and Indiana. Of busy men he became about the busiest, not for a greed of gain, but because he had an instinct of activity and a fondness for business. Without an interest in the outward forms of religion, he led a practically good life. His friendships were many, his acquaintance very large, and his taking away in February, 1875, in the seventy-sixth year of his age, was widely regretted by all among whom he was known. E. W. Bramble lived with his parents until he was twenty-eight years of age, where he received a good education and assisted his father in all of his business. In 1870 embarked on life's rugged pathway by trading in Kentucky. In 1873 he married Miss Loraine Megibben, a daughter of Hon. T. J. Megibben, of Harrison County, and in 1876 became a partner in the firm of Megibben, Bramble & Co., the largest distillers of Harrison County. He and wife are members of the Baptist Church. In politics he is a Democrat.

JAMES A. COOK, deceased, was a distiller in Cynthiana, born in York County, Pa., 1830; son of Stephen B. and Lydia Cook, who were the parents of four sons and five daughters. Our subject remained with his parents in Pennsylvania, and emigrated with them to Clark County, Va., in 1847, continuing with them several years on their farm, but in 1855 returned to Pennsylvania and located near Carlisle. In 1861 he came to Kentucky, and for a short time remained in Lexington, but finally located in Cynthiana, where he engaged in the distilling business; was also engaged in the manufacture of woolens, flour, &c. In 1867 he moved to Chicago and engaged in the real estate business for several years, but his health failing, he returned to Kentucky, where he remained until his death, which occurred in June, 1873. In York, Pa., April 18, 1859, he married Miss Sarah Wolford, daughter of Peter and Mary A. (Carl) Cook, all natives of the Keystone State. Two children have blessed this union: Charles W. and Mary, who is the wife of James W. Frazer, of Mt. Sterling. Mr. Cook was, and his widow is, a Presbyterian; he was a Democrat.

C. B. COOK, Jr., miller and distiller; P. O. Cynthiana; was born near Richmond, Ky., Feb. 19, 1860, son of C. B. and Parmelia (Knight) Cook; he born in Lancaster County, Pa., March 31, 1823, was a millwright and distiller by occupation, coming to Kentucky in 1858, served as Magistrate at Richmond and was Mayor and Councilman several terms, dying Nov. 16, 1880. His wife was born in Hagerstown, Md., Dec. 9, 1828, where she was married in 1844; they had one son and four daughters. Our subject received his education in Cynthiana. He is and has been for some time, of the firm of C. B. Cook & Co., distillers, millers, &c., at Cynthiana. Mr. Cook has served as Chief of the fire department one term. One of the sisters of Mr. Cook is Mrs. Laura Musser, another is Mrs. Cora V. Addams, and the other two, Lillie and Hattie, are at home. His wife is a member of the Christian Church, and he is a Democrat.

MRS. MARGARET CRENSHAW; P. O. Cynthiana; is the widow of Henry Crenshaw, who was born in Virginia in 1802, anddied in 1879. He was the son of John and Hannah (Madison) Crenshaw, who came to Kentucky, at an early day, from Virginia, he dying in 1855. They have had five sons and four daughters. Mr. Crenshaw, the husband of the lady whose name heads this sketch, was educated in the district schools of his native county, and began life in moderate circumstances; was a carpenter by occupation, but subsequently began farming, and, at the time of his death, owned nearly four hundred acres of land. He was a Democrat. June 15, 1854, he married Miss Margaret Allen, who was born in Woodford County, Ky., Nov. 8, 1812; daughter of John and Alice (McKay) Allen; he, born in Virginia, Dec. 17, 1765, and dying Sept. 4, 1847; she, born Feb. 1, 1772, and dying May 3, 1815. Mrs. Crenshaw is a Presbyterian, and owns a handsome residence in Cynthiana, where she lives.

R. M. COLLIER, County Sheriff; P. O. Cynthiana; is one of Harrison County's self-made men. He is the grandson of William Collier, and son of Robert and Catharine (Moore) Collier, the latter daughter of William Moore, of Harrison County. The father of R. M. was raised in Nicholas County, Ky., and devoted his life to farming. He died in Springfield, Ohio, in 1849, leaving a family of five children, of whom our subject was the second eldest, and born Oct. 18, 1844. At the age of sixteen years Mr. Collier entered the Confederate army; was with Humphrey Marshall and Col. E. F. Clay's regiment; and spent ten months of his service as a prisoner of war in Camp Morton, Indianapolis, Ind. Returning from the army, he engaged in farming. In 1870 he was elected assessor of Harrison County, and in 1878 he was appointed Deputy Sheriff, held the office until 1880, when he was elected by the Democratic party to the office of Sheriff of Harrison County, which office he now holds. Mr. Collier was married in June of 1874, to Miss Eliza Ewalt, daughter of John H. Ewalt. Two children have been born to them: Thomas A. and William M. Mrs. Collier is a member of the Christian Church, and he is member of the order of A. F. and A. M., in which order he is a Sir Knight.

MRS. ADELIA COX, is a daughter of Joseph and Evaline Wiglesworth, of Virginia, and was married in Cynthiana in 1848, to Henry Cox, by whom she had eight sons and one daughter. Henry Cox, the husband of our subject, who departed this life Dec. 7, 1880, at the age of sixty-four years, ten months and eighteen days; was the son of William and Lucy Cox, who emigrated to America from a small sea-coast town in England, in November, 1815, coming to Kentucky from Virginia, where they sojourned for a short time, and in 1816 Henry was born. When Henry was only fourteen he connected himself with the Christian Church, and before he was twenty-one years of age he set up in the cabinet-making business, which trade he had learned with his father He worked at his trade in Cincinnati and Lexington; he also started business at Centerville, but not finding it up to his expectations, he was induced to move to Cynthiana and open business. After a few years in the cabinet making business with his brother, he sold out and opened a small grocery store, which he continued with improving success until 1861, when the war coming on, he sold out and moved to the country; after a residence in the country several years, having engaged in the manufacture of woolen goods, he removed to Cynthiana, where he dealt largely in the productions of the Covington factory, in which he had become a partner. He also bought the house and business of C. G. Land, which he continued several years, and then sold out and turned his attention to farming and trading, doing an extensive business. Mr. Cox was a man of marked decision of character, and possessing more than ordinary ability and energy. For many years he was the largest buyer of stock of all kinds in the county; was well posted in values, of great discrimination, and yet was just in all his dealings with his fellow man. In his family relations he was a model, being invariably kind and attentive to those around him, and to friends always courteous and considerate. In the death of Mr. Cox, Cynthiana lost a citizen whose void is difficult to fill.

JAMES W. CROMWELL, farmer; P. O. Cynthiana; is a native of Harrison County, and son of H. F. Cromwell. He was born Aug. 31, 1840, in Cynthiana. The first seventeen years of his life were spent in attending and receiving an education from the high school at his native town. At the expiration of that time he became apprenticed in his father's machine shop at Cynthiana, where he remained three years. In 1860 he married Mary E. Nichols, who has borne him four children, three of whom are now living, viz.: John M., Lillie L., and Sally C. In the same year he removed to the farm of Maj. Ben. Desha, where he remained tilling the soil until 1862, when he removed to the farm of his father-in-law, Maj. Nichols, where he remained until 1869, when he bought the farm upon which he now resides, having 210 acres of land, situated one mile from Cynthiana, called "Locust Grove." He is the owner of the prize stallion, "Harrison Chief," and is the owner of the two stallions, viz.: "Maj. Nichols," and "Abdallah Membrino." He was the owner of the valuable team which was bought by a gentleman from New York for the late James A. Garfield. Himself and family are members of the Christian Church at Cynthiana. He is a Democrat.

THOMAS CURRENT, farmer; P. O. Cynthiana; is a native of Bourbon County, Ky., and the son of John and Elizabeth (Amos) Current; he was born in 1811; his father was a native of Bourbon County, and the son of Thomas and Margaret Current; he followed the occupation of farmer, and also kept hotel at Ruddel's Mills. He was a Major in the war of 1812; a member of the Methodist Church and the Masonic Order at Millersburg. He died Jan. 18, 1837. Thomas, our subject, lived with his parents in his early life, receiving an education and assisting in tilling the soil of his father's farm. He has been twice married; in 1835 he married Miss Priscilla Fisher; a native of Bourbon County, and the daughter of Nathaniel Fisher; she died Oct. 1, 1877, aged sixty-three years. In 1879 he married Mary E. Lindsay, a native of Bourbon County. By his first marriage he had twelve children, seven of whom are living, viz.: H. C., Martha H., America E., Jasper N., Mollie J., William C., and Mattie. Mr. Current followed farming in Bourbon County until 1855, when he removed to Nicholas County, and in 1871 removed to Harrison County, on the same farm he now resides. He is the owner of the best farm in Harrison County; it contains 300 acres, and has it appropriately named "Locust Grove"; it is situated on the Cynthiana and Ruddel's Mills Pike. Upon his farm he makes the raising of short-horn stock a specialty. He is a quiet, unassuming man, and bears a name and reputation which is beyond reproach; previous to the war was a Whig, but now unites with the Republican party.

SAMUEL CALHOON, farmer; P. O. Cynthiana; born in the State of Ohio, in the year 1831; his father was William B. Calhoon, who died in 1833, at the age of forty-five years; his grandfather, Matthew Calhoon, was of Scotch-Irish birth; his mother, Elizabeth Matthews, was from Pennsylvania. Samuel Calhoon married Miss Mandy Smith, of Harrison County; daughter of Martin Smith; and by this marriage he has three children, viz: Albert Sidney, Arthur Lee, and Mary Eliza. He owns 175 acres, one and three-quarter miles from Cynthiana, on Cynthiana and Leesburg Pike; and on this farm he is breeding a nice lot of short-horns. He is a member of the Orders of Oddfellows and Working Men, and a staunch Democrat; and his wife a member of the Christian Church at Cynthiana.

DUDLEY B. CONWAY, merchant; P. O. Oddville. Miles Conway, father of this gentleman, was born in Fayette County, near Lexington, in the year 1792; his father, John Conway, and his mother, Elizabeth, were natives of Virginia. The mother of our subject, Dudley (Berry) Conway, was the daughter of Geo. W. Berry, a native of Virginia; she was born in Kentucky in 1799 and died in 1823. Miles died in 1864. They were the parents of three childien, of whom was our subject, Dudley B. He was born in Mason County, Ky., Sept. 26, 1820. At the age of fifteen he commenced business for himself by farming in his native county, which he continued until 1839, when he commenced in the milling business; in 1861 he removed to Harrison County, where he continued the milling business until 1865, when he again resumed the occupation of farming, continuing the same until 1878, when he embarked in mercantile business, which he still continues at Oddville. In Harrison County, Feb. 26, 1861, he married Miss Margaret M. Haviland, the daughter of Robt. S. and Mary C. (Stuart) Haviland. She was born in Harrison County, April 17, 1835. They are the parents of three children, viz: Robt. H., Fanny P. and William E. His wife is a member of the Beaver Baptist Church, and he is an A., F. & A. M., Thos. Ware Lodge, No. 340, of Claysville, and in politics is a Republican.

AMERICUS CRAIGMYLE, farmer; P. O. Robertson's Station; was born in Harrison County, near Cynthiana, May 19,1816; son of James and Susan (Duley) Craigmyle; he, born in Pennsylvania, March 10, 1770, a farmer and cabinet-maker, who came to Kentucky with his father in 1780, settling in Scott County; she, a native of Maryland, born Oct. 16, 1781. James died in 1844, and his wife in 1842, leaving eleven children. After receiving an ordinary education in the schools of his native county, he began farming, which he has continued throughout his life. He owns a farm of 250 acres of excellent land. April 12, 1838, he married Hannah Newell; born March 4, 1821; daughter of Hugh and Sally (Blair) Newell; he, of Bourbon County, born in 1793, and dying in 1875; she of Harrison County, born in 1795, and dying in 1853. Mrs. Craigmyle died Jan. 26, 1880, leaving four children: Hugh N., James W., Joseph H., and Sally M. Mr. Craigmyle is a member of the Baptist Church and a Democrat.

B. F. COLVIN, farmer; P. O. Oddville; was born in Pendleton County, Ky., March 29, 1843, son of R. F. and Sarah W. (Wright) Colvin; he, born in Pendleton County, Dec. 24, 1811, a farmer, and son of Henry and Margaret Colvin, who came from Virginia at an early day; she, born in Pendleton County, in 1815, daughter of Lewis and Agnes Wright, natives of Virginia. R. F. and Sarah had six children, subject being the fourth. He, R. F., died in 1876, and his widow still resides in Pendleton. Mr. Colvin received his education in the common schools of Pendleton County, and was raised to the life of a farmer, which occupation he has continued through life, and which he is at present engaged in, owning and cultivating a farm of 100 acres of land. Nov. 7, 1867, he married Miss Sarah A. Douglas, born in Harrison County, Ky., Oct. 3, 1847, daughter of John R. and Sarah Ann Douglas; he, a native of Bourbon County, Ky.; she, of Ireland. Mr. Colvin has been blessed with a family of three children, viz.: Emma A., Nancy M., and Carrie V. He and wife are members of the M. E. Church, and he is a Republican in politics.

LEONARD DRANE, farmer, P. O. Cynthiana; was born in Shelby County Ky., May 9, 1835, son of Stephen T. and Bertha (Ford) Drane, who had five sons and one daughter. Our subject was educated at Eminence College, and began life as a farmer, but has been engaged at various times in hotel keeping and stock-yard business at Louisville; has also merchandised and dealt in wool. Mr. Drane enlisted in the Federal Army—Ninth Kentucky Cavalry, and served six months, being wounded in both hands at the battle of Perryville, in consequence of which he was discharged; was First Sergeant of his company when he left the service. Oct. 3, 1876, he married Anna E. Shawhan, daughter of Henry E. Shawhan, of this county, which union has been productive of two children: Henry Shawhan and Maggie Lyne. Himself and wife are members of the Christian Church, and he is a Mason and a Jeffersonian Democrat.

CHRISTIAN T. DELLING, clothing and furnishing goods; P. O. Cynthiana; was born in Saxony, Oct. 10, 1823, and came to the United States in 1848. He is the only son of Christian A. and Ernestine W. Schneider, both natives of Saxony, and both dead. His parents had one other child: a daughter, Matilda. Our subject learned the trade of a silk and wool weaver, and after he came to this country remained one year in Pennsylvania; then six months in Ohio; then to Kentucky in 1850, locating first in Grant, then in Bourbon, and thence coming to Cynthiana in 1852, where he has resided ever since. Sept. 4, 1861, he married Mrs. Louisa (Taber) Ormsby, principal of the first female school in Cynthiana; a native of Duchess County, N. Y., born March 30,

1823, daughter of Andrew and Louisa (Whitting) Taber; he a native of Connecticut, and dying in 1838; she, still living, in her ninety-fourth year, at Galion, Ohio. One child has been born to our subject: Fannie L., born Nov. 22, 1865. Himself and wife are members of the Methodist Church, and the daughter is an Episcopalian; he is a Mason and a Republican. During Morgan's raid in 1862, Mr. Delling met with a loss of about $1,000, and in 1864, a loss in goods of about $7,000. He is the oldest Protestant foreigner in Cynthiana, being a Lutheran. Mr. Delling is the owner of a fine collection of mineral and geological specimens, and antiquities. Among them are old and rare books, viz: 1645 to 1650, containing full trials of King Charles I, 1648; also the trial of the twenty-nine Regicides, which took place Oct. 12, 1660; also trial of William Penn for street preaching, Sept. 20, 1670, before the Lord Mayor of London; and a written manuscript of over 200 pages, by Jacobi de Paradiso, Tractatus de Erroribus et Moribus Christianorum. A beautiful written manuscript of the fifteenth century, 1465 to 1472. One pre-historic Indian female mold, found a quarter of a mile north of Cynthiana, at the time the C. & L. R. R. was built; also two coins connected together, a relic from a Catholic French Missionary, who no doubt had been murdered and burned by the Indians in that part of Cynthiana, now called Wilsontown. One of them represents the shape of a heart, with the holy images thereon. The other is oblong and grants the Missionary 1080 indulgences for truth, fidelity, and prayer to the Holy Ave Maria. He has also one large copper coin AVRELIVS CAESAR, AVG., who died, A. D. 275.

JAMES E. DICKEY, U. S. Store Keeper; P. O., Cynthiana, Ky.; was born in Ohio County, West Va., July 28, 1823; and is a son of John G. and Eliza (Ewing) Dickey. He was born in Pennsylvania in 1788, is a farmer and merchant by occupation, and is still living. His wife was a native of Virginia, and died in 1836. The subject was educated in the public schools of Virginia, and commenced his career in life as a carriage maker. Was for several months census taker, and served six months in the State service during the war. In 1871 he was appointed United States Store Keeper, in which capacity he still serves. He was married, June 24, 1849, in Wheeling, West Va., to Miss Sarah J. Jordan, who was born at Bellaire, Ohio, in 1826. They have seven children, viz: Mary E., Joseph J., Emma, John, George, James and Mattie. Mrs. Dickey was a daughter of Joseph Jordan. He was a native of Virginia and died in 1861. His wife, Marian Cordell, was also a native of Virginia, and died in 1881. Mr. and Mrs. Dickey are members of the Presbyterian Church at Cynthiana. He is also a member of the Independent Order of Odd Fellows; is an energetic and prosperous man, and highly respected by all who know him. In politics he is a Republican.

WILLIAM M. DILLS, farmer; P. O. Cynthiana; is a native of Harrison County, and son of David and Lydia (Broadwell) Dills. He was born July 22, 1827. His grandfather, Abraham Dills, was among the early settlers of Harrison County; he died in 1850, aged seventy-seven years. His father was also a native of Harrison County, and during his lifetime followed the occupation of farmer; he died in 1877, aged eighty-three years. He was a member of the Methodist Church. He was politically a Whig, and was the President of the First Agricultural Society of Harrison County. His mother was a native of Harrison County, and daughter of William Broadwell; she died in 1872, aged seventy-five years. She was a member of the Methodist Church. They were the parents of six children. William, the subject of our sketch, spent the first thirty years of his life with his parents, the first fifteen years were spent in receiving such an education as he could gain from the common schools of his native county. At the age of fifteen he became the manager of his father's farm, which he continued for fifteen years. In 1866, he married Miss Rosa Austin, a native of Lexington, Ky. and who previous to her marriage, was a teacher in the high schools of Louisville, Ky. They were married by the Rev. Dr. Craig, at Louisville. They are now the parents of five children, four of whom are now living, viz.: Florence, Lena M., Mattie B., and Clara. Three years previous to his marriage, he bought the farm he now resides on, having 150 acres of the best land of Harrison County, called "Glenwood." Upon his farm he makes the breeding and raising of horses a specialty. He was the owner of the celebrated stallion, "Indian Chief," and is now the owner of a fine horse, "Gov. Wilkes," by "George Wilkes," dam "Daisy Burns," by "Indian Chief;" he now is under the training of Lee Doble, of Pittsburgh, Pa. Himself and family are members of the Episcopal Church. He is a Democrat.

JOHN R. DOUGLAS, farmer; P. O., Oddville; was born in Harrison County, Ky., March 28, 1814; son of Richard and Martha (Ames) Douglas; he, born near Fredericksburg, Va., a farmer by occupation, and dying in 1856, aged 76 years; she, born also in Virginia, and dying in 1862, aged 76 years. They had sixteen children. Our subject received his education in the common schools of Harrison County, and began life as a farmer. Dec. 18, 1842, he married, in Harrison County, Ky., Miss Sally Ann Lang, born in Ireland, April 16, 1822 ; daughter of William and Sarah (Ross) Lang, both natives of Ireland, and by which union there are three children living and two dead. Those living are Sarah A., Martha and John W. He owns 200 acres of choice land. Himself and wife are members of the M. E. Church, and he is a member of the ancient and honorable fraternity of Free Masons, and a Democrat.

NOE DILLS, farmer; P. O. Cynthiana; was born in Cynthiana Precinct on the place where he now resides, and is the son of David and Lydia (Broadwell) Dills; he born June 25, 1795, in Harrison County, a farmer, and dying in 1877, aged 82 years; she, born in 1800, and dying in 1872, being the daughter of Samuel and Anna Broadwell, of Harrison County. They (David and Lydia) had six children. Our subject was educated in the schools of his native county, and began life as a farmer, which occupation he has followed through life, at present owning a fine farm of 175 acres of land, his place being called "Woodland Lawn." He has a very fine brick residence on his farm, and his land is under a high state of cultivation. Stock raising is a specialty with Mr. Dills, horses and sheep being more especially attended to, he raising some of the finest animals produced in the county. Nov. 12, 1872, he married, in Augusta, Bracken County, Ky., Anna P. Diltz, daughter of Milton L. Diltz, of Bracken County. Himself and wife are members of the Methodist Church, and he is a Democrat.

DR. N. C. DILLE, deceased ; was born in Cuyahoga County, O., May 21, 1819. He was a son of Calvin Dille and Naomi Hendershot, both of the State of Virginia ; the former born April 11, 1785, the latter August 15, 1784. While still a youth he went to West Virginia, where he remained several years. He afterwards entered the High School at Bardstown, Ky., to which institution he was indebted for his general education. He chose the science of medicine as his profession, and after receiving his diploma from the University of Louisville, returned to his home in Harrison County, where he built up an extensive and lucrative practice. On the 16th of August, 1849, he married Miss Mildred F. Varnon, daughter of John and Elizabeth (Williams) Varnon ; the former of Delaware, the latter of Virginia. Four children were born to them ; one a boy, Lycurgus, who died, and three daughters, Adelaide, Eugenia and Elizabeth. The Doctor was a liberal patron of education, and his daughters are accomplished and refined. He represented Harrison County twice in the lower house of the General Assembly of Kentucky, and acquitted himself in a statesmanlike manner. He was successful in business and leaves a very handsome estate of 300 acres, called "Mount Ida." His friends were numerous, and he was noted for his kindness and acts of charity. On the 2d of January, 1881, he was borne to his final resting place by the Knights Templar of Cynthiana, he having been a member of the Commandery in good standing. His widow is a member of the Christian Church at Buena Vista.

FREDERICK A. EVELETH, saddler and harness maker; P. O. Cynthiana; was born in Boston, Dec. 13, 1813; son of Isaac and Alma (Taggert) Eveleth; he, born in Rhode Island, Aug. 25, 1779; was a book-keeper, and died April 4, 1858; she, a native of England, born about 1783, and dying in 1826. They had seven children, three sons and four daughters, all of whom grew to maturity, and all of whom are dead with the exception of Frederick A., our subject, and two sisters. Mr. Eveleth received his education at New Harmony, Ind., and early learned the trade of saddler. As an incident of interest in the life of our subject, he relates that in 1836, with a friend, he came near losing his life: He and this friend, while crossing a river in New Jersey about dusk, were carried out into the Atlantic by wind and tide, and a storm coming up suddenly, they were tossed about without much ceremony on the part of Old Neptune, but were fortunately cast ashore and were rescued, with what might be termed "fisherman's luck." Mr. Eveleth, in addition to his regular business of saddle and harness making, has at times kept a grocery, and a livery stable awhile. He is a Mason of long standing and has held the responsible position of Treasurer for twenty-three years, during which time he has handled thousands of dollars and never had a discrepancy of a penny. He has also several times represented his Lodge in the Grand Lodge. In Ohio, Oct. 22, 1838, he married Miss Hester Ann Hoffner, born in Hamilton County, Ohio, July 13, 1822, daughter of John Hoffner, a native of Maryland, of German descent. Ten children have blessed this union. George, the oldest, was killed in the Confederate army; Francis died in infancy; those living are: Thomas W., John A., Alonzo G., Harriet L., Mary S., Alma T., Ada and Maggie. Himself and wife are Methodists and he is a Democrat.

HARRY D. FRISBIE, freight and passenger agent; P. O. Cynthiana ; was born in New York, Feb. 28, 1843, son of H. F. and Statira (Gibbs) Frisbie, both natives of the Empire State ; they have six children, Harry D., being the youngest son. Our subject received his education principally in Chicago. He commenced early in life railroading, and has also been engaged in merchandising and dealing in horses, coal, etc. He superintended the building of about 100 miles of telegraph for the Western Union through West Virginia. Mr. Frisbie, when he began his business life was in very moderate circumstances, but by good management and industry, has prospered to a competency. In 1863, he was taken prisoner by Morgan's men, while on duty at Cynthiana, and after being held a short time was released. June 8, 1865, he married Oteria E. Day, born in 1845, daughter of Judge Day, by whom he has had four children, three sons and one daughter, viv.: Harry, Shirley, Raymond and Hattie. He is an A. F. & A. M., a Knight Templar, and member of the A. O. U. W. and Knight of Honor. Self and wife are members of the Methodist Church, South, and he is a Democrat.

T. T. FORMAN, lawyer; P. O. Cynthiana. The grandfather of this gentleman was Ezekiel Forman, who came from New Jersey to Kentucky in 1789, and located in Mason County, where he afterward owned an extensive farm of 1,000 acres or more of land. His son, Rev. E. Forman, was born in 1819. He is a prominent minister of the Presbyterian Church, and at present resides in Richmond, Ky. His wife was Miss Ellen, daughter of David Russell of Danville, Ky. Their son, T. T. Forman, was born in Richmond, Ky., Dec. 29, 1852, and is consequently just thirty years of age. He studied for a while at Centre College, Danville, and afterward entered the University of Virginia, where he graduated with distinction in 1871. After leaving college he taught school for a year, preparatory to studying law, which he began and finished under the tutelage of J. Q. Ward, in Cynthiana. Obtaining license from the Court of Appeals, he began practice in the city of New Orleans, La., in the winter of 1873–4, but soon returned to Cynthiana, where he has continued to practice with gratifying success. Mr. Forman was married in October, 1876, to Miss Lelia Campbell Donoho, daughter of M. Donoho, of Bardstown, who has borne him two children, viz.: Russell D., and Thomas V. He is a member of the Presbyterian Church, a Master Mason, and stands high in the estimation of the people as a lawyer and a gentleman. His political views are in accord with the principles of the Democratic party.

D. A. GIVENS, breeder of Jersey cattle ; P. O., Cynthiana ; was born in Harrison County, Ky., May 18, 1831; son of Alexander and Mary (Steele) Lamme; he, a farmer by occupation, a native of Bourbon County, filling the position of Colonel of Militia of Harrison County for many years, and dying in August, 1840; she, a daughter of Samuel and Nancy A. (Steele) Lamme ; natives of Virginia, but of Scotch descent. They had ten children. The grandfather of our subject, Samuel Lamme, came to Milford, near Cynthiana, about 1783, and was one of the brave and honored patriots who served in the Revolutionary army. He was one of the first Trustees of the schools of Cynthiana. January 19, 1855, Mr. Givens, the subject of this sketch, married Miss Margaret Keller, born in 1839, in Harrison County ; a daughter of Abraham and Polly A. Keller. One child has blessed their union—Lamme Steele Givens, born Jan. 14, 1866. Mr. Givens received his education in the schools and Academy at Cynthiana, and commenced business in the mercantile line in 1850, which he followed for many years, including a term as railroad agent, about 1855, but is now giving attention to farming and the breeding and sale of Jersey cattle, being the only breeder in that line in Harrison County, and his herd of Jersey cattle the only herd of Jersies in his county, about sixty in number, having at its head the bull Rex Alphea (4509). His Nelida represents the Niobe (99) family—Favorite of the Elms, Pierrott, Duke of Darlington, Uproar, Pansey, etc. He owns 175 acres of land, his home consisting of 25 acres, being called "Elmarch." Himself and wife are members of the Presbyterian Church, and he is a Democrat.

HUGH N. GARNETT, farmer; P. O. Cynthiana; was born in Harrison County, Ky., Sept. 2, 1850, son of William and Margaret (Newell) Garnett; he, born in Harrison County, where he and his wife still reside upon a large farm upon which he has a fine brick residence. The grandfather of Mr. Garnett, our subject, Hugh Newell, was a very prominent man in his day, he having represented Harrison County in the Legislature several terms. Mr. Garnett has been a farmer all his life, he having been raised one, and to which he naturally inclined, after receiving an education in the schools of his native county. He owns a fine farm of 140 acres of land, upon which he raises principally corn, wheat and tobacco. In 1875, in Harrison County, he married Miss Ada Lancaster, born in Parkersburg, Va., in 1850, daughter of Ransom and Lucy (Hard) Lancaster. His wife is a member of the Methodist Church South, and he is a Democrat.

LARKIN T. GARNETT, farmer and stockraiser; P. O. Cynthiana; was born in Harrison County, Ky., April 1, 1848, son of William and Margaret (Newell) Garnett, both natives of Harrison County, who were the parents of five children. After the ordinary education attainable

"CEDAR DALE" RESIDENCE OF L. VAN HOOK, CYNTHIANA, KY.

in the schools of his native county, our subject entered into the life of a farmer, to which he had been reared and has followed that occupation steadily ever since, making stock raising for some years past a specialty. He owns an excellent farm of 200 acres, his place being known as "Cottage Home." In April, 1881, he married in Harrison County, Miss Lillie King, born in Harrison, May 22, 1861, daughter of George Thomas and Susan (Craigmyle) King, of Harrison County. He is a Democrat.

GEORGE HOWK, grocer ; Cynthiana. George Howk, Sr., was born in Bracken County in 1822. He conducted the business of a general grocer for a while, when he removed to Covington, where he remained for six years, when he came to Cynthiana in 1865, and opened a large establishment of the same character. He accumulated a handsome estate, and died in October, 1881. His wife was Mary Chowning, daughter of John Chowning, of Harrison County. George Howk, jr., was born in Kenton County, Oct. 6, 1859. He received his education in Cynthiana, and upon attaining his majority, entered the grocery, queensware, and furniture business. He now has one of the largest and best stores of the kind in Central Kentucky. He was married in August, 1880, to Miss Mattie O'Neal, daughter of George O'Neal, of Paris, Ky. They have one child, George Barrett, born Sept. 23, 1881. In politics Mr. Howk is a Democrat.

THOMAS HINKSON, farmer, distiller and wholesale liquor dealer ; P. O. Cynthiana, Ky. Among the prominent self made men of Harrison County, we would mention the name of Thomas Hinkson, who was born in the county on March 12, 1819. His grandparents were natives of Ireland. His father, Samuel Hinkson, was born at Bullitt's Lick, and when quite young moved to Harrison County, and settled near what is now called Trickum, where he died about 1837. He married Susan Lyons, of Bourbon County; they had eight children born to them, six of whom were raised to maturity, four sons and two daughters. The fourth son, Thomas, of whom we write, enjoyed but very limited educational advantages; to use his own language, when asked where he was educated, he replied, "I never had any." He began life as an humble farmer without any means, and on Aug. 16, 1860, was married to Susan, daughter of John and Julia (Ecklar) Richardson, of Harrison. This union has been blessed with four sons, viz.: John, Wm., Sterling, and Wyatt, living, and Bennie, who died Nov. 14, 1877, in his fourth year ; and one daughter, Oteria. Mrs. Hinkson is a member of the Christian church. Our subject has never had any political aspirations, and consequently never filled any county office. He is however a member of the City Council of Cynthiana at this time, and has been affiliated with the Democratic party since the War. He has ever been an active, thoroughgoing business man, possessed of indomitable energy, and is regarded by all who know him as a man possessed of more than ordinary business capacity. In *his* case we have a fine example of what can be accomplished by perseverance and economy in a life time, beginning without a dollar, and worse than this, without educational advantages, and at this date (1882) owns 1200 acres of land in this county, 300 in Kansas, fine brick residence in Cynthiana; twenty shares of National Bank Stock, $15,000 or $20,000 worth of whisky distillery property, &c., &c.

CAPTAIN JOHN HAMILTON, farmer; P. O. Cynthiana. Capt. Hamilton was born near Gettysburg, in York County, Penn., in 1766, and died in 1863. His father, Wm. Hamilton, was born in County Tyrone Ireland, and emigrated to America several years prior to the Revolution, and settled at the place now called Ginger Hill, in Washington County, Penn. It was then called a frontier settlement. He married Mollie Bitener, also of County Tyrone, Ireland. She died about the year 1814. The fruits of this marriage were eight children, but one of which died under eighty years of age. His educational advantages were very limited, only having an opportunity to attend school about three months. He afterward learned to write his name on the head of a whisky barrel while distilling. His first business was in clearing up the forest and watching the Indians. Capt. H. was married in Bourbon County, in 1795, to Rachel Cook, who was born in Virginia about 1770, and died in 1813. Her parents were John and Peggy (Blair) Cook, both of Virginia birth. Subject was a Captain in the war of 1812. Commanded a company of volunteers, mounted riflemen, under Gen. Hopkins. His first march was to Fort Harrison, commanded by Maj. Zachary Taylor. Being but ten years of age when Independence was declared, he was too young to take any part in the Revolution, except, toward the close, he carried dispatches. He had born to him two sons, (Septimus, born 1805, and John in 1808), and five daughters (Peggy. born 1796; Polly, 1798; Sally, 1800; Nancy, 1803; and Caroline, in 1810). Capt. H. came to Kentucky in 1785, then in his nineteenth year. He and a few companions took a large canoe and came down the Ohio River to the mouth of Limestone Creek, now Maysville; from that they went to Ruddel's Station by way of the Buffalo trace. He remained in Kentucky till the whisky insurrection broke out in Western Pennsylvania, at which time he returned there by the wilderness route, and, arriving, found an army camped on his brother's farm, to put down the insurrection. His brother refused to pay the tax on his still, and hid to prevent being arrested, and had made up his mind to allow his still to be confiscated. At this juncture our subject went after dark, took the still out of the furnace and carried it to the Monongahela, which was some three miles distant, concealed it there, returned and secured the cap and worm, which he took to the same place, until he was ready to start. A few days later our subject, in company with a Mr. McCoons, procured a large canoe, loaded their distilling apparatus and brought the same down the Ohio to Limestone; they again hid it, and made their way to Ruddel's Station, where they got an auger and axe and made a rough log sled, to which they hitched a horse, and returned to Limestone and hauled their still, etc., to the Station. The following year they raised some corn and rye and manufactured the same into whisky, which was perhaps the first of that article ever made in the county, although the credit has been claimed by other parties. He only *doubled once a week*, and the men would come in every Saturday from the neighboring stations and drink as much as they could, and carry the *balance* home with them to supply their wants till the next Saturday. His yield was from six to eight gallons per week. He voted for George Washington at his second election to the Presidency of the United States, and voted at every Presidential election afterwards to the time of Abraham Lincoln's election. He also voted for a delegate to represent Kentucky in Virginia.

JAMES M. HODSON, farmer; P. O. Oddville; was born in Butler County, Ohio, Aug. 10, 1827; son of Joseph and Mary (Ramey) Hodson; he, born in Delaware in 1797; she, born in Nicholas County, Ky., in 1797; both now living in Indiana; they had eight children, James M. being the third in order of birth. Mr. Hodson received his education in the schools of his native county and at Cincinnati. He began his business life by learning the painter's trade, at which he worked for some years, but in 1868 commenced farming. In 1872, he entered into merchandising at Oddville, which he left in 1878, and has continued farming since, owning a fine productive farm of 200 acres. In Cincinnati, Oct. 2, 1849, he married Elizabeth C. Phillips, born in Bristol, England, Oct. 1, 1827, daughter of Peregine and Elizabeth (Chapman) Phillips; he, born in Bristol, England, June 30, 1800; she, born in London, England, Nov. 25, 1807. James M., our subject, has been blessed with but one child, James P., married and living at Oddville. He and wife are members of the M. E. Church South. He is an Odd Fellow and an Independent Democrat.

THOS. C. HAYS, deceased; was born in Bourbon County, Dec. 12, 1811, and died May 5, 1881; son of Walter and Catharine (Kendall) Hays; he, a native of Maryland and a farmer; she, of Bourbon County, Ky. They had nine children. Our subject received his education in the schools of Nicholas and Bourbon Counties, and, when a lad, learned the shoemaker's trade, in connection with which occupation he pursued farming until his death. At Oddville, Harrison Co., Dec. 6, 1838, he married Miss Rachel C. Whitaker, born August 24, 1815, at Oddvile, daughter of Joseph and Sukey (Horrey) Whitaker; he, born in 1779, in Harrison County; she, in 1781, in Bourbon County, Ky. Mr. Hays had nine children born to him, seven of whom are living: Sudie, Wm. T., Gusta A., Lucius, Joseph L., Abbott B. and Eva C. Sudie is the wife of Wm. H. Mathers; Wm. T. is married and living at Oddville; Gusta A. is the wife of Abraham Lingenfelter; Joseph also is married. Mrs. Hays has a fine farm of 110 acres. Mr. Hays was a member of the Patrons of Husbandry, a Good Templar and a Democrat. Mrs. Hays and her entire family are members of the Methodist Church.

BENJAMIN HUMPHREY, farmer; P. O. Robinson Station; was born in Bourbon County, March 9, 1813; son of Gilford and Nancy (Martin) Humphrey; he, a shoemaker by trade; born in Virginia in 1791, and dying in 1879; she, also a native of Virginia, born in 1791, and dying in 1872. They had nine children, Benjamin being the oldest. Mr. Humphrey, the subject of this sketch, attended school in Bourbon and Harrison Counties, and then entered into the life of a farmer, at which occupation he has continued ever since, at present owning a fine farm of 123 acres of land. Oct. 17, 1837, in Harrison County, he married Deborah Brannock, born in that county, Dec. 7, 1819, daughter of Robert and Elizabeth (Myers) Brannock; he, born in Delaware in 1772, dying in 1853; she, born in Maryland in 1789, dying in 1850. Mr. Humphrey has been blessed with a family of fourteen children, eight of whom are living: Enoch; Benjamin Franklin and Deborah, twins; Elizabeth; Sally; Laura; David A.; and Batson A. The family are members of the Methodist Church, South. Mr. Humphrey is a Democrat.

W. S. HAVILAND, farmer, P. O. Cynthiana. There are but few families of the Northern belt of the Blue Grass region who are able to trace the genealogy of their ancestry back to the seventeenth century; and of these few the name of Mr. William S. Haviland is worthy of more than passing mention in this history. His great grandfather, James Haviland, was born in New York, May 25, 1740, and died Nov. 25, 1786. He was a farmer, and married Miss Ann Hanniwell; seven children were the issue of their union, of whom was Israel Haviland, born March 12, 1765, in Harrison Purchase, Westchester County, N. Y. He was married to Miss Jane Anderson, Oct. 12, 1788, and died Oct. 23, 1819, in New York City, where for many years he had resided, engaged in the manufacture of boots and shoes. There were born to them fourteen children, of whom Robert S., father of our subject, was the second son; he was born Nov. 11, 1796, and emigrated to Kentucky in 1818. April 6, 1820, he married Miss Mary C. Stewart; his death occurred Aug. 8, 1858, at Havilandsville, Harrison County, Ky. He was educated for a sea captain, but spent most of his life in Kentucky. Of the nine children born to them, William S., our subject, was the second son. He was born March 22, 1823, in Harrison County, and Dec. 30, 1845, he married Mary E. Whitehead, whose death occurred April 13, 1849. He was married a second time on June 13, 1854, to Miss Mary Ellen Jones. His children are by his first wife, Mary F., born Jan. 17, 1847; Bettie, born April 11, 1849, and by his second wife, Charles B., born April 19, 1855; Robert S., born Dec. 23, 1857; Carrie, born June 30, 1863. Mr. Haviland is one among the best known and prominent citizens of Harrison County, a native of the county by birth; he has always taken a very active part in her development, aud has assisted largely in those enterprises which mark the progress of civilization. His early life was spent in assisting his father to conduct a large mercantile and manufacturing business in Havilandsville, at which place he at the age of twenty-one years embarked in the manufacture and sale of cabinet-ware on his own account. He continued this business until 1850, when he engaged in establishing the legality and collecting claims in the United States and foreign countries. He is the owner of one of the finest houses in Harrison County, located two miles north of Cynthiana on the Cynthiana and Falmouth Pike. His farm consists of 200 acres of choice land, and the brick residence erected by his design, is spoken of as the finest farm residence in Harrison County. He has always been an energetic and enterprising citizen, and bears a name and reputation of which his children may well be proud. Now, in the latter years of his life he is surrounded with those comforts and enjoying those pleasures that are ever the result of honesty, industry and economy.

J. H. HOLDING, farmer; P. O. Lair's; native of Scott County, born in 1818. His father was James Holding, who died in 1762, at the age of seventy-five. His grandfather, William H., was a native of Maryland, emigrated here early and settled in Scott County, and his great-grandfather emigrated here from England. His mother was Nancy Barnett, a daughter of Joseph Barnett, of Harrison County, who came from Virginia, she died in 1827. He married Mrs. Elizabeth Hill, daughter of David Jewett, of Bourbon County, and they have two children, named James David and Lair Belle. His son, James W., was in Capt. Jim Cantrill's Co. of Gen. John, H. Morgan's command during the war and returned home in 1865. Mr. Holding is a breeder of high grade stock, and belongs to the Masonic fraternity, and a Democrat, and he and his wife are members of the Methodist Church at Cynthiana, he being one of the stewards of the Church; he was also Lieutenant in Militia.

LEWIS A. JONES, deceased, was a farmer and blacksmith; born in Bourbon County, July 15, 1815, and came to Cynthiana when twenty-one years old, dying May 12, 1881. He was the second son of a large family born to Marshall and Cynthia (Reno) Jones, of Bourbon County. Lewis A. began life by learning the trade of blacksmith, and, although in very moderate circumstances, by attention to business soon acquired a good property in Cynthiana, which he sold out and purchased a farm in Nicholas County, where he remained some ten years, then bought at Scott's Station; there selling out, he bought a snug little farm three miles east of Cynthiana, where he died. He was a member of the Christian Church and a Granger. May 2, 1844, he married Sally E. Douglas. born June 16, 1817; daughter of John and Elizabeth (Strother) Douglas, both natives of Virginia. Mr. Douglas died Sept. 5, 1851, and his wife Feb. 20, 1850. The union was blessed with three sons and seven daughters. The widow of our subject, Mrs. Sally A. Douglas, and her daughters are members of the Christian Church.

ELIJAH J. JOHNSON, farmer; P. O. Oddville; was born in Harrison County, Ky., Oct. 2, 1838, son of David C. and Polly Ann (Mattox) Johnson; he, born in Clark County, Feb. 28, 1815, a farmer, and son of John and Betsey Johnson, natives of Virginia, who emigrated to Kentucky at an early day; she, born in Harrison County, Ky., in 1822, daughter of Elijah and Martha Mattox, natives of Kentucky. David C. died in March, 186[illegible], and his wife, Polly Ann, surviving him until March, 1876; they had four children, Elijah J., our subject, being the oldest. He received his education in the common schools of his native county, and was raised to farming, which he still continues. He was married in Harrison County, Feb. 22, 1859, to Susan Whalin, born May 30, 1839, daughter of Stephen and Eliza Whalin, which union has been productive of seven children, six of whom are living, viz.: Daniel R., Annie E., Effie, Crawford, Willie and John Q. Mr. Johnson has been School Trustee for a number of years, and Overseer of Roads. He owns a farm of 120 acres, his place being called "Crow Farm." Himself and wife are members of the Baptist Church, and he is a Democrat.

CHARLES R. KIMBROUGH, farmer and stockraiser; P. O. Cynthiana; was born near Cynthiana Dec. 7, 1834; son of Mager and Margaret A. (Redmon) Kimbrough; he, born in Virginia in January, 1800, was a blacksmith and farmer, and died Feb. 19, 1879; she, born in Harrison County in 1810, and died in June, 1857; they had two sons and three daughters, Charles R. being the oldest child. Mr. Kimbrough, our subject, received his education in Cynthiana, under the tuition of Prof. Smith and Rev. Carter Page, and he began life farming, in addition to which he has made stockraising and stockhandling a specialty. Director and Vice President of the A. & M. Association, now Agricultural, Mechanical and Live Stock Association. April 2, 1857, he was married to Mary A. Roberts, daughter of Benson and Mary (Russell) Roberts, and four children have blessed the union, two of whom are now living: John W. and Ida May. He is a Presbyterian and a Democrat; she a Methodist.

PAUL KING, dealer in ice, insurance agent and book-keeper Farmers' National Bank ; P. O. Cynthiana; was born in this county, Dec. 15, 1841, son of Paul and Sarah B. (Bell) King ; he, a native of Harrison County, born Aug. 18, 1806 a farmer by occupation, and dying March 8, 1872 ; she, born Jan. 24, 1822, and died Aug. 19, 1859. They had twenty-one children born to them, of whom seven died; those remaining were seven sons and seven daughters. Our subject received his education at the district schools at Mt. Zion, and was raised to farming. From 1869 to 1871 he was in the grocery business, but since the later date he has been engaged in the ice and insurance business, and has also filled the position of book-keeper for three years of the Farmers' National Bank. He resides on Main street, Cynthiana, where he has a fine two-story brick residence. In 1861 he enlisted in the Confederate Army, and served three years. Dec. 14, 1865, he married Miss Sallie E. Garnett, born Sept. 29, 1845, daughter of Capt. William and Margaret (Newell) Garnett, of this county, which union has been blessed with four children, viz.: Willie G., Lawrence Erwin, Lizzie Felix, and Gracie Marguerite. Mr. and Mrs. King are members of the Baptist Church, and he is a member of the A. O. U. W., and Knights of Honor, and is a Democrat.

JOHN W. KIMBROUGH, farmer and trader; P. O. Cynthiana; was born in Harrison County, Ky., May 30, 1822, son of Mager and Rachel (Kelso) Kimbrough, who were the parents of three sons and three daughters, John W. being the oldest. He was educated in the schools of his native county, and was raised to farming, in which occupation he is at present engaged, and in trading. In August, 1847, he was married in Nicholas County, to Eliza Victor, born in September, 1827, daughter of John and Elizabeth (Rule) Victor, and from which marriage there has resulted four daughters: Alice, Evie, Mattie, and Addie. Himself, wife and one daughter are Methodists, and two daughters are Baptists; he is a Democrat.

ROBERT KIMBROUGH, farmer; P. O. Cynthiana; was born in Harrison County, Ky., Sept. 25 1809, son of William and Elizabeth (Walton) Kimbrough; he, born in 1767, in Louisa County, Va., came to Kentucky in 1783, settling in Nicholas County, a farmer, and dying in 1852, at the age of eighty-six years; she, born in 1778, near Baltimore, Md., and dying in 18[illegible]3. They had six children. The grandfather of our subject, was Samuel Kimbrough, a native of England, who was brought to Maryland at an early day, and emigrated to Kentucky in 1783. Mr. Robert Kimbrough, after attending school the period ordinarily given the youth of his day, began farming, in which occupation he has continued ever since, and now owns a farm of 190 acres of land. Aug. 27, 1839, our subject married in Cynthiana, Miss Elizabeth Frazer, born in Harrison County, July 5, 1809, daughter of James and Kate (Hendricks) Frazer; he, a native of Pennsylvania, born 1768; she, of North Carolina, born 1780. Eight children have been born to Mr. Kimbrough; the names of those living are as follows: Mary, Eliza, James, Joseph, Ellen, Robert. Self and wife are members of the Reform Church, and he is a Radical.

POLLY ANN KELLER, farmer ; P. O. Cynthiana ; she is the wife of Abraham Keller, who was born May 4, 1809, and died in 1876 ; he was the son of Abraham Keller, who came from Pennsylvania. Mrs. Keller is the daughter of Hugh and Mary (Ewalt) Miller, and is the mother of ten living children, viz. : Hugh M., Margarget Givens, of Cynthiana; William Henry, who died in 1838 ; Mary, who died in 1843 ; Elizabeth Frazier, Alice Vanhook, Sarah E. Jones, James M., Abraham, Noah, Nannie, and Billy. She is the owner of 162 acres of fine land, two and a half miles from Cynthiana on the Cynthiana and Lair's Road, called " Pleasant Home," and she is a member of the Christian church at Mount Carmel.

J. G. KENNARD, farmer; P. O. Cynthiana; is a native of Mason County, Ky., and the son of William and Jane (Hunter) Kennard ; he was born in December, 1819 ; his father was a native of Northampton Tp., Pa., born Jan. 30, 1788 ; he was a farmer ; his wife, the mother of our subject, was a native of Lexington, Ky.; born Dec. 7, 1778. They have both been dead several years. They had eight children, of whom was our subject, J. G. Kennard. He received his education in Harrison County. In 1856 removed to Cooper County, Mo.; in 1859 returned to Harrison County, where he has since remained engaged in farming. He has a snug little farm, called "Locust Grove," pleasantly located on the Oddville and Cynthiana Pike. He was married, Oct. 30, 1856, to Miss Susan Thompson, a native of Harrison County, and the daughter of Robert and Emily (Lindsey) Thompson ; she was born March 28, 1813. Mr. and Mrs. Kennard have five children : Laura, born Sept. 22, 1857 ; Ida, born Oct. 22, 1860 ; Arthur, born Jan. 11, 1863 ; Nany, born July 12, 1865 ; and Robert, born Jan. 14, 1871. Mr. Kennard is a Democrat and a demitted member of the order I. O. O. F. at Cynthiana.

W. W. LONGMOOR, Clerk of the Circuit, Chancery and Criminal Courts of Harrison County ; was born June 21, 1840, in Kenton County, Ky., near the city of Covington. His father, George Longmoor, was a farmer, born in Bourbon County, but moved to Kenton County, where he resided till his death, in 1847. His mother, Amanda Hammett Longmoor, was a native of Mason County, and daughter of Samuel Hammett, a farmer of that county. His grandfather, Hugh Longmoor, was born in Scotland, and in early infancy moved with his parents to Ireland. Hugh Longmoor always called himself an Irishman. In early manhood he emigrated to America and settled in Bourbon County, Ky. He returned to Ireland once, on business, after he had settled in this country. He was married in Bourbon County to Miss Sarah Elizabeth Eaton, who was a native of New Jersey. He died in 1810, a rigid Puritan. George Longmoor, father of W. W. Longmoor, was born in Bourbon County, Ky., July 30, 1803. He married Miss Amanda Hammett, daughter of Samuel Hammett, in Kenton County, then called Campbell County, on the 18th of March, 1830. Samuel Hammett was born in Virginia ; came to Kentucky when young, and settled in Mason County ; married Mary Adamson in that county, where his daughter, Amanda, was born on the 15th of March, 1813. He subsequently moved to Kenton County. Mrs. Amanda Hammett Longmoor died in 1856. Mary Adamson, her mother, was also a native of Mason County, but her last residence was in Kenton County. W. W. Longmoor, the subject of our sketch, left the farm in 1854 to attend school in Cincinnati, where he remained three years, and two more were spent at the Farmers' College at College Hill, Hamilton County, Ohio. In 1859 he took a course of instruction at Bartlett's Business College, in Cincinnati, and afterwards spent some time in the office of Haven & Co's foundry, of that city, the senior member of which firm was his brother-in-law. In 1861 he enlisted in Company H. 2d Kentucky C. S. Infantry, but remained in the regiment only three months, being compelled to return home by injuries received in a fall. After his recovery he assisted in organizing two companies under the command of Captain Corbin, of Boone County, and accompanied them as far as Mount Sterling, when they were routed and several of the number killed by the Federals, who were concealed in the Court House and in the dwellings of the town. In attempting to escape he was captured by the Winchester Home Guards and confined in the Clark County jail ; thence he was sent the next day to Lexington, afterwards to Covington and Cincinnati, and then removed to Camp Chase, and finally to Johnson's Island ; and after several months' imprisonment was exchanged, in the fall of 1862, at Vicksburg. He then made his way to Murfreesboro, Tenn., and reported to Colonel Hanson, of the old Second Infantry ; thence proceeded to Alexandria, Tenn., and joined Company B. Second Cavalry, Colonel Basil Duke commanding, and remained with that regiment till the battle of Cynthiana, June 11, 1864, when he was permanently disabled. Up to this time he had participated in all the raids and engagements of the regiment, was captured in the Ohio raid, and after one month's imprisonment at Camp Chase, and then three months at Camp Douglas, he made his escape and joined his regiment at Wytheville, Virginia, after a most dangerous trip through Ohio and Kentucky. On the 11th of June, 1864, however, at the battle of Cynthiana, his career as a soldier came to an end, unless long and severe suffering may be reckoned a part of the soldier's professional life. He was wounded in the thigh in such a manner that amputation at the hip joint became necessary. For about two years he was unable to leave his bed, and so critical was his condition that the Federal post commander of Cynthiana, by request of General Morgan a few days after the battle, received orders from his superiors at Lexington to permit Mr. Longmoor to be removed to a private residence at

Cynthiana for more careful treatment. He was taken to the house of Dr. Abram Addams, then living near the Methodist Church, and all that skill, kindness, and unwearied attention could do was put in requisition. About four weeks after this arrangement was made a drunken Federal captain, on his own authority, intruded upon this private residence, and with a posse of negroes, carried the desperately wounded man, under a July sun, to the extemporized hospital, situated where the Christian Church now stands. On learning the facts of this outrage all parties were indignant, none said to be more so than the Northern officers themselves. But a month elapsed before it was thought safe to move the wounded man back to the hospitable mansion of Dr. Addams. Six months thereafter he was paroled, through the influence of Colonel Robert Kelley, now of Louisville, and removed, still on his back, to the residence of his brother-in-law, Mr. Augustus Haven, about six miles from Covington, Ky. Eight or nine months after this removal it was found unavoidable to amputate the wounded limb at the hip joint, an ordeal the peril of which all surgeons well know. The operation was performed by Dr. George C. Blackman, of Cincinnati, assisted by Dr. John Dulaney, of Kenton County. Four months after this operation, to the surprise of everybody, Mr. Longmoor was able to move about on crutches. At the battle of Cynthiana Mr. Longmoor was the advanced vidette, and received his injury when in the act of charging the Rankin House, in which a Federal regiment had taken refuge. The Federal colonel was fatally wounded, the regiment captured, and the Rankin House, now the Smith House, was taken. In 1866 Mr. Longmoor actively engaged in the dry goods business at Burlington; after eight months came to Cynthiana and embarked in the hardware business with his brother; and in 1868 he went into the furniture trade, in which he continued until 1874. In that year he was elected Clerk of the Circuit and Criminal Courts of Harrison County, a position which he still holds. Mr. Longmoor was married on Feb. 5, 1867, to Miss Louisa Addams, daughter of Dr. Abram Addams, deceased, of Cynthiana, and granddaughter of Major William K. Wall. One son, a bright boy, ten or twelve years old, cheers their pretty residence on Main street.

JOHN K. LAKE, lawyer; P. O. Cynthiana; was born Nov. 29, 1851, in Harrison County. His parents were William and Mary (Renaker) Lake; both of whom were born and raised in this county. Mr. Lake was a prosperous and well-to-do farmer. He died in 1855. Mrs. Lake was a daughter of Jacob Renaker; she died in 1851, when John K. Lake was an infant. He entered Wesleyan University at Millersburg, Ky., where he completed his course and received a diploma in 1871. He graduated in law from Washington and Lee University, Virginia, in 1872, and immediately entered upon the practice of his profession at Cynthiana. He owns 500 acres of good land, and resides in sight of Cynthiana; he divides his attention between the farm and the bar. He has never been an office-seeker, but served for a time as City Attorney. He was married, April 27th, 1876, to Miss Mattie Broadwell. The union has produced one child, Dawson. She was born Jan. 24, 1877. He is a member of the M. E. Church South, and holds the office of steward. He is a prominent member of the Masonic Fraternity, and has taken the Commandery Degree. He holds the office of Grand Sword Bearer to the Grand Commandery of Kentucky. Mr. Lake adheres to the tenets of the Democratic faith in polit cs.

W. T. LAFFERTY, lawyer; P. O. Cynthiana. This promising young man was born March 1, 1856, in Harrison County. His father, John A. Lafferty, a native of the county, served as sheriff for six years, besides filling numerous positions of minor importance. His wife the mother of our subject, was Frances E., daughter of John Henry, of Harrison. His father, James Laff rty, was a Pennsylvanian, and came to the Virgin State of Kentucky about the year 1802. W. T. Lafferty, after attending the common schools of the county, entered the A. & M. College of Kentucky University at Lexington, where he pursued his studies for a couple of years. His course through college was marked by plodding industry, and a determination to make his mark in the world. Returning from Lexington to Cynthiana, he began reading law with A. H. & J. Q. Ward. By dint of hard study he was enabled to pass an examination, and was admitted to the bar, Dec. 1, 1879. He has now a growing practice, and has been honored by the Democratic party with the nomination for County Attorney. He is a member of the Christain Church and is regarded as a model young man.

REV. RANSOM LANCASTER, minister, M. E. Church; P. O. Oddville; was born in Madison County, Ky., April 15, 1818; son of Littleton and Nancy (Hays) Lancaster; he a native of Spartansburg, S. C.; born in 1794; a farmer by occupation, who came to Kentucky with his father, Jeremiah Lancaster, in 1798, and died in 1838; she, born in Madison County, Ky., daughter of Solomon and Nancy Hays; they (Littleton and Nancy) had 11 children. Our subject received his education in the common schools of Daviess County, Ky., and began preaching the Gospel at the age of 21 years, which he has since continued, as a minister of the Methodist Church. He was admitted to the Kentucky Conference in 1842, and has been stationed in Virginia and Kentucky ever since; was Presiding Elder of the Greenbriar District for three years; on the Falmouth Circuit two years, and at present is on the Oddville Circuit. Mr. Lancaster was married in Scioto County, Ohio, May 13, 1845, to Miss Lucy White Hard, born July 19, 1818; daughter of Jonathan and Sophronia (White) Hard; he, born in Vermont, in 1791; she, in New Hampshire, in 1798. Five children have been born to Mr. Lancaster, one of whom, Wm. Wirt, died at the age of one year; those living are: Wesley A., Edgar B., Adelaide V., Mary E. He is the owner of 81 acres of fine land, which he works himself, his place being called "Sleepy Hollow." He is a Knight Templar and a Democrat.

JOSEPH LAKE, farmer; P. O. Cynthiana; was born in Pendleton County, Ky., April 13, 1827, son of Joseph and Mary A. (Smith) Lake, both natives of Scott County, Ky.; he, dying in 1829, and she in 1842; they having had six children. Mr Lake after receiving an education in the schools of his native county, continued farming, to which occupation he was reared, and has continued the same ever since, owning a farm of forty-one acres of excellent land. He was a soldier in the Mexican War, and has filled the position of Justice of the Peace in Pendleton, and is at present (Feb. 14, 1881,) a candidate for the same position. Dec. 22, 1852, he was married in Harrison County, to Miss Hannah A. King, born in 1833, in Harrison, daughter of George and Sally B. (Garrett) King; he, a native of Culpepper County, Va., who came to Kentucky in 1809, dying in 1874, aged 65 years; she, a native of Harrison County, and now living in Cynthiana. In 1865, Mrs. Lake died, having borne her husband seven children, five of whom are now living, viz.: Sally G., Felix, Carrie B., Joseph W. and John T. July 25, 1872, Mr. Lake married Josephine King, born April 12, 1838, daughter of John and Mary (Rankin) Keller, by whom he had two children, Harry H. and Keller. The father of the present Mrs. Lake, came to Harrison County in 1809, and settled on what is now known as the Oddville Pike. Self and wife are members of the Methodist Church, and he is an A. F. & A. M., and a Democrat.

MATTHIAS LAIR, Sr., farmer; P. O. Lair's Station; is a native of Harrison County, and son of Charles and Sallie (Anderson) Lair. He was born Sep. 5, 1813. He lived his earlier life with his parents, receiving his education from the common schools of his native county, and assisting in tilling the soil of his father's farm. In 1835 he married Roanna Lair, a native of Harrison County, and daughter of Matthias C. Lair. She has borne him eleven children, eight of whom are now living, viz: Charles F., John H., M. L., Matthias, Franklin P., Sally, Roanna, and Joseph. He is the owner of 122 acres of choice land, called "Locust Hill," upon which he raises all the principal crops and all kinds of stock. He is a member of the Grangers' Lodge, No. 154, at Cynthiana. He has held the office of Justice of the Peace for four years, and has been a school trustee for about thirty years. He is a Democrat. Mr. Lair is a man of good ability and knowledge, and is most respected by his neighbors, having taken a great interest in the welfare of his country as well as that of his fellow men.

JOHN M. LAIR, farmer; P. O. Cynthiana; is a native of Harrison County, Ky., son of Matthias C. and Jane (Anderson) Lair. He was born on South Licking, near Lair's Station, Oct. 7, 1820. His grandparents John A. and Sarah (Custard) Lair, were natives of Virginia, they emigrated to Kentucky in 1791, and settled in Harrison County at Houston's Fort. His father was a native of Harrison County, and during his life followed the occupation of farmer; he died in 1860, aged sixty years; he was a Democrat. His mother was a native of Harrison County, and daughter of William and Elizabeth (Miller) Anderson; she was a member of the Methodist Church; she died in 1868, aged eighty-three years. John M., the subject of this sketch, received his education from the common schools of his native county; at the age of eighteen, on account of his father's failing health, he became the manager of his farm. In 1869 he bought the old homestead farm, and remained on the same until 1876, when he sold it and bought the farm upon which he now resides, of George Redmon, having 167 acres of choice land, situated one mile from Cynthiana, on the Cynthiana and Lair's Station Pike, and is called "Sunnyside." He has been quite an extensive stock raiser of cattle, mules, sheep, and hogs. He was married in 1866 to Miss Mary S. Grimes, daughter of David and Zerilda (Hedges) Grimes. She has borne him two children; one of whom is living: Zerilda A. His wife died in 1879, aged eighty-four years. She was a member of the Christian Church at Leesburg, Harrison Co. He is a Democrat and a member of the Grangers' Lodge at Cynthiana.

JOHN LAIR, farmer; P. O. Lair's Station; native of Harrison County, and son of Charles and Sallie (Anderson) Lair. He was born in 1825. His father was a native of Virginia, and son of Matthias and Sallie (Rush) Lair. He received his education from the common schools in Virginia. In 1791 he emigrated with his parents to Harrison County, Ky. One year after their arrival in Kentucky his father died, leaving the burden of the family upon him. During his lifetime he followed the occupation of farming and also carried on a distilling business. He died in 1860, aged 86 years. His wife and mother of our subject, was a native of Harrison County, Ky., and daughter of Wm. Anderson; she was born in 1781 and died in 1860, aged seventy-nine years. They were the parents of twelve children, living to arrive at man and womanhood. John received his education in his native county, living with his parents to the time of their death, and is now still residing upon the old homestead. In 1850 he married Emily Redmon, a native of Clark County, Ky., and daughter of Robert Redmon. She died in October, 1854, aged twenty-eight years. By this union they had two children, one of whom is now living—Robert Wm. She was a member of the Baptist Church. He was married a second time, to Miss Maria S. Varnon, a daughter of Benjamin Varnon, and a native of Bourbon County, Ky., near Millersburg. She has borne him four children, two of whom are now living: Sarah E. and Laura, both living at home. His family are members of the Methodist Church at Cynthiana. He is the owner of 740 acres of choice land called "Evergreen Valley." Upon his farm he makes the raising and breeding of short horn cattle a specialty. He is a member of the Grangers' Lodge No. 154 at Cynthiana. He is a Democrat.

WILLIAM L. LOWRY, deceased; was born in Harrison County, April 17, 1837, and died March 28, 1877. His father, William Lowry, was born in South Carolina, and died July 4, 1869. His mother was Rebecca Stevenson, who was born Feb. 19, 1773. William L. Lowry was educated in Harrison County, and began life with farming. He was married in Harrison County, Jan. 4, 1871, to Elizabeth Bassett, who was born Aug. 6, 1829. She is the daughter of Jonathan Bassett, who was born in 1801, and Elizabeth Disher, who was born Dec. 13, 1803. He was twice married, and by first wife he had four children, viz.: William E., Kate, Anna and Scott. His surviving wife is a member of the Baptist Church, and she has a farm of 270 acres of land, four miles from Cynthiana on Connersville Pike, called "Hollow Spring." Mr. L. was in politics a Republican.

HON. T. J. MEGIBBEN, capitalist, P. O. Cynthiana, whose portrait and a view of whose residence and distillery appears in this history, is undoubtedly the most public-spirited citizen that ever figured in the history of Harrison County. Kentucky does not present a more striking exemplification of the old maxim, "Industry brings its own reward," than in the life of this gentleman, who, by his own efforts has become the most prominent farmer, distiller, thoroughbred stock breeder, etc., of Harrison County, and indeed, among the first of Central Kentucky. To follow this remarkable man from his first venture in business upon his own resources, step by step, along his very successful career, to the present time (1882) will certainly be full of interest, to the many enterprising and ambitious young men of the present generation. He was born March 28, 1831, in Clermont County, O. His father, William Megibben, was a native of Pennsylvania, and was born on June 4, 1808, near Brownsville. Early in life he moved to Clermont County, O.; engaged in farming, and continued the same until his death, which occurred July 1, 1845. He was married in Clermont County, to Miss Emily Galvin, who was born May 26, 1811, and died Nov. 5, 1857. There were born to them five sons: Thomas J., (our subject), William Jr., John W., Jeremiah and James K., and three daughters: Martha, Elizabeth, and Eliza J. At an early age, the subject of this biography was found among the pupils of the common schools of Neville, O., where he remained until sixteen years old, his attention then being turned to the more difficult pursuit of making his own living. On leaving school in 1847, he first engaged as a common hand in a distillery, at Neville, where he remained about two years. On the 6th of January, 1849, he came to Harrison County, Ky., and began work for the distilling firm of Findley & Foley, near Broadwell, his position being assistant chief distiller. After spending one year in this capacity, he took charge of the establishment as chief distiller, and operated it for the proprietor until about 1853. In 1854 Mr. Megibben engaged in agricultural pursuits. This year has since been remembered as the "dry year," and on account of the failure of crops there was no distilling done in Harrison County that season. In the Fall of 1855, in connection with J. L. Shawhan and James Snell, he leased what was then known as the Brannon & Shawhan distillery, with 75 acres of land attached, for a term of three years, which time proved very profitable to the firm, and before the expiration of said lease Mr. Megibben became the purchaser of the farm and distillery, and all the appurtenances thereunto belonging, and from that time to the present has been running the same successfully. In 1859 he bought the farm upon which he now resides, containing about two hundred acres, with comfortable improvements, and has since added to it from year to year, until now he owns 2,800 acres; being

H. E. Shawhan

the largest land owner in Harrison County. Different from most of our land kings, he usually cultivates and grazes all his lands himself. While he has added to his possessions in real estate, Mr. Megibben has also gradually taken a prominent stand as a breeder of fine stock. He purchased his first short-horns in 1868, and from that time to the present he has been one of the most successful breeders in the State. Among the most noted animals purchased by him may be mentioned the "10th Earl of Oxford," of Gov. Cornell, of New York, for $10,000; "Second Duke of Oneida," at New York Mills sale, at a cost of $12,000; and at the same sale, he and Mr. E. G. Bedford, of Bourbon County, bought in partnership the two-year-old heifer "4th Duchess of Oneida," at the enormous price of $25,000. Besides these, he has bought quite a number from the most celebrated families, at a cost ranging from $3,000 to $5,000 per head. His herd now numbers 100 head, selected from the best families in the country, and has the reputation of being one of the finest herds in the United States. In 1872 he purchased his first thoroughbred horse, since which time he has been running and breeding with moderate success. He now owns 50 head of this class of horses, besides about 100 head of trotters and roadsters. In Cotswold and South Down sheep Mr. Megibben also ranks among the leading breeders. He made his first importation of Cotswolds in 1854. His interest in breeding has led him to take an active part in the different associations pertaining to the development of these interests. He has been President of the Harrison County Agricultural and Mechanical Association for the past ten years. He has also been President of the Kentucky Trotting Horse Breeders' Association, of Lexington, Kentucky, since its organization in 1873. Strongly in favor of gravel roads, he agitated this question, and invested in one year $10,000 in turnpike building. While growing in prominence as a breeder of fine stock, he has also become one of the most liberal and enterprising distillers of the State, and now owns in whole or in part, and is operating six distilleries, among which is the famous Edgewater distillery, selected as an illustration for this history. He has at present about 12,000 barrels of whisky on hand. With such a magnitude of business on hand, it would seem there was but little time for him to devote to the political issues of the day, yet, for the past ten or twelve years, his name has been familiar to the people of Kentucky, as a man possessing unusual ability and tact as a politician. He represented Harrison County in the House of Representatives in the session of 1871-'72 and 1872-'73, and by being always vigilant and watchful, regarding the best interests of his constituency, and singularly prompt in devising measures best adapted to their wants, he was very justly honored with a re-election to the same position in the session of 1875-'76 and 1876-'77. In 1879, he was elected to the State Senate, and served during the sessions of 1879-'80 and 1881-'82, and is at the present time a member of that honorable body. So extensive is the business of Mr. Megibben, and so vast his resources, that he has extended the trade of his liquors to all parts of the United States, and even largely to Europe ; and has become the most widely known influential distiller and short-horn breeder, who has et lived in Central Kentucky. His liberality is by no means an uncommon subject of discussion. Those interested in the cause of religion and education in Harrison County and vicinity, are largely indebted to his generosity. The poor and needy find no cause for complaint when applying to him. Those, however, who are probably most largely the recipients of his favors, are that class of honest young men who may apply to him for assistance when struggling to establish themselves in business. Such men as Mr. Megibben will naturally be one of the marked features of any community, and his vast business transactions and great success have given him additional weight and distinction. He has always been a man of fine personal and business habits, with a high sense of social and business integrity. His great fortune is the legitimate result of uncommon business ability and judgment. His whole career presents one of the finest instances of a successful self made man, any where to be found in the history of the State. Mr. Megibben was married in Harrison County, June 23, 1853, to Miss Elizabeth J., daughter of Simon and Nancy (Brown) David ; the former born in Harrison County in 1811, and died November, 1849 ; eight children have been born to them, four sons, James W., John T., Perry R. and David C., and four daughters, Mary L., wife of E. W. Bramble ; Mattie J., wife of J. M. Kimbrough ; Nannie W. and Birdella. Mrs. Megibben is a lady of most exemplary character, pleasing address, and good judgment, and well worthy to be the life companion of one who is justly entitled to the good will and wishes of all those who know him—the Hon. Thomas J. Megibben.

JOHN W. MUSSELMAN, farmer, trader and wholesale liquor dealer; P. O. Cynthiana, was born in Harrison County, Oct. 2, 1838; son of William and Martha (White) Musselman; he, born in Harrison County, Ky., in 1797, a farmer, and dying Feb. 9, 1852; she, born in Daviess County in 1801, dying July 31, 1853; they had three children, J. W. being the youngest. Our subject began life as a farmer, which occupation he is engaged in at present, beside dealing in liquor and trading. He was married March 14, 1861, to Mary Rowland, born in Harrison, Jan. 10, 1842, daughter of Harvey and Matilda (Dills) Rowland, and from which union have resulted three children: William, Ettie and Maud. Himself and wife are members of the Christian Church, and he is a Democrat.

CAPTAIN W. C. MUSSELMAN, miller and Stamp deputy; P. O. Cynthiana; was born near Rutland, Harrison Co., Jan. 29, 1839; son of James and Eleanor (Stewart) Musselman; he, born in Harrison County, in 1799, a farmer, and dying in 1872; she, a native of this county, and dying in 1851. Captain Musselman received an education in the schools of his native county, and taught school and merchandised for some time, but since the war has been engaged in the Revenue service. In 1866 he ran on the Republican legislative ticket, but was defeated, as his party was in the minority, although running ahead of his ticket; General Green Clay Smith being his competitor. He enlisted in the Union Army on Oct. 9, 1861, as a private, and on the organization of his company was elected first lieutenant; was afterwards promoted to the captaincy of another company, and served throughout the war, participating in several hot engagements, among which may be mentioned Shiloh, Perryville, Wilson's Cross Roads, Atlanta Campaign, serving on staff duty with General Strickland, and fighting from Chattanooga to the sea; was captured at Lebanon and paroled. The Captain is one of the firm who purchased in January, 1882, the Licking Valley Mills, and are now running the same. Nov. 28, 1868, he married Kittie Sallie, born in Jessamine County, Oct. 7, 1840, daughter of Jacob Price; from which union there have born two children: Sidney Forrest and Helen. Captain Musselman and wife are members of the Baptist (Missionary) Church and he is a Republican.

B. F. MARTIN, farmer; P. O. Cynthiana; was born in Harrison County, July 20, 1835, son of James H. and Mary (Vanderen) Martin; he, born Aug. 31, 1803, a farmer, and dying in July, 1880; she, a native of this county, now dead. They had four sons and two daughters. Our subject received his education at Cynthiana and began life as a farmer, in which business he has continued in addition to that of trader. May 9, 1871, he married Mary E. Victor, born in September, 1839, daughter of James I. and Margaret B. (Rutter) Victor, which union has been productive of two daughters: Rillie Lee, and Flora Rutter. Self and wife are members of the Christian Church, and he is a Democrat.

WM. H. MARTIN, M. D,, farmer; P. O. Poindexter; was born at Robertson's Station, Harrison County, Ky., April 25, 1830; son of William and Catharine (Perrin) Martin. He, a native of Maryland, a carpenter and farmer, dying in 1831; she, born in Harrison County, and dying in 1865. Our subject, after receiving the education afforded by the schools of his native county, took a course in Transylvania College, Lexington, and then a course at Jefferson Medical College, Philadelphia, from which institution he graduated in 1851, and immediately began the practice of his profession; was at Claysville in 1857; at Cynthiana in 1858; Robertson's Station in 1868; when he moved to Poindexter, where he has remained. In 1853 the Doctor married Mary T. Whitehead, who died in 1855. In 1867 he married Jennie Garnett, daughter of Thomas T. Garnett, a native of Virginia. The following children have been born to Dr. Martin: Harry, Charley, Josephus, and Marian D. He has a farm of 425 acres of land, upon which he has erected a fine brick house, after his own designs. He has paid considerable attention to the breeding of shorthorns. Self, wife and family are members of the Baptist Church, and he is a Mason and a Democrat.

F. M. MILLER, dentist; P. O. Cynthiana. Rev. Alex. Miller, a Presbyterian minister, was born in Antrim, Ireland; educated at Edinburgh, Scotland; graduate. He emigrated and settled in Virginia, and was one of the pioneers of the Presbyterian church in this country. He was brought to a premature death by being thrown from his horse. His son John M., was born in 1749, in Rockingham County, Va.; moved to Kentucky in about 1807 or, 8. He served 3 years as an officer of the Militia vs. the British. He married Margaret Hicklin, of Augusta County, Va., who was of English descent. The result of this union was eight sons and two daughters. The third son, Dr. Alex. Miller, was born on the 26th of November, 1782, in Augusta County, Va. He studied medicine with Dr. P. Harrison of Virginia. He left his home in Virginia for Kentucky, on April 3, 1806, and opened an office in Richmond, May 15, same year. He was married Oct. 13, 1807, to Elizabeth, only child of Col. James Barnett, an officer of the American army in the war of the Revolution. (See other part of sketch in 1811. After his marriage he was induced by his wife's parents, to sell out his property in Richmond, and purchased a farm on Silver Creek, where he farmed and practised his profession for many years. By this marriage there were four sons and one daughter. The youngest son, Dr. Fayette M. Miller was born, 16th June, 1823, on Silver Creek. He studied medicine with Drs. Walker & Scott, of Richmond, Ky., and graduated at the Medical Department, of the old Transylvania College, at Lexington, Kentucky, in 1846, and afterwards took a course, and graduated the following year at the University of Pennsylvania, at Philadelphia. He returned to Richmond and began the practice of his profession in 1848, where he continued about 6 years, and in 1854 he purchased a farm in Jackson County, near Independence, Mo., where he immediately moved and continued his practice in connection with his farm, till the civil war broke out. He was among the first to enlist in the Confederate cause, under Capt. Holloway, a former citizen of Kentucky, and graduate of West Point. He died of typhoid fever in the army of Missouri, on April 29, 1863, in his 39th year. He was married on March 31, 1846, to Carrie W. Embry; she was born Dec. 26, 1826, in Richmond, Ky. By this marriage there were three sons and two daughters, our subject is the youngest son. After the death of Dr. Miller, his wife with her five children sold their farm, and in October, 1863, again returned to Kentucky, and settled in Richmond, where Mrs. Miller died on March, 1878, in the same room where she was born and married. Her father Talton Embry, emigrated from Raleigh, N. C., in Sept. 1781, to Richmond, Ky., and was one of the companions of Daniel Boone. Our subject was born near Independence, Mo., Nov. 27, 1856; came to Richmond, Ky., in 1863; was educated at Richmond High School under Profs. Chenault and Breck; after, engaged in the drug business at Richmond, for several years; abandoned that and studied dentistry, and graduated at Pennsylvania College, Philadelphia, Feb., 1880, and located at Cynthiana, the 19th of April, 1880, where he still practices his profession and enjoys the confidence and respect of his numerous acquaintances and friends in the county. Col. James Barnett, was one of the first magistrates of Madison County, in 1786, and in charge of the spies in 1784–5; he had been a Captain in the revolutionary war, in the Virginia line, on the continental establishment, and was Colonel of one of three regiments, under Gen. Geo. Rogers Clark, on his last expedition vs. the Indians, which proved abortive. He was also County Lieut. under the State of Virginia. He with Col. John Miller, Col. John Snoddy and one Mr. Adams, held the first court ever held in Madison County, represented the County in Legislature, and built the first mill in the County, and died the 27th of August, 1835, aged 87 years.

J. P. MADISON, physician; P. O. Cynthiana; was born near Cynthiana, Feb. 16, 1821; son of Robert and Rachel (Hayden) Madison; he, born in 1795, in Virginia, a farmer, was in the war of 1812, came to Kentucky and died in 1860; she, born in Harrison County, Ky., in 1797, and died in 1840; they had ten children. Our subject received his primary education principally in Harrison, Ky., after taking a medical course in Botanico-Medical College of Ohio, at Cincinnati, graduating from that institution, Feb. 24, 1843. He began the practice of his profession shortly after his graduation, in Elmira, Missouri, where he remained until 1848, when he returned to Kentucky, and practiced in Harrison County, locating in Cynthiana in 1863. In 1845, in Elmira, Missouri, he married Miss Eveline Hayden, who was born in 1830, and died in 1863, having borne her husband four children, three of whom are living: John R., Maude and Willie N. He married, as his second wife, Miss Helen McShane, born in 1845, a native of Ohio.

LOUIS M. MARTIN, attorney; P. O. Cynthiana. The ancesters of this gentleman on the maternal side came from Maryland. His grandfather, William Martin, reached Harrison County at an early day, and settled down to farming. His father, M. D. Martin, is also a substantial and reliable farmer who represented the county in the Legislature in 1868–9. His mother, Zerilda Sellers, daughter of David Sellers, was born and raised in the county. Louis M. Martin received his education in the Harrison Academy, and graduated from the graded school of the city in 1873. He then entered the law school of Kentucky University from which he received a diploma in 1874. He began the practice of his chosen profession in Cynthiana soon after his graduation, and now has a large and growing practice. He is a member of the Christian Church, and a Democrat in politics. Mr. Martin is of a modest and retiring disposition, but studious and energetic, and possessing the confidence and esteem of the intelligent and appreciative community in which he resides; it is safe to predict for him a future marked by much that will be gratifying to his friends.

J. H. McILVAIN, farmer and stock raiser; P. O. Cynthiana; was born in Harrison County, Ky., Sept. 9, 1812; son of Samuel and Elizabeth (Nesbett) McIlvain; he, born in Virginia in 1780, a farmer by occupation, and dying in 1852; his wife having preceded him in 1829. They had five children. After concluding his education in the common schools of his native county, our subject learned the trade of cabinet-making, which he followed for many years, but since 1865 has given his attention to farming, making a specialty of stock raising. His farm consists of ninety-nine acres of land. In 1834 he married Rebecca Humble, of Harrison County; born in July,

1814, daughter of Esquire and Katie (Bean) Humble· Mrs. McIlvain dying, Mr. McIlvain married in 1847 Lucinda Buzzard; born in 1811, and who died in 1871. In 1872 he married Lizzie Walter; born in 1829, in Bracken County, Ky. Six children have been born to Mr. McIlvain, three of whom are living: Sarah E. Martin, Lucy A. Dunn, and John W.; the two first by the first wife, and the last by the second. Himself and wife are members of the Methodist Church at Mount Zion, and he is an A. F. & A. M., and a Democrat.

J. A. McKEE, farmer and fruit raiser; P. O. Cynthiana; was born in Bourbon County, Ky., in May 1829; son of John and Eliza (Wilson) McKee. He, a native of Bourbon County, Ky., born Feb. 6, 1804; she, born in Fayette County, March 8, 1807. Mr. McKee, after receiving a primary education at the schools of his native county, took a three years' course at College Hill near Cincinnati, graduating in 1852, when he commenced farming, making that occupation, in connection with fruit raising, the business of his life. In fact, fruit raising is his specialty, he having upon his choice farm of 200 acres, known as "Cynthiana Nursery," 5,000 peach and 1,000 apple trees, besides sixteen acres in grapes, and ten acres in strawberries. His fruit is of the best varieties, having been selected with extreme care, both in regard to quality and adaptation to soil and climate. Mr. McKee has also paid some attention to fine stock raising, but is now devoting himself, as stated above, almost entirely to his nursery business. In 1854, he married Lydia J. Beatty, of Butler County, Ohio, who died in 1870, aged thirty-six years, leaving three children: John B., Anna E., and Elwood D. Mrs. McKee was the daughter of David E. Beatty, an advanced agriculturist of Butler County, Ohio. Mr. McKee, in 1874, married Mary R. Butler, daughter of Robert and Paulina (Findley) Butler, of Fleming County, Ky. Himself and wife are members of the Presbyterian Church, and he is a member of the Patrons of Husbandry, of Cynthiana, having been Secretary of the Grange at the point named. Is a Democrat.

JOSEPH MARTIN, SR., farmer; P. O. Cynthiana; was born in Harrison County, Sept. 6, 1811, son of Jonah and Rebecca Martin, both natives of Virginia, and the parents of eight children. Our subject received a limited education, after which he went to farming, having been raised to that occupation, and has continued in it ever since, until at present he owns a farm of 600 acres of land. In 1834, he married Miss Lucinda Taylor, born in Harrison County, in 1812, daughter of Tapley and Lavinia (Duncan) Taylor, natives of Virginia. Oct. 4, 1870, Mrs Martin died, having borne her husband ten children, eight of whom are living: William F., Lavinia, Rebecca J., Tapley T., James W., Mary, Sally, Harvey. Mr. Martin is a Democrat.

WILLIAM MAGEE, deceased; was born in Harrison County, Ky., Feb. 25, 1812, and died March 23, 1870. He was a farmer and the son of William Magee, of Virginia, who was the father of eleven children. Feb. 29, 1852, Mr. Magee, our subject, married Miss Margaret Doyle, daughter of Simon and Eliza Doyle, of Harrison County, and four children were born: William S., born Dec. 6, 1852; Edward L., Jan. 31, 1854; Eliza C., July 8, 1856; John H., Aug. 5, 1860. Mr. Magee held the position of Magistrate for some years, and was a Democrat. Mrs. Magee, the relict of our subject, received her education at the Cooper Institute, at Dayton, Ohio. Since the death of her husband, Mrs. Magee has continued the management of the farm herself, which is an excellent tract of 200 acres, her place being known as Locust Grove. Her great grandfather, Edward Doyle, came to Lewis County at a very early day, and accumulated a very large fortune. Her great uncle, John Doyle, was in the Revolutionary war. And died at the age of 116 years. Her grandfather and grandmother were natives of Harrison County, and her grandfather was in the Revolutionary war. Mrs. Magee is a member of the Methodist Church. Her husband was a Democrat.

JOHN J. McCLINTOCK, farmer; P. O. Cynthiana; was born July 7, 1826, in Bourbon County, Ky.; son of Samuel and Elizabeth Martin, a sketch of whose lives, written by Mrs. Martin, appears in another place in this section of this work. After receiving his education, our subject began farming, which he has followed throughout life. He was married in May, 1866, in Harrison County, to Nancy Scott, born in Harrison County, April 13, 1843, daughter of Thomas and Elizabeth (McShane) Scott, and four children have been born to them, three of whom are living, viz.: William T., Effie and Samuel. Mr. McClintock has a farm of eighty-four acres, and makes stock raising a speciality. Self and wife are members of the Christian Church, and he is a Republican.

JOHN McKEE, retired farmer; P. O. Cynthiana; was born in Bourbon County, Ky., Feb. 6, 1804, son of John and Betsey (McClintock) McKee; he, a native of South Carolina, born in 1779, came when an infant to Bourbon, and was the owner of Ruddel's Mills, dying in 1848; she, born in Bourbon County in 1783, and dying in 1874. They had ten children. Our subject received but an ordinary education, but began when young working in Ruddel's Mills. In 1833 he bought a farm in Harrison

County, upon which he lived for many years, and in 1875 moved to his residence one mile from Cynthiana, where he has a farm of 108 acres of land, his place being known as "Poplar Hill." In 1827 he married Eliza Wilson, born in Lexington, Ky., March 8, 1807, daughter of James and Elizabeth Wilson; he a native of Ireland, and she of Pennsylvania. Three children were the result of this marriage, two of whom are living: John A. and James W. In 1839 Mrs. McKee died, and in 1841 he married Nancy Thorn, by whom there has been one child, Miles S., who is engaged in handling agricultural implements in Cynthiana, being the largest dealer in that line in his section. His store is on Main street. Mr. John McKee has retired from active farm life, but is one of the leading citizens of the county, as is also his son, Miles S. The family are Presbyterians, and Mr. McKee is a Democrat.

JAMES W. McKEE, farmer; P. O. Cynthiana; is a native of Harrison County, and son of John and Eliza (Wilson) McKee. He was born March 26, 1836, and in 1856 married Miss Jane M. Turney, a native of Illinois, and daughter of William Turney, of Bourbon County, Ky. By this union they have had eleven children, ten of whom are now living, viz.: William T., now living in Bourbon County; Eliza W., wife of Joseph A. Thorn, of Bourbon County; Chas., Julia, Alice, Lizzie, George, Frank, Jesse and Turney living at home. His wife died in 1879, aged thirty-eight years; she was a member of the Presbyterian Church at Cynthiana. Mr. McKee attended the common schools of Bourbon County until he was seventeen years of age, when he attended the Farmers' College on College Hill, near Cincinnati, Ohio, remaining there three years. In 1856 he began farming and trading, which he has since followed, now having 580 acres of land upon which he makes the breeding and raising of sheep and mules a speciality. He is a member of the Presbyterian Church at Cynthiana. He is a Democrat.

DANIEL McSHANE, farmer; P. O. Cynthiana; is a son of Daniel and Nancy (Talbert) McShane; his father was a native of New Jersey, and the son of Edward and Catharine (Dunham) McShane, who emigrated to Virginia when Daniel was ten years of age, where he remained with his parents until he was seventeen years old, when he removed to Harrison County, Ky., in the year 1798, when he commenced business for himself by following the occupation of farming, continuing the same to the time of his death, which occurred in 1856. In about the year 1802 he was married to Miss Nancy Talbert, a native of Virginia, who bore him six children, of whom was Daniel, our subject. He was born in Harrison County, Ky., April 19, 1832, and in 1867 married Miss Mary Martin, a native of Harrison County, and daughter of Edmond and Elizabeth Martin. By this union they were blessed with one child—Minnie F., now living at home. His wife died in 1872, aged twenty-four years. Mr. McShane has always been a hard working man, and has succeeded in getting a good property. He is the owner of 385 acres of choice land. He is a member of the Presbyterian Church, and is a Democrat.

ELIZABETH MARTIN, P. O. Cynthiana. The grandfather of Elizabeth Martin, Richard Waits, emigrated from Pennsylvania to Harrison County, Ky., at an early date, her father, John Waits, born May, 1778, remained in Harrison County, Ky.; his father, Richard Waits, and family moved to the State of Ohio. The grandfather on her mother's side, Edward McShane, emigrated from Virginia to Harrison County, Ky., 1797 or '98, and died a few months after; he had bought land with a small improvement on it, as was common in that day, small improvements and large scopes of timberland between. This is the same farm her father purchased after his marriage with Mary McShane. It lies five miles east of Cynthiana on the head waters of Indian Creek. Her mother was born 1778, and married Sept. 27, 1798. Her father was a farmer, a man of good habits, good principles, and good mind; was a great reader, never better satisfied than when he had a book in his hand and a pipe in his mouth; he filled the Magistrate's place over twenty years, which entitled him to a term of Sheriffship according to the laws of that day; this he had filled by Deputy, as he did not wish to ride; he had never studied surveying, but to show his ingenuity, he made a compass and chain all complete, and surveyed with them to the satisfaction of those who employed him; they had twelve children, five of them still living, three sons, Richard Watts, born 1801; Edward Waits, born 1810; Charles Waits, born October, 1820; all are farmers and own farms and are men in good standing, members of the Christian Church. Mrs. Martin has one sister living in Indiana, Catharine Stewart, born Nov. 16, 1804, member of the Christian Church; her mother was a pious, good and industrious woman, did much for the comfort of her family and others, and had great sympathy for the poor and afflicted. They among many other good things, taught their children the worth of truthfulness and honesty, and they did not depart much from it through life. Her father remained on the farm where he first settled, till death; died 1855. Her mother died in 1850, both buried in the church yard at the Indian Creek Church. Elizabeth Martin grew up with the rest of the family, and was educated in the common schools. She recollects the cardingof cotton and wool on hand cards, for clothing; this was her first spinning. Her grandmother carded cotton and she spun. She came through the bulk of sugar making times; this was a sweet season with many bitters attached to it, but when she looks back and think of the children gathered around a sugar kettle, with a little wooden paddle in one hand and a cup in the other, making wax balls and eating them, looking like they never would want anything more to make them happy. She thinks she would like to be there again. Time rolled on and brought her to the year 1825; at this time she was married to Samuel McClintock, in Bourbon County, near Paris, and remained in Bourbon County till his death, July 14, 1827; he learned the gunsmith trade in Paris, followed it till his death; he left a son, John James McClintock, born in Bourbon County, 1826, raised and remains in Harrison County. 1833, she was married to Edmund Martin, born in Maryland. 1745, emigrated with his father, Joseph Martin, at an early date to Harrison County, Ky.; he settled on the head waters of Indian Creek, four miles east of Cynthiana, purchased more land joining, and remained on the same farm till death; he was a farmer, himself and wife attached themselves to the Christian Church in Cynthiana in 1840; a short time after there was a church organized at Indian Creek, and for convenience they moved their membership there. They had four daughters, Eliza Jane, born Jan. 31, 1835, and died in 1850; her father followed in 1851; they were buried at Indian Church. She remained on the farm with her three little girls till they grew up and married, and all died in their twenty-second year; Matilda Ann, born Feb. 27, 1840, married Dr. William C. Gragg, left a son, Eugene Walter Gragg; Nancy Elizabeth, born May 25, 1845, married James H. Waits; Molly Kate was born Oct. 31, 1847, married Daniel McShane, left a daughter, Minnie Frost McShane; these three daughters were members of the Christian Church. It is often said we have lost our friends, but Mrs. Martin feels like saying, they are not lost but gone before —that

"Like the last withered rose,
I must stand here alone;
Until God my life will close,
And I be taken home."

She has remained on the farm thirty years since her husband's death, and had it cultivated to make a support for herself and family. Mrs. Martin says: "Now as I am writing these lines, I see I have followed my life down to my eightieth year."

JAMES K. MEGIBBEN, distiller and farmer; P. O. Lair's Station; was born in Clermont County, Ohio, May 15, 1844, to Wm. and Emily (Gelvin) McGibben. His father died when he was but an infant; was taken care of and supported by his older brother. In 1854, at the age of ten years, he came to Harrison County and began to work for himself by doing such work as his strength and age allowed, principally on a farm; at the age of nineteen began working in the distillery of John Shawhan, and continued the same until 1866, when he married and began farming, in partnership with his brother, T. J. Megibben; followed the same for about one year, when he, with his father-in-law, J. L. Shawhan, bought a distillery in Scott County, near Stamping Ground. In 1868 he sold out his business in Scott County and became a partner in the distillery business with his brother. In 1868-9 he built the distillery known as the "Excelsior No. 38." He is now the owner of an interest in two large distilleries, and is building a large distillery and flouring-mill at Lair's Station; has a farm of about 350 acres of the best land of Harrison County, pleasantly situated at Lair's Station, on the K. C. Railroad and the Cynthiana and Lair's Station Pike. Upon his farm he has a fine brick residence, which is spoken of as one of the finest residences of Harrison County. In 1866 he married Miss Mary E. Shawhan, a native of Harrison County. He is a Democrat. He has been a prominent member of the order of A., F. & A. M. at Cynthiana for a number of years. He is a thorough and energetic business man, always first in any public enterprise, and is well worthy of the high esteem in which he is held.

G. H. PERRIN, retired physician; P. O. Cynthiana; whose portrait appears in this book, was born near Crab Orchard, Lincoln County, Ky., Nov. 9, 1794, and is the son of Josephus and Elizabeth Perrin. They were the parents of twelve children, of whom the Dr. was second eldest. His paternal grandfather, Josephus Perrin, Sr., removed from Charlotte County, Va., in 1774, and with his family settled near the Crab Orchard in Lincoln County, Ky. This was long before the organization of the State, and during the most perilous times of the "Dark and Bloody Ground" and while every male settler was compelled to act in the double capacity of farmer and soldier. The mother of Dr. Perrin was also a Perrin; her father, George Perrin, having been a farmer in Charlotte County, Va., and in 1784 removed with his family and settled in Edgefield district, South Carolina. He raised a family of eight children of whom the mother of this subject was the eldest daughter. Both these Perrins, together with two other of their brothers, entered variously into the army during the Revolution, and were soldiers during the entire war for Independence. The father of Dr. Perrin, Joseph Perrin, Jr., accompanied his father and family to their new home in Kentucky, and, although young, soon became conspicuous among the new settlers for his activity and boldness in aiding to expel the roving bands of Indians who from time to time made incursions into the new settlements. After the defeat of Gen. Harmer at the battle of Chillicothe, he aided in raising a company of volunteers, and as first lieutenant, marched with his company to the aid of Gen. St. Clair, and was actively engaged in the battle that terminated in his inglorious defeat. Some years after, having married in March, 1799, he removed with his family to Harrison County and located on the south fork of the Licking river, about eight miles below the town of Cynthiana. He there cleared and opened a farm, on which he reared a large family, and where he resided until his death, in his seventy-third year. He early took an active part in the political affairs of his State, and for over twenty years served his country in the Legislature of the commonwealth having been repeatedly elected to the Senate and Lower House, and took an important part in the proceedings. G. H. Perrin, the subject of this sketch, remained on his father's farm until his sixteenth year, in the meantime having the advantages of the common schools of his neighbourhood. During 1811 and 1812, he attended a select school in Scott County, under Rev. Thomas Smith. In 1813 he entered Transylvania University, at Lexington, in which institute he remained until he completed his literary, classical, and medical education. In 1814, while the war with England was still in progress, he left the university and volunteered for a six months tour in the army; joined the 16th regiment, and marched with it to join the army of the North-West, at that time commanded by General McArthur. He was in no general engagement, but had frequent encounters with the Indians. The war with England having terminated in 1815, his military life at once came to a close. On leaving the army, and when receiving an honorable discharge, he was highly complimented by his commander, General Gratiot, for the efficient manner in which he had discharged the very onerous duties of such a campaign. In compensation for military service then rendered, he has long been in reception of a pension from the Government. In the Spring of 1815, he returned to his home in Kentucky, and not long after he again returned to Transylvania University, and there remained until he had completed his medical education, and the last year of this term he was a private student of the professor of anatomy of the institution, the justly celebrated Benjamin W. Dudley. Late in the fall of 1817, by the urgent request of his relatives, he began practice in Edgefield District, S. Car., remaining there in practice for eight years. At the end of that time, in consequence of the climate, and his own health having been completely broken down, he determined to move back to Harrison County, in which he had been raised, and settled in Cynthiana. For two years he was unable to engage in the practice, only to a limited extent. As soon as his health was restored he gradually acquired a large and lucrative practice, which he retained until near 1840, when his health again failed. Having, however, accumulated a competency for life, he abandoned forever the practice of medicine. In November, 1819, he was married to Miss Arabella, daughter of Mr. John Edwards, of Bourbon County. Her paternal grandfather, Col. John Edwards, upon the organization of the State, was elected by the Legislature one of the two senators first sent by the State to the Congress of the United States. Her maternal grandfather, Colonel James Garrard, had fortunately become the possessor of a patent that had been located on 10,000 acres of the richest land in Kentucky, and which secured to him a large fortune for life. He was eight years Governor of Kentucky. With his wife, who still remains to him, Dr. Perrin has lived a happy life of over sixty years; both of them, long years ago, became members of the Protestant Episcopal church, and have ever since remained consistent communicants of the same, and he, by his extensive charities and large liberality, was among the most efficient members in originating and placing on a permanent basis the Church of the Advent, Cynthiana. Having no taste for it, he never engaged in politics; was a Whig, and voted with that party until its dissolution; in the late war between the Northern and Southern States he sympathized strongly with the South, and during the war and since, has voted uniformly with the Democratic party. His first presidential vote was for James Monroe. Having hitherto led a very active life, after his retirement from the practice of medicine,he engaged actively in agricultural pursuits, and by his untiring energy soon became one of the model farmers of the county. He took great delight in raising fine stock, and was among the first farmers to introduce into Harrison County the highly prized and valuable short-horn Durham, which he bred extensively, frequently competing successfully at the different fairs, with the most approved breeders of Bourbon and Fayette Counties. For twenty years he enjoyed the pleasures of a farmer's life, and counts those the happiest years of his life. But, on the close of the war between the North and South, he, with a large number of Kentuckians, suffered heavy pecuniary losses by the emancipation of the negroes; and, being advanced in life, he determined to bring to a close his agricultural life as a farmer. He consequently sold his splendid farm of nearly 500 acres, lying adjoining Cynthiana. Not long afterward he purchased a handsome home within the limits of Cynthiana, where he now resides, highly esteemed by all who know him as a gentleman and a Christian.

A. PERRIN, lawyer; P. O. Cynthiana; was born Christmas day 1840, in Harrison County, near Robinson Station, K. C. R. He is a son of Josephus and N. E. (Baldwin) Perrin, daughter of Jonah Baldwin, of Springfield, Ohio. His father is a native of the county, a prosperous farmer, who still lives to enjoy the confidence of his neighbors, and the companionship of his faithful wife. The grandfather of our sketch was Josephus Perrin. He attended the common schools of the county, until he had acquired the rudiments of a common English education, when he entered the Kentucky Military Institute, from which he was graduated in the class of 1861. He then taught school for a year, when, the war breaking out, he enlisted in Col. E. F. Clay's Battalion of Confederate Cavalry, and was desperately wounded the very next day, at the battle of Cynthiana, and was confined to his bed until the close of the war. He read law with W. W. Trimble, and was admitted to the bar in 1868. He was elected County Attorney in August, 1870, and re-elected in 1874. Served as Master Commissioner of the Harrison Circuit Court for ten years. In October, 1881, Mr. Perrin renewed the publication of the Cynthiana *Democrat*, which had been suspended, and of which he is now the editor and proprietor. He was married in 1868, to Miss Mary E. Perrin, who died June 2, 1875. He is a member of the Presbyterian church, and stands high in the estimation of those who know him.

J. W. PECK, banker; P. O. Cynthiana; was born Nov. 7, 1819, in St. Lawrence County, N. Y., and is the son of Hiram and Wealthy (Kilburn) Peck. Mr. Peck came to Cynthiana as a school teacher, and subsequently engaged in the dry goods business. Time proved him to be a financier of no mean ability, and in the mercantile and manufacturing business he has been one of Cynthiana's leading spirits. He has engaged in the whole sale and retail grocery trade; distilled for six years, and run a woolen factory and flouring mill, all of which have been conducive to the general welfare of the public, in the disbursement of money to employes. Retiring from active business, Mr. Peck is enjoying the fruits of his industry and economy.

O. J. POINDEXTER, farmer; P. O. Cynthiana; was born in Harrison County, Ky., near Poindexter's Station, July 16, 1817; son of James and Martha (Ammon) Poindexter; he, born in Louisa County, Va., July 6, 1787, a miller by occupation, who came to Kentucky when six years of age, with his parents, and died in 1865; she, born in Bourbon County, May 11, 1789, and died in 1863. They had seven children After receiving an education in the schools of his native county, our subject began clerking in the store of his father at Poindexter Station. This was in 1832, but in 1836 he commenced the milling business, which he continued until 1839, when he removed to Missouri and engaged in farming. In 1841 he returned to Harrison County and again entered the milling business. In 1848 he purchased the farm upon which he now resides, having remained there since its purchase. His farm comprises 300 acres of choice land, and he makes a specialty of raising tobacco. Poindexter Station, on the Kentucky Central Railroad, was named from the family of our subject. Nov. 5, 1857, Mr. Poindexter married Malinda J. Haviland, born Nov. 17, 1828, in Harrison County, daughter of Robert S. and Mary C. (Stewart) Haviland, of Harrison, from which union there have been born six children, five of whom are living: James R., Mattie E., John W., Henry H., and Maggie E. Self and wife are members of the Methodist Church. He is a member of the Grangers' Lodge, Mt. Zion, No. 250, and a Democrat.

FRANK PARKS, farmer and trader; P. O. Cynthiana; born in Harrison County, April 8, 1835; his parents were from Maryland, and died soon after emigrating to Kentucky. At the age of fifteen he learned the blacksmith's trade, having had little opportunity to prosecute his education. He has been engaged in farming and trading most of his life, in which business he has been very successful. On Nov. 14, 1865, he married Mattie, daughter of James and Jane (Hamilton) Carroll; the former of Scott and the latter of Fayette County. Five children have been born to them, two lovely little girls, of whom survive, Minnie, born Aug. 20, 1868, and Jennie, born Feb. 3, 1871. Mr. Parks is a Democrat in politics. He is a member of the Cynthiana Commandery of Knight Templars. Of late he is paying considerable attention to the breeding of short-horn cattle. Mr. Parks is in communion with the Christian Church at Cynthiana. He served during the late war in the 1st Ky. Mounted Riflemen.

"WOOD LAND HALL" RESIDENCE OF NOE DILLS, NEAR CYNTHIANA, KY.

GEORGE REDMON, farmer; P. O. Cynthiana; was born on the old homestead of the family, March 29, 1816, son of (Charles and Mary (Reibolt) Redmon; he, born above Pittsburg in 1779, and emigrated with his parents to Bourbon County, and learned the saddler's trade at Millersburg. Settled off South Fork of the Licking, and afterward moved to the farm, one and a half miles from Cynthiana, where he died; his wife was a native of Lexington, born about 1782, and died in 1856; they were the parents of eight children. Our subject was in the clerk's office for eighteen months, with Samuel Endicott, Clerk of the County, but has followed farming since 1870, at present owning 183 acres of land, for which he gave $18,300 cash, a nice residence in Cynthiana, and a vacant lot that cost $4,000. In 1870, he was elected Police Judge of Cynthiana for four years, which position he filled creditably, and to the entire satisfaction of his fellow citizens. Previous to his removal to his magnificent farm, Mr. Redmon had sold goods in Cynthiana for about eight years. Nov. 14, 1839, he married Eliza Lair, born Oct. 12, 1820, daughter of Charles Lair, a native of Rockingham County, Va., by which union there were two daughters, one of whom died in 1859, and the other married Joseph Cosby. Mrs. Redmon dying in 1847. Mr. Redmon married, Jan. 2, 1855, Mrs. Ruth T. McGee, danghter of Henry and Eliza (Miller) Warfield, who died in 1875, having borne one child, which died in infancy. March 13, 1877, he marrred Miss Mattie E. Martin, daughter of William and Delilah J. (Brannock) Martin, of Harrison County. Mrs. Redmon is a member of the Methodist Church. Mr. Redmon was a Union man during the war, and he is a Republican.

CAPTAIN B. T. RIGGS, miller and grain dealer; P. O. Cynthiana; was born in Paris, Feb. 25, 1839, son of Benjamin M. and Agnes W. (Wilson) Riggs; he born in Kentucky, Jan. 6, 1799, and dying in 1839; she born in Falmouth, Jan. 14, 1801 and dying in 1874; they had three sons and three daughters. Our subject was educated in Falmouth and was engaged in clerking from 1858 till 1861, when he enlisted in the Federal Army as a private, from which he was promoted to a second lieutenancy, then to first lieutenancy, and in 1863 to a captaincy; the last two months of service being spent on the staff of General Absalom Baird. Captain Riggs participated in several warm engagements, among which may be mentioned Richmond, Ky., Hoover's Gap, and Chickamauga; was taken prisoner and confined in Libby Prison seven months, and other prisons, from which he escaped and gained the Federal lines at Savannah, after many hardships and much weary night travel. From 1869 to December, 1881, he was engaged in revenue service, having been previously engaged in merchandising in Williamstown for about four years; was also member of the Council in Williamstown. April 26, 1866, he was married to Kate M. Kerr; born in Fayette County, Ky., Oct. 31, 1840; daughter of John and Rachel (Fry) Kerr, both of whom are dead. Two children have been born to Captain Riggs: Edna W. and Kerr Tunis. Himself and wife are Presbyterians, and he is an I. O. O. F., A. Y. & M., and a Republican.

MILTON J. RANKIN; P. O. Cynthiana; was born in Harrison County, Ky., July 7, 1825; son of Samuel and Mary (Hamilton) Rankin; he, born in this county, Dec. 4, 1792, a farmer and trader by occupation, and dying in May, 1868; she, also born in this county, Dec. 2, 1792, and dying March 15, 1857; they had six children. Our subject married in Harrison County, March 1, 1853, Miss Lydia A. Veach, born March 19, 1833; daughter of David and Mary (Broadwell) Veach; he born Dec. 9, 1792; she, May 22, 1799, all of this county.

JOHN W. RENAKER, druggist; P. O. Cynthiana; was born in Harrison County, Ky., August 22, 1844, son of William B. and Martha (Bennett) Renaker; he, a farmer, born in Harrison County, and dying in Cynthiana in 1881, aged 58 years; she, also of Harrison County; they had seven children. Our subject received his education at Millersburg College, Ky.; was raised a farmer. but left that occupation and commenced the drug business in 1867. May 14, 1867, Mr. Renaker married Miss Kate Houston, daughter of Wesley and Matilda Houston, of Cynthiana, and from which union there have been born four children, only one of whom is now living—Houston, born August 10, 1878. Mr. Renaker is one of the firm cf Renaker Bros., the leading druggists of Cynthiana, located on Main street. He and wife are members of the M. E. Church, South.

WILLIAM T. REDMON, farmer; P. O. Cynthiana; is a native of Harrison County, and son of Charles and Mary (Rybolt) Redmon; he was born June 17, 1805 His father was a native of Pennsylvania, and brought to Bourbon Counry, Ky., by his parents when he was quite young, and settled on the place known now as Flat Run. He remained with his parents to the age of twenty-one, when he removed to Cincinnati and engaged in the saddler's business, which he followed for three years, at the expiration of that time, he returned to Kentucky, settling in Harrison County, on a farm one and a half miles from Cynthiana, having 900 acres of land. He was born in 1787, and died in 1851. His wife was born in Lexington, Ky., and with her parents settled on Flat Run, Bourbon County; she died in 1856, aged seventy-two years; they were the parents of twelve children, eight of whom living to the age of maturity. William Redmon, the subject of our sketch, lived his earlier days with his parents, receiving his education and assisting his father in tilling the soil of his farm. In 1833, he married Susan Williams, the oldest daughter of Squire John Williams, of Harrison County, Ky.; she has borne him four children, three of whom are now living, viz.: Sally W., Nancy H., and Mary S. His wife died in 1847, aged thirty years. She was a member of the Christian Church. In 1851, he married his second wife, Amanda F. Berry, daughter of John Berry, of Harrison County; she has borne him three children, viz.: Eva, William B. and Fannie P. Mr. Redmon first commenced farming upon the same farm he now is living on, having seventy acres of choice land, called "Elm Wood." Self and family are members of the Christian Church at Cynthiana. He is a Democrat. He was County Surveyor of Harrison County for nearly thirty years.

THOS. RORER, deceased; was born in Philadelphia, Pa., Jan. 16, 1824, and died Oct. 29, 1878. He was the son of Thomas Rorer, who was born in Philadelphia in 1796, and died in 1867. His mother was Elizabeth Caster, born in 1791, in Pennsylvania, and being a third cousin of General Washington. They had six children. Our subject received his education in Philadelphia, and began life by learning the trade of plasterer, after which he went into merchandising for a while, and then to farming and running a saw-mill. June 1, 1851, in Harrison County, he married Miss Frances McLean, born March 11, 1826, daughter of Robert and Cynthia (Lewis) McLean; he, of Mason County, Ky.; she, of Harrison County. Mr. Rorer's union with Miss McLean produced nine children, seven of whom are living: William, Elizabeth, Thomas, Annie, Charley, Francis and Johnny. Mr. Rorer served in the Federal army as Captain, being in the 40th Kentucky Regt. The widow of Mr. Rorer owns a snug farm of 150 acres of excellent land, the place being called "The Heights." She and family are members of the Methodist Church. Mr. Rorer was an Odd Fellow and a Republican.

MILTON J. RANKIN, farmer; P. O. Cynthiana; was born in Harrison County, July 7, 1825. His father, Samuel, was born in Harrison County, Dec. 4, 1791. He followed the occupation of farmer and trader in Harrison County until 1856, when he removed to Bath County, also following farming to the time of his death, which occurred in May, 1826. His wife, and mother to our subject, was born in Harrison County and died in 1854, aged fifty-eight years; they were the parents of six children. Milton J., our subject, lived with his parents his earlier days, receiving his education and assisting in tilling the soil of his father's farm. At the age of twenty-one he began farming on his own account, which he has since continued to follow. In 1853, in Harrison County, he married Miss Lydia Veach, a native of Harrison County, and daughter of David and Mary Veach. They are the parents of three children, two of whom are now living, viz: Sally B., wife of Horace Benton, living in Clark County, Ky., and Comes V., living at home. He is the owner of a well improved farm of 140 acres of choice land, called "Walnut Hill," situated three miles east of Cynthiana, on the Cynthiana and Millersburg Pike. Upon his farm he makes stockraising a specialty, as horses, cattle, sheep and hogs. He was at one time a U. S. Storekeeper and Gauger. His wife is a member of the Methodist Church, and in politics he is a Republican.

P. S. REEVES, revenue collector; P. O. Cynthiana; born in Ross County, Ohio, Dec. 18, 1842; his father, William Reeves, was a native of Ireland, where he was born in 1799; he married Julia Ann Ryan, who was born in Scotland in 1800; they emigrated to Ohio in 1840, and raised a family of twenty-one children; P. S. Reeves whose name heads this sketch, received his early education from the public schools of Kenton County, Ky.; he afterwards attended the Herald College of Cincinnati, from which institution he was graduated with honor in 1866; during the "late unpleasantness" he was Captain of Co. G., 23d Kentucky troops, and served with distinction during the war; after graduating from college, he engaged as a clerk in Cincinnati mercantile firm; Nov. 10, 1880, he married Elizabeth, daughter of Berry and Isabella (Edwards) Kennedy, of Woodford county; one child has been born to them, which died in infancy. Mr. Reeves is a Republican in politics, and a member of the Masonic fraternity.

HENRY E. SHAWHAN, deceased. Henry E. Shawhan, late president of the National Bank of Cynthiana, farmer, and prominent business man of Harrison County, was born Nov. 20, 1805, and died at his residence, one mile west of Cythiana, March 4, 1882. His parents were Joseph and Sallie (Ewalt) Shawhan. His grandfathers, Daniel Shawhan and Henry Ewalt, were both from Alleghany County, Pa. His father, Joseph Shawhan, was born in that County, and emigrated to this State with his parents in 1788, and settled in Bourbon County. In 1816 he removed to Harrison, where he died on Sept. 15, 1871. He was a soldier of the war of

1812; was for several terms a member of the Kentucky Legislature; followed agricultural pursuits; was of Scotch-Irish extraction; and was one of the most influential and valuable men in his county. At the time of his death he owned and had interest in several of the largest distilleries in the country, and owned more land than any man in Harrison County. He was married in the year 1800 to Sallie, daughter of Henry and Elizabeth Ewalt, of Bourbon County. The result of this union was seven children, only one now living, Mrs. Margaret Miller, who lives with her son, William Miller, in Bourbon County. She is well stricken in years. Sallie Ewalt, our subject's mother, was of German origin, but was a Bourbon County woman by birth, and also belonged to one of the old pioneer families of the State. Her son, Henry E., of whom we write, was raised on the farm, his education being confined to the country schools as organized in his boyhood days. He was actively engaged on the farm till 1838. In that year he turned his attention to the making of whisky, and built a distillery in Harrison County, four miles from Cynthiana; and from this time till 1869, in connection with his farming interests, he continued distilling, and buying and selling whisky of various distillers in the county. In 1864 he took an interest in the grocery house of Shawhan & Jewett, of Cynthiana; the following year formed a partnership with J. Shawhan in the same business; in the following year bought the interest of his partner, and has since been sole proprietor of one of the largest grocery businesses in Cynthiana. In 1874 he became one of a number of capitalists who undertook to build a narrow gauge railroad from Mount Sterling to the Mountains, or the coal and iron region of Eastern Kentucky. Several miles of this road are in actual operation, and its great local importance is now largely felt. It is the ultimate purpose of the originators of this valuable enterprise to terminate the road at Cynthiana. Mr. Shawhan was for several years one of the directors of this road, and was largely interested in the stock and the future success of the road. In 1871 he was elected president of the National Bank of Cynthiana, which position he ably filled to the time of his death. He has always been a Democrat, and during the rebellion, his sympathies were strongly with the cause of the South. He was a man of sterling qualities, unmarred by deep prejudices; of plain, unaffected, honest manners; moved through life without show or pretense; was of irreproachable integrity of character; and was a man of great physical endurance. Mr. Shawan was three times married: Oct. 20, 1835, to Mary Varnon, daughter of John Varnon, a Bourbon County farmer; she died in 1842. Two years afterwards he was married to Mrs. Sallie Pugh (*née* Cantrill), who died in 1857. In 1859 he was married to Mrs. Sallie Cult, a native of Bourbon County, and daughter of John Ravenscraft, a farmer of that county. He is the father of eight children by these marriages.

C. M. N. STODDARD, jeweler; P. O. Cynthiana; was born in Portage County, Ohio, in December, 1837; son of Henry and Amelia Stoddard; he, a native of Connecticut, and a bridge builder by occupation; died in 1845; she, a native of New York State. They had seven children. Our subject received his education in the schools of his native county, Portage, Ohio, and began life as a farmer, but in 1861 opened in the watch and jewelry business in Circleville, Ohio, where he remained for some years, and finally, in 1877, removed to Cynthiana, Kentucky, opening in the same business that he conducted in Ohio, and at once taking the position of the leading jeweler of Cynthiana. He is one of the best workmen in the State, or anywhere else, for that matter, and keeps constantly on hand a fine stock of goods in his line. In 1878, in Carlisle, Ky., Mr. Stoddard married Miss Lizzie M. Webb, born in Harrison County, Ky., daughter of Newton Webb, Esq., by which union there has been one child, which is now dead. His wife is a member of the Christian Church, and he is a Democrat.

J. H. SMISER, M. D.; P. O. Cynthiana; was born in Harrison County, Ky., July 27, 1638, and is the son of Denos Smiser, who was born in Harrison County, July 4, 1814, and is now a farmer in Bates County, Mo.; and grandson of George Smiser, who was born in Maryland, and emigrated to Kentucky as early as 1795; the Doctor's mother was Miss Louisa Smith, daughter of Michael and Mary Smith, of Harrison County; the Doctor received his literary education in the common schools of Harrison County and at Eminence, and graduated as an M. D. in Missouri, in 1868, beginning practice in Cynthiana the same year; he began life as a farmer; followed that business eight years, but gave it up for the study and practice of medicine, in which his natural talent and ability have been proved by his success; in 1870, the Doctor was married to Miss Mary, daughter of John H. Ewalt, of Bourbon County; four children have been born to them, viz: Hunt A., Louisa H., Todd, and Earle. The doctor is a member of the Christian Church, is a Democrat, and a Master Mason.

CHARLES W. SHARP, farmer; P. O. Shady Nook; and son of John W. and Lucy (Collier) Sharp; he was born July 17, 1844. His father was born March 11,

1803, in Scott County, Ky., and was brought to Nicholas County, Ky., when but four years of age. He has lived in Headquarters Precinct, Nicholas County, for seventy-four years, and during that time has followed the occupation of farming; he has a farm of 250 acres. In 1834 he was elected member of the Legislature, being the first one elected in Nicholas County by the Whig party; he is now a Republican. He was at one time U. S. Gauger and is now U. S. Deputy Collector. He and his wife are members of the Christian Church at Indian Creek. Charles W. lived with his sister in Illinois, where he received his education; in 1865 he taught school. In 1866 he bought a farm in Harrison County of 100 acres. In the same year he married Susan P. Wilson, who has born him four children, viz: Lulu, Margaret, John M. H., and Eliza W. In 1871 he commenced merchandising at Scott Station, which he followed until August, 1873, when he was appointed U. S. Storekeeper and Gauger. He now is the owner of 112 acres of land. He is a Republican, and himself and family are members of the Baptist Church at Indian Creek. He is a member of the order of A., F. & A. M. at Headquarters, of Nicholas County, and of the order of I. O. O. F. at Ruddel's Mills.

REV. J. A. SAWYER, P. O. Oddville; was born in Norfolk, Va., July 10, 1845, son of Samuel and Elizabeth (Hastings) Sawyer; he, a native of England, being killed on the coast of North Carolina by robbers, in the spring of 1858; she, also, a native of England, and dying in North Carolina in 1854; they had seven children, J. A. being the sixth in order of birth. Our subject received a portion of his education at Georgetown College, Scott County, Ky., and at West Point military school, Virginia, and began teaching school near Lexington, Ky., which he followed for some time, and was afterward a professor in Laurel Seminary, London, Laurel County, Ky. In 1866 he began preaching as a minister in the M. E. Church, South, which holy calling he has continued ever since. May 30, 1867, he married, in Fayette County, Miss Mattie Horene, daughter of Horatio Nelson, a native of Mercer County, Ky., which union resulted in two children, John Horatio and Mattie Horene. His wife dying in 1870, Mr. Sawyer married, in 1877, Sally A. Hardin, a native of London, Laurel County, Ky., born Oct. 26, 1857, daughter of Mark and Emily Pearl Hardin. Mr. Sawyer is a Mason, an Odd Fellow, and a Democrat.

WILLIAM N. SCOTT, M. D.; P. O. Cynthiana; was born in Harrison County, Ky., in September, 1840, son of Francis and Matilda (McClintock) Scott; he, born in 1804, in Muhlenburg County, Ky., was a blacksmith and died in Bourbon in 1865; she, a native of Bourbon, born in 1810, and now living with her son, the subject of this sketch; they have three children. Dr. Scott received his primary education in Fayette County, after which he took a course in medicine and surgery, at Starling Medical College, Columbus, Ohio, from which institution he was graduated in 1863, since which time he has practiced his profession in his native county, being located at Scott Station, where he has a large and growing practice, and having a reputation for assiduity and ability which makes him respected by all. The doctor was married in Pulaski County, Ky., in November, 1860, to Miss Ellen Gragg, born in December, 1840, daughter of Hiram and Lucy Gragg; he, a native of Virginia, and she of Kentucky, and three children have been born to them, viz: Maria, Ella and Otis. Self and family are members of the Methodist Episcopal Church, and he is an A., F. & A. M. and a Republican.

JOSEPH SHAW, deceased; was born in Paris, Bourbon County, Ky., March 22, 1825, son of John and Hannah (Cox) Shaw; he, a native of England, a manufacturer of cotton goods, who emigrated to Kentucky, an an early day, and settling in Maysville; she, also a native of England; they had eight children. Our subject attended the schools of Bourbon County, after which he went into the milling business, running a flouring mill for some time, and then began farming, which he continued until his death, that event occurring in 1870; in 1853 the deceased married Miss America Jett, born in Bracken County Ky., Nov. 25, 1830, daughter of William and Rachel (Howard) Jett, both natives of Bourbon County, and from which union there were born nine children, all living: William, John T., Edward C., Joseph W., James, Benjamin F., Hannah J., Albert, and Ira N. Mr. Shaw was a Republican and a member of the Independant Order of Odd Fellows; the family are members of the Christian Church, and their farm consists of 147 acres of choice land, the place being known as "Valley View."

G. R. SHARPE, farmer; P. O. Lair's Station; is a native of Harrison County, and son of George and Elizabeth (Ruddel) Sharpe; he was born in 1810. His father was one of the early settlers of Bourbon County; was born in Virginia, and at the age of twenty, in the year 1779, he moved to Bourbon County, Ky., where he remained till the time of his death, which occurred in 1846. His wife was the daughter of Arch Ruddel, of Virginia; she died in 1840, aged seventy-seven years; they were the parents of nine children, one of whom is our subject, G. R. He was born and raised in the same house in which he now resides. In 1844, he married Miss Caroline Eeles, a native of Harrison County, and daughter of James Eeles; by this union they have had six children, two of whom are now living, viz: George R. and James E. His wife is a member of the Christian Church at Ruddel's Mills. He is the owner of 120 acres of land, called "Spring Farm." He is a Democrat. He was at one time a magistrate, and President of the Harrison County Agricultural Society. Mr. Sharpe has alw tys taken a very active part in the progress of his native county, and to-day bears a name and reputation which is beyond reproach, and is most respected by those who best know him.

JAMES SIMS, farmer; P. O. Cynthiana; is a native of Bourbon County, and son of John and Ellen (McNeer) Sims. He was born March 19, 1818. His father was born in Virginia, in the District of Columbia. During his life he followed the occupation of farming. In 1815, he removed to Bourbon County, Ky., where he remained to the time of his death, which occurred in October, 1843, aged 57 years. His wife, the mother of our subject, was also a native of Virginia, and daughter of Wm. McNeer. She was born 1789, and died 1875, aged 86 years. They were the parents of eleven children. James lived with his parents to the age of 29 years, receiving an education and assisting in tilling the soil of his father's farm. In 147 he married Miss Louisa Hibler, native of Bourbon County, and daughter of S. M. and Cynthia A. Hibler. By this union they have had five children, three of whom are now living, viz: Caroline F., Mary F. and John K. In 1847 Mr. Sims began farming upon the farm of his father-in-law, near Ruddel's Mills, where he remained until 1848, when he bought a farm of 100 acres, remaining upon and working the same until 1858, when he bought the farm upon which he now resides, having 213 acres of the choicest land of Harrison County, called "Ashland," upon which he makes stock raising a specialty. Himself and family are members of the Christian Church at Indian Creek. He was at one time a member of the I. O. O. F. Lodge at Ruddel's Mills; resigned from the same at the time of the war. In politics he is a Democrat.

LEONARD STUMP, farmer; P. O. Cynthiana. Among the early settlers of Harrison County was Leonard Stump, father of him whose name heads this sketch. Born in Maryland in 1769; he emigrated to Harrison County in 1787, and after being a very useful man died in 1859. His wife, Sarah Kinston, was also born in Maryland in 1779; surviving her husband six years; died in February, 1865. The result of this union was six children, Leonard being one of them; he was born in Harrison County, June 9, 1814, receiving his education at the county schools of Harrison County. He began life with farming, and was married in Harrison County in 1837 to Susan Crenshaw, who was born in Harrison County, May 5, 1816, who was the daughter of John Stump, of Virginia, who died in 1855, at the age of eighty-seven years; and Hannah Madison, his wife, was also born in Virginia, and died in 1833, at the age of fifty-two years. Mrs. Susan Stump is a member of the Methodist communion at Cynthiana, and in politics Mr. Stump is a Democrat. He has a farm of 180 acres of choice land two miles from Cynthiana, on Ashbrook Pike, called "Locust Grove."

HENRY C. SMITH, miller; P. O. Poindexter; born in Bourbon County, Nov. 24, 1824; his father was Michael Smith, who was born in Harrison County in 1805, and died in 1826; his mother, Sallie David, was born in Bourbon County in 1807, and died in 1825; they had two children. Henry C. Smith received his education in the county that gave him birth, began business with farming, which he followed until 1860, when he commenced milling, which he has followed ever since. He was married in Harrison County in 1846 to Miss Mary E. Boyers, who was born in September, 1826; and she, the daughter of Jacob and Eliza (Smith) Boyers, of Harrison County; by this union they have had five children, three of whom are now living, Margaret E., Isabella, and Lee. Mr. Smith and family are members of the Presbyterian Church; he is a Democrat in politics. He has a large milling business at Poindexter Station, and is making a superior brand of flour.

THOMAS E. SPARKES, farmer; P. O. Lair's. Among those who came early from Virginia was James Sparkes, having a son born in 1811, by name of Silas H. Sparkes, who married Miss Isabella Givens; who was born in 1813, and died in 1863; the husband surviving the wife three years, and dying in 1866, leaving seven children, viz: Ruth J., Richard C., Sarah C., Martha E., Silas G., a resident of Missouri; Thomas E, whose name heads this sketch; William W., and Belle. They are the owners of 194 acres of fertile land a quarter of a mile south of Lair's Station. Silas Sparkes is a Mason, and all of the family are members of the Christian church at Mount Carmel, in Bourbon County, Richard Sparkes being one of the deacons.

H. H. TEBBS, farmer; P. O. Cynthiana; was born Dec. 21, 1851, son of James J. and Rebecca (Allen) Tebbs. Our subject received his education in the schools of his native county, and began life farming, at which he has continued throughout li e, owning at the present time a fine farm of 148 acres of land, his place being known as "Stony Point." Oct. 16, 1877, he married Lizzie G. Ammerman, born Sept. 23, 1852, daughter of Wesley, and Louisa (Bassett) Ammerman, all of Harrison County. Mr. Ammerman died in 1877, aged fifty-two years. Two children have been born to Mr. Tebbs, one of whom is living, Wesley H., born Dec. 27, 1878. Mrs. Tebbs is a member of the Christian Church, and he is a Democrat and a Granger.

JAMES J. TEBBS, farmer and stock-raiser; P. O. Cynthiana; was born in the year 1814; his father, Daniel Tebbs, who came from Virginia, was born in 1771, and died in 1846. The grandfather of our subject was also named Daniel, and spent his life in Virginia. The mother of James, Alice Taylor, was born in 1790 and died in 1855, and, through her father, Hubbard Taylor, was also of Virginia ancestry. Our subject married Miss Rebecca Allen, of Harrison County, daughter of Daniel Ammerman, of Harrison County. The names of the children are as follows: Daniel A., Tabitha Alice, Foushee J., Hubbard H., Joel Philip, Sarah Lizz e, Rebecca Enfield, Lucy Crittenden, Eusebia Catharine, who died May 27, 1861, Mary Gour, Ida and Helen. He owns 450 acres of land, two miles from Cynthiana, on the Cynthiana and Connersville Pike, and his farm is styled "Never Failing," from the fact that it has never failed to produce crops. Mr. Tebbs is a breeder of short-horn cattle, merino sheep, which he claims are superior to any other breed, while the rest of his stock are all of high grade; he has had at the head of his herd, Imported Bullion and Birmingham, who was also out of imported stock. Mr. Tebbs is a Granger. His wife is a member of the Christian Church at Cynthiana. He has resided on his present place ever since 1825.

A. A. TAYLOR, tobacco dealer; P. O. Cynthiana; was born in Harrison County, Feb. 14, 1822; son of Hillery and Melinda (Alexander) Taylor; he, born in Baltimore, Sept. 22, 1792, a wheelwright by trade, dying in Robinson County, Ky., Oct. 25, 1881; she, born in Virginia, Aug. 1, 1874. Hillery and Melinda Taylor had ten children. Our subject was educated in the common schools of Harrison County, and commenced life as a farmer, but at present is dealing in tobacco, buying and selling quite largely. Oct. 24, 1854, he was married, in Cincinnati, to Lizzie M. Glenn, born in Harrison County, Ky., April 17, 1835, daughter of Peter and Sarah (Ashcraft) Glenn; he died in 1853, aged forty-two, and she in 1841, aged thirty-two. Mrs. Taylor died June 20, 1878, having borne her husband seven children, four of whom are living: Wm. F., Laura G., Omer P., and Mary H. In 1881, Mr. Taylor married Fannie Hickman, a native of Harrison County, born in 1849; daughter of C. and Anna Yarnall, of Harrison County. Mrs. Taylor is a member of the Beaver Baptist Church, and Mr. Taylor is a Freemason and a Democrat.

T. L. THOMPSON, farmer; P. O. Cynthiana; was born in Harrison County, Ky., May 8, 1850, son of Robert and Emily (Linsey) Thompson; he, born in Harrison County, Sept. 9, 1802, and now in his eightieth year; she, also a native of Harrison County; they had ten children. After receiving in the schools of his native county his education, Mr. Thompson began farming, which occupation he has followed ever since, owning a farm of seventy-two acres of choice land. Oct. 5, 1876, in Cynthiana, he married Miss Lura Violett, born in Texas, May 12, 1855, daughter of Dr. George Violett, who was born in Kentucky, and died in 1869, aged thirty-eight years; her mother, also born in Kentucky, died in August, 1881, aged forty-four years. One child, Violett, born Sept. 17, 1879, has blessed the household of Mr. Thompson. Mrs. Thompson is a member of the Episcopal Church, and Mr. Thompson is a Democrat. The father of Mrs. Thompson is a Mason, and in his younger days, was a very active member of the honorable fraternity.

NEWTON P. TAYLOR, farmer; P. O. Robertson's Station; was born in Harrison County, Ky., Dec. 31, 1832, son of Tapley and Lavina (Duncan) Taylor; he, a farmer, born in Virginia, and dying in 1846, aged fifty-seven years, his wife having died in 1832. They had fourteen children; Mr. Taylor attended the schools of his neighborhood during his youth, after which he began farming, which he has continued, also, runing a saw mill; he owns a farm of 450 acres of land, and has been a School Trustee. March 8, 1857, he married Sarah J. Shanks, born in Bourbon County, Ky., May 27, 1840, daughter of David and Mary (Brannock) Shanks; he a native of the State of Delaware, and she of Harrison County, Ky.; Mrs. Taylor bore her husband eight children, seven of whom are living: James W., born March 11, 1858; Lorena, born Oct. 8, 1859; Frederick D., born Aug. 23 1861; Ida J., born Sept. 7, 1863; Benjamin N., born Aug. 11, 1865; Edward W., born Sept. 2, 1867; Virginia M., born Jan. 19, 1873; Gertrude, born Aug. 3, 1875. Mrs. Taylor is a member of the M. E. Church South, and he is a Democrat.

WILLIAM M. TAYLOR, farmer; P. O. Robertson's Station; was born in Robertson County, Ky., Jan. 15, 1814, son of Tapley and Lavina (Duncan) Taylor; he, a native of Virginia, a farmer by occupation, and dying in 1846, aged fifty-seven years; his wife having preceded him in 1832; they had fourteen children. Our subject received his education in the schools of Harrison County, and began life as a farmer, in which occupation he has continued, owning a splendid farm of 290 acres of the best land of Kentucky. In 1834 he married Nancy Shanks; born in Bourbon County in 1810, daughter of David and Nancy Shanks, natives of Delaware; and from this union there were born ten children, seven of whom are living: Tapley A., Frances A., Elizabeth, Arbell, David W., Martha, and Susan. Mrs. Taylor died in 1864, and after remaining a widower ten years, Mr. Taylor, in 1874, married Elizabeth King; born March 19, 1844; daughter of Joseph and Catharine King; and by this union there have been born two children: Ada H., and Sally E. Mrs. Taylor is a member of the Methodist Episcopal Church, and her husband is a Democrat.

GEO. W. TURNER, farmer and stockraiser; P. O. Poindexter Station; was born Dec. 21, 1829, in Harrison County, Ky.; son of Thornton and Elizabeth (Van Deren) Turner; he, a farmer, born in Virginia in 1799, and dying in 1859; she, born in Harrison County, Ky., and dying at the age of thirty-seven years, in 1841, leaving seven children. The grandparents of our subject came to Kentucky at an early day, and were among those brave and hardy pioneers who helped to turn the wilderness into the garden spot now known as the Blue Grass region. Mr. Turner, our subject, after receiving a moderate education, began farming, and has continued in that occupation since. In addition to farming, Mr. Turner has made a specialty of stockraising, breeding horses, mules, cattle and hogs, and producing some of the finest animals raised in the county. He owns a farm of 160 acres of fine land. In 1861 he married Julia B. Thompson, born in Harrison County in September, 1840, daughter of Robert and Emily (Linsey) Thompson, natives of Harrison County, Ky. Mr. Turner and family are members of the Baptist Church, and he is a Democrat.

F. D. TAYLOR, farmer and stock raiser; P. O. Cynthiana; was born March 12, 1839, in Harrison County, Ky.; son of Tapley and Lavina (Duncan) Taylor; he, a native of Virginia, a farmer, and dying in 1846, his wife preceding him in 1832; they were the parents of fourteen children. F. D. received his education in the schools of Harrison, after which he began farming, and has continued at the same ever since. He has a farm of two hundred acres, which he cultivates, making stock raising a speciality. In 1853, he married Mary A., daughter of Daniel and Ann Buzzard, who died in 1856, when he married in 1857, Rebecca J., daughter of Wyatt and Nancy Martin. Eight children have blessed Mr. Taylor's house; their names are: Preston, Mary D., Nora, J. L., John W., Leon L., William W., Lucinda. Mr. Taylor and wife are members of the Methodist Church South, and he has been a Granger, and is a Democrat.

LUTHER VAN HOOK, banker and distiller; P. O. Cynthiana; among the most active and energetic business young men of Harrison County; we would mention the name of L. Van Hook, who is now and has been since its first organization, in October, 1877, cashier of the Farmers National Bank, at this place, and also one of its charter members; he is a native of Harrison County, and was born July 25, 1840; his father, Samuel Van Hook, was also a native of this county, and married Elizabeth J. Veach, by whom he raised two sons, Luther and Lewis, and one daughter, Serena; Samuel Van Hook followed the occupations of farming and merchandizing, and died in 1849; Luther was educated at Cynthiana, and began life as a merchant, which he followed very successfully for some time; afterwards engaged in the manufacture of woolen goods; since that time he has engaged in the various occupations of milling, distilling, grain, and stock dealing, etc. He has held several municipal offices, among them we would mention City Councilman, Vice President School Board, and is now Notary Public of Cynthiana; he was married near Cynthiana, Feb. 16, 1865, to Alice Keller, who was born in Harrison County, in July, 1844; her father, Abraham Keller, was a native of Bourbon, but moved to Harrison many years ago, where he acquired considerable property and prominence. Mr. Van Hook has an interesting family of six children, three sons, Keller, Luther, and Roger Peck, and three daughters, Lyda, Maggie and Serena; his wife is a member of the Christian Church; he belongs to the Knights of Honor, and is politically Democratic. Mr. Van Hook is one of our most thorough going, upright business man, and is distinguished for his courtesy and politeness towards those with whom he has had business relations; he is a man of rare judgment, excellent business ability, and enjoys the confidence and respect of his fellow citizens.

ALFRED VAN DEREN, farmer; P. O. Cynthiana; was born in Harrison County, Dec. 16, 1825, son of James and Sarah Van Deren; he, born in Virginia, Oct. 7, 1780, coming to Kentucky with his parents in 1789, a farmer by occupation, dying Jan. 9, 1867; she, born in New Jersey, Aug. 10, 1790, now living with our subject; they had thirteen children. Mr. Van Deren received his education in the schools of his native county, and began life as a farmer, at which he has continued, with the exception of three years in the mercantile business, until the present time. He owns a farm of 175 acres of good land. Mr. Van Deren is a member of the Baptist Church, and a Republican.

JAMES VAN DEREN, farmer; P. O. Cynthiana; was born in Harrison County, Ky., Oct. 18, 1821; son of James and Sarah Van Deren; he, born near Winchester, Va., Oct. 7, 1780, and emigrated with his parents to Bourbon County, Ky., in 1789; was a farmer, and died Jan. 9, 1867; she, born in New Jersey, Aug. 10, 1790; now living with her son Alfred, whose sketch appears in another portion of this work, and aged ninety-two years; they had thirteen children. Mr. Van Deren received his education in the common schools of his native county, and began life as a farmer, which he has continued throughout life, owning at the present time 465 acres of land, known as "Cedar Grove." His grandfather, Barnard Van Deran, was a native of Virginia, and emigrated to Bourbon County about 1789. May 13, 1856, Mr. Van Deren married Sarah E. Waits, daughter of Edward and Elizabeth (Parker) Waits, from which union there have been born seven children, six of whom are living: Edward F., Anna F., James G., Willie S., Harry P., and Lizzie A. Self and family are members of the Christian Church, and he is a Republican.

JAMES I. VICTOR, deceased, was born in Nicholas County, Ky., in 1806, son of William and Ellen (Ingalls) Victor; he, a native of Virginia, a farmer, and dying in in 1845, aged seventy-five years; she, a native of Nicholas County, Ky., dying in 1856, aged seventy-eight years; they had eight children. Mr. Victor received his education in the schools of Nicholas County, after which he began teaching school, which he followed for some time, and then went to farming, at which he continued until his death, which occurred in 1868, at the age of sixty-two years. The deceased in 1838, married Margaret Rutter; born in Harrison County, Aug. 22, 1818; daughter of Alexander Rutter; born in Harrison County, in 1791, and dying in 1855; and Margaret (Moore) Victor, born in 1793, and dying in 1879. Five children were born to James I. and Margaret Victor: Mary E. (Martin), Rillie T. (Whaley), Alexander R., Ellen (Hedges), and J. W. Mrs. Victor's son, J. W., was the owner of the celebrated stallion "Indian Chief," and is now engaged in raising stock of all kinds. He has produced some of the finest stock ever bred in the county, and his ability in training horses is well known and acknowledged far and wide. Since the death of her husband Mrs. Victor has remained on the farm, which consists of 250 acres of choice land, and is managed with ability and care. The family are members of the Christian Church. Mr. Victor was a Democrat.

LEWIS VEATCH, farmer; P. O. Cynthiana; whose portrait appears in this work, was born in Harrison County, Nov. 23, 1804; his father, Thomas Veatch, was born in Pennsylvania, April 19, 1770; emigrated to Kentucky in about the year 1785, being among the first settlers of Sellers Run; he was a farmer; he died in Sept., 1842. His wife, Jane Huff, the mother of our subject, was of German descent, born in Virginia in 1765, and died in 1841; they had nine children. Lewis Veatch was born on the same farm that he now resides, has always been a hard working man; by his economy and industry, he succeeded in gaining a good property, and is now the owne of one of the best farms of Harrison County. Sept. 1 1881, in Harrison County, he married Mary A. Lewis, native of Harrison County, and the daughter of Almon and Dicy (Dean) Lewis; she was born Feb. 6, 1840. Mr. Veatch is a strong Republican, and a personal frien' and acquaintance of Gen. U. S. Grant.

RICHARD J. WHITEKER, farmer and trader; P. O. Oddville; was born July 14, 1832, son of Peter and Ann (Dunn) Whiteker; he, born in Maryland, in 1793; died in Kentucky, in 1856; she, born in Harrison County, in 1798, and died in 1862, having been the second wife of Peter; they had seven children. Our subject was reared to the life of a farmer, and has followed that principally throughout life, although he was engaged in the mercantile business six or eight years. He served as Constable five years and as Magistrate six years, which position he has filled ably and acceptably. Mr. Whiteker began life without a dollar to his name, but by persistent enonomy and well-applied industry has acquired a competency for approaching old age, he owning a fine farm of 150 acres of land, comfortably improved, and two valuable houses in Cynthiana. Feb 10, 1851, he married Ruth E. Beckett, born Nov. 21, 1833, daughter of John and Alice (Hickman) Beckett, of Harrison County. Mr. Whiteker and wife are members of the Methodist Church South, and he is a Mason, an Odd Fellow, a Good Templar, and a Democrat.

JACOB A. WOLFORD, liquor dealer and distiller; P. O. Cynthiana. Among the enterprising young men of Cynthiana, there are few who surpass the subject of this sketch, J. A. Wolford, son of Peter and Mary A (Carl) Wolford; was born in Pennsylvania on the third day of December, 1841. His parents were both natives of Pennsylvania, but now live at Minneapolis, Minn.,

F. G. Ashbrook

where his father, Peter Wolford, is successfully engaged as Broker and Banker. Out of a family of five children, two sons and three daughters, Jacob A. is the elder son. His younger brother was named William L., and his sisters were: Sarah, Henrietta and Jennie. Our subject was educated at Tuscarora, Pa. After leaving school he accepted a position as clerk in his father's bank. He next went to Memphis, Tenn, where he engaged in the mercantile business for a few years. In 1863, he came to Cynthiana, and commenced the manufacture of woolen goods. In addition to this in 1864, he began running a distillery, and in 1865 he discontinued the manufacturing business altogether, and devoted his entire attention to his distillery, which business he has followed very successfully ever since. He was married in Harrison County, Ky., on the 14th of November, 1867, to Miss Josephine Cook, who was born in Pennsylvania, June 9, 1845. Her father, Stephen B. Cook, was also a native of Pennsylvania, and was born March 1, 1797, and died in Kentucky, on the 10th of March, 1874. His widow, Lydia (Beecher) Cook, was born in Lancaster County, Pa., June 10, 1805, and now lives quietly in the city of Cynthiana, near her children. Mr. Wolford's marriage has been blessed with one son, Louie C., and two daughters, Mary L. and J. Albertie. Mrs. Wolford is a member of the Episcopal Church. Our subject has no political aspirations, but always acts with the Democratic party. He is also a member of the Order K. H. By his close attention to business he has accumulated sufficient means to enjoy any reasonable luxury that himself or family should desire.

JOHN S. WITHERS, banker; P. O. Cynthiana; is one of Cynthiana's oldest as well as most prominent residents, being a native of the place, and born Sept. 4, 1830. He is the son of William A. and Eliza (Perrin) Withers. The former was born in Virginia, subsequently became a merchant of Cynthiana, and was killed by a stray shot at the battle of Jacksonville; the latter was the daughter of Archie Perrin. They were the parents of three children. John S. was educated in the public schools of Cynthiana and at the University of Missouri. Mr. Withers first began business in the mercantile line with his father. In 1856, he was married to Miss Kate Remington, daughter of George Remington. Their union has been blessed with three children, viz.: Ida, Lizzie and Rodney. In 1853, Mr. Withers succeeded his father in business, he also retiring from the mercantile business in 1856. In 1857, the charter was obtained for the Deposit bank.

J. Q. WARD, lawyer; P. O. Cynthiana; was born Aug. 29, 1838 at Oxford, Scott County, Ky.; he is a son of Cary A. Ward, who was born July 5, 1808, in Harrison County; he was a printer by trade, and was for a while editor of a paper at Oxford, Ohio, and subsequently engaged in farming and merchandizing; he died April 8. 1861; Joseph Ward, a native of Fauquier County, Va., was the grandfather of our subject; he married Margaret Cotter, and came to Kentucky when a young man; J. Q. Ward spent his early days upon the farm, and after attaining the proper age, entered Georgetown College, from which he graduated in 1858; the class of 1858 was composed of men, most of whom have attained prominence, among whom may be mentioned Lt-Gov. James E. Cantrill, Richard Reed, of Mt. Sterling, and others; Mr. Ward studied law under the guidance of M. Polk, of Georgetown, and was admitted to practice in September, 1866; he served in the office of School Commissioner, for many years, and for four years as County Attorney; he was elected to the Legislature in 1873–4; he was married Nov. 30, 1868, to Miss Mary E. Miller, daughter of James Miller, of Harrison County; the couple have three children, viz: Miller, Anna Cary, J. Q.; he is a member of the Presbyterian Church, a Master Mason, and in politics is a Democrat. Mr. Ward is regarded as one of the best lawyers in this section of the State; he is a man of commanding presence, a forcible speaker and is undoubtedly one of the coming men of Kentucky.

ANDREW HARRISON WARD, lawyer; P. O. Cynthiana; was born Jan. 3, 1815, in Harrison County, near Cynthiana; his parents were Andrew and Elizabeth (Heddington) Ward. His father was a Virginian and came to Kentucky when a boy with his parents, and settled in Jessamine County; in 1800 removed to Harrison, where he remained until his death in 1842; was a soldier in the war of 1812, and the subsequent Indian War; and was a soldier under General Harrison when "Harry Ward," as he is familiarly called, was born, and for whom he was named. Both of his grandfathers, Ward and Heddington, were soldiers in the Revolutionary War, and among the early and valuable pioneers of Kentucky. Elizabeth Heddington, his mother, was born in Baltimore, and came with her parents at an early day to Harrison County. Our subject was brought up on a farm and usually spent his winters in the country schools. He finished his education at Transylvania University at Lexington. In 1837 he took a position as clerk on a steamboat on the Tombigbee River, where he remained several years. In 1842 he began the study of law, and prepared for his profession under Major James R. Curry, of Cynthiana; was admitted to the bar and began practice in 1844. He was elected to represent Harrison County in the Legislature in 1863. In 1865 he was the Democratic candidate for Congress from the sixth district, but was defeated by the Federal soldiers being allowed to vote. In 1866 however, he was re-nominated for Congress and elected to fill the vacancy caused by the resignation of General Clay Smith, to accept the Governorship of Montana. He served one term in Congress and was distinguished for his opposition to the reconstruction measures of the Republican party. At the expiration of his term he resumed the practice of his profession in Cynthiana with his usual brilliant success. His first vote was cast for Henry Clay and his last before the war for Bell and Everett. During the war he was a Constitutional Union man; since that time he has been a Democrat; he is an able lawyer and an extremely popular speaker.

JOHN WHITE, farmer and trader; P. O. Cynthiana; is a son of Nicholas and Frances (Green) White, and was born in Harrison County, Ky., on Nov. 7, 1829. His paternal grandfather, Thomas White, was a native of Georgia, and his maternal grandfather, Martin Green, was from North Carolina. They emigrated at an early day, and were among the first settlers of Madison County, Ky., near Richmond. His ancestors on his father's side, were principally Baptists, while those on his mother's side were Methodists, and had a house of worship erected on their farm, known as "Green Chapel." Nicholas White (father of our subject) was born in Georgia, in 1789, and when five years of age came to Kentucky with his parents, and settled in Madison County. He served as a soldier in the war of 1812. His wife, Frances Green, was born in the year 1800, and was married to Mr. White in 1817. They subsequently settled near Sharpsburg, in Bath County, where they remained about two years, but in consequence of a heavy financial loss Mr. White sustained at this place, by going security, he sold his farm and purchased a tract of land in the forests of Harrison County, seven miles northeast of Cynthiana. He and his wife were members of the Baptist church, but, early in the Reformation, united with the Christian denomination. He soon became a leading member, and she, being a truly pious woman, they led a very exemplary life. He died in 1858, and his wife followed him in 1860. They were the parents of nine children, John being the sixth child. Perhaps there are but few things more indellibly stamped upon John's memory, than the rudely constructed benches, made of slabs and without backs, he found at the first old log school house he attended; being then only six years old. His opportunities for attending school were quite limited, as he was required to assist in clearing the woods and tilling the land, except on rainy days, and such other time as his parents thought they could conveniently dispense with his services at home. When John was seventeen, his father hired a blacksmith to run a shop on his farm, and John was put to work in the shop to learn the trade; he made such rapid progress that after the first year's apprenticeship he was considered competent to take charge of the shop, which he continued to run for his father about two years, then went to work for himself; after working as journeyman for one year he opened a shop of his own, which he run very successfully until he was twenty-five years of age, at which time he found, by enonomy and prompt attention to his business, he had accumulated about $2,000; in 1854 he married Nannie A. Cheatham, daughter of John and Harriet Cheatham, of Nicholas County, Ky.; he then purchased 100 acres of land near his father's place, where he removed and at once engaged in agricultural pursuits and dealing in stock, which business he has followed ever since. After living at this place about two years, he sold out and moved to a farm of 100 acres on Indian Creek, about five miles south-east of Cynthiana; he has added to his farm here from time to time until he now owns 350 acres, upon which he has erected a commodious residence, and has his farm otherwise very well improved; he also possesses other property and means not here mentioned. Mr. and Mrs. White have an interesting family; they have had born to them six children, four of whom are living, viz: Jennie, Evaline, Adelia, and William A.; the family are all members of the Christian Church; politically he is Democratic; he has been a strong advocate through life, for education in its various departments, and spares no effort or means to give his children such educational advantages as are within his reach, thus preparing them for the coming duties of life; the old adage of "industry brings its own reward" has been very beautifully exemplified in the case before us, and should be a source of encouragement to any young man who may chance to read this sketch, especially if it is his lot to venture out upon his own resources without capital.

JOHN H. WHEELER, tobacco dealer; P. O. Oddville; was born in North Carolina, Aug. 25, 1825; son of Ozias and Sarah (Fults) Wheeler; he born in Vermont, a farmer, and dying in 1869, aged sixty-six years; she, born in North Carolina, in 1799, and dying in 1867; they had seven children, John H. being the oldest. He received his education in the common schools of Harrison County, and commenced farming at the age of twenty-one years, which he continued until 1864, when he commenced dealing in tobacco, in which business he has been quite successful, doing an extensive trade, handling on the average 100,000 pounds of tobacco yearly, the amount in 1881 being about 175,000 pounds. May 14, 1845, he married in Harrison County, Miss Alcinda Mahoney, born in Harrison, May 9, 1825, daughter of Henry and Catharine (Corder) Mahoney, natives of Virginia, and which union resulted in eight children, six of whom are living: Nancy C., Sarah A., Margaret E., Thomas S., Louisa and Mary J. Mr. Wheeler is the owner of 200 acres of land. Himself and family are members of the M. E. Church, and Mr. Wheeler is a Republican.

ASA F. WHITEKER, farmer; P. O. Oddville; was born in Harrison County, Ky., April 16, 1824; son of Peter and Nancy (Dunn) Whiteker; he, born in Harrison County in 1783, was a Methodist minister, and died Sept. 22, 1856, his parents being John and Nancy Whiteker, natives of Maryland, who came to Kentucky at an early day; she, born in Harrison County, and died in 1862, at the age of sixty years, daughter of Archie and Elizabeth Dunn, of Maryland. Peter and Nancy Whiteker had thirteen children. Asa F. received his education in the schools of his native county, and at the age of twenty-one years began farming, at the same time working at the carpenters' trade, which he continued until 1857, when he engaged in the mercantile business at Oddville, where he remained until 1869, when he removed to Cynthiana and also sold goods. In 1877 he returned to Oddville, and again engaged in selling goods until 1879, since which time he has been engaged in farming, he owning a snug little farm of sixty acres of choice land. In August, 1844, he married Frances J. White; born in Harrison County, Jan. 10, 1825; daughter of Nicholas and Frances White, natives of Madison County, Ky. Mrs. Whiteker died March 7, 1860. June 10, 1860, Mr. Whiteker married Mary E. Duncan, daughter of Robert and Cynthia (McLean) Duncan, of Ohio; from which union there have been born three children, two living: Mary L. and Susan J. Mr. Whiteker has been Postmaster at Oddville for sixteen years, and was Coroner of the county eight years. He is a Knight Templar and an Odd Fellow, having filled all the chairs in the latter; he is a Democrat, and himself and wife are members of the Methodist Episcopal Church South.

JAMES H. WAITS, farmer; P. O. Cynthiana; was born in Harrison County, Ky., June 30, 1842; son of Richard and Sarah (Van Deren) Waits; he, a native of Nicholas County, Ky., born July 12, 1801; she of Harrison County, born Jan. 10, 1818. Mr. Waits received his education in the common schools of his native county, and began life as a farmer, which occupation he has continued throughout life, and now owns a beautiful and productive farm of 200 acres of land. He was married in Harrison County, Nov. 29, 1864, to Nancy E. Martin; born in Harrison County, May 25, 1845; daughter of Edmond and Elizabeth Martin, both natives of Harrison County. Mrs. Waits died July 4, 1866. Sept. 16, 1875, Mr. Waits married Mary Elliott, born Jan. 24, 1844, in Fayette County, Ky.; daughter of A. Smith Elliott, of Fayette. Two children have blessed this union: Martha E., born Aug. 6, 1877; and Sally L., born Oct. 15, 1878. Mr. Waits is a member of the Christian Church, and his wife is a Presbyterian. He is a Republican.

JAMES M. WHITE, farmer and blacksmith; P. O. Cynthiana; was born in Harrison County, Ky., April 21, 1832, son of Nicholas and Frances (Green) White; he, born in Georgia, Aug. 7, 1789, a farmer and blacksmith, and dying in 1861; she, born in Madison County, Ky., in 1800, and dying in 1862; were the parents of nine children. Our subject was educated in the schools of his native county, and when a youth learned the trade of blacksmithing, at Oddville; and after working at that business five years began farming, and is at present following both occupations, he having a sung little farm of fifty-five and one-half acres of good land. In 1855, in Owen County, Ky., he married Miss Evelina Lucas, born in Ohio, March 30, 1838, daughter of John B. and Mary (Robb) Lucas, natives of Pennsylvania, he dying in 1851, aged forty-four years, and she in 1845, aged thirty-nine years. Eleven children have gladdened the household of Mr. White, eight of whom are living: William G., Eliza E., Laura B., Eveline, Mary F., James E., Adie, Mattie M. Mr. White, wife and entire family are members of the Methodist Church. He is a member of the Honorable Fraternity of Ancient, Free and Accepted Masons, and a Democrat.

N. B. WILSON, farmer; P. O. Cynthiana; is a native of Harrison County, and son of John C. and Corrilla (Durbin) Wilson; he was born January, 1837; he lived with his parents to the age of twenty-one, receiving an education from the schools of his native county, and also attended the Farmer's College at Cincinnati, graduating from the same in 1856; after his return from college he taught school for two terms of nine months each; in 1860 he married Mary E., a native of Harrison County, and daughter of Richard and Sarah (Van Deren) Waits;

they are the parents of six children: Robert D., Hattie L., Maggie, Durbin, Sally V., and Richard N.; one year previous to his marriage, he bought the farm upon which he now resides, having 162 acres of choice land; himself and family are members of the Christian Church at Indian Creek, he being an elder of the same; he is a member of the Grangers Lodge, No. 154, at Cynthiana, and now is one of the executive committee of the Kentucky State Grange; he has been a deputy surveyor and deputy clerk for several years, and in politics is a Democrat.

JOHN C. WILSON, farmer; P. O. Cynthiana; is the son of Rob't and Sally (Sweeney) Wilson. He was born in Harrison County, one half mile from his present residence, in 1810. He spent his earlier days with his parents in receiving a limited common school education, and assisting in tilling the soil of his father's farm. In 1835 he married Miss Corrilla Durbin, a native of Harrison County, and the daughter of Daniel and Betsey Durbin. She was born in 1813 and died in 1845. By this union they were blessed with four children, one of whom still living, viz.: N. B. Wilson. In 1850 he married a second time to Miss Jane Trimble, a native of Harrison County and daughter of John Trimble. She was born in the year 1800 and died in 1854. In 1807 he married his third wife, Mary L. Hamilton, the daughter of Samuel and Mary Veach. Mr. Wilson has followed the occupation of farming during his life, and is now the owner of 350 acres of choice land, called "Cedar Avenue." He is an enterprising citizen of his native county, and bears a name and reputation which is beyond reproach; now in the later years of his life he is surrounded with those comforts and enjoying those pleasures that are ever the result of honesty, industry and economy. He and his wife are members of the Christian church at Indian Creek, and in polities he is united with the Democratic party.

J. W. WORNALL, farmer; P. O. Cynthiana; born in Harrison County, December, 1834; is a son of Thomas Wornall, of Clark County, and a grandson of Thomas Wornall, Sr., a native of Virginia. Thomas Wornall, Jr., married Rebecca Bean, daughter of John and Eva Bean, of Virginia, by whom he had three children. J. W. Wornall, the subject of this notice, received his education from the common schools of Harrison County, spending his early life upon the farm. On April 21, 1857, he married, in Bourbon County, Sophia M., daughter of Major John and Elizabeth (Keller) Edwards. A more complete sketch of Major John Edwards will be found in the history of Bourbon County. Mr. Wornall was for two years engaged in the distilling business, but has returned to farming, which he prosecutes with success. He is a Democrat in politics. Mrs. Wornall is a member of the Presbyterian Church.

RICHARD WAITS, farmer; P. O. Cynthiana; was born in Nicholas County, July 12, 1801. He is the son of John Waits (see sketch of Elizabeth Martin. He received his education from the common schools of Harrison County. At the age of 21, began farming on his own account, which he still continues. He has been twice married; in Bourbon County, Nov. 4, 1830, to Miss Mary Parker, of Bourbon County, born in 1811, and died in Aug. 10, 1833; in 1839, in Harrison County, he married Miss Sarah Van Deren, a native of Harrison County, born Jan. 10, 1818. They have five children: Mary E., James H., John L., Maggie and Alfred V. He and family are members of the Christian church. He is a Republican. Mr. Waits is a man of sterling qualities, which has endeared him to the community, of which he has been a member so long. He has always been a hard-working man; now in the later years of his life he is surrounded with those comforts, and enjoying those pleasures, that are ever the result of honesty, industry and economy.

SYLVAN DELL PRECINCT.

SAMUEL W. CRACRAFT, farmer; P. O. Sylvan Dell; born in Mason County, March 11, 1818; his grandfather, Thomas Cracraft, came from Ireland and settled in Virginia; removed to Kentucky very early, when the Indians were still troublesome; died in Kentucky upwards of four score years of age; his father, Joseph Cracraft, came from Virginia; he was a cooper by trade as well as farmer; died in Robertson County, aged about 84 years. Our subject, Samuel W. Cracraft, was raised a farmer; he also now deals pretty extensively in leaf tobacco; in the year 1842 he married Elizabeth, daughter of Wm. and Fannie (Griffin) Smith, of Bourbon County; he is the father of seven children, six of whom are living, viz: Mary Ellen, married first to Wash Taylor, and now to James Smith, of Nicholas County; Sarah, married to Jno. McGuire, of Robertson County; William, living in Texas; Thomas, married to Frances Minor; and Fannie, married to John Argo; both himself and wife are members of the Irvinsville Baptist Church; enlisted in the Southern army in the fall of 1861, under Capt. Cameron, 1st batallion of Kentucky Cavalry, Humphrey Marshall's Division. Was in the two engagements at Middle Cut and Princeton, Va.; at this time, being over age, he got discharged and returned home; is a Democrat, a member of Fair Play Grange, and a demitted member of the Mt. Olivet Masonic Lodge.

LAFAYETTE J. DAVIS, farmer; P. O. Cynthiana; born in Harrison County, Sept. 15, 1834; his grandfather, James Davis, came from Virginia or Pennsylvania when quite small; he died March 1, 1857, aged seventy-one; he was a member of the Christian Church for forty-five years, being one of the first to embrace the doctrine of that sect. William Mc. Davis, father of our subject, was born Dec. 26, 1811, and was raised as a farmer and cooper; he served as Magistrate of Sylvan Dell Precinct from 1858 to 1862; he held a responsible office in the State militia; he died July 3, 1874. L. J. Davis was married Oct. 1858, to Mary E., daughter of Peter and Agnes (Beaton) Pope, and granddaughter of John Beaton, all of Harrison County; four children have blessed their union, all of whom still live, named and aged respectively: John W., born Oct. 17, 1859; Sarah A., Feb. 18, 1861; Wright, March 17, 1865; Mary A., May 23, 1867. Mr. Davis now holds the positions of Deacon and Clerk of the Republican Christian Church, of which his wife and daughter are likewise members; he is now Chaplain of Fair Play Grange; he was appointed to fill out the unexpired term in the magistracy of N. C. Marsh, who was elected in 1874, and resigned in 1876; his suffrage has always been exercised in aid of the Democratic party.

GREEN D. EVANS, farmer; P. O. Sylvan Dell; was born in the house where he now resides, April 10, 1826. His grandfather, Walter Evans, came from Maryland, and settled at Summit Station, in Nicholas County, where it was not safe for settlers to reside except when banded together for mutual protection. When the Indians made an attack upon Summit Station, Walter Evans was one of the party who followed them to the Ohio River, where they discovered them in the act of crossing the river in their canoes. He died in Harrison, June 20, 1846, aged eighty years. David Evans, father of our subject, was born in Nicholas County, in 1795. He was serving apprenticeship as blacksmith in Cynthiana at time of war of 1812-15. He stood three drafts, and drew clear each time. He died in 1865. G. D. Evans was raised as a farmer. On Dec. 13, 1855, he married Emeline, daughter of James and Elizabeth (Lennox) Davis, of Harrison County, who has borne him eight children, five of whom are living; James D., Sallie K., David, Elizabeth, and Luther Green. Mr. and Mrs. Davis are members of the Republican Christain Church. He is now Treasurer of Fair Play Lodge of the Order of Patrons of Husbandry. In politics, he is a Democrat.

HENRY H. HARDING, farmer; P. O. Shady Nook; born in Harrison County, Jan. 31, 1831; his grandfather, Thomas Harding, came from North Carolina at an early day, and settled in Nicholas County, near Hooktown, where he resided till he fell a victim in 1833 to that dreaded scourge, the cholera; his father, Wm. Harding, survived the year of the great epidemic, and was carried off in 1835 by consumption. Henry H. Harding was raised on a farm and acquired the trade of cooper before he reached his majority; he married first Nancy E., daughter of William and Mary (Maffit) Bishop, of Harrison County; four children were born to them, two of whom, Napoleon B. and Samantha Ann, are living; he next married Elizabeth, daughter of Jno. and Visa (Friman) Florence, of Harrison County; they have eight children, all living, named and aged respectively: Thomas McF. 20; Berry M. 18; Jno. W. 15; Visa W. 13; Ira Ecty 12; Luther 7; Nannie M. 5; Henry N. 2; self and wife members of Republican Christian Church. Mr. Harding is a member of the Orient (Masonic) Lodge, of Nicholas County, in which Lodge he now holds the office of Junior Warden; in 1861 he was elected Constable by the Republican party and served for five years.

JOSEPH MUNTZ, Jr., farmer, P. O. Oddville; born in Harrison County, Oct. 1, 1842. His grandfather, Jacob Muntz, was a native of Prussia, and served in the Austrian Lancers against Napoleon. His father, Joseph Muntz, Sr., is a native of Baden, Germany, where he was born June 21, 1809; came to New Orleans in 1836, and married Lavinia Davis, of Pennsylvania. Volunteered for the Mexican war in 1846, but as the troops were all cavalry and he had never ridden a horse, he could not go. He and his wife are still living with their son. Joseph Muntz, Jr., of whom we write, enlisted in the Union Army, July 12, 1862, under Capt. Wm. Bradley, Co. D. 7th, Ky. Cavalry. Six days after, and before he had been sworn in, he was taken prisoner at the first Battle of Cynthiana, by Morgan's men and paroled; was afterward sent to Camp Chase, Ohio, for exchange, but returned eighteen days after, walking the entire distance home. Remained in Harrison County till June, 1863, when he left to join his regiment. He was regularly mustered into service in October 1863, in the same company in which he enlisted at Nashville, Tenn. Was in several engagements in East Tennessee, among them Mossy Creek, Beaver Dam and others; was in Resaca, Ga., when Hood attacked the place. At Chattanooga, Ga., had his feet badly burned while asleep before the fire, having them encased in a gum blanket. After remaining in the hospital ten days, he again joined his company at Nashville, Tenn., came to Louisville with them, where they were re-equipped with horses and sent back to Nashville. He remained in the South till the close of the war, was in many skirmishes, endured several forced marches, in one of which they covered three hundred miles in six days. Was in Forsythe, Ga., with a scouting party of eighteen when a special train arrived bearing Gen. Cobb and staff, with flag of truce indicative of the surrender of the Southern Army. Was afterwards among the party detailed for the purpose of capturing Jefferson Davis. Returned home and was mustered out July 10, 1865. In May, 1867, he married Armilla White, daughter of James and Elizabeth (Lenox) Davis, who had two children at the time of her marriage, Wm. Yancy, and Mary J. By her he is the father of six children, all of whom are living; Joseph A., born Aug. 21, 1868; James Louie, April 29, 1871; Laura E., Oct. 9, 1872; Roy Harlan, June 18, 1874; Geo. Nicholas, Feb. 20, 1878; Walter F., Jan. 23, 1880. His wife died Oct. 2, 1881, and was a member of Salem Christian Church. Although opposed to secession, he has always been a Democrat in principle. He now holds several important positions of honor and trust, among which is the presidency of the Oddville and Beaver Baptist Church Turnpike Company. He is a member of the Fair Play Grange.

NICHOLAS C. MARSH, farmer; P. O. Oddville; was born in Harrison County, Aug. 4, 1833; his grandfather, Thomas Marsh, came from Maryland, near Baltimore, in the latter part of the eighteenth century, and settled in Bourbon County; afterwards moved to Nicholas, thence to Harrison, where he died at the advanced age of eighty-four. Nathan C. Marsh, father of our subject, was born in Bourbon County, April 22, 1808; was elected Magistrate of Harrison, under the old Constitution, about 1849; he is still living, now a resident of Bracken County. Nicholas C. Marsh married, April 22, 1856, Mary G., daughter of Augustus F. and Sally Ann (Browning) Holton; they have five living children, named and aged as follows: Augustus F., born May 5, 1862; Matilda F., April 29, 1865; Thomas, July 8, 1870; John D., Dec. 1, 1872; James H., July 24, 1879; himself and wife are members of the Republican Christian Church; he is a member of the Blue Lodge (Masonic) at Cynthiana, and is also a Royal Arch Mason in the Chapter Lodge at the same place; was appointed by the Governor to fill out the unexpired term of Squire Whittaker's magistracy; at the expiration of this time he was elected by the people to the office for four years; served two years and resigned; he has also filled the local offices of School Trustee, etc.; he votes the Democratic ticket.

DAVID H. RAYMOND, farmer; P. O. Oddville; was born in Harrison County, Aug. 18, 1818; his grandfather Raymond came from England and settled in Virginia; his father came from Culpepper County, Va., and settled in Mason County, Ky.; he served five years in the Revolutionary war for the Independence of the United States; he was at the battle of Yorktown, and witnessed the surrender of Cornwallis; he served as Magistrate for several years, and had four sons that held the same office; he received the office of Sheriff under the old constitution, being the oldest Magistrate in the county; on his farm, now occupied by his son David H., there are apple trees still bearing which were set out before he moved to the place, ninety years ago. David H. Raymond, the subject of this sketch, was raised a farmer, which occupation he still follows; he married, Sept. 24, 1840, Mary Ann, daughter of Martin and Sallie (Hardin) Van Hook, of Harrison County, by whom he had eight children, five of whom survive: Sarah, Charles M., Amanda F., John D., and Annie D. B.; his wife died March 25, 1881; she was a member of the Republican Christian Church, while he is in communion with the Beaver Creek Baptist Church. His career as a servant of the people began in 1840, when he was elected Constable; he served one year and resigned on account of other business; in 1851 he was elected as Magistrate in his own precinct over several opponents; this was the first election under the new constitution; he was elected by the Know-Nothing party to represent Harrison County in the Legislature; he was a candidate for the same honor against Dr. Beale, but was defeated; he was a candidate for Deputy Sheriff in 1854 with George Lemon, and carried the east side of the river by about 300 majority; he suffered defeat, however, his opponent, John Berry, carrying the west side by perhaps six hundred votes. In politics, he is Democratic.

DAVID ROSS, farmer; P. O. Shady Nook; is a native of Harrison County, where he was born Dec. 5, 1823; his grandfather, James Ross, was a native of Ireland, whence he emigrated about 1787, and settled in Harrison County; he was one of its first settlers; his father, David Ross, Sr., was but two and a half years old when he came to Kentucky; being in the vigor of manhood when the war of 1812–15 broke out, he was among the first to enlist from Harrison County; he escaped unhurt, and lived till 1852. David Ross, Jr., was raised on a farm; he learned the carpenter's and cooper's trades; he gained a common school education by his own industry; on the 2nd of Oct., 1851, he married Dulcena, daughter of Thomas and Margaret (Orr) Paxton, and granddaughter of Jno. Orr, Esq., of Nicholas County; he has five living children: Mary, born June 23, 1852, and married to W. H. Pope; Jno. T., Sept. 10, 1854; Granville, May 3, 1857; Wm. Yancey, April 10, 1863; Victor, Nov. 30, 1869. In 1846, Mr. Ross enlisted in the Mexican war, under Capt. Jno. Shawhan, Col. Humphrey Marshall's 1st Kentucky Cavalry, and served twelve months; he was in the battle of Buena Vista, under Gen. Taylor and acted principally as scout and guard; in 1878, he was elected to the Magistracy of Sylvan Dell Precinct, over Lafayette Davis, which office he now holds; he is a member of the Republican Christian Church; politics, Democrat.

JACOB TAYLOR, farmer; P. O. Oddville; was born in Harrison County, June 15, 1818; his grandfather, Jacob Maybrier, was a foreigner, and weaver by trade; he came to Kentucky very early, and enlisted while here in the war of 1812-15; he was in one engagement. His father, Jacob Taylor, came to Kentucky from Ohio, and died in Harrison County in 1818, aged about thirty-five; his son Jacob, whose sketch is here recorded, passed his youth as a farmer's boy; he married Elizabeth, daughter of Benjamin and Rebecca (Padgett) Allen, of Mason County, by whom he was the father of six children, four of whom are living: 'Benjamin, aged forty-two; William, forty; John, thirty-three; Rebecca Ellen, thirty-five; he has fourteen living grandchildren. Mr. Taylor has been a widower since Feb. 18, 1848; is a member of Salem Christian Church and Democratic in politics. About the year 1840 he was thrown from a horse and suffered a fracture of the left thigh bone, which, from having been improperly set by the attending physician, has never united, and now presents the peculiar feature of a joint between the knee and hip; being unable to sustain his weight upon that limb it has rendered him a cripple for life. During the war he was arrested for the crime of being a Southern sympathizer. Two of his sons were in the Confederate army; one returned, the other died at Harper's Ferry of small-pox, near the beginning of the war.

P. P. WYLES, farmer, P. O. Oddville; born in Mecklenburg County, Va., April 7, 1844. His grandfather Hebbon Wyles, was Scotch-Irish descent and married an English lady. His maternal grandfather, Peter Puryear for whom our subject was named, was a native of France, whence he emigrated after the French Revolution and married a Virginia lady; he took an active part in the war of 1812–15. His father, Leroy B. Wyles, was a native Virginian; was in the Confederate army in the late war; had also three sons in the same army, of whom P. P. was the youngest; had command of a wagon train; was killed by a falling tree about 1875. P. P. Wyles, the subject of this sketch was raised on his father's farm, receiving the rudiments of an education from the common schools. When the war broke out in 1861 he was among the first to enlist in the cause of the South, being at that time but little over sixteen years of age. His company, the Clarksville Blues, was the first southern troops that went from Mecklenburg County, and was commanded by Capt. George Hedges. They were placed in the 14th Virginia Regiment, under Col. Hodges, Armstead's Brigade, Pickett's Division of Lee's army of Northern Virginia. They were in several skirmishes, and fought their first regular battle at Seven Pines. At the battle of Malvern Hill, thirty days after, our hero lost his right arm by a shell. He was conveyed to the rear in an ambulance, but could not get his arm amputated until twenty-four hours after. He remained in the hospital at the Old Union Hotel in Richmond, for two weeks, when he went home on an indefinite furlough, and was never in active service again, though he visited his old regiment on several occasions. He was present when Dahlgren and Kilpatrick attempted to liberate the prisoners at Richmond. After the war he began to feel the neccesity of an education and to perfect it he entered Randolph Mason College, of his native County, which he attended for two and one-half years, defraying his expenses by teaching in the prepartory department. At the end of the two and a-half years, the site of the college was moved from his county, and not having the necessary means to follow it, he was obliged to give up school. About this time he came to Kentucky, in answer to an advertisement for a teacher at Lair's Station in Harrison County. He secured the position and has been engaged in teaching every year since up to 1879. In 1878 he was elected School Commissioner of Harrison County, which office he now fills. In 1870 he married Meribah daughter of Joseph and Charlotte (McCauley) Sipe, of Harrison County. Five children have been born to them, the dates of whose births are as follows: Herbert, Oct. 25, 1871; Leroy, Sept. 30, 1873; Joseph W., Feb. 11, 1876; Emma A., March 6, 1878; Jno. P., Feb. 15, 1881. Himself and wife are members of Beaver Baptist Church. He is also a member of Beaver Lodge of Good Templars. Politics, Democrat.

John McKee

RICHLAND PRECINCT.

SMITH ARNOLD, farmer; P. O. Oddville; is a native of Harrison County, Ky., and the son of Wm. and Polly Arnold. He was born Dec. 15, 1836. His father is a native of Virginia. He was born in 1807. In 1815 he removed to Harrison County, Ky., with his parents, where he received his education. In 1834 he married Polly A. King, who has borne him twelve children, eleven of whom are living. He is now living upon his farm. Smith Arnold lived with his parents until he was 18 years of age, when he married Nancy Whalin, who has borne him seven children, six of whom are living, viz.: Joseph, Polly A., William, Clarinda F., Emma, and Nancy S. The first three years of his married life were spent upon a rented farm. In 1858 he bought a farm of 52 acres, and has since added to it, now having 610 acres. Upon his farm he makes stock raising a specialty. In connection with his farm he carried on mercantile business for four years. He spends part of his time in buying and selling leaf tobacco. In the year 1880 he bought and sold over 325,000 pounds, for which he paid about $32,-000. He is a Democrat. His wife is a member of the Methodist church. He commenced life a poor man; when he first bought his farm, he was compelled to give his only horse and hog to get possession, and to work one day himself, to gain the use of a horse for one day in clearing his premises. By his hard work, and studied economy he has gained a good property, and a name and reputation which is beyond reproach.

WILLIAM B. ARNOLD, miller; P. O. Havilandsville; is a native of Harrison County, Ky., and son of Elijah and Anna (Hickman) Arnold. He was born in 1827, and in 1853 married Miss Anna M. Henry, a native of Bourbon County, Ky. They are the parents of eight children: Lulu L., John P., Amanda, Ida, Sarah, Elijah, Henry and Betty. The first seventeen years of our subject's life was spent in receiving an education and assisting in tilling the soil of his father's farm; in 1854 he commenced farming, which he followed for about nine years, when he purchased the steam grist mill and wool factory at Havilandsville, which he continues to be the successful manager of, employing a number of men and doing a large business; his wife died in 1879, and his father died when he was quite young, leaving him dependant upon his own resources, and by his studied economy and business habits he has succeeded in gaining a good property, and a name and reputation which is beyond reproach. Now, in the later years of his life, he is surrounded with those comforts and enjoying those pleasures that are ever the result of honesty, industry and economy.

JOHN ASBURY, farmer; P. O. Antioch Mills; is a native of Harrison County, Ky., and son of Clayton and Nancy (Mattox) Asbury. He was born Jan. 13, 1845. He lived with his parents up to the time of the war, when he enlisted in the 40th Regt., Co. G, K. V's, of the Confederate Army. In 1865 he followed the occupation of farming upon a rented farm. In 1867 he bought twenty acres of land, which he tilled until 1869. At that time he married Nancy E. Whitteker, who has borne him six children: Minnie E., Robert E., Anna J., John W., Emma F., and Benton S. He spent the first year of his married life upon his father-in-law's farm. In 1871 he bought 150 acres of land, and in 1880 added to it 187 acres, now having 337 acres, upon which he now resides. Upon his farm he raises all of the principal crops, and is making stock-raising a specialty, his attention in this department being turned principally to the thoroughbred "short horn." He is a Republican, and cast his first presidential vote for James A. Garfield. He is a member of the Christian Church at Antioch. His wife is a member of the Methodist Church at Mt. Vernon.

ALFRED BARLOW, farmer; P. O. Oddville; was born in Harrison County, Ky., Oct. 30, 1815, and is the son of Eliphalet and Mildred (Barlow) Barlow. His father was born in Virginia June 1, 1777, and raised in Wilkes County, N. C. In the year 1800 he became a resident of Scott County, Ky., and in the year 1801 was married to the lady named. Nine children were born to them, four of whom are now living: Lewis, Tompkins, Elizabeth and Alfred. Mr. Barlow followed farming and carpentering in Scott County for 2 years, and then removed to Nicholas County, and there engaged in farming until 1807, when he removed to Harrison County, where he resided until his death, which occurred in 1868, on March 20. His mother was a native of Virginia; she became a resident of Nicholas County by the removal of her parents to Kentucky, and died in Harrison county in 1863. The early life of Alfred was spent on his father's farm. Jan. 22, 1839, he married America Barnes. But two of the five children of this union are now living, viz: Tompkins and Lauretta. In 1849, his wife died. In 1850, he married a sister to his first wife, Miss Nancy A. Barnes. Six children were the fruits of this marriage, four of whom are now living, viz: Stephen E., Henry B., America F., and Maria E. Mr. Barlow has been a farmer by occupation, and now owns a farm of 170 acres. Himself and family are members of the Methodist church, and he is a member of Lodge No. 199, of the Grange organization. In politics he is a Democrat, and he has held the office of Justice of the Peace for eleven consecutive years. The church of which he and family are members, is known as the Barlow Church, and the school in his district also bears his name. He is an active, public spirited man, and much of the improvement in his neighborhood is due to his enterprise and liberality.

D. F. BRANNOCK, M. D., farmer; P. O. Antioch Mills; is a native of Harrison County, Ky., son of James and Elizabeth (Shanks) Brannock. He was born Feb. 21, 1823. His father, James Brannock, was also a native of Harrison County. He was born 1796. During his earlier days worked at the trade of stone mason, and afterward followed farming until the time of his death, which occurred in 1871, aged seventy-five years. His wife was born December, 1800, in Bourbon County, Ky.; is now living in Missouri. His father, Robert, was one of the first settlers of Harrison County. He was born in 1770, and died in 1850. D. F. Brannock lived with his parents in Harrison County till the age of twenty-two, going to school and assisting his father in farming. In 1844 he was married to Susan K. Ginn. He then commenced studying medicine and attending lectures at the Transylvania University, Lexington, Ky. Since his graduation he has practiced medicine until 1876, when he gave his attention to his farm of 385 acres, upon which he now resides. He is a Democrat; himself and family are members of the Methodist Church. His wife has borne him six children, five of whom are now living: James L., married and living in Brown County, O.; William H., M. D., married and living in Brooksville, Ky.; Benjamin B., M. D., married and living in Washington County, Ind.; George and David N., now residing at home with their parents.

GEO. CUMMINGS, farmer; P. O. Antioch Mills; is a native of Harrison County, Ky., and son of Joseph and Lydia (Fleming) Cummings. He was born Aug. 8, 1810. His father was a native of Maryland. When quite young he moved with his parents to Bourbon County, Ky., who were among the earlier settlers. He was then married to Lydia Fleming, who bore him thirteen children, all of whom are now living, and having large families of their own. He followed farming to the time of his death, which occurred in 1833, aged eighty-seven years. His wife died in 1824, aged fifty years. Geo. Cummings lived his earlier life with his parents, working on the farm and hunting. In 1831 he married Sarah Adams, who was a native of Harrison County, Ky. She was born in 1808 and died in 1866. She bore him thirteen children, seven of whom are living, viz: Joseph F., Catharine E., Lydia M., Sarah J., John, Robert and Thomas. He bought his farm in 1835, still continuing the management of it. In 1875 he again married, to Sarah McLaughlin, who has borne him one child, Anna W. He has a farm of 343 acres, raising all the principal crops, making tobacco a specialty. During his younger days he took great delight and made great success in hunting; he is a member of the Christian Church; he is a Democrat.

JOHN CRISWELL, farmer; P. O. Richland; was born Nov. 17, 1826, in Henry County, Ky., and is the son of William and Catharine (Lurrson) Criswell, the former born in Scott County, Ky., in 1802, and has followed farming during his life. He now resides in Harrison County, and with his wife, they make their home with their sons, John and David. John resided with his parents until 1844, when he left home and began work by the month, on a farm in Harrison County. In 1849 he bought a farm of 300 acres, which he worked until 1858, when he removed to Illinois, but in 1859 returned to Harrison County, where he bought a farm of 167 acres, which he at once began improving, and to which he has since added, until he now has 638 acres. In 1848 he married Miss Lucinda Rankin. Eleven children have been born to them, nine of which are living, as follows: Willis, Nancy R., Sarah C., James W., David A., Henry N., John T., Robert L., George N., beside their adopted child, Lucy N. Lawson. Politically, Mr. Criswell is a Democrat, and has taken quite an active part in political affairs. Himself and family are members of the Methodist Church. When first becoming a resident of Harrison County, Mr. Criswell was a poor man, but by his studied economy and excellent business habits, coupled with a firm determination to succeed, he has accumulated a fine property, and has won the esteem of the community where he resides.

DAVID CRISWELL, farmer; P. O. Richland; was born Jan. 27, 1827, in Henry County, Ky., and is the son of William and Catharine (Lawson) Criswell; his father was born in Scott County, Ky., in 1802; he subsequently moved to Harrison County. His mother was born in

Henry County, Ky., in 1802. The old people are still living, and make their home with Joseph and his brother John. In 1856 Joseph was married to Miss Polly Right, who bore him six children, four of whom are living: William T., John L., Lucinda A. and Luther. Mr. C. has a farm of 275 acres, and makes the growing of tobacco a specialty. Himself and family are members of the M. E. Church, and in politics he is a Democrat. They trace their genealogy back to the old pioneers of Kentucky, and stand in the community now, as they did then, honorable, industrious and respected people.

WM. T. CASEY, farmer; P. O. Havilandsville; is a native of Harrison County, Ky., and son of Wm. H. and Nancy (King) Casey. He was born in 1839; his father was a native of Harrison county, Ky.; he was always a farmer; he died in 1868, being 72 years of age; his wife was also a native of Harrison County; she bore him 12 children, all of whom are living; she died in 1849, aged 58 years. Mr. Casey spent his boyhood days upon his father's farm, receiving his education and assisting in tilling the soil. In 1860 he married Anna F. Blackburn, who has borne him nine children, eight of whom are living, viz: James T., John H., William S., Mildred, David, Sidney J., Adia, and Joseph D. In 1866 he bought a farm of 160 acres, upon which he raises all of the principal crops, making tobacco a specialty. Himself and family are members of the Baptist Church; he is a member of the order of A., F. & A. M. of Claysville Lodge; he is a Democrat.

DAVID H. COLVILL, farmer; P. O. Havilandsville; a native of Bourbon County, Ky., and son of William and Mary (Hunter) Colvill; was born Feb. 29, 1832. William, his father, was born in Pennsylvania, and in 1790, being three years of age, moved with his parents to Harrison County, Ky., who followed farming until the time of their death. He died in 1855, aged 59 years; his wife died in 1871, aged 60 years. His father was one of the early settlers of Harrison County. David received his education in Mason County, and until he was twenty-four years of age assisted his father in farming. In 1857 was married to Lydia F. Miller; he bought a farm of 141 acres, upon whieh he is now living, and continues the management of the same. Having no children of their own, they have adopted and raised six orphan children. He is a Democrat. His wife is a member of the Methodist Church near Havilandsville.

HENRY ECKLER, farmer; P. O. Richland; was born Feb. 5, 1820, in Harrison County, Ky., and is the son of John and Elizabeth (Macneese) Eckler. He lived with his parents until the age of 21, when he began working on a farm by the month, at which he continued until 1843; then rented a farm till 1847, when he bought a farm, selling the same in 1849. In 1857 he repurchased his farm by reason of failure of the buyer to pay for it. In 1858 he married Mrs. Elizabeth Hodges, who has borne him one child, John R. In 1860 he bought a farm of Wm. Warner and lived on the same until 1874. In 1876 he bought the farm of 184 acres, where he now lives. His principal productions are wheat, rye and tobacco. Himself and family are members of the Baptist Church, and he at one time was a member of the Granger organization. Politically, he is a Democrat. Mrs. Eckler was formerly Miss Elizabeth Arnold, daughter of Samuel and Rebecca (Hetch) Arnold. She is a native of Harrison County, and was born March 31, 1822, and was married to Thomas Hodges, who died in 1853, and in 1858 she married Mr. Eckler, as above stated.

W. D. HICKMAN, merchant; P. O. Havilandsville; is a native of Harrison County, Ky., and son of J. B. and Susan Hickman. He was born in November, 1842. His boyhood days were spent at home, receiving an education and assisting his father in the duties of his farm. In 1862 he married Jane D. Garrett, and commenced work for himself by teaming and farming. In 1871 he commenced mercantile business in Havilandsville, where he now lives, and continues his business in the store. He is politically a radical. His wife is a member of the Methodist Church. They are the parents of seven children, viz: Nora, Jesse, Wm. G., Susie, Lotta, Walter and Mattie. Mr. Hickman has, by his business habits and fair dealing, established a trade and a reputation which is an honor to himself and to the citizens in the community of which he is a part.

JAMES A. HAVILAND, farmer; P. O. Havilandsville; was born in Harrison County, Ky., May 6, 1821; son of R. S. and Mary C. (Stewart) Haviland. He is a native of New York State; removed to Harrison County, Ky., in 1818, and taught school for about ten years, when he removed to Lexington, and then back to Harrison County, and followed, many years previous to his death, the woolen manufacturing business and merchandising, dying at Havilandsville, Aug. 8, 1858. He had eight children. The grandfather, Israel Haviland, and great-grandfather, James Haviland, were both natives of New York; the first a dealer and manufacturer in boots and shoes, and the latter a farmer. James A., after receiving his education, became superintendent of his father's manufacturing business, and followed farming for twenty years. Our subject is a brother of W. S. Haviland, whose sketch appears in the Cynthiana sketches.

PAUL C. KING, farmer; P. O. Antioch Mills; is a native of Harrison County, Ky., and son of Joshua and Elizabeth King; he was born March 3, 1830; he lived with his parents until he was twenty-three years of age, receiving an education and assisting in tilling the soil of his father's farm. In 1854, he married Miss Mary Simpson, who has borne him seven children, viz: John A., Washington, Paul, James W., Cordelia A., Ella and Elizabeth. His wife died in 1872, aged 35 years. In 1878, he married a second time, Miss Elizabeth Owens; since 1854 he has followed the occupation of farming, and is now the owner of 143 acres of land. Himself and family are members of the Reformed Church, and is politically a Republican. Though not so old a resident of Richland Precinct as some of his neighbors, there is little doubt of Mr. King's being one of the leading spirits in that part of Harrison County.

LUCINDA MATTOX, farmer; P. O. Havilandsville; daughter of James and Elizabeth Meck; was born in Carroll County, Ky., in 1815. Her parents also natives of Kentucky, were of pioneer families of Scott County. Lucinda was left motherless at the age of five years; her father, a farmer, died in 1832, aged 52 years. The daughter married, in 1832, Tobias Mattox, a farmer, owner of 60 acres of land, who died in 1871, aged 60 years, a member of the Methodist Church, to which his widow also belongs. Her son, Oscar M., born Nov. 11, 1851, in Harrison County, has always lived on the home farm, receiving a good education; marrying in 1872 Mattie S. Rankin, and taking charge of his mother's farm. He, too, is a Methodist, a member of Lodge 317 A., F. & A. M., and a Democrat. He has two children, Carrie W. and Claude B.

J. WARREN SMITH, farmer; P. O. Antioch Mills; is a native of Clark County, Ky. He was born July 24, 1821, and is the son of Patterson and Jane (Darnel) Smith. His father was born in Montgomery County, Ky., in Dec. 1793, and died in 1853. His business had been farming until fifteen years previous to his death, when he began preaching. He was a soldier in the war of 1812, and a man highly respected by his fellow citizens. His mother was also a native of Montgomery County. She was born in 1798, and was the daughter of Smith Darnel. She died in 1836. The early life of J. Warren was spent at hard work; he remained with his parents until he was twenty-one years old, and then began work for himself by hiring out as a farm hand. In 1844 he was married to Miss Amanda Rankin, who bore him three children, but one of whom is living, viz., Thomas Jefferson. His wife died in 1851, and in 1852 he was married to Miss Hester Mitchell. Four children were born of this union, three of whom are now living: Joseph W., Mary J., and John W. His second wife died in 1859, and in 1861 he married Miss Martha Mattox. Six children are the result of this marriage: Elza, Anson, Sadie, Anna, Edward, and Euphrasia. Mr. Smith and family are members of the Methodist Church, and politically he is a Democrat. He owns a farm of 150 acres, and has been an honest, upright citizen. His reputation is that of a man whose honesty and industry are not questioned, and his word or promise once pledged is as good as many a richer man's bond.

A. SELLARS, miller; P. O. Antioch Mills; is a native of Harrison County, and son of John and Lucinda (Craig) Sellars. He is descended from a family who traces their genealogy back to the early settlement of Harrison County. His father was a native of the county, born in 1835; spent his life at farming, and died in 1864. Our subject was born in 1850; received his education and assisted his father while he remained a resident of the old home. In 1871 he left home and began as salesman in a dry goods store. In 1875, he was married to Miss Katie Jones, who has borne him two children. About this date he also engaged in business on his own account, by purchasing a partnership with his old employer, Mr. E. W. Martin. In 1876, he bought a flouring mill, and run the same until 1878, when it was destroyed by fire. He then bought his partner's interest in the mercantile business, and has since conducted it alone. He is an enterprising, energetic young man, and is following in the footsteps of the wealthiest men of Harrison County, viz: depending upon his own industry, economy, and good financiering to accumulate a fortune, and establish a good business.

L. F. STRUVE, merchant; P. O. Richland; was born April 14, 1832, in Germany, and is the son of John H. Struve. In 1835 he was brought to the United States by his parents, who settled in Clermont County, O., There he grew to manhood, assisted his father at farming and received his education. In 1853 he embarked in the mercantile business in East Liberty, O., and in 1855 removed to Pleasant Corners, O., but left there in the fall of the same year, and removed to Pendleton County, Ky., and there engaged in business also. In 1858 he removed to Harrison County, Ky, and began at selling goods. He has also purchased land in different parts of the county, and at present owns 613 acres. He is a Democrat and a Knight Templar of the order of A., F. and A. M. Lodge, No. 16, of Cynthiana. He is a thorough-going business man, and has taken an active part in all things pertaining to the general welfare of the community where he resides. In 1852 he married Miss Julia A. Carpenter, who has borne him eleven children, six of whom are living: John M., Lewis D., F. Kirby, Maggie N., Calvin and Leon.

GEORGE L. TRUAX, physician; P. O. Antioch Mills; is a native of Virginia, and son of John and Mary (Galbreith) Truax; he was born in 1841; his father, John Truax, is of German descent, and a native of Vermont; he was born in 1780; when quite a young man he moved with his parents to Virginia, and in 1842 to Toronto, Ca., where he died in 1877; he was in the war of 1812. George L., when a child moved with parents to Toronto, Ca., there attending school until 1857, when he went to the Victoria College, studying medicine, and graduated in 1861; he then located in Lexington, Mich., and began the practice of medicine; in 1863 he enlisted in the Confederate army, and acted as Assistant Surgeon. At the close of the war he moved to Harrison County, Ky., and married Lucinda Craig; they have two adopted children: Wm. Truax and Minnie Hutchinson. He still follows the practice of medicine, in which he has been very successful; he is a Democrat.

JOHN WOOLERY, farmer; P. O. Antioch Mills; is a native of Harrison County, Ky., and son of Joseph and Elizabeth (Stump) Woolery. He was born Jan. 2, 1822. His father, Joseph, was born in Bourbon County, Ky., in 1793. He was always a farmer. He died in 1838. Elizabeth, his wife, was born in Pennsylvania; died aged seventy-three years. John Woolery lived with his parents, receiving his education until twenty-one years of age. In 1843 he married Fannie Scott, who has borne him ten children, viz.: Robert S., James, Mary F., John T., Bettie, Henry J., William A., Annie E., Joseph F., and Joseph, the eldest, who at the age of nineteen enlisted in the Confederate army, holding the office of Sergeant. He was killed at the battle of Chickamauga. John Woolery, by the death of his parents, inherited sixty acres of land, and since has added to it, now having 140 acres. He was born on the farm on which he now lives. He is a Democrat; has always taken an active part in politics; at one time held the office of Justice of the Peace, and now is deputy County Clerk, which office he has held for twenty-five years. Himself and family are members of the Christian Church at Antioch.

JOHN T. WYATT, farmer; P. O. Havilandsville, is a native of Pendleton County, Ky., and son of John and Delia (McKinney) Wyatt. He was born June 29, 1836. His father is a native of Pendleton County, Ky.; was born in 1812. He is following the occupation of farmer in his native county. He is a Democrat. His wife is a native of Clark County, Ky.; she was born in 1812. Mr. Wyatt spent his earlier days with his parents, in receiving an education and assisting his father in farming; in 1857 he married Frances Lennox, who bore him four children, three of whom are living, viz: James R., William O., and George M. His wife died in 1869, aged thirty-three years. In 1859 he bought a farm of sixty acres in Pendleton County, Ky., which he improved and afterward sold. In 1865 he moved to Harrison County, and bought farm of 145 acres, upon which he now resides. In 1870 he married Anna E. Lennox, own sister of his first wife, who has borne him five children, viz: Sidney W., Emma F., John F., Lizzie B., and Carrie H. His wife is a member of the Christian Church. He is a Democrat; he now holds the office of Constable; he has always taken a very active part in politics.

BERRY'S STATION PRECINCT.

A. M. BASKETT, farmer; is a native of Nicholas County, Ky., and the son of Jesse S. and Edy (Victor) Baskett. He was born in December, 1843. His people were among the early settlers of Nicholas County, his father having been born there in 1802. He was a trader before his marriage, after which he engaged in farming, and continued the same until his death, which occurred in 1877, when he was 75 years of age. His mother was born in Nicholas County in 1816; she is still living, and makes her home with her son, the subject of this sketch. A. M., was four years of age when his parents moved to Harrison County. He has spent his life at farming, and now has a farm of 124 acres. In 1873 he was married to Miss Minerva Stanley; one child has been born to them, Jesse S. His wife and mother are members of the Baptist Church, and in politics he is a Democrat. Though a comparatively young man, Mr. Baskett, by his energy and good business habits, has acquired a fair property and he is a man of good name and reputation in the community.

J. B. CROUCH, merchant; P. O. Berry; is a descendant of Harrison County's old pioneers. He being of the third generation of his people who have been residents of the county. He was born Sept. 20, 1829, and is the son of Wm. and Nancy (Barlow) Crouch; the former, a native of Harrison County, and son of John Crouch, the pioneer. William was born in 1803; received his education in his native county, and spent his life in the occupation of farming; he died June 17, 1873. The mother of J. B. died in 1834, aged twenty-five years. The early years of Mr. Crouch's life were spent with his parents, where he received his education, and assisted his father in the duties of farming. In 1850, he married Miss Mary Crouch, who bore him five children, four of whom are living, viz: Martha, Nancy, Samuel, and Louisa. His wife died in 1868, and in 1871 he was married to Mrs. Eveline G. Dills, daughter of Thomas A. Rankin. One child has been born to them. Being raised on a farm, Mr. Crouch in 1850 began farming on his own account, owning and working a farm of 140 acres; in 1865, however, he engaged in the mercantile business, to which he has since devoted his time; he began in Colmansville, as successor to L. M. Hume, and in 1866 removed to Berry's Station, remaining, however, but six months, and then he returned to Colmansville and engaged in business in the Masonic Hall building, which burned in 1869; he fortunately saved his goods, and removed to the building where he first entered trade; in 1878 he again removed to Berry's Station and engaged in business with a vigor, honesty, and determination that has won him success. He now carries a stock of about $10,000, and does an annual business of about $25,000. His store is 100 feet deep by 20 feet frontage; the first floor is occupied as a general salesroom, and the second is given up to boots and shoes, hats and caps, ready made clothing, &c. In all respects Mr. Crouch's place of business would do credit to many of the larger cities of the Blue Grass region. Politically, Mr. Crouch is a Democrat, and himself and family are members of the Baptist Church, in which he is a deacon; he is a member of Taylor Lodge No. 164, A., F. & A. M., in which he is at present acting as W. M.

E. C. CRENSHAW, farmer; P. O. Berry; was born in Scott County, Ky., July 7, 1805, and is the son of Joel and Millicent (Sutton) Crenshaw, both natives of Virginia and brought by their parents to Scott County when children; he was born in 1780; was a soldier in the war of 1812, and died in 1838. Mrs. Crenshaw died in 1869, aged seventy-six years. E. C. remained with his parents until thirty years of age; he received his education in Scott County, and spent the early years of his manhood assisting his father at farming; in 1835 he was married to Miss Lizzie Goddard, who has borne him four children, two of whom are living: Mary E., now wife of I. N. Walker, and George, who married Miss Keturah Walker, and who now resides with his parents. In 1835 Mr. Crenshaw began farming on his own account in Scott County, and in 1836 also run a brickyard near Georgetown. In 1837, he removed to Fayette County; he farmed there for two years, and then returned to Scott County; in 1842, he removed to Harrison County; bought a farm of 260 acres, and has since been engaged in agricultural pursuits and stock raising, and has added to his farm until he now ownes 510 acres. He is considered one of the substantial thorough-going men of the county, and is in every way worthy of the good name and reputation he bears.

Y. H. DOAN, farmer; P. O. Berry; was born in Harrison County, Ky., Dec. 19, 1812, and is the son of Benjamin and Mary (Burks) Doan. They were among the old pioneers of Harrison County; he was a native of North

Carolina, and she was born in Virginia; he was a farmer by occupation, and at the age of nineteen years became a resident of Fleming County, Ky., but subsequently moved to Harrison County, where he died in 1852, aged eighty-four years. His wife survived him but two years, she dying in 1854, aged seventy-eight years. Mr. Doan lived with his parents until their death, having for ten years previous to their death cared for and supported them. In 1832 he was married to Miss Nancy Henry; thirteen children have been born to them, six of whom are living, viz.: William B., John B., Elizabeth J., Lucretia R., Nancy M., and Margaret A.; his family are members of the Christian Church. Mr. Doan has spent his life in Harrison County, engaged in farming; he has a farm of 220 acres, and is considered one of the substantial, enterprising citizens of the community in which he resides.

A. J. HICKS, farmer; P. O. Robinson; was born in Harrison County, Jan. 28, 1820, and is the son of James and Millie (Adams) Hicks, who were among the early pioneers of Harrison County. The former was a native of South Carolina, and born in 1785; he removed to Wayne County, Ky., after having arrived at manhood, and subsequently to Harrison County, where he died in his seventy-eighth year. The mother of A. J. was born in Virginia, and died shortly after they became residents of Harrison County, her death occurring in 1815, in her twenty-second year. A. J. was thrown upon his own resources at the early age of ten years, and as is usual in many similar instances, his success in life seems to have been increased by his early hardships. In 1838 he married Miss Polly Ashbrook. Six children were born of this marriage, three of whom are now living: Anna E., James J., and George. In September, 1852, his wife died; his second marriage was to Miss Elizabeth Craig, and of the eleven children born of this marriage six are now living, viz.: Edward, Hugh, Alvin, Doctor, Jacob, and Clark P. About the time of his first marriage Mr. Hicks bought his present farm of 154 acres, since which his time and labor have been spent in its improvement and cultivation. Mrs. Hicks is a member of the Christian Church, and in his political views, is a Democrat.

W. B. HILDRETH, blacksmith; P. O. Berry; was born in Bourbon County, Ky., and is the son of Jonathan and Ann (Crutchfield) Hildreth. His father was a native of Virginia, and was brought to Bourbon County by his parents when but a child. He followed farming as a business, and moved to Harrison County during his early manhood, where he resided until his death. W. B. became a resident of Harrison County at the time of his parents' removal from Bourbon County. He followed farming during his early manhood, but at thirty-five years of age he began work at blacksmithing, which he has since continued. In 1846 he married Miss Martha M. Penn, who has borne him six children, only two of whom are now living: Margaret, now wife of T. B. Stone, and Mary B., who still resides with her parents. Mr. Hildreth is a Democrat, and a member of Taylor Lodge No. 164, A., F. & A. M., of Berry's Station. He is an honest, hard working man, who bears a worthy name and reputation.

J. L. JUETT, hotel; P. O. Berry; was born in Harrison County, Ky., Jan. 1, 1847, and is the son of Adam and Elizabeth (Reneker) Juett. The former is a native of Grant County, Ky.; he has followed farming, and is now a resident of Harrison County. The mother of J. L. died in 1852, aged thirty-two years. J. L. lived with his parents until he was eighteen years old, when he entered the Confederate army, enlisting in the 6th Kentucky Cavalry, in which he served two years and four months; he was wounded three times, from the effects of which he has never recovered; after leaving the army, he spent about two years at his old home, and shortly after bought a farm of 100 acres, which he conducted successfully until 1880, when he sold his farm and moved to Berry's Station and engaged in keeping hotel; he has the only public place of entertainment of the place. By careful management and a study of the needs of the traveling public, he is making a success of this business; in 1867, he was married to Miss Susan E. King. Five children have been the issue of this union, three of whom now are living, viz: Millie C., Nancy S. and Howard. Mr. Juett is a Democrat, and he and Mrs. Juett are members of the Baptist Church; he is a stirring, energetic man, who has been careful to dabble in no business to bring his name into disrepute, and as a consequence he enjoys an honorable name and reputation.

CHARLES LAIL, farmer; P. O. Berry; was born in Harrison County, Ky., Nov. 28, 1846, and is the son of Charles and Louisa (Douglas) Lail. He is descended from one of Harrison County's old pioneers. His grandfather, John Lail, was born while his parents were en route from Pennsylvania to Kentucky. They settled in Harrison County, where John Lail subsequently married Miss Mary Williams, who bore him ten children, among whom was Charles Lail, the father of our subject. He was born in Harrison County in 1805, and followed farming as a business; he married Louisa Douglas as above stated, who bore him eight children, all sons, and six of whom are still living. He died in 1861, and his wife, who was born in 1814, died in 1880. Charles Lail, whose name heads this sketch, spent his early life with his parents; received his education while with them, and assisted his father at farming. In 1869 he was married to Miss Anna Clifford; but three children of the seven born to them are now living: Evelyn, Edgar, and Leslie. In 1880 Mr. Lail bought a farm of seventy-five acres. He is a Democrat, and his wife is a member of the Baptist Church; he is also holding the office of Justice of the Peace. Daniel Boone was great uncle to his mother, and his great grandfather, Capt. Bryant, was the settler and founder of Bryant's Station, the place which figured so conspicuously in the early Indian wars of the blue grass region.

WILLIAM McMURTRY, farmer; P. O. Robinson; was born in Harrison County, Ky., in 1812, and is the son of James and Nancy (Bryan) McMurtry. His father was a native of Virginia, and at the age of eight years was brought by his parents to Mercer County, Ky. There he grew to man's estate, and became the owner and manager of a tannery, and continued this business for forty years, being at the same time interested in farming; he was the father of eleven children; a member of the Baptist Church, and in his political views a Whig. His death occurred in 1853, his wife having died as early as 1832. William lived with his parents until he was grown to manhood. In 1852 he married Miss Anna Robertson, who has borne him six children, five of whom are living, viz.: James, Frank, Sally, William, and Susan. Mr. McMurtry became the manager of his father's tannery, conducting the same until 1855; in 1859 he removed to his present home, where he has a farm of 400 acres; he is doing a general farm business, though his specialty is breeding fine stock; he and his family are members of the Christian Church, and in politics he is a Democrat.

JAMES M. ROLLINS, farmer; P. O. Boyd; is a Virginian by birth, and son of John and Polly (Monroe) Rollins; he was born March 25, 1817; his parents were also natives of Virginia; his father was a farmer, and removed from his native State to Logan County, O., to carry on this business; he remained a resident of that county until his death, which occurred at the ripe old age of eighty-six years. His mother died in Virginia as early as 1810. At the age of fifteen years James M. left his home and became a resident of Guernsey County, O.; he remained there about eighteen months, and then removed to Nicholas County, Ky., where he remained until 1837, engaged in repairing the Maysville and Lexington Pike; he subsequently became a resident of Council Point, Ark., where, on account of sickness, he remained about eighteen months; in the spring of 1845 he returned to Nicholas County, Ky., and took charge of the farm of Mr. John Holliday; in 1846 he married Miss Elizabeth J. Summitte, who bore him two children: Mary L. and Frances A. About the time of his marriage he removed to Schuyler County, Ill., where he began farming; he remained there, however, but one season, and then returned to Kentucky and settled in Harrison County, buying the farm where he now resides, which now consists of 250 acres. In January of 1852 his wife died, aged twenty-six years, and in 1853 he married Miss Mary J. Swinford, by whom he had six children, viz.: Allie E., Addie, Agnes, Mary L., James W., and Charles. Mr. Rollins and family are members of the Christian Church, and in politics he is a Democrat.

B. M. SWINFORD, farmer; P. O. Berry; was born in Harrison County, Ky., June 7, 1815, and is the son of H. H. and Mickie (Perrin) Swinford. His father was a native of Harrison County, and born in 1789; he worked for many years at the blacksmithing business, and then engaged in farming, in which he was interested at the time of his death, which occurred in 1840; politically he was a Democrat. The mother of B. M. died in 1847; both his parents were members of the Christian Church; Mr. Swinford lived with his parents until he was 20 years of age, and then learned the trade of a carpenter and millwright; he followed this business until 1848, and then began farming on Sycamore Creek, near Cynthiana; he remained there until 1853, and then removed to Lair's Station, where he resumed farm business, and continued the same for two years, when he removed to Covington, Ky.; there he began merchandising and did some carpenter work; he continued a resident of Covington until 1859, and then returned to Harrison County; resumed mill building, which he followed until 1862. He then went to Bourbon County for three years, and then became a resident of Cynthiana for about seven years; in 1871 he made his final move, and settled on the farm he now owns of 140 acres. In 1845, Mr. Swinford was married to Miss Polly Young, who bore him six children, one of whom now lives, James H.; his wife died in 1851, aged thirty-nine years, and in 1871 he married a Mrs. Emily Blair, who was the mother of two living children by her former husband, viz: Joseph and Edward. Both the parents and children are members of the Christian Church, and Mr. Swinford is a Democrat.

"Colville" Residence of John T. Talbott, Bourbon County, Ky.

RUTLAND PRECINCT.

THOMAS F. BUTLER, farmer; P. O. Hinton, Scott Co.; born in Scott County, at Muddy Ford, on the South fork of Eagle Creek, Oct. 4, 1808; his grandfather, James Butler, was an Englishman by birth, and in company with his two brothers, Pierce and Charles, was brought to America by his parents in 1734; they settled in Culpepper County, Va., and all three of the brothers were soldiers in the Revolutionary war; James was killed in a duel while in the army; the circumstances which brought about this unfortunate affair were as follows: he received word that his youngest son, James, had been drowned in James River; he procured a limited furlough and went home to attend the funeral; he overstayed his time three or four days, and upon his return was accused of cowardice by one of his comrades; he immediately challenged him and received a wound which proved mortal. Cornelius Butler, the father of our subject, was born in Culpepper County, Va., June 17, 1772, and in company with his brother Charles, his mother, and three step-brothers (one of whom, Wm. Brissy, is still living in Owenton, aged 93), came to Kentucky in 1792 and settled on Stoner Creek, near Paris; Cornelius worked on a farm, also worked in distillery of Col. Robt. Russell, at Russell's Cave, in Fayette County, from 1801 till 1804; he moved to Muddy Ford, in Scott County, in 1806, where he lived until his death, in 1850. Thos. F. Bu ler, of whom we write, led a roving life till he was thirty-three years of age, having traveled in thirteen States, Mexico, and the province of Texas, where he found himself located at the time it declared its independence. During his travels he had frequent encounters with wild beasts; upon one occasion, while in Mississippi in 1839, overseeing a plantation for a man by the name of Bookout, he was followed by a panther; the animal followed him until they came to a small opening, upon which six oxen were grazing; he attacked one of the oxen, lacerating its haunches terribly with its sharp claws; Butler, though armed, was unable to get a shot for fear of killing one of the oxen, but he was spared the trouble of shooting the panther, for the other five oxen rushed upon the savage brute and literally gored him to death. During the same year, while the hands were burning cotton stalks, Bookout, fearing that the gin might be in danger of catching fire, came down about dusk, and was standing by one of the fires, when a panther appeared on the opposite side of the fire; he was apparently aiming to catch a dog that was in the company, and being intent upon prey, he seized Bookout, when they both rolled over in the fire, and both came out badly burned; Butler shot at the panther twice, but in the uncertain light did not kill him. On June 8, 1843, he married Harriett, daughter of Thomas and Betsey (Wickhoff) Riley, both of Culpepper County, Va.; his wife died about six months after their marriage of consumption; on the first of May, 1845, he married his present wife, Melvina, daughter of Asher and Nancy (Mitchell) Hinton, of Virginia, by whom he is the father of four children, all boys, three of whom are living. The oldest, Benjamin T., born Oct. 10, 1846, and married, first Frances Havicus, second Kate Patterson, and third Adelaine Beatty, of Atlanta, Ga.; this son entered the Southern army when only sixteen, and served throughout the war under Caantrill, Buford and Morgan; he was captured while with Morgan in his Ohio raid, and put into Camp Douglass, where he remained for sixteen months; he was released upon a special order of President Lincoln, obtained by his father in a personal interview. About this time, the Federal troops threatened to hang Mr. Butler, whereupon he fled to Richmond, Va., where he had the privilege of shaking hands with the President of the Southern Confederacy, whom he had formerly known in Mississippi; his second son, George Braxton, married Mary Fightmaster, and is now residing at Hinton Station, in Scott County; his third son, Mitchell F., seems to inherit the wandering disposition that characterized his father's boyhood, having traveled through nearly all the Gulf and Atlantic states. Both Mr. and Mrs. Butler are members of Mt. Olivet Christian Church in Scott County.

P. S. BROOKS, farmer; P. O. Hinton, Scott Co.; is a native of Harrison County, where he was born Oct. 8, 1837; his great-grandfather, Wm. Brooks, was a soldier of the Revolution; his grandfather, Wm. Brooks, and his father, James Brooks, emigrated from Tazewell County, Va., in 1815, and settled in Fleming County; he removed to Harrison in 1816, and settled near the head waters of Raven. Creek, James Brooks is still living with his son, P. S. Brooks, the subject of this sketch. P. S. Brooks and Mary Brooks, his first cousin, daughter of Colby and Any (Henry) Brooks, were married in 1860; they have eight children, all of whom are living: James C., born Oct. 12, 1861; Mary J., born March 16, 1864; Julia Ann, born

Oct. 16, 1865; Rhoda, born July 17, 1866; Wm. P., Jno. A., born May 20, 1875; Henrietta, born Dec. 13, 1876; Alice, born Feb. 13, 1879. Mr. Brooks joined the order of Free Masons in 1865, first uniting with the Mullin Lodge at Rutland, where he remained till the organization of the Raven Creek Lodge, in 1875; since that time his membership has been with the latter body, and he has filled the several offices pertaining to that institution with credit; he is now Senior Warden; in politics his sympathies are with the Republican party.

LEWIS COLLINS, farmer; P. O. Rutland; is a native of Jessamine County, Ky., where he was born Oct. 16, 1826, near Keene, on Sinking Creek; his grandfather, John Collins, was born in Orange County, Va., and in company with Mr. Allen, the maternal grandfather of our subject, was in the battle of Bunker's Hill, where both were wounded; he was also at the surrender of Cornwallis, at Yorktown, having served through the entire war; he often related to his family the joke that a darkey passed on the noted English commander at the time of the surrender. Upon being told that Cornwallis had surrendered, he replied: "He no more Cornwallis, Massa; he Cob-wallis now." After the Revolutionary war he came to Kentucky, passing over the Alleghanies, and continuing his journey down the Ohio River in a flat boat; he landed at May's Lick; came through to Central Kentucky; their party camped at the Lower Blue Licks two or three days after the battle at that place, which decided the fate of so many of the Kentucky brave pioneers. He and his son William were detailed as a guard at this place while the others slept; they passed through Lexington when it consisted of only a few log cabins, and settled on South Elkhorn, in Fayette County; he leased 200 acres of land from Col. Bowman, and was offered a title to it for a wagon and team, but refused; he worked it during his lifetime, and had it in good condition, but his lease expiring with his life, his family could reap no benefit from his labor; he died in Fayette County in the sixty-sixth year of his age, and was buried in the graveyard of the old Baptist Church, at South Elkhorn. Whitfield Collins, son of John and father of Lewis, was born in Orange County, Va., April 16, 1782; he was about six years old when his father moved to Kentucky. When a small boy, he and his brother went to Ryman's Mill; being compelled to remain over night, their horses were placed in a lot adjoining the mill, while they stood guard from the mill window. When about twenty-four years of age he entered the ministry of the old style Baptist Church, in which he labored until his death, Feb. 18, 1871. His career as a minister was a noted one, extending for a period of sixty-four years, having as his associates Ambrose Dudley and his son Thomas P., Matthias Gossett, William Conrad, and others. Like most of the pioneer preachers of his time, his work was scattered over a large territory, embracing churches in most of the counties of Central Kentucky. On the 1st of February, 1804, he married Sarah, daughter of David Allen, of Pennsylvania, by whom he had thirteen children, and with whom he lived for more than sixty years, she dying Jan. 5, 1865, in the eighty-second year of her age. Lewis Collins, the subject of this sketch, came to Harrison County with his father when three years of age, and settled at Rutland, where he now resides. His brother, Meredith Collins, twenty-one years his senior, was the first resident of Rutland. Lewis worked with his father till he was twenty-seven years old, when he married Martha Ann, daughter of Samuel and Rachel (Boyers) Eckler, receiving from his father at that time thirty-seven acres of land, a part of his present farm; his early education was quite limited, and after his marriage, while erecting the house in which he now lives, he was taught at night by Joseph Miller, the stonemason who assisted him in his work; he has a family of seven children, the oldest, Samuel, born July 21, 1854, an active member of the Cynthiana Commandery of Knights Templar; his second child, Sarah, has been afflicted since her eleventh year, and is now confined to her bed all the time, and has not spoken a word for three years; Eliza, born Dec. 17, 1857, married to William Hannah; Mary Elizabeth, Jan. 19, 1859; Lewis W., Dec. 15, 1861; Alice G., July 1, 1864, and Martha Ann, April 28, 1870. He stood three drafts for the late war; was ordered into the ranks by Col. Landrum during the first battle of Cynthiana. Himself and wife are both members of the Mill Creek Baptist Church; in politics he is a Republican.

WM. P. CROSTHWAIT, farmer; P. O. Rutland; was born in Harrison County, Oct. 20, 1814; his grandfather died in Virginia under the old British law, hence all the property was inherited by his oldest brother, Shelton. This brother was a wholesale merchant, and very wealthy; upon one occasion he gave a dinner to some of his friends, and was accidentally shot by one of his guests. Wm. Crosthwait, the father of our subject, was born in Virginia, and came to Kentucky about 1793, being then about twenty-one years of age; he settled on Mill Creek, about two and one-half miles west of Cynthiana, where he engaged in farming and working at the carpenter's trade; he was a soldier of the war of 1812–15; he died in 1833, aged about sixty years. W. P. Crosthwait, for whom this sketch was prepared, married first, Jane, daughter of Thomas and Ellen (Robinson) Faulconer, of Harrison County, whose birth occurred the same date of his own; they had four children, named respectively, Louisa, Mary E., Wm. T. and Susan; his wife died April 24, 1842, and July 7 of the same year, he was married to Emily, daughter of John and Elizabeth (Rodgers) Hutcherson, of Harrison County; by this wife he had six children, named, respectively: Sarah, Elizabeth, Lizaett, Jno. P., James M., Henry F. On the 9th of April, 1860, he was afflicted with the loss of his second wife, and on the 3rd of Oct. of the same year, he married Maria Trimble, of Virginia, who bore him two children: Louisa E. and Maggie M.; he is now a widower for the third time; he has had thirty-nine grandchildren, thirty-six of whom are living; he was elected to the Magistracy of his precinct in 1859; he resigned in 1861; he is a Democrat, also a member of the Baird Presbyterian Church, of Scott County.

THOMAS S. FAULCONER, farmer; P. O. Hinton, Scott Co.; was born in Harrison County, Jan. 31, 1882. His grandfather, Reuben Faulconer, came from Culpepper County, Va., in 1810, and settled on Raven Creek. His life was devoted to teaching; he was noted for his piety. When a small boy he was bitten by a mad dog, and in his declining years was subject to spasms, which probably caused his death in June, 1845, at the advanced age of fourscore. Edmund Faulconer, father of our subject, was born in Virginia in March, 1798, and was consequently twelve years of age when he came to Kentucky. He married Elizabeth, daughter of Jonathan Hedger, who was a soldier of the war of 1812, and Mary Caplinger. He died Jan. 7, 1875. T. S. Faulconer received his education as a farmer from the excellent precepts of his father. He married Jane Faulconer, daughter of Jno. and Melissa (Faulconer) Jones, and relict of W. N. Faulconer, all of Harrison County. She had three children when married the second time, viz: Jno. C., Annie M., and Nathaniel. T. S. Faulconer has six children: Sarah E., married to Jno. Matthews; James E.; Susan E., married to Spencer Faulconer of Kenton County; Thomas G. and Lucy. Mr. Faulconer has been a member of the Mullin (Masonic) Lodge, at Rutland, since its organization; is a thorough Democrat, and much devoted to field sports. He has traveled from Canada to Georgia, on account of his delicate health.

EDMUND P. FAULCONER, farmer; born in Harrison County, on the south fork of Raven Creek, Oct. 7, 1834; his two grandfathers, Richard Faulconer and Edmund Pollard, both came from Culpepper County, Va., while the prowling Indian still roamed this delightful hunting ground. Richard Faulconer was a farmer by occupation; he died in Harrison County, aged seventy. Benjamin Faulconer, father of our subject, was born in Harrison County; was a farmer; married first Emily Pollard, by whom he had nine boys; he then married Nancy Hawkins, of Scott County; his third wife was Mary J. Skinner, of Harrison, by whom he had three children; he died in Harrison in July, 1859. Edmund P. Faulconer was raised a farmer; he married Lucy Faulconer, daughter of Nathaniel Faulconer, who was an old soldier of the war of 1812, and whose father was one of the first settlers of Shelby County, having built the first mill that was ever built on South Elkhorn; he married Mary Straughan; four children were born to them; Robert H., April 15, 1867; Emily F., Nov. 26, 1870; Mary W., June 28, 1873; Sallie J., Nov. 19, 1879. His right of suffrage has always been exercised for the furthering of the interests of the Democratic party.

JNO. K. GRAY, farmer; P. O. Broadwell; his grandfather, Wm. Gray, came from Pennsylvania at an early day and settled in Harrison County, near Cynthiana, giving name to the stream known as Gray's Run, which rises near Leesburg and flows into South Licking, at Cynthiana. Having been an extensive trader in hogs and cattle, he was known very familiarly over the greater part of central Kentucky. His son, James Gray, the father of Jno. K., is still living at his home near Broadwell, in the enjoyment of a ripe old age (see Biog). On the 15th Nov., 1860, when in his twenty-fourth year, Jno. K. Gray was united in marriage to Marietta, daughter of James and Susan (Dewett) Henry, of Harrison County. Their union has been blessed with three children: James H., born Oct. 28, 1861; Mary S., born Aug. 6, 1863; Margaret Ann, born Jan. 14, 1868. Their home was invaded May 12, 1875, by the stern messenger of death, who bore away their youngest. Mr. and Mrs. Gray have for many years been in communion with the Silas Baptist Church, of Bourbon County. Both the children are also members of the same denomination—the daughter at Silas and the son at Friendship, on Raven Creek. Mr. Gray devotes his entire attention to farming and stock raising, being the owner of about 260 acres of good blue grass land. During the progress of the Grange Lodge at Broadwell, he was one of the leading members. His suffrage has always been exercised for the support of the Democratic party.

WM. T. GOODMAN, farmer; born in Pendleton County, June 11, 1833. Grandfather Zachariah Goodman came from Virginia, about 1800, and settled in Pendleton County, where he died at an advanced age. Lafayette Goodman, father of our subject, was born in Pendleton County about 1801. He followed farming, and died in 1841. Wm. T. was raised a farmer; married Elizabeth, daughter of James and Anna (Dewett) Redd, of Harrison County. They have had ten children, seven of whom are living, the dates of whose births are as follows: Jno. J., Dec. 6, 1858; Allen B., Sept. 12, 1861; Anna, April 24, 1863; Zachariah, July 12, 1865; William, Sept. 27, 1868; Effie, Feb. 28, 1871; Mattie, June 24, 1874; politics, Democrat. Mrs. Goodman is a member of the Christain Church at Stringtown, in Grant County.

THOMAS W. HARDY, farmer; P. O. Rutland; born in Greenup County, July 15, 1837. His grandfather, Thomas Hardy, was a native of Scotland, whence he emigrated and settled in Virginia; he was a soldier of the war of 1812–15, at the close of which he moved from Virginia and settled near Chillicothe, Ohio, where he died. Rev. John C. Hardy, father of our subject, was born at Chillicothe, and was educated for the Methodist ministry. At the age of twenty-one he was stationed on the Greenup Circuit. He is still living in Lewis County, but owing to an affection of his throat he is compelled to desist from his ministerial labors. When quite young, he was a soldier of the war of 1812, but never engaged in any regular battles. T. W. Hardy was taken by his father to Mason County, where he was raised. In 1859 he came to Harrison and settled near White Oak Meeting House. He married Sarah F., daughter of James W. and Sarah (Lair) Berry, by whom he has four children, aged as follows: Lena T., thirteen; Charles M., twelve; Albert B., ten; Julia E., seven. Mr. Hardy was the first Master of Raven Creek (Masonic) Lodge, having taken an active part in securing the dispensation for said Lodge; he is also a Knight Templar of the Cynthiana Commandery, and now holds the position of Junior Warden in the same. Himself and wife are members of the Methodist Church at Mt. Zion; he was elected a delegate to represent the Kentucky Conference in the general conference which met at Louisville in 1877. In August, 1880, Mr. Hardy was elected Magistrate of the Rutland Precinct as the regular nominee of the Democratic party. In September, 1862, he enlisted in the Southern army under Humphrey Marshall. When Marshall left Kentucky he held the office of Captain; he afterwards acted as Adjutant and scout under Forrest; he served throughout the war; was in several engagements; at the battle of Chickamauga he was wounded; afterward taken with small-pox at Louisville, where he remained till close of the war, literally wearing out the disease by his strong constitution.

G. W. HINTON, farmer; P. O. Hinton; was born in Scott County, Aug. 29, 1829; his grandfather, Wm. Hinton, came from Culpepper Court House, Va., in 1794, and settled at Turkey Foot, in Scott County, taking up one thousand acres of land; his family and effects were transported from Virginia in wagons; he was one of the first settlers of Turkey Foot, which takes its name from the faot that three streams unite at that point, forming a figure which bears some resemblance to the shape of the foot of that remarkable Western bird. During those early days they were much troubled with Indians and wild beasts, and had to keep their sheep and cattle in pens to protect them from the ravages of wolves and panthers. The father of our subject was born in Virginia in 1784, and was ten years old when the family moved to Kentucky. G. W. Hinton lived with his father till twenty-two years of age, when he removed to Harrison County and run a sawmill, in partnership with his brother-in-law, T. F. Butler; Sept. 6, 1857, he married Millie, daughter of Capt. John and Catharine (Lemon) Rennaker, of Harrison County; he is the father of three children, namely: Jno. T., born Oct. 6, 1858, married to Miss Jeffers, of Grant County; Mary E., born Feb. 7, 1860, married to J. T. Stone, of Scott County; and Wm. A., born Feb. 2, 1872; was elected Magistrate of Rutland precinct in 1865 and served four years; was re-elected in 1869, receiving at this time the largest vote that has ever been given to any man in Rutland Precinct. Mr. Hinton has devoted his life to farming and trading; he is the owner of 375 acres of land lying in Harrison and Scott Counties, and is a prudent and successful business man; himself and wife are members of the Christian Church at Mt. Olivet, in Scott County, where he has been an Elder since the organization of the church, in 1868; he votes with the Democratic party.

NEWTON HENRY, farmer; was born in Harrison County, Nov. 5, 1822; his grandfather, Thomas Henry, came from Virginia very early, and settled on the middle fork of Raven Creek; his life was spent in pursuing the peaceful avocation of husbandman; his death occurred about the year 1820. James Henry, father of Newton, was born in Virginia, and came out with his father, settling near him in the same part of Harrison County. He bore an honorable part in the war of 1812–15, but was spared to his family for more than half a century after its close. He died in the county, where most of his life had been spent, Nov. 3, 1866. Newton Henry spent his boyhood upon his father's farm, receiving what education could be gleaned from the country schools of that day. He married Elizabeth, daughter of Pollard and Louisa (Crosthwait) McKenney, of

Harrison County, by whom he had three children; the only surviving one, James, was born Aug. 15, 1846. Mr. Henry has always been an ardent Republican. During the year 1864 he enlisted under Capt. Thomas Musselman, of the Harrison County Home Guards.

GEORGE HAMPTON, farmer; P. O. Corinth; his grandfather, Andrew Hampton, paternal uncle of Gen. Wade Hampton, of South Carolina, came to Kentucky about the year 1790, and settled on the middle fork of Raven Creek. He engaged in farming, and through a long and useful life commanded the esteem of his fellow men. His remains repose in the old burying ground of Raven Creek. Thomas Hampton, the father of our subject, was born in Kentucky, about the time or shortly after his father's settlement. Besides farming, he acquired the trade of gunsmith, which he carried on with success for several years. He died at his home in Harrison County, May 9, 1837. Geo. Hampton was born Feb. 18, 1832, and received his early training upon his father's farm. In the year 1857, he married Paulina, daughter of Crockett Evans, of Wales, Great Britain, by whom he has four children, named and aged respectively: Asa, 17; Lucy, 15; Lena, 6; Gen. Wade, 5. In politics, Mr. Hampton is a staunch Democrat. Mrs. Hampton is a member of the Methodist Church, at Laton's Chapel, in Grant County, Ky.

HENRY HILES, farmer; was born in Scott County, Jan. 22, 1825; his grandfather, Christopher Hiles, was a native of Germany; he emigrated to Kentucky, and settled on Eagle Creek, in Scott County; he was a soldier of the war of 1812-15; he died about 1833. Jno. C. Hiles, father of our subject, was born in Scott County in 1799; he served several days in his father's stead in the war of 1812, not being old enough to enlist regularly; he was a farmer; he married Ruth, daughter of Henry Chappell; he died March, 1877. Henry Hiles was raised in Scott County, and married Ellen, daughter of Edmund and Elizabeth (Hedger) Faulconer, of Harrison; he moved to Harrison and settled where he now lives, in 1853; he was one of the first members of the Raven Creek Lodge, assisting in its erection. Mrs. Hiles is a member of the Methodist Church at Mt. Zion.

LEWIS M. HENRY, farmer; born in Harrison County about the year 1816. His grandfather, John Henry, came from Virginia very early and settled on the Middle Fork of Raven Creek, where he died about the year 1820. Jas. Henry, father of Lewis, came out from Virginia when quite small; he followed farming for an occupation; he was in the war of 1812-15; he died at home, aged sixty-five. Lewis M. Henry married Elizabeth, daughter of Thomas and Lucy (Matthews) Hampton, of Harrison; had nine children, eight of whom are living: Nellie J., James T., Richard H., George, Andrew, John, Lewis, and Allen. Mr. Henry is a member of the Friendship Baptist Church; his right of suffrage has always been exercised in the interest of the Democratic party.

GREENBERRY KINMAN, farmer; P. O. Hinton; his grandfather, William Kinman, came from Pennsylvania about 1800, and settled on the South fork of Raven, where he had two small distilleries for peach and apple brandy; he took great delight in hunting, and a relic of one of his expeditions is still preserved by his grandson in the shape of an elk horn. David Kinman, the father of our subject, was but nine years old when his father came from Pennsylvania; he engaged chiefly in farming and transporting merchandise from the Ohio River to the interior of Kentucky; he died June, 1855, aged sixty-three years. Greenberry, when only seven years of age, went with his father and several others to the town of Augusta, and brought back salt on horseback; this was before a wagon road had been cut to that place from Cynthiana. On Sept. 4, 1843, he married Eliza, daughter of Edmund and Betsy (Hedger) Faulconer, by whom he had no children; on June 13, 1871, he married Elizabeth, daughter of Richard and Phoebe (Hedger) McKenney, of Harrison County. Himself and wife are members of the Methodist Church at Boyer's Chapel; in politics Mr. Kinman was formerly a Whig, but since the disruption of the Know-nothing party he has cast his lot with the Democrats.

JAMES S. KINMAN, farmer; born in Pike County, Indiana, April 23, 1824; his grandfather, James Kinman, came from Georgia and settled in Indiana very early; Elijah Kinman, father of our subject, came from Georgia, and with his father, settled in Indiana, where he died in 1827, aged about fifty years. James S. Kinman, of whom we now write, came to Kentucky with his mother when about six years old, and settled on the middle fork of Raven Creek. He married Elizabeth, daughter of Alex. and Delilah (Fightmaster) Dungan, of Harrison County. He was elected Constable of Rutland Precinct in 1853, and served nine months; in 1864 he was appointed by the county court to fill out the unexpired term of W. N. Matthews, and elected to same in 1865; he served two years. Mrs. Kinman is a member of the Raven Creek Baptist Church. In politics Mr. Kinman is a Democrat.

C. P. KINMAN, farmer; was born in Indiana, Oct. 20, 1827. (For history of ancestry, see biography of his brother, James S. Kinman.) He married Louisa, daughter of Thos. and Lucy (Matthews) Hampton, of

Harrison County, by whom he has had seven children, five of whom survive, viz: Jesse, born March 3, 1861; Elijah, born May 1, 1863; Mary A., born July 31, 1866; Elizabeth, born Jan. 18, 1872; Daniel M., born Aug. 23, 1879. Mrs. Kinman is a member of the Raven Creek Baptist Church. Politically, Mr. Kinman is a Democrat; was for a number of years an active member of the Raven Creek order of Patrons of Husbandry.

W. N. MATTHEWS, farmer; P. O. Hinton; was born in Harrison County, June 22, 1837; his grandfather, Richard Matthews, came from Virginia at an early day, and settled in Harrison County, where he engaged in farming; also had copper distillery on his place, in which he worked up the produce of his own and adjoining farms. He died at an advanced age, and is buried on the farm now occupied by his grandson. The father of our subject is still living, in the eighty-eighth year of his age, stout and active. W. N. Matthews was raised as a farmer, which occupation he has successfully prosecuted, being the owner of 325 acres of good land, lying on the middle fork of Raven Creek. On the 30th of September, 1858, he married Eunice, daughter of Isaac and Eunice (Coulston) Ramey, of Harrison County, by whom he has eight children, four boys and four girls, named respectively: Mary E., Lucy E., Alfred R., Robert B., George C., Eva J., Flora B., and James T. In 1863 he was elected Constable of Rutland Precinct, but resigned in 1864, to enlist in the Federal army; he was elected Captain of Co. I, 1st Kentucky State Guards, under Col. E. P. Hawkins, and Lieut. Col. J. J. Craddock; he served till the close of the war, receiving his discharge in 1865. After the war he was nominated by the Republican party for the office of Magistrate, but was defeated by John Burgess, the Democratic nominee. In 1869 he was elected Magistrate as an Independent candidate, over A. J. Perkins, the champion of the Democratic party; was elected to the same office again in 1879, as an Independent candidate, over John Burgess, his first opponent; is a member of Raven Creek (Masonic) Lodge; has filled every office in it, from Tyler to Master; is Treasurer at the present time. Till the outbreak of the war he was a Democrat; his opposition to secession accounts for his present political views.

RICHARD MATTHEWS, farmer; P. O. Hinton; was born in Harrison County, Feb. 25, 1839; his grandfather, Richard Matthews, came from Virginia at an early day, and settled in Harrison County; he married Susan, sister of Whitfield Collins; he died in Harrison County in 1837, upwards of three score and ten years of age. Lewis Matthews, father of our subject, was born in Harrison County, in 1817; he was a farmer; he married Jane, daughter of Thomas and Betsey (Kendall) Redd; he was noted for his fondness for hunting, and other out-door sports; he perhaps killed more deer than any other man of his day; he was an exceptionally good marksman, and at the outbreak of the Mexican war he was Captain of a rifle company. Richard Matthews spent his early life upon his father's farm; when nineteen years of age he married Fannie J., daughter of Colby and Ann (Henry) Brooks, by whom he had six children, four of whom are living, aged as follows: Annie S., twenty-one; Thomas, eighteen; Jane, sixteen; Ollie, thirteen; his wife died Feb. 21, 1870; he next married Rosa, daughter of John F. and Mary (Woollums) Linn, by whom he is the father of four children, three of whom survive, viz: Mary E., aged nine; Levie, six; Effie, four, and Maggie, two; he is a member of Friendship Baptist Church; politics, Democrat.

LORENZO McKENNEY, farmer; he was a native of Harrison County, where he was born Oct. 28, 1842. His grandfather, Traverse McKenney, of Virginia, was one of the early settlers of Harrison County. Pollard McKenney, father of our subject, was twelve years of age when he accompanied his father, Traverse, to the then unsettled wilds of Kentucky. A quarter of a century ago he was familiarly known in Scott, Harrison and Owen counties, where he carried on an extensive and lucrative trade in cattle and hogs; he died in 1876, aged sixty-eight. Lorenzo McKenny, his son, and the subject of this sketch, spent his early life upon his father's farm. On the 3d of Sept. 1863, he married Louisa, eldest daughter of William P. and Jane (Faulconer) Crosthwait, of Harrison County, who has borne him seven children, the dates of whose births are as follows: Martha E., Dec. 24, 1875; Louisa, Oct. 11, 1867; Wm. P. Aug. 2, 1869; Thos. N., Sept. 28, 1871; Mary E., June 13, 1874; Richard F., April 26, 1877; Maggie E., April 17, 1880. For several years both himself and wife have been in communion with the Methodist Church, South, holding their membership at Boyer's Chapel. In politics Mr. McKenney has always identified himself with the Democratic party.

W. H. MARTIN, Jr., farmer; P. O. Corinth; born in Harrison County, April 28, 1826, being the oldest of nine children. The longevity of his family is rather remarkable; his grandfather, Benjamin Martin, being over one hundred years of age at the time of his death, and all of his children being still alive but one. Benjamin Martin was among the first of those who left the soil of Old Virginia and sought a home in the land of cane. He made his first settlement in Bourbon County, and took an active part in those early struggles which fell to the lot of every frontiersman, and served with honor throughout the war of 1812. In company with his family, among whom was William Martin, Sr., the father of our subject, he moved to Harrison County about the year 1825, and settled near where Casey's mill now stands, on Raven Creek. W. H. Martin, Jr., of whom we write, was raised a farmer, and notwithstanding his limited education, has managed his affairs with economy and foresight; he finds himself now in possession of a good farm of 140 acres, which he is constantly improving and enlarging. His staple crop is tobacco, the handling of which he understands to advantage. He married Zerelda, daughter of Richard and Elizabeth (Johnson) Johnson, of Clark County, Ky., by whom he has had eleven children, seven of whom are living: John William, aged 24; Mary Ann, 23; Edward and Almi, 22; Martha, 19; Ida, 17; Andrew, 13. Mrs. Martin is a member of the Crooked Creek Baptist Church, of Grant County. In politics Mr. Martin is a Democrat.

JACOB PERKINS, farmer; P. O. Hinton; was born in Harrison County, Ky., April 15, 1848; is the son of Eli Perkins, and the grandson of John Perkins, both natives of Harrison County; his father has been engaged in farming all his life, and is still living in Scott County, aged about sixty years. In 1867 Jacob Perkins was married to Cannarissa, daughter of Calton and Margaret (Hinton) Bailey, of Scott County; five children have been born to them, four of whom still survive: George W., born April 17, 1869; Mary E., born Feb. 26, 1871; Josie A., born March 30, 1873; Leathy, born Sept. 5, 1879. Himself and wife hold their church membership at Byer's Chapel; politically, he has always been identified with the Democratic party.

JNO. S. SCOTT, farmer; was born in Sussex County, Del., May 8, 1821; his grandfather, William Scott, was one of five brothers who emigrated from Ireland and settled in Virginia; in 1781, he came from Virginia and settled on Boyd's Run, near Newtown, in what is now Bourbon County; he took an active part in the early struggles with the Indians; he was Captain of a scouting party, and one of the number who followed to the Ohio River the murderers of the Shanks family; about 1794 he moved to Harrison County and settled on Gray's Run, near Cynthiana, where he died in 1831, aged eighty-six. Jno. Scott, father of Jno. S., was born in Virginia, Sept. 1, 1773, and was hence eight years old when his father came to Kentucky; went with his father in pursuit of Indians who killed Shanks' family; in 1808, he freed about thirty of his slaves; in 1806, he married Lavina Stafford, of Harrison County, by whom he had one child, James, who afterwards took a boat load of whisky and flour to New Orleans, and was murdered there; in 1808, he moved to Delaware, where he married Annie Handy, of Delaware, his first wife having died in childbirth; in 1812, he enlisted in the war, during which he rendered some valuable services; in 1814 he took the first ship load of lumber to Washington, to be used in the erection of the Capitol Building; he returned to Kentucky in 1826, living one year each in Pittsburg and Cincinnati, on his way back; upon his arrival in Kentucky he settled at Leesburg and started a store; in 1830, he moved to Leeslick; in 1841, he moved to Raven Creek and bought a farm; in 1850, he went to Grant County; thence to Leeslick in 1853, engaging in merchandising in both places; in 1855, he came to live with his son, Jno. S., where he continued to sell goods till his death, which occurred Oct. 11, 1860, he then being in his eighty-eighth year. Jno. S. Scott came to Kentucky with his father, and lived with him till he was twenty-four years old; March 7, 1844, he married Sarah, daughter of Captain James and Annie (Webber) Burgess; they have eight living children: James T., born Dec. 25, 1844; Wm. W., June 8, 1846; Jno. B., April 10, 1848; Sarah, March 10, 1854; Louisa, April 9, 1856; Effie J., Sept. 24, 1860; Henry, May 17, 1863; Charles, June 15, 1865. Mr. Scott was one of the first members of Mullin (Masonic) Lodge, at Rutland, now a member of Raven Creek, which lodge was dedicated by him; in 1854, he was elected Magistrate and served four years; since 1858, he has been Deputy County Clerk, except the seven years that he sold goods; has been a farmer all his life; owns 320 acres of land on Raven Creek; in the way of curiosities, he has now in his possession a quilt which was pieced by his mother in 1812; the calico was bought while the embargo act was in force, and cost from seventy-five cents to one dollar per yard. Mr. Scott is a member of the Methodist Church at Mt. Zion; in politics he is a thorough Democrat.

JOHN SWINFORD, farmer; P. O. Rutland; was a native of Harrison County, where he was born March 17, 1837. His grandfather, John Swinford, came from North Carolina very early and settled in Harrison County; he died at advanced age of seventy years. His grandfather on mother's side, Edmund Pollard, was a soldier in the Revolutionary war. His father, Matthew Swinford, was born in Harrison County, in the year 1800; he was a cooper by trade, but farming was his principal occupation; he died in native County, aged seventy years. John Swinford, the subject of this sketch, was early trained to till the soil. He married Nancy, daughter of

Thomas and Caroline (Garnett) Rose, of Harrison County; has four children, named and aged respectively: Thos. N., eleven; James D., eight; Cora F., six; Edmund F., three. Both himself and wife are members of the Methodist Church at Boyer's Chapel. Politically he is a Democrat.

HON. W. A. WEBBER, farmer; P. O. Rutland; whose portrait appears in this work, is a native of Jessamine County, Ky., where he was born March 4, 1817; his paternal grandfather came from Virginia to this State about 1795, and settled in Jessamine County, where he resided up to the time of his death, which occurred about 1815. His widow, Sarah (Anderson) Webber, removed with her family, consisting of five daughters, one son, and grandson (subject) to Harrison County, in 1817; Annie W., the eldest, and widowed daughter, who was mother of our subject, after coming to Harrison County, married James Burgess, by whom she raised three sons and three daughters, and died in 1834; her son, W. A. Webber, like many other young men of that early day, enjoyed but limited facilities for an education; being the eldest son, he was compelled to remain at home the greater portion of his time, and attend to the duties of the farm, such as going to mill, caring for the stock, &c., &c.; when but fourteen years of age, he relinquished the idea entirely of securing even a fair education, and at once turned his attention to making a living for himself; his first venture was to hire out to a neighbor by the month, for which service he received the very limited salary of $3.50. However, by carefully saving this paltry sum, and adding to it little by little, in a few years he found himself possessed of sufficient means to purchase and pay for a small tract of ten acres of land. About this time he had a dissipated neighbor, who owned about 100 acres of land, and who was accustomed to sell from five to ten acres annually for the purpose of defraying his expenses, and our subject by industry and economy managed to save money enough yearly to buy these small strips, and in a few years he possessed the entire farm. In 1841 Mr. Webber had increased his farm to 150 acres, and on Dec. 21 of this year, he was married to Lucinda Jane, daughter of James and Nancy (Blair) Baird, and to the help and counsel of this most estimable wife and companion, Mr. Webber attributes much of his future success. This union was blessed with one son, James Henry, who was born on the 29th of January, 1843; when in his twentieth year this only son left his parental roof and started to join the Southern army, but being of a very delicate constitution, he was taken sick a few days afterward at Lexington, Ky.; his parents hearing of this, they at once sent and had him brought home, where he died on the 16th of January, 1863. In 1853 Mr. Webber sold his entire farm, then containing 300 acres, and removed to Rutland, where he engaged in the mercantile business for twelve months, in partnership with John Mullin; at the end of this year they sold their store to William Laughlin, and our subject exchanged his other Rutland property for 200 acres of land lying about one mile west of that place, where he moved in 1855, and again engaged in agricultural pursuits; in 1860 he again sold out and bought an undivided one-half interest in what was then known as the Kendall farm, and upon which he still resides; this farm contained 845 acres. At the close of the third year on this place he purchased the other half; in 1870 he added 170 acres more to his farm, which made him one of the largest land owners in his end of the county; besides this he owns good property at Williamstown, Grant Co. and also at Glencoe, on the Short Line Railroad; 300 shares in the Farmers' National Bank of Cynthiana, and much more than this amount loaned out to his neighbors and friends; thus showing to the rising young men of his county what can be accomplished by industry, economy, and close application to business; he is a Director of the Harrison County Agricultural Association, also of the Farmers' National Bank of Cynthiana, dating his connection with both corporations from their foundation. In 1877 Mr. Webber was elected by the Democratic party to represent his county in the Lower House of the Legislature, which office he filled with credit to himself and entire satisfaction to his constituency. He and his wife, who is now an invalid, have been prominently connected with the Methodist Church for many years.

W. A. Webber

UNITY PRECINCT.

SAMUEL J. ASHBROOK, farmer and distiller; P. O. Cynthiana; was born in Harrison County, Ky., Jan. 13, 1831; son of Aaron Ashbrook, who had seven children. Our subject received what education the pioneer log school houses afforded in the early times, and, being raised a farmer, has followed that occupation in addition to distilling. He began life in moderate circumstances, but by economy and industry has acquired a competency, he owning at the present time 400 acres of land, and a half interest in a distillery. Mr. Ashbrook has been a director of the Harrison County Agricultural and Mechanical Association for twenty years; a director of Farmers' National Bank since its organization; President and Treasurer of Ashbrook Mills Road; also Treasurer Trickum Road, and School Trustee in District No. 7, for several years. May 8, 1856, he married, in this county, Susan R. Robertson, born near Cynthiana, in August, 1835, daughter of James Robertson, and from that union there have been born three children: Aaron, George and Minnie. Self and family are members of the Christian Church, and he is a Democrat.

COL. THOMAS T. GARNETT, farmer and trader; P. O. Cynthiana. Among the early emigrants to Kentucky was Larkin Garnett, who was born in Virginia about 1782, and came to this State in 1807 and settled near Cynthiana, Harrison County, where he spent the remainder of his days. He married Elizabeth Bell, also of Virginia birth, by whom he raised six sons and six daughters. He was a farmer and mechanic, and by close application to business he managed to accumulate considerable property. He ranked among the prominent men of his day, and died in October, 1856, respected by all who knew him. His eldest son, Thomas T., who is the subject of this sketch, was born in Virginia, on the 15th of May, 1806, and when only about one year old was brought by his parents to Harrison County, Ky., where he was reared and educated, and where he still resides. When he arrived at the age of maturity his father gave him a good horse, with which he ventured out upon his own resources, full of energy and ambition. On the 4th of Oct., 1840, Col. Garnett was married to Louisa Wiglesworth, who was born in the county in 1819, and was the daughter of John and Jane (Bush) Wiglesworth, who were also residents of Harrison County. In the early days of this county's history our subject was elected Captain of a militia company, and subsequently promoted to major and colonel, which latter title he still bears. He was also elected justice of the peace in his district, an office he filled very acceptably. He has had born to him two daughters, both of whom are now married and settled in life. His elder daughter, Jane E., is the wife of Dr. W. H. Martin, and Mary F. the wife of Col. William Moore. Col. Garnett has been a very "wide-awake" business man through the early part of his life, being possessed of rare judgment and quick to see a bargain; he has succeeded in acquiring handsome property, consisting of about 1,000 acres of land, upon which he has erected, according to his own plans and designs, one of the best residences in the county (a view of which graces the pages of this work), fronting the K. C. R. R. at Garnett Station, which station was named in honor of our subject. He and his family are all members of the Baptist Church, and he is a straight Democrat in politics.

JNO. A. LAFFERTY, farmer; P. O. Cynthiana; was born in Harrison County, Ky., Feb. 13, 1832, and is the son of James and Susan (Smith) Lafferty, the former a native of Pennsylvania, born Jan. 7, 1790, and died July 15, 1866, and the latter born in Bourbon County, Ky., April 8, 1801, and died Sept. 5, 1838. James Lafferty was a farmer, which business he continued till his death, and at which he learned Jno. A. the duties of self support. Our subject received a common school education, and on May 23, 1855, he married Miss Fanny E., daughter of John and Elizabeth Henry, both natives of Virginia. They have a family of eleven children: W. T., D. N., Tera, Susan E., James F., Francis E., Minnie, Mary E., Purlie, Meddie and Jno. A. Politically Mr. Lafferty has taken quite an active part in the home contests of Harrison County; he filled the office of Constable in Unity Precinct, in 1867–'68, and was elected Sheriff of Harrison County in 1870, and was honored by being reelected, in 1874, and again in 1876, each term being for two years of service. During the war he enlisted in Jno. Shawhan's Battalion, C. S. A., at Prestonburg, Ky., in 1861, and did not return home until 1865; he is a Democrat, a Granger, and a member of the order of A. F. & A. M. Quite an exciting episode in the life of our subject occurred in 1849, while he and his father were on their way to Cincinnati with a team and wagon. When within about twenty miles of the city they were, while eating their dinner by the roadside, set upon by two robbers. In the early part of the conflict, his father was hit upon the head and partially disabled, and though Jno. A. at that date, was but a boy, he fought with the coolness of an old trooper and the fierceness of a tiger. The result of the fight was the death of one of the robbers and the flight of the other. He now enjoys the respect and confidence of the community in which he resides.

GEO. V. NORTHCUTT, farmer and tobacco dealer; P. O. Trickum; was born in Harrison County, Ky., near Rutland, June 5, 1837; son of John and Agnes (Knox) Northcutt; he, born in 1806, in Harrison County, a farmer and son of John Northcutt, who came from Virginia; she, born in Virginia, and came to Kentucky when seven years of age, dying in 1876. They have four sons, and six daughters, our subject being the eldest. George V. received his education in the schools of his native county, and began life as a farmer, continuing at the same vocation till the present time. He began life in moderate circumstances, and by industry and economy has acquired a competency, owning a fine farm of 152 acres of land. He has been a successful producer of tobacco and dealer in the same for eighteen years. Feb. 3, 1859, he married, on Twin Creek, Millia Catharine Juett, born in Harrison County, in January, 1842, daughter of Adam and Susan (Renaker) Juett, and by this union there were born four sons and five daughters: Lewis, George T., Adam, James H., Agnes E., Susan A., Cordelia, Catharine and Alice. Mr. Northcutt and wife are members of the Baptist Church, and he is a Democrat.

LEESBURG PRECINCT.

THOS. B. ARNETT, farmer; P. O. Connersville. Born in Bourbon County in 1825; his father, James Arnett, came from Virginia, and died young, being only forty-seven years old. His grandfather was Zachariah Arnett, a soldier in the war of 1812. His mother, Sarah Woodgate, is still living at the advanced age of eighty-two; she was the daughter of Jonathan and Sarah Woods, of Fayette County. Mr. Arnett has been twice married; first, in 1848, to Miss Susan McDaniel, a daughter of George McDaniel, of Harrison County; she died in 1855, leaving two living children, viz: Sarah L. Mathews and Eliza Jane Cason, and Wm. B. died in 1871; then in 1867, he married Miss Maria McDaniel, sister of the first wife. He owns twenty-two acres of land one mile from Broadwell, but lives one-half mile south of Leeslick. He and wife are consistent members of the Christian Church at Leesburg, he being an Elder, and a member of the Masonic fraternity; he is a Democrat, and was first elected a Justice of the Peace in 1866 and has been three times elected to the same office from Leesburg Precinct; he had, prior to this time, served nine years as Constable of the same precinct. He has one thing to be proud of: having never offered for an office without being endorsed by the people of his precinct. In 1881, he offered for the nomination of County Judge against two popular and well known gentlemen, yet he was endorsed by the people of Leesburg Precinct by a large majority.

DAVID ALLEN, farmer; P. O. Cynthiana; in the primitive days of our Commonwealth, there came many families from Virginia and other States, to occupy some of the fine country of Central Kentucky; among that number were David Allen and Elizabeth Wright, who came when quite young with their parents. Settling near each other they grew up together, loved each other and were married. Among the children of that marriage was David, whose name heads this sketch, being born in Bourbon County in the year 1805. He has been three times married; first to Miss Emily Talbott; daughter of Samuel Talbott, she dying without children. Was married second time to Miss Ellen Berry, daughter of Benjamin Berry; by this wife he has nine living children, named Joseph, Bushrod, Julia Ann, Sarah, Mary, David, Columbus, Martha and Clara. The second wife dying, he was married the last time to Mrs. Maria Way; by this union he has no children. He is owner of 300 acres of good land eight miles from Cynthiana, near Cynthiana and Leesburg Turnpike, and a member of the Methodist Church at Pleasant Green.

CORNELIUS AMMERMAN, farmer; P. O. Cynthiana. Among the early pioneers to Bourbon County was Philip Ammerman, from Maryland. His son, Daniel Ammerman, married a Miss Reed, daughter of Jonathan Reed, of Bourbon, who died in 1864. Philip Ammerman died in 1844. Cornelius Ammerman was born in Bourbon County in 1817, and was married to Miss Elizabeth Renaker, daughter of Jacob and Francis (Bennet) Renaker. By this union they have seven children, named Sarah F. Lydick, Martha Ellen Henry, wife of Thos. Henry, Daniel, Loulie Forsythe of Mercer County, Jacob H., Lizzie W., James L. He is the owner of 307 acres of land five and one-half miles from Cynthiana, near Lexington and Covington roads. He is a Granger, and he and wife are among the leading members of the Methodist Church at Mt. Hope; and he is a good solid citizen.

LUKE ADAMS, farmer; P. O Connersville; a native of Bourbon County, born in 1816. His father was Francis Adams, who came from North Carolina. His mother was America Brennen, daughter of Mr. T. Brennen, who died in Georgetown. Mr. Adams has been three times married, first to Miss Frances Jane Furnish, in 1844. She died in 1857, leaving six children, viz: Wm. F., America Courtney, T. L., Rebecca E., who died in 1875, Anna and McKenny. Then in 1863, he married Emily Courtney. She died in 1865, and in 1866 he married Mrs. Elizabeth Goodnight, of Harrison. He is the owner of 235 acres of land two miles west of Connersville. He is a member and ruling Elder in the Presbyterian Church at Beards, in Scott County, and his wife is a member of the Methodist Church at White Oaks, in Harrison County.

BUSHROD TEMPLE BOSWELL, P. O. Leesburg; farmer and stock raiser; was born Jan. 14, 1811. His father was William Elliott Boswell, born Jan. 8, 1772, and died May 22, 1828. His grandfather was George Boswell, who died near David's Fork in 1817. His mother was Hannah Hardage Smith, daughter of Temple Smith, of Harrison, she being born Aug. 5, 1781, and died Feb. 12, 1863. The father and mother were married in 1810. Our subject was married in 1844, to Miss Susan Smith, by whom he had one child, which died in infancy. Mrs. Boswell dying in 1846, Mr. Boswell, in 1852, married Miss Susan Penn, of Scott County, by whom he has had eight children: William Gustavus, James Lane, Joseph, Sallie Hunter, Lizzie Hardage, Mollie, John, Temple. Mr. Boswell followed farming until 1839, when he commenced selling goods at Leesburg, which he continued until 1861, since which time he has been engaged in farming, owning at the present time 215 acres of land half mile from Leesburg, where, in addition to general farming he raises a high grade of stock. Mr. Boswell volunteered for the Sabine War in 1836, and was Lieutenant of Captain Coleman's company, but was disbanded by proclamation of President Jackson before marching to the front. From 1846 to 1848 he was General of Militia. His father and a brother were in the war of 1812–14. The father of Mr. Boswell came to Kentucky in 1790, from Loudoun County, Va., and was a member of the first Legislature from Harrison County in 1793, serving in the same capacity till 1806; was also a member of the Constitutional Convention in 1799. He commanded a regiment in the war of 1812, and was in the battle of Fort Meigs, in 1813. His wife and two of his children, James and Sallie, are members of the Baptist Church at Silas, and he is a Democrat.

JOSEPH BARKLY, M. D.; P. O. Leesburg. Matthew Barkly, a native of the "Emerald Isle," came to Woodford County at so early a period that the few scattering settlers of the surrounding country had often to take refuge in the fort at Lexington to escape being massacred by the Indians. On one occasion, Mr. Barkly and his family fled to Lexington, and the fort being so crowded with the panic-stricken pioneers that there were no accomodations for them inside the cabins, he and his family had to stand all night against the wall of the fort in a heavy falling rain. They had a son, Robert, who was born soon after their arrival in Woodford County; he grew up to man's estate, married Mary Cooper, lived a long and exemplary life, and died in 1858. Of this union comes he whose name heads this sketch; he was born in Scott County in 1820, and inherited from his ancestry those qualities which adorn, and give tone and strength to life. His grandfather, on the maternal side, was Samuel Cooper, an Englishman by birth, who came to America and settled in Maryland, where he married Jane McClure. The young couple soon after emigrated to Kentucky, settled in Lexington, and helped to build the first frame house in that place. Dr. Barkly was married to Miss Mary E. Kimbrough, of Harrison County, who has borne him the following children: Mary Owings, Ann Eliza, Rachael Cooper, Lizzie, Paul, Martha and Minerva (twins), Charles M. and Robert M. He was graduated from Transylvania University at Lexington, in 1847, and soon thereafter began the practice of medicine at Roanoke, Mo. Here he remained not quite a year, yielding to his inclinations to make the State which gave him birth the theater of his future career; he returned to Kentucky and began the practice of his profession at Leesburg, Harrison Co., where he still remains, enjoying a remunerative practice, and the partiality of a large circle of friends. Dr. Barkly is a member of the Masonic fraternity; himself and wife are communicants of the Methodist Church. In politics he is in accord with the dominant party of the State—the Democracy.

JAMES T. BROCK, farmer; P. O. Leesburg, is descended from good old Virginia stock. His grandfather, Joseph Brock, came from the "Old Dominion" at an early period of Kentucky's history, where he remained for some time, but longing for the scenes of his boyhood, he returned to Virginia, where in due course of time he was gathered to his father's, full of honors and of years. His son, James Brock, continued to reside in the State. He married Miss Nancy Anderson, daughter of Reuben Anderson, who was a faithful and loving companion to him until his death in 1840. She survived him until 1873, when she died at an advanced age. Our subject, a scion of this union, was born in 1832, and is consequently fifty years old. He chose as his partner in the joys and cares of life, Miss Susie Bars, daughter of J. V. Bars, of Boone County, Ky. In 1862, Mr. Brock, catching the spirit of the times, enlisted like thousands of other young Kentuckians, in the Confederate service, and remained until the close of the war, without even returning home during the time. He first entered Co. I., of Col. Basil W. Duke's Regiment, of Gen. John H. Morgan's command, which was subsequently transferred to Col. W. C. P. Breckinridge, to form the nucleus of his Battalion, which was afterwards known as the 9th Kentucky Cavalry. When Lee surrendered at Appomattox, and the stars and bars went down to rise no more, Mr. Brock returned to Harrison County, and began farming on the Leesburg Pike, eight miles from Cynthiana, where he now owns 104 acres of land. Himself and wife are both communicants of the Baptist faith, being members of the Silas Church, Bourbon County. His political affiliations are with the Democracy.

J. M. BOYER, farmer; P. O. Connersville. Among the early settlers of Harrison County was Jacob Boyer. He was a man of great usefulness in his day, and dying left a son named John, who married, and the union producing J. M. Boyer, the subject of this sketch, in 1845. His parents dying when he was five years old, he underwent an orphanage, and has had to struggle for a place in life. How well he has succeeded will be understood when we tell that he is now the owner of 337 acres of land two and one-half miles northeast of Connersville, handsomely improved, and fine productive soil. He married Miss Sarah E. Allen, daughter of David Allen, of Harrison County. By this union they have eight living children, viz: Mary E., Johnnie, Alice C., Perry David, Jacob, Emma; Mattie died in 1877; Allen and Sarah E. He and his wife are worthy and consistent members of the Christian Church at Leesburg. He affiliates with the Democratic party, and as an evidence of the confidence and esteem in which he is held by his neighbors, he was made, and served in the office of Treasurer, of the Grange of which he was a member for a long time.

RICHARD BRAND, farmer; P. O. Cynthiana. About 1780, Richard Brand, grandfather of our subject, emigrated from Scotland and settled in Bourbon County, where he was a practicing physician. His son Richard bought a farm in Harrison County, and married Miss Fannie Brand, daughter of David Brand, of Staunton, Va. Of this union Richard Brand was born in 1833. In 1865 his father died, and the son has been living on the same place since. It is situated seven miles from Cynthiaina, on the Cynthiana and Leesburg Turnpike, and contains 180 acres of land, which he calls "Locust Grove." He is a member of the Methodist Church South, at Pleasant Green, in Bourbon County, and his wife a member of Silas Baptist Church, Bourbon County. She was Miss Fannie Hendricks, a daughter of Esquire Hendricks and Sarah (Falconer) Hendricks; by this union they have five children, named Fannie Dills, wife of Sidney Dills, near Cynthiana, Kentucky. Robert, who is at present at Georgetown Baptist College, Kellar, Edward and Leslie. He is a Democrat and an honorable, upright citizen.

THOMAS D. BASSETT, farmer; P. O., Cynthiana; is a native of Bracken County, having been born there in the year 1837; the son of Jonathan S. Bassett, who was a native of Harrison County, who emigrated to Bracken and died in the year 1862. His grandfather was Amos Bassett, who came from New Jersey to Harrison County at an early day. His mother was Elizabeth Disher, who was of German ancestry. He married Miss Sallie Stockton, daughter of Preston and Mary (Hardin) Stockton, of Franklin County, Ky. By this marriage they have four children living, named Bessie, Harry P., Katie L., and an infant unnamed. He is owner of 133 acres of fine land, five miles from Cynthiana, along the Turnpike that leads from Cynthiana to Connersville, and in this Pike Mr. Bassett holds stock and is one of its directors. He votes the straight Democratic ticket, and his wife is a member of the Free Will Baptist Church.

JOHN CRAIG, farmer; P. O. Cynthiana; is a native of Harrison County, having been born in 1803. His father, John Craig, emigrated here at an early day, being among the early settlers of Harrison County, coming from North Carolina, he underwent many of the hardships of the early pioneers to the "dark and bloody ground." After living to a ripe old age he died in 1841. His mother was Miss Nancy Patterson, of Tennessee birth, who survived the husband just ten years, dying in 1851. When twenty-nine years old, Mr. Craig married Miss Isabella Gray, and for fifty-two years they have enjoyed the joys and divided the sorrows of life together. By this union they have three living children, named Francis, James and William; is the owner of 300 acres of fine blue grass land situated five miles from Cynthiana, on the Leeslick dirt road. He votes always the Democrat ticket and is a good, solid citizen.

JOHN L. CONNER, farmer; P. O. Connersville; was born in Harrison in 1827. His father was John Conner, who died in 1864. His grandfather was a Baptist preacher of the old school; coming from Virginia he settled near where Mr. John L. Conner now lives. His name also was John; having preached for twenty years; he died of cancer in the full assurance of faith. John L. Conner's mother was Mahala (Haden) Conner, daughter of Jerry Haden, of Harrison County. He married Miss Emily Penn, of Scott County, in 1852, and by this union they have no children. He owns 120 acres of land one mile southeast of Connersville. He is a member of the Presbyterian Church, at Beards, Scott County, and his wife is a member of the Methodist Communion, at Mt. Gilead, Scott Co., Ky. Mr. Conner is a man of even habits and is well thought of by his neighbors.

LEWIS L. CONNER, farmer; P. O. Connersville. Among the early settlers of Harrison County, was Rev. John Conner, who emigrated here from Virginia, bringing with him his son Lewis, who, growing to manhood's estate, took as his wife Miss Elizabeth Falconer, daughter of Joseph Falconer, of near Lexington, Kentucky, and she died in 1859, her husband having died just died just ten years preceding her in 1849. Lewis L. Conner married Miss Rebecca Furnish, daughter of William Furnish, of Harrison County, in 1836; have three living children, viz: Eliza Jane, Alpheus,

Sarah Elizabeth. He is owner of 250 acres of land one-fourth mile southeast of Connersville. He is the breeder of all kinds of high grade stock. Both he and wife are members of the Presbyterian Church at Beards, Scott County, in which Church he is a Ruling Elder.

W. K. GRIFFITH, farmer; P. O. Cynthiana; is a native of Harrison County, where he was born at his present residence in 1828. His grandfather, William Griffith, was a native of Virginia, whence he emigrated at an early day, and figured conspicuously in those pioneer struggles which were the common lot of all of Kentucky's early settlers. He was noted for his uprightness and candor, and soon became possessed of the confidence and esteem of his fellow men, having been elected as a delegate to the convention which met at Danville in April, 1792, to frame the first constitution of Kentucky. The father of our subject, Burrell Griffith, married Harriet King, daughter of John King, of Bourbon County, Ky. After a brief period of wedded life the connubial tie was severed by the death of the wife in 1829. The husband survived her eight years, dying in 1837. W. K. Griffith married Miss Margaret Spears, daughter of John K. and Emily Spears, of Bourbon, and is the father of four children: Wm. B., Emma H., Hubert F. and John K. He is the owner of a very fine estate of 1,360 acres of superior blue grass land, located on Cynthiana and Leesburg Pike, five miles from Cynthiana, and called "Silver Lake" from a very fine lake which covers an area of about two acres and adjoins his residence. Mr. Griffith has for several years past been a successful breeder of short-horn cattle and Cotswold sheep, having at the head of his herd "Victor 2nd," by Duke of Broomfield. (American Short Horn Register, Vol. 19, No. 37,192.) His politics are identified with the Democratic party, of which he is a warm and valiant supporter. Mrs. G. is a member of the Christian Church at Leesburg.

JAMES GRAY, farmer; P. O. Cynthiana; a native of Harrison County, born in the year of 1804; his father, William Gray, came from Pennsylvania in 1797 and located in Harrison County, near where his son, James, now lives; his grandfather was also named William; his mother was Jane Craig, daughter of James and Hannah (McCoy) Craig. In 1828 he married Miss Jane McCory, daughter of James McCory, of Bourbon County, Ky.; she died in 1831, leaving one child, now Sarah J. Lail. In 1832, he married Miss Mary Keiser, of Bourbon County, and daughter of John Keiser; she died in 1869, leaving ten children, viz: Susan R., who is dead; Elizabeth, now the wife of Mr. Ammerman, of Harrison County; John K., Margaret, now the wife of Mr. Megibben, of Harrison County; Nancy Umston, Martha Gray, Menory Tucker, Letitia Gray, Addie and Fannie. He is the owner of 350 acres of land five miles from Cynthiana along the line of the Cynthiana and Leesburg Pike. He is the breeder of a high grade of stock. He is a member of the Presbyterian Church of Mt. Pleasant, and by honest toil he has amassed a handsome fortune.

JOHN W. GALBREATH, farmer; P. O. Cynthiana. Benjamin Galbreath and Miss Clara Hall, a daughter of Daniel Hall, of Harrison County, were united in the holy bonds of matrimony; by this union they have a son John W. Galbreath, who was born in Bourbon County, Sept. 23, 1836. His grandfather was John W. Galbreath, who was a Revolutionary soldier, and was killed in the battle of River Raisin. John W., who heads this sketch, married Miss Mary E. Fry, a daughter of William and America Fry, and by this marriage, they have six children, named: Mary Alice, George William, Rosa Lee, Mildred Ann, James Woodford, and Melinda Belle. He is the breeder of high grade stock, and a Democrat in politics.

W. C. HOBSON, farmer; P. O. Connersville; he was born in Clermont County, Ohio, in 1834; his father was William Hobson, who was born in Ireland, and died in Ohio in 1860. His mother, Mary N., was the daughter of Covington Nelson, of Virginia. She died in 1850. He married Miss Wiley, of Harrison County, daughter of B. B. Wiley, who died of cholera in 1850. By this union they have five living children, viz: Emerald W., John B., Lulu A., William A., and Nelson L. He is the owner of ninety-two acres of land, situated some seven miles from Cynthiana on the Cynthiana and Georgetown road. He is a member of the fraternity of A., F. & A. M. His wife is a member of the Christian Church. He is a Republican.

G. T. JOHNSON, farmer; P. O. Connersville; native of Scott County, having been born in that County in 1846; his father, Garland Johnson, died in 1878; his mother, Thirzah (Payne) Johnson, is still living at the advanced age of seventy-four; his grandfather, John R. Johnson, emigrated to this country from Ireland. G. T. Johnson married Miss Amanda Coppage in 1869, daughter of Wesley and Lucinda (Carter) Coppage, of Harrison County; by this union there are five children viz: Ada, Garland, Mollie T., James T. and Asa. He owns 125 acres of land known as the "Minteer" farm, one and a-half miles from Leeslick in a northeast direction, and on the Leeslick and Scott County road. He and wife are members of the Christian Church at Turkey Foot, Scott County, and he is a member of Gilead Grange in Scott County, and an active and uncompromising Democrat.

J. L. LOGAN, farmer; P. O. Connersville; was born in Harrison County in the year 1849; his father, James F. Logan, is still living, at the age of seventy-nine years, having been born in 1802; his grandfather, James Logan, came from Pennsylvania; his mother was Catharine (Thompson) Logan, who died in 1849. J. L. Logan married Miss Mary E. Carter, of Harrison, daughter of John and Adeline Carter, and has six children, named: Catharine, Charley W., Ora, James F., Ernest and Joseph E. He is owner of 625 acres of fine land eight miles from Cynthiana, in sight of Leeslick, handsomely improved and well stocked. He is a Mason, belonging to the Commandery at Cynthiana, also a Granger, belonging to Gilead Lodge, Scott County, Ky. He and his wife belong to the Presbyterian Church at Beards, in Scott County, he being a Ruling Elder. He affiliates with the Democratic party, and in all the walks of life is regarded as an honorable, upright citizen.

E. D. McADAMS, farmer ; Cynthiana. The subject of this sketch was born in Fleming County, Kentucky, in 1814 ; a son of Armstrong McAdams, who died in 1857, and grandson of John McAdams, who was of Scotch birth. His mother was Nancy Purcell, who died of cholera during the fearful rage of that fell destroyer in 1833, she was the daughter of William Purcell, an Englishman by birth who emigrated to this country and resided for a long while in Bourbon County. When advanced in years he moved to Harrison County, and after living a life of great usefulness, he died in 1826. In 1849, E. D. McAdams and Miss Rebecca Ann Ammerman, a daughter of Joseph and Rebecca Ammerman, of Harrison County, were united in the holy ties of matrimony. By this marriage they have five children, named : Joseph A., James W., John W., Franklin R., and Hettie A. By honest toil and close attention to business, he is now the owner of a nice tract of good land, containing 115 acres, three miles from Cynthiana, lying immediately along the Cynthiana and Leesburg Turnpike, which he calls Sugar Grove. Father, wife, and son Joseph, are members of the Christian Church at Cynthiana.

JAMES L. PATTERSON, farmer ; P. O. Cynthiana. Among the leading and successful farmers of Leesburg Precinct, none are better or more popularly known than him whose name heads this sketch. He was born in Harrison County, in the year 1815. His father was Joseph Patterson, who was brought from Virginia when an infant, by his parents, and died in the year 1849. His mother was Susan Smith, a daughter of Eliza Smith, from Pennsylvania, who died in the same year of her husband, being in 1849. James L. Patterson married Miss Margaret J. Miller, of Harrison County, in the year 1841, just forty-one years ago, a daughter of Hugh and Mary (Ewalt) Miller. Her father died in 1821, and her mother in 1866. By this marriage they have no children. He is the owner of a magnificent body of land, containing in all 1460 acres. His home tract is situated in the fertile valleys of Silas Creek, seven miles from Cynthiana, near the Bourbon line, and he has given it the appropriate name of "Rural Choice," upon this farm he has fine stock of every description, such as short-horn cattle, Cotswold sheep, etc. He is the owner of twenty-eight brood mares, from which he raises principally mules, which he generally sells at one year old. In politics, he is identified with the Democratic party, and he and his wife are consistent members of the Christian Church at Mount Carmel. Beginning life poor, and by patient industry and economy, he has amassed a handsome estate, and to which we can point the ambitious young man of the present day, as an example worthy of imitation.

HIGGINS C. SMITH, M. D.; P. O. Leesburg; son of F. C. and Agnes (Chinn) Smith, born in 1847. His father, Francis C.; was born in 1814, and he and wife are still living. She being the daughter of John Chinn and Mildred (Higgins) Chinn; the former was born August 2, 1766, and died March 8, 1839, and the latter was born July 24, 1776, and died July 20, 1819. His grandfather, John Smith, was one of the most prominent citizens of Harrison County in his day; filling at one time the office of Justice of the Peace, and for several years Sheriff of Harrison County. Dr. H. C. Smith was a student at the colleges of Georgetown and Harrodsburg in this State, and graduated in medicine in the class of 1869, at Bellevue Hospital, New York. In 1870 he began the practice of his profession at Georgetown, Kentucky; remained there one year, then located at Leesburg, where he has since been in active practice, and is regarded by his neighbors as a physician of ability. His father resides eight miles from Cynthiana on the Lexington and Cynthiana Pike, and is engaged in farming, being the breeder of short horn cattle and Cotswold sheep. Dr. Smith has four living brothers. Samuel L. is a broker at No. 40, Wall Street, New York. Francis B. is a farmer of Harrison and is interested in fine stock. Marcus A. is a practicing attorney at Tombstone, Arizona Territory, and James J. is in Colorado. Mother and all of her sons are members of the Christian Church at Leesburg.

JAMES H. SHROPSHIRE, Jr., farmer; P. O. Leesburg; a native of Bourbon; having been born in that County in the year 1850. His father, James H. Shropshire, Sr., is an active and energetic farmer of Bourbon, and his grandfather was Abner Shropshire. His mother was Miss Maria Louisa Harcourt. Mr. Shropshire married Miss Mary A. Crenshaw, of Bourbon County, and by this union they have two children, named Fannie Pearl and Jessie. Both he and wife are leading and consistent members of the Christian Church at Leesburg, taking part in every good work that tends to elevate and ennoble mankind. He has become an active and leading member of the Good Templars at Leesburg. In politics he is identified with Democracy.

THOMAS D. URMSTON, farmer; P. O. Cynthiana; born in the State of Ohio on the 12th of February 1801. His father, Benjamin Urmston, was one of the founders of the now thriving city of Chillicothe, Ohio. He spent his life in doing good deeds and died in 1820. His mother was Miss Ann Magee. He was twice married, first in 1825 to Miss Eliza Harcourt, who died in 1855, leaving two children, Wm. D., who lives near Lair's Depot, and John W. is farming seven miles from Cynthiana on the Cynthiana and Leesburg Turnpike. Then in 1856 he was married again to Miss Ann G. Hurst, who died in 1878, leaving no children. Mr. Urmston has been a man of considerable enterprise, running at one time a tannery and currying shop; attached also is a country store which he is now carrying on. In addition to this he is running his farm of 140 acres of good land seven miles from Cynthiana on the Cynthiana and Lexington road, which is well stocked with all kinds of high-grade animals, and is known as Union Villa. He is a Democrat and a prominent member of the Presbyterian Church at Mt. Pleasant, located at Broadwell; having been a member of the Presbyterian Church for sixty-four years and an elder in the same church for fifty years. Growing old, yet with his faith unshaken in the friend of man, he has asked the church to excuse him from the eldership, and looking back upon a life well spent with a ripe old age upon him he only awaits the call of his blessed Master to go hence.

JAMES W. WREGG, farmer; P. O. Leesburg; was born in Scott County, September 20, 1818. His father, Samuel Ray, an Englishman by birth, came to America when eleven years old. Both of his parents died six months after he came to Kentucky. Himself and brothers were " bound out" until he was twenty-one years of age when he began life for himself as a blacksmith. He died in Mississippi in 1870, aged ninety-seven years. His wife was Mary E. McKenzie, daughter of Reuben and Susan McKenzie. Reuben McKenzie assisted in building the fort at Lexington. He participated in the battle of Blue Licks, and though desperately wounded, escaped with his life. Mr. Wregg married Miss Angela Price, daughter of Isaiah Price, who served through the war of 1812. They have seven children, viz: Mrs. Mary E. Carroll, Samuel I., Hulda A., Kelly B., Susan E., Fanny and Lena. He owns 166 acres of land three-fourths of a mile west of Leesburg where he breeds high-grade stock and farms in a general way. He is a Mason, and he and his wife are members of the Christian Church at Leesburg. He is a Democrat in politics.

CLAYSVILLE PRECINCT.

W. T. ASBURY, farmer and merchant; P. O. Claysville; son of Obannan Asbury, a native of Nicholas County, Ky.; was born in Robinson County, Ky., in 1832, where he received his education and then commenced his work in life by assisting in tilling the soil of his father's farm. In 1861 he was married to Anna M. Hatch, who has borne him two children, the oldest, Maria N., now the wife of H. C. Fightmaster, of Cynthiana, and Obannan N., now eight years of age. In 1862, Mr. Asbury moved to Mason County, Ky., and in 1863 removed to Harrison County, and there buying a farm of 150 acres and also starting in the mercantile business, which, at the present time is the principal one of Claysville; he is politically a Radical, and has held the office of Magistrate for nine consecutive years. Mr. Asbury has been dependent on his own resources, and by his studied economy and industry has accumulated a good property, and his name and reputation is above reproach.

T. S. BECKETT, farmer; P. O. Claysville; a native of Harrison County, Ky., and son of John and Jane (Fleming) Beckett. He was born in 1818. His father was born in Maryland, and removed to Virginia with his parents; afterward removed to Harrison County, Ky., where he died, aged seventy-six years. His mother was born in Virginia. T. S., our subject, is one of Claysville's most respected men; he is a temperate man, and has been a member of the Methodist Church for thirty years. In 1838, he married Miss America Scott. They were the parents of eleven children, viz.: Robert, Melissa, Jane, John, Frances, Thomas, Joseph, America, James, Lucy and Mary. He is the owner of 211 acres of land, upon which he makes hog-raising a specialty. His family are members of the Christian Church.

STEPHEN W. BARNES, farmer; P. O. Claysville; is a native of Harrison County, Ky., and son of John and Polly (Godman) Barnes; he was born Aug. 26th, 1817. In 1845, he married Miss Frances Quigley, a native of Ohio; she died May 17, 1879. They are the parents of nine children: Wm. H., Sarah, Elizabeth, Mary, Emily, Stephen, Anna, Ellen and John. He is the owner of 200 acres of land, upon which he still resides; he is a member of the Christian Church. His father was born in Bourbon County, Ky., and at the age of five years was brought to Harrison County by his parents, where he remained, following the occupation of farmer and cooper; he died aged eighty-four years. His mother was a native of Harrison County.

DAVID DUCKWORTH, farmer; P. O. Claysville; is a native of Montgomery County, Ky., and son of William and Susan (Legget) Duckworth; he was born April 24, 183[illegible]; his father was born near Charlotte, Mecklenburg County, N. C. When but four years of age he emigrated to Montgomery County, Ky., with his parents, where he remained and received his education and following the occupation of farming during his life; in 1828 he married Miss Susan Leggett; they were the parents of seven children. The mother of our subject was born and raised in Montgomery County, Ky. David, our subject, lived his earlier life with his parents, receiving an education and assisting in tilling the soil of his father's farm; in 1849 he removed to Harrison County, where he has since remained, following the occupation of farming. Dec. 11, 1873, he married Miss Sarah J. Stewart, who bore him one child, George B., now eight years old. His wife died April 12, 1881. He is the owner of 236 acres of land, principally located in Harrison County; he is a member of the A., F. & A. M., Lodge No. 243, at Claysville; a member of the Christian Church and a Republican.

LOUISA FLETCHER, farmer; P. O. Claysville; a native of Harrison County, Ky., in which she now lives, was born in 1828, and was married to B. F. Fletcher in 1857. Five children were born to them, viz.: Oliver, Jefferson, John, Henry and Arthur. B. F. Fletcher was first married to Elzira Dicky, who bore him six children: Anna, Robert, Carolina, Vishti, Frances and Dora. Mr. F. lived about thirty years in Harrison County, and was always a hard-working man, and by so doing succeeded in getting a farm of 130 acres. He was a soldier in the Confederate Army for three years, and died soon after his return home from the war. Mrs. F. has lived to witness many of the changes in the development and improvement of the country surrounding her home, and has reared a family of children, whose promise of honorable man and womanhood is an honor to her in her old age.

WILLIAM HUNT, farmer; P. O. Smitsonville; is a son of H. D. and Charlotte Hunt, both natives of Kentucky, and traces the genealogy of his family back to one of the first settlers of Kentucky; his grandfather, Mr. Robertson Hunt, came to Kentucky with Daniel Boone, where he remained a resident until his death, which occurred at the extreme old age of one hundred and four years. William was born in Montgomery County, Ky., in 1842, and at the age of six years, his parents moved to Harrison County, Ky., where he received his education. In 1859, the family removed to Texas, settling in Harrison County of that State; there William engaged in work at the trade of carpenter and at carrying the United States mail from Marshall, Tex., to Keatchie, La. Within one year after the arrival of the family in Texas, his father and mother died, leaving three children younger than himself to his care. In 1860, he returned to Harrison County, and settled on the farm he now owns. In 1861, he enlisted in the Confederate Army, and at the close of the war, on his way home, he walked from Abingdon, Va., to Mt. Sterling, a distance of two hundred miles, in five days. Upon his return he at once engaged in agricultural pursuits, which he has since followed, in connection with which he runs, during the winter season, a saw mill, owned by him, and built in 1810, by one —— Miller. Here, by his own energy and industry, he has built for himself a comfortable and pleasant home, his house being at the time of its erection, the finest between Augusta, Bracken County, Ky., and Cynthiana. In 1870, Mr. Hunt was married to Miss Lizzie Botts; they are the parents of six children: Hattie, Annie, Amanda, Sidney, Nettie, and Mamie. In religious faith he is a Baptist, he and family being members of the Beaver Church; he is also a Democrat, as was also his father, and although a young man, he has already a good business, and a worthy name and reputation in the community where he resides.

SUSAN HICKMAN, farming; was born in Nicholas County (Ky.), February 18, 1817. She lived with her parents, in Nicholas County, to the time of their death. Her father died when she was but six weeks old, and her mother when she was 17 years old. After the death of her parents she lived with her relatives until she was 23 years of age. In 1840 she was married to Jesse Hickman and removed to Harrison County, where they spent nearly 40 years of happiness together. Mr. Hickman died in 1878, aged 67 years; he was a man of good morals and a christian. The community in which he lived mourns the loss of such a good citizen. There was born to them 10 children, seven of whom are living, viz.: David, Benjamin, John, Mary, Henry, Amanda and Nany. Mrs. Hickman's grandfathers were both ministers of the Gospel. She is a woman of indomitable energy and perseverance, and enjoys the highest esteem of the community in which she lives.

BEN. C. HICKMAN, farmer; is a native of Harrison County, and the son of Jesse and Susan Hickman. He was born in 1844. His early life was spent in receiving an education and assisting in the tilling of the soil of his father's farm. In 1865 he embarked in business for himself by carrying on a mercantile business at Havilandsville with his brother, W. D. Hickman. In 1878 he sold his interest in the business at Havilandsville to his brother; bought a farm of 170 acres, and began farming, which business he still continues. In 1878 he married Miss Emma Casey, a native of Harrison County. Although a young man, he has, by his honesty, economy and industry, succeeded in gaining a good property and a name and reputation which is beyond reproach. He is a Republican, a member of the order I. O. O. F. Lodge No. 191, at Cynthiana, and, with his wife, united with the Baptist Church.

JOHN HULS, farmer; P. O. Claysville; he was born in Montgomery County, Ky., in 1803, June 30; he received his education from the common schools of his native county, and at the age of twenty-one began farming, which he followed in Montgomery County until 1849, when he removed to Harrison County, Ky., where he has since remained and followed the occupation of farming and working some at the trade of shoemaking. In 1827, September 18, he married Miss Louisiana Fletcher, who has borne him thirteen children, eleven of whom are still living, viz: Garrett F., Pleasant, Andrew J., Achilles, Jerusha, Winifred, Sally, John, Nimrod, Elizabeth, and Naomi. He had held the office of Magistrate for four years; he is a member of the Christian Church, and is a Democrat. Mr. Huls is one of the oldest citizens of Claysville Precinct, and bears a name and reputation of which his children may well be proud.

J. M. HOBDAY, farmer; P. O. Claysville; a native of Gordonsville, Virginia, and son of Edward and Sarah P. Hobday; he was born in 1825; his father was born in Virginia, and removed to Pendleton County, Ky., where he followed the occupation of farming; he died aged eighty-five years. His mother was born in Charlottesville, Va., in 1796, and is now residing in Harrison County, Ky. J. M., the subject of our sketch, received his education in Pendleton County, Ky., and at the age of twenty left home and began first by teaching school in Harrison County, which he followed for eighteen years, during that time he bought a farm and managed it. In 1872, he married Rebecca M. Jackson; she was born in Bracken County, in 1842. His children by his first wife are James H., and by his present wife Charles B., Thomas M., and Howe. He is the owner of 600 acres of land; he is a member of the Masonic Order, Taylor Lodge, No. 164, at Berry's, Ky.

WINDER KINNEY, farmer; P. O. Claysville; is a native of Harrison County, and son of Isaac and Rutha (Fields) Kinney; he was born in 1839; his father was born in Bracken County, in 1813, and now resides in Illinois, following the occupation of farming. His mother was also born in Bracken County, and died at the early age of twenty-three years. Winder, our subject, lived his earlier life with his uncle, W. Kinney, where he received his education. In 1865 he married Frances Beckett, who has borne him six children, viz: Joel, Susan J., Melissa, Thomas S., William, and James A., named from our assassinated President, James A. Garfield. In 1865, he bought a farm of sixty acres, which he continues to till, raising all the principal crops. He enlisted in the Federal Army, 20th Reg't, Co. I, K. V., as a private, and returned as First Lieutenant. He is a Republican.

T. J. LANGLEY, farmer; P. O. Claysville; was born in Harrison County, Ky., February, 1834, and, is the son of Abraham and Anna (Scott) Langley. He is descended from one of Harrison County's old pioneers. His grandfather, Isaac, was born in Virginia, and in crossing the Dix river en route for Kentucky, was drowned; his wife, with her one child, Abraham, father of our subject, continued their journey alone, and settled on Beaver creek in about the year 1798, and in 1815 Abraham married Miss Anna Scott, who bore him twelve children, of whom was T. J. Langley, the subject of our sketch. He spent his earlier days with his parents in receiving an education and assisting in tilling the soil of his father's farm. In 1855, he married Miss Melissa Beckett, a native of Harrison County, Ky, and daughter of T. S. and America (Scott) Beckett. They are the parents of eight children, five of whom are now living, viz: Corrilla, Maggie, Abraham, Ida and Artinsa. Mr. Langley has always resided at his present residence, having 228 acres of land. The Christian Church in his neighborhood was founded and named from the family; also the school which is called Langley School. His family are members of the Langley Christian Church.

CORNELIUS McLEOD, farmer; P. O. Claysville; is a native of North Carolina, and son of Duncan and Barbara McLeod. He was born June 12, 1821, in Moore County; his grandparents were both natives of Scotland, and emigrated to North Carolina before the Revolutionary War. The father of our subject was born in North Carolina in 1799, and in 1826 removed to Knox County, Ky., where he followed the occupation of farming to the time of his death, which occurred in December, 1861. Cornelius, our subject, spent his earlier days with his parents in Knox County, Ky., where he received his education, and assisted in tilling the soil of his father's farm. In 1842, he removed to Estill County, where he engaged in the manufacture of salt until 1844, when he removed to Harrison County, where he took contracts for sinking wells for salt. In 1846, he engaged in the lumber business, buying and shipping to Cincinnati. In 1847, he married Miss Martha J. Kinney, a native of Harrison County, and daughter of Wyander and Sarah Kinney. In the same year, he removed to Clay County, where he followed the occupation of farming. In 1852, he removed to Harrison County, again farming until 1861, when he enlisted in the Federal Army, 20th Reg., Co. I, K. V. He was discharged from the army Jan. 17, 1865, when he returned home to Harrison County, and engaged in the mercantile business at Claysville, which he continued until 1867, when he kept hotel, remaining in the same until 1873, when he was appointed by U. S. Commissioner of Internal Revenue as U. S. Gauger, which office he held until 1878, when he again resumed farming, and has since followed it. He has the following children, viz: John, Mary M., William A., Belle, Harry and Winder. He is a Republican.

ELIJAH MOORE, farmer and miller; P. O. Claysville; a native of Bracken County, Ky.; was born 1809. His father, Levi Moore, was born in Pennsylvania; he was a farmer, and died aged eighty-two years; he was a Whig, and in his life-time held the offices of Constable and Magistrate for several years. His wife, Jane Truax, was a native of Pennsylvania; she died aged forty years. The subject of our sketch is among the most prominent men of his precinct; he is the owner of 600 acres of land, upon which he raises all the principal crops, making tobacco and stockraising a specialty; he also is the owner and manager of a grist-mill; in 1870 he married Miss Parmelia Jackson. He is the father of ten children, viz: Nimrod, Ann S., Levi H., Susan H., Isaac C., John, Elijah, Stilwell S., Artinsia and Mary. Mr. Moore has by his studied economy and business habits, succeeded in gaining a good property, and bears a name and reputation which is beyond reproach.

THOS. A. MONTGOMERY, farmer; P. O. Claysville; was born Feb. 15, 1850, and is the son of James Montgomery, a native of Dauphin County, Pa., who was the owner and successful manager of a leading woolen-mill; he was born in 1806, living to the age of fifty-six years. One year after his death his son, Thos. A., moved to Harrison County, Ky., and there studied for an education until 1871, when he bought a farm of 177 acres upon which he raises the principal products as corn, wheat, rye and tobacco, and at one time made the breeding of hogs a specialty. In 1877 he was married to Fannie Curran, who has borne him two children; James M., now being three years old, and Thomas W., two years old. Mr. M. is a Democrat; he is a member of the Masonic Lodge of Claysville, No. 243, and is now holding the office of Secretary. Though a young man, he has taken more than an active part in the local affairs, and, by his business habits and integrity, is one esteemed by the citizens in this community.

ROBERT F. MILLER, farmer; P. O. Claysville; is a native of Wabash County, Ind., and son of Adam S. Miller; he was born in 1849. His father was born in Indiana in 1820; he was always a farmer to the time of his death, which occurred in 1864. Robert lived with his parents to the age of twenty-one, receiving an education and assisting in tilling the soil of his father's farm. In 1870, he removed to Harrison County, buying a farm of 118 acres, upon which he now resides. In 1871, he married Miss Celia A. Miller, a native of Harrison County, and daughter of James H. Miller; she was born Feb. 16, 1851. Her father was born April 7, 1818, in Harrison County. She is a member of the Methodist Church. He is a Democrat. They are the parents of five children, viz.: John J., George L., Willie A., Bruce A., and Charlie H.

T. A. ROBERTSON, farmer; P. O. Smitsonville; is the son of Richard H., and Mary T. (Samuels) Robertson, and was born June 9, 1832, in Shelby County, Ky.; his father was a native of near Richmond, Va., and came to Kentucky about the year 1803, a young man of twenty-three years of age; he settled first in Garrard County, and then removed to Shelby, and subsequently to Harrison; he was a Democrat and a man possessed of a high sense of honor, and though he died in November, 1858, he predicted with wonderful accuracy. as subsequent events proved, the near approach of the late civil war. The mother of T. A. died when he was a child. Arriving at man's estate, Mr. Robertson, in 1854, was married to Miss Lucy A. Hickman, a native of Harrison County. For about three years following this event he was engaged in buying, selling and shipping stock; quitting the business at the close of this period a poorer, and perhaps a wiser man, he moved to Cincinnati, where he spent the two succeeding years. Returning again to the old homestead, he spent about two years at farming and milling, and then purchased his present farm of 175 acres, located on the extension of the Cynthiana and Claysville Pike. In 1867 his brother was elected Sheriff of Harrison County, holding the office until 1870. In 1873 and 1874 he filled the same responsible position, and during his whole term of service T. A. acted as his deputy, and though a Democrat, and his long service as deputy thoroughly fitting him for the office, he sought no political preferment at the hands of the people. In 1879 he began agitating the question of the extension of the Cynthiana and Claysville Pike, from its terminus (Oddville) to Claysville. Succeeding in securing the granting of a new charter for the extension, he was made the first President, but accepting a contract in the building of the road, in which he is the heaviest stockholder, he resigned his office. Though not so old a resident of Claysville Precinct as many of his neighbors, there is but little doubt of Mr. Robertson's being one of the leading spirits in that part of Harrison County. When he was twenty-two years of age he joined St. Andrews' Lodge A. F. & A. M.; subsequently he was dimitted and became one of the charter members of Thomas Ware Lodge No. 340, of Claysville, which he represented at the Grand Lodge four times as W. M. of Thomas Ware Lodge, and once by proxy. His wife, oldest daughter, and himself, are members of the Christian Church. Ten children have been born to Mr. and Mrs. Robertson, eight of whom are living, viz.: Richard Henry, Fannie, now wife of W. H. Zilor; two deceased, Frank W., Laura, Cora, Hattie, Blanche, and Stella.

WILLIAM H. ROUTT, farmer; P. O. Claysville; is a native of Bracken County, Ky., and son of Nimrod and Elizabeth (Howard) Routt. He was born Dec. 10, 1817. His father was born in Virginia, in 1786, and died in 1860, aged seventy-four years. His mother was born in Maryland in 1793, and died in 1865, aged seventy-two years. William, our subject, lived with his parents to the age of twenty-four; receiving an education and assisting in tilling the soil of his father's farm. In 1841 he married Miss Jane Moore, a native of Bracken County, Ky.; by this union they had nine children, eight of whom are still living, viz: Maria, Clara, Lucius, Temple, John, Fannie, Ada and Willie. In 1862, he removed to Harrison County; buying a farm near Claysville, where he remained three years, he then returned to the old homestead, which was willed to him by his father, remaining there until 1867, when he returned to Harrison County, and since remained there, following the occupation of farming. He is the owner of 141 acres of land. His family are members of the Baptist Church. He is a Democrat, and for a number of years in Bracken County, he has held the office of Justice of the Peace.

NICHOLAS COUNTY.

CARLISLE CITY AND PRECINCT.

G. W. ADAIR; D. D. S., Carlisle; son of Richard and Mary (Tarr) Adair, (see Robert Tarr's history, in Millersburg Precinct), the paternal ancestry of Scotch-Irish descent, but a native of Maryland, emigrated to Nicholas County about 1815, where he resided the principal part of the time until his death. His occupation was that of tanning, which he followed during his lifetime, in connection with agricultural pursuits. He died at 77 years of age, leaving a large family of which our subject was the youngest, and an estimable wife, who followed him to the grave in the winter of 1875, aged 81 years. Three sons of the family have received a degree of notoriety in the dental and medical professions. R. M. Adair, now of Mt. Sterling, one of the first dentists of the blue grass region, a graduate of the Baltimore Dental College; J. J., now deceased, also a graduate of the Baltimore College, and of the Louisville Medical College. Our subject was born Aug. 16, 1838; received a common school education, and remained on the farm until about the age of twenty years, when he began the study of dentistry with his brother R. M., at Mt. Sterling; thence to Cincinnati with Dr. J. Taft, one of the professors in the Cincinnati Dental College; here he remained a short time, subsequently returning to Mt. Sterling. He began the practice of his chosen profession in 1858, locating a short time subsequent in Carlisle, where he has since been doing a large business. He was married Oct. 29, 1861, to Miss Mary H. Henry, daughter of Richard Henry, and his wife, a Miss Henshaw, both of Harrison County. By this marriage there have been two daughters—Sally B. and Lucy, O. He has held for a number of years the office of town trustees, is a member of the Masonic Order and Knights Templar, now filling the position of Commander of Carlisle Commandery, No. 18, and an esteemed and an honored citizen, and with his family belongs to the Baptict Church.

W. B. ALLEN, merchant, Carlisle; son of F. W. Allen, he a brother to J. Banks Allen (see Allen's history under the head of Millersburg Precinct, Bourbon County), F.W. Allen, cashier of the banking firm of Allen, Harbeson & Co., of Augusta, Ky.; was sheriff of Bath County for eight years, then started the banking house of Smith, Wilson & Co., at Flemingsburg, where they carried on business successfully for a number of years, then to his present business. He was married to Maria Herndon, a native of Kenton County, Ky., by whom he had four children (two daughters died in infancy). The two sons now living, Thomas M., the eldest, engaged in business with his father, and the subject of this sketch, who devoted himself to study in the common schools, until 15 years of age, when his passion for an active business life led him, first, to engage in the drug business with Dr. Benj. Derrett, at Flemingsburg; after which he entered the dry goods store of Geo. V. Morris. Subsequently he engaged in trading and various business speculations, the last of which resulted disastrously; but with that firm determination (characteristic of his people), he began again, and soon made for himself a place among the foremost business men of his community. Sept. 1, 1878, he came to Carlisle, where he engaged in the clothing business, at the head of which branch he stands first in Nicholas County. He was married May 27, 1875, to an estimable young lady, Miss Julia F. Wood, daughter of Bela Wood and a Miss Royce, both of which are among the first families of Nicholas County. They have one child, Ida Belle. He is a member of the Masonic order, and one of the euterprising men of Carlisle.

A. W. ALLEN, farmer; P. O. Moorefield; son of David and Susanna Thompson, who were married Nov. 20, 1833; she a daughter of David Thompson. David Allen was born in Loudon County, Va., Oct. 5, 1794, and the fourth of ten children, eight sons and two daughters, the eldest of whom was born in 1788; four are now living: James, Joseph and Louisa, widow of James Boardman, residing in the State of Indiana, and Douglas, in Iowa. The father of our subject, who is still living, is a son of Joseph and Fannie (Wright) Allen, who came to Bourbon County, settling near North Middletown, in the year 1799, subsequently resided in Clark and Scott Counties, thence removed to Bath County, where they both died. David lived with his parents until his first marriage, when he engaged in business for himself. This union was blessed with five children, two of whom are now living: our subject, and Martha A., wife of John W. Brown, who reside in Saline County, Mo., Henry, deceased, married and left heirs in Nicholas County. His second marriage was to Lucretia Neff, deceased, Oct. 10, 1833, by whom he had also five children, of which number four daughters are living: Louisa C., wife of Charles Potts, residing in Boone County, Mo. The others are in Nicholas; Elizabeth, unmarried; Amanda, wife of Wm. Caldwell, and Adeline, wife of Joseph Wilson. The subject of this sketch was born Dec. 18, 1825, and has always been engaged in farming, with his father. He was married, Dec. 13, 1877, to Rosa Cook, who was born in Helena, Mason County, Ky., April 28, 1846, to John and Margaret (Weaver) Cook; he a native of Nicholas, where he died while on a visit to his daughter, in May, 1878; she still living. By this marriage, there has been born to them one child, John D., Nov. 29, 1878. He is in politics a Democrat, and, with his family, are connected with the Presbyterian Church at Moorefield.

JUDGE A. J. BANTA, Judge of the County and Quarterly Courts; P. O. Carlisle; was born in Bourbon County, Aug. 2, 1824 (see Peter Banta's history); he received a common school education, assisting his father until the year 1842, when he engaged in farming on his own account, removing to Nicholas County in February, 1846. He was married on Oct. 5, 1846, in Flat Rock, to Elizabeth Johnson, of Bourbon County, where she was born in November, 1824, to John and Lettie (Call) Johnson, natives of Bourbon. Her parents both died in 1833 of cholera. By this union there have been four children, two of whom died in their infancy; those living are: Letitia J., wife of M. A. Glenn, a farmer, of Nicholas; and John P., farming in Bates County, Mo. Mr. Banta and family are of the Christian faith, religiously, and Democratic politically. He was Sheriff of the county at the breaking out of the late war, but was compelled by order of the Federal troops to relinquish his office, which proved disastrously to him in a financial point of view. He espoused the cause of the Confederacy, enlisting in 1862 in the 9th Kentucky Regiment, was made First Lieutenant of Company B., but on account of bad health was appointed to the commissary department for general supplies for the Southern Army, in which he served until the close of the war, when he returned home and engaged in farming and distilling. He is now engaged in various other pursuits besides his judicial duties.

ABRAM BANTA, farmer, P. O. Carlisle; youngest son of Henry Banta's (see Peter Banta's history); he was born April 18, 1805, and attended school about three months, during which time he received his theoretical education. He remained with his parents until in the year 1839, when he came to the farm upon which he now resides. He was married in 1828, to Miss Dorcas Hedges, born July 28, 1806, to James and Annie (Forman) Hedges, who were heirs in the famous "Hedges Estate." The Bantas and Hedges are among the early settlers in the "Region," and noted for their longevity. Mr. Banta is the father of eight children, all of whom grew to maturity. They were: Scythia A., born Dec. 24, 1829, was wife of Samuel Fulton, and James H., born Aug. 14, 1831; both are residing at Ridge Farm, Vermillion County, Ill.; Margaret L., born May 28, 1833, wife of Thomas Campbell, residing in Headquarters Precinct; Andrew J. died a prisoner at Camp Morton, Aug. 20, 1864, aged twenty-nine years; Sarah F., born April 4, 1839, died March 19, 1877, leaving one child, Nannie; J. M., the father, Edwin Collins, engaged in business at Carlisle; William F., born May 28, 1841; farming in Edgar County, Ill.; Elizabeth, a twin sister to William F., wife of Lon Campbell, of Carlisle; Amie Maria, born Aug. 9, 1847, wife of Henry Bogart, of Vermillion County, Ind. The parents are vigorous old people, highly esteemed citizens of the community in which they live, and with their family belong to the Christian Church.

DR. H. C. BURROUGHS; P. O. Carlisle; is a native of Nicholas County, and a son of Alexander and Betsy (Hutchings) Burroughs, who came from Virginia very early in the history of the State; he is one of twelve children, ten of whom are living, namely: George W., Molly P., wife, James W. Dalzell; Eliza J., wife of William Norton; William M., Susan A., Elizabeth F., wife of William Spencer; Keder D., Dr. H. C., Mattie L., wife of James Ringo, and Nannie R. Dr. Burroughs received a limited education, his father dying in 1865, when he was only thirteen years of age; on Jan. 1, 1869, he engaged as a clerk in the mercantile firm of Adair & Bro., where he remained until the fall of 1872, at which time he entered the College at Millersburg; being compelled to retire from this institution on account of failing health, he engaged in January, 1874, with J. J. Taylor, of Millersburg in the merchandising; in the fall of 1875 he entered the University of Louisville having prepared himself for that institution by private reading during his spare hours; after being graduated in 1877, he located in Carlisle, and commenced the practice of his profession, which he continued with success until March, 1881, at which time he formed a partnership with Mr. Adair, purchasing the half interest of Mr. Brewington; on Aug. 6, 1878, he married Miss Lizzie, daughter of John and

Cynthia (Gardner) Dallas, of Nicholas County; two children have been born to them, only one of whom, John Bell, survives; himself, wife, father, mother, and all of his brothers and sisters were identified with the Christian Church, in which society he holds the office of Deacon.

WM. H. BROWN, deputy sheriff; P. O. Carlisle; was born near Mt. Olivet, in what was then Nicholas County (now Robertson), April 4, 1844. His father, John Brown, was a native of Pennsylvania, and came to Nicholas County about 1830, where he followed farming and carpenting until his death in 1848. The mother, Mary Tatman, was a native of Bracken County, Ky., and a daughter of Vincent and Sarah (Williams) Tatman. Her death occurred in 1860 at about the age of forty-seven years. She had by her first marriage two sons and one daughter, all of whom are now living: James E., farming at Mt. Olivet; Bettie, wife of Dr. Riley Wells, who is practicing his profession at Mt. Olivet; and the subject of this sketch. Her second marriage was to Mathew Throckmorton, also deceased. By this marriage there were three children: George and La Fayette, in Mt. Olivet, and Mathew, in Nicholas County. Mr. Brown received a district school education, and has, since his boyhood, devoted the principal part of his life to farming. His marriage occurred in 1865 to Matilda J. Linville, who was born in Bracken, May 25, 1850, to John R. and Mary (Cooper) Linville, both of whom were natives of Bracken County; he born in 1809; she in 1830; both are now living in Nicholas County. Upon the 10th of October, 1862, he enlisted in Company A, 1st Kentucky Mounted Riflemen, under Capt. Joe Hardin, Col. Zeke Clay, and Major John B. Holliday. He was engaged in several closely contested battles, among them those of Murfreesboro, McMinnville, Jonesboro, and Farmington, where he was captured and sent to Camp Morton, where he remained for fifteen months, when he took the oath of allegiance, and returned home in January, 1865. A short time after entering the service, he was captured at Owingsville, Ky., but was soon after exchanged, and returned to his command at Abingdon, Va. In the summer of 1863 he was transferred to Wheeler and Forrest's Cavalry; was in the forty days' forced march from Knoxville, through Tennessee and Georgia, also in the seven days' skirmish at Cleveland, Tenn. By his marriage he has five children: Nannie, born March 7, 1866; John, Jan. 20, 1869; James F., Oct. 16, 1871; Hattie L., Sept. 5, 1875; and Millie, Jan. 5, 1878. They are members of the Christian Church, and in politics he is Democratic.

EDWARD B. BOYD, merchant, Carlisle; was born in Greenfield, Highland County, O., May 10, 1834, to John and Mary R. (Bryan) Boyd; he, a native of Pennsylvania, died in 1868; she, born in Bourbon County, Ky., in 1813, and is still living; they had six children, of whom, Edward, our subject, was the second. He received his education in Ohio, and entered upon his career in life as a clerk in a dry goods store, at Chillicothe, O. Later, he entered into the employ of the Adams Express Company, as express messenger, and ran on the Fort Wayne and Chicago Railroad six months; on the Pan Handle, from Pittsburg to Cincinnati, one year, when he became bill clerk in the office at Columbus, O., where he remained one year. He followed the fortunes of war during the Rebellion, from the beginning to its close, and filled the position of A. Q. M. at Mobile, Ala., for one year after the close of the war. He entered the service as private in the 63d O. V. I., and became Quartermaster, then a Captain of same. He was also A. Q. M. in the 1st Division of the 17th Army Corps, under Gen. Frank P. Blair, and eventually was commissioned Major in A. Q. M., and was mustered out as such in July, 1865. He was married at Zenia, Greene County, O., in 1871, to Miss Annie E. Trader, a native of that place, and who died in 1872. She was the mother of one child, a boy, which lived to be four months old. Mr. Boyd's second marriage occurred in Highland County, O., April 16, 1875, to Miss Emma Guthrie, who was born in Leesburg, O., September, 1831, and was a daughter of Capt. L. C. and Elizabeth (Boran) Guthrie, natives of Ohio. In the year 1874, Mr. Boyd moved to Carlisle, and became one of the firm in the New York Cash Store, known as Boyd & Co., and later Boyd & Beck. He is now a silent partner in the dry goods business with J. W. B. Lee. He is an energetic and enterprising business man; began life a poor boy, and the first money he ever earned for himself was by driving cattle from Bainbridge, O., to Philadelphia, Pa., for Chas. Robbins, of Ross County, O.; was about eight months on the road, and returned by canal. He is a man of generous disposition, obliging manners, and merits the high esteem in which he is held. Himself and wife are members of the M. E. Church at Carlisle. Politically, he is a Republican.

ALEXANDER W. BLAIR; farmer; P. O. Carlisle; was born at the "Valley Mills" in Nicholas County, Dec. 28, 1818. His father, Wm. Blair, died upon that farm formerly owned by the son, Dec. 24, 1822, aged thirty-four years; he was born in Jessamine County, near Versailles; was a son of Alexander Blair, who was born in the County Derry, Ireland; died Jan. 8, 1847, aged eighty-four years. He was a son of Thomas Blair, who came with his family to this country in the year 1777, settling in Pennsylvania, where he died. He was compelled on account of poverty to sell his older children (of which Alexander was one), to pay their passage across the ocean. His children were John, William, unmarried, drowned in the Mississippi river at an early date; Thomas, Alexander and James. Mary was the wife of a Mr. Clark, and Hannah wife of Elijah Adams, and Nancy, wife of Moses Scott. He settled in Pennsylvania, where he resided till about 1784, when he came to Boone Licks, where he worked at salt making, subsequently renting the works and carrying on the business for himself. About 1790 he went to Jessamine County, where he was married to Mary Black, a native of Pennsylvania. He engaged extensively in stock raising, and came at an early date to Cane Ridge, Bourbon County, because of the unlimited stock forage of young cane; he subsequently came to Nicholas County, where he engaged in milling, which proved disastrous to his fortune, but by persistent energy he was enabled, after years of hard labor and anxiety, to pay all honorable claims against him. He served two terms in the Kentucky Legislature from Nicholas County; also held the office of High Sheriff, receiving the position through the magistracy. He was in his religious belief, a Presbyterian of the strictest sect; he attended school 14 days during his lifetime, and from the lowest depths of poverty, without advantages for accumulating knowledge or property, he started out with a mattock and axe and a determination to succeed, and brought himself to the high position which he afterward held in the county. Our subject received moderate educational advantages in his youth, one year being spent at Hanover college. In the year 1841, August 5th, he was married to Miss Mattie Moore, a native of Nicholas County and daughter of John A., and Nancy (Berry) Moore, she a daughter of "old Col. Berry," of Indian fame. John A. Moore was a native of Georgetown, and son of Samuel and Mary (Archer) Moore, he from North Carolina; her family from Virginia. Mr. Blair by this marriage had nine children—William, a member of Company H., 18th Kentucky Federal troops, died at Cynthiana, Feb. 23, 1862; John G. (see history); James was also in Federal service; was assassinated upon the 4th of July, 1876, in Carlisle, and died upon the day following; Harlan A. married Lou T. Champ, of Millersburg, Dec. 11, 1873. She died May 8, 1875, leaving one child; Willie A. Parks, a lawyer at Carlisle; died Jan. 13, 1879. Joseph, Martha A., wife of James T. Clay (see hist.); Robert A., married June 20, 1878, Miss Annie E. Arrowsmith, died Aug. 22, 1879; and Wallace M. Mr. Blair in 1862 enlisted in the 18th Kentucky Federal Regiment, in which he held the office of Quartermaster under Col. Metcalf, and in 1863 he went into the 7th Cavalry, in which he was made Quartermaster; was taken prisoner upon July 16, same year, at Cynthiana; was exchanged in the fall and left the service. He was Sheriff of Nicholas County from 1863 to 1867, inclusive, and in 1868 was appointed by the government as Gauger, afterwards Store-keeper, and in 1878 was made Store-keeper and Gauger, which position he now holds at Oakland Mills. He is a strong Republican, and member of the Presbyterian Church.

MRS. MARY C. BELL, proprietress of Kimbrough House, Carlisle; was born in Bourbon County, Ky., Feb. 1, 1839, to Benjamin and Mary (Current) Bowen; he was born in Bourbon County, Oct. 7, 1794, and died Oct. 6, 1881; his father was a native of Virginia; his mother of Maryland, and they were among the first to enter upon pioneer life in Kentucky. Mary Bowen, the mother of our subject, was born in Bourbon County in 1808, and is still living; she was the mother of six children, of whom Mary, the subject, was the fourth. She was educated in a private school in Bourbon County, and was married in the same county, Nov. 20, 1855, to Mr. Joshua Kimbrough, who was born in Harrison County, Sept. 15, 1821, to William and Elizabeth Kimbrough (see history). During the Rebellion Mr. Kimbrough entered the service, and eventually became attached to the 25th City Battalion of Richmond. While there he was taken sick, and at the time Richmond was evacuated, he was conveyed to Amelia Court House, Virginia, where his death took place, April 12, 1865. He was the father of two children, viz: Luella, born May 14, 1857, wife of Oscar Ham (see history); and Henry Clay, born Jan. 25, 1860, an energetic and enterprising young man, of fine social and business qualities. During the year 1869, Mrs. Kimbrough bought the hotel known as "The Nicholas Exchange," of Carlisle; had the same repaired and enlarged, and changed the name to that of "Kimbrough House," in which she acted in the capacity of proprietress. Her second marriage occurred June 16, 1870, to Dr. William H. Bell; born to Hosea and Malinda (Davis) Bell, Jan. 21, 1841, and who died July 25, 1871, leaving her a second time a widow. She is a lady of indomitable energy and perseverance, kind and generous, with tact and forethought in business principles, and possessing the highest of womanly graces. Religiously, she and family are connected with the Christian Church at Carlisle.

J C Herndon M.D.

E. M. BUNTIN, farmer; P. O. Carlisle; was born near his present home, Nov. 27, 1842, to John J. and Theresa A. (McDaniel) Buntin, who were married in March, 1837; she was a daughter of John McDaniel, a very early settler in Nicholas County ; John J. had by her three children, viz.: the first died in infancy; John W. residing in Union precinct, and E. M.; the mother died April 22, 1846; the father remarried Elizabeth A. West, March, 11, 1847, who is still living, and a daughter of Adam and Mary (Wills) West, she a daughter of David and Margaret (Goram) Wills, who were natives, the father a native of Ireland; the West family were from the State of Delaware, the Wills from Pennsylvania, and both were very early settlers in the State of Kentucky; Adam West was a son of Isaac and Nancy (Heney) West; by this second marriage there was one child : Margaret S., a maiden lady; Mr. Buntin died Feb. 20, 1880; was born Jan. 6, 1812; John J. Buntin was a son of William Buntin, who was three times married, first to a Miss Hill, second to a Mrs. Howard, from whom sprang this branch of the family; their children were John J., Susan, who married Joshua Dale and settled in Missouri, where they left a family; Henry, residing in Boone County, Ind., and Byers, in Nicholas County ; the third marriage was to Susan Grimes, by whom he had three children, the first died young ; Margaret and Elizabeth married brothers, John and James Darrow, at the same place and under the same ceremony, and reside in Boone County, Ind.; William Buntin was a native of Nicholas County; was a son of William, who, with his family was the second settler at the town of Harrodsburg, Ky.; he was a brother-in-law of Major McGeary, who was killed at the battle of the Blue Licks; William was also killed by the Indians; the subject of this sketch is engaged with his step-mother in general agriculture and stock raising business; they are members of the M. E. Church; he is a member of the Masonic order; in September, 1862, he enlisted in Company B., 9th Ky. Cavalry, under General Morgan, and served gallantly as a soldier until in 1864, when he returned home.

JOHN G. BLAIR, farmer, P. O. Carlisle ; was born upon the homestead in 1843, Aug. 30th, to Alexander W. Blair (see history); he received a common school education with the additional attendance upon the Springfield, Ohio, high school during the winters of 1859-60, when, at the outbreak of the Rebellion he was compelled to remain at home to render assistance to the family, while his father and older brother united their fortunes with the Federal forces ; and in June, 1864, he too entered the service, connecting himself with Comp. I, 1st Ky. I; he served until the end of the struggle, when he received his discharge, and was immediately appointed by the government as Assistant Assessor of the 7th Dist., having charge of Nicholas and Robertson, and later Clark counties ; this position he held for a number of years, or until the law, requiring that office, was repealed. He then went to Kansas, where he engaged in real estate business until the spring of 1874, returning each winter and engaging in trading through the South. In 1875, May 6th, he was married to Miss Lydia A. Thomas, born Oct. 20th, 1852, in Nicholas Co., and daughter of Daniel R. and Rachael A (Bryan) Thomas ; she a daughter of Jas. Bryan and a wife of Nobel ; he a son of Erasmus and Lydia (Fishback) Thomas. They have had 2 children: Marion Custer, born Nov. 19, 1877 ; Gertrude Thomas, March 13, 1880. He and family are members of the Christian Church ; a Republican politically, and member of the I. O. O. F. He is the possessor of 206 acres of land, which, with his beautiful residence, makes one of the finest and most valuable farms in the county. In 1875 he made the race in Nicholas and Robinson Counties for the Legislature against John D. Durham and Wesley Robins; he left his own county with 170 odd majority and reduced the popular majority of 800 to about 200. In 1878 he made the race for County Judge, with Judge Banta, cutting a 500 majority down to about 200. He is an energetic and enterprising young business man.

JESSE T. BERRY, clerk ; P. O. Carlisle ; was born in Bath County, Ky., March 28, 1851, to Samuel and Elizabeth (Rennick) Berry ; he was born in Nicholas County, Ky.; is a farmer by occupation, and still living. She was born in Bourbon County, and is still living; they have six children, of whom Jesse, our subject, is next to the oldest. He received a common school education, and assisted his father in the livery business, and stage driving for a number of years, when he became clerk in a hotel, and is now engaged at the Kimbrough House in Carlisle ; he is a man of generous disposition and obliging manners, and merits the esteem in which he is held. He was married at Aberdeen, Ohio, Feb. 8, 1877, to Miss Annie E. Call, who was born in Nicholas County, Dec. 11, 1857; they have one son, Harry Foster, born May 27, 1880. Mrs. Berry was a daughter of Henry and Mary E. (Ralls) Call. He was born in Virginia, and died in September, 1867 ; she was also born in Virginia, and is still living. Owing to his industry and economy, Mr. Berry is now the owner of a pleasant home in Carlisle, the house having been constructed on a plan of his own design. His political sympathies are with the Democratic party.

JOHN A. CAMPBELL, County Clerk, Carlisle; was born in Lewis County, Ky., July 13, 1827, near Flemingsburg. His father, Edward Campbell, was of Scotch origin, and a native of Mason County, where he was born May 22, 1801. After marriage he lived in Lewis County until the death of his wife in 1837. After his second marriage he went to Fleming County, and died in Mason County in 1844. The mother, Mary Lewis, of Welsh extraction, was born in Lewis County in 1803, and died in 1837; her parents were Stephen and Julia (Griffith) Lewis. The parents of John A. had seven children; four are now living: Our subject; S. R., of Fleming County; Lee L., in Jefferson County, Ill., farming; Rebecca, wife of a Baptist minister, in Jefferson County, Ill. Mr. Campbell worked on the farm until seventeen years of age, when he began learning the trade of wagon making, which he finished with a Mr. Miley at Murphysville, Mason County, Ky.; then came to Carlisle, where he carried on a shop for eleven years. At the time of beginning his trade he could not write his own name, having attended school but about six weeks during his life. He perfected his education by diligent study during his apprenticeship, thus fitting himself for the responsible position he now occupies. He is a remarkably fine penman, having acquired the art by copying letters from printed matter, and his books are marvels of neatness, beauty and accuracy. He was elected to his present position in 1858, which position he has held since, with the exception of a few months in the year 1862, when he was displaced by the soldiery. He was married March 2, 1847, in Fleming County, to Miss Malinda J. Story, a native of Fleming County, where she was born Feb. 22, 1825. Her parents were James E. and Rebecca (Summitt) Story. By this marriage there were seven children, viz: Silas W., a farmer in Nicholas; Mary J., wife of George W. Moore, of Mt. Sterling; James B., an artist and merchant, Carlisle; John M., Deputy Clerk; Virgie, Ida and Annie. He is a Democrat politically, and a member of the Odd Fellows' fraternity.

JAMES A. CHAPPELL; Carlisle. The subject of this sketch was born near Carlisle, within one mile of Old Concord Church, on the 11th day of Sept., 1823. He was named James Augustus, in honor of his grandfather James, and uncle Augustus W. Chappell. Received a fair English education, under such excellent teachers as his father, Elder John Rogers, and one or two others. At the close of the year 1837, James entered the dry goods store of John McMahan, upon the modest salary of $15.00 per year. If this sum should seem small, let it be borne in mind that the sales of his employers did not reach $5,000 per annum. In this service he remained during the years 1838 and '39. At the close of '39, he was succeeded by Willis Sims, and James A. went home to again enter school. But on the first day of April, 1840, he again left home, and for the last time, and took position with Mr. J. F. Tureman, the leading dry goods merchant of Carlisle, at a salary of $100 per annum. In this position he remained until July 1, 1845, when through the kindness of his employer, and Mr. Willis L. Parker, of Philadelphia, a clerkship was secured for him in the wholesale dry goods house of Sparing, Good & Co., 138 Market Street, Philadelphia, at a salary of $600 per annum. This situation was held but a few months, for on returning to Carlisle on the 9th of November, same year, to travel in the interest of his house, he was offered a partnership by his old friend and employer, Mr. Tureman, which he accepted at once. January 1, 1846, a partnership was formed with Mr. Tureman, J. A. Chappell and Joseph M. Tureman, son of the former, under the firm name of Jas. H. Chappell & Co. This firm continued in business during the years 1846, '7 and '8. At the beginning of 1849, the elder Mr. Tureman retired, and the firm became Chappell & Tureman (Jas. A. Chappell and Jos. M. Tureman). The sales of this firm rose rapidly in succession, from less than $9,000 in 1848, to over $27,000 in 1854. On the ninth of Oct., 1848, Mr. Chappell was married to Miss Ellen Bruce, daughter of Mr. Geo. S. Bruce, of Fleming County. By this marriage he had two children born: Henry Bruce Chappell, Aug. 26, 1849, and Ellen N. Holt, now Mrs. Wm. S. Spencer, Sept. 18, 1850. On the morning of Feb. 1, 1851, the faithful and beloved wife died after a lingering attack of typhoid fever. Feb. 8, 1853, he married Lucy P. Bruce, sister of his first wife, a lovely, beautiful, young girl, then only a little over seventeen. Five children were the fruits of this marriage: Ada Lena, born Dec. 7, 1853, died of scarlet fever, in Carlisle, Dec. 23, 1862; the second, Sabina B., now Mrs. P. B. Powers, of Augusta, Ky., on the 7th of May, 1855; the third, Thomas Taylor, born May 26, 1858, and died July 17, 1858; the fourth, Sallie Thomas, born April 27, 1864, died in Carlisle, June 29, 1865; the fifth, Lillian, born Nov. 14, 1869. On the 1st of Jan., 1855, the firm of Chappell & Tureman was dissolved, J. A. Chappell retiring, Mr. J. M. Tureman continuing with Mr. Chas. W. McIntyre, as J. M. Tureman & Co. It was during this year that Mr. Chappell edited the Carlisle *American;* but in September of that year he and his brother-in-law, William P. Bruce, opened a new dry goods house on Front street, under the firm name of Chappell & Bruce. July 1, 1856, Mr. J. M.

Tureman sold out to Chappell & Bruce, and they, together with Mr. Charles W. McIntyre, formed a copartnership under the firm name of Chappell, Bruce & McIntyre. This new combination proved to be the most successful firm which ever did business in Carlisle, their sales reaching in 1864, to nearly $60,000, and returning a net profit of near $6,000 each year of its continuance. On the 1st of January, 1865, the members of the firm having sold their stock of goods and s tore house to B. F. Adair, E. M. Ewing and S. M. Waugh, and retained an interest themselves, J. A. Chappell, C. W. McIntyre and Mr. Geo. S. Bruce, moved to the cit y of Cincinnati, leaving Mr. Wm. P. Bruce in Carlisle to superintend their interest in the new firm of W. P. Bruce & Co. The new and handsome store room, No. 144 West Fourth street, Cincinnati, was secured, at an annual rental of $4,200. Here a wholesale dry goods house was opened with J. A. Chappell, W. P. Bruce, Geo. S. Bruce, Chas. W. McIntyre, Stephen G. Chapman and Robert T. Armstrong, as partners, under the firm name of Chapman, Bruce & Co., with a cash capital of $100,000. But scarcely had Mr. Chappell began purchases in New York for his firm, when news came that Mr. S. G. Chapman was found to be a confirmed inebriate ! This of course would never do, and Mr. Chapman was summarily ejected from the firm, and the name of Mr. Chappell placed at the head. The firm of Chappell, Bruce & Co. at once took high rank among the jobbing houses of the city, their sales for the first year reaching $1,250,000. On the 1st of January, 1866, the firm was augmented by the addition of Eli M. Bruce, Esq., and the name changed to Chappell, Bruce & McIntyre. Heavy losses on stock and ruinous losses by bad debts in the South, melted away the capital of the partners like dew before the morning sun. To add to their calamities, Mr. E. M. Bruce died of heart disease, sitting in his chair at the Southern Hotel in New York in the Spring of 1867. This last sad event was the "coup de grace" to the firm ; they paid one hundred cents to the dollar on their liabilities but nothing was left of their capital. January 1, 1868, James A. Chappell and John T. Allen organized upon the ruins of the former house, Mrs. E. M. Bruce having kindly loaned the firm $25,000 of the stock held by her as principal creditor of the house of C., B. & M. Mr. Allen having a like sum, a firm was opened as Chappell, Allen & Co. But within two months after, the firm of Embry & Fisher was consolidated with that of Chappell, Allen & Co., and the new firm became Chappell, Fisher & Allen. This firm, with a nominal capital of $100,000, opened out at 116, West Third Street, Cincinnati. The first six months' business of the new firm seemed to indicate a prosperous career, but it was not long after the July statement was made, before it was discovered that the senior partner, W. W. Embry, Esq., was seriously involved. This was a stunning blow to the firm, and especially to Mr. Chappell, who felt that under the new regime—having already passed through one ordeal, the result of the collapse which followed the close of the war—he had now hoped that the storm was over, and that a more auspicious day was dawning upon his fortunes, which had met with such cruel reverses since leaving his native town, Carlisle. But the die was cast; under the severe financial storm, deserted by the captain of the vessel, Mr. Embry, there was no help for the firm but to strike their colors and succumb to destiny. The firm of Chappell, Fisher & Allen were compelled to close and seek a compromise with their creditors. Chappell and Allen essayed to hoist the flag once more, but the force of the tide was too strong ; thoroughly disheartened with his city venture, with the loss of everything but honor, integrity, and energy, Chappell determined to return to his native town, and cast in his lot with the people among whom he had been so long identified. Resolving to take nothing with him, but to leave all behind him, he wrote to his former friend, F. E. Congleton, cashier of the Deposit Bank at Carlisle, to loan him one hundred dollars, upon which to move his family back to Carlisle. Mr. Congleton with that liberal kindness which has always distinguished him, very promptly sent his check for the amount, and upon Aug. 14, 1869, James A. Chappell with his wife and two daughters, returned to Carlisle after an absence of nearly five years. Without capital, with nothing in fact but hope left, he opened a dry goods store, backed by the kindness of his old friend H. M. Stitt. Through the years 1870 and '71, he managed to pull through with the additional help of his old friends, John Clay, Col. Robert Sims, and E. M. Ewing, until Jan. 1, 1872, when his brother-in-law, F. M. Peale, moved to Carlisle, and took the financial helm with J. A. Chappell, under the firm name of F. M. Peale & Co. But the trials of the Chappell family were no yet ended ; on the morning of Jan. 5, 1873, the store occupied by F. M. Peale & Co. was burned to the ground, with a net loss of nearly ten thousand dollars, and not a dollar of insurance. It now seemed as if it was almost useless to struggle with adverse fortune ; but the firm of Peale & Co. met with much kindness and encouragement, and so the partners, Peale & Chappell, once more flung their war-worn banner to the breeze and opened out, February, 1873, in the new and handsome three story frame, built near the K. C. R. R. depot. Fortune once more for a while smiled upon the Chappell star. Business, which at first was slow and fitful, gradually increased until towards the middle of May, the sales of the house rose to $200 and $250 per day. But the force of misfortune was not yet fully spent. On the morning of the 28th of May, less than five months from the preceding fire, the firm were burnt out again. This time they were insured for $6,000, but their loss on stock, loss of time, and other sources, could not have been short of $3,000. Amidst all these losses, enough to have discouraged many better men, the firm still presented a bold front, resolved still to conquer or perish in the attempt. The firm held bravely on its way, until Jan. 1, 1882, when the firm name was changed to Peale & Chappell, with every indication of a safe, if humble, career before them. In the year 1874, Chappell wrote a short story for his friend, John B. Scudder, and published in the Carlisle *Mercury*, entitled the "Lady in Black." This little romance of five chapters was dedicated to Mrs. Julia Neal, of Carlisle, and was quite favorably received. Having for some years been painfully afflicted with hemorrhoids, and not knowing when he might be compelled to give up the active and onerous duties of the mercantile business, Mr. Chappell felt that the time might come when he should have to resort to his pen for the means of a livelihood for himself and those whom he so devotedly loved. Accordingly the "Lady in Black" was soon followed by a more elaborate work, of twenty-five chapters, entitled "The New Overseer." This met with indifferent success from the public. The following year another story from his pen followed, entitled "Addie Raymond, or Love in a Street Car," and the next year, that which proved his best and most successful one, entitled "Lucy Walton, a Romance of the Blue Lick Springs." In closing this article, we may say that the religious element has always predominated in the life of Mr. Chappell. He was converted when but a mere child, but never joined the church until February, 1861. He has been a deacon in the Baptist church nearly twenty years; has held the office of President of the Nicholas County Sunday School Union for several years, and at this writing bids fair for several more years of active and, we trust, useful and honorable life.

NANCY COLVILLE, farmer; P. O. Carlisle; wife of Daniel Colville, deceased, who was born in Bourbon County, Ky., July 17, 1828, to John and Martha (Summers) Colville. He was born in Virginia, Aug. 27, 1778, and came to Bourbon County, in 1800; was a farmer by occupation, and died May 28, 1835. His wife, Martha, was born near Washington, Pa., Jan. 20, 1794, and died June 26, 1852. The result of their union was three sons, viz.: Sanders, Daniel and Samuel. Daniel, the second son, was married Sept. 4, 1851, to Nancy McClure, the subject of this sketch, who was born in Bourbon County, April 8, 1831. The husband of our subject died March 29, 1866, leaving to her care three children, viz.: John S., born June 18, 1852; William M., Jan. 29, 1861, and Martha Ann, Jan. 17, 1865. Mrs. Colville was a daughter of William and Elizabeth McClure. He was born in Bourbon County, in the year 1807, and died Feb. 22, 1847. His wife, Elizabeth, was born in Montgomery County, June 9, 1809, and died June 8, 1844. They had four children, viz: James, Nancy, Sarah and Elizabeth. Nancy, our subject, received her education in the common schools of Montgomery County; she is a member of the Christian Church, at Carlisle, and is a lady of intelligence and highly respected by all who know her.. She has a farm containing 175 acres of choice farm land, which is kept in a high state of cultivation by her sons. Samuel Colville, a widower and brother of Daniel Colville, deceased, resides with the family. He was born in Bourbon County, July 30, 1823, and on May 25, 1858; was married to Sarah McClure, the sister of our subject, who was born Aug. 31, 1834, and died Sept. 13, 1866. Mr. Colville is at present a Democrat, and for twelve years filled the office of County Assessor. He has supported himself since he was eight years of age, when he became a farm hand and worked his way up in the world, by his own energy and industry. On the 11th of May, 1848, by the accidental discharge of a gun, while climbing a fence, he was wounded in the leg, which injury resulted in amputation. He is a very energetic and enterprising man, and highly esteemed by all.

JOHN W. CAMPBELL, merchant, Carlisle; was born in Nicholas County, Ky., Aug. 4, 1822, to Hugh and Elizabeth (Waugh) Campbell; he was born in Virginia, 1776, came to Kentucky, and settled in Fayette County, in 1790; he was a farmer by occupation, and died July 3, 1843; she was a native of Nicholas County; died July 20, 1843; the result of their union was five children, viz.: Luther C., died at the age of seventeen; John W., Mary Ann, died at the age of ten; James B., and Leonidas B.; John W., the subject of this sketch, is the oldest child now living. His educational privileges were limited to the common schools of the county. He entered upon his career in life by taking upon himself the duties of a farm life, and dealing in stock. He was married in Nicholas County, May 2, 1843, to Miss Elizabeth Myers, daughter of Jacob and Priscilla (Adair) Myers; she was born in July, 1824, and died in January, 1870; she was the mother of eight children, viz.: Priscilla, wife of George W. Roberts; Jacob H., Elizabeth, wife of J. W. Swartz; Luther W., William T., Mary, John F., and Hallie; the latter died at the age of five and a half years. Mr. Campbell was married again to Miss Emma Swinney, who was born in Bath County, in May, 1836, and daughter of John and Minnie (Metier) Swinney, natives of Bath County. She has borne to him two children, viz: Minnie and Walter; the latter died when two years old. Mr. Campbell has served the county in different capacities for a number of years, having been Constable one year, Sheriff four years, and has represented the Republican party in the Legislature two terms, the duties of which position he performed with marked zeal and ability. During the Rebellion he served five months as first quartermaster in the 7th Kentucky Cavalry, when he was promoted to the rank of Major, which position he subsequently resigned to take his seat in the Legislature. He has engaged at different times in several different enterprises, and commenced merchandising at Carlisle, where he is still engaged in business. His wife is a member of the Presbyterian Church; himself a Methodist. He has been a prominent member of the Masonic order at Carlisle, and has attained the Royal Arch and Council degrees; politically he is a Republican.

G. W. CLARK, farmer; P. O. Moorefield; was born upon the 14th of Jan., 1822, in Nicholas County, on the south fork of Somerset Creek, upon the site of the birth of his father, Thomas Clark, who was born Aug. 2, 1797; also an older brother at the same place in 1793, and all other members of the family born at same place. The Clarks were among the earliest settlers in Nicholas County, and the ancestry of Thomas Clark came to America at a very early date from England. The father of Thomas Clark had six children: Samuel, who settled in Mason County, Ky.; Jack, who was an aid-de-camp to Gen. Harrison, went to the West; Thomas remained at the old homestead; Prudence went to Indiana, where she married; Nancy married David Grimes, and settled in Putman County, Ind.; and Herman, who settled in Boone County, Ind. Thomas Clark married Polly Grimes, and died upon the old homestead May 15, 1875; was the father of twelve children, four of whom died young; the others grew to maturity: Aaron, residing in Woodford County; George W.; Zerilda, wife of George Grimes, living upon the old homestead; John, in Nicholas; Elgiva, deceased, wife of David Barnes, who resides in Boone County, Ind.; Jerry (deceased), left family in Nicholas; Sarah, wife of Geo. Shrout; and Mary, unmarried, residing in Union Precinct. The subject of this sketch remained with his father until his marriage, which occurred Sept. 4, 1842, to Sally A. Forgy, daughter of John Forgy, of Nicholas County; she a native of Bourbon County. By her there were six children: a daughter died at the age of fifteen years; William A., in Montgomery County, Ind.; Mary, wife of James Ralls, in Henry County, Mo.; Margaret, wife of Geo. Ison, in Montgomery County, Ind.; Thomas, in Nicholas; Lizzie, wife of Allen Boys, of Fleming County. The mother of the above died Oct. 27, 1859. Mr. Clark was remarried Dec. 25, 1862, to Mrs. Louisa (Higginbotham) Green, widow of R. B. Green; by him she had three children, only one of whom is now living, Mrs. Margaret Davis. By the second marriage there were four children: a son died in infancy; John, Joseph and Lulu, all at home. Mr. Clark served in the 1st Kentucky Reg. Mounted Cavalry, under Capt. Thomas and Col. Bradly, commanding. He enlisted in 1861, remaining until near the close of the war in the Western Department, commanded by Gen. Marshall. After about fifteen months' active service, he was stationed at Liberty Hill in charge of wagon repairing; he and wife are members of the M. E. Church.

THOMAS C. COLLIVER, farmer; P. O. Millersburg; was born in Montgomery County, Ky., July 13, 1843, and is a son of Presley O. and Elizabeth (Congleton) Colliver. He was born in Montgomery County Jan. 19, 1821; was a school teacher by profession. He was married in 1842, to Elizabeth Congleton, who was born April 2, 1820, and died Feb. 10, 1875, (see hist. F. E. Congleton.) They had two children, viz.: William, deceased, and Thomas, our subject; he attended the common schools of Montgomery County for several years, and completed his education at the Millersburg College; after which he commenced merchandising at Weston, where he remained until 1869, when he bought a farm and turned his attention to farming; he was married April 12, 1871, to Mary Bell Hutchins, who was born Aug. 26, 1852, to Daniel J. and Julia A. (Hall) Hutchins, native of Nicholas County; he born Jan. 23, 1831, and still living; she died April 2, 1860. Mr. Colliver is a very energetic and enterprising business man, and a practical farmer; he owns a fine farm containing 238 acres of choice farm land. In addition to growing the usual farm crops, he deals extensively in high grade stock, his specialties being Cotswold sheep and Poland China hogs; he is a prominent member of the Baptist Church and society, and enjoys the highest esteem of the community at large; politically he is a Democrat.

F. P. CLARY, telegraph operator and station agent, P. O. Carlisle; was born in Mason County, Ky., June 18, 1854, and is a son of Joshua and Eliza (Prather) Clary. He was born in Fleming County, Ky., in Dec., 1818. He is a blacksmith by trade, and is still living; has been married three times. He was married the first time in Mason County, in March, 1842, to Miss Eliza Prather, the mother of our subject. She died in Oct., 1859. His second marriage occurred in Illinois, in Nov. 1865, to Mary Y. Hamson, who died in Oct. 1867. In 1869 he married Rebecca Anna March, in Orangeburg, Mason County, Ky. He is the father of 13 children, of whom F. P. the subject of this sketch, was the 7th. He received a common school education, and in 1874 began the study of telegraphy at Cynthiana, where, by his energy and strict attention to business he soon became proficient in that, and two years later took charge of the Station and Telegraph office at Carlisle. He was married in Carlisle Oct. 4, 1881, to Miss Fannie Conway, who was born in Pike County, Ky., May 20, 1861, and was a daughter of Washington and Rhoda L. (Piper) Conway, both natives of Nicholas County. He born Aug. 27, 1832; she, April 17, 1839. Mr. Clary is a man of fine personal, social and business habits, and one of the most substantial young men of the town. Politically, he is identified with the Democratic party.

GREENBERRY CHEATHAM, Hotel Keeper, P. O. Carlisle; born in Nicholas County, December 5, 1832; his grandfather, John Cheatham, and wife, Elizabeth Harper, came from Culpepper County, Va., very early, and settled in Montgomery County, whence they afterwards moved to Nicholas County. He started life as a very poor boy, but by industry and frugality acquired a position of independence. John Cheatham, Jr., the father of Greenberry, married Harriet Garrett, of Montgomery County, of a family noted for its longevity, a member of it having attained the age of 117 years. He had seven children, five sons and two daughter, viz: William, (deceased); Richard, now in southern California; Greenberry, Nancy A., married John White, of Harrison; John, now in Missouri; Boone, and Armilda, married to James Long. Our subject received a limited education, remaining with his father till twenty-one years of age. In 1863 he engaged in distilling, which he followed for ten years, when he resumed farming. In 1881 he built in Carlisle the large and commodious hotel which he now occupies and manages in an energetic and business-like manner, for the entertainment of the traveling public. In 1852 he married Melvina Stoker, daughter of Thomas Stoker, by whom he had five children: Emma, married to James Turley; William F., Harvey, Annie, wife of Martin Brayfield, of Carlisle, and Dixie. In 1863 he married his present wife, Miss Melvin Mann, daughter of Col. David Mann, of Nicholas County. Three children have blessed their union: Lucian, Ora and Herman.

JOHN W. CLAY, farmer; P. O. Carlisle; was born near Carlisle, February 25, 1840, to John and Mary (Arnold) Clay; she a daughter of Lewis and Mary (Throckmorton) Arnold. John Clay, is a son of Isaac Clay, distant connection of the Clays of Bourbon County. The father of our subject died November 27, 1876, in his sixty-eighth year; the mother, August 6, 1869, in her sixtieth year. They had ten children, eight of whom are now living: Joseph, Mary, wife of Benjamin Staples, in Shelby County, Ky.; Maria, wife of Robert Rogers, residing in Henry county, Mo.; Matthew, John W., James T., Sally, a maiden lady, and Samnel C.; all are in Nicholas County, except the two daughters as above mentioned. Mr. Clay is engaged in general agriculture; is a member of the Masonic order, and also a member of the Baptist church; is a young man, interested in the welfare of his community, in public improvements, the advancement of schools and churches, and of the farming interest of the county.

F. E. CONGLETON, banker; P. O. Carlisle; is a member of a family of eight children; his father was William Congleton, a farmer of Bourbon County; his mother, Mary Rule, also of Bourbon. The Congleton family are decendants of the Old Holland Dutch, and heirs to the famous "Anneke Jans" estate. Mr. Congleton was born Sept. 9, 1829, in the above named county. He began life as a merchant, and was married at Sharpsburg, Ky., Dec. 16, 1852, to Hannah C. Cummings, of Mercer County, Ky. He was made cashier of the Deposit Bank of Carlisle, at its organization in August, 1869, which position he has since held. In his political tenets, he is a Democrat; he is a prominent member of the Masonic Order at Carlisle. By his marriage he had two children; one only of that number survives; she, a Mrs. Horace M. Taylor. The family are connected with the Presbyterian Church.

JAMES T. CLAY, farmer; P. O. Carlisle; was born near Carlisle, Nov. 16, 1846, to John Clay (see hist); he lived with his father until attaining his majority, securing in the meantime the advantages of a common school education, and rendering what assistance he was able on the farm; he then engaged in farming, and from the years 1874 to 1879, was engaged with his brother in horse and mule trading during the winter season in the Southern States; his marriage occurred Nov. 10, 1880, to Miss Martha A. Blair (see hist. of A. W. Blair), after which he located at his present home, where he is engaged in a general agriculture and stock raising; he has acted as adminstrator for several estates, and in the discharge of his duties has won the confidence of the citizens of the community in which he lives; he is an energetic and enterprising young man, a Democrat politically, and highly esteemed by his fellow men.

THOMAS A. DORSEY, lumber merchant, contractor and builder; P. O. Carlisle; was born near Flemingsburg, Jan. 5, 1828; his father, John I. Dorsey, was an extensive farmer, and born in Maryland, near Hagerstown, in 1873, and died in Nicholas County in 1846; his parents were Leakin and Mary (Ingram) Dorsey, who came in 1879 to Stockton's Station; their children were Sally, wife of Thomas Wallace; Rachel, wife of Charles Anderson; Edward, John I., Joseph and Amelia, wife of Thomas Andrews; the youngest of the family was born in Fleming County, the others in Maryland; all are now deceased. Edward was a prominent physician in Fleming County. The mother of Thomas A., was Nancy Spiers, a native of Maryland, settled at Bryan's Station with her parents, Greene and Mary Spiers, who were of German descent; she died in 1871, aged seventy-six years, leaving a family of ten children, six of whom are now living, four sons and two daughters, two of the former in Missouri and one in Indianapolis; a sister, Mrs. David Stewart, of Maysville; and Mrs. Martha McClure, of Paris; a sister, now deceased, was the wife of Col. T. S. Parks. Thomas A. received a very good education in the Flemingsburg schools, and at about twenty years, or at his father's death, engaged in the avocation of farming in Nicholas County, in which capacity he continued until the year 1868, when he became one of a firm which had taken the contract to build the Ky. C. R. R., from the Licking River to Paris, finishing the same in the year 1871, since which time, by the assistance of other parties, he has built the mill at Parks' Ferry, of which he is superintendent, in connection with his contracting and other business. He was married Feb. 15, 1855, in Nicholas County, to Miss Maggie Griffith, born Dec. 20, 1832, in Nicholas County, and a member of one of its early families; her parents were William A. and Cynthia (Mathers) Griffith, she a daughter of William Mathers; by this marriage there have been eight children, four of whom died in childhood. Those living are: Willie, Nannie, wife of N.W. Yelton, freight agent at Crittenden Station, on the Cincinnati Southern R. R.; the youngest are Mattie and Eddie. The family are members of the M. E. Church. He was formerly an old live Whig, now a member of the Democratic party, and a member of the Masonic order.

MALCOLM DILLS, physician; P. O. Carlisle; born in Harrison County, Sept. 9, 1849; he is a son of B. F. Dills and S. M. Bradley, daughter of William Bradley, who came to Harrison County from Virginia very eariy. William Bradley married a daughter of George Kirkpatrick, a native of Ireland. B. F. Dills was a son of David and Lydia (Broadwell) Dills--the Broadwells being among the earliest and most wealthy settlers of Harrison County. The subject of this sketch was the eldest of four children, three surviving his sister Nora, who is unmarried, and his brother Sydney being a prominent farmer of Harrison County. Dr. Dills received a liberal education, graduating from the Miami University at Oxford, Ohio, before he was nineteen years of age. In the fall of 1869, he entered the Ohio Medical College of Cincinnati, taking a three years course. He was graduated in March, 1871, and after spending a short time in Bath County, located in Carlisle the same year. where by his superior ability and affable manners he has won for himself an extensive and lucrative practice. On Oct. 1, 1872, he married Miss Allen Mann, daughter of James Mann, of Carlisle. He is a member of the Carlisle Commandery of Knights Templar, and with his wife is a member of the M. E. Church South. He has made homœpathy a study, and makes a partial use of it in his practice. He is the possessor of an extensive miscellaneous library.

MRS. MARGARET DONNELL, farmer; P. O. Carlisle; widow of Samuel M. Donnell, who died in June, 1878, in his 70th year. He was born in Bourbon County, upon the farm which is now occupied by his son, James L. His parents were James and Mary (Quilt) Donnell, who came to Nicholas County, which was then Bourbon, in the year 1791. His father was a native of Ireland, but came to America at an early date. The mother of our subject was a daughter of James and Catharine (Wasson) Quilt, who were at an early day residents of Pennsylvania. The families above mentioned, were among the early settlers of this section of Kentucky, and were people held in high esteem and having the respect of the best families throughout the different generations. Mrs. Donnell, since the death of her husband, has continued the farming, with the assistance in part of her family. By her marriage with Mr. Donnell, there were four sons and four daughters born to them.

Three of the sons and one daughter are still living. She is a lady of intelligence, and held in the highest esteem by her neighbors.

MISS SARAH DINSMORE, farmer; P. O. Carlisle; was born on the place where she now lives, April 9, 1810; her father was John Dinsmore, who was of Irish descent, a native of Westmoreland County, Pa., and a farmer by occupation; he was a son of Samuel and Margaret (Yost) Dinsmore. John came very early to Nicholas, where he died about 1828, aged about 70 years. His wife was Catharine Van Meter, also a native of Westmoreland County; died in 1856, aged 94 years. She was a daughter of Capt. John Van Meter, who served in the revolutionary war. Mr. Dinsmore was married, and had three children before coming to Kentucky, in 1792. He settled near Paris, then became one of the earlier settlers of Nicholas. They had, in all, eleven children, five sons and six daughters, viz: Henry, Elizabeth, Margaret, John, Samuel, Jane, Mary, James, Catharine, William, and Sarah, the latter the only one living. Four of the daughters were unmarried, the others left heirs in Ohio, Illinois, Missouri, Indiana and Kentucky. Miss Dinsmore has been carrying on farming for many years, although a cripple for eleven years, by an accident. Her nephew, Thomas Dinsmore, is residing with her, lending his assistance in farming. She is a member of the Christian Church.

DR. WM. W. FRITTS, druggist; Carlisle; is a son of Henry and Lucy (Adams) Fritts, she a native of Spottsylvania County, Va., but came to Clark County, N. Y., with her parents, when about five years of age, or in the year 1805. The Adams family is related to the illustrious statesmen, John and Samuel Adams of Virginia. Henry Fritts, (originally Fri z), was a native of Pennsylvania, born in 1797, to Valentine Fritts, a native of Germany, but came to Pennsylvania at an early date, thence to Southern Ohio. Henry served his time at the hatters trade, in Winchester, Kentucky, where he became acquainted with and married his wife, by whom he had five children, two of whom died in infancy. Our subject, the only son and eldest of the family, was born Oct. 28, 1816; two daughters, Catharine, wid w of Wm. Ogden (a nephew of Gov. Metcalf) emigrated to northern Iowa, where she now resides; Sarah, now the wife of Wm. P. Harris, a resident near Waverly, Iowa. The mother died in 1844. The father again uniting himself in marriage to a Miss Edward, who now resides in Indiana with her only child, Volney O. Fritts, an eminent minister in the Baptist church. Our subject received very limited educational advantages, learning at an early age the hatters' trade with his father. He came to Carlisle in 1836, where he plied his trade and studied, with his open books upon the bench, and attendance upon night schools, he acquired an ordinary education. In 1843, in connection with J. F. Tureman, he opened a drug store and studied medicine with Dr. John F. McMillan, a very talented preceptor In 1848, he entered the University of Louisville, taking an advanced course and graduating therefrom in 1853. He and one other member of a class of eighty received the honors in the publication of their thesis. He then formed a partnership with his former preceptor with whom he continued until 1870, when, on account of ill-health, be was compelled to give up the practice of his profession. In 1871, in company with his eldest son, he opened the large and commodious drug store, which they now occupy. He was married April 11, 1837, to Miss Sarah Hamilton, daughter of John and Catharine (Rule) Hamilton, which family was quite prominent in Virginia, and among the early settlers of Bourbon County. By this marriage there were six children, three of whom died in infancy. Those living are William H., who was married to Miss Sue Clark (now deceased), of Bourbon County; left one son, Edward C. Fritts; John R., a practicing physician of Centreville, Bourbon County; and Martha Alice, at home. They are staunch Republicans, both sons serving in the Federal army. William H. holds the position of Postmaster of Carlisle. Dr. Fritts and family are members of the Baptist Church, in which he has for many years held the office of Deacon and Superintendent of the Sunday School. He is one of the school of self-made men, and holds a position of love and honor in the hearts of his fellow citizens.

ELIJAH D. FOSTER, farmer; P. O. Carlisle; was born in Nicholas County, Jan. 1, 1826, and is a son of George R. and Harriet M. (Daisey) Foster; he was born in Virginia, Nov. 10, 1801; a tailor by trade and farmer by occupation; died Feb. 26, 1875. His wife, Harriet, was born in Nicholas County, Nov. 11, 1805, and died Nov. 10, 1877. The result of their union was three children, viz.: Millia, deceased wife of James E. Secrest, Elijah D. and Jeremiah P. The subject of this sketch was educated in the common schools of Nicholas County, and commenced his career in life as a farmer; he was married in Bourbon County, Jan. 16, 1856, to Miss Jane E. Sanders, who was born in Bourbon County, Nov. 5, 1832, and died Jan. 31, 1875; four children were born to them, viz.: Hattie A., George R., James S., and Jeremiah C., one of whom, James S., died when six years of age. Mrs. Foster was a daughter of James R. and Martha

(Smith) Sanders; the former was born Oct. 1, 1779, and died April 18, 1871; his wife was born Oct. 26, 1814, and died Aug. 1, 1864. Mr. Foster is an energetic and prosperous farmer, having by his industry accumulated a large property, and at the present time owns a farm containing 255 acres of choice farm land, well stocked with high grade and thoroughbred stock. He is a member of the Christian Church at Millersburg, and also a prominent member of the Masonic order at Carlisle. In politics he is a Republican.

ISAAC FEEBACK, farmer; P. O. Oakland Mills; was born in Nicholas County, Ky., Oct. 26, 1842, son of John T. and Rachael (McDaniel) Feeback; he a farmer, born in Nicholas and still living; she also a native of Nicholas. They had six children. Our subject received a common school education, and early began the life of a farmer, in which occupation he has continued since, at present owning 260 acres of choice land, in one of the best sections of the best land on this continent—the famous "Blue-Grass region." May 9, 1862, he married Miss Minerva Smith, daughter of Jesse and Martha Smith, all of this county, and from which union has sprung the following children, living: Jesse, Bettie and Rosa. The grandfather of Mr. Feeback was in the war of 1812, and he himself was the first Postmaster of Buffalo Trace. Self and wife are Methodists; he, a Republican.

JOHN T. FEEBACK, farmer; P. O. Bartersville; was born in Nicholas County, Aug. 3, 1829; his father, Gilbert Feeback, was born in Nicholas County, in 1802, and died in 1878; he was in the war of 1812, and his brother, Mathew, in the Mexican war; the mother of John T. Feeback was Millie Richey, born in Nicholas County, in 1807, and died March, 1879; she was the mother of fourteen children, the subject being the third son; he was educated in the common schools of Nicholas County, and is a farmer; he was married Aug. 2, 1848, to Rachel Baker, who was born in Nicholas County, Sept. 3, 1833; she was the daughter of John Baker, of Bourbon, and Lucy McDaniel, of Nicholas County; they have five children: Isaac, Mary J., James, Green, and Lucy; they are both members of the Methodist Church; he is a Mason at Carlisle, and a Republican.

MITCHELL GRIMES, retired farmer; P. O. Carlisle; was born at Poplar Plains, Fleming County, Ky., Feb. 22, 1827; his father was Dr. Avery Grimes, who was born near Clintonville, Bourbon County, about 1790, and expired in 1868, after having lived a long and useful life, serving in the war of 1812, and practicing in Esculapian arts for over forty years, or until a few years before his death, when he engaged in farming; he, a son of Avery, Sr., who came to Bourbon County from the South branch of the Potomac, in about 1782, and by persistent effort secured a home for himself and family, after having paid for the same three times, through false titles and unprincipled agents. The mother of our subject was Maria Mitchell, who was born in Georgetown, D. C., and at a tender age was left an orphan by the death of her father, when she was taken and raised by her uncle, Richard Butler, of Mason County, the wife of whom was a Lovejoy, and sister to the mother of Maria Mitchell. Dr. Avery Grimes by his marriage had seven children, four of whom are living: James, in Fleming County, Mrs. T. D. Byram, of Nicholas, and the wife of Rev. John T. Enan, of Fleming County. Mr. Grimes received a common school education, and read law two years with Judge Andrews, of Flemingsburg, studying also the Latin language, in which he became quite proficient; he was a young man of energy and industry in his studies, through which he acquired a valuable education. He began life as a farmer and trader, shipping extensively to all parts of the country, having several droves of stock of different kinds on the road at the same time; in this business he continued more than forty years. He was married Jan. 22, 1850, in Montgomery County, near Mt. Sterling, to Elizabeth Frances Smith, who was born near Mt. Sterling, Dec. 22, 1830, to Enoch Smith, Jr., who was born near Mt. Sterling, in September, 1793; he, the only son now living of Enoch Smith, Sr., who came from Virginia at a very early date, settling at Mt. Sterling, surveying and laying out the town. He settled about 4,000 acres at that place, many acres of which he gave to families who would come in and improve the country with him; his wife was Frances Wren; Enoch, Jr.'s wife was Sally Grimes, daughter of James Grimes, and Sally Bryant, who was a niece of Daniel Boone's. They had twelve children, eight daughters and four sons; seven are now living: Dr. Thomas J., in Fayette, County, Mo.; Amelia, wife of Rev. Joslin, of Linn County, Mo.; Anna E., wife of a Mr. Carter, of Lafayette County, Mo.; the wife of our subject, Mrs. Dr. J. C. Waugh, of Fleming County, the widow of Barton W. Stone, Jr.; Mattie B., wife of Silas Marshall, of Kansas City, Mo.; Loretta, wife of George Whiting, who reside at the old homestead, near Mt. Sterling, and Virginia C., wife of Roy Stone, of Bath County. Mr. Grimes by his marriage had two children, one of whom died at two years, the other at twenty-one years of age. Mr. Grimes is in political ideas, Democratic, and a member of the Masonic order.

WILLIAM F. GILLESPIE, farmer; P. O., Carlisle, was born in Montgomery County, Ky., Nov. 2, 1833, to Calvin and Cythia (Hedges) Gillespie; he was born in Madison County, Ky., Dec. 25, 1809; is a farmer by occupation, and still living; his wife, Cythia, was born in Bourbon County, and died in April, 1840; to them was born nine children, of whom, William, our subject, was the second. He was educated in the common schools of Montgomery County, and when twenty-one years of age entered upon the duties of a farm life. He was married in Nicholas County, Oct. 26, 1854, to Miss Lucretia Boardman, who was born in Nicholas County, Sept. 29, 1833, and died July 22, 1861, leaving to his care two children, viz: James and Nancy; Mrs. Gillespie was a daughter of Abner and Mary (Cross) Boardman; he was born in Bourbon County, April 16, 1801, and died Aug. 29, 1875; his wife, Mary, was also born in Bourbon County, Jan. 3, 1806, and died Jan. 30, 1878. Mr. Gillespie was married again in Nicholas County, Jan. 15, 1863, to Miss Harriet Sparks, who was born in Nicholas County, June 17, 1831; they have three children, viz.: Robert L., Joseph and Elizabeth; the present Mrs. Gillespie was a daughter of William and Catharine (Knox) Sparks, both natives of Nicholas County; the former was born July 30, 1793 and died March 20, 1864; his wife was born Dec. 3, 1797, and died Jan. 11, 1845. Mr. Gillespie commenced life a poor man, but owing to his natural business tact and persistent energy, has become a successful farmer, and now owns a farm containing 275 acres, which, "being a practical farmer," he keeps under a high state of cultivation, and well stocked. He is a man well worthy of the high esteem in which he is held by the community. In connection with his wife, he is a member of the Christian church at East Union. He is also a prominent member of the Masonic order at Carlisle. In politics he is a Democrat.

THOMAS COLLINS HERNDON, physician and farmer; P. O. Carlisle; whose portrait appears in this work, is the oldest practitioner in Nicholas County, was born near Blair's Mill, on Licking river, on the 22nd of April, 1817, and named for his grandfather, T. C. Herndon, who was a native of Fauquier County, Va., and came to Mason County about 1812, and to Nicholas in 1816. His wife was Mary Ann Seal, daughter of Captain John Seal, of revolutionary fame. She was born and raised in Alexandria, on the Potomac; her mother was Sally Jarvis, who, with her husband, died in Virginia. The grandfather of our subject by his marriage had five sons and three daughters, viz: Priscilla, married Geo. M. Campbell, and reared family in Nicholas County; Solomon resided in Virginia; William left family in Nicholas, went West, and was never heard from; John M. reared a family in Boone County, Ky.; finally settled in Dearborn County, Ind.; James W. reared a family in Nicholas, was a very prominent man in the county, and held the office of Colonel in the State Militia at the time of his death of cholera in 1833; Sarah J. married Jeffrie Bartlett and settled in Indiana; Francis married Lawrence McCowan and settled in Boone County, Ind.; and George W. reared a family in Nicholas. The father and four oldest sons were soldiers in the war of 1812. Our subject received a limited common school education, but engaged in teaching, the proceeds for which he applied in further education, and graduated from the Louisville Medical College in 1844, when he spent one year at Elizaville, then came to his present location, where he has since resided and built up a large practice and a reputation in Nicholas and adjacent counties. He was married to Miranda J. Craycraft on the 19th of Nov., 1846; she a daughter of Zadock and Annie Hendricks. By her he had three children: W. W., Mary A., wife of Walter S. Potts (see hist.), and William E. (see hist.). Both sons are graduates of the University of Louisville, and are practicing physician in Nicholas County. The mother of these died March 27, 1860, when the Doctor was remarried upon the 9th of May following to Mary Ann Craycraft, a sister to his first wife; by her he has one child, Thomas C. The Doctor, in connection with the practice of his profession, is extensively engaged in the breeding of all the principal strains of the Bates family of shorthorns; also fine horses and Cotswold sheep, and is carrying on general agriculture upon his large and beautiful farm, "Herndon Ranch." They are members of the Missionary Baptist Church at Locust Grove.

WILLIAM TELL HENRY; P. O. Carlisle; was born in Carlisle May 16, 1833; his father, Richard D. Henry, was born near Paris, April 5, 1804; died Dec. 7, 1874; he was for many years a resident of Carlisle, where he won the esteem of the people in his several avocations, of cabinet making, mercantile pursuits, and farm life, also among the foremost in the village government; his early ancestry were from Ireland. The mother of our subject was Rhoda Ogden, daughter of Henry and Lucy (Metcalf) Ogden; she a sister to Govenor Metcalf; she was born Oct. 15, 1810, and died Sept. 21, 1839. Richard D. by two marriages had five children: Louisa, died in early childhood; John, in the Mexican war, at nineteen years of age; William Tell and George W., born Feb. 13, 1836;

second marriage to Mary Crenshaw, of Harrison County, and Henry Crenshaw. By her he had one child, Mary, born Aug. 29, 1842, now wife of Dr. G. W. Adair (see history). Mr. Henry received a limited education in the early Carlisle schools, and began life in 1855, in the furniture and undertaking business, in which he continued about ten years, then engaged in farming and trading, on account of his health, dealing largely in real estate and various other enterprises. On the 8th of Nov., 1855, in Nicholas County, he was married to Nancy T. Hall, who was born in Carlisle May 26, 1832. Her father, Robert C. Hall, was born in Virginia in 1783, and came with his father, Caleb Hall, to Bourbon County in 1793; after arriving at maturity, his opinions became of importance in the affairs of Nicholas County, on account of which he was made Judge; also represented the same in the State Legislature. His wife was Frances Banton, of Garrard County, Ky., daughter of John Banton, also a native of Virginian. Mr. Henry by this marriage had two daughters: Lizzie, who died at twenty-three years of age, and Fannie, now the wife of Hon. Thomas A. Webster, of Carlisle ; he a son of Dr. Thomas A., of Green County, Ky. Our subject has been among the prominent men of the village and county, and during the late war was made Provost Marshal of Nicholas County, ill health keeping him from active duty at the front. He is a Republican in political faith, and with his family belong to the Presbyterian Church.

JOHN HAMILTON HAM, dealer in real estate, Carlisle, was born in McBride's Run, Nicholas County, Ky., Dec. 22, 1821, to Samuel and Elizabeth (Hamilton) Ham ; he died in April, 1837, at the age of fifty (see history of M. K. Ham) ; she was a daughter of John and Elizabeth Hamilton, and died at the age of fifty, in 1852 ; she was the mother of five children, viz : Leann, wife of Thomas M. Mathews, residing in Orange County, Ind. ; John H., William W., Jacob A., married, died and left a wife and three children (two sons and a daughter,) in Orange County, Ind. ; and Samuel W., also deceased ; John H., the third child and subject of this sketch, began his career in life as a farmer, and followed the same until a few years since, when he engaged in the real estate business. He was married in Carlisle, Nov. 9, 1848, to Elizabeth McCune, born in Nicholas County, July 15, 1830, to John and Elizabeth (Mathers) McCune, natives of Nicholas County ; he born in 1796, she in 1806, to Thomas Mathers, born in 1759, and Elizabeth, his wife, born in 1768 ; John McCune, a son of John, born in 1762. Mr. Ham, by this marriage had three children, viz : R. Edgar, born Nov. 17, 1849 ; Oscar, born Sept. 6, 1852, and Elizabeth, died in infancy. Mr. and Mrs. Ham are members of the Church at Carlisle, of which he served as Deacon several years ; he is neutral in politics. His youngest son, Oscar, was married Oct. 28, 1879, to Miss Luella Kimbrough (born to Joshua and Mary (Bowen) Kimbrough) May 14, 1857 (see history of Mrs. M. C. Bell). After marriage he engaged in business with his brother-in-law, Mr. H. C. Kimbrough, at the hotel, and continued his stock interests and trading. They are the owners of the famous trotting horse, "Pegasus." In business, they are enterprising, energetic, and are highly esteemed by the people of the county.

WILLIAM SMITH HOWSE, farmer ; P. O. Millersburg, proprietor of Rising Sun farm, was born near Rockville, Montgomery County, Md., Sept. 19, 1814; he came with his parents to Nicholas County, in 1818, settling about three miles from where he now lives ; his parents were John and Elizabeth (Smith) Howse ; she, a daughter of Daniel and Anna (Holland) Smith. The latter named people were prominent in the local politics of Montgomery County, Md., and among the early settlers of Kentucky; John Howse, a son of John, Sr., the subject of this sketch is the eldest son and third child of four daughters and three sons, and the only one of the sons now living. Two daughters younger than himself are still living : Sarah, widow of (John Letton), (Thomas Blackamore), and (Joseph Winfrey) ; and Loraday, wife of William H. Gage, a farmer in Missouri. Mr. Howse received a limited education ; worked with his father on the farm until his death, which occurred in 1835 ; he then engaged in driving stock for a number of years. In July, 1844, he was married to Eleanor D. Willett, a native of Bourbon County, and daughter of Silas and Barbara (Fisher) Willett ; she, a daughter of William Fisher ; by her he had two sons, Edwin R., married and farming in Nicholas County ; Silas L. died April 10, 1873, in his twenty-third year, married Dec. 5, 1872, to Miss Molly Bryan, a native of Hancock County, Ind., was brought by her parents at a very early age to Nicholas, thence to Bourbon ; she the only daughter of Henry Bryan, near Plum Lick, and niece of Anson P. Bryan. Mr. Howse is an intelligent, social gentleman, having acquired a practical education by his extensive travel. His wife died April 5, 1869. He possesses good business qualifications, is a solid Democrat and an esteemed citizen.

MICHAEL K. HAM, farmer; P. O. Carlisle; was born on the old homestead near where he now lives, Feb. 14, 1822, to John Ham the second, who was born on the line of Berkeley and Loudoun Counties, Va., June 13, 1782, and died May 17, 1867; he was a farmer by occupation, and came to the farm now owned by Robert Letton, in 1794; he a son of Jacob and Catharine (Kime) Ham, the latter a native of Pennsylvania; Jacob, a son of Jacob and Barbara (Tull) Ham; the two latter gentlemen were also natives of Virginia, and served with transportation wagons in the Revolutionary war; the mother of our subject was Chloe T. Jones, born in Maryland, Jan. 26, 1785, married in, 1806, on Cane Ridge, Bourbon County; by Barton W. Stone, died Oct. 19, 1860; she a daughter of John and Johanna (Richards) Jones, who came to Cane Ridge in about 1796 ; Johanna, a daughter of William Richards and a Miss Letton; John Ham by his marriage had eleven children, all of whom grew to maturity; the youngest of three deceased, Caleb, Jacob, and William R.; the family of first two in Nicholas, the latter in Morgan County, Ill., lived to be fifty-six years of age; they were: J. J. and Berton R., in Clay County, Mo.; Willis C., in Morgan County, Ill.; Sarah, wife of John T. Johnson, in the same county; Solomon W., Michael K., Brice W., and Johanna K., wife of Jonathan Johnson; all are in Nicholas, except as above mentioned; Michael K. after receiving a limited education, engaged in farming in which he has continued all his life; he has been twice married, first Aug. 25, 1842, to Elizabeth Miller, who died June 21, 1853, she a daughter of Henry and Mary (Johnson) Miller, who were natives of Nicholas; by her he had five children, two of whom died in infancy, and Mary E., deceased, wife of John Hamilton; Henry, at home and Monroe in Ill.; second marriage, Jan. 10, 1856, to Isabella Hamilton, a native of Nicholas, and daughter of John Hamilton; by her there were three children: Tabitha, a wife of Brice Ham; Emerine, and Willis. Mr. Ham in political sentiment is Democratic.

W. T. INGELS, farmer; P. O. Millersburg; proprietor of Mt. Pleasant farm, is a Parisian by birth, being born in the Metropolis of Bourbon County, July 13, 1819. His father was Boone Ingels, who was born in 1784 in what was then Fayette County, now upon the line of Bourbon. His grandfather was the owner of a small tract of land in Philadelphia, which he leased for a given time before coming to Kentucky. The land subsequently became very valuable, but the records having been lost, the rightful heirs were kept from the possession of their property. The wife of Boone Ingels was Elizabeth Reed, a native of Lexington and a member of one of the oldest families of that place. They had nine children; five sons only are living: James, in Paris; Thomas, farming near Pleasant Hill, Mo.; W. T., Dr. Edward, and George, in Cincinnati. The Ingels were related to Daniel Boone, hence the name Boone in the family. The father of our subject was a hatter by trade and an extensive manufacturer in his business in Paris. He was an early settler in the place; carried on his business till near his death, amassing quite a fortune. The subject of this sketch received the advantages of a subscription school until fifteen years of age, when he was engaged in the dry goods store of Hugh Brent, in Paris, for one year, thence to Lexington, where he engaged in merchandising until 1854. From 1848 until the close of his mercantile career he was in partnership in the hardware business with his brother Boone (deceased). Since 1854 he has been engaged in agriculture and the raising of thoroughbred Cotswold sheep in Bourbon and Nicholas Counties. In 1872 he received the appointment as Storekeeper for the Government; afterward held the different offices of Special Deputy, Storekeeper and Gauger, which offices he held for a number of years. He was married, Dec. 3, 1846, to Mary R. Vimont, daughter of B. F. Vimont (see hist.). They had nine children; two died in infancy. Those living are: F. B., at home; Gertrude, wife of Thomas Savage, of Millersburg; Sue B., widow of F. R. Jaynes, of Paris, who was burned to death while impersonating "Santa Claus" at a Christmas tree, Dec. 25, 1879; Alice, wife of Will Judy, of Millersburg; John V. and Edward, clerking in Millersburg; and Owen W., at home. Mr. Ingels is a staunch Republican, and with his family are members of the Christian Church.

WILLIAM MASON JOHNSON, farmer; P. O. Millersburg; was born in the room in which he now lives, was the youngest child of Jonathan and Rachael (Dills) Johnson; she, a daughter of Isaac Dills, of Harrison County. Jonathan Johnson was a native of Pennsylvania, born in May, 1780, and was brought by his parents to "Irish Station" when eight years of age; his father, Laban, was the earliest settler in the section where subject now lives. Jonathan was for a time a resident of Scott County; was married and moved at a very early date to the farm where William M. now resides. He had three sons and two daughters, John C., born Oct. 14, 1804; he was twice married—first to Aby Tennants, of Mason County, second to Sally Victor; he had seven children who resides in Bourbon, viz.: Nancy, born Nov. 25, 1806, married Elijah Summit; left eight children, those living are in Nicholas County; Betsey, born March 8, 1810, married Rolland Steers; they had four children, one son, William, in Missouri, and one daughter in Harrison County, now living; Harmon D., born Dec. 13,

1811, residing in Missouri; and William Mason, born June 1, 1824, who when eighteen years of age, with his brothers, sisters and parents, seven persons in all, aggregated 1,477 lbs., or an average of 211 lbs. each; only the two youngest of that number are now living. Mr. Johnson was married Nov. 27, 1845, to Martha Victor, daughter of John and Betsey (Rule) Victor, who were residents of Nicholas County; they had five sons, viz.: Bruce, born Sept. 27, 1846, farming near Carlisle; Charley M., born May 26, 1851; Victor, born Jan. 14, 1853, died Aug. 31, 1859; Stewart, born Nov. 24, 1855; and Oscar M., born Aug. 17, 1858; all are farming in Carlisle Precinct. His wife died May 8, 1872. Mr. Johnson is a man of thorough business habits, and honorable in all his dealings; he lived fifty-two years without giving a note or running an account of any kind. He is strictly temperate and highly respected by the citizens of the county in which he lives.

THOMAS KEHOE, editor of the Carlisle *Mercury*, published at Carlisle, Nicholas County, Ky., was born in the city of Cincinnati, Ohio, May 1, 1850, and removed from that city to Lewis County, Ky., with his parents, at the age of two years, since which time he has continued to make his permanent home within the borders of the State of Kentucky. His early boyhood days were uneventful, and were spent with his parents upon a modest farm in the vicinity of the famous Esculapia Springs, in Lewis County, where the family continued to reside until Thomas had reached the age of nine years. The educational facilities of Lewis County in those days were extremely meager, and in 1859, his parents, finding their children growing up around them without the advantages of schooling, sold their home in Lewis and removed to a farm in Mason County, in the immediate vicinity of the city of Maysville, where he attended school a part of the time. In 1861 the family removed to Maysville, and he continued to attend school. In 1862 the unaccountable course of human events left him without a father's care, and left his mother with a family of eight children, and without means for their support. He had now attended school altogether about one year, and could read and write. The unfavorable turn of events compelled him to quit school, and, together with those of his brothers who were old enough, to go to work for the support of the family. Possessing a desire for knowledge, he continued to apply himself in his leisure moments to reading and other studies, and each succeeding space of time brought with it its reward of useful knowledge gained. June 12, 1863, at the age of thirteen years he enlisted in Captain F. H. Bierbower's Company A., of the 40th regiment of Kentucky volunteers, being probably the youngest soldier ever regularly mustered into the army of the United States; the regiment was organized at Falmouth, Ky., and participated in numerous scouts and skirmishes in Kentucky, Tennessee and Virginia, and was the leading regiment in the battle with the famous John Morgan at Mt. Sterling, Ky., June 7, 1864, and again it led in the battle of Cynthiana, which, though lasting but a few hours, was one of the severest battles of the war; in the fall of 1864, the 40th regiment participated in the battle of Canton, on the Cumberland River; later in the same year the regiment participated in the battles of Abingdon and Saltville, Virginia, and in December of the same year was mustered out of the service; its time having long since expired; at this time Thomas had served eighteen months in the army, and was yet but little over fourteen years of age. During his service in the army he had applied himself to study and returned home with his education much improved. Business at this time was in a very precarious condition, and not being able to find remunerative employment, and having cultivated a taste for adventure he again joined the army, enlisting in Company I, Fifty-fifth Regiment, Kentucky volunteers, at Covington, Ky., on March 8, 1865, before he was fifteen years of age, and was elected an officer of the company. The Fifty-fifth Regiment served to the close of the war, but was not engaged in battle during its term of service, and was mustered out at Louisville, Ky., Sept. 27, 1865. April 5, 1866, at the age of sixteen years, he began the trade of a marble cutter, in Maysville, Ky., at which he served an apprenticeship of three years. He worked at his trade in various parts of the country, his skill as a workman commanding ready employment and the highest wages. In 1870 he went to Helena, Ark., where he secured a situation in an engineer corps then being organized for the purpose of surveying the Helena and Iron Mountain Railroad. In April, 1871, he resigned his position in the engineer corps and went to St. Louis, much improved in health. From St. Louis he went to Kansas City, returning to St. Louis in a short time, and from that city went to Owensboro, Ky., where he accepted a situation as foreman of the Owensboro Marble Works, which position he held for three years, during which time he executed in Italian marble a monument, the design of which took the prize offered at Chicago in 1872 for the best design produced by any American or Canadian Sculptor. In 1873 he engaged in the marble business at Owensboro on his own account. In 1875, on July 5, he was married to Miss Fannie Maddox, daughter of B. F. and Mary L. Maddox, of Daviess County. Mr. Kehoe continued in the marble business in Owensboro until November, 1879, when, finding his health again impaired, he sold out his business and traveled for some time in Colorado. In August, 1881, in connection with his younger brother, Dr. H. C. Kehoe, he assumed editorial control of the Carlisle *Mercury*—the latter retiring shortly after to enter the practice of medicine. He is the eldest of six brothers and the second of a family of eight—the children of James and Nora Kehoe. In regard to the brothers and sisters of Mr. Kehoe, we will make brief reference in the order of their ages. Mary, the eldest, was born in New Orleans, La., and was raised in Kentucky. In 1866 she was married at Nashville, Tenn., to Captain James T. Harahan, who is at this writing President of the Ponchartrain Railroad and Superintendent of the Louisville and Nashville Railroad, and resides in New Orleans. Wm. J. Kehoe, stenographer and editor, was born in Lewis County, and raised in Mason County, Ky.; learned the printing business, and for several years was a compositor in the office of the Cincinnati *Commercial*. In 1877, he formed a partnership with Prof. T. C. H. Vance, and purchased the Carlisle *Mercury*, Mr. Vance shortly after retiring. Mr. Kehoe continued its publication and under his management it became the boldest Democratic journal in Eastern Kentucky. He was a warm friend of Judge Thomas F. Hargis, and was instrumental in nominating him for Criminal Judge of the district of which Nicholas County was a part, and through the columns of the *Mercury*, was first to mention that gentleman for the office of Judge of the Court of Appeals. He took a leading part in the Owingsville Convention, in which Judge Hargis was nominated for Appellate Judge, and was Chairman of the District Convention at Flemingsburg. In August 1881, he retired from the *Mercury* to accept a lucrative position as stenographer in the offices of the Louisville & Nashville Railroad Company, at New Orleans. J. D. Kehoe, printer, editor and statesman was born in Lewis County, and raised in Mason County, Ky.; he began the printing business in Maysville, Ky., at the age of ten years and soon developed a remarkable talent as a fine job printer; went to Cincinnati when about twelve or thirteen years of age and became foreman of a printing establishment and afterward returned to Maysville where he became foreman of the office of the Maysville *Republican*, which position he continued to hold for a considerable length of time; resigning his position in the *Republican* he opened an office in the city of Maysville on his own account; was elected and served as Clerk of the City of Maysville; at the age of twenty-four he received the unanimous nomination of the Democratic party, for the office of Representative. In 1881 he again received the unanimous nomination of the Democratic party for Representative, and was elected without opposition. In 1882, while a member of the Kentucky Legislature he was nominated for the office of Public Printer of Kentucky, by Hon. W. J. Hendrick, of Fleming County, and received a strong vote but withdrew on the second or third ballot. Mr. Kehoe is at this writing a leading member of the Kentucky Legislature, and is Chairman of the Committee on Printing, a member of the Committee on Military Affairs and represents the 10th District of Ky. in the Committee on Apportionment. Mark F. Kehoe, cigar manufacturer and merchant, was born in Lewis County, Ky., and raised in Mason County; learned the business of cigar-making at an early age, and at the expiration of his apprenticeship, established himself in business at Union City, Ind., from which place he removed to Owensboro, Ky., and afterward to Maysville, Ky., where he has carried on the business of a cigar manufacturer for a number of years. He is a high-toned gentleman of refinement and good education, and is strictly a self-made man. H. C. Kehoe, editor and physician; was born in Lewis County, and was raised in Mason County, Ky. Learned the printing business at an early age, and developed superior skill as a printer, and in 1877 became foreman and manager of the mechanical department of the Carlisle *Mercury* office, which position he held until 1881, when he became a partner in the business of the office, and editor of the paper in connection with his brother, W. J. Kehoe, and afterward his brother Thomas. During his connection with the *Mercury*, his leisure time had been devoted to his self education, and to reading medicine in the office of Dr. M. Dills, of Carlisle. When the town of Carlisle received a city charter, he was elected first City Clerk, and was elected Collector of City Taxes. In 1881, he retired from the *Mercury* and attended medical lectures at Pulte Medical College in Cincinnati, Ohio, and is at this writing, just entering upon the practice of medicine, at the age of twenty-three years. Jennie M. Kehoe, was born in Mason County, Ky., and was raised in the City of Maysville, where at this writing, she resides with her mother; she was educated at the Academy of the Visitation in that city. James N. Kehoe, printer; was born in the City of Maysville, Ky.; learned the printing business under his brother, Hon. J. D. Kehoe, and is a work man of superior genius. At the age of seventeen he became foreman and manager of the office of the Clark

County *Democrat*, published at Winchester, Ky., but returning to Maysville, he is at this writing manager of the business of J. D. Kehoe, printer and publisher of *Kehoe's Annual*. He is the youngest of the Kehoe family, and is endowed with rare mental abilities, which give promise of a brilliant future. Mrs. Nora Kehoe, the mother of this family of self-made men, is a native of Queen's County, Ireland, and is closely related to the ancient patriotic families of Moores and Lalors, of Ireland; she was married to James Kehoe, of Wicklow County, Ireland, in 1847, and came to America in 1848, with her husband, at the age of eighteen years, with whom she shared the joys and sorrows of life, until 1862. She is an intelligent lady of strong religious principles and is strictly conscientious. She is at present a resident of the city of Maysville, Ky., where she has lived for twenty-two years, and where she reared her large family of children, bringing them up to maturity, in honor, and with credit to herself. Mrs. Mary Conroy, the mother of Mrs. Kehoe, was born in Ireland, in 1798, and now resides at Connersville, Ind., with her daughter, at the age of eighty-five years. She is the seventh daughter of Colonel Dooney, a Commander of the Irish Patriots in the rebellion of 1798. He was killed in the massacre, on the Curragh, Kildare, Ireland, in the rebellion of '98, under the following circumstances: It was the custom of the brutal British to murder their Irish prisoners, and a surrender of the patriots having been agreed upon, under conditions of immunity from death, a large number of the Irish patriot force had preceded his command, surrendering their arms and marching into an enclosure, but none of those going in had come out. When it came his turn to enter he refused to do so until he understood what was to be the fate of those entering. His refusal was immediately followed by the British opening fire upon his command and upon the unarmed prisoners inside the enclosure, and the massacre was one of the most terrible in history, all or nearly all the prisoners inside being butchered. A great number of his command escaped, but he was killed early in the massacre. Of the paternal ancestors of the Kehoe family, it may be said that the name has been associated with the efforts for Irish liberty from the days of "Strong Bow" to "Buckshot" Forester. It is one of the oldest Irish names, and some one bearing it has figured on every battlefield from the Boyne to Vinegar Hill, and down to the present day, they are found among the 600 "Suspects," who are now languishing in British dungeons for daring to advocate the cause of liberty.

JUDGE JAMES MADISON KENNEY, retired farmer, P. O. Carlisle; was born near Paris, on the Stoner, April 5, 1810. His father was James, born at same place. His mother was Edith Johnson, born upon the south branch of the Potomac, but at a very early age came with her father Andrew and her mother, who was before marriage, a Miss Gregg, and made their settlement upon Green Creek. The parents of our subject had nine children all of whom grew to maturity: Mrs. Alexander Robinson, of Seymour, Ind., and James M., the only two now living. He received but about two weeks' schooling on account of the death of his father, the duty of supporting a large family and widowed mother then falling heavily upon him. According to his statement "he got his education a-running." At twenty-five years of age he could not write his own name, but by persistent energy he acquired a good education, being thus enabled to fill some of the most responsible positions of the county in later years. He began life as a farmer in which he has continued, adding to his possessions from year to year. Was twice married: in September, 1833, to Mary Parish, who died May 4, 1848; was a daughter of Nathaniel Parish; his second marriage occurred Feb. 8, 1849, to Harriet B. Dunnington, born in Charles County, Md., June 2, 1819; came to Nicholas County in 1838. Her father was James Dunnington, born in Charles County, Md., March 29, 1781, died May 31, 1852. Her mother was Sally Payne, born in Fairfax County, Va., March 18, 1786, died April 17, 1865. The Paynes related to the one who had a difficulty with Gen. Washington, also, to the Brents, who claim a relationship to Pocahontas. Mr. Kenney served as constable eleven years, from 1840. In 1856 was elected magistrate, serving twelve years, and in 1872 was elected County Judge, filling the unexpired term caused by the resignation of Judge Hargis, after which he was elected for four years to fill the office of Public Administrator. He had by his second marriage five children: William, James M., Ella and Hattie. The fourth child, a daughter, died in young-womanhood. His wife and others of the family are members of the Baptist Church, he of the Presbyterian Church, a christian gentleman, a highly esteemed citizen, and "born a Democrat."

ROBERT KINCART; jailer; Carlisle; was born in Carlisle, Ky., Jan. 14, 1825, and at the present time, there is but one person now living in Carlisle that was born at that place, older than himself. The father of our subject was born in Washington County, Va., in the year 1782; came to Kentucky in 1807; and at one time owned all the land where Carlisle now stands. His father was buried in the now Court House yard. He was married in 1817, to Miss Isabella Packston, who was born in Carlisle in 1780, and died in 1869; and her husband followed her two years later, Jan. 18, 1871. The result of their union was nine children, of whom Robert, the subject of this sketch, was the third. He never attended school to exceed ten days, and got his education by his own industry and by observation. He entered upon his career in life as a farmer and machinist. He has always been a prominent Democrat, and, in 1874, the Democratic party substantiated their appreciation of him by electing him Jailer, which position he still retains. During the rebellion he held the position of 2nd Lieutenant, in Co. B., of the 5th Kentucky Mounted Riflemen, with Capt. John Holliday. He remained in the service four years. He was married in Nicholas County, Oct. 7, 1847, to Miss Elizabeth Ishmael, who was born in Nicholas County, Jan. 24, 1823. They have four children, viz.: Nancy, George, Maria, and Harrison. Mr. Kincart is a very energetic and enterprising man; owns a farm of 156 acres, and devotes his time to its cultivation in connection with his duties as jailer. In connection with his wife, he is a member of the Christian Church at Carlisle. He has also been a prominent member of the Masonic Order, at the same place, since the year 1863.

WILLIAM J. KENNEDY, farmer and tobacco dealer; Carlisle; was born Feb. 12, 1843, to Alfred J. and Sally Ann (Hillock) Kennedy (see hist). Our subject received his education in the common schools of Nicholas County, and commenced his career in life at merchandizing at Headquarters, where he remained sixteen years, and during the last half of that period dealt largely in tobacco. In 1882 he bought 200 acres of land of A. W. Blair, and turned his attention to farming in connection with his tobacco business. He was married in Nicholas County, Nov. 21, 1865, to Miss Eliza J. Smith, who was born April 10, 1845. They have six children, viz.: Esle H., James S., Claudia, William E., Harvey M. and Warren R. Mrs. Kennedy was a daughter of Samuel and Annie (Cook) Smith (see hist. of Granville C. Smith). Mr. Kennedy is a member of the Masonic Order at Headquarters, and Chapter at Carlisle. He is a thorough business man, and highly esteemed by the community, and is always first in any public enterprise. He is a good neighbor, a kind husband and an indulgent father. In addition to his other enterprises, he deals extensively in stock of all kinds. In his political ideas he is Democratic.

JUDGE CHARLES LYTLE, youngest son of Robert and Rebecca Maranda Lytle, was born in the city of Cincinnati, Ohio, Sept. 26, 1847, during a temporary residence of his parents at that place. Robert Lytle, the father of the subject of this sketch, was the oldest son of William Lytle, who emigrated from the Highlands of Scotland and settled in Pennsylvania. There he met and married Lydia Thompson, only child of John and Lydia Thompson, who emigrated from Londonderry, Ireland, when Lydia was only twelve years of age. They afterwards located in Kentucky, near the mouth of Bracken Creek, in what is now Bracken County. There Robert Lytle, the father of Judge Lytle, was born, raised and married to Rebecca Maranda, the oldest daughter of Samuel and Polly Maranda, who had emigrated from the eastern shore of Maryland, and located in Ohio, on the river, one mile west of where the town of Higginsport now stands. Samuel Miranda, the maternal, and William Lytle, the paternal grandfather of Judge Lytle, were soldiers in the war of 1812, and also in the Mexican war, and both were gun and locksmiths, by trade. Robert Lytle's early life was spent in flat and steamboating on the Ohio river. He was the pilot of the first regular packet that ran between Maysville and Cincinnati. He was a thrifty river trader in the early days of flat and steamboating, but in 1845 had the misfortune to wreck three boats, on that terrible wrecker of fortune the Ohio river falls. After this he quit the river and went into the milling business, at Augusta, Ky., where he still resides, and within two and one-half miles of the place where he was born, married and has lived all his life. The only education Judge Lytle received, was such as could be obtained at the common public schools in the town of Augusta (which were not so well organized as at present,) and one term at the Augusta College. He hired out and worked on a farm during the summer months, and attended school during the winter. He studied law in Augusta, Ky., with the late lamented Judge Joseph Doniphan, and Francis L. Cleveland, who were partners at that time; he would read and recite to these gentlemen during the summer months, and in the winter taught a district school; after obtaining his license to practice in March, 1872, he spent the summer in the office of Hon. John B. Clark, late Congressman from the 10th Congressional District, at Brookville, Bracken County; the following fall he taught a district school in the southern portion of Bracken County, and in March, 1873, located in Mt. Olivet, Ky., the county seat of Robertson County, where he began to practice law in earnest; here he succeeded well, and soon built up a lucrative practice, and by his honest and straightforward manner of doing business, gathered around him a host of staunch friends, and in a

very short time obtained the confidence of the people to such an extent that he was twice appointed to the office of County Court Judge over a very worthy competitor; he was married to Flora B. Wilson, youngest daughter of Henry L. and Nancy Wilson, of Mt. Olivet, in May, 1875, who died of consumption in June, 1880; he was a candidate for re-election to the Judgeship in 1876, at a time when Grangerism was on the boom, and at its most formidable period in Kentucky; his opponent was a wealthy farmer, and a master of one of the strongest Granges in the county, and with the combined agencies of money, and the organized strength of the Grangers throughout the county, he was only defeated by one vote, and that being his own; he voted for his opponent, and his opponent failed to vote for him; as a judge, perhaps the youngest in the State, he was regarded able and impartial, and managed the finances of the county with great success; Mt. Olivet being a small town, he sought a broader field for work, and located in Carlisle in 1878, where he practiced his profession alone until July, 1880; he formed a partnership with Judge W. P. Rose, one of the oldest and most experienced attorneys in that section of the State; he was married again in 1881, to Fannie P. Nichols, an adopted daughter of Dr. R. J. R. and Anna E. Tilton; he still retains a lucrative practice in Robertson County, where he is deservedly popular; he is quite a young man yet, and his friends predict for him a successful and brilliant future.

JOHN LONG, farmer; P. O. Carlisle; was born in what is now Nicholas County, near Millersburg, in the year 1800, Nov. 28. He has always lived in the county and been identified with its interests. His parents were Eliakim and Jemima (Victor) Long, natives of Maryland, near Snow Hill, where he learned the trade of shoemaking; she was a daughter of John Victor, who died in Maryland; his wife, Hannah (Brewington) Victor, came to Nicholas County in 1790 with four sons and three daughters, all of whom married and settled in the county; Eliakim is a son of Delves Long, who only had two sons and a daughter, who married John McCauley, and finally moved to Kentucky; they had two sons, both of whom left children in Ohio. Wm. Long, an uncle to our subject, was killed by a horse; he had two daughters, who married and located in the West, and a son, who went to sea and was not heard from. The father of John was married about 1796, and had eleven children, the oldest born in 1798; there were nine sons and two daughters; all had children but two sons. William, deceased, settled in Harrison County; Polly, now the widow of Parish Jones, residing in Vermillion, Ill.; James, deceased, settled in same county; Nancy, deceased, wife of John C. Cassidy, left children in Missouri; Levi, residing in Vermillion County, Ill.; Littleton (see hist.) Eliakim, in Putman County, Ind.; Samuel, in Kansas. The subject of this sketch received a very limited education, and worked on the farm with his father until of age. In 1825, he was married to Nancy Young, whom he buried after eight weeks of married life. On the 6th of Sept., 1827, he was again married, to Nancy Nesbit, who was born upon the farm where they now reside, April 26, 1800; she a daughter of Nathan and Sarah (Huston), who were natives of Pennsylvania, near Carlisle, but settled in Bourbon County in 1788; some of the family were among the original settlers of Bourbon; Sarah was a daughter of Joseph, who was a prominent man in Pennsylvania; Nathan was a son of John. By this marriage Mr. Long had two children: Sarah J., born Sept. 4, 1837, now the wife of Charles Wise; John W., May 9, 1841, married Elizabeth F. Victor, Dec. 20, 1866; she born Aug. 23, 1845, an only child, who lived to maturity, of George and Sarah (Hedges) Victor, who were natives of Kentucky. They have one child, George Victor, a daughter, born June 28, 1869. They are devoted to a general agriculture and stockraising; religiously, they are connected with the Presbyterian Church.

WILLIAM W. LETTON, farmer, P. O. Carlisle; was born in Bourbon County, Ky., November 25, 1809, to Michael and Isabel C. (Jones) Letton; he was born in Maryland, and was one of the early settlers of Bourbon County; he died June 29, 1839; his wife Isabel, was born Feb. 7, 1773, and died Feb. 7, 1852; the result of their union was seven children, of whom, William, our subject, was next to the youngest. His education was limited to such as could be obtained in the common schools of that early day. He commenced his career in life as a farmer; was married in Bourbon County, October 17, 1833, to Miss Lucy Ann Williams, who was born May 1, 1809, and died December 19, 1863; she was the mother of six children, viz: Burton R., Martha I., Mary E., Laura W., Elton R. and Tabitha A.; Mrs. Letton was a daughter of Joseph and Elizabeth L. (Jones) Williams. Mr. Letton has served the county as Constable for a number of years; he is a practical farmer and has 135 acres of land which he keeps in a high state of cultivation; he has been a member of the Masonic order at Carlisle for several years; his political sentiments are with the Democratic party.

COL. DAVID MANN, farmer; P. O. Carlisle; was born March 14, 1809, in the house in which he now lives, to Peter and Barbara (Jones) Mann; she a daughter of

Jacob and Susie (Earlywine) Jones; the two latter families were among the earliest settlers of what was then Bourbon, now Nicholas County; Peter was a son of Geo. and Elizabeth Mann, who came from Rockingham Co., Va., to Nicholas County about 1790, and purchased 500 acres of land, being in part, the home where Col. Mann now lives; he had seven sons and one daughter; George, the eldest, died in the Revolutionary war; Jacob settled in Clinton County, Ohio; John, died in Nicholas County; Peter, accidentally killed by the fall of a tree in the year 1852, in his eightieth year; Henry, settled in Greene County, Ohio; Charles, David, and the daughter, who married Adam Shillenger, also settled in the above county. The parents of our subject had six sons and one daughter, four of the former; Jacob left a large family, who are scattered throughout the country; Elizabeth, wife of David Trimble, both of whom are deceased; William and family, all deceased but one son, LaFayette, residing in Nicholas; David, and Amos, residents of Nicholas; Emanuel, near Millersburg, and Peter J. in Cooper County, Mo. The subject of this sketch received a limited education, and spent his life working on the farm and at different trades, until 1845, since which time he has been engaged in farming. Upon Jan. 26, 1832, he was married to Olive Stoker, daughter of Edward and Elizabeth (Currant) Stoker; he a son of Edward, or "Old Stoker," as he was commonly called; one of the first settlers of Nicholas County and a Revolutionary soldier; he, by this marriage, had eight children, three of whom died without issue. Those living are, Melvina, wife of G. Cheatham (see history); Lucian; Maria A., wife of Solomon Robertson, of Nicholas; Pickett T., wife of Joseph Mays, in Nicholas; Rozella, wife of Winfield Buckler, a lawyer at Mt. Olivet, Ky.; they are all members of the Christian Church; Lucian enlisted in October, 1862, in Co. B., 9th, Ky. Mounted Riflemen, under Capt. J. G. Neal, Col. Breckinridge and Gen'l Morgan, subsequnetly under Gen. Wheeler and Cols. Grigsby and J. S. Williams; the principal contests in which he was engaged were at Hartsville, the raid on the Louisville and Nashville R. R., raid through Kentucky, Dug's Gap, Atlanta, and in the long Skirmish with Gen. Sherman; at the close of the war he returned home, and on November 28, he was married to Miss Emma Layson, daughter of Martin Layson, of Millersburg; by her he has four children: Carrie Lee, Minnie Noble, Robert T. and David L.; he is a member of the K. T.; for several years a tradesman in Carlisle; was in the Rocky Mountains engaged in mining; also, in Illinois, farming; he was one of the soldiers who assisted in guarding the much-talked-of treasure held by Jeff Davis, at one time during the war.

NELSON H. McNEW, physician; Carlisle; was born near Knoxville, Tenn., Sept. 11, 1840; he is of Scotch-Irish descent; his father, Isaac McNew, having emigrated from Washington County, Va., to Tennessee, about 1820; his mother, whose maiden name was Parmelia Halffinger, was a native Virginia lady; she died in Tennessee in 1842, her husband having died ten years previous; the doctor is the eighth of nine children, seven of whom are still living; when only two years of age, he lost his mother, but received a good education, his father having married twice; the second time to Mary Arnwine, a sister of his eldest daughter's first husband; he taught school for several years, devoting his spare time to the study of medicine; in 1858, he entered the University of Nashville, taking a medical course; upon being graduated by that institution in 1861, he immediately entered the Confederate service under Captain Churchill, of the 1st Arkansas Mounted Riflemen; he remained in private service till after the battle of Pea Ridge, when he was promoted to the post of Assistant Surgeon of his regiment, which position he filled till the close of the war in 1865; in May, 1864, he married Miss Jerusha Yeary, daughter of Henry Yeary, a prominent farmer of Tennessee; she died in 1874, having borne him four children, two of whom, Nannie Lee and Carrie, are still living; after the war he located in Sherburn, Fleming County, where he soon acquired the esteem and confidence of the people; he was favorably mentioned by the people of that county for the Legislature just before his departure in 1874; in 1876, he removed to Carlisle, where he is highly esteemed as an able and careful physician; he is a member of the Masonic fraternity, having held all the principal offices, and is a correspondent of several of the most prominent newspapers of the Southwest.

FITCH MUNGER (deceased); died March 26, 1866, in the forty-ninth year of his age; he was no ordinary character, but the highest type of a gentleman of the old school, with the energy of the new. Mr. Munger removed from Lewis County, N. Y., the place of his nativity, to Kentucky, upon his arrival at the years of manhood, without means, a stranger in the midst of strangers, unaided, save by his own indomitable energy, and irreproachable morals and habits. From the humble though honorable calling of school teacher, he soon joined the ranks of the legal profession, and settled at Carlisle; his integrity and sense of honor were of the highest type; he laid contributions on and brought to the aid of an unflagging industry the most rigid rules of punctuality, system and order. Before these fine qualities, his native strength of intellect and the best social qualities, all difficulties and obstacles in the way of his progress vanished. Honored by the citizens of Mason and Nicholas Counties with a seat in the Kentucky Senate, his usefulness took a more exalted and general range, and the inestimable qualities mentioned made him one of the best of legislators. His services reflected high credit upon his constituency, the general good was advanced, and his right to public favor and esteem fully assured. He was a son of Roswell and Marvin (Palmer) Munger, natives of Copenhagen, N. Y.; she a daughter of John Palmer and a Miss Usher. He was married Feb. 7, 1844, to Miss Mary Summers, who was born in Montgomery County, Feb. 8, 1820, to Archibald and Margaret (Payne) Summers, natives of Fairfax County, Va.; she a daughter of Benjamin C. and Jane (Campbell) Payne, she a native of Scotland, he of Virginia. Mr. Munger by this marriage had two sons: Charles W. (see history), and Harry, born Oct. 13, 1857; he was married May 8, 1880, to Miss Carrie Nichols, a native of York State, and daughter of Rev. W. B. and Harriet (Munger) Nichols; he a prominent divine in the M. E. Church of that State. He and his mother are carrying on a general farming and stock raising at their beautiful home in the suburbs of Carlisle. They are a family highly respected by the citizens of their community.

REV. MILTON MANN, farmer; P. O. Carlisle; proprietor of Sumach Grove Farm; was born upon the farm which is his present home, Nov. 25, 1828; he is a grandson of John Mann, and the youngest of three children: James, a local preacher in the M. E. Church, South; Fanny, deceased, wife of John Shaw, who still resides in Nicholas County, and the subject of this sketch, who received very few advantages in early life. but worked hard upon the farm until the fall of 1851, when he entered Asbury University, where he remained four years, then returned home and entered the ministry, from which time it is said, he has raised more money for the Bible cause, built more churches, and taken more people into the church, than any other man in the Kentucky Conference; his itinerancy continued until 1876, since which time his life has been principally devoted to farming. He has been four times married; first upon the 31st of May, 1855, to Margaret Ricketts, daughter of Wm. Ricketts, of Nicholas; by her he had three children, only one of whom are living: Fletcher, who married Mary Jones of Carlisle, by whom he has three children: Horde W., James M., and Bruce; first wife died May 26, 1862, at Mt. Olivet, Ky.; second marriage to Jenny Ricketts, a sister to his first wife, July 15, 1862; by her he had two children: E. G. B., and L. E.; the mother died June 23, 1867; third marriage Dec. 4, 1867, to Louisa E. Williams, daughter of Byrd Williams, of Nicholas; by her he had five children, the two eldest died in infancy; those living are: Pearly H., Allie and Lumie D.; wife died July 9, 1877; fourth marriage Feb. 12, 1878, to Elvira Hughs, daughter of Esq. Grason Hughs, of Nicholas. He has been especially favored in being called upon to perform marriage ceremonies, uniting as many as five couples in one day, and two and three couples under one ceremony; he deserves much credit for the education of himself under adverse circumstances, and the amount of good he has done for the promotion of Christianity, the improvement of stock, sheep, cattle and horses, owning some very fine animals of each kind. He bred and now owns the famous Mambrino Le Grand stallion, who took twelve premiums in the fall of 1881, and for beauty stands next to the Mambrino King, said to be the finest horse in the world. Mr. Mann is a prominent man in his community, interested in public improvements, and is treasurer of the Board of Directors of the Forest Retreat and Panther Creek Turnpike.

CHARLES M. MAY; teacher; P. O. Carlisle; was born in Vermont, Aug. 12, 1833, to Gen. Benjamin and Jerusha (Gilbert) May. He was a merchant by occupation; was born in Vermont, in 1799, and died in 1838. She was also born in Vermont, in 1805, and is now living in Washington, D. C. The result of their union was four children, viz.: Daniel, Louis, Mary, and Charles, our subject. He was educated at the Middlebury College, Vermont, where he graduated in 1853, and three years later, was made A. M., since which time he has been engaged in teaching school. He was principal of the school at May's Licks, for several years, and then took charge of the Minerva Seminary, in Mason County, where he remained four years. He also had charge of a school at Flemingsburg, and was connected with the Augusta College three years, and after severing his connection with the latter institution, he removed to Carlisle, and is now engaged in teaching a private, high grade school, which numbers about forty students, members of the best families of Carlisle. He was married at Minerva, Ky., Aug. 29, 1874, to Miss Asenath Dinwiddie McIntire, who was born to James and Miss (Hunt) McIntire, in Oct. 1838, and died Oct. 18, 1878, without issue. Mr. May is a thoroughly educated man, and ranks high in his profession, and socially enjoys the highest esteem of the whole community. Although a strict and thorough teacher, he possesses the faculty of obtaining the love and respect of all his students. Politically, he is a Republican.

COL. R. E. MANN, grocer, Carlisle; is a son of James and Bettie (Stoker) Mann, both from Virginia, and early settlers of Nicholas County. He was born near Forest Retreat, Nicholas Co., July 21, 1846; is one of eight children, four of whom are now living: Leonidas, R. E., Alice, and Sherman. Col. Mann received his education in the town of Carlisle. He was appointed by the Legislature upon the staff of Governor Leslie, and in the same year was appointed by the Governor as one of the four commissioners from Kentucky to the Vienna Exposition. On account of the death of his sister, about the time of starting, he was compelled to decline the appointment. In 1876 he started the only wholesale grocery in Carlisle, which he is now running in connection with eight other stores in different counties. On the 29th of June, 1876, Col. Mann married Miss Phœbe, daughter of Dr. J. J. and Pickett (Metcalf) Taylor, of Lexington, Mrs. Taylor being a neice of Governor Metcalf, and a sister-in-law of James Metcalf, who was Secretary of State under Governor Powell, and represented Nicholas County in the Legislature two terms. Colonel Mann has two children: Horace and Madge H.

CHARLES W. MUNGER, lawyer, Carlisle; was born in Carlisle, April 9, 1849, son of Fitch Munger, deceased (see hist.) The subject of this brief sketch received a liberal education, attending the school at Lexington, Va., under the preceptorship of Robert E. Lee; also spent two years at the University at Lexington, Ky., graduating from the law department of that institution in February, 1871, when he began the practice of his chosen profession in the city of his present location. He was married Oct. 19, 1869, in Newport, Ky., to Miss Virginia Stiff, a native of New Orleans, daughter of Dr. Richard Stiff, deceased, a prominent physician of New Orleans and Newport. His wife was Cassandra Pauline, of Mercer County, now the wife of Richard Taliaferro, of Newport. Mr. Munger was elected to the office of Mayor, of Carlisle, in June, 1880, being the first to receive that honor under the new constitution. By his marriage there are three children, as follows: Fitch, Ida, and Ada, twin daughters. He is a Democrat, politically, and a member of the Grand Encampment I. O. O. F.

JOSEPH NORVELL, Ex-Circuit Clerk, Carlisle; was born in Carlisle, Nov. 13, 1842 (see J. P. Norvell's history); he received a liberal education, attended the preparatory school, taught by Rev. James Hendricks, where he studied the Latin and Greek languages, preparatory to entering the College at Danville, Ky.; he subsequently studied law with his father, but before being admitted to the bar, he enlisted in Company A, of the original squadron under Gen. Morgan, in which he served until that command was cut to pieces at Lebanon, Tenn.; subsequently, in the re-organization, he served for a short time as a private, in Co. B, 9th Ky., under Col. Breckenridge, he was there promoted to the position of Second Lieutenant; subsequently, by a special order from the war department, that officers should be examined in military tactics, by a special board appointed for that purpose; he received the appointment as Captain of the company, which position he held until the close of the war. The captaincy of the company was made vacant by the resignation of Captain Neal, and Mr. Norvell's promotion over a superior officer, was on account of proficiency in military tactics. He served in all the principal contests with his command, some of which were those of Shiloh, Stone River, Chickamauga, Stony Fork, Resaca, Peach Tree Creek, the salt works of Virginia, and skirmishes in front and rear of Sherman's march to the sea. He was four times a prisoner; the first time he was captured he escaped from Camp Morton; the second he leaped from the car window while being transported from Louisville to Camp Douglas; the third, while under guard in the woods in Tennessee. The longest that he was away from his command was four months, when he was imprisoned at Johnson's Island. From 1865 till the spring of 1868, he was engaged in the mercantile business in Cincinnati with Chappell, Bruce & McIntyre. In 1868 he was elected to the office of Circuit Clerk, which position he held until in August, 1874, where for a considerable time he was engaged in the Kimbrough and St. Cloud Hotels. He was married Oct. 18, 1869, in Sharpsburg, to Miss Belle Wilson, who was a native of Fleming County, and a daughter of Harvey T. Wilson, Past Grand Master of the Masonic Order for that State of Kentucky. He is a native of Fleming County; was an extensive pork packer in Covington, Ky., during the war. He now resides in Kenton County. His wife, Margaret (Serency) Wilson, also a native of Fleming County. Mr. Norvell, by this marriage has had five children, four of whom are now living, viz.: Alva, Annie, Lucy and Mary. He is a Democrat and a Master Mason.

WILLIAM NORTON, farmer; P. O. Carlisle; was born a tthe old homestead, near Hinkston River, Jan. 11, 1828; his father, Hiram Norton, was born in Bourbon County in 1797, and there resided until in 1822, when he came to the house now occupied by his widow; he was a great business man at the time in which he lived; raised a large family, and died in 1871. His wife, who is still living, was Nancy Spencer; born Jan. 19, 1802, in Clark County (see Spencer history). The grandfather of our subject was John Norton, one of the early settlers from Virginia to Bourbon County, and died at rather an early age, leaving the care of the family upon the eldest, Hiram. William Norton received an education such as could be obtained in the early common schools of Nicholas County, then engaged in farming, remaining with his father until in 1847, when he purchased ninety acres of land, a part of the Old Ham farm, to which he has added since that time, and is now the possessor of over 300 acres of choice land, and a beautiful home. His first marriage occurred in 1847, to Nancy A. Squires, who died in February, 1873 ; she was the mother of eight children, five of whom died young; those living are : Jesse, Willie, and Charley. His second marriage was to Eliza J. Burroughs, Aug. 12, 1875 ; she, a sister to Dr. Burroughs ; by her he has a pair of twins, Harry and Harvey. Mr. Norton is a Republican in politics, and with his family connected with the Christian Church at Carlisle; has been a member of the Masonic order since 1848, and is now connected with the Commandery at Carlisle ; is liberal in public improvements, religious, and educational matters, and commands the high esteem of the citizens of the community in which he lives.

JOHN P. NORVELL, attorney, Carlisle ; was born in Carlisle, Dec. 31, 1850 ; his father, William Norvell, was born in Garrard County, Ky., Nov. 10, 1803; died Sept. 5, 1875; he was one of the best and most prominent men of Carlisle, where he was an attorney for nearly fifty years. The mother was Emily G. Summers, still living, who was born in Montgomery County, in 1822, and married in 1836; she was a daughter of Archibald Summers, a prominent citizen of Montgomery and Nicholas Counties. They had thirteen children, six of whom are now living, viz. : Mary, wife [illegible] William George, D.D., one of Kentucky's favorite [illegible] w loca[illegible] the State of Texas ; Joseph (see [illegible] Judge Hargis, Judge of Court [illegible] nnie, and Alice. The others [illegible] a, who was the wife of Wm. [illegible] inent merchant of Carlisle, [illegible] lendale, O. The father of [illegible] n Nicholas County to the [illegible] terms; also held the posi- [illegible] ter Commissioner of the [illegible] this sketch received a [illegible] udied law with Judge. [illegible] actice of the profes- [illegible] of the Legislature, [illegible] ; he immediately entered into partnership with Judge Hargis, continuing until the year 1878, when the Judge was elected to his present position. Mr. Norvell is now of the firm of Norvell & Tureman. He was married in Paris, Jan. 14, 1879, to Ella M. Steele, a native of Bourbon County, and daughter of Dr. William and Julia (Wood) Steele, both of whom are now living near Hutchinson Station, Bourbon County.

FRANK M. PEALE, merchant; P. O. Carlisle; a native of Highland County, Ohio; by the removal of his parents to Cincinnati in 1844, while he was two years of age, he became early in life a resident of that city, where he enjoyed the advantages of the primary and high schools, graduating from the latter in 1860. He then became a teacher in the first intermediate school, retaining that position until in 1864; he was then made principal of the Eighth District, where he remained until 1868, when he resigned to accept the junior partnership in the hat and fur house of C. B. Camp, where he remained until in 1872, when he came to Carlisle and engaged in merchandising. The firm now of Peale & Chappell, the largest dry goods and carpet house in Nicholas County. He is a gentleman of pleasing address and marked ability, and has been thoroughly identified with the business interests of State and County. He was married in 1870 to Miss Mattie L. Bruce, daughter of George S. Bruce and Sabina Metcalf, a niece of Governor Metcalf. By this union there has been one child, Ada B. He is a member of the Baptist Church, also of the order of Masons, K. T. and Odd Fellows. During the summer and fall of 1864 he was a non-commissioned officer of Gen. Butler's Division, in and around Petersburg and Richmond. His father was Samuel Peale, a native of Pennsylvania, near Harrisburg; the paternal grandparent a native of the central portion of England, and came at an early date to Pennsylvania. The wife of Samuel Peale was Margaret Crissey, a native of Cincinnati in its early history; her father was a native of Scotland, was married in Connecticut, and immediately removed to a place then near Cincinnati. By this marriage there were nine children, seven of whom are still living—four sons and three daughters: T. P., William C., F. M., T. F., M. Etta, Sally C., wife of D. George Cheesman, of Slate Lick, near Pittsburg; Arzelia, wife of Charles Liddell, a manufacturer of fancy soaps and perfumes in Cincinnati; T. F., engaged in a general merchandising at New Vienna, Ohio. The two eldest sons engaged in mercantile business on Central avenue, Cincinnati, after the retirement of their father, who was for many years a prominent wholesale merchant on Main street, Cincinnati.

JOSEPH S. PARKS, (deceased), an older brother to Col. T. S. Parks, see history by Col. Parks. He was married in Bath County, Ky., in the year 1825, to Elizabeth Gordon Frank, who was born in Fayette County, Ky., in 1810, to John and Nancy (Smith) Frank ; she a daughter of Gideon and Jemima (Shelton) Smith. The mother of Gideon Smith was Elizabeth Powell, of noble birth and a descendant of the Rollins family, of England. John Frank was born in Fayette County, to Robert and Elizabeth (Gordon) Frank. These families were among the early and prominent families in Fayette County, from Va. Mr. Parks, by his marriage, had 10 children, two of whom died in infancy. Those living are, John, J. B., a widower engaged in business with the Sheppard Book Publishing House, of New York City; James E., married and in business at Carlisle ; Richard M., married, formerly Freight Agent and a prominent business man of Carlisle; W. E. W., engaged in farming; Mattie, Katie and Belle. The mother of these died March 5, 1880; the father, April 26, 1868, in the 73d year of his age. Mr. Parks, although a cripple, was a man of indomitable will and energy, trusted and honored by the citizens of his county, on account of his integrity, energy, kindness and superior knowledge, which was a source of pleasure and instruction to his neighbors. He was instrumental in the construction of the prosperous school which still stands, and designated as "Harmony Seminary." Honesty was the ruling principle of his life, and by that he was impelled to take upon himself a debt of the family, which led him through many trials and reverses ; all of which he conquered. He held positions of honor and trust, meriting the highest confidence of the people and many were the heartfelt regrets at his death. W. E. W. Parks is engaged in raising thoroughbred short-horns, of the principal families, such as Cambrias, Bates and Hilhurths ; also horses of the Abdallah and Joe Downing strains. He is the owner of "Downing Abdallah," bred by James Talbott, of Bourbon County ; a fine horse and sire of Lady Martin, a famous trotter in the East, and others of notoriety.

ZACH. TAYLOR PIPER ; farmer ; P. O. Carlisle; was born in Nicholas Co., Ky., March 27, 1848, and is a son of Samuel and Elizabeth (Smith) Piper. He was born in Nicholas Co., Sept. 6, 1806 ; was a farmer by occupation, and died Aug. 31, 1876; his wife, Eliza, was born in Bourbon Co., May 6, 1807, and died May 22, 1866. They had ten children, of whom Zach., the subject of our sketch, was next to the youngest. He obtained his education in the common schools of Nicholas Co., and at the Wesleyan College at Millersburg. He has followed farming and trading all his life with the exception of two years, when he was engaged in merchandising at Carlisle. He was married in Bourbon Co., Feb. 22, 1872, to Miss Ida Steele, who was born in Bourbon Co., April 5, 1849 ; they have two children, viz.: Samuel and Steele ; Mrs. Piper was daughter of William and Julia (Wood) Steele. He was born in Bourbon Co., in Oct., 1808, and died Jan. 15, 1882. Julia, his wife, was born in Nicholas Co., in 1828, and is still living. Mr. Piper is a model farmer, and one of the most enterprising men in the county ; he is liberal in all public improvements and enterprises. In connection with his wife he is a member of the Presbyterian Church at Carlisle. He owns 200 acres of choice farm land and deals in all kinds of stock. In politics he is a Democrat.

BENJAMIN W. PRATHER, farmer; P. O. Carlisle; was born in Bourbon County, Ky., Nov. 25, 1815, to Benjamin and Priscilla (Willet) Prather, natives of Maryland. He was born in 1783, died in April 1868. She was born in 1788, died 1863. They were among the early settlers of Bourbon County. The result of their union was ten children, of whom the subject of this sketch was the oldest. He received a common school education in Nicholas County, and commenced his career in life as a farmer. He was married Dec. 20, 1838, to Miss Sarah E. Edwards, who was born to Robert and Frankie (Marshall) Edwards, in September, 1820. They have two living children, viz. : Ann, born April 23, 1855, wife of John H. Renn, of Bourbon County ; Mary E., born Oct. 25, 1860, wife of R. McClure; also, Priscilla and William, deceased. Mr. Prather is one of the most energetic and enterprising farmers in the County. He has a farm of 210 acres of choice farm land, which, "as a practical farmer," he keeps in a high state of cultivation, and in addition to growing the usual farm crops, makes a specialty of breeding high grade cattle. In 1879, he erected a large and beautiful residence, after his own design, and one of which he may well feel proud. Religiously, himself and family are connected with the Baptist Church. His political sympathies are with the Democratic party.

ROBERT W. POTTS, farmer and trader; P. O. Carlisle; is a son of William Potts, who was born in Nicholas County, Sept. 5, 1800; he of William, Sr., born June 27, 1763, and died Oct. 27, 1828; he came to Nicholas County with his goods on jack horses, about the year 1795, from Iredell County, N. C. He had the following children: Priscilla, born May 15, 1788, married John Sweeney; remained in Nicholas, where she died of the "cold plague," March 19, 1813; Henry, born Sept. 6, 1790; Sarah, Jan. 1, 1793, married a Mr. Hall, and went to Indiana; James, born July 15, 1795; Margaret, Feb. 14, 1798, died without issue; William as above, and Jesse, June 26, 1803, died when a boy, of the "cold plague." The mother of these was Margaret Purviance, born Feb. 17, 1768, and died about two years after her husband. The mother of our subject was Palmyra Hall, daughter of Robert, he of James Hall, who was one of the first settlers of Nicholas County. She had nine children: Robert W., Jesse, who died in infancy; Mary, wife of George Talbott, of Cynthiana, no children; Sarah, wife of S. F. Stores, near Moorefield, (see hist.); Margaret, wife of J. H. Blair, of Fleming County, no children; Walter S. and Henry T. (see histories); Sue, wife of Charles Talbott, of Bourbon County (see hist.), and Cynthia A., wife of Garrett Allen, of Elizaville. Mr. Potts was born Feb. 15, 1830, in the same house of the father, and being the eldest of a large family, was deprived of even moderate educational advantages; he remained with his father until twenty-five years of age, when he was married to Miss Grizzell Burns, daughter of Wesley Burns; by her he had a son and a daughter, both of whom died in infancy, the mother following them to her final resting place, in 1880. Mr. Potts was sheriff of the county during the years 1867 and '68. He has been for many years one of the leading stock shippers of the county, a prominent Democrat, and among the first in the enterprises of the county, and in the hearts of his fellow men.

LEE T. POTTS, farmer; P. O. Carlisle; was born Nov., 4, 1847, to Henry T. and Lorana (Alexander) Potts (see hist. of Jesse Potts of Union Precinct, also that of Robert W. Potts, of Carlisle). He was the sixth of nine children, and received the advantages of a common school education. He remained at home until about twenty-three years of age, when he was married upon the 5th of May, 1870, to Tabitha Donnell, daughter of Milton and Margaret (Parker) Donnell (see hist.). They have had three children: Henry M., born March, 1871; Edna Louisa, Oct. 3, 1875, an infant deceased. Mr. Potts came to his present home in February, 1876, where he has since been engaged in a general agriculture, tobacco raising, and the breeding of short horns, to a limited extent, of some of the most popular strains, such as Imported Elizabeths, Bates, etc., also Cotswold sheep and Berkshire hogs. He and family are members of the Christian Church, an industrious, enterprising young man, and a prominent citizen of the county.

WALTER S. POTTS, farmer; P. O. Carlisle; was was born March 9, 1840, upon the old homestead, and shared the fate of the older members of the family in educational advantages. He engaged in farming with his father until his marriage, which occurred Feb. 20, 1866, to Miss Mary A. Herndon, daughter of Dr. J. C. Herndon (see hist.). After his marriage he immediately settled upon the farm which is his present home, and a part of the lands settled by his grandfather upon coming to this county at a very early date, and where he endured all the trials of early pioneer life, in the dense cane brake and heavy timber. Our subject, since removing to his farm has carried on a general farm life in connection with extensive trading through the Southern States. Like the other members of the family he enjoys the profoundest respect and esteem of the citizens of the community in which he lives. He and wife are members of the Christian Church, at Carlisle.

HENRY T. POTTS, farmer and trader; P. O. Carlisle; was born Feb. 15, 1842; staid with his father until his death in 1873, assisting in the business upon the farm, and receiving, in the meantime, very poor educational advantages. His marriage occurred upon the 25th of November, 1875, to Miss Kitty Metcalf, daughter of Col. Leonidas and Sarah (Victor) Metcalf; she a daughter of Ambrose and Eliza (Sturgis) Victor. By this marriage they have had two children: Ada, born May 27, 1877, and Lillian, born June 22, 1880. Mr. Potts is engaged in a general farming, and is extensively engaged in shipping horses and mules to the Southern markets. He is one of the most enterprising and energetic men of the county, in which he is held in the highest esteem on account of his hospitable and affable manners. He is a member of the Masonic Order, and, with his estimable wife, belongs to the Christian Church.

JUDGE WILLIAM P. ROSS, a prominent lawyer and banker of Carlisle, is a son of Greenberry and Martha (Parks) Ross (see Parks' hist). He was born Aug. 11, 1825, at Carlisle. His father was a native of Bourbon County, but settled in Nicholas 1818, where he lived until his death, March 29, 1859. He was a tailor by trade; subsequently a farmer. The grandfather of the Judge was Samuel Ross, a Pennsylvanian of English extraction, who settled in Bourbon County at an early date. The subject of this sketch attended the best schools of the county, and worked upon the farm a considerable portion of the time until his twenty-first year, when he turned his attention to teaching. During the same year, 1846, he began reading law, and prepared for the legal profession at Carlisle under Fitch Munger, a prominent lawyer of the town. In 1848 he was admitted to the bar and entered upon the practice of his profession at Carlisle, where he has since resided. He established a large and successful practice, taking a foremost position at the bar, and became one of the most valuable business men of the county. In 1851 he was elected the first Judge of Nicholas County under the workings of the new Constitution; he also held the office of Master Commissioner for a number of years, but has never held a political office, strictly speaking. He is a stockholder in the Deposit Bank of Carlisle, of which he has been president since the year 1870. He belonged to the old Whig party of the State until its dissolution, since which time he has been independent in politics. During the Rebellion he was an ardent Union man. Religiously, he is connected with the Presbyterians, is an elder in that denomination, and a prominent man in the affairs of the church. He is a man of fine personal, professional and social habits, of great integrity of character, and is one of the most substantial and useful men in his community. Mr. Ross has been twice married; in February, 1853, to Miss Columbia Neal, daughter of John Neal, of Nicholas County. She died Jan. 29, 1857, leaving one child, John N., born Nov. 28, 1853; was married Nov. 28, 1876, to Miss Ida Adair. He is a member of the large grocery house of Adair & Son. In 1862 he was again married to Miss Elizabeth Davis, a native of Woodford County, and daughter of John W. Davis and America Gaines. By her he has six children: Columbia T., born June 6, 1863; Henry E. and Mary E., Oct. 5, 1864; William P., Jr., Jan. 9, 1867; James B., July 27, 1871; Mattie, Sept. 28, 1874.

SOLOMON ROBERTSON, merchant and tobacco-dealer; P. O., Carlisle; was born in Bourbon County, Ky., Dec. 26, 1843, and is a son of William and Maria (Nevins) Robertson; he was born in 1803, and is now living in Illinois. His wife, Maria, was born in New York, in 1809, and died Sept. 11, 1878. She was the mother of thirteen children, of whom Solomon, the subject of this sketch, was the eighth. He received his education in the common schools of Indiana, where his parents removed when he was a small child; as soon as his school days were over he learned the trade of a plaster mason, and followed the same about fifteen years, when he began merchandising near Blue Licks, but afterward sold his stock of goods to his brother and a Mr. Overby, and engaged in dealing in tobacco, which business he still follows. He was married March 4, 1869, to Maria Ann Mann, who was born in 1844. They have two children living, viz.: Nettie May and Olie Frank, and Daisie, who died at the age of three years. Mrs. Robertson was a daughter of Col. David and Olie (Stoker) Mann. (See hist.) Mr. Robertson is an energetic and thorough business man, and ranks high in the esteem of the community. He has served the people of Carlisle several years as councilman, and is the present postmaster of Ellisville. Religiously, himself and wife are members of the Christian Church of Carlisle. He is also a prominent member of the Masonic order at the same place. Politically, he is a Democrat.

B. H. ROBINSON, County Attorney; P. O. Carlisle; a native of Carlisle, and son of James R. Robinson, who died in Georgia in 1876, to which place he had gone with stock, having been engaged in that capacity through the South for over thirty years. He was a son of William Robinson, a native of Maryland, but who settled in Pendleton County, Ky., at an early date; there the father of our subject was born, in 1809. His early life was spent in Lexington, serving an apprenticeship and working at the trade of carding. He subsequently engaged in trading, in which he suffered heavy losses during the war. His wife was Adeline Hughs, a native of Nicholas County, and daughter of Jesse Hughs; she a sister to J. M. Hughs, of Paris. They had nine children: Thomas (deceased), Mary J., wife of David Hughs, of St. Joseph, Mo., Carrie Lou, Georgia (deceased), wife of Capt. John H. Seeley, of the Federal army, Robert H., of Carlisle, Aggie, wife of Dr. X. M. Sayre, of Lexington, B. H., and Eva. The subject of this sketch received the advantages of the Carlisle schools, with a short time at Hanover College. In 1873, at twenty-one years of age, he began the study of law with Judge Thomas F. Hargis and J. P. Norvell. He was admitted to the practice of his chosen profession in September, 1875. By the death of his father soon after, and leaving the family in destitute circumstances, he engaged in teaching, that he might obtain subsistence for himself, unmarried sisters and deceased sisters' children. In April, 1878, he received the nomination for County Attorney, at the Democratic primary convention, held in that month, and was elected to the office the following August. In October of the same year, he was elected to the office of School Commissioner for two years, and at the expiration of the terms of each office he was re-elected, the people of the County showing in that an appreciation of his talents, which may in the future be of valuable service to the people of his County and State.

HENRY CLAY REED, farmer and stock raiser; P. O. Carlisle; was born near Clintonville, Bourbon County, upon the 20th day of March, 1848, came to Nicholas County in 1854, and in 1858 to his present home. His father was Wm. Reed, who was born in Bourbon County, March 18, 1816, and died Sept. 9, 1871; he was a farmer

by occupation, and a son of John and Catharine (Starr) Reed; John a son of George Reed, a native of France and an exile from that country; his wife was a Rennig. The mother of our subject was Sarah J. Dawson, born near Clintonville, also, and daughter of Armstrong and Sarah (McKinney) Dawson; she a daughter of John McKinney, of Lexington, of wild-cat fame. Wm. Reed had two children, our subject and Katie, who died without issue, at about twenty-two years of age, having been married about one year. Henry C. received a liberal education in the schools adjacent to his home and at Carlisle; he studied surveying, and subsequently spent three years in the study of medicine, and attended one course of lectures at the University of Louisville, but on account of the death of his father, he was compelled to return to the farm and take upon himself the duties of the father, which deprived him of the completion of his medical education. He was married upon the 13th of Nov., 1874, near Mt. Sterling, the native place of his wife, Emma Dooley, who is the daughter of Jabez and Rebecca (Scobee) Dooley; by this marriage there are three children: Wm. H., Nannie Maud and Mary Kate. Mr. Reed is a farmer and stock raiser of considerable note, owning a half interest in one of the finest bred colts of that region, "Abdallah Chief." He was elected as one of the magistrates of the county in 1879, which position he now holds. He is a member of the Christian Church and one of the trustees of "Old Concord," and a member of the Carlisle Commandary; he is interested in public improvements, the advancement of education and religion, and is a highly respected citizen of the county.

JEROME B. SANFORD, farmer; P. O. Carlisle; was born in Sumner County, Tenn., Feb. 26, 1826, and is a son of Muse and Elizabeth (Scott) Sanford. He was born in Orange County, Va., March 15, 1780; was a farmer by occupation, and died Dec. 9, 1863. His wife was also born in Orange County, Va., Jan. 1, 1770, and died March 21, 1868. They lived in Tennessee for a few years, and in 1829 moved to Kentucky, and settled near Lexington. They raised a family of twelve children, of whom Jerome, our subject, was the ninth. Owing to the limited school privileges at that early day, his education was confined to what he could obtain in the common schools. In 1852 he purchased property in Bethel, Bath Co., with a view to keeping a hotel, but the house and contents were burned down on the sixth day after he took possession. He then turned his attention to farming—first in Rowen County, where he remained one year, and then moved to the place he now owns. He was married in Bourbon County, near Ruddel's Mills, July 23, 1852, to Miss Elizabeth Knight, who was born in Bourbon County, Dec. 22, 1833. The result of their union is twelve children, viz.: William M., Mary Ida, Maud, Paris, Beauregard, Jerome, Kate, Mark and Mettie, twins, the latter of whom died in infancy; Charles, Lizzie and Bessie, the latter of whom also died in infancy. Mrs. Sanford was a daughter of Isaac and Mary (Howard) Knight, both natives of Kentucky. Mr. Sanford is a man of noble impulses, a generous disposition, and noted for his hospitality. He is an enterprising and prosperous farmer, and owns 116 acres of choice farm land. He has been a prominent member of the Masonic order at Carlisle for a number of years. Politically he is a Democrat.

THOMAS H. SAMMONS, City Marshal; P. O. Carlisle; was born in Genevieve, New York, Feb. 22, 1853, and is a son of Patrick and Mary (McGuinnis) Sammons. He was born in Ireland, and went to Cape of Good Hope, Africa, where he held a Government station three years; he emigrated to America in 1850, and lived nine years in Kentucky. During the war he entered the service, and was captured at the battle of Chickamauga, and died in Libby prison, in 1863. His wife, Mary, was born in Ireland, in 1826, and is still living. They had five children, of whom Thomas, our subject, was the second. He was educated in the schools of Cleveland, Ohio, and Carlisle, Kentucky. He learnt the saddler's trade, in Mt. Sterling, Kentucky., and in 1877, located at Carlisle; three years later he took into partnership Augustus Laubley, with whom he is now engaged in business. He was married in Bourbon County, May 15, 1872, to Miss Lizzie Fallon, who was born in Bourbon County, July 29, 1857. They have one girl, Mary H., born July 29, 1880. Mrs. Sammons was a daughter of Patrick and Mary (Mallon) Fallon, both natives of Ireland. Mr. Sammons is an energetic and enterprising man, and highly respected by all who knew him. Jan. 6, 1882, he was appointed by the town Council of Carlisle as City Marshal, which position he still retains. On the death of his father, the duties of supporting his widowed mother and his younger brothers and sisters devolved upon himself and older brother, and which duties they have faithfully fulfilled to the present. Himself and wife are members of the Catholic Church, at Carlisle. His political sympathies are with the Democratic party.

HENRY STEWART, farmer; P. O., Carlisle; was born Feb. 23, 1830, to Wm. and Olivia (Ogden) Stewart; she a daughter of Henry and Lucy (Metcalf) Ogden, a niece of Gov. Metcalf. The Stewart and Ogden families were from Virginia; Henry is the only son, and the only one of the family now living; three daughters grew to womanhood, but died without heirs in perpetuation. Mr. Stewart received a common-school education; was brought up in a blacksmith shop, where he learned the trade with his father, at which he worked about twenty-five years. At seventeen years of age he enlisted in Capt. Metcalf's company, under Col. M. V. Thompson, for the Mexican war; being under age he was removed after a short service. In the spring of 1848 he assisted in taking a drove of cattle to New York City, walking all the way, spending 67 days on the road. In the spring of 1849 he started for California; was severely wounded in the hip by a half-ounce rifle-ball accidentally discharged from a gun in the hands of a comrade. The wound was received 140 miles from Fort Laramie; he was hauled to that place in an ox-wagon, where he remained more than two months, when he returned home. In the years 1856 and '7 he made two trips to Minnesota, where he settled land-claims near St. Peter. Subsequently he returned home, remaining until October, 1861, when he enlisted in J. B. Holliday's company, under Gen. Williams' and Gen. Morgan's command; was at the battle of Shiloh, but on account of health he connected himself with Kirby Smith's division in 1862, and went to Texas and Mexico, where he remained until the close of the war; when he returned home and was married Sept. 25, 1862, to Mrs. Sarah (McCormick) Robinson, by whom he has two sons and two daughters, viz.: Minnie, Robert, Lindsey (deceased), Berry and Nellie. He followed smithing until the year 1880, when he engaged in farming. He is a member of the I. O. O. F.; a Democrat politically, and member of the Christian Church. His father is one of the oldest, most prominent, honorable, and highly esteemed citizens of the county.

JAMES SPENCER, farmer; P. O. Carlisle; first saw the light of this world at Stony Point Church, Bourbon County, Nov. 10, 1799. His father, William Spencer, a native of Maryland, settled at the above named place at a very early date. His mother was Mary Tellett, a Virginian, who gave birth to six children, three sons and three daughters: William H., in Fort Scott, Kansas; Mrs. Nancy Norton, of Nicholas, and the subject of our sketch, are living. Mr. Spencer received a very limited education, walking a long way through the woods to accept the very meager advantages which surrounded him at that early day. He staid with his father, working on the farm, until about thirty years of age. On Nov. 10, 1830, in Clark County, Ky., (where his parents had lived for many years,) he was united in marriage to Miss Elizabeth Chevis, who was born in Caroline County, Va., July 21, 1811, to Henry and Patsey (Minor) Chevis of that State. Soon after marriage, or in May, 1831, Mr. Spencer came to his present home, where he has since resided, engaged in general farming and stock raising. By his marriage there were thirteen children born: Laura died at twenty-three years of age; William in Bourbon County; Patsey, wife of Benjamin I. Taul, residing in Clay Conty, Mo.; Mary, wife of James Terry in Nicholas; Sarah, wife of Burton Terry, at Flat Rock; Nancy, wife of Robert Hamilton in Clay County, Mo.; John, in Nicholas, married Prather; Louisa, widow of James H. Burroughs, had one child; Maud A.; Betsey, and Kate, at home; Rhoda, wife of James Donnell, of Bourbon; Alice wife of Joseph Huffstetter, of Nicholas; Jennie, wife of Frank Huffstetter, on Cane Ridge. Twelve children and parents members of the Christian Church at Carlisle. Democratic, politically; interested in education, advancement of religion, and public improvements.

WILLIAM N. SANFORD, farmer and high-grade stock-raiser; P. O. Carlisle; was born in Rowan County, Ky., Nov. 27, 1853, and was brought by his parents, when about six weeks old, to the County of Nicholas (see history of Jerome Sanford). The subject of this sketch was the eldest of twelve children, in consequence of which his education was very limited. He applied himself closely to study, and at an early age was enabled to enter upon life as a teacher, the remuneration for which he applied to the advancement of his education. He was married, in Lexington, on March 6, 1879, to Miss Ella D. Wood, of Nicholas County, and sister to the wife of W. B. Allen (see history). By this marriage there has been born to them two children, the eldest of whom died in infancy; the younger, Roy Lee, born Sept. 7, 1881. In political sentiment he is Democratic. He is a member of the Masonic Lodge at Carlisle, is a young man of practical common sense, interested in public improvements and the advancement of education, religion and Sunday-School work; a highly respected and esteemed citizen of his community, and with his estimable wife belong to the Christian Church at Carlisle.

HEZEKIAH SMART, farmer; P. O. Carlisle. Born in Nicholas County, April 11, 1823; is a son of Polly Myers and Humphrey Smart, a Pennsylvanian by birth, and who was a soldier of the war of 1812 from Kentucky, having come to that State at a very early day; he was a farmer and trader; died in October, 1869. Our subject was one of eleven children; received his education from the common schools of Nicholas County, spending most of his time upon his father's farm. On the

26th of April, 1855, he married Catharine, daughter of Harry Foster, of Nicholas County. Three children have been born to them: Sarah Catharine, Luvina M. and Hezekiah T. Himself, wife and both daughters are members of the Methodist Church at Carlisle; for several years he has been connected with the Masonic Lodge at Carlisle and during its progress was also identified with the Patrons of Husbandry at that place; in politics he is an unswerving Democrat.

JOSEPH SMART, farmer; P. O. Black Hawk ; born in Nicholas County, April 11, 1819; is a son of Wm. Smart and Sarah Myers, both natives of Nicholas County. Wm. Smart was a soldier in the war of 1812, and an early settler and highly respected farmer of Nicholas County; he died about the year 1829. Joseph Smart, whose name heads this sketch, was married, March 16, 1851, to Matilda, daughter of David and Betty (Trahune) McIntire, of Nicholas County. They have had three children, all of whom are living: Francis, John and David B. Mr. Smart has been a widower since April 11, 1869; is a member of the Christian Church, and a sterling Democrat. He enlisted in the Mexican war under Col. Metcalf, and accompanied that distinguished leader to the city of Mexico, arriving, however, after its capture.

P. T. THROOP, lawyer, Carlisle ; was born in Carlisle, Oct. 19, 1854. His father was Phares Throop, born in Alexandria,Va., in the year 1809; died in March, 1860 ; he was a son of Rev. Phares Throop a native of the above named place, and for long years a prominent divine in the States of Kentucky and Virginia. The children of Rev. Phares Throop were: Susie wife of Judge R. H. Stanton, of Maysville; Mary, deceased wife of Hon. Thomas P. Throop, of Covington ; Hannah, wife of Hon. D. K. Weis, of Ashland, Ky., Hon. Thomas Throop, of Flemingsburg, who died ten days before the election for Representative to Congress, for which he was making the race; Judge French, who was nominated in his stead, being overwhelmingly elected on ten days' notice by the popularity of Mr. Throop; Dr. Benjamin T., who died in Texas soon after the war; Joseph, a merchant at Poplar Plains, Fleming Co., Ky., and the father of our subject, who came to Flemingsburg in 1832,where he engaged in mercantile business; subsequently studied medicine, and graduated at the medical college in Cincinnati, about 1835. While there he was married and had five children, all of whom died in infancy. After graduation he located at Mays Lick, where he plied his profession for several years. His second marriage occurred in Missouri to Arabella Williams, daughter of Thaddeus Williams, a brother of General Samuel and Dr. Charles Williams, two prominent men in the country. She died in 1856 at the age of about 30 years, being the mother of seven children, three of whom are now living: Abbie T., wife of Judge A. E. Cole, Circuit Judge of the 14th Dist.; Mary A., a maiden; and the subject of this sketch. Phares Throop, Sr., located in Carlisle in about 1842, where he plied his profession until in 1857, when he located at North Middletown, where occurred his third marriage to Amanda Harris, daughter of Charles Harris, of Bourborn. By her he had one child, Myrtle V., who resides with her mother, now a Mrs. W. R. Gorham; he a merchant of Louisville. The Throops are descendants of one Earl Adrian Scroope, one of the Regicides, who came to this country and changed his name to Throop. The subject of this sketch was raised by his uncle, Joseph, until about 13 years of age, when he went to live with his sister, Mrs. Cole. In 1869 he entered the Kentucky University, where he remained until March, 1872, when he (without seeking it) received the appointment from the 10th Congressional Dist. as a cadet to West Point, but was rejected in the examination on account of physical debility. He then engaged in teaching, at which he continued until in April, 1881. During that time he acted as School Commissioner of Fleming Co. for three years, and read law with Judge Cole and was admitted to the practice of the profession at Maysville, Jan. 14, 1881 ; he located at Carlisle in Oct. of the same year. He was married Nov. 6, 1875, to Miss Maria B. Kenner, of Flemingsburg, daughter of L. W. and Mary H. (Bell) Kenner; by her he has one child, Abbie Holten, born May 5, 1880. He is a member of the I. O. O. F. at Flemingsburg, and of the Grand Lodge of the State. He and wife are members of the M. E. Church.

WILLIAM W. TUTTLE, carpenter ; P. O. Carlisle ; is a native of Moorefield, where he was born Jan. 21, 1822, to Peter and Elizabeth (Calvert) Tuttle ; she a daughter of Jesse Calvert, who was a native of Virginia, but came at an early date to Mason County. Peter Tuttle was a cabinet maker, and plied his trade in Mason County and at Moorefield. He died in 1859, at the age of seventy-seven years, in Johnson County, Mo., whither he had gone in 1851 ; his wife died in the year 1880, at the extreme age of ninety-six years. He was a son of John, who died in Virginia. Peter was the father of ten children : Ambrose D., in Nevada, California ; Saphronia and James, died unmarried ; Eliza J., deceased, wife of Leroy Day, left family in Mercer County, Mo. ; Angeline, wife of James M. Myers, residing in Johnson County, Mo.; Harriette N., wife of Isaac Wallen residing in Platte County, Mo.; William W., Nancy, wife of John Roberts, in Johnson County, Mo.; Preston M. S., in Omaha, Neb.; Helen M., wife of Samuel Grinstead in Johnson County, Mo. Mr. Tuttle learned the trade with his father, when a boy, and received but very limited educational advantages; his life has been devoted to mechanics, mercantile business and farming. He was married in 1847 to Nancy A. Roberts, a native of Nicholas County, and daughter of Col. Henry and Susan (Daugherty) Roberts; he a native of Virginia, she of Maryland. He held the offices of Lieutenant and Captain in the war of 1812, and was afterward made Colonel in the Kentucky Militia. He also represented Nicholas County in the Legislature; was Sheriff of the county many years, and held various other offices. Mr. Tuttle, by his marriage, has two children, Susan E. and Helen J. who are teachers of high standing. He is a member of the Masonic order at Carlisle, and member of the Baptist Church, in which he holds the office of Moderator.

ELIJAH WEST, who died June 3, 1877, was born in the year 1804, upon the farm where the family now reside; his father was Amos West, a native of North Carolina; subsequently removed to Maryland, where he was married to Elizabeth Robbins, and came to Nicholas County before 1800; they had ten children, of which number the subject was the fourth; he was married to Maria B. Smoot, a daughter of one of the first merchants of Millersburg; she died in 1863, at fifty-two years of age; her children were thirteen in number, six of whom died childless; those living are: Sarah A., widow of Col. R. A. Stewart, residing at Orange Lake, Fla.; William H. at the old homestead; Mary G., wife of John W. Parker, in Vermillion County, Ill.; Lizzie A., wife of Rev. Henry W. Abbott, of Monmouth, Kan.; George B. at Wichita, Kan.; Laura T. and Emma R. unmarried. Mr. West was again married in 1863, to Mrs. Rosanna Hughes, widow of Jesse Hughes. He began life as a merchant, learned the carpenter's trade, and carried on farming. He was a Magistrate in the county for many years, also held the position of County Judge for a considerable period. Mrs. Sarah A. M. Blackford, widow of Merritt Blackford; is the daughter or Mary W., eldest daughter of Amos West; she married Enoch Conyers, and in 1832, moved to Quincy, Ill., where both died; they had eight children, three of whom are now living, viz.: Millicent A. P., a twin sister to the above, married William P. Burns, at Portland, Or.; and Enoch W., residing in Columbia County, Ore. Mr. Blackford was born Oct. 22, 1821, at Lebanon, Ohio, to Allen and Nancy (Merritt) Blackford. He was married Oct. 9, 1854, in Quincy, Ill., to Sarah A. M. Conyers, by whom he had five children: Emma A., has been thrice married; first, to Horace Ludwig, by whom he had three children; Oscar, Willie, and John, the two eldest in Missouri; her second marriage to Lou B. Hamilton; third, to William West, who resides near Carlisle. The second child of Merritt Blackford, is John M., married, and living in Pike County, Ill.; Enoch C., married, and living in Princeton, Ill.; Allen W. and George L. B., single. Mr. Blackford enlisted in October, 1861, in Company D., 50th Illinois Infantry; he was made Second Lieutenant, and died July 15, 1863, after three days sickness; he was in the Army of the Cumberland under Col. Dr. Bain, of Payson, Ill.; he was a good soldier, and gallant leader during his short military career. Before entering the service, he was a mechanic of considerable note, and a worthy and highly esteemed citizen.

S. M. WAUGH, dry goods merchant, Carlisle; born Nov. 28, 1838; his father was Archer S. Waugh, born in Nicholas county in the year 1801, and died Jan. 5, 1871; he was a man held in high esteem by the citizens of the county, which was manifested by conferring upon him the honors connected with the offices of Sheriff, Coroner, Constable, and other positions of trust, all of which he held about thirty years. The mother of our subject, who is still living, was, as maiden lady, Miss Matilda Piper, born in Nicholas County in September, 1803, to James R. Piper, Sr., an early and prominent farmer of said county. Archer S. Waugh by this marriage had eight children, who grew to maturity; four are now living, viz.: Eliza, wife of John Wright, of Nicholas County; Wm. H. (see history), James H., a banker, in Columbia, Mo.; Samuel who received a limited district school education, beginning in the mercantile business early in life as a clerk in the dry goods house of Chappell, Bruce & McIntyre, where he remained four years; he then formed a partnership in business under the firm name of Campbell, Waugh & Metcalf, thence into the firm of W. P. Bruce & Co.; then became a member of the firm of Adair, Waugh & Ewing, from which he returned to the firm of Chappell & Co., now with the business house of Peale & Chappell. He is Democratic, politically, and a member of the Presbyterian Church.

WILLIAM H. WAUGH, farmer; P. O. Carlisle; a native of Nicholas County, where his birth occurred in 1825, a son of Archer S. (see history of S. M.) Waugh; he began life as a farmer, in which he has always been engaged; in the year 1856 he was married, in Nicholas County, to Mary Tune, also a native, where she was born in 1833, to Samuel T. and Mary (Hutson) Tune, who were natives of Virginia. Mr. Waugh was drafted during the late war but took no part in the service. They are members of the Presbyterian Church at Carlisle; he is independent in political matters, believing in the policy of voting for the best men to fill the responsible positions in office. He is a member of the Masonic order, a highly esteemed citizen of the community in which he lives, and an energetic and enterprising business man, having by his own industry and frugality accumulated a good farm of 145 acres, upon which he is engaged in general farming and high grade stock raising of all kinds.

THOMAS WADE, farmer; P. O. Millersburg; born Jan. 20, 1850, to John Wade, near Carlisle. He received a limited education, working upon his father's farm until twenty-three years of age, when he was married Nov. 7, 1873, to Molly Anderson, daughter of Hugh and Louvisa (Miller) Anderson; she a daughter of John Miller, of Lancaster, Ky.; her parents are now residing in Mt. Sterling; the father a saddler by trade; some of the Andersons also reside in Cynthiana and vicinity. Mrs. Wade is the eldest of four daughters and three sons, all of whom are living. By this union there are six children: Henry, Emma L., Benjamin F., John, Hugh M. and Anna L. He came to his present home, "Bowden Farm," in the fall of 1878, purchasing 140 acres of choice land, upon which he is engaged in stock breeding and agriculture. He is Democratic politically, and with his family members of the M. E. Church at Carlisle.

LOWER BLUE LICKS PRECINCT.

LINCOLN ABNEE, miller and mill-wright; P. O. Blue Licks; was born in Clay County, Ky., May 10, 1826, and is a son of John and Pamelia (Watts) Abnee. He was born in Clay County; died in 1852; she a native of Perry County, Ky.; died in 1844. She was the mother of six boys and three girls. Lincoln, the subject of this sketch was the oldest boy. He was educated in the common schools of Clay County, and commenced his career in life as a farmer, but a few years later he turned his attention to milling, which business he still follows at Blue Licks in a mill built on Licking river. He was married in Fleming County, Oct. 3, 1853, to Miss Margaret Evans, who was born in Fleming County, Sept. 19, 1836. They have had ten children, viz: Serilda, Robert, John M., Francis, William H., James, Charles, Effie, Clarence and Lee; the latter died when four years of age. Mrs. Abnee was a daughter of Rafe R. and Mahaley (Bartlett) Evans; he a native of Montgomery County, still living; she a native of Nicholas County, deceased. Mr. Abnee is a prominent man in the precinct, and has served the people several years as Magistrate. He is energetic and enterprising in business, and well worthy of the high esteem in which he is held. In connection with his milling interests he is interested in a merchandising store with his sons. Politically he is a Democrat.

GEORGE D. BRIGGS, teacher; P. O. Pleasant Valley; was born in Bennington County, Vt., Sept. 20, 1842, to Nelson and Jane (Seeley) Briggs; both still living in Michigan. He, born in 1811; she, born in Erie County, Pa., in 1808. They have six children, of whom George, our subject, is the third. He was educated at Hiram, Portage County, O., and entered upon his career in life as a farmer. During the rebellion he entered the service in Co. A, of the 42d O. V. I. with Capt. J. S. Ross, under Gen. Jas. A. Garfield, and remained in the service four years, and in 1868 removed to Kentucky and engaged in teaching school; 2 years later, on April 23d, he was married to Miss Annie Rowe, who was born to Cornelius M. and Emeline (Stanfield) Rowe, July 11, 1852. They have five children, viz: Eva J., Hoy, Norton, Webster, Clay, Irena Bell, and Elberon Garfield. Mr. Briggs possesses the qualifications necessary in gaining the good will of all, and socially ranks very high in the esteem of all who know him. Religiously, himself and wife are connected with the Christian Church.

WM. A. FOWLE, farmer; P. O. Lower Blue Licks; a native of Bourbon County and the youngest of a family of 13 children; was born July 20, 1832. His father Isaac Fowle, a native of Vermont, where he was born March 24, 1791, was a hatter by trade, and came to Bourbon County in 1816, having served in the war of 1812; he died Dec. 30, 1879. His wife, Caroline Green, was born in Virginia, March 25, 1793, and died Sept. 20, 1879. The subject of this sketch began life as a farmer, and was married in Nicholas County, July 25, 1852, to Susan Robertson, who was born in Bourbon, March 8, 1834, and died March 14, 1869; she was a daughter of William Robertson. By this marriage there were the following children: Rufus, June 5, 1853; died July 10, 1854; Sarah Eliza, born Sept. 9, 1854; now the wife of Dr. Wells (see hist.); Wm. Isaac, June 26, 1856, graduated at Bible College, Lexington, and upon that occasion delivered the valedictory; he is now preaching at Chaplin, Nelson County, Ky.; Nathaniel W., born Sept. 12, 1858. Mary E., Sept. 28, 1860. In June, 1867, Mr. Fowle was again married to Cassandra (Maston) Kenton, widow of Wm. Kenton, and daughter of Caleb and Hannah (Ellis) Maston). They are members of the Christian Church at Blue Licks. He is, in political faith, a Democrat. In agriculture he raises the usual crops, and is considered one of the substantial men of the precinct.

SIMON KENTON, farmer; P. O. Blue Licks, was born in Nicholas County, Ky., Sept. 16, 1817, to William and Jane (Burden) Kenton, natives of Kentucky. She died in 1855; he in 1857; he was a son of Mark Kenton, brother to Simon Kenton, the noted Indian fighter. Simon the subject of this sketch was the second of a family of ten children. His education was limited to such as could be obtained in the common schools at that early day. He entered upon the battle of life, by taking upon himself the duties of a farm life, which he has always followed, with the addition of trading extensively in mules and horses, and later, shipping tobacco. He is one of the most prominent and enterprising farmers in the precinct, and owns 500 acres of choice farm land, situated on the banks of Licking river. He was married in Nicholas County, Jan. 26, 1841, to Hannah Bishop, who was born in Harrison County, in Sept. 1820, to Josiah and Elizabeth (Watton) Bishop, natives of Maryland. By this marriage he is the father of eight children, viz., William

J., Nancy J., Eldridge, Elizabeth, Mahulda, Thomas B., Lafayette and Simeon B. Mr. Kenton is a member of the pioneer association of the county, and was one of the committee to represent that association before the Legislature at Frankfort, in the interest of the monument about to be erected in commemoration of the battle at Blue Licks. Religiously, himself and family are connected with the Methodist Church at Blue Licks. He is also a member of the Masonic Order of that place. Politically he is a Republican.

GEORGE M. LINVILLE, farmer; P. O. Blue Licks; was born in Mason County, Ky., Aug. 4, 1835, to John R. and Matilda (Galbraith) Linville; he was born in Bracken County, Aug. 27, 1809, is a farmer by occupation, and still living; she was born in Mason County, and died in 1842. George, the subject of this sketch, was the oldest of a family of four children; he obtained his education in the common schools of Bracken County, and commenced his career in life, by taking upon himself the duties of a farm life, and which he still follows, and has, by his industry and energy, accumulated a large amount of this world's goods, and now owns a farm containing 200 acres of choice farm land, well stocked and well cultivated; he was married in Nicholas County, Jan. 11, 1857, to Mary Ann Ashpaw, who was born in Nicholas County, Nov. 26, 1842; the result of their union was twelve children, viz: J. Horace, Thomas, Helen, Joseph, Charles, William, Jacob, Albert, Matilda, Faney, Jessie, and Solomon. Mrs. Linville was a daughter of Joseph and Effie (Rankin) Ashpaw; he a native of Harrison County, she of Nicholas County, and both living. Mr. Linville is one of the most prominent farmers in the precinct, and is held in the highest esteem by all who know him, and in connection with his wife, is a member of the Christian Church; his political sympathies are with the Democratic party.

JOHN LAREN, landlord; P. O. Lower Blue Licks, proprietor of the "Laren House" at the famous summer resort, "The Blue Licks," was born in Mason County, Ky., Feb. 18, 1820. His father, a millwright and farmer, was born in Virginia upon the 19th of February, 1780, and came to Bracken County, Ky., among its earliest settlers; his death occurred in October, 1846; his wife was Elizabeth Robinson, a native of Maryland, who died in 1863. By these parents there were five children, of which number our subject was the youngest, and received his education at Lewisburg, Kentucky. At the latter place he began life as a merchant, where he continued about three years, then located at Mayslick, remaining five years, thence to the Blue Licks, where he continued about two years, then turned the mercantile business over to his sons and took charge of the hotel which he is now running. His marriage occurred Sept. 30, 1846, in Mason County, to Miss Corrilla Humphreys, a native of Mason County, born June 25, 1826; she was a daughter of Robert and Harriet (Waters) Humphreys, natives of Mason County. By the above marriage there are seven children: Hattie, wife of George Preston of Covington; Charles C., John A., Frank W., Tillie, Elizabeth and Alice. They are members of the Baptist Church, at Lewisburg. Mr. Laren is a Democrat politically, and a man of prominence in business circles. He was postmaster at North Fork, Lewisburg, six years. He is running a livery stable in connection with his hotel, the latter having a capacity of 100 guests.

JEREMIAH PRATHER, farmer; P. O. Pleasant Valley; was born in Fleming County, Ky., Oct. 27, 1837, to James and Nancy (Casiday) Prather, natives of Fleming County; he, born Nov. 4, 1811, and is still living; she, born in May, 1814, died May 25, 1870. Jeremiah, the subject of this sketch, was the second in a family of seven children. His education was limited to such as could be obtained in the common schools of the county. He entered upon his career in life as a farmer, and in connection with the duties of a farm life, he also worked at blacksmithing. He was married in Fleming County, June 4, 1857, to Sarah J. Collins, who was born to J. Russell and Miss (McCrackin) Collins, natives of Fleming County, July 15, 1837, and died Oct. 14, 1870, leaving a family of six children, viz: Nancy M., Charles M., William A., Jeremiah M., Barbara L. and James R. Mr. Prather's second marriage occured Aug. 7, 1873, to Mary J. Bentley, daughter of George B. and Sarah Jane (Graves) Bentley, she was born in Fleming County, Nov. 9, 1854, by this marriage he has three children, viz: R. B., Allie B. and Joseph. Mr. Prather is a very energetic and enterprising man, and one of the most prominent farmers in the precinct, and is well worthy of the high esteem in which he is held by the community. He owns a fine farm called "Pleasant Hill," containing 160 acres of choice farm land, which, "as a practical farmer," he keeps in a high state of cultivation. Himself and wife are connected with the Pleasant Valley Christian Church. Politically he is a Democrat.

HENRY BISHOP SAMPSON, farmer; P. O. Blue Licks; was born in Fleming County, Ky., March 23, 1824, to Abraham and Mary (Warren) Sampson, natives of Fleming County; he died in 1862; she in 1866. Henry, the subject of this sketch, was the oldest of a family of eight children. His educational privileges were limited to the common schools of Nicholas and Fleming Counties. He commenced his career in life as a farmer, and removed to Missouri, where he remained two years and returned to Kentucky. He was married in Nicholas County, in Sept., 1853, to Miss Eliza McCabe, who was born in 1830, and died in Jan., 1857, without issue. She was a daughter of Josiah and Miss (Bartlett) McCabe, natives of Nicholas County. Mr. Sampson's second marriage occurred Dec. 25, 1867, to Miss Armilda M. Allison, who was born in Nicholas County, Feb. 8, 1840. By her he has four children, viz: Edward R., born July 25, 1870; George B., born Sept. 12, 1874; R. M., born June 28, 1872; Irwin Garfield, June 29, 1880. Mrs. Sampson was a daughter of David G. and Sally Allison, natives of Nicholas County; he was born in 1812; died in 1870; she was born in 1809; died in 1850. Mr. Sampson is an energetic and enterprising farmer, and aside from raising the usual farm crops and tobacco, is a breeder of high grade sheep, and tra les in stock of all kinds. He owns a fine farm containing 244 acres, situated on Licking River. His house is built on an eminence overlooking the surrounding country with a commanding view. Himself and wife are members of the Christian Church at Blue Licks; he is also a member of the Masonic Order at that place. In politics he is a Democrat.

JAMES A. SPARKS, farmer; P. O. Blue Licks; was born in Nicholas County, Ky., May 12, 1847, to Charles and Mary A. (Barnett) Sparks. He was born in Nicholas County, Dec. 25, 1817, and is the present toll-gate keeper at Blue Licks, on Maysville and Lexington Pike. She was born in Bourbon County, Jan. 15, 1819. They have seven children, of whom James, the subject of this sketch, was the fifth. He obtained his education in the common schools of the County, and entered upon a farm life. He was married in Nicholas County, to Miss Martha J. Bowen, who, was born July 1, 1848, to W. F. and E. J. Bowen. He was born Feb. 23, 1825; she, Jan. 9, 1823. By this marriage, Mr. Sparks has six children, viz.: Jennie L., Charles D., Bettie F., Walter W., Lulie B. and Mattie R. Mr. Sparks is an energetic and enterprising man, and, socially, ranks high in the esteem of the community. He has served the people, since 1878, as Constable, and performed the duties of the office with zeal and integrity. Religiously, himself and family are connected with the Christian Church. He is also a member of the Masonic Fraternity at Blue Licks. In politics he is a Democrat.

ELIAS WESTFALL, farmer; P. O. Blue Licks; was born in Prussia, March 8, 1844, to Philip and Elizabeth Westfall, natives of Prussia. He was born in 1812, died Aug. 11, 1872; she was born in 1814, died Aug. 13, 1874. They emigrated to America in November, 1856, and settled in Nicholas County. They had thirteen children, of whom Elias, the subject of this sketch was the youngest. He received a common school education and learned the trade of a shoemaker, which he worked at for a number of years, and eventually turned his attention to farming, and which occupation he still follows. He was married in Nicholas County, Dec. 27, 1865, to Miss Sarah Harney, who was born Feb. 1, 1846. Their union resulted in seven children, viz: Phillip, Nicholas, George, Charles, Perlie, Daniel and Lizzie, the latter died in infancy. Mrs. Westfall was a daughter of Willoughby and Mahaley (Harrington) Harney, natives of Nicholas County. Mr. Westfall is an energetic and enterprising man, and a practical farmer, and one well worthy of the high esteem in which he is held. He has filled the office and performed the duties of Deputy Clerk for a number of years. He owns a farm containing 200 acres of land, and in addition to growing the usual farm crops, makes the raising of tobacco his specialty. He is a prominent member of the Masonic fraternity, at Blue Lick's. In politics he is a Democrat.

JOHN M. WELLS, physician; P. O. Blue Licks; the youngest son of a family of four sons and three daughters, is extensively engaged in tobacco raising upon his well kept farm of 140 acres, and in connection with his agricultural pursuits has a large and lucrative practice in his profession; he attended the common schools of his neighborhood and the high school at Carlisle, he subsequently attended the medical department of the University of Louisville, and received his diploma upon March 1, 1876. He was born in Nicholas County, Jan. 4, 1854, and married Sarah Fowle in the County of Nicholas, Oct. 31, 1878; she born in the above county, Sept. 9, 1854, to William and Susan (Robinson) Fowle (see history.) The result of this union is two sons, Herman L. and Leslie T. His father who is still living and a prominent agriculturist, was born in Nicholas County, Nov. 27, 1811. His mother, Lucinda Collins, was born in the same county, in the year 1816, and died in 1862. Dr. Wells is a Republican of prominence in his county, and with his family is connected with the Christian Church.

HEADQUARTERS PRECINCT.

MARQUIS D. L. BURRIS, store keeper and gauger; P. O., Headquarters; was born in Fleming County, Ky., Nov. 23, 1846, to Hiram and Elizabeth (Biddle) Burris. He was born in Fleming County, May 3, 1799, and died Nov. 13, 1854. His wife, Elizabeth, was also a native of Fleming County, born Feb. 1, 1807, and died Nov. 18, 1864. The result of their union was ten children. Marquis, our subject, was next to the youngest. He was educated in the common schools of Nicholas County, and entered upon a clerkship in a store at Headquarters. Two years later he turned his attention to farming. In 1869 he was appointed U. S. Gauger, and is now serving the government as gauger and store-keeper. Was also postmaster at Headquarters a short time. He was married in Nicholas County, June 6, 1872, to Miss Elizabeth Brooks, who was born in Nicholas County, Jan. 18, 1851. They have three children, viz: William H., Harry E. and Robert B. Mrs. Burris was a daughter of Anderson and Susan (Evans) Brooks. (See hist.) During the war Mr. Burris enlisted in Co. A. of the 145th Illinois regiment, under Captain Chapman, but remained in the service only five months. In connection with his wife he is a member of the Methodist church at Headquarters. He has also been a prominent member of the Masonic order at Headquarters for a number of years. He is a very energetic and enterprising business man, and socially ranks very high in the esteem of the community. In politics he is a Republican.

ANDERSON BROOKS, farmer; P. O. Headquarters; was born in Nicholas County, Ky., Feb. 18, 1815, and is a son of Zachariah and Frances (Overby) Brooks, who were among the first settlers in Nicholas County, Ky.; he was born in Virginia, in 1767; was a farmer by occupation, and died Jan. 2, 1857; his wife, Frances, was also a native of Virginia, born in 1797, and died Sept. 14, 1839; there was born to them eight children, of whom Anderson, our subject, was next to the youngest; his education was limited to the common schools of the county; he commenced his career in life as a farmer, was married in Nicholas County, Nov. 3, 1843, to Miss Susan Evans, daughter of Gillead and Anna (Trigg) Evans. (See hist.) Mrs. Brooks was born in Nicholas County, Sept. 18, 1826; the result of their union is ten children, viz: Nathan O., Eveline, William F., Sarah E., Mary L., Albert, Carrie, Ann Eliza, Gillead F., and Elmira, the three latter of whom are dead. Mr. and Mrs. Brooks are both members of the Mt. Carmel Methodist Church; in his political ideas, he is unsettled, and, as he expresses it, votes for the best man; he is a very energetic and enterprising man, and a prosperous farmer; owns 226 acres of choice farm land, and, besides raising the usual farm crops, deals largely in high grade stock of all kinds.

R. H. COLLIER, farmer; P. O. Morning Glory; was born in Nicholas County, Ky., March 17, 1831; his father, C. A. Collier, was a native of Virginia, and was born about 1790; he was a farmer by occupation, and emigrated to Kentucky some time prior to the war of 1812, and settled in Nicholas County; he was a soldier in the 1812 war, and was captain of a company; was taken prisoner at the battle of the River Raisin; after the war closed, he returned to Nicholas County, Ky., where he died in 1855; his wife was Catharine Howerton, also a native of Virginia, born about 1806, and died in 1866. They raised two sons, viz: Robert H. (subject) and William J.; his sons received a moderate education in the country schools of Nicholas County; Robert H. was married in Nicholas, in 1849, to Eliza Peterson, a daughter of Henry and Annie Peterson; his wife, Eliza, was born in 1832; they have three sons: Coleman A., Samuel R., and William H. Mr. Collier has always been a farmer since he was large enough to work; he however run a mill about six years in connection with his farm; in 1879, he was elected Magistrate of his precinct for a term of four years, an office he holds at this time; he was a soldier in the Federal army about two years, belonging to the 18th Kentucky regiment; he has also been a member of the Masonic order for twenty-nine years, and himself and wife are members of the Baptist Church; politically, he is a Democrat; like many others he began life without any means whatever, but by industrious habits and close application to his business, he is now in very comfortable circumstances.

GILLEAD EVANS, farmer; P. O. Headquarters; was born in Delaware, July 4, 1794, and is a son of John and Rachael (Taylor) Evans, who were among the first to enter upon pioneer life in Kentucky; the former was born in Delaware in 1774, and died 1809. His wife, Rachael, was also born in Delaware in 1774, and died in 1825. Gillead, our subject, was their only child, and his opportunities for receiving an education was very limited, there being very few schools at that early day. Early in life he entered upon a farmer's life; served six months in the war of 1812 ; was married March 9, 1817, to Miss Anna Trigg, who was born in Virginia, Jan. 10, 1794, and died in Sept., 1864, leaving to his care two children, viz.: Susan, wife of Anderson Brooks (See Hist.), and Elizabeth, the wife of Oscar Orr, and now living in Missouri. Mr. Evans was married again July 6, 1873, to Mrs. Rose Ann Sanders, widow of James Sanders, and daughter of John and Rose (Mitchell) Cook. Mr. Evans has always been an enterprising farmer and a thorough business man, is a member of the Methodist Church; in politics he is a Democrat.

SAMUEL R. FISHER, physician; P. O. Headquarters; was born in Sharpsburg, Bath County, Ky., Dec. 12, 1852, and is a son of Ambrose and Susan F. (Rogers) Fisher; he was born in Bourbon County Dec. 24, 1824, to Thomas and Terricia (Ruddle) Fisher. He was born in Bourbon County, in 1795, and died Sept. 1, 1865; she born in Bourbon County in 1799, and died in February, 1867. They had five children, of whom the father ot our subject was the third. He was married in Aberdeen, Ohio, July 10, 1850, to Miss Susan F. Rogers, who was born April 24, 1830. The result of their union was eight children, viz: Samuel R., Mary E., John Q., J. Williamson, Lucinda J., Lydia M., Clifton H. and Lottie L.; the latter died Aug. 12, 1880, at the age of fourteen. Mrs. Fisher was a daughter of Samuel and Elizabeth (Irvin) Rogers. He was born in Virginia Nov. 6, 1789; died June 23, 1877; she was born July 8, 1792; died in March, 1868. Samuel R., the subject of this sketch, was educated at Carlisle, and attended the Medical College at Louisville, Ky., one year; he also attended the Ohio Medical College at Cincinnati two years, and received his diploma at the latter place in March, 1876. He located at Headquarters, and began the practice of his profession the same year, and has, by the thorough knowledge of his business and strict attention to his calling, built up a large and steadily increasing practice. He was married in Harrison County, Oct. 16, 1877, to Miss Laura Kinnard, who was born in Missouri, Sept. 23, 1857. One child, Irene Thompson, is the result of their union. Mrs. Fisher was a daughter of Garrison and Susan (Thompson) Kinnard; he a native of Mason County; she a native of Harrison County. Mr. Fisher is a man of energy and enterprise, and possesses all the social qualifications necessary in gaining the good will of all with whom he associates. He is a prominent member of the Masonic order at Headquarters and of the I. O. O. F. at Carlisle.

ALFRED J. KENNEDY, farmer; P. O. Headquarters; was born in Nicholas County, Ky., Dec. 26, 1821, to William and Nancy (Brooks) Kennedy; he was born Nicholas County, September 6, 1797; was a farmer and stone mason by occupation; and died Dec. 11, 1831. His wife, Nancy, was born in Nicholas County, Aug. 15, 1805, and is still living. Alfred, our subject, is the oldest of six children. He received a common school education, and commenced the battle of life as a farmer. He was married in Nicholas County, Dec. 23, 1841, to Miss Sally Ann Hillock, who was born in Nicholas County, Jan. 2, 1822. She is the mother of six children, viz.: William J., Mary S., (deceased), Betty F., John F., Winfield S., and Harvey M., (deceased). Mrs. Kennedy was a daughter of James and Susie (Snapp) Hillock. Mr. Kennedy served the County as Constable six years. He is an energetic and enterprising farmer, and, socially, ranks high in the esteem of the community. He has always been a prominent Republican, and is a member of the Methodist Church at Headquarters.

LITTLETON LONG, farmer; P. O. Shady Nook; was born in Nicholas County, Ky, Jan. 25, 1813, to Eliakim and Jemima (Victor) Long, natives of Maryland, near Snow Hill. Littleton, our subject, was the seventh of nine children. He received a common school education, and commenced the battle of life as a farmer. He was married in Harrison County, Feb. 18, 1840, to Miss Nancy Maffett; who was born in Harrison County, Dec. 23, 1821. They had two children, viz: Marion and James R. (see history). Mrs. Long was a daughter of William and Nancy (Killum) Maffett (see history of John H. Maffett). Mr. Long is a man of noble impulses and a generous spirit, and is well worthy of the high esteem in which he is held by the community. He is a very energetic and enterprising farmer, and a thorough business man. He commenced life a poor boy, but by making good use of his abilities has accumulated a good property. He now owns a farm of 120 acres of choice farm land. In connection with his wife he is a member of the Christian Church at Indian Creek. Politically he is a Democrat.

JAMES R. LONG, farmer; P. O. Headquarters; was born in Nicholas County, Ky., May 13, 1848, to Littleton and Nancy (Maffett) Long. (See hist.) James is the youngest child. He received his education in the common schools of Harrison County, and began his career in life as a farmer. He was married in Nicholas County, Feb. 13, 1868, to Miss Armilda Cheatham, who was born in Nicholas County, Nov. 7, 1850. They have three children, viz: Floyd, Carl and Eva. Mrs. Long was a daughter of John and Harriet (Garrett), Cheatham. He was born Nov. 2, 1804, and died Sept. 14, 1857. His wife Harriet was born in August, 1808, and is still living. Mr. Long is a member of the Christian Church at Indian Creek. Mrs. Long is a member of the Baptist Church at Irvinsville. Mr. Long has also been a prominent member of the Masonic Order at Headquarters for a number of years. He is an energetic and enterprising farmer and business man; owns 75 acres of choice farm land, which, "as a practical farmer," he keeps in a high state of cultivation. He is also a dealer in high grade stock, and has in his possession a very fine horse named Chief Justice. In politics he is a Democrat.

MARION LONG, farmer; P. O. Shady Nook, was born in Nicholas County, July 26, 1825, to Littleton and Nancy (Maffett) Long. (See His.) Marion the subject of this sketch received a common school education in Harrison County, and began life as a farmer. He was married in Harrison County, March 11, 1866 to Miss Sarah M. Ravenscraft, who was born April 6, 1846. They have four children, viz., Lena M., Ada M., William L. and Ila M. Mrs. Long was a daughter of William and Margaret (Anderson) Ravenscraft, both now living in Bourbon County. Mr. Long is highly esteemed by all who know him. He is a very energetic farmer and business man, and liberal in all public enterprises. He owns a farm of eighty acres which is well cultivated, and on which he raises the usual farm crops and tobacco. In connection with his wife he is a member of the Christian Church at Indian Creek. He is also a member of the Masonic Order at Headquarters. In politics he is a Democrat.

JOHN H. MAFFETT, farmer; P. O. Headquarters; was born in Harrison County, Ky., March 8, 1824, and is a son of William and Nancy (Killum) Maffett. He was born in Pennsylvania in 1781; was a farmer and shoemaker by occupation, and died in April, 1853. His wife Nancy was a native of Maryland and died in August, 1852; they had eleven children, of whom John, our subject, was the eighth. He received his education in the common schools of Harrison County and then took upon himself the duties of a farm life. He was married in Nicholas County, Dec. 18, 1851, to Miss Hepsey A. Turley, who was born in Nicholas County, in 1830, and died Oct. 6, 1863, leaving to his care five children, viz: LaFayette, John W., Susan A., Jane A. and Hamlet F. Mrs. Maffett was a daughter of John and Susan (Griffith) Turley. Mr. Maffett was married again Nov. 9, 1865, to Miss Elizabeth A. Gaffin, who was born in Nicholas County, June 1, 1824, and was a daughter of Otho and Anna (Munford) Gaffin. The former was born April 17, 1785, and died June 6, 1858; the latter was born Jan. 11, 1789, and died April 14, 1863. During the war, Mr. Maffett was drafted into the service, but being a widower with five small children, he hired a substitute. He is a member of the Christian Church at Indian Creek. Is an energetic and enterprising farmer and business man. In politics is a Republican.

JOHN A. PORTER, merchant; P. O. Barterville; was born in Nicholas County, Ky., May 23, 1847, to Henry and Elizabeth (Brady) Porter (see hist.). John A. is the oldest child. He was educated in the common schools of Nicholas County, and commenced his career in life in a saw and grist mill, at Shakerag, (now Ellisville), where he remained six years. In 1880, he erected a building at Helena, and opened a general merchandising store, where, by his pleasing manners and kind attentions to his customers, he has built up a large and rapidly increasing trade. He was appointed Post Master at Barterville, (Helena), Dec. 13, 1880. He was married in Nicholas County, July 6, 1869, to Miss Charlotte Q. Burnett, who was born Oct. 22, 1848. They have three children, viz.: Lulie E., James H., and Bettie F. Mrs. Porter was a daughter of James A. and Elizabeth (Glasscock) Barnett. He was born in Nicholas County, July 14, 1809, and died May 4, 1879. His wife, Elizabeth, was born Sept. 15, 1806, and is still living. During the war Mr. Porter served thirteen months in the service, in Co. B, of the 14th Ky. Cavalry, under the command of Col. H. C. Lilly, with Capt. W. D. Craig. He is a thorough business man, and highly respected by all who know him. He is a prominent member of the Masonic Order at Greenbush. Politically, he is a Republican.

JAMES RANKIN, merchant; P. O. Morning Glory; was born in Nicholas County, Ky., Dec. 6, 1847, to Nicholas and Elizabeth (Fryman) Rankin; he is a native of Nicholas County, she of Harrison, and their parents were among the early settlers of Nicholas County. The result of their union was eight children, of whom James, the subject of this sketch, was the second. He was educated in Nicholas County, and entered upon his career in life as a school teacher, which occupation he followed four years, when he began merchandising at Irvinsville, in partnership with his brother Oscar, and later with his father. He is still engaged in the business, and by his promptness in business relations, and kindly attention to his customers, he has built up a large and steadily increasing trade. He was married in Nicholas County, Nov. 20, 1878, to Miss Emma Lawson, a native of Nicholas County, born in 1859. By this marriage they have two daughters, viz: Maud and Blanche. He is highly respected as a citizen, and in connection with his wife is a member of the Baptist Church at Irvinsville. His political sympathies are with the Democratic party.

JOHN W. SHARP, farmer; P. O. Headquarters; was born in Fayette County, March 11, 1803, and is a son of John T. and Sophia (Nicholson) Sharp, both natives of Sussex Co., Del. The former was born March 26, 1773. His wife, Sophia, was born Jan. 6, 1774. They were among the first to enter upon pioneer life in Kentucky, and settled in Fayette in 1801, where they remained six years, then moved to Nicholas County and were the first settlers on the farm now owned by Benjamin Thomas. A few years later they again sought a new home, this time in St. Louis County, Mo. where Mr. Sharp died, Aug. 3d, 1840. His wife survived him six years and died Nov. 4th, 1847. The result of their union was nine children, of whom John W. our subject, was the fifth, and is now the only one living. He was left in Kentucky by his parents without a relative or friend, and nothing but his hands with which to enter upon the battle of life. His education was very limited, he never having the opportunity to attend school to exceed six months, but being possessed with a stout heart and an energetic spirit, he determined to make his own way in the world. He engaged with Mr. Daniel Thompson as a farm hand, receiving a compensation of ten dollars per month. His persistent energy and strict performance of his duties won him many friends, and when but 19 years of age he was elected to a captaincy in the State Militia. He was married in Nicholas County, March 29, 1832, to Miss Lucy F. Collier, who was born in Charlotte County, Virginia, May 30, 1811. She bore him six children, viz: Elizabeth M. born Dec. 25, 1832. She now lives in Virden, Ill. She was married Feb. 12, 1850, to Willis Sims, who died in 1880. Ann E. was born Nov. 1, 1834, and married in 1854 to Lafayette Rollen, now living in Virden, Ill. John W., born May 28, 1839, died Oct. 30, 1861. Thomas M. born Jan. 5, 1842; a farmer; now living in Nicholas County. He has held the offices of Constable and Magistrate for a number of years. He was married Sept. 15, 1868, to Miss Louisa E. Smith, who was born Feb. 3d, 1844. They have two children, viz: Carrie and Maud. Charles W., born July 17, 1844. (See history.) Ellen M., born Sept. 2, 1848, and died Nov. 17, 1850. Mrs. Sharp died June 20, 1851. She was a daughter of William and Elizabeth (Williams) Collier, both natives of Charlotte County, Virginia. Mr. Sharp was married again Dec. 1, 1857, to Miss Charity C. Baskett, who was born in Nicholas County, Nov. 11, 1827. They have three children, viz: Hamlet C., born Dec. 31, 1858. (See history.) Lucy F., born May 26, 1860. She is a lady of marked ability as a scholar and in art, having produced several works deserving of merit. James Mc., born August 12, 1864. He is still at home, assisting his father on the farm. Mrs. Sharp was a daughter of Jesse and Charlotte (Williams) Baskett. He was born in Virginia, March 30, 1768 and died in March 1833. His wife, Charlotte, was born in Maryland, July 28, 1785, and died Oct. 30, 1881. Mr. Sharp soon after his first marriage, moved upon the farm he now owns, and a part of which he purchased in 1840, since which time he has continued to add to his possessions, until he now owns a farm containing 231 acres, which, "as a practical farmer," he keeps in a high state of cultivation. He has served the county for a number of years in different offices, viz., Constable, Magistrate, Coroner and County Commissioner, and was appointed by the Government as Gauger and Storekeeper, which he subsequently resigned in favor of his son. In 1838, the Whig party substantiated their appreciation of his abilities, and the high esteem in which he was regarded by the people, by electing him to a seat in the Legislature, the duties of which he performed with marked ability, zeal and integrity. On account of his business qualifications, he has been employed numerous times, by large stock dealers to make shipments for them to different parts of the country. He is a man of noble impulses, generous spirit, and noted for his hospitality; is a prominent member of the Masonic Order, and a charter member of the Orient Lodge at Headquarters. He has always been a prominent Republican and the proudest feature of his political career, is the fact that he never asked for an office without receiving it.

GRANVILLE C. SMITH, farmer; P. O. Headquarters; was born in Nicholas County, Ky., Feb. 10, 1843, and is a son of Samuel and Annie (Cook) Smith; he was born in Madison County, Ky., June 20, 1809, is a farmer by occupation, and is still living; his wife, Annie, was a native of North Carolina; they had ten children, of whom Granville, our subject, was next to the youngest; he received his education in the common schools of Nicholas County, and at the Wesleyan College, at Millersburg; he commenced his career in life, as a clerk in a general merchandise store, at Headquarters, but tiring of that, he turned his attention to farming; he was married in Nicholas County, Jan. 13, 1870, to Miss Eva Brooks, who was born in Nicholas County, Nov. 11, 1848;

they have four children, viz: Charlie, Roy, Addie, and Rainie. Mrs. Smith was a daughter of Anderson and Susan (Evans) Brooks, (see hist). Mr. Smith served the county as deputy sheriff and constable, two years each; in connection with his wife, he is a member of the Methodist Church at Mt. Carmel; he is also a prominent member of the Masonic Order at Headquarters; he is one of the most enterprising and energetic men of the county, and held in the highest esteem by the community on account of his hospitable and affable manners; he commenced life a poor man, but owing to his natural business ability and strict attendance to business, has continued to add to his possessions until he now owns a farm containing 240 acres, and keeps the same in a high state of cultivation and well stocked. His political sympathies are with the Democrats.

JAMES A. SMITH, farmer; P. O. Headquarters; was born in Bourbon County, Ky., Jan. 25, 1831, and is a son of William and Jane (McNear) Smith. He was born in Virginia, Sept. 8, 1804, was a farmer by occupation; died April 27, 1871. His wife Jane, was also born in Virginia, Feb. 11, 1802, and is still living. The result of their union was nine children, of whom James was the third. He obtained his education in the common schools of Bourbon County, and commenced his career in life as a farmer. He was married in Nicholas County, Oct. 29, 1873, to Mary S. Kennedy, who was born Oct 9, 1845, and died March 9, 1879, leaving to his care three children, viz: Anna May, Luella and James Kennedy. Mrs. Smith was a daughter of Alfred and Sally (Hillock) Kennedy, (see hist.) Mr. Smith was married again Nov. 25, 1879, to Mrs. Mary E. (Craycraft) Taylor, who was born in April, 1845. By her first husband she had one child: George W., and has borne to Mr. Smith one son: Thomas M. Mrs. Smith was a daughter of Samuel and Mary (Smith) Craycraft, both natives of Kentucky; subject and wife are members of the Christian Church; he is also a member of the Masonic Order of Headquarters. Mr. Smith is an enterprising farmer, and by the close application of his business abilities, has continued to add to his possessions till he now owns 210 acres of choice farm land. In addition to his farm duties, he is engaged extensively in raising stock and trading. He is a good neighbor, a kind husband and indulgent father. He is a Republican.

STILES STIRMAN, farmer; P. O. Headquarters; was born in Harrison County, Ky., Feb. 19, 1841, and is a son of Silas and Nancy (Dills) Stirman. He was born in Nicholas County, Sept. 1, 1809; was a farmer by occupation, and died June 5, 1874. His wife, Nancy, was born in Harrison County, March 1, 1819, and is still living. The result of their union was ten children, of whom Stiles, our subject was the oldest. He attended the common schools of Harrison County, and completed his education in the college at Jacksonville, Ill., where he took upon himself the duties of a farm life. He was married in Harrison County, Dec. 13, 1864, to Miss Mary J. Kennard, who was born near Lexington, La Fayette County, Mo., Feb. 9, 1843. They have four children, viz.: Eliza E., Addie P., Anna P., and Walter B. Mrs. Stirman was a daughter of Hartwell B. and Eliza A. (Brown) Kennard. He was born in Mason County, Ky., March 5, 1816. His wife, Eliza, was born in Harrison County, April 4, 1820; both still living. Mr. Stirman is a thorough business man, an energetic and enterprising farmer, and, socially, ranks very high in the community. He owns eighty-five acres of choice farm land, on the Headquarters and Steel Run Pike. He has been a prominent member of the Masonic Order at Headquarters. His political ideas are Democratic.

WILLIAM S. SMITH, farmer; P. O. Morning Glory; was born to Paterson and Jane (Darnall) Smith, natives of Montgomery County, Ky., Nov. 3, 1816, and was the oldest of ten children. He received a common school education, and in 1838 bought land and entered upon the duties of a farm life. He was married in Nicholas County, Aug. 14, 1845, to Elizabeth Ann, daughter of Thomas and Elizabeth Ann (Collier) Blackmore. Mr. Smith is one of the most prominent farmers in the precinct, and owns a farm containing 140 acres of choice farm land, which he keeps in a high state of cultivation. He was in the employ of the Government two years as Storekeeper, and has also served the county as Magistrate. Although not regularly enlisted into the service, he was connected with the Federal Army in the battle at Cynthiana. He is an energetic and enterprising man, and socially enjoys the esteem of the entire community. In connection with his wife he is a member of the Baptist Church at Irvinsville. Politically he is a Republican.

ELLISVILLE PRECINCT.

B. T. ASBURY, farmer; P. O. Oakland Mills; was born in Harrison County in 1842. His father, Franklin, was born in Nicholas in 1820; he was a farmer, and died Aug. 29, 1862. The maiden name of his mother was Lucinda Mattox, who was born in Nicholas in 1828, and died Oct. 3, 1859; they were the parents of nine children. Our subject was educated in Harrison County and began farming in the fall of 1865; he was married in Nicholas County, Sept. 28, 1865, to Miss Roda J. Mann, who was born May 14, 1848, and was the daughter of John Mann, who died in 1869. At the beginning of the civil war in August, 1861, Mr. Asbury enlisted in company K, Fourth Ky. V. I., U. S. A., and went all through the engagements of the Army of the Cumberland until the close of the war, in 1865. He is the father of eight children, seven of whom are living, viz.: Martha, Ellen, Mary, Thomas, William, Elizabeth, and Minnie. His wife is a member of the Methodist Church at Bald Hill, and in politics he is a Republican and a Mason, being a member of Blue Lick Lodge, No. 495. He is the owner of seventy-three acres of land, on which he produces tobacco, wheat and corn, chiefly.

ABRAHAM S. BARR, farmer; P. O. Ellisville; was born in 1819, son of Robert and Polly Belle Barr; he, a native of Maryland, born April 1, 1784, a farmer, and dying Oct. 10, 1869; she, born August 14, 1790, dying Dec. 8, 1872. They had ten children. Our subject was raised to farming, and is engaged in that occupation at the present time, owning 97 acres of land. He raises some fine trotting stock, in addition to doing general farming. Mr. Barr is an Elder in the Christian Church at Stony Creek, and was liscensed to marry and exhort. He has been a Justice of the Peace since 1866, except about six years, and is at present filling that office. In 1841, in Nicholas County, he married Catharine Sears, born in 1820. Eleven children have been born to Mr. Barr, six of whom are living, viz: Robert, Elizabeth, John J., Mary R., Julia Ann, George W. Mrs. Barr dying in 1855, Mr. Barr married Susan P. Alexander, daughter of George and Mollie Alexander. The last two children named are by the present wife; are members of the Christian Church, and he is a Democrat.

GILBERT FEEBACK, farmer; P. O. Oakland Mills. Among the old and prominent citizens of Ellisville, precint, none stand higher than Mr. Feeback. He was born in Nicholas County, Nov. 11, 1813. His father was of Virginia birth, following the occupation of a farmer all his life, and died in 1872; the maiden name of his mother was Elizabeth Earlywine who died in August, 1862. They were the parents of nine children. Our subject was educated in Nicholas County, and began life with farming, and was married in Nicholas County, Feb. 26, 1835, to Miss Elizabeth Dewitt, who was born May 26, 1812; she being the daughter of Jacob Dewitt, who was born in Pennsylvania, and Elizabeth Mann, who was born in Nicholas County. They have been the parents of nine children, five of whom are still living, viz: Mary, Malinda, Sarah, Margaret and Jonathan. He and his wife are both consistent members of the Baptist Church at Bald Hill, and in politics he is a Republican. He is the owner of 170 acres of fertile land, seven miles from Carlisle, on Cynthiana and Ellisville road.

MRS. HANNORA HOLLAND, farmer; P. O. Ellisville; was of Irish birth, being born in Ireland in 1837. Her father was John Holland, who was born in Ireland and died in 1879. Her mother was Mary Burgoin, who was born in Queens County, Ireland, and died in 1875. They were the parents of nine children. She was married in Mason County, Ky., in 1855; and her husband began life working on public works. The maiden name of Mrs. Holland was Delaney. She is the mother of ten children, seven of whom are living, viz: Michael, John, Mary, Annie, Joseph, Lucy, Serrilda. She is a member of the Catholic Church at Carlisle. She is the owner of 180 acres of land, ten miles from Carlisle, near Cynthiana and Ellisville road.

RALPH LAWRENCE, farmer; P. O. Oakland Mills; was born in Nicholas County, March 10, 1851; son of John and Fidella (Caldwell) Lawrence; he a native of Mason County and she of Nicholas; they had eight children. Our subject, as was his father, was raised to the life of farming, and has continued in that occupation throughout life. He received his education in the schools of his native county, and commenced the battle of life at an early age. He is a member of the Christian Church at Stony Creek; is a democrat, and a member of Blue Lick Lodge.

D. T. MORRIS, Miller; P. O. Ellisville; was born in Bourbon County, Ky., in 1844, son of Captain John and Catharine (Turney) Morris; he, born in Bourbon County in 1793, a farmer, and dying in 1871; she also a native of Bourbon, born in 1803 and still living; they were the parents of fourteen children. Our subject, after receiving an education, began farming in 1868; he owns forty-five acres of land six and one-half miles from Carlisle, on the Maysville Pike, where he raises high-grade stock. He is engaged extensively in milling, running the grist, saw, and shingle mill, built by John Porter in 1876. Mr. Morris is an energetic business man, and a citizen that is highly respected. September 10, 1868, he married, in Nicholas County, Miss Sarah Anderson, daughter of William and Sarah (Kelley) Anderson, natives of Ireland, and four children have blessed his union: W. A., Sarah Catharine, Rebecca Anderson, and James Robinson. Mr. Morris entered the service of the Confederate States, and served as a member of Giltner's regiment, Morgan's command. Is a member of the Christian Church at Blue Licks; is a Mason and a Democrat.

HENRY HARRISON PORTER, farmer; P. O. Oakland Mills; was born in Maysville, Dec. 1st, 1812; his father, Wm. Porter was born May 10, 1784. He was a merchant, and died in Carlisle May 27, 1837. His mother was Hannah Martin; she was born in Virginia August 24, 1791, and died Aug. 10, 1851. They had ten children, only one of whom is now living. Henry Harrison Porter was educated in Nicholas, and was by occupation a farmer. He was married in Mason County, Nov. 5, 1835, to Margaret Davis Mason, who was born Oct 21, 1813; she was the daughter of Samuel Davis, and Nancy; unto the marriage was born three children, all of whom are dead. On June 25, 1846, the subject was united in marriage to Elizabeth Brady, daughter of Patrick Brady. They had two children, named John A. and Henry E. Mr. Porter is identified with the Republican party. Himself and wife are both members of the Christian Church, himself holding the office of Elder. He owns fifty acres of land, six and one-half miles from Carlisle, on Maysville Pike.

F. M. RANKIN, general farmer; P. O. Oakland Mills; was born where he at present resides, June 29, 1848, and is the youngest child born to John and Nancy (McMahill) Rankin. John Rankin, the father of our subject, was born in Lewis County, Ky., May 4, 1804, and was an extensive farmer; he also kept a hotel on the Maysville Pike, for the accommodation of stage travel; he was a highly respected citizen and a member of the Carlisle Lodge of Free Masons; he died July 19, 1870; his wife, Nancy McMahill, was born Aug. 26, 1809, daughter of William and Polly (Curtis) McMahill, all natives of Kentucky. John and Nancy were the parents of eight children. Our subject received a liberal education for the time at Carlisle, and began life as a farmer, following the same to the present time, having a farm of 300 acres well stocked and improved; Dec. 30, 1880, he married Miss Mattie Armstrong, born in Fayette County, June 26, 1855, daughter of James and Elizabeth (McDaniel) Armstrong, natives of Nicholas County; one child has blessed this union, James Wady, born Oct. 30, 1881. Mr. Rankin is a Democrat.

G. W. SIBERT, wagonmaker; P. O. Oakland Mills; was born in Clay County, Ky., Feb. 10, 1822; son of Daniel and Sally Sibert; he, a native of Virginia, who followed boating on the Kentucky river; and she a native of Kentucky; they were the parents of nine children. Our subject received an ordinary education in his native county, and began at an early age to learn the coopering trade. He owns three acres of land, six and one-half miles from Carlisle, on which he has a cooper shop. He has served as Constable for several years. July 27, 1848, he married Mary A. Sadler, born in 1829, daughter of Jessie Sadler, of Bourbon County, and eight children have been born to them, five of whom are living: Johnnie, Sallie, Julia, Mollie and Bobbie. Those dead are Jennie, Joseph aud Mary. Mrs. Sibert is a member of the Baptist Church at Ellisville, and he is a Republican.

THOMAS VAUGHN, farmer; P. O. Blue Licks; was born in Lewis County, Ky., November 10, 1822, son of Thomas and Elizabeth (McDaniel) Vaughn. Thomas Vaughn, senior, came from Pennsylvania at an early day and settled in Lewis County, Ky., where he passed through all the hardships incident to the life of the early pioneer, and where he prospered and died. He was the father of ten children, eight of whom are living. Our subject received the educaton afforded by the schools of his native county, and began life as a farmer, in which occupation he is engaged at present, owning a snug farm of ninety-eight acres. April 2, 1846, he was married in Nicholas County, to Elizabeth Wilson, born in March, 1828, daughter of Thomas and Catharine (Croce) Wilson, of Virginia. His wife is a member of the Christain Church at Stony Creek, and he is a Republican, and a member of Blue Lick Lodge.

JAMES VAUGHN, farmer; P. O. Oakland Mills; was born in Lewis County, Ky., April 23, 1825, son of Thomas and Elizabeth (McDaniel) Vaughn, additional notes of whose life appear in the sketch of Thomas Vaughn, the brother of our subject. Mr. Vaughn began life as a farmer and has so continued throughout life. In 1851, he married in Nicholas County, Miss Mary A. Campbell, daughter of David and Matilda (Wills) Campbell. Mr. Vaughn and wife are members of the Methodist Church, and he is a Republican.

S. G. WASSON, farmer; P. O. Carlisle; was born in Nicholas County, Ky., April 17, 1837, son of Charles J. and Nancy (Waugh) Wasson; he, a farmer and carpenter, dying in 1866, aged sixty-six; she, a native of Nicholas County; they were the parents of seven children. Our subject began life as a farmer, in which he has continued; has served as School Trustee. Sept. 6, 1871, in Carlisle, Mr. Wasson married Miss Pencila McCuan, daughter of Robert and Rachel (Campbell) McCuan; five children have blessed this union, viz: Mollie P., Thomas M., Annie M., Eliza B. and Nancy Ange. Self and wife are members of the Christian Church, and he is a Democrat.

UNION PRECINCT.

WILLIAM S. ATKINSON, farmer; P. O. Moorefield; was born in Nicholas County, Ky., Aug. 2, 1858, and is a son of Albert and Maria (Templeman) Atkinson. He was born in Nicholas County March 12, 1834; was a farmer by occupation, and died April 30, 1864. His wife was born in Bath County Oct. 25, 1840, and is still living. The result of their union was three children, of whom our subject was the eldest. He was educated in the common schools of Nicholas County, and commenced his career in life as a farmer. He was married in Aberdeen, O., Dec. 29, 1877, to Miss Florence Stephenson, who was born in Nicholas County, Ky., Oct. 16, 1857. They have two children, viz: Charles A. and Katie M. Mrs. Atkinson was a daughter of David and Nancy (Bradshaw) Stephenson. He is a native of Nicholas County, and was born Aug. 8, 1827, and is still living. His wife, Nancy, is a native of Bath County, Ky., and was born Oct. 9, 1832. Mr. and Mrs. Atkinson are members of the Christian Church. He is the owner of some fine stock, including some choice grades of sheep. He is an ambitious and enterprising young man, and bids fair to win a high rank in life's race. In politics he is a Democrat.

MINERVA ADAMS, farmer; P. O. Moorefield, was born on the place where she now lives, in Nicholas County, Ky., July 20, 1818, and is a daughter of John and Elizabeth (Kincade) Banister; Mr. Banister the father of our subject, was born in Virginia, June 20, 1791, and died Sept. 22, 1864; his wife was born in Garrett County, Ky., in 1792. The subject of this sketch received a common school education in Nicholas County; was married in Bath County, April 27, 1841, to Samuel Adams, who was born in Nicholas County, Oct. 18, 1818, and died March 28, 1878, leaving to her care four children, viz: Elizabeth, Nancy, Millard and Statire. Mr. Adams was a son of John and Mary (Pinter) Adams, both natives of Nicholas County, Ky. Mrs. Adams is a member of the Presbyterian Church at Moorefield; owns ninety-nine acres of land, which is tilled after her directions; she is a woman of intelligence and well worthy of the high esteem in which she is held by the community in which she lives.

MILFORD BERRY, farmer; Moorefield, was born in Bath County, Ky., near old Springfield Church, Oct. 20, 1817, and is a son of John and Polly (Coons) Berry; he was born in Tennessee, in 1796 was a farmer by occupation, and died April 15, 1867; he was brought to Kentucky by his parents in 1804; his wife Polly, was born in Montgomery County, Ky., in 1799, and died Jan. 15, 1845; the result of their union was nine children, of whom Milford, our subject, was one; he received a common school education in Montgomery County, and commenced his career in life as a farmer; he was married in Montgomery County, March 20, 1839, to Miss Elizabeth Howard, who was born in Montgomery County, in 1822, and died July 15, 1840, she was a daughter of John and Elizabeth (Anderson) Howard, both natives of Montgomery County Ky. Mr. Berry was married again July 7, 1842, to Miss Frances Ann Hendricks, who died July 15, 1851, leaving to his care two children, viz: Mary Frances and Lucy Harriett. Mrs. Berry was a daughter of Levi and Rebecca (Hart) Hendricks, natives of Bath County, Ky. On Aug. 28, 1855, Mr. Berry was married to Eliza Ann Robertson, widow of William Edward Robertson, and daughter of John and Susan (Burroughs) Judy; she was born in Clark County, Dec. 25, 1823; they have three children, viz: James W., Ida and Elizabeth; Mr. Berry is a member of the Christian Church at Bethel, and is also a prominent member of the Masonic fraternity at Carlisle. By his industry and persistant energy, he has accumulated a large property and now has in his posession 360 acres of land, which, being a practical farmer, he keeps in a high state of cultivation, and well stocked; he is highly esteemed by the community, and is a warm advocate of the Democrat party.

ALVIN BRANCH, farmer; P. O. Moorefield; was born in Bath County, Ky., May 22, 1840, to James R. and Sarah (Whaley) Branch. He was born in Bath County June 16, 1816; is a farmer by occupation, and is still living. His wife, Sarah, is also a native of Bath County, born in May, 1819, and is still living. She has borne to him eight children, of whom Alvin, our subject is the second. He received his education in the common schools of Nicholas County, and commenced his career in life as a dry goods clerk at Bethel, where he remained for a period of seven years. He was married in Nicholas County, Sept. 11, 1861, to Miss Lizzie Adams, who was born in Nicholas County July 1, 1842. They have four children, viz: Eliza, Maggie, James and Millard.

Mrs. Branch was a daughter of Samuel and Minerva (Banister) Adams (See history). In 1867, Mr. Branch purchased 100 acres of land, and entered upon the life of a farmer, at which he still continues. He also owns five acres of village property, containing the house in which he now lives. Owing to his persistent energy and careful attention to business, he has gained the good will of the community at large, and has served the people as Deputy County Clerk and Examiner for fifteen years, which position he still holds, conforming to the duties of the office to the full satisfaction of the public with accuracy and dispatch, exhibiting that honor and integrity characteristic of the highest type of manhood. In his political belief, he is a Democrat, and is also a prominent member of the Masonic Order.

SAMUEL HOWE DALZELL, farmer; P. O. Moorefield; was born in Nicholas County, Ky., near where he now lives, May 1, 1837. His father, Robert Dalzell, was born in Nicholas County, in 1798, was a farmer by occupation, and died in 1876. His wife, Catharine Roberts, was born in Montgomery County, Ky., April 4, 1810, and is still living. They had eight children, of whom, Samuel our subject, was the third. He received a common school education, and remained on the homestead with his parents until he was twenty-four years of age, when he commenced farming on his own account. He was married in Nicholas County, Nov. 27, 1860, to Miss Laura A. Wasson, who was born in Nicholas County, May 10, 1844. They have eleven children, viz: Harriett C., Clifton H., Robert W., Cora M., Benjamin F., Jessie N., Joseph W., Anna R., Ettie, Fred and Hollis. Cora died when twelve years of age. Mrs. Dalzell was a daughter of William and Harriet (Stoakes) Wasson. He was born in Bourbon County Ky., May 6, 1804, and died Jan. 2, 1853. His wife, Harriett, was born in Nicholas County, Jan. 29, 1820, and is still living. In October, 1862, Mr. Dalzell enlisted in the Ninth Kentucky Cavalry, under Morgan, and remained in the service till the close of the war. He is an enterprising and energetic business man and a practical farmer; is a member of the Christian Church at East Union. In politics, he is a Democrat.

JOHN B. DURHAM, farmer; P. O. Moorefield; was born in Boyle County, Ky., March 9, 1818, to Benjamin and Margaret (Robertson) Durham. Mr. Durham, Sr., was a native of Virginia, a farmer and blacksmith by occupation, and died in 1847. His wife, Margaret, was also a native of Virginia, and died Feb. 26, 1855. She was the mother of ten children, of whom John B., our subject, was the eighth. He received a common school education in Boyle County, and entered upon the life of a farmer. He was married in Nicholas County Dec. 7, 1840, to Miss Jane Wilson, who was born in the same county, March 27, 1820; she has borne to him three children, viz: Charles W., William A. and Emma W. Mr. and Mrs. Durham are members of the Methodist Church. He is a member of the Masonic Order at Bethel. By his persistent energy he has amassed a goodly amount of this world's goods, and now owns 285 acres of choice farm land, to which he has given the name of Cedar Grove. He is an ambitious and prosperous farmer, always first in every public enterprise, fair and honorable in all his dealings with his fellow men, and prominent for his sterling business qualifications. His political sympathies are Democratic.

JAMES A. DUNCAN, farmer; P. O. Moorefield, was born in Montgomery County, Ky., Feb. 1, 1819, and is a son of Traverse and Lucy (Rogers) Duncan. He was born in Virginia, and died Nov. 26, 1846. Was a farmer by occupation. His wife Lucy was born in Fayette County, Ky., Nov. 26, 1796, and died July 22, 1873. The result of their union was seven children, of which our subject was the second. He received his education in the common schools of Montgomery County, and commenced business for himself as a farmer. On the 17th of July, 1842, he led to the altar Mary Ann Wilson, who was born in Montgomery County, June 13, 1820. They have eight children, viz: Joseph, William, David, John, Granville, George, Susan and Elizabeth. Mrs. Duncan was a daughter of David and Elizabeth (Johnson) Wilson, both natives of Montgomery County. The former died April 29, 1871; the latter, Feb. 8, 1879. Mr. and Mrs. Duncan are members of the Christian Church. He is also a member of the Masonic Order at East Union. He is an energetic and enterprising man and a prosperous farmer, owner of 100 acres of good farm land. In politics is a Democrat.

GEORGE W. GRIMES, farmer; P. O. Moorefield, was born in Nicholas County, Ky., Aug. 30, 1815, to David and Nancy (Clark) Grimes; he was a native of North Carolina, a farmer by occupation, and died in 1832; his wife, Nancy, was born in Nicholas County, Ky., and died in 1864; they reared a family of eight children, of whom our subject was the second; he was educated in the common schools of Nicholas County, Ky., and in the State of Indiana; he commenced his career in life in a saw and grist mill, where he remained eight years, and then turned his attention to farming, which he still follows; he was married in Nicholas County, Ky., May 10, 1843, to Miss Serelda Clark, who was born in Nicholas County, June 3, 1827; by this marriage they have had the following children: Nancy, Thomas, John, Laura, Jerry, William, George, Warner, David, Francis, and Sarah, six of whom are still living. Mr. and Mrs. Grimes are both members of a church, but of different denominations; he is a Presbyterian, she a Methodist; he has thirty-four acres of land, on which he grows the usual farm crops; he is a man, never weary in well doing, looking to the interests of those around him, as well as his own, and is universally held in high esteem by all who know him; in his political ideas he is Democratic.

HUGH GILVIN, farmer; P. O. Moorefield; was born in Virginia March 25, 1810, and is a son of Hugh and Sally (Scott) Gilvin. Mr. Gilvin, the father of our subject, was born in Virginia, and died March 19, 1858; his wife, Sally, was also a native of Virginia, and died in 1852. They emigrated to Adair County, Ky., when our subject was five years of age. He received a common school education, and commenced his career in life as a farmer and teamster; was married Aug. 2, 1840, to Miss Sally Dallas, who was born in Bourbon County, Ky., March 25, 1807. They have one child, Fannie. Mrs. Gilvin was a daughter of William and Elizabeth (Harris) Dallas. He was born in New Jersey, July 11, 1780, and died March 19, 1849. His wife Elizabeth was born in Princeton, N. J., July 6, 1779, and died Dec. 18, 1848. Subject owns 139 acres of land, on which he has lived forty-two years; is highly esteemed by all who know him; is an energetic and enterprising farmer; in politics he is a Democrat.

MRS. SUSAN A. GRAVES, farmer; P. O. Moorefield; was born in Virginia, Nov. 17, 1792, and is a daughter of John and Margaret (Helvy) Breckenridge. Mr. Breckenridge is supposed to have been born in Ireland, and died Aug. 27, 1824; his wife, Margaret, was born in Pennsylvania, and died May 5, 1825. Our subject was educated in the common schools of Kentucky, and was married Sept. 1, 1806, to David A. Graves, who was born in Virginia, Sept. 9, 1781, and died June 6, 1821. They had three children, viz.: Barton, John and Louisa. Mr. Graves was a son of Richard and Sarah (Arnett) Graves, both natives of Virginia. Subject is a member of the Christian Church, owns eighty acres of land, on which she now lives in her declining days, receiving the kindly attentions she merits from her children. Having been a woman of persistent energy, and a life-long Christian, she richly deserves the high esteem in which she is held.

ROBERT T. HILL, physician; P. O. Moorefield, was born in Wilson County, Tenn., Feb. 5, 1838, to Robert and Eliza (Harrison) Hill. Mr. Hill senior, was born in Virginia in 1778, and died in 1850. His wife was born in Wilson County, Tenn., Nov. 29, 1813, and is still living. Of the eight children born to them, Robert, our subject, was the third. He received his education at Lebanon, Tenn., and attended lectures at the Medical University at Nashville, Tenn., during the winter of '59 and '60, and graduated in the hospital service in connection with General Bragg's army, during the late rebellion. He reeived his diploma from the Jefferson Medical College, of Philadelphia, Pa., in 1865, and began the practice of medicine at Howard's Mills, Montgomery County, Ky., the same year, where his thorough knowledge and strict attention to his profession was the foundation of a large practice. He was married in Montgomery County, June 22, 1869, to Miss Mary B. Berry, who was born in the same county, April 7, 1854; she has borne to him five children, viz: Louisa, Mary E., John B., Robert W., and William P. Mrs. Hill was a daughter of John F. and Mary E. (Phelps) Berry. He was born in Montgomery County, Nov. 26, 1832, and is still living. His wife, Mary, was also a native of Montgomery County, born in 1830, and died July 20, 1863. In August, 1872, our subject purchased a house and lot in Moorefield, Nicholas County, where he moved with his family, and is still devoting his time to the duties of his calling in that locality. Outside of his profession he is a man of prominence, and was acting Deputy Clerk of the county for one year. In connection with his wife, he is a member of the Christian Church, at Bethel. He is also a prominent member of the Masonic Order. In politics he is a Democrat.

WILLIAM H. HOWE, merchant; P. O. Moorefield; is a son of Dunlop and Antha (Hall) Howe. He was born in Fleming County, Ky., in January, 1801; was a merchant by occupation, and died June 30, 1852. His wife, Antha, was born in Bourbon County, Ky., and died Aug. 15, 1875. The result of their union was five children, of whom William H., our subject was one. He was born in Nicholas County, Ky., May 14, 1842, received his education at Millersburg, Ky., and commenced his career in life as a merchant at Moorefield, Ky., where he still remains in the business. His pleasing manners, kind attention to customers, and natural business qualifications, have been the means of building up a large and steadily increasing trade. In addition to merchandising, he also deals largely in seeds, general produce and wool, and is post master at Moorefield, which position he has held several years. He was married Dec. 4, 1862, to Miss Mary F. Robertson, who was born Sept. 2, 1844. They have two children, viz: Edna and William D. Mrs. Howe was a daughter of William Edward and Eliza N. (Judy) Robertson. The former was born in Bath County, Ky., March, 1817, and died July 13, 1851. His wife, Eliza, was born Dec. 25, 1824, is still living, and is now the wife of Milford Berry (See Hist.) Mr. and Mrs. Howe are members of the Christian Church at Bethel, Bath County, Ky. Mr. Howe is an energetic and enterprising business man; is a man of noble impulses, generous spirit, and always first in any public enterprises. His political ideas are Democratic.

WILLIAM E. HERNDON, physician ; P. O. Moorefield, Nicholas County; was born at Weston, Nicholas County, Ky., Feb. 21, 1856, to Thomas C. and Miranda J. (Craycraft) Herndon, (see history.) William E., our subject, received a common school education in Bourbon and Nicholas Counties, and in 1876 entered upon a three years course in the Medical University at Louisville, Ky., where his diligence and close attentions to his studies, soon made him a general favorite and placed him at the head of his class, which position he maintained throughout the course, and at the time of receiving his diploma, March 1, 1879, he was one of the number called upon for the honors of the class, which numbered 350. In May of the same year, he located at Moorefield, and entered upon the duties of his profession with the same zeal that characterized all his efforts, and soon gained a position that can only be attained by a thorough knowledge and strict attention to his calling. He has gradually grown in the favor of the community, and now has an extensive practice, the duties of which would fall heavily upon the shoulders of a man many years his senior. During three years practice, he has lost but two patients. He was married Dec. 18, 1879, to Miss Edna A. Howe, who was born in Moorefield, Nicholas County, Ky., Sept. 7, 1863, to William H. and Mary F. (Robertson) Howe, (see history.) Our subject owns the house and lot in Moorefield where he resides. He is a very energetic and enterprising man, and possesses all the natural qualifications necessary in gaining the good will of all. His political ideas are Democratic.

MRS. MARY E. HOWE, farmer; P. O. Moorefield, Nicholas County; was born in Nicholas County, Ky., April 31, 1835, and is a daughter of James and Nancy (Hayden) Thomas; Mr. Thomas was born in Virginia, Nov. 12, 1799, was a farmer by occupation and died June 15, 1873; his wife, Nancy, was born in Nicholas County, Ky., Jan. 6, 1804, and died June 16, 1877. Our subject is the youngest of eight children, she received her education in Nicholas County, was married in the same county, May 16, 1855, to Mr. William W. Howe, who was born in Nicholas County, Jan. 31, 1819, was a farmer by occupation; died Aug. 1, 1871 ; the result of their union was three children, viz: Thomas E., James M. and William R. Mr. Howe, the husband of our subject, was a son of Ezra and Anna (Dalzell) Howe; he was born in Nicholas County, Oct. 7, 1785, was a farmer and school teacher, and died Sept. 26, 1820; his wife Anna, was born Sept. 19, 1792, and died Sept. 6, 1853. The subject of this sketch owns a house and lot in Moorefield, also 258 acres of land situated in Union Precinct, which is cultivated under her own management; she is a member of the Presbyterian Church at Moorefield, is a woman of intelligence, and ranks high in the esteem of the community where she lives.

GEORGE D. KNOX, farmer; P. O. Moorefield; was born in Bourbon County, Ky., Sept. 29, 1831, to David and Rebecca (Baxter) Knox. He was born in Bourbon County, Feb. 13, 1804, was a farmer by occupation, and died Sept. 27, 1879. He was a son of Samuel and Margaret (Donnell) Knox, both natives of Pennsylvania. The former was a pioneer preacher, born in 1775, died in 1865, and a son of David and Hannah (Wasson) Knox, natives of Dublin, Ireland. Rebecca (Baxter) Knox, the mother of our subject, was born in Bourbon County, Ky., Feb. 13, 1804; died Feb. 26, 1848, and was a daughter of Edward and Rebecca (Davis) Baxter. He was born in Maryland, Dec. 5, 1750, and died April 2, 1826. His wife, Rebecca, was born July 12, 1767, and died Jan. 10, 1818. The subject of this sketch was the oldest of seven children; he received a common school education in Nicholas County, and then took upon himself the duties of a farm life. He was married in Nicholas County, Nov. 5, 1856, to Miss Amanda Boardman, who was born in Nicholas County, Sept. 12, 1831. The result of their union was five children, four of whom died while young, and are buried in the old family graveyard, situated on the farm now owned by Abner Boardman. Their only living child is a daughter, Nancy L. Mrs. Knox was a daughter of Abner and Mary (Crose) Boardman. He was born in Bourbon County, April 16, 1801, and died Aug. 29, 1875. His wife, Mary, was also a native of Bourbon County, born Jan. 3, 1806, and died Jan. 30, 1878. In connection with his family, Mr. Knox is a member of the Christian Church at East Union. He has a farm of 186 acres of choice farm land, and devotes his time to growing the usual farm crops and breeding fine stock. He is an energetic and enterprising farmer, prominent in the community for fair and honorable dealings with his fellow men, a kind father and devoted husband. In politics he is a Democrat.

ALLEN MOLLER, farmer; P. O. Sharpsburg; was born on the farm where he now lives, Jan. 27, 1818, and is a son of Joseph and Elizabeth (Welty) Moller. He was born in Georgia, in 1780, and was one of the early settlers in Kentucky, where he died in 1825. His wife, Elizabeth, was born in North Carolina, in 1783, and died in 1870. The result of their union was eleven children. Allen, our subject, was educated in the common schools of Nicholas County, and entered upon his career in life as a farmer. He was married in Bourbon County, Oct. 17, 1867, to Mrs. Matilda Bramblett, widow of Henry Bramblett, and daughter of Covington and Sarah (Crouse) Utterbach. He was born in Virginia, and died July 20, 1864. His wife was born in Bourbon County, and died Jan. 15, 1879. Mrs. Moller was born in Bourbon County, Aug. 19, 1830. Mr. Moller is a member of the Christian Church at Sharpsburg; has also been a prominent member of the Masonic order for a number of years. He owns a farm of seventy-five acres, and is an energetic and enterprising farmer. He is a Republican.

JESSE B. POTTS, farmer; P. O. Moorefield, Nicholas County; was born in Nicholas County, Ky., Aug. 30, 1839, and is a son of Henry and Lorana (Alexander) Potts. The father of our subject was born in North Carolina, Sept. 6, 1790; was a farmer by occupation, and died Dec. 24, 1872. For further information see history of Robert W. Potts. His wife, Lorana, is a native of Nicholas County, Ky., born in January, 1813, and is still living. The subject of this sketch was educated in Nicholas County, and commenced his career in life as a school teacher, and later turned his attention to farming. He was married Dec. 22, 1874, to Miss Ellen Ferguson, who was born in Lewis County, Ky., Feb. 24, 1854. They have two children, viz: Roger F. and Nimrod S. Mrs. Potts was a daughter of Birthod and Eliza (Crosby) Ferguson. He was born in Montgomery County, Ky., June 11, 1814, and is still living. His wife, Eliza, was born in Ripley, Ohio, and died in 1861. In 1879 Mr. Potts was elected Assessor in Nicholas County, which office he still holds. In connection with his wife he is a member of the Christian Church. His farm contains ninety acres of good farm land, and in addition to raising general farm crops, he breeds a choice grade of sheep. The appearance of his farm and stock indicates the careful attention they receive, proving him to be a man of energy and enterprise, and well worthy of the high esteem in which he is held. He is a Democrat. His brother, Nelson F. Potts, is also a prominent young farmer. He was born in Nicholas County, Oct. 29, 1852. In order to add to the stock of knowledge he obtained in the common schools of Nicholas County, he also attended Center College, at Danville, Boyle County, Ky., after which he took upon himself the duties of a farm life on the old homestead, and the support of his widowed mother. He has a farm of 70 acres; he is ambitious and industrious, and socially, ranks very high. In politics he is a Democrat.

CALEB RATLIFF, Jr., farmer; P. O. Moorefield; was born in Caldwell County, Ky., Feb. 25, 1818, and is a son of Joseph and Keziah (Stone) Ratliff. Mr. Ratliff, the father of our subject, was born in Virginia, Nov. 23, 1783; was a carpenter and farmer by occupation, and died Oct. 5, 1827, and was a son of Zephaniah and Philadelphia (Stone) Ratliff, the former supposed to have been born in England, Feb. 25, 1753, and died June 8, 1831; the latter born in Virginia. The mother of our subject was born at Boonesboro, Ky., and died in 1862, leaving a family of 11 children, of which our subject was the sixth; received his education in the common schools of Bath County, Ky.; at the age of fourteen he hired out as a farm hand, and continued in that manner for ten years, when he purchased 48 acres of land in Bath County of James Moffet, on the condition that he should pay for the same in hemp, at the rate of 800 lbs to the acre, which he succeeded in doing in the specified time. On Feb. 2d, 1842, he was married to Miss Elizabeth Whaley, who was born in Bath County, Ky., April 7, 1825, and died Sept. 20, 1846, leaving to his care two children, viz.: Mary L. and Enos B., the latter of whom died fifteen months after birth. Mrs. Ratliff was a daughter of James and Margaret (Cannon) Whaley; the former a native of Virginia, the latter of Kentucky, and both still living. Mr. Ratliff was again married on July 2, 1847, to Miss Elizabeth Baird, who was born on Bethel Ridge, Bath County, Ky., Jan. 31, 1830. They have had nine children, viz.: Samuel J., Arrilla, Henry C., Leander C., Wallace B., John W., Charles, Eldred D., Kate and Caleb C. Samuel, the eldest, died at the age of 16. Mrs. Ratliff was a daughter of ——. Ratliff and Sally (Harden) Baird. He is a native of Bath County, and still living. His wife Sally was born in Virginia, and died in September, 1859; Mr. Ratliff is entirely a self-made man, having by his energy and industry, accumulated 400 acres of land, originally known as "Old John Carter's store stand," which has been in his possession 22 years. He is now engaged in farming and handling mules, the latter in partnership with two of his sons. He is a member of the Baptist Church, at Poplar Grove, Bath County. His wife is also a member of the same church. Mr. Ratliff is an enterprising and prosperous farmer, and is held in high esteem by all who know him. He is a Democrat in politics.

JOHN NEWTON REED, farmer; P. O. Moorefield; was born in Bourbon County, Ky., Oct. 25, 1834, to George and Livinia (Dean) Reed; he was born in Bourbon County, Nov. 5, 1804, and died March 7, 1868; was a physician by profession; he was married in Clark County, Nov. 22, 1826, to Miss Livinia Dean, who was born Feb. 18, 1805, died June 30, 1835; she was the mother of five children, of whom the subject of this sketch was the youngest. He obtained his education in the common schools of Bath and Nicholas Counties, and entered upon his career in life as a farmer. During the Rebellion he served two years in the Confederate service with Capt. Neal, under John Morgan's command. He was married in Hendricks County, Ind., Sep. 22, 1857, to Miss Asenath C. Wilson; who was born in Montgomery County, Ky., March 3, 1836. The result of their union is ten children, viz: Mary E., George, Livinia U., Kate, John W., Henry, Belle, Josiah, Elizabeth, and Emma. Mrs. Reid was a daughter of Uriah and Mary (Gillespie) Wilson; he was born in Bath County, in September, 1804, died in October, 1838; she was born in Montgomery County, Dec. 11, 1812, and is still living. Mr. Reed ranks high among the prominent farmers of the county, and enjoys the esteem of the entire community. He is a thorough business man and a practical farmer, and owns a fine farm of 207 acres, near East Union, on Summerset Creek. Himself and wife are members of the Christian Church at East Union. He is also a prominent member of the Masonic Order of the same place. Politically he is a Democrat.

WALLACE B. RATLIFF, Merchant; P. O. Moorefield, Nicholas Co., was born in Bethel, Bath County, Ky., Feb. 6, 1855, and is a son of Caleb and Ellen (Baird) Ratliff. (See Hist.) Aside from his common school education, our subject attended school two years at Lebanon, Ind. In February, 1875, he opened a general merchandising store at Moorefield, where his natural business ability, strict attention to business, and his courteous and obliging treatment of customers, soon won him the highest esteem of the community, which is now manifested by his largely increasing trade. He was married in Moorefield, Sept. 21, 1876, to Miss Amanda B. Howe, who was born in Flemingsburg, Nov. 9, 1858, and died Jan. 18, 1880, leaving to his care their only child, Amanda B. Subject is a member of the Christian Church at Bethel, and is also a member of the Masonic Order at East Union. He is an energetic and enterprising business man, and well worthy of the high esteem in which he is held. His political ideas are Democratic.

S. F. STONE, farmer; P. O. Moorefield; born in Bourbon County, Jan. 6, 1832. His grandfather, James Stone, was raised probably in Jessamine County, and married in Bourbon County, Annie Talbert. His maternal grandfather, Hugh Forgey, of Ireland, came very early to Bourbon County, and settled near North Middletown, where he engaged in farming. Asa L. Stone, the father of our subject, was a native of Bourbon County, where he died in 1853, after a useful and well spent life; he had been married twice, the first time to Elizabeth Forgey, who died in 1836, and the second time to her sister, Ludice Forgey. Our subject was raised on the farm, receiving a common school education. On Jan. 9, 1854, he married Sarah J. Potts, daughter of William and Elmira (Hall) Potts, of Nicholas County. They have had seven children, six of whom are living: Robert married Ida Berry; Fannie married John McCray, of Bourbon; Charlie, Lulie, Gano, Walter, William died in infancy. Mr. and Mrs. Stone are both members of the Christian Church at Bethel in Bath County. In politics he was a whig till the outbreak of the Civil War, since which time he has been a Democrat. He has been a farmer and trader for twenty years in cattle and hogs, and is a partner of J. R. McVey in the horse and mule trade.

ANDREW THOMPSON, blacksmith; P. O. Moorefield; was born in Nicholas County, Ky., Feb. 9, 1846, to Pierson M. and Cynthia Ann (Grass) Thompson. He was born in Ohio, March 26, 1811; was a blacksmith by occupation; and died May 26, 1867. His wife, Cynthia, was born in Virginia, Feb. 14, 1815, and is still living. The fruits of their union were eleven children, of whom our subject was the fourth. He was educated at Mt. Olivet, Robinson County, Ky. He commenced the battle of life in a saw and grist mill, where he continued six years; he then turned his attention to farming, and followed the same three years, when he followed in his father's footsteps, and took up the trade of blacksmithing and carriage-making. His persistent energy, careful attention to business, and superior workmanship, soon won him scores of friends, and was the means of building up a large business, at which he still continues, and now owns a house and lot, and a large shop, situated in Moorefield. He was married in Bath County, Ky., March 30, 1871, to Mary Ann Purvis, who was born in Ireland, Feb. 17, 1854. She has borne him four children, viz.: John B., Mary, Lela and Lenora. Mrs. Thompson was a daughter of John and Mary Ann (Holland) Purvis. He was a native of England;

his wife was born in Ireland, and is still living. During the late rebellion, Mr. Thompson joined Company E, 10th Ky. Cavalry, in Morgan's division, and remained in the service three years. He is a member of the Christian Church, at Bethel, Bath County, and is also a member of the Masonic Order at the same place. He is an enterprising business man, a skillful mechanic, and is highly esteemed by the community at large. He is a Democrat.

ERASMUS THOMAS, farmer; P. O. Moorefield; was born in Nicholas County, Ky., May 18, 1826, to James and Nancy (Hayden) Thomas; he to Erasmus and Lydia (Fishback) Thomas, in Virginia, Nov. 12, 1799, and died Jan. 5, 1873. Nancy, his wife, was born in Bourbon County, Jan. 6, 1804, and died June 16, 1877. She was the mother of seven children, of whom Erasmus, our subject, was the oldest. His education was limited to such as could be obtained in the common schools of that early day. He began his career in life as a farm hand, and by his energy and economy earned and saved money, with which he purchased fifty acres of land, which he sold two years later and bought 130 acres. He traded extensively in young cattle, and, as he expresses it, made the most of his property by the use of blue grass. He was married in Nicholas County, Jan. 24, 1850, to Miss Elizabeth Boardman, who was born in Nicholas County, Sept. 12, 1828. They have six children, viz: Mary L.; Nancy L., wife of William Gore; Amanda F., wife of E. Ralls; James A., William and Erasmus. Mrs. Thomas was a daughter of Abner and Mary (Crose) Boardman, natives of Bourbon County. He was born April 16, 1801; died Aug. 29, 1875. She was born Jan. 3, 1806; died Jan. 30, 1878. Mr. Thomas is one of the most prominent and enterprising farmers in the precinct, and owns 500 acres of choice farm land, which, as a practical farmer, he keeps in a high state of cultivation, well stocked and well seeded with blue gràss, which his father was the first to bring into notice and use, in the region of Summerset Creek, in the year 1828. Mr. Thomas was at one time a prominent member of the Grange. Politically he is a Republican.

UPPER BLUE LICKS PRECINCT.

M. R. CLAY, farmer; P. O. Moorefield; born in Nicholas County, Sept. 20, 1838. His maternal grandfather, Lewis Arnold, served as Circuit Clerk for about twenty-five years under the old constitution; died about 1850 having attained a good old age. John Clay, father of M. R., was born in Fayette County, near Boonesborough; was a successful farmer and trader; came to Nicholas when about twenty-two years of age, and married Mary, daughter of Lewis Arnold. Served as Sheriff of Nicholas County for a number of years under the old constitution; was elected the first Sheriff of the county under the new constitution, and served two years as Deputy for an additional term. He died in November, 1875; aged about sixty-nine. M. R. Clay, whose sketch is here recorded, was raised a farmer. He married first Mary, daughter of George Campbell, of Fleming County, by whom he had seven children, six of whom survive, viz: John W., aged fifteen; Charles, fourteen; Matthew, ten; Silas, eight; Virgil, seven; Lizzie, six. He married the second time Lizzie, daughter of Andrew and Sallie (Highland) Shrout, of Nicholas. Has one child, Oliver S., aged three years. Mr. Clay is a dimitted member of Daugherty (Masonic) Lodge at Carlisle, and a thorough Democrat. Mrs. Clay is a member of the Christian Church at Mt. Zion.

R. J. COLLIVER, farmer; P. O. Moorefield; born in Nicholas County, Ky., May 1, 1855. His grandfather, James Colliver, came from Pennsylvania at an early day and settled in Montgomery County. His father, Elijah Colliver, was born in Montgomery County; farmer; moved to Nicholas after his marriage with Nancy Johnson; died in Nicholas aged sixty-three. R. J. Colliver was raised in Nicholas; farmer; married Fannie, daughter of Edwin Nichols of same county. Has one child, Eddie B., born Jan. 19, 1880. Mr. Colliver has been a member of Fitchmonger (Masonic) Lodge for four years. Himself and wife are members of the Christian Church at Mt. Zion. In politics he is a Democrat.

G. C. FARIS, farmer; P. O. Moorefield; is a native of Madison County, Ky., where he was born Oct. 12, 1827. His ancestors were of Scotch-Irish descent, emigrating to Virginia very early in the history of that State. In 1780 his grandfather, Michael Faris, came to Kentucky and settled on the waters of Silver Creek in Madison County, where he engaged in farming, dying at an early age. Michael Faris, Jr., the father of our subject, was born in Madison County in 1789; was a soldier of the war of 1812, was in the battle of Dudley's Defeat; had two brothers in same war, Isaac and Dudley, the latter captain of a company. In 1815 Michael Faris married Lucy, daughter of John Herndon of Madison. His death occurred at the age of sixty-eight. G. C. Faris was raised in Madison County upon his father's farm, beginning his medical education in his brother's office. In 1848 he moved to Bath County, and there on the 16th of May of that year he married Nancy L., daughter of Dewey B. and Lydia (Jones) Boyd, who died childless. In 1851 he moved to Nicholas County; attended two courses of lectures at the Cincinnati Medical Institute in 1852–55; practiced medicine for one year, and then went to farming, which he has followed to the present time. On the 20th of May, 1868, he married Elizabeth J., daughter of Wm. B. and Elizabeth P. (Whisner) Hopkins, of Nicholas County. In 1855 he was elected on the American ticket to represent Nicholas County in the Legislature, and served one term. Mr. Faris has been a member of the Masonic Order since coming of age, and for twenty-five years has been a member of R. A. Chapter at Carlisle. Politically he is a warm supporter of the Democratic party.

JAMES GARRETT, farmer; P. O. Moorefield; was born in Montgomery County, May 18, 1832; his grandfather of same name was a native of Virginia, whence he emigrated very early, being one of the first settlers of Montgomery County. He was a soldier in the Revolutionary war for Independence, and lived to the advanced age of one hundred and ten years, a lease of life seldom enjoyed by men of the present day. Sanford Garrett, father of our subject, was also a native of Virginia, having been born in that State in 1795. He married Nancy Reed, of Kentucky, who is still living in her seventy-eighth year. They raised ten children, all of whom obtained their majority. James Garrett married in Montgomery County, Jan. 17, 1855, Miss Mary Call, daughter of William Call and Mary Beckett, of Bourbon County. Six children have been born to them, named respectively: Eliza B., Nannie J., Horace B., Sarah, Joseph, and Eudora. Mr. and Mrs. Garrett are members of the Baptist Church at Poplar Plains, in Bath County; in politics he is a Democrat.

JOHN HERRIN, High Sheriff of County, and farmer; P. O Carlisle; was born near North Middletown, Bourbon County, March 20, 1826. His father was Thomas Herrin, who was born in Virginia, in 1793, and at an early day settled in Bourbon County; he was a farmer by occupation, and died in 1853. The mother was a Miss Sarah Douglas, a native of Tennessee, where she was born, in 1795; her death occurred at about 70 years of age, having been the mother of 11 children, two sons and two daughters, who are now living. Mr. Herrin received his education at the primitive log school house of that day, upon the subscription plan; the time, however, of his attendance upon even those meagre facilities, was about ten months. After arriving at maturity he attended school for a short time, and utilized his spare moments in study, which yielded him a practical education. He started in life a poor boy, choosing agriculture as his life avocation, and by energy and industry he has made for himself a home, and has won the esteem and confidence of the men of his county, who in 1876 elected him to the office of Deputy Sheriff, which he held two terms; his first election was by one majority over a large number of candidates; the second election by 450 majority. In 1880 he was a candidate for High Sheriff, and receiving a majority of 44 votes, was declared elected. He was married September 13, 1853, in Nicholas County, to Amanda J. Blount, who was born in Nicholas County in August, 1835, to Wm. and Lucinda (West) Blount, who were very early settlers at Lexington, and the Blounts old residents of Nicholas County. By this marriage there are 8 children:—Sarah A., wife of John C. Blount; Lucinda F., wife of R. B. McVey; Margaret, wife of Wm. H. Bevard; Wm. T., James S., Mary E., Daniel and Leora. He is a member of the Grange, a Democrat politically, and with his family, is connected with the Christian Church.

PRESTON KENDALL, farmer; P. O. Blackhawk; was born in Bath County, April 17, 1841. His ancestors originally came from England. Sandford Kendall, his father, was a native of Culpepper County, Va., whence he emigrated to North Carolina, thence to Bath County, Ky., where he died in June, 1878. Our subject was one of ten children, and received a limited education. On the 20th of December, 1873, he married Miranda Swart, daughter of Amos and Sarah Swart, by whom he has one child, Lettie, a bright girl of six summers. At the outbreak of the civil war, then in his twentieth year, he enlisted in the United States army, under Col. Grigsby; he was in the several engagements of Pittsburg Landing, Shiloh, Knoxville, Resaca, Perryville, etc. At Knoxville he was wounded in the shoulder. He is a Republican in politics. His wife is a member of Humphrey's Chapel, on Cassidy Creek.

J. R. McVEY, farmer; P. O. Moorefield; born in Nicholas County Nov. 9, 1829. His ancestors originally came from Scotland; his grandfather died in Virginia. John McVey, the father of our subject, was born in Virginia, and when quite a small boy came out to Kentucky, traveling most of the way on a pack-horse; he settled in Nicholas County, where he married Sallie Perrin; they raised a family of nine children. His brother, James McVey, was a soldier of the war of 1812, and is now living in Indianapolis. J. R. McVey was the seventh child of his parents, and spent his early life upon a farm, where he also engaged to some extent in trading. On the 12th of October, 1854, he married Lydia McClary, daughter of Robert and Fannie (Summers) McClary, of Mason County. Four children have been born to them; Charles (deceased) married Miss Fannie Hawkins; Robert married Miss Willie Conway; Sallie married Charles M. Hopkins, of Bourbon County, who died June, 1877; and Fannie. Mr. McVey is a member of the Masonic Lodge at Carlisle, and himself and family are members of the Christian Church at Mt. Zion. Till the war he was a supporter of the Whig party, and his suffrage is now exercised in the interest of the Democrats. For many years he has engaged in trading South, and by industry and diligent attention to business has acquired quite a handsome property. His early education was of the most limited character, having learned to read and write from his wife and children. His father before him was a trader and stock driver, having piloted 1,600 head of stock to Mexico during the Mexican war.

CHARLES T. NEAL, farmer; P. O. Davidson; was born in Nicholas County, Dec. 9, 1836. His grandfather, John Neal, came from Virginia about 1820, and settled in Bath County, as a farmer; he died in Nicholas about 1845, aged eighty. Henry Neal, father of Charles T., came from Virginia when sixteen years of age; married Martha Powell, now living in Nicholas, aged seventy-eight. Charles T. Neal married, Oct. 24, 1861, Helen C., daughter of Thomas and Kitty (Wilson) Vaughan; he has four children: Pickett B., aged seven; Nora V., five; James W., three, and Addie H., one. He served one month with John Morgan in the late war; he is a member of Fitchmonger (Masonic) Lodge, in which organization he holds the position of Secretary. Himself and wife are members of the Christian Church at Mt. Zion, and politically he is a Democrat.

THOMPSON S. PARKS, farmer. The history of Nicholas County would be incomplete without a sketch of this, the oldest resident representative of a family that has figured in the history of the county for nearly a century. His grandfather, John Parks, came to Pennsylvania from the North of Ireland, about the year 1740, being at that time about seven years of age; he married a Miss Galbreath, who was of Scotch birth, and who bore him six children, five sons and one daughter. He was a tailor by trade; served throughout the Revolutionary War; came to Kentucky in 1788, and settled at the mouth of Steele's Run, near Millersburg. James Parks, the father of our subject, was born in Pennsylvania, May 6, 1763; came to Kentucky in 1788, having married in Pennsylvania, Miss Jane Entrikin, of a very old and noted Scotch family. Before he became of age, he was sent to carry some clothing to his father in the Revolutionary war, and did not return till the close of the war. Upon his arrival in Kentucky, he settled at the mouth of Steele's Run, where he remained for a short time. Moved to Carlisle in 1800, and engaged in farming and distilling; removed to Licking River in 1804, locating at what is now termed Park's Ferry, where he engaged in milling, pork packing and general merchandising (see history of Fleming Creek and Cassidy Creek Mills). He was a man of remarkable business capacity, and did more perhaps, than any other man of his day in developing the natural resources of his county. He was not without political honor, having been elected by the people of Bourbon County, to the Lower House of the General Assembly, in 1798. He was in the Senate from Fleming County continually, from 1806 to 1822, and was once afterward in the Legislature from Nicholas, and once in the Senate from Nicholas and Bracken. He died May 6, 1836, aged exactly seventy-three years. T. S. Parks, whose portrait appears in this work, was born and raised where he now resides, at Park's Ferry. Received his early education at the academy in Paris, under the instruction of Ebenezer Sharp; was a fair English, and at that day considered a good Latin scholar. Upon leaving the academy, he taught school for a couple of years. In 1828, he hired himself to George Robinson, to manage a drove of hogs to Richmond. In 1831, in connection with John N. Congleton, he purchased a half interest in the store of his brother-in-law, John Carter, at Gill's Mills, in Bath County; he afterwards located at his present farm, a magnificent estate of some 300 acres. In his seventy-seventh year, as President of the Washington Manufacturing and Mining Company, he assumes a great part of the labor in managing their extensive business. Our subject was the eighth son and eleventh of fourteen children. On the 11th of January, 1838, he married Elizabeth Ingram Dorsey, daughter of John and Nancy Spires Dorsey, of Fleming County. They have four children, all living, viz: Nancy Jane, Nancy Pickett, married Rev. Joseph M. Scott, from Virginia, now living in Waverly, Missouri; Cora B. married James T. Layman, prominent hardware merchant of Indianapolis, Ind., of the firm of Layman & Cary; John Steele married Elizabeth Howell, of Carlisle. Col. Parks represented Nicholas and Fleming Counties in the Legislature, in 1851 and 1853; elected again in 1867, and served two years, at which time he secured an appropriation of $75,000, to pay for and remove the dams from Licking River, and thus cleared it for navigation. Had his views upon this subject been carried out, it would no doubt have been of great benefit to the counties lying adjacent to that stream. Mr. Parks is a thorough Democrat. He claims the Presbyterian Church as his choice, in which his father held the office of elder for forty years, and of which all his family are members.

JOHN B. SHANNON, farmer; P. O. Blackhawk; was born in Nicholas County, Nov. 27, 1827; he is a son of Robt. Shannon, who was raised in Kentucky; was farmer, trader, and merchant, and died Oct. 4, 1877, and Frances Berry, daughter of Col. Robert Berry, who took an active part in the early struggles with the Indians. John B. Shannon was one of ten children; he received a limited education in Nicholas County, and up to the present time has devoted his attention to farming. He married, Feb. 2, 1851, Elmira Campbell, daughter of Joseph and Elizabeth (Robinson) Campbell, of Nicholas County. They have had ten children, six of whom survive: Robert, Emerson W., John W., Samuel, Thomas J., and Mary F. Mr. Shannon is a Republican in politics, and his wife is a member of the Christian Church at Mt. Zion.

T. M. TOUT, farmer; P. O. Davidson; born in Hendricks County, Ind., Dec. 4, 1833. His great-grandfather was an Irishman, and marrying an English lady, they came to Kentucky and settled in Fleming County. Basil Tout, grandfather of T. M., was born in Fleming County, and was a soldier of the war of 1812. His son, Abram Tout, was also in that war. Basil Tout was a bricklayer and farmer; moved to Indiana in 1833, and died in that State about 1854. Andrew Tout, father of our subject, was born in Fleming County; married Rebecca Powell; sold out in 1833 and moved to Indiana. Taught school for several years; served for several years as Constable, and afterwards elected Sheriff of Hendricks County. He also served as Assessor of same County from 1854 till the war; elected Captain of a Militia Company, and died in Indiana, 1880, aged seventy. T. M. Tout was raised in Indiana as a farmer, also learning the trade of engineer and surveyor. He came to Kentucky in 1858 and ran a sawmill in Fleming County. Came to the Upper Blue Licks in 1858, and in Sept., 1859, married Martha Ann, daughter of Elijah Colliver of Montgomery County. Has nine children, all of whom are living; named respectfully, Nannie R., John T., Andrew E., Sarah E., George, Hattie L., Mary A., Fannie R., and Willie A. He had four brothers in the late war, three of whom were in the Union army and one, John L., in the Southern army under Humphrey Marshall. Mr. Tout has been a member of Fitchmonger (Masonic) Lodge for nine years. Both himself and wife are members of the Christian Church at Mt. Zion. Politically he is a Democrat.

H. C. THROCKMORTON, farmer; P. O. Pleasant Valley Mills; born in Nicholas County, Dec. 21, 1830. His great grandfather came from Virginia and settled on Johnson Creek. His grandfather, John I. Throckmorton, came also from Virginia when quite a youth. The father of our subject, also named Jno. I., was raised in Nicholas County, farmer, died in May, 1853; his wife, Lucy Holladay, survived him two years. H. C. Throckmorton received most of his education from the academy at Millersburg, under the tutorage of Richard Todd and other teachers of that day. March 11, 1852, he married in Nicholas County Parmelia, daughter of Grayson and and Ellen (Cook) Hughes of Nicholas County. They have two children, Ellmore and Robert. Mr. Throckmorton, has devoted his life to agricultural pursuits and by industry and economy has acquired quite a handsome estate; his farm contains some 400 acres in Nicholas County, most of it located in Pleasant Valley, and unexcelled in point of fertility. He is an ardent Democrat; his wife is a member of the Christian Church at Stony Creek.

T. W. VAUGHAN, farmer; P. O. Davidson; born in Fleming County, April 14, 1848. His grandfather, James Vaughan, was raised in Nicholas County; farmer, died about 1830. Thomas Vaughan, father of T. W., born and raised near the Upper Blue Licks; farmer, died June 20, 1873. T. W. Vaughan married Feb. 2, 1873, Fanny, daughter of John and Lucinda (Chrisman) Clark, of Fleming County. He is the father of two children, one of whom, Willie T., died in infancy, the other is still living, a bright boy of two summers. Mr. Vaughan is part owner of the Upper Blue Licks Mill, a history of which appears elsewhere. He is a member of Fitchmonger (Masonic) Lodge. Himself and wife are members of the Christian Church at Mt. Zion. Politics, Democrat.

WM. S. WILLS, farmer; P. O., Moorefield; born in Montgomery County, Oct. 31, 1824. His grandfather, Wm. Wills, came from Virginia about the year 1800, and settled on the waters of Slate Creek in what is now Menifee County, where he devoted his attention to farming. He was a man quite noted in military history, though his humbler positions have made him less famous than many whose deeds are no more worthy of record. He began his soldier life under Gen. Braddock when only thirteen years of age, and was a witness of the disastrous failure of that haughty commander. He bore an honorable part in the war of the Revolution, and when we were involved with England a second time in 1812, he did not consider himself too old to render all assistance in his power—serving under Gen. St. Clair, of whom he was an ardent admirer. He died in Menifee County about 1836. Wm. S. Wills, the subject of this sketch, was the oldest of seven children. His opportunities for obtaining an education in youth were very limited, having been compelled to work to support himself and mother till he was twenty-six years of age. In 1850 he married Eliza, daughter of Robert and Sarah (Whaley) Stone, of Bath County, by whom he has seven children, all living, namely: J. C., John S., Albert M., Louisa, Leroy, Laura and L. W. At the time of his marriage, according to his own statement, he had but fifteen cents left after paying his fee. He bought 500 acres of land on Slate Creek for $900, and by almost superhuman exertion, managed to pay for the same within four years, teaching school and working for wages during the day and working on his house at night. At the outbreak of the Civil war, he was led into a debate with a Methodist preacher upon the subject of slavery, from which time he was marked as a rebel. His location between the Union troops and the lawless raiders who took refuge in the mountains of Kentucky, was an unfortunate one for him. He was elected Captain of a company, but was soon captured by order of Col. Wm. Craig and thrown into prison at Mt. Sterling. He took the oath and endeavored to live a citizen, but his well known political principles made him a target for those in power. His thrilling adventures and hair-breadth escapes during that four years would fill a volume in itself, and need not be detailed here. In June, 1862, he bought the store and stock of goods of L. M. Stone, at Bald Eagle, in Bath County, for $3,500, and carried on a good trade for a while. In 1863 the store was robbed and he moved to Little Flat, in Bath County, on Licking river. In the course of three or four years he accumulated sufficient to purchase his present farm of 120 acres, where he has resided since. In 1869, he was elected Magistrate of his precinct, and served four years, refusing a re-election. He is a member of the Chapter (Masonic) Lodge at Carlisle, was also elected President of the Grange Council during its existence. He is a sterling Democrat, and with his wife is in communion with the Christian Church at Mt. Zion.

JOSEPH B. WOODS, farmer; P. O. Moorefield; was born in Nicholas County, Dec. 6, 1825; his great grandfather probably came from Ireland to Virginia, thence to Kentucky, before the Revolutionary war, and entered land in Mercer and Jessamine Counties; returned to Virginia and died. Thomas Woods, grandfather of Joseph B., came to Kentucky in 1784, and settled in Jessamine County, living for a time in Wilson's Station. He served as an independent scout in the Revolution for five years; died in 1845, aged eighty-four. Joseph Woods, father of our subject, was born in Wilson's Station, July 7, 1784; moved to Nicholas County in 1815; married, the second time, Dorcas Buckhanan, daughter of George Buckhanan; he left nine children, three of whom are living. Joseph B. Woods, of whom we write, was raised a farmer. On Sept. 12, 1868, he married Margaret, daughter of L. A. and Elizabeth (Huddleson) Brown, of Bath County; has no children; he served during the late war as an independent skirmisher, principally to suppress horse thieving; is a member of the Presbyterian Church at Moorfield, in which he has served as Elder since 1870; has been President of the Moorfield and Upper Blue Licks Turnpike Company since its organization in 1866. In politics he was an old-line Whig till the Rebellion, since which time he has been in sympathy with the Republican party.

DAVID WILSON, farmer; P. O. Davidson; born near Lexington, Ky., Nov. 19, 1790. His father, Jeremiah Wilson, and his mother, Katie Cooper, were both from the State of New Jersey. They were among the first to brave the dangers of the Western wilderness, taking their share of the hardships common to the early pioneers of this land of cane. David Wilson was reared on a farm. He suffered in his youth an attack of the white swelling, which made him a cripple for life. His education, like that of most of his contemporaries, was of a very limited character. He married, in Bourbon County, in 1815, Sarah, daughter of William and Cassander (Tippet) Newman; has eight living children: William, Matilda, Abbie, Ephraim, Sophia, Joseph, David and Kitty Ann. Mr. Wilson is now the oldest man in this precinct, and has for many years filled the eldership of Mt. Zion Christian Church. His political suffrage is exercised in behalf of the Democratic party.

ADDENDA.

Biographies too Late for Insertion in Proper Place.

PARIS—Bourbon County.

HENRY CLAY, deceased, whose name stands among the list of the first pioneers of Bourborn County, and whose portrait appears in this history, was born in Virginia, Sept. 14, 1779, and was the son of Henry and Rachael Clay. He came to Kentucky in 1787 with his parents, who settled in Bourbon County. He spent his early youth on his father's farm, and acquired such education as the school system of the time afforded. He engaged in business for himself at the age of eighteen years at growing tobacco. He was a very successful financier and energetic worker, and left at his death a farm to each of his eleven children. He was also extensively engaged in the stock business. He was a man of strong mind, and took more or less an active part in the political issues of the day, and was honored by being elected a member of the State Senate of Kentucky. During the war of 1812 he served under Gen. Harrison as a second lieutenant. When eighteen years of age he was married to Miss Peggy Helm, of Lincoln County, Ky., who was the daughter of Joseph Helm, who, with a party of settlers, came to Kentucky in an early day, and on their way were attacked by a band of Indians and nearly all killed. Twelve children were born to them, one of whom died in infancy, viz.: Henry, John, Sally, Joseph H., Letitia, Henrietta, Rebecca (died in infancy), Elizabeth, Samuel, Mary, Francis and Matt. Henry Clay was a man of religious principles and a member of the Primitive Baptist Church for many years. His death occurred in his 84th year.

JOHN GIVENS CRADDOCK, was born in Harrison County, near the Bourbon line, and about nine miles from Paris; during his boyhood his father resided part of the time in Bourbon and part in Harrison, without changing neighborhood. His father, Richard Clough Craddock, was a Virginian, born in Amelia County; his mother, Ruth Givens, was born in Mecklenburg County, N. C.; his father lived to be called, as he was, an old bachelor before marrying; while traveling from his Virginia home to some lands owned by him in the Green river country, Ky., he stopped for the night with an old Virginia friend near the Bourbon and Harrison County line, who said to him "Craddock, why don't you marry? The best woman I ever knew in my life lives just over the way; she is of a highly respected family, her husband, Maj. John Givens, having died while a member of the Legislature, and although she has six children, there is an ample estate to take care of them." The old bachelor so little thought of ever marrying that he had given a great part of his estate to his widowed sister and her children; especially did he feel that he would as soon think of suiciding as marrying a widow with six children; he had his horse caught to pursue his journey, when a storm came up and prevented his leaving, causing him to stay over; that afternoon he met the widow, and at once surrendered; he felt that she was the woman that the Lord intended him to marry; had there been sixteen children instead of six, it would have made no difference. They married, and had two children born to them; the first one a daughter, Anna Craddock, died a young lady; the second, John G., resides in Paris, Ky., and is editor and proprietor of the Paris *True Kentuckian*. His father died suddenly, at the homestead, March 4, 1849, aged seventy-two years; his mother died in Paris, in 1852. In religious faith she was Presbyterian, but followed her husband into the Methodist Church, caring little for sects, but cherishing the spirit of Christianity to the end of life. John G. Craddock was educated chiefly in the schools and academies in his vicinity, and commenced the study of medicine in conjunction with a favorite friend, John Sidney Smith, born in the same neighborhood, on the same night as himself, and by agreement of parents were both named John, and pledged as friends for life; while attending lectures at the medical college in Lexington, the second call for volunteers for the war with Mexico, was published; he at once volunteered, and was made an officer in a company organized by the then Lieutenant Jno. H. Morgan, who at a later day became the famed General Morgan; but the company, in the lottery by which companies were drawn for service, failed to win a place. He then came to Paris and was mustered into Capt. W. E. Simms' company of volunteers ; went with it to Mexico, served through his time and was safely returned ; taking up his residence in Paris shortly afterwards, and having a decided predilection for journalism; he passed several years in reading, and making voluntary contributions to the papers of the day. In 1857 he was associated with Col. W. E. Simms in conducting and publishing the *Kentucky State Flag*, at Paris. The paper was discontinued at the commencement of the late civil war; after the termination of that unhappy conflict, and the minds of the people began to settle into business channels, Mr. C. established the Paris *True Kentuckian*, the first number of which was issued Feb. 22, 1866 ; he has been editor and proprietor from its commencement, and has secured for it a circulation and influence far surpassing any other county newspaper ever published in the State. He has never been connected with any church organization, though a friend and patron of every denomination. At the late meetings of Rev. Geo. O. Barnes, held in Paris, he was the first person to advance and make confession, and is an enthusiastic admirer of the great evangelist.

JOHN T. HINTON, furniture dealer and undertaker, of Paris, is descended from an old and well respected family, who trace their genealogy back to English ancestry. Three brothers, William, Spencer and Henry, emigrated from the "mother country" and settled in Lancaster County, Va., shortly after the war of the Revolution. Of these, William was the great-grandfather of John T. Two sons were born to William, viz: Richard and John; the former was the grandfather of our subject; he married Miss Mary Ingram, and to them were born five sons and four daughters; of the former, Richard E. was the father of John T. His parents dying about the year 1812, he was left dependent upon his own resources; he came West in 1817, and first located in Jessamine County, Ky., but soon changed his home to Danville, Kentucky, where he learned the trade of a hatter; he remained in Danville about five years, and then removed to Paris, Bourbon County, arriving in August, 1822; he was born April 10, 1797, and is yet well preserved, for one of his years. In October, 1823, he was married to Miss Betsey Maston, who was born and raised in Baltimore, Md.; she was the daughter of John Maston, a sea captain, who was lost at sea. To Richard E. Hinton were born eleven children, viz: Richard, Joseph, William, James, John (deceased infant), John T., Loretta, George, Mary, Charles and Taylor. Of these George and Joseph died while in the Confederate Army. There are now living of the eleven only William and John T. The latter was born in Paris, Jan. 29, 1837, and has since been a resident of his native place. He received a good business education, and in 1860 embarked in the furniture trade and undertaking business, which he has since continued with marked success. Though in 1863 he lost everything by fire, he immediately rebuilt and continued the business. Gradually climbing to the position of one of the leading business men of the town, he was for a number of years a member of the City Council, and in 1880 he was honored by being elected Mayor of the city of Paris, and re-elected in 1881. He has also taken an active interest and been a member of the Board of the Agricultural and Mechanical Association. April 10, 1860, Mr. Hinton was married to Miss Elmetia, daughter of Henry Hamilton. She died Jan. 24, 1874, leaving four children: W. O., Edward, Albert and John T. His present wife is the daughter of Elisha and Kittie (Thomas) Brown. Mr. and Mrs. Hinton are members of the Christian Church. He is a member of the community whose loss would be deeply felt, and is now enjoying the fruits of a well established business, which is wholly the result of his own energy, industry and good financiering.

WILLIAM KELLY, merchant and banker ; was a leading citizen of Paris in the early years of the town. He was born at High Park Lodge, County Galway, Ireland; and when about sixteen years of age, lost an eye from the kick of a colt. Being of a very sensitive nature, his mortification at this disfigurement made him resolve to leave home, and he ran away and came to America ; first stopping in the West Indies, and finally landing on the quay, in Philadelphia, with only a few shillings in his pocket. Mr. Kelly, a prominent merchant of that city, attracted by his appearance, questioned him, took him to his home and wrote to his parents. The lad refusing ever to return home, Mr. Kelly was requested to take charge of him, and money was sent for his expenses. He entered upon a mercantile career, and soon after the town of Paris was established, about 1791 or '92, he came to Kentucky and settled there as a merchant. He made numerous trips to Philadelphia for goods, bringing them over the Alleghanies on pack-mules, and from the Ohio to Limestone, now Maysville, on flat boats, about six months being required for the whole journey. He was first associated with the firm of Owings, Langhorne & Co., and afterwards formed a partnership with Hugh Brent. The firm of Kelly & Brent was, up to the time of his death, one of the most considerable mercantile establishments in that part of the State, and did the first banking business in Paris. After some years residence in Paris, he married Anna Maria Webb, born Smith, widow of Dr. Edward Webb; there were born to them three children, Thomas, William and Helen; Helen died in childhood, William in 1839, and Thomas in 1862. Mr. Kelly took an active interest in the public affairs of the town; he was a member of the first board of Trustees, organized the first Friday in March, 1797; was one of the first Trustees of the Bourbon Academy, established by special act of the legislature, Dec. 22, 1798; a member of the first board of Directors of the Public Library in 1808, and a member of the first Fire Company which was organized in 1810. He was the owner of the first brick house erected in Paris, and died in 1813, in the 50th year of his age, in the house now occupied by the Citizens' Bank, which belonged to him. He was an acute and enterprising business man, and left what was a large fortune for those days. His widow subsequently married Hugh Brent, his partner. Mr. Kelly was of medium height, of very dignified manner and courteous bearing, and noted for extreme neatness and precision in dress. He was fond of literature, a great reader, and an energetic friend of education; he had great force of character, and left a decided impress upon the society and business of the town.

THOMAS KELLY, was a merchant and banker of Paris, the son of William and Anna Maria Kelly, born Feb. 20, 1803, and died March 28, 1862. His father died when he was little over ten years of age, and he was reared in the family of his stepfather, Hugh Brent. He was educated at the Bourbon Academy, of which his father was one of the founders, and at Transylvania University, Lexington, Ky., where he graduated in 1820 or 1821. Dec. 24, 1824, he married Cordelia Morrow, daughter of Col. Robert Morrow, of Bath County, and his wife, Margaret Trimble Morrow. He was in early life actively engaged in mercantile affairs, carrying on mercantile establishments at Paris, Mt. Sterling and Owingsville, a woolen mill at Paris and a furnace in Bath County. He met with heavy financial reverses in the troublous times of 1843, and devoted his life to securing an honorable extrication from them. He became connected with the branch of the Northern Bank of Kentucky, at Paris, on its first organization, and was for many years, and at the time of its death, its cashier. He was a man of the kindliest disposition, of the strictest honor, and the staunchest devotion to his principles and his friends, and few men had more or better friends. He was a firm friend of the Union, and the outbreak of the civil war was a great grief to him. Five of his sons served in the Union army, and in attendance upon the death bed of one of them, Lieut. Nicholas M. Kelly, 4th Kentucky Infantry, he contracted the disease of which he died. His widow survived him only a few years, dying Oct. 31, 1864.

JUDGE MATT TURNEY, attorney; Paris; is descended from one of Bourbon County's early pioneers named Daniel Turney, who moved from the Shenandoah Valley, of Virginia, to Bourbon County, Ky., when but one house was standing on the ground where now stands the city of Paris; he engaged in farming in Bourbon County and continued the same until his death; among the children born to him in Bourbon County, was the father of Judge Amos Turney, who also spent his life in agricultural pursuits; he married Miss Lucinda McIntyre, whose people were also early settlers of Bourbon County, though her grandparents first settled in Nicholas County. The early life of the Judge was spent on his father's farm; he is one of a family of eight children, most of whom are well known to the people of Bourbon County; he began the study of law when he was twenty-one years old, with General Croxton, of Paris; he then attended law school in Cincinnati, where he graduated in April, 1861; he began practicing in Paris, directly after quitting college, where his success has been of a nature sufficiently inducing to keep him from seeking a new location; he has been, for many years, prominently identified with the political history of his native county; in 1866 he was elected by the Democratic party, with which party, since becoming a man, he has affiliated, to the office of County Attorney, for a four years' term; in 1877 he was elected to fill the unexpired term of Judge R. Hawes, as County Judge of Bourbon County; at the end of his services, he was re-elected to the same office for four years, and is at present engaged in the discharge of his duties; he is now the nominee of the Democratic party for re-election. Judge Turney was married in 1867, to Miss Mary L. Goodman, of Bourbon County; they have but one child living, who bears the name of his father, Matt; their oldest child, a boy, was burned to death, on Nov. 30, 1872, by his clothing accidently catching on fire. To whatever height Judge Turney may have climbed in the estimation of the citizens of Bourbon County, is due to his own energy and hard study; his position of honor and trust before the public, for so many years, is the best of evidence of the justice of his verdicts, and the careful observance of his duties.

J. M. THOMAS, dealer in lumber and general merchandise, Paris; was born at Flat Rock, Bourbon County, Ky., Sept. 5, 1833. He was named James after his maternal grandfather, and Mason after the family of his maternal grandmother. The father of our subject, Esquire David Thomas, died when J. M. was but fourteen years old, and the lad being delicate, he was not forced in his studies, but had a natural fondness for books. He received the rudiments of his educational training under Hugh B. Todd at his academy in Mt. Sterling. He began housekeeping before he was eighteen years of age, and joined the Christian Church about the same time. In July, 1853, he married Annie E. Rogers, the youngest child and only daughter of Esquire William Rogers, of Cambridge, and settled at Cambridge where he lived as a farmer until the war, when, his sympathies being with the South, he raised a company and entered the service of the Confederate States. He and company were under Generals Humphrey Marshall and John S. Williams until they were mustered out, some two years after entering the service; was in several engagements in Kentucky and Virginia. After being mustered out in 1862 and returning home, he went to Canada, where his family joined him; remained in Canada in the lumber business, in Windsor, until 1866, when he returned to Paris, where he has continued in the lumber, general merchandising, and manufacturing and building interests. Mr. Thomas has always thrown his influence on the side of religion, education and the material interests of his native county. He has five children living: William Rogers, Richard Philemon, Robert Lee, Mary Windsor and Baby Tom. Mr. Thomas is an elder of the church of which he is a member, superintendent of the Sunday-school, and chairman of the city Board of Education.

RUDDEL'S MILLS PRECINCT—Bourbon County.

F. E. BAIRD, farmer, life insurance agent, &c.; P. O. Cynthiana. Among the pioneer farmers of Harrison County, was James Baird, a native of New Jersey, born Sept. 5, 1788, and when seven years old was brought to Kentucky, by an uncle, who placed him in the family of David Ellis, a Bourbon County farmer; with him he remained till he arrived at manhood. James then left the home of his adoption and came to Harrison County, where he married Nancy Blair, daughter of Samuel and Polly (Russell) Blair, who lived on Twin Creek, in this county. Soon after his marriage he bought and settled on a small farm on Raven Creek. His wife was born June 9, 1791, and died March 31, 1839. This union resulted in ten children, three sons and seven daughters; eight of the children are still living and are all married, and with one exception they all reside in their native county. They rank among the leading and most prominent families of their part of the county. James Baird's second marriage was to Mrs. Nancy Garnett, who survived him but a few years. He lived to see all his children married, after which he expressed himself as being then ready to die, having been spared long enough to see his large family all settled in life. He died Dec. 25, 1857, aged sixty-nine years. Perhaps there was no man in the county held in higher esteem, or was more popular among his fellow men and neighbors. His whole career through life was characterized by honesty and undoubted veracity and integrity. Notwithstanding he was abundantly supplied with the necessaries of life, yet he never cherished any disposition to accumulate propperty or wealth, and consequently died, comparatively speaking, a poor man, leaving but little to hand down to his children, save the rich legacy of an untarnished name and an unimpeachable character. Samuel Baird, the eldest son of the above family, was born July 14, 1817. The early part of his life was spent upon his father's farm. Owing to the very poor educational facilities in his vicinity in those early times, he was obliged to commence his career in life with but a very limited store of knowledge. His learning, therefore, was necessarily confined to the plain rudimentary branches, and the study of these could only be pursued in the spare time snatched from the more pressing duties of the farm. When twenty-one years of age, with no capital whatever, save a strong constitution and a willing mind, he determined to venture upon his own resources and endeavor to make a living for himself. His first effort was to purchase a small tract of land, all in woods, on one of the tributaries of Twin Creek, and by his own labor the same was developed. From time to time he has added to his original purchase, till he now owns about 200 acres comfortably improved, and some surplus otherwise invested. Through the early part of his life, he was a very industrious, hard-working man, and what possessions he now enjoys are the true reward of industry and and economy. Samuel Baird has been thrice married. His first union was with Emmaline, daughter of Francis and Sarah (Hutchinson) Edwards, of Harrison County. This mar-

riage occurred on Oct. 28, 1838. She was born Feb. 17, 1821, and died Sept. 18, 1848. His second marriage was on June 12, 1849, to Eleanor Edwards, sister to his first wife; she was born Oct. 12, 1818, and died June 1, 1865. His third marriage was to Leah Conrad, who was born in 1824, and is the daughter of Benjamin Conrad, a native of Virginia, and one of the early settlers of Harrison County. Samuel Baird has five living children. By the first wife there are two sons, James T. and Francis E.; by the second wife there are two sons, Samuel P., and Russell B., and one daughter, Sallie Ellis. Francis E., who is the subject of this sketch, was born in Harrison County, Oct. 16, 1846. His boyhood days were spent about the homestead, working on the farm and attending the district schools, where he acquired a good practical knowledge of such branches as are usually taught in our common schools. When about nineteen years of age his father sent him to the Kentucky Wesleyan College, at Millersburg, Bourbon County, where he finished his education. He left school without any means, and at once began teaching for a livelihood, a profession he followed about three years, during which time he ranked among the leading and most popular teachers in Harrison and Bourbon Counties. His last school was a ten month's term at Kiser's Station, 4 miles north of Paris, on the K. C. R. R. Discovering that the confinement to which a teacher is necessarily subjected, was seriously affecting his health, he heeded the counsel of a medical friend, in whose ability and judgment he had implicit confidence, and at once quit the school room to embark in some branch of business that would admit of more freedom and recreation, if not prove more remunerative. For some time after this, our subject, engaged in various kinds of traveling business; and in the spring of 1872, bought a small store in Ruddel's Mills, Bourbon County, where he engaged in merchandizing. On Oct. 10th, 1872, he was married to Miss Maggie F. Howard, only daughter of Eli Howard, a prominent farmer of Bourbon County. Maggie F. was born Jan. 25, 1856. The spring following his marriage, Francis E. sold out his store and engaged in agricultural pursuits. In the fall of 1876, he bought a little place of 124 acres, on the Colville Pike, in Bourbon County, known as the Alex. Patton farm, and moved to the same in March, 1877. After devoting his entire attention to farming here for two years, he was induced to engage in the life insurance business, in which he was very successful. In 1880, he was promoted to the position of State Agent for one of his companies, and was given exclusive control of Tennessee, where he succeeded in establishing the merits of his Company upon such a basis as to attract the attention of all similar institutions trying to operate in that State. In the spring of 1881, he bought what was known as the Dr. Bright place, located on the same pike and less than a mile of his other place, where he immediately moved and continued farming in connection with his other business. In the fall of 1881, when a corps of historical writers were induced to undertake the publication of a history of several Counties of the famous blue grass region of Kentucky, our subject was recommended to the managers of the enterprise as a man every way suitable and competent for the various and difficult duties connected with a work of that character. In this new field of labor he began with that same zeal and energy that has characterized his successful career thus far in life, and to-day it is universally conceded by his co-laborers, that he ranks among the most careful and efficient writers belonging to the force. He has been prominently connected with the the Masonic Order since he was old enough to become a member; has filled all its offices; has been Master of his lodge, and its honored delegate to the Grand Lodge for six or seven consecutive years, and is thoroughly conversant with the esoteric work and masonic jurisprudence. He and his estimable wife are connected with the M. E. Church South, and in politics he is a Democrat. In his marriage, Mr. Baird realizes that he has been extremely fortunate, having obtained for a life companion a lady of most exemplary character, pleasing address, and rare good judgment, and one, withal, of whom it may be truly said, she knows her every duty and how best to fulfil it.

GEORGE W. BOWEN, farmer and distiller ; P. O. Shawhan ; was born Oct. 18, 1828, near Ruddel's Mills, Bourbon County ; he is the son of Benjamin and Mary (Current) Bowen, both natives of Bourbon County; two sons and three daughters were born to them, of whom George W. was the oldest son. He received a fair education at the district schools near Ruddel's Mills, and remained with his father until he had grown to man's estate. From 1852 to 1856 he was engaged in the mercantile business in Ruddel's Mills, and then fitted up and run the old Spear's Cotton and Woolen Factory as a flouring mill, which he run about one year, and then converted the same into a distillery, and has since been operating it successfully. He entered the Confederate Army in 1862, and was First Lieutenant of Company C., of H. Smith's Regiment, and Buford's Brigade. On the Ohio raid in July, 1863, he was taken prisoner; he was first taken to Johnson Island, where he was held about four weeks, and then sent to Allegheny City, Pa., and there placed with

115 others in the State Penitentiary, remaining in confinement about eight months; orders were then received for all officers ranking from lieutenant and higher, to be removed to Camp Chase, Ohio; there he was also confined for eight months, and was then released through the influence of friends. Mr. Bowen now has 670 acres of fine land, well improved, and for the past five years he has devoted much time and study to the breeding of thoroughbred horses, of which he now owns about eighty head. Notable among sales made by him, may be mentioned: Runymede, two years old, bred upon his farm, and sold in 1881 for $10,000; Wallenstein, sold for $9,000; Quito and Elias Lawrence, the two for $5,000. Mr. Bowen now has on hand ten or twelve fine two-year olds, and thirty-seven brood mares. His progress and judgment in breeding have brought him rapidly to the front in this industry. About 1875 he engaged in the hardware trade in Paris, Ky., under the firm name of Ford & Bowen. In addition to the above, Mr. Bowen owns one-twentieth of a tract of 500,000 acres of mountain land, rich in timber, coal, and iron ore. In the legitimate acquirement of the property mentioned, Mr. Bowen has been entirely dependent upon his own resources; his career only shows what can be attained by well directed diligence, good judgment and economy. His beautiful residence, a view of which appears in this history, was designed by himself, and built according to his plans. He was married March 23, 1852, near his home, to Miss Lucy J. Wyatt, a native of the same place, and born Feb. 19, 1832, her parents being Fleming R. and Martha (Rogers) Wyatt. They have one son and three daughters living: Warren W., and Callie, now wife of Alexander Keller; G. Ida, now wife of Dr. Arthur Keller; and Miss Belle M. There eldest son, John T., was killed by the cars in 1880.

LARKIN MONSON, farmer; P. O., Ruddel's Mills; is a son of Moss and Susan (Sims) Monson, and was born near Robinson Station, Harrison County, Jan. 21, 1843. Moss Monson is also a native of Harrison, and was born near Indian Creek in 1809; about the year 1830 he was married to Susan Sims, and in 1847 moved to the place upon which he now resides, near Robinson Station, containing about 120 acres, with good, comfortable improvements. He reared a family of six sons and one daughter; this daughter died when twenty-two years of age, and the eldest son is also dead. Their fifth son, Larkin Monson, who is the subject of this sketch, received a limited education in the common schools of his county, and after remaining with his father at the old homestead till he arrived at his maturity, where he received a good practical knowledge of general agriculture, he ventured out upon his own resources without any capital whatever. In 1864 subject was married to Nancy J. Brown, daughter of John and Mary Brown, of Harrison County. His wife was born on the 13th of May, 1845, and died May 2, 1870, leaving one daughter, Mary Susan, born the 4th of March, 1866. On the 5th of February, 1874, our subject again married, this time to Evaline, daughter of George Million, of Harrison County. The result of his second marriage was two children; one died in infancy; the second child, Elbert Elwoodie, was born on the 17th of March, 1879. Mr. Monson, as above stated, began life without a dollar, and by industry and economy managed to get a few hundred dollars surplus, when affliction and death visited his family and took away his wife, and again almost reduced him to the point from which he started. But possessing indomitable energy and perseverance he soon was on foot again, and to-day he owns a good comfortable little home in Bourbon County, where he is considered one of the best tillers of the soil in his neighborhood. He and wife and daughter are members of the Christian Church; politically he is a Republican.

BERRY PRECINCT—Harrison County.

MRS. SARAH K. ALLEN, farmer; P. O. Berry's Station; was born Feb. 28, 1832, and is a daughter of William and Frances (Falconer) Kendall. Mr. Kendall was born in Bourbon County, Ky., Dec. 22, 1796; was a farmer by occupation, and died Dec. 13, 1875. His wife, Frances, was born in Orange County, Va., Sept. 18, 1801, and died Jan 16, 1863. The subject of this sketch was educated at the Methodist Institute, at Cincinnati, O. She was married in Harrison County, Oct 11, 1861, to Joseph Ingels, who was born in Harrison County in April, 1825, and died soon after his marriage. He was a son of James and Mary Ingels, hoth natives of Bourbon County, Ky. Our subject was again married Nov. 6, 1865, to Rev. W. H. Forsythe, of Mercer County, who died Sept. 22, 1868. On May 6, 1875, she was again married, to A. J. Allen, of Bourbon County, who died

Aug. 22, 1878, leaving her once more alone. From her last husband she inherited 200 acres of land, on which she still lives, and portions of which rents out, the balance being cultivated under her management. She is a member of the Christian Church at Lexington, Ky.; is a woman of rare intelligence, and is highly esteemed by all who know her.

JAMES S. BARNES, stone mason, P. O. Berry's Station; was born in Bourbon County, Ky., April 26, 1827, and is a son of Daniel and Mary (Hubbard) Barnes. Mr. Barnes, senior, was born in Virginia, June 2, 1792; was a stone mason by occupation, and died Jan. 22, 1862. His wife, Mary, was also a native of Virginia, born May 12, 1790, and died July 27, 1862. James, our subject, received his education in the common schools of Missouri, into which State his parents had moved when he was nine years of age. He followed in his father's footsteps and learned the trade of a stone mason; also held the position of clerk in a grocery store for three years; was married in St. Louis, Oct. 27, 1862, to Miss Mary Frances Barnes, who was born in Harrison County, Ky., July 12, 1844. They have five children, viz.: William T., James M., John K., Elizabeth J., and Arthur B. Mrs. Barnes was a daughter of W. B. and Eliza (Redd) Barnes. He was born in Harrison County, Ky., July 12, 1818, and is still living. His wife, Eliza, was also born in Harrison County, in 1816, and is still living. In 1850, Mr. Barnes emigrated to California, where he remained nine years, engaged in mining for gold, and teaming. He eventually returned to Harrison County, and again took up his trade as stone mason, and by his energy and industry has purchased a house and lot, located at Berry's Station, Ky. He is a member of the Masonic order. In politics he is a Democrat.

FRANCIS G. CRAIG, distiller; P.O. Berry's Station; was born in Harrison County, Ky., June 2, 1838, and is a son of John and Isabella (Gray) Craig; he was born in Harrison County, Ky., Feb. 22, 1803; is a farmer by occupation, and is still living; his wife, also a native of Harrison County, was born in 1813, and is still living. The subject of this sketch was educated principally in the public schools of Woodford and Harrison Counties, although he attended school for a short time at Versailles, Ky. Early in life he commenced trading in stock, in which business he remained until the year 1861, when, in company with his uncle, H. Gray, he started a copper still in Harrison County; he remained in partnership twelve years, when he again commenced business for himself at Lair's; in 1880 he moved to Berry's Station, where he now is conducting a large distillery. He was married Nov. 15, 1866, to Miss Kate Sparks, a native of Harrison County, Ky., who was born Sept. 25, 1848. They have three children, viz.: Annie Isabella, George, Francis and Dille. Mrs. Craig was a daughter of Wesley Sparks; he was born Oct. 4, 1805, in Bourbon County, Ky., and died March 3, 1873; his wife, Jane Gibbings, also a native of Bourbon County, was born May 20, 1809, and died Aug. 1, 1858. Mr. Craig is a member of the Masonic Fraternity, at Cynthiana, and is also a Knight Templar; he is a man of prominence in his precinct, and is energetic and enterprising in business. He is a Democrat in politics.

JAMES D. DUDLEY, farmer; P. O. Berry's Station; was born in Bourbon County, Ky., Jan. 22, 1819, and is a son of Robert and Margaret (McClanahan) Dudley; he was a native of Virginia, one of the early settlers in Bourbon County, a farmer by occupation, and died in January, 1842; his wife was also a native of Virginia, and died in September, 1847. Mr. Dudley (the subject) was educated in the public schools of Bourbon and Harrison Counties, and began his career in life as a farmer, which he still follows; he was married May 7, 1852, to Miss Ann Pulum, a native of Harrison County, Ky., who was born Feb. 9, 1830; they have six children, viz.: Margaret, Mary, James, Robert, Liddie and Albert. Mrs. Dudley was a daughter of Abel and Liddie (Rallen) Pulum, both natives of Harrison County, Ky. Subject owns fifty-two acres of land, and is an energetic farmer and business man; he is a Democrat in politics.

THOMAS J. DUNAWAY, farmer and stock-raiser; P. O. Berry's Station; was born in Bourbon County, Ky., July 8, 1821, and is a son of James and Rebecca (Kennedy) Dunaway; he was born in Virginia in 1788, and died May 17, 1879; his wife was born Feb. 14, 1799, and is still living. Mr. Dunaway (the subject) was educated in Harrison County, and began his career in life in a saw and grist mill, where he continued for four years; since then he has been engaged in trading, merchandizing, farming and stock-raising—the two latter of which he now follows. He was married April 19, 1852, to Miss Amanda C. Bagley, a native of Kenton County, Ky., who was born Aug. 5, 1832; they have eleven children, viz: Madison G., Albert, Rufus, Mary, Ida, Ella, Hattie, Edon, Eva, Susie and Robert; Mrs. Dunaway was a daughter of Robert Bagley, who was born Ang. 1, 1790, and died Nov. 14, 1839; his wife, Mary E. Hansford, was born Feb. 16, 1799, and died Nov. 11, 1881. Subject owns 400 acres of land, and is an energetic and prosperous farmer and business man. He is a Republican in politics.

MORTIMER D. MARTIN, farmer; P.O. Robertson's Station; was born on the farm where he now lives Dec. 5, 1822, and is a son of William and Catharine (Perrin) Martin. He was born near Hagerstown, Maryland, Jan. 4, 1790; was a farmer and carpenter by occupation, and died in September, 1831. He was married March 7, 1822, to Miss Catharine C. Perrin, who was born April 5, 1802, in Harrison County, and died June 10, 1865, leaving a family of six children, of which Mortimer D., our subject, is one. He received his education in the common schools of the county; began his career in life as a farmer, but has at intervals during his life engaged in merchandising and school teaching. He was married Nov. 16, 1843, to Miss Terrilda Ann Sellers, who was born Dec. 26, 1825, in Harrison County, and was a daughter of David and Susannah (Ehlat) Sellers. He was born in Harrison County, Oct. 23, 1799, and is still living; his wife, Susannah, is also a native of Harrison County, and was born Jan. 7, 1805, and is still living. Mr. Martin is the father of ten children, viz.: Edwin W. U., Ellen, David A., Louis M., William J., Katharine C., George P., Sue, Emma and Belle. He is a member of the Christian Church, and helped to organize the Christian Church at Robertson's Station. Mr. Martin is a member of the Grange, and has also been a member of the Masonic fraternity for a number of years; was an old Whig until 1861, when his sympathies were with the South; took no part in the war other than what he could do to relieve the Southern soldiers in prison and for the relief of their families. Is a man of prominence in his precinct, having served as Justice of the Peace for a term of nine years. In 1867 was elected by the Democratic party of Harrison County to the lower branch of the Legislature, where he remained one term. Mr. Martin is a very energetic man, always first in any public enterprise, and is a model farmer. In politics he is a Democrat.

MRS. MARY A. RANKIN, farmer; P. O. Berry's Station; was born at Cynthiana, Harrison County, Ky., March 21, 1819, and is a daughter of Martin and Sarah (Spears) Smith; he was born in Pennsylvania, Aug. 29, 1787, was a farmer by occupation, and died Sept. 21, 1871; his wife, Sarah Spears, was born in Bourbon County, Ky., May 25, 1791, and died Aug. 3, 1854; she was the mother of nine children, of which the subject of this sketch is one; she was married in 1837 to Jonas Lyter, who was born Nov. 26, 1814, in Bourbon County, Ky., and son of Henry and Barbara Lyter. Mr. Lyter, the husband of our subject, died Aug. 14, 1846, leaving to her care three children, viz.: John M., A. D. and J. C. Lyter, the result of their union; she was again married Feb. 11, 1851, to Thomas A. Rankin, son of Robert and Jane Rankin, natives of Harrison County, Ky. Mr. Rankin was a miller by trade, and owner of a saw and grist mill, which was a few years later destroyed by water; when he turned his attention to farming, purchasing a farm containing 176 acres of land, on which is situated the "Old Elm Spring," by tradition a favorite camping ground for the Indians at an early day. Death again entered her home circle, leaving her once more a widow, with the addition of six children, viz.: Sarah J., Thomas H., Mary E., Henry Clay, Robert McLellan, and Ann M. To add to her misfortune, her house was consumed by the flames, on Feb. 5, 1866; being a woman of energy and ambition, however, she did not give up to despair, and on April 17, of the same year, moved into a new house erected by her own design, where she still resides in her declining years, surrounded by a large family of children; she is a lady of intelligence, highly esteemed by the community where she lives, and is, with several of her children, connected with the Christian Church, at Colemansville.

CYNTHIANA PRECINCT—Harrison County.

T. WIGLESWORTH, farmer; P. O. Poindexter; was born near Poindexter Station, Harrison County, Oct. 10, 1830. His father John Wiglesworth, was born in Spotsylvania County, Va.; was by occupation a farmer, and died in 1846, at the age of 64. His mother, Jane Bush, was born March 16, 1792, in Clark County, Ky., and died in Harrison County, Jan. 21, 1851, aged 58 years. Our subject, who was one of thirteen children, received his education in the common schools of his county, and began life for himself as a farmer. He has since engaged in the distilling business, and is now running a large distillery, with Wiglesworth Bros. He was married in Harrison County, Dec. 21, 1870, to Ella Martin, who was born in the same county, Aug. 31, 1846. They have the following children: John, Katie, Tandy, Anna Dell and Louise. Mrs. Wiglesworth belongs to the Christian Church. Her husband is a Democrat, and possesses 360 acres of land and a fine brick residence, and his is one of the finest farms in this county.

GEORGETOWN—Scott County.

BEERI CHRISTY GLASS, Farmer and Capitalist, was born December 4, 1804, six miles from Georgetown, in Scott County, Kentucky, and died at his home in Georgetown, June 20, 1874. His father, William Glass, was a native of Pennsylvania, emigrated to Kentucky at an early day, and became one of the most substantial and successful farmers of Scott County. Beeri C. Glass received a good education in the best schools and academies then existing in his native county, and made his first step in life as a teacher; and although he probably taught school at intervals for several years, it does not appear that he had any design of pursuing that avocation as a profession. January 20, 1846, he was appointed agent of the McCracken Fund. He resided on his father's farm until 1847, and was actively engaged with him in the various interests of the place. Under the old State Constitution, he was several years Sheriff of Scott County, but had little desire for political position. In 1847 he removed to Georgetown, where he continued to reside during his life. May 17, 1848, he was appointed one of the commissioners to lay out Scott County into eight election precincts. November 19, 1849, he was appointed County Treasurer. He was one of the founders of the Farmers' Bank of Georgetown, and remained in its directory until his death. He had accumulated considerable means, having been remarkably successful in everything he undertook with earnestness, before settling in Georgetown, and mainly occupied his time for years in loaning and speculating on his capital. His name was associated with all the important interests of his community. He contributed largely to the organization and building of Georgetown College, and was one of its most active managing trustees, and was connected with the Board of Trustees during his life. He was a leader in every movement of advantage to the town, and was one of its most active, influential, and successful business men. In politics, he was always a Democrat; had strong convictions and adhered to them at all hazard, but was courteous and deferential when any personal feeling or principle of individual honor was involved. When the civil war broke out, he espoused the cause of the South, and, had his health and age permitted, would have entered the army in defense of his principles. In 1852 he united with the Baptist Church, and, until his health and hearing failed, he was one of its most active and valuable members. On November 15, 1858, he resigned both the agency of the McCracken Fund and the office of County Treasurer. He was one of the Trustees of Georgetown for several years, and held various positions of trust in the community; lived an exemplary, active life; was open-hearted and charitable; started out in life as a poor boy, and, by superior judgment. business ability, and unyielding perseverance, succeeded, mainly unaided, in accumulating a fortune. He was a man of fine habits; of strong, sympathetic nature; was strongly devoted to his family; was a man of fine sentiment and feeling, which he displayed liberally in his home and in his personal friendships; and died universally regretted and respected, leaving the world better by his having lived in it. Mr. Glass was married in 1847, to Miss Margaret A. Kenney, daughter of Joseph B. Kenney, a prominent citizen of Georgetown, a lady of great personal and social worth, who still survives him. Their only child, Victor Kenney Glass, married Miss Bettie Force, of Georgetown, and resides in that place.

VICTOR KENNEY GLASS, Farmer, P. O. Georgetown; son of B. C. Glass, Esq., whose life is sketched in the preceding biography, was born July 18, 1848, near the city of Georgetown, Ky. He received a collegiate education; began life as a farmer; was married January 24, 1867, to Bettie Force, who was born in Scott County, Ky., in 1849, daughter of A. W. Force, of Henry County, Ky., and Martha (Beaty) Force, who was born in Scott County. Mr. and Mrs. Glass have been blessed with four children—J. Force, George, Augustine and Bettie. Mr. Glass continues to engage in farming, and has held no political offices, though taking an active part in politics. He is a member of the Presbyterian Church, a Freemason and a Democrat.

BIG EAGLE PRECINCT—Scott County.

J. T. JOHNSON, physician ; P. O. Oxford ; was born in Scott County, Feb. 8, 1836. His father was Garland W. Johnson, whose occupation was that of a farmer, and who was born in Rockingham County, Va., in 1805, and died in 1878, having come to the State of Kentucky at the age of four years. The maiden name of his mother was Thirzah Payne, who was born in Woodford County in 1811. His parents had ten children. He was educated in Georgetown, at the Burton Stone Academy, and began life in the capacity of a school teacher ; was married in Georgetown, Scott County, Dec. 1, 1868 ; maiden name of his wife was Nannie M. Mallory, born in Scott County in 1845. His wife's father was G. S. Mallory, who was born in Scott County in 1816. Her mother being Mary E. Emison, born in Scott County in 1823. He has been engaged in the practice of medicine. In 1868 he removed to Liberty, Mo., and there practiced medicine for ten years, returned to Kentucky and remained but a short period, when he removed to Hot Springs, Ark.; returned again to Kentucky in 1879, and resumed the practice. He has two children, whose names are Lucien McAfee and Garland Savage. He is a member of the Christian Church ; politics, Democratic; belongs to the Masonic fraternity, and is a member of the State Medical Association of Missouri. Dr. Johnson, after several years of practice in this State, removed to Missouri, locating in Clay County. He acquired a very extensive practice there, and ranked among the leading physicians of that State. It was during his practice there that he made the treatment of hemorrhoids and fistula a specialty, and is now considered the most eminently successful physician in the State, in this branch of the profession.

PARIS—Bourbon County.

FRANCIS LEWIS McCHESNEY, editor of the *Western Citizen*, was born in Georgetown, District of Columbia, December 7, 1829. His father, David McChesney, was a native of New Jersey, and came from an old Revolutionary stock. His great-grandfather was born in Edinburgh, Scotland; when four years old he was brought to America by his parents; attended Princeton College; was elected to the Continental Congress, but died on his way to take his seat, and, it is said, his property was confiscated by the British Government. David McChesney, the father of the subject of this sketch, was a soldier of the War of 1812, and, we are informed, was on shipboard with Francis Barton Key, when he wrote the "Star-Spangled Banner." A few years after the war he was married in Georgetown, D. C., to Ann Wise Webster, of Prince George's County, Md. Her great-grandmother, whose name was Stephens, was, with her children exiled from Holland, after the beheading of her husband. Her mother's maiden name was Lynn, and the family came to Maryland among the early settlers with Lord Baltimore. Among the near relatives on the mother's side was General George W. Childs, who was a conspicuous soldier in the war with Mexico, and for many years a prominent officer in the regular army. In 1832, the family came to Kentucky, and located at the Grand Crossings, in Scott County. Here they remained until 1837, when they moved to Frankfort. David McChesney died August 24, 1839, aged about fourty-four years, his wife surviving with six children, of whom Lewis (the subject) was the youngest. Left at the age of less than ten an orphan, he was deprived of the advantages of an early education, and he does not know when or where he learned to read or write. He was never taught either of them in any school, but somehow or other he picked them up. In 1841, he entered the Presbyterian Sunday School at Frankfort, and each year, for three years, bore off the highest prize among the boys for reciting the largest number of verses from the Bible. From 1841 to the anniversary in 1842, he recited 2,953 verses; from 1842 to 1843, 2,600 verses; and from 1843 to 1844, 2,650 verses. The last two years the scholars' lessons were limited to fifty verses each Sunday, and during that time young McChesney was not absent a single Sabbath. He learned during these three years the New Testament by heart, and also a portion of the Old Testament, and this, he believes, was the foundation of all his after education. He was in the habit of sleeping with the New Testament under his pillow, and each morning before rising he would read over the next Sunday's lesson ten times. As early as in 1840 he took a deep interest in political matters, and the next year, being only eleven years old, made an arrangement with a neighbor, Orlando Brown, Esq., son of U. S. Senator Brown, to go to the post office each day for the *Louisville Journal*, the agreement being that he should first read the paper, and then take it to Mr. Brown. Of course this was an invaluable source of political information. In 1845, Mr. Brown also befriended him, not only in proffering the use of his splendid library, but also in advising him as to the proper course of reading he should pursue, and for several years he availed himself of these great advantages. By the time he was fifteen years old, he became a Sunday School teacher, and to this time, after the lapse of thirty-seven years, he still retains a class. He was a member of debating societies with Justice John M. Harlan, now of the Supreme Bench, Senator George Vest, of Missouri, Judge James Harlan, of Louisville, Col. S. I. M. Major, now of the *Yeoman*, Col. Thomas B. Monroe, Jr., the editor of the *Lexington Statesman* before the war, and who was killed at the Battle of Shiloh. In 1846, he was elected first Presiding Brother of an organization called the Younger Brothers of Temperance. His successor was James Harlan; he was succeeded by John M. Harlan, he by Edward H. Taylor, Jr., now Mayor of Frankfort, and E. L. Samuel, now Cashier of the Bank of Kentucky at the same place. In 1847, the lodge had a public celebration, with procession, music, etc., and on this occasion he was the orator of the day, and made his first public address, being then about eighteen years of age. He subsequently attended, for a short time, Mr. B. B. Sayre's Classic School, and afterward the school taught by Rev. Jno. R. Hendrick, recently deceased. In 1851, he entered the Junior Class of Centre College, Danville, then under the Presidency of Rev. Dr. John C. Young. Here he was gaining some reputation as a speaker, winning every question he discussed, when he was stricken down by a severe sickness, which lasted nine months, and which completely broke him down, and he was forced to abandon his studies. When less than fourteen years of age, in 1843, for nine months, he had worked at the case in the *Yeoman* printing office, Frankfort, and after the failure of his health at college, in 1853, he went to Louisville, and became a compositor in the office of the *Daily Times*, then conducted by William Tanner and Cols. J. T. Pickett, Theodore O'Hara and W. W. Stapp. He afterward worked at Hull & Brothers, and also at the *Democrat* office. In 1855, he was elected President of the Louisville Typographical Union. In 1856, he went to Cynthiana, where he became one of the publishers of the *Age*, then edited by Jabez H. Johnson, afterward well known as "Yuba Dam." In 1857, he was chosen as Mr. Johnson's successor as editor of the *Age*. In January, 1858, he married Miss Eliza Belle Remington, of Cynthiana, youngest daughter of Mr. Greenup Remington, the oldest citizen of that place. In December of the same year he went to Washington City as the correspondent of the *Louisville Daily Courier*, and remained there for several months. In April, 1859, he purchased an interest in that paper and moved to Louisville, and in a short time became its political editor. His connection with the *Courier* was severed in 1860. As a part of the political history of that day, it may be stated that Mr. McChesney was the first editor in the State to take position in favor of the protection of slave property in the Territories. This position he first took in the *Cynthiana Age*, and, subsequently, in the *Louisville Courier*. It is proper also in this connection to state, that the *Louisville Journal*, then edited by the able journalist, George D. Prentice, advocated the same doctrine with equal zeal, and with great ability; and also that Justice John M. Harlan, and others equally prominent, also were conspicuous in their extreme pro-slavery views at that time, and on this question "out-Heroded Herod." In 1861, the civil war began, and Mr. McChesney was known as a sympathizer with the South in its unequal struggle. He had been educated to believe in the right of secession, and he aimed always to follow his principles wherever they might lead. As far back as 1852, when no one dreamed of a dissolution of the Union, in Chamberlain Society, at Centre College, he had made his first speech, in debate, in favor of the right of secession, and, when the proposition was submitted to a vote of the members of the society, his side won the question. Immediately afterward, however, when the question was debated as to whether the citizens of Lexington were justifiable in the suppression of Cassius M. Clay's Abolition paper, the *True American*, he took ground against their action, and so earnest and vigorous was his effort on this occasion, that at one time his remarks would be received with hisses, followed by wild applause, and on this question, too, he carried the day. In September, 1861, he abandoned his home at Cynthiana, to which he had returned; but being assured, that he would not be molested, he again returned. But, in a very short time, a squad of Federal soldiers came to his home, and he was marched through the streets by a file of soldiers and taken to Camp Frazier. He met there W. W. Cleary,

Esq., then a member of the Legislature, who had also been arrested for disloyalty. These arrests caused much excitement, and large numbers of citizens were starting off, intending to go to the South, fearing that, if they remained, they would be sent to Camp Chase, or to some other Northern prison. The Federal authorities soon discovered that they had made a mistake, and, in order to quiet the fears of the people, through the influence of Judge W. W. Trimble and J. W. Peck, two prominent Union citizens of Cynthiana, both Cleary and McChesney were unconditionally released, and their release caused universal rejoicing. For several months he was left undisturbed. But, in the following June (1862), he was again placed under arrest, and made his escape, going at once to Canada. He remained a few weeks at Toronto, and, being without means, it became necessary for him to obtain some employment. A position was secured on the Montreal *Daily Advertiser*, as local editor, which he held for about one year. In August, 1863, at the solicitation of leading Southerners in Canada, he went to Richmond, Virginia, going overland through the Federal lines. The object of his mission was to induce the Confederate Government to organize an expedition for the release of the prisoners on Johnson's Island. He presented this subject to the Government, and the proposition met their approval, and an expedition was organized to accomplish this purpose, under command of Lieutenant Wilkinson, of the Confederate Navy, and the sum of $100,000 was appropriated to carry out the project. The men placed in charge of the expedition were among the flower of the Confederate Navy, including Lieutenant Bradford, and others. Owing to the treachery of some one, after the party started, the attempt was a failure. A similar enterprise met with a like fate the next year. In October, Mr. McChesney returned from Richmond, crossing the Potomac River at Britain's Bay, and taking the public conveyance to Washington City, passing the Federal pickets at the Navy Yard Bridge, and escaped without being arrested. Had the object of his mission become known, and had he been arrested on his way from Richmond to Canada, it is not unlikely that his life would have paid the forfeit for his devotion to the Confederate cause. But he had counted the cost, and willingly and cheerfully took his life in his hands, trusting that thereby the release of the prisoners at Johnson's Island might be effected. In October, 1864, at the request of Mr. John Porterfield, then of Montreal, before the war a prominent banker at Nashville, Tenn., Mr. McChesney went to Toronto, and met Hon. Jacob Thompson, the Confederate Commissioner to Canada. The object of his mission was to ask Mr. Thompson to entrust to Mr. Porterfield, without security, the sum of $100,000, the latter agreeing to go to the city of New York, and with that sum purchase gold for shipment abroad, with a view of breaking down the price of greenbacks, and thereby injuring the credit of the Government. To some extent, the effort was successful. The money was given to Mr. Porterfield; he went to New York, and early in November, 1864, as can be seen by reference to the New York papers at that time, several million dollars of gold was exported, and gold advanced from thirty to forty cents within the same time. General B. F. Butler was then commander in that city, and several bankers were arrested, but the true party was not discovered. It required the expenditure of less than ten thousand dollars to produce the large advance in gold from 215 to 254. The balance of the $100,000 was returned to the Confederate Commissioner. In assisting escaped prisoners, in visiting the sick, Mr. McChesney, although without means himself, was always successful; and among the mementoes of the past which he retains, and will hand down to those who come after him, is a splendid gold watch, the gift of twenty-one young men (Confederates), in recognition of his services in their behalf. In other matters in Canada he took an important, but not conspicuous part. His labors, however, were none the less effective; and of all his friends at this time, those who stick closer to him than a brother, are those who were in trouble in Canada. To illustrate: early last year, he met one of these friends, of whom he had never asked a favor, and after the usual greetings were over, his friend told him that he had thought much of him during the last few years, and then he asked him how he was getting along in the world. He had been greatly blessed, "and you," he said, addressing McChesney, "were a friend to me when I needed a friend, and now I authorize you whenever you need any money to draw on me at sight, I am rich,—I will never feel it." And then he continued, "Perhaps you may need something at this time," and with that he wrote out a check for $500 and handed it to him, saying, "you can't conceive the pleasure it gives me to hand you that check. I am willing to divide my last crumb with you." Subsequently he furnished a larger amount, and within a few months, unsolicited, offered to guarantee that Mr. McChesney, if elected to the position of State Printer, should have all the means necessary to carry on the work, and this guarantee involved the advance of not less than $20,000. This is given as an illustration of the appreciation of Mr. McChesney's services by those who knew him best in times of darkness and of trial. Mr. McChesney has been a consistent Democrat all his life. His first vote was cast in 1851, Lazarus W. Powell for Governor, and John C. Breckenridge for Congress. In 1855, on "Bloody Monday," in Louisville, he was one of the fourteen hundred who voted the Democratic ticket against the Know Nothings. In 1856, he made the opening speech in the canvass in Harrison county against the Know Nothings. In 1866, he returned from Canada to Kentucky, and became connected with the *True Kentuckian* office at Paris. While connected with that paper he conducted an animated controversy on the subject of "Woman's Rights," with Elder David Walk, a minister of the Christian Church of some note. The discussion excited much interest at the time. Mr. McChesney, in the preparation of these articles, prepared them while at the case, without writing them, in that way combining the mental with the mechanical in their composition. And this he does very frequently, and thinks the articles he prepares in this way are usually his best productions. He remained with the *True Kentuckian* until the first of February, 1868, when, with L. T. Fisher, he became one of the publishers and editor of the *Western Citizen*. His connection with this paper has been continued more than fourteen years. During this period important questions have arisen, upon all of which he has taken position. Under his control the *Citizen* has advocated every measure believed to be for the interest of the people and the development of the resources of the State. He has also spoken a good deal upon questions of public interest. But at best, the life of a country editor is not attractive or desirable. The press is regarded almost as common property, to be used by the aspiring to promote their individual aims; to be the party organ; to make great men out of small material; to labor unceasingly for party, and to receive no reward, except in the consciousness of duty faithfully performed and principles conscientiously adhered to. Of him it may be said, as it has been of the literary man, "That he is like the candle which, in illuminating others, consumes itself." At the age of fifty-two Mr. McChesney is still in the editorial harness, and still writes about as well as at any period of his life. He is a ready writer, an easy, off-hand speaker, and has made addresses to the people on very frequent occasions. As age advances on him he loses very little of the buoyancy of his younger days. He frequently, in the social circle and in literary societies, and sometimes on public occasions, gives readings, being equally at home in the rendition of selections from Shakespeare as in imitation of the Dutch and Negro dialects. He has only one son, James R. McChesney, born in 1862, who is associated with him in the publication of the *Citizen*.

By: Mrs. Ella E. Lee Sheffield,
Texas City, Texas